Praise for *Mac OS X Help Line*

"*Mac OS X Help Line* is the reference book to keep on your desk … at all times. If there would be one book that I would be allowed to buy when someone would put me in a room with a Mac OS X system and tell me I can't consult any other work to make the thing do what I wanted to do, it would be his 1000-plus pages troubleshooting book."

—IT-Enquirer (www.it-enquirer.com)

"I've got to add *Mac OS X Help Line* to the canon of best OS X books. … If there's an OS X question that you or I could pose, it'll most probably have the answer. … I can't speak highly enough of this book. MyMac rating: 5 out of 5."

—David Weeks, MyMac.com

"The book is an extraordinarily well-written and well-organized compendium of practical knowledge. *Help Line* … will provide you with everything you need to take care of all the OS X machines in your life."

—MacDirectory (www.macdirectory.com)

"Trouble? No one shoots it better than Ted Landau. If you've got the use and enjoyment of Panther down but want a single source for preventive maintenance and help should oddities occur, then *Mac OS X Help Line* is the book to get."

—Think Secret (www.thinksecret.com)

"This invaluable compendium covers just about any technical problem you're likely to encounter. Mac OS X Help Line is the book I'm most likely to take along on Mac consulting calls. Time after time, it delivers the goods. Very highly recommended."

—Mug One (www.mugone.com)

"One of your best resources is Ted Landau's *Mac OS X Help Line*. Just about every nook and cranny is covered in exquisite detail."

—Mac Night Owl (www.macnightowl.com)

"It is a phenomenal piece of work. I would've paid three times the price just in recognition of the amount of work it must've taken to write this opus. It's an essential book for any OS X user. It's the first book I recommend to students in my OS X classes, and the one I recommend to IT managers responsible for Macs on their networks."

—From Amazon.com

"If you only buy one book for your Mac—this is the one to get! … Apple should include a copy with every Mac. This book should be owned by every Mac user."

—From Amazon.com

"An instruction guide that truly instructs and guides. This book isn't a dry tech-manual. It is a 'this is how you use it' book. And it was fun to read too! If you don't have a tech-type at your beck-and-call 24/7 … get this book." Five-star rating.

—macCompanion (www.maccompanion.com)

Mac OS X
Help Line

Tiger Edition

Ted Landau

with Dan Frakes

 **Peachpit Press**

Mac OS X Help Line, Tiger Edition

Ted Landau with Dan Frakes

Peachpit Press

1249 Eighth Street
Berkeley, CA 94710
510/524-2178
800/283-9444
510/524-2221 (fax)

Find us on the World Wide Web at www.peachpit.com.
To report errors, please send a note to errata@peachpit.com.

Peachpit Press is a division of Pearson Education.
Copyright © 2006 by Ted Landau

Project editors: Clifford Colby and Elissa Rabellino
Production coordinator: Myrna Vladic
Copy editor: Elissa Rabellino
Compositors: Rick Gordon and Debbie Roberti
Indexer: Valerie Perry
Cover design: Nathalie Valette with Mimi Heft

ISBN 0-321-33429-9

9 8 7 6 5 4 3 2 1

Printed and bound in the United States of America

To Naomi

Acknowledgments

My biggest thanks go first to my wife, Naomi. It has been a difficult few years for us. Among other things, we made a move from Michigan to California that took almost two years to complete (I could probably write an intriguing book just describing all the ups and downs of that adventure!). Trying to revise *Help Line* in the midst of all this often seemed an impossible task. Yet somehow it got done. It would not have been possible without Naomi's encouragement, support, and willingness (sometimes understandably reluctant) to take a back-seat to these other demands.

Another very big thanks goes to Dan Frakes, who has been an immeasurable help in writing this book for the past few editions. His role grows with each new revision. For this Tiger edition, he wrote the initial revised drafts for Chapters 2, 3, 7, 10, and 11, as well as doing a technical edit of the entire book.

For help with the Unix chapter, Dan and I enlisted James Bucanek. If Chapter 10 appears to be written by a Unix expert, it's because of James's contribution.

Having to go over copyedited text is not the most fun-filled part of writing a book. But my copy editor, Elissa Rabellino, made it as pleasant as possible, and the book clearly benefited from her efforts.

A very warm thanks to all of the gang at Peachpit (and a special nod to Cliff Colby, Nancy Ruenzel, Marjorie Baer, and Gary-Paul Prince). If there's a better bunch of people in the publishing industry, I have yet to find them. It's been a joy to work with them over the years.

I also want to express a heartfelt thank-you to my son, Brian. His enthusiasm and support for all things Macintosh, including my own accomplishments, have made him my unofficial partner. It would all have been far less fun without him.

Sadly, my mother died this past year. If there is such a thing as an afterlife, I am confident she is there, and still proudly showing off copies of my book to all who will listen.

Finally, thanks to all the readers of this book who have continued to support this effort—by buying the book, by recommending it to others, and by offering me feedback. Without you, this edition would never have been written.

Ted Landau
E-mail: ted@tedlandau.com

Contents at a Glance

Contents

Preface

What's new in this edition?

Welcome to *Mac OS X Help Line, Tiger Edition*. How does this edition differ from the previous *Panther Edition*? The primary answer should come as no surprise: The book has been completely updated to cover all the new features in Mac OS X 10.4 Tiger. This includes full coverage of Tiger's new Spotlight file searching, Automator scripting, RSS feeds in Safari, enhancements to Unix, and all the rest. These changes affect almost every page of the book.

Readers familiar with the previous edition will find other notable changes to the organization and content of the book:

- Chapter 6's coverage of disk-related issues (such as problems mounting hard drives and burning CDs) has been expanded.

- Chapter 8 (previously titled "Troubleshooting Networking: File Sharing and the Internet") was by far the longest chapter in the Panther edition. In this Tiger edition, it has been split into two chapters: Chapters 8 and 9. The first is called "Troubleshooting Networking." It covers the Network System Preferences pane, as well as associated network-related setups (Bluetooth, AirPort, routers, and so on)—and, of course, troubleshooting issues related to these topics. The second chapter, called "Troubleshooting File Sharing and the Internet," focuses primarily on issues surrounding the setup and use of the Sharing System Preferences pane, as well as the Network Browser and the Connect to Server command. Network security issues, including firewalls, are also discussed here. Finally, it offers troubleshooting advice for the two most common categories of Internet software: e-mail applications and Web browsers.

- In the previous edition, Chapter 9 was devoted to using Classic. Because of the declining use of Classic over the years, and because *Mac OS X Help Line* was already reaching the limits of its maximum page count in the Panther edition, I decided to drop Chapter 9 from this edition. Instead, I have posted the Panther version of Chapter 9 on the Mac OS X Help Line Web site (www.macosxhelpline.com). As very little about Classic has changed between Panther and Tiger, the Panther chapter remains current.

- Chapter 11 ("Troubleshooting the iApps") has been completely revised and updated. This has less to do with Tiger than with the fact that these applications have been substantially overhauled since the last edition of this book.

Finally, from the day the Panther edition of *Mac OS X Help Line* was published, and all the way through the release of Mac OS X 10.4 and after, I have continued researching and recording new troubleshooting tips and hints. The results of this research are reflected in the dozens of new and expanded topics in this book.

Overall, Tiger is not as overwhelming a change from Panther (Mac OS X 10.3) as Panther was from Jaguar (Mac OS X 10.2). Which is just as well. To keep up with that degree of change in the OS—and at a rate of a new OS version every year—was getting to be exhausting. Still, packing all the new information into this book was hardly a vacation. I hope you are pleased with the result.

Why buy this book?

Another way of phrasing this question is, "How is *Mac OS X Help Line* different from other Mac OS X books? What makes it unique?" My answer zeros in on three key points:

- *Mac OS X Help Line* focuses on troubleshooting. More than anything else, this is what separates the book from others that might seem similar. When something goes wrong with your Mac, this is the book you want to turn to first. And with it weighing in at more than 1100 pages, I am certain that there is no other book that covers troubleshooting in as much detail.

- *Mac OS X Help Line* covers more than just troubleshooting. It has always been my belief that the best way to effectively troubleshoot is to understand what is going on, rather than blindly following a set of steps that fix the problem. Therefore, this book goes into detail about the fundamentals that lie behind the troubleshooting solutions. You'll learn about what happens during the Mac's startup process, what hides inside Mac OS X packages, what the contents of Mac OS X's Library folders do, how Mac OS X's permissions work, and much more. Again, it is doubtful that you will find as much depth on these topics in any other book.

- Although *Mac OS X Help Line* spends a healthy amount of space on Unix and troubleshooting solutions that depend on Unix, it does not attempt to provide in-depth coverage of the Unix software that lies beneath Mac OS X. I view this as an asset. I think that, as much as possible, fixing common problems on your Mac should not require knowledge of Unix. Further, much of what is covered in books that have a greater emphasis on Unix is of little interest to all but the smallest minority of Mac users. It is interesting, for example, that you can use Unix to set up a mail server on your Mac or do Perl scripting, but those are not things that most Mac users will ever attempt—and certainly they should not be needed for troubleshooting.

In the end, *Mac OS X Help Line* is not a beginning-level introduction to Mac OS X. Neither is it a book to answer all your Unix-related questions about Mac OS X. But if you are seeking a book that explains the underpinnings of how Mac OS X works, that can take you from a beginning user to an advanced one, and that can provide the tools to solve almost any troubleshooting problem you may confront, then this is the book you want.

Mac OS X versions covered

It's hard enough to cover just the problems associated with the most recent versions of Mac OS X. To cover problems with older versions (many of which have been fixed or made irrelevant by changes to the software) would require two volumes! For this reason, *Mac OS X Help Line* assumes you're using Tiger (Mac OS X 10.4). The book includes coverage through Mac OS X 10.4.3.

However, except in regard to new features specific to Tiger, most of what is contained here applies equally well to Panther (Mac OS X 10.3). Where key differences exist, I try to point them out. (This edition drops almost all references to earlier versions of Mac OS X.)

As already indicated, this edition also eliminates almost all coverage of Mac OS 9, whether accessed via using Classic or by booting from Mac OS 9 or earlier (for those with older Macs that can still do so).

Sidebars

This book contains two main types of sidebars:

- **Take Note.** These sidebars contain background information that may not relate directly to the problem at hand or fit easily into the flow of the main text but is still relevant to the main topic. For example, in a section where the main text refers to Xcode Developer Tools software, a Take Note sidebar tells you exactly what's included in the Xcode Developer Tools and how to obtain it. Consider these sidebars to be as essential as the main text.

- **Technically Speaking.** These sidebars cover more technical and/or advanced topics than the Take Note sidebars. You can usually skip them and still understand and apply the advice in the main text; however, if you do read them, you'll have an even more complete understanding of the topics at hand. They are, in essence, a bonus for more advanced users.

Cross-references

Often the same advice or information can be applied to several different situations, coverage of which may be scattered across a number of chapters. To avoid doling out the same advice again and again, I frequently refer readers to information already covered elsewhere—hence the copious cross-references!

Still, too many cross-references can disrupt the flow, forcing you to thumb back and forth between chapters just to follow a topic. For this reason, I do repeat information at times.

Styled text

Sometimes my instructions for fixing problems include text or commands that you must type from the keyboard—particularly when I'm discussing the command-line interface of the Terminal application. To make these instructions as clear as possible, I've used the following text styles:

- **Monospaced text.** This indicates text that you input from the keyboard. For example:

  "To move to the Applications directory, type `cd /Applications`."

  A few additional notes: A period that comes at the end of a command, if that command is at the end of a sentence, should not be included in what you type. Quotation marks in commands, however, *should* be typed. Unless otherwise indicated, all commands are to be typed on a single line, even if they take more than a line to print in this book. Assume that a space exists at the end of every printed line, where the command continues to the next line. Finally, assume that you need to press Return at the end of each command in order to run the command.

- **Monospaced bold text.** This indicates text that the Mac generates in response to what you type. For example:

  "If, when trying to move to a new directory, you enter the name of the directory incorrectly, you will see the following response in Terminal: **No such file or directory**."

- **Monospaced italicized text.** Used in conjunction with input text, italicized text indicates that you should not type the text as written but rather substitute what the italicized text implies. With output, it similarly means that the actual output text will be a specific case of the general italicized term. For example:

  "To view the contents of a text file in Terminal, you can type `cat` *filename*."

  Sometimes the italicized text, if it is several words, is enclosed in brackets, such as {*name of application*}.

Getting more help: On the Web

Certain troubleshooting information, of necessity, could not or should not be covered in this book—in particular:

- Time-sensitive problems (for example, bugs that get fixed by updates released within weeks of their discovery)

- Problems not discovered until after the book was published

For these matters, I recommend the MacFixIt Web site (www.macfixit.com). This site—which I created ten years ago, though I no longer own the site or produce its daily content—is devoted to Mac troubleshooting and provides extensive coverage of Mac OS X. The homepage and forums are free; you must pay an annual fee to access its archives. I believe it offers the most comprehensive Mac troubleshooting information available on the Web.

My alternate choices for the latest in Mac OS X troubleshooting are Apple itself (especially its Support site, located at www.apple.com/support) and Mac OS X Hints (www.macosxhints.com).

Finally, I will be posting occasional online updates to this book on the Mac OS X Help Line Web site (www.macosxhelpline.com). Here you will find any corrections or clarifications to the text—issues that were discovered too late to be included in the printed copy. This site will also include new information that was not available at the time the book was printed.

Obtaining software mentioned here

Throughout this book, I mention third-party products (mainly shareware utilities) that can assist you in troubleshooting Mac OS X. You can download all of this software from the Web; however, you don't have to search the Web to find each program. Instead, you can get the latest versions simply by going to the VersionTracker Web site (www.versiontracker.com), which includes links to just about every Mac program in existence.

In addition, you can obtain a list of *my* favorite Mac OS X utilities—which include most of the ones mentioned here—from the Mac OS X Help Line Web site.

1

Why Mac OS X?

The focus of this brief chapter is a look at the history of Mac OS X and an overview of the ups and downs of troubleshooting the OS.

In previous editions of *Mac OS X Help Line*, this chapter began with an explanation of why Apple decided to move from Mac OS 9 to Mac OS X. Mac OS X was not merely an incremental change in the Mac OS; it was more like a quantum leap. It was essentially an entirely new operating system. So an explanation of the rationale for such a radical change seemed important.

However, Mac OS X is now more than five years old. Almost all Mac users are familiar with it, and recent converts to the Mac have never used anything other than Mac OS X. Therefore, the rationale behind the change no longer seems necessary to explain, so I have omitted it from this edition.

In This Chapter

A Brief History of Mac OS X

The road to Mac OS X was not an easy one. It was filled with detours, dead ends, delays, and surprises.

What we now call Mac OS X began as Mac OS 8—*not* the Mac OS 8 that was eventually released but a different OS entirely, which never saw the public light of day.

The original Mac OS 8 was intended to serve as a radical upgrade of what was then the current OS: System 7. (Back then, Apple used the word *System* to describe the OS.) Code-named Copland, Mac OS 8 included many of the critical features that are now part of Mac OS X, such as preemptive multitasking and protected memory (features that form the basis of Mac OS X's superior performance and stability, as covered more in Chapter 4).

After working on Mac OS 8 for several years, Apple finally announced it publicly in 1994, and development versions soon began to ship. CDs that took users on a demo tour of the new OS were handed out at Macworld Expos. The final-release version was scheduled for 1996.

Unfortunately, all this was going on at the same time that Apple hit its financial nadir. During this period, Apple's sales and market share plummeted, and articles about the "death" of Apple began appearing in the media with the regularity of weather reports.

It was in this atmosphere that Apple took a hard look at the status of Mac OS 8 and realized it would require too much time and money to finish. The result: In 1996, Apple killed Copland.

In the meantime, the Mac OS 8 that *was* eventually released was a much more modest update. It added some significant new features to System 7 but was essentially the same OS.

Back at the drawing board, Apple realized it couldn't entirely abandon its plans for a new OS. But if not Mac OS 8, what? The company had to do something fast. Apple had promised to announce its new strategy by January 1997. Having decided that it could no longer afford to design a new OS itself, Apple decided to purchase one. The focus quickly narrowed to two choices:

BeOS. On the surface, BeOS seemed to be the logical choice. Be Inc. had already released versions of BeOS that ran on Mac hardware. The compact, fast code often exceeded the capabilities of the Mac OS itself, and its user interface was sufficiently similar to the Mac OS so as not to be a shock to long-time Mac users. But BeOS had two strikes against it. First, many essential components (such as its printing and networking capabilities) were lacking. Second, Be Inc. demanded more money than Apple was willing to pay. The latter turned out to be the decisive strike. Be was out.

NeXT. NeXT was the company Steve Jobs started after he left Apple in 1986. The original NeXT product was a combination of hardware and software, much like the Mac itself. By 1996, however, all that was left was the software, called NextStep, which ran only on Intel processors. It eventually evolved into an open operating system called OpenStep, developed jointly with Sun Microsystems. OpenStep was a more mature OS than BeOS; it already had almost all of the features that Apple was looking for. The main problem was that it lacked the familiar Mac user interface. In fact, it didn't even run on Apple hardware. Nonetheless, Apple decided to tie its future to NeXT. In December 1996, the two companies announced their intention to merge.

The primary initial benefit of the merger was that Steve Jobs returned to Apple. This eventually led to the iMac and the subsequent "supercool" hardware that allowed Apple to rise from the ashes and become a profitable, thriving company again.

At the same time, work proceeded on converting OpenStep to the next-generation Mac OS. Initial plans centered on Rhapsody, the code name for a project that was largely a direct port of OpenStep to the Mac. The problem was that no existing Mac software would run in Rhapsody, so all Mac applications would have to be completely rewritten. Developers let it be known that they would abandon the Mac before doing this.

So Apple returned to the drawing board one more time. Rhapsody evolved into Mac OS X (the roman numeral *X*, pronounced "ten"). In this version of the OS, existing Mac software would be able to run with just minor modifications—a process Apple called "updating the software for *Carbon.*"

Mac OS X's Unix core, Library-folder structure, and many development tools have their origins in OpenStep. But the most distinctive feature of Mac OS X— the Aqua interface—came from Apple itself and was unveiled with great fanfare at Macworld Expo in January 2000. Apple also added the capability to run Mac OS 9 within Mac OS X via a feature dubbed *the Classic environment* (or just Classic for short). With these pieces in place, Mac OS X had reached its final stages.

A public beta version of Mac OS X was released in September 2000. The official release, labeled Mac OS X 10.0, came in March 2001. This first release still had some significant limitations, such as no AirPort or DVD support. But these problems were largely addressed in Mac OS X 10.1, released in September 2001. This release was the first version of Mac OS X that was truly ready for prime time.

Almost a year later, in August 2002, Apple released Mac OS X 10.2, also known as Jaguar. This represented yet another quantum leap in the evolution of Mac OS X, introducing Sherlock 3; iChat; Ink; Rendezvous; and a significantly refined, bug-fixed interface.

In early 2003, Apple sounded the death knell for Mac OS 9: New Mac models would no longer be able to boot into Mac OS 9. The only way to run Mac OS 9 software would be via Mac OS X's Classic mode.

By the middle of 2003, Apple had released iTunes 4 (and the iTunes Music Store), the Safari Web browser, and iChat AV—all now-important components of Mac OS X.

In October 2003, Apple released yet another major update to Mac OS X: Panther (Mac OS X 10.3). This version introduced numerous new and revised features, including these troubleshooting-related highlights:

- **Activity Monitor.** Called Process Viewer in Jaguar, this utility underwent such a major overhaul that Apple gave it a new name.

- **Exposé.** This allows you to instantly tile all your open windows so that you can locate and select the one you want.

- **Fast User Switching.** This allows your Mac to have multiple accounts logged in at the same time and allows users to switch from one to the other without closing any open files and applications. Fast User Switching is a boon to troubleshooting: When you need to determine whether a symptom occurs with only one account, this makes it a snap to do so.

- **Faxing capability.** This is now built into the Printing software.

- **FileVault.** This security feature allows you to encrypt your entire home directory.

- **Font Book.** This utility provides font-management options similar to the basic features found in third-party software such as Suitcase.

- **Restore.** This feature of Disk Utility allows you to back up and restore the data on your hard drive.

Apple also made dozens of smaller (but troubleshooting-relevant) changes to the underpinnings of the OS. Panther was such a huge update that it just about required that Jaguar-based Mac OS X books be tossed out and rewritten from scratch!

Over the course of 2004, Apple released several updates to Panther. It also released several major updates to its iLife software, starting with iLife '04 (which included GarageBand). The iLife package was updated to iLife '05 at the start of 2005.

In March 2005, Apple released Tiger (Mac OS X 10.4). Happily for trouble-shooters, Tiger does not require as much unlearning of what you already know, as did Panther. Most troubleshooting-relevant components of Tiger are similar or identical to what they were in Panther. Of course, there are still numerous significant new features in Tiger. Troubleshooting-related highlights include the following:

- **Spotlight.** This is Tiger's biggest new feature. It is a super-fast, global search capability for locating items on your drive. It has been described as "Google for Mac OS X." It will search not only files and folders, but also e-mail messages, address contacts, and more. And it can do "intelligent" searches, such as finding all QuickTime movies on your drive when you enter the word *movie* as the keyword.

- **Dashboard.** Dashboard is a programming environment intended for small, limited-use applications (called *widgets*) that can be made to appear or disappear when needed. The best part is, since these applications are written in JavaScript, third-party developers will easily be able to create their own widgets, extending what Dashboard can do. Initial widgets shipping with Tiger include a date book, a calculator, an iTunes controller, and Stickies.

- **Safari RSS.** Safari now has the ability to handle RSS feeds built-in. This allows you to monitor Web sites that provide headlines via news feeds—text summaries of articles, updated whenever new articles are posted. This makes it easy to track what's happening on all the Web sites you want to check, and go to a site only when a headline piques your interest. The new version of Safari also lets you save a Web page as an *archive* so that all images and links are included. Previously, you could save a page only as an HTML text document; no images were included, and relative links did not work.

- **Automator.** Using Automator, you can create a sequence of events to perform repetitive tasks. Want to change all the JPEG images in a folder to TIFF images with new names? Automator will let you do it. Although based in part on AppleScript, Automator uses a simple visual interface that allows any user to create these *workflows* without needing to learn a scripting language.

- **Migration Assistant.** Introduced in later versions of Panther for use with Apple's latest hardware, this is now a built-in feature of Mac OS X. When you purchase a new Mac, this utility facilitates the transfer of the data on your old Mac to your new one. This is important because simply copying the contents of one drive to the other using the Finder does not create a working duplicate. Setup Assistant simplifies what used to be an annoying hassle.

- **Keychain Access.** This utility has been beefed up with a new interface and additional support for working with certificates.

- **Unix additions.** Apple has improved Mac OS X's Unix software in several ways. The most significant for troubleshooters is the inclusion of Access Control Lists (ACLs). This allows administrators to assign permissions to any item on a user-by-user basis. For example, you could give Jane permission to read a file, while letting John modify it.

There's still more, including revamped unexpectedly quit dialogs, changes to the startup sequence, and new firewall features. All the details are contained within the pages of this book!

It's been a long road, but the hard part is over. It's been over 20 years since the introduction of the Macintosh, whose original OS set the standard for elegance and ease of use. Mac OS X sets that standard all over again.

Unix and Mac OS X

For most Mac users, the biggest potential hurdle in mastering Mac OS X troubleshooting will be the Unix basis of Mac OS X's core functions. Unix uses a command-line interface (CLI)—which means it's an entirely text-based OS. You type in a command and press Return to execute that command; the OS then gives you the appropriate feedback. If this arrangement sounds old-fashioned and quaint, that's because it is. It harks back to a style of computing that was in use before graphical user interfaces (GUIs) and mouse input were available. Unix dates back to the mammoth, clunky mainframe computers that were in use before desktop computing was born.

Thus, you might reasonably ask, "How does using Unix represent a step forward for Mac OS X?" Here's how:

- As an easily extensible operating system, Unix has largely kept pace with changes in the computer world. Although, for better or worse, it retains its command-line interface (which some users actually find preferable for certain tasks), it's a much faster, sleeker, and more powerful OS than it was years ago.

- Unix is immensely popular for running multiple-user servers (such as those at universities, where a central server regulates traffic on a network of client computers). Because of its speed and stability, many Web sites also favor Unix (MacFixIt.com, for example, runs on a Unix server). Variants of Unix are even becoming increasingly popular on personal computers, as is Unix's popular cousin, Linux.

- By basing Mac OS X on Unix, Apple instantly acquired all the power and benefits of this mature OS. Mac OS X's Web Sharing feature, for example, is based on the Apache Web server included in Unix and far exceeds the Web-sharing capabilities of Mac OS 9. If Apple had been forced to start from scratch in building all this functionality into Mac OS X, it probably would have taken another decade for the OS to reach the same level as Unix.

- Mac OS X is not merely a shell for Unix. Although some people have mischaracterized it as a graphical interface for accessing Unix, this is most certainly not the case. Mac OS X can do many things that would be other-wise impossible in Unix. (For example, AppleWorks could never run under Unix.) And although Mac OS X uses Unix for some of its core features, it expands upon those features extensively. It is this combination of Unix and the unique features of Mac OS X that makes Mac OS X the success that it is today.

Still, in some cases, using Unix in Mac OS X *will* feel like a step backward. Unix can be intimidating for those who expect the Mac to work the way it always has. This is especially true for the typical users in Apple's prime markets: home users, small-office users, and students. For this reason, Apple designed Mac OS X so that most users don't even need to know that Unix exists in Mac OS X. The OS succeeds at this most of the time.

And for many cases where you would otherwise need to access Unix directly, via the Terminal application, third-party developers have come to the rescue with shareware applications. These provide a graphical Mac-like alternative to the Unix commands. I mention these utilities throughout the book.

Unix exists as an operating system independent of Mac OS X. Numerous large books about Unix have been written, and there is no way I can provide a thorough background on Unix here. Instead, throughout the book I will present specific "cookbook" examples, as appropriate. I will also present a primer on Unix for Mac OS X troubleshooters in Chapter 10.

Bottom line: Although casual users may almost never need to confront Unix on Mac OS X, troubleshooters will need to become familiar with it. This doesn't mean you must become a Unix *expert* to be an expert Mac trouble-shooter, but it does mean that you can't be an expert troubleshooter without at least a basic knowledge of Unix.

Mac OS X: The End of Troubleshooting?

In its ads, Apple touts Mac OS X's stability, claiming it never (or almost never) crashes. Apple makes a good point: Mac OS X is indeed incredibly stable. In Mac OS 9, it was not unusual to experience multiple system crashes each day, forcing you to restart your Mac every time. In Mac OS X, you can go weeks or even months without having to restart your Mac.

However, this *does not* mean that troubleshooting is less important in Mac OS X than in Mac OS 9. In fact, I would say just the opposite is true.

Serious crash-and-burn problems may be less common in Mac OS X, but the number of more minor problems has multiplied dramatically. And these problems often have very specific cures (such as deleting or editing an obscure file) that make it difficult to create a *general* set of troubleshooting rules.

An install of Mac OS X includes tens of thousands of files. In addition to the main Library folders (especially /System/Library, with all of its frameworks files), there are the invisible (to the Finder) Unix directories. This means that when something goes wrong, it can be a major effort just to locate the source of the problem. It could be a .plist or cache file that needs to be deleted. It could be a bug in a framework file that requires another OS update to fix. A folder may have incorrect permissions that need to be modified. A Unix config file may need to be edited. Or you might need to modify a Unix variable via a command in Terminal. Often, users just give up and reinstall the entire OS.

Adding to the complexity, many problems affect only certain systems (such as G3 Macs, or Macs with an attached USB floppy drive, or Macs with a particular third-party application installed as a startup item). These things happened in Mac OS 9 as well, but they seem to be more common in Mac OS X.

More and more, troubleshooting Mac OS X is becoming a process of gathering and remembering specific fixes to specific problems, rather than learning a few general principles. Still, mastering general principles is an important first step to understanding how and why to apply specific fixes.

Again, none of this is meant to suggest that Mac OS X is prone to problems. It's far more stable than Mac OS 9 ever was and is a knockout winner in comparison with Windows. However, things can and do go wrong, and understanding why and what to do about them is not always simple—which is why I wrote this book. So enough introduction—let's get to work.

TAKE NOTE ▶ **Intel Inside**

In June 2005, Steve Jobs announced that the next generation of Macintosh computers, due out in 2006, will shift from the PowerPC processors in current Macs to Intel processors. Yes, this is the same brand of processors that have long been used in PCs running Windows. This same brand of processors will now be used to run Mac OS X.

In a perfect world, this change would have little or no effect for the average end user—any more than changing the brand of hard drive or RAM inside a Mac would have a noticeable effect. However, the processor has more influence on how software works than any other hardware component does. Therefore, you can expect that there will be at least a minimum of problems during the transition period.

For starters, some programs that run fine on current Macs may not run directly on an Intel-equipped Mac. To solve this, Apple will include something called Rosetta with the next-generation Macs. This will enable older, otherwise incompatible software to run in an emulation environment.

More-specific effects of the shift to Intel are still a bit hard to predict at this time. However, I have read that Intel-based Macs will no longer support the Classic environment or Open Firmware (a topic covered in Chapter 5). I expect we will discover numerous other changes and problems after these new Macs finally hit the streets.

Whatever happens, it is certain that this shift will require some significant modifications to how you troubleshoot a Mac. So stay tuned.

2

Using Mac OS X:
An Overview

If you're largely unfamiliar with Mac OS X, this chapter should bring you up to speed. You'll take a basic tour of the major features in the Mac OS X Finder, Dock, and Desktop.

Even if you are familiar with Mac OS X, however, don't be too eager to skip to the next chapter. This chapter also contains a variety of tips and technical information that even experienced Mac OS X users may not know.

It is not intended as a comprehensive overview, but rather as a selective survey of the topics that are especially relevant to troubleshooting. Later chapters will make frequent reference to topics covered here.

In This Chapter

TAKE NOTE ▶ Mac OS X vs. Mac OS X Server

Mac OS X Server is a special version of Mac OS X that includes the software required to set up the computer as a central server for a large network of client computers. For this book, I assume you're using the standard (client) version of Mac OS X, not the server version.

However, the distinction between Mac OS X client and server is really quite small. Nearly all of the software included in the client is also included in the server—and in exactly the same version. In fact, if you're willing to put a bit more effort into managing tasks, you can use the client as a server as well.

The primary differences between the two OS versions are that (1) Mac OS X Server includes some additional utilities (designed specifically for managing servers); and (2) some applications included with both client and server have options enabled when run in the server that are not enabled in the client. In the latter case, it's interesting to note that the software is the same, even if you don't see the enabled option in the client. The software simply checks (by looking for a file located in the CoreServices folder in the System/Library folder) to see if you're using the server before displaying server-only options.

The Dock

The first time you arrive at the Mac OS X Desktop, the predominant item is the Dock—Mac OS X's primary navigational tool. Regardless of where you are in Mac OS X, you can almost always access the Dock—it's always visible unless you've chosen to "hide" it (in which case moving the pointer to the edge of the screen causes it to appear) or a full-screen application has hidden it (in which case quitting the application reveals the Dock again).

Figure 2.1

The Dock.

Dock basics

The Dock itself is quite straightforward. Icons in the Dock represent items on your drive. However, the Dock is divided into two parts, which hold different types of items: All applications appear on the left side, while the right side holds icons for folders, documents, and anything else, along with the Trash. A line divides the two regions.

The Trash is where you place items when you want to delete them. You also use the Trash to eject media and unmount servers and external drives, as well as to begin the process of burning CDs and DVDs. To burn a disc, you drag it to the Trash icon, which then changes to an Eject or Burn icon.

To launch an application or open a document via the Dock, simply click its icon. If an application is currently running, a triangle appears below its icon. Clicking an already-open application makes it the active application, bringing all of its windows to the front.

Dock icons aren't necessarily static; while an application is opening, its icon bounces. Similarly, the icon for an open application bounces to alert you that it requires your attention. An e-mail client's icon, for example, bounces if the client has received e-mail in the background while you are working in another application. The bouncing stops as soon as you make the e-mail program the active one. Dock items also provide menus that offer additional functionality (see "Dock menus," below).

When you move the pointer over a Dock icon, its name pops up in text (which is helpful when the item's icon is not familiar to you). No clicking is needed for this feature.

Adding and removing items to and from the Dock

Adding items to the Dock. To permanently add an item to the Dock, just drag its icon from the Finder to the Dock. Keep in mind, however, that you cannot place an application icon on the *right* side of the Dock, nor can you place other types of icons on the left side of the Dock. Otherwise, you can put Dock icons pretty much where you want. You can even rearrange the icon order by dragging an icon to the desired location.

When you launch an application whose icon is not already permanently in the Dock, the icon appears there only temporarily—when you quit the application, the icon disappears from the Dock. However, if you move the application's icon to a different location in the Dock while the application is running, the Dock assumes you want it to remain in the Dock permanently. Thus, it will remain there even after you quit the application. You can also click-hold (or Control-click) an application's Dock icon to bring up its menu (see below), where you can select Keep in Dock.

Removing icons from the Dock. To remove a "permanent" icon from the Dock, simply drag it off the Dock. You will see a "poof of smoke" animation before the icon disappears. Don't worry—removing a Dock icon does not delete the item it represents from your hard drive; it just removes the icon from the Dock. The Dock icon serves as a pointer to the actual item; the item still exists and can be accessed via the Finder. (In Tiger, you can also click-hold or Control-click the item's Dock icon to bring up a menu containing the option Remove from Dock.)

Note that because all running applications appear in the Dock, you cannot remove the icon of an application that's running. If an application is not "permanently" part of the Dock, its icon will disappear from the Dock once the application quits. If you want to remove a permanent item from the Dock that is currently running, drag its icon off the Dock; you won't see the "poof," and the icon will remain until the application quits, but once it does quit, the icon will no longer appear in the Dock.

Minimizing windows to the Dock. By clicking the yellow minimize button in a Finder or application/document window (discussed in "The Finder," later in this chapter), you can minimize a window to the Dock. This means the window shrinks from its full-size location on the screen to become a representative icon in the Dock (always on the right side of the Dock, of course). The name of the window appears when you pause the pointer over its minimized Dock icon, allowing you to tell what's what when you have several windows in the Dock. In addition, the icon for a window contains a mini-icon of the application that created the window. When you click the icon in the Dock, the window returns to its normal size. (An animation effect typically accompanies this movement.)

Dock menus

If you click an item in the Dock and hold down the mouse button (or Control-click the item, or right-click it if you have a multibutton mouse), a menu will pop up. The contents of the menu depend on the nature of the item. At a minimum, you should see two items: Show In Finder, which will open a new Finder window displaying the folder in which the item is located; and Open at Login, which will add the item to your list of Login Items (as covered in the section on the Accounts System Preferences, later in this chapter).

Figure 2.2

The Dock menu for iTunes.

For open applications, the menu is likely to include at least a few additional items. The Quit command does exactly what its name suggests (that is, it quits the application). As discussed in the previous section, if the item is not a permanent member of the Dock, there will also be a

Keep In Dock selection; if it is a permanent member, this item will instead read Remove from Dock. You'll also probably see a Hide item—choosing this item will hide the application and all of its windows; clicking the item's Dock icon again will reveal it. Depending on the application, you may see additional items, intended to provide convenient access to specific features. When iTunes is open, for example, you can control playback from its Dock menu. Finally, the Dock menu for most applications will also include a list of all open windows in the application. For example, the Dock menu for Microsoft Word lists all open Word document windows. Selecting a window from the menu will bring that window to the front.

For folders, the Dock menu also includes a list of every item contained within the folder itself. If the folder contains subfolders, you will get hierarchical submenus containing the contents of those subfolders. Drag the pointer to any item in the menu and release the mouse, and you will "open" that item (actually, you *open* a folder or document but *launch* an application), as appropriate. This works even if an item in a Dock menu is actually an alias to a folder.

SEE: • "Aliases and Symbolic Links," in Chapter 6, for more on this topic.

This means that if you drag the icon of your hard drive to the Dock, you will be able to access a hierarchical menu listing every item on your drive! (Note that the Dock menus for both folders and files also include the Show In Finder and Remove from Dock commands.)

Finally, the menu for the Trash item offers the Empty Trash option: You use this command to delete the contents of the Trash. Before you empty the Trash, however, you can always click the Trash icon to open its window and drag any items out (should you decide you've placed them there in error).

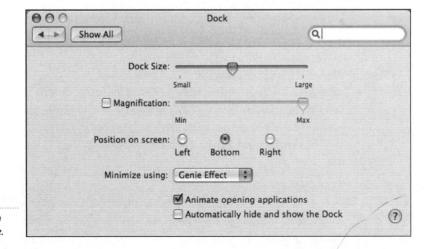

Figure 2.3

The Dock System Preferences pane.

Dock preferences: Customizing the Dock

You can customize the Dock's appearance as well as the way several of its features work.

For example, if you move the pointer over the Dock's white separation line, the pointer changes to a bar with arrows on either side. If you move the pointer in the direction of either arrow, the entire Dock gets larger or smaller.

If you press and hold the Control key while the arrow pointer is visible, it brings up a special pop-up menu. From here, you have several options:

- **Turn Hiding On/Off.** With this option enabled, the Dock vanishes from the screen until you move the pointer to the edge where the Dock resides—convenient if you need extra screen real estate.

- **Turn Magnification On/Off.** With this option enabled, the Dock icons directly under the pointer are magnified—convenient if the Dock is set very small by default, or if you have a large number of items in the Dock, causing it to shrink to fit everything.

- **Position on screen.** This option lets you place the Dock on the left, right, or bottom edge of the screen.

- **Minimize using.** This option lets you determine what type of animation effect is displayed when windows are minimized to the Dock: Genie or Scale. Genie is slower with a more dramatic effect; Scale is faster and simpler.

- **Dock Preferences.** Choose this option to open the System Preferences pane for the Dock. (I discuss System Preferences in more detail later in this chapter.) For the Dock, this simply provides a way to the same options I just described—along with a few extras—from a single-window layout rather than a menu.

You can also access various Dock settings in two other ways:

Dock System Preferences pane. You can access the Dock System Preferences pane directly (that is, without going through the Dock's pop-up menu) by choosing System Preferences from the Apple menu or the Dock and clicking the Dock icon in the list of preference panes. The Dock pane contains some options that are not available in the Dock's pop-up menu, such as a slider for adjusting the magnification effect and an option to disable the "bouncing icon" effect when an application is launched.

Dock command in the Apple menu. Apple wants to make sure you can find these Dock options, so a Dock command is also included in the Apple menu. If you choose this command, you get a hierarchical menu with a few of the same options found in the Dock's pop-up menu, as well as a Dock Preferences item that opens the appropriate System Preferences pane.

Dock troubleshooting tips and hints

The Dock is quite reliable. Occasionally, however, problems may occur.

If you click an item in the Dock and it either doesn't launch or doesn't function correctly, the first thing you should do is remove the offending item from the Dock and then put it back in by dragging the original item from the Finder to the Dock. This should fix 90 percent of Dock-related problems. For the other 10 percent, here are some tips that should help you get out of any remaining trouble.

Question-mark icon in the Dock. When a Dock icon has a question mark superimposed over it—or there is a blank spot in the Dock containing a question mark—it means the Dock is unable to locate the item that the icon represents. In some cases, the item may have been deleted. If, however, the item is still on your drive, the solution is simple:

1. Place the pointer over the question-mark icon.

    The name of the missing file appears; make a note of it.

2. Drag the question-mark icon off the Dock.

    The icon disappears.

3. Locate the missing file in the Finder and drag its icon to the Dock.

    Problem solved!

If you delete an item from your Mac that had been "permanently" added to the Dock, the question mark will not appear in the Dock until the Dock is relaunched (typically after a logout or restart) or until you try to open the item. In other words, the Dock won't immediately reflect the fact that the item is no longer available.

Figure 2.4

A Dock icon with a question mark.

The Dock fails to function as expected. Very rarely, the Dock may appear to stop functioning altogether—that is, clicking a Dock item has no effect.

To fix this problem, you need to quit and relaunch the Dock. However, because the Dock is a special application, there's no easily accessible Quit command. Even if you use Mac OS X's Force Quit window (by pressing Command-Option-Escape, as discussed in Chapter 5), the Dock will not be listed.

The solution is to launch Activity Monitor, a program included with Mac OS X and located in the Utilities folder. This utility shows all running processes (an application is a type of process), even ones that are not accessible directly from the Finder. In the Activity Monitor window that appears, do the following:

1. From the Show pop-up menu, choose My Processes (if it's not already selected).

2. Scroll the list of processes to locate the Dock item; then select it.

3. From the View menu (the Process menu in older versions of Mac OS X), choose Quit Process (Command-Option-Q).

4. When a dialog appears asking whether you really want to quit, click the Force Quit button.

   The Dock should quit, vanishing temporarily. It will then relaunch, and all should be normal again.

Poof does not evaporate. When you drag an item out of the Dock, a poof of smoke appears; however, occasionally that poof may linger on the screen, refusing to disappear. Everything else works normally, but you don't really want to stare at that poof. Logging out and logging back in will fix this problem, but it forces you to close all open applications. Don't despair—there's a better way! Simply quit the Dock (as described in the previous section), and the poof will disappear (with no ill effect).

Application fails to open or quit. Occasionally, you may click a Dock icon but its application refuses to open, leaving the Dock icon to bounce indefinitely. Alternatively, you might quit an application, but its Dock icon remains—even though it's not a permanent icon (and the application appears to have quit successfully). In either case, the problem is with the application itself, not the Dock. Thus, you usually can fix these problems by force-quitting the application.

In some cases you can force-quit directly from the Dock by holding down the Option key while accessing the application's Dock menu (in other words, click-hold the icon while pressing the Option key, or Control-Option-click the icon). When you do this, the Quit command should change to Force Quit; choose it. If this command does not work (the application will appear to be running, and its Dock menu will say, "Application not responding"), you can still try to force-quit by pressing Command-Option-Escape, as described previously.

SEE: • Chapter 5 for more on the Force Quit option.

TAKE NOTE ▶ Dock and Finder Shortcuts

Keyboard shortcuts provide an alternative method for accessing various commands and features. If you look at the menus of almost any application, such as the Finder, you will see shortcut equivalents for many of the commands. In the File menu, for example, you will see that Command-W is the equivalent of the Close Window command.

Some mouse-related shortcuts are less obvious, however, because they're not conveniently listed in menus. One example is the Control-click option for accessing the Dock menu from its separator line (which I described earlier in the chapter). I recommend that you experiment on your own by clicking your mouse button and/or holding down the Command, Option, Control, and Shift keys in various combinations and in various locations. See what happens.

To help you get started, here are some of the most common and useful shortcuts for the Dock and Finder (beyond those I've already covered in the main text or that are listed in Finder menus).

Dock shortcuts

Command-click. This is equivalent to choosing Show In Finder from an item's Dock menu. If you hold down the Command key and click an item in the Dock, a new Finder window opens, showing that item.

Command-Option-click. If you hold down Command-Option and click an application in the Dock, that application becomes the active application, and all open windows for other applications become hidden.

Clicking the Dock icon for any hidden item makes its windows visible again. To get everything back at the same time, from the Finder menu (or a similar menu for whatever application is active) choose Show All.

Finder window shortcuts

Option. If you hold down the Option key when you double-click a folder, the folder opens in a new window, and the previous window closes.

Command. When the toolbar is visible in a Finder window, double-clicking a folder icon in that window usually replaces the contents of the current window with those of the folder you just chose to view—that is, a new window does not open. If you hold down the Command key when double-clicking a folder, the folder opens in a new window, leaving the previous window untouched. (The Finder will always open a new window if the toolbar is not visible.)

Finder selections

Command. If you want to select several items from a list that are not contiguous, hold down the Command key while you make the selections—this is especially useful in List view.

Shift. To quickly select a contiguous group of items, click the first item in the list, hold down the Shift key, and then click the last item.

continues on next page

TAKE NOTE ▶ Dock and Finder Shortcuts *continued*

Finder copy and move shortcuts

Option-drag. Normally, when you drag an item's icon to a different folder on the *same* volume, it moves the item to that location rather than copying it. (That is, the item no longer exists at its original location; it exists only where you moved it.) If you hold down the Option key when doing this, however, you make a copy of the item rather than moving it.

Command-drag. Normally, when you drag an item's icon to a *different* volume from the one in which it resides, the Finder copies the item rather than moving it. If you hold down the Command key when doing this, however, you will move the item rather than copy it.

Note: These last two commands may not work as described if you do not have sufficient permissions to make the desired move or copy. (See Chapters 4 and 6 for more information on permissions.)

More shortcuts

Command-Tab. If you press and hold down the Command key, you will bring up a translucent overlay that contains icons of all your currently running applications. If you continue to hold down the Command key while repeatedly pressing the Tab key, you will cycle through the highlighted applications. When you release the keys, the highlighted application becomes the active one. Command-Shift-Tab (or Command-~) cycles through the applications in the opposite direction.

Command-~ and Command-Shift-~. In most Mac OS X applications, you can cycle forward and backward through open document windows in the current application by pressing Command-~ (tilde) and Command- Shift-~ , respectively. In Cocoa applications, this feature is automatically enabled; however, some Carbon applications may not support this feature. (See Chapter 4 for definitions of Carbon and Cocoa.)

See the following Apple Knowledge Base article for a long list of Mac OS X shortcuts, including ones that work at startup (most of which are covered in Chapter 5): http://docs.info.apple.com/article.html?artnum=75459.

The Finder

The Finder is the application in Mac OS X that you use to navigate through files and folders on your mounted volumes. Whenever you click the Desktop background, you make the Finder the active application. Similarly, clicking any open Finder window or the Finder icon in the Dock makes the Finder active. In this section, I'm going to take you on a tour of the many things you can do in the Finder.

SEE: • "Take Note: Finder Folders vs. Unix Directories," in Chapter 4, for an explanation of the use of these two important terms.

TAKE NOTE ▶ Windows in Applications Other Than the Finder

Most applications use windows. An open document in a word processor, for example, is presented in a window.

Document windows vs. Finder windows. The options and actions available in document windows sometimes differ from those in Finder windows. Here are two examples:

- If you have unsaved changes in a document, a dot appears in the red close button in the top-left corner of the document window, indicating that recent changes have not been saved. If you click the close button (in other words, attempt to close the window), a dialog will appear, warning that you have not yet saved your changes. Finder windows do not include this option.

- Document windows generally do not have the toolbar and sidebar features of Finder windows (though there are exceptions).

Applications with no open windows. If you close the last open window in an open application, in most cases the application remains open. It does not work this way, however, for many Mac OS X utilities. For example, if you close the System Preferences window, the System Preferences application immediately quits. Apple's theory seems to be that in applications that work with separate document windows, closing the last window doesn't quit the application, whereas if the entire interface of the application is contained in a single window, closing the window is equivalent to saying "I'm done." I guess this helps prevent the accumulation of open applications that you're no longer using; still, it would be nice to have an option to toggle this behavior; there are times when I would prefer to close a utility's windows but still have it running.

Finder windows

To see a typical Finder window, click the Finder icon in the Dock. If no Finder windows are currently open, this action will open a new window. (Depending on how you've configured your Finder Preferences, the window will open to the area generically referred to as Computer, which lists all mounted volumes, or to your own home directory. If your new window is opened to Computer view, choose the Home item from the Go menu to switch that window to home view.) Using your home window as an example, I will now walk you through the major features of Finder windows. For the moment, I'm assuming you're viewing Finder windows in the Icon view. (If not, choose "as Icons" from the View menu.)

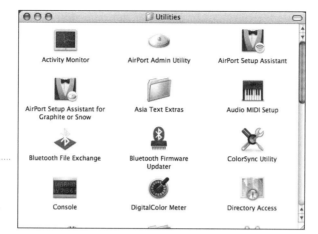

Figure 2.5

A typical Finder window, in Icon view, without the toolbar, sidebar, or status bar visible.

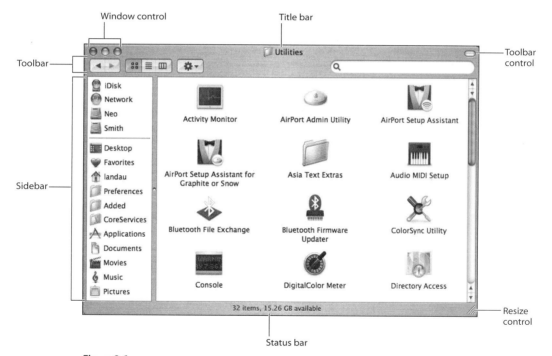

Figure 2.6

The same Finder window as in Figure 2.5, but with the toolbar, sidebar, and status bar now visible.

Window controls. The top section of the Finder window is called the *title bar*. If the toolbar is visible (as explained below), the title bar blends in with the rest of the window because they share the same metallic background; if the toolbar is not visible, the title bar is a separate bar. In the top left corner of the title bar are three jewel-like buttons called *window controls*. If you move the pointer over these buttons (from left to right), an *X*, a minus sign (–), and a plus sign (+) appear on each button in turn. If you click the left (red, *X*) button, you close the current window. If you click the middle *minimize* (yellow, –) button, the window is minimized to the Dock (see "The Dock," earlier in this chapter, for more on this feature). The right *zoom* (green, +) button changes the size of the window, alternating between a larger and a smaller size. (This button is often called the *maximize* button, to complement the *minimize* button. However, in most cases it doesn't actually "maximize" the window; instead, especially in the Finder, it usually resizes the window to fit all of the items in that window.)

Toolbar control. In the top-right corner of the window is an oval button. If you click it, you toggle between displaying and hiding the toolbar and the sidebar.

Window title. In the middle of the title bar are the title of the window and an icon representing the contents of the window. If you Command-click the title, a menu pops up, showing all folders that are higher up in the directory hierarchy than the window itself (all the way back to the Computer level). Select any one, and go directly to that window. (This feature also works in document windows in many applications.)

If you click-hold the icon in the title bar, you can drag the icon to another location in the Finder or to an application icon. This moves the contents of the folder to the new location or, in the case of an application, "opens" the folder in that application. Option-drag copies, rather than moves, the contents to the new location. Command-Option-drag creates an alias to the folder.

Tip: If you click a window in the background and it does not become the active foreground window, try clicking the title portion of the window. This typically does the trick.

Toolbar. Below the title bar in a Finder window is the *toolbar* (assuming you set it to be visible). I discuss this in more detail below. You can toggle this toolbar on and off via the Show/Hide Toolbar command (Command-Option-T) in the View menu or by clicking the toolbar control, as described above.

Sidebar. The sidebar, which borders the left side of each Finder window, is divided into two sections. The upper section of the sidebar lists mounted volumes (according to your settings in Finder Preferences). Click an item to switch the view of the current window to the root level of the clicked volume. If any of the volumes are removable media, an eject icon appears next to them. Click an eject icon to eject that item.

This upper section of the sidebar can also contain icons for your iDisk and the local network if you've enabled these options in Finder Preferences. Click the iDisk icon to mount your iDisk. Click the Network icon to view all currently mounted network volumes as well as aliases to local volumes available for mounting.

SEE: • Chapter 8 for more on the iDisk and Network options in the sidebar.

The lower section of the sidebar lists various files, folders, and applications on your drive. A selection of folders, including that for your home directory (with the home icon and your short name) and the Applications folder, are included here by default. You can also add or subtract items simply by dragging their icons into or out of the sidebar. (The first item I add to my sidebar is the Utilities folder!) You can similarly drag items to rearrange their order.

Click any folder to view its contents in the current window, or click an application or file to open it. If you Command-click a folder or volume in a sidebar, a new window will appear listing that item's contents; the current window will retain its current view.

You can adjust the width of the sidebar by click-holding the vertical divider along the right border of the sidebar and then dragging it left or right. If you double-click the sidebar border, it will disappear completely. As you add more items to the sidebar, their icons will get smaller to allow more to fit, but eventually you may find that the height of your window is too short to accommodate all of your sidebar items. If so, a vertical scroll bar will appear to let you scroll through the items.

Status bar. If the toolbar is visible, the bottom of the window will include a *status bar* that displays the number of items in the current folder (as well as the number of items selected, if applicable) and the space available on the current volume. If the toolbar is hidden, the status bar will appear near the top of the window, just below the title bar. (If the status bar is not visible, choose Show Status Bar from the Finder's View menu.)

Depending on the window, you may also see symbols at the left end of the status bar. A pencil icon with a line through it, for example, means that the current window's contents are read-only.

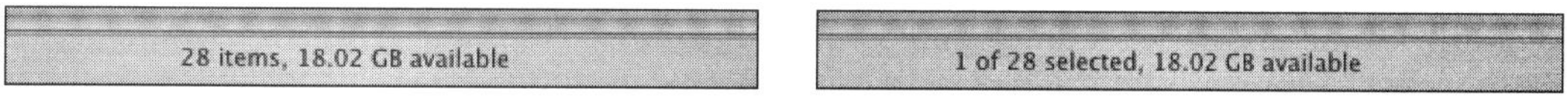

| 28 items, 18.02 GB available | 1 of 28 selected, 18.02 GB available |

Figure 2.7

Left, *the status bar in the Finder without any item selected;* right, *the status bar with an item selected.*

Scroll bars and resize control. If you cannot see the full contents of the current window, *scroll bars* on the right and bottom allow you to bring other items into view. While the pointer is within a window, you can also drag the mouse to the borders of the window to scroll its contents (and thus move the scroll bars).

In the bottom right corner of the window is the *resize control* (several lines forming a triangle). Drag this box to resize the window as desired.

Window contents. Windows contain files (applications and documents) and folders. To select an item in a window, click it once. The item's shading will change to indicate that it's selected, and its name will be highlighted (using the color you choose in Appearance preferences).

To open a file or launch an application, double-click its icon. To open a folder, double-click the folder icon. By default, opening a folder causes the selected folder's contents to replace the contents of the current window; you can change this setting so that folders open in a new window, as discussed later in the chapter.

SEE: • "Take Note: Dock and Finder Shortcuts," earlier in this chapter, for variations on opening a folder.

In Icon view, you can edit the name of an item in a window by clicking the name below the icon. After a second or so, a box should appear around the name and the text should be highlighted to indicate that you can edit it. (You can also press Return when an item is selected to enable editing of its name immediately.) If the name is too long to fit on one line, it will wrap to a second or even a third line as needed. To rename an item in List and Column views, you need to click the item once to highlight it, then wait a moment and click its name again to make it editable. (Just be sure not to click twice too quickly, or the Finder will think you want to open the item.) Alternatively, you can click once and then press Return to make the name editable.

If an item's name is still deemed too long to display when it's not the selected item, an abbreviated version of the name will appear. If you pause the pointer over the shortened name for a few seconds (or hold down the Option key and place the pointer over the icon to get an instant response), the full name will appear in an expanded text window.

Spring-loaded folders. To use this feature, drag an item to a folder's icon and hold it there. After a brief delay (which you can adjust via the Finder's Preferences dialog), the folder will spring open. You can then place the item in the folder (by releasing the mouse button), spring open a subfolder (by similarly dragging the item to the subfolder's icon), or simply move the pointer away from the folder (causing the folder to close with no other change). Note that if you press the spacebar while holding an item over a folder, it will instantly spring open—even if you've disabled spring-loaded folders in Finder Preferences.

Toolbar and Finder views. Finally, in this tour of Finder windows, you return to the toolbar. In its default state, moving from left to right, here's what you'll find:

- **Back.** Click the Back arrow button to go back to the folder that was previously visible in this window. This works if you have replaced the original contents of a window by double-clicking a folder within it.

- **Forward.** Click the Forward arrow button to reverse the effect of clicking the Back button. Alternatively, to go forward in a different path, double-click any folder icon in the window being displayed.

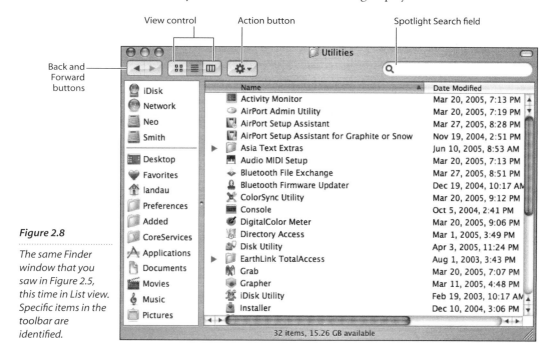

Figure 2.8

The same Finder window that you saw in Figure 2.5, this time in List view. Specific items in the toolbar are identified.

- **View control.** The View control is really three separate buttons, each of which affects how the contents of the window are displayed:

  Icon view. This is the traditional view, in which every file is represented by an icon with a name below it. You can move icons by dragging them.

  List view. In this view, all items are in a text list, with each item in its own row. The contents of a row are identified by the columns listed at the top. On the far left side is a column of icons and names for each file. This column typically is followed by columns for last modification date, file size, and kind (such as application, document, or folder). Clicking any column title sorts the window by that column. Clicking the same column again reverses the sort order.

  You can resize the width of a column by dragging the dividing line between two column headers, and move a column by dragging the column header itself. (You can choose which columns are displayed for a selected window via the dialog that appears if you select Show View Options from the Finder's View menu.)

  To the left of each folder in the list is a *disclosure triangle.* Click the triangle to reveal a subdirectory list of the folder's contents within the current window (as opposed to opening the folder in its own window). If, instead, you double-click a folder, you open the window, replacing the current contents displayed.

Column view. In this multicolumn view, the contents of a folder appear in the left-most column. If you click a folder in that column, its contents appear in the column to the right. This arrangement can continue until there are no more folders to open (at which point the selected item is previewed in the final column, as described below).

You can use the horizontal scroll bar to slide back and forth among columns if they don't all fit within the current window.

If you click an item that is not a folder, the column to the right typically displays summary information about the file (such as its name, kind, size, version, and modification date). For documents, you may see a preview of the document's contents.

You can drag the small double vertical bars at the bottom of each column divider to resize the column widths.

Figure 2.9

Top, *a Finder window in Column view;* bottom, *a similar Column view, this one showing a file preview in the right-most column.*

- **Action button.** Click-holding this button reveals a menu from which you can select context-sensitive commands. If no item in the folder window is selected, the Action menu lists commands for the folder itself. If an item is selected, the Action menu's commands refer to the selected item.

  The contents of the Action menu are identical to or a subset of the list of items found in contextual menus.

  SEE: • **"Take Note: Contextual Menus (and Folder Actions)," later in this chapter.**

- **Search field.** This is where you enter text to search the contents of your drive. You'll learn more about this in the "Spotlight" section, later in this chapter.

Customizing items in the toolbar. To add an item (such as a folder or application) to the toolbar, simply drag its icon to the bar. (In most cases, I recommend using the sidebar for this purpose.) To remove an item, Command-drag its icon off of the toolbar. You can rearrange the left-to-right order of items in the toolbar by Command-dragging them.

If you have more items in the toolbar than you can see in the window, an arrow will appear at the right end. Click it to access a pop-up menu of the remaining items.

To further customize the toolbar, from the Finder's View menu choose Customize Toolbar. The Customize Toolbar dialog includes options available only via this dialog, such as a Get Info option (which opens the Get Info window for the selected item in the Finder window) and an Eject option (as discussed in "Take Note: Eject Options," later in this chapter).

Note that if you Command-click the toolbar control in the upper right of a Finder window, the toolbar display cycles through the six possible modes: small text only, large text only, small icon only, large icon only, small text and icon, and large text and icon.

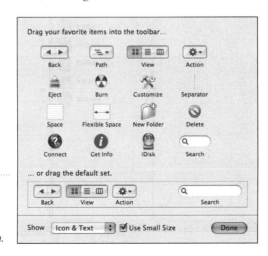

Figure 2.10

The dialog that appears when you select Customize Toolbar from the Finder's View menu.

Finder menus

The following provides a tour of the key items in the menus you can access when the Finder is the active application.

Apple menu. This menu is visible in all applications, not just the Finder. From here, you access a variety of universally available features. The About This Mac item provides info on your Mac (described in detail in "Take Note: About This Mac"). You can also use the Apple menu to access various system settings, via menu items for the System Preferences application, the Software Update System Preferences pane, the Dock System Preferences pane (or various Dock options directly via a submenu, as discussed earlier in the chapter), and Network Location options (covered in Chapter 8).

You can access recently used applications, documents, and servers via the Recent Items submenu, and when you're finished with your work, you can choose Sleep, Log Out, Restart, or Shut Down to tell your Mac to perform the respective action. Because of the stability of Mac OS X and the low power consumption of Sleep mode, most users will not need to restart or shut down very often. Note that the Log Out command lists the name of the current user (for example, Log Out Ted Landau). This is because you can have multiple users logged in at the same time via Fast User Switching (described later in this chapter).

Finally, you use the Force Quit command to quit applications that don't quit when requested to via the application's own Quit command.

SEE: • **Chapter 5 for more on the Sleep, Log Out, Restart, Shut Down, and Force Quit commands.**

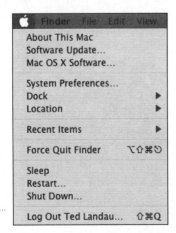

Figure 2.11

The Apple menu.

TAKE NOTE ▶ About This Mac

The Apple menu's About This Mac command opens a window that tells you a number of important details about your Mac and its software. Just beneath the Mac OS X logo is your Mac's operating system version number (such as Mac OS X 10.4.1). Conveniently, you can click the Software Update button to launch the Software Update application and check for new updates; this bypasses the need to access Software Update via the Software Update pane of System Preferences.

If you click the version number, you get something called the *build number*. A version of Mac OS X may have numerous builds, including prerelease builds and, occasionally, post-release builds. The build number changes whenever you update Mac OS X. For example, the build number of the initially released version of Mac OS X 10.2 Jaguar was 6C115. After the upgrade to Mac OS X 10.2.1, it changed to 6D52.

However, note that you can't necessarily use the build number to see if an update has been installed. For example, shortly after Panther (Mac OS X 10.3) shipped, Apple released two security updates. Installing these updates did not change the build number of Mac OS X. For this reason, the best way to check to make sure you're running the latest version of the OS is still to run Software Update and see if a newer version is listed.

If you click the build number again, you get the serial number for your computer, which can be handy if you ever have a problem and need to call Apple for tech support.

Below the Software Update button are three other bits of useful info. The processor line tells you the speed and type of your Mac's processor(s). The memory entry displays the amount of installed RAM. Finally, the Startup Disk line indicates which volume contains the version of Mac OS X you're currently booted into; this can be useful if you've got multiple startup volumes, as it's faster than launching System Preferences and checking the Startup Disk preference pane.

The last item in the About This Mac window is the More Info button. Clicking this button launches the System Profiler utility, which provides detailed information about your Mac, including installed hardware and software.

Figure 2.12

The About This Mac window.

Application (Finder) menu. The menu immediately to the right of the Apple menu is officially called the *application menu*, because it provides a way to access options common to most applications, such as About, Preferences, Services, Hide/Show, and Quit. However, its name is always the name of the active application, so you always know what application those options apply to. (In other words, you know you're quitting Safari if the Quit item is contained in the Safari menu.) In the case of the Finder, this menu is called Finder.

Figure 2.13

The application menu—in this case, for the Finder.

Note: Unlike most application menus, the Finder's application menu does not include a Quit command. Since the Finder normally runs constantly, the Quit command is not listed (though there are various methods, such as an option in Marcel Bresink's TinkerTool (www.bresink.de/osx/TinkerTool.html), to add this command—later in the book I'll discuss reasons why you might *want* to quit the Finder).

The Finder's Preferences command brings up the Finder's Preferences window. In the toolbar at the top, you can select from among four panes: General, Labels, Sidebar, and Advanced.

In the General pane, you can select among the following options:

- **"Show these items on the Desktop."** You select which types of volumes are shown as icons on the Desktop—"Hard disks," "CDs, DVDs, and iPods," and "Connected servers." If none of these options are selected, you access these items primarily via the Computer view in a Finder window (accessible via the Finder's Go menu by choosing Computer) or via any Finder window's sidebar.

- **"New Finder windows open."** You choose, from the pop-up menu, whether a new Finder window shows the Computer view, the startup volume, your iDisk, your home directory, your Documents folder, or any other volume or folder of your choice.

- **"Always open folders in a new window."** You decide whether to open a new folder, by default, within the existing window or as a new window.

- **"Open new windows in column view."** This does precisely what its name implies: With this option enabled, new Finder windows will default to Column view.

- **"Spring-loaded folders and windows."** Checking this option enables spring-loaded folders: When you drag a file or folder over a folder icon in the Finder, that folder will eventually open, allowing you to drop the dragged item into any subfolder; if you drag the item over a subfolder, it will eventually open; and so on, allowing you to "dig down" into your hard drive until you find the place where you want to drop the item. Use the slider here to adjust the delay time for spring-loaded folders (how long you need to hold an item over a folder before it "springs" open). (Note that even if you disable this option, you can access spring-loaded folders on a case-by-case basis by pressing the spacebar as you drag an item over a folder or volume.)

The Labels pane is used to assign names to the different file label colors. (The Color Label command itself is in the Finder's File menu, as described below.)

The Sidebar pane is used to enable or disable the items that show up, by default, in Finder window sidebars. Note that you can also add other items to the sidebar, and remove items from it, by dragging those items into or out of the sidebar, respectively.

Finally, in the Advanced pane, you can enable the following options:

- **"Show all file extensions."** You decide whether to show file extensions of names displayed in the Finder (discussed more in Chapter 4).
- **"Show warning before emptying the Trash."** You choose whether you want to see a warning message when you choose Empty Trash.

Just below the Preferences command in the Finder menu, the Empty Trash command tells Mac OS X to delete the contents of the Trash. As mentioned earlier, items you place in the Trash are not actually removed until you manually empty the Trash. Also note that each user maintains his or her own separate Trash. Thus, any items left in your Trash cannot be deleted by other users. Such items will remain in your Trash until you specifically empty it. (Alternatively, if you click the Trash icon in the Dock, this opens a window showing the current contents of the Trash. You can drag an item out of the window before emptying the Trash if you decide it was placed there in error.)

In Panther and later, you also have the option of choosing the Secure Empty Trash command, which deletes items in the Trash in such a way that it's virtually impossible for them to be recovered—even by utilities that claim to be able to undelete files.

Note: Some undelete utilities, if installed on your drive prior to using Secure Empty Trash, may preserve a second, separate copy of the file that survives a secure delete. If this is of concern to you, check out how your undelete utility works—use Secure Empty Trash to delete a test file and then attempt to recover that file.

SEE: • Chapter 6, for help in troubleshooting problems with deleting files.

The Finder (as well as most other applications) also includes a Services command in this menu. I discuss this more under "Services," later in this chapter. Finally, like most application menus, the Finder's application menu contains commands for showing and hiding it and other apps. The Hide Finder item hides the Finder and any open Finder windows; you can show it again by clicking its icon in the Dock. The Hide Others command does the opposite—it hides everything but the Finder. The Show All command unhides any applications that are currently hidden.

File menu. This menu contains many of the Finder's most commonly accessed features, including the following commands: New Finder Window, New Folder, New Smart Folder, New Burn Folder, Open (files and folders), Open With, Print, Close Window, Get Info, Duplicate, Make Alias, Show Original (of an alias), Add to Sidebar, Create Archive (of item or items), Move to Trash, Eject (removable media or mounted server volumes), and Burn Disc (to burn a CD). You will also find the Find and Color Label commands here.

All of these items are discussed in more detail elsewhere in the book.

SEE: • "Spotlight," later in this chapter, for more on the Find and New Smart Folder commands.
  • "Get Info," in Chapter 4, for more on the Get Info command.
  • Chapter 6, for more on most of the other options, including opening files (and using the Open With command), deleting files, creating aliases, and ejecting media.

Although most of these menu commands are self-explanatory, a few deserve more discussion:

• **New Burn Folder.** Use this command to create a Burn Folder. Dragging items onto this folder creates aliases to the original item inside the folder; you can keep the Burn Folder, or even multiple Burn Folders, around until you're ready to burn a copy.

  SEE: • "Burning Discs: CDs and DVDs," in Chapter 6, for more details.

• **Add to Sidebar.** This command adds the selected item to the sidebar. It replaces the Add to Favorites command in Mac OS X 10.2.

• **Create Archive** {*of item*}**.** This command compresses the selected item using the Zip format. A new file with a .zip extension is created in the same location as the original file. The original file is not deleted. If you double-click one of these Zip files, it is decompressed using a background process called BOM Archive Helper (located in /System/Library/CoreServices). These features eliminate the need for StuffIt Expander and DropStuff for basic archiving and expanding of files on your drive; you'll also want to use the Archive feature when sending files to Windows users. However, you'll still find these Aladdin utilities useful for working with other compression formats, such as .bin and .sit, as found on the Internet.

• **Color Label.** This command allows you to assign a color (and text) label to individual items in the Finder. You can sort items by Label in List view in the Finder, and Tiger's Find feature includes a Label criterion, allowing you to search for all items with a particular label. Choose *x* to remove the label from an item.

Edit menu. This menu, which like the application menu also appears in all applications, contains commands relating to the editing of content, and generally contains the Cut, Copy, Paste, and Undo commands. In most applications, the *content* is text, graphics, and so on. However, in the Finder, these commands can also apply to files and folders. For example, you can select an item in the Finder, choose Copy {*name of item*} from the Edit menu, and then navigate to another location and choose Paste {*name of item*} to create a copy of the file at that location. This allows you to move an item from one window to another, for example, without having both windows open. The Undo command in the Finder lets you "undo" Finder actions (such as moving files to the Trash) and supports multiple levels of undo. Other common commands are the Select All command, which selects all the items in a list or in a Finder window; the Show Clipboard command, which displays the contents of the clipboard in a small window; and the Special Characters command (discussed in "Fonts," in Chapter 4).

TAKE NOTE ▶ Contextual Menus (and Folder Actions)

If you Control-click an item in the Finder (or right-click if you have a multibutton mouse), you bring up a *contextual menu* for that item—so called because the contents of the menu change based on the *context* in which the menu is displayed and the item(s) being clicked (for example, a file versus a folder). Common menu commands include Open, Open With, Get Info, Move to Trash, Duplicate, Make Alias, and Copy {*name of item*}.

You can also install third-party contextual menus to extend the functionality of Mac OS X's stock menus. If the software does not include an installer that handles the task, all you need to do is drag the {*CMname*} plug-in file to one of the Contextual Menu Items folders, located in the Library folder of your home directory or (allowed only if you are administrator) the Library folder at the root level of your drive.

Note: If you are having problems with a third-party contextual menu item not working (or causing more general problems accessing contextual menus), the solution is to reverse this procedure: remove the item from its Contextual Menu Items folder. Also see "Take Note: Launch Services Files and Beyond," in Chapter 6, for related information.

In Panther and later versions of Mac OS X, the Action menu (accessed from the Action button in Finder window toolbars) lists most of the same commands found in the Finder's contextual menu for a selected item. However, some commands appear only in contextual menus. The commands to Enable and Configure Folder Actions, for example, appear in an item's contextual menu but not in the Action menu. The same holds true for custom (third-party) contextual-menu items you've added.

continues on next page

TAKE NOTE ▶ Contextual Menus (and Folder Actions) *continued*

Folder Actions. In Panther and later, contextual menus for folders include several commands used for implementing Folder Actions. With Folder Actions, you can have Mac OS X run an AppleScript every time some action is taken with a particular folder. For example, you can set this up so that every time a TIFF graphic file is dragged to a given folder, the file is converted to a JPEG file. This requires writing the relevant AppleScript (discussed briefly in "Take Note: AppleScript," in Chapter 4). Once you've done this, follow these steps:

1. From the folder's contextual menu, select Enable Folder Actions. This command toggles with Disable Folder Actions.

2. Again from the contextual menu, select Attach a Folder Action to select the desired script. This opens a Choose a File window, which typically defaults to /Library/Scripts/Folder Action Scripts. (To check for more built-in scripts, navigate to /Library/Scripts/Folder Actions and ~/Library/Scripts/Folder Action Scripts.)

You can also add more than one script. To do so (as well as to remove or edit existing scripts), from the folder's contextual menu select Configure Folder Actions. This launches the Folder Actions Setup application, located in /Applications/AppleScript.

You can access Folder Actions (and get a wider range of scripts) by enabling the Script menu (as described in "Enabling or disabling Menu Extras," later in this chapter).

Alternatively, the contextual menu for a file includes an Automator command. If you select Create Workflow from its submenu, it automatically launches the Automator application (discussed more in Chapter 4) with the file listed as the initial component of a workflow. Automator workflows can mimic the effects of many folder actions.

Figure 2.14

A contextual menu.

View menu. This menu's options in large part overlap with those in the stock toolbar, allowing you to switch between Icon, List, and Column views, for example. You can also select Customize Toolbar and Hide Toolbar from here. Selecting Hide Toolbar hides both the toolbar and the sidebar—the same thing you would accomplish by clicking the toolbar control in the top right portion of the window (as you will recall from our earlier discussion). If the toolbar is hidden and you want to hide or show the status information bar, choose the Hide/Show Status Bar command.

You can choose the Clean Up command to line up and space all icons in the active Finder window (which may be the Desktop) according to an invisible grid. Or you can choose Arrange By (plus an item from its submenu, such as Name) to arrange all icons according to the selected criterion as well as push them to the top left corner of the current Finder window (the top right if the Desktop is active).

If you select a subset of the items in a window, the Clean Up command changes to Clean Up Selection, allowing you to clean up just the selected items.

One caveat: Mac OS X still seems to have some problems with cleanup. More than occasionally, icons in a window you've "cleaned up" will return to their messy state on a subsequent visit. This is especially true for items on the Desktop. On the other hand, if you unintentionally select to "clean up" or "arrange by," a program called Desktility (www.desktility.com) can save and restore your original arrangement.

Figure 2.15

Left, *the Finder's View menu;* right, *the options available for Show View Options (for an Icon view).*

The Show View Options command brings up the Finder's View Options window, which includes a number of options that vary according to whether the current window is in List, Icon, or Column view. For example, for an Icon-view window, it lets you select options such as the size of the icons and whether you want the icons to snap to a grid. For List-view windows, it lets you select which columns you want to display. The following are some particularly interesting items available in View Options:

- **Text size.** This adjusts the size of Finder filename text.

- **Show icon preview.** Accessible when Icon view is selected, this changes the icons of graphic files (such as JPEG or TIFF graphics) to thumbnails of the actual graphic images rather than the generic document icons of the applications in which the document will open.

- **Label position.** Accessible when Icon view is selected, this allows you to specify whether an item's name is listed at the bottom of or to the right of its icon.

- **Show item info.** Accessible when Icon view is selected, this adds various tidbits of information to items. For example, for folders, it adds a line of text that lists how many items are in the folder. For volumes, it lists the capacity of each volume and how much of that capacity is still free. For QuickTime movies, it shows the length of the movie in minutes and seconds.

Go menu. As its name implies, the Finder's Go menu is used to go to specific locations. At the top are Back and Forward commands (which work the same as the buttons in Finder-window toolbars). This menu also includes an Enclosing Folder command, which takes you to the parent folder of the currently displayed folder. This is convenient if the Back button would take you to some other location (as might happen if you use a command to open a folder other than one located within the currently open folder).

Figure 2.16

The Finder's Go menu.

The following provides an overview of the remaining items in this menu.

- **Computer.** Choosing this item takes you to a window that shows all mounted volumes, including hard drives, CD-ROMs, and iDisks.

  SEE: • "Take Note: Computer and Root-Level Windows," in Chapter 4, for more details on this window and its contents.

- **Home.** Choosing this item takes you to the top level of the home directory of the current user. Your home directory is the one with your name on it, located within the Users folder.

  SEE: • Chapter 4 for more information on the home directory concept.

- **Network.** This opens the Finder's Network view, just as if you had selected Network in the sidebar of a Finder window.

- **iDisk.** This command has three subcommands: Choosing My iDisk mounts your own iDisk as a volume in the Finder, assuming you're connected to the Internet, have a .Mac account, and have entered your .Mac account information in the .Mac pane of System Preferences. The Other User's iDisk and Other User's Public Folder commands let you access another user's iDisk—either the entire disk, assuming you have the user's user name and password, or just his or her Public Folder.

  SEE: • ".Mac," later in this chapter, and "Using .Mac," in Chapter 8, for more information on iDisk.

- **Applications.** Choosing this item takes you to the Applications folder, located at the root level of the Mac OS X startup volume. This folder houses all of the applications initially installed by Mac OS X, as well as any other applications that may have been installed there.

- **Utilities.** Choosing this item takes you to the Utilities folder, located within the Applications folder.

- **Recent Folders.** This item simply lists folders you have recently visited. Select one to go there directly. Note: To go to a recently used document, application, or server, you would instead use the Recent Items submenu of the Apple menu.

- **Go to Folder.** This command lets you go directly to a specific folder; if you know the exact path to a folder, you can use this option to access folders that would otherwise be invisible. I provide several examples of this feature, such as getting to the /private/tmp folder, in Chapter 3.

  SEE: • "Technically Speaking: Where Does Software Update Hide the Software It Installs?" in Chapter 3.

- **Connect to Server.** This command lets you connect to other volumes on a local network or over the Internet. You can access any volume, remote or local, by typing its URL in the Server Address field. However, you can also access computers on your local network by clicking the Browse button to open a new Finder window to Network view.

  SEE: • Chapter 9 for much more information on Network view, Sharing, and Connect to Server.

Window menu. This menu, which exists in most applications, offers a number of features for managing windows in the current application. The Minimize command lets you minimize the active window—that is, move it to the Dock. (Clicking a minimized window in the Dock restores it to full size in the Finder.) The Zoom item does the same thing as the green zoom button in a window. The Cycle Through Windows command, more conveniently accessible by pressing Command-`, does just what it says—it switches between windows in the current application; the Bring All to Front command brings all of those windows to the front, so that none are hidden behind the windows of other applications. Finally, the bottom of the Window menu lists all open windows and lets you choose one to bring it to the front.

Help menu. When in the Finder, you can choose Mac Help from this menu. This opens Mac OS X's Help Viewer application (located in /System/Library/CoreServices). Given the sparse documentation that comes with your Mac, this option is an important one. Exactly what you see when selecting a command from the Help menu depends on the application you're using and the command you've selected (the menu may include more than one command). After selecting Mac Help from the Finder, you can find the help you seek in one of three primary ways:

- Click any of the links in the first pane that appear to go directly to the information you desire (for example, What's New in Tiger?, Top Customer Issues, and so on).

- Click a specific Help library from the Library menu to browse or search topics in that library. These libraries generally relate to specific technologies (AirPort, Bluetooth, AppleScript) or to specific applications (DVD Player, iPhoto, or even third-party applications).

- Type keywords in the search field in the toolbar. By accessing the magnifying-glass pop-up menu, you can choose to search just the current Help file (Mac OS X in this case) or all available Help files. Type format disks, for example, if you want to learn how to do that. Press Return to initiate a search. In the results list that appears, double-click the item(s) you want to see. More information will appear.

Click any links within a displayed page to go directly to the selected link. You can also navigate forward and back using the arrow buttons in the toolbar to go to any previously viewed page and back again. Click the Home icon to instantly return to the initial page (or click and hold the Home icon to access the Library list). You can also navigate from Help Viewer's Go menu.

When accessing help for a specific Mac OS X application, the initial pane will be different from the main one described here. Typically, you will get an overview description of what the application does and a link to more information.

Note: If you enable the Include Product Support Searches option in the Help Viewer menu, Help Viewer will also search for Help-related information over the Internet, if possible. For example, if you search for help on an Apple product with this option enabled, Help Viewer will also search Apple's Service & Support Web site.

Not all software supports Help Viewer; the developer must specifically create Help Viewer files. For this reason, the Help menu's contents may vary in applications other than the Finder. In some cases, the Help menu may include nothing more than a link to the vendor's Web site. In other cases, selecting the Help command for an application will open a different help system (provided by the application) or HTML-formatted help files in your preferred Web browser.

Beyond Help. In many applications in Mac OS X (including the Finder), if you pause the pointer over a command, button, item listing, icon, or just about any other application component, a yellow tool tip box appears, providing additional details about the item beneath the pointer. This, of course, depends on whether the developer has provided this supplemental help—though it's quite common in software from Apple. Experiment to see what appears.

For further help, you have two primary options: You can either (1) go to a Web site (especially Apple's support site or a troubleshooting site such as MacFixIt.com); or (2) purchase a book on the Mac (such as the one you're now holding!).

Figure 2.17

Help Viewer: top, *the pane that appears when you select Mac Help in the Finder;* bottom, *the results of a search for the term* filevault.

TAKE NOTE ▶ Getting Help for Help

Most Mac OS X utilities are located, appropriately, in the Utilities folder. Help Viewer is an exception: It's located in /System/Library/CoreServices.

If Help Viewer is crashing on launch, the most likely cause is third-party Help aliases, primarily located in ~/Library/Documentation/Help or /Library/Documentation/Help. To alleviate such crashes, delete these aliases. If this fails, try deleting the ~/Library/Caches/com.apple.helpui folder. A new folder, without the problem items, will be re-created as needed.

Note: Double-clicking an alias file (in the Finder) to a particular Help folder may do nothing— say, for example, if the original folder has been deleted. Similarly, choosing Show Original from the alias's contextual menu may not work, either. In this case, the reason could be that the original Help file is located within an application package (the Finder will not locate an original that's inside a package).

If Help Viewer launches, but very slowly, its speed should pick up after several launches. Apple states that this slowness (especially if the stall occurs while the word *Retrieving* appears on the screen) is due to Help Viewer's downloading updated information from online sources.

Spotlight

When it comes to locating files and folders on your local or networked volumes, and searching the contents of files, Tiger differs significantly from previous versions of Mac OS X. In those earlier versions, you had two search options: the Search field of Finder windows, which simply searched the filenames of files located in a specific location, and the Finder's Find window, which allowed you to search both files and their content according to specific criteria. In Tiger, all searching is performed by a technology called *Spotlight*. Spotlight is sort of a cross between Mac OS X's traditional Find functionality, Unix's locate program, and a detailed database of your computer's files and their contents. Aside from speed, the most noticeable difference between Spotlight and Panther's Find function is that Spotlight finds and displays much more data. For example, it can search for content in PDF files, and it can search for and display images of a given format. In addition, developers can write Spotlight plug-ins that allow Spotlight to search for file metadata specific to the developer's application, thereby expanding what Spotlight can find.

Spotlight is always active on your Mac, indexing the contents of hard drives, removable volumes, and even network volumes. As a result, when you perform a search in Tiger, the results are nearly instantaneous—you rarely have to wait for your search to finish as you did in previous versions of Mac OS X. (The exception is volumes that haven't been indexed; for example, if you mount a network file server for the first time and then search it, the process will take longer than a local search because the file server hasn't yet been indexed. It will also take a bit of time for Tiger to index your boot drive the first time you start up in Tiger.)

Spotlight's technology—and thus your ability to find information—can be found in a number of different implementations:

Spotlight searching from the menu bar. If you click the Spotlight (magnifying-glass) icon on the right-hand side of the menu bar (or press Command-spacebar), a Spotlight Search field will drop down. Begin typing the word or phrase for which you want to search, and as you type, a drop-down menu will appear showing applications, System Preferences panes, documents, folders, images, PDF documents, and any other supported file types that contain that word or phrase, either in its name, its contents, or its metadata—Spotlight even searches information such as Keywords in iPhoto images and EXIF data in digital photos. As Spotlight indexes all mounted volumes, you'll even see results residing on network volumes.

Figure 2.18

Spotlight's Search field menu.

Click an item in the menu (or use the arrow keys to highlight the item and then press Return), and that item will be opened. In the case of an application, the application will be launched (or made active, if it's already running). In the case of a document, the document will be opened in the appropriate application. But if that application is Spotlight-aware, you'll also see the results of a search within the application. For example if you type `Apple` into the Spotlight Search field, and then choose a PDF document from the results menu, when that document is opened in Preview, Preview will automatically perform a search for all occurrences of *Apple* within the PDF!

Note that if there are many results for your search term, the results menu will display only the first few for each type of file. The first item in the menu will then be "Show All (#)" where # is the total number of search results; choosing this item will open a Spotlight window listing the complete search results. (See the next item for more details.)

Spotlight searching from the Spotlight window. If you choose the Show All item from the Spotlight menu search results (or if you press Command-Option-spacebar at any time), a Spotlight search window will appear. Depending on how you accessed it—via an existing search in the Spotlight menu or via the keyboard shortcut—it will either show the results of the current search or be empty, waiting for you to search. In either case, this window searches just like the Spotlight menu—you simply type your search query and Spotlight will immediately return all matching results. The difference is that in the Spotlight window, you have more control over the results that appear. Within each file type, you can choose to show just the top five results or all matches, and you can click the "i" button next to an item to view detailed information about that file, including a preview. In the case of images and PDF files, you can also switch between List view and Icon view.

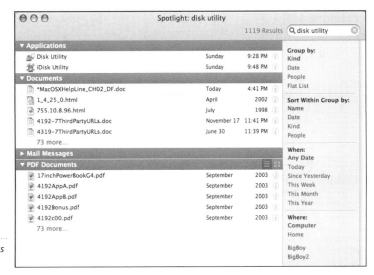

Figure 2.19

The Spotlight results window.

Even more useful are the options listed along the right side of the window, which let you group results (by kind, date, or people); sort within the groups (by name, date, kind, or people); filter by time (today, since yesterday, this week, this month, or this year); and filter by location (your home directory, your hard drive, or Computer—the latter includes all mounted volumes).

Spotlight searching via the Finder window Search field. If the toolbar is displayed for a Finder window, one of the toolbar items is a Search field; this field uses Spotlight. If you start to type a search word or phrase in the field, the window will switch from displaying the files located in the current folder to displaying the results of your search. (You can return to the folder view at any time by clicking the Back button in the toolbar.)

Once the window displays search results, you'll notice that just below the toolbar are at least four buttons: Servers, Computer, Home, and Others. If you were browsing a folder in the Finder when you started your search, that folder will also be listed. Clicking a button limits the search results to items found in that particular location (connected servers, all volumes, just your home directory, or Others, respectively).

If you click the Others item, a "Search in" dialog drops down that lists particular locations; you can add folders and/or volumes to the list by dragging them into the window, and you can delete a location by selecting it and pressing the Delete key. You can also use the Add (+) and Delete (–) buttons at the bottom of the dialog to add or delete items. Locations that are checked will be searched when the Others button is clicked.

Modifying and saving Finder window searches. The results you see in a Finder window search are similar to those you see in a Spotlight window search, with two significant differences. First, when you select an item in the list in a Finder window search, the bottom of the window will show the path to the file itself. Second, you don't get the same search limits and filters as you do with a Spotlight window search. However, Finder window searches provide three significant other options.

- **Additional search parameters.** When you click the Add (+) button (to the right of the Save button in the location bar that appears after initiating a search), a bar with two pop-up menus containing search criteria will appear directly below; your current search results will remain. These criteria allow you to further narrow your search. The default criterion is Kind, Any.

  If you instead start a search by choosing Find (Command-F) from the Finder's File menu, an empty search window will open. It will include two default criteria: Kind=Any and Last Opened=Any Date.

  In either case, you can modify these criteria to further restrict your search or change to different criteria. Each item (Kind, Any, Last Opened, and Any Date) is one choice from a pop-up menu of options. Just click-hold the menu on the left to see the other options. For example, you can change Kind to options such as Keywords or Name. Doing so changes the options in the menu on the right appropriately. Thus, if you change Kind to Name, the Any choice changes to Contains, and a text box appears to the right. The Any option can be shifted to Text or Images, among several other options.

The last item in the first (Kind) pop-up menu is Other. Choosing this provides you with a list of more than 100 special criteria that apply to documents, applications, folders, photos, music files, URLs, contacts, and much more. Suffice it to say that you can make your search as specific as you want. You can also choose to add an item to your Favorites. If you do, the item will be listed in the pop-up menu in the future, without your having to choose the Other option.

To add search-criterion rows, click the previously mentioned Add button again (or click the plus button located at the end of the criterion row). To delete a row, click the Delete button at the end of that row.

Note: You can perform a search using any of these criteria, even if no text entry is made in the Search field (with the magnifying-glass icon) in the toolbar.

- **Saved searches.** If you plan on performing the same search again in the future, click the Save button. Specify a name for your search (for example, "Movies over 100 MB") and a save location (the default is the Saved Searches folder in your Library folder, but you can save search documents anywhere), and the search parameters are saved for later use. The next time you want to perform the search, double-click the saved search file to see the results. Note that the results will be *current* results, updated in real time, not saved results; you saved only the search parameters.

- **Smart Folders.** When you save a search, one of the options is Add To Sidebar. If you enable this option, your search will be saved normally, but a new folder called a Smart Folder will be added to the sidebar of Finder windows. Much like Smart Playlists in iTunes and Smart Albums in iPhoto, Smart Folders are actually saved searches that are updated in real time. Whenever you click a Smart Folder in the sidebar, the Finder window will display updated results of that search. So, for example, you could create a Smart Folder search that lists all Microsoft Word documents in your home directory that have been created or modified in the past week—and presto! You've got your own, constantly updated, list of in-progress Word documents. (The documents aren't actually moved into the Smart Folder; it just provides you with a search-results window listing the documents.)

Spotlight searching in Open and Save dialogs. Since one of the places you're most likely trying to find a file is an Open dialog or a Save dialog, Spotlight is also available in these dialogs. Click in the search field (or press Command-F) and type your search term; the search results will be listed in the dialog window just as they are in a Finder window. The location bar gives you options to filter your search by computer, home, or the directory you were in when you started to search.

Spotlight searches in other applications. Spotlight searches are also available in other applications. Mail, for example, uses Spotlight to provide instantaneous searches of your mail messages. (You can even create saved searches, called Smart Mailboxes, that work like Smart Folders in the Finder.) Developers can create Spotlight plug-ins that enable a Spotlight search to also search the contents of files created in the developer's applications.

Spotlight Get Info Comments. Spotlight will search anything you add to the Spotlight Comments section of a file's Get Info window (described in more detail in Chapter 4). You can use this to group a collection of files so that they will come up together in a search (for example, use the term *tax stuff* to get all your tax-related files to appear).

Spotlight in System Preferences. The System Preferences application showcases a way of using Spotlight that truly justifies its name. In the Spotlight text field that appears in the upper right corner, start typing a term you are looking for (such as *security*). Immediately, a menu will drop down that lists all the System Preferences panes (and tab panes within each pane) that are relevant to this word. In addition, a literal "spotlight" will surround the icon of each of the System Preferences panes that match your search term.

Spotlight's System Preferences pane. Although Spotlight is, for the most part, a feature that provides functionality without much user interaction (other than specifying what to search for), it does have a few settings, accessible from the Spotlight pane of System Preferences.

In the Search Results pane, you choose the types of items searched by Spotlight; unchecking a file type excludes it from Spotlight search results. The order of file types here determines the order in which results appear in any of Spotlight's results lists—if you'd rather that found documents be listed above found applications, simply drag the Documents item above the Applications item in this list.

In the Privacy pane, you can prevent—for privacy reasons—Spotlight from searching particular folders or volumes. To add a folder or volume to the list—which prevents it from being searched—either drag the item into the window or click the Add (+) button and navigate to it. (You can remove an item from the list by selecting it and pressing the Delete key or clicking the Delete [–] button.)

Using the fields and pop-up menus at the bottom of the Spotlight preference pane, you can also choose the keys used to activate the Spotlight menu-based search and the Spotlight window-based search. By clicking the menu arrow button, you can choose any function key from the menu that opens; however, if you click in the shortcut field itself to highlight the existing shortcut, you can press a custom keyboard combination to save it as your preferred shortcut.

Spotlight with compressed files and disk images. Spotlight cannot search the contents of a compressed file (such as a .zip file) or an unmounted disk-image file (a .dmg file). If you wish to have Spotlight search the contents of such files, you must first expand compressed files and mount disk images, respectively.

Figure 2.20

Top, *a Finder window after selecting Find (Command-F) with a home directory folder the active window;* bottom, *the same window after searching for documents of the kind Text that contain my name (ted landau).*

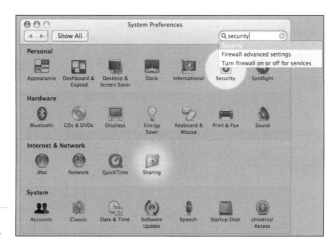

Figure 2.21

Using Spotlight in System Preferences.

Spotlight search limitations. There are certain locations in which Spotlight does not look. These are separate from the list of excluded folders in the Privacy pane of the Spotlight System Preferences pane.

By default, Spotlight searches all files in your home directory (including files in your Library folder), files at the top level of other users' home directories, as well as the /Applications, /Library/PreferencePanes, and /System/Library/PreferencePanes folders. It will also index and search the contents of external drives that you may mount. Note: To see a detailed list of exactly what Spotlight does and does not search, check out this Apple Knowledge Base article: http://docs.info.apple.com/article.html?artnum=301533.

As mentioned above, Spotlight will not look inside the contents of package files (such as application bundles, which end in .app). It will also not include items in the invisible Unix folders (such as /var and /etc) or any other invisible folders, even if items within the folder are themselves visible.

In addition, it will not search folders owned by other users (such as folders within another user's home directory). It is also limited to searching folders for which you have Read & Write access. This means, for example, that it will not search the contents of the root-level System folder, even if you're an administrator. For a standard user, it will not even search the contents of the root-level Library folder.

Note: Much of the software and settings files for content indexing are located in the /System/Library/Find directory. For example, a file there called SkipFolders includes a list of all the folders that are skipped over when doing content indexing.

SEE: • "Take Note: Spotlight Tips" and "Technically Speaking: Spotlight Indexes," below, for related information, including how to search for items that Spotlight normally would skip.

• Chapter 3, for more on package files.

• Chapter 4, for more on root access and permissions.

• Chapter 6, for more on invisible files.

• Chapter 10, for more on using Terminal and Locator.

TAKE NOTE ▶ Spotlight Tips

Here are some tips on using Spotlight that go beyond the basics covered in the main text:

Show item instead of opening it. If you Command-click an item in a Results list rather than double-clicking it, or use the arrow keys to select it and then press Command-Return, the item will be revealed in a Finder window, rather than opened.

continues on next page

TAKE NOTE ▶ Spotlight Tips *continued*

Searching where Spotlight normally does not go. Spotlight doesn't normally search inside many locations on your drive, as outlined in "Spotlight search limitations," in the main text.

You may be able to work around some of these limitations by using the Others option in a Finder-window search. To do so, drag the folder you want searched to the "Search in" window that appears when you click the Others button. Make sure the check box for the item is checked; then click OK. You are now set to search in just those checked locations. Note: I have not found this to be 100 percent successful—sometimes Spotlight still appears not to search in a selected location.

This feature can also be used to search the contents of packages: When you Control-click an application or other package and choose Show Package Contents, a Finder window will open showing the contents of that package. Drag this Contents folder into the "Search in" box so that Spotlight can then search it.

Another alternative: If the active window is the folder you wish to search when you press Command-F in the Finder, the name of the folder will be one of the buttons listed in the location bar below the toolbar. It should be the selected choice; if not, click it. You will now search the contents of that folder, even though Spotlight does not normally search them.

However, you still won't be able to use these techniques to search the contents of another user's home directory (unless you first log in as the root user).

More generally, if all these techniques still fail to get results, you can do a complete search of all files on your drive via Terminal commands (such as locate) or third-party utilities (such as Sebastian Krauss's Locator; www.sebastian-krauss.de/software).

Searching invisible items. If you click the criterion pop-up menu (such as the menu that typically states Kind when you first open a Find window) and choose Other, one of the options will be Visibility. If you select this and click OK, you will have the option to search for invisible items on your drive. Oddly, Apple states that Spotlight currently does not index metadata for invisible items. This would lead you to think that you will not see invisible items in a search result, regardless of what you select. You would be right. I am not sure if this is a bug or an oversight or what, but if you want to search for invisible items, you will need to use another utility (such as SkyTag Software's File Buddy; www.skytag.com).

Reindexing Spotlight (the easy way). If Spotlight stops working or behaves strangely, or seems to have an unusually high level of processor usage, it may be that its database has become corrupt. A simple way to fix this is to force Spotlight to rebuild its database. To do so, drag and drop the icon for your startup volume to the Privacy list in Spotlight's System Preferences pane. This tells Spotlight that you no longer want it to search any part of the volume. The result is that the index for the volume is erased. Next, remove the volume from the list. A new index will be created (if you do not see Spotlight begin a new indexing, evident when you select the Spotlight menu in the menu bar, you may need to restart your Mac).

continues on next page

TAKE NOTE ▶ Spotlight Tips *continued*

Changing default search criteria. This last tip is a technical one; it requires an understanding of packages and .plist files, as covered in Chapters 3 and 4. As noted in the main text, when you press Command-F in the Finder, a window opens with two default criteria (Kind and Last Opened). These defaults are determined by settings in a file buried within the Finder application package. To view the file contents, go to /System/Library/CoreServices; then open the Finder.app package and navigate to Contents/Resources. In this folder is a file called default_smart.plist. It can be opened in Property List Editor.

You can change the default criteria by modifying the contents of this file (assuming you know what changes to make!). However, there is a simpler alternative: If you create and save a Spotlight Smart Folder (as described in the main text), you can rename it *default_smart.plist* and use it to replace the file in the Finder.app package. The criteria in your custom Smart Folder will now be the new default criteria. However, be cautious about doing this, as you are making changes to a critical System folder file. At the very least, make sure you have backups of the original default_smart.plist file and the Finder, in case something goes wrong.

Accessing Spotlight within documents. Suppose you want to use a word in an open document as the search term for Spotlight. No need to copy and paste, at least for documents of Cocoa applications. You can select the word and either (a) Control-click to get a contextual menu and then select Search in Spotlight, or (b) press Command-Shift-F (the shortcut for selecting the Spotlight item in the Services menu).

More tips. See Apple's Spotlight Tips Web page (www.apple.com/macosx/tips/spotlight.html).

SEE: • "Using the Finder's Find command," in Chapter 6, for related information.

TECHNICALLY SPEAKING ▶ Spotlight Indexes

This sidebar covers some additional "under-the-hood" tips to those covered in the "Take Note: Spotlight Tips" sidebar. In particular, there are several Unix commands that can similarly assist in your working with Spotlight. I discuss some examples of their use here. (I am assuming some understanding of Terminal commands, using Property List Editor, and permissions issues.) More general information can be found in Chapter 10 in "Finding files: The find, locate, and mdfind commands" and "Running Mac OS X software from Terminal."

The .Spotlight_V100 directory. When Spotlight indexes your hard drive for files, folders, and file contents, it stores an index of that information on your hard drive. More specifically, it stores the index for each mounted volume's files in a folder called .Spotlight-V100 at the root level of that volume. This means you have one of these invisible folders for each mounted volume.

continues on next page

TECHNICALLY SPEAKING ▶ Spotlight Indexes *continued*

Reindexing Spotlight (the not-so-easy ways). As an alternative to the method described in "Take Note: Spotlight Tips" for forcing a reindexing of your volume, you can delete the actual .Spotlight_V100 folder. To do so, first make invisible files visible, as described in Chapter 6, and drag the index folder to the Trash (giving your password when the authenticate dialog appears). Or you can use the `su rm -R` command, in Terminal, to delete the folder.

Another method is to use the `mdutil` command in Terminal. The `mdutil` command is used to manage the metadata indexes where Spotlight's data are stored. You can use it with the `-E` option to erase an index, forcing it to be rebuilt, just as you would using the Privacy list feature. In particular, to erase the index for the current startup volume, you would type the following:

```
sudo mdutil -E /
```

The / symbol indicates the startup volume. If you want another volume re-indexed, enter its path instead.

Ideally, you should turn Spotlight off before erasing the index and turn it back on afterward. To do so, type `sudo mdutil -i off` to turn Spotlight off and `sudo mdutil -i on` to turn it back on.

Searching where Spotlight normally does not go. You have no access to the contents of the .Spotlight-V100 folder by default (for example, it has a no-entry icon on the folder). However, you can gain access to its contents via Terminal or by logging in as root (as covered more in "Accessing other users' folders" in Chapter 6). If you do, one of the files you will find within is _rules.plist. This file, which can be opened with Property List Editor, provides yet another route to get Spotlight to index a folder it would not normally index. Specifically, to "include" a folder not normally searched by Spotlight, use the New Child command in Property List Editor to add a new "child" to the `INCLUDE` array; add the folder's absolute path as the string value.

The `mdimport` command can also be used to import metadata from files. That is, it, too, can be used to force Spotlight to search in locations where it would normally not search. To do this, type

```
sudo mdimport -f {absolute path of location you want searched}
```

As with several other aspects of Spotlight, I have not had 100 percent success with this method, although many users have found that it works just fine.

Expanded search criteria. The `mdls` and `mdfind` commands allow you to list the metadata attributes of a specified file and search the database, respectively. What is especially valuable about the latter command is that it allows for searches on complex criteria that the standard Spotlight interface does not support. However, you can enter these same "raw" commands directly from Spotlight by accessing the Kind pop-up menu from a Find window and choosing the Raw Query item. Check out the `man` files for these two `md` commands in Terminal for more details, including the syntax for these raw searches.

continues on next page

TECHNICALLY SPEAKING ▶ Spotlight Indexes *continued*

Smart Folders and queries. Spotlight's Smart Folders are not really folders. They are actually XML-formatted files with a .savedsearch filename extension. Each file is stored in ~/Library/ Saved Searches by default. The file's data contains the instructions to Spotlight as to what to search. In fact, if you choose the Finder's Get Info command for a .savedsearch file, the search instructions are viewable in the Query field in the General section of the window. These instructions are the same sort as used by the mdfind command.

Disable Spotlight. There may be times when you want to turn off Spotlight. This might be because you find it is causing an unusual amount of CPU activity and slowing your Mac down. Also, it is a good idea to turn Spotlight off for the destination volume of a backup. To disable Spotlight for a specific volume, you can use the Privacy pane in Spotlight's System Preferences pane. However, to completely turn off Spotlight, you need to modify the hostconfig file in the Unix /etc directory. In particular, change the line that reads SPOTLIGHT=-YES- to SPOTLIGHT=-NO-. Then restart your Mac. You should use this only as a temporary measure, as it disables virtually any type of search command that depends on Spotlight (normally not what you would want to do). To reverse the procedure, change the NO back to a YES and restart again. A third-party utility from Fixamac Software (www.fixamacsoftware.com), called Spotless, performs these changes for you automatically. Note: If your hostconfig file does not have a SPOTLIGHT entry, Spotlight is still probably on by default. In this case, you will need to add the complete line of text to get Spotlight to turn off.

Spotlight folders. There are folders named Spotlight in /System/Library and /Library. The folder in /System/Library contains .mdimporter packages that were created by Apple and included in Mac OS X. The /Library folder contains .mdimporter packages created by third-party applications. In some cases, an application's .mdimporter package may be contained within a Spotlight folder inside the application package itself (Delicious Monster's Delicious Library; www.delicious-monster.com) does this, for example). In brief, these .mdimporter packages contain the information needed for Spotlight to be able to search (and potentially use application-specific search criteria for) files created by the named application. Thus, Keynote.mdimporter is what allows Keynote to work with Spotlight. Ditto for QuickTime.mdimporter and QuickTime. In some cases, these .mdimporter packages may contain a file called schema.xml. These files contain the special search criteria for a given application; they are the items you would find listed when you select Other from the criterion pop-up menu (as covered in the main text).

Note: The text descriptions of these criteria do not always identify the application they work with. This can get confusing. You may, for example, select a criterion you think will apply to all applications when in fact it only works with a specific one.

Note: The schema for the built-in choices in Mac OS X are mainly contained in schema.xml and schema.strings files located within various frameworks in /System/Library/Frameworks and /System/Library/PrivateFrameworks.

SEE: • "Finding files: The find, locate, and mdfind commands," in Chapter 10, for more on more on mdls and mdfind commands.

Services

As noted in the previous section, the application menu contains an item called Services. From its hierarchical menu, you can select an assortment of actions to be applied to the currently selected text, content, files, or folders. The options that appear (and whether they actually work within a given application) depend on the Services support of the currently active application. For example, although Services work by default in Cocoa-based applications, in Carbon applications the developer must manually code support for Services into the application. In addition, some Services only work in certain applications. (For example, an item that manipulates text might not be active in an application that does not permit any text editing.) An item that does not work for a given application will be either absent from the menu or dimmed.

The Finder's Services options include Make New Sticky Note, Open URL, Mail, and more. If you select some text and then choose the Service called Search with Google, the Google Web site will be launched in Safari, with your currently selected text as the search term. Other interesting options include Speech (to speak selected text) and Summarize (a fascinating feature that condenses the selected text to a brief—but surprisingly accurate—summary, which it displays in a separate process called SummaryService, located in /System/Library/Services).

Another service—available if you install the Developer software (as covered at the end of this chapter)—is FileMerge, which allows you to compare the contents of two documents and report the differences (if any). This can be useful for comparing two versions of the same text document, for example. Third-party software may also add items to the Services menu (Startly's QuicKeys [www.startly.com]and Rainmaker's Spell Catcher [www.rainmakerinc.com] are two such examples).

To get an idea of using Services beyond the Finder, open a document in TextEdit, select a paragraph of text, and from the TextEdit menu select Services. Now select Make New Sticky Note. The Stickies application will launch, and the selected paragraph will appear in a new note.

Troubleshooting Services. Beginning with Mac OS X 10.2.6 and later fixed in Panther, a bug existed in which having more than 70 Services (the number seems to vary depending on the installed software) caused the Services submenu to fail in some applications. Unfortunately, avoiding this bug could be tricky because it's not easy to figure out exactly how many Services you have. Mac OS X provides a number of Services by default, many applications provide Services, and you may have manually installed third-party Services packages. For example, one extremely useful set of third-party Services, WordService.service, provides more than 30 new text-related Services. Many users found that installing WordService.service "broke" their Services menu, while other users had no problems. In the end it was determined that the problem was not due to WordService.service itself but rather to the fact that for some users, these 30-plus new Services pushed them over the more-than-70 number, thus "breaking" their Services menus.

As a general quick fix, if you are having a problem with a Service, or one that you believe may be related to a Service, go to the /System/Library/Services or ~/Library/Services folder, locate the offending Service, and remove it. Then log out and back in.

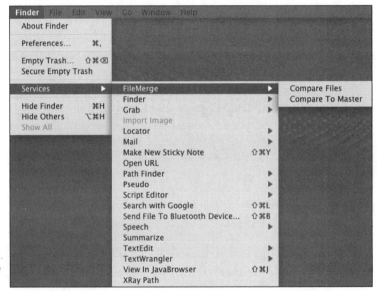

Figure 2.22

A list of Services with FileMerge selected.

SEE: • **"Technically Speaking: Understanding Services," in Chapter 4, for more details on this feature.**

Menu Extras

Menu Extras (sometimes called *menulets*) are the items that appear on the right side of the menu bar. They remain, regardless of which application is currently active. The Extra itself is typically an icon: Simply click the icon to reveal its menu options.

Common Menu Extras provided by Mac OS X or Apple software include the following: Volume (when clicked, it reveals a slider that allows you to adjust speaker volume), Displays (used to change your display resolution and color depth), and iChat (used to select your current iChat status). Other Extras indicate the current date and time, a laptop's battery status, an AirPort card's signal strength, whether your dial-up modem is currently connected, and more.

A few Menu Extras appear by default when you install Mac OS X. For the rest, you need to select an option to enable them. Some items are only relevant (and only accessible) if you have the appropriate hardware. For example, the Battery Extra will be available on notebooks but not on desktop Macs. The AirPort extra is available only if you have an AirPort card installed.

Enabling or disabling Menu Extras. In most cases, you add or remove Extras by selecting an option in the relevant System Preferences pane. (I discuss System Preferences a bit later in this chapter.) To add the Displays Extra, for example, you check the box for "Show displays in menu bar" in the Displays pane of System Preferences. To remove the Extra, uncheck the box. Similarly, to activate the Clock Extra, go to the Clock pane of the Date & Time System Preferences pane and check the box next to "Show the date and time," then click the View in: Menu Bar radio button. Available in Panther and later is a menu bar item for Classic, which you access by checking the "Show Classic status in menu bar" item in the Classic System Preferences pane.

You can also remove any Extra by holding down the Command key and dragging the Extra's icon off the menu bar. You can rearrange the left-to-right order of Extras by clicking an Extra icon with the Command key held down and dragging the icon to the desired location.

Most Menu Extras files are located in the /System/Library/CoreServices/Menu Extras folder. The items there all have a .menu extension. Thus, the Volumes Extra is called Volume.menu. If you cannot locate the check box for adding a specific Extra to the menu bar, go to this folder. Drag the desired .menu file from this folder to the menu bar (or simply double-click the Extra) and the Menu Extra will appear. The Eject Extra is one that needs to be enabled in this way (that is, it's not accessible via System Preferences). This only works, however, if your Mac supports the feature referenced by the Extra. You cannot, for example, add the AirPort Extra to the menu bar of a Mac that does not have an AirPort card installed.

Note: In early versions of Mac OS X, .menu items may appear as folders in the Finder. In Panther or later, they are likely to appear as documents identified as MenuExtra plug-ins. In either case, they are actually packages. Thus, even if they look like folders, you'll find that if you double-click them, they do not open a new window (as folders would) but instead launch. You can access their contents by using the Show Package Contents contextual-menu item. In Panther and later, this is most easily accomplished by clicking the .menu item and then choosing the command from the Actions menu.

Note: When VoiceOver is enabled (in the Universal Access System Preferences pane), some items may appear twice in the Apple menu. This is not exactly a bug. It happens so that VoiceOver can be used with the Apple menu.

SEE: • **"Understanding Image, Installer Package, and Receipt Files," in Chapter 3, for more on packages.**

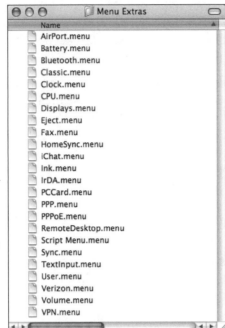

Figure 2.23

Top, *the contents of Tiger's Menu Extras folder;* bottom, *the Menu Extras selected to display in my menu bar. From left to right, these are: Keychain, Bluetooth, AirPort, Battery, Volume, Input (from the International System Preferences pane), and Date & Time.*

Some Menu Extras are stored in locations other than the Menu Extras folder. One example is Keychain.menu, used to access some of the features of the Keychain Access application. This menu is hidden within the Keychain Access application package. To view it, use the Show Package Contents command for Keychain Access and go to Contents/Resources. (See "Keychain Access," later in this chapter, for more on using this Extra.) You can also enable the menu from within the Keychain Access application.

Check the following Apple Knowledge Base document for a complete list of all Mac OS X Menu Extras, their locations, and how to enable them: http://docs.info.apple.com/article.html?artnum=75466. Although the list was originally written for Mac OS X 10.2, much of the information still applies.

TAKE NOTE ▶ Eject Options

Mac OS X offers numerous choices for ejecting and unmounting devices (such as CDs, DVDs, and external hard drives).

Eject Menu Extra. You can install and use the Eject Menu Extra (located in /System/Library/CoreServices/Menu Extras). Select an optical drive listed here, and its tray will open (regardless of whether it's empty or contains media).

Eject key. You can use the Eject key on the Apple Pro keyboard (F12 on other Apple keyboards) to eject the internal CD/DVD tray. If you have a desktop Mac that includes two internal optical drives, press Option-Eject to select the second drive.

Note: When using F12, you need to hold down the key for a few seconds before it will eject the media. This is to prevent an accidental pressing of the key resulting in an eject. You will know you've held it long enough when a translucent Eject symbol appears on the screen.

Finder's Eject command. You can add the Eject item to the Finder's toolbar (via the Finder's Customize Toolbar command). This item works similarly to the Eject command in the Finder's File menu. However, unlike the Menu Extra, the toolbar item ejects, opens the tray of, or unmounts virtually any device, including a hard drive. The simplest way to use this option is to open the Computer window, click the icon for the item you want to eject, and then click the Eject button. If the item cannot be ejected (for example, if it's the startup volume), the Eject button (and File menu command) will be dimmed.

Note: When you eject one partition of a drive, all other partitions also get unmounted (except for the startup partition, of course).

iTunes and DVD Player. iTunes and DVD Player both include an Eject button for CD/DVD drives.

Disk Utility. You can mount, unmount, or eject volumes from the Option menu in Disk Utility.

Third-party Menu Extras. Some items in the Extras region of the menu bar may come from third-party software. Typically, these are installed when you install the associated software, and some may appear only when the application is open and active. In some cases, there may just be a Menu Extra equivalent with no associated application. QuicKeys and StuffIt Deluxe are two examples of software that include Menu Extras. However, you will not find their Menu Extra files in Mac OS X's Menu Extras folder (it only contains Extras that are part of Mac OS X). Instead, you'll find them with the application software. For example, StuffIt Deluxe's MagicMenu.menu is located in the same folder that contains the StuffIt Deluxe application.

SEE: • "Technically Speaking: Third-Party Menu Extras Not Welcome in Mac OS X," below, for related information.

TECHNICALLY SPEAKING ▶ **Third-Party Menu Extras Not Welcome in Mac OS X**

Starting with Mac OS X 10.2, Apple has reserved menu-bar real estate for itself. Thus, some non-Apple Menu Extras that predate Jaguar no longer function. The good news is that you can re-enable many of these banned Menu Extras via a utility called Menu Extra Enabler, by Unsanity (www.unsanity.com/haxies), which is installed in the InputManagers folder of the ~/Library folder. For the record, Apple warns against using this utility, stating, "Apple does not recommend, endorse, or provide technical support for use of such solutions or for complications arising from the use of such solutions." However, I believe Apple is blowing smoke here: There appears to be no harm in doing this, and should a problem occur, you can always change your mind and disable the utility.

Some developers have found their own way around Apple's prohibition. In these cases, they get menus to appear without using the Menu Extras technology. For example, a menu may get added when the application is launched. To get the menu to appear automatically at login, you must add the software to the Login Items list.

System Preferences

The System Preferences utility provides a central location from which you can set up or customize a variety of Mac OS X features. In most cases, these features are not linked to a particular application and are not accessible by any other means. In some cases—especially with background applications and applications that don't otherwise include their own menus—this window is also where you're likely to find an application's preferences settings. Preferences are organized by topic; each set of related preferences is found in what is called a *preference pane*.

Figure 2.24

The System Preferences window.

You can access System Preferences from a variety of locations. The System Preferences Dock icon is probably the most common way. You can also choose System Preferences from the Apple menu or double-click the System Preferences application icon in the Applications folder. Whichever method you choose, you wind up in the same place.

System Preferences overview

After launching System Preferences for the first time, which displays icons for all the available panes, check out the View menu. In addition to a list of all System Preferences panes, you'll find the following four commands (at the top of the menu): Show All Preferences (Command-L), Organize by Categories, Organize Alphabetically, and Search—these commands refer to the display of panes. The Categories option is the default. Experiment to see which of the two organization methods you prefer. Clicking an icon switches the System Preferences display to that particular pane and allows you to access the settings contained in that pane.

New in Tiger is the Search feature. By typing in a few words related to the setting you're looking for, Mac OS X's Spotlight feature will determine which preference pane (or panes) most likely contains those settings. For example, if you type password, you'll get a pop-up list of topics containing the word *password*, and the Security, .Mac, Network, and Accounts icons are highlighted.

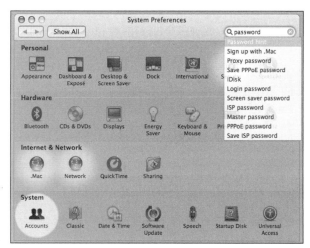

Figure 2.25

The System Preferences Spotlight search on the word password.

At the top of the System Preferences window is the toolbar. However, unlike many toolbars, the System Preferences toolbar in Tiger cannot be customized and contains only three options: Back and Forward buttons to navigate between panes you've accessed; a Show All button that returns the System Preferences display to the list of all panes (listed either alphabetically or by category, as per your selection); and the search field.

The remaining portion of the window lists all of the preference panes. If you've chosen to sort them by category, you see the following: Personal, Hardware, Internet & Network, and System. There may also be a fifth category called Other, which is used for third-party panes not installed by Mac OS X. As mentioned above, click any icon, and the window shifts to a pane showing that particular set of preferences. To go to another preference pane, choose its name from the View menu, type a search query in the search field, or click the Show All button and select the desired icon from the full display.

Tip: To use the keyboard to quickly open any System Preferences pane from the Show All view, press Tab until the desired icon is highlighted, and then press the spacebar to open the pane.

All the panes installed by Mac OS X are located in the PreferencePanes folder of /System/Library. Third-party panes may be installed in the PreferencePanes folder of the Library folder at the root level of your drive—which makes them available to all users—or in the PreferencePanes folder in the Library folder in your home directory (which limits their use to your account).

Some of the preferences can be set only by administrative users. If you're not an administrator, either these options will be dimmed or you will receive an explanatory message when attempting to access them.

System Preferences locked? Some System Preferences panes, such as Network and Accounts, have a padlock icon in their lower left corner. If this icon is locked, you cannot make changes to the pane's settings. To unlock it, click the icon and enter your admin-level user name and password when requested. To lock a pane that is unlocked, click the padlock icon.

If you unlock one pane, you unlock them all—unless you selected the option in the Security pane that reads, "Require password to unlock each secure system preference."

Following are brief descriptions of all the standard System Preferences panes, by category. Some of these are covered in more detail in subsequent chapters (when I explore the topics for which they're used). For additional information, from the Help menu choose System Preferences Help.

Personal

System Preferences panes in the Personal category include the following:

Appearance. This is where you set a variety of basic preferences relating to the look and feel of Mac OS X, such as the color of buttons and highlighted text. (Font-smoothing settings are discussed in more detail in Chapter 4, in "Font smoothing.")

Mac OS X 10.3 and later provides a check box that allows you to "Minimize when double clicking a window title bar." This option is on by default, but you can turn it off. This feature is vaguely similar to the WindowShade feature of Mac OS 9, which "rolled up" a window into its title bar when you double-clicked the title bar. In Mac OS X, with this box checked, double-clicking the title bar of a window instead minimizes the window into the Dock. (In most versions of Mac OS X, Option–double-clicking the title bar of any Finder window causes all currently open windows to be minimized.)

For those of you who want the WindowShade feature back, there's a great alternative: the WindowShade X shareware System Preferences pane, available from Unsanity (www.unsanity.com).

Dashboard & Exposé. This pane contains settings for two related, although quite different, aspects of Mac OS X.

- **Exposé.** Exposé, which debuted in Panther, lets you use a function key (or other user-defined key combinations, or even a *hot corner*, which is activated when the pointer is moved to that corner of the screen) to temporarily display all of your open windows simultaneously (in reduced sizes so they don't overlap). When you're in this view, the name of each window appears as you move the pointer over the window. Click any window, and it becomes the new active window as all other windows return to their original positions (ending the Exposé display). As you can imagine, this can be a great convenience when you have many open overlapping windows. This default behavior is Exposé's "All windows" mode.

  You can also set Exposé to show only windows belonging to the current active application ("Application windows" mode) or to move *all* windows out of the way, showing only the Desktop and its contents ("Desktop" mode). By default, the F9, F10, and F11 keys, respectively, are used for these three functions.

  Note: If you click-hold an item before invoking Exposé or in the middle of an Exposé session, the item remains in your view and can be dragged to any window in the Exposé display. Just release the mouse button when you've moved or copied the item to the new location.

- **Dashboard.** Dashboard is a new feature in Tiger. You can activate it by clicking the Dashboard icon in the Dock. This brings another layer—called the Dashboard—onto the screen, overlaying existing windows. The Dashboard contains a number of useful "one-trick-wonder" applications that provide services such as a mini-address book, a calculator, a weather reporter, a dictionary, an iTunes controller, Stickies, and much more. These applications, called *widgets*, are the kind of quick-reference apps that you're likely to need to use for only a few seconds or so; when you're done, you press the Dashboard keyboard shortcut (or access its hot corner) again and the Dashboard disappears. (You can also click any "blank" area of the screen to dismiss the Dashboard.)

TAKE NOTE ▶ Dashboard Usage and Tips

Here are some tips on using Dashboard that may not be immediately apparent (or, in some cases, not apparent at all!):

- When the Dashboard is activated (typically when you click the Dashboard icon in the Dock or press an F-key shortcut), all your previously opened widgets become visible. You can customize the layout of these active Widgets by dragging them around the screen.

- When the Dashboard is active, an Add (+) icon appears at the bottom left of the screen. If you click the plus icon, a *widget bar* appears at the bottom of the screen, listing all of the widgets installed in one of the Widgets folders (see below). To add one to the Dashboard, simply click it. In fact, you can add the same widget twice, thus allowing you, for example, to have two Weather widgets open at the same time describing the weather in two different locations.

  When the widget bar is visible, the + icon becomes an X icon. Click it to close the bar.

- Most widgets have a "back side"—providing more information about the widget or even settings to customize the widget—accessible via a small *i* button somewhere on the widget's face.

- When you download a widget from the Web via Safari, you will likely get a warning message stating that the widget is an application and asking if you are sure you want to download it. This is a security precaution, as covered more in "Downloaded widgets and security" in Chapter 9.

- Installed widgets are typically stored in ~/Library/Widgets. To install a new widget that did not get automatically placed in the ~/Library/Widgets folder, drag it there yourself.

  Note: Widgets preinstalled by Mac OS X are located in /Library/Widgets.

- You can run a widget not installed in a Widgets folder (such as a widget on your Desktop) simply by double-clicking it. Mac OS X will ask you if you want to install it; if you do, it will automatically be moved to ~/Library/Widgets. The Dashboard will appear, and the new widget will launch inside a "testing" area. You can then confirm that you want to keep the new widget
  or choose to delete it.

- Most open widgets can be closed by clicking the X icon that appears when the widget bar is visible. If no X is visible, which typically happens if the widget bar is not visible, hold down the Option key and the X should appear when you move the pointer over the widget.

- Starting in Mac OS X 10.4.2, you can use the Widgets widget to disable or delete widgets. Access this widget by clicking either the Widgets icon in the widget bar or the Manage Widgets button that appears just above the bar, to the right of the X icon. This widget manager presents you with a list of all installed widgets. From here, you can enable/disable any widget by toggling the check box to the left of its name. A disabled widget is removed from the widget bar, although it remains in ~/Library/Widgets. By clicking the Delete (–) button to the right of a widget, you are prompted to move the widget from the Widgets folder to the Trash. (Note: You are not given the option to delete widgets installed as part of Mac OS X.)

continues on next page

TAKE NOTE ▶ Dashboard Usage and Tips *continued*

Alternatively, in any version of Mac OS X 10.4, to remove a widget (that you have installed yourself) from the widget bar, go to the ~/Library/Widgets folder. Locate the widget you want to get rid of and drag it out of the folder; if you want to delete the widget completely, drag it to the Trash.

You can also manage widgets via third-party utilities. For example, Downtown Software House's Widget Manager (www.downtownsoftwarehouse.com) allows you to enable, disable, or remove any widget via a System Preferences pane. You can also use it to reload the entire Dashboard. Marcel Bresink's TinkerTool (www.bresink.de/osx/TinkerTool.html) is another useful utility for modifying Dashboard; for example, you can use it to disable Dashboard entirely.

- Having problems getting a widget to work properly? Try reloading it. To do so, click anywhere on the widget to select it and then press Command-R. Watch the neat animation as it reloads!

- Do you have a frozen widget that will not even reload? If so, you can force-quit it (a procedure described in more detail in Chapter 5). Unfortunately, individual widgets do not appear in the Force Quit window (as accessed from the Apple menu). However, they do appear as separate processes in Activity Monitor. If a widget appears frozen, you can force-quit it in Activity Monitor.

  To quit and restart all widgets at once, force-quit the Dock in Activity Monitor. This works because the Dock is the parent process of all widgets.

- To entirely disable the Dashboard (perhaps to conserve memory if you rarely or never use Dashboard), launch Terminal and type `defaults write com.apple.dashboard mcx-disabled -boolean YES`. Then open Activity Monitor and force-quit the Dock (see Chapter 5 for how to do this, if needed). This will relaunch the Dock with the change in effect. To undo the change, enter the same command in Terminal, except change YES to NO. Relaunch the Dock again.

- If you have a favorite widget, perhaps you would like to make it available even when Dashboard is not active. Happily, you can do this. First, you have to modify the preferences (.plist) file for Dashboard (as described in general terms in Chapter 4). Specifically, launch Terminal and type `defaults write com.apple.dashboard devmode YES`. This enables the *debug* mode for Dashboard (primarily intended to provide features that assist developers in testing widgets). Next, log out and log back in. Now, activate Dashboard and start dragging the widget you wish to "move out" of Dashboard. While still dragging the widget, deactivate Dashboard (by pressing the Dashboard F-key, F12 by default). If you did all of this correctly, the widget you were dragging should be accessible on the Desktop, even without Dashboard active. (The third-party utility Amnesty Widget Browser, from Mesa Dynamics [www.mesadynamics.com], provides this functionality without your having to use Terminal.)

- Widgets are written in HTML and JavaScript, the languages of Web pages. This makes them much easier to create than traditional applications. Anyone who can create a Web page can learn how to create a widget.

You use the Dashboard & Exposé System Preferences pane to modify the keys used to invoke these functions, as well as the hot corners, if any, used to activate them. The screen corner options can also be set to start or stop Mac OS X's screen saver.

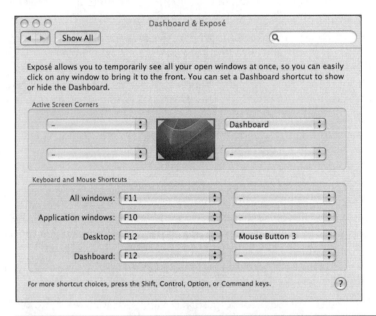

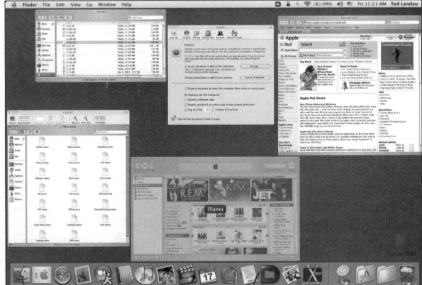

Figure 2.26

Top, *the Dashboard & Exposé System Preferences pane;* bottom, *the Mac display with Exposé activated (and the pointer over the iTunes window).*

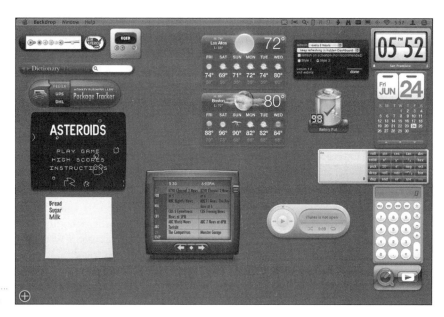

Figure 2.27

Widgets on display.

Desktop & Screen Saver. You use this pane to set the Desktop background and to select a screen-saver module. Note that if you want to require a password for the computer to wake up from a screen saver, this option is located separately in the Security System Preferences pane.

Dock. I covered this pane previously in this chapter under "Dock preferences: Customizing the Dock."

International. This pane includes options for adjusting the language and format capabilities of your Mac to match conventions used in different countries. It contains three main tabs:

- **Formats.** In this pane, you can change number, time, and date formats. Selecting a region from the Region pop-up menu automatically sets all formats to default values for that region; however, if you don't like the defaults for your region, you can customize them via the Customize buttons and Calendar and Currency pop-up menus. (In the Customize dialogs, you can create your own format by typing and dragging format elements into the field at the top of the dialog.)

- **Language and Input Menu.** You use these panes when setting up a Mac to work with foreign languages. These options determine the language used for menus and dialogs. The order of languages in the Languages pane tells Mac OS X your preferred order of language support. For example, if you move Español to the top of the list, and place English second, applications that provide Spanish support will use Spanish; those that don't will use English. (Keep in mind that to switch languages within third-party software, the developer must have built in the needed support.) The Input Menu pane lets you choose which keyboard layouts appear in the input menu; you can switch between keyboard layouts using the menu or a keyboard shortcut. This is also where you access Keyboard Viewer and Character Palette.

SEE: • **"Working with Fonts," in Chapter 4, for more on the Language and Input Menu options of the International System Preferences pane.**

Security. As its name implies, this System Preferences pane combines several options relating to the security and safekeeping of your Mac.

- **FileVault.** In the top half of the Security pane are the controls for Mac OS X's FileVault feature, available in Mac OS X 10.3 Panther and later.

  Enabling FileVault creates an encrypted version of your entire home directory (using Advanced Encryption Standard with 128-bit keys [AES-128]). The purpose of FileVault is to protect the data in your home directory in the event that your computer is lost or stolen. With FileVault enabled, it will be virtually impossible for anyone to access the encrypted files (regardless of their file-recovery tools)—unless they have your account password or your Mac's *master password*. (Note: This also assumes you are not logged in to your account, as covered more in "Technically Speaking: Inside FileVault," later in this chapter.)

  Before you enable FileVault on an account for the first time, you must set a master password. To do this, click the Set Master Password button. This password is intended as a safety net, in case you (or any other user) forget your own login password. With the master password, you can unlock any FileVault account on the computer. Thus, the security value of the FileVault protection is essentially eliminated if unauthorized people know the master password, so only administrators on the computer should be given it. Once a master password is set, the button reads Change; you can then click it to change the password. However, you can change the password only if you know the old password. If you forget the old password, there is no method, even as an administrative user, to reset and start over.

  After creating a master password, to enable FileVault, do the following:

  1. Click the Turn On FileVault button. This brings up a dialog that states: "You are now ready to turn on FileVault protection." The reminder of the dialog provides warning information about this process.

  2. Decide whether or not to click the "Use secure erase" button at the bottom of the dialog (as covered in the "Technically Speaking: Inside FileVault" sidebar, later in this chapter).

  3. Click the Turn On FileVault button.

     You are now logged out. A FileVault window appears; it is similar in appearance to the Login window. FileVault creates the encrypted version of your home directory and deletes the unencrypted files. When the process is complete (and it may take quite a while), you are allowed to log back in.

  4. After logging in again, if you return to the Security System Preferences pane, the Turn On FileVault button will now read Turn Off FileVault. Click it to reverse the process, if and when desired.

With FileVault enabled, the icon for your home directory changes from a house icon to a house icon with a combination lock inside. Your home directory is now encrypted. In most cases, however, you won't notice any difference while you're logged in. All files appear in the Finder just as if they weren't encrypted, and the Finder automatically decrypts them as needed—transparently and speedily behind the scenes. Ideally, you should not notice any delay due to these processes.

Note: To enable FileVault, you need administrative authorization as well as the affected user's login password. Non-administrative users will be prompted to enter both passwords when enabling FileVault.

Note: The same FileVault options appear in the Security section of each user's account in the Accounts System Preferences pane.

SEE: • **"Technically Speaking: Inside FileVault," for more details about this feature, including recommendations about "Use secure erase."**

Figure 2.28

The Security System Preferences pane.

Figure 2.29

The FileVault dialog. Note the "Use secure erase" option at the bottom left.

- **The rest.** The bottom half of the Security pane includes options for set-ting whether a password is required when waking your Mac (including from a screen saver set in Desktop & Screen Saver) and whether a pass-word is needed to unlock secure System Preferences (ones that require administrative status).

  Note: Requiring a password to "wake" from a screen saver is a relatively weak form of security. For example, any administrative user with an account on your Mac can use his or her name and password, rather than yours, to wake a screen effect activated by you. That user is then returned to *your* Desktop, just as if the screen effect had never been activated. Of course, administrative users can access your account in other ways as well; I just wanted to make it clear that this is a far-from-bulletproof form of a security.

  The Security pane is also where you choose "Disable automatic login." Automatic login is enabled in the Login Options section of the Accounts System Preferences pane for a selected user. When that user starts or restarts his or her computer, he or she is automatically logged in (that is, without seeing the Login window or having to enter a password). When you disable this option here, it is similarly disabled in the Accounts pane.

  You can also choose to have your Mac automatically log out—returning to the Login window—after a user-defined period of inactivity.

  Finally, the last option in the Security pane is "Use secure virtual memory." With this option disabled, it's possible—though not very likely, especially if you're a home user—for someone to surreptitiously obtain sensitive information that has been temporarily stored in Mac OS X's virtual-memory swap files. With this option selected, your swap files are encrypted, closing this security hole.

TECHNICALLY SPEAKING ▶ Inside FileVault

The following provides details about what happens when you turn FileVault on or off—includ-ing numerous caveats about its use.

Turning FileVault on for your account. When you turn on FileVault for your account and log back in to your account, the following changes occur:

- An alias with the name of your home directory is created in the same Users folder where your unencrypted home directory would otherwise be. If you select Show Original from the contextual menu of the alias, you will be taken to the Computer window. You will not see an original directory there, however.

- If you go to the /Users directory, you will find an invisible folder named *.username* (that is, the name of your home directory but preceded by a period). One quick way to see this item is to launch Terminal and type ls -a /Users (see Chapter 6 for more on how to view invisible items). If you double-click this folder, you will find a file inside called *username*.sparseimage. This is the encrypted version of your home directory—it is in fact a disk image, much like one you can create using Disk Utility (as discussed later in this chapter). This file gets updated every time you change the contents of your home directory.

continues on next page

TECHNICALLY SPEAKING ▶ Inside FileVault *continued*

FileVault on for other accounts. What if FileVault was turned on for an account other than the one that is currently logged in? What do you see when you look inside the other user's home folder (assuming the user is not logged in at the moment) from within your own account? You see a single file, called *username*.sparseimage, that represents the entire encrypted home directory of the user. (If you go up one level to the Users folder, you will find a folder with the name of the user, as expected.) If you double-click the user's encrypted image file, a dialog appears asking you to enter a password. If you enter the login password of the user, the home directory will mount as if it were an external volume. You will now have complete access to all of that user's files.

However, if the other user is logged in at the same time as you (via Fast User Switching), you will see an alias for his or her home directory. You will not be permitted to access its contents (other than the user's Public Folder, as expected).

Turning FileVault off. When you turn off FileVault for your account, the encrypted disk image is mounted; its contents are moved back to a new user folder inside /Users; and then the disk image is deleted—basically, your drive returns to its state prior to using FileVault.

FileVault and Public folders. The Public folder in your home directory is intended to be available to any user who has network access to your computer, even if you are logged out. No password is needed to access this folder. However, if your account has FileVault enabled, access to this folder is denied. The only way to provide such access is either to turn off FileVault or be logged in to your account.

FileVault and Secure Erase. If you enable the "Use secure erase" option in the FileVault dialog, the files making up the unencrypted version of your home directory are securely erased (as opposed to being erased normally), just as is done with files when you choose the Secure Empty Trash command from the Finder's Finder menu.

If you select this option, it is critical that you not interrupt the subsequent encryption and secure-erase process. Doing so may prevent you from logging in to your account and may lead to a loss of files.

If you enable FileVault without a secure erase, a status message appears that tells you approximately how long the encryption process will take. If you enable the secure erase, this status message does not appear. Instead, you'll see a message that says simply, "Deleting old Home folder." It is at this point that you should not interrupt the process. Wait until it is done, even if it seems to be taking an unusually long time.

If you do interrupt the process, and can no longer log in to your account as a result, you will need to either log in via another account (and delete your now hopelessly corrupted account) or reinstall Mac OS X (you can use an Archive and Install option, but do not preserve user accounts). In either case, the data in your old account is now lost, unless you had a backup.

continues on next page

TECHNICALLY SPEAKING ▶ **Inside FileVault** *continued*

Forgot your password? If you forget your master password, all may not be lost. See "Take Note: Forgot Your Password?" in Chapter 5, for details.

More FileVault caveats. When deciding whether or not to enable FileVault, take note of the following:

- Your files are protected only if you're not logged in. That is, if a person steals your computer while you're logged in (such as when your Mac is asleep, but your account is logged in), he or she will have access to your home directory even if FileVault is on. The solution is to make sure you are logged out whenever you leave your computer unattended.

- With FileVault on, various other processes may have trouble accessing your home directory, especially when you're not logged in. These include accessing your files via file sharing, and backing up your data. There is no work-around for this other than to turn FileVault off.

- When backing up a volume, the home directory of each user who has enabled FileVault (except the currently logged-in user) will be encrypted as a single .sparseimage file (as described above). The entire file will need to be backed up, even if only one unencrypted file has changed and even if you have your backup utility set to only back up changed files. This can make the backup take much longer than would otherwise occur (and makes for very inefficient backups!).

- More generally, to facilitate recovering data from a backup, I recommend turning FileVault off for all user accounts on your drive, other than the one currently logged in, before backing up the entire drive.

- FileVault is not compatible with setups where you move your home directory to another volume. As described more in Chapters 3 and 6, moving your home directory is typically something you would do to improve performance or to allow you to erase and reinstall your drive without losing your home directory.

- If FileVault is enabled for your home directory, operations such as copying files to your Desktop from another volume may take significantly longer—despite Apple's claim that this should not be the case. The reason for this is that every file copied to your home directory has to be encrypted during the copy operation. The work-around here is to turn off FileVault.

- Encrypting a home directory requires creating a temporary file equal in size to the home directory. Thus, make sure you have enough free space to do this.

- If you have Fast User Switching turned on, you will not be able to open the home folder of a user who is also logged in and who has FileVault enabled. That user's home folder icon will be an alias and will appear with a Network icon. If you double-click it, you will get a message that states you do not have "sufficient access privileges."

- A user cannot turn FileVault on or off when more than one user is currently logged in via Fast User Switching.

- You should not attempt to delete an encrypted account until you turn FileVault off for the account.

continues on next page

TECHNICALLY SPEAKING ▶ Inside FileVault *continued*

- When logging out of an account for which FileVault is on, you may receive a message stating that Mac OS X wants to "reclaim unused space." In early versions of Panther, accepting this request could result in the loss of files in your home directory, including preferences files and even music files in your iTunes Library. Updating to Mac OS X 10.3.1 or later fixed this bug. In later versions of Panther (and now in Tiger), the message also only appears when reclaiming space is needed, instead of on every logout. However, a similar loss of data can still occur if you lose power or your Mac crashes during logout.

- Having FileVault enabled can reduce the performance of programs like iMovie and Final Cut. The solution is to either turn off FileVault (at least when using these multimedia applications) or move the document files for these programs to a location outside of your home directory.

Bottom line: Given all these caveats, I recommend *extreme caution* in deciding whether or not to use FileVault. If you're traveling with a laptop that includes sensitive data, FileVault makes sense. Otherwise, I'd probably skip it. In any case, always make a backup of your home directory, to an external media such as a CD-RW or DVD-R, before using FileVault for the first time.

Spotlight. I covered Spotlight earlier in this chapter; the Spotlight preference pane is where you customize Spotlight's search settings.

Hardware

CDs & DVDs. This pane is where you select default actions that occur when you insert a CD or DVD. When you insert a blank CD-R, for example, you can specify whether the Mac will do the following:

- "Ask what to do." (This option causes a dialog to appear when you insert a CD, from which you make your choice.)
- "Open Finder."
- "Open iTunes."
- "Open Disk Utility."
- "Open other application." (For example, Toast.)
- "Run script."
- "Ignore." (That is, do nothing.)

If you choose to have the blank CD-R open in the Finder, it directly mounts the disc with the name Untitled CD. If you decide you don't want to burn anything to the CD, you can choose Eject rather than Burn in the dialog that appears when you drag the CD icon to the Trash.

SEE: • "Burning discs: CDs and DVDs," in Chapter 6, for more details.

Figure 2.30

The CDs & DVDs
System Preferences
pane.

Displays. This pane is where you set the resolution and color depth of your monitor (via the Display pane) as well as select (or create) a ColorSync profile to match your display (via the Color pane).

If you have multiple displays, you also use this pane to select how the displays will work together. For example, will one display mirror the other, or will the displays act as one large Desktop area that spans both? (If the latter, you also use it to arrange the displays relative to one another so that Mac OS X knows where on one screen the pointer should appear when it moves off the edge of the other.)

Energy Saver. This is where you set the options that determine when the Mac goes to sleep and how it manages power-related settings.

If you are using a notebook Mac, the default view will show just two pop-up menus, one called "Settings for" and one called Optimization. The first lets you choose your preferred Optimization settings when using the power adapter and when using the battery. Those optimization choices include Better Energy Savings, Normal, Better Performance, and Custom. The default choice is Normal, which lets the Mac decide what it thinks is best to do at a given moment. Choosing Custom is the same as clicking the Show Details button, discussed below.

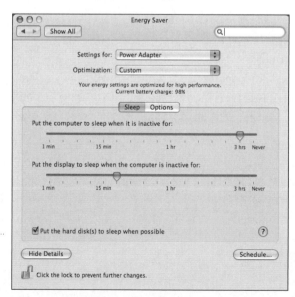

Figure 2.31

The Energy Saver
System Preferences
pane as selected in
my PowerBook.

The bottom of the Energy Saver pane also has a Schedule button; this button brings up a dialog that lets you select times for the computer to automatically start up, wake up, and/or shut down.

Finally, at the bottom of the pane is a Show Details button. Select this to get access to the full set of Energy Saver options. The button will then toggle to read Hide Details.

None of the above options appear on desktop Macs. For these models, the Details mode is the only available mode.

On desktop Macs or after selecting Show Details or Custom on laptop Macs, you will find the following two tabs:

- **Sleep.** In this pane, you can set customized times for display and computer sleep. You can also select whether the hard disk will sleep. If you're using a laptop, you can access the "Settings for" pop-up menu to create separate settings for Battery Power and Power Adapter.

- **Options.** This pane presents you with several options, including whether to have your Mac automatically restart after a power failure and, on some newer PowerBooks, whether or not to activate the automatic screen-brightness sensor. In addition, if you have a laptop, from the Processor Performance menu you can choose between Reduced and Highest. Choose Reduced if you want to maximize battery life. Note: The Power Mac G5 as well as newer PowerBooks and iBooks include an additional setting in this menu: Automatic. If you select this setting, performance shifts between Reduced and Highest modes, as needed, via a process called *slewing*. This allows for maximum speed when you're actively using your Mac, and reduced power (and extra battery life on laptops) when the Mac is mostly idle.

In this pane, if you are using a laptop, you can also enable "Show battery status in the menu bar." If you enable this option, you can then choose the Show command in the Battery menu to determine whether the battery status is viewed in terms of Icon Only, Time, or Percentage (where 100% equals fully charged). Note: If you select Percentage and the number gets stuck shy of 100% when charging (for example, remaining at 94% indefinitely when the laptop is plugged into AC power), the solution is to let the battery drain (to below 50%), then recharge; it should now go to 100%. (In Tiger, the battery-status menu also lets you switch between Optimization settings.) Tip: To go as long as possible before you need to recharge your laptop battery, minimize activities that drain battery power. For example, dim the screen to the lowest acceptable level, minimize use of the CD/DVD drive, and turn off AirPort and Bluetooth if you're not using them.

TAKE NOTE ▶ Sleep Problems

Computer *sleep* (or *deep sleep*) is the low-power mode in which the Mac appears to be off, except for the pulsing light on the Power button and/or on the monitor on desktop Macs—or similar locations on notebooks. If your Mac is not going to sleep as expected, the first thing to check is your Energy Saver settings: Make sure that automatic sleep is indeed selected for the time period you want.

No deep sleep. In certain cases, the Mac may refuse to enter deep sleep. Typically in such cases, the Mac's fan and possibly the hard drive remain on—even after you've selected Sleep from the Finder or waited for automatic sleep to occur. This is a form of sleep, but it is not deep sleep.

A common cause of this problem is a peripheral device that does not support deep sleep—such as a SCSI PCI card or a USB scanner. In some cases, the problem can be fixed by software or hardware updates (such as a firmware and/or driver update for a SCSI card). To determine whether such a fix is available, check the Web site for the vendor of the suspected hardware. (You can often determine the vendor via the Hardware section of the System Profiler window.) If your SCSI card or other peripheral was part of the original equipment from Apple, check with Apple regardless of vendor.

Otherwise, as a work-around for a peripheral device such as a scanner, simply disconnect the device and then reconnect it. Sleep will now likely work until the next time you use the device.

For devices you cannot easily disconnect, such as a SCSI card, you may be able to get around the problem by disabling the device's associated kext files (located in the /System/Extensions folder). For example, for a sleep problem caused by an Adaptec SCSI card, log in as a root user and disable all kext files with the word *Adaptec* in their names—either by moving them to a folder you create called "Extensions (disabled)" or by removing them from the System folder altogether. Alternatively, you can disable these files via a third-party utility such as Infosoft's MOX Optimize (http://fly.to/infosoft), eliminating the need to log in as the root user. The downside is that you will not be able to use the card (and thus any SCSI devices) once the extensions are disabled. However, if you only rarely need this capability, you can re-enable the extensions when you need them. After making a change here, restart your Mac to make sure the change takes effect.

In other cases, a sleep problem may be caused by a bug in Mac OS X itself and possibly also involve a conflict with third-party software. In early versions of Mac OS X 10.2.x, for example, enabling Personal File Sharing, Printer Sharing, or Internet Sharing (via the Sharing System Preferences pane) prevented automatic sleep as set by Energy Saver. Similarly, when you disconnected a FireWire or USB hard drive, the Mac would not go to sleep automatically after the idle period specified in Energy Saver.

To work around this, from the Apple menu choose Sleep, or disable the feature that's causing the problem, or restart the Mac (which may restore the automatic feature).

continues on next page

TAKE NOTE ▶ Sleep Problems *continued*

Some causes of this problem are eventually fixed with updates to Mac OS X. However, if the problem remains, the ultimate solution is to wait for and then get the update to the third-party software that fixes the problem.

Wake for administrators. The Options pane of Energy Saver includes an option to "Wake for Ethernet network administrator access." Note that this feature works only for computers connected to an Ethernet network; it does not work via AirPort. In addition, Apple states, "Applicable routers must be configured to allow directed broadcast of the wake-on-LAN (WOL) packet, also known as a *magic packet*. To remotely wake an eligible computer from sleep, use one of these applications: Apple Remote Desktop; Wake550, by Five Fifty Software; Wakeonlan."

Wake-from-sleep problems. There are a host of potential problems that can occur when waking from sleep—the most common of which is a crash, where the screen remains black, as described in Chapter 5.

SEE: • "Take Note: Miscellaneous Crashes," in Chapter 5, for advice on dealing with wake-from-sleep crashes and related problems.

TECHNICALLY SPEAKING ▶ Hard-Drive Sleep

You cannot set a specific time for hard-disk sleep from Energy Saver preferences in Mac OS X. Instead, your only option is to select "Put the hard disk(s) to sleep when possible." This uses a default setting of 10 minutes before spinning down the drive.

If you still want to regulate the timing for hard-drive sleep, however, you can do so via the `pmset` command, run as root in Terminal. To set a hard-drive sleep time to occur after 60 minutes of inactivity, for example, type `sudo pmset -a spindown 60`. You can use this command to spin down the hard drive before deep sleep is set to occur. The `sudo` command is needed because you must have root access to make this change. Spin-down settings changes work here even if you don't check the "hard-disk-to-sleep" box in Energy Saver.

For drives connected to your Mac after startup, spin-down may occur after 10 minutes even if the "hard-disk-to-sleep" box is not checked. In this case, type `sudo pmset -a spindown 0` to prevent any spin-down. Keep in mind, however, that this prevents spin-down for your startup drive as well. For more details on how this command works—including options for setting hard-drive sleep separately for battery (`-b`) and charger (`-c`) power on a laptop—type `man pmset`.

These settings are saved in a file called com.apple.PowerManagement.plist. In Panther and later, this file is located in /Library/Preferences/SystemConfiguration. As an administrator, you can make changes to this file by opening it in Property List Editor. For hard-drive sleep, change the value of Disk Sleep Time to the number of minutes you want until sleep occurs (to a maximum of 180).

continues on next page

TECHNICALLY SPEAKING ▶ **Hard-Drive Sleep** *continued*

For problems related to Energy Saver and sleep, a last resort is to delete this PowerManagement file entirely and restart. A new one with default settings will be created. In most cases, the problem will be fixed.

Note: If you have installed Tiger's Developer Tools software, you can accomplish these same changes via a utility called SpindownHD (located in /Developer/Applications/Performance Tools/CHUD/Hardware Tools).

SEE: • "Root Access" and "Preferences Files," in Chapter 4, for more on root access and using Property List Editor.

• "Using Unix to delete files," "Item cannot be placed in Trash or Trash cannot be emptied," and "Invisible Files: Working with Invisible Files," in Chapter 6, for related information.

Keyboard & Mouse. This pane is used mainly for adjusting keyboard and mouse settings. It has up to five main tabs:

• **Keyboard.** You can use this pane to set the Key Repeat Rate and Delay Until Repeat intervals. Laptop Macs have additional options. If you've got a PowerBook with a backlit keyboard, you can enable this feature and choose a "sleep" timer for it. In Mac OS X 10.3.3 and later, this pane also provides a new "Use the F1-F12 keys for custom actions" option. If it is selected, you will need to hold down the Function (Fn) key to use these keys for special system features (brightness, Exposé, volume, and so on); otherwise, the function keys will act as function keys. With this option disabled, the keys' behavior will be reversed.

  This pane has a very useful option called Modifier Keys. Click this button, and you'll see a dialog that lets you swap the functionality of four modifier keys: Caps Lock, Control, Option, and Command. This is handy if you're using a Windows-centric keyboard with your Mac, as the Windows (Command) and Alt (Option) keys are backward in that situation.

  On laptops, you'll also have the option to "Use the F1-F12 keys to control software features." With this option chosen, you can use the function (F) keys as standard keys; to access volume, brightness, and other hardware controls, you'll need to hold down the Fn key. (This option basically reverses the standard behavior.) Finally, PowerBooks that have an illuminated keyboard will also show settings to enable this feature and to turn the lighting off after a period of inactivity.

• **Trackpad.** (Only visible if your computer has a trackpad.) This pane is where you set tracking and double-click speed for your PowerBook or iBook trackpad. In addition, you can choose whether to use the trackpad itself (rather than just the trackpad button) for clicking and dragging. You can also choose to ignore accidental trackpad input—basically, any trackpad activity that occurs while you're typing—and to ignore the trackpad completely if a mouse is connected to your laptop.

- **Mouse.** (Only visible if a mouse is connected to your computer.) You can use this pane to set tracking and double-click speed for the device. If your mouse has a scroll wheel, you can also set the scrolling speed. In Tiger, you can swap the left and right buttons on a multi-button mouse—a nice option for left-handed users.

- **Bluetooth.** (Only visible if your Mac has Bluetooth functionality.) From here, you can set up a Bluetooth keyboard or mouse (and monitor the battery level if it's an Apple-branded model). You also have the option to allow Bluetooth devices to wake your Mac from sleep. These options work in conjunction with several other Bluetooth components of Mac OS X, including the Bluetooth System Preferences pane, Bluetooth Setup Assistant, and Bluetooth File Exchange. I sort out all the details in Chapter 8.

- **Keyboard Shortcuts.** In this pane, you can reassign the shortcut keys for any of Mac OS X's shortcuts. For example, if you want to change the shortcut for a screen capture from Command-Shift-3 to something else, you can do so. You can even create your own shortcuts for menu commands—simply click the Add (+) button; in the Application pop-up menu in the dialog that slides down, choose All Applications or a specific application, and then type your title and shortcut in the Menu Title and Keyboard Shortcut fields. (Note that the menu title should be the name of the menu command, spelled and punctuated exactly.) Finally, you can select how you want the Tab key to affect the keyboard "focus" in windows and dialogs. In particular, you choose whether it should be active for "Text boxes and lists only" or for "All controls."

Print & Fax. This is the System Preferences pane used for adjusting settings related to (surprise!) printing and faxing. For more on this pane, see Chapter 7.

Sound. This pane is where you select an alert sound and volume. It's also where you determine the audio input (microphone) and output (speakers) you're using. Finally, it allows you to enable or disable "interface sound effects"—the sounds Mac OS X makes when you perform actions in the Finder.

Note: There is no option in this preferences pane to record sounds from a microphone. You will need additional third-party software to do this.

Ink and Bluetooth. Some Hardware System Preferences—notably, Bluetooth and Ink—appear only if the required hardware is attached or preinstalled. To see and use the Ink handwriting-recognition pane, for example, you need to have a graphics tablet attached. To use Ink, you also need to install drivers for the tablet that are new enough to recognize the Ink software. Otherwise, even if the Ink pane appears, you won't be able to use it.

SEE: • "Using Bluetooth," in Chapter 8, for more on Bluetooth.

Internet & Network

.Mac. This pane is where you adjust settings related to Apple's optional .iMac service. It includes four main tabs:

- **.Mac.** In this pane, you enter your .Mac name and password (assuming you've signed up for .Mac). If you haven't signed up for the service, there is a Join Now button you can use to do so. (The Sign Up button reads Account Info if you've got an account and have entered your information.)

- **Sync.** In Panther and earlier, you set up iSync to synchronize .Mac-related data in the iSync application; in Tiger, you set such preferences, and initiate syncs, here. You choose which information—Safari bookmarks, iCal calendars, Address Book contacts, Keychains, and Mail accounts and other info—you want to sync, and then choose how often you want it synchronized (hourly, daily, weekly, manually, or automatically).

- **iDisk.** In this pane, you can check to see how much iDisk storage space you have left, determine the level of access allowed for your iDisk Public folder, and (in Mac OS X 10.3 and later) create a separate local copy of your iDisk. With this last option, you can make changes to your iDisk content locally—with no Internet delays (and without the need to be connected to the Internet)—and then have those changes updated to the actual iDisk later.

- **Advanced.** This pane lets you see which Macs are set up to synchronize data to your .Mac account. You can also use this pane to unregister a computer, which means it will no longer sync.

    SEE: • ".Mac System Preferences," in Chapter 8, for more details.

Network. This System Preferences pane is essential if you plan to use the Internet or access another computer (even just another Mac connected via an Ethernet cable). Whether you have devices connected via Ethernet, AppleTalk, or AirPort—and whether you use a dial-up modem, cable modem, DSL modem, or Bluetooth—you will need to configure this System Preferences pane.

SEE: • "Setting Up Network System Preferences," in Chapter 8, for more details.

QuickTime. This System Preferences pane is where you determine the settings for QuickTime Player (used to play multimedia files) and the QuickTime Plug-in that works with Web browsers (for example, to view movie trailers posted online) and other QuickTime-enabled applications. Apart from a few mentions in Chapter 11, I don't spend much time discussing QuickTime in these pages. The following, however, is a brief list of notable features:

- **Browser pane.** Check the "Save movies in disk cache" box to allow saving of movies that you play in your Web browser.

- **Streaming pane.** If you check the Enable Instant-On box, Internet streams, such as movie trailers, will begin to play immediately; however, this also makes them more susceptible to skips and stops, since it requires a steady stream of data. Obviously, the faster your overall connection, the better this will work—you should have a broadband connection for starters. For Instant-On to work effectively, the Transport settings (which you can configure via the Transport Setup pop-up menu in the Advanced pane) should be UDP and Port 554. (If you choose Automatic, these are likely to be the settings you will find selected.) You can also choose how "instantly" playback begins, using the slider. Completely disabling this option causes QuickTime to cache the stream before playback begins.

- **Advanced pane.** Click the MIME Settings button to see a list of all the different media formats supported by the QuickTime Plug-in. Note that the list includes AAC (Advanced Audio Coding encoding, which is a specific type of MPEG encoding). This compresses much more efficiently than formats such as MP3 while delivering "CD-quality" audio. With QuickTime 6.2 or later, you can listen to AAC files in iTunes 4.

Note: The QuickTime Player application itself is in the Applications folder. When you launch QuickTime Player, click the "Click here for more content" button to view a variety of QuickTime content available via the Internet.

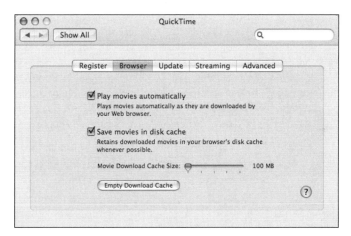

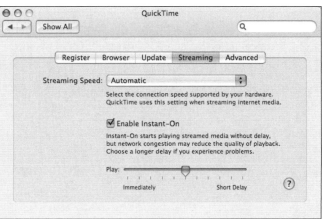

Figure 2.32

The QuickTime System Preferences pane: top, the Browser pane (whose settings determine what happens when you access QuickTime from a Web browser); bottom, the Streaming pane with the Enable Instant-On option selected.

Sharing. This pane is where you set the options for sharing access to your computer with other machines. You also set your Computer Name (and, via the Edit button, your Bonjour name—I talk about Bonjour in Chapter 8) here. This pane includes three main tabs:

- **Services.** Settings here are used to enable or disable various sharing services, such as Personal File Sharing, Personal Web Sharing, FTP Access, Remote Login, and Printer Sharing.

  For example, enabling Personal File Sharing makes it possible for other users to access your computer over a network, and enabling Printer Sharing allows you to share USB printers among several computers on your local network.

- **Firewall.** Settings here allow you to restrict incoming access to your computer to the ports specifically enabled in this pane. Thus, if you start the firewall, your computer will be accessible only via the ports with check marks next to them in this pane. This provides protection against unsolicited attempts to access your computer.

- **Internet.** Settings here allow you to share an Internet connection among several computers. You can select options, for example, to set up a Mac that has an AirPort card to share its Internet connection (obtained over Ethernet via cable modem, for example) with other AirPort-equipped Macs. This is often referred to as a Software AirPort Base Station; it bypasses the need for an actual AirPort Base Station. More generally, setups such as this can be used as an alternative to getting a hardware router. The main disadvantage, compared with having a router, is that the Mac must be on for other computers to have Internet access.

SEE: • "Printer Sharing," in Chapter 7, for more details on this feature.

  • "Setting Up System Preferences: Sharing," in Chapter 9, for more details on this System Preferences pane.

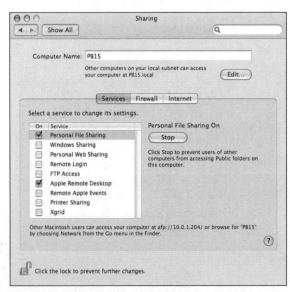

Figure 2.33

The Services pane of the Sharing System Preferences pane.

System

Accounts. This critical System Preferences pane seems to receive a redesign with each major new version of Mac OS X. The descriptions here apply to Mac OS X 10.4.x (Tiger).

Direct access to Mac OS X on your computer requires a user account. When you install Mac OS X, the Setup Assistant software requires that you set up a User account for yourself. This first account is set up, by default, for an administrative user. If you want to modify the data you entered, or if you want to add, delete, or modify additional user accounts, you do so via the Accounts System Preferences pane.

Each account created on your Mac has its own folder in the Users folder. The logged-in user's folder becomes the home folder (directory) for that session—an arrangement that allows each user to maintain customized preferences. This arrangement is also how Mac OS X determines each user's access privileges. If your computer has multiple users, you enter the name and password for your account when you log in (unless you assigned your account for automatic login).

In the left column of the Accounts pane is a list of all accounts currently set up on the system. The top account (labeled My Account) is for the currently logged-in user. In the examples discussed here, I will assume that this user is an administrator. You can always access most options for your own account (such as changing your password). However, an administrator can also access a few options for other accounts as well. Simply click the name of an account, and the settings in the right side of the pane shift to represent those of the selected user:

- **Password.** Each user is assigned a name, short name, password, and (optionally) password hint. You can modify these settings in the Password pane.

  The *short name* is a nickname or shortened version of the full name. When you create a new user, a new folder is created in the /Users directory, with the user's short name appearing as the folder name. The short name can be as many as 255 characters. When you create a new account, a short name is actually suggested *for you* by Mac OS X, and it's likely to be 8 characters long. You can accept this suggestion or replace it with your preferred short name. (Keep in mind that you're likely to have to enter this short name fairly often, especially as an administrator, so having a 255-character "short" name may be a bit of a hassle!)

  To change the password for your own account, click the Change Password button. You'll be asked to provide your current password, and then to provide and verify the new password. You can also enter a password hint. When viewing the pane for another user, this button changes to Reset Password.

This option is mainly useful if a user forgets his or her own password. If your account has administrative access, you simply provide and verify a new password—you don't need the user's old password. (Note: This is also a good reason to limit who has administrative access on your Mac.)

New in Tiger is easy access to Mac OS X's Password Assistant. Just click the key icon next to the New Password field; Password Assistant opens in a separate window. It can suggest passwords, of varying complexity, for you, or can tell you how secure the password you're considering is.

On the Password pane for your own account, you'll also see an Address Book Card Open button. Clicking this button opens Address Book to your own contact entry—the one designated as My Card).

Finally, this pane also includes an "Allow user to administer this computer" check box. Be cautious in giving other users administrative status. As an administrator, a user will have virtually the same access to the computer that you have, including the ability to access other users' data. The only exception is that the account of the original administrator (presumably you) cannot be modified by other administrators (though there may be bugs that allow you—or someone else—to circumvent even this exception).

- **Picture.** In this pane, you select a picture to be associated with your account. You can choose from among Apple's included pictures or browse for one of your own. If you have chosen to show the list of users at login, these pictures will appear next to each user's name.

- **Login Items** (called Startup Items in Panther). This pane is available only for the user currently logged in and viewing Accounts preferences. It provides a list of all processes and applications that automatically launch at login for that user. For example, if you have QuicKeys installed and want it to launch automatically at each startup, you would add it to this list. Some software automatically adds itself to the list when you install the software. Virex does this, for example, which is why the Virex application launches with each login.

  You can add or delete items from the list with the Add (+) and Delete (–) buttons at the bottom of the pane. If you see an item you don't recognize, pause the pointer over the item's name; a label will appear showing the complete path to the item's location on your hard drive. This should give you a better idea of where it came from.

  SEE: • **"Disabling login items" and "Take Note: Solving Problems with Login Items," in Chapter 5, for troubleshooting advice related to login items.**

Figure 2.34

The Accounts System Preferences pane: Login Items pane.

- **Parental Controls** (called Limitations in Panther). This pane is available only when an administrative user accesses the account settings of a "normal" (nonadministrative) user. From here, you can limit the type of access such users may have. For each topic area—Mail, Finder & System, iChat, Safari, and Dictionary—you can decide whether or not to limit access or functionality. For example, you can configure iChat and Mail so that the user can only "chat" or exchange e-mails with particular people. You can also limit the Finder with two options, Some Limits and Simple Finder. With Some Limits activated, you can decide whether a user is allowed to access System Preferences, modify the Dock, burn discs, and, if desired, you can limit what applications he or she can use. Simple Finder provides a simplified Dock that allows access only to those applications contained in the My Applications folder, which appears in the Dock. You determine which applications are in this folder by way of this Simple Finder option.

Figure 2.35

NetInfo Manager with the users:landau fields visible at the bottom of the window.

Near the bottom of the left column of the Accounts pane you'll see a Login Options button. (If the button is dimmed, you need to unlock the Accounts pane by clicking the padlock at the bottom of the window, providing your administrator user name and password when prompted.) If you click the Login Options button, the right side of the pane displays a set of options that apply regardless of who logs in. In particular, you can select from among the following options:

• **"Automatically log in as {*name selected from pop-up menu*}."** If you choose this option and select a user from the pop-up menu, Mac OS X will be automatically logged in to that account at startup, bypassing the Login window, where you would normally choose a user and enter that user's password. Obviously, you can set this item for only one user. (To bypass auto-login at startup, hold down the Shift key after seeing the gray startup screen and until the Login window appears.)

• **"Display login window as."** If you choose "Name and password" rather than "List of users," the names of users with accounts on your Mac will not be displayed. Instead, you'll be provided with a pair of blank boxes in which to enter a name and password. This offers a bit more privacy and security than showing the full list of users.

Note: If you have selected the "List of users" option, there may be times when you want to enter a login name not in the list (such as ">console" or "root," as described more in Chapter 4). If you have enabled the root user (again as described in Chapter 4), an Other option should appear in the Login window list, allowing you to do so. If the Other option does not appear, you are out of luck, until you log in and either enable the root user or shift to the "Name and password" option. In Panther there was another alternative: Press Option-Return and click the name of any listed user. This doesn't work in Tiger.

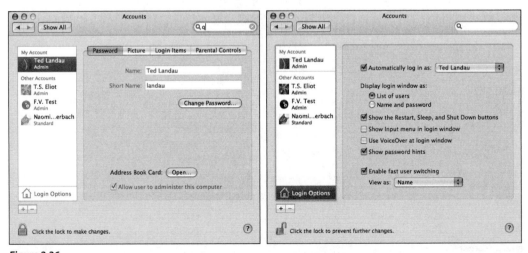

Figure 2.36

The Accounts System Preferences pane: left, my account with Password selected; right, the Login Options pane.

TAKE NOTE ▶ Adding or Deleting a User

To add a new account, simply click the Add (+) button at the bottom of the Accounts pane. A folder with the short name of the new account will be added to the Users folder. This is the home directory of the newly added user.

To delete an existing account, click the Delete (–) button. A message will appear giving you two options for deleting the account. If you click Delete Immediately, the account, including the entire user folder for that account, will be deleted on the spot. If you instead click OK, the message explains what will happen: The account will be deleted and the user folder for that user will automatically be converted to a disk-image file named {*deleted_user*}.img. This image will be stored in a Deleted Users folder located in the Users folder at the root level of the drive. (This Deleted Users folder is created automatically if you're deleting an account for the first time.) At any point, an administrative user can either open the disk image (to access files you may want to save) or delete the image file.

Important: *Never* attempt to move any folders (for active accounts) from the Users folder to another location. If you do, those accounts will no longer be accessible. Similarly, do not relocate the Users folder itself.

Figure 2.37

The message that appears when you select to delete an account from the Accounts System Preferences pane.

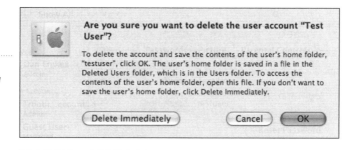

Figure 2.38

The user menu that appears when you enable Fast User Switching.

- **"Show the Restart, Sleep, and Shut Down buttons."** This item lets you show or hide these buttons in the Login window. Hiding them is, in essence, a security measure, used to limit access to these options when the Mac is in a public location.

- **"Show Input menu in login window."** With this option selected, the Input menu (which you configure in the International pane of System Preferences, as discussed earlier) will be displayed in the Login window. This is a useful option if you use a keyboard layout different from the default language you've selected for Mac OS X—you can choose your keyboard's layout from the Input menu and then use your keyboard to type your name and password.

- **"Use VoiceOver at login window."** This option enables Tiger's VoiceOver feature, which speaks relevant portions of the interface. For example, at the Login window, your Mac will speak the name of the highlighted user name (or the names of text fields); if you choose a user from the list of users, it will read the user name and say "Enter secure text" (that is, your password).

- **"Show password hints."** When this option is selected, if a user enters the incorrect password at login, the login window will display the user's password hint. If the user again enters the incorrect password, the Login window will request your Mac's Master Password; if you enter it correctly, you'll be allowed to provide a *new* password for the user.

- **"Enable fast user switching."** This option, added in Mac OS X 10.3, allows multiple users to log in at the same time and lets you easily switch between these logged-in user accounts without having to log out. This means, for example, that you and your spouse could both log in to the same Mac—using the *User menu*, which appears in the upper-right corner of the menu bar when this option is enabled—without either one of you having to log out.

  To switch to another account, you simply select that account from the User menu. If the to-be-switched-to account does not have a password (as set up in Accounts preferences), the switch occurs instantly. Otherwise, you will be requested to enter the user's password before the switch can occur.

  To log in a user not listed in the menu, or to return to the Login window (thus locking your account) without logging out, choose Login Window from the menu. This takes you back to the Login window without logging anyone out. You can use this to log in as the root user, for example, while keeping your own account logged in. Note that the Login window will display the words "Currently logged in" below the name of any currently logged-in user.

New in Tiger is a Fast User Switching "View as" pop-up menu; this menu lets you choose to display the User menu as a generic user icon, the current user's short name, or the current user's full name. The advantage to using the icon method is that it uses significantly less menu-bar real estate.

TAKE NOTE ▶ Problems with Fast User Switching

The ability to have more than one user logged in at a time is definitely cool. However, it also raises the possibility of problems that wouldn't occur with just a single user. These include the following:

- **Insufficient memory.** Multiple logged-in users mean that additional memory is being used—applications, including the Finder and other user-level services, are being run in multiple accounts at the same time. If you plan to use this feature regularly (especially for more than two users at a time), make sure you've installed sufficient physical memory. If everything starts to slow down, it means you don't have enough memory to support multiple logins.

- **Denied access.** A severe crash in one account may prevent access to other logged-in accounts, forcing you to restart the computer.

- **One user's error affects *all* users.** Because multiple users are sharing processes that load prior to login, an error by one user (such as one that causes the loss of an Internet connection) may similarly affect other logged-in users.

- **Single-account processes.** Some processes cannot be open in more than one account. One example of this is Classic: If you try to start Classic in one account while it is already running in another, you will get a message stating that you cannot do this.

- **Restart/Shut Down.** If you select to Restart or Shut Down while multiple users are logged in, you will get a message asking you to enter an admin name and password (authorizing the logging out of all users and thus permitting the restart or shutdown). This means that a non-admin user will not be able to restart or shut down if another user is currently logged in.

- **USB printing prohibition.** With some USB printers, you may find that only the first user to log in can print.

    SEE: • "Logging in as root," in Chapter 4, for related information.

    • "Restarting and shutting down with Fast User Switching enabled" and "Logging in as another user," in Chapter 5, for more on Fast User Switching.

    • The Classic chapter, online at Mac OS X Help Line (www.macosxhelpline.com), for more on Fast User Switching and Classic.

TAKE NOTE ▶ Accounts Problems

The following describes a couple of issues that may crop up when using the Accounts System Preferences:

- **User short name.** You cannot change the short name of any user (including yourself) from the Accounts System Preferences pane. If you need to change a user's short name, you must do so with NetInfo Manager. Launch NetInfo Manager and click the padlock icon (and then enter your password when requested): You now have permission to make changes. Once you've done this, you will need to change virtually *every instance* of the short name in the database to the new name.

For starters, in the Directory Browser choose "users" and then click the name you want to change. (For the name *tedmac*, for example, you would go to users:tedmac.) In the fields that now appear in the bottom area of the window, change every instance of the old name to the new name. Then, change the name listed in all groups of which the user is a member (such as groups:admin and groups:wheel). Because it's easy to overlook something in this process—and thus fail to get the change to work (or even mess things up so that *nothing* works)—and because there are other settings not included here that may be affected if you use such a procedure, I recommend not changing a user's short name unless it's absolutely necessary. Overall, it's easier to create a new account with the name you want to use and then transfer the files to that account.

Actually, the complete instructions for changing a short name are even more involved than I've suggested here. For a complete set of instructions, see the following Apple Knowledge Base document: http://docs.info.apple.com/article.html?artnum=106824. Another alternative is to use the utility ChangeShortName, available at www.macosxpowertools.com.

Whatever you do, *do not* try to change a short name by simply changing the name of the directory in the Users folder in the Finder. Assuming you have sufficient permissions to make the change, doing so can prevent subsequent login to the account!

- **Editing as the root user.** In one situation, my account mysteriously lost its administrative-user status. Because I was the only administrator on the system, no one else could log in and restore my status. Fortunately, I had previously enabled the root user account, which meant that I was able to log out of my account and then back in as a root user and access the Accounts System Preferences pane. From here, I was able to re-enable my administrative status.

SEE: • "Root Access," in Chapter 4, for more on root access.

• Chapter 5, for more on the Login window and startup issues in general.

• Chapter 9 for more on Accounts and file sharing.

Classic. This pane is used for settings related to running the Classic environment, which allows you to run Mac OS 9 from within Mac OS X. It includes three tabs:

- **Start/Stop.** In this pane, you select the Mac OS 9 System Folder to be used for Classic. You also launch Classic from here or quit Classic if it is already running. You can choose to add the Classic status menu to the menu bar.

- **Advanced.** This pane provides useful troubleshooting features, such as the option to disable extensions at startup or rebuild the Desktop.

- **Memory/Versions.** This pane provides a graphical display of running Classic applications and their memory use, similar to what you would see in the About This Computer window if you had booted into Mac OS 9.

    SEE: • **The Classic chapter, online at Mac OS X Help Line (www.macosxhelpline.com), for more details on these options, including the "Use Mac OS 9 preferences from your home folder" option (in the Advanced pane).**

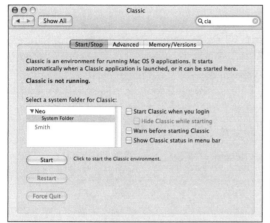 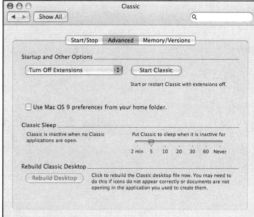

Figure 2.39

Left, *the Start/Stop pane of Classic System Preferences;* right, *the Advanced pane.*

Date & Time. This pane is where you set preferences for the date and time. It includes three tabs:

- **Date & Time.** In this pane, you can set the current date and time manually or elect to have it set automatically via a network time server. The automatic option makes sense only if you have an always-on Internet connection (such as a cable or DSL modem).

- **Time Zone.** From here, you select your local time zone, either by choosing a zone from the pop-up menu or by clicking your location on the world map.

- **Clock.** This is where you set how the time is displayed onscreen. For example, you can select whether to display the time in the menu bar or in a window on the Desktop. (In Jaguar, the Desktop clock is available from a separate Clock application rather than this preferences pane.)

    The "Use a 24-hour clock" option here applies specifically to this clock. For more general date and time format settings (including 12-hour versus 24-hour clocks), especially as they apply to settings used for different countries, use the Formats pane of the International System Preferences pane.

Software Update. The choices you make in this pane determine how your computer checks for new Mac OS X software that Apple makes available over the Internet. There are two main tabs:

- **Update Software.** From here, you set if and how often you want Mac OS X to automatically check for available updates. If you check the "Download important updates in the background" box, it will automatically download updates it deems important. (However, it does not *install* them automatically; it simply downloads them to your hard drive for later installation.)

  Alternatively, you can click the Check Now button at any time to manually check for possible updates.

  In all cases, to actually check for updates, a separate application called Software Update launches. This is the application that lists the new software and provides the options for you to install it.

- **Installed Updates.** From here, you get a list of all updates installed with the Software Update application (though not updates you've installed by other means, such as a direct download from Apple's Web site).

Figure 2.40

The Software Update System Preferences pane. Click the Check Now button to launch the Software Update application that actually lists the available updates.

SEE: • **Chapter 3 for more details on how Software Update works.**

Speech. This pane contains the settings that determine Mac OS X's ability to recognize speech input and provide spoken feedback (such as Talking Alerts). It is rarely relevant for troubleshooting issues; thus, I don't discuss it further in these pages.

Startup Disk. This is where you select the startup volume. If your Mac can still boot Mac OS 9, you can use this pane to switch between Mac OS 9 and Mac OS X. If you have more than one volume that can mount Mac OS X, this is where you would select the desired startup volume. (There are other ways to switch startup volumes as well, which I discuss in Chapter 5.)

This pane also includes a Network Startup option for NetBooting (if you're connected to a server that supports this option).

New in Tiger is a button to restart your computer in Target Disk Mode—in this mode, your Mac acts as a FireWire hard drive that can be connected to any FireWire-capable computer.

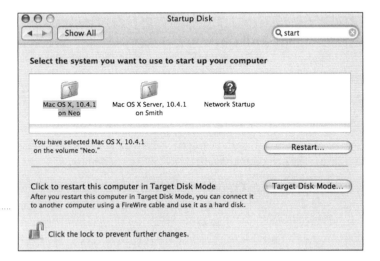

Figure 2.41

The Startup Disk System Preferences pane.

Universal Access. This pane contains four tabs: Seeing, Hearing, Keyboard, and Mouse. These options are designed primarily to assist people with physical disabilities; a few are of more general troubleshooting interest. Here are three examples:

- **VoiceOver.** You access this option in the Seeing pane. Alternatively, you can press Command-F5 to toggle this option at any time. It enables various audio feedback features, such as announcing the name of each menu item as you move the pointer over it. Customization of VoiceOver, including what type of voice to use, is done through the VoiceOver Utility, which you can launch by clicking the Open VoiceOver Utility button in this pane.

- **Zoom.** You access this option in the Seeing pane. Alternatively, you can press Command-Option-8 to toggle the option at any time. With this enabled, press Command-Option-+ (plus sign) or Command-Option- – (minus sign) to increase or decrease the zoom effect, respectively, in the pane.

- **"Enable access for assistive devices."** This option is at the bottom of the pane. It must be selected for certain other applications to work correctly, especially ones that automate access to menus and buttons. For example, QuicKeys X requires this to be selected for recording macros.

Other

Third-party software can also use the System Preferences interface. If you've installed any non-Apple System Preferences, these panes will appear in the Other section. SharePoints and WindowShade X (discussed elsewhere in this book) are just two examples of the many popular System Preferences panes that you may decide to install here.

Installing third-party preference panes. If you download a third-party preference pane from the Internet, or copy it to your computer from a CD or another computer, you'll generally have one of two options for installing it. If the preference pane is provided in the form of an installer, running the installer will place the preference pane file(s) in the appropriate location(s). If you simply see an icon that looks like a preference pane, double-click it; System Preferences will launch and then ask you if you want to install the preference pane for just your account or for all user accounts.

Where System Preferences pane files are stored. The System Preferences pane files that Mac OS X installs are stored in /System/Library/PreferencePanes. There, you will see files with names like Classic.prefPane and Displays.prefPane. In the Get Info window, these files are listed as Mac OS X Preference Pane. In most ways, however, they function just like ordinary applications, with the exception that their interface is in fact the System Preferences window, so launching them also launches the System Preferences application.

Third-party System Preferences panes will be most likely stored in the ~/Library/PreferencePanes folder (in your home directory). As a result, installed third-party preference panes will be available only for the user in whose account the file resides. If you have created more than one user account and want all users to have access to a specific preference, you will need to install it in each user's directory or, alternatively, install it in the PreferencePanes folder in the Library folder at the root level of your drive (/Library/PreferencePanes). Some installers for third-party panes automatically place the file in this latter location.

SEE: • **Chapter 4 for more on the /Users directory and its function.**
     • **"Technically Speaking: How Mac OS X Selects a Document or Application Match," in Chapter 6, for troubleshooting information regarding preference panes.**

If user-installed preference panes do not appear in System Preferences. If user-installed third-party preference panes don't show up in the Other section of the System Preferences window, here is what to do:

1. Quit System Preferences.

2. Go to the Library/Caches folder of your home directory and locate the file named com.apple.preferencepanes.cache.

3. Delete the file.

4. Relaunch System Preferences. A new version of the cache file will be created. Ideally, the previously missing panes should now appear.

This should also fix problems in which the same pane appears twice or the icon for a preference pane is not correctly displayed in the System Preferences window.

Remove a user-installed preference pane. To remove a pane listed in the Other section, Control-click its icon to access a contextual menu. Select Remove from the menu. Alternatively, you can quit the System Preferences application and then remove the pane from the appropriate PreferencePanes folder.

If, when trying to do this, you get a message that states "The '%@' preferences pane could not be removed because an error occurred," go to the appropriate /Library/PreferencePanes folder and remove it directly.

Figure 2.42

System Preferences panes not installed by Tiger get listed in the Other section.

Applications

Mac OS X installs numerous programs in the Applications folder (as well as in the Utilities folder within the Applications folder). In this and the following sections, I provide a brief overview of the programs that are most relevant to troubleshooting. I also return to most of these programs again elsewhere in the book (when discussing troubleshooting problems for which they're used). In addition, I cover many of the applications *not* mentioned here later in the book. For example, Safari and Mail are covered in Chapter 9, and most of the i-software (iPhoto, iMovie, iCal, iSync, and so on) is covered in Chapter 11.

I start here by describing six programs of general importance located in the Applications folder: Automator, Font Book, Preview, Sherlock, Stickies, and TextEdit. Then I move to the all-important Utilities folder.

Automator

New in Tiger, Automator lets even beginning users automate repetitive tasks. I talk about this application in Chapter 4.

Font Book

In some respects, much of the functionality of Font Book, which made its first appearance in Panther, is accessible from within other applications. For example, in TextEdit you can view detailed font information by choosing Format > Font > Show Fonts. Font Book simply makes these features accessible systemwide.

However, there are a few significant features in Font Book that are unavailable from Show Fonts: First, you can enable and disable Fonts and Collections. You can use this feature to restrict which font collections (as well as individual fonts within a collection) are listed in the Font panels of applications (such as TextEdit) that use this Mac OS X feature—without actually deleting the font and/or collection. Second, you can validate fonts. You can use this feature to check for corrupt fonts.

When you double-click a font file in a Finder window, Font Book will launch to allow you to view the font.

SEE: • **Chapter 4 for more details on Font Book and related features.**

Preview

Preview opens graphics files of various formats. You can use it to view the GIF and JPEG files that are common on most Web pages, for example. You can also use Preview's Save As command (Export in earlier versions) to convert a graphics file from one format to another: Choices include BMP, GIF, JPEG-2000, JPEG, PDF, Photoshop, PICT, PNG, QuickTime Image, SGI, TGA, and TIFF. (If you create a new graphic in Preview, which automatically pastes the contents of the clipboard, the default choice depends on the type of data on the clipboard.)

Preview also opens PDF documents. PDF, which stands for Portable Document Format, is the native format used by Adobe Reader and is also Mac OS X's "native" file format for graphics.

Preview includes a thumbnail view, as well as the capability to zoom and rotate figures via buttons in its toolbar. There is also a Tools menu (from which you can make a graphic selection of part of a page or select text to copy it to the clipboard), a Find command, the ability to crop images, active Web links, and the ability to play animated GIFs.

The Tiger version of Preview adds a slide-show feature to view multiple images in sequence, bookmarks, keywords, PDF layout options, annotations, support for PDF forms, image-correction tools, screen-capture commands (in File > Grab) and a number of other options. This is one application that gets significantly more useful with every release.

Note: Adobe Reader still has some options that Preview does not—which means you shouldn't be in a hurry to throw out your copy of Adobe Reader just because Preview is available.

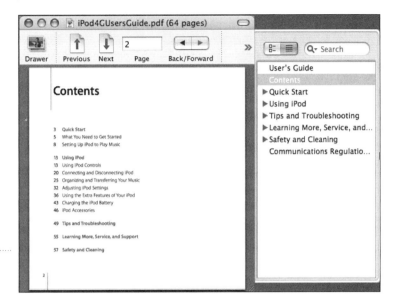

Figure 2.43

The Preview application with a document open.

Figure 2.44

The PDF and Preview buttons in a Print dialog.

One unique feature of Preview is the link to it in the Print dialog of almost any application that works with documents. Specifically, the Print dialog includes two related buttons:

- **Preview.** If you click the Preview button in a Print dialog, the Preview application launches and opens the document "to be printed" as a PDF file. The document should look virtually identical to how it looked in the application in which it was created. In any case, it should show exactly how the document will look when printed, including page breaks, even if the creating application does not show this. This option may also be useful for occasions when you can't get the document to print from the application in which it was created.

- **PDF.** If you click-hold the PDF button in a Print dialog, a menu of options appears. The one you are most likely to use is Save as PDF. Once you've done this, you can open the saved document in any application that can view PDF files, including Preview itself or Adobe Reader. This option can be very useful for exporting documents to platforms (such as Windows) that would not otherwise open the original files. Because a Windows version of Adobe Reader is available, Windows users will be able to open the PDF file.

Additional options include the ability to fax a PDF, mail a PDF, or save the PDF to iPhoto. Finally, you can choose Edit Menu to add more options. The default installed options are located in the /Library/PDF Services folder. Each item is actually an Automator workflow document. You can use Automator to create your own.

Troubleshooting tip: If a document in Preview does not appear correctly (for example, text looks blurry or blocky), go to the PDF pane of Preview's Preferences and uncheck the "Anti-alias text and line art" option. Also, try lowering the "Greeking threshold" in the same Preferences pane.

SEE: • "Automator," "Technically Speaking: Type/Creator vs. Filename Extensions vs. Others," and "Take Note: Filename Extensions," in Chapter 4, for related information.

• "Opening and Saving: Problems Opening and Saving Files," in Chapter 6, for a more extended discussion of opening and saving documents.

• Chapter 7 for more information on printing and additional PDF options.

Sherlock

Sherlock is essentially a specialized Internet search tool. The initial window contains a toolbar from which you can select a *channel*—a specific Web location with which Sherlock interacts to display its information. You can also select a channel from the Channel menu.

If you choose Show All Channels from the Channel menu, or click the initial Channels icon in the toolbar, you get an overview of all the available options. A Collections sidebar, along the left side, includes five items: Toolbar, Channels Menu, Apple Channels, Other Channels, and My Channels. (The first two items duplicate the lists in the toolbar and the Channel menu, respectively.) Click a collection to display its list of channels in the right side of the window. You can drag items from other collections to these names in the sidebar to add a new channel to the toolbar or the Channels menu. Doing this does not remove the channel from its original location; it just adds it to the new location—in this respect, these collections are much like playlists in iTunes or albums in iPhoto.

The Apple Channels collection lists all of the channels that Apple officially supports. The Other Channels collection is used for third-party channels. An initial collection of third-party channels (such as one for VersionTracker.com) is generated the first time you choose this command (assuming you are connected to the Internet at the time). My Channels starts out empty; you drag channels to it to create your own customized list.

Channels. Two of the most commonly accessed channels are

- **AppleCare.** This channel is of special significance for troubleshooting because it provides a way to search Apple's Knowledge Base documents. Simply enter your search criterion, click the magnifying-glass icon to search, and then select an article from the results list. The bottom half of the window will now show the complete contents of the selected article just as if you were viewing it from a Web browser. This feature is often more convenient than going to Apple's Web site (unless you need its additional features, such as the ability to limit searches by date).

   Note: Make sure that the Accept Cookies Always option is enabled in Sherlock's Preferences; otherwise, the contents of Knowledge Base documents will not appear.

- **Movies.** Another cool channel you should be sure to check out is Movies. Click the Movies icon, and you can search for what's playing in the theaters in your area, including showtimes.

Customizing Sherlock's toolbar. Sherlock's toolbar lists most or all of the Apple-supported channels. Similar to how the Finder's toolbar works, Sherlock's toolbar can be customized with the Customize Toolbar command in Sherlock's View menu. (You can also customize it by dragging channels to and from the Toolbar collection on the left.)

Creating shortcuts. You can save a channel as a file by opening the channel in Sherlock, then choosing the Make a Shortcut command in Sherlock's Channel menu. After doing so, simply double-click the file to directly launch that channel at any time.

The created file is an XML document that contains the URL for the given channel. For example, the shortcut for the Movie channel contains the following URL in its XML code: http://si.info.apple.com/sherlock3s/channels/movies.xml.

Adding channels. To add a channel in Sherlock, go to the Web site that offers a channel and click the link provided to add the channel. In most cases, Sherlock will present a dialog explaining that a channel is being adding, giving you the option to proceed, cancel, or get more info (which displays the originating URL). If you want to add the channel, select the collection to which you want to add it, then click the Proceed button.

TECHNICALLY SPEAKING ▶ **Sherlock Under the Hood**

Sherlock stores the information about which channels to display in the com.apple.Sherlock.plist file in ~/Library/Preferences. Notable keys here include Sherlock Channels, SherlockChannelCache, SherlockChannelOrganization, and SherlockSubscriptions. These keys provide details of the names, URLs, and category organization of all the channels that Sherlock currently tracks. Channels for which subscriptions exist are automatically updated when Sherlock is launched. All Apple-supplied channels (including the initial list in Other Channels), for example, are subscription-based. Thus, when Apple updates its channels, this .plist file is updated accordingly. The default list of subscriptions is found in the DefaultChannelSubscriptions property in the .plist file.

The ~/Library/Caches/Sherlock folder is where cache data for Sherlock is located. In particular, check the contents of the CheckPointCache.plist file, which also lists all currently tracked channels. Most of the actual Sherlock software is located in /System/Library/PrivateFrameworks/SherlockCore.framework.

The version of Sherlock in Tiger (and Panther) is 3.x. This differs substantially from versions of Sherlock (for example, 2.x) in earlier versions of Mac OS X. Oddly, if you open the Sherlock 3 application package via the Show Package Contents contextual-menu command, you will find a folder in Contents/Resources called Channels. Inside this apparently obsolete folder is a subfolder for each of the main channels used in Sherlock 2!

If you want to know how to create a Sherlock 3 channel for your own Web site, check the following URL: http://developer.apple.com/macosx/sherlock.

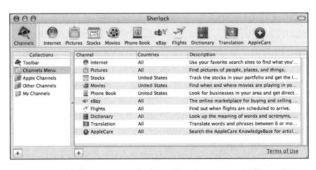

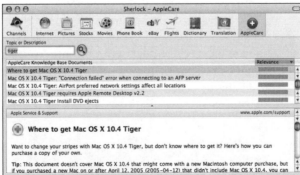

Figure 2.45

Sherlock: top, *the Channels menu;* bottom, *the AppleCare channel selected.*

Stickies

Stickies software allows you to save notes in colored windows that resemble Post-it Notes. (The application version of Stickies is different from the Stickies widget available in Dashboard, and the two do not share notes.) One troubleshooting-related note about this program: The information you create and save in Stickies is stored in a file called StickiesDatabase, located at the root level of the Library folder in your home directory. It's a good idea to back up this file as protection against accidentally losing all of your Stickies notes. (Although if you're backing up thoroughly, you're backing up your Library folder anyway.)

TextEdit

TextEdit is Apple's generic word processor. It can open plain-text files and Rich Text Format (.rtf) files. It can also display numerous types of graphics files and save them in a special type of Rich Text Format document. Starting in Panther, TextEdit can directly open and save Microsoft Word files. It can even save native TextEdit files in Word format.

In Tiger, TextEdit can also read XML files and export documents in HTML and Microsoft Word XML formats. In addition, check out TextEdit's Format > Text menu. New options here include Link (for creating Web links); List (for creating outline-like lists); and Table (for generating user-customizable tables).

SEE: • "Working with Fonts," in Chapter 4, and numerous sections in Chapter 6 for more on TextEdit.

Utilities

The Utilities folder—which is contained within the Applications folder at the root level of your volume—contains a wealth of troubleshooting utilities. Starting in Mac OS X 10.2, most of these utilities employ a similar toolbar format, bringing a welcome consistency to their user interfaces. In this section, I provide an alphabetical overview of the most important of these utilities for general troubleshooting purposes. (I'll return to both these and other utilities throughout the book, as relevant.)

SEE: • Chapter 4, for coverage of Directory Access, a Utilities folder utility not mentioned here.
• Chapter 8, for more on network-related utilities and related software such as Internet Connect, Mail, Safari, AirPort Admin Utility, Bluetooth File Exchange, and Network Utility.

Activity Monitor

Activity Monitor is a critically important troubleshooting utility that can be used to view information about every open process. Although an application is, by definition, a process, many processes that can run in Mac OS X are not traditional Mac applications.

Activity Monitor's most important feature for troubleshooting purposes is that it can force-quit any process, even ones that aren't listed in the Force Quit window (which opens when you press Command-Option-Escape). It's also useful for monitoring performance-related statistics for open processes.

Activity Monitor is such a feature-rich utility that I'm presenting only an overview of it here. You'll find more details as well as discussions of additional features later in the book, as they relate to various troubleshooting topics.

Activity Monitor window: The process list. This list is able to display every open process. You can filter which processes are listed at any given time with the Show pop-up menu in the toolbar, which includes the following choices:

- **My Processes.** This shows all processes for which you are the User. These are generally either applications you launched or background processes launched at login. Most applications with custom icons next to their names are also listed in the Force Quit window. Note: Dashboard widgets are one exception.

- **Administrator Processes.** For these processes, the system is the User (that is, root is the name listed in the User column). In general, these processes monitor essential and maintenance activities of the OS, such as those initiated at startup prior to logging in, those responsible for net-working and printing, and so on.

- **Other User Processes.** If more than one user is logged in, via Fast User Switching, this window will show processes assigned to other logged-in users. Note: At a minimum, the mdimport and WindowServer processes are listed here even when no other users are logged in.

- **Active Processes and Inactive Processes.** These choices display processes currently in Active and Inactive Memory, respectively. The Active Processes view is a particularly good option for troubleshooting. It allows you to narrow your focus to just those processes that are the most likely culprits.

- **Windowed Processes.** These show all processes that can be launched from the Finder (and typically that can display windows in the Finder).

- **All Processes and All Processes, Hierarchically.** These display every open process.

You can also filter the list of processes—in effect, search for a particular process—by entering text in the Filter text box in the toolbar. Only those processes that contain the text you type will be shown.

The process list provides information about each process (beyond its name), including its Process ID, its percentage of CPU usage, and the amount of real versus virtual memory it is using. You can also view additional columns—showing information such as CPU time, number of ports, private and shared memory, and system messages sent and received—via the View menu's Columns submenu. All of this data is updated in real time (as determined by the time period you designate in the Update Frequency command in the View menu).

Quit Process button. To quit or force-quit any listed process, click the name of the process and then click the Quit Process button in the Activity Monitor window's toolbar (or choose Quit Process from the View menu). In the dialog that appears, choose Quit (or Force Quit).

SEE: • "Force-quitting," in Chapter 5, for more on Force Quit and Activity Monitor.

Performance monitors. In the bottom section of the Activity Monitor window are five tabs: CPU, System Memory, Disk Activity, Disk Usage, and Network. Click any of these to get data on the respective topic. (I'll show you how to interpret these data later in the book.)

SEE: • "Technically Speaking: Dividing Up Mac OS X's Memory," in Chapter 4, for more on the System Memory pane of Activity Monitor.
   • "Utilities for monitoring and improving performance," in Chapter 6, for details about all of these options.
   • "Technically Speaking: Terminal Commands to Monitor and Improve Performance," in Chapter 10, for more details on Terminal commands and third-party utilities related to performance.

The View menu. You will find several useful commands in this menu:

• Choose Dock Icon and then choose among the options in its hierarchical submenu to replace the Activity Monitor icon in the Dock with one that displays real-time performance data (such as CPU usage).

• Choose Send Signal to Process, and then choose from among the options in the dialog that slides down. Mainly, they offer a greater variety of ways to quit an application using Unix "sig" commands such as Hangup (SIGHUP), Quit (SIGQUIT), Abort (SIGABRT), and Kill (SIGKILL). These are alternatives to issuing these commands in Terminal.

SEE: • "Killing processes from Terminal," in Chapter 5, for related information.

- Choose Show Deltas for Process for a selected process to shift the listing for that process to display changes relative to the time you selected the command. Thus the amount of virtual memory listed for a process will shift to 0 bytes initially, and then change as its memory usage changes. The color of the process name changes from black to green when you are showing delta values for that process.

- The Filter, Inspect, and Sample Process items are alternatives to similar buttons in the Activity Monitor window. (Sample Process is found in the Inspect window, as described below.)

The Window menu. This menu also includes a few useful items, some of which were part of a separate utility in Jaguar called CPU Monitor but are included as part of Activity Monitor in Panther and later:

- Choose Activity Monitor to display the Activity Monitor window, should you ever close it.

- The CPU Usage and CPU History items show floating windows that display CPU usage and history, respectively.

- The Show Floating CPU Window's submenu provides the option to view a small vertical or horizontal monitor that shows real-time CPU usage.

Note: If you show CPU usage in the Dock icon, you cannot display the CPU Usage window via the Window menu.

SEE: • "Utilities for monitoring and improving performance," in Chapter 6, for related information.

Inspect icon. If you select a process and click the Inspect icon in the toolbar (or select Inspect from the View menu), the Inspect window opens. From here, you can get details about each process beyond what's shown in the process list. This window contains three tabs: Memory, Statistics, and Open Files and Ports.

Selecting the Memory or Statistics tab provides detailed performance data specific to the selected process. The Open Files and Ports pane displays a list of all shared files (primarily frameworks in the System folder) that the selected process may call to accomplish its tasks.

Clicking the Sample button at the bottom of the Inspect window brings up a snapshot of the functions the process is executing at a given moment. This (like most Activity Monitor features) is actually a graphical front end for a Unix function. Thus, if you launch Terminal and type man sample, you'll be provided with much more detail about what the Sample feature does.

In my view, however, the information provided by the Inspect options (especially the Sample feature) goes well beyond what most end-user troubleshooters need to know.

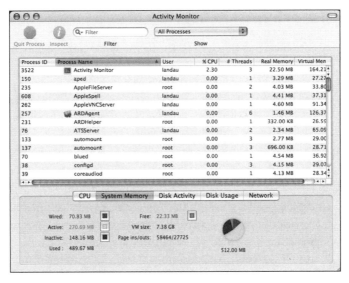

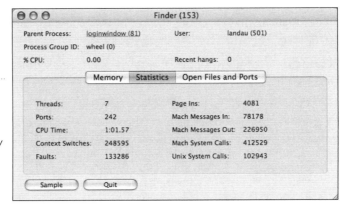

Figure 2.46

Activity Monitor:
top, *showing All
Processes and
System Memory;*
middle, *showing My
Processes and CPU;*
bottom, *Activity
Monitor's Inspect
window.*

ColorSync Utility

ColorSync Utility includes a Profile First Aid button, which you can use to verify and repair ColorSync profiles. These profiles are used to make sure that the colors you see on your monitor match those produced on peripheral devices, such as printers. The other options available for this utility are beyond the scope of this book (that is, only graphics professionals are likely to need them).

SEE: • Chapter 7 for more on ColorSync and printing.

Console

Console provides access to the log files that your Mac maintains. These files track various events—especially errors that occur while using your Mac. Viewing these log files can be useful, especially to software developers but also to troubleshooters, in diagnosing the cause of a problem such as a system crash. For example, my Console log file kept reporting a failure to delete a file, even though nothing was in the Trash at the time. It turned out that the file was in an invisible folder used by a third-party delete utility called Data Recycler X. Alerted by the log message, I located and deleted the problem file.

The log that appears by default when Console launches is called console.log and is stored in a folder that has the same name as your account's user ID (UID), located in /Library/Logs/Console—for example, /Library/Logs/Console/501/ console.log. This log focuses on events specific to your particular login session. Whenever you open or quit an application, for example, the log notes this. Various minor errors, most of which you can ignore, are also listed here.

A second important log is system.log, which is located in the Unix /var/log folder. This log focuses on system-wide events—that is, events that occur independently of any users who are logged in. However, many events are tracked by both console.log and system.log.

If you close either window, you can reopen it by selecting the appropriate Open command from Console's File menu. You can also use the Open Quickly submenu to open any log in the most common log file locations (~/Library/Logs, /Library/Logs, and /var/log).

Each log window displays a toolbar (by default) with four icons and a Filter text box:

- **Logs.** Clicking the Logs icon opens a sidebar from which you can access any available log file. The first two items are used to directly access the console.log and system.log files. The remaining three items are folder locations for the same three log file locations accessible via the Open menu's Open Quickly submenu: ~/Library/Logs, /Library/Logs, and /var/log. Click the disclosure triangle next to each name for a list of that location's logs and subfolders.

Of special importance are the two CrashReporter subfolders (one in each of the two Library/Logs folders). These contain log files created or updated each time an application crashes. Each one is named {*application name*}.crash.log. The information they contain can be critical for developers trying to debug the cause of a crash.

Note: Use Console's Preferences to customize what to do when an open log is updated.

- **Clear.** This icon clears the display of all log text. However, it *does not* erase the log file being viewed, even though it may appear to do so. Simply click the Reload icon to view the log's contents.

- **Reload.** This icon reloads the log from disk (entering any items that have been updated since you first loaded the file).

- **Mark.** This icon time- and date-stamps the file. (Since newly logged information is appended to the end of a log, the date/time stamp is placed at the bottom of the log file. New information will appear after the stamp.)

- **Filter.** This feature works similarly to the search field in many Mac OS X applications: Only those lines containing the filter text will be displayed.

Note: You can add features to the toolbar, such as "Delete log file" and Mail Log, by selecting Customize Toolbar from the View menu.

SEE: • "Technically Speaking: What and Where Are the Unix Files?" and "Take Note: Finder Folders vs. Unix Directories," in Chapter 4, for more on accessing Unix folders such as /var/log and understanding pathname notation.

• "Application quits," in Chapter 5, for more information on Console, especially for using CrashReporter logs.

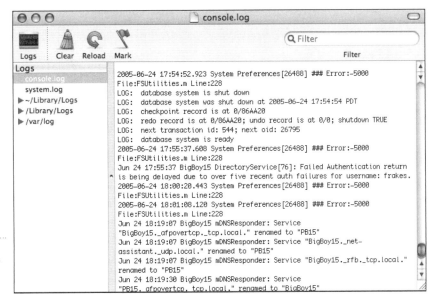

Figure 2.47

A Console window for console.log with the Logs list shown on the left.

Disk Utility

Disk Utility combines a variety of related functions into one application. The following provides a brief overview of this important utility.

Sidebar and main window. The sidebar on the left side of the Disk Utility window lists all currently accessible volumes. Typically, your first step, before doing anything else in Disk Utility, will be to select a volume (a drive or a partition of a drive) or a disk image from this list. Depending on what you select, different options will appear on the right side of the window. If the volume is unmounted, you will typically want to select Mount Volume from the File menu (or click the Mount icon in the toolbar).

If you select a physical drive (for example, a hard drive), you will be presented with five tabs from which to choose: First Aid, Erase, Partition, RAID, and Restore. If you select a partition of a volume, you will be offered only three or four of these choices: First Aid, Erase, Restore, and possibly RAID. If you select an image file, the options vary according to image type; at minimum, First Aid and Restore should appear. The following is a summary of these panes' functions.

- **First Aid.** The First Aid pane is the main repair component of Disk Utility. From here, you can repair a volume and (for Mac OS X volumes) its disk permissions.

  The ability to run First Aid from the Mac OS X Install CD (as described in Chapter 3) is important, because the Repair Disk component of the First Aid pane of Disk Utility cannot repair the drive currently running the OS. Thus, if you start up from a hard drive, you cannot use Disk Utility to repair that drive. However, you *can* use the Repair Disk Permissions component when booted from your hard drive.

  SEE: • **"Performing repairs with Disk Utility (First Aid)," in Chapter 5, for more on First Aid.**

- **Erase.** In the Erase pane, you can erase (also called *initializing* or *reformatting*) any writable media: a partition of a disk, an entire disk, or even a rewritable optical media disc (such as a CD-RW).

  If you have an older Mac that can still boot from Mac OS 9, and you intend to do so, remember to check the Install Mac OS 9 Drivers option before erasing the drive (assuming you even see this option; it may not be available in Tiger).

  If you click the Security Options button, a dialog appears with a number of options for erasing data. Don't Erase Data does a basic initialization—the volume's directory is erased, making the OS think the volume is empty, but the data remains in place. This is fine for environments where data security is not an issue, but it means that data is potentially recoverable with the right tools. Zero Out Data, 7-Pass Erase, and 35-Pass Erase offer diminishing chances of recovery—it's highly unlikely that anyone who gains possession of your hard drive would be able to recover data, even using utilities that claim to be able to recover data off erased or damaged drives—but increase the amount of time needed to complete the erasure process. For example, the 35-Pass Erase option will take 35 times longer than the Zero Out Data option, which itself will take much longer than the Don't Erase Data option.

If you click the Erase Free Space button, you get a similar set of options. However, it will only erase those portions of the drive that are currently unused. This is of potential value as a security matter because such areas may still contain data from deleted files that could otherwise be recovered.

When erasing most volumes, the options in the Volume Format pop-up menu include Mac OS Extended, Mac OS X Extended (Journaled), and possibly UNIX File SystemFile System. If you select a drive (not a partition of a drive), additional format options appear: Mac OS Extended (Case-sensitive), Mac OS Extended (Case-sensitive, Journaled), and MS-DOS File System. Use the latter option to format a drive to be compatible with Windows. Such drives will also mount on your Mac.

- **Partition.** The Partition pane is where you can partition the drive as well as determine the type of drive formatting you want to use (for example, Mac OS Extended) for each partition. Note that partitioning a volume also erases it. If you're erasing an entire disk, you can use the Partition pane to divide it into separate partitions. Note: This option does not appear if you select a partition of an already formatted drive.

- **RAID.** The RAID (Redundant Array of Independent Disks) pane is only of use if you have multiple hard drives that you wish to set up as a RAID set. In brief, RAID coordinates the drives so that they act almost as if they were one larger drive, or uses multiple drives as a single same-size drive that offers better performance. It can also provide automatic data backup. Since RAID sets are used primarily in institutional setups, I will not be covering them further here.

- **Restore.** From here you can create a backup version of a volume or restore a drive from a previous backup, especially a disk image.

    SEE: • "Backing Up and Restoring Mac OS X Volumes," and "Technically Speaking: Case-Sensitive HFS Formatting," in Chapter 3, for more on these topics.

Images menu. You use this menu primarily to verify, modify, and burn disk images. These are the files (typically with a .dmg extension) that, when opened, mount a virtual volume on your Mac that acts almost identically to a true external volume. You use the Burn command to burn images to a CD or DVD—especially useful for making an exact complete copy of a volume (which cannot be done by simply dragging files to a CD-R mounted in the Finder).

Toolbar. In large part, the icons here duplicate commands accessible elsewhere—the toolbar simply makes them more convenient. Included are icons for creating, converting, or verifying an image; mounting, unmounting, and ejecting volumes; as well as enabling journaling for a volume.

New beginning in Panther is the Info feature. Select a volume and click this icon to open a window that provides a detailed list of the characteristics of the volume. From here, you can learn, for example, whether a volume is bootable, whether you can repair permissions on the volume, whether journaling is on, and how many files and folders are on the volume.

New in Tiger is a Preferences dialog that provides options for pre-processing and post-processing images and volumes, as well as an option for using Keychain for remembering disk-image passwords.

SEE: • **Chapter 3 (especially "Image (.dmg) files," "Creating an Emergency Startup Volume," and "Technically Speaking: Internet-Enabled Disk Images,") for more on using Disk Utility, including details on how to make a bootable copy of a startup CD.**

• **Chapter 5 for more on the First Aid component of Disk Utility and details about journaling.**

• **"Burning discs: CDs and DVDs," in Chapter 6, for more on disc burning.**

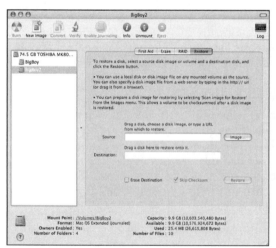 

Figure 2.48

Disk Utility: left, *the Restore pane;* right, *an Info window.*

Grab

Grab creates screen captures—that is, pictures of your screen just like those that illustrate this book. Personally, I find Grab to be a bit of a kludge; however, it has one saving grace: a Timed Screen capture, useful for those occasions when you can't access Grab the moment the screen is ready to be captured. This makes it easy to take a picture of a pop-up menu, for example. Beyond that, Grab is inconvenient to use and too often prevents you from getting the shot you want.

Fortunately, there are alternatives, as described in "Take Note: Screen Captures."

TAKE NOTE ▶ **Screen Captures**

In addition to the Grab utility, the main Mac OS X methods for taking screen snapshots (also called *captures* or *screen shots*) involve pressing Command-Shift-3 and Command-Shift-4 (both of which work similarly in Mac OS 9).

Command-Shift-3. This key combination allows you take a snapshot of the entire screen.

Command-Shift-4. Command-Shift-4 allows you to select a portion of the screen for capture. Simply drag the crosshair pointer to define the selection borders. Just as with Command-Shift-3, captured files are saved to the Desktop.

However, if you press the spacebar before selecting a region, you get a special option: The pointer changes to a Camera icon. Now whatever window, icon, or other specific interface element the pointer is over is selected automatically (and changes color to indicate this status). Click the mouse, and you get a snapshot of the selected item. When you want to capture just a window, this method eliminates the need to try to line up the selection borders with the window border.

Note: You cannot use these commands to take pictures of anything that requires that you hold down a key or the mouse button to display. To take pictures of pull-down menus, for example, click the menu name in the menu bar, so that the menu remains visible even when you're not holding down the mouse button.

Canceling a capture. If you've activated the Command-Shift-4 screen-shot mode, pressing the Escape key (or Command-period) *before* you click any item cancels the capture.

Saving to the Clipboard. If you hold down the Control key while pressing Command-Shift-3 or Command-Shift-4, the screen capture will be saved to the clipboard instead of as a file. You can then paste it into any graphics application or use Preview's File > New From Clipboard command to open the screen shot in Preview. The advantage of this is that you can then export it to any supported graphics format.

Screen-capture file format. The above commands save the capture as a PNG document to the Desktop named Picture 1. Subsequent saved captures are named Picture 2, and so on.

Note: In Panther, captures are saved in PDF format.

Note: If you're in a Classic application, the files are saved as PICT documents at the root level of the volume containing the Classic application.

You can change the default format for saved captures to any other supported format (which includes most or all of the formats supported by QuickTime Player or Preview) by typing a command in Terminal that creates and/or edits the needed preferences file. The file is com.apple.screencapture.plist (located in ~/Library/Preferences). For example, to have files saved in PDF format by default, type

```
defaults write com.apple.screencapture type pdf
```

Log out of your account and log back in for the change to take effect.

continues on next page

TAKE NOTE ▶ Screen Captures *continued*

You can also make these changes by using a utility such as Property List Editor (as covered more in Chapter 4) to open and edit the .plist file directly. Finally, several third-party utilities, such as TinkerTool (www.bresink.de/osx/TinkerTool.html), provide an option for making this change. Especially convenient, TinkerTool includes a pop-up menu of all the available format choices, saving you the hassle of remembering them.

As an alternative, you can open your PNG screen-shot file in Preview and use Preview's Save As command to change the file's format. You can similarly use the Control option when taking a screen shot (as mentioned above) to save the screen shot to the clipboard, select the New From Clipboard command in Preview's File menu, and then save the document to the desired format.

Screen capture from Preview or Grab. After launching Preview, go to the Grab item in the File menu. From the submenu, you can select Selection, Window, or Timed Selection. These commands do what their names imply. Try them. After selecting and using one, the screen capture automatically opens in Preview. If you select to save it, the file is saved as a TIFF file by default.

Similarly, the Grab application saves screen captures as TIFF documents.

Screen capture from Terminal. You can take screen captures from Terminal via the screencapture command. To learn more about its use, type screencapture and press Return. This essentially duplicates the features of Command-Shift-3 and Command-Shift-4.

Snapz Pro X. If you want more features than Grab or screen-capture shortcuts provide, try the shareware utility Snapz Pro X, from Ambrosia Software (www.ambrosiasw.com). Among other options, it allows you to select a default graphics format for saving captures and to create movies from your screen actions.

Installer

Installer is the utility that launches when you open an installer package file.

SEE: • Chapter 3 for complete details regarding this utility and installing software in Mac OS X.

Keychain Access

Keychain Access allows you to interact directly with keychain files. These files store passwords for, and regulate access to, applications, e-mail accounts, and Internet sites that use passwords.

Default keychain files. A default keychain, called login.keychain, is created for each account when the account is created. It is stored in ~/Library/Keychains. (Note: In older systems, or ones upgraded from older systems, the name of this keychain may be the user's short name.) A system-wide keychain called

System.keychain and located in /Library/Keychains is created when you first start up your Mac under OS X and is shared by all users. Keychain Access can be used to modify these two keychains and/or create new ones (see below).

The login keychain is assigned, by default, the same password as the password for the account—this allows the keychain to be unlocked automatically when you log in. However, if an administrator changes another user's account password, the keychain password is *not* changed—you must manually change the login keychain password to match the new password (as explained below), or the user's keychain will no longer automatically open at login!

Creating and setting up Keychain files. To use Keychain Access, you must have at least one keychain file. Almost certainly, you already have at least two keychain files (as previously noted): the default login and System keychain files.

The login keychain is typically unlocked and displayed by default when you launch Keychain Access. This keychain file is used for your personal items, such as passwords you create or store while logged in to your account.

Note: If you don't see a list of all the keychains to which you have access, click the Show Keychains button in the bottom left corner of the Keychain Access window. The button then toggles to read Hide Keychains.

You can create additional keychain files by selecting New Keychain from the File menu. To add an existing keychain to the list, from the File menu select Import.

You can also lock and unlock keychain files. If a file is locked, you will be asked to provide the keychain file password before you (or any application, as explained below) can access any data within the file. You can lock and unlock the selected keychain via padlock icon in the toolbar or the Unlock/Lock (Command-L) command in the File menu.

To change a keychain file's password, from the Edit menu select "Change password for Keychain *name*." Keep in mind that the password for the login keychain will automatically be changed if you change your login password in the Accounts System Preferences pane. (However, if an admin user changes another user's account password, this may *not* update that user's keychain password; in such cases, users have to make the change themselves.)

The Keychain Access window. The Keychain Access window layout has been redesigned in Tiger. On the left side is a column with two sections: Keychains (if you have clicked the Show Keychains button) and Category:

- **Keychains.** This is a list of the keychain files to which you have potential access. Most likely, the only one you will need to interact with is the login keychain, as already discussed. Other keychains in the list should include the System keychain (which holds root-level passwords, such as the ones used by an AirPort Base Station) and an X509Anchors keychain. The X509Anchors keychain is a repository of the certificates installed by Mac OS X. Certificates are a way of determining authenticity, used mainly to assess the trustworthiness of documents received over the Internet (as covered in "Take Note: Certificates," in Chapter 9).

To display the contents of any keychain file, simply click its name in the Keychains list.

- **Category.** Use the terms here to filter a list of keys in a keychain file. For example, to just see Password items in a list that contains both password and certificate keys, select Passwords.

To the right of these columns is the main section of the window. The lower portion is a list of all the keys in the selected keychain file. If you select a keychain item from the list, the top of the window provides information about that item: kind, account/name, where (the application, site, or application that uses it), and modified date. You can delete a selected item via the Delete option in the Edit menu.

If you double-click a keychain item, or select it and click the Info (i) button at the bottom of the window, you'll be presented with an info window for that item that contains two tabs: Attributes and Access Control:

- **Attributes.** The Attributes pane lists the basic information for a key. For example, to see the actual password stored in a keychain item, open its info window, and in the Attributes pane check the "Show password" box. A window will appear that asks you to enter your keychain file password. Do so and click the Allow Once or Allow Always button, and the requested password will appear. If you select Allow Always, you will not be asked for the keychain file password on subsequent requests—obviously reducing your security protection.

  The Comments field lets you add comments about the item.

- **Access Control.** The Access Control pane is where you choose whether or not you want Keychain Access to require you to provide your keychain password each time an application asks for that item's password. If you choose "Confirm before allowing access," you will be requested to enter the keychain password (perhaps in addition to the application password) each time you launch the application.

  You can also choose to allow particular applications to always have access to the item by adding those applications to the "Always allow access by these applications" list. This is essentially the same as selecting the Allow Always option when the password window appears within the given application. However, it's rare that you would need to do this; it's better to let the application request to add itself, at which point you'll see the access dialog mentioned above.

Keychain Access also includes a search field that lets you search the text of the Comments fields of keychain items.

Confirm Application Change dialog. If you install a new version of an application (or install an update to Mac OS X that may include new versions of several applications), the first time you launch an updated application, you are likely to get a Confirm Application Change dialog. It asks whether you want the new version to have access to the same keychain items that the old version could access. Normally, you would agree to this (by clicking Change All). However, if you believe that you did not install a new version of the application, or you are otherwise suspicious of what is going on, click Don't Change and investigate further. Although unlikely, a suspicious occurrence could signal a virus infection. Running antivirus software would be recommended.

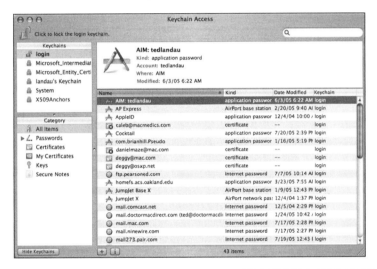

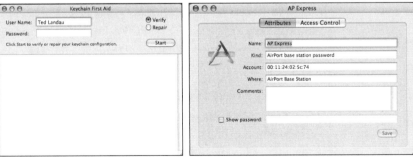

Figure 2.49

Keychain Access: top, Main window; left, First Aid dialog; right, info window.

Using keychain files. One way you can use Keychain Access is as a database for storing sensitive information: You can manually store information in Keychain Access at any time. For example, to store a new password linked to an application or Web site, choose New Password Item from the File menu (or click the Add [+] button at the bottom of the window). Similarly, you can store information unrelated to your Mac, such as a credit card number, by choosing New Secure Note Item from the same menu.

You can also use Keychain Access with keychain-aware software to automatically enter your password when it's required—thus eliminating the need to remember multiple passwords. If an application is keychain aware, it will typically include a check box to "remember" your password (the option will be available in the window where you enter the password). If you choose this option, the application will store the data in your login keychain file and retrieve it when needed. Most Mac OS X applications that use passwords are keychain aware; however, there are exceptions (Microsoft Internet Explorer being one).

Keychain First Aid and Keychain Access Preferences. If you have problems getting Keychain Access to work as expected—for example, if your e-mail client continues to ask for your mail password, even though you've provided it multiple times, checking the "remember password" box each time—select Keychain First Aid from the Keychain Access (Application) menu. This feature verifies and repairs (if necessary) a variety of potential problems. The following are some examples of the types of problems it addresses:

- Your .Mac password is not retained in the Internet System Preferences pane.
- Mail and iChat continue to prompt users for their passwords after saving them in the keychain.
- Applications are unable to retrieve items from a keychain file located on a network volume.

An administrative user should also be able to repair the keychain file of another user; however, the administrator will not be able to see the exact errors that were repaired.

If you choose Preferences from the Keychain Access menu, and select the First Aid tab, you will find additional options. Most important are "Synchronize login keychain password" and "Set login keychain as default." These must be selected if you want your login keychain to automatically unlock when you log in to your account (enabling Mac OS X to automatically recognize the passwords stored in the file). In the General pane, you can also click the Reset My Keychain button. This will create a new empty keychain, leaving your old one still in place, but no longer active.

Finally, if you check the Show Status in Menu Bar box in Keychain Access's Preferences window, a Lock menu is added to the menu bar. You can use this menu to lock or unlock any keychain file. One surprise in this menu is the Lock Screen command: If you choose it, your Mac will launch whatever effect you have selected in the Desktop & Screen Saver System Preferences. However, you will now need to enter your login password before you can get the screen effect to stop. This is an alternative to permanently requiring the use of a password via the option in the Security System Preferences pane, and this feature works regardless of your settings in the Desktop & Screen Saver pane of System Preferences.

Keychain Access and changing passwords. If you change your own account password, the password for login.keychain is automatically changed as well. This allows the keychain to continue to open automatically at login. However, if you (as an administrator) change another user's password in the Accounts System Preferences pane, the login.keychain password is not changed; the user must do this. However, to do so, the user must first enter the original password—if he or she can't remember it, there's no back door to get into the keychain file. The best the user can do in such situations is to open Keychain Access Preferences and then click the Reset My Keychain button (as just noted). However, this new keychain will be empty—there's no way to retrieve the information in the original keychain without the original password. The old file is not deleted but rather saved in the Library/Keychains folder of the user's home directory. Alternatively, you can delete the problem keychain. To do this, select Keychain List from the Edit menu. Then select the keychain and click the Delete (–) button. A new empty default keychain file will be created the next time you log in.

Sharing Keychains. New in Tiger is the ability to share a keychain file between users. For example, you can share a keychain containing login information for financial Web sites with your spouse. To do so, create the new keychain (preferably with a unique password), then choose Keychain List from the Edit menu. Check the Shared box next to the keychain you wish to share; it will then appear in the keychain lists of other users. They'll need to enter the keychain's password to access it, but after that they should be able to access the shared keychain just like any other. Caution: I had trouble getting this feature to work in the initial version of Tiger; there may be a bug that Apple will need to fix.

SEE: • "Take Note: Forgot Your Password?" in Chapter 5, for related information.

NetInfo Manager

The NetInfo Manager utility lets you access and modify the database that stores much of the critical information used by Mac OS X, including the details of each user's account (passwords, short names, and so on). Several components of Mac OS X software, such as the Accounts System Preferences, access this database. NetInfo Manager allows you to access it directly, though it provides little user-friendly help on how to use it.

SEE: • "NetInfo and NetInfo Manager" and "Root Access," in Chapter 4, for more on NetInfo Manager.

Network Utility

Network Utility tests and troubleshoots network connections. If you are having trouble with an Internet connection, this utility can help you diagnose the problem.

SEE: • Chapter 8 for details on Network Utility and network issues in general.

Printer Setup Utility

Printer Setup Utility is where you set up printers and manage print jobs. You need printer-driver software for a given printer to be present before you can set up the printer via Printer Setup Utility. Mac OS X ships with a large number of printer drivers already installed; others may be available from the printer manufacturer or third parties. To print to a given printer, you must first add the printer to Printer Setup Utility's Printer List.

Two notable features of Printer Setup Utility are Desktop Printers and Faxing.

Desktop Printers are icons on your Desktop that can be created by Printer Setup Utility and represent specific printers. You can directly view a printer's status (for example, what documents are being printed, which are on hold, and so on) by double-clicking the icon. You can also drag a document to a desktop printer to initiate printing of the document.

Printer Setup Utility contains a Fax List of devices from which you can send and receive faxes. It works in conjunction with the Fax command in Print dialogs and the settings you configure in the Print & Fax pane of System Preferences. The first time you click the Fax button in a Print dialog, the internal modem will be automatically added to the Fax List (assuming your Mac has an internal modem).

SEE: • Chapter 7 for details on Printer Setup Utility and printing and faxing issues in general.

System Profiler

System Profiler provides details about the software and hardware on your Mac. You can launch System Profiler by double-clicking its icon in the Utilities folder or by clicking the More Info button in the About This Mac window.

You view information by selecting from among the following three major headings in the left sidebar (choose Full Profile from the View menu to get the full list):

- **Hardware.** Selecting the main Hardware item provides you with a general hardware overview in the pane to the right. This overview lists such basics as CPU type and speed, amount of memory, bus speed, and firmware (Boot ROM) version.

Clicking the Hardware disclosure triangle reveals a list of hardware sub-categories that includes Memory, PCI Cards, ATA, USB, and FireWire. When you click any item, the right-pane display shifts to reveal details regarding that item. For example, Memory displays the size, type, and speed of each memory card you have installed. There is no option to list devices connected via an Ethernet network (such as a printer).

If you're having problems with any external device, these items are a good place to check first. If the device is not listed, the Mac doesn't recognize it as being connected.

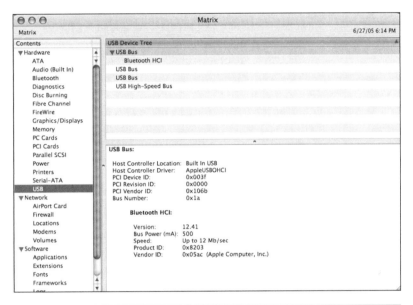

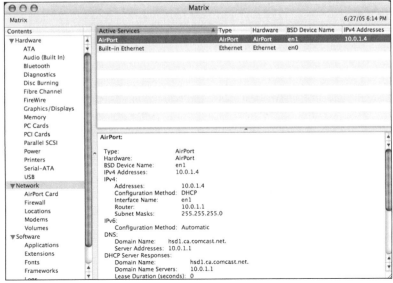

Figure 2.50

System Profiler: top, the USB list; bottom, the Network list.

- **Network.** The main Network item displays in a list to the right all possible network interfaces on your Mac. Select one of those interfaces, and the bottom of the window provides detailed information about it.

  The individual Network subheadings—AirPort Card, Firewall, Locations, Modems, and Volumes—provide summary information. For example, the Locations item displays a summary of your Network Locations (as defined in Network preferences), including all of the settings for each Location.

- **Software.** Click the Software item to see an overview of your Mac's system software in the pane to the right. This overview displays the System version (including build number), the kernel (Darwin) version, and the names of the boot volume, computer, and current user.

  Clicking the Software disclosure triangle reveals a list of software subcategories, including Applications, Extensions, Fonts, Frameworks, Logs, Preference Panes, and Startup Items. Click any item, and the right-pane display shifts to reveal information regarding that item.

  For example, Applications provides a list of all applications on your drive and their version numbers; Extensions provides a list of all kernel extensions (items that are mostly located in /System/Library/Extensions, and described in Chapter 5), their version numbers, and whether they loaded at startup; and Frameworks lists all the items in the /System/Library/Frameworks and /System/Library/PrivateFrameworks folders (as well as framework items possibly added by third parties in the /Library folder). The Logs item displays a few important log file names at the top of the window; selecting one shows its current contents at the bottom of the window.

  SEE: • "Frameworks," in Chapter 4, for more information about this topic.

  SEE: • Chapter 4 for background information on logs and extensions—particularly "Technically Speaking: Log Files and cron Jobs," for more on logs.

Terminal and X11

Terminal and X11 both directly access Mac OS X's underlying Unix software.

Terminal. This is the application that lets you access Mac OS X's Unix command-line environment. From here, you can enter Unix commands just as if you were using a traditional Unix computer.

Terminal offers two potential advantages for Mac users:

- In some cases, Unix represents the only way (or at least the most reliable way) to solve certain troubleshooting problems and to access otherwise hidden features in Mac OS X.

- It opens the door to a wide range of Unix features; use of Perl, PHP, and Sendmail; and much more.

Although I provide many examples of using Terminal to troubleshoot problems, I've tried to emphasize *non-Terminal* solutions whenever possible, because this book is targeted at users who want to become proficient at troubleshooting Mac OS X *without* having to become Unix experts as well. Still, with minimal effort, you can learn enough Unix basics to use Terminal as an effective trouble-shooting tool. This book provides those basics. Using Unix for such matters as advanced Web server setups, FTP server setups, and the use of Sendmail, how-ever, is beyond the scope of this book.

X11. Unix was originally a text-only environment. Although this may not be a significant limitation for such tasks as troubleshooting and server adminis-tration, it made Unix noncompetitive (in comparison with the Mac OS and Windows) when it came to dealing with such productivity tasks as word pro-cessing and spreadsheets—and especially when dealing with anything for which graphics are a requirement (such as editing graphic image files). XWindowing systems (often called X11 systems) were created to deal with this limitation, providing a graphical interface for Unix. There now exists a healthy collection of software written for X11—from productivity suites to games. Mac OS X's X11 allows you to run these programs on your Mac.

In some cases, software will need to be modified by the developer in order to port it to Mac OS X's X11. You will also need to know how to install it on your Mac so that it runs. Details about this process can be found on various X11 Web sites, such as the XFree86 Project, Inc. (www.xfree86.org).

To run an X11 program, add it to the X11 list (using the Customize Menu command in the application menu). Once you've done this, simply choose the application's name in the application menu; the program will open in windows that feature a Mac OS X–like interface—you may not even be able to distin-guish it from "regular" Mac software.

In a sense, Mac OS X itself is a graphical user interface (GUI) for Unix—which would make X11 unnecessary on a Mac, and indeed I suspect most Mac OS X users will never employ X11. However, X11 software is often free, or much cheaper than comparable software running in Mac OS X, and thus offers a cost-saving alternative to standard Mac software.

X11 is not installed by default when installing or upgrading to Panther. To install it, you need to select a custom installation and then select the X11 item. Alternatively, you can install X11 separately via the software available from Apple at www.apple.com/macosx/features/x11/.

SEE: • Chapters 1 and 4 for background on Unix.
   • Chapter 10 for details on how to use Terminal for troubleshooting.

TAKE NOTE ▶ Gone but Not Forgotten

Two applications have been dropped from Tiger that had been included as part of the Mac OS since before the release of the first version of Mac OS X:

• **StuffIt Expander.** The Finder's Archive command can compress files in the .zip format. Apple offers this as the alternative to Allume's compression utility. StuffIt offers more features, including a variety of different archiving formats. If you want it, you can still get it free from Allume's Web site.

• **Internet Explorer.** Microsoft stopped updating the Mac version of its Web browser after Apple released Safari. Up until Tiger, Apple included both browsers with Mac OS X. Apple has finally dropped Internet Explorer altogether. Although I wouldn't recommend using it anymore, if you really want it, you can still obtain it from Microsoft's Web site.

TAKE NOTE ▶ Developer Software

Mac OS X comes with a collection of developer software called Xcode Tools.

If you purchase a retail copy of Mac OS X on CD, this software comes on a separate CD, called Xcode (or Developer Tools). If your copy of Mac OS X came on a DVD, the software install package can be found in a folder called Xcode Tools, visible in the window that opens by default when the disc mounts. If you purchase a Mac, the installer package files for the developer software are located in the Installers folder inside the Applications folder at the root level of your drive. Should you need to reinstall the Installers folder, you can do so via the Restore Software option (as described in Chapter 3).

If none of these options apply to you, you can still get the software by going to Apple's Developer Connection Xcode Web site (http://developer.apple.com/tools/xcode/index.html). You need to be an ADC member to download the software; happily, the online membership category is free and includes permission to download the developer software. Even if you already have the software, you should check here occasionally to see if newer versions are available.

From the perspective of a nondeveloper troubleshooter, the software remains similar to the older Developer Tools. The main addition in Xcode Tools is the Xcode application itself, which is designed to facilitate creating and compiling programming code.

For troubleshooting purposes alone, I would not bother installing most of the software on this CD. Instead, I would do a Custom Install and install just the first item in the list: Developer Tools Software. Deselect any other items that are enabled by default.

continues on next page

TAKE NOTE ▶ Developer Software *continued*

After installation, the Xcode Tools software is located in a folder called Developer at the root level of your Mac OS X volume. This folder has two subfolders of particular interest to troubleshooters:

- **Applications.** This is where programs such as Property List Editor (inside the Utilities folder) and Interface Builder are located.

- **Tools.** This is where Unix commands such as CpMac and SetFile are located. Applications here are Unix executable files and work via the Terminal application.

You will find examples of using this software throughout the book.

Note: Should you later want to uninstall Xcode Tools, you can use the uninstall-devtools.pl command, located in the Tools folder.

SEE: • **Chapters 3 and 4 for several examples of using Property List Editor.**

  • **"The Mac OS X Install disc(s)," in Chapter 3, for more background on installing software.**

  • **"Take Note: Unix Executable Files and TerminalShellScript Files," in Chapter 10, for details on how and why to run the software in the Tools folder.**

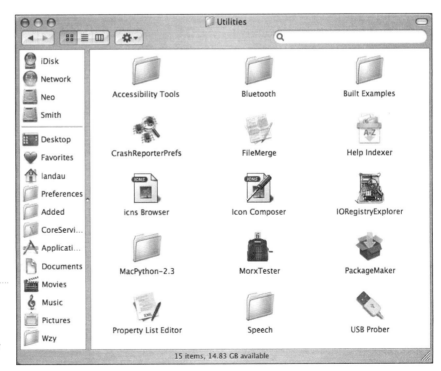

Figure 2.51

The software in /Developer/ Applications/ Utilities. This is where Property List Editor is located.

Third-party utilities

As rich as the programs in the Utilities folder are, they do not come close to providing all the troubleshooting help you might want. Fortunately, third-party software developers have jumped in to fill the gaps, providing an array of useful utilities. These programs run the gamut from freeware to shareware to commercial. They include utilities such as XRay, BootCD, SharePoints, Pseudo, Locator, LaunchBar, and DiskWarrior. Rather than list and describe them all here, I cover them in my discussions of the topics for which they are intended.

3

Installing, Upgrading, Backing Up, and Restoring Mac OS X

Chances are, you were using Mac OS X even before you bought this book, since few Macs sold in the past few years can boot into anything else. And even if you own an older Mac, the fact that you're reading this volume means you've probably already installed Mac OS X on it!

For that reason, I provided an overview of Mac OS X (in Chapter 2) *before* this description of how to install the operating system, believing that most of you are already up and running in Mac OS X. Even if that's the case, though, you may someday be called upon to install Mac OS X on an older Mac that's still running Mac OS 9. Or, even more important, you may need to *re*-install Mac OS X (to fix problems). Finally, as new versions of Mac OS X are released, you will need to upgrade your OS. For all of these occasions, this chapter explains what needs to be done (and why) and offers solutions to a variety of potential problems.

I start off by providing background information on installing Mac OS X for the first time, moving on to give more general information about installing, reinstalling, and restoring Mac OS X software. You'll also learn about upgrading Mac OS X and find recommendations about how best to back up Mac OS X.

In This Chapter

What You Need to Install and Run Mac OS X

Well, for starters you need the Mac OS X Install CDs or DVD. Beyond that, keep reading…

Which Mac models can run Mac OS X?

Apple's official position is that only Macs with the following specifications can run Mac OS X 10.4.x (Tiger); older and newer versions of Mac OS X may have different requirements:

- PowerPC G3, G4, or G5 processor
- Built-in FireWire ports
- At least 256 MB of RAM (although the more, the better)
- A built-in display or a display connected to an *Apple-supplied* video card supported by your computer (in other words, Apple doesn't officially support a Mac running a third-party video card)
- 3 GB or more of free hard-drive space (4 GB or more if you install the Xcode Developer Tools)

Older versions of Mac OS X supported older Power Macs, iMacs, and PowerBooks. Tiger does not.

If you're uncertain of your own Mac's processor, select About This Mac from the Apple menu and check the Processor line.

Figure 3.1

The About This Mac window shows that this Mac is a Power Mac G5 with 2 GB of RAM and is running Mac OS X 10.4.2.

Does this mean that you absolutely cannot use Mac OS X on an older Mac—even one that's been upgraded to include a G4 processor (such as a Power Mac 7500 with a processor upgrade)? Apple's position remains firm: You cannot run Mac OS X on these Macs. However, some users (who won't take no for an answer!) *have* found ways to run Mac OS X on at least some of these older Macs. If you're willing to give it a shot, the utility XPostFacto, from Other World Computing (http://eshop.macsales.com/OSXCenter/XPostFacto), provides a good starting point. Be aware, however, that if you have any problems running Mac OS X on these systems, Apple will not help you solve them. For that reason, I strongly recommend that if you want to run Mac OS X, get a Mac that's sanctioned to run it.

How much memory do you need?

If you know your Mac can run Mac OS X, your next step is to make sure it has enough memory (RAM) installed. Without sufficient RAM, Mac OS X may run, but performance may be unacceptably slow—to the point where the OS may seem to freeze at times.

Apple says you need at least 256 MB of memory to use Mac OS X. Consider this figure to be a bare minimum. To get the best performance from Mac OS X, I recommend at least 512 MB—more, ideally.

Every Mac can accommodate more memory than the minimum that ships from Apple. Typically, you add memory by purchasing a memory module and inserting it into the designated RAM slot(s) on your Mac. Each Mac model comes with instructions on how to do this, and Apple makes sure that the process is easy (the Mac mini is an exception here; just opening the case is a bit tricky).

How much hard-drive space do you need?

Apple says you should have a minimum of 3 GB of free space on your hard drive before attempting to install Mac OS X (4 GB if you intend to install the developer software). (Note: The amount of "available" hard-drive space on a volume is shown in the status bar of the Finder window for any folder on that volume.) However, Mac OS X runs best when

36 items, 19.56 GB available

Figure 3.2

The amount of disk space available for a volume, as viewed in the status bar at the bottom of a Finder window.

you have a good deal *more* unused space. Given the size and price of today's hard drives, I recommend that you make sure you have at least 6 GB of unused space on your Mac OS X volume *after* Mac OS X and any additional software have been installed.

We'll return to the issue of hard-drive space later in the chapter when I cover the pros and cons of partitioning a drive.

Will you be installing Mac OS 9?

Mac OS 9 applications are able to run seamlessly within Mac OS X—a capability derived from Mac OS X's Classic-environment feature (which you can learn more about in the online Classic chapter). To take advantage of this capability, however, you must have Mac OS 9 installed somewhere on your drive. If you're running Mac OS X 10.2 Jaguar or later, you need Mac OS 9.2.x installed.

If you don't know which version of Mac OS X is installed on your computer, just choose the About This Mac item from the top of the Apple menu. The window that opens provides this information. Similarly, to determine the version of Mac OS 9, select About This Computer from the Apple menu that appears when a Classic application is active in Mac OS 9 or when your computer is booted from Mac OS 9. Otherwise, you can check the version number by opening the Mac OS 9 System Folder, selecting Get Info (Command-I) for the System or Finder file, and checking the version information. If Classic is running, you can also get this information from the Memory/Versions pane of the Classic System Preferences.

Currently shipping Macs do not come with a Mac OS 9 System Folder preinstalled. If you want to install Mac OS 9, you'll need to use a Mac OS 9 Install CD (if you have one) or the disc containing Mac OS 9 that came with your Mac (which may be called Software Restore, Additional Software & Apple Hardware Test, or Mac OS 9 Install Disc, depending on your Mac model).

SEE: • "Restoring Mac OS Software" and "What About Mac OS 9?" later in this chapter.

Other requirements

Check the Read Before You Install file for more information that may be relevant to your particular setup. This file is included as a text document on the Mac OS X Install CDs (or DVD). The contents of the file are also presented when you run the Install utility.

SEE: • "Cannot select a volume to install" and "Software installs but fails to work," later in this chapter, for related information.

• "Take Note: Startup Failure When Starting Up from an External Device," in Chapter 5, for more details.

Installing or Reinstalling Mac OS X

There are three situations in which you will want to install or reinstall Mac OS X:

- Mac OS X has never been installed on your Mac. Presumably, you purchased a retail version of Mac OS X, and you now want to install it.

- You erased a drive on which Mac OS X was installed (perhaps because it contained corrupted data you could not fix), and you now want to reinstall Mac OS X.

- Mac OS X is installed on your drive, but you want to upgrade to a major new version (such as when going from Mac OS X 10.3 Panther to Mac OS X 10.4 Tiger), or you want to reinstall a version already installed (perhaps in hopes of eliminating suspected problems with the currently installed copy).

The primary way to install or reinstall Mac OS X is via the Mac OS X Install CDs (or DVD)—which either came with your computer or you purchased separately. In some cases, you may also want to use the Restore Software CDs/DVD that came with your computer. (Note: On newer Macs with DVD drives, you will have only a single DVD that serves as both a Mac OS X Install disc and a Software Restore disc.) Finally, in those cases where you are installing an updated version of Mac OS X over an existing version, you may be using a Mac OS X Update CD instead of an Install CD. I discuss all of these variations in the sections that follow.

The Mac OS X Install disc(s)

The Mac OS X Install software is provided on either CD or DVD. For Mac OS X 10.4 Tiger, the retail version is sold only as a DVD. If you need to have a CD version, you can order it from Apple for $9.95 (see this Web page for details: www.apple.com/macosx/upgrade). Note that at the time of this writing, Apple had an official deadline of December 22, 2005, to make such an exchange. However, that was an extension of a previous deadline of July 9, 2005, so it's possible that Apple may end up further extending the deadline. On newer Macs—which come with optical drives that can read DVDs—Apple ships a bootable DVD that contains both a Mac OS X installer and a more comprehensive installer that will restore all the original software (including the OS and third-party applications) that came with your Mac.

Older Macs—especially those that didn't include an optical drive that can read DVDs—include similar Install content on three or four CDs: Install Disc 1, Install Disc 2, Install Disc 3, and possibly Install Disc 4. The main installation of Mac OS X software takes place from Disc 1. Disc 2 includes numerous additional .pkg files in its Packages folder—including those that contain the software for iCal, iMovie, Microsoft Internet Explorer, iPhoto, iSync, iTunes, and StuffIt Expander—as well as files for additional printer drivers and for foreign language support. Disc 3 contains the X11 software, Additional Speech Voices, more printer drivers, and a few other components.

Figure 3.3

This is the window that appears when you launch the Install Mac OS X application from a Mac OS X Install DVD.

The rules for using the DVD versus CD version of the Install disc(s) are largely the same. The major exception is that if you are installing from CDs, after installing Mac OS X from Disc 1 and restarting your Mac you will be prompted to insert the remaining discs to finish the installation. Note: If you do a Custom Install (as described later in this chapter) and deselect the software contained on Discs 2 and 3, you will not be prompted to insert these discs.

In the discussions that follow, I typically assume you're using an Install DVD.

Xcode Tools. The retail version of Tiger includes the Xcode Tools installer package on the Install DVD. However, it does not get installed as part of the general Tiger installation. You need to install it separately. Because some of the software is of general value beyond the needs of developers, I recommend installing it.

SEE: • "Take Note: Developer Software," in Chapter 2, for more details on obtaining and installing this software.

Startup from the Mac OS X Install disc

As you would expect, you start the installation process by using the Mac OS X Install DVD (or Disc 1 of the CD set). To do so, insert the DVD and wait for it to mount. Next, double-click the Install Mac OS X icon, which should be visible in the window that opens by default when the disc mounts. (Note: On Restore discs, it's in the Welcome to Mac OS X folder that's visible in this window.) In the window that appears, click the Restart button. Next, assuming you're running Mac OS X already, you will be prompted to give your administrator password. Do so, and your Mac will restart, booting from the Install disc.

Alternatively, you can start up from the DVD by accessing the Startup Disk System Preferences pane, selecting the DVD, and clicking the Restart button. Finally, you can boot directly from the CD by inserting it at startup and holding down the C key.

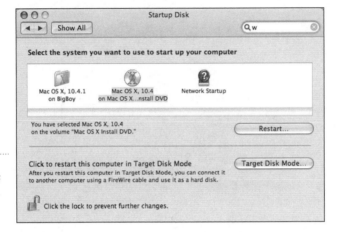

Figure 3.4

The Startup Disk System Preferences pane with a Mac OS X Install DVD highlighted.

On restart, the gray Apple logo screen will appear, followed by a blue screen and the launch of the installation process. (Note: If you have a Mac with built-in Bluetooth, and your Mac doesn't detect a mouse or keyboard connected to the USB port, you'll first see the Bluetooth connection utility; after pairing with your Bluetooth mouse and/or keyboard, the installation process will begin.)

As the first step of the installation process, the Installer asks for your preferred language. This determines the language used in the remaining windows as well as the main language used by Mac OS X after it is installed. After selecting it, you'll see the text "Preparing installation," followed by the launch and appearance of the Installer utility's Introduction ("Welcome to the Mac OS X Installer") pane.

Before you go any further, look at the menus available in the Installer utility. A number of them provide options that are of special interest.

TAKE NOTE ▶ Installing Mac OS X *Without* Starting Up from the Install Disc? Maybe...

To install Mac OS X on a volume other than the current startup volume, you don't necessarily have to restart from the Mac OS X Install disc. Instead, mount the disc and go to the /System/Installation/Packages folder (not found in the System folder on a hard drive running Mac OS X), which contains all the .pkg files used by the Mac OS X Install disc. From within this folder, locate the OSInstall.mpkg file and then double-click it to launch the Installer utility. You should now be able to install the software.

Note, however, that you do this at your own risk: I've seen cases where it hasn't worked. The safest bet is to start up from the disc.

The Installer menu

Only one command is important in this menu:

Quit Installer. If you select this command before you install Mac OS X, a window will appear, asking if you are sure you want to quit the Installer. Your choices are Restart, Startup Disk, and Don't Quit. Choosing Startup Disk launches the same pane that appears when you choose the Change Startup Disk command from the Utilities menu (below). If you choose Restart, your Mac will simply restart without any changes being made to your hard drive.

The File menu

The File menu also contains only one important command:

Show Files. You may not be able to choose this command from the initial Installer display; instead, you can only access it later—exactly when will depend upon the installation you're performing (that is, full install or update). The command is *likely* to be active by the time the Select a Destination pane appears and certainly no later than after the installation has completed (and before you restart).

If you choose this command, you will get a list of every file that gets installed by the current Installer setup and the exact folder locations in which each file will be placed. You can save this list as a text document. Although this information is not critical for the initial installation, it will become of more interest when you update the OS and want to see what files the updater installed.

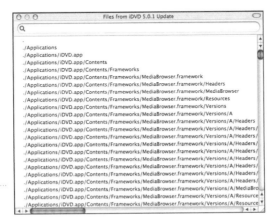

Figure 3.5

A Show Files listing in an Installer.

The Utilities menu

The Utilities menu that appears when using current Mac OS X Install discs combines a number of utilities found in the Installer menu of older discs, as well as a few new items of particular interest to troubleshooters. Choosing an item from this menu launches one of the separate utilities located on the disc; to exit any utility and return to the main Install pane, choose the Quit command from the application menu. The included utilities are the following:

Startup Disk. This utility, which functions much like the Startup Disk pane of System Preferences, comes in handy if you can't get your Mac to start up from a particular hard drive or get it to shift to an alternative bootable hard drive as its default choice. By selecting this command, you can specify any currently available bootable drive as the default. Once you've done this, click Restart to reboot the Mac using that drive.

Reset Password. If you've already installed Mac OS X, you can use this command to enter a new password for any Mac OS X user on any mounted Mac OS X volume—an important back door of last resort in case you cannot recall your own password. Click Save to save your changes.

This arrangement also represents an obvious security weakness, since it means that anyone with a Mac OS X Install disc can change your password to gain access to your system (although you can set an Open Firmware password to prevent this, as described in Chapter 5). The security risk is the tradeoff for the ability to recover from a forgotten password.

To change a password, you first need to select the volume containing the user account whose password you wish to change. The resulting user list (the pop-up menu) includes all of the user accounts you've set up, plus the root user (if enabled). After choosing a user, enter a new password (twice, for verification) and, if desired, a new password hint. Then click the Save button to save the new password. When finished, quit the Reset Password utility.

You can access the Reset Password command only if you're starting up from an Install disc. If you launch the Installer application from a hard drive, this option will not appear. In addition, you cannot launch the Reset Password utility directly and use it—it can be used only if your computer is booted from the Install disc.

> **SEE:** • "Logging in as root," in Chapter 4, for more on the Reset Password command.

Disk Utility. This command launches the same Disk Utility application that you'll find in the Utilities folder on your Mac OS X volume. After choosing a volume on the left, you can select First Aid (used to repair a disk) or a variety of other options to reformat or partition your drive. I cover Disk Utility in more detail later in this chapter and again in Chapter 5. For an overview of what is available via Disk Utility, see "Disk Utility" in Chapter 2.

In general, you will not need to use Disk Utility at this point—with one exception. The default setup for a drive, as shipped from Apple, is to have one partition. Should you want to have two or more partitions, you will need to use Disk Utility to set up the additional partitions.

SEE: • "Take Note: Why and How to Partition," below, for information on how and why you would want to partition a drive when using Mac OS X.
• Chapter 5 for more on startup issues, including using passwords and Disk Utility.

System Profiler, Network Utility, Terminal. These commands, like Disk Utility, launch their respective utilities from within the Installer. As with Disk Utility, it's rare that you would need to use any of these utilities during an installation of Mac OS X. The primary reason for their inclusion here is for subsequent troubleshooting, especially if your problem prevents you from starting up from your hard drive.

SEE: • "System Profiler," in Chapter 2, for more information on this utility.
• Chapter 8, for more on Network Utility.
• Chapter 10, as well as numerous other places throughout the book, for coverage of Terminal.

TAKE NOTE ▶ Why and How to Partition

Partitioning a hard drive means dividing it into two or more separate volumes. Each volume in turn mounts separately when you launch your Mac. In most respects, the volumes behave just as if you had two (assuming you made two partitions) separate hard drives (rather than just one). The only times it will be apparent that just one hard drive is at work are when the hard drive fails or if you need to reformat it.

All drives ship from Apple with just one partition. Thus, if you want two or more partitions, you must create them yourself. Using Mac OS X software, changing the number of partitions on a drive requires erasing its contents. Thus, anything on your drive that you want to save will need to be backed up first—which is precisely why I recommend partitioning a drive the day you unpack your new Mac. There will be nothing to back up because you haven't used it yet—which means the process will be simplified considerably.

Why partition?

A primary benefit of partitioning is that if you make both volumes startup volumes (in other words, you install Mac OS X on both partitions), you have two ways of starting up your Mac from the same drive. If you're having trouble with volume A, for example, and you need to restart from another volume to fix the problem, volume B is ready to go. You don't necessarily need to seek out a CD or other external medium.

You can also use a second partition to install a different version of Mac OS X. For example, if you're currently running Panther, you could install Tiger on a second partition, to test it out, before deciding whether to install it on your main partition.

Even if you don't choose to make the second partition bootable, you can still use it to store backups of important personal files (such as documents and photos) that are stored on the first partition. Or (as I discuss more in Chapter 6), you can choose to store Mac OS X's virtual-memory swap files or even your entire home directory on the second partition (to protect them from problems with the boot volume).

continues on next page

TAKE NOTE ▶ Why and How to Partition *continued*

Note: The best and safest backup option is to move or copy these items to another drive altogether, not just another partition of the same drive. If the drive fails completely for some reason, such a failure is likely to affect both partitions.

In any case, you can erase one partition (for example, via the Installer's Erase and Install option) without erasing any others. The day may come, for example, when Mac OS X files get so messed up that the only solution is to erase the volume and start over. With two partitions, you can erase the boot partition without losing whatever is on the second partition.

Mac OS 9 on the second partition. If you have a Mac that's still capable of booting from Mac OS 9, you can make the second partition a Mac OS 9 boot volume. In fact, the ideal arrangement is to maintain two Mac OS 9 System Folders: one on a separate partition from Mac OS X and a second on the same partition as Mac OS X. Since some files work in Mac OS 9 directly but not in Classic (primarily extensions and control panels—for more on this, see the online Classic chapter), with only one copy of Mac OS 9 installed, you may have to choose between giving up on these programs so that you can use Classic in Mac OS X or keeping them and giving up on Classic. Having two Mac OS 9 System Folders allows you to use one version of Mac OS 9 (typically the one on its own partition) when you want to boot from Mac OS 9 and the other (the one on the Mac OS X partition) when you want to launch Classic—you can have your cake and eat it, too!

A related benefit: If you hold down the Option key at startup (as discussed in Chapter 5), you can select a startup volume. If Mac OS X and Mac OS 9 reside on the same partition, however, only the most recently booted OS will appear. If you cannot start up from Mac OS X, for example, you will not be able to use this method to switch to starting up from Mac OS 9, because the Mac OS 9 System Folder will not be listed as an option. Your only option is to start up from a CD or DVD. With Mac OS 9 and Mac OS X on separate partitions, the Mac OS 9 choice would be available, and you could bypass the need for the disc—helpful if you need to boot in Mac OS 9 to back up files before erasing a troublesome Mac OS X volume.

Mac OS X on the second partition. Alternatively, especially for Macs that cannot boot from Mac OS 9, you can have the second partition be a second Mac OS X boot volume—for example, populated with maintenance and repair utilities. (In this case, I would boot from the second partition only in emergencies, since regularly switching back and forth between two Mac OS X installations can lead to confusion and problems, such as permissions errors that prevent files from opening.)

Bottom line: I recommend partitioning a drive as long as your hard drive is large enough to accommodate more than one partition. If you hard drive is 60 GB or more, you should have more than enough room for at least two partitions.

How to partition?

The following are some general instructions for dividing a drive into two partitions. Remember: Doing so will erase all existing data on any and all current partitions for this drive.

1. After starting up from a Mac OS X Install disc (as described in the main text), from the Utilities menu select the Disk Utility command.

continues on next page

TAKE NOTE ▶ Why and How to Partition *continued*

2. Select the drive you want to partition from the list in the left column of the Disk Utility window.

3. Click the Partition button.

4. From the Volume Scheme menu, select "2 partitions" (assuming you want only two partitions).

5. Drag the divider between the partitions to adjust their sizes as desired.

    Mac OS X works best when you have a healthy amount of unused hard-drive space on the boot volume. Thus, in choosing a partition size, make sure that you'll have at least several gigabytes of unused space *after* you've completed the installation. If this is not the case, I recommend getting a larger hard drive or not partitioning.

6. Click the first of the two partitions. In the Volume Information section, enter a name in the Name text box and select a drive format—most likely Mac OS Extended (Journaled).

    Now click the second partition and repeat the process.

    Note: If you intend to boot from Mac OS 9, make sure the Mac OS 9 Drivers Installed option is selected, if such an option is present. If your Mac cannot boot from Mac OS 9 (as is the case for all currently shipping Macs), you will not get this option.

7. Click the Partition button.

8. Now that the partitions have been created, the next thing you'll likely want to do is install Mac OS X on one partition, including restoring all the additional software that was on your Mac when it first arrived. Mac OS 9 may not have been installed on your drive at that time. Still, it should be available via the Restore software. Refer to the sections on installing and restoring software, in the main text of this chapter, for details.

9. Finally, after restarting from your newly installed Mac OS X volume, if you want Mac OS X on the second partition, don't drag and drop the Mac OS X System software from one partition to the other. This will not result in a bootable partition. To install Mac OS X on the second partition, use the Installer a second time.

    If you instead want Mac OS 9 on the second partition, copy a Mac OS 9 System Folder—as well as the Applications (Mac OS 9) folder, if you want—to the second partition, via drag and drop, so that you have a separate copy of the System Folder there. You can delete the original Mac OS 9 software after you've copied it, should you want only one Mac OS 9 system on your drive.

Partitioning without erasing. There are now utilities—such as Prosoft's Drive Genius (www.prosofteng.com)—that can partition a drive on the fly or even modify the size of an existing partition without requiring that you erase its contents. Always back up your drive before using one of these utilities, in case something goes wrong. I can tell you that I have used Drive Genius and it worked just fine.

Note: These utilities are at least partly based on Apple's Unix pdisk command, included as part of Mac OS X.

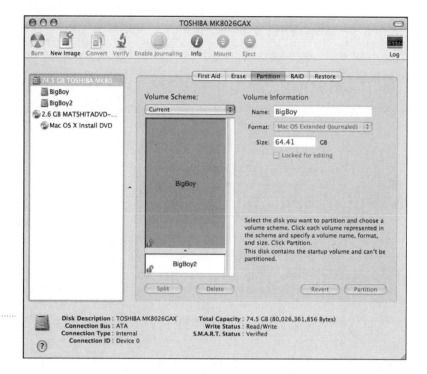

Figure 3.6

The partition options of Disk Utility.

The Window menu

The Window menu contains one last command of note:

Installer Log. If you choose this command, a log window will open, displaying all actions and errors (if any) that occur while Mac OS X is being installed.

In most cases, you can ignore any reported errors, because they don't imply that you won't be able to install Mac OS X. If you really trip over a show-stopping error, you will almost certainly be warned about it directly, via a message alert in the Installer window. In other words, you won't need to check the log. The log may prove useful as a diagnostic aid, however, if a problem occurs for which no other explanatory message appears. You can choose at any time to save the log to your hard drive by clicking the Save button.

Introduction

Returning to the main Installer window, you begin with the Introduction pane, which contains important information about the requirements for installing Mac OS X and what you need to do before installing it. For example, it is likely to warn you about checking for firmware updates. Read the brief message and click Continue. You have now completed the Introduction.

License

Next up is the License pane, which provides the Software License Agreement for the software you're about to install. Agree to the terms and then move on.

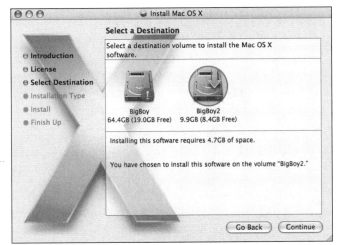

Figure 3.7

The Select a Destination pane of the Installer, with a volume selected on which to install Mac OS X.

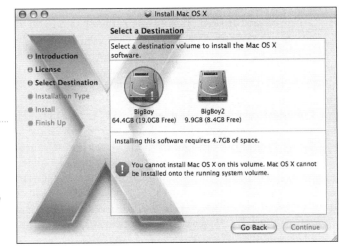

Figure 3.8

Installer refuses to install. The error message on the bottom appeared when trying to install Mac OS X on a volume that is currently the startup disk.

Select a Destination

Finally, we get to the first of the two critical panes for installing Mac OS X: Select a Destination.

In this pane, you will see an icon for every mounted volume (that is, each drive or partition of a drive). Some icons may include a symbol (such as an octagon with an exclamation point) indicating that you cannot currently install Mac OS X on that volume. If you do click the volume, a message will appear at the bottom of the window, indicating what the problem is and what you can do about it. One problem, for example, might be insufficient free disk space.

Once you've selected a volume, click the Options button at the bottom of the pane. A dialog will appear, providing the following installation options. Choose and then click OK:

- **Upgrade Mac OS X or Install Mac OS X.** This option will read Upgrade OS X if your selected volume includes an updatable version of Mac OS X; using this option will install the necessary newer files on top of the existing installation. If you do not have an updatable version of Mac OS X installed, the option will read Install OS X; this will install a new copy of Mac OS X on the volume. Typically, the appropriate choice here is the default option—which means, for example, that you can bypass this Options pane if you know you intend to upgrade an existing Mac OS X installation. However, in some cases, such as if there is insufficient disk space to upgrade, this option will be dimmed and you will have to choose one of the remaining two. In addition, you may prefer to use one of the remaining options even if the Upgrade/Install option is available (see below).

  With either option (but especially the Upgrade option), the Installer just installs or replaces the OS files that are new or updated. Thus, any documents you created or third-party software you added should be preserved.

- **Archive and Install.** This option is the one you will want if you are having any trouble with your current Mac OS X installation. Actually, you may want to use it instead of upgrading (I do!) as a way of preventing potential problems. Used for a volume that already contains some version of Mac OS X, archiving moves the existing OS software (essentially the System, Library, and Applications folders, plus all the invisible Unix folders) to a new folder named Previous Systems, located at the root level of your drive. One exception: Third-party software in the original Applications folder is not moved to the Previous Systems folder; instead it is transferred to your new Applications folder (which is typically what you would want!). The first time you do an Archive and Install, all the moved software is placed in a folder named Previous System 1 inside the Previous Systems folder. If you repeat this process, a Previous System 2 will be created and used, and so on. A new copy of Mac OS X software is installed in place of the moved copy.

This process also moves the Developer folder (if one is present) to Previous Systems. To replace this folder, you need to install the Developer Tools software separately.

A key sub-option here is Preserve Users and Network Settings. With this option selected, both the contents of the /Users folder (which contains your home directory!) and your Network settings are preserved. In almost all cases, I recommend selecting this option; if you don't, you'll have to re-create your accounts from scratch. About the only reason you wouldn't choose it would be if you thought files in your home directory were causing a problem, which you didn't want to carry over to the new installation.

In addition to preserving the contents of your /Users folder, this option also preserves your Network System Preferences settings. It may also preserve third-party software that would not get preserved via a standard Archive and Install (such as certain software in the Applications folder).

Note: This option does not preserve *all* system settings, just *most* of them. For example, it does not preserve the following: settings pertaining to whether a network time server is used; the list of configured printers (stored in /etc/printers.conf); the computer's time zone (stored in /etc/localtime); the resolution of your display(s), and other settings if more than one display is connected, such as arrangement (stored in the com.apple.windowserver.plist in /Library/Preferences and ~/Library/Preferences/ByHost/); and Sharing preference pane settings (stored in /etc/hostconfig). Most of this is minor stuff and can be easily reset if lost.

Note: If you proceed past the Select a Destination pane and then use the Back button to return, the Preserve Users and Network Settings option may be dimmed and unselectable. If so, select another volume (if possible) and then return to the original volume. Otherwise, you'll need to restart the Installer to reselect the option.

> SEE: • "Take Note: Why and How to Use Archive and Install," later in this chapter, for more details on this option.

- **Erase and Install.** This option erases your drive and gives you the opportunity to reformat the volume as Mac OS X Extended (Journaled) or (the rarely used) Unix File System.

  Obviously, you shouldn't choose this option if you're installing Mac OS X on a drive that includes software you don't want to erase.

  Typically, you would select the Erase and Install option only if you suspected such severe drive problems that even a Mac OS X Archive and Install would be unable to fix them. In such cases, you would want to save any critical data on the drive before erasing it. To do this, start up from another hard drive or partition (assuming you can do so) and back up anything you want to save from the problem volume. Then relaunch the Install CD and perform an Erase and Install.

  Avoid using Unix File System (UFS) unless you know you need it—and you almost certainly won't! For starters, Mac OS X Extended is the same format that Mac OS 9 uses. If you select UFS, you will not be able to use that partition for Mac OS 9. UFS drives also prevent some Mac OS X applications from working correctly. About the only people who might prefer UFS formatting are the select few running Mac OS X Server and thus working primarily with the Unix software in Mac OS X, not the Aqua applications.

Note: Alternatively, you can use Disk Utility to erase any volume (other than the current startup volume) at any time. To do so, launch Disk Utility, select the desired partition or disk, and click the Erase button. In the pane that appears, select a name and format for the volume, and click Erase. You can then use the Installer's Install Mac OS X option. This would be the approach you'd take if you wanted to use Disk Utility's "secure" erasure features (described in Chapter 2).

Some users recommend that you always select the Erase and Install option when you move to a major new OS version (such as from 10.3 to 10.4); however, I have not found this to be necessary.

SEE: • "Disk Utility," in Chapter 2, for more details on using Erase, including additional format options available from here.

• "Performing repairs with Disk Utility (First Aid)," in Chapter 5, for more on what *journaled* means.

TECHNICALLY SPEAKING ▶ Case-Sensitive HFS Formatting

If you're using Tiger (client or server) or Panther (server version only), when you format a drive you will be presented with an additional Format option: "Mac OS Extended (Case-sensitive)" (in Tiger) or "Case-sensitive HFS Plus (+)" (in Panther Server).

This format is exactly like the ordinary Mac OS Extended format, except that all file and folder names are case sensitive. That is, a folder with the name *My Memos* is seen as distinct from one named *My Memos*. In contrast, these names would be seen as the same name in standard Mac OS Extended—in fact, you couldn't even create two folders with these names in the same parent folder; instead, you would get a message saying the name already exists. (Note: Standard Mac OS X Extended remembers that the *M* in *Memos* is uppercase; however, the name is not treated differently in searches or file databases from one with a lowercase *m*.)

The main rationale for this is that Unix is case sensitive. By setting up a server to be similarly case sensitive, it eliminates some potential problems and inconsistencies between Mac OS X's Unix base and the higher-level user interface.

However, although it may make sense for certain server setups to use this format, you shouldn't use it in a client system unless you've got a specific reason to do so and are aware of the risks. Although most third-party disk utilities have been updated for compatibility with case-sensitive file systems, not all have, and using an incompatible one could result in data loss. A repair utility that is unaware of the case-sensitive format may assume that My Memos and My memos, if in the same location, are the same folder and delete one of them. In addition, few Mac OS X applications understand case-sensitive file systems.

TAKE NOTE ▶ Why and How to Use Archive and Install

The Archive and Install feature in Mac OS X is similar to the old Clean Install feature of Mac OS 9. Rather than updating an existing installation, it in essence creates an entirely new installation of system software.

Why Archive? You would use the Archive option for either of the following reasons:

- **The Installer refuses to update or reinstall Mac OS X, or you need to install an older version, and you don't want to reformat the drive.** This option is especially helpful when reinstalling Mac OS X from the disc would be a downgrade from the existing OS version (say, because you updated to Mac OS X 10.4.1 via Software Update after installing 10.4.0 from the CD—you can't do a standard install of an older version of the OS). In Mac OS X 10.1.x, Apple strongly advised against doing any sort of downgrade installation, even if it seemed to be permitted by the Installer. At that time, Apple claimed that a downgrade could lead to the presence of files (especially Unix files and /System/Library files) from multiple OS versions in the same system—a potential source of conflicts. Apple's unwelcome solution was to erase your drive if you wanted or needed to do a downgrade installation. The Archive feature of newer versions of the Mac OS X Installer solves this dilemma. Now you can downgrade without erasing by using Archive and Install to install the older version and then update the new installation to the latest version.

- **You want to preserve files from the previous OS version.** In some cases, you may worry that a simple upgrade will overwrite existing files that you may wish you had saved. For example, the Installer may install a new version of an application that contains a new bug. Going back to the old version may work around this bug until the inevitable bug-fix update is released. With the Archive function, the old application version is still in your Previous Systems folder and can be returned to active duty—assuming it works in Mac OS X. Similarly, you may want to replace some modified settings files—especially in the Unix software—with the new ones installed by Mac OS X, as detailed later in this sidebar.

For minor upgrades, such as from Mac OS X 10.4 to 10.4.1, the Options button is not available, meaning you cannot choose Archive and Install. Instead, your only option is Upgrade. However, if you're performing a major reference upgrade (that is, where there is a change in the first number after the decimal, such as from Mac OS X 10.3.x to 10.4.x), you will be presented with a choice of options. In this case, I recommend using the Archive and Install option and preserving the /Users folders, as described in the main text. There's very little downside to this option, other than the additional disk space required to store the archived software.

Reinstalling software and resetting preferences after an Archive installation. After an Archive and Install, you may need to reinstall some third-party software to get it to work properly. You may also need to reset some serial-number registrations. For example, I needed to re-enter my QuickTime Pro serial number.

As noted in the main text, you may also need to re-create some Mac OS X System Preferences settings. For example, when upgrading from Mac OS X 10.2.x to 10.3, I needed to reset the time zone in Date & Time, because it reverted to the Pacific time zone. I also had to re-enable the Network Time check in the same preferences pane.

continues on next page

TAKE NOTE ▶ Why and How to Use Archive and Install *continued*

Moving files after an Archive installation. After an Archive clean install, the archived OS software (in the Previous Systems folder) may contain a few files that you want to return to the now-current OS. As a general rule, I wouldn't move anything back until you discover that a setting or feature is missing and you can't re-create it easily by entering new settings. This way, you avoid the problems that can occur if you replace a needed newer file with an older one. That being said, included among the items you may want to move back are the following:

- **Files and folders in the old /Library folder.** Files and folders that exist in your archived /Library folder but not in the updated /Library folder may contain additions and preferences files that you want to preserve. One example would be receipt files for third-party software in the Receipts folder. Another would be the StuffitEngineShell.cfm file, contained in the CFMSupport folder in /Library, which provides support for StuffIt Expander. Also, if you're running a Web server from your Mac but are storing your files in the system's Web directory rather than your user-level Web directory, you should transfer any custom contents of /Library/WebServer/Documents. Third-party items in the StartupItems folder are also not moved.

  Note: Sometimes, simply moving files from the old /Library folder to the new one doesn't work. For example, moving startup items from the previous /Library/StartupItems folder to your new /Library/StartupItems folder doesn't always work. You may need to reinstall the related software to install new copies of the StartupItems files. Another specific example: Some Palm Desktop users upgrading from Jaguar to Panther via Archive and Install found that after the upgrade, syncing no longer worked. The reason was that the HotSync Library files, located in /Library/CFMSupport, were not moved. Moving them manually did not fix the problem, either; the Palm software had to be reinstalled.

- **Certain applications.** Some applications that require a password or registration code to function may not offer the option to re-enter the password. Instead, you may need to transfer an application's password/serial-number file from the Previous Systems folder. Otherwise, you may need to reinstall the application software.

If you do decide to transfer files back, you may be blocked from moving certain files due to insufficient permission access. In such cases, you will need to use techniques to modify permissions or authenticate the moves (such as those described in Chapter 6) so that you can bypass this blockade.

Deleting files after an Archive installation: Help files. You may want to delete some files that were carried over from the old home directory to the new one. If you are having problems with Help Viewer, for example, check out "Take Note: Getting Help for Help," in Chapter 2.

continues on next page

TAKE NOTE ▶ **Why and How to Use Archive and Install**   *continued*

Transferring Unix files. Finally, you may have reason to move back some directories and files in Unix's invisible /private directory. In particular, you may want to move the following files and folders:

- **/etc/hostconfig.** If you've set up Sendmail on your Mac, this file is important and probably should be restored from Previous Systems to the current Mac OS X folder. (Note, however, that Panther and later versions of Mac OS X use Postfix as their default Unix mail server, which means that this may be a good opportunity to switch, since Postfix has a much better reputation than Sendmail.)

- **/etc/httpd/httpd.conf.** If you edited your Apache configuration (used for Web server preferences beyond those you can set up via the Sharing System Preferences pane), move this file back.

- **/var/log.** This folder contains archives of system-level log files. If they're valuable to you, copy them over.

- **/var/root.** If you enabled the root user in Mac OS X, this folder is the root user's /User folder: It contains the Desktop, Documents, and user-level Library directories, as well as any other files and folders that may have been created or saved to your home directory when you were logged in as root or using an application as root. If this folder contains any files you want to save, transfer them back.

You may need to log in as a root user or launch a file utility as root to make some of these changes.

Using the Previous Systems folder. One weakness of the Archive option is that the archived system is not bootable. In addition, the Installer does not offer a "switch back" option. Thus, if you decide that upgrading was a mistake (which is very unlikely!) and you want to return to the previous version of Mac OS X, there's no easy way to do a reverse exchange. For that reason, make sure that your Mac OS X volume is backed up before doing the upgrade. Then if you decide to go back, you can restore the old Mac OS X version from your backup.

Note: A third-party back-up program, Shirt Pocket's SuperDuper! (www.shirt-pocket.com), has a feature that offers the ability to switch back to a prior installed version of the OS.

Note: The application software in the Previous Systems folder—all older versions of "stock" Mac OS X applications that have been replaced by newer versions—remains functional. Thus, if you double-click a document that uses one of these applications and a newer version is not available elsewhere, the document will attempt to launch via the application in the Previous Systems folder.

Preserve Users and Network Settings. As I stated in the main text, I generally recommend using the Preserve Users and Network Settings option when doing an Archive and Install. But what if you *did not* use it and later wish you had? Good news: You can still restore your home directory; it will just be more work to do so. The directory is preserved in the /Previous Systems/ Users folder. What you will need to do is create a new account for yourself, using the same short name as your old account. You can then copy files from the old account into the new one. You may need to reset permissions of some files, making yourself the owner, before you can use them. You can repeat this for any additional accounts you may have that you want to re-create.

continues on next page

TAKE NOTE ▶ Why and How to Use Archive and Install *continued*

Deleting Previous System (#) folder. After updating, you may eventually decide you no longer need any of the files stored in the Previous System 1 (or 2, and so on) folder and want to delete the folder to regain the disk space. If your account has administrator status, you can simply drag the folder to the Trash; if you're asked to authenticate, provide your user name and account password.

SEE: • "Ownership & Permissions," in Chapter 4, for more on setting permissions.

 • "Opening and Saving: Permissions Problems," and "Copying and Moving: Permissions Problems," in Chapter 6, for more on setting permissions.

 • "Modifying invisible Unix files from Mac OS X applications," in Chapter 6, for related information.

 • "Take Note: Deleting SystemConfiguration Folder Files," in Chapter 8, for more on where network settings are preserved.

TECHNICALLY SPEAKING ▶ Custom Config Files After a Mac OS X Update

When you make custom changes to a config file, the changes may be wiped out when you update to a new version of Mac OS X. This is because the update often replaces the customized config file with an updated default copy of the file. It will appear that all of your customized changes have been lost. In some cases, the Installer nicely preserves the customized file in the same directory, adding an extension to the filename, as in httpd.conf.applesaved or hostconfig.old. This allows you to recover your changes and add them back to the new file. Alternatively, you can swap the files so that the inactive file is returned to active duty. For example, for the httpd.conf files, give the active httpd.conf file a name like httpd.conf.base and rename the applesaved file as *httpd.conf*. Doing this httpd.conf change requires root access and should be done with Personal Web Sharing turned off.

However, starting with the installer package for the Mac OS X 10.2.5 Update, Apple reversed what happens when an update is installed, at least for the httpd.conf file. In describing this, Apple states, "Mac OS X 10.2.5 and later updates have a different installation method for the new httpd.conf file. The Installer checks to see if you have modified the existing httpd.conf file. If you have not, then it automatically replaces it with the new version. If you have modified it, then your modified file is left in place, and the new file is written as /etc/httpd/httpd.conf.default. At your leisure, you should add your modifications to the new file and retire the old one."

SEE: • "Modifying invisible Unix Files from Mac OS X applications," in Chapter 6, for related information.

TAKE NOTE ▶ Mac OS X Install Disc vs. Upgrade Disc

Major Mac OS X upgrades (typically defined as one in which the first digit after the decimal point changes, such as from 10.3 to 10.4) almost always require a new full-installation Mac OS X disc (a DVD or several CDs)—specifically, one that you must pay Apple to obtain. From this disc, you can install a new, full version of Mac OS X, even on an empty volume.

Between major updates, however, Apple releases minor updates. These free updates are available via Software Update or by downloading the update file from the Web. Such updates, however, can be applied only to already installed versions of Mac OS X (and sometimes only to the most recent prior version).

In some cases, Apple may offer an upgrade disc, such as via the Mac OS X Up-To-Date program (www.apple.com/macosx/uptodate), that differs slightly from the full install disc.

In the most extreme case, both the Install Mac OS X and Archive and Install options will be disabled on the upgrade disc. You will be able to upgrade only from an existing older version of Mac OS X. This limitation is significant, as it prevents you from using one of the key install features of Mac OS X: Archive and Install.

Tiger upgrade discs do include an Archive and Install option. However, it works only to upgrade a volume that is presently running Panther. You could not use this option, for example, to downgrade from Mac OS X 10.4.1 back to 10.4.0. You still cannot use the upgrade disc to install Mac OS X on a volume that does not already have an earlier version of Mac OS X installed. For such cases, you need the full Install disc.

SEE: • "Cautions regarding extracting files from update packages," later in this chpater, for related information.

Installation Type, Install, and Finish Up

Finally, you'll reach the pane where you actually initiate the installation. By default, the Easy Install pane appears (unless your drive has insufficient disk space). If you're installing via CD, this pane informs you of whether you need Disc 2 and/or Disc 3 for the installation. At this point, you can simply click the Install (or Upgrade) button and then sit back and relax. You have now reached the Installation stage. The installation may take 20 minutes or so to complete, during which time a variety of status messages appear, informing you of what is happening at each stage. Unless something goes wrong and the installation fails, you're finished with the installation process. However, before you click the Install/Upgrade button, I recommend at least taking a look at the customization options, accessible via the Customize button.

Custom Install. Rather than doing an Easy Install, you can click the Customize button to bring up the Custom Install pane. From here, you can enable or disable individual components of the installation—which means you can disable options you don't need in order to save drive space or simply reduce clutter. This is also how you install software that would otherwise not be installed.

Custom Install options include the following:

- **Essential System Software.** You cannot disable this option when installing Mac OS X; you can only do so when upgrading. And even then, I strongly advise against it—unless the only reason you're upgrading is to obtain a minor component of Mac OS X that you didn't install initially (such as a set of printer drivers).

- **BSD Subsystem.** (Only an option in Panther and earlier installers.) The BSD Subsystem is made up of optional components of the otherwise essential Unix software at the core of Mac OS X (as discussed in Chapter 4). Although these components are technically optional, some applications may not run correctly without them. Again, other than for the reasons described above, I would never disable this option. (In Tiger and later installers, this option isn't even available—the BSD Subsystem is always installed.)

- **Additional Applications.** (Only an option in Panther and earlier installers.) If you choose this option, you can omit the installation of specific applications such as Microsoft Internet Explorer.

- **Printer Drivers.** From here, you can elect to omit specific printer drivers (such as those for particular brands of printers you do not own or expect to use). Panther also includes the option to install additional Gimp-Print drivers, used for adding Mac OS X support to otherwise unsupported printers (as covered in Chapter 7). (The Gimp-Print drivers are installed by default in Tiger.)

- **Additional Speech Voices.** (Only an option in Panther and earlier installers.) This option installs more voice choices for Mac OS X's text to-speech options.

- **Additional Fonts.** If you enable this option, fonts used by such languages as Chinese, Korean, Arabic, Hebrew, and a number of other non-Roman-alphabet languages will be installed.

- **Language Translations.** These options provide the localized files and fonts that Mac OS X needs to support languages beyond English. If you're confident you don't need this support, disable these options. Doing so saves a significant amount of disk space—over 1 GB! I always choose a Custom Install over an Easy Install when I install Mac OS X for just this reason. If you want to just install files for one or two additional languages, you can do so; click the disclosure triangle for Localized Files and choose the languages you want installed.

- **X11.** This installs the Unix X11 windowing system (see "Terminal and X11," in Chapter 2). This option is disabled by default, so you will need to do a Custom Install if you want to install it.

When you select a Custom Install option in the list, the bottom of the window shows a description of that item; to the right of the item you can see how much space it will require on your hard drive. When you're done configuring your Custom Install, click the Install button to begin installation. (If you change your mind and want to do an Easy Install instead, click the Easy Install button.)

Restarting. When installation is complete (and you reach the Finish Up pane), you can choose to restart by quitting the Installer. If you don't, the Installer will restart automatically after a brief delay.

When you restart, the Mac should start up from the volume where you just installed or upgraded Mac OS X. If it instead boots from the Install disc, restart again and hold down the Eject key (or mouse button) until the disc ejects. (If Disc 2 and/or Disc 3 are needed, you will be prompted to insert them at this point. The additional software on these discs is then installed.) If this is the first time you've installed Mac OS X (or if you did an Erase and Install or an Archive and Install without preserving user accounts), you will be prompted to set up an account for yourself, as well as Internet access, before you can log in. Otherwise, the Login window will appear or you will be automatically logged in, depending upon your preferences.

Checking for updates. Even if you've just installed Mac OS X, there may be minor updates that are newer than the installed version. For this reason, once you've successfully installed Mac OS X, you should run Software Update to check for and then install any updates. (If you're connected to the Internet on login, Software Update may launch automatically.)

Alternatively, if you previously downloaded the update files, you can install them directly from the .pkg files.

At this point, you can also install the Developer software from the Xcode Tools folder on the Install DVD. Updates to the Developer software are not listed in Software Update. Instead, you must check Apple's Developer Web site (http://developer.apple.com/tools) for updates to this software.

SEE: • "Take Note: Developer Software," in Chapter 2, for more details.

• "Updating Mac OS X," later in this chapter, for more on updating.

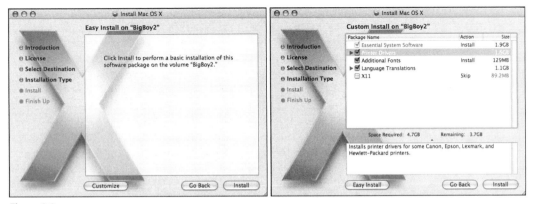

Figure 3.9

Left, *the Installer's Easy Install window;* right, *the Custom Install window.*

Restoring Mac OS Software

The Mac OS X Install disc installs the latest versions of the standard Mac OS X applications. However, your Mac may have come with a number of other applications, such as the iLife suite, games, and even Mac OS 9. If you erased your drive prior to installing Mac OS X, or if one or more of these applications or Mac OS 9 has become damaged or corrupt, you'll probably want to get them back. To do this, you will need the Restore feature included with the disc(s) that came with your computer. Exactly what disc(s) you get, whether it is a series of Restore CDs or a single DVD (that combines Install and Restore options), and how it all works, varies as a function of the Mac model you purchased. In this section, I will focus mainly on how it works for the newest Macs (released in 2005). For older Macs, consult the documentation that came with your machine.

Note: The only thing that will not get restored by this method is the collection of music files included on some iMacs and iBooks. If you want to save these, you must back them up first. A Restore also may not reinstall software that comes on its own CD, such as the World Book software.

To restore software on the latest Macs, which include a DVD (more likely two DVDs, Install Disc 1 and Install Disc 2) that combines the Mac OS X Installer and the ability to restore bundled software, you have two choices:

- **Install Mac OS X and Bundled Software.** This icon, when double-clicked, will ask you to restart and will then boot from the DVD. You'll be presented with a standard Mac OS X Installer that behaves just as I described earlier in this chapter. However, the Custom Install pane will also include options for bundled software.

- **Install Bundled Software Only.** This icon will launch the standard Mac OS X Installer utility and give you the option, in the Custom Install pane, to choose the bundled software you wish to install.

Note: On some older Macs, an Install and Restore DVD will have icons for two options: Install Mac OS X and Install Applications & Classic Support. Launch both to completely restore all the preinstalled software on your Mac.

When you're finished restoring your software, use Software Update to check for and install any more recent updates to the applications you just reinstalled. Alternately, if you've already downloaded the updates to your drive, just open the .pkg files directly and install them.

Note: The core software used to run Software Restore is actually the Unix command asr (for *Apple Software Restore*), which you can access directly from Terminal. The cool thing about asr is that you can use it to restore anything, not just the files on the Software Restore CDs.

SEE: • "Technically Speaking: More About Disk Utility's Image and Restore Features," later in this chapter.

Figure 3.10

A look at the contents of a Mac OS X Install and Restore DVD that comes with a Mac. Note the Install Mac OS X and Bundled Software icon and the Install Bundled Software Only icon.

What About Mac OS 9?

From the moment Apple released Mac OS X, it began plotting the demise of Mac OS 9. For starters, it has stopped all development of new versions of Mac OS 9.

No more booting from Mac OS 9. Starting in January 2003, new Mac models could no longer boot Mac OS 9. Only Mac OS X booting was supported. (Note: This is limited to Mac models *introduced* after January 2003, not to all Macs sold as "new" after this time. This distinction is important because Apple continued to sell a few "older" models after January 2003, specifically because those models could still boot into Mac OS 9.)

Thus, if you bought a Mac model released in 2003 or later, you cannot boot from Mac OS 9, either via a Mac OS 9 System Folder installed on a hard drive or via a Mac OS 9 CD.

No more Mac OS 9 preinstalled. Starting in June 2004, Macs no longer came with Mac OS 9 preinstalled, even for use in Classic.

Still, you may wish to use Classic to run some Mac OS 9 software that you still have. Happily, you can do so. You just need to make sure that Mac OS 9 winds up installed on your drive. Exactly how to do this varies as a function of which Mac model you have and when you purchased it.

This is because Apple seems to keep changing how it handles Mac OS 9 with each new Mac model it releases. That's also why I hedge some of my statements on this subject. And whatever I write may be at least partially obsolete in a few months!

Getting Mac OS 9 onto your Mac OS X Mac

If you have an older Mac that came with Mac OS 9 preinstalled (for use with Classic), as long as you don't plan to erase your drive or move Mac OS 9 to another partition, you're already set to go. In addition, newer Macs still ship with software to install Mac OS 9, either with a separate Mac OS 9 Install CD or as part of the Restore software (noted in the previous section).

On the other hand, the retail version of Mac OS X no longer includes a Mac OS 9 Install CD. This can be a minor hassle if you want to install Mac OS 9 on your drive.

The following represent some potential ways to get Mac OS 9 installed:

- Some newer Macs include a separate Mac OS 9 Install Disc. You can use this CD to install a copy of Mac OS 9 to use with Classic.

- If you have a Power Mac G5, an iBook, or an iMac G5 that shipped with Mac OS X 10.3.4 through 10.3.7—Apple is quite specific about this!—the Additional Software & Apple Hardware Test disc that came with your Mac provides a means to install Mac OS 9. On my Power Mac G5, for example, there is an icon named Install Additional Software. If you double-click it, it will install Classic Support.

- On Macs that include a combined Software Install and Restore DVD, there will be two separate icons: Install Mac OS X and one called either Install Applications & Classic Support or Install Bundled Software Only. Double-click whichever of the latter icons appears, to access an option to install Classic.

- If Mac OS 9 and Mac OS X are installed on the same volume and you want to move Mac OS 9 to a separate volume, you can simply copy the Mac OS 9 System Folder to the alternative volume.

- On older Macs that came with a series of Software Restore CDs, there should be an invisible folder called .images on the first CD. Use a utility such as Mac4ever's InVisibles (www.mac4ever.de/invisibles) to make it visible. Inside this folder will be a disk-image file called OS9General.dmg. Copy this file to your hard drive and mount the image. The files contained within the image include a Mac OS 9 System Folder. To install Mac OS 9 on a volume, copy the System Folder on the image to the volume.

Selectively Installing Mac OS X Files

Suppose at some point you accidentally delete an application that is included as part of Mac OS X or that came preinstalled on your drive. Or perhaps the application somehow gets corrupted and no longer launches. Even worse, you never made a backup copy of it. What can you do? You have several choices.

Do a Custom Install/Restore

A Custom Install ideally allows you to reinstall just the software you want, without having to do a complete reinstall of Mac OS X. With a complete reinstall, you run the risk of overwriting a file (possible a newer version of the file) that you don't want to modify—not to mention the fact that you're reinstalling thousands of perfectly OK files to get the one file that's missing (or *not* OK). As always, exactly how to do a Custom Install varies as a function of the Mac model you have.

To do a Custom Install on Macs that come with an Install DVD that includes an Install Bundled Software Only icon, start by double-clicking this icon. When you get to the Installation Type pane, click the Customize button. From here, you will be able to select which applications you want to reinstall. If the software you want is not listed, quit the Installer and instead double-click the Install Mac OS X and Bundled Software icon. Restart your Mac when requested and similarly check the Customize options.

Alternatively, you may be able to locate and launch a specific desired .pkg file (such as iPhoto.pkg) from an Install/Restore disc that allows you to install just the particular software you want. To find most of the packages you might want, go to /System/Installation/Packages on the initial Install 1 DVD.

Note: Some package items are in an invisible folder called .packages located inside the Packages folder(s). To see these items, use a utility such as InVisibles to make invisible items visible. Or use the Finder's Go to Folder command and type the path to the desired folder. For example, for the Install Disc 1 DVD, you would type /Volumes/Mac OS X Install Disc 1/System/Installation/Packages/.packages. Installing from an application's .pkg file is almost the same as installing the software via a Custom Install from the "full" Mac OS X Installer. One advantage of the separate install is that you may not need to restart your Mac from the Install disc in order to install. Also, you may be able to locate and install a .pkg file that is not listed separately in the Customize pane of the full Installer.

Note: In some cases, a .pkg file (especially an .mpkg file) may serve only to redirect the Installer to other .pkg file(s) where the software is actually located.

Note: If you install a version of an application from your Mac OS X Install disc, and a later update to Mac OS X—or just to that application—had previously updated the application, you'll need to go back and reinstall the update(s) to make sure you've got the latest version of the application.

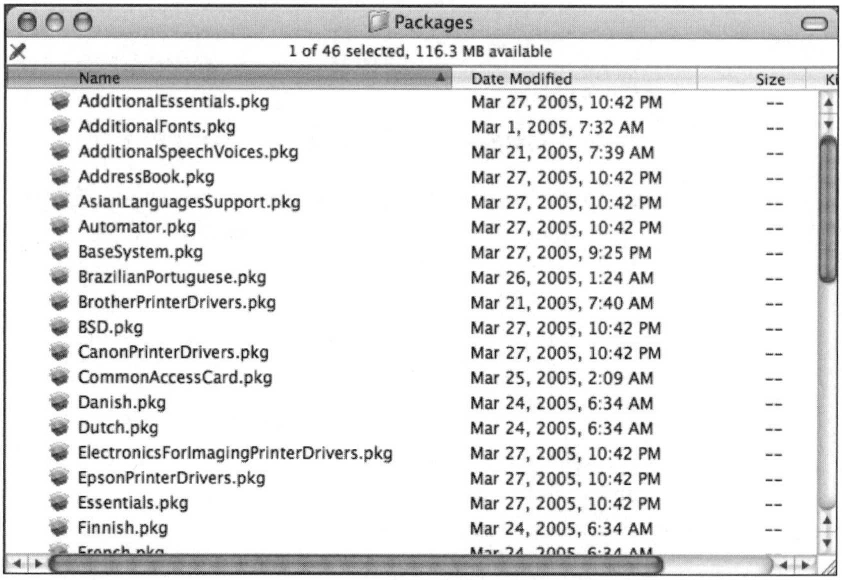

Figure 3.11

The /System/Installation /Packages folder on a Mac OS X Install Disc.

Copying from the Mac OS X Install discs

If the latest version of the file you want is on the Mac OS X Install discs, as an accessible file, you can copy it directly from the disc.

On some Install Disc 1 discs, for example, check inside the System folder at the root level of the disc. Here you will find a Library folder that contains copies of some files (such as Fonts) that eventually get installed in /System/Library on your drive. Should you need to replace one of these files (perhaps because you tried a hack on one of the files, and it failed and you don't have a backup), you can use the copy here. One caution: Occasionally, a file used on an Install disc will differ from that used on a hard drive. Overall I would be cautious about using this method and recommend performing a Custom Install instead.

The /Applications/Utilities folder contains working copies of applications such as Disk Utility and Installer.

Reinstalling from a Web download

If you cannot or do not wish to reinstall software from the Install disc(s), you may be able to download a separate installer from the Web. Check Apple's Web site to see if one is available.

Extracting from an expanded .pax.gz file

If the file you want is contained within a .pkg file—for example, MacOSXUpdateCombo10.4.3.pkg—you will most likely need to extract the file from the larger update. Here's one way to do so:

1. Locate the .pax.gz file (for example, Archive.pax.gz) inside the Installer package file. (To view the contents of the package file, Control-click it and then select Show Package Contents from the menu that appears; then open the Contents folder.)

2. Make a copy of the .pax.gz file and move it to the Desktop. (Although this step is not required, it serves as a good precaution against damaging the only copy.)

3. Decompress the copied file.

   If the current version of StuffIt Expander does not decompress the file, use the shareware application OpenUp, by Scott Anguish (www.stepwise.com/Software/OpenUp). For large update packages, expect this output to take up a healthy amount of disk space (since it contains every file in the update).

4. Locate the desired file and use it to replace the original.

   You may need root access to do this. You can delete the remaining expanded files or save them in case you need to do this again someday.

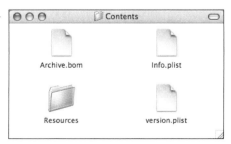

Figure 3.12

Top, *inside the package file of a Keynote Updater;* bottom, *the receipt file for the same updater. Note that the .pax.gz file is missing from the receipt file.*

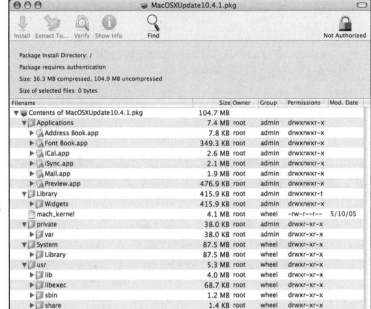

Figure 3.13

This Pacifist window displays the contents of a Tiger Mac OS X update file. Clicking the disclosure triangles reveals subdirectory contents.

Use Pacifist

A simpler (and thus better) alternative to the previous procedure is to use a shareware utility called Pacifist, by CharlesSoft (www.charlessoft.com). Simply open a package (.pkg or .mpkg) file from within Pacifist, and you will see a complete list of all files in the .pkg file. You can then choose to extract a single file (or more, if you wish)—either to its intended destination location or to any location you select.

Note: On the Mac OS X Install CD, most of the to-be-installed software is stored in .pkg files. For example, inside the System folder at the root level of the CD is a folder called Package, which contains several .pkg files (most notably Essentials.pkg) that include the bulk of the Mac OS X software. You can open these packages via Pacifist to extract individual files. In fact, Pacifist has an Open Mac OS X Install Packages button that will provide a list of all packages on a Mac OS X Install disc along with the contents of each.

Of course, if you have a newer version of Mac OS X installed on your hard drive than the version on the Install CD, check any Update .pkg file(s) you have to see if there is a newer version of the software than the version on the Install CD—unless you specifically intend to downgrade as part of some trouble-shooting work-around (in which case you want the version on the Install CD).

SEE: • "Understanding Image, Installer Package, and Receipt Files," later in this chapter, for more details.

Cautions regarding extracting files from update packages

Two cautions about using Pacifist or otherwise extracting software from a .pax.gz file:

- **Related files may not get extracted.** Sometimes the software you want to replace is part of a related set of files. For example, an application may require a file in an Application Support folder and/or an update to a Framework in order to function correctly. In such cases, if the additional files are not already present on your drive, just installing the application may not be sufficient. A complete reinstall of Mac OS X then becomes a better choice. You will know this is a possibility if the application does not work after the installation.

- **The extracted file may be incomplete.** Starting with Mac OS X 10.3.4, Apple began releasing three different versions of most OS updates: *Combo*, *Delta*, and *Patch*.

  Combo updates contain all the changes made, from the original major version of the OS to the most recent minor update. For example, the Mac OS X 10.4.3 Combo Update can update any version of Mac OS X 10.4, from 10.4.0 to 10.4.2.

  Delta updates typically contain only the changes from the immediately previous version. For example, the Mac OS X 10.4.3 Update can only update systems running Mac OS X 10.4.2.

  Patch updates are similar to Delta updates. However, to keep the size of the update .pkg file to a minimum, they typically include only those files within application packages (and any other bundles) that have been modified in the update. Thus, a patch update that contains a new version of Safari may only include the files in the Safari package that have been changed. The extracted Safari application package would thus be incomplete and would not run.

  Patch updates can be used only by certain installations of the previous update. They are only available as a download via Software Update because Software Update must first see if your installation of Mac OS X is eligible to use the Patch version. Because a Patch version of an update does not contain complete versions of most software, you should not use a utility such as Pacifist to extract parts of the update.

  You can see if an update package you've downloaded is a Patch version by looking at its name—if so, the name will end in *Patch.pkg*.

I would hesitate to use Pacifist to extract files from anything but a Combo update package or, even better, a full Mac OS X Installer package.

Upgrading Mac OS X

The terms *upgrade* and *update* are often used synonymously. In the context of Mac OS X, however, they carry important distinctions: An *upgrade* refers to moving from one major version of Mac OS X to another—such as *upgrading* from Mac OS X 10.3 Panther to Mac OS X 10.4 Tiger. An *update*, in contrast, refers to moving from one minor version to another—such as *updating* from Mac OS X 10.4.1 to Mac OS X 10.4.2. For upgrades, the number after the first period changes; for updates, the number after the second period changes. As you might expect, updates represent mostly minor changes (such as bug fixes), whereas upgrades typically introduce dozens of major new features.

Another important distinction is that upgrades are rarely free (unless you qualify for a free upgrade because you purchased your Mac a few weeks before the upgrade was released; check with Apple to see if this is the case). For example, the upgrade to Tiger cost $129 even if you purchased Panther just a couple of months before.

Updates, on the other hand, *are* typically free.

Upgrading to a new version of Mac OS X always requires installing Mac OS X from a new Mac OS X Install DVD (or set of CDs). Thus, the procedure for doing so is exactly as described earlier in this chapter for installing Mac OS X the first time. Updates are usually handled via a single update .pkg file.

This section discusses upgrading; the next section covers updating.

Upgrade oddities. If you have an earlier version of Mac OS X installed, you may decide to use the Installer's Archive and Install feature; however, if you have not been too aggressive in customizing your Mac OS X environment and if you follow the procedures covered in the next section, the standard upgrade, as opposed to the Archive and Install, is likely to work well.

There are, however, a few odd glitches that may occur when doing a standard upgrade—and even when doing an Archive and Install in some cases. This is because each major upgrade may change a few default system settings and/or software. For example, as discussed in other chapters, Panther changed the default shell in Terminal from tcsh (its Jaguar default) to bash. Panther also changed the default group for files you create from "staff" to a new group with the same name as your user account, and changed your personal keychain file name from {*your username*}.keychain in Jaguar to login.keychain in Panther. However, when you upgrade—or do an Archive and Install where users are preserved—from Jaguar to Panther, these settings may retain their Jaguar status for existing accounts. On the other hand, new users that you create will follow the Panther rules instead. This can get confusing. If you want your account to use the new Panther settings, you can do an Archive and Install without select-ing the Preserve User option (and then copy any needed files from the Previous Systems folder to your newly created account folder in the /Users folder). Otherwise, you can do a standard upgrade and change the default set-tings in the relevant config/preferences files (seek additional advice from Web sites, books, or knowledgeable users, as to what files to change, if needed).

SEE: • **"Installing or Reinstalling Mac OS X" and "Take Note: Why and How to Use Archive and Install," earlier in this chapter, for more details.**

•   **"Document opens in the 'wrong' application," in Chapter 6, for details of other oddities.**

Before you upgrade

Before you insert the Mac OS X Install disc and begin the installation process, you should make sure you're prepared for any problems that may result. Here are the main things you should do before upgrading:

Back up. In the event that something goes wrong, you can still return to your pre-upgrade state using your backup copy.

SEE: • **"Backing Up and Restoring Mac OS X Volumes," later in this chapter.**

Remove or update software that's likely to be incompatible with the upgrade. Once you've upgraded, you may find that software that worked perfectly previously no longer works. Although any third-party software on your drive could turn out to be a problem here, be especially wary of third-party System Preferences as well as items in your Login Items list.

Ideally, you want to take care of these software conflict issues *before* you upgrade (rather than discover the problem afterward). The best and most common fix for such problems is for the third-party developer to release an upgrade that addresses the conflict. If an update that fixes the problem is already available, install the update before upgrading the OS. Otherwise, you may have to disable, remove, and/or uninstall the problem software until an update gets released.

How do you find out which software needs to be updated? To some extent, you can self-diagnose. That is, items that modify the system (such as WindowShade X, which changes how the Finder minimizes windows) are those that are most likely to need an update. Check with the developer's Web site for confirmation regarding these likely candidates. In most cases, the developer will have information about compatibility within a day or so of a new OS's release. Otherwise, check various Web sites (such as Apple's own Web site and MacFixIt [www.macfixit.com]) for news of compatibility problems.

TAKE NOTE ▶ The Migration Assistant and Moving Data to a New Computer

Beginning with Macs that shipped in June 2004, Apple includes on all Macs a utility called the Migration Assistant; this utility is also included with Tiger. The purpose of the Migration Assistant is to help you transfer data—user accounts and files, applications, system settings, and the like—from an old computer to a new one. For example, it is run by the Setup Assistant on a new Mac to see if you have accounts and data on an old Mac that you want to transfer. If so, you can transfer those accounts to the new Mac instead of setting up new ones—your new Mac will look much like your old one with minimal effort.

I mention this here for two reasons. The first is that it answers the age-old Mac OS X question of "How do I get my stuff from my old Mac to my new one?" Assuming your old Mac has a FireWire port, you simply place your old Mac in Target Disk Mode (discussed more in Chapter 8) and connect it to the new Mac, and the Migration Assistant walks you through the process. The Migration Assistant will also transfer data from a mounted external drive as long as Mac OS X is installed on it.

Once the two Mac installations are connected, you decide which accounts, complete with all files and settings (the entire /User folders, actually), will be transferred. You then choose if you want to transfer the contents of /Library, /Applications, and/or files and folders at the root level of the "old" volume. (If the same application is found on both Macs, the Migration Assistant is smart enough to keep or copy the newer version.) If the old Mac has additional volumes (such as second or third partitions), you can choose to have the contents of those volumes copied to new folders at the root level of the new Mac's hard drive. Finally, you can choose to "migrate" your old Mac's network, time, and sharing settings.

Migration Assistant and upgrading Mac OS X. The Migration Assistant is also potentially useful if you're upgrading to a new version of Mac OS X on the same Mac. I mentioned in the main text that many people elect to back up their Mac's hard drive and then perform an Erase and Install installation, later copying their important files back. The Migration Assistant can also perform its migration magic using a second volume on the same Mac—for example, a second partition or a DVD containing your files—or using an external hard drive. The only caveat is that the Migration Assistant recognizes only volumes with Mac OS X installed. So you can back up your hard drive to another partition or volume, perform an Erase and Install, and then use the Migration Assistant to populate your new installation with all of your previous accounts, settings, and files.

Updating Mac OS X

Once you have installed and (if necessary) initially updated to the latest version of Mac OS X, you will want to keep it up to date. Apple regularly releases software updates (as opposed to *upgrades*, as covered in the previous section) and makes them available via both the Software Update System Preferences pane and the Apple Web site. Because Software Update is the simplest and fastest way to stay current, I recommend using it. I gave a brief overview of how to use Software Update in Chapter 2; the following provides some additional details.

Apple releases three categories of updates, almost all of which are available via Software Update:

- **General updates to Mac OS X.** These are the Combo, Delta, and Patch updates, as described previously in "Cautions regarding extracting files from update packages."

   Note: In no case do these updates contain the complete set of software you need to run Mac OS X. For this, you need a Mac OS X Install disc.

- **Security updates to Mac OS X.** These updates, with names like Security Update 2005-05, modify the OS to plug various security leaks, but do not alter the version number of the OS.

- **Separate updates to specific components of Mac OS X as well as to software not included as part of Mac OS X.** For example, you may see a QuickTime update, an iPhoto update, or a Pages update.

   SEE • "Take Note: About This Mac," in Chapter 2, for more on Mac OS X version and build numbers.

Although I generally recommend installing updates—Apple provides them to fix bugs and to add new features—I also recommend waiting a few days after an update has been released to do so. Use this time to check the Web (for example, the MacFixIt site) to make sure the software doesn't contain any significant bugs that weren't discovered until *after* its release. And always make backups of critical files before installing an update.

How and why things can go wrong. After installing software, it's possible to start getting permissions errors when trying to launch various applications, including applications unrelated to the one(s) you just installed. In extreme cases, the system may even become unusable. How can this happen simply as a result of running the Installer utility? The answer is two-pronged: When installing software, you're typically asked to enter your administrative password, which gives the Installer temporary root access. In addition, script files within an Install .pkg that are run as part of the installation can contain instructions to modify permissions of files and folders—or even to delete certain files. These script files, typically located in the Resources folder inside the package file, have names like "preflight," "postflight," and "postinstall." If these scripts contain errors that cause permission changes or file deletions that should not occur, you can wind up with serious problems.

Basically, you just have to trust that the software developer has not made such an error. And usually your trust is well placed—such mistakes are rare. Although the risk rises slightly with software that does not come from Apple, even Apple can make a mistake here.

Here's one example: When Apple initially released iTunes 2.0 as a free upgrade on the Web, it was supposed to delete any older version of iTunes found on your drive before installing the new version. Unfortunately, the installer .pkg file contained a nasty quirk: Due to an error in how it was set up to work, the installation sometimes failed to install iTunes at all. Even worse, when attempting to remove an older version of iTunes, the installer sometimes also removed much of the data on your drive! This horrendous bug was fixed the same day via another iTunes update—but not before hundreds of users lost files.

In general, if an installer causes a serious mistake, you will need to reinstall Mac OS X to fix it—and then restore any lost files from your backups.

TAKE NOTE ▶ **Unexpected Differences Between Updates and New Installs**

Ideally, assuming that all goes well with the installation, there should be no differences between how a newly installed version of Mac OS X works, whether you upgraded (or, in some cases, even did an Archive and Install) from an older version of Mac OS X or you erased your drive and started over with an entirely new installation. Indeed, this is how things typically work.

However, there are exceptions. These exceptions occur in certain cases where the new version changes the way an existing feature worked in the older version. In these cases, the older method may be preserved in the update. For example, as covered in "Upgrading Mac OS X," earlier in this chapter, if the new version changes the default shell used in Terminal, you may find that Terminal still uses the older default shell after an upgrade. If you want to shift to the new methodology, there are usually ways to do so without having to resort to a completely new install. I provide details for some specific cases, as relevant, in remaining chapters of this book.

Updating from Software Update

The simplest way to check for and install updates is to select Software Update from the System Preferences window, the Apple menu, or the About This Mac window.

SEE: • Chapter 2 for more on System Preferences.

Software Update System Preferences pane. As discussed in Chapter 2, the Software Update System Preferences pane includes two tabs, each of which accesses a separate pane:

- **Update Software.** In this pane, you can choose the "Check for updates" option—at daily, weekly, or monthly intervals. With this option selected, you can also choose the option to "Download important updates in the background." With this selected, updates that Apple deems important will be downloaded without the system's first asking your permission (though you will still be asked for confirmation before the software is installed).

  Alternatively, you can manually check for updates at any time by clicking the Check Now button.

  If you click Check Now and there are no new updates, a message will appear telling you that you are currently up to date. Otherwise, you will have the option to install new uninstalled software, as described in "Software Update application," below.

- **Installed Updates.** This pane presents you with a list of everything you've installed via Software Update (though the contents may get wiped out each time you upgrade to a new version of Mac OS X). Alternatively, you can view this listing from a log file by using the Open as Log File button.

  SEE: • "Installed Updates does not list previously installed updates," later in this chapter, for related information.

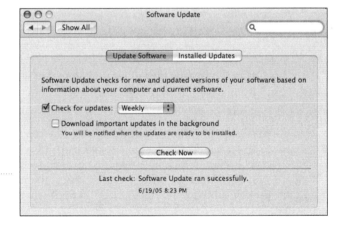

Figure 3.14

The Software Update System Preferences pane.

Software Update application. A separate application, also called Software Update (located in /System/Library/CoreServices), is launched after any of the following have occurred: You clicked Check Now in the Software Update System Preferences pane; an automatic check was initiated (assuming new software is available); or you clicked Software Update in the About This Mac window. The Software Update window displays a list of all available updates. Note, however, that it lists only Mac OS X and application software from Apple and occasional third-party software (such as StuffIt Expander) that is included with Mac OS X.

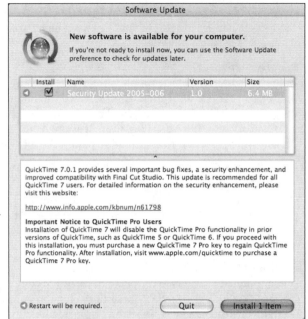

Figure 3.15

The Software Update application: The main window shows a needed update—select it and click the Install 1 Item button to install it.

Figure 3.16

Software Update's Update menu.

To install the software listed in the Software Update application, you simply check the box(es) in the Install column for each item you want to install. Then click the Install Item(s) button. Alternatively, after selecting the items to install, you can go to the Update menu and select one of the following four commands:

- **Download Only.** This downloads the update file (typically a .pkg file, referred to as a *stand-alone update*) to a folder named Packages, located in the root-level Library folder. The folder is automatically opened in the Finder when the download is complete. You must then manually open the .pkg file (which launches the Installer application) when you're ready to install it.

  This option is useful if you want to retain a copy of the .pkg file after installing the software. One reason to do this would be so that you can reinstall the update later (should you erase your drive, for example) without having to redownload it. Another reason would be to install the update on multiple machines without having to download the update from the Internet each time. Also, if the update provides any Custom Install options, running the Installer manually is the only way to access them.

  If you use this option but do not install the software, Software Update will not "remember" that you downloaded the file. Instead, Software Update will continue to list the downloaded file as an uninstalled update until you actually install it. In fact, if you subsequently select the Install command, it will redownload the update, rather than using the copy you previously downloaded.

- **Install.** This is just like clicking the Install Item(s) button: It both downloads and installs the selected update(s). Onscreen messages inform you of Software Update's progress, from downloading to installing.

  The downloaded .pkg file(s) are kept hidden in the Finder. They are automatically deleted the next time you restart—making it difficult to save them for future use.

  The Install option is especially convenient for installing multiple items that require restarting the Mac. With the Download Only option, you would have to run each update separately (although you can have them all open in the Installer utility at one time). With Software Update, all updates are installed before any restart is requested. The Software Update option is also the simplest because it requires no further action on the part of the user.

  If you select this option and it stalls while installing the software (after having downloaded it), force-quit Software Update. Next time, select Download Only and manually install the software. This often works around the problem.

  SEE: • "Technically Speaking: Where Does Software Update Hide the Software It Installs?" later in this chapter, for further details.

- **Install and Keep Package.** This option combines the previous two options: It automatically installs the software, plus it saves a copy of the update package in the Packages folder. This is the option I typically choose.

- **Ignore Update.** If you select this option, the update is removed from the list. You will not be notified again of this update or of any subsequent updates for the same software. You may end up choosing this option for software you don't need (such as an iPod update if you don't own an iPod). Should you change your mind and want to get the update later, you can select Reset Ignored Updates from the Software Update menu.

  If you don't choose to ignore an update but don't go ahead and install it either, this same software update will be listed again the next time you check for updates.

If an update requires administrator approval, you will be asked for your admin-level user name and password before the update will install.

If an update requires that you restart your Mac, a restart symbol will appear to the left of the update name.

Some updates appear only in Software Update if certain prior updates have been installed. For example, Apple at one point released an update to the Installer application itself. No newer updates would appear in Software Update until after the new Installer had been installed. For this reason, once you've installed an update, return to the Software Update System Preferences Pane and click Update Now again. Keep doing this until no new updates appear. Actually, you should no longer have to do this in Panther or later, because Software Update does this rechecking automatically until no new updates appear.

After reinstalling Mac OS X via an Archive and Install, Software Update may not list the more recent updates because it erroneously believes they are already installed. Thus, as a safeguard, check Apple's Web site for recent updates regardless of what Software Update says.

Note: In Jaguar or later, you can no longer update Mac OS 9 by running Software Update via Classic.

SEE: • "Ownership & Permissions," in Chapter 4, and "Opening and Saving: Permissions Problems" and "Copying and Moving: Permissions Problems," in Chapter 6, for details on checking and setting permissions.

TECHNICALLY SPEAKING ▶ Where Does Software Update Hide the Software It Installs?

If you were wondering where Software Update hides the .pkg update file it downloads prior to installing if you don't choose to save the update package, here's the answer:

When using Software Update to install files, the .pkg file is temporarily (until you restart) stored at /private/tmp/501/Temporary Items. This location is normally invisible from the Finder; however, you can access it via the Finder's Go to Folder command or via Terminal.

Note: The 501 number is your user ID (UID). It may be different from 501 if you're not the original administrative user for your Mac. You can check your user ID via NetInfo Manager: To do so, select Users in the middle column and then the name of your account to the right. Your UID will be one of the items listed in the bottom window (actually under gid). You can also find your UID by opening Terminal and typing id; the first item will be your UID.

Updating from the Installer package (.pkg) file

You can install a software update by first downloading the .pkg file from the Web (such as from Apple's Web site at www.info.apple.com/downloads or via the Download Only option in Software Update). These stand-alone updates open in the Installer utility and proceed in a manner similar to how Mac OS X itself was installed from the Install CDs or DVD. The main difference is that you don't need to boot from a Mac OS X Install CD (or any other CD) to install these updates. You can do so while running Mac OS X, directly from your drive. You will be asked to enter your administrative password before you are allowed to perform the installation.

Recall that you can use the Show Files command, in the Installer, to view and save a list of all files that the update will install.

This method is essentially the same as using Software Update and selecting the Download Only option; however, there are three differences of note:

- Downloaded update files typically download as .dmg files. The actual .pkg file is on the mounted .dmg image.

    SEE: • "Understanding Image, Installer Package, and Receipt Files," later in this chapter, for more on this matter.

- Occasionally, updates (even those from Apple) are available only via Web download, with no Software Update option.

- A potential advantage of using Software Update to download the file is that it often lists the latest updates even sooner than Apple's Web site.

- Software Update will always download the smallest version of the update; for example, if Software Update determines that you only need the Patch version, you can't download the Delta version or the Combo version. Some people prefer to always use a Combo version of the update; to do so, you need to download the update from Apple's Web site.

TAKE NOTE ▶ **Interrupted Downloads**

If you're using a dial-up (rather than broadband) connection to the Internet, downloading large updates can take a very long time. Even worse, you may occasionally get disconnected before the download is complete. If this happens, you may be able to resume the download from where you left off—avoiding the frustration of having to start completely over. This should automatically happen with Software Update, if you have not restarted your Mac in the interim.

Otherwise, your best bet is to download updates from Apple's Web site using an application that permits an auto-resume of a partial download. Safari, for example, supports this feature. To access it, open its Downloads window and locate the name of the partially downloaded file. Ideally, there should be an icon to the right of its name with a circular arrow. Click this icon to resume a download. This should work as long as the partially downloaded file has not been moved from its original location. Actually, if you locate this file in the Finder, you can also resume an interrupted download by double-clicking the file.

TAKE NOTE ▶ **Updating or Adding QuickTime Components**

Although updates to Apple's QuickTime software are generally provided via Software Update, they are also available via a separate QuickTime Updater system accessed via the QuickTime pane of System Preferences. In addition, third-party QuickTime software (such as QuickTime Plug-ins) is also often available via the QuickTime Updater system.

To access this system, open the QuickTime preference pane and click the Update tab. By checking the "Check for updates automatically" box, you instruct the Updater system to check for new versions of the main QuickTime software each time you use that software (by launching QuickTime Player, for example). You can also manually check for new QuickTime software by clicking the Update button (for Apple updates) or the Install button (for third-party updates).

Skip the restart?

After you've completed your software installation, either via the Installer or Software Update, some installations will insist that you restart your Mac before continuing. You should follow this advice, especially if you intend to use the installed software immediately. However, on occasions in which it's not convenient to restart immediately (say, because you want to finish work or save documents in another application), you can simply switch to a different application and finish up. When you're ready, return to the Installer application and click Restart.

Alternatively, you may want to install a second or third program before restarting, so you don't have to restart each time. With Software Update, this is not an issue; it does all selected installations before requesting that you restart. If, instead, you are using the Installer application, you can accomplish the same goal by launching all desired Installer .pkg files without quitting the Installer application. This works because, starting in Panther, the Installer can have multiple packages open at the same time. However, you cannot actively install more than one at time; you must do each install sequentially (waiting until the optimization stage is completed for each one)—just don't click the Restart button for any installation until all are finished. This allows you to install multiple packages before restarting.

Alternatively, you can quit by choosing Quit (or, if needed, Option-Quit) from the Dock menu of the Installer or Software Update applications. Any of these options bypass the Restart request.

SEE: • Chapter 5 for more on force-quitting.

Downgrading and Re-upgrading Mac OS X

Occasionally (though hopefully not often), you may decide that you need to downgrade to an older version of Mac OS X—perhaps due to a bug in the latest update.

Similarly, you may sometimes need to start over with a fresh installation of Mac OS X. Most likely, you will want to attempt this when you begin to have general problems running Mac OS X for which you can find no easier solution. In most cases, doing this means downgrading to an older version of Mac OS X and then re-upgrading back to the current version.

Archive and Install, then re-upgrade

The best way to handle downgrades and re-upgrades is to start with a complete reinstall of Mac OS X, using the Installer's Archive and Install feature, which you can access when starting up from a Mac OS X Install disc. If your Install disc doesn't include this feature, you should erase your entire volume and reinstall from whatever Install disc you do have.

Note: You cannot do a direct downgrade from Apple's Installer, even for a minor upgrade. For example, if you tried to install Mac OS X 10.4.1 on a volume running 10.4.2, the Installer would not allow it.

After doing an Archive and Install from the Install disc, you will likely be back at an older version of Mac OS X than the one you were previously running (for example, you may be back at 10.4.0, when you had been running 10.4.3).

To re-update to the current version of Mac OS X, use Software Update; it automatically lists the needed update(s). Software Update should also list any updates beyond Mac OS X itself that you may need to reinstall as a result of the Archive and Install—and allow you to install them all in one step (while you leave to have lunch!).

Alternatively, assuming you want to re-update to the latest version of the OS, download the most recent Combo Mac OS X updater (as described in "Updating Mac OS X," earlier in this chapter) from Apple's Web site. Not only is using the Combo updater simpler and faster than downloading and installing multiple individual Mac OS X updates, but it's also more likely to remedy whatever symptom led to your decision to reinstall.

SEE: • "Software installs but fails to work," later in this chapter.

The main advantage of using a Web download rather than Software Update is that if you don't wish to return to your current version (perhaps you were running Mac OS X 10.4.3 but now want to downgrade to 10.4.2), you can do so by selecting the appropriate update file from the Web.

Of course, you cannot downgrade "lower" than the version installed by the Install disc. Thus, if you want to downgrade from Tiger back to Panther, you would need to use a Panther Install disc.

Warning: If you do an Archive and Install of an earlier major Mac OS X version (for example, 10.3) over a newer major version (for example, 10.4) *preserving* user and network settings, you may not even be able to log in. The work-around is to *not* preserve user and network settings. In addition, Apple has documented (at http://docs.info.apple.com/article.html?artnum=25508) an issue where "downgrading" in this manner may result in applications' not opening documents, unexpectedly quitting, or refusing to launch at all. Their "fix" is to re-update back to the version of Mac OS X you were running prior to the

Archive and Install—which, of course, defeats this particular purpose for doing an Archive and Install—or to at least update affected applications to the latest versions.

SEE: • "Select a Destination," earlier in this chapter, for more on Archive and Install.

Uninstalling Mac OS X

Suppose you want to uninstall Mac OS X—because you no longer want to use it, or you no longer want it on a particular volume, or you're having such problems getting the OS to start up that an uninstall followed by a fresh installation is the only possible solution. How do you go about it?

By far the most direct approach is to erase the entire volume. Of course, you'll first want to back up any personal files (most of which will be located in your home directory) that you want to save.

Manual uninstall?

In some cases, you may be reluctant to erase the volume. Perhaps you also have Mac OS 9 software installed on the volume and don't want to erase it. Or perhaps you don't have a full backup of all the files you want to save (and you're not prepared to back them up at the moment). In such cases, you would prefer to just delete all files associated with Mac OS X and leave everything else intact. This is also likely to take less time than erasing the volume and restoring saved files from your backup. Can this type of uninstall be done?

The answer is yes—but with difficulty. Apple offers no officially supported uninstall method. To do so requires starting up from another volume and manually deleting all Mac OS X–specific folders from the desired volume. Many of the Unix software folders (such as dev and var) remain invisible even when starting up from another volume, so you will need to either make them visible in the Finder or use Terminal to delete them. The fastest way to get an overview of what needs to be deleted is to launch Terminal and type ls -a /. This lists all files and folders, invisible and visible, at the root level of your current Mac OS X startup drive. Use this command to make a list of all the items you intend to delete. The list should include .hidden, .vol, Applications, Library, Network, System, Users, Volumes, automount, bin, cores, dev, etc, mach, mach.sym, mach_kernel, private, sbin, tmp, usr, and var—as well as any other items you know you want to delete. But I would use such an approach only as a very last resort. Given the low cost of FireWire and USB hard drives today, you'd be much better off backing up your important files and then doing an Erase and Install.

SEE: • Chapter 6 for more information on Mac OS X and invisible files and folders.

• Chapter 10 for more information on Unix and invisible files and folders.

Using DesInstaller?

DesInstaller (http://krugazor.free.fr/software) is a shareware utility that can be used to uninstall any software that has a receipt file in the Receipts folder. It uses the information in a receipt file to remove all of the software that was originally installed—even if the software has been modified. It can archive the removed files and create a reinstaller for future use. You can also create a reinstaller without removing the software—which can be useful for software for which you do not have the Installer .pkg file.

DesInstaller is not really useful for a complete uninstall of all Mac OS X software, but it can be great for selective uninstalls of updates.

Keep in mind, however, that it's also a potentially dangerous tool. If it makes an error and uninstalls more or less than it should, you could wind up with an unstable system. For example, I would not use this utility to remove Mac OS X updates, as it might delete critically needed files. Ultimately, a complete reinstall of Mac OS X may be needed. So use at your own risk!

Understanding Image, Installer Package, and Receipt Files

The previous sections of this chapter made occasional reference to receipt, image, and package files, which I refer to elsewhere in this book as well. This section provides essential background on exactly what these files are and how they work.

TAKE NOTE ▶ What Happened to Disk Copy?

Disk Copy is a well-known Mac utility, a version of which has been around through many iterations of the Classic Mac OS as well as previous versions of Mac OS X (up to and including Jaguar). In Panther and later versions of Mac OS X, however, it's conspicuously absent. What happened?

In Panther, Apple took most (but not all!) of the functionality of Disk Copy and split it up into two new locations.

To create new image files or edit existing ones, you now use the Images menu in Disk Utility.

continues on next page

TAKE NOTE ▶ What Happened to Disk Copy? *continued*

To mount image files, you simply double-click the file to launch a background application called DiskImageMounter. This program is located in /System/Library/CoreServices. If you go there, you will see that it still retains the old Disk Copy icon!

Unlike Disk Copy, DiskImageMounter gives no sign that an application has launched (for example, no icon gets added to the Dock). This streamlines the process of mounting images a bit, which I suppose is the rationale behind the change.

If you use Terminal, Panther and Tiger still include the `hdiutil` command, which is the Terminal equivalent of the former Disk Copy application. This provides access to all of the old Disk Copy features, even the ones not included in Disk Utility's Images menu.

SEE: • "Technically Speaking: More About Disk Utility's Image and Restore Features," later in this chapter, for related information.

• "Preferences Files," in Chapter 4, for more on editing preferences files.

Image (.dmg) files

Many files that you download from the Web (in fact, almost all Apple files and a healthy minority of non-Apple files) arrive in the form of image files. These files typically have names that end in .dmg (also called a *UDIF format*). However, you may see image files that end in .img; these are carryovers from an image format originally used in Mac OS 9. Over the past few years, .img files have begun to disappear from the Mac OS X scene; thus, I'm omitting further coverage of them from this book. Some image files may be self-mounting (with an .smi extension) and thus should work even if a mounting application is not available.

Note: For a more technical background on the history and nature of disk-image formats, launch Terminal and type man `hdiutil`. Then press Return until you reach the sections on compatibility and history.

If you double-click an image file, the image file will *mount* (more technically referred to as *attach*). That is, a virtual volume appears, much as if you had mounted some sort of removable media, such as a CD. This generally happens thanks to Mac OS X's DiskImageMounter, a background utility that handles disk-image mounting, although some third-party software, such as StuffIt Deluxe, can also mount image files.

Note: When downloading software from the Web, the image file may self-mount and the original .dmg file may be automatically moved to the Trash, as discussed in "Technically Speaking: Internet-Enabled Disk Images," later in this chapter.

The name of the mounted image may differ from the .dmg file itself, though there's usually some similarity. Double-click the mounted image's icon, if a new Finder window doesn't automatically open, to view its contents and access it from the Finder.

For Apple software updates, the contents of the mounted volume will typically be a package (.pkg) file. A Read Me file or other documentation may also be included. For third parties, the contents may similarly be a .pkg file or a separate third-party installer utility. A VISE Installer is currently the most popular alternative to .pkg files; it makes no use of Apple's Installer utility. Alternatively, the disk image may contain a fully functional version of the software in question, sans installer.

If the image contains an installer package file or some other form of install utility, the next step is to launch the install package or utility. Typically, you can do this by double-clicking the file directly from the image. If this does not work, try copying the file to your hard drive first.

When you've finished doing what you need to do, you unmount the virtual volume (by dragging the Volume icon to the Trash or by clicking the Eject icon next to the image's name in the sidebar of a Finder window). You can also delete any install software you dragged to your drive, as well as the downloaded image file itself (if you don't want to save it as a backup).

If the image file contains a fully functional newer version of the software in question rather than an installer, you simply replace the previous version of that software on your hard drive with the new version on the image.

Note: As I discuss later in this chapter, you can use Disk Utility to create image files—a convenient way to make exact copies of folders, discs, and other items you want to transfer over the Internet.

SEE: • **Running Mac OS X software from Terminal," in Chapter 10, for more on the** hdiutil **command.**

Figure 3.17

The DiskImageMounter application, highlighted in the CoreServices window.

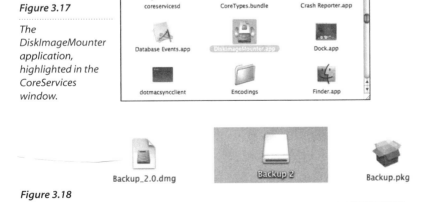

Figure 3.18

From image file to package file in three steps: left, *an image file downloaded from the Web;* middle, *the virtual volume that appears when you mount the image;* right, *the package file contained in the volume.*

Image files vs. compressed files

When you download software from the Internet, it often arrives in compressed and/or encoded format. Such files typically have a .zip, .sit, .sitx, .bin, .gz, or .tgz suffix. In this case, the first step is to decompress and/or decode the file. You do this either via Mac OS X's "built-in" decompressing software or (if Mac OS X's software is not up to the task) via third-party software such as Stuffit Expander. In many cases, your Web browser is preconfigured to automatically launch Expander if needed.

In some cases, the expanded file will be an image (.dmg) file. If so, the image file will likely mount its virtual volume automatically. (If it doesn't, double-click the image file to mount it.) The resulting software (such as an Installer .pkg file) will now be accessible. You then proceed as described in the previous section.

In many cases, however, the decompressed file will be the "final" software itself, such as an installer or another application. You can use this directly.

TECHNICALLY SPEAKING ▶ Internet-Enabled Disk Images

Beginning with Mac OS X 10.2.3, Apple has simplified the procedure of working with downloaded disk images. For starters, .dmg files that are created as compressed (and read-only) are flat files that can be directly downloaded from the Internet. This eliminates the need to download a file as a .bin or .sit file and then expand it to a disk image—which in turn allows the user to skip the step that requires Expander.

To make things even simpler, the person who creates the disk image (.dmg) file can make it an *Internet-enabled* disk image. When you download an Internet-enabled disk image, some or all of the following occurs:

- The image is automatically mounted when the download is complete.

- The contents of the mounted image are copied to the user's drive—in the same location as the .dmg file itself or in a folder created at that location.

- If the mounted image contains a .pkg file, the Installer application may automatically launch and open the file, prompting you to install the software.

- The image is then unmounted, and the .dmg file is placed in the Trash.

The net result is that the user is left with the downloaded software ready to run or install—no additional steps required.

To save a .dmg file that has been moved to the Trash—for example, for archival purposes—just drag it out of the Trash before you next choose Empty Trash. Alternatively, in Tiger you can prevent these types of images from being moved to the Trash after they've been mounted via Disk Utility's preferences; select the option "Don't move Internet-enabled images to Trash."

continues on next page

TECHNICALLY SPEAKING ▶ **Internet-Enabled Disk Images** *continued*

Tip: Would you find it quicker and more convenient to access Disk Utility's Preferences via a System Preferences pane? You can do it. Just go to /System/Library/PrivateFrameworks/DiskImages.framework/Versions/A/Resources. Here you will find a file called DiskImages.prefPane. Double-click it to install it as a System Preferences pane. Done.

Note that the Internet-enabled feature is cleared after the first time the image is mounted. This means that, after retrieving a .dmg file from the Trash, if you mount the image a second time, the automated actions will not occur.

Creating an Internet-enabled disk image. The Disk Utility application currently does not include an option to create an Internet-enabled disk image. If you want to create one yourself, you must use the `hdiutil` command in Terminal. In particular, type the following:

```
hdiutil internet-enable -yes {path to disk image}/imagename.dmg
```

In the above command, *imagename.dmg* is the name of an existing *read-only* disk image. If you now double-click the image file, it should behave as described above.

Substitute no for yes in the above command to remove an already-present flag.

Note that this feature is dependent on the Web browser you are using. That is, it will work as described here only if your Web browser supports this feature. Obviously, Safari includes this support, and you will see it in action when downloading software. However, I have had trouble getting the above command to work when double-clicking an image file from the Finder.

TAKE NOTE ▶ **Image Files That Won't Mount**

Occasionally, if you double-click a .dmg file, it may open as text in a text editor or otherwise fail to open. This may happen because the file is corrupted. If you downloaded it from the Web, the solution may be to simply download it again.

More likely, however, the problem is that the Finder doesn't know what application is needed to open the file. In this case, if instead of double-clicking the file you drag it to the DiskImageMounter icon (in /System/Library/CoreServices), it should mount just fine.

If you want to fix the file so that double-clicking works, you can use the Open With section of the Get Info window for the file. Basically, you just change the selected application from whatever it is to DiskImageMounter. Then click the Change All button to apply the change to all future image files.

SEE: • Chapter 4 for more details on using the Get Info window.

Installer package (.pkg) files

A *package* (also referred to as a *bundle*) is really a folder in disguise. In this guise, it acts as though it were a single file rather than a folder containing a collection of files. These folders are disguised this way to simplify the user's experience of working with them.

The Installer utility uses one type of package file to install updates. These files typically have a .pkg extension at the end of their name (such as MacOSXUpdateCombo10.3.9.pkg), though you may occasionally see one with an .mpkg extension. This latter type of extension represents a *meta-package*, which is the first file launched in an installation involving several .pkg files. Launching this file will not result in a successful installation unless all of the additional .pkg files are also in its folder.

One key advantage of this approach to OS updates is that the user sees what looks like a single file rather than the dozens of files scattered among several folders that Mac OS 9 updates typically require. When you double-click this item, it launches the Installer and you're on your way.

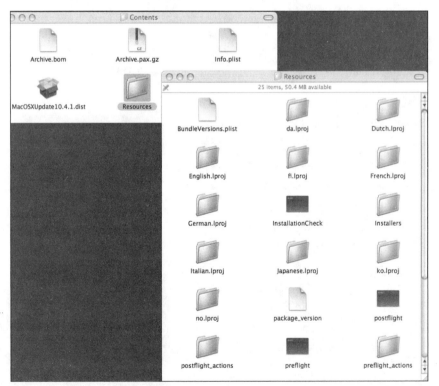

Figure 3.19

Inside the Mac OS X 10.4.1 update .pkg file: the Contents folder and the Resources folder.

TECHNICALLY SPEAKING ▶ Inside Packages

Installer package files (as described in the main text) represent just one of several types of package files in Mac OS X. Receipt files (stored in /Library/Receipts) represent another type of package file and are very similar to Installer packages.

Most Mac OS X applications are also packages. Such files have an .app extension. The Finder hides the extension, however, so all you see is a single file called AppleWorks, as opposed to a file called AppleWorks.app—or, more properly, a folder called AppleWorks.app. The application file itself, as well as various accessory files used by the application (such as international language support), are stored within the package.

Inside the Mac OS X System folder, you will find .framework and .bundle files or folders. These are also considered packages and are covered in more detail in Chapter 4.

Viewing package contents. If you want to view the contents of a package from the Finder, simply Control-click (or right-click on a multibutton mouse) the package icon and choose Show Package Contents from the contextual menu. The same command is also accessible from the Action menu in Finder window toolbars. If that menu choice does not appear, the file is not a package.

Although the Finder is designed to see a package as a single file, other applications may play by different rules. For example, the Open and Save dialogs of some applications—especially older applications that don't understand the package concept—allow you to view a package as a folder and navigate within it. As a rule, you should not attempt to add new files to packages or delete or modify files within packages via this route unless you're confident of the consequences and specifically intend to do this (as in some hacks).

Search package contents. The Finder's Find/Search function does not search the contents of package files by default. If you want to do a volumewide search to locate an item inside any package, I recommend that you get the shareware utility Locator, which is a front end for the Unix `locate` command. To use it, first update the locate database (as Locator will request you to do on launch), type / (meaning the root level of the volume) in the In text box, and then type your search term in the Locate text box. Click Start, and you should find what you seek. Just remember that search terms are case sensitive (unless you check the Case Insensitive box).

To search the contents of an individual package, you can use the Show Package Contents command to enter the package and then enter the desired text in the Search field in the Finder window's toolbar. Alternatively, you can do a Finder search, but in the location bar click the Others button and then drag the package's Contents folder to the Search In list.

continues on next page

TECHNICALLY SPEAKING ▶ **Inside Packages** *continued*

Another way to quickly navigate your volumes so that you can see inside packages, as well as all the normally invisible Unix directories and files, is to type file://local in your Web browser. In most browsers, this displays a list of the items at the root level of your startup volume. Each directory name is a hypertext link to the contents of that directory (assuming you have permission to view it). You can even display the contents of certain text documents via this method. However, in Safari this command simply opens a Finder window for the root level of your startup volume; thus, in Safari the command offers no advantages over using the Finder directly.

What's inside a package? If you use the Show Package Contents contextual-menu command to open a package file, the first thing you will typically see is yet another folder, called Contents. Inside most Contents folders is an Info.plist file.

The Info.plist file is a key file: It contains all of the critical information that the Finder and other system software needs to understand what the package contains and how the package's files should be treated. You can look at this .plist file (and similarly structured files) with any text editor (I recommend the free TextWrangler, from Bare Bones Software[www.barebones.com]). Even better, use the Apple Developer Tools utility called Property List Editor (covered more in Chapter 4).

Some packages also include a PkgInfo file, which contains a subset of the Info.plist data; the Finder uses it for quicker access.

If the package is an application, the top level (where the Contents folder resides) also sometimes contains an alias file to the actual executable code file, which is more deeply nested within the package.

Depending on the type of package, the Contents folder may include MacOS and MacOS Classic folders (where the actual applications are stored) and a Resources folder, which contains graphics and other accessory items, as well as information for multiple-language support (in .lprog folders).

What's inside an Installer package? Given that this chapter is about installing software, I want to note two files of particular interest that are included within Installer packages:

- **Archive.bom.** The filename extension .bom stands for *bill of materials*. This file contains the list of everything that the Installer will install; it creates the list that appears when you choose Show Files from the Installer's File menu. You may also see a matching file with the extension .bomout. This file contains essentially the same data, but in a form that can be read by any text editor, such as TextEdit, included in Mac OS X.

  Note: Receipt files left in the Receipts folder after an installation also contain an archive.bom file. This allows Mac OS X to check the .bom file for information as needed (such as when repairing permissions via Disk Utility).

  SEE: • "Technically Speaking: Repair Disk Permissions and Receipts," in Chapter 5, for more details.

continues on next page

TECHNICALLY SPEAKING ▶ Inside Packages *continued*

- **Archive.pax.gz.** The .gz and .pax extensions refer to separate compression schemes designed to reduce the size of this file, which contains all the files to be installed by the update.

    SEE: • **"Extracting from an expanded .pax.gz file," earlier in this chapter, for more details.**

Filename extensions and packages. In most cases, adding the appropriate extension to a folder's name is enough to convert the folder to a package. For example, if you take an ordinary folder and change its name from *foldername* to *foldername*.pkg, you will get a message that says, "Are you sure you want to add the extension 'pkg' to the end of the name? If you make this change, your folder may appear as a single file." If you click the Add button, the folder will now appear as a package file and launch the Installer if you double-click it. Of course, the Installer will ultimately fail to open this pseudo-package, as the contents do not conform to what the Installer expects to find.

You can make this same package conversion using the .app extension. In this case, the folder will adopt the generic application icon. If you double-click it, it will attempt to launch but ultimately fail to do so (as your folder is not really an application).

Can you reverse this process? Yes. You can take any file with a .pkg or .app extension and remove the extension. When you do this for an .app file, for example, you will get a message that says, "Are you sure you want to remove the extension '.app'? If you make this change, your application may appear as a folder." However, you cannot typically remove the extension directly in the Finder. Doing so simply prevents the extension from appearing in the Finder; it does not actually delete the extension. To truly delete it, open the Finder's Get Info window for the file and click the disclosure triangle for Name & Extension. Delete the extension from the name as it appears here. Then click the disclosure triangle again. At this point, the message described above will appear.

Note: To be safe, I advise that you *not* try these tricks unless you're experimenting with files you've backed up elsewhere or don't care if they get ruined.

SEE: • **"Name & Extension," in Chapter 4, for more details.**

Bundle bits and packages. Another way the Finder determines whether a folder is treated as a package lies in something called *Finder attributes* (or *bits*). These bits determine whether a file is locked, for example. One of these bits is called the *bundle bit* (or *package bit*). Before the invention of packages (back in the Mac OS 8 days), this bit was relevant only to applications and had no effect on folders (whether on or off). Typically, the bundle bit was enabled for applications: It instructed the Finder to check the application for information about the type of documents the application creates. Starting in Mac OS 9, Apple decided to use the bundle bit with folders to indicate that a folder should really be treated as a package. Mac OS X similarly continues to use this bundle bit for folders.

continues on next page

TECHNICALLY SPEAKING ▶ Inside Packages *continued*

Although bits are intended primarily for developer manipulation, numerous shareware utilities, such as Rainer Brockerhoff's XRay (www.brockerhoff.net/xray) and Gideon Softworks' FileXaminer (www.gideonsoftworks.com),make it possible for anyone to manipulate them. Turn the bundle bit on to indicate a package; turn it off to indicate a normal folder. In this case, enabling the bit for an ordinary folder will typically result in the folder's adopting a document icon. However, if you double-click it, the item will still open as a folder. In most cases, assuming you have any need as a troubleshooter to make these conversions, I would recommend using the name extension method rather than fiddling with the bundle/package bit.

Creating a package. Creating a functional package (one that truly operates as an installer file or an application), as opposed to one that looks like a package but does nothing, requires more than just converting a folder to a package: You must set up the contents of the package accord- ing to specific guidelines described in Apple's Mac OS X documentation for developers. Apple's PackageMaker utility (available as part of Apple's Xcode Developer software) provides a conven- ient graphical interface for automating most of this process. You can only use it, however, to create new package files or to open an existing package template (.pmsp or .pmsm) file. You cannot, for example, download a package file from the Internet and open the file in PackageMaker with the intention of modifying the contents. Further details on using PackageMaker exceed what you need to know for typical troubleshooting.

Receipt files

Receipt files, as their name implies, are used by the OS to maintain a record of what the Installer application has installed. A receipt file is created each time you install new software via a package file. It's stored in a folder called Receipts, located in the root-level Library folder (/Library/Receipts).

When viewed from the Finder, a receipt file appears identical to the matching package file that was used to install the software. In fact, both files have identi- cal names and share the same icon and description ("Installer package") in the Kind line of their Get Info windows. Indeed, if you use the Show Package Contents contextual-menu command to look inside a receipt package, you will see only minor differences between its contents and the contents of its match- ing Installer package. The biggest difference is that the Archive.pax.gz file, which contains the actual updated software (as noted above in "Technically Speaking: Inside Packages"), is missing from the receipt file. This is why the receipt file is so much smaller than its Installer package sibling—and why you can't use the receipt file to install an update.

In Panther, if you double-click a receipt file, it will initially launch Installer (just as an Installer file would). However, the launch is soon interrupted by an error message stating, "The Installer package {*name of file*} cannot be opened.

The selected package is a receipt." Oddly, Apple appears to have eliminated this helpful alert in Tiger. In Tiger, it lets you go all the way through to where you click the Install button. You then get an error message that says: "There were errors installing the software. Please try installing again." The log files, however, correctly note that the installation failed because the Installer could not extract the appropriate files from the package.

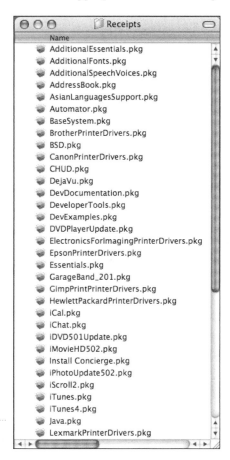

Figure 3.20

The contents of a Receipts folder.

What are receipt files used for? Receipt files are primarily used by Mac OS X to track the updates you've installed. In theory, this is relevant in several situations:

• Software Update may use receipt files to determine what software has yet to be installed and, thus, what updates appear in the Software Update window.

• The Installer application uses receipt files to determine whether a given installation should be listed as a new (full) installation or as an upgrade of an existing one. If it finds a relevant receipt file, it considers the installation to be an upgrade.

- The Installer application may similarly use these files to check whether a given update can be installed on your computer (that is, it checks to see if the prerequisite software is installed).

- The First Aid portion of Disk Utility uses the information stored in these receipt files to check the default permissions of files installed by updates so that they can be restored when using Repair Disk Permissions (as described in Chapters 5 and 6).

In reality, however, when I tested the "rules" of how receipts are used, I found the process to be less than completely predictable:

- In no case did the presence or absence of a receipt file prevent a stand-alone installer from reinstalling an update.

- A receipt file did sometimes affect whether or not Software Update listed an update, but it did this mainly for non-OS updates (such as for iPod software). For updates of the OS itself, such as an update to Mac OS X 10.3.9, Software Update checks the OS version in a way that does not depend on receipt files. Mainly, it uses information stored in the SystemVersion.plist file, located in /System/Library/CoreServices.

Removing receipt files. If you remove a receipt file in hopes of bypassing Mac OS X's refusal to list or install a given update, don't count on it working. In general, I recommend leaving these receipt files in place; ideally, you want Mac OS X to correctly track what you've installed.

You may, however, occasionally need to remove a receipt file to solve a problem with reinstalling a particular piece of software. For example, suppose you have software such as Apple's Keynote application on your drive. You decide to delete it and reinstall it via a Keynote.pkg file. If the Installer does not permit this reinstall, it's probably because you did not delete the receipt file of the same name from the Receipts folder. If this is the case, follow these steps:

1. Drag the receipt file for the problem software from its /Library/Receipts folder location to the Trash. (You need to be an administrator to do this.)

   Do not delete the file just yet: Deleting certain receipt files without successfully reinstalling the same software can cause problems (including failure to start up on restart).

2. Attempt the problem reinstallation again.

3. After the software has been successfully reinstalled, a new receipt file is created. You empty the Trash to delete the old receipt file.

If, after doing this, the install still fails, the receipt file is not the cause. Drag the receipt file back to its original location before restarting your Mac. Check for other causes, as described elsewhere in this chapter.

Note: Receipt files are created only by software installed via Apple's Installer utility.

SEE: • "Technically Speaking: Repair Disk Permissions and Receipts," in Chapter 5, for related information.

Backing Up and Restoring Mac OS X Volumes

Here's some advice you should already know: Back up the files on your drive(s)—and do so often! If a file on your drive gets corrupted or accidentally deleted and you don't have a backup, you may not be able to retrieve it. When this happens, you'll be glad you had a backup.

The danger posed by a lost or corrupted file may not seem serious if the file in question is a freeware program you downloaded from the Web. In that case, you can just download it again. Even here, though, if a problem destroyed a folder containing hundreds of such programs, it would be a real pain to remember everything you lost and then reacquire all of the software. More serious is the loss of irreplaceable files such as the near-final draft of a novel you spent the last two years writing.

To prevent such disasters, it's usually sufficient to back up just the files you've acquired, and, especially, the documents you've created. For these purposes, you don't need to back up your entire drive but instead can restrict your backup to your home directory.

If you've installed applications in the Applications folder or added fonts to the /Library/Fonts folder, you may also want to back them up—especially if the software didn't come on a CD that could serve as a backup. But remember: Reinstalling applications from their installers is often better than just saving a backup of the application itself because an installer utility will install any accessory files (including invisible files), which you would not save by backing up just the application.

Note: If you've been using Classic, you may also want to back up your Mac OS 9 folders—System Folder, Applications (Mac OS 9), and (especially) Documents—to save any critical files and simplify a restore later.

There is, however, a good reason for maintaining a complete backup of your entire drive: If it becomes damaged in such a way that you need to either erase and reformat it or get a new drive, the simplest and fastest way to get up and running again is to restore the drive in its entirety from a current backup.

That being said, restoring a Mac OS X startup volume presents some unique obstacles, the most critical of which is making sure your backup and restored volumes are bootable. Unlike what you can do with Mac OS 9 volumes, you can't create a bootable copy of a volume via drag and drop in the Finder. If you try to do so, the following problems occur that prevent the copy from booting (or even from being a complete copy!):

- File permissions are not preserved correctly.
- Invisible files, especially the critical Unix software, are not copied.
- Unix symbolic and hard links are broken.

TAKE NOTE ▶ Backing Up and Restoring a Home Directory

Even if you decide not to maintain a complete, bootable backup of your Mac OS X volume (because it takes too long or requires costly additional hardware and software), you should at least maintain a backup of your home directory. Since it should contain almost all of the files you've added and created since installing Mac OS X (except perhaps some programs in the Applications folder and some systemwide settings and add-ons stored in the main Library folder), creating a backup of it should at least prevent you from losing irreplaceable data. You can perform this type of backup in several ways, all of which I describe in the text that follows.

Using the Finder

Backing up. Here's one simple method that uses the Finder and thus does not require any third-party software (though it won't copy invisible files in the copied directories):

1. If there's something you want to save that's not yet in your home directory, copy it there. (Most of what you want to save should already be there.)

2. Copy your entire home directory to your backup location.

    Your home directory (as well as those of other local users) is located in the /Users directory at the root level of your drive.

    SEE: • Chapter 4 for more on the directory structure of Mac OS X.

    Ideally, your backup location should be a removable medium such as a CD-RW, a DVD-R, an external hard drive, or an iPod. Alternatively, you could use an online server such as Apple's iDisk, which Mac OS X fully supports (see Chapter 8).

    The medium you select will depend on what types of storage you have available and how much space the backup requires. A small directory can fit entirely on a CD-R disc. Larger ones will require DVD-Rs or an additional hard drive.

    SEE: • "Backing up Mac OS X: Hardware strategies," later in this chapter, for more details.

Do this often, so that your backup remains current. If you plan on erasing your Mac OS X volume, perform this type of backup just before you erase the drive.

You are now set to restore individual files from your backup, as needed.

continues on next page

TAKE NOTE ▶ Backing Up and Restoring a Home Directory *continued*

Restoring. Should you ever need to erase your entire drive and reinstall or restore Mac OS X, you will want to restore your entire home directory (as well as any other user directories you backed up). To do this, you need to create new home directories, ideally with the same names as the ones you backed up. As part of reinstalling Mac OS X, a fresh home directory will be created for you, as the default administrative user. Use the Accounts System Preferences pane to create accounts and, therefore, home directories, beyond the one automatically created for you.

To restore your home directory:

- Copy the contents of each backed-up directory to the new folder of the same name. In some cases, such as the Desktop, you may need to copy directly from one subfolder to the other.

  To replace the contents for users other than yourself, you must be an administrator and use root access (as described in "Root Access," in Chapter 4).

  Warning! Do not copy a home directory to the /Users folder, by simply dragging the folder icon to the /Users folder. Similarly, do not create a new folder in the /Users directory via the Finder's New Folder command. These methods will not work because Mac OS X will not recognize the folder as a valid /Users folder. You can set up a system so that your active home directory is on a volume separate from your Mac OS X software, but that's a different issue.

  SEE: • "Technically Speaking: Moving Your Home Directory to a Separate Partition," below, for details.

  If you're concerned that some preferences files, fonts, or other files in the Library folder of your old directory may be corrupt, you can bypass copying any or all files from the old Library folder.

  You can always copy these files later if you find that you need them and cannot re-create them.

Note: The following Apple Knowledge Base article includes information about how to back up and restore an entire /Users directory (which contains all users' home directories) using the Finder and Terminal: http://docs.info.apple.com/article.html?artnum=106941. Another article has more information specific to Tiger: http://docs.info.apple.com/article.html?artnum=301239, including how to back up specific files such as your Safari bookmarks, Address Book database, and Mail data. Of note, Address Book and iCal now include Back Up commands in their File menus.

Note: If FileVault (which is described in Chapter 2) is enabled for a home directory that is not the currently logged-in user's, the directory will be encrypted. Ideally, you should unencrypt it before backing it up.

continues on next page

TAKE NOTE ▶ Backing Up and Restoring a Home Directory *continued*

Using backup utilities

Synchronization utilities. You can use a variety of utilities, such as Qdea's Synchronize Pro! X (www.qdea.com) or Benjamin Rister's Synk (www.decimus.net/synk), to "synchronize" two folders. When you do this, the utility updates both folders so that they always contain the same data— useful when backing up your home directory because just the new or modified files get backed up (as opposed to everything in the folders). Synchronizing is also useful for maintaining a backup of a folder whose contents change often (such as the contents of a Web site you maintain).

Some synchronize utilities can also serve as full volume-backup utilities. Check the utility's documentation for details.

Apple's Backup utility. If (and only if) you have a .Mac account, you can use Apple's Backup utility to back up selected files to your iDisk storage or to CDs, DVDs, and (for some backed- up items) hard drives. The utility has been completely revamped for version 3.0 (released in September 2005). Backup offers five templates to use for backup plans: Home Folder (backs up the entire contents of your home folder); Personal Data & Settings (backs up Address Book contacts, iCal Calendars, and so on); iLife (backs up all your iLife data, such as your iTunes and iPhoto Libraries); Purchased Music (backs up music purchased from the iTunes Music Store); and Custom. Choosing the Custom template opens a window from which you can specifically select what you want to back up—from a list of QuickPicks (such as Application preferences) to any file or folder on your drive. This means you can use Backup for files beyond your home directory, up to and including an entire volume!

Once you have selected items to backup, you can set a schedule, so that backups are made automatically at predetermined intervals (such as every day or every week). You can create more than one backup plan, so that some items are backed up daily while others are weekly, for example. You can similarly have different backup destinations for each plan.

Backup 3.x performs incremental backups, saving newer versions of previously backed-up files, without deleting the older versions. To start over with a new backup, without any accumulated incremental backups, select Full Backup from Backup's Plan menu. To delete all previously backed up data from the Backup folder on your iDisk, select Remove iDisk Backups from the Backup menu.

Backup, of course, also includes a Restore function, for when you need to replace data from your backup.

continues on next page

TAKE NOTE ▶ Backing Up and Restoring a Home Directory *continued*

Backup is an easy-to-use and powerful utility. However, the utility has some significant limitations. In particular, you cannot use Backup to create a bootable backup of your drive; for that, you need a backup utility such as EMC Dantz's Retrospect (www.dantz.com) or Prosoft's Data Backup (www.prosofteng.com). In addition, using Backup with your iDisk can get expensive if your backup plans include a large amount of data; this is because you will need to pay for additional storage space (beyond the initial 1 GB that comes with your .Mac subscription).

Check out Backup Help from the utility's Help menu for more tips and problem-solving information.

.Mac. Once again, if (and only if) you have a .Mac account, you can use the Sync options in the .Mac System Preferences pane to back up selected items from your home directory (such as Safari Bookmarks, iCal database, and Mail data) to your iDisk. As covered more in Chapters 8 and 11, this not only serves as a backup, but it also allows you to synchronize these data across multiple computers. In addition, as with the Backup utility, it provides a safe "offsite" storage location for your data.

Disk Utility. You can use the Disk Image from Folder command, in the New submenu of Disk Utility's File menu, to create a disk image of your home directory. When you're finished, select Scan Image for Restore, from the Images menu, to verify that the image is OK to use for restoring. This can be a convenient and space-saving way to make a backup—especially if you've created a compressed image. You would later mount the image to access the files for restoring. Alternatively, you could use the Restore feature of Disk Utility to back up and restore an entire disk. Note that in order to back up files safely, you would want to store the backup in a location other than the volume containing the files being backed up—on a CD, DVD, or external hard drive, for example.

More help from Apple

Apple has several Knowledge Base articles that cover issues related to backing up and restoring your home directory. In particular, check the following articles, as relevant to your needs:

- Mac OS X: How to back up and restore your files: http://docs.info.apple.com/article.html?artnum=106941.

- Mac OS X: How to recover a home folder (directory): http://docs.info.apple.com/article.html?artnum=302150.

- How to get files from a previous home directory after Archive and Install: http://docs.info.apple.com/article.html?artnum=107297. This article is especially useful if you want to recover data from a home directory after doing an Archive and Install where you forgot to select the "Preserve Users and Network Settings" option.

  SEE: • "Backing up Mac OS X: Utilities for volume backups," later in this chapter, for related details.

Figure 3.21

Left, *Apple's .Mac's Backup utility;* right, *the Sync options from the .Mac System Preferences pane.*

TECHNICALLY SPEAKING ▶ Moving Your Home Directory to a Separate Partition

As described in "Take Note: Backing Up and Restoring a Home Directory," you can easily copy your home directory to a separate partition via the Finder, where it serves as a useful backup for your personal files (should you ever need to erase your Mac OS X volume and reinstall the OS from scratch).

However, if you want to *move* your home directory to a separate partition and have it function from there as your active home directory, you cannot do so simply by dragging the folder to the separate partition.

Why would you even want to do this? Some users prefer this arrangement, as it reduces the hassle of erasing their Mac OS X startup drives and reinstalling Mac OS X because they don't have to worry about backing up and later restoring items in their home directories. This arrangement can also free up space on the Mac OS X startup volume, which can improve performance if space is getting tight. That said, I doubt that many users will derive sufficient value from this to make it worth the bother.

If, despite my reservations, you still want to move your home directory to a new location and use it as your active directory, there are several ways to do so. The following method requires Terminal. Note: Each command is one line in Terminal even if it appears as two lines in this text. Where a command is split into two lines here, enter a space before continuing to type the second line.

continues on next page

TECHNICALLY SPEAKING ▶ **Moving Your Home Directory to a Separate Partition** *continued*

1. Launch Terminal and type the following:

```
sudo ditto -rsrc "/Users/username" " /Volumes/volumename/Users/username"
```

volumename is the name of the partition or volume where the new home directory is to go. username is your user name and thus the name of your home directory.

This copies your home directory, including all invisible files, to a /Users folder on the separate volume; the `-rsrc` option ensures that all resource forks are copied.

2. Next, type the following:

```
sudo niutil -createprop / "/users/username" home "/Volumes/volumename/Users/username"
```

This command reassigns your home directory from the original location to the new location.

Note: Alternatively, you can accomplish this step via NetInfo Manager. To do so, launch the application and go to users/*username*. Then, in the lower portion of the window, scroll down until you see the home line. Change its value from its current location (for example, /Users/*username*) to the new location (for example, /Volumes/*volumename*/Users/ *username*). However, I have found that using Terminal instead is less likely to precipitate any problems.

3. Check that the newly created directory is working by logging out and logging back in (or, if the user you're modifying is a different account, by logging in to that account—you can even use Fast User Switching to log in without logging out of your own account).

4. Repeat the previous two steps for any additional home directories you want to move and save.

5. If all seems well, return to Terminal and type the following:

```
sudo rm -dr "/Users/ username"
```

This command removes the old directory. (Repeat this step for each account you've moved.)

6. Now type the following:

```
sudo ln -s "/Volumes/volumename/Users/username" "/Users/username"
```

This command creates a symbolic link (similar to an alias) in the /Users directory on the boot volume that points to the newly created home directory on the new host volume. This creates the illusion that your home directory is still in its expected location in the /Users folder on the boot volume. (Repeat this step for each account you've moved.)

If you erase and reinstall your Mac OS X volume, you presumably can reconnect to this alternate directory via Steps 2 through 5.

continues on next page

TECHNICALLY SPEAKING ▶ **Moving Your Home Directory to a Separate Partition** *continued*

If the host volume is a removable volume or one that you sometimes unmount, you *must* either shut down or log in with a user not on the external volume before you can disconnect the external volume. Actually, in Tiger the volume should be automatically unmounted when you log out of the account. Once the device is physically disconnected from your Mac, you can connect it to another similarly set up computer—both computers can thus share the same home directory.

Note: If you intend to use Mac OS X's FileVault security feature, you should not move your home directory as described here.

SEE: • "Security," in Chapter 2, for more on FileVault.

• "Aliases and Symbolic Links," in Chapter 6, for more on this subject.

• Chapter 10 for more on using Unix commands.

Backing up Mac OS X: Utilities for volume backups

Fortunately, the problems with backing up and restoring a Mac OS volume can be easily solved with a number of readily available utilities. These are especially good at creating a full, bootable "clone" of your startup volume.

SEE: • "Take Note: Backing Up and Restoring a Home Directory," earlier in this chapter, for related information, especially for details regarding Apple's Backup utility.

Third-party backup utilities. Although you can back up and restore volumes using just the software that came with your Mac, the best, most reliable methods employ third-party software. Thus, I'll begin my discussion with these.

• **Prosoft's Data Backup** has an exceptionally clear interface that allows you to choose different types of backups, such as the following:

    Clone. Creates an exact duplicate of the drive—the best option if you want a complete, bootable copy of the drive. Older files present on the backup but no longer present on the main drive will be deleted from the backup.

    Incremental. Adds new files to the backup but does not delete old ones—best if you want to keep old versions of documents and applications as an archive.

    Synchronize. Ensures that two folders or volumes are "in sync," copying in both directions, always preserving the newer version of a file. Note that if you delete a file from your main drive, it will also be deleted from the "synchronized" volume; similarly, if you delete a file from the backup, it will be deleted from the main drive. A variation of this approach, a *unidirectional synchronization*, is essentially the same as a clone (or mirror).

- **EMC Dantz's Retrospect for Mac OS X** is the Mac OS X version of the gold standard of Mac OS 9 backup utilities. It includes numerous features that other backup utilities do not; however, one consequence of being more powerful is that it is also not quite as easy to use. One especially nice feature: It allows you to restore files while you're booted from the Mac OS X volume that's the intended destination.

- **Carbon Copy Cloner** is a shareware utility that uses Unix's ditto command to make backups. The author's Web page (www.bombich.com/mactips/image.html) provides many more details about backing up Mac OS X volumes via Unix.

- **SuperDuper!** is another excellent shareware utility. It features a unique safety clone feature that allows you update to a new version of Mac OS X while keeping the ability to quickly revert back to the prior version, should you need to do so.

Disk Utility. If you want to make a full backup of a volume using just Mac OS X utility software, use Disk Utility's Image and Restore features, which provide you with two options: You can back up and restore a volume directly, or you can create an image file for backup and restoring.

To back up and restore a volume directly:

1. Launch Disk Utility, and in the window that appears, click any volume from the list at the left, and then click the Restore tab.

2. From the list in the left column, drag the volume you wish to back up to the Source text box. Although your currently active startup volume *can* be used as the source, I would advise against it (that is, you should start up from another volume instead). For example, the active startup volume may impose permissions restrictions that prevent a successful complete backup.

3. From the list in the left column, drag the volume you wish to contain the backup to the Destination text box.

    Note: Make sure the Ignore Ownership on This Volume option is not selected in the Finder's Get Info window for the Destination volume.

4. Check the Erase Destination box.

    If you do not select Erase Destination, the restore will add to the existing contents of the Destination volume rather than replace it—typically not what you would want.

5. Click the Restore button at the bottom of the window.

    If you have permissions problems when creating a backup (for example, you get a "Permission denied" error or other problem), log out and log in as the root user (or simply launch Disk Utility as root, using a utility such as Pseudo, as described in Chapter 4), and then try the above again.

Assuming that both volumes you selected were hard-drive volumes, this should back up the source volume to the destination volume.

If the source volume was bootable (for example, it was a volume from which you could start up in Mac OS X), the backup should be bootable as well (see Chapter 5 if you're having problems booting).

To restore from the backup you created, reverse the above procedure—that is, start up from the backup copy you made and restore to your original volume location.

To back up to and restore from a disk image:

1. Launch Disk Utility, and from the list in the left column select the volume you wish to back up.

2. From the File menu choose New, and from the submenu select Disk Image from {*name of selected device*}. The name of your selected volume should appear as the device name; however, it may appear as something like "disk0s3 (*volumename*)."

3. In the Convert Image window that appears, do the following:

    A. Enter a name for the image.

    B. Choose an Image Format. "Read-only" is the best choice overall; however, you should choose "compressed" if you need to create a smaller image so that it will fit on the destination volume.

    C. Leave Encryption set to None (unless security of the image is a concern).

    D. Select a destination volume via the Where pop-up menu (or navigate to the desired destination location if you've expanded the dialog to view the file browser). This volume must be large enough to contain the image (plus temporary storage that may be needed while creating the image, which means the volume should have at least twice as much free space as the image itself will need).

4. Click Save and wait for the image to be saved.

    If you run into permissions problems when attempting to create the image (for example, you get a "Permission denied" error or other problem), log out and log in as the root user (or simply launch Disk Utility as root, using a utility such as Pseudo, as described in Chapter 4). Try the above again.

5. From the Images menu, select Scan Image for Restore. In the window that appears, select the image you just created and click Open. This verifies that an image can be used for restoring.

    The image is now saved and ready to be restored.

If desired, you can burn the image contents to a CD or DVD (assuming they fit) by selecting the image and clicking the Burn icon in the toolbar. This copies the "mounted" contents of the image to the CD or DVD, not the actual .dmg file itself. You can also copy just the .dmg file without using Disk Utility: Drag the .dmg file's icon to a mounted, unused CD-R or DVD-R in the Finder and burn the disc.

To restore from the image file:

1. Launch Disk Utility, and in the window that appears, click the Restore tab.

2. If the image you created is in the left column, drag it to the Source text box. If not, click the Image button, and then locate and select the image.

3. Drag the name of the volume to be restored from the left column to the Destination text box. Keep in mind that this cannot be the current startup volume, because if it is, the destination volume will be erased.

4. Check the Erase Destination box.

5. Click the Restore button at the bottom of the window.

The volume should now be restored. Wait until restoration is complete; then restart from the restored volume.

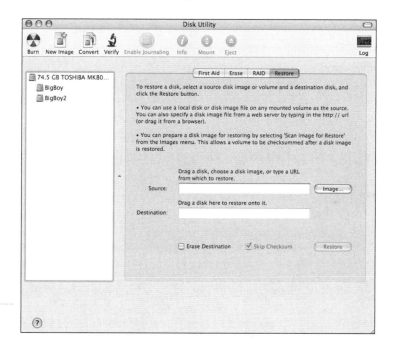

Figure 3.22

Disk Utility's Restore pane.

Figure 3.23

Left, *Disk Utility's File > New submenu;* center, *Images menu; and* right, *New Blank Image dialog (accessed through File > New > Blank Disk Image).*

TECHNICALLY SPEAKING ▶ **More About Disk Utility's Image and Restore Features**

The Image and Restore features in Disk Utility debuted in Panther. The following provides some background information to help you understand how they work.

The **asr** and **hdiutil** commands. Disk Utility's Restore features are actually a front end for the asr (Apple Software Restore) command in Terminal, and its image commands are similarly based on the hdiutil command. As discussed earlier in this chapter, asr is also the basis of the Software Restore application used to restore Macs to the factory-set configuration.

Type man asr and man hdiutil in Terminal to get the documentation (manuals) for these commands. The following are the opening comments from the documentation for asr and hdiutil:

"*asr* efficiently copies disk image contents onto volumes. The asr command can also accurately clone volumes. In its first form, asr copies source (usually a disk image) to target. In its second form, asr prepares a disk image to be restored efficiently, adding file by file and whole-volume checksum information.

"*hdiutil* uses the DiskImages framework to manipulate disk image files."

As usual with Unix commands in Mac OS X, the above commands provide more options than are available via their front-end utility (Disk Utility, in this case).

Restore features and system administrators. Although end users can take advantage of Disk Utility's Restore features for their own backups (as described in the main text), Apple emphasizes the value of these features for system administrators—for example, in classrooms with computers. An administrator can create an image file of a default installation; place it on a CD, DVD, portable hard drive, or server; and then use the image to restore the status of the machines in the lab after they've been modified by student use.

In the "How to use asr" section of the man asr documentation, Apple offers step-by-step instructions for using a combination of Disk Utility and Unix commands in Terminal to do this. In particular, it notes how you may want to initially create a read/write image so that you can eliminate the admin account used to set up the machine and any machine-specific (for example, by host) preferences from the image before using it for a multimachine installation.

Image from Folder vs. Image from Device. To create a backup clone of a volume, the man asr documentation recommends using Disk Image from Folder rather than Disk Image from *Device* (as can be chosen from Disk Utility's File > New submenu)—at least for pre-Tiger versions of Mac OS X. It states the following:

"If you create an image from a device, you will not be able to block restore it (pre-10.3.x) to any volume larger than the one you created the image on. Creating an image from folder/volume is slower, but will give a better result (stretchable, defragmented). Beware that either operation (on OS versions before 10.4) requires two times as much free space on the volume to which you are saving the image as you have data on the source."

continues on next page

TECHNICALLY SPEAKING ▶ More About Disk Utility's Image and Restore Features *continued*

Despite all of Apple's advice, I've had problems using Image from Folder. In particular, I've received an "Operation not supported" error when using this option, whereas Image from Device succeeded. In addition, when making a copy of a bootable CD, as described in the main text, it's generally recommended that you select Disk Image from *Device* instead of Disk Image from Folder—because the device image selection ensures that all of the mass-storage-device components (partition maps, drivers, and so on) that are required for the volume to be bootable are copied.

I go with what works for me and use Disk Image from *Device*, when backing up entire volumes.

Note: The reason why Apple stated (pre-10.4.x) that the imaging operation required twice the free space of the image to be saved was that, when creating an image, Mac OS X first created a temporary file equal in size to the image file. This is no longer done in Tiger.

Segmented images. In Jaguar, the Disk Copy application includes an option to segment a large disk image, such as into 630 MB segments, allowing you to back up a large image to multiple CDs. (Note: If backing up to a hard drive or a DVD, you could pick a size as large as 2 GB.) This segmenting option is not included in Disk Utility's Images options in Panther and later. However, the *segment* option remains available via the hdiutil command in Terminal. Segmenting requires having enough free space on a single drive to hold the complete set of disk images you will need to create.

Mounted images. Disk-image files will appear in the bottom of the left-hand column of the Disk Utility window. If you mount an image, the attached volume will appear as a subhead under the image file. These listings will remain in the column as long as the files or volumes are available. If an image you want to use is not listed, drag its icon from the Finder to the column.

Blank image. When you create a new blank image via the Blank Disk Image command in the File > New submenu, you select the image size from the Size pop-up menu. You have numerous choices: For example, if you want to create a disk image that perfectly matches the size of a CD or DVD, there are specific options for these media sizes.

When creating a new blank image, the only options available in Format are "read/write disk image" and "sparse disk image." Not to worry: You can always change the format after you've created the image, using the Convert command from the Images menu. From here, you are presented with the same Format and Encryption options that you get when you select to create an Image from Folder or Device: read/write, read-only, compressed, and CD/DVD Master.

A new blank image should start out as read/write or sparse because the whole point of it is to be able to add content to the image file after it has been created. To do this, mount the image and drag the desired files to the window of the mounted volume. If you create a blank read/write image of a given size, the size is fixed. Even as a blank image, the image is the size you set. If you create a sparse image file, it starts out at a minimal size (usually around 10 MB to 14 MB) and grows to the maximum you specified in the Size option as you add files to the mounted volume. This allows you to create an image file that is never any larger than you need. In either case, you cannot add files that would exceed the maximum size you set.

continues on next page

> **TECHNICALLY SPEAKING** ▶ **More About Disk Utility's Image and Restore**
> **Features**   *continued*
>
> To burn a disc from a blank image, add the content you want to the mounted volume, unmount
> the volume, select the image, and click the Burn icon in the toolbar (or select Burn from the
> Images menu).
>
> **Checksum.** The checksum is a calculation based on all the data on a volume. Thus, the check-
> sums for a volume and an image created from that volume should be the same. The checksum
> thus provides a means of verifying the accuracy of an image you create. See the Disk Utility Help
> file for more details on checksum.
>
> SEE: • "Burning discs: CDs and DVDs," in Chapter 6, for more on this topic.
>
>   • "Running Mac OS X Software from Terminal," in Chapter 10, for more details on using
>   the asr and hdiutil Unix commands.

Using Terminal. If you're comfortable with using Terminal, you can back up
a volume with Unix commands. The following provides an overview of what
you need to know:

- **ditto.** The ditto -rsrc command copies directories (and their contents),
  correctly maintaining all permissions settings and copying any resource
  forks. As a result, ditto is a good choice for making a clone backup of an
  entire volume—one that will be bootable, if necessary. In fact, Carbon
  Copy Cloner is a front end for the ditto command, bypassing the need
  to use this command in Terminal.

  Note: Make sure you are using a version of Carbon Copy Cloner that
  has been updated to work with Tiger. This applies to any third-party
  backup utility.

  SEE: • "Unix: Copying, Moving, and Deleting," in Chapter 10, for more
     details on ditto and related copy commands.

- **rsync.** The rsync command acts as a directory synchronization tool.
  Compared with ditto, rsync adds the option to copy *only* files that are
  new or that have changed from an existing backup, thereby reducing
  the time needed to complete the task. Its disadvantage is that, like cp,
  it does not preserve the resource fork. The solution here is a variation
  on rsync that copies resource forks: RsyncX, from MacEnterprise.org
  (www.macosxlabs.org/rsyncx/rsyncx.html).

- **asr.** As noted in "Technically Speaking: More About Disk Utility's Image
  and Restore Features," the asr command may be used to "clone volumes"
  (that is, make full bootable backup copies). You can use it instead of Disk
  Utility's Restore feature.

  SEE: • "Technically Speaking: Type/Creator vs. Filename Extensions vs.
     Others," in Chapter 4, for related information.

TAKE NOTE ▶ Backups of Bootable Volumes Don't Boot

If you back up a complete Mac OS X volume with the intention of using it as a bootable copy (such as by using Retrospect's Duplicate command), you may find that you can't boot from the backup volume once you're finished. In some cases, you may get an error during the backup attempt, which prevents the backup from completing.

The most likely cause of such an error is that the "Ignore ownership on this volume" option (located in the Ownership and Permissions section of the Get Info window for the volume) is selected. If that's the case, *uncheck* the box for this option and try the backup again. Then try to boot from the backup; it should work.

In addition, I've found that the most reliable way to boot from a newly created backup is to use the Startup Disk System Preferences to select the backup as the startup disk. Alternatives, such as holding down the Option key at startup (as described in Chapter 5), may not work until you've successfully started up via the System Preferences method.

Otherwise, depending on your Mac OS X version, Mac model, and external drive (SCSI, USB, or FireWire), you may have problems starting up due to issues with the drive itself, as noted later in this chapter (see "Troubleshooting Tips and Hints: Installing Software").

In any case, a word of advice: Always check to see that your backup clone can re-create a bootable volume—before you need it to do so. When disaster strikes is not the time to discover that your backup does not work as expected.

SEE: • "Take Note: Blessed Systems and Starting Up," in Chapter 5, for related advice.

Backing up Mac OS X: Hardware strategies

Over time, the preferred backup hardware has changed, just as the common backup media has shifted (for example, from floppy disks to DVDs) and typical hard-drive capacity has increased (for example, from 20 MB to 100 GB and more). Backup hardware also varies as a function of the type of data you're backing up (a few files versus an entire disk).

Here are my current preferred backup choices. (You may find that using a combination of them provides the best option of all!)

- **CD-RW or DVD-RW drive.** You use a CD-RW or DVD-RW drive to back up data to CD-Rs or DVD-Rs—primarily for a limited subset of your data (in particular, data that doesn't change often or that you would not be able to replace). In general, you can use the Finder to perform these types of backups. This method is perfect, for example, for backing up your MP3 music library, your collection of family digital photos, or the manuscript of that novel you're working on. It provides the most reliable way to store these files without risk of the backup itself becoming damaged or inaccessible. You can use this method (especially DVD-R) to back up an entire drive, though you won't want to do so often because it's likely to be very slow. You can also use RW discs in order to perform later backups with the same media; however, I recommend against this because writing to these discs is significantly slower than to the write-once media, and the discs are also more prone to becoming unreadable at some later point.

If you're using CD-Rs (or similar media of limited size) and are unable to fit the entire contents of a directory onto one disc, you can divide the contents across as many discs as needed. Your only problem would be if you had a single file too large to fit on one disc. In that case, you might want to use a utility like StuffIt Deluxe, which can create a segmented archive of the file; each segment can then be stored on separate media. Apple's Backup application can also back up across multiple CDs. Additionally, you can create a segmented set of .dmg files (as noted in "Technically Speaking: More About Disk Utility's Image and Restore Features," above). However, I recommend using media that can contain the entire file or volume (if possible): It's much faster and less tedious.

- **Tape drive.** A tape drive used to be a great choice for maintaining a regularly updated backup of an entire volume. However, with FireWire drives adding greater capacity for less money every year, it is often more economical (and certainly faster) to back up to another hard drive. Still, if you have a large amount of data that you want to archive and store, tape can be the preferred choice.

  With a tape drive and Retrospect, it's also easy to perform incremental backups. That is, you can instruct Retrospect to only back up files that have changed since the last time you backed up (saving time over a complete backup), and you can have it so that Retrospect does not overwrite old versions of files when adding new ones. This latter option is especially useful for frequently changing files: If you discover that an old "deleted" version of a document contains a passage you want to retrieve, you may still be able to recover that particular version of the document.

- **Hard drive: Individual file backup.** If you've got an external hard drive—for example, one that connects via FireWire or USB—you can use it to quickly and easily back up individual files and folders. You simply connect it to your computer, drag the files and folders you want to back up, and then disconnect it.

- **Hard drive: Full backup.** You can also do a full "mirrored" backup of a volume to another hard drive. This is especially useful if all you want to do is back up the internal drive in a single Mac. You can use Retrospect for this task (in exactly the same way that I described for tape drives); however, Retrospect includes *another* option, called Duplicate, that I recommend instead. Here's what to do:

  1. Get an external FireWire drive equal to or larger in size than your internal drive.

  2. Format it with the same number and sizes of partitions as your internal drive.

  3. Use Retrospect's Duplicate option to create a duplicate of the drive. (You will have to do this separately for each partition.)

With this method, instead of storing your data in a Retrospect archival file format, Retrospect creates a duplicate of each file, much as the Finder would do. Unlike the Finder, however, Retrospect copies all files (including invisible files) and maintains all permissions and links correctly. The result is an exact duplicate of your hard drive. You can even boot from it.

Do this backup as often as you feel necessary.

With Retrospect and a hard drive (or multiple hard drives), you can do regularly scheduled incremental backups—great for users who need to back up an entire volume every day, or even every few hours.

You can also use the previously mentioned utilities (such as Data Backup X and Carbon Copy Cloner) to do a mirrored backup of a hard drive.

- **Internet.** You can back up to a server on the Internet. Apple's .Mac, especially in combination with its Backup utility, is the best-known example of this for Mac users. Although it is slow (and potentially expensive for large backups), it has the advantage of being off-site. If disaster strikes (such as a theft or fire in your home), these Internet backups will still be available. Unless you maintain physical backups somewhere else (such as by placing backup CDs in a safety deposit box or storing them at a friend's or relative's home), this is the only protection you will have against such disasters.

    SEE: • "Take Note: Backing Up and Restoring a Home Directory," earlier in this chapter, for more on the Backup utility.

See also the following Web pages for more background on the Unix backup commands: "How to Create a Bootable Backup of Mac OS X (Cloning Mac OS X discs)" (www.bombich.com/mactips/image.html) and "Learning the Mac OS X Terminal, Part 5" (www.macdevcenter.com/pub/a/mac/2002/07/02/terminal_5.html).

Creating an Emergency Startup Volume

Troubleshooters often find it useful to have a startup disk other than the one that's normally used—typically, the Mac's internal drive. Alternative startup disks can be convenient when you're doing something that cannot be done to the current startup drive (such as disk repairs with some utilities). They become especially valuable if the data on your default drive gets corrupted in such a way that your computer cannot start up from the disk. At these times, a bootable emergency disk becomes an essential tool for repairing the problem drive, or at least recovering data from it.

Because the Mac OS Install disc is bootable and provides access to Disk Utility, you can use it as an emergency boot disc. Third-party repair utilities also typically come on their own bootable CDs. Still, these discs may prove less useful as updated versions of the software are released, for which you do not have a CD. (In addition, as new models of Macs are released, it often takes time before an updated version of a third-party utility's CD, modified to start up the latest Macs, is released.) In any case, it's convenient to be able to create your own custom bootable emergency disk—one that contains all the software of your choosing.

In past years, emergency bootable volumes took the form of floppy disks or (more recently) CD-Rs or Zip disks. More recently, that emergency volume could have been a portable FireWire hard drive. In this section, I discuss how to set up an emergency volume using several different media. Of special interest are the procedures for making a custom bootable CD.

Creating a bootable volume in Mac OS 9 was about as simple as it could possibly be: You just dragged a copy of a System Folder to the volume, and (assuming the software was recent enough to run on the Mac in question) you were able to start up your Mac from that drive. This method worked with hard drives as well as most removable media (such as Zip disks). CDs, however, presented a special problem: A CD needed some special boot code for the Mac to recognize the disc as a startup volume at a point in the startup process when it typically would not yet have loaded the code needed to recognize CDs in the first place! This problem was solved by utilities such as Roxio's Toast, which created a bootable CD with the needed special code from any original that contained a System Folder. Even Mac OS X's Disk Utility can burn a bootable Mac OS 9 CD if you first create a disk image of a bootable CD for it to copy.

Creating a custom bootable Mac OS X volume presents considerably more difficulties. The primary reason is that the essential System files are not all in the Mac OS X System directory. In addition, numerous invisible files, mostly related to the underlying Unix OS, need to be copied as well. And there is the potential issue of setting up a default user account.

Thus, you cannot simply copy a Mac OS X System folder to a Zip disk, for example, and expect it to function as a startup volume. In fact, given that Zip discs max out at 250 MB, and a typical Mac OS X system can require more than 600 MB, it's unlikely that you'll be able to use a Zip disk as a Mac OS X startup disc under any circumstances.

Bootable hard drive

If you've divided your internal hard drive into several partitions, the simplest way to create an emergency startup volume would be to use a Mac OS X Install CD to install Mac OS X on more than one partition. You could then use the second Mac OS X installation as your emergency partition. One weakness of this approach is that if the entire hard drive fails, you will not be able to start up from any partition.

A better alternative is an external hard drive. Especially convenient when traveling are small, portable FireWire drives.

Bootable CD or DVD

For troubleshooters, by far the most useful and commonly used bootable disc is a bootable CD or DVD. So, if you own a CD or DVD burner (Apple's SuperDrive will make things go most smoothly), can you create one of these bootable discs yourself? Yes, with some limitations.

You can certainly create an exact copy of a bootable CD or DVD that will also be bootable, but making a useful customized bootable disc is not as simple.

Making a duplicate bootable CD/DVD. If all you want is to make an exact copy of a bootable disc (such as the Mac OS X Install disc) for use as an emergency disk, it's relatively easy to do.

However, don't expect to use the Finder's Burn Disc command (in the File menu) to accomplish this feat. At least as of Mac OS X 10.4, you could not create a copy of a bootable disc using this feature.

Toast, a commercial disc-burning application, can make a bootable Mac OS X disc—and using it is as simple as clicking the Copy tab, inserting the disc to be copied, and clicking the red Record button. This works especially well if you have two optical drives (only one needs to be RW)—one for the blank CD-R or DVD-R and another for the Mac OS X Install disc. If this doesn't work for some reason, first create a .dmg of the Install disc and then use Toast to copy the unmounted image file to the blank disc. You could do this by creating the image file via Disk Utility in Mac OS X. However, if you need to go this route, you might as well skip Toast altogether and just use Disk Utility.

To create a bootable copy of a Tiger Mac OS X Install DVD with Disk Utility:

1. Booting from your hard drive, insert and mount the Mac OS X Install DVD.
2. Launch Disk Utility.

3. In the left-hand column, the Mac OS X Install DVD will be listed in the following manner: At the top of the hierarchy will be the name of the drive itself (for example, 2.6 GB PIONEER DVD-RW DVR-117D); the subheading under that name will be either Mac OS X Install DVD or Session 1; if the latter, the subheading under that name will be Mac OS X Install DVD.

4. Select Mac OS X Install DVD (or, if Session 1 is listed, select it instead).

    Note: For multisession discs, each session would be listed separately. To create a multisession disc, check the "Leave disc appendable" box in Disk Utility's Burn Disc dialog (in Step 9, below). Otherwise, the instructions here assume you have a single-session disc.

5. From the File > New submenu, choose "Disk image from {*name of device*}." The name of the device should be something like "disk1s3 (Mac OS X Install DVD)."

6. In the Convert Image dialog, name the image. For Image Format, typically choose either "read-only" or "DVD/CD master" (which is what I recommend). Leave Encryption as "none."

    Note: The "read/write" format should be used if you intend to modify the contents of the image (which we are *not* doing here) before burning it. With this format, you can later mount the image and drag files to or from the mounted volume. Changes you make are saved to the image (.dmg) file. You then unmount the image before burning the image to a disc. Ideally, you should still choose DVD/CD master, read-only, or even compressed (if needed to conserve space) when setting up to burn the modified image.

7. Click Save.

8. Returning to the left-hand column of the Disk Utility window, select the image you just created. Click the Burn icon in the toolbar or select Burn from the Images menu.

9. Insert a CD-R or DVD-R at the prompt in the Burn Disc dialog that appears. At this point, the Burn button in the dialog will become undimmed. Click it and wait for the burn to complete.

Making minor changes to the exact procedures and selections I have described here may still produce a successful bootable disc. I have not tried them all. But I have tried several different combinations, and this was the one that worked best for me. Feel free to experiment with other combinations if you don't share my success.

Note: In some cases, you may be able to download a .dmg file of a bootable disc from a Web site. Or you may create your own image with software other than Disk Utility. If so, you can drag the image file to the lower half of the left column of Disk Utility (where image files are listed). Once the image file appears in the list, you can go directly to Step 8 above.

SEE: • **"Burning discs: CDs and DVDs," in Chapter 6, for more on multisession discs and related issues.**

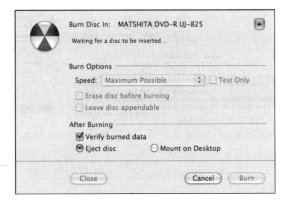

Figure 3.24

Disk Utility's Burn Disc dialog in Tiger.

Making a modified copy of a bootable disc. The above procedure is all well and good. But what if you want to make a customized disc with your own utilities on it?

It may at first seem that the solution is to create a read/write image from the Mac OS X Install disc (as described in the previous section), and then add your own utilities to the image (deleting unneeded and nonessential files already on the image, if necessary). The problem is, a bootable disc created in this way does not load the Finder. In fact, the Finder is not even on the disc. Instead, the disc boots directly into the Installer utility, which is the only way the disc can start. Thus, although you may have other utilities on the drive, you would have no way to access them. Could you get the disc to boot into another utility instead of the Installer? It's possible to modify the rc.cdrom file (located in the /etc directory of a bootable CD) to get it to boot into another utility, but doing so is tricky enough that I wouldn't bother.

Apple has created software that developers can use to create custom bootable CDs. It is this software that the developers of programs such as Alsoft's DiskWarrior (www.alsoft.com) and Micromat's TechTool Pro (www.micromat.com) use to create the bootable discs. However, Apple has not made this development tool available to the public. In fact, Apple even limits its availability to "qualified" developers who can demonstrate a need for making such discs. Clearly, Apple does not want to encourage the creation of custom bootable discs. And even in these cases, the discs typically do not include a Finder and thus cannot access the Desktop.

So what can you do here? Get the shareware utility BootCD (which can also be used to make a bootable DVD).

Making a custom bootable CD with Boot CD. BootCD (www.charlessoft.com) allows you to create a bootable CD that contains a Finder and a Dock. The Dock can be set up to contain any applications you choose. Here is an overview of how to use it.

1. Launch BootCD. Type in the desired name in the Volume Name field.

    Note: If you are going to make a bootable DVD, change the Disk Size here from the default of 650 MB to the size of the DVD (typically, 2600 MB). Otherwise, leave this value alone. Although this should work to make the disc bootable, it will still install only the same limited system software that it would install on a CD.

    If you want to change the RAM Disk Size, you can also do so; however, there should rarely be a need to so this, so I don't recommend it.

2. Click the Create Bootable CD Image button.

3. Give a name to the .dmg file that BootCD will create; then click Save.

4. Choose which applications you would like to include on the CD and put in the Dock that is used when you boot from the CD. You do this via a file-browser window that appears. Typically, you would add utilities that you might need for repair or recovery in an emergency. Click Open to add a utility. Click Cancel when finished. Disk Utility, Console, and Terminal are automatically included, so you don't need to select them.

5. Quit BootCD, launch Disk Utility, and burn a CD of the disk image you created.

To use your newly created bootable CD, insert it into your CD/DVD drive and then restart. Boot from the CD (by holding down the C key at startup). When startup is complete, you should be at the Finder. There will be a Dock that contains all the utilities you selected (plus Disk Utility, Console, and Terminal). Your startup-drive volume/partitions will also be mounted. You have root user status at this point. (BootCD has the root password set to *BootCD*.)

With the full contents of the hard drive now accessible, you can work with most applications on the drive (in addition to the emergency utilities on the CD). I could run the Chess game or create a document in TextEdit, for example. However, since the CD is read-only, you won't be able to save documents to the CD or to save preferences to applications.

The Restart, Shut Down, and Log Out commands in the Apple menu do not work on a CD created with BootCD. To reboot again from your hard drive, use the reboot command in Terminal. To make sure you don't reboot from the CD, hold down the Eject button on your keyboard until the CD ejects.

Note: The steps in this section are accurate for the Panther version of BootCD. This version is *not* compatible with Tiger! A Tiger version of BootCD was still in development as of this writing. The new version may, of course, work a bit differently than described here, so be sure to read the documentation.

See "Creating a Mac OS X Bootable CD" (www.bombich.com/mactips/bootx.html) for more technical information on creating a bootable CD.

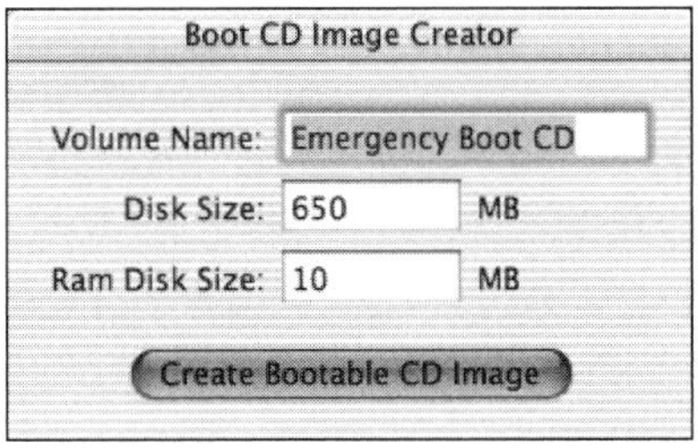

Boot CD Image Creator

Volume Name: Emergency Boot CD

Disk Size: 650   MB

Ram Disk Size: 10   MB

Create Bootable CD Image

Figure 3.25

Making a bootable disc with BootCD.

Troubleshooting Tips and Hints: Installing Software

Most Mac OS X installations go quite smoothly. As with any OS, however, problems can occur. The following covers most of the things that may go wrong, as well as what to do to get things right again.

Can't start up from Mac OS X Install CD

Some users are unable to get the Mac OS X Install disc to act as a startup disc for their Mac, getting the following error message instead: "Startup Disk was unable to select the install disc as the startup disk. (-2)." In other cases, the disc simply stalls at some point in the startup sequence, with or without displaying an error message. In the most extreme cases, the Mac drops into Open Firmware.

Problems like these are often caused by defective discs. However, if the disc fails in some Macs but works in others, a defect is not the likely cause. In one case, the culprit was a third-party CD-ROM drive that replaced the internal drive that came with the Mac. The drive worked in general but not for the Mac OS X Install CD. In this case, if you were up to the task, you could reinstall the original CD drive and see if that worked. Or you could borrow or buy an external CD drive and try that.

SEE: • Chapter 5 for more information on Open Firmware and on startup problems in general.

By the way, if you installed an internal CD or DVD drive, you need to be careful about its settings. In particular, the drive, which is an ATA device, should be set for the *master* position, not the *slave mode* position. Users have reported that drives in the slave position do not work in Mac OS X. If you don't have a clue what I'm talking about here, don't worry—unless you decide to install an internal CD or DVD drive and start having problems. At that point, check my *Sad Macs* book, the documentation that came with the drive, or Apple's support Web site for more help.

In any case, because starting up from the disc is a requirement for installing Mac OS X, you cannot ignore symptoms like those described above. Apple advises that you follow these steps if you're unable to start up from a Mac OS X Install disc:

1. Inspect the Mac OS X disc.

    Verify that the shiny side of the disc is relatively clean (no particles, smudges, or other abnormalities).

2. Make sure that current firmware is installed.

    Your computer may require a firmware update for best Mac OS X compatibility. Check Apple's Web site for possible upgrades.

3. Disconnect peripheral devices connected to your computer except for the Apple keyboard and mouse, including USB devices, FireWire devices, SCSI devices, and PCMCIA cards.

4. Remove third-party hardware upgrades such as third-party memory (RAM) and third-party PCI cards.

    SEE: • "Kernel panic," in Chapter 5, for a description of a problem with a third-party video card that may occur when trying to install Mac OS X.

After doing all of this, try starting up from the disc again. If it still fails, especially if the Mac drops into Open Firmware, you probably have a damaged CD/DVD. Contact Apple to replace the disc.

Cannot launch Installer successfully

If you're running Mac OS X from your hard drive rather than from a CD/DVD, you may find that the Installer application refuses to launch. Most likely, this will be a general issue that will occur no matter what software package file you attempt to use. In such cases, try the following until one works:

1. Quit all open applications. Make sure Classic is disabled as well. Try again. Do not attempt to perform any other actions on the Mac while the install is proceeding.

2. Restart the Mac and try again.

3. Disconnect all peripheral hardware devices, restart, and try the installation again.

4. Use Disk Utility's First Aid (or a similar third-party utility) to check whether disk repairs are needed.

    SEE: • Chapter 5 for more information on disk and permissions repairs.

5. Use Disk Utility's First Aid tab to repair disk permissions on the volume.

6. Create a new administrative user, and install from the new user's account.

    If the installation succeeds, you can delete the newly created user account when you're finished.

SEE: • "Take Note: Adding or Deleting a User," in Chapter 2, for more information on creating and deleting additional users.

7. Reinstall the Installer application itself, either by extracting it from the Mac OS X package (via Pacifist) or from a backup of a working copy, or by reinstalling Mac OS X altogether.

Cannot select a volume to install

When installing software via the Installer utility, the Installer may launch successfully, but when you get to the Installer's Select a Destination pane, you may find one of the following problems:

- The volume that you intended to use to install your selected software is not displayed.
- The volume icon is displayed but dimmed, so it cannot be selected.
- The volume icon is displayed, but a Stop Sign symbol with an exclamation point overlaps the volume icon, indicating that you cannot install the software on that volume.

Typically, a text message appears lower in the window, explaining the reason for the prohibition (see Figure 3.8, earlier in this chapter). The message, however, is not always very informative. One common explanation, for example, states, "You cannot install {*name of software*} on this volume. This volume does not meet the requirements for this update." Another reads, "You cannot install this software on this machine."

The end result in all of these cases is that the Install button is not available for the volume you wish to use. Here are some potential causes and solutions.

Make sure you meet the minimum requirements. The read-me file that accompanies the software to be installed should supply the minimum requirements. For starters:

- Make sure you have at least the minimum installed RAM and free hard-drive space for the installation to proceed.
- You may need to have certain software installed for the current install to proceed. As an obvious example, you can't install any updates to Mac OS X 10.4 until 10.4 itself is installed. The solution here is to go back and install the needed software and then return to the problem installation. It should now work. Similarly, for update .pkg files, make sure that the required prior version of Mac OS X is on the destination volume. You can check your current version from the About This Mac window, which you access from the Apple menu.

Reinstall and downgrade problems. If you want to reinstall the same version of software that already exists on your drive (perhaps because you believe the software on your drive is corrupted), or to downgrade to an older version of the software, the Installer is not likely to allow it. If this happens (and the software to be installed is a single application), drag the application and its receipt file (in /Library/Receipts) to the Trash. Now try again.

To do this for an installation of or update to Mac OS X itself, you will need to do an Archive and Install back to the version that came on your Mac OS X Install disc, and then re-update from there.

SEE: • "Downgrading and Re-upgrading Mac OS X," earlier in this chapter, for related information.

External drives. Mac OS X often will not install on an external SCSI drive. It also has problems installing or booting from some external FireWire and USB drives.

The problem is sometimes due to the specific external drive. In such cases, the solution may be to get a firmware update for the drive or to abandon the drive altogether. Other times, the problem may be with the Mac OS X software, requiring an update from Apple before the drive will work. Check with the drive vendor for exact recommendations. The drive vendor's name is available from the Apple System Profiler listing. Otherwise, check with Apple's support pages or MacFixIt.com for the latest details as to which drives work with Mac OS X.

Note: If you can't install Mac OS X on a drive and/or start up from a drive with Mac OS X installed, you can still use the drive as a non-startup volume.

SEE: • Chapter 5, for more on startup problems, especially issues regarding blessing of Mac OS X volumes.

Update disc. If the drive is listed but its icon is dimmed so that you cannot select it, make sure you're not using an Update disc and trying to install the OS on a volume that does not have a prerequisite version of Mac OS X already installed.

If you have moved, deleted, or modified files in the /System/Library folder, it's possible that the Installer may not recognize the OS as the correct version, even if it is. In this case, unless you can move everything back correctly, you will likely need to start over with a reinstall from a full Mac OS X Install disc.

iPod. Apple's iPod (except for the iPod Shuffle) is basically a FireWire hard drive. In principle, if you have a FireWire Dock connector cable, you can install Mac OS X on the drive and use the iPod as a portable emergency startup drive. To do so, you must enable iPod's FireWire Disk Use option, which you access via the iPod options in iTunes.

However, you may not be able to install Mac OS X on an iPod via the Mac OS X Install disc. Exact symptoms may vary, but in my case, for the Jaguar Install CD, the Installer utility simply refused to display the iPod's icon in the Select a Destination pane. When starting from the Panther Install CD, however, the iPod showed up just fine. If you do have problems here, you should still be able to work around the glitch by using a backup utility (such as Carbon Copy Cloner) to copy a preinstalled bootable copy of Mac OS X from another drive onto an iPod, though this is not as convenient as using the Install disc.

Note: After installing Mac OS X from an Install disc, installing further minor updates (for example, from 10.3 to 10.3.1) should work without any problems.

Note: After installing Mac OS X software on an iPod, you may not be able to update the iPod software.

Warning: Apple warns against using the iPod as a full-time startup disc, as the hard drive inside the iPod can overheat when used in this manner; I would recommend using your iPod as a startup disc only for short periods of time— for example, as an emergency utility drive.

SEE: • "Troubleshooting the iPod," in Chapter 11, for more details on these problems.

Checking console.log. If an update installation (not a full installation done when booting from a CD or DVD) fails, despite checking all of the above, launch the Console utility and check the Console log file that appears. The most recent entries are likely to refer to what went wrong when the installation failed. The information *may* give you a clue as to how to solve the problem. For example, I've seen several reports where the problem made reference to a preferences file on the drive. Deleting the named preferences file and retrying the updater led to success.

Check the Web. Check the Web for late-breaking information about problems and solutions not covered here. Also see this Apple Knowledge Base document: http://docs.info.apple.com/article.html?artnum=106692.

Java Update 1.4.2 will not install

Many users have found that they are unable to install the Java Update 1.4.2 update. The easy fix for this problem is to delete the QuickTimeJavaUpdate.pkg receipt from /Library/Receipts and then attempt the installation again.

Software Update does not list or install an update

If you believe a software update is available (perhaps you read about it on a Web site), but Software Update does not list it, you have several options:

• Make sure you have a working Internet connection.

• If you get a "server busy" error or are otherwise unable to get Software Update to work as expected, there's probably a problem at Apple's end. Try again later (ideally in a day or so).

- If you get a message that says, "Your software is up to date," it may be that the desired software cannot be downloaded via Software Update. Apple sometimes provides certain updates only through its Web site. Or it may simply be that the update is not available; try again the next day to see if it is now listed.

- If multiple users are logged in via Fast User Switching, do not attempt to switch to another account while Software Update is running. Ideally, log out of all but one account prior to running Software Update.

- Make sure the file you want is really newer than the one you already have. For example, if you're trying to obtain Mac OS X 10.3.8, make sure you don't already have Mac OS X 10.3.9 installed. To check the current installed version, select About This Mac from the Apple menu.

- If the problem occurs because you reinstalled an older version of Mac OS X and now want to reinstall subsequent updates (that you had previously installed), check to see if the receipt files for those subsequent updates are still in the /Library/Receipts folder. If so, remove the receipt files and try again.

  SEE: • **"Receipt files" and "Downgrading and Re-upgrading Mac OS X," earlier in this chapter, for more details.**

- If you recently downloaded and installed software via Software Update, try running Software Update again. The desired software may appear only after the initial software has been installed.

  As noted earlier in the chapter, Software Update in Panther and later automatically checks for newer updates after it completes an installation, assuming you chose to install the software rather than just download it.

- The software may not be needed for your computer: For example, a DVD Player update may not appear if you do not have a DVD drive.

- Needed hardware may not be accessible. For a PowerBook with a removable DVD drive, for example, installing a DVD Player update will not work if the DVD drive is not currently inserted in the expansion bay.

- Make sure the software is in its original location. In general, when Mac OS X software is installed (such as to the Applications folder), it is best to leave it where it is. Moving it to a different folder can cause problems when updating the application or when you later try to use it.

  SEE: • **"Relocation problems," later in this chapter.**

In some cases Software Update may list an update but fail to successfully install it. You may get an error message such as one that says, "Some of the checked updates couldn't be installed. Software Update could not expand the package correctly." In the Software Update window, an exclamation-point icon will appear to the left of the name of each update that was not installed. If this happens, remove any package and receipt files for prior versions of the problem software (prior updates to iTunes, for example, if that is what you are updating) from the /Library/Packages and /Library/Receipts folders. Then try again.

Otherwise, choose Download Only, to have Software Update just download the update package to your Desktop. Then double-click the package to launch Installer, which will hopefully succeed where Software Update failed.

If problems persist, your last resort is to completely reinstall Mac OS X.

Software Update quits unexpectedly

In a very specific incident, Panther versions 10.3.0 through 10.3.4 can exhibit an issue where the Software Update application quits unexpectedly if an update includes a license agreement (the software license agreement that sometimes pops up and requires you to "agree" before the update will install). According to Apple, the cause of this bug is the third-party Times RO font. You can work around this bug by deleting the font and then restarting; however, an easier fix, especially if you need this font, is to download the Mac OS X 10.3.5 (or later) Update from Apple's Web site and install it manually.

Installed Updates does not list previously installed updates

The Installed Updates list in the Software Update System Preferences pane may not list updates you previously selected and installed. You may encounter a similar problem in the log file maintained by Software Update. If this happens, try the following:

* **Make sure you really installed the update via Software Update.** If you installed an update by downloading it from Apple's Web site or by using Software Update's Download Only option, the Installed Updates pane will not list it. This pane only lists updates actually installed by Software Update.

* **Check the permissions settings for the relevant log file (Software Update.log in /Library/Logs).** In Panther and later, you (that is, your user name) should be the Owner, and admin should be the Group. Owner should have Read & Write access. Group and Others should have Read Only access. Note that in Jaguar, the owner is System, and both System and admin have Read & Write access. If your settings are different, edit them to match those described here.

    SEE: • "Ownership & Permissions," in Chapter 4, for details on how to make these changes.

* **If the problem began immediately after you upgraded to Tiger, open the Software Update.log file in a text editor.** Delete all lines referring to updates installed *prior* to installing Tiger, and then save the file.

    Once you've done this, Installed Updates should list updates correctly.

    SEE: • "Updating from Software Update," earlier in this chapter, for more on this feature.

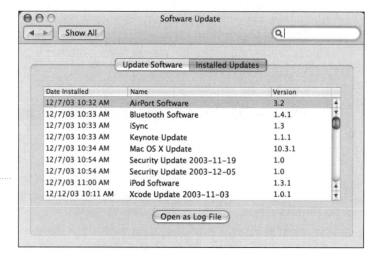

Figure 3.26

The Installed Updates pane of the Software Update System Preferences pane.

Install and Keep Package option doesn't keep

I've found that if I use the Install and Keep Package option in Software Update—which should install an update and then save the update package in /Library/Receipts—and there's already an update package in the Receipts and/or Packages folder with the same name as the update being installed, the new update package typically won't be saved. For example, I saw this issue with iTunes and AirPort software updates. This could be prevented if Apple would provide unique names to all update packages; in the meantime, to ensure that this problem does not prevent future packages from being saved, I've started checking on packages saved to /Library/Receipts, and if their names do not include version numbers, I add them.

SEE • "Receipt files," earlier in this chapter, for related information on removing receipt files.

Installation is interrupted

Whether you're attempting to install Mac OS X from the Install disc(s) or installing updates at some later point, the process may bog down during the installation. Here are some common causes and cures:

- If you are using Mac OS X Install CDs, rather than a single Install DVD, you will reach a point where you're asked to restart after the first CD has finished its work. However, a problem may occur where the request for a second or third CD never comes. If software on these CDs is not needed (because you removed the relevant options via a Custom Install), this is expected, and all is well. However, if the CD really is needed, the restart typically fails at this point, though it may sometimes proceed without asking for the second CD. In either case, the needed software is not installed.

There appears to be more than one possible cause for this. In some cases, when trying to install Mac OS X on an external FireWire drive, there's a conflict between Mac OS X and the drive—in which case the solution is to hope that an upgrade to Mac OS X or the drive's firmware will fix the problem. If not, you won't be able to use the drive to install Mac OS X.

On one occasion, the problem was with the Mac OS X Install CDs themselves. When another set of the CDs was tried, the problem did not occur.

- In general, when installing updates while running Mac OS X from your hard drive, turn off any settings in Energy Saver and Screen Saver System Preferences that automatically put the Mac to sleep or shift to a screen saver. Otherwise, the onset of sleep could halt the update process.

- If an installation of a Mac OS X update via Software Update gets interrupted, such as by a power failure, get the stand-aione version of the Installer—via either Software Update's Download Only command or Apple's Web site. Use the downloaded and saved Installer package to try again to install the update. Note: If you try to use Software Update, it may report incorrectly that you no longer need the update, in which case deleting the receipt file for the update (in /Library/Receipts) may fix the problem. On the other hand, with a bit of luck, Software Update may recognize that an installation was partially completed and pick up the process where it left off.

- When using Software Update, if you get an error message that says an update "could not be installed," choose Download Only to get the stand-alone updater and try again. If you're already using a stand-alone updater and it too "unexpectedly quits" or otherwise reports an "error while installing," run the installation yet again. There is a good chance it will now work. If not, the update file itself may be corrupted. In this case, download a new copy of the updater and run the install again. If this fails, log in as a different user and try the install again.

- If the update fails at the point where it says, "optimizing drive," don't worry too much—you've already completed the actual installation process. The only problem may be that you might have slower overall performance than you otherwise would get. To fix this, trying running the Installer again, or run the /update_prebinding command in Terminal.

- In general, if an installation fails, open one of the relevant log files (located in /var/log), either in Console or a text editor. These logs will often indicate the nature of the problem.

    SEE: • "Technically Speaking: Checking Logs After an Installation Error," below, for more details.

    • "Defragmenting/optimizing Mac OS X volumes," in Chapter 5.

    • "Technically Speaking: Terminal Commands to Monitor and Improve Performance," in Chapter 10.

TECHNICALLY SPEAKING ▶ Checking Logs After an Installation Error

If an alert box appears with a message stating, "There was an error while installing," check the relevant log files for clues to a possible cause. There are three main log locations to check:

- **Installer log.** If you're using Apple's Installer utility, from the Window menu select Installer Log. If the information in the log window is not immediately helpful, check the Show More Detail box.

- **Software Update log.** If you're using Software Update, click the Installed Updates tab of the Software Update System Preferences. The same log information is also available as a log file, which you can access by clicking the Open as Log File button in the Installed Updates pane.

- **Console log and system log.** Use the Console utility to check other potentially relevant logs used by Mac OS X, especially console.log and system.log. Look for messages containing the word *Install* or ones that appeared around the time of the installation.

With some luck, information in one or more of these locations will help you diagnose what went wrong with the installation and thus help you figure out how to fix it.

SEE: • Chapters 2, 4, and 5 for more on Console and logs.

Software installs but fails to work

In some cases, a Mac OS X update may install successfully (or at least appear to), but after you restart (if necessary) or attempt to use the new software, you discover problems that had not occurred previously. In the worst case, you may not be able to start up at all. The advice that follows focuses on installing Mac OS X updates, but much of it applies to installing any software update in Mac OS X (including third-party updates).

Bugs. Most often, problems with updates can be traced back to a bug in either the package file used for the installation or the software that was installed. If such a bug affects all Macs, it would almost certainly be discovered *before* the package file's release—which is exactly why most such problems affect only a small subset of users (ones who have a particular, often older, Mac model, for example). Unfortunately, sometimes the only fix is to go back to the previous version of Mac OS X and wait for Apple to release an update that corrects the problem. Otherwise, you may find a work-around posted to Web sites (such as MacFixIt.com) shortly after the update is released.

The unfortunate truth is that Mac OS X has become so complex that whenever Apple releases a new update, at least some users will report having problems with it that they did not have before. Some (although by no means all) of these reported problems are due to bugs remaining in or introduced in the update. Common post-update problems include an inability to start up the Mac, date and time not being maintained correctly, external volumes not being recognized, an inability to maintain dial-up connections, an increase in kernel panics, an inability to add new printers or print to existing ones, wake-from-sleep crashes, and more.

Rather than wait for specific causes of and solutions to these bugs to be worked out (assuming that ever happens), your best bet is to try to avoid the problem in the first place. Here's some standard advice for avoiding these frustrations:

- **Use the Combo updater.** If you're running the Mac OS X version immediately prior to the current update (for example, you're running Mac OS X 10.4.2 and updating to 10.4.3), the update package you are using especially if you downloaded it via Software Update—typically works only with that (immediately prior) version. The alternative, if you're running an even older version of Mac OS X, is to use a separate Combo updater file (as discussed earlier in this chapter).

  However, you can use the Combo updater for 10.4.3 even if you're already running 10.4.2, for example. Though doing so may be of little benefit over running the Delta or Patch 10.4.3 update, some users report better success with Combo updaters, even in these situations.

  What's more likely to help avoid upgrade problems is to start over and re-upgrade with the Combo updater. For example, if your Mac OS X Install disc contains version 10.4.0, reinstall Mac OS X from the disc, using the Archive and Install feature, and then run the Combo updater to get to 10.4.3. If this seems like a hassle—which it is—wait to see if you have problems after updating via the non-Combo updater, and use this method only if problems occur.

  In such cases, it is also recommended that you download the updater and run it from your hard drive rather than let Software Update do the install.

- **Repair Disk Permissions.** Immediately after installing a Mac OS X update and restarting, access Disk Utility's First Aid and select Repair Disk Permissions. This is known to prevent a number of symptoms, including applications' failing to launch, that might otherwise occur.

  Note: Occasionally, repairing disk permissions may cause a problem itself, especially with third-party software that does not follow Apple's rules for setting permissions via an Installer. Therefore, some experts recommend *not* routinely repairing permissions. Rather, do it only if you have a problem that you hope it may fix. Personally, I have never made a problem worse by repairing permissions. If you have any symptoms that you think may be permissions related, it's worth giving it a try.

- **Delete cache and preferences files.** If the problem is specific to a single application, delete any preferences or cache files associated with that application. You may also want to use a utility, such as Northern Softworks' Tiger Cache Cleaner (www.northernsoftworks.com) or Maintain's Cocktail (www.maintain.se/cocktail), to more generally delete potentially corrupt preferences and cache files.

  If all of this fails, do a search for files that include the name of the problem application, and delete any that show up. Then reinstall the application and re-update it as needed.

If none of these suggestions help, check the sections that follow for more specific advice. Otherwise, your main option is to seek a solution elsewhere (such as a support Web site). If everything you try fails, you probably have a bug that was introduced in the new update or a conflict between the update and installed third-party software. If the problem is with third-party software, either remove it or upgrade to a compatible version (if one exists). For bugs in the OS itself, you'll have to learn to live with them (at least until Apple provides a fix) or downgrade back to the previous version of Mac OS X.

SEE: • "Downgrading and Re-upgrading Mac OS X," earlier in this chapter, for related information.

• Chapter 5, for details on Repair Disk Permissions, preferences, and cache issues.

Startup problems. If your Mac crashes immediately after installing a Mac OS X update or upgrade, consider the following:

• **SCSI.** On older Macs with built-in SCSI ports, or newer Macs with SCSI PCI cards, the most common cause of these crashes is SCSI devices. *SCSI* refers to a technology for connecting peripheral devices, such as hard drives, to a Mac. No current Mac comes with a SCSI port as part of the logic board; instead, all new Macs use USB and/or FireWire as alternatives. The main places where you will still find SCSI are older Macs and newer Power Macs that have a separate SCSI card installed in one of the PCI slots. In some cases, the SCSI PCI card itself is incompatible with Mac OS X and may lead to startup problems. Fixing this problem may require a firmware upgrade of the card or, at the very least, a software driver upgrade.

In other cases, the problem may be with a device connected to the card or the way in which multiple devices are chained together, mainly involving what's called *SCSI termination*. This term refers to how SCSI devices are connected in a chain when you have more than one device. Mac OS X is much more sensitive to SCSI termination, so technically incorrect setups that did not cause a problem in Mac OS 9 may cause a problem in Mac OS X.

Check with the card's vendor (or Apple, if your Mac came with a SCSI card) for specific recommendations. Apple has an update for its Apple Ultra Wide SCSI PCI card (http://docs.info.apple.com/article.html?artnum=25176); you need this update if you intend to use the card with Mac OS X.

• **Memory.** In some cases, a Mac will not start up in Mac OS X due to a problem with a third-party memory (RAM) module. If you get a black screen immediately at startup, I would suspect this problem. To check, remove the extra installed memory (especially memory not purchased from Apple) and try again. If startup succeeds, contact your memory vendor about getting a replacement.

SEE: • **"Checking for 'bad' memory (and other hardware problems)," in Chapter 5, and "Utilities for monitoring and improving performance," in Chapter 6, for more advice on how to test for bad memory.**

- **Firmware.** A firmware upgrade alters a special modifiable component of the hardware on the Mac's logic board. Before installing Mac OS X (especially if you have an older Mac), make sure your computer has the latest firmware installed. Failure to update firmware prior to installing Mac OS X, or even just a newer version of Mac OS X, may lead to serious problems, including startup failures.

   If you plan on erasing your drive before installing Mac OS X, do the firmware update before erasing.

   SEE: • **"Take Note: Firmware Updates," in Chapter 5, for details on firmware updates.**

   • **Chapter 5 for coverage of startup problems beyond those that immediately follow a Mac OS X installation.**

Note: After Panther was released, a problem was discovered in which certain external FireWire drives could get hopelessly corrupted if they were mounted when restarting or shutting down from an internal startup volume running Panther. The primary solution is to upgrade the firmware for these drives. (You get the updates from the drive vendor, *not* Apple.)

SEE: • **"Take Note: Startup Failure When Starting Up from an External Device," in Chapter 5, for related details.**

• **"Mounting and unmounting/ejecting media," in Chapter 6, for more specific information on this Panther-FireWire issue.**

Relocation problems. Sometimes an update installation works correctly only if the prior version of the software is in its correct default installed location—especially with older versions of Mac OS X. In these cases, the problem is that the Installer expected to find Mac OS X–installed applications (like Mail) in their default locations (such as at the top level of the Applications folder). If, for example, you were to move Mail from the Applications folder—to, say, a subfolder called "Internet apps"—and then install a Mac OS X update that updated the Mail application, Mail would not get updated properly. Instead, the Installer would place a nonfunctional (even non-launchable!) copy of Mail in the Applications folder. This copy would contain only the subset of files that make up Mail's .app package that were actually updated. Meanwhile, your relocated copy of Mail would remain unchanged. The result would be one copy of Mail (in Applications) that did not work and another copy (located elsewhere) that was not updated. You would not receive any warning message from the Installer that a problem had occurred.

If you're comfortable working inside packages, you could fix this problem by dragging the updated files in the .app package at the default location to their respective folders within the application package of the original version, replacing the older versions as needed. The process is a pain, but it should work.

Alternatively, you can use Pacifist (as covered earlier in this chapter) to separately reinstall an individual application. However, an easier approach is to simply return the application to its default location and try reinstalling the update.

Apple states that, starting with Mac OS X 10.2.2, this problem no longer occurs. The Installer should locate the needed files wherever they may be (as long as they're on the boot volume) and update them correctly. However, there have been a number of reports—relating to various updates—that indicate this is not consistently the case. I recommend playing it safe here by *not* moving Apple-installed files from their default locations.

With third-party installers, especially ones that allow you to choose the folder where the installed software should go, this should not be an issue.

External drives do not boot. If you have a bootable external drive (such as a FireWire hard drive), you may not be able to start up from the drive when it's attached to a Mac newer than the Mac OS X version installed on the drive. This may be because the new Mac requires an updated version of the operating system that includes the needed support files for its newer ROM. In some cases, the version of Mac OS X on your external drive and on the new Mac may be the same—leading you to believe that there should be no problem. However, the build number may be different. In any case, the solution is to update (or do a complete new install, if the Installer refuses to do the update) the version of Mac OS X on your external drive to the version that came with the new Mac (or a newer version).

SEE: • "Take Note: Backups of Bootable Volumes Don't Boot," earlier in this chapter, for a related issue.

• "Take Note: Startup Failure When Starting Up from an External Device," in Chapter 5, for other reasons why you may have problems starting up from external devices.

Third-party software will not install

If you're trying to install third-party software that uses an installer utility (either Apple's or a competing one), and the install fails due to an unspecified error, this is almost always a permissions-related problem. The failure may occur during installation or on the initial launch of the application after installation. Specifically, the problem is that the installer attempted to install some file into a folder for which it did not have permission to do so.

The most common solution is to repair disk permissions with Disk Utility (as described in Chapter 5), and then attempt the installation again.

You can also log in as the root user and perform the installation from there. As root user, you avoid any permissions hassles. In some cases, after completing the install and logging back in as yourself, you may need to adjust the permissions (including owner and group names) of the newly installed software (probably located in the Applications folder) to match those of other applications in the same folder. If the installer created a new folder with several files and folders within it, you can use a utility like ArbySoft's BatChmod (http://macchampion.com/arbysoft) to make the changes to all items in one step.

If you are using a VISE Installer utility, make sure you disconnect from any remote networks before running the installer. Otherwise, the utility may search all computers and servers on the network prior to initiating an install. This could take sufficiently long that it will appear as if the utility has frozen.

If none of this works, check the vendor's Web site. It should either offer a specific work-around or indicate that the software has a conflict with the current version of Mac OS X (which the developer is presumably working to fix).

SEE: • Chapter 4 for more on root access and Chapter 6 for more on BatChmod.

Can't install a Classic application

If you're still using third-party Mac OS 9 software, you may occasionally need to upgrade this software to a newer version. In some cases, upgrading requires running an installer utility that, of course, runs only in Mac OS 9. In general, this is not a problem. If you launch the installer utility, it will load Classic, and the installation will proceed as if you had booted from Mac OS 9. However, there are a few installers that will work correctly only if you boot from Mac OS 9.

The solution here—if you have an older Mac that can still boot in Mac OS 9—is to reboot in the older OS and do the installation. Otherwise, you will have to get more creative. For example, you may need to find an older Mac, do the installation there, and then copy the updated installed files to your Mac.

Video issues warning

When Mac OS X 10.2.5 was released, Apple warned: "On certain computers, you should set the Displays preferences to the native resolution before installing the Mac OS X 10.2.5 Update. If you do not, temporary video issues may occur when the computer wakes from sleep." The affected computers were the PowerBook G4 (17-inch); the iMac (17-inch 1 GHz); and the Power Mac G4 with an nVidia GeForce 4MX or nVidia GeForce 4 Titanium display card connected to an LCD display.

Even if your Mac is not on that list, and even if you are upgrading to Tiger, if you're using an LCD display, I would play it safe: Shift to the native resolution (via the Displays System Preferences) before installing an update. Typically, the native resolution is the highest one listed in Displays.

If you read this suggestion after the problem has already occurred, change the resolution to anything that works and restart. After restarting, you can select the desired resolution successfully.

A collection of basic tips

In conclusion, I offer a summary of the most frequently needed advice for installation woes:

- Make sure you have enough disk space for the installation (and that you meet all other requirements listed in the read-me file that accompanies the software).
- Make sure you have administrative status and know your password.
- Disable Screen Effects and Energy Saver sleep before performing an installation that may take long enough that these are invoked before it's complete.
- Turn off Classic (if it's running).
- Don't attempt other computer activities during an installation.

For further, more technical details on software installation, check out Apple's developer documentation at the following location: http://developer.apple.com/documentation/DeveloperTools/Conceptual/SoftwareDistribution.

4

Mac OS X in Depth

There's more than one way to divide a pizza. There's the familiar method of cutting it into slices, of course, but you could also divide it into layers of toppings, cheese, sauce, and crust, or—theoretically—distill it into its basic ingredients of flour, water, tomatoes, garlic, and milk. The way you think about dividing that pizza will depend on what you plan to do with it.

The same holds true for Mac OS X. You can look at it and take it apart any number of ways, each of which contributes to your understanding of the OS. Taking apart and examining the components of Mac OS X is the subject of this chapter.

In This Chapter

Aqua

Aqua is what most users think of when they think of Mac OS X: its user interface, the Finder, the Dock, the windows, the translucent buttons, the high-resolution icons, the menus, and all of the other things you *see* when you look at the screen. In fact, many users never pursue their understanding of Mac OS X beyond its Aqua layer.

At its core, the Aqua interface works pretty much the way the Mac has worked since its beginnings: You still double-click icons in the Finder to launch their applications; you still choose Save from an application's File menu to save a document; and you still open a folder icon to see its contents.

However, there is much that has changed and continues to evolve—both on the surface (such as Spotlight) and under the hood. It's the more under-the-hood stuff that I'll be focusing on in this chapter.

Figure 4.1

The layers of Mac OS X.

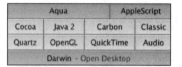

Application Environments

The main thing you do in Aqua is use applications. On the surface, most Mac OS X applications function similarly: You launch them; you use commands from their menus; you quit them. However, Mac OS X accommodates several—fundamentally different—types of applications. As a troubleshooter, you need to understand these categories.

Cocoa

The Cocoa environment is unique to Mac OS X. This means that software developed in Cocoa uses Mac OS X–only programming tools, and Cocoa applications run only in Mac OS X. The advantage of Cocoa-based software is that it can benefit from all of Mac OS X's built-in features without much additional effort on the part of the developer. Take, for example, the TextEdit application that comes with Mac OS X: Its Font panel window, spelling checker, and ability to let users access Services from the TextEdit menu (via the Services submenu) are all made possible—at least in part—by the fact that TextEdit is a Cocoa application. Only Cocoa applications can access Services by default; other applications need to be specially written to do so. Similarly, Cocoa applications are the only ones likely to use the Font panel; others generally use the more traditional Font menu. Thus, non-Cocoa applications are less likely to include these and other features.

Apple encourages all Mac OS X software to be Cocoa-based. As time since the initial release of Mac OS X has passed, this has certainly been the trend. However, there are still some applications (primarily ones initially developed for Mac OS 9 and converted to run in Mac OS X) that do not use Cocoa. This is because converting an older application to Cocoa is the most time-consuming method to make the transition.

Carbon

The Carbon environment was first used for applications designed to run in the Classic Mac OS (such as Mac OS 9). However, applications written for the Carbon environment still run "natively" in Mac OS X. In fact, in most cases you will be hard-pressed to distinguish between Cocoa- and Carbon-based applications—Carbon-based applications can offer all the basic Aqua features (such as the look and feel of Aqua windows), so you can't often determine whether an application is Cocoa- or Carbon-based by looking at it.

Developers can, however, determine how much of the Aqua interface they wish to support in their own Carbon-based applications. As a result, some Carbon applications may look and feel more like Mac OS X applications than others.

The primary rationale for Carbon's existence is that it reduces the time it takes to rewrite existing Mac OS 9 applications to work in Mac OS X. That's why major Mac OS 9 applications such as AppleWorks and Microsoft Office are Carbon-based applications rather than Cocoa ones. In addition, some developers find Carbon preferable even when creating applications from scratch. REALbasic, for example, is a programming language that creates Carbon-based applications for Mac OS X.

There are two distinct subcategories of Carbon applications, and the differences between them depend on an OS feature called a *library manager*. The function of this special type of program is to prepare other, more ordinary programs (such as user-launched applications) to be run. Carbon applications in Mac OS X can use two types of library managers:

- **CFM (*code fragment manager*)** is essentially the same as the CFM used in Mac OS 9. It works with an application's executable binary code, which is in a format called PEF (for *preferred executable format*). Unfortunately, this format is *not* preferred in Mac OS X.

- **dyld (*dynamic link editor*)** is the library manager that only Mac OS X uses It works with an executable binary-code format called Mach-O, which is what Mac OS X's kernel uses. Mach-O is derived from Unix.

If the above descriptions contain more jargon than you can decode, don't worry. Exactly what all of these managers and formats do, and how they differ, need not concern most users. What does matter is the following:

- **CFM is not optimized for Mac OS X**. Mac OS X is a native dyld platform. This means that for CFM-based programs to work, they must bridge to the dyld platform via Carbon routines. This bridging step takes time, resulting in a performance penalty that does not occur with dyld-based software—that is, CFM-based software will not run as fast in Mac OS X as if the same program had been written to use dyld instead.

  The most visible sign of this bridging can be found in the LaunchCFMApp application (itself a Mach-O application), which is located in /System/Library/Frameworks/Carbon.framework/Versions/A/Support. This file (which is an updated version of the Mac OS 9 CFM) is used every time you launch a CFM-based application. In fact, prior to Mac OS X 10.2 Jaguar, if you launched Process Viewer (now called Activity Monitor) and looked at the list of open applications in User Processes, you wouldn't see any CFM-based applications by name; instead, you would see multiple instances of LaunchCFMApp. Although Mac OS X 10.2 and later now display the CFM-based applications by name, the LaunchCFMApp process is still used to launch them, and this process is still what appears (instead of the name of the application) in the output of certain Unix commands.

  In addition, some CFM applications still use the single-file format common in Mac OS 9 rather than Mac OS X's package approach. Thus, if you open the contextual menu for an application and no Show Package Contents command is listed, the application is almost certainly a CFM application. dyld software will always use the preferred package format.

  SEE: • "Understanding Image, Installer Package, and Receipt Files," in Chapter 3.

- **dyld (Mach-O) software cannot run in Mac OS 9**. Because Mac OS 9 does not provide the dyld library manager, software written using dyld will not run in Mac OS 9 at all.

Given that CFM applications are generally slower and are not optimized for Mac OS X, you're probably wondering why developers bother with CFM at all. Two reasons: First, it may be easier to convert an existing Mac OS 9 application to its CFM-based cousin than to a dyld one. Second, CFM-based programs run equally well in Mac OS 9 and Mac OS X. Thus, you need only one application for both environments. Software based on dyld runs only in Mac OS X. (By the way, Cocoa-based software also uses Mach-O and, of course, runs only in Mac OS X.)

For those who want a dyld-based Carbon program for running in Mac OS X but also want the program to run in the Classic environment (or even in an older Mac running Mac OS 9), the solution is to create two versions of the application, a CFM version and a dyld version. You can then combine these versions into an application package that appears as a single file in the Finder. When the application is launched in Classic (or when booted from Mac OS 9), the CFM version will be used; when it's launched in Mac OS X, the dyld version will run. This situation allows each OS to use the version optimized for it. (This type of division is more common when Classic and Carbon software versions are included in the same package, as you'll learn more about in this chapter.) With newer Macs no longer booting in Mac OS 9, the need for this versatility is on the wane.

As a side note, when a program is said to be Mac OS X–native, this generally means that it's either a Cocoa program or a dyld Carbon one (though some people consider any Carbon application to be native).

TAKE NOTE ▶ Faceless Applications

Typical applications are launched via a double-click of their icon in the Finder. These applications include their own menus and windows.

However, some applications have no user interface. You double-click their icon and they appear to launch, but nothing else obvious happens. As they have no menus, there will be no immediate way to quit the application. With luck, you can quit the application via a force-quit (as covered in Chapter 5).

Some applications run even more unobtrusively. They run without an icon in the Dock or without being listed in the Force Quit window. Such applications are often called *faceless* or *background* applications or processes because they run without a user interface. The loginwindow application, which you'll learn more about in Chapter 5, is one example. Most of the administrative processes listed in Activity Monitor are similar examples of faceless processes.

As a troubleshooter, you need to be aware of background processes, as they are often important for solving problems with Mac OS X. Numerous examples appear throughout this book.

Note: Faceless applications are different from applications that are hidden via the Hide command in application and Dock menus. The Hide command temporarily hides the user interface of an otherwise "normal" application. Truly faceless applications are always "hidden."

Figure 4.2

The Hide iTunes command in iTunes' application menu.

> **TAKE NOTE ▶ Identifying Application Formats**
>
> Suppose you need to know whether a given application is Cocoa, Carbon-cfm, Carbon-dyld, or Classic: What's the fastest way to find out? A utility called GetInfo for App (http://saryo.org/basuke/osx/getinfo4app/index.html) works great—if it works (in the most recent versions of Mac OS X it kept crashing on me). Just drag the application in question to the GetInfo for App icon, and a window opens, revealing the information you need.
>
> For TextEdit, for example, you will see that the Framework is Cocoa and the Binary Kind is Mach-O. On the other hand, if you select Microsoft Internet Explorer, the window will say Carbon for the Framework and CFM for the Binary Kind.
>
> As an alternative, you can use the ever-handy XRay (www.brockerhoff.net/xray/). Although it doesn't distinguish between CFM and Mach-O, it does distinguish between Cocoa, Carbon, and Classic applications.

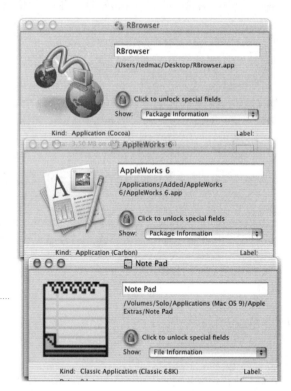

Figure 4.3

Three applications as listed in XRay. Note the Kind line distinction of Cocoa, Carbon, and Classic 68K.

Classic

Mac OS 9 programs that have not been rewritten to run in Mac OS X's Carbon environment may still be able to run in Mac OS X, but it requires a trick: Mac OS X needs to launch what is called the *Classic environment*. For a detailed discussion of this topic, see the Web-only chapter on Classic at Mac

OS X Help Line (www.macosxhelpline.com). For now, here's the short version of what happens when you launch Classic: A working version of Mac OS 9 (including extensions and control panels) is loaded; the Mac OS 9 application then runs in this environment. In many ways, going back and forth between the two environments is almost seamless. You can cut and paste from a Classic program to a Mac OS X one, for example. Classic can even borrow your Mac OS X Internet and printer settings so that Classic applications can retain their access to the Web and your connected printers.

Still, running a program in Classic has a huge disadvantage: You aren't really using Mac OS X, and thus you get almost none of its advantages. Running an application in Classic is like running it in Mac OS 9—or perhaps not quite as good, since it is likely to run slower and have more potential conflicts than if you had simply booted from Mac OS 9. The sole advantage of Classic is that it allows you to run Mac OS 9 programs that you could not otherwise run in Mac OS X. As time goes by, however, you will want to find Mac OS X alternatives to these applications (or hope that Mac OS X versions of them become available) so that you can eliminate your reliance on Classic.

Java

Mac OS X can also run programs written in Java. If you're like most users, you probably think of Java as something that certain Web sites use and your Web browser accesses. However, Java software can be created to run independently of a browser, and Mac OS X is able to run such applications. Apple has even provided a means for developers to incorporate Mac OS X's Aqua interface into Java code so that their Java applications look and feel like typical Mac OS X applications. For programmers, the main advantage of Java is that it's platform independent—that is, the same Java software (with some minor modifications to accommodate the platform's user interface) can run on any computer that supports Java, including Windows PCs. At present, few Java applications are available for Mac OS X, so the jury is still out as to whether Java will play a significant role in Mac OS X.

Even Java programs meant to be run from Web browsers can be run separately. For example, for Java applications normally accessed via Web pages, you can use Java Web Start (located in /Applications/Utilities/Java) to automatically install and run the applications from your drive. See the Apple Developer Connection page "Java Web Start on Mac OS X" (http://developer.apple.com/java/javawebstart) for details.

Putting it together

All of these application environments are unified within the Aqua interface. There may be visible signs—some subtle, some obvious—when you shift from

Classic to Carbon to Cocoa to Java; however, one of the great successes of Mac OS X is that you can switch among these environments almost effortlessly. And at least most of the time, it all works as Apple intended.

There is one other type of application that can run in Mac OS X: Unix software. For a detailed discussion of Unix, see "Darwin," later in this chapter.

Graphics Services

Running underneath the application layer is another layer of core technologies that create the elements you see on the screen: fonts, graphics, movies, and so on. As a troubleshooter, you need not be concerned with the inner workings of this layer; however, you should be familiar with its terminology.

Quartz

Quartz—the Mac OS X technology used to create all two-dimensional images (including text)—is quite different from the QuickDraw technology used in Mac OS 9. Some of the most spectacular differences show up when you work with text. First, Quartz uses PDF (Portable Document Format) as a native format for documents. This format is the one employed by Adobe Reader, which means that almost anything you create—in any application—can be easily saved as a PDF document. This in turn makes it easy for anyone to view these documents, even on Windows PCs, with all their fonts, formatting, and graphics intact. Because PDF is a PostScript-aware format, PDF documents can easily be rendered to PostScript printers. Quartz is also responsible for the fact that virtually all text in Mac OS X has a smoothed (anti-aliased) look.

Also of relevance is Apple Type Services (ATS), a technology that unifies the display of fonts (regardless of format, be it TrueType, PostScript, or whatever) and provides the basis for multiple-language support.

Multimedia: OpenGL and QuickTime

Three-dimensional graphics use Mac OS X's OpenGL software, which comes into play mainly with 3D game software.

Mac OS X also supports QuickTime for multimedia. This software is used for playing QuickTime movies, such as the popular movie trailers available on Apple's QuickTime Web site.

On a related note, Mac OS X supports a variety of graphic, audio, and video formats and technologies. These are part of Mac OS X's "Core" components: Core Image, Core Audio, and Core Video. They can be used by third-party developers to easily add these Mac OS X features to their programs.

TECHNICALLY SPEAKING ▶ **ATSUI and Unicode**

Some more Apple jargon:

ATS (Apple Type Services) manages fonts in Mac OS X. It checks for all fonts in Mac OS X's Library/Fonts folders as well as in the Classic System Folder and prepares (rasterizes) them for use in Mac OS X applications.

ATSUI (Apple Type Services for Unicode Imaging) is the technology used for printing and displaying Unicode text in Mac OS X.

Unicode is the font technology Mac OS X uses for multiple-language support. Unicode, for example, allows you to use multiple languages in applications such as Mail, TextEdit, and the Finder. Thanks to a single worldwide character set that works with most of the world's languages, Unicode-enabled programs allow text characters to be displayed consistently, regardless of the language and language software selected for display.

The Unicode standard supports 917,631 different characters. One practical implication of this is that you no longer necessarily have to shift to a separate font to access symbols or dingbats—they can be incorporated into the font itself. How this all works will depend on (a) whether the font is a Unicode font; and (b) whether the application in use supports Unicode fonts. You can use Mac OS X's Character Palette to see and access all of the characters available in a given font.

SEE: • **"Font Formats," "Viewing and Managing Fonts," and "Working with Fonts,"** later in this chapter, for more information on fonts.

Darwin

Now you're ready to delve into the deepest layer of Mac OS X—the core, if you will. The umbrella name for this layer is *Darwin*. Because Darwin uses open-source code (that is, code that's publicly available—in this case, at Apple's "Darwin" page [www.publicsource.apple.com]), developers are able to study, modify, and improve it. Darwin is sometimes more generically referred to as the Mac OS X kernel environment.

The Darwin kernel consists mainly of the FreeBSD 5 and Mach 3.0 technologies. Darwin also includes various core services, such as those involved in networking and device drivers, which we'll examine in detail in Chapter 5 as I walk you through the startup sequence of events. Beyond that, as an end-user troubleshooter, you need to be aware only of the two key kernel components.

In discussing the layers of Mac OS X, how do you determine whether something is considered to be at a higher or a lower level? As a general rule, a component at a lower level is used by all higher-level layers. However, the converse is not necessarily true. Thus, an application, whether it's Carbon or Cocoa, uses the core Darwin technology; however, Darwin itself doesn't require any additional layers to run.

Mach

As a troubleshooter, you will rarely, if ever, work directly with Mach code. Nonetheless, it's important that you understand its basic concepts. Mach code not only handles the most fundamental aspects of Mac OS X (for example, the processes that enable the Mac to boot and recognize attached hardware), but also is responsible for several of Mac OS X's most touted benefits:

Preemptive multitasking. This term describes Mac OS X's ability to schedule its processor activity among different open applications or processes. (Note: All applications are considered processes, but not all processes are user-accessible applications. For example, there are many background processes that make up the actual operating system.) As a point of comparison, Mac OS 9 uses *cooperative multitasking*, which is not very intelligent. In Mac OS 9, unimportant but CPU-intensive background events can take up so much of a processor's time that more important foreground activities become sluggish and unresponsive. Neither you nor the OS can do anything about this situation. Mac OS X's Mach is much more flexible in the way it handles these matters. In essence, it can preempt any running process, giving another process more attention. It can intelligently determine which activities are in the foreground and make sure that they get the lion's share of attention. Developers can also write hooks in their software to increase (or decrease) the priority that their software should get. As a result, operations that need the most processor activity at any moment should get it, enhancing overall performance. This is a good thing.

A related benefit of Mac OS X's multitasking capability is called *multithreading*. In Mac OS 9, when you launch an application, you typically must wait for it to finish launching before you can do anything else, even in other applications—a process that can take a minute or two. Mac OS X doesn't have these waiting games; as soon as a program starts to launch, you can begin another activity—for example, you can check your e-mail while waiting for Classic to launch and Adobe Photoshop to open.

Protected memory. Metaphorically, *protected memory* means that the memory assigned to each running process is entirely separate (*protected*) from that of every other running process. The result is that systemwide crashes should almost vanish from the landscape. If and when an application does crash, the rest of the operating system should remain functional. In the event that a program freezes (such as when you get an endlessly spinning wait cursor), you will be able to switch to a different program (such as the Finder) and continue to work as normal, even while the problem application remains frozen. This would be impossible to do in Mac OS 9. Protected memory also means that you should almost never need to restart the Mac to recover from a crash.

Shared memory. The exception to the "rule" that one crashed application will not affect other open applications in Mac OS X comes in programs that use shared memory. As its name implies, *shared memory* refers to memory used by more than one process—typically to share certain resources, such as graphics or sounds, that would consume large amounts of memory if loaded separately by each process. The problem, as Apple describes it, is that "shared memory is fragile; thus, if one program corrupts a section of shared memory, all programs that reference that shared memory will also be corrupted."

Virtual memory. Virtual memory allows you to simulate memory (RAM) via special files—called *swap* files—on your hard drive. The main advantage of virtual memory is that if you don't have sufficient physical (built-in) RAM for your purposes, virtual memory may be able to provide the "additional" RAM you need.

In Mac OS 9, you can choose to turn virtual memory on or off. Because virtual memory tends to slow performance, it is typically wise to turn it off if your physical RAM is adequate for your needs. In Mac OS X, virtual memory is always "on." The good news is that until you really start pushing its limits (by having way too many applications open at the same time, for example), you should not notice a performance hit.

Still, you can't have too much physical RAM, and given the current low prices of memory, I recommend buying as much RAM as you think you will ever need—or more.

Dynamic memory. In Mac OS 9, the amount of memory assigned to an application is fixed (or *static*) when the program is launched. You assign this fixed amount via the Memory settings in the application's Get Info window. If, after an application has been launched, it needs more or less memory than was assigned to it, Mac OS 9 can't do much about the situation. You can add a limited amount of RAM to an application via an OS feature called *temporary memory*, but not all programs are able to use this feature, and even for those that can, it doesn't solve the problem completely.

As a result, you wind up getting "out of memory" error messages in Mac OS 9 when you technically have enough memory for the task at hand. Mac OS 9 simply can't shuttle the memory to where it's needed at a particular moment.

In Mac OS X, memory assignment is dynamic, which means that the amount of memory assigned to an application is automatically increased or decreased as needed. Thus, if an application is idling in the background and hogging unused memory, the OS can grab some of this memory for another application that needs it more. Or it can reassign that memory to the pool of "free" memory so that it's available to applications that have yet to be launched.

Similarly, the total amount of memory available as virtual memory is adjusted on the fly in Mac OS X. In Mac OS 9, on the other hand, if you want to change the total amount of virtual memory, you have to restart your Mac.

This combination of dynamic memory assignment and Mac OS X's virtual memory means that you should almost never see an "out of memory" error and encounter fewer memory-related system freezes and crashes.

Mac OS X manages all of these tasks and also allocates memory intelligently from physical and virtual memory to maximize the performance of each application. The result is that, within reason, each application "feels" as if it has almost infinite memory, no matter how little physical memory you've actually installed.

Still, as I implied earlier, memory availability in Mac OS X is *not* infinite. If you push your Mac to its memory limits, you will start noticing an overall decline in its performance. One reason for this is that Mac OS X attempts to keep a certain minimum amount of physical memory "free" at all times. If the free memory falls below a certain threshold value (which varies depending on how much physical memory you have installed), Mac OS X refills it from memory assigned to currently open applications that have not been accessed recently. The next time you go to access a previously "dormant" application, there is likely to be an initial delay in its response. However, you will not receive an error message, just a slowdown in performance. This process is called *paging* (as covered in the following "Technically Speaking" sidebar). This problem lessens as you install more physical memory—which is why getting more physical RAM still makes sense.

Note: As described in more detail later in this chapter (in "Get Info"), Mac OS X's Get Info window still includes a Memory tab for Classic applications, needed because Classic applications do not take advantage of Mac OS X's dynamic-memory feature.

Figure 4.4

A graphical display of Mac OS X's memory divisions, as seen in Activity Monitor.

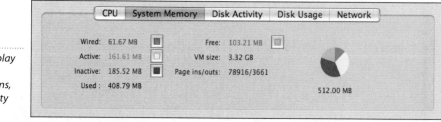

TECHNICALLY SPEAKING ▶ Dividing Up Mac OS X's Memory

You can view Mac OS X's memory usage via the System Memory section of the main Activity Monitor window. Several third-party utilities, such as Matt Neuburg's MemoryStick (www. tidbits.com/matt) also enable you to monitor memory visually.

If you use a utility to view your Mac's memory usage, it will typically reference different categories of memory use. These categories refer to the way in which the installed physical memory interacts with Mac OS X's virtual memory. In particular, they refer to the portion of the memory in use and whether the items in memory can be *paged out* to the swap file(s) located in /var/vm on your hard drive (and used by virtual memory). Because it takes longer to access items that are paged out, the Mac tries to avoid paging out the most essential and actively used resources.

The following provides an overview of the different types of memory:

- **Wired memory.** This is memory that contains resources essential for the Mac to run. Items here are never "paged out" to the swap file(s) on your hard drive—they must always be in physical RAM. User processes cannot assign wired memory; only administrative processes can do this.

- **Active memory.** Items in active memory are currently being used (or were used very recently) by open processes. As such, they will not be paged out.

- **Inactive memory.** Items here have been used less recently and are not immediately required for any open processes. As such, they may be paged out. For example, if you have several applications open, and one of them has not been the active application for quite some time, it would likely be placed in inactive memory. If you were to select a window from that application, the needed resources would be moved back to active memory. If the information had been paged to disk, it would be accessed first from there.

- **Free memory.** This is the memory not currently in use. Ideally, you want a healthy amount of free memory because this is what's used instead of paging items to disk. If free memory becomes too low, paging will occur.

When you quit an application, its resources may remain in inactive memory for a while—which means that the increase in free memory size will not match the resources you freed up by quitting the application. Thus, if free memory occasionally gets low and some page-outs occur, it may not be a source of concern. Wait a while to see if the situation improves as inactive memory is returned to the free-memory pool. However, if you frequently run low on free memory, and get numerous and frequent page-outs (especially if Mac OS X creates a second or third swap file—these files are also located in /var/vm), this is a sign that you need to install more physical memory.

Occasionally, frequent page-outs may be caused by a memory leak in an application or an unusually memory-intensive application. In such cases, even installing more memory may not alleviate the problem—you might just have to wait for the developers to fix the problem.

SEE: • "Maximizing Performance," in Chapter 6, and "Technically Speaking: Terminal Commands to Monitor and Improve Performance," in Chapter 10, for related information.

BSD (Unix)

BSD, which stands for *Berkeley Software Distribution*, used to be called the Berkeley version of Unix. For all practical purposes, for Mac OS X, "BSD" can be used interchangeably with "Unix." BSD code is also used for a portion of the Mach code. In all cases, the code has been customized for Mac OS X.

SEE: • "Unix and Mac OS X," in Chapter 1, for more on Unix's inclusion in Mac OS X.

Mac OS X's Unix integration represents a significant change from Mac OS 9. In Mac OS 9, the System Folder *is* the OS. Except for a small number of invisible files (such as the Desktop files), all OS files are in the System Folder, where they are easily accessible. In Mac OS X, by contrast, the entire Unix layer remains largely invisible from the Aqua Finder. Thus, Mac OS X has a sort of secondary OS hidden beneath the visible OS.

Occasionally, troubleshooting will require that you access or modify these hidden Unix files. You access Unix commands and files in Mac OS X in three main ways:

- **Terminal.** In essence, the Terminal application (included with Mac OS X) provides a command-line environment where most Unix commands will work just as if they were being executed in a "pure" Unix environment rather than in part of the Mac OS. Still, Terminal lets you know right away that you're in Apple's implementation of Unix, via its "Welcome to Darwin!" greeting. Any changes you make in Terminal, such as renaming or deleting files, will be reflected in the Aqua environment, as well, so you need to be careful.

- **Finder and text editors.** Tasks such as moving or deleting Unix files can often be done directly from the Finder. You can also modify some Unix files with text editors such as TextEdit and Bare Bones Software's TextWrangler (www.barebones.com/products/textwrangler). This will often require root user access and/or use of a utility that makes invisible files visible.

- **Aqua utilities.** Many third-party utilities let you use an Aqua-based interface to do what would otherwise require Terminal. In essence, such utilities simply run Terminal commands behind the scenes, providing a more user-friendly graphical user interface (GUI), or front end, to the user.

    SEE: • "Root Access," later in this chapter, for more information on this subject.

    • "Technically Speaking: Log Files and cron Jobs," later in this chapter, for an example of accessing Unix files from the Finder and/or via GUI utilities.

    • Chapter 6, for other examples of how to access the invisible Unix files from the Finder.

    • Chapter 10, for more information on Unix and Terminal.

TECHNICALLY SPEAKING ▶ What and Where Are the Unix Files?

The Unix-based software at the core of Mac OS X is located at the root level of the Mac OS X boot volume. You can see these invisible directories and files from the Finder by using a utility, such as Marcel Bresink's TinkerTool, to make invisible files visible (as described in greater detail in Chapter 6). In addition, you can typically access files and folders within these directories (even when they're invisible in the Finder) by using the Go to Folder command. (For example, entering /var/db in the Go to Folder text box opens a Finder window that displays the contents of this folder.)

You can also use Terminal to view these files. To do so from Terminal, type the following: cd /. Now type ls. This will return a list of root-level contents.

The following is a sampler of the Unix directories and files found at the root level:

- **bin** is the directory where most of the main Unix commands (or *executables*) are stored. These are the equivalent of Mac OS X applications. **sbin** is a similar directory of executables.

- **dev** is where device drivers are stored. Your computer needs these files in order to interact with other hardware, such as external drives.

- **etc** (actually an alias to /private/etc) contains a collection of administrative files. This is the location of the *periodic* directory (used by the cron and launchd software), the cups directory (used by the CUPS printing software), the master.passwd file, and various important configuration files, such as hostconfig and inetd.conf.

- **tmp** (actually an alias to /private/etc), as its name implies, contains files created by programs that are only needed temporarily. Unfortunately, some programs may forget to delete these temporary files, so you may find some files here permanently.

- **usr** is another place where critical Unix OS commands are found. For example, the ditto and open commands are stored in /usr/bin. In addition, the /usr/local directory is a common storage location for third-party software (that is, software installed after the initial installation of Mac OS X).

- **var** (actually an alias to /private/var) is yet another important location for essential files. For example, this is where the home directory of the root user (/var/root) is located. The db directory, located within var, contains the netinfo database. The log directory, as implied by its name, contains the various system log files.

- **mach_kernel** and **mach.sym** make up Unix's *kernel*, or the core code of the operating system. This is a file, not a directory. As noted in the main text, this kernel is the software equivalent of the Mac's CPU, the central processing location for all Unix commands. Without mach_kernel and mach.sym, nothing else would work.

Note: The etc, tmp, and var items at the root level are actually aliases (symbolic links, as described in Chapter 6) to directories in /private. Thus you can typically access these directories by typing either /private/{directory name} or just /{directory name}. Either way, you wind up in the same place. These aliases—which are needed by Mac OS X to work with Unix software—are not standard Unix components.

Figure 4.5

A list of the Unix directories and files (for example, usr, bin) located in the root directory, as viewed from Terminal, left, and the Finder, right (with normally invisible items made visible).

TAKE NOTE ▶ Finder Folders vs. Unix Directories

In Finder windows, you will see many icons that resemble folders, and indeed this is the Desktop metaphor for what they are: containers that hold items (documents, applications, or other folders).

Folders vs. directories. In the Unix world, folders are referred to as *directories*. Because Mac OS X has a Unix basis, I sometimes refer to its folders as directories—especially when I'm in a Unix environment such as the Terminal application. Even in the Finder, I occasionally refer to folders as directories. For example, I typically refer to a user's home *directory* rather than home *folder* because of the home directory's special significance in Unix. (This directory is the default location when you log in via Terminal, for example.)

Thus, an Aqua folder is best viewed as—and, in reality, is—a graphical representation of a Unix directory. Moving an item into or out of a folder in the Finder changes the contents of the underlying directory in Unix. The terms *folder* and *directory* are sometimes used interchangeably when the distinction is not relevant.

Note that not all Unix directories are displayed in the Finder. In fact, most of those that contain Unix-related files (such as /bin, /etc, and /var) remain invisible to the Finder because typical Mac OS X users rarely, if ever, need to manipulate these files—and modifying them accidentally can lead to serious problems (including ones that can take down the system). Still, throughout this volume I will cover the essentials of how to access these files for troubleshooting purposes.

continues on next page

TAKE NOTE ▶ Finder Folders vs. Unix Directories *continued*

Pathnames. A *pathname* is what Unix uses to define the location of a file or directory. An *absolute pathname* starts at the top, or root, level of the hierarchy and works its way down. /System/Library/Fonts/Geneva.dfont, for example, is an absolute pathname. Slashes separate directory names; thus, an initial forward slash indicates that you are starting at the root level. This setup is important, for example, in distinguishing otherwise-identical fonts in multiple Fonts folders (such as /Library/Fonts versus /System/Library/Fonts).

A *relative pathname* is the path starting from your current location. Thus, if you were already in the /System/Library directory, the relative path to the same font file would simply be Fonts/Geneva.dfont.

The ~ (tilde) symbol means to start at the top of the current user's home directory. Thus, ~/Library/Fonts means to look in the Fonts folder inside the Library folder inside your home directory.

Because the forward slash is used in all of these designations, you should not use this character in file or folder names in Mac OS X. The OS may treat the slash as a directory designator rather than as part of the file or folder name. In some cases (for example, when naming files in the Save dialog), Mac OS X will prohibit you from entering a forward slash (much as Mac OS 9 does not permit colons in file and folder names).

Mac OS X Domains

Having dissected Mac OS X's layers, we're now going to take the OS apart from a different perspective. In this section, you'll learn why Mac OS X has multiple Library folders and directories, as well as the functions of each. You'll also get an overview of the files and folders they contain.

First, though, a bit of background: Mac OS X was conceived in 1997 when Apple acquired the NeXT OS (often referred to as OpenStep) at the time when Steve Jobs (founder of both Apple and NeXT) returned to Apple. As a result of this deal, much of the higher-level Mac OS X software was based on NeXT code. In fact, it's not unusual to peek inside a Mac OS X system software file and find a reference to NeXT or OpenStep.

At a practical level, this reliance on NeXT code means that the System Folder of Mac OS 9 is gone from Mac OS X, as are the control panels and extensions that populated the System Folder. Instead, in Mac OS X you have the Library folder—or, more precisely, a multitude of Library folders. This is because Mac OS X is inherently a multiple-user system, and different Library folders correspond to different domains or levels of the OS. At the top level (System), for example, changes affect all users of the Mac in question. At the bottom level (User), changes affect only the individual user who is logged in.

Levels of users. There are three main levels of users in Mac OS X. These levels are related to the nature of the domain and library structure of the OS.

- **Standard/ordinary.** These users can access files only in their own home directories (unless an administrator specifically grants them access to other files).

- **Administrative.** These users (often called *admin users* for short) are able to access sections of the OS designed to be shared among all users, such as the Applications folder and the root Library folder. An ordinary user cannot add to or remove anything from the Applications folder; however, an administrative user can. By default, even administrative users are denied access to areas used by the system that are considered essential to running the OS (such as /System). Administrators can, however, access these files via temporary root access.

- **Root/System.** This user, or level of access, is the only one that can modify and access the essential system software needed to keep the OS running, as well as anything else on the boot volume. This user is also sometimes referred to as the *system administrator*.

  SEE: • "Take Note: Multiple Users: Why Bother," "Ownership & Permissions," and "Root Access," later in this chapter, for related information.
  - Chapter 6 for solving troubleshooting problems that require modifying permissions settings.
  - Chapter 9 for more information on file sharing.

TAKE NOTE ▶ Multiple Users: Why Bother?

All of these domains, libraries, and permissions may seem a bit overwhelming, especially to a new Mac user. At this point, you may be wondering, "Why bother?" (especially if you are the only person who ever uses your Mac). Indeed, the idea of preventing certain users from accessing particular files was irrelevant in early versions of the Classic Mac OS. But it is critical to the functioning of Mac OS X.

When you install Mac OS X, you set up an initial account for yourself and are automatically assigned administrator status. The OS also, by default, turns off the requirement to log in at startup. (You can change this setting via the Login Options in the Accounts System Preferences pane.) Thus, when the OS starts up, you are not required to enter a password, making it appear that security of multiple users is not being enforced—even though it is!

coninues on next page

TAKE NOTE ▶ **Multiple Users: Why Bother?** *continued*

In Mac OS X, even as an administrator, you're no longer at the top of the heap: The user called System is higher than you. This means that if the System owns a file, you can't modify its permissions. Similarly, if you've set up users besides yourself, you can't access the files in their User directories. The result is that Mac OS X may tell you that you don't have permission to move or delete certain files or to add files to certain folders. The truth is that you don't own Mac OS X; Mac OS X owns Mac OS X. You're just a privileged visitor.

Bear in mind that Unix was created as an OS for large networked systems. As such, it needed to allow hundreds of people to log in to the same system. At the same time, it needed to maintain a level of security that prevented users from accessing other users' data. Just as important, it needed to restrict access to the main system software so that no user could deliberately or inadvertently bring down the entire system.

Mac OS X adopts the same Unix-based security features.

This setup can be annoying if you're the only person using your Mac, forcing you to deal with overhead and complexity. The upside, though, is that if you do need a multiple-user setup, Mac OS X is equipped to handle it right out of the box. And there are ways that admin users can circumvent these restrictions (more on this later in this chapter).

You can also take advantage of multiple user accounts, even as the only user of your Mac. For example, by creating a "troubleshooting" account that you use only in emergencies, you log in to that account to determine if a problem you're experiencing is isolated to your regular account or affects the entire system.

Note: There can be more than one administrator on a Mac setup. All admin users have equal status. The only exception is that the password of the original administrator (the account established when Mac OS X was first run) cannot be changed by other administrators.

System domain

The first Library folder on our tour is located in the System folder at the root level of the Mac OS X volume. There are several ways to get to it.

One way is to choose Computer from the Finder's Go menu (Command-Shift-C). Among several items you may find in the window that appears will be a drive icon with the name of your current startup volume: Double-click it (or click it in column view), and you're at the root level of the Mac OS X volume. Here you will find a folder called System (which should have an X on its folder icon). Double-click this folder to view its contents; you will now see a folder called Library—the first stop on our tour!

Another way to get to this window (assuming you have selected to Show hard disks on the Desktop) is to double-click the icon for your startup volume.

Still another way to get to this folder is to Command-click the window name in the title bar of any Finder window (assuming the folder being viewed resides on the boot volume) and, from the pop-up menu that appears, choose the name of the startup volume—it should be the next-to-bottom item. If your startup volume *is not* listed here, choose the bottom name (your computer name) to bring up the same Computer window I described in the previous paragraph. From here, you can similarly navigate to the /System/Library folder.

Finally, in the General pane of the Finder's Preferences, you can select what you want to appear by default when you open a new Finder window (via the "New Finder windows open" pop-up menu). If you choose the name of your startup volume from the menu, you will be taken to the root level of your Mac OS X volume whenever you select New Finder Window (Command-N).

SEE: • Chapter 2, especially "Toolbar and Finder views," for more background on navigating Finder windows and using the toolbar.

TAKE NOTE ▶ Computer and Root-Level Windows

The Computer window. To open this window, from the Finder's Go menu choose Computer. In the resulting Finder window you will find a list of all currently mounted volumes, including hard drives, CD-ROMs, and iDisks. It also includes the Network icon, as described elsewhere in this chapter. (The term *volume* refers to a drive, a partition of a drive, or anything else that can be mounted in Mac OS X.) The name of the Computer window will not be *Computer* but rather the name you assigned to your computer when you first set up Mac OS X. You can access and edit this name in the Sharing System Preferences pane. A hard drive can be divided into multiple *partitions*, each of which effectively functions as though it were a separate drive—it has its own listing in this window.

The icons at the Computer level are also represented by identically named icons on the right border of the Desktop (assuming you enabled the feature to show these icons on the Desktop via the Finder's Preferences). The Network icon is an exception; it does not appear on your Desktop.

Note: The Computer window is a bit odd. For example, if you choose Go to Folder from the Go menu and type /, you will be taken to the Computer window, just as if you had chosen Computer from the Go menu. However, if you instead type /Applications, you will be taken to the Applications folder at the root level of the startup volume (as described next)—a folder that is not in the Computer window. Odd? Indeed. In almost all cases, the / symbol refers to the root level of your startup volume rather than the Computer window; however, the result of typing / in Go to Folder is the exception. The Computer window is a special window created by the Finder that doesn't really exist as a folder anywhere on your drive. To go to the root level of your startup volume via Go to Folder, type //.

continues on next page

TAKE NOTE ▶ Computer and Root-Level Windows *continued*

Note: Items in the Computer window may also be listed in Finder windows in the top section of Finder window sidebars. Even the Computer view itself may be listed here. You determine what items are shown via settings in the Sidebar pane of the Finder's Preferences.

The root level of the startup volume. If you double-click the icon of the current Mac OS X startup volume in the Computer window or on the Desktop, you are taken to the root level of that volume. The window that appears will contain at least four folders:

- **Applications.** This folder houses all of the applications initially installed by Mac OS X, as well as any other applications that may have been installed there by you or by third-party installers. The Utilities folder is also within this folder.

- **Library.** This folder contains *local domain* (see "Local domain," below) Mac OS X software.

- **System.** This folder holds core Mac OS X software.

- **Users.** This folder contains the home directory for each user with an account on the volume. The Shared directory is also located here.

If Mac OS 9 is installed on this volume, there will also be a folder called System Folder, which may or may not have a *9* in its icon. This folder is *not* the Mac OS X System folder. There may also be a folder called Applications (Mac OS 9). This folder contains application software installed by Mac OS 9, such as SimpleText and QuickTime Player.

If you installed the software from the Developer Tools (Xtools) CD, a folder named Developer is also located at the root level.

Finally, the Unix directories discussed in the main text (normally invisible in the Finder) are located here as well.

The root level of other volumes. Clicking any of the other volume icons in the Computer window will similarly take you to the root level of those volumes. The contents, of course, will depend on the nature of the volume. It could be another Mac OS X volume, a Mac OS 9 volume, or simply a volume that stores files (with no OS software at all).

In the structure of Mac OS X, the root level of the startup volume has a special status. For example, in Terminal (as covered in Chapter 10), *root level* refers only to the Mac OS X startup volume's root level. Other volumes are structured differently. If you choose the Finder's Go to Folder command and type /Volumes, you will be taken to the Unix Volumes directory, located at the startup volume's root level. Here you will see a list of all the partitions on your drive as well as any other volumes that are currently mounted (or may have been mounted previously).

SEE: • **"Technically Speaking: What and Where Are the Unix Files?" earlier in this chapter.**

• **Chapters 2 and 9 for more on Sharing System Preferences and the Users folder.**

• **Chapter 3 for more information on partitioning a drive.**

Figure 4.6

The Computer window.

Figure 4.7

The root level of a Mac OS X startup volume (with invisible items invisible and with Mac OS 9 and Developer software installed).

The Library folder here contains the bulk of the files (aside from Unix files) that are essential to the operation of Mac OS X. Nearly every file in this folder is installed by the Mac OS X Installer (or another Apple-supplied updater). The contents of the Library folder are rarely modified, other than by an update to the OS or, occasionally, by a third-party kernel extension. In fact, Apple specifically warns against modifying the contents, because doing so can result in failure to start up the computer. If you even attempt to make a change to this folder, you will typically be blocked—either by a message stating that the item can't be moved because "the Library cannot be modified" or by one asking you to "authenticate" (that is, enter your administrative name and password) before the OS will allow you to make the change.

SEE: • "Using the Finder's Authenticate dialog," in Chapter 6, for related information.

In rare circumstances, you *will* want (or need) to modify files in this folder—and, in fact, I provide some examples elsewhere in this book. However, by and large, I concur with Apple's assessment: Troubleshooting will rarely require that you modify the contents of this folder.

Local domain

If you return to the root level of the drive, you'll see a folder called Library. Inside it is an assortment of folders—some of which have the same names as the ones in the /System/Library folder.

This Library folder also gets its initial contents when you install Mac OS X. However, unlike files in the /System/Library folder, most files here *can* be directly modified by any administrative user. Some files, such as those in the Preferences folder, offer read-only access even for administrators—meaning that administrators can view the contents but not modify them. However, even these can be modified if an administrator has root access.

This Library folder is intended as a repository for all the "modifiable" resources shared by the *local* users of a particular computer. A local user is anyone who has physical access to the computer and an account that enables him or her to log in directly.

User domain

Next, click the button with your short name in a Finder window's sidebar or choose Home from the Finder's Go menu. This will take you to the top level of the directory for the person who is logged in (presumably you!).

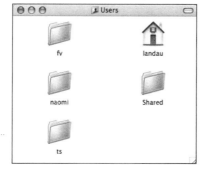

You can also get to your home folder by opening the Users folder at the root level of Mac OS X. Inside the Users folder, you will see at least two folders:

- **Shared.** The Shared folder houses files that any user can access.

- *Username*. This folder will have the short user name you assigned when you set up the OS (in my case, "landau"). If you've created more than one user, you will find additional folders with those user names. Your folder (if you are the logged-in user) will have a house icon; the others will have a generic folder icon. If you open your own folder, you will be at the same place you would be if you had chosen Home from the Go menu.

    SEE: • Chapters 6 and 9 for more information on the Shared folder and file sharing.

Inside your home folder you'll find a third Library folder. Every user will have his or her own Library folder. These user-level Library folders contain resources specific to each user. Any personal preferences you set for an application will be stored here. That way, when you log in, those preferences will be in effect. When another user logs in, his or her preferences will be in effect instead.

Network domain

Your drive has a fourth level. To access it, return to the Computer window (via the Computer command in the Go menu) and double-click the globe icon called Network. (Alternatively, you can directly select Network in the Go menu or click the Network icon in the sidebar of a Finder window.) In the window that appears, you should at least see an alias icon called Servers.

This Servers item is particularly relevant if you're on a network that's connected to a central server—such as a computer running Mac OS X Server software. If you double-click this icon, you will see a list of servers to which you can connect or to which you are already connected, allowing you to access these servers without using the Finder's Connect to Server command. You will most likely find this sort of setup in a university or large corporation, where the central server is accessible by all users and regulates what those users can do on the network. If you can access a network server volume in the Servers folder, you may find a Library folder located on the server. The Network domain Library folder contains resources available to all users of a local area network, typically via a server as set up and implemented by a network administrator.

I'm not going to tell you how to troubleshoot server networks in this book; that job is best left to server administrators. For that reason, I will not be discussing any possible Library folders that appear in this Network folder.

Finally, a few additional tidbits regarding networks, servers, and Library folders:

- If you start up via NetBooting (as covered in Chapter 5), you're actually using a central server as your startup volume.

- Typically, even if you are not connected to any server, there will still be at least one item in the Servers folder. It will be named as the local hostname of your computer: {*name of computer*}.local. Double-click this item and you are taken to the root level of the current Mac OS X startup volume.

- The Network window will also display icons for any computers that are on your local network to which you can connect via file sharing. These are separate from the volumes contained in the Servers folder. If these local computers are running Mac OS X, they will contain Library folders just as your Mac does.

- If you have a .Mac account and you mount your iDisk, you will find a Library folder on your iDisk. (Note that iDisk is not listed in the Network window; instead, it's listed separately in the Computer window.)

- The software largely responsible for the automatic mounting of items in the Computer and Network windows is the Unix `automount` command together with the items in the invisible automount folder at the root level of your startup volume. For more details, type `man automount` in Terminal.

> **SEE:** • Chapters 8 and 9, for more on file sharing, iDisk, and other networking issues.

TAKE NOTE ▶ Multiple Folders of the Same Name in Multiple Library Folders

As noted in the main text, several folders (such as Fonts and Sounds) appear in more than one Library folder. The reason for the presence of these multiple folders, including the multiple Library folders themselves, lies in the different level of access that each folder provides. To make this arrangement clear, here is an overview that uses the different Fonts folders as an example.

- **User (~/Library/Fonts).** The fonts here are accessible only to the user whose home folder they reside in. That user can add fonts to or remove fonts from this folder as desired. This is the method by which non-administrative users can install new fonts.

- **Local (/Library/Fonts).** Any local user of the computer can *use* fonts installed in this folder. (A set of these fonts is installed by the Mac OS X Installer; however, the OS does not require these additional fonts for system operation.) An admin user can modify the contents of this folder, and this folder is the recommended location for installing fonts that are to be shared among users.

- **System (/System/Library/Fonts).** This folder contains the essential fonts required for the OS to run (such as the ones needed for creating menus and dialog text). These fonts should not be altered or removed.

- **Classic (/System Folder/Fonts).** This folder contains fonts used by the Classic environment. If more than one Mac OS 9.x System Folder is present, only fonts in the System Folder selected in the Classic pane of System Preferences are used. Mac OS X applications can use these fonts even when the Classic environment is not active. These fonts can be accessed even if they are in locations other than the Fonts folder.

  Classic applications can only access fonts in the Classic System Folder, *not* those stored in Mac OS X Fonts folders. An exception: The third-party software Suitcase, by Extensis (www.extensis.com), includes an extension called Suitcase (or Classic) Bridge. When installed in the Classic System Folder, this extension allows fonts activated in Mac OS X to be available to Classic applications.

Application-specific font locations. Fonts may also be stored in association with specific applications. Inside the Office folder of the Microsoft Office X folder, for example, is a folder called Fonts, which contains an assortment of fonts that are installed with Office. The fonts are copied to the Fonts folder of your home directory the first time you launch Office.

Similarly, Adobe applications may install fonts in any of several special locations, including ~/Library/Application Support/Adobe/Fonts, /Library/Application Support/Adobe/Fonts, and /Library/Application Support/Adobe/PDFL/6.0. Only Adobe applications access these fonts.

Note: Mac OS X may use fonts found in the Fonts folders on mounted Mac OS X volumes that are not the current startup volume. Mac OS X can also find fonts, and list them in Font menus, even if they're placed within a subfolder of a Fonts folder (such as /Library/Fonts/MyFonts).

More generally, when Mac OS X searches for something (fonts or otherwise) in Library folders, it typically does so in the following order: User, Local, Network, and then System. Note: The Network domain contains the resources available to all users of a local area network, typically via a server as set up and implemented by a network administrator.

SEE: • "Take Note: Problems with Duplicate Fonts in Fonts Folders," later in this chapter, for related information.

Mac OS X: /System/Library

It's now time to take a closer look at the contents of each of the main Library folders in Mac OS X. There are far too many files and folders in any of these Library folders for us to cover even a bare majority here. Instead, I'm limiting the list to the ones that are most relevant to troubleshooting. Feel free to open these folders and browse around yourself: There's no fee for looking!

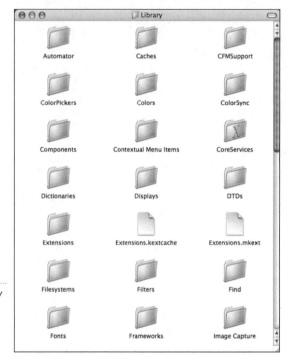

Figure 4.9

The /System/Library folder (partial view showing items beginning with A through I).

The /System/Library folder contains the essential OS software. Here's a sampling of the folders you'll find within.

CFMSupport

CFMSupport contains software used for running Carbon applications. The CarbonLib file is in this folder, for example.

CoreServices

CoreServices is the most critical folder in the /System/Library folder. Like the System folder itself, it has an *X* on its icon to denote its special status. It contains the BootX file, which is required for starting up from Mac OS X (as described in Chapter 5).

This folder also contains many files with obvious functions, such as the Classic Startup, Dock, Finder (an invisible file in Tiger), Help Viewer, and Software Update applications.

It also contains some equally important files and folders with less obvious functions, such as loginwindow (covered in Chapter 5), Menu Extras (covered in Chapter 2), and SystemVersion.plist file (which determines what Mac OS X version is listed in the About This Mac window).

There is also a fake Mac OS 9 System file, simply called System, created so that Carbon applications that expect to see this Mac OS 9 file will "see" it. Yes, you will see the word *Fake* used in the Version description in the file's Get Info window.

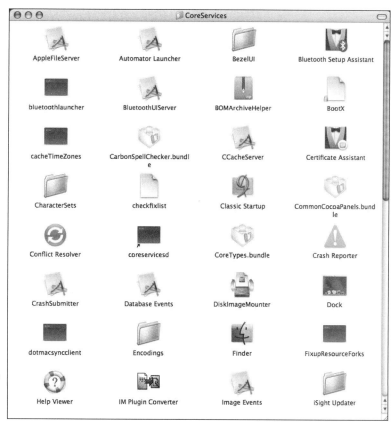

Figure 4.10

Some of the files and directories in the CoreServices folder.

Extensions

This folder contains the *kext* (short for *kernel extension*) files that load at startup, primarily acting as driver software for hardware peripherals. As their name extensions imply, kext files are extensions of the basic kernel software that loads at startup (as covered in Chapter 5).

Fonts

This is one of several Fonts folders in Mac OS X. This one contains the fonts that are considered to be essential for Mac OS X.

SEE: • "Take Note: Multiple Folders of the Same Name in Multiple Library Folders," earlier in this chapter.

Frameworks

Frameworks are an important component of Mac OS X; however, you will have little reason to work with them directly in troubleshooting.

Briefly, *frameworks* are the Mac OS X equivalents of Mac OS 9's dynamic shared libraries, which means they are executed only when needed (dynamic) and contain code that can be used by more than one application simultaneously (shared). The code might be Unix executable software or even a Mac OS X application. The basic idea is to eliminate the need to repeat code used by multiple applications.

Although frameworks appear to be ordinary folders and can be opened without using the Show Package Contents contextual menu, they are structured as package files. A framework package can contain multiple versions of the shared software; applications that require the newer version can access that version, and those that are incompatible with the newer version will be able to access the older version.

Frameworks can also be found in locations besides the /System/Library directory. The ones in this directory are simply the ones that are most essential for the OS.

Frameworks vs. private frameworks. Most frameworks are available for third-party developers to use. For example, if you wanted to write an application that could burn CDs, you would likely want to use Mac OS X's DiscRecording.framework. Among other things, a DevicePlugIns folder within this framework includes a separate device plug-in file for all supported CD-R drives.

However, some Mac OS X–installed frameworks are not available to third-party developers. These private frameworks are found in /System/Library/PrivateFrameworks. Only Apple is able to use these.

Frameworks and troubleshooting. As a troubleshooter, you usually won't need to bother with frameworks. However, there are a few exceptions.

In general, when Apple releases a Mac OS X update that alters Mac OS X applications such as the Dock, Preview, or the Finder, the improved code may not reside in the specified application itself. Instead, it may reside in a framework that the application accesses. For example, some improvements to the

Finder may be contained in ApplicationServices.framework, which itself contains several subframeworks, including HIServices.framework (where *HI* stands for *human interface*) and LaunchServices.framework. A related framework is the HIToolbox.framework located within the Carbon.framework.

Here's one example of a troubleshooting problem resolved by accessing a framework: If an outdated version of the Developer Tools software is installed on your drive, an alert with error 1634955892 may appear when you open DVD Player. The solution is to rename or remove the no-longer-needed HIServices framework installed by the Developer Tools package. To rename the framework, enter the following two commands in Terminal:

```
cd /System/Library/PrivateFrameworks/
sudo mv HIServices.framework HIServices-old.framework
```

SEE: • **"Understanding Image, Installer Package, and Receipt Files," in Chapter 3, for more details on packages.**

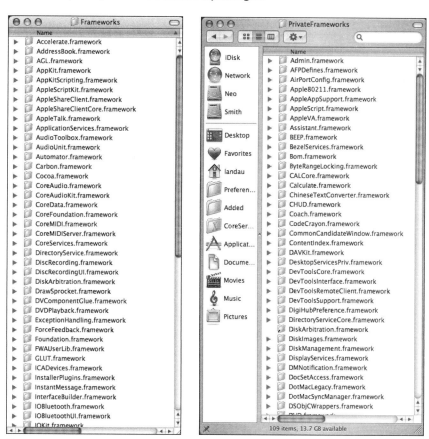

Figure 4.11

Partial contents of the /System/Library/Frameworks folder, left, and the /System/Library/PrivateFrameworks folder, right.

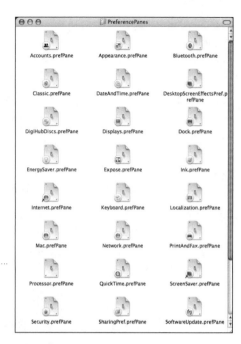

Figure 4.12

Partial contents of the /System/ Library/ PreferencePanes folder.

PreferencePanes

This folder contains the stock (Apple-provided) preference panes that you access via System Preferences.

SEE: • "System Preferences," in Chapter 2.

Printers

This folder contains some of the files needed for printers to work with Mac OS X. Among other things, it contains the PPD files required for LaserWriter printers in Mac OS X.

SEE: • Chapter 7, for more information on printing, including details on PPD and other printer-related files.

QuickTime

This folder contains QuickTime-related software, such as the QuickTime Updater application.

Screen Savers

This folder contains the Apple-provided screen-saver options (Beach, Forest, and so on) that you can access in the Desktop & Screen Saver System Preferences pane.

Services

This folder contains Apple-provided plug-ins for Mac OS X's Services feature (which allows you to access features of one application while in another). In Mac OS X 10.4 Tiger, you will find at least five such services stored here: AppleSpell, ImageCapture, SpeechService, Spotlight, and Summary.

You typically access services via the Services command in the active application's menu. This menu will typically have many more options than just the five in this folder. Most of them will be specific to a given application. For example, via the TextEdit > New Window Containing Selection option, you can open TextEdit with the selected text of the frontmost application already pasted into an untitled TextEdit document. These options work only for applications that support Services technology. If a service is not supported by a particular application, the item will be dimmed in the Services menu when that application is active.

Some services may also be incorporated directly into any Cocoa application (without use of the Services menu). With AppleSpell, for example, a developer can include a spelling-checker feature in an application without having to write the code for it.

TECHNICALLY SPEAKING ▶ Understanding Services

If you check the application menu of most applications (including the Finder), you will find an item called Services. In the Services submenu will be a list of functions you can choose. Mac OS X comes with a default set of services built in. What else appears here will vary depending upon whether or not you have installed third-party software that installs its own Services items or standalone Services plug-ins.

Some items may be dimmed, preventing you from choosing them. This varies as a function of the type of application (Carbon applications, although they can be written to work with services, often do not) and whether or not the service "makes sense" in the context of the application (for example, a service that manipulates files is not designed to work with a selection of text in a word-processing document).

What are services? Most services are linked to an application and are designed to access the features of one program from within another. For example, Mac OS X includes a service that automatically copies selected text from an application document and pastes it into a new Stickies note. Other services are not directly linked to any specific application. Such services could act as spelling checkers or text cleaners, for example.

If an application supports more than one service item, the application name will appear in the Services menu, with each service listed as a submenu from the application name.

continues on next page

TECHNICALLY SPEAKING ▶ **Understanding Services** *continued*

In either case, services work by passing data back and forth between the active application and the selected service, via a shared *pasteboard*.

How does Mac OS X "know" to include an item in the Services menu? The service code itself is contained within the application code. However, a list of an application's available services is contained in the NSServices property array of the application's Info.plist file. The Info.plist file is located within the application package ({*ApplicationName*}.app/Contents/Info.plist).

In some cases, especially for services that are not part of a matching application, a separate service plug-in file exists. These files have a .service extension and are stored in Services folders inside Library folders (for example, ~/Library/Services).

Whenever you log in, Mac OS X checks the contents of the Applications folder (looking at the Info.plist files of applications) and all Services folders. Any services it discovers are added to the Services menu. This has several implications:

- If you install a new service, it is not likely to show up in the Services menu until you log out and log back in again.

- Services within applications that are not stored in the Applications folder may not appear in the Services menu. (However, I have personally found that such services often do appear, despite Apple's indication that they should not!)

- If you wish, you can remove a service that is included as part of an application. To do so, open up the application's Info.plist file (such as with Property List Editor, as discussed more later in this chapter). From the NSServices sub-items (dictionary items labeled numerically from 0, 1, 2, and so on), cut the entire dictionary item that contains the name of the Services item you want to delete. Save the change. This service will no longer appear in the Services menu the next time you log in.

Sounds

This folder contains the default sound files (in AIFF format) that are listed in the Alerts pane of the Sound System Preferences pane.

Note: AIFF is one of several sound formats supported by Mac OS X. Others include the well-known MP3 format and the newer ACC format, commonly used for music files stored on your drive and used by iTunes and the iPod.

StartupItems

This important folder contains some of the various protocols and processes that load at startup while you wait for the Login window and/or Desktop to appear. These items include Apache, AppleShare, Networking, and NetworkTime.

SEE: • **Chapter 5 for more information on the startup sequence.**

Mac OS X: /Library

As I explained earlier in this chapter, this folder stores files that are available to all local users and can be modified by an administrative user. The following are some of the folders you'll find inside.

Figure 4.13

Partial contents of the /Library folder.

Application Support

This folder contains accessory software and support files for various applications. Support files will be in folders named for the base application or the application's software vendor. For example, if you've installed Adobe software, there will be an Adobe folder. Among other things, this folder contains a Fonts folder that holds fonts required for use with Adobe software.

ColorSync

The profiles you create via the Calibrate feature in the Displays System Preferences pane are stored here.

Contextual Menu Items

This folder contains third-party software that adds items to Mac OS X's contextual-menu feature (accessed by Control-clicking an item).

Desktop Pictures

This folder contains the default background pictures you can select via the Desktop System Preferences pane.

Documentation

Some programs that provide read-me files and other documentation (which you access via commands within the application, such as Help) store their documentation files here.

Fonts

This folder is similar in function to the Fonts folder in /System/Library; however, these fonts are not considered essential. As an administrator, you can add fonts to or remove fonts from this folder.

SEE: • "Take Note: Multiple Folders of the Same Name in Multiple Library Folders," earlier in this chapter.

Internet Plug-Ins

This folder stores plug-ins used with your browser, such as QuickTime and Macromedia Shockwave.

Modem Scripts

This folder holds the modem scripts that you can choose from the Modem pop-up menu in the Modem settings of Network System Preferences.

SEE: • "Take Note: Modem Scripts and Terminal Scripts," in Chapter 8, for more information.

Preferences

A few systemwide preferences (.plist) files are stored here, such as those for loginwindow. In general, you'll have little reason to modify preferences files in this folder. However, the files inside the SystemConfiguration folder do appear on the troubleshooting radar from time to time—as does com.apple. AppleFileServer.plist.

SEE: • "Preferences Files," later in this chapter, for more information on .plist files.
• Chapter 5 for more information on the loginwindow application.
• Chapter 8 for more on the SystemConfiguration files and Chapter 9 for more on the com.apple.AppleFileServer.plist files.

Printers

This folder is where you will find support software for printers (in addition to the LaserWriter support files located in /System/Library/Printers). In particular, drivers for most third-party printers are stored here.

SEE: • Chapter 7 for more information on printing.

Receipts

Every time you install a Mac OS X update, a receipt .pkg file for the update is stored in this folder. In certain situations, as discussed in Chapter 3, the OS (especially Software Update) uses these files to verify that a given update has been installed.

SEE: • "Understanding Image, Installer Package, and Receipt Files," in Chapter 3, for more information.

StartupItems

This folder is the equivalent of the StartupItems folder in /System/Library. The main difference is that this folder is used for third-party software, as opposed to the preinstalled Mac OS X items stored in the /System/Library folder. In fact, the folder may not even be present unless you have third-party items that need it. For example, if you install Netopia's Timbuktu Pro, it will install a Startup Item in this folder called TimbuktuStartup. This item is needed for the Timbuktu software to be active at startup, no matter which user logs in. The actual Timbuktu application is located elsewhere, most likely in your Applications folder. Similarly, the Dantz Retrospect backup software also installs a folder, called RetroRun, in the StartupItems folder.

TECHNICALLY SPEAKING ▶ Log Files and cron Jobs

Mac OS X maintains numerous log files that record events (mainly errors) that occur while your Mac is running. Referring to these files can sometimes help in diagnosing a problem.

Log files and Library folders. The following is an overview of the main log files used by Mac OS X and their locations.

- **Console.log in /Library/Logs.** This log file opens by default when you launch Console. The actual file is located in /Library/Logs/Console/*username*; this folder contains a separate folder for each user account. Each Console log maintains a record of recent activity (especially error messages) specific to the named account. Many of these errors are too minor to overtly affect your work—in fact, you probably wouldn't even know they had occurred if you hadn't checked the log. Therefore, you can often ignore these errors. However, if you do start to have problems, checking for errors here may point to the solution.

- **System.log and other log files stored in /var/log.** The system.log file is similar to the console.log file except that it focuses on systemwide processes that are independent of a specific user. This file is stored in the invisible /var/log directory, along with numerous other log files.

- **CrashReporter log files in Library folders.** Both the /Library/Logs folder and the ~/Library/Logs folder contain a folder called CrashReporter. Contained within are log files, named for applications (or processes), that record what happens each time the named software crashes. The /Library/Logs folder also includes the panic.log file, which records information about kernel panics. CrashReporter logs will mainly show up in your home directory's Logs folder. However, if Mac OS X cannot determine who is the owner of the crashed process, or if the root user (System) owns the process, details will wind up in the /Library/Logs folder.

continues on next page

TECHNICALLY SPEAKING ▶ **Log Files and cron Jobs** *continued*

The easiest way to access any log file (visible or invisible) is via the Console utility. After launching Console, click the Logs button on the left side of the toolbar. From the list that appears in the sidebar, locate and open any desired log file.

SEE: • "Console," in Chapter 2, and "Crash.log files" and "Kernel panic," in Chapter 5, for more details.

Doing log maintenance with cron jobs. The Unix system periodically compresses log files to save space, in the process deleting the oldest ones. This maintenance, along with other tasks (such as updating various Mac OS X databases), is performed by running special shell scripts, which are normally scheduled to be run by a utility called launchd (cron in Panther and older versions of Mac OS X). Running these scripts is a Unix operation—launchd schedules (formatted as .plist files) are located in /System/Library/LaunchDaemons, and the cron schedules (called crontabs) are stored in Mac OS X's Unix directories.

If you're comfortable using Unix commands, you can run these maintenance scripts from Terminal via the periodic command. For those who prefer to avoid Terminal, get a shareware utility called MacJanitor, from Brian Hill (http://personalpages.tds.net/~brian_hill/macjanitor.html). This Aqua-based utility makes it easy to run the daily, weekly, and monthly maintenance scripts.

Why might you need to use MacJanitor? One problem with the default schedule for mainte-nance scripts is that they're typically set to run at night—between 3 a.m. and 6 a.m., depending on the script. Thus, if you turn your Mac off each night, these tasks may never get run. In truth, this probably won't matter much; however, it can lead to very large log files (or a very large number of log files) that never get cleared.

A similar utility, called Macaroni, from Atomic Bird (www.atomicbird.com), provides the added benefit of being able to verify if cron jobs have been run as scheduled and, if not, run them automatically. This means that even if you turn off your Mac at night, the scripts will get run via Macaroni.

Note: You can change the times these events occur or even create your own system-level jobs via LaunchDaemon .plist files (in Tiger) or by editing the system-level crontab via a third-party utility such as CronniX. However, I suggest not making any changes unless you know what you're doing.

SEE: • Chapter 6 and Chapter 10, for more on the periodic, launched, and cron commands.

Mac OS X: /Users/Home/Library

The home folder or directory is where you go when you click the home icon in a Finder window sidebar or enter ~ (a tilde) in the Finder's Go to Folder window. The abbreviated path to your home directory's Library folder can thus be written as ~/Library. This Library folder contains files that are accessible only to—and used only by—the logged-in user. Each user account has a separate folder of this kind.

This Library folder is actually stored in /Users/*username*, where *username* refers to the name of the home folder of the currently logged-in user. The folder's name is the user's short name. For example, the full pathname for my home Library folder would be /Users/landau/Library.

The following list of this folder's contents is selective, emphasizing folders that do not have duplicates in the Library folders that I've already discussed. For those that *do* have duplicates, their purposes are the same as those located in /Library, except that they apply only to the user in whose home directory they reside.

Note: Some of these folders get created only when needed to hold the items they contain. That is, rather than having an empty folder, you may have no folder at all.

Figure 4.14

Partial contents of my /Users/ landau/Library folder.

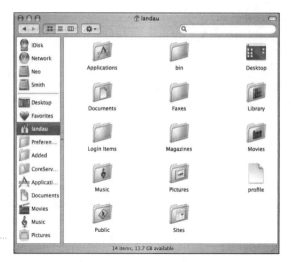

Figure 4.15

My home directory.

TAKE NOTE ▶ Other Folders in the Home Directory

The home folder/directory for each user contains standard folders (installed by Mac OS X) besides the Library folder. Of particular interest for troubleshooting are the following:

- **Public.** This folder is used for anything you want to make publicly available. Any user who can access your computer, via a local network or even the Internet, will be able to access what's in the Public folder. Although these users won't be able to modify anything, they will be able to copy the files to their own folders (locally) or drives (remotely).

- **Documents.** This is where you will save most documents that you create in applications (since most applications select this folder as the default location for saving documents). Some applications also install important data for using the application in this folder (for example, AppleWorks installs an AppleWorks User Data folder here containing information about the list of starting points that appears when you launch the program).

- **Desktop.** This folder contains all the files and folders that are scattered about the Desktop. Because each user has his or her own Desktop folder, what appears on the Desktop will change depending on who is logged in.

   SEE: • "Take Note: The Location of Desktop Folders," later in this chapter.

Application Support

This folder serves the same purpose as the Application Support folder in /Library, except that items in it are available only to the owner of the home directory in which it resides.

This folder has become popular with developers: I currently have support folders for about two dozen applications, including Adobe (for several Adobe software products), LaunchBar, Spell Catcher, and Jedi Knight II (it's where Jedi stores saved games!).

Caches

Cache files, such as the cache files created by Microsoft Internet Explorer (selected in the Advanced pane of Internet Explorer's Preferences), are located here. To see these Internet Explorer files, check the MS Internet Cache folder.

Contextual Menu Items

This folder is where third-party contextual-menu items are typically installed (assuming you have any; otherwise you may not see this folder). There is a similar folder in /Library.

Favorites

This folder contains Internet Location files that are created via the Favorite Servers option in Connect to Server.

Other third-party software that includes a Favorites feature may store aliases here for favored locations (such as for the Documents folder in your home directory); selecting an item from a Favorites list takes you to the original location of the selected alias item.

FontCollections

Open a Cocoa application (such as TextEdit), and from the Font submenu of the Format menu choose Show Fonts; the Font panel appears. The names in the Collections column on the far left side of the Font panel are stored in this folder. You can edit Collections items in the Font panel.

SEE: • "Font panel," later in this chapter, for more information on the
        Font panel.

Fonts

This folder is the third item in the main trio of Fonts folders. This one is used for fonts that are accessible only to the owner of this particular ~/Library folder.

Note: I copy third-party fonts from my Classic System Folder and place them here if I intend to use them in Mac OS X. This method seems to result in fewer problems than if I access the font from the Classic Fonts folder. (Mac OS X uses a font in a Mac OS X folder before it uses the same font in the Classic folder.) If you know you won't need these fonts for Classic applications, it's best to delete them from the Classic System Folder.

SEE: • "Take Note: Multiple Folders of the Same Name in Multiple Library
        Folders," earlier in this chapter.
     • "Viewing and Managing Fonts," later in this chapter.

Keychains

Your keychain file, named login.keychain (which you access from the Keychain Access application in the Utilities folder), is stored here. A keychain file is a convenience feature that stores passwords for any number of applications and services (as long as they support Apple's Keychain technology). If it's working, when entering or creating a password, you may encounter an option that says something like, "Add password to keychain." If you check the box, the password will be added to the keychain data. In the future, you will not need to re-enter the password.

Note: Another Keychains folder, which contains a systemwide keychain file, named System.keychain, is stored in the /Library folder.

SEE: • "Keychain Access," in Chapter 2.

PreferencePanes

System Preferences panes that appear in the Other section of the System Preferences window are installed here. Typically, if you download a third-party preferences pane, you install it simply by dragging it to this folder. The next time you launch System Preferences, the new pane will be listed.

Preferences

As a troubleshooter, you are likely to access this folder most often. It contains the preferences files created by most applications you use—which means that it stores any customized changes you make via the Preferences command of these applications. Some OS-related preferences files are also stored here (such as the ones used by the Finder).

When something goes wrong with an application, a common early trouble-shooting step is to delete its preferences file, since such files can get corrupted when modified. If this is the cause of the problem, deleting the corrupted preferences file will fix it. The application automatically creates a new default version of the file the next time it launches.

Note: Don't be too eager to delete preferences files: A few of them contain important information that you can't easily re-create after Mac OS X has created a new default version. The Favorites.html file (inside the Explorer folder in the Preferences folder), for example, contains all the URLs listed in Internet Explorer's Favorites menu. To be safe, make a backup copy of any file you intend to delete so that you can restore it if it turns out not to be the source of your problem.

Most of the preferences files you will work with have the .plist extension.

SEE: • "Preferences Files," later in this chapter, for more on preferences files.

• "Technically Speaking: Type/Creator vs. Filename Extensions vs. Others," later in this chapter, and "Deleting or removing preferences," in Chapter 5, for related information.

Application-specific folders

Even though Apple makes it clear that application-related files should be stored in the Application Support folder, some applications may instead install their support folders at the root level of the Library folder.

TAKE NOTE ▶ Library Folders, Applications, and Accessory Files

One of the cited advantages of Mac OS X is that it ends the proliferation of application-related files, scattered in numerous locations, that often plagued Mac OS 9 users. This proliferation made it more difficult to troubleshoot problems (because you often couldn't find all of the relevant files!) and to copy applications to other locations (because if you failed to copy needed accessory files, an application might not work).

The Mac OS X solution is the application package (.app). The package concept allows developers to place the actual application together with its associated files in one location. The truth, however, is that there remain many locations in Mac OS X beyond the application package where an application's accessory files may get placed.

If an application you're using begins to develop odd symptoms—especially if simply replacing the .app file doesn't fix the problem—ferreting out these files and reinstalling or deleting them may help. This is because these files may have become modified in a way that prevents their expected use. Deleting often works because many of these files (such as .plist files) are self-regenerating—a new default copy is created the next time the application is launched. For non-regenerating files, reinstalling the entire application (from its installer) or getting a backup copy from your backup files is the most common way to replace a suspected problem file. In some cases, however, modifying the ownership/permissions or editing the content of an accessory file may fix the problem. I cover specific examples of troubleshooting accessory files throughout this book, especially in Chapters 5 and 6.

Look for folders containing accessory files in both the /Library and ~/Library folders. An application's installer utility will place a file in the /Library folder if it wants all local users to be able to access the file. It will place the item in your home (~) Library folder if it expects that only you will be accessing the file(s). Sometimes an installer will give you a choice of which way to go. The majority of accessory files, however, will be in your home directory.

continues on next page

TAKE NOTE ▶ Library Folders, Applications, and Accessory Files *continued*

Here is a short list of the most common Library folders that may contain application accessory files:

- Application Enhancers
- Application Support
- Caches
- Contextual Menu Items
- Documentation
- Fonts

- Individual iApp folders (for example, iTunes)
- InputManagers
- Internet Plug-Ins
- Preferences
- PreferencePanes
- StartupItems (found only in /Library)

The Library directories can also contain folders with application names. These, too, contain accessory files. For example, there is a Safari folder in ~/Library used by Apple's Safari Web browser. In some cases, the application-named folder may be within one of the above folders. For example, you'll find an Explorer folder inside the ~/Library/Preferences folder, and within this folder are several important files used by Internet Explorer, including the Favorites.html file that Internet Explorer uses to create the list of items in its Favorites menu.

Other home-directory folders. Besides files in the ~/Library folder, folders in the root level of the home directory may also contain accessory files. The most common example is the Documents folder, where you'll find the AppleWorks Users Data folder, the Microsoft User Data folder (used by Microsoft Office applications, especially Entourage), and the iTunes folder. Again, if these files are deleted or are not present, the application typically creates a new default version when the application is launched.

SEE: • "Installer package (.pkg) files" and "Technically Speaking: Inside Packages," in Chapter 3, for more details on package files.

• Chapter 5 for details about startup items.

TAKE NOTE ▶ The Location of Desktop Folders

Desktop folders in Mac OS X. Anything you place on your Desktop in Mac OS X is actually stored in a folder in your home directory called, appropriately enough, Desktop. To confirm this, navigate to your home directory (such as by choosing Home from the Finder's Go menu) and open the Desktop folder in the window that appears. Inside you'll see every file and folder on your Desktop. Any changes you make in this folder will be reflected on the Desktop as well. That's because this folder *is* your Desktop (just as in Mac OS 9 an invisible folder called Desktop Folder contains the contents of your Desktop).

This setup means that when a different user logs in to your computer, he or she will neither see nor have access to the files on your Desktop. Instead, this user will see the contents of the Desktop folder in his or her own home directory. There is no systemwide Desktop folder whose contents are visible to everyone. Thus, things that you want to make accessible to everyone need to be placed in shared locations, such as the Applications folder, the Public folder in your home directory, or the Shared folder in the /Users directory.

continued on next page

TAKE NOTE ▶ The Location of Desktop Folders *continued*

Mac OS 9 Desktop folders and Mac OS X. As mentioned above, in Mac OS 9, items placed on the Desktop are maintained in an invisible folder, located at the root level of the drive, called Desktop Folder.

In Mac OS X, especially if you have a Mac that no longer boots in Mac OS 9, there are not likely to be any items on a Mac OS 9 Desktop—in which case, the Mac OS 9 Desktop Folder might not even get created.

If the Desktop Folder does exist on a Mac OS X volume—and it contains items—it remains invisible even when you're running Mac OS X. Further, as implied in the previous section, none of the items in this invisible folder appear on your Mac OS X Desktop. Thus, there's no direct way to access the contents of this invisible Desktop Folder. Mac OS X solves this problem by creating a special alias file (actually a symbolic link) called Desktop (Mac OS 9). This folder contains the items that would be visible on the Desktop if and when you were to boot from Mac OS 9.

If a Desktop Folder with items exists, this folder will automatically appear at the root level of *any* volume with Mac OS X installed, *not* just the Mac OS X startup volume. There is one problem, however: If you double-click the alias icon, you're always taken to the Desktop Folder of the current startup volume, not the volume where the icon is located. This means you cannot use these aliases to access the contents of a Desktop Folder other than the one on the current startup volume.

For volumes that have a Desktop Folder but do not have Mac OS X installed, this problem is avoided. The Desktop Folder appears as a visible folder icon at the root level of the volume when running Mac OS X from another volume. No alias icon is used or needed.

For volumes that do have Mac OS X installed and also have this Desktop (Mac OS 9) alias, the easiest work-around (to access the contents of the Desktop Folder on the non-startup volume) is to use the Finder's Go to Folder command. For example, to access the Desktop Folder contents on a secondary volume called R2D2, enter the following in the Go to Folder window: `/Volumes/R2D2/Desktop Folder`.

If all items in a Mac OS 9 Desktop Folder are removed or deleted, the linked alias is removed automatically the next time the computer restarts. The alias has its permissions set so that it cannot be deleted in normal use. If the alias is deleted somehow, it will be re-created after the next restart.

The root user Desktop. If you log in as the root user, you also have a Desktop. Because there is no *root* folder in the /Users folder, however, a question arises: Where is the Desktop folder for the root user?

This folder is located in an invisible location at /var/root/Desktop. You can view the root folder icon by typing /var as the path in the window that opens when you choose the Finder's Go to Folder command. You will not be able to open the folder, however, because you do not have root access.

continues on next page

TAKE NOTE ▶ The Location of Desktop Folders *continued*

To see the contents of the folder, you can log in as root. Once you've done this, you can move or delete the files located in the folder.

If you're an administrative user, you can also use Terminal to view the contents of this folder— even when you're not logged in as root. To do so, type the following commands:

sudo -s (then enter your admin password when requested)

cd /private/var/root/Desktop (to move to that directory location)

ls (to list the contents of the Desktop directory)

SEE: • **"'Desktop (Mac OS 9)' file is a symbolic link,"** in Chapter 6, for related information.

• **"Desktop folders in Mac OS 9/Classic vs. Mac OS X,"** in the Classic chapter, online at **Mac OS X Help Line (www.macosxhelpline.com),** for more information.

TAKE NOTE ▶ The Locations of Trash Folders

As is the case with the Desktop folders, each user in Mac OS X maintains his or her own Trash (actually a folder, just like the Desktop). Thus, the contents of your Trash will not be visible or accessible in another user's Trash. Likewise, other users can't delete items you've left in the Trash. (Mac OS X has no universal emptying of the Trash, as does Mac OS 9.)

.Trash. The files that you place in the Trash in Mac OS X are actually stored in an invisible folder in your home directory called .Trash. Each user's directory (including the one for the root user, located at /private/var/root) has its own .Trash folder.

.Trashes. If you've mounted partitions or volumes in addition to the Mac OS X startup partition, anything you drag to the Trash from these additional volumes will still appear in the Trash window you access by clicking the Trash icon in the Dock. If you empty the Trash, those files will be deleted. However, the files are not stored in the .Trash folder in your home directory; each is stored in an invisible .Trashes folder on the volume on which the file resides. These .Trashes folders have default write-only privileges; thus, you would need to change the privileges (as described in "Ownership & Permissions," later in the chapter) to view their contents, such as via the list (ls) command in Terminal.

There is actually a .Trashes folder for the startup volume. However, it's unlikely to be used unless you reboot from another volume and mount the now-former startup volume as a secondary volume.

continues on next page

TAKE NOTE ▶ The Locations of Trash Folders *continued*

Network Trash Folder. There may also be a Network Trash Folder, located at the root level of your startup volume, for trashing files over a network.

Mac OS 9 Trash. Items placed in the Trash while running Mac OS 9 (assuming you have a Mac that can still boot into Mac OS 9!) are stored in the invisible Trash folder used by Mac OS 9. There is one such folder at the root level of every volume that contains Mac OS 9.

Note: If you boot from Mac OS 9, files you left in the Trash while in Mac OS X will not appear in the Mac OS 9 Trash (and vice versa). To access the Mac OS X Trash contents and try to delete them from Mac OS 9, you will need a utility that allows you to view and modify the contents of invisible folders (File Buddy, for example). Then you will need to navigate to the directory in the /Users folder containing the .Trash file that you want to empty.

Seeing invisible Trash folders. You can "see" invisible Trash folders via the Terminal utility. To see the .Trash folder for your home directory, for example, simply launch Terminal and type ls -a. This command lists all files, including invisible ones, in the current directory.

If you prefer not to use Terminal, try TinkerTool (or a similar utility) to make normally invisible files visible in the Finder. To do so with TinkerTool, select the Show Hidden and System Files option in the Finder section of TinkerTool. Then relaunch the Finder via TinkerTool's Relaunch Finder button. You can undo the change in TinkerTool to make invisible items invisible again.

SEE: • "Deleting: Problems Deleting Files," "Invisible Files: What Files Are Invisible?" and "Invisible Files: Working with Invisible Files," in Chapter 6, for more information on these subjects.

• Chapter 10 for more on using Terminal.

Get Info

This section—together with all the remaining sections of this chapter—forms a category that I refer to as *advanced basics*. If this term sounds like an oxymoron, that's because it is. But here's what I mean by it: There are some topics in Mac OS X that the average user doesn't need to know much about but are so essential to understanding the way the OS works that you can't get far in troubleshooting without some basic knowledge of them. That's why I consider these topics advanced basics.

The starting point for any Mac OS X advanced-basics tour must be the Finder's Get Info (also referred to as just Info) windows. As you will remember from Chapter 2, you access a Get Info window by selecting an icon in the Finder and pressing Command-I (or choosing Get Info from the icon's contextual menu or from the Finder's File menu).

The window that appears will contain several sections. For a document icon, these sections include the following:

- Spotlight Comments
- General
- More Info
- Name & Extension
- Open With
- Preview
- Ownership & Permissions

The contents of each section may or may not be visible when you open an Info window. Typically, the General section is visible by default. To view other sections, you need to click the disclosure triangle to the left of a section's name. Any sections you reveal this way remain revealed in subsequent Get Info windows that you open (a real time-saver when comparing multiple windows).

The sections that appear differ if you are viewing an application, folder, or volume, rather than a document. (You can even see the Get Info window for the Desktop by pressing Command-I when no item is selected!) In the sections that follow, I will list the full set of options.

Multiple Info windows. You can have multiple Get Info windows open at the same time. Just click Command-I for each. Or select multiple items in one group and press Command-I. (Note: If you select 11 or more items, a Multiple Item Info window, as described below, will appear instead.)

Old-style Inspector. The user interface of the Finder's Get Info window (called Show Info in Mac OS X 10.1.x) was overhauled in Mac OS X 10.2. To bring up the old Mac OS X 10.1.x Inspector-style window, press Command-Option-I. You can even have both the old-style and new-style windows open at the same time. One advantage of the old-style window is that if you click a different Finder icon while the old-style window is open, it shifts to display the information for that item. Thus, you cannot have two Inspector-style windows open at once—a convenience when you want to view information from several files in succession (you don't have to press Command-I for each and have several windows open) but inconvenient when you want to compare two Get Info windows side-by-side.

Multiple Item Info window. Using the Inspector mode (Command-Shift-I), you can select multiple items and then choose Get Info for all of them. This reveals one Get Info window representing all of the items you selected. Any change you make here will affect all of the items simultaneously. When you're working in "batch mode" like this, you're limited to the options that are available for *all* of the selected items. If, for example, a folder does not include an option that's available for a document, you won't be able to access any of the document options if your multiple-item selection includes a folder. You can also access this window by highlighting 11 or more items and invoking the Get Info command—Mac OS X assumes that with that many items selected, you really don't want individual Get Info windows for each item.

Except for batch mode, you'll almost always be working with the newer style of Get Info window. Thus, that's the only style I'll be discussing here.

Because the options available in the Get Info window are critical to so many troubleshooting tasks, I describe each in detail in the following sections (for the most part, following the order of appearance in the Get Info window).

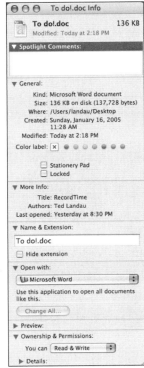
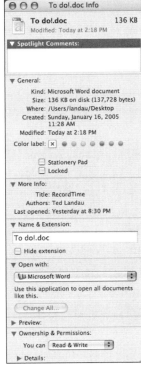

Figure 4.16

The Info window after selecting Get Info, left, versus Show Inspector, right. The difference in appearance is in the title bar.

Spotlight Comments

In this section, you can type in any comments about the item that you wish—these comments will be searched by Spotlight. For example, if a document was e-mailed to you by your friend Alice, you could add a note that says "From Alice; she thought it was funny." These comments get included in the Spotlight database. Then, for example, if you later use Spotlight to search on the word *Alice*, the commented document will appear in the results, even if *Alice* doesn't appear anywhere in the file's name or contents.

General

The General section of the Get Info window appears by default when you open the window. It provides basic information such as item type (application, document, folder, volume, or alias), item size, item location, version number (if the application provides one), and item-creation and modification dates. It also lets you view and modify the item's color label.

Note: A folder's modification date changes only when its contents change, not when items within it have been modified. Thus, if you were to modify and save a file within a folder, the folder's modification date would not change. However, if you were to add or delete a file to or from the folder, the folder's modification date would change.

If the file is a document, the Kind line typically identifies its type (that is, the application used to create it). For example, a Microsoft Word document will say just that: "Microsoft Word document." However, the Kind line for an AppleWorks document will read, "com.apple.appleworks.document." Although this may seem an odd way to identify it, you still know that the document was created by AppleWorks.

If the item is a volume, such as a hard drive, the General section will list the capacity of the volume and how much of it is presently used versus unused (available).

If you have multiple drives, each subdivided into partitions, the Where line will not identify which is the drive of origin for a selected partition. To determine this, check the left-hand column in Disk Utility.

If the file is an alias, the General section will tell you where the original is located.

SEE: • "Aliases and Symbolic Links," in Chapter 6, for more information on aliases.

At the bottom of the General section for a document, you may see one or more options with check boxes, one of which will be Locked. If this option is selected, you are prevented from deleting the file. In fact, if you try to place it in the Trash, you will get a message stating that you don't have sufficient privileges to do so.

SEE: • Chapter 6 for more information on problems with locked files and with deleting files in general.

For some documents, you will also have a Stationery Pad option. If this option is enabled, opening the document opens a *copy* of the document rather than the document itself. This allows you to make changes in the copy and still preserve the original. As its name implies, this option is useful for documents in which you have some element (such as a name and address) that you want to preserve for use in future documents (such as letters you are writing).

There are some applications that you can open in either the Classic environment (Mac OS 9) or Mac OS X. By default these applications usually open in Mac OS X; however, if for some reason you want one of these applications to open in Mac OS 9, choose the Open in the Classic Environment option in the General section of the Get Info window. If this option is not available, it probably means the application you're using is not a switch-hitter—that is, it can open in only one environment. (Note: As described in the Classic chapter— online at www.macosxhelpline.com—some applications, such as AppleWorks 6, can open in either Classic or Mac OS X even though the Open in the Classic Environment option does not appear.)

If the application can open in Classic, there will also be a Memory section that you can use to allocate the amount of memory assigned to the app when opened in Classic.

Finally, the icon of a file or folder is visible in this window.

TAKE NOTE ▶ Changing and Troubleshooting Finder Icons

Changing the icon for a file or folder is usually done more for aesthetic reasons than true need.

Changing icons via Get Info. In most cases you can copy the icon in the Get Info window of any item and paste it into the Get Info window of another item. The other item will then display that icon in the Finder. To do this, follow these steps:

1. First, determine whether the destination file already has a custom icon, and if it does, delete it: Open the Get Info window for the destination file, click the icon, and then from the Edit menu choose Cut (Command-X).

   When you cut (Command-X) a custom icon, you're left with either a default icon (as assigned by the Finder, based on the file's creator or filename extension) or a blank icon.

2. If you did delete a custom icon, log out and log back in. This is really only necessary if the destination file is on the Desktop, but to be safe, you can do it in any case. If you don't, the icon you paste may not "stick."

3. Open the Get Info window for the file with the desired icon.

4. Click the icon in the Get Info window, and from the Edit menu choose Copy (Command-C).

5. Open the Get Info window for the destination file.

6. Click its icon, and from the Edit menu choose Paste (Command-V).

   Pasting a custom icon works for most document files. It also works for applications, folders, and volumes.

continues on next page

TAKE NOTE ▶ Changing and Troubleshooting Finder Icons *continued*

If you're curious about where custom icons are stored, the answer is that it varies by file type:

- The icon for a volume is stored in an invisible file called .VolumeIcon.icns, located at the root level of that volume.

- A custom icon for a folder is stored in an invisible file called Icon? that's created within the folder when you add its custom icon.

- For .app application packages, the custom icon is stored in an invisible file called "icon," located at the root level of the package.

Changing package-file icons. Although you can add a custom icon to an application package, the default icon obviously remains. That is, if you cut the custom icon, the default icon returns. Similarly, the information needed to assign the correct icons to documents created by the application remains. Where is all of this default information stored? And can you change it?

Here are the answers:

You need to have the desired icon in the form of an .icns file rather than a graphic on the clipboard. You can download .icns files from the Web, create them via icon-editing utilities, or "borrow" them from existing package files. For example, to place the .icns file from one package in another, you would do the following:

1. Select the application with the icon you want to copy and Control-click it to access its contextual menu. If a Show Package Contents item appears, the application is a package. (Note: Not all applications will be packages in Mac OS X.)

2. Choose Show Package Contents. In the window that opens, navigate to the Contents/ Resources folder, where you will find at least one .icns file. Look for the one named {*name of application*}.icns. (Note that the file may have a slightly different name. For example, NetworkConnect.icns is the name of the relevant .icns file for the Internet Connect application.) Whatever name it goes by, this is the file that's used to create the Finder icon for that application.

   The remaining .icns files, if any, are typically ones used for documents created by the application.

   Note: If you double-click an .icns file, it will open in Preview. This can help determine if you have the "correct" .icns file.

3. Option-drag this .icns file to the Desktop to create a copy of it there.

4. Select the application where you want the icon to go and, using the Show Package Contents contextual menu, go to the same Resources folder inside the package (as described in Step 2).

5. Rename the .icns file on the Desktop to match the name of the one in the destination package's Resources folder.

6. Drag the renamed file to the Resources folder of the destination package and click OK when asked if you wish to replace the file already there.

continues on next page

TAKE NOTE ▶ Changing and Troubleshooting Finder Icons *continued*

7. Close all opened folders.

8. Relaunch the Finder (for example, by holding down the Option key when accessing the Finder's Dock menu and choosing Relaunch). In some cases, for this or the alternate method described next, relaunching the Finder may not be sufficient; if so, you will need to restart the Mac.

Another way to do this would be to try the following:

1. After obtaining the .icns file you wish to use (as described in Steps 1 through 4 above), go to the Contents folder inside the destination package.

2. Using Property List Editor, open the Info.plist (or Info-macos.plist) file, as appropriate.

3. Change the value of the CFBundleIconFile key to the name of the new .icns file (do not include the .icns extension in the name). Save the change.

4. Move the new .icns file into the package's Resources folder. With this method, you don't overwrite the original .icns file or change the name of your newly added one. However, if you have problems getting the new icon to "take effect," you will likely have to remove the old .icns file from the application and relaunch the Finder.

Note: I recommend working with copies of the applications involved so that you don't have to worry about doing permanent harm if things don't go as planned. Be aware, however, that there's a bug in Mac OS X that affects this method: When you copy a package file, you may not be able to open the Contents folder within the copy of the application package immediately after making the copy. This in turn means you won't be able to access the needed .icns file. The solution seems to be simply to log out and log back in again. Once you do this, you should be able to open the Contents folder.

Where to get icons. If you don't want to copy an icon from an existing item, you can create your own. One way to do so is with the IconComposer utility that comes with Developer Tools software. Third-party utilities like Iconographer X also work well and are more user-friendly. For folder icons, check out Folder Icon X. Another alternative would be to obtain icon files downloaded from the Web and paste them as custom icons. You might even be able to paste graphics other than icons, such as images opened in the Preview application (though they won't look as good as a graphics specifically designed as icons).

One simple way to generate icons is to use the `tiff2icns` command in Terminal (as covered in "Running Mac OS X software from Terminal," in Chapter 10). This turns any TIFF image into an .icns file.

Note: An .icns file inside an application package typically contains several variations of the same icon (you can see these variations if you open up the .icns file in Preview; you will see 128-by-128, 32-by-32, and 16-by-16 versions of an icon, for example). Replacing this file with a simple .icns file that has only one version of the icon may result in the icon's appearing "incorrectly" in certain situations, such as when you resize the icon or highlight it. The `tiff2icns` command creates a file with three versions: 128-by-128 and two 32-by-32 variations.

continues on next page

TAKE NOTE ▶ **Changing and Troubleshooting Finder Icons** *continued*

Mac OS X System icons. Many of the icons used by Mac OS X itself—such as the ones for the Applications folder, your home directory, and the Finder itself—cannot be changed by simply pasting a custom icon into the item's Get Info window: Mac OS X will not permit this. Still, with some extra effort you can change these icons.

These icons are stored in /System/Library/CoreServices/CoreTypes.bundle (in Panther, you'll find them in /System/Library/CoreServices/SystemIcons.bundle). To access them, view this package's contents and navigate through Contents/Resources until you find a collection of system icons, such as ClippingText.icns, FinderIcon.icns, FullTrashIcon.icns, and iMac.icns. With root access, you can change these icons in the same way I described above for application icons.

For more icon-editing capabilities, you can use a third-party utility like the Iconfactory's CandyBar (www.iconfactory.com/cb_home.asp). And if you have Apple's Developer software installed, check out icns Browser and Icon Composer.

Opening an icon in Preview. In an item's Get Info window, select its icon and copy it to the clipboard. Now launch Preview and select the New from Clipboard command from the File menu. The icon will open in Preview, revealing not only the basic icon itself, but all the different size and resolution variations that are "built in" to the icon's .icns file.

Troubleshooting: Icons that move. You may find that icons, especially ones on your Desktop, occasionally reposition themselves—often as a result of changing your monitor resolution via the Displays System Preferences. In addition, some games automatically change monitor resolution, in which case you might see this symptom even if you didn't change the resolution manually. Icons can reposition themselves at other times as well—for example, after waking from sleep. The basic solution here is to simply move the icons back to their desired positions. In addition, some utilities, such as SwitchResX (www.madrau.com) or Desktility (www.desktility.com), may enable you to save and restore icon positions.

Note: Finder icon positions are stored in the invisible .DS_Store file in each folder. Other information about Finder windows, such as size, whether they're in Icon or List view, and other options set via the Show View Options command in the Finder's View menu can be found primarily in the com.apple.finder.plist file. Suffice it to say that Finder window information settings are overly complex and not altogether bug-free. If you find that when you close and later reopen a window, it's not always the way you left it, you're not alone. One example: After copying a folder to a different volume, I found that the folder's settings had changed (for example, a List view had reverted to an Icon view).

SEE: • "Preferences Files," later in this chapter, for more on using Property List Editor.

  • "Take Note: Filename Extensions" and "Technically Speaking: Type/Creator vs. Filename Extensions vs. Others," later in this chapter, for related information on things that can affect what icon an item displays.

  • "Take Note: Launch Services Files and Beyond," in Chapter 6, for yet more related information.

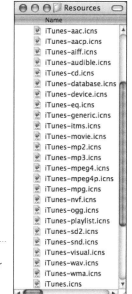

Figure 4.17

The .icns files inside
the Resources folder
of the iTunes.app
package.

More Info

This section of the Get Info window displays additional information about a
file. The information is automatically updated as appropriate. The most common data you will find here, for example, is the date and time that the file was
last opened. However, some documents provide much more detailed information. For example, a Microsoft Word document will list the Title and Author of
the document. If there is no available "more info" for the file, the section will
be empty (displaying two dashes to indicate "no info").

Name & Extension

This section of the Get Info window displays the name of the file and its
extension (if any). All applications have the filename extension .app. Other
files, especially documents, may have extensions that identify their type (such
as .gif to identify a file as a GIF graphic). Since Mac OS 9 does not use filename extensions, converts from that OS may find it inconvenient or confusing
to see these extensions listed in the Finder. This is why the .app extension is
almost always hidden for applications. You can similarly choose to hide an
extension for a given filename by checking the Hide Extension box in the
Name & Extension section of files that have extensions.

SEE: • "Technically Speaking: Type/Creator vs. Filename Extensions vs.
     Others," later in this chapter, for further details.

     • "Technically Speaking: How Mac OS X Selects a Document or
      Application Match," in Chapter 6, for related information.

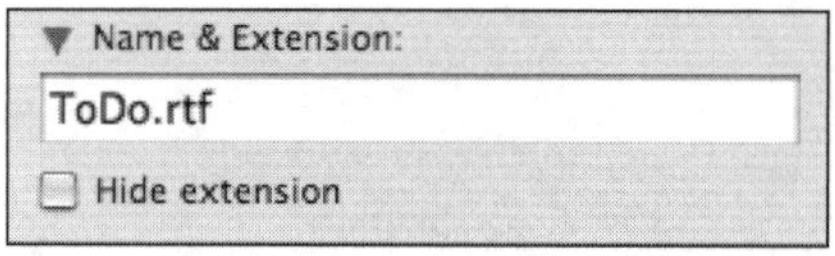

Figure 4.18

*The Name &
Extension section of
a Get Info window.*

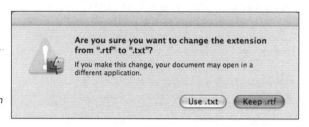

Figure 4.19

*An error message
that may appear
when you try to
change an extension
in the Finder.*

TAKE NOTE ▶ Filename Extensions

Filename extensions have a wide range of effects and can be modified from a variety of locations. Here's what you need to know about them:

What is the function of filename extensions? Filename extensions are abbreviations appended to the end of a file's name—for example, .jpg in picture.jpg. In this case, the .jpg extension indicates that the file is a JPEG document. Mac OS X uses filename extensions to determine file types. For documents, this type can determine what application opens the document if you double-click the file's icon in the Finder. The type can also determine which icon the document displays.

If an application can save files in more than one format, it may assign a different extension to each format. Thus, when Word saves a document in its own Word format, it uses the extension .doc; if it saves it in plain text, the extension will be .txt; if it saves it in Rich Text Format, the file will have an .rtf extension.

Showing vs. hiding extensions. In addition to the Hide Extension option in the Get Info window, most applications' Save dialogs include a Hide Extension option (though the exact wording may vary). This option pretty much duplicates the effect of toggling the Hide Extension setting in the Name & Extension section of the Get Info window. Another option that may appear in a Save dialog is Append File Extension. This is a bit different: Toggling it determines whether an extension is included in the filename, not merely whether it's visible in the Finder.

In addition, you can choose to hide or show virtually all file extensions in the Finder. To do this, open the Finder Preferences window, and in the Advanced section, deselect or select "Show all file extensions."

The following are some additional details about how these options work:

- If Hide Extension is selected, a file's extension will not be shown in the Finder unless you enable "Show all file extensions" in Finder Preferences. That preferences setting overrides the Get Info setting.

continues on next page

TAKE NOTE ▶ Filename Extensions *continued*

- If Hide Extension in the Get Info window is disabled, a file's extension is always shown, regardless of the setting in Finder Preferences.

- In general, if "Show all file extensions" is disabled, the option you choose in the Get Info window or the Save dialog will determine whether the file's extension is visible in the Finder.

   That is, even when the "Show all file extensions" option is not selected, you can display an individual file's extension in the Finder by deselecting the Hide Extension option in the Get Info window's Name & Extension section. This option is not always available, however. For example, prior to Tiger (Mac OS X 10.4), the application extension .app was always hidden and typically never shown in the Finder. Still, you could see the .app extension listed in the Name & Extension section of the Get Info window for the application. Starting with Tiger, if you select "Show all file extensions" in the Finder's Preferences, the .app extension is now also shown.

- In some cases (for example, with Microsoft Word), if you do not choose the "Append file extension" option in the Save dialog, the Mac does not merely hide the extension; it doesn't add one at all. Thus, you create a file with no extension. In this case, the Hide Extension box in the Get Info window is checked, and the option is dimmed so that you cannot uncheck the box (because there is no extension to show). Even in this case, you can choose to add your own extension in the Finder after you've saved the document. For the Word document, you can add .doc to the end of the document name. Now the Hide Extension box in the Get Info window will be unchecked, and you can check it again if you want.

Problems with filename extensions. Whether you choose to hide or view filename extensions, the system has more than its share of problems. The following describes some of these problems as well as ways of dealing with them.

General advice: To confirm the true name of a file at any time, check its name in the Name & Extension section of the file's Get Info window. To be certain that the change you're making to a file's extension sticks, make that change in the Get Info window as well. When you close the Get Info window, a warning dialog will appear if Mac OS X considers your change ill-advised: You can click OK or Cancel. Don't expect changes you've made in a Save dialog to yield the results you anticipated.

More specifically:

- The fact that an extension can exist but remain invisible in the Finder is one source of confusion. For example, suppose a file's extension is hidden and you try to add one (such as changing *sample* to *sample.txt*), either in the Finder or in a Save dialog: If a .txt extension exists but is hidden, you could end up changing the file's name to *sample.txt.txt* without even realizing it.

- Even if you choose to hide extensions, this setting will be overridden for files downloaded from the Internet. If a downloaded file was named fileone.rtf, it will remain that way. If you later change the name to myfile, however, the Finder will change the name and hide the .rtf extension (because you didn't type it). Thus, the .rtf extension will still be in the Name & Extension pane of the Get Info window; you just don't see it in the Finder. Similarly, you can wind up with a situation in which one .rtf file downloaded from the Web includes a visible extension but another that you created with TextEdit does not.

continues on next page

TAKE NOTE ▶ Filename Extensions *continued*

- Complications can occur when you save files using extensions. Mac OS X–compliant applications typically add the appropriate extension for their document type when you save a new document, even if you don't type the extension. Thus, when you save an AppleWorks word-processing document, AppleWorks will add .cwk to the name of the file. Although AppleWorks shows that it is adding this extension, other applications may do so without indicating it. Even if you delete the extension from the name in the Save As dialog, the extension still gets added.

  The application should also warn you against trying to assign an invalid extension (such as .jpg to an AppleWorks .cwk file). If you try to do this, you will have the option to append both extensions to the name (such as name.jpg.cwk), but the Finder will look only at the .cwk extension when it decides how to treat the file.

- When you save a document in an application, it should respect whether you've specified for extensions to be hidden in the Finder; however, some applications do not. Extensions may be visible in a saved file's name even if you chose to keep extensions hidden, and vice versa.

- Another complication involves the interaction of filename extensions with the "Open with" section of the Get Info window. In particular, changing the application used to open a document and then choosing Change All will change the default application associated with that extension. Files with the extensions .txt and .rtf, for example, are opened by TextEdit by default. If you choose Change All for a .txt file, the Finder will open all .txt files in the new application you select. This system also respects type and creator codes. Thus, if the .txt file is specifically indicated as having been created by AppleWorks, Mac OS X will change only .txt files created by AppleWorks. If no creator is listed, Mac OS X will change all .txt files that have no creator listed.

- The Finder's Find feature "sees" filename extensions even if they're not visible in the Finder. Thus, if you have a file called picture.jpg, but the .jpg extension is hidden, all you will see in the Finder is *picture*. However, if you search for a file that ends in *ture*, this file will not appear in the results, because Find sees *jpg* (not *ture*) as the end of the file's name.

It's hopeless to try to cover every possible extension-related permutation here. Extensions are not among Mac OS X's most logical features. To make matters worse, the filename extension is not necessarily the only method Mac OS X uses to determine what document goes with which application. The OS can also use the type and creator information used by Mac OS 9 (if that data is present in the file). In fact, if a creator is present, the Mac will use the creator setting in preference to the extension.

Editing file extensions and warning messages. You can edit a filename in the Name & Extension section of the Get Info window; in fact, you can even add or remove an extension. Similarly, you can do this directly from the Finder by clicking on the file's name field. There is, however, one twist: If you delete an extension visible from the Finder, you will only hide it, *not* delete it. This is why it's generally better to edit extensions in the Get Info window. In addition, to make sure you're actually removing (not just hiding) an extension, uncheck the Hide Extension box before you make the change.

continues on next page

TAKE NOTE ▶ Filename Extensions *continued*

Be careful, however: If you add, delete, or change an extension, you will typically get an alert box that asks whether you're sure you want to do this—and warns of the consequences of doing so when you should not.

For example, editing or deleting an .app filename extension may change the application into a folder. Thus, if you confirm your change by clicking Yes at the alert, you will no longer be able to launch the application—that is, until you undo the change.

If changing a document's extension merely alters which application the Finder uses to open it (and the new application is able to open the file), your change should be fine. But if changing an extension makes the Finder think you've changed the file's format (when you have not), problems are likely to occur.

For example, if you change an extension from .doc to .txt, you haven't really changed the document's format from a Microsoft Word file to a plain-text document; however, the Finder may mistakenly think you have. Similarly, changing a file's extension from .jpg to .gif doesn't really alter the graphic format of the file; it just changes what the Finder *thinks* the file is—that is, the Finder will now be in error.

Troubleshooting tip: Sound files and extensions. Any sound file in the AIFF format that you place in your ~/Library/Sounds folder can be used as an alert sound via the Sound System Preferences pane. However, this will work only if the .aiff extension is included in the name of the file. It has to be exact—even .aif will not work.

TECHNICALLY SPEAKING ▶ Type/Creator vs. Filename Extensions vs. Others

Mac OS X identifies file types by either their filename extensions (introduced in Mac OS X) or their type and creator (a carryover from Mac OS 9). There's some controversy over which is the better approach.

Resource forks and data forks. In Mac OS 9, most files are made up of two components: a resource fork and a data fork. In the case of applications, most of a file's contents are stored in its resource fork. You can view (and even modify) this information (which includes application icons, dialogs, error messages, version info, and more) via Apple's ResEdit utility.

For documents, the data fork is more significant because it typically holds their essential data (for example, the words you type in a word-processing document). Most documents, such as text documents, need only a data fork. The resource fork does not usually contain actual user data.

Because Mac OS X has moved away from using resource forks (for reasons discussed later in this sidebar), Mac OS X–native applications store all this information in the data fork. In fact, these native files lack a resource fork altogether.

continues on next page

TECHNICALLY SPEAKING ▶ Type/Creator vs. Filename Extensions vs. Others *continued*

Type/creator. In Mac OS 9, every file is identified by a type and a creator. *Type* refers to the type of file (that is, application, system extension, AppleWorks document, and so on), and *creator* refers to the application that the Finder considers the creator of a document. The information in the Kind line of one of these files' Get Info windows is typically determined by the type and creator code for the file.

Type information and creator information is essentially two separate four-letter codes. Each creator (application) has a unique code, and separate codes exist for different file types (for example, applications all have the type APPL). In Mac OS 9, this information was stored in an application's resource fork. In Mac OS X (with the exception of older software that still maintains the data in its resource fork), this data is stored in an application's Info.plist file (described next) and, for documents, in the volume directory.

Although Apple provides no utility for changing creator and type codes in a standard installation of either Mac OS 9 or Mac OS X, many third-party utilities fill this gap. In Mac OS X, for example, you can use utilities such as XRay or Gideon Softworks' FileXaminer (www.gideonsoftworks.com/filexaminer.html). You can also change these codes via the SetFile command in Terminal, included as part of Developer Tools.

The creator code is especially important for documents that can be opened by several applications. When a plain-text document is double-clicked in the Finder, it opens in SimpleText (in Mac OS 9) if SimpleText is listed as the creator. The same file opens in AppleWorks if AppleWorks is listed as the creator.

The type code can also affect how documents are treated. Read-only SimpleText documents (the ones with the newspaper icon) have a type of ttro, whereas read-write SimpleText documents have a type of TEXT (case matters!). You can change a read-only file to an editable one simply by changing this type. In both cases, the creator for SimpleText should be ttxt. (Note: In TextEdit—Mac OS X's equivalent of SimpleText—you can change an editable document to a read-only one via the Prevent Editing/Allow Editing toggle commands in the Format menu.)

As a result of this type/creator system, no matter what you name a file, the Finder will always be able to figure out its type and (for documents) what application it should open in, simply from the type and creator information.

An application's Info.plist file. In Mac OS X, creator and type information for a native application—which doesn't have a resource fork—are stored in its information property list (Info.plist) file, located inside the application package. This Info.plist file is where the Finder goes to determine what codes to assign to documents created by that application. This is consistent with Mac OS X's move away from storing this information in a resource fork. You can use Property List Editor (as covered later in this chapter in "Modifying a .plist file") to open the .plist file. Look for CFBundlePackageType and CFBundleSignature as the keys for the file type and creator.

continues on next page

**TECHNICALLY SPEAKING ▶ Type/Creator vs. Filename Extensions
vs. Others** *continued*

This information will be listed in the Value column of the row of that name. If the column says, "????," no type and/or creator has been assigned. You can also view and edit this information via third-party utilities such as XRay.

The Info.plist file also lists the filename extensions that the application recognizes as document types it can open; this information is stored in the CFBundleDocumentTypes property. If more than one application lists the same extension, the Finder uses predetermined rules of precedence to determine which to use with which application. For example, it will use a Cocoa application in preference to a Carbon one and a Carbon one in preference to a Classic one. At the top of the hierarchy are any preferences you have made via the Open With command in the Finder's File menu or in the Get Info window for the document. Selections made here are stored in the com.apple.LaunchServices.plist file in the ~/Library/Preferences folder.

Note: Info.plist files include information beyond the focus of this sidebar. These are mainly of interest to developers. For example, the LSPrefersCarbon versus LSRequiresCarbon key determines whether certain applications must run in Carbon versus Classic, or let the user decide which environment to use (via an option in the Get Info window).

Metadata locations. Type/creator information is an example of a file's *metadata*. (Metadata is often described as "data about data"—in other words, information *about* a file, rather than the file's actual data.) Whereas type/creator information for an .app application is stored in the application's Info.plist file, you may wonder where this information is stored for the documents created by these applications. The answer is, it's stored in the volume directory (the same area that Disk Utility's First Aid checks for making repairs). Thus, it is not nearly as accessible as the Info.plist data.

Some other remaining metadata are stored in the invisible .DS_Store file located within every folder.

Problems with type/creator. Mac OS X can use the same type and creator information that Mac OS 9 does, but it does not require it. In fact, Apple prefers that developers no longer depend on it. And documents created by many of Mac OS X's own applications, such as TextEdit, include no type or creator code.

Why has Apple gone this route? First and foremost, no platform except Apple uses this dual-fork file structure—most platforms have trouble with dual-fork files. For example, when you send a file from the Mac to the Windows platform, its resource fork—and thus its type and creator data—is typically lost. Conversely, files created on Windows machines and sent to a Mac do not include a resource fork, and thus do not contain this data. Similarly, Unix does not support type and creator data—which means that a Mac OS X drive formatted with UFS (see Chapter 3) would not be able to use this data to identify files. Files on all of these other platforms consist only of data forks—a direction in which Mac OS X is moving as well.

continues on next page

TECHNICALLY SPEAKING ▶ Type/Creator vs. Filename Extensions vs. Others *continued*

Extensions. Apple's "solution" to the type/creator problem has been to move to filename extensions (as described in "Take Note: Filename Extensions")—in essence, to use the same approach as other platforms. In fact, the improved cross-platform compatibility of such an approach is Apple's main rationale for the shift.

Advantages of type/creator (as compared with filename extensions). Type and creator codes still have a few advantages, however. In addition to the basic problems with filename extensions noted earlier in this chapter, here are a few other issues with filename extensions:

- It's much easier to accidentally change the name of a file—and, possibly, its extension—than it is to change a file's type or creator. For example, if you were to assign a .jpg extension to a word-processing document, the Finder might mistakenly think you have a .jpg file, when in reality the file is *not* a JPEG and *will not* open in applications designed to work with .jpg files.

- Eliminating an extension can make it very difficult to figure out a document's type and what application to use with it.

- By relying on just one bit of information (filename extension) rather than two (type *and* creator), you lose significant flexibility. With type and creator, you can have two JPEG files with different creators. One may open in Preview; the other may open in AppleWorks. You can't do this with file extensions. All JPEG files open in the same application by default unless you override the setting in the file's Get Info window.

For all of the above reasons, there has been considerable backlash against Apple's use of file extensions instead of type and creator. Many feel that Apple took something that worked very well and substituted something more likely to have problems. Regardless of your opinion, however, if you're a Mac OS X user, you're stuck with Apple's decision; you might as well get used to it!

MIME types. MIME types provide yet another way to identify file formats. MIME types are used primarily for identifying files in Web browsers or when files are downloaded to your drive from the Internet. Certain applications beyond Web browsers, such as QuickTime Player, also use them. MIME types actually use filename extensions, as well as type and creator codes, to map the MIME type of a particular file. However, MIME types are not a way that the Finder typically identifies file formats, so I am omitting discussion of them here.

UTI: Happy ending or another layer of complexity? New in Tiger, Apple has added yet another way of describing file formats, called *Uniform Type Identifiers* (UTIs). UTIs offer greater flexibility and customizability than the other methods described here. They also promise to be a way to standardize file-format identification in Mac OS X, so that there is no longer this hodgepodge of several methods used at once. As Apple states: "A UTI provides a consistent identifier for data that all applications and services can recognize and rely upon, eliminating the need to keep track of all the existing methods of tagging data."

continues on next page

TECHNICALLY SPEAKING ▶ Type/Creator vs. Filename Extensions vs. Others *continued*

The problem for now is that this method is restricted to internal use by applications. There is currently no user interface for viewing these settings, nor any end-user utilities for manipulating them. I expect that will change as time goes on. For now, let me just provide a brief introduction.

UTIs describe formats in a somewhat user-friendly terminology that is similar to the notation used for preferences (.plist) files. UTIs are organized in a hierarchy, where types lower down in the hierarchy inherit the properties of their parents, and then add more properties. The *public* domain is reserved for common or standard types that are of general use to most applications. Here is one hierarchical sequence: public.content (used for all documents) > public.text (used for most plain text documents, such as .txt TextEdit documents and HTML documents) > public.rtf (used for .rtf TextEdit documents). Developers can create UTIs for their applications and add them to the list that Mac OS X understands.

Whether this turns out to be the ultimate solution for the complexities of file identification in Mac OS X, or just another brick in an already confusing wall, remains to be seen.

SEE: • **"Technically Speaking: How Mac OS X Selects a Document or Application Match," in Chapter 6, for related information.**

    • **"Troubleshooting Internet Applications," in Chapter 9, for more on MIME types.**

Figure 4.20

Partial contents of the Info.plist file for TextEdit. Note the lines below CFBundleTypeExtensions that indicate .rtf (TextEdit documents) and .doc (Microsoft Word documents), two of the extensions that TextEdit recognizes.

  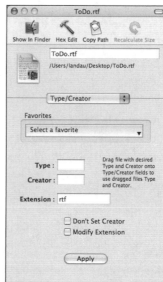

Figure 4.21

Type and creator codes for three documents, as viewed in FileXaminer: left, a Preview document in TIFF format (with type and creator codes plus a .tiff extension); center, a Microsoft Word document (with type and creator codes but no extension in this case); right, a TextEdit document (with no type or creator codes but an .rtf extension).

Open With

The "Open with" section appears only when you open the Get Info window for a document. The main reason you will use this section is if double-clicking a document's icon does not open the document with the application you expected (or does not open the document at all). This section includes two options:

- **Pop-up menu.** The default choice here (visible in the menu before you click it) is the application that will currently open the document. In fact, the word *default* may appear in parentheses after the application name. You can choose another application from the pop-up menu. In most cases, the menu will list all applications that can potentially open the document; simply choose the one you want, and you're finished.

  If an application you believe *should* work with the document is not listed, choose Other from the pop-up menu. A Choose Other Application window opens, providing access to all applications on your drive(s). Initially, Recommended Applications will appear in the Enable pop-up menu at the top of the window, and only those applications will be selectable. However, you can select All Applications from the Enable menu.

  Below the file browser is a check box labeled Always Open With. When this box is checked, the document should always open with the selected application (which I'll discuss more in a moment); however, I've seen cases where it appeared to have no effect. When you've made your selection, click the Add button.

As a result of your changes, your document will now open in the newly selected application (until you make additional changes). This does not alter the default choice for other documents of this type; it just changes the effect for this particular document. Remember, changing this option doesn't ensure that you can successfully open the document with the selected application. It just means that the application will try. For example, if you attempt to open a QuickTime movie with the Calculator application, it won't work.

Note: When you make a change here, the document's icon may change to reflect the new application (though documents from some older Carbon applications may not do this). However, if you make additional changes, the icon is unlikely to reflect them. To get the new icon to appear, click the icon itself in the upper left of the Get Info window and from the Edit menu select Cut.

- **Change All button.** The lower part of the "Open with" section contains a Change All button, which is enabled when you make a change via the pop-up menu. Clicking Change All changes the default choice for similar documents to your changed selection—meaning that *all* documents of the type you just modified will open in the newly selected application. Before the change takes effect, you will get a warning message asking if you're sure this is what you want to do and stating which documents will be affected by the change. For example, when I did this for an Internet Explorer archive document, my message stated, "This change will apply to all Internet Explorer documents of the type 'WAFF.' " This information refers to the document's creator (Internet Explorer) and type (WAFF). Depending on the document's characteristics, the message may refer to files of a certain extension rather than type.

  SEE: • "Technically Speaking: Type/Creator vs. Filename Extensions vs. Others," earlier in this chapter, for further details.

  One reason you might want to use Change All is if all files in a certain graphics format (say, JPEG files) open in Application A by default but you would rather they open in Application B. Or perhaps all documents of a certain type are opening in a Classic version of an application, and you would prefer to use a Mac OS X version.

Open With (from Finder and contextual menus). The Get Info window is not the only place where you can choose an Open With option. You can also do so via the Open With command in the Finder's File menu or via the Open With item in the contextual menu for the document (accessed when you Control-click the document icon). Both options work similarly to the "Open with" pop-up menu in the Get Info window—with one exception: If you access the Open With option from the Finder or a contextual menu, it uses the selected application only for that single launch. The next time you double-click the document, it will still launch the original default application. To make the change "permanent," hold down the Option key while selecting the Finder or contextual-menu option. This changes Open With to Always Open With. However, this will not affect other similar documents. To apply your changes to all similar documents, you still need to use the Change All button in the Get Info window.

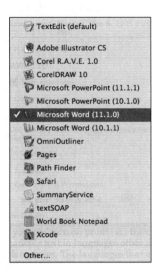

Figure 4.22

Left, Get Info's *"Open with" section, indicating TextEdit as the default application;* right, *the "Open with" pop-up menu, indicating a shift to Microsoft Word.*

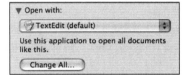

Preview

The utility of the Preview section of the Get Info window ranges from completely worthless to minimally useful. For applications, it's mainly worthless, as all it shows is the Finder icon of the file. For text documents, it displays a snippet of the text from the beginning of the file. For graphics files, it provides a miniature version of the graphic content. For QuickTime movies and many media formats (such as MP3 and AAC), you can actually view or listen to the file's contents right in the Preview window. This can be useful if you don't want to have to launch QuickTime Player just to check the contents of a movie file, or you'd like to quickly listen to an audio file without having to launch iTunes and add the file to your iTunes Library.

Languages

If the item you've selected is a Mac OS X application, its Get Info window is likely to include a Languages section. From here, you can turn on or off (via the check box by each language name) the ability to display the application's text in languages other than the default choice. You can also add or remove additional languages. The languages that appear here depend on what language-support files are included within the application package. Whether or not you can use them depends on what languages (accessed via the International System Preferences pane) you installed with Mac OS X.

SEE: • **"International language support: Basics," and "International language support: Troubleshooting," later in this chapter, for more details.**

Plug-ins

Some applications may also include a Plug-ins section (iPhoto and Disk Utility are two examples), used to add modules (including ones from third-party developers) that provide additional features. As with languages, you can turn plug-ins on and off as well as add or remove them. Apple encourages developers to use this method instead of any other plug-in management method.

For an interesting example of how this works, select Get Info for Disk Utility. You will see modules (all with .dumodule extensions) for each of the main functions available from Disk Utility. If you deselect a module (don't click the Remove button; just uncheck its check box) and then launch Disk Utility, the disabled module's tab no longer appears. For example, if you uncheck the box for RAID.dumodule, the Raid tab no longer appears when you select a drive.

You can ignore the settings in this section of the Get Info window unless you have a module that you want to add (or remove for some reason). For third-party modules, the instructions that came with the software will provide further explanation.

Figure 4.23

The Plug-ins section of iPhoto's Get Info window.

Memory (Classic applications only)

Memory allows you to set the amount of memory (RAM) used by Classic applications. This option appears only for applications that can run in Classic (for those that can run either as Mac OS X or Classic applications, the settings here apply only when the applications are run in the Classic environment). This section lists a suggested size and allows you to set a preferred size and a minimum size. The application will not open unless the amount of memory in the Minimum Size setting is available. Thus, you should almost never change this setting to be lower than the default. The Preferred Size setting is how much memory the application typically uses (assuming the amount is available). This setting is usually the same as the suggested size, though you can make it larger if you feel the program is not working well (running slowly, for example) due to the preferred size being insufficient.

Mac OS X programs are not assigned any preset level of memory because the OS itself allocates the appropriate amount of memory dynamically as needed. That's why this option doesn't appear for Mac OS X applications. The Mac OS X approach is much more flexible because it permits on-the-fly adjustments that Mac OS 9 does not allow.

SEE: • **The Classic chapter, online at www.macosxhelpline.com, for more on memory and Classic applications.**

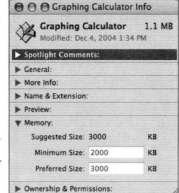

Figure 4.24

Get Info's Memory section (available for applications that run only in Classic).

Ownership & Permissions

Ownership & Permissions is a section of the Get Info window where you can modify a file's permissions and ownership settings. If you ever get a message indicating that you cannot do something (such as move, open, or delete a file) because you don't have sufficient permission or privileges, this is the first place you should go to solve the problem. Beware, however: The permissions for Mac OS X's essential software are set so that you cannot easily move or delete those files. This is as it should be: Bypassing these restrictions could result in a nonfunctioning OS. Still, there are many cases where modifying permissions is perfectly appropriate, such as for files in your home directory.

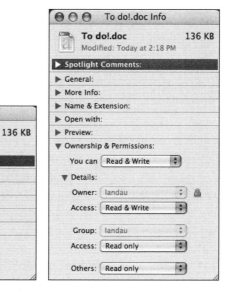

Figure 4.25

The Ownership & Permissions section of a Get Info window: left, without details shown; right, with details shown.

When you first access the Ownership & Permissions section, there will be two items:

- **"You can."** This pop-up menu tells you what type of access you currently have to the file (for example, Read & Write, Read Only, or No Access). If you own the file, the menu is active and you can modify the settings. Otherwise, the menu is dimmed. The following sections of this chapter explain how your access here is determined.

- **Details.** Click this disclosure triangle to reveal the full set of Ownership & Permissions options.

  The Details subsection of the Ownership & Permissions section includes five pop-up menus: an Owner and Access pair, a Group and Access pair, and Others (which is an Access menu). Permissions settings appear for all types of items: documents, applications, folders, and volumes. Exactly what they imply, however, varies depending upon the type of item you've selected. In most cases, you will be working with permissions of document files—which is what I'll emphasize here.

Owner, Group, and Others. These three categories represent the different levels of permissions settings. Thus, the owner of a file can have settings that are different from everyone else's. There may also be a collection of users that form a group. (Mac OS X has numerous predefined groups.) You can separately assign permissions to the group. Finally, everyone other than the owner and the members of the selected group is considered to be Others.

TECHNICALLY SPEAKING ▶ Ownership & Permissions: Mac OS X vs. Unix

The permissions settings in the Get Info window of Mac OS X are actually determined by—and are a subset of—the more complex permissions settings of the underlying Unix base of Mac OS X.

In Unix there are three main attributes, somewhat different from those in the Get Info window: Read, Write, and Execute. Further, unlike those in the Get Info window, choices are not mutually exclusive. In Get Info windows, you can choose between Read Only versus Read & Write, for example. In Unix, Read and Write are two separate settings; each is turned on or off independently. Similarly, to eliminate all access (the equivalent of No Access in Mac OS X), you turn off all permissions in Unix. Thus, there are six possible combinations of settings, from all off to all on. In addition, some special options—such as setuid, setgid, and sticky bit—have no corresponding options in the Get Info window. Also, the Execute (sometimes referred to as the *search*) permission does not apply directly to Aqua-based applications—that is, you can run an Aqua application even with this setting off. It does, however, apply to Unix commands and programs. It has a special meaning when applied to folders. In particular, you must have Execute access for a folder in order to view the content listing of the folder. Read Only or Read & Write access is not sufficient.

When you make a change in the Get Info window, you're actually changing the corresponding Unix permissions settings. To make changes that do not fit into the subset of possibilities included in Get Info, you need a utility such as FileXaminer or XRay, both of which have options for editing owner and group names, privileges settings, and type/creator settings. They even include options for editing more obscure permissions settings (such as setuid and setguid).

SEE: • "Take Note: Multiple Users: Why Bother?" earlier in this chapter.

  • Chapters 6 and 10 for more background on privileges and permissions.

Figure 4.26

Permissions settings as viewed in Get Info, left, and XRay, right. (See also Figure 4.5 for how permissions [rwx] are listed in Terminal.)

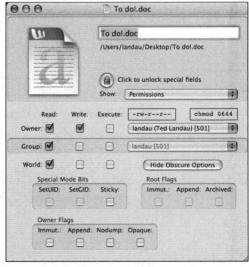

What determines the owner of a file? A file's owner is typically the user who created it. Thus, when you create and save a new document in AppleWorks, you are the owner of the file. You also own files that you copy to a drive—for example, files you download from the Web or copy from a network volume to your Mac's hard drive.

With a few exceptions, you own all of the files in your home directory. One notable exception: If you move a file into your home directory (such as from the Applications folder), it retains its original ownership. If you instead copy the same file (so that the original remains in its original location), the copy will inherit the properties of the folder where it now exists—that is, you will own the copy in your home directory. Thus, copying a file can change its ownership.

Modifying Ownership & Permissions settings. By default, the names of the Owner and Group are dimmed, signifying that they can't be changed. However, if you are an administrative user, you *can* modify the Owner and/or Group. To do so, click the padlock icon to the right of the Owner name; the Owner and Group menus should now be enabled.

Even with the Owner and Group menus enabled, you still can't change Access menu settings unless you own the item. You can make yourself the owner by choosing your name from the Owner pop-up menu. Once you've done this, you can make Access menu changes. When you're finished, you can return Owner to its prior setting, if desired.

By changing both Owner and Access settings, you (as an administrative user) can give yourself access to any file on your drive. For example, if the owner of a file is *system* and you have no write access to the file, you can unlock the padlock, change the owner to yourself, and grant yourself Read & Write access. You can now do whatever you want to the file. If you're modifying the text of a Mac OS X System file, however, you'll probably want to change the settings back to the originals when you're finished. This avoids any possible problems that might occur if the system can't access the file later when needed.

Access permissions. If you're listed as the owner of a file, the short name of your account should appear as the owner name. If this is the case, you can easily change Access settings for yourself, the group, and others. These settings determine which type of file access you have:

- **Read & Write:** You can view and modify a document file's contents. If the file is an application, you can run the application.
- **Read only:** You can view but not modify the contents of a document file. If the file is an application, you can run the application. The Others category will typically be limited to "Read only" permissions.
- **No Access:** You can neither view the file (if it's a document) nor run it (if it's an application).
- **Write only (Drop Box):** This option appears only for folders and volumes. It means that you can add files to the folder but not view the folder's contents.

You may find it surprising to learn that even if you have no access privileges to a file, you may still be able to delete it. This is because the ability to delete a file is a function of the permissions settings of the *folder* that contains the file (rather than of the file itself). If you have Read & Write access for the folder, you should be able to delete a file within it, regardless of the file's settings.

Typically, a file's owner has Read & Write access to the file—which makes sense. If you own the file, you should be able to modify it, and even delete it, if you want. In fact, the owner of the file is the only person who can change the Access settings.

One more example: The Group setting for the /Applications folder is "admin"; its access has been set to Read & Write. That same folder's Others setting has "Read only" access. This is why administrative users can add or delete applications, while non-administrative (standard) users can run applications in this folder but cannot add files to or delete files from it.

Note: A user's access is determined first by whether he or she is the owner, then whether or not he or she is in the chosen group, and finally by the Others setting. This means, for example, that if you are in the listed group for a file, your access is limited to that of the group—even if Others has greater access than Group!

Owner and Group. When you click the Owner menu, you get a list of a file's potential owners—one of whom will be yourself, of course. The list will also include any other local users that have been set up, as well as a special user named "system" (which is the same as the root user). Additional owners listed here—conveniently set off by a separator line—are for various system processes and can typically be ignored.

When you click the Group menu, you get a similar list of potential group selections. Those that are of the most interest include the following:

- **{*Your short user name*}.** For each user account, Mac OS X creates a group with the same owner name—in both cases, the short name of the user account. In my case, for example, this group name is "landau."

  The group with your name is assigned by default to files you own. You are the sole member of this group.

  Note: In Jaguar, the default group for files you own is "staff." The same is true for all other local accounts on your Mac. Thus, all local users are members of this group. This group still exists in Panther and Tiger; however, it no longer acts as the default assigned group, and no accounts are assigned to it by default. If you upgrade from Jaguar to Panther or Tiger, however, existing accounts may still use staff as the default; newly created accounts will use the new user name group.

- **Admin.** All admin users are members of this group.

- **Wheel.** The only officially listed member of this group is the root user. Membership in this group is typically needed for access to processes restricted to the root user. While admin users are not a member of this group, they can get temporary root-level access via the su or sudo command in Terminal (as covered more in "Technically Speaking: Group Settings Explained" and in the next section, "Root Access").

Putting it together. A user's access is determined first by whether he or she is the owner of the item and/or in the listed group of the item. If not an owner or a group member, the Others setting determines access. This means, oddly enough, that if you are in the listed group for a file, your access is limited to that of the group—even if the Others setting shows greater access than Group! As another example, if you are a member of the admin group (which all administrators are) and the admin group has Read & Write access to a file, you will have Read & Write access to the file, even if you do not own the file.

SEE: • "Root Access," later in this chapter, for more details.

TECHNICALLY SPEAKING ▶ Group Settings Explained

If you take a look at the Get Info window for the Applications folder, you'll see that the folder is owned by the System. Does this mean that all applications within it are owned by the System? And if so, how is it that you can work with these files almost as if you owned them?

Admin. The reason is that the Group setting is Read & Write, and the group name is "admin." If you're an administrative user (which you certainly are if you set up Mac OS X initially), you're part of the admin group—and thus have read/write access to the files in the Applications folder. All administrators have admin group privileges to any file that is assigned to the group admin.

Wheel. Another group, one that is more important in Unix systems than it is in Mac OS X, is the "wheel" group. Typically, files with wheel as their listed group offer read-only access to members of the wheel group. Thus, a member of wheel can look at and use these files but not modify them. In Mac OS X, most of the files in the /System/Library directory employ this setting.

Wheel vs. admin. As noted in the main text, an admin user is not a member of the wheel group, so changes to the wheel group's access will not directly affect an admin user's access. Instead, it's the Others setting that affects admin users' access to files owned by the System. Typically, Others access is also restricted to "Read only." You can test this by making changes to the access settings in the Get Info window and watching how the "You can" access shifts as a result.

This means that if a wheel or admin member (or any user with read-only access to System files) wants to modify a file in /System/Library, the person must do one of the following: (a) change the file's ownership (for example, via the Get Info window); (b) get root access (for example, by employing the sudo command in Terminal), or (c) authenticate in the Finder when attempting to move an item (if the Finder allows it). These restrictions are designed to protect the files from being mistakenly moved or modified—an obvious safety precaution when you consider that they are essential to the operation of the OS.

continues on next page

TECHNICALLY SPEAKING ▶ **Group Settings Explained** *continued*

The wheel group no longer plays an active role in Mac OS X 10.3 and later—even though some System files and folders in Tiger may still list wheel as their assigned group. Instead, wheel's role has been taken over by the admin group. In Unix, wheel group membership is needed to use the su command. In Mac OS X, such root user access is now almost never needed in the Finder, as the admin user can perform almost all actions—via authentication dialogs—that might otherwise require root access. Apple states: "The only thing the administrator is prevented from doing is directly adding, modifying, or deleting files in the system domain."

"Unknown" group. Occasionally, you may find that a group is listed as "unknown." This is not necessarily an error; it simply means that the OS cannot determine the group—usually because one hasn't been assigned—which is typically the case with folders and files on a Mac OS 9 partition or on many forms of removable media. In some cases, however, a file is listed as part of an unknown group because an error has occurred—that is, its intended group name has been "lost." This can spell trouble—especially if such files are in the /System/Library or /Library folder—leaving you unable to access files you should be able to access. For more specific examples, as well as instructions for how to fix them, see Chapter 6.

Who's in a group? To find out whether you're a member of wheel, admin, or any other group, you can use NetInfo Manager. Simply launch this utility and select the "groups" item in the first column in the window that appears. In the next column on the right, you will see a list of all groups (more than you might think, most of which are used by Unix and need not concern you). Scroll to find the group "admin," for example. Click it. In the section at the bottom of the window, you will see a property called "users." The names associated with this item, in the Value(s) column, are the users who are part of the admin group. (Note: You can alternatively open a Terminal window and type the command groups; any groups to which you belong will be listed.)

Note: For all *username* accounts as listed in NetInfo Manager (for example, landau, in my case), no group members are listed. However, the group ID (GID) number is the same as your user ID (UID) number (for example, 501). In Mac OS X's version of Unix, this makes you a member of your self-named group. Thus, I am a member of the "landau" group even though I am not listed as such in NetInfo Manager.

Note: GIDs and UIDs are numerical representations of group and user names. The IDs can often be used interchangeably with names (for example, when entering commands in Terminal). To find out any user's UID via NetInfo Manager, select the users category in the left-most column and then select the desired user name from the middle column. The output at the bottom of the window will include a property called "uid," the value of which will be the UID number. Similarly, to find out a GID for a group, select the groups category, select the desired group name, and look for the "gid" property in the output at the bottom of the window.

continues on next page

TECHNICALLY SPEAKING ▶ Group Settings Explained *continued*

As an administrator, you can use NetInfo Manager to create new groups or make changes to the membership of existing groups. These modifications are rarely necessary for Mac OS X client users. Instead, they are mostly of value to administrators of large networks (who will most likely be using Mac OS X Server). For example, if you were a network administrator at a university, you might want to create a separate group for each faculty department. If, as a Mac OS X client user, you do have a need to edit group settings, I recommend using SharePoints as a more user-friendly solution (as covered in "Take Note: Using SharePoints," in Chapter 9).

SEE: • "Root Access," later in this chapter, for related details.

• "Technically Speaking: Access Control Lists and Extended Attributes," in Chapter 10, for new options for setting permissions in Tiger.

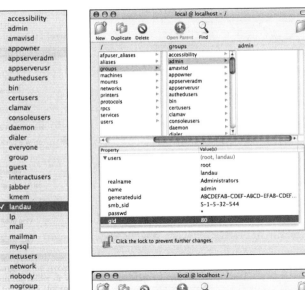

Figure 4.27

Groups: left, the list of groups selectable in the Get Info window; top right, NetInfo Manager shows the Property listings of the admin group—indicating that root and landau are the sole members; bottom right, NetInfo Manager shows the Property listings for my landau group.

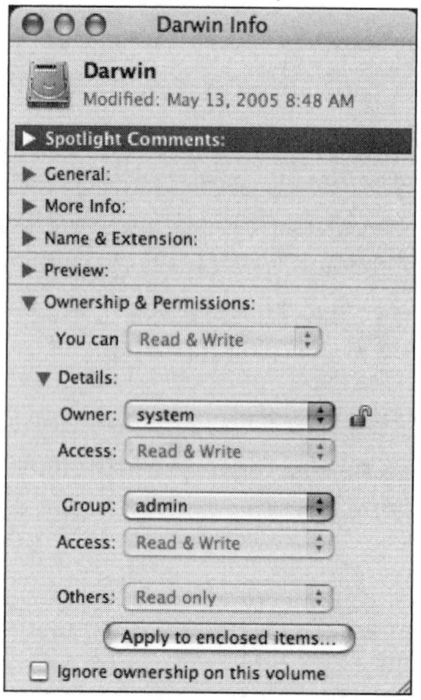

Figure 4.28

The "Apply to enclosed items" button and the "Ignore ownership on this volume" option, as seen for the Darwin volume.

Special options for folders and volumes. At the bottom of the Ownership & Permissions section for folders and volumes, you will see a button called "Apply to enclosed items." If you click this after making a change to the Access settings, it will apply the chosen Access settings to all items contained within the folder or volume. However, it will apply changes only to files that you have permission to modify (for example, files you own). In addition, it will *not* apply changes to user or group ownership.

Finally, for nonstartup volumes, the Ownership & Permissions section contains a check box labeled "Ignore ownership on this volume." This option is primarily necessary for accessing external third-party storage devices, letting you bypass permission security that might otherwise prevent you from accessing the contents of the volume. Although this may seem like a security weakness, it's a necessary one. Basically, the OS assumes you did not steal the drive; therefore, if you can connect it to your Mac, the owner of the drive must have given you permission (or the drive belongs to you). As discussed in Chapter 3, you should deselect this option when using the volume to create a bootable backup of a Mac OS X volume. In general, don't select this option unless you need to access files on the drive. The "Ignore ownership" option can be used on nonboot internal volumes, not just removable media, but doing so will increase the risk of unauthorized access to data on these volumes.

Bottom line. An understanding of Ownership & Permissions settings will help you solve all kinds of Mac OS X mysteries. If, for example, you try to move something from /System/Library, you'll typically find that you've copied rather than moved the item because (by default) you can't make changes within the System directory. Conversely, if you try to move something into the /System directory or drag something from the /System directory into the Trash, you may be prevented from doing so, instead getting an error message explaining that you can't do this because the item is owned by root. (You could also get a more general error message stating that you don't have sufficient privileges.) When you understand the implications of the Ownership & Permissions settings, this arrangement begins to make sense.

Note: Starting in Panther, you can bypass many of these prohibitions via a dialog that appears, asking you to *authenticate* (that is, enter your admin name and password). Once you've done this, you're permitted to carry out the action.

SEE: • Chapter 6, especially "Using the Finder's Authenticate dialog," for more on the Authenticate dialog.

      • "Unix: Modifying Permissions," in Chapter 10, for using Terminal to modify permissions.

Root Access

Mac OS X can make you feel like a guest on your own computer—and in a sense you are! But as an administrator, you can also give yourself *root access*. Doing so makes you the equivalent of the System user—meaning you can do pretty much anything you want (which is no doubt why root is sometimes referred to as the *superuser*).

To briefly review: Different levels of users have different levels of access. For example, an ordinary user can modify the files in the Library folder of his or her home directory but not any *other* Library folders. An admin user can modify the files in the Library folder at the root level of the drive but not in the /System/Library folder. The root user (or an admin user with root access) can modify anything.

In Tiger, many actions (such as deleting a System-owned file) that require root access are handled by the Finder's Authenticate function. For situations where this is not sufficient, you will need to separately obtain root access. There are several ways to do so, each with advantages and disadvantages. Three of them are covered here.

SEE: • "Using the Finder's Authenticate dialog," in Chapter 6.

Mac OS X utilities

The easiest and most user-friendly method of obtaining root access is via a third-party utility that offers temporary root access. In essence, you log in as you normally would and then launch the utility. Typically, when you attempt to make a change that requires root access, the utility will ask you for your password. If you give it (and you're an administrator), you'll be granted temporary root access and allowed to make the change. As soon as you quit the application, your root access will be denied. Several utilities use this method—including those used to change files' permissions settings (for example, FileXaminer and XRay), as well as many others (such as Cocktail and Retrospect).

The main disadvantage of this approach is that it only allows you to do precisely what the application is designed to do. Want an option that's not included? You either need to find another utility or give up. Still, for the Unix-phobic user or anyone who values ease of use in a familiar GUI interface, this method is the way to go.

Pseudo. This shareware utility, by Brian Hill (http://personalpages.tds.net/ ~brian_hill/pseudo.html), works a bit differently from those mentioned above: It lets you open just about any application as "root," even if that application doesn't directly support this. Simply drag an application to the Pseudo icon, and it launches with root access (you'll be prompted to enter your password). By letting you launch applications as root, Pseudo makes it possible for you to open and modify documents you couldn't otherwise—for example, allowing you to modify the contents of System Folder files (not something I recommend in most cases). Property List Editor (included as part of the Developer Tools software) is one utility that works well for this purpose (since it's designed to work with the preferences (.plist) files used by Mac OS X, some of which are owned by root).

Note: When an application opened via Pseudo is active, the Log Out command in the Apple menu will say Log Out System Administrator rather than Log Out {*your name*}, providing a quick way to determine if an application is running with root access. *Do not*, however, choose this Log Out System Administrator command: It won't work in this instance. Instead, either quit the application and then log out as you normally would, or simply make another application active first.

SEE: • "Modifying invisible Unix files from Mac OS X applications," in Chapter 6, for related information.

Terminal

Anything you can do with Unix in Mac OS X, you can do via the Terminal application—the command-line interface utility that accesses the Unix underpinnings. Likewise, any Unix action that requires root access can be performed in Terminal via the sudo command. To use it, type sudo followed by whatever command you want to use, all in the same line. This gives you root access for that one command. (Technically, you retain sudo status—and thus the ability to perform actions that require root access—until you have gone 5 minutes without using it. This makes it convenient to issue a number of commands in sequence as root without having to type sudo before each one.)

Note: You can duplicate Pseudo's effect, for many applications, by typing sudo -b followed by the path to the application that's in the .app package of the application. For example, to open TextEdit this way, type the following:

```
sudo -b /Applications/TextEdit.app/Contents/MacOS/TextEdit
```

SEE: • "Unix: The sudo and su Commands" and "Take Note: Opening Mac OS Applications from Terminal," in Chapter 10, for more details.

Logging in as root

If you want (or need) to ignore the preceding advice about keeping your root access to a minimum, you can log in as the root user. You remain in the familiar Aqua environment, except that you now have the power accorded to the root user. This means you can freely add or delete files to or from the System folder, for example, or access the home directory folders of all the users on the drive.

Before you can log in as a root user, however, you need to enable root user access. There are two main ways to do this.

Use Reset Password. This option is available when you start up from the Mac OS X Install CD/DVD. Follow these steps:

1. Start up your computer from the Mac OS X Install CD/DVD.

   To do so, insert the CD/DVD and double-click the Install Mac OS X icon. In the dialog that appears, click Restart.

2. When you see the Installer window, choose Reset Password from the Utilities menu.

3. In the dialog that appears, select the Mac OS X volume (assuming that more than one is listed) for which you want to set up a root password.

4. From the "Select a user" pop-up menu, choose "System Administrator (root)."

5. Enter the desired password in the text boxes. Also enter a password hint, if you wish.

6. Click Save.

7. Choose Quit Installer from the Installer menu. In the dialog that appears, click Restart (or click Startup Disk, if you first want to confirm that the Mac will boot from the desired volume).

Use NetInfo Manager. You'll find this application in the Utilities folder on your hard drive. Launch it and then follow these steps:

1. From the Security menu, choose Authenticate.

2. In the dialog that opens, enter your administrator password at the prompt.

3. From the Security menu, choose Enable Root User.

   If you're using this method for the first time, you will get a message stating that the password field for the root user is blank. You will be asked to set a password; do so.

From this same menu, you will later be able to change the root password (via the Change Root Password command) or disable root access (via the Disable Root User command). (Note: You can also change the root password via Terminal by using the passwd command, as described in "Take Note: Forgot Your Password?" in Chapter 5.)

At one time, I used the same password for root as I did for my own admin account—even though this practice entails a slight security risk. It keeps things simple and is generally all the protection most people need in home and small-office environments. However, I now use separate passwords. This helps me know for sure if I am logging in as root or as admin. And if you expect more than one person to log in as root, you should definitely use a unique password.

Note: Even if you never intend to log in as the root user and do not intend to enable the root user, you should still create a password here. This will prevent another admin user from creating a root password and thus obtaining root access, possibly without your authorization to do so.

Figure 4.29

NetInfo Manager's Security menu.

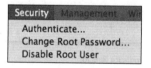

SEE: • "Take Note: Securing Mac OS X," in Chapter 10, for related information.

Log in. After you've enabled the root account (using either of the previously outlined methods), you can log in as root. To do so, follow these steps:

1. From the Apple menu choose Log Out to log out.

   Note: If Fast User Switching has been enabled, you can alternatively choose Login Window from the Fast User Switching menu in the upper right corner of the screen.

   Even after you've logged in as root, the System Administrator (root) user does not appear in this menu. This means that if you log in as System Administrator (root) and then switch to another user, you will have to return to the Login window to return to the System Administrator account.

Note: I've had problems logging in as the root user via Fast User Switching. In particular, when I've tried to do so while another user was also logged in, the Desktop typically appeared but the Finder and the Dock never launched. The only thing to do at this point is restart the Mac. To avoid this problem, log all other users out before you attempt to log in as the root user.

2. What you see will depend upon whether you chose "Name and password" or "List of Users" as the "Display Login Window as" setting (in the Login Options pane of the Accounts System Preferences pane).

   If you chose "Name and password," simply enter root as the user name and the root password in the respective text fields.

   If you chose List of Users, an Others option should appear at the bottom of the list. Click it. Then enter root and the selected password in the text fields that appear.

3. Click the Log In button.

Now you're logged in as the root user. Note that any items on your usual Desktop, or additions you've made to your Dock, will not be visible: The Mac now considers you to be a different user—the root user—so you use the settings for that account.

As root user, you have the keys to the kingdom. Use them wisely! Remember: You want to log in as root only as a last resort. Whenever possible, you should use a more temporary method of gaining root access (such as those described previously) to minimize the chance of making a change you end up regretting. As soon as you've completed the task at hand, log out of the root user account.

Note: If you expect to log in as root regularly, for whatever reason, you may wish to uncheck the "Automatically log in as" box in the Login Options section. This will make it quicker to log in as the root user on initial startup because the Login window will appear by default.

"Other" does not appear in the Login window. As of this writing, there is a bug in Mac OS X that occasionally prevents the Other option from appearing in the List of Users in the Login window, even though you have enabled the root user. If this happens, do one or more of the following:

• Press Option-Return and then click a name. The blank Name and Password fields should now appear. If this does not work, try Shift-Option-Return. Once the fields appear, enter the root name and password as described above.

• To address the problem permanently, go to NetInfo Manager. You will probably find that the Enable Root User command is active, even though you previously enabled the root user. Further, if you choose the command, it will not work. That is, you cannot get it to toggle to Disable Root User. If this happens, quit NetInfo Manager and restart your Mac. Now return to NetInfo Manager. You should be prompted to create a new root user password, as if you had not done so before. After doing this, everything should work as expected; the Other option should now appear in the Login window.

- Apple has stated that enabling NetInfo in the Directory Access application fixes this problem, although doing so can lead to a longer startup time. I have not found this to work on my Mac. But if nothing else has worked, give it a try.

SEE: • **Coverage of the Accounts System Preferences pane in Chapter 2, for more details.**

• **Chapter 5, especially "Login," "Alternative Mac OS X Startup Paths," and "Login crashes and failures," for more on logging in.**

• **Chapter 10 for more information on Unix and Terminal.**

NetInfo and NetInfo Manager

NetInfo Manager is a Mac OS X utility located in the Utilities folder. It provides access to the NetInfo database, allowing you to view and even modify the data that the database contains. The NetInfo database is a database for network and administrative data in Mac OS X, keeping track of user accounts, printers, servers, and access.

Apple states: "NetInfo is the directory service database that is built into computers running Mac OS X and Mac OS X Server. NetInfo facilitates the management of administrative information used by Mac OS X computers. For example, NetInfo lets you centralize information about users, printers, servers, and other network devices so that all Mac OS X computers on your network, or only some of them, have access to it. It helps you set up and manage home directories for Mac OS X users on multiple, integrated Mac OS X Servers. And it simplifies the day-to-day management of administrative information by letting you update information that's used across the network in one central place. Every Mac OS X computer has a local directory domain called NetInfo. Only local applications and system software can access administrative data for this local domain. It is the first domain consulted when a user logs in or performs some other operation that requires data stored in a directory domain."

Every time you log in to your account or create a new user account, Mac OS X accesses the NetInfo database (for example, to confirm the login password or to store the new account information).

As discussed earlier in this chapter, NetInfo Manager is also where you go to enable root user access. In fact, apart from this, most Mac OS X users will rarely need to deal with the NetInfo database directly. You're more likely to use the NetInfo database if you use Mac OS X Server—for example, creating new group categories here.

However, there are occasions when accessing and even modifying the data here can be of troubleshooting value. For example, you can easily check a user's ID number (UID) from here by selecting /users/{*name of user*} from the navigation columns and checking the value for the "uid" property that appears in the bottom part of the window.

You can use NetInfo Manager to move your entire home directory to a different volume, as covered in "Technically Speaking: Moving Your Home Directory to a Separate Partition," in Chapter 3. You can also change the short name of your account in NetInfo Manager. As noted in "Take Note: Accounts Problems" in Chapter 2 and again in Chapter 5, this is something you cannot do in the Accounts System Preferences pane and should not try to do by renaming the account in the Finder—doing so could result in an inability to log in to your account the next time you try!

You can even change passwords in NetInfo Manager, including getting an account to use the newer, more secure *shadowhash* method of password encryption, which is used starting in Panther. However, for accounts upgraded from Jaguar, the older encryption is maintained. Among other things, this difference can lead to problems if you are asked for a password when working with the CUPS printing Web interface (as covered more in Chapter 7).

Figure 4.30

NetInfo Manager, with the listing shown for me (user = landau).

NetInfo and Unix. Mac OS X users can access and modify the NetInfo database via either NetInfo Manager or ni commands in Terminal. For example, the general-purpose utility nicl mimics many of NetInfo Manager's functions; the niload command loads information from standard input (such as a file) into a given NetInfo domain; the nidump command does the reverse. In Terminal, type man and the name of the command for more details.

NetInfo itself, however, stems from Mac OS X's NextStep heritage, *not* its Unix one. In a pure Unix system, much of what is handled by the NetInfo database would be handled by something called lookupd—which also exists in Mac OS X and works with NetInfo Manager. Actually, lookupd acts as a superset of NetInfo, getting information from other sources (such as a DNS server). It is beyond the scope of this book to go into much detail about this feature.

The NetInfo database is stored in the Unix directory /var/db/netinfo. The BSD Unix configuration (database) files accessed via lookupd are located in Unix's /etc directory.

Starting with Jaguar, Apple began to move away from NetInfo, relying instead on other database systems, such as the BSD files. In Tiger, the database is used only within a local network. Even locally, it is sometimes possible to bypass NetInfo and use the files in the /etc directory instead. If you're on a server, the data accessed by the server is either the BSD configuration files or other (not NetInfo) databases as determined by the setup in the Directory Access utility. In fact, Apple has already started to refer to NetInfo as Mac OS X's "legacy" database.

SEE: • "Technically Speaking: Restoring and Replacing NetInfo and Directory Access Data," later in this chapter, for more details.

• "Directory Access," later in this chapter, for more on this utility.

TAKE NOTE ▶ NetInfo Manager: Mac OS X Server vs. Mac OS X Client

As mentioned previously, Mac OS X Server is basically the same operating system as the Mac OS X you use on your own computer—with two major differences: First, the Server version of Mac OS X comes with server-specific administrative tools (such as NetBoot, Apple File Services, Macintosh Manager, and Web Objects) that aren't typically required in a desktop OS. Second, Mac OS X client can run both Carbon and Classic applications, whereas Mac OS X Server runs only Mac OS X–native applications. Thus, even the desktop version of Mac OS X can function as an adequate server in many situations. In fact, the two versions of Mac OS X use many of the same administrative databases and tools. One of these tools is the NetInfo database.

Although most Mac OS X client users will rarely deal with the NetInfo database directly, administrators of the Mac OS X client system will find it helpful to understand what NetInfo is and how to use it to their advantage. For information beyond what I cover in the main text here, Apple offers a document titled "Understanding and Using NetInfo" (http://docs.info.apple.com/article.html?artnum=106416).

TECHNICALLY SPEAKING ▶ Restoring and Replacing NetInfo and Directory Access Data

Restoring NetInfo from automatic backup. The NetInfo database file is located at /var/db/netinfo/local.nidb. A backup copy is maintained at /var/backups/local.nidump. You need root access to enter these directories and access these files.

The backup copy is updated each time Mac OS X's daily Unix maintenance script is run (at 3:15 a.m., assuming your computer is turned on at that time). However, it's a good idea to maintain an additional current copy of the database on another volume. This way, you can restore it if your current database is corrupted or you mistakenly make changes to it (especially critical if the automatic backup has not been recently updated or it, too, has become corrupt).

As a last resort, you can replace a corrupt version with the default version that came with Mac OS X; however, you will lose all the changes that were made to the database as a result. Even so, because a corrupt database can prevent Mac OS X from starting up, replacing one with a default version can be preferable to erasing your drive and reinstalling Mac OS X.

The details of how to back up and restore a NetInfo database are covered in the Apple Knowledge Base at http://docs.info.apple.com/article.html?artnum=107210. Similar advice is given on other Web sites, such as NetInfo Recovery Techniques (www.afp548.com/Articles/system/netinfobackup.html). The following provides an overview of what you need to do to restore a corrupt database from the automatic backup file:

1. Start in single-user mode (as described in Chapter 5). Then type the following two commands:

   ```
   /sbin/mount -uw
   /sbin/fsck -yf
   ```

   Note: The first line is especially important if journaling has been turned off (another topic described in Chapter 5).

2. Rename the current local NetInfo database and replace it with the archived copy, using the following two commands:

   ```
   mv /var/db/netinfo/local.nidb /var/db/netinfo/local.nidb.bad
   /usr/libexec/create_nidb
   ```

   Note: These commands replace the current copy of the NetInfo database with the archive created by the daily Unix maintenance script; to replace it with a backup copy you created manually, type mv {*name of backup*} local.nidb and then restart your Mac. You can then skip Steps 3 and 4.

3. Start the network and the NetInfo system, and load the local database with the backup data, using the following command:

   ```
   /usr/bin/niload -d -r -t / localhost/local < /var/backups/local.nidump
   ```

   Note that the above command is applicable to only Mac OS X 10.4; for earlier versions of Mac OS X, see the Apple Knowledge Base article referenced above.

continues on next page

TECHNICALLY SPEAKING ▶ **Restoring and Replacing NetInfo and Directory Access Data** *continued*

4. Restart the computer by typing the following:

```
reboot
```

If you don't have a good backup or if you just want to start over, you can restore from defaults. To do this, skip Step 3 and instead remove the AppleSetupDone file by typing the following:

```
rm /var/db/.AppleSetupDone
```

This sets your computer back to a default NetInfo configuration (the way it was when you first installed Mac OS X). When the computer finishes starting up, Setup Assistant will appear.

Setting Directory Access back to defaults. The Directory Service settings are stored in a folder called DirectoryService, located in /Library/Preferences. If files in this folder are corrupted, they may prevent your Mac from starting up, especially if Mac OS X is set to access an LDAP server at startup. The solution is to set the Directory Access configurations back to their default values:

1. After restarting in single-user mode, type

```
/sbin/fsck -yf
```

followed by

```
/sbin/mount -uw
```

2. Then type (all in one line):

```
mv /Library/Preferences/DirectoryService /Library/Preferences/DirectoryService.old
```

3. Finally, type

```
reboot
```

On a related note, various Apple Knowledge Base documents provide solutions to other problems with starting up or logging in caused by incorrect Directory Service settings. For example, see http://docs.info.apple.com/article.html?artnum=107536 for coverage of an LDAP issue.

Directory Access

Directory Access (called Directory Setup prior to Mac OS X 10.2), located in the Utilities folder, is not something you're likely to use if you're not part of a larger network maintained by a central server or servers. Directory Access settings determine what directory services your computer checks at startup, as well as your ability to access them.

As Apple states: "When the user logs in to a Mac OS X computer, Open Directory (Apple's open-source, standards-based directory system) searches the computer's NetInfo database for the user's record. If NetInfo contains the user's record (and the user typed the correct password), the login process proceeds, giving the user access to the computer. This is the default behavior, but it can be changed by specifying an alternate search path in the Directory Access application."

In other words, if you are not connected to a central server, you can usually ignore this application altogether. If you are connected to a server, you will typically follow the specific instructions given to you by the network administrator—I would not randomly experiment with the options here. For this reason, I simply provide some general background in this section.

As noted in the previous section, Apple is moving away from its use of the NetInfo database. As this process continues with each upgrade of the OS, the importance of the Directory Access application increases. For additional background, choose Directory Access Help from the application's Help menu.

Directory Access includes three main tabs: Services, Authentication, and Contacts. Each opens a different pane.

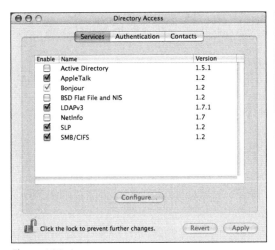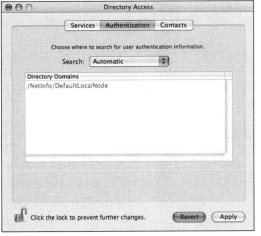

Figure 4.31

The Directory Access application: left, *Services;* right, *Authentication.*

Services. There are two categories of services listed here: (1) those that contain the database of user and administrative information that Mac OS X might use to check such things as passwords and group memberships; and (2) the types of services Mac OS X can discover on a network. This latter category accounts for the inclusion of AppleTalk, for example. Check or uncheck a service's check box to enable or disable access to the service.

For nonlocal networks, instead of using the local NetInfo database for storing data, Mac OS X uses and accesses the remote directories for the services listed in this pane. These directories are located on the respective servers, not on your client machine.

SEE: • **Chapters 7 and 8 for more on file and print services such as AppleTalk and SMB.**

Note: Disabling a service only affects whether or not Mac OS X attempts to access its directory automatically (for example, at startup). If you know the specific address of a server, you can still connect to it regardless of whether the directory service for that type of server is on or off. For example, you can do this via the Connect command in the Server menu of Directory Access.

In some cases, the Configure button for a service is enabled when you select a specific service. Clicking this allows you to enter specific settings for the directory server to which you want to connect.

Here are a few points of interest about some of the services listed:

• **NetInfo.** This is the local directory service used by Mac OS X. It's what you access when you open NetInfo Manager.

  If this box is checked, Directory Access will check for additional NetInfo databases on other Macs and servers in a larger network. You can uncheck this box and still use the NetInfo database on your local Mac. (In fact, the box is unchecked by default for this very reason.)

  From the Configure options, you can select how your Mac searches for a NetInfo database on a network. If no such databases exist on the network, don't select any options here: Doing so will only slow startup for your Mac as it searches for databases it will never find.

• **BSD Flat File and NIS.** This refers to the files in the Unix directories (/etc) that Unix uses in place of NetInfo on non-Mac Unix systems. Again, you need to enable this option only to access nonlocal databases.

  However, if you click the Configure button, you will see the following message: "The node /BSD/local must be added to the Authentication and/or Contacts tabs for the information in /etc /to be used." This means that if you want your local system to check for password and contact information in the BSD files on your own drive (instead of NetInfo), you need to add the relevant information in Authentication and Contacts (as described in the next section).

• **LDAPv3.** Mac OS X Server now uses *LDAP* (*Light Directory Access Protocol*), an open standard that can be used by Macintosh, Windows, and Unix systems. If you logged in to a Mac running Mac OS X Server, you would likely be accessing its LDAP database instead of the NetInfo database on your drive.

  Note: Some applications (such as Mail and Address Book) may connect directly to an LDAP directory. In this case, you configure LDAP settings in the preferences window of the application rather than through Directory Access.

- **SMB/CIFS.** This is a protocol used by Windows (and some Unix) machines for file sharing and printing. This is one place where a Mac user, even though not logged in to a server, might want to use Directory Access. You can use it to change the workgroup selected for SMB on a network. As stated by Apple: "A workgroup is to Windows File Sharing what an AppleTalk zone is to AppleTalk. It is a way network administrators can group related computers into smaller subgroups with meaningful names." The default workgroup for SMB is WORKGROUP. To change this:

    1. Select SMB/CIFS in the Services pane of Directory Access and click the Configure button.

    2. Select a new Workgroup name (and WINS Server, if needed) in the dialog that drops down.

    3. Click the Apply button. Wait a few minutes for the change to take effect.

Authentication and Contacts. These sections of Directory Access designate where your Mac searches for password (authentication) and contact information. If the list contains more than one node, the Mac searches in the order in which the nodes are listed.

The Search pop-up menu offers three choices: Automatic, Local Directory, and Custom Path.

All three choices start by checking the local directory, typically the local NetInfo database (/NetInfo/DefaultLocalNode). This means that even if you're connected to a server and a different database is accessed, your Mac is still set by default to check your local NetInfo database at login to see if your password is correct. Without this setup, you would not be able to log in to your Mac when not connected to the server.

Automatic (the default choice) additionally checks certain LDAP directories if available. If you choose Custom Path, you can create your own list of directories to check. For example, to add the /BSD/local option for authentication, as noted in the previous section, you would do the following:

1. Click the Authentication button.

2. From the Search pop-up menu, choose Custom Path.

3. Click the Add button; /BSD/local should appear as an available directory.

4. Click the Add button.

5. If you want /BSD/local to be searched before /NetInfo local, drag that node to the top of the list.

6. Click the Apply button.

Note: Unless you're directly accessing the more advanced features of Unix, it's unlikely that you would want or need to make this change.

SEE: • "Technically Speaking: Restoring and Replacing NetInfo and Directory Access Data," earlier in this chapter, for related information.

• Chapter 9, for more on file sharing.

Preferences Files

Preferences files refer primarily to those files that store the customized changes you can make to an application, most commonly through an application's preferences window. These preferences files are separate from the preference panes accessed via the System Preferences application. Throughout this book, I refer to ways you can use these files for troubleshooting. The following provides an overview of what these files are, where they're located, and how they work.

Format

The most common preferences files in Mac OS X are files that end in .plist (such as com.apple.finder.plist). The .plist extension stands for *property list*. All preferences files that end in .plist are thus also property list files. The term *preferences file* refers to the function of the file, whereas *property list file* refers to the format of the file. Thus, there are files that also end in .plist that are not preferences files (that is, they serve a function other than modifying preferences of an application). These files are also briefly noted in the following sections.

Most .plist files in Tiger are written in binary format. Prior to Tiger, these same files were written in XML (*Extensible Markup Language*) format, which is still supported by Tiger. The rationale for the switch is that binary formatted files are generally smaller and thus load faster.

Note: XML is essentially a superset of the HTML used for most Web pages. In fact, some property list files will have an .xml extension rather than .plist. In either case, the Kind description of the file (as viewed in the Get Info window) will be XML Property List File. For those familiar with XML, the document type declaration (.dtd) file for property lists is PropertyList.dtd and is located in /System/Library/DTDs.

SEE: • The section on the `plutil` command in "Running Mac OS X software from Terminal," in Chapter 10, for related information.

Why the com notation? You'll notice that most .plist files begin with the abbreviation *com*. This is Apple's way of making sure that each application has a unique preferences file. Suppose two developers created applications called SuperText, and you had both of them on your drive. If both .plist files were named supertext.plist, how would the applications tell them apart? To deal with this problem, Apple has requested that developers format preference files with their Web sites' domain-name information—formatted in reverse—followed by the application name. Because no two domain names are identical, this setup ensures that each file will have a different name. For example, Apple's Web site is http://www.apple.com, which converts for .plist purposes to com.apple. A .plist file for Apple's Finder is thus com.apple.finder.plist.

Locations

When it comes time to locate a preferences file, here's where to look:

- **~/Library/Preferences.** Most preferences files are located in the ~/Library/Preferences directory (in each user's home directory). The files here are specific to each user. This is why when different users log in, they can have different preferences settings.

  Most files in this folder are standard Mac OS X preferences files ending in .plist. The loginwindow.plist file, for example, contains the list of items that you selected in your Login Items list in the Account System Preferences pane. You may also find Mac OS 9–type preferences files and folders in this folder, however. And a few files don't fit into either category.

- **~/Library/Preferences/ByHost.** A few preferences files are likely to be tucked into the ByHost folder within the Preferences folder. In this folder, all filenames are structured as follows: {*com name*}.{*Ethernet address*}.plist. The Ethernet address is the MAC address (described more in Chapter 8) that you find in the Network System Preferences pane. For example, a .plist file for Software Update may look like this: com.apple.SoftwareUpdate.00806466c832.plist. These ByHost files define preferences that are specific to a particular host machine (for example, the one with the listed MAC address).

  Files here could be used for those cases where your machine is part of a network and an application on your machine is run from another machine. In such cases, the preferences in this folder would be ignored.

  More generally, if you copy your Mac OS X software from one machine to another, preferences here with the Mac address of the source machine would be ignored on the destination machine. They should thus be deleted.

- **/Library/Preferences.** Several preferences files are stored in the Preferences folder of the /Library directory. Because these files can be accessed by all local users, they're typically ones that, if they can be changed at all, are restricted so that only administrators can change them (such as preferences files corresponding to System Preferences panes that have the "Click the lock to prevent further changes" option).

  SEE: • Chapter 8 for details on the SystemConfiguration folder files and Chapter 9 for more information on the com.apple.AppleFileServer.plist file located in /Library/Preferences.

- **/System/Library folder.** Occasionally, system-level preferences files—most of which are created by Mac OS X—can be found in locations scattered throughout the /System/Library folder. The SystemVersion.plist file in the CoreServices subfolder, as noted in Chapter 3, is one example.

- **Unix directories.** There are files that use the property list format and are located in the invisible Unix directories on your drive. Go to the /etc/mach_init.d folder for several examples (such as DirectoryService.plist). You will rarely need to access these files.

Note: Assorted other files are also included in these Unix folders, such as config files (especially in the /etc directory) that act like preferences files for Unix software. This is not the place to explore config files in any detail. I do cover some specific examples in "Modifying invisible Unix files from Mac OS X applications," in Chapter 6.

Figure 4.32

A partial view of the Preferences folder in my home directory.

Content

Preferences files contain "nonessential" information. By this, I mean the application should still be able to launch even if its preferences file is deleted; it simply creates a new default .plist file. Likewise, deleting a .plist file shouldn't delete important user data—other than a user's personal settings or perhaps a registration code. Initial default preferences are obtained from data stored within the application itself (most commonly in a file called defaults.plist, located in the Resources folder of the application package).

Each .plist file is primarily a list of items, called *keys* or *properties*, that can have different values. By changing the value of a key, you modify a given preference.

Viewing the content. Given that .plist stands for *property list*, it should come as no surprise that you can open and edit .plist files in an application called Property List Editor. This application is located in the /Developer/Applications/Utilities folder (if you installed Developer Tools). Feel free to move it to a more convenient location.

Prior to Tiger, as stated above, the default format for .plist files was XML. Therefore, these files could be opened in any text editor (such as TextEdit or BBEdit) in addition to specialized applications such as Property List Editor. However, the binary formatted .plist files, as used in Tiger (such as for the ones located in ~/Library/Preferences), are not suitable for viewing and editing in standard text editors. If you try, the file will open but the text will include odd, indecipherable characters.

Fortunately, these files still appear correctly when opened in Property List Editor. In addition, Property List Editor provides a graphical interface for the file's contents that makes it easier to read and modify the file (as well as preventing you from making XML syntax errors). Most third-party .plist editing utilities, such as Plist Edit Pro (http://homepage.mac.com/bwebster/plisteditpro.html), have been updated to open binary .plist files correctly as well. Still, in this book, I use Property List Editor in almost all discussions of viewing and manipulating .plist files.

If you prefer to have your .plist files in the old XML text-based format, you can do so. Just open a .plist file in Property List Editor, select the Save As command, and save the file as an XML Property List File (via the File Format pop-up menu). The XML file can subsequently be opened by any text editor. It will still function correctly if stored in a Preferences folder, although that may result in a slight performance decline in the application—for most applications, so slight as to be imperceptible.

As another alternative, as covered later in the chapter in "Terminal's defaults command," you can view and edit the contents of a .plist file via the defaults command in Terminal.

SEE: • The section on the plutil command in "Running Mac OS X software from Terminal," in Chapter 10, for related information.

Hidden properties. Applications sometimes include "hidden" preferences settings—by this I mean settings for which there's no user interface (such as an option in the application's preferences) to modify the setting. In most cases, such hidden properties are listed in the application's .plist file. Thus, the primary (and sometimes only) way to modify the setting is by changing the value in the .plist file—typically by using Property List Editor. Occasionally, a third-party developer will create a utility that allows you to make changes to specific "hidden" items; the utilities TinkerTool and Cocktail are examples. However, the value of Property List Editor is that it allows you to make any changes, not just those the third-party utility permits.

In some cases, a property is so hidden that it doesn't even show up in the .plist file. Such a property simply remains set to its default value; the only way to modify its value would be to first add it to the .plist file. But how can you add a property when you don't even know it exists? Typically, you find out about such properties when the news gets spread via Macintosh Web sites (such as Mac OS X Hints [www.macosxhints.com])—or by reading a book like this one. In addition, Apple occasionally provides information about such properties in its Knowledge Base articles or in documents on its Developer Connection site.

SEE: • "Technically Speaking: Completely Hidden Properties: Changing the Finder," later in this chapter, for an example of a completely hidden property.

Properties that do not appear in .plist files until changed from their default values. In some cases, a preference setting appears in an application's user interface but the property for that setting does not appear in its .plist file until the setting has been modified from its default value (typically by changing a setting in the relevant application's preferences dialog). In this case, when you open the .plist file prior to changing the default setting, the property will not appear. Should you ever change the preferences value from its default, the property will automatically be added to the .plist file. Should you later change the setting back to the default value, the added property typically remains in the .plist file.

Note: The other way to get such properties to appear in a .plist file is to add them to the file directly—typically via Property List Editor (as described later in the chapter).

Note: In some cases, the .plist file itself is not created until after you launch the relevant application for the first time and change at least one default setting.

Troubleshooting: Changes in application not saved to .plist file.
Whenever you make a change to a preferences setting from an application's preferences options, the corresponding .plist file should get updated. However, occasionally problems occur. For example, several Microsoft applications store their Internet-related preferences in the same file—com.apple.internetconfig.plist—which can cause a glitch where changes you make don't get saved. For example, suppose you have Internet Explorer and Entourage open at the same time, and you make a change to Internet Explorer's preferences—say to its "auto-fill" settings. Now quit Internet Explorer and then Entourage, and then relaunch Internet Explorer: Your changes have vanished! What appears to have happened is that when you quit Entourage, it "updated" the preferences data and overwrote the change you made via Internet Explorer. Thus, if you need to change settings that will get written to com.apple.internetconfig.plist, make sure to quit all applications other than the one in which you plan to make the change.

Modifying a .plist file

In most cases, you can modify the contents of a preferences (.plist) file without working with the .plist file directly. To do so, select the Preferences (or similar) command of the application that uses the file. Any changes to preferences settings you make in the application will modify the application's .plist file. However, you can also make the same change by editing the application's .plist file directly in Property List Editor. This conversely changes the settings as viewed from the application's Preferences command. If a property is hidden (as described above), you will need to use Property List Editor (or a third-party alternative) to make changes.

The following are two examples of how this all works.

Editing com.apple.Terminal.plist. This example shows how to use Property List Editor to edit a value that also could have been changed from the application's preferences settings.

1. In the ~/Library/Preferences folder, double-click the com.apple.Terminal.plist file.

2. If you're asked what application you want to open this document with, choose Property List Editor. (If Property List Editor is installed, the document will most likely open in it directly.)

3. Click the disclosure triangle next to the word *Root* to display the list of items/keys.

   If you've launched Terminal only once and made no preferences changes, you will find a very limited list of properties in this .plist file. In my case, I found just two: FirstRun and StartupFile. If this is the case for you, close the .plist file and launch Terminal. From the File menu, select Show Info (Command-I) to open the Terminal Inspector. In the Terminal Inspector window, click the Use Settings as Defaults button. This command adds all of the current settings as properties to the .plist file. Now reopen com.apple.Terminal.plist. You will find several dozen properties listed (I found 58). This is one example of how properties get added to the .plist file as a function of what you do in the application itself.

4. Scroll down to the TerminalOpaqueness item. Note its value. Its initial default value is 1.00000 (which means the Terminal window is completely opaque).

5. Close the .plist document.

6. Launch Terminal.

7. Open the Terminal Inspector (via Command-I). Select Color from the pop-up menu at the top of the window.

8. Move the Transparency slider all the way to the right. The Terminal window is now completely transparent.

9. Click the Use Settings as Defaults button.

10. Quit Terminal and reopen the com.apple.Terminal.plist file. Return to the TerminalOpaqueness item. Its value should now be changed, most likely to 0.050000.

As you can see, changing an application setting modified the value of a property in its .plist file. You could conversely change a setting by modifying its value in the .plist file itself. For example:

1. In the com.apple.Terminal.plist file, as opened in Property List Editor, type in a new value for TerminalOpaqueness, such as 0.600000. (You must first double-click the value to make it editable.)

2. Save the change and quit Property List Editor.

3. Launch Terminal and return to the Color item in the Terminal Inspector. The Transparency slider should now have moved to near the middle.

As you can see, you changed the transparency level without launching Terminal.

Editing com.apple.finder.plist. The following demonstrates how to use Property List Editor to modify an application's hidden .plist item (that is, a setting not accessible from the application's preferences). In this case, you will change the Finder's Preferences so that normally invisible files are visible in the Finder.

1. Open the com.apple.finder.plist file, located in ~/Library/Preferences, in Property List Editor.

2. Click the disclosure triangle next to the word *Root* to reveal the list of keys.

3. Scroll down to find the property called AppleShowAllFiles.

It will either have a Class of String and a Value of 0 or a Class of Boolean and a Value of No. The advantage of the Boolean class is that the Value choices appear in a pop-up menu and are thus easier to figure out.

If this property is not present, you will need to add it (as covered in "Adding and deleting keys in Property List Editor," later in this chapter.)

4. If the item's value is No, click the pop-up menu and change the value to Yes. If the value is 0, double-click the value and change the 0 to a 1.

5. Save and close the .plist file.

6. If invisible files are not yet visible, choose Force Quit from the Apple menu, select Finder from the list of applications, and click Relaunch.

You could alternatively use a utility such as TinkerTool to make invisible files visible—you would use the command "Show hidden and system files." All TinkerTool does is provide a user interface to make the same change you just made in Property List Editor.

Note: Other items in com.apple.finder.plist are directly linked to Finder Preferences settings. For example, the WarnOnEmptyTrash key is what gets changed via the setting in the Advanced section of the Finder's Preferences. Note, however, that this key may not be included in the .plist file if you haven't changed the setting from its default selection.

Warning: Bug in Property List Editor. Apple has acknowledged a bug in Property List Editor, present in Panther (I am not certain if it has been fixed in Tiger), that may prevent a property from appearing in an opened .plist file. If you suspect that a property is missing from a file, you can check for this bug by saving the file in XML format and opening the file in TextEdit instead. The property, if present, should appear in TextEdit even if it does not appear in Property List Editor.

SEE: • "Take Note: The Location of Desktop Folders" and "Take Note: The Locations of Trash Folders," earlier in this chapter, for more information on invisible files.

• "Invisible Files: Making Invisible Files Visible (and Vice Versa)," in Chapter 6.

• "Modifying or deleting the .GlobalPreferences.plist files," in Chapter 6.

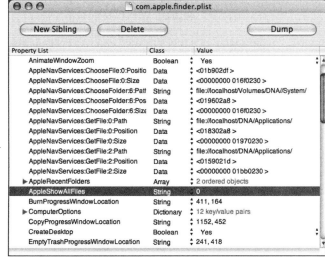

Figure 4.33

Property List Editor showing the contents of the com.apple.Terminal. plist file, top, and the contents of the com.apple.finder. plist file, bottom.

TECHNICALLY SPEAKING ▶ Completely Hidden Properties: Changing the Finder

The com.apple.loginwindow.plist contains settings that affect what happens when you log in. However, there is at least one property that does not appear in this file by default. This property is the one you use if you want to replace the Finder as the application that launches at login. To modify this property from its default setting, you will need to create a new key. Although most users will never have any reason to do this, you could use it to replace the Finder with a third-party Finder alternative (for example, PathFinder, by Cocoatech; www.cocoatech.com/pf.php) or with Terminal (if you're a Unix geek and prefer not to deal with the Aqua interface).

1. In ~/Library/Preferences, open the com.apple.loginwindow.plist file.
2. Click the Root line and then click the New Child button.
3. In the Property List column, locate the newly created child and name it *Finder*.
4. In the Value column, enter the path of the application that you wish to substitute for the Finder. It should be sufficient to enter just the path to the application package (such as /Applications/Utilities/Terminal.app, to substitute Terminal for the Finder). However, if that does not work, enter instead the path to the executable process within the package (typically located in the Contents/MacOS folder inside the package file). Thus, for the Terminal application, you would enter /Applications/Utilities/Terminal.app/Contents/MacOS/Terminal. If you're unsure how a path should appear, launch Terminal and drag the desired icon to the Terminal window; its path will appear. You can then copy it and paste it into Property List Editor.

The next time you log in, the selected application will launch instead of the Finder. Even though the Finder won't load at login now, you can still launch it manually by clicking its icon in the Dock.

Troubleshooting: If Property List Editor cannot save changes. In some cases, you may be able to open a .plist file in Property List Editor but not be able to save changes because you have insufficient permissions. This situation is most likely to occur with .plist files that are not in your home directory. If you want to modify one of these files, all you need to do is open Property List Editor with root access, using Pseudo (as explained in "Mac OS X utilities," earlier in this chapter).

As a rule, avoid making changes in such cases, especially if the file is somewhere in the System folder. Changing files in this folder is always risky: You may do more harm than good, perhaps even rendering your system unbootable. In any case, changes you make here are likely to get wiped out the next time you update the OS (sometimes even the next time you restart).

Note: I once had a .plist file for which changes could not be saved, even though permissions were set correctly. Eventually, I made a copy of the file in the Finder and was able to make changes to the copy. However, I still couldn't discover any differences between the two files that would account for the inability to save the original, so I just dumped the original, made the changes to the copy, and substituted it for the original file.

SEE • Chapter 6, for more on problems saving files.

Adding and deleting keys in Property List Editor. To add a new key to a .plist file, click the New Sibling button (it's called New Child if you first select the Root item). You can now name the property and assign its value. To delete an existing property, select it and click the Delete button.

SEE: • "Technically Speaking: Completely Hidden Properties: Changing the Finder," above, for an example of adding a key.

Terminal's defaults command. You can use the `defaults` command, in Terminal, to access and modify the same data that Property List Editor does. This command also provides access to parameters that may not be listed in .plist files, such as the position of a window. Users comfortable with Unix may prefer this alternative. For details on how to use this command, type `man defaults` (or `defaults usage`).

For example, to view the value for AppleShowAllFiles in the Finder, you would type the following:

```
defaults read com.apple.Finder AppleShowAllFiles
```

Note that *.plist* is omitted from the name of the file.

As a second example, to launch Terminal at login rather than the Finder (as described in "Technically Speaking: Completely Hidden Properties: Changing the Finder"), type the following (on one line):

```
defaults write com.apple.loginwindow Finder
/Applications/Utilities/Terminal.app
```

To modify files that you do not have permission to do so, use `sudo` (such as: `sudo defaults write...`).

Property list files: More locations

Files that have a .plist (or sometimes an .xml) extension show up in other standard locations beyond those already described. These files located elsewhere are typically not meant to be edited by the end user. Here are two examples.

Info.plist and other package .plist files. All application packages contain at least one essential .plist file: Info.plist. This file is located within the Contents folder inside the application package, and it contains, at minimum, the following information:

- Name of application (displayed by the Finder)
- Bundle Package Type (for example, APPL is the type for applications)
- Version string
- Descriptive information (displayed by the Finder)
- Documents handled by this application, including their names, icons, role, types, and extensions
- URLs handled by this application, including names, icons, and schemes

If the Info.plist information is specific to Mac OS X or Classic, the OS name will be embedded in the filename—for example, Info-Macos.plist or Info-MacosClassic.plist. A related version.plist file contains summary information about the name and version number of the application. An InfoPlist.strings file (located in Contents/Resources/*language*.lproj) contains information used by Info.plist that has been localized for different languages. The Finder uses these files to determine how it interacts with the application, such as what documents go with what applications.

Installer package files also typically contain these .plist items.

StartupParameters.plist. Startup items (which are described in more detail in Chapter 5) include a StartupParameters.plist file, which provides information about when, in the sequence of loading startup items, a given item should load.

SEE • "Technically Speaking: Understanding Services,""TakeNote: Changing and Troubleshooting Finder Icons," and "Technically Speaking: Type/ Creator vs. Filename Extensions vs. Others," earlier in the chapter, for more on Info.plist files.

Interface Builder

Interface Builder is an application that's included with Mac OS X's Developer Tools (Xcode) software. You'll find it, along with all of the other developer applications, in the /Developer/Applications folder (assuming you have installed the Developer Tools, that is). Because Interface Builder is designed to help developers build Aqua interfaces for their software, you'll have little use for it as a troubleshooter. There are, however, a few instances in which it might be helpful.

For example, if you don't like the brushed metal windows in Apple's Safari Web browser, you can change them in an instant with Interface Builder. To do so, follow these steps:

1. Select Show Package Contents for Safari. (Make sure Safari is not currently running.)

2. Go to Contents/Resources/English.proj and double-click Browser.nib. It should open in Interface Builder (assuming you have installed the Developer Tools software).

3. In the Browser.nib window, select the Instances tab and single-click the Window item.

4. From the Tools menu, select Show Inspector (Command-Shift-I).

5. From the pop-up menu, choose Attributes. If a list of attributes does not appear, click the Safari window template that should be in the background.

6. Go to the bottom section of the Attributes list and uncheck the Has Texture box.

7. Save the change. Now when you open a new window in Safari, the brushed metal appearance is gone.

When you save the changed option, a new file called Browser~.nib is added to the English.proj folder. It contains the original settings—useful if you forget what you did and want to return to the default settings.

Using almost the same procedure, you can add scroll bars to documents in the Stickies application. To do so:

1. Select Show Package Contents for Stickies. (Again, make sure Stickies isn't currently running.)

2. Go to Contents/Resources/English.proj/ and double-click StickiesDocument.nib. It should open in Interface Builder (assuming you have installed the Developer Tools software).

3. In the StickiesDocument.nib window, select the Instances tab and single-click the Window item.

4. From the Tools menu, select Show Inspector (Command-Shift-I).

5. From the pop-up menu, choose Attributes.

6. In the list that appears, look for an item called Show Scroller. If it does not appear, click the Stickies window template in the background. This should shift the Inspector from StickiesWindow to NSTextView. The Scroller option should now be there.

7. Check the Show Scroller box.

8. Save the change. Now, when you next launch Stickies, each document will have scroll bars along its right border.

Many shareware and freeware utilities that add features to or otherwise modify an application take advantage of "tricks" like this. That is, the utility does not make its changes via some unique code written by the utility's programmer; rather, it takes advantage of functionality already built into Mac OS X. In essence, the utility does the grunt work for you: All you need to do is run it and make your selection. But now you know how to do these things yourself.

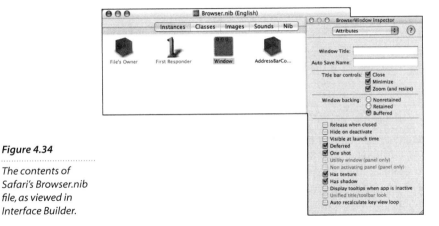

Figure 4.34

The contents of Safari's Browser.nib file, as viewed in Interface Builder.

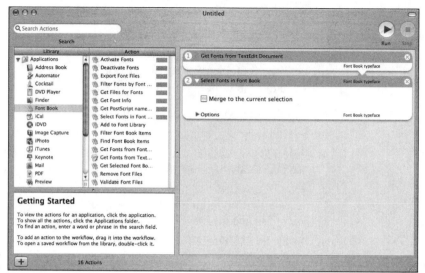

Figure 4.35

Automator in action.

Automator

New in Tiger is an application called Automator. Essentially, it does what its name implies: It provides a way to automate a sequence of steps. Such programs, often called *macro utilities* (a third-party program called QuicKeys being one well-known example), are especially useful for creating one-step shortcuts for what would otherwise be a much longer sequence of steps that you intend to perform over and over. They save time and hassle.

Automator ships with a built-in collection of useful steps, called Actions. Most of them are organized by application. Thus, there are collections of actions that work with the Finder, the OS itself, iTunes, Safari, TexEdit, and more. Many of the actions are not all that useful by themselves; they are designed to be combined with other actions into a workflow. Here is one simple example:

1. Launch Automator. Select Applications in the Library column list.

2. From the Action list, select Get Fonts from TextEdit Document. The description at the bottom of the window informs you that this action "returns the fonts used in the frontmost TextEdit document."

3. Drag the action to the workflow area to the right, or simply double-click the action item. This adds the item to the workflow.

4. The contents of the Action list will now shift. The most relevant items to add next will be at the top of the list. In this case, all of the top items should refer to the Font Book application.

5. From the listed Font Book actions, double-click Select Fonts in Font Book. This adds the item as the next action in the workflow.

6. Launch TextEdit and create a new document that uses two or three different fonts. Select all the text in the document.

7. Return to Automator and click the Run button in the upper right corner. Your workflow will run. The result will be that the fonts that you used in your TextEdit document will now be selected in Font Book.

8. Once you are satisfied with a workflow, you can save it via File > Save. You can save it as either a Workflow document or an Application. A saved workflow document will open in Automator when you double-click it; from here, you can edit it or run it. If saved as an application, it simply runs when you double-click it. Whichever way you run the workflow, you could use it to put the selected fonts in a new Font Book Collection, for example.

   Note: There is a command in the Services menu, Font Book > Create Collection from Text, that performs a very similar action. The set of steps presented here was designed only as an example of how to use Automator.

Some additional tips about using Automator:

- Many actions can be customized after they are added to a workflow. For example, the Finder's Create Archive action lets you select a default name for the to-be-created archive as well as optionally (via checking the Show Action When Run box in the Options section of the action) allow for the location of the archive to be selected when the workflow is run.

- Instead of Save, you can choose File > Save As Plug-in. In this case, the dialog that drops down includes a "Plug-in for" pop-up menu. Choices include: Finder, Folder Action, Print Workflow, Script Menu. The selection you make here determines how and where the workflow is saved. For example, if you select Finder, the workflow will be accessible from the submenu of the Automator item in the contextual menus of Finder items. Selecting the workflow causes its action to be applied to the active Finder item. Thus, if the workflow modifies the names of all files in a folder, you could select this workflow from the contextual menu of the folder whose files you wanted to change. The workflow itself is saved in the ~/Library/ Workflows/Applications/Finder folder. (Note: The Automator contextual menu item's submenu also includes a Create Workflow command. Choosing this launches Automator and creates a new workflow with the active Finder item as the initial listing in a Get Specified Finder Items action.)

- When a workflow is running, you should see feedback in the menu bar describing its action. When the workflow is done, the feedback will state, "Workflow completed." If a workflow appears to get stuck and never completes, you can cancel it by clicking the Stop icon to the right of the feedback text. If even that fails to work, launch Activity Monitor and quit the Automator Launcher process.

There's a rich array of workflows you can create from Automator's actions. At some point, however, you may wish there were an action that does not exist in the list. For example, I wanted to use Automator to automate filling in a form in Safari. But there were no actions to enter text on a Safari Web page. Can you fill this gap by creating your own actions? Yes. But this is considerably more difficult than simply creating a workflow. You will need Apple's Developer software for doing so. See Apple's "Working with Automator" page for more details (http://developer.apple.com/macosx/tiger/automator.html). Another alternative is to download Automator actions created by other people. Apple provides a library of such actions on its "Automator Actions" page (www.apple.com/downloads/macosx/automator), and you can find others on sites such as VersionTracker.com (search for *automator*).

There is much more you can learn about how Automator works. For starters, select Automator Help from Automator's Help menu or select Display Automator Website from the Automator menu.

Some people have characterized Automator as "AppleScript for the rest of us." That is, much of what you can do with Automator could already be accomplished—prior to Tiger—with AppleScript. The problem is that AppleScript has always existed in a sort of limbo between a user-friendly utility for all Mac users and a developer tool for just advanced users. It never achieved the popularity that Apple had hoped. Automator is much easier to use and should get the much more widespread use that AppleScript never was able to.

Is Automator just a simpler GUI for AppleScript? No. AppleScript can be the basis for an Automator action, but so can Objective-C programming. For people who still prefer AppleScript, or for actions that cannot be easily programmed with Automator, AppleScript remains an active part of Mac OS X, running much the way that it did in Panther.

SEE: • "Take Note: AppleScript," below, for more background on what AppleScript is and how it works.

TAKE NOTE ▶ AppleScript

Although AppleScript is an incredibly useful tool, it's not particularly helpful for troubleshooting—which is why I don't pay a lot of attention to it in this book. Still, you should at least know the basics of its use—which is precisely what follow here!

AppleScript is akin to a programming language; however, it uses an English-like syntax that makes it much easier to learn than most programming languages. It's used primarily to automate repetitive actions (like a macro utility). Thus, if you wanted to convert dozens of JPEG files to TIFF files, give each a new name, and move all of them to a new folder, you could create an AppleScript to carry out these tasks. In fact, you could set up the AppleScript as a Folder Action, so that the conversion takes place automatically when you drag a JPEG file to a folder.

If you know Unix, you'll be happy to learn that you can even call Terminal commands from within an AppleScript. AppleScript also includes conditional commands so that scripts can adjust their decisions to the situation (for example, you could create the previously suggested script so that a JPEG file created more than a year ago would be deleted rather than converted).

continues on next page

TAKE NOTE ▶ AppleScript *continued*

Script Editor is the application used to create AppleScripts. Beginning with Panther, AppleScript also supports GUI scripting—which means you can access buttons and menu commands (via the System Events application) even in applications that don't directly support AppleScript. Check Apple's "GUI Scripting (System Events)" page for more details (www.apple.com/applescript/uiscripting).

System Events—which resides in /System/Library/CoreServices—drives much of AppleScript's functionality. For example, when a script sends a command to the Finder or when a Folder Action is called, System Events is spurred into action.

Creating a script. To create a new AppleScript, locate the AppleScript folder (in /Applications) and launch Script Editor. If you know AppleScript commands, you can begin writing a script immediately. If not, you can record a sequence of actions (just click Record and start performing!) and have your actions automatically converted into a script. Click Stop when you're finished. This isn't as powerful as actually writing a script (because it doesn't allow for conditional statements); however, it does provide a quick way of getting started. Unfortunately, many applications (including many that otherwise support AppleScript) don't support recording. If nothing appears in Script Editor when you try to record a script, this is probably why.

To save a script, choose Save As from the File menu and then choose a name and format for the file. In most cases, your selected format will be either Script (if the compiled script is to be an item in an application's script menu) or Application (for double-clickable AppleScript files that function much like ordinary applications). In either case, the files can still be reopened in Script Editor. With the help of AppleScript Studio (which requires the Developer Tools), you can make a script look and act just like a professional Mac OS X application—users wouldn't even be able to tell it had been created in AppleScript.

You can test a script before you save it by clicking the Run button in the toolbar. Click the Event Log tab in the bottom of the window before clicking Run, to view a record of the script as it actually executed (that is, with actual values substituted for all variables).

Checking the dictionary. One limitation of AppleScript is that it works primarily with applications that have been specifically written to include AppleScript support. To determine what such applications are, choose Open Dictionary from Script Editor's File menu. You can now scroll through the list of all supported applications. If you double-click the name of an application, it will reveal a list of all the actions in that application that can be scripted. Click an action to view the details of how to use it in a script.

Using existing scripts. Even if you don't ever intend to write a script yourself, AppleScript can still be a great bonus. This is because you can make use of scripts that other people have written. For starters, go Apple's "Scriptable Applications" page (www.apple.com/applescript/apps). Here you will see a list of all applications included with Mac OS X that work with AppleScript.

continues on next page

TAKE NOTE ▶ AppleScript *continued*

In many cases, clicking an application leads to a new page from which you can download a set of scripts, provided by Apple, that work in that application. In some cases (such as for iTunes), to use such scripts you need to correctly install them. Here's how:

1. Open the folder with the same name as the application, located in your home Library folder (for example, ~/Library/iTunes).

2. If a folder called Scripts already exists, open it. If not, create a new folder with that name. Now drag the downloaded scripts to this Scripts folder.

3. Launch the application. On the right side of the application's menus (probably just to the left of the Help menu) will be an AppleScript icon. Click it to select the menu and see the list of scripts now available to you.

Third-party applications may also include a script menu option. For example, to add scripts that work with Microsoft Entourage, add them to the Entourage Script Menu Items folder in the ~/Documents/Microsoft User Data folder. To find scripts that work with Entourage (or other applications), check Web sites such as VersionTracker.com.

You can also enable the Mac OS X Scripts menu with its collection of many useful basic scripts. To do so, launch the AppleScript Utility application (located in the same AppleScript folder as Script Editor, and described more below) and then check the box for "Show Script Menu in menu bar." Note: If you want to open one of these scripts in Script Editor rather than execute it, hold down the Option key when selecting the script.

Folder Actions. Folder Actions work via AppleScripts attached to a folder. To attach an action script to a folder and enable the action, access the contextual menu for the target folder and choose Enable Folder Actions (if it's not already selected). Next, choose Attach a Folder Action from the same contextual menu. This opens a Choose a File window, from which you can select the script to attach to that folder. By default, the dialog takes you to the ~/Library/Scripts/Folder Action Scripts directory. You can also select items from the /Library/Scripts/Folder Actions directory. Items from this latter directory are selectable via the AppleScript menu, if it's installed (oddly, the similarly located Folder Action Scripts folder does not appear in this menu).

AppleScript Utility. New in Tiger is an application called AppleScript Utility, located in the same AppleScript folder as Script Editor. From here, you can enable the GUI Scripting feature noted above. You can also set up Folder Actions and enable/disable the Script Menu.

Download AppleScript software. Finally, you can download AppleScript-created software from the Internet. Such software is typically meant to run as either an application (double-click it to launch it) or a droplet (drop a file on the icon to launch the script and process the file).

To learn more about AppleScript, including how to write your own scripts, start at Apple's AppleScript page (www.apple.com/applescript).

SEE: • "Menu Extras" and "Take Note: Contextual Menus (and Folder Actions)," in Chapter 2, for more details.

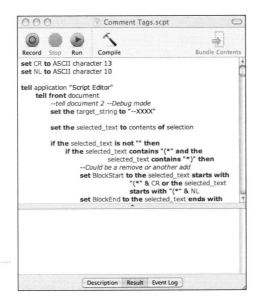

Figure 4.36

AppleScript's
Script Editor.

Figure 4.37

AppleScript
Utility's window.

Font Formats

Given the complexity of the task, Apple has done a great job of implementing fonts in Mac OS X. For the casual Mac OS X user, working with Mac OS X's fonts is as simple as selecting and using them. In addition, it's easier to switch among languages than it was in Mac OS 9. But for users who want to add and delete their own fonts, who have problems getting certain fonts to work, or who are experiencing problems that may be font related, this section provides the background information required to get to the heart of the problem.

You can use more than one type of font on a Macintosh. Because font formats are not a Mac OS X–specific issue, I'm not going to provide detailed coverage of them here. Instead, I'll simply present a brief overview—especially useful for those new to the subject.

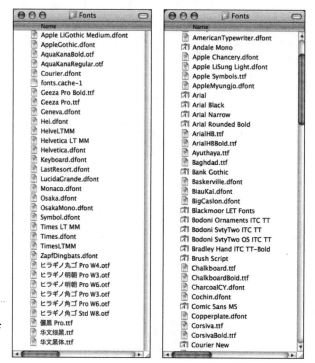

Figure 4.38

Left, *my /System/ Library/Fonts folder;* right, *my /Library/ Fonts folder.*

TrueType fonts

TrueType fonts are Apple's preferred font for Mac OS X. Most or all of the fonts that ship with Mac OS X are TrueType fonts. With TrueType, the font displays and prints smoothly (with no irregular jagged edges) no matter what size (for example, 10 points versus 13 points) or style (for example, plain text versus bold) you select.

For this feature to work, you need only a single font file for a given TrueType font. However, individual font files will often provide separate style variations (such as Times Italic and Times Bold). If such variations *aren't* present, you won't be able to select different styles for a given font in most Mac OS X applications.

Windows PCs can also use TrueType fonts; however, Windows TrueType font files employ a format that's slightly different from that of Mac TrueType fonts. Fortunately, Mac OS X recognizes the following Windows versions of TrueType fonts: TrueType fonts (with the extension .ttf) and TrueType collections (with the extension .ttc). (Note: The .ttf extension may also be used for Macintosh TrueType fonts.)

PostScript fonts

These font files contain the PostScript instructions needed to print to PostScript-supported printers. If your printer doesn't support PostScript, you should avoid PostScript fonts and stick with TrueType fonts (if possible). No PostScript fonts ship with Mac OS X, but you may have some in your Mac OS 9 System Folder, or you may have added them (or had them added by third-party software installers) to your Mac OS X System folder.

Because PostScript fonts are printer font files that contain instructions only for printing the text to a PostScript printer, in Mac OS 9 you could not display PostScript fonts on the screen—a matching screen font version (either bitmap or TrueType) was needed to display them. This screen/printer font pairing didn't always work well. Often what you saw on the screen was different from what appeared on the printed page. This situation improved significantly, however, with the release of Adobe Type Manager (ATM). This utility uses the PostScript printer's font instructions to display the fonts on the screen.

ATM doesn't work in Mac OS X; however, it's not really needed. Whereas Mac OS 9 used a technology called QuickDraw to display fonts, Mac OS X uses Quartz. And the Quartz technology is able to display PostScript fonts without the use of additional software (such as ATM). (Note: ATM still works for displaying text in Classic applications.)

You typically still need at least one matching TrueType or bitmap screen font (font suitcase) to get PostScript fonts with a type of LWFN to be listed in Font menus. However, PostScript fonts of the SFNT type may work without separate matching screen fonts.

Multiple Master fonts. PostScript Multiple Master fonts (font files that end with MM) are supported in Mac OS X 10.2 and later. You cannot create them in Mac OS X, but you can correctly use existing ones. To create a new Multiple Master font, you need software from Adobe, which must be run under Classic.

OpenType fonts

Microsoft and Adobe jointly designed this relatively new font format, which boasts the advantage of allowing the same font file to work on both Mac and Windows platforms. Microsoft created OpenType to free itself from its dependence on Apple's TrueType—so in a sense the formats are competitors. At the time of this writing, most Mac users were still using TrueType fonts rather than OpenType fonts (which typically have an .otf extension).

Bitmap fonts

This, the oldest font type, is rarely used anymore. With this font type, each size requires a separate file (Times 10, Times 12, Times 14, and so on). If you select a size that doesn't have a separate file, the font will appear jagged.

Although you may get these fonts to work in Mac OS X, especially when you're working in Classic they are not officially supported, so you should avoid them. Especially avoid older bitmapped versions of Chinese-, Japanese-, Korean-, and Vietnamese-language fonts; they will not work in Mac OS X at all. Also unsupported are older bitmapped fonts of the type FONT. Meanwhile, fonts of the type NFNT are supported for Classic/QuickDraw applications but ignored by applications based on Cocoa (such as TextEdit).

TAKE NOTE ▶ TrueType Fonts, Data Forks, and the .dfont File Extension

Mac OS X TrueType and .dfont. In Mac OS 9, a font file (like most Mac OS 9 files) has both a resource fork and a data fork. A file's main data (such as the text of a text document) resides in the data fork; its metadata (type and creator information, icon, and so on) is stored as separate resources in its resource fork. Mac OS X prefers to avoid resource forks, instead keeping everything in the data fork. Apple claims this arrangement makes it possible for fonts to work in other operating systems, such as Windows, that do not recognize resource forks.

Data fork–only TrueType font files have the filename extension .dfont. They may also have the file type dfon.

Essentially, a .dfont file is a TrueType font with all the resource-fork info moved to the data fork so that only the data fork remains. Mac OS X can read both old-style TrueType fonts and the new .dfont type. Apple, however, clearly prefers the. dfont type, so that's primarily what gets installed by Mac OS X. Old-style TrueType fonts may still be installed by third parties.

Note: Mac OS X's dfonts will not work in Mac OS 9. Thus, if you need to print a document that uses these fonts via Mac OS 9, it may not print correctly. To work around the problem, in the Mac OS X Print dialog select the Save as PDF option. This saves the file as a PDF, which you can then print from within Mac OS 9.

OpenType and Windows TrueType. OpenType fonts and Windows TrueType fonts also store all of their data in the data fork and don't have the additional resource fork of Macintosh fonts. The data fork for the Mac OS X TrueType format, however, is different from the data fork for the TrueType font format used by Microsoft Windows. The difference is that data-fork Mac OS X files contain all of the resources associated with a Macintosh font, including FOND and NFNT resources, which are used with QuickDraw Text. OpenType and Windows TrueType fonts do not include this information. Windows TrueType fonts have the extension .ttf.

Want more info? If you're unfamiliar with terms like *FOND* and *NFNT resources*, you can check this Apple Developer Technical Note from 1991: http://developer.apple.com/technotes/te/te_02.html.

Identifying font formats

You open a Fonts folder and see an assortment of fonts: How do you tell which are TrueType, which are PostScript, and which are OpenType? There are several ways.

Font icon and Kind line in Get Info. Starting in Panther, almost all fonts have icons indicating that they are Font Book files. Font Book is Mac OS X's font-management application, and—with the exception of PostScript fonts—all font files open in Font Book when you double-click them.

In addition, if you look closely at each font icon, you will see that it includes either the four-character type code or the extension name of the font's format. What's more, if you view the Get Info window for a font, the Kind line will fully describe its format. For example, a dfont will display *DFONT* on its icon, and the Kind line of its Get Info window will include the description "Datafork TrueType font." Similarly, a PostScript font's icon will display the letters *LWFN*, and its Kind line in the Get Info window will say, "PostScript Type 1 outline font."

Filename extensions. As discussed earlier, if a font file's name includes an extension, this extension can indicate font type—for example, .otf is used for OpenType fonts.

Figure 4.39

Font file icons: an FFIL font file and a DFONT font file.

Arial

Geneva.dfont

Type/creator utilities. As you will learn more about in Chapter 6, numerous Mac OS X utilities are able to list a file's type and creator information. In Mac OS 9 every file needed to have these codes assigned; in Mac OS X this information is optional. Most files (including most fonts), however, still include this information. In addition to the already noted font types such as FONT, NFONT, SFNT, and LWFN, suitcase font files will have a type of FFIL and a creator of DMOV.

Utilities that can display type and creator data include XRay and FileXaminer.

Font utilities. If you open Font Book and from its Preview menu choose Show Font Info (Command-I), you will see font information (including font type and format) for the selected font displayed beneath the font sample. Third-party font utilities, such as Suitcase, will also show font formats.

SEE: • "Take Note: Font Book: An Overview," later in this chapter.

• "Technically Speaking: Type/Creator vs. Filename Extensions vs. Others," earlier in this chapter, for more information on type and creator codes.

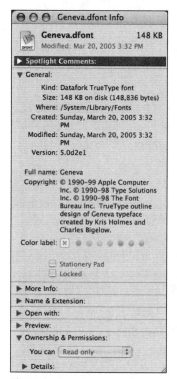

Figure 4.40

The Get Info window for the Geneva.dfont file.

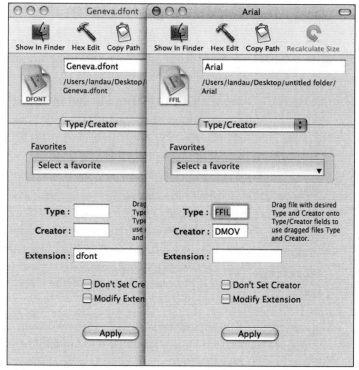

Figure 4.41

The FileXaminer utility, showing type, creator, and extension fields for the two fonts shown in Figure 4.39.

TAKE NOTE ▶ Font Suitcases

In Mac OS 9, a font could exist as an individual file or as one of several different font files combined into a font *suitcase*. TrueType and bitmap versions of the same font could be combined in the same font suitcase. A single suitcase could even hold entirely different and unrelated fonts (such as Helvetica and Times).

Mac OS X recognizes these suitcases (which have a file type of FFIL and a Kind of Font Suitcase when viewed in a Get Info window); however, Mac OS X much prefers single font files or, at the very least, no mixing of multiple font types in the same suitcase. Mac OS X finds mixed font suitcases confusing because their names are unlikely to divulge clues about their contents.

In Mac OS 9, if you wanted to add or remove a font file to or from a font suitcase, you could double-click the suitcase icon to open a window displaying its contents. Then you simply dragged a font file from the suitcase to remove it or dragged a file into the suitcase to add it.

continues on next page

TAKE NOTE ▶ Font Suitcases *continued*

You cannot do this in Mac OS X. In Mac OS X, these suitcases are displayed as a single file, and double-clicking them may not reveal their full contents.

If the font suitcase appears correctly as an FFIL file with a Font Book icon, double-clicking the font should cause it to open in Font Book. If the font suitcase still has the old Mac OS 9 "suitcase" icon, double-clicking it is likely to result in the suitcase's attempting to open in the now-obsolete Font/DA Mover application. It almost certainly will not find this application, so the font will not "open" at all. To fix this, you can use Get Info's "Open with" option to shift the default application to Font Book.

For a suitcase that contains mixed fonts, the simplest way to separate them out is to reboot in Mac OS 9 (if your Mac can still do so) and modify it there via the Finder. Otherwise, you may find utilities that let you do this from Mac OS X (either in Mac OS X itself or via Classic), but I haven't found any good ones so far.

As a result, although mixed fonts may work well in most cases, they are another potential source of trouble in Mac OS X. My advice is to restrict mixed suitcase files to the Mac OS 9 Classic System Folder, assuming that you need to use them at all. If possible, before upgrading to Mac OS X, convert all of your font suitcase files to individual font categories (that is, isolate each font, such as Times or Helvetica, into a separate file). You can do this most easily by duplicating the mixed font file and then deleting fonts from each copy so that only one type remains in each.

In general, it's wise to avoid Mac OS 9 font files whenever possible. These older fonts remain a too-common source of problems.

SEE: • "Checking fonts," in Chapter 5, for more on troubleshooting font problems.

Figure 4.42

Left, *a font suitcase icon, and* right, *a TrueType font file icon, as viewed when booted in Mac OS 9.*

Arial Black suitcase

Arial Black

Viewing and Managing Fonts

Apple persists in overhauling the way Mac OS X works with fonts in each major upgrade. For that reason, the following sections assume you are using Tiger, unless otherwise indicated.

TAKE NOTE ▶ Font Book: An Overview

Font Book is Mac OS X's font-management utility. It allows you to do the following:

- **View fonts.** Font Book lets you preview each font as well as get more information about the font (such as its format).

- **Add and delete fonts and collections.** You can use Font Book to install new fonts. Once installed (by simply placing the font file in the appropriate Fonts folder within a Library folder), a font is immediately available for use in applications.

  Similarly, Font Book lets you group fonts in *collections*—subsets of the entire list of installed fonts. In applications that support collections (like TextEdit), you can select a collection in the Font panel. This restricts the list of fonts to those in the collection. The idea here is that you can create different collections for different tasks (for example, preparing a newsletter versus working on a report).

  You can also disable and/or remove fonts and collections. Whether disabled or removed, the font and/or collection is removed from applications' font lists. The difference between disabling and removing is that a disabled collection or font remains listed in Font Book and can be re-enabled. A removed item, in contrast, is moved to the Trash.

  Note: At the top of the Collection column is an item called All Fonts, which you cannot disable or remove. As its name implies, it lists all of your fonts. Below the All Fonts category are several subcategories: User (fonts in ~/Library/Fonts), Computer (fonts in /Library/Fonts and /System/Library/Fonts), and (if present) Classic Mac OS (fonts in the Classic System Folder).

- **Resolve Duplicates and Validate Fonts.** Two important troubleshooting features in Font Book are the ability to resolve problems due to the presence of duplicate fonts installed on your Mac and the ability to check for corrupt fonts.

The sections on fonts in the main text of this chapter provide details regarding these features.

SEE: • "Font Utilities," at the end of this chapter, for information about additional font utilities.

Figure 4.43

The main Font Book display, with the Preview > Show Font Info option selected.

Viewing fonts

A font file in the Finder won't tell you anything about how the font looks when used in a document. To see this, you need a separate utility, either Mac OS X's Font Book utility or a third-party alternative.

Font Book. If you double-click a font file in the Finder, it opens Font Book in one of three ways:

- If the font is installed in any of your active Fonts folders, the main Font Book window opens with the double-clicked font selected and displayed.

  Note: Font Book even lists fonts in Fonts folders located on nonstartup volumes with Mac OS X installed. However, it may not list fonts in other locations, such as the folder used by Adobe applications to store the fonts installed by its software.

  SEE: • "Take Note: Multiple Folders of the Same Name in Multiple Library Folders," earlier in this chapter.

- If the font is not installed in any of your active Fonts folders (for example, if you double-click a font you just downloaded from the Web that is located on your Desktop), a separate window opens with the name of the font and a sample of the font's text. (This is actually a special feature of Font Book, which is the active application when this window appears.) At the top of the window is a pop-up menu from which you can choose different styles of the font (if there are any).

- If the file is a PostScript outline font, Font Book launches, but the file is not selected. Font Book cannot directly display PostScript font files; however, it does list the display font (for example, bitmap or TrueType) linked to the PostScript font files.

Third-party utilities. You can also view fonts in third-party utilities. In fact, if you have a third-party font utility (such as Suitcase or Insider Software's FontAgent Pro) and want fonts to open there rather than in Font Book when you double-click them, you can use the "Open with" options in the Get Info window to change the default application from Font Book to your choice.

You still can't open a suitcase file in Mac OS X and see a list of all its fonts (as described more in "Take Note: Font Suitcases," earlier in this chapter).

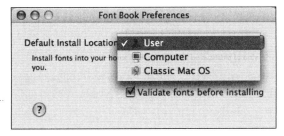

Figure 4.44

Font Book's
Preferences options.

Installing fonts

To make a font available in your application's Font menus, you need to install it. In essence, this means placing it in one of the Library/Fonts folders that Mac OS X uses when checking for fonts. There are several ways to do this.

Double-clicking an uninstalled font to access Font Book. As described above, if you double-click an uninstalled font file in the Finder, it opens a special Font Book window for that font. At the bottom of this window is an Install Font button. Clicking this installs the font in your home directory's Fonts folder (by default). The original of the font file is moved rather than copied (unless the original location is another volume or a location from which you do not have permission to delete files, in which case the original is copied).

You can change the default behavior of the Install Font button via Font Book's Preferences. From here, you can choose among the following options for where you want the font installed: User (the initial default choice; fonts are installed in the Fonts folder of your Library folder and are available only to you), Computer (fonts are installed in the /Library/Fonts folder and are available to all users on the computer), and Classic Mac OS (fonts are installed in the Fonts folder of the Classic Mac OS System Folder).

Using Font Book directly. From Font Book's File menu, you can choose Add Fonts (or click the Add [+] button at the bottom of the Font column). This opens a window from which you can select to install a font from among the same choices that are listed in Font Book's Preferences.

Note: If you install a font in your own Fonts folder (~/Library/Fonts) and later wish to make it available to all users (that is, by moving it to /Library/Fonts), you can do so from Font Book: Simply drag the font from the All Fonts collection (or the User collection) to the Computer collection. (You can do the reverse as well.)

You can similarly create a new font collection by choosing New Collection from the File menu (or clicking the plus button at the bottom of the Collection column). A new collection is empty by default. To add fonts to a collection, select All Fonts and then drag the font(s) you wish to add from the Font column to the collection name in the Collection column. This does not move the font's location in the Finder; it simply adds it to the list of fonts in that collection. Collection information is maintained by files with a .collection extension in the FontCollections folder of your /Library folder.

Performing a "manual" install. You can install a font "manually" from the Finder by dragging it to the desired Fonts folder (for example, ~/Library/Fonts). Of course, you can also drag a font out of one of these Fonts folders to uninstall it.

Note: For PostScript font files, you have no choice *but* to manually install them from the Finder (since you can't install them directly via Font Book).

However, there is an exception: If you have both a font suitcase file (FFIL) for a PostScript font and the PostScript font files (LWFN) that work with it, you can install the suitcase file. When you do this, it will automatically install all the PostScript font files that are in the same location. When viewed in Font Book, the font will be correctly listed as a PostScript font (in the Font Info display). The available style variants will depend on the PostScript files you installed.

Using third-party utilities. With third-party font utilities, such as Suitcase, you can also activate and install fonts—including making active fonts that are not in any Library/Fonts folder.

Disabling and removing fonts

If you've installed fonts that you don't use or that you otherwise want to remove (possibly because you suspect they're corrupt), you can disable or remove them. The following describes how.

Using Font Book. To *disable* a font (or entire font family) using Font Book, simply choose the name of the font (or font family) in the Font column of the Font Book window and click the Disable button at the bottom of the column.

Note: This will also remove the check mark from the Disable button, leaving just a blank box. The button has now toggled to an Enable button; clicking it will enable a selected font (or font family). Alternatively, you can disable a font by choosing "Disable {*font name*}" from the Edit menu.

To disable an entire collection of fonts, as listed in the Collection column, select the name of the collection and then choose "Disable {*collection name*}" from the Edit menu. You can use the latter method, for example, to easily disable all Classic Mac OS fonts. Such fonts can be re-enabled later by selecting the fonts or collection and then choosing "Enable {*collection or font name*}."

To completely *remove* a font or collection, highlight the item and choose "Remove {*font name*}" or "Delete {*collection name*}" from Font Book's File menu. When fonts are removed, they're placed in the Trash.

Note: If you try to *disable* all the fonts in the Computer collection, essential System fonts such as Geneva and Lucida Grande still remain enabled. You should almost never attempt to *remove* fonts from this collection.

Performing a manual uninstall. Any user can manually remove a font from the Fonts folder in his or her ~/Library directory. As an administrator, you can also remove fonts from the /Library/Fonts folder and the Fonts folder in the Classic System Folder.

To remove fonts from the /System/Library/Fonts folder, you need either (a) root access, (b) to Authenticate (if the dialog to do so appears), or (c) to change the ownership of the font and/or Fonts folder from System to yourself (via the

Get Info window). However, you will rarely want or need to remove a font from /System/Library/Fonts.

If you're using Font Book to manage fonts, I recommend not moving fonts from one folder to another in the Finder because doing so can cause problems within Font Book. For example, if you go to the Finder to remove a disabled font from its Fonts folder, it gets listed as enabled again in Font Book.

Using third-party utilities. With third-party font utilities, such as Suitcase, you can also deactivate and uninstall fonts.

Installing and removing fonts: Troubleshooting

In most cases, you won't have problems installing or uninstalling fonts. However, for the occasional problems that crop up, note the following:

Fonts that should not be removed. In general, you should not move or otherwise deactivate system-critical fonts (that is, those in /System/Library/Fonts). In fact, you shouldn't even rename fonts in the /System/Library/Fonts folder or Mac OS X–installed fonts in /Library/Fonts. If you do, Mac OS X may not be able to locate the fonts when it needs them.

If you remove LucidaGrande.dfont, for example, your system won't boot.

Another example of what can happen if you don't heed this advice: Removing the TrueType HelveticaNeue.dfont (as some users do to substitute a PostScript version), installed by Mac OS X in /Library/Fonts, will cause some versions of iCal to crash on launch. You may be able to avoid this by immediately substituting the replacement font after removing the Mac OS X–installed one. However, many users have not found this to be the case.

That being said, if you decide to disable a font in the /System/Library/Fonts folder, you should be OK as long as you replace it with another font (in another Fonts folder) of the same name (such as to change from a TrueType version of a font in the System folder to a PostScript version that you prefer to use instead).

Fonts that sometimes should be removed. The Times RO font is one that can cause unexpected grief. For example, in older versions of Mac OS X, it can cause Safari to unexpectedly quit. The work-around is to disable or remove the font. However, this problem should no longer occur in Mac OS X 10.3.4 or later.

Font changes and open applications. When installing or removing fonts, some currently open applications will not recognize the change until you quit the application and relaunch it. Others, in contrast, can "auto-update." If in doubt, quit all open applications before making changes to fonts.

Resolving duplicates. From the Collection column, select All Fonts. If you see an alert or bullet symbol next to the name of a font family (or an individual font), it means you have more than one copy of the font installed. To remedy this problem, you can use the Resolve Duplicates command from Font Book's Edit menu. There are two ways to use this command:

- Select the Font family that contains duplicates (that is, the one with a bullet next to its name) and then choose Resolve Duplicates to disable all duplicates within that family. If, for example, you had two sets of Verdana fonts (Regular, Italic, Bold, and Bold Italic), one complete set would be disabled (because all of the variants are contained within the single Verdana font suitcase file).

- Click the disclosure triangle next to the Font family name to reveal the full list of fonts. Assuming there are just two copies of each font, one of each pair will have a bullet next to its name. Click any font of the set you wish to remain enabled, then select Resolve Duplicates; the other set will be disabled.

    Why would you ever need to use this second method? Here's why: When you use the first method, Font Book automatically selects which duplicate font (or font set) to disable. It is the set with the bullet next to its name. In most cases, it makes the "wise" choice—that is, if one set resides in your home directory and the other is located in the System directory, it disables the one in your home directory. This makes sense because fonts in the System directory are often required for certain applications to function properly. Disabling these system fonts could thus cause more problems than those you would solve by disabling the duplicate.

    If, however, Font Book incorrectly disables a System font—or if you intentionally want to disable a System font—you can manually select which font to disable via the second method.

    Note: The flip side of all this is a troubleshooting tip: If, after using Remove Duplicates, you start having unexpected problems in applications, check to see that you did not inadvertently remove the "wrong" duplicate.

    How can you tell where each font is located, so you can decide which one you want to disable? Hold the pointer over the font name in the list; a yellow tool-tip box will appear that provides the font's complete pathname and version number. Alternatively, from Font Book's File menu, you can choose Show Font File (Command-R); this will take you to the location of the font in the Finder.

Whichever method you use, after you choose Remove Duplicates, the disabled fonts will be dimmed in the list and the word *Off* will appear next to their names.

Finally, to re-enable a font disabled via Resolve Duplicates, simply select the font and click the Enable button at the bottom of the column. Conversely, you can use the Disable button, rather than Resolve Duplicates, to disable an active duplicate font; it has the same effect. Remember, though: Disabling a font does not remove it; it just prevents the font from appearing in Font menus.

Note: One time when I launched Font Book, it listed fonts in Fonts folders on a second mounted partition with Mac OS X installed (in addition to correctly listing all fonts on the startup partition). As a result, numerous duplicates were listed. Oddly, when I tried to replicate this later, the external volume fonts were no longer listed. I'm not sure what went on here, but a word of warning: If this happens to you, avoid using the Resolve Duplicates command to disable fonts—especially if you could wind up disabling fonts on your current startup volume as a result.

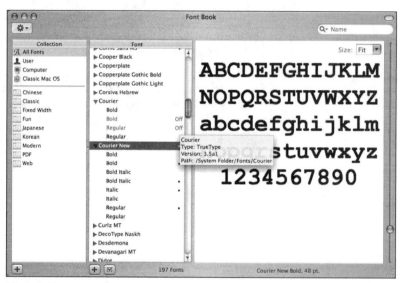

Figure 4.45

In Font Book, the bullets next to several of the Courier New fonts indicate that they are duplicates. A similar conflict between two of the Courier fonts was addressed using the Resolve Duplicates command—which is why the fonts are listed as disabled (Off). (Note: Tool tips, such as the one seen in the figure, provide information about the type [for example, TrueType] and location [such as /System Folder/Fonts] of a selected font.

TAKE NOTE ▶ Problems with Duplicate Fonts in Fonts Folders

If you have two versions of the same font in different Fonts folders, how does Mac OS X decide which one to use? In general, it follows the typical Library hierarchy: first checking for and using the font found in the Fonts folder of your home /Library directory, and then (as needed) checking in the /Library directory, the Network Library (if one is present), the /System/Library, and, finally, Classic's Fonts folder.

Although it's usually OK to have two versions of the same font in different Fonts folders, *do not* place two versions of the same font in the same Mac OS X Fonts folder. This will almost certainly cause problems, especially with Carbon applications. The most likely symptom is that the application will crash when attempting to display the font or, sometimes, immediately upon launching. This has been known to affect the font-management utility Suitcase, Microsoft Office applications, several Adobe applications, and more.

continues on next page

TAKE NOTE ▶ Problems with Duplicate Fonts in Fonts Folders *continued*

How or why would you wind up with two versions of the same font in a Fonts folder? It could happen by accident, such as if a Mac OS 9 font suitcase containing several different fonts were to be copied to a Mac OS X Fonts folder (most likely the Fonts folder in your home directory, at ~/Library/Fonts). If one of the fonts in the suitcase had a name identical to one of the fonts already in the Fonts folder, this could trigger the problem.

Less often, problems occur if the same font is in two *different* Fonts folders—most commonly seen when there's a duplicate between a TrueType .dfont in the /System/Library/Fonts folder and a PostScript version of the same font that the user has installed in either /Library/Fonts or ~/Library/Fonts. (For example, the problem has been reported after installing an Adobe Helvetica PostScript font.) In this case, in addition to potential crashes, there may be oddities when displaying the font.

Problems occur here because an application must, of necessity, choose one or the other version when deciding how to display the font. If different versions of the same font appear in multiple Library/Fonts folders, the more "local" version generally takes priority. Thus, if you place in your home directory's Fonts folder a font that is different from the same-named font in the /System/Library/Fonts folder, the version in your home directory should be used in applications' Font menus. However, there is at least one situation where this does not occur. In particular, if there are multiple font versions available, several Adobe applications will choose the version with the most glyphs (visual displays of font characters)—which could be the system TrueType version in the System directory rather than the PostScript version in the home directory. The result is that you may have fewer style variations available than you had expected by installing the PostScript font. That is, if the TrueType version does not include an italics font, you may not have italics available (because Mac OS X does not create an italics display on the fly from the plain version, as Mac OS 9 can do).

A solution to this problem, assuming you wanted access to the PostScript version of the font, would be to delete the corresponding TrueType font from the /System/Library/Fonts folder.

Alternatively, the Suitcase utility includes an option (in its preferences) called "Allow Suitcase to override system fonts." Be similarly cautious when using this option.

SEE: • "Take Note: Multiple Folders of the Same Name in Multiple Library Folders," earlier in this chapter, for related information.

Corrupt fonts: Troubleshooting/validating

New in Tiger, Font Book includes a feature to *validate* fonts. Essentially, this checks for potentially damaged or corrupt fonts. Mac OS X itself should not corrupt any fonts (since it doesn't modify them); however, fonts originally used in Mac OS 9 or modified by font utilities can become corrupt. Such fonts can result in garbled text in a text document or, in extreme cases, cause an application to crash.

Font Book can check to see if a font is corrupt. To do this, select the font (or fonts) you wish to check, by highlighting them in Font Book's Font column list, and select Validate Font(s) from the File menu.

The resulting window that appears will indicate whether the selected font(s) are OK (Passed), have minor problems, or have serious problems. If a font has "serious problems," you should remove it. You can do this directly in the Font Validation window: Check the box next to the font name and click the Remove Checked button.

Font Book also allows you to validate an uninstalled font. To do so, choose Validate File from Font Book's File menu. Then navigate to and select the font file you wish to validate. You can use this to confirm that a font is OK prior to installing it. If it passes inspection, you can then install it. To do so, check the box for the font and click the Install Checked button in the Font Validation window.

You can have a validation check performed automatically, when installing fonts, by checking the box for "Validate fonts before installing" in Font Book's Preferences options.

Several third-party font utilities (such as those described at the end of this chapter) can help you isolate, and possibly even repair, corrupt fonts. Otherwise, you will need to use trial and error to locate the problem font and remove it.

Note: Mac OS X has a built-in validation process whereby it checks the integrity of a font prior to displaying or printing it. If it detects that a font in use in a document is corrupt, it should automatically deactivate it.

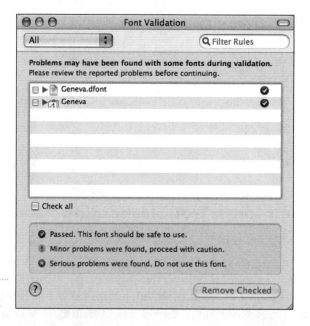

Figure 4.46

Font Book's Font Validation window.

Corrupt font caches: Troubleshooting

Occasionally, you may have problems with fonts that extend beyond a problem with the font files themselves. In particular, a font cache file may get corrupted. These cache files maintain information about what fonts are currently installed and where they are located. Because these files are frequently updated and modified, they are vulnerable to corruption. Symptoms of a corrupt cache file include garbled text in documents and font names that are not listed correctly (or not listed at all) in Font menus.

Fixing corrupt font cache files. The easiest solution for corrupt font cache files is to delete them. To do so, simply drag them to the Trash (in some cases, you will need an administrator password to do this). New files will be created automatically the next time they are needed.

Alternatively, you can use a third-party utility such as Mark Douma's Font Finagler (http://homepage.mac.com/mdouma46/fontfinagler). This utility creates a list of all the relevant cache files on your drive and then lets you delete them with the click of a button.

Here is a list of the names of most font cache files and folders, and their locations:

- **com.apple.ATS.plist.** This file is located in ~/Library/Preferences. Among other things, it contains information about what fonts you've disabled via Font Book. Thus, deleting this file will likely reactivate disabled fonts. That's the price you have to pay if the file is corrupt.

- **com.apple.ATS.** This folder is located in /Library/Caches. Cache files are contained within it. In particular, check in this folder for subfolders that have your user ID (UID) number in their name. If you're the only or first user to have an account on the system, for example, your UID will be 501. Inside these folders are your font cache files. Deleting these files may, for example, fix a problem where Suitcase is not activating fonts correctly.

- **fontTablesAnnex.** This file is located in /System/Library/Caches and, if corrupted, is the single most likely cause of garbled text.

- **Office Font Cache and Word Settings.** These files are located in the ~/Library/Preferences/Microsoft folder. Delete them if your font troubles are restricted to Microsoft Office applications. The primary trouble you would have here is that the name of the font listed in the Formatting palette or toolbar is not the same as the font selected and displayed in the document text.

Also consider deleting any other files that include *.ATS* or *font* in their name that are inside the /System/Library/Caches folder. The com.apple.ATS.System.fcache and com.apple.ATSServer.FODB_System files are the most critical ones to worry about. But it can't hurt to get rid of all of them.

If you want to be cautious, move the files to the Trash but do not empty the Trash until you see that the symptom is gone. This way, you can return the file(s), if their removal had no effect. This can potentially save you some hassle (such as having to reactivate fonts in Font Book).

Some applications, such as those from Adobe and Microsoft, may maintain their own font caches. For problems in these applications, try deleting their caches. For example, if you have a problem in Microsoft Word where displayed text is of a different font than the one you selected, quit Word and try deleting the Office Font Cache (10 or 11) file in the ~/Library/Preferences/Microsoft folder. Also consider deleting the Word Font Substitutes and Word Settings (10 or 11) files, located in the same folder. Relaunch Word; the problem should now be gone.

More generally, to check for a potential problem with preferences and cache files, log in as another user. If the problem vanishes, you probably have a corrupted preferences or cache file.

SEE: • "Logging in as another user," in Chapter 5, for more details.

LastResort.dfont. There is a font in /System/Library/Fonts called LastResort.dfont; however, it's not listed in any application's Font menus. This is because it's used only if a font is having problems displaying a particular Unicode character (possibly due to corruption of the font or possibly because the font does not contain the needed information). The appropriate gylph from LastResort is then used instead. With luck, the clue from LastResort will allow you to determine what font you need in order to get the glyph to display as intended.

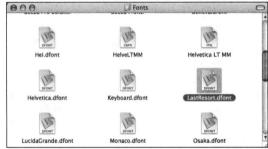

Figure 4.47

The LastResort.dfont file in the /System/ Library/Fonts folder.

Working with Fonts

This section covers issues pertaining to using fonts in applications.

Character Palette

In the Edit menu of all applications that ship with Mac OS X (and other software that supports this feature) is an item called Special Characters. Certain older Carbon-based applications, such as AppleWorks 6.x, do not have this command.

If you choose this command, a window called Character Palette appears. The Unicode-based Character Palette, which works in most Mac OS X applications (especially Cocoa ones), is used to locate and insert special non-alphanumeric characters into applications that accept text (word processors being an obvious example). The following provides an overview of how it works. The easiest way to follow along here is to open a TextEdit document and access the Character Palette.

1. The Character Palette contains a View menu at its top. From here, you select the desired basic display options. A common selection is Roman. This provides a list of most of the symbol characters available to you. Other options you may wish to explore are All Characters, Code Tables, PIFonts, and Glyph.

   In truth, the details of the Character Palette options take us far afield of troubleshooting issues. That's why the steps here provide only an overview. If you are into designing your own fonts, using foreign-language fonts, taking advantage of the symbol and glyph options normally hidden from view in an application's Font menus, or examining Unicode tables, you will want to learn more about the Character Palette than I cover here.

2. Just below the View menu is a set of tab buttons. Exactly what buttons appear varies as a function of what View item you select.

   If you select Roman, as an example, the two tabs will be "by Category" and "Favorites."

   If you select "by Category," the left column immediately below the tabs will contain a scrollable list of character categories, such as Arrows, Currency Symbols, Crosses, and Greek. Make a selection, and you will see a graphical display of all characters in that category to the right.

3. Select the character you wish to insert and click the Insert button (or simply double-click the character). If things work as intended (and they sometimes do not), the character will appear wherever the insertion point is located in your document.

   The character will appear in whatever font is current at the insertion point. If the current font does not contain the character you selected, the character is shifted to one of the fonts that do contain the character.

   You can search for a particular type of character from the seach field at the bottom of the window. Enter arrow to see a good example of how this works.

4. To select a particular font for use with a character (especially helpful if the font in your document does not include the character), click the Font Variation disclosure triangle. From the Collections pop-up menu, choose "Containing selected character." Scroll through the list of fonts and select the one you want. The Insert button will change to Insert with Font; click it, and the character will be inserted in the document in the selected font.

   Note: If a font supports glyph variants (such as a rotated version of the character), they will be listed at the bottom of the window after you've selected a character. You can further select the variant you want.

5. For a list of related characters for a selected character, click the Character Info disclosure triangle. In some cases, when you click a related character, the top of the palette will shift. The tabs will now read Unicode Blocks, Unicode Tables, and Favorites. These provide even more character options; however, the details for these are well outside our troubleshooting focus.

   Also in the Character Info section is an enlarged view of the selected character. You can drag this item to any text insertion point in your document as an alternative to using the Insert button.

6. Finally, there are several options available from the Action menu at the bottom left of the window. In particular, if you choose Add to Favorites, the selected item will be added to your personal Favorites list. You can view and edit the list by selecting the Favorites tab at the top of the window. If you choose Manage Fonts, Font Book will launch.

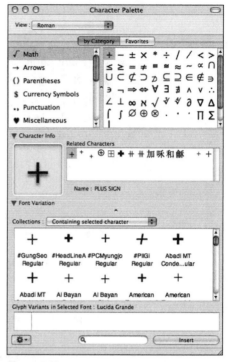

Figure 4.48

The default options of the Character Palette window.

Font panel

The Font panel is where Mac OS X applications display font choices. In Mac OS X 10.1.x, only Cocoa applications could use this palette. However, beginning with Mac OS X 10.2, Carbon applications are now able to access it as well (if they have been updated to do so). Most Carbon-based applications running in Mac OS X, including AppleWorks and Microsoft Office, continue to offer font choices in the same way they did in Mac OS 9—that is, via the same Font menus (which means there's no Mac OS X Font panel).

TextEdit is an example of an application that does use the Font panel. To access the Font panel in TextEdit, from the Format menu choose Font > Show Fonts (Command-T). If you've already explored Font Book, you know that the Font panel has a lot in common with the Font Book window. Font Book has columns labeled Collection and Font (with the typefaces for each font family accessible via disclosure triangles for the specific font). And the Font panel has columns labeled Collections, Family, and Typeface, and Size. Both windows have similar slider and text box options for adjusting font size. As you might suspect, changes in one window (such as enabling or disabling a font in Font Book) are reflected in the other window.

Note: Exactly what appears in the Font panel depends on how you resize the window; some options are hidden as the window gets smaller. To see all of the options described here, enlarge the window as needed.

Here's a closer look at the Font panel:

Columns. The Font panel contains four main columns:

- **Collections.** Use this column if you want to restrict the listed fonts to a subset of the total fonts installed. This method may be advisable when you're working on a project that will use only certain fonts and you don't want to be bothered with seeing the rest. Initially, you will see collections for All Fonts, Favorites, and Recently Used. There may also be additional preinstalled collections (such as Fun and Web). You can add or delete a collection by using the Add (+) and Delete (–) buttons at the bottom of the window.

  To add a font to a particular collection, select All Fonts. From the Family column, select the font you want to add and drag it to the name of the collection. To remove a font family from a collection, drag the family name to the Desktop, where it will vanish in a poof.

- **Family.** The fonts included in a selected collection appear in the Family column to the right of the Collections column. You can search for a specific family by entering text in the text box at the bottom of the window.

- **Typeface.** If you select a font in the Family column, its available typefaces appear in the next column over. The typefaces that appear (italic, bold, and so on) will vary by font.

- **Size.** You can choose different sizes for a font via the Size column. If you choose the Edit Sizes command from the Action menu, you can modify which sizes appear in this column or switch to using a slider.

Figure 4.49

The Font panel as accessed from TextEdit's Show Fonts command. The Action menu is shown at the bottom.

Dingbats, Symbols, and other graphic fonts. Whatever font you select in the Font panel will be applied to the newly selected text in your TextEdit document. One exception: You cannot directly select the Symbol or Zapf Dingbats font (or other similar graphic fonts) in the Font panel. If you try, the font selection reverts to another text font (such as Lucida Grande). To use the characters in these graphic fonts, select the Character Palette and enter the characters directly.

Why this difficulty in using graphic fonts? The answer lies in Mac OS X's use of Unicode in applications like TextEdit (see "Technically Speaking: ATSUI and Unicode," earlier in this chapter). More specifically, this is what Apple has to say on the matter: "In Mac OS 9, the Symbol and Zapf Dingbats fonts acted like other fonts, as if they worked with the usual alphabetic and numeric characters, when in fact they contained symbol characters. In a Unicode system, the special characters in the Symbol and Zapf Dingbats fonts have their own unique Unicode character codes. Typing a character like 'A' does not work when these fonts are used with Unicode, as the fonts don't contain an 'A' character."

Similarly, if you're using the .dfont version of these fonts (for example, /System/Library/Fonts/ZapfDingbats.dfont), the text document is not likely to display these Unicode-based fonts correctly when viewed from Mac OS 9. To avoid this, use the PostScript version of these fonts instead of the .dfont version. Doing this may require a utility, such as Suitcase, that lets you select which version of a font to use.

Another, similar, problem may occur when importing a Word document from a Windows PC to the Mac. Certain Unicode symbols (such as fractions) that appear correctly on the PC will not appear in Word X for the Mac (because Word X is not yet Unicode savvy). To see these characters correctly, you would need to open the document in TextEdit.

Font panel's Action menu

At the bottom of the Font panel is a pop-up menu with the same icon as the Action menu in Finder windows. The following provides an overview of the most troubleshooting-relevant items available from this menu:

- **Add to Favorites** adds the selected font to the Favorites collection.
- **Show/Hide Preview** opens (or collapses) a section at the top of the Font panel where a sample of text in the selected font appears.
- **Show/Hide Effects** adds (or removes) an Effects toolbar above the main part of the Font panel. From here, you can select various text attributes, such as underline, strike-through, and color. To see what each item does, pause the pointer briefly over the item; a yellow tool tip should appear. For example, the controls at the right end of the row are all for shadow effects (shadow opacity, shadow blur, and so on).

- **Color** opens a palette in which you can choose a color for the text you have selected. The color palette accessible from here is the same one you get if you click the Text Color button in the Show Effects toolbar or if you choose Show Colors from the Font submenu of the Format menu in TextEdit.

- **Characters** opens the same Character Palette accessible via the Special Characters command in the Edit menu of the application.

- **Typography** offers advanced typography options such as the ability to add spaces before or after characters via sliders.

- **Edit Sizes** allows you to select whether you want the Font panel to show a fixed list of selectable font sizes, an adjustable slider that changes font sizes automatically as you move it up and down, or both.

- **Manage Fonts** opens Font Book.

Input menu

The Character Palette can be accessed more generally (in any application, even ones whose Edit menus do not include the Special Characters command) via an optional Input menu. To enable it, follow the steps outlined below:

1. Launch System Preferences and open the International pane. Select the Input Menu tab.

2. From the list that appears, check the box for Character Palette (it should be the top item).

3. Optionally, you can also select Keyboard Viewer a few items down.

   Note: The U.S. option should be selected by default (assuming that U.S. English is your default language for Mac OS X). Otherwise, you can ignore this and the other items in the list for now; I'll return to them later in this chapter.

4. Check the "Show input menu in menu bar" box and close the pane.

The menu bar should now include a menu (on the right side) with an icon matching the default language of your Mac OS X installation—this is the Input menu. If you access it, you will be presented with the following two choices (among others):

Show Character Palette. To open the same Character Palette already covered, choose Show Character Palette from the Input menu.

Note: Although the Character Palette will work in applications (such as AppleWorks) that do not offer full Unicode support, it will not work as well as it does in applications like TextEdit. When using a program such as AppleWorks, after you click the Insert button in the palette, an incorrect (non-Unicode) character may appear in the document. In some cases, you can fix this by selecting the character in the document, going to the application's Font menu, and selecting a font that contains the character (for example, Symbol or Zapf Dingbats). However, it's probably easier to select the font from the application's Font menu and bypass the Character Palette altogether. Overall, you should reserve use of the palette for applications that support Unicode.

Show Keyboard Viewer. If you choose this option, a small window opens containing a keyboard layout. The characters on the keys change depending on what font you choose from the pop-up menu and whether or not you're holding down modifier keys (such as Option). If you have a text document open, whichever character keys you click will also appear in the document. In case you were wondering, yes, this feature replaces the former Key Caps utility from Jaguar (which dates back to Mac OS 9). The Key Caps feature does not exist in Panther or Tiger.

Other inputs. Some third-party software may work via the Input menu. Spell Catcher, for example, is turned on or off from this menu. When you choose Spell Catcher, an additional Spell Catcher menu appears in the menu bar.

This menu is also where you select to display keyboard layouts for different languages.

SEE: • **"International language support: Basics," later in this chapter, for information on keyboard layouts.**

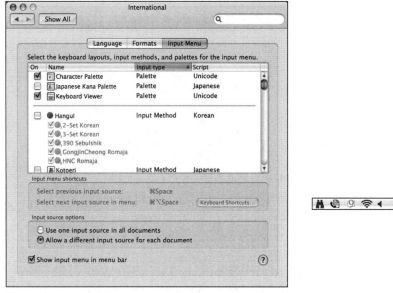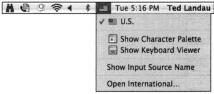

Figure 4.50

Left, the International System Preferences pane's Input Menu pane; right, the menu that appears in the menu bar after you select items from the list.

Figure 4.51

The Keyboard Viewer.

TAKE NOTE ▶ TextEdit: Format Options Beyond Show Fonts

TextEdit is Mac OS X's basic word-processing application (as covered initially in Chapter 2). Here is some basic troubleshooting advice for working with TextEdit and fonts. Some of the advice applies to text and font issues in general in Mac OS X.

Rich text vs. plain text. The default format for files saved in TextEdit is Rich Text Format (RTF). Files saved in this format have the .rtf extension. Rich Text Format allows you to include the specialized font, justification, stylized text, and other options that TextEdit is capable of producing. You can also open RTF files in applications such as Microsoft Word.

Some applications (a number of e-mail programs, for example) may not be able to understand Rich Text Format. In such cases, you may need to save the file in plain text format (which has the filename extension .txt). To do so, from the Format menu choose Make Plain Text and then save the file. Once you've done this, virtually any application should be able to read the file.

You can make the text revert back to Rich Text Format by using the Make Rich Text command (which you access from the Format menu when viewing plain text files). Keep in mind, however, that any RTF formatting you applied will not return.

.rtfd. If you paste graphics into an .rtf document and then try to save it, you are likely to get an alert box stating, "You cannot save this document with the extension 'rtf' at the end of the name. The required extension is 'rtfd.'"

An .rtfd file is actually a package that combines text and graphics data as separate elements. Should you decide to remove the .rtfd extension from the file's name in the Finder (such as via the Name & Extension section of the Get Info window), the file will revert to a folder. Adding back the .rtfd extension should get it to appear as a document file again.

Note: You can place more than graphics into an .rtfd document. Try dragging an application icon from the Finder to a TextEdit document; you'll see that this creates a copy of the application inside the .rtfd package. In the document itself, a small icon of the application appears. You can similarly copy QuickTime movies and sound files to a TextEdit document, and then play them from within the document. Try it!

Read-only. TextEdit's Format menu also includes an option to save a file as read only, via the Prevent Editing command. You may want to employ this option when creating the read-me files that accompany applications. Conversely, if you open a read-only file, the command in the Format menu will change to Allow Editing.

Saving SimpleText documents. You can use TextEdit to open and edit documents created in Mac OS 9's SimpleText application. However, when you try to save a modified SimpleText document, you will get an error message that states, "Please supply a new name. TextEdit does not save SimpleText format; document will be saved as rich text (RTF) instead, with a new name." If you click OK, you will be given the chance to save the document with a new name.

continues on next page

TAKE NOTE ▶ **TextEdit: Format Options Beyond Show Fonts** *continued*

Wrap. The Format menu has a command that toggles between Wrap to Window and Wrap to Page. If text continues beyond the right border of a window (so that you cannot read it), choosing Wrap to Window will readjust the text so that you can read it all. Alternatively, to make sure that the text prints in a readable size, select the desired paper size in the Page Setup dialog; then select Wrap to Page.

Font Styles. TextEdit supports styles—a broader use of the term *style* than merely changing the look of text to italics or bold. A style here refers to a full collection of type characteristics (font type, font size, font style, alignment, spacing, and so on). If you want to format text in a style you've used before in your document, simply highlight or place the pointer within text to which the style has already been applied, and from the Font submenu choose Copy Style. Now select the text you want to modify and select Paste Style from the same submenu.

Even better, the TextEdit toolbar at the top of each document now includes a Styles pop-up menu. Every time you make a change to a style element in your document, TextEdit remembers it. To see this, from the Styles menu select Other. A window appears where you can rotate through every style change in your document and then apply the one you want to use to selected text. If you expect to use this style again, you can save it as a Favorite.

Working with Word documents. You can directly open and save Microsoft Word documents in TextEdit. If you've created a new TextEdit document, you can also choose Word Format from the File Format pop-up menu in the Save As dialog, and save the document as a Word document. The conversion won't always be perfect (since Word supports features not found in TextEdit), but it's quite good.

Plain Text Encoding. If the entire text of a document appears incorrect, it may be that it does not use the default encoding method selected. To select a different one, close the document and select the Open command. Now select the desired encoding from the Plain Text Encoding pop-up menu.

Ignore Rich Text Commands. If an HTML document opens as if it were displaying in a browser, rather than revealing its HTML code, check the "Ignore rich text commands" box (located below the Plain Text Encoding pop-up menu in the Open dialog) before opening the document.

Note: You can change the default selections in both of the Plain Text Encoding and Ignore Rich Text commands via the Open and Save section of TextEdit's Preferences.

Spelling. TextEdit supports Mac OS X's spelling-checker service. You can access it via the Spelling command in the Edit menu. If you Control-click a misspelled word, it will bring up a contextual menu with suggested alternatives.

SEE: • **"Technically Speaking: Type/Creator vs. Filename Extensions vs. Others," earlier in this chapter, for more on SimpleText and TextEdit documents.**

Figure 4.52

The Save Warning message that appears when you attempt to save an RTF file after pasting a graphic into it.

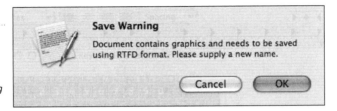

Figure 4.53

Inside the package of the .rtfd file (with graphic) that generated the warning in Figure 4.52.

TAKE NOTE ▶ Font Styles and Copy/Paste

In most Mac OS 9 (and Carbon-based Mac OS X) text applications, a Style menu allows you to change the style of text from plain to italics to bold and so on. Although the situation gets a bit more complicated with PostScript fonts, these menu options generally allow you to change a font's style even if the font file itself has only the regular (plain) variant. In essence, the application uses built-in OS routines to create a good estimate of the style variation. Mac OS X Cocoa applications such as TextEdit, however, only support styles that exist in the font file itself. Thus, if a font file contains only regular and bold styles, only those styles will appear in TextEdit; you can't display that font in italics. As a result, even if you were to paste text of that font that had been italicized in another application, the italics would be lost when you pasted the text into TextEdit.

This behavior can have unintended consequences. For example, if you add a version of a font to the Fonts folder in your home directory, it will generally take precedence over versions of the same font in other Fonts folders (as covered more in "Take Note: Problems with Duplicate Fonts in Fonts Folders," earlier in this chapter). If the newly added font contains different style variants than the preexisting font, the styles accessible in programs such as TextEdit will change.

Font smoothing

Even without any special font-smoothing effects, Mac OS X is able to display PostScript and TrueType fonts quite smoothly.

Anti-aliased text. Mac OS X, via its Quartz layer, includes a font-smoothing option called *anti-aliasing*. This feature modifies font edges to eliminate the inevitable "jagginess" of their display (which is due to the fact that an edge— especially an oblique edge—is a string of square pixels rather than a true line).

Anti-aliasing fills in the gaps left by the pixels with various shades of gray pixels. The human eye views this display as a smooth line (unless the magnification level gets so high that you start seeing the gray shades).

Although anti-aliased text generally looks superior to non-anti-aliased text (which is why the technology exists!), it may not work as well for smaller fonts, which can end up looking more blurry than smooth (making them even harder to read).

For this reason, Mac OS X lets you turn off anti-aliasing for small font sizes. To do so, follow these steps:

1. Launch System Preferences and open the Appearance pane.

2. From the "Turn off text smoothing for font sizes {#} and smaller" pop-up menu, choose your preferred font size limit. Your choices are point sizes 4, 6, 8, 9, 10, and 12.

   Thus, if small fonts are too blurry, choose a higher number to turn off smoothing for more font sizes. Conversely, if large fonts are too jagged, choose a lower number.

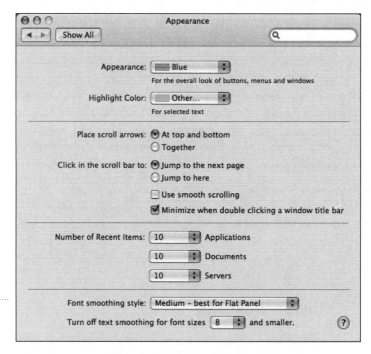

Figure 4.54

The Appearance System Preferences pane.

The Appearance pane does not allow you to disable font smoothing for sizes larger than 12 points.

The Appearance pane also includes an option called "Font smoothing style." Typically, you should select Automatic (which will in general equate to Standard for CRT monitors and Medium for flat-panel displays). All but the Standard option use a technique called *subpixel rendering*, which employs colored pixels, rather than shades of gray, to achieve the smoothing effect. However, this technique only works well with flat-panel displays.

Carbon applications and Silk. In general, in Mac OS X 10.1.5 and later, font smoothing works in Carbon applications as well as Cocoa ones—without the need for third-party software. However, the application needs to be updated to hook in to this feature. A work-around for non-updated programs is to use a third-party program called Silk, from Unsanity (www.unsanity.com), which enables text smoothing for all Carbon applications.

However, Carbon support for text smoothing may cause problems (such as text that disappears) in some applications. Microsoft software, such as Internet Explorer and Office applications, appears to be especially prone to text-smoothing problems. In such cases, turning off the smoothing feature from within the application should solve the problem. In Internet Explorer, you would deselect the "Enable Quartz text smoothing" option in the Interface Extras pane of Internet Explorer's Preferences window. Finally, add the problem application to Silk's "exclude" list, if you're using this utility.

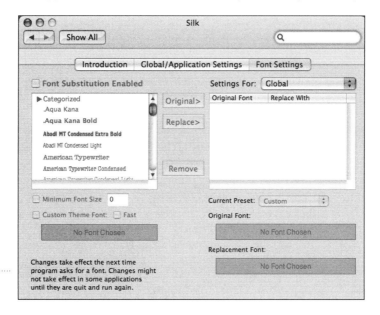

Figure 4.55

The Silk System Preferences pane.

Modifying default fonts

You can use a third-party utility called TinkerTool to change the default font settings (such as the font and the size) that Mac OS X uses for its system font and applications. To do so, click the Fonts button in TinkerTool's toolbar and make changes to the list of fonts, as desired. You cannot access these modifications from any Mac OS X–supplied System Preferences pane. Not all applications will use these changes, however, and the changes will not affect the menu-bar font.

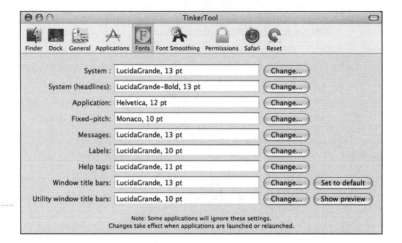

Figure 4.56

*TinkerTool's
Fonts dialog.*

International language support: Basics

Mac OS X lets you change the language used in its menus and dialogs. You can also use these international language characters in text you create in applications. For this book, I'm sticking primarily to troubleshooting in English (there's more than enough to cover!); however, it still pays to be aware of some basics of multiple-language support.

International System Preferences pane. To get your Mac to display its menus, dialogs, and most other standard elements in a language other than English, your first stop is the International System Preferences pane. Here's what to do:

*   In the Language pane, select the order of the languages listed by sliding them to their desired locations. Once you've done this and logged out and back in, a given application will display its menus and text in the first language in the list if that language is available and enabled for the application. If the application does not support the first language in the list (or that language has been disabled, as described below), it will display in the next language on the list. And so on.

    If a language you want is not listed, click the Edit List button to select it. If it is not listed here (or does not appear after being selected), it probably means support for that language was not installed with Mac OS X (that is, you probably chose, via a Custom Install, not to install the support) or you subsequently deleted the files (there are various third-party utilities that can do this).

*   From the "Order for sorted lists" pop-up menu, you can choose a language. This affects only non-Unicode applications. In essence, for a set of languages that share the same alphabet (for example, Spanish, French, Italian,

and English), you can select which language behavior you want. This causes text to be sorted according to the specifics of the selected behavior.

- Having the language displayed correctly is all well and good. But what if you want to type in that language? Different languages are often matched with keyboards specific to that language. To type text in a given language, you may thus need to select a keyboard layout or input method specific to that language—especially important for Asian and Middle Eastern languages.

To set up for this, go to the Input Menu tab and select the keyboard layouts for all languages you may use. To enable a selection, check the box next to its name. You can then switch among any of your selected languages via the Input menu in the menu bar—or via keyboard shortcuts as defined in the Keyboard & Mouse pane. As you switch, the flag icon in the menu bar shifts to that of the selected country and the keyboard layout changes to match that of the keyboard for that country.

Keyboards listed as Unicode in the Script column of the Input menu pane are available only in Unicode-compatible applications, such as Mail, TextEdit, and the Finder. When you're typing within an application, the availability of these keyboards in the Input menu indicates whether that application works with Unicode.

SEE: • "Input menu," earlier in this chapter, for more on setting up and using this menu.

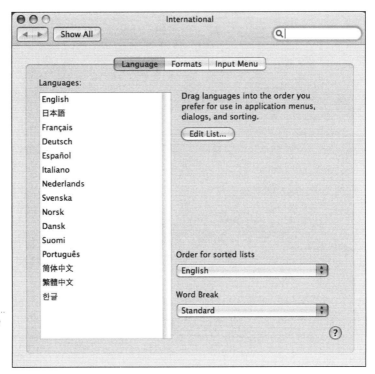

Figure 4.57

The Language pane of the International System Preferences pane.

Having done all of this, you still won't see use of languages other than English unless the specific applications you use support additional languages. Here are the details:

Multiple-language support files. Support for multiple languages in the OS itself (such as the Finder) or in any application that runs in Mac OS X is determined by whether or not the files needed for any additional language(s) are included with the application.

Using iTunes as an example (since it includes excellent multiple-language support), we're going to explore how all of this works:

1. In the Finder, select the iTunes icon.

2. Control-click the icon, and from the contextual menu that appears, choose Show Package Contents.

3. In the window that appears, open the Contents folder and then the Resources folder within the Contents folder.

Here, you'll find numerous folders that end with the extension .lproj (such as English.lproj and French.lproj). Each of these folders represents the required support for iTunes to run in the named language.

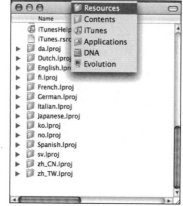

Figure 4.58

The .lproj folders in the Resources folder of my copy of iTunes.app.

Disabling or removing language-support files. The language-support files in iTunes take up most of the iTunes application (around 20 MB). Thus, eliminating these files (assuming you don't need additional languages in iTunes) can save a considerable amount of space.

To do this, you can simply remove the undesired .lproj folders from the iTunes package and drag them to the Trash (or anywhere else, should you want to save them). Or, if you don't care about space and want to keep the files within iTunes but not have them accessible for display, drag them to the Resources Disabled folder in the Contents folder (you may need to create this folder if it doesn't already exist). Note that you should not remove or disable the English.lproj folder; iTunes will not run without it.

Alternatively, if you don't want to delve into package contents, you can do the same thing via iTunes' Get Info window. Follow these steps:

1. In the Finder select the iTunes icon.

2. Press Command-I to bring up its Get Info window.

3. Click the disclosure triangle next to the Languages section.

4. To *disable* a language, simply uncheck the appropriate check box; this action moves the language into the Resources Disabled folder.

   or

   To delete the language resource (which is what you need to do to reduce the size of iTunes), select a language and click the Remove button. You cannot, however, remove a language that has been disabled. To remove a disabled language, you must first re-enable it. If the Remove button is still dimmed when you select an enabled language, force-quit the Finder and try again.

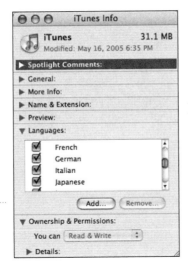

Figure 4.59

The Languages section of the Get Info window for iTunes.

Choosing to remove a language places its .lproj folder in the Trash. Until you empty the Trash, you can drag the language folder from the Trash and save it elsewhere. In this way, you can use the Add button to return it to the list later, should you want to. Note: You will have to close the Get Info window and reopen it before it will show that you have added a language.

Finally, you can use the third-party utility DeLocalizer, by Mike Bombich (www.bombich.com/software/local.html), to remove unwanted language files.

Reinstalling language-support files. If you entirey deleted language-support files (or if you never installed them when you initially installed Mac OS X), a time may come when you want to add some or all of these files back. The easiest way to do so is to use the Mac OS X Install DVD for Tiger. Double-click the Optional Installs package (located at the root level of the disc) to open the package in the Installer application. Click Continue until you get to the Custom Install pane; click the disclosure triangle next to Language Translations. From the list that appears, choose just the languages you want; then click the Install button.

International language support: Troubleshooting

The following describes a couple of problems (and their solutions) that can arise when using multiple languages in Mac OS X.

Additional software needed. Some languages may require additional software. Apple writes: "For example, Mac OS X includes script bundles for Cyrillic and Central European languages. However, such a script bundle does not activate unless at least one font for that script is present. Installing a font that is compatible with the script bundle will activate it. Keyboard layouts associated with the activated bundle then appear in the International Preferences panel."

Localized OS needed. Some languages work only if you have a region-specific, or *localized*, version of the Mac OS installed. Thus, you may not be able to use these languages with a typical North American English Mac OS X system; you may instead need to install the version of Mac OS X specific to the language in question. Apple now releases each version of Mac OS X in a variety of localized versions.

Note: For languages that use non-Roman-alphabet characters, you may also need to make sure that the needed Additional Fonts were installed when you initially installed Mac OS X.

Font Utilities

For many users, Font Book (covered earlier in the chapter) is the only font utility they'll ever need or use. However, a variety of other font-related utilities are available for tasks that go beyond Font Book's capabilities. The following is a small selection of what you can find:

Extensis's **Suitcase** (www.extensis.com), which I've mentioned throughout this chapter, allows you to view, activate, and deactivate individual fonts separately for Cocoa, Carbon, and Classic applications. This utility can be especially useful when two fonts conflict or when a font causes a problem with a specific application. In such cases, you can use Suitcase to deactivate the problem font. There's a great deal of overlap between the features in utilities like Suitcase and those found in Font Book (with Suitcase offering more features). In general, you should use one or the other, but not both.

Insider Software's **FontAgent Pro** (www.insidersoftware.com) is another font-management utility similar in function to Suitcase.

FontDoctor (included with Suitcase) finds and repairs an assortment of font problems, including damaged and corrupted fonts, missing fonts, duplicate fonts, and font ID conflicts.

Pixits's **FontExampler** (www.pixits.com) displays all of your installed fonts in WYSIWYG mode in a single window. You can also see how any font looks at different sizes.

Stone Design's **FontSight** (www.stone.com) adds a font menu to Cocoa applications such as TextEdit. This eliminates the need to access the Font panel just to change the font of selected text (which I find to be a much less convenient method than using a font menu).

Marcel Bresink's **TinkerTool** (www.bresink.de/osx/TinkerTool.html) allows you to change the default fonts used in many Mac OS X locations, such as window title bars (as described in "Modifying default fonts," earlier in this chapter.

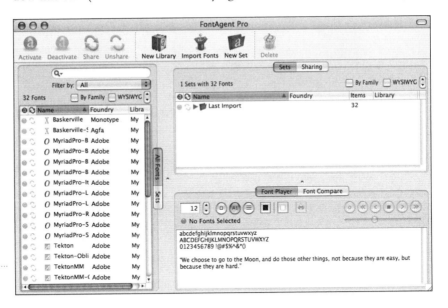

Figure 4.60

A view of FontAgent Pro.

5

Crash Prevention and Recovery

Of all the things that can go wrong with a computer, the one that users typically want to avoid most is a crash. Actually, the words *crash* and its first cousin *freeze* are generic terms that cover a wide range of symptoms and causes, some far more serious than others.

Relatively low on the seriousness scale is an application crash or freeze. In the simplest case, the application quits itself (often referred to as an *unexpected quit*). You may have trouble relaunching the application at this point, but your computer is likely to run just fine otherwise. A bit more frustrating is the *hang*, or freeze. In this case, the application remains open and visible, but nothing works. In some cases, until you thaw things out, other programs may also be inaccessible.

More serious is a crash or freeze that's not limited to a single program but rather brings almost everything on your Mac to a halt, forcing you to restart. For obvious reasons, the most serious of these situations is a crash that occurs during startup, thus preventing you from even beginning to use your Mac.

In this chapter, I'll cover all of these variations of crashes and freezes. I'll tell you how best to recover from them and offer some tips on how to prevent them.

One bit of good news: The more serious crashes, the ones that bring down your entire system, occur much less often in Mac OS X than they did in Classic Mac OS versions (Mac OS 9 and earlier). To learn why, see "Protected memory," in Chapter 4.

In This Chapter

Uh-Oh!

What causes crashes and freezes?

Most crashes and freezes can be attributed to one of three things:

Software bug. Errors in programming code often cause application crashes. Sometimes these errors are referred to as "pure" bugs—that is, they occur independently of other software or hardware. For example, an error in the code of a word-processing application that causes the program to crash every time you try to save a file with italicized text—regardless of what other software you're running—is a pure bug. However, bugs can also be caused by the way particular programs interact with one another. For example, an application may crash on launch, but only if another particular program is open as well. The problem then is determining which program is the culprit. Ideally, at least one of the developers will agree to fix the code in order to resolve the conflict.

Corrupt file. Occasionally, a file on your drive will become modified to either include data from another file, lose vital data of its own, or include "nonsense" code. Say you saved a word-processing document just before a power failure occurred, resulting in a partial save of the file: The next time you open the file, you're likely to get a crash. Alternatively, in a critical OS file that gets updated periodically (such as one in the System folder), an error can occur when the file is being written to disk, causing the file to stop working—another situation that can lead to a crash, which in this case may prevent you from starting your Mac. Corrupt preferences files are also common sources of system crashes. These files are usually updated quite frequently, increasing the odds of a copy error.

Hardware conflict. A problem with a hardware component, either external or internal, can also lead to a crash. A circuit can burn out on the logic board, or your memory may have been defective from the day it shipped. Conversely, your hardware might not be compatible with your particular Mac. For example, RAM comes in many speeds and sizes, but most Mac models work with only specific types. Although two RAM modules may look identical (and may even both fit in your Mac), one could be the wrong type—and that would lead to a startup crash or seemingly random freezes or crashes while using your Mac.

Finally, hardware components that *should* work with your Mac may not, due to software problems. In particular, certain devices (such as printers, scanners, and other peripherals) require that driver software be present on your startup drive in order to work. Some devices use drivers built into Mac OS X, whereas others require that you install driver software provided by the manufacturer.

Bugs in the driver software can result in crashes, just as other software bugs can. Hardware devices can include firmware. Representing a sort of middle ground between software and hardware, firmware is software code that resides in a component of the hardware itself. Typically, you can upgrade firmware by running a special firmware-update program. Often, as new Macs and OS updates come out, hardware devices will require these firmware updates to remain compatible.

General strategies for fixing crashes

Most crashes are limited to specific applications—meaning you can continue to use your Mac despite the crash. You'll often even be able to relaunch the offending application. If the crash doesn't occur the next time you attempt the procedure (you may need to restart your Mac to stop the crash from recurring), you may well decide to ignore it—and hope that it's a one-time-only thing or that it happens so infrequently that it's not a problem. Otherwise, your goal will be to locate the cause of the crash and fix it. In general, the exact fix will depend on the type of crash.

For crashes caused by corrupt files, the solution may be as simple as deleting the file. If the problem is a preferences file, for example, you can simply delete the file and a new version will be created automatically the next time the relevant application is launched. The default file should be free of whatever corruption caused the crash. You'll need to reinstate any changes you made to the preferences file, but at least the crash won't occur again.

Similarly, if you have a corrupt document—especially if you have a backup of the file—you can simply delete the corrupt version and start again with your backup. You can even delete and replace corrupt OS files, assuming you know where and how to get the replacements (for more on this, see Chapter 3). In some cases you'll need a disk-repair utility, such as Apple's Disk Utility or Alsoft's DiskWarrior (www.alsoft.com). And reinstalling the OS software can also provide a cure. (In the worst-case scenario, you may need to erase your drive before reinstalling the system software.)

For buggy software, you simply have to hope that the company provides a bug fix—and in the meantime find a work-around to prevent the crash.

Because so many problems occur as a result of something going wrong at startup (including a startup crash itself), we're going to take a look at the startup sequence of events before I go into detail about crash types and their solutions.

The Startup Sequence of Events

After you turn on your Mac, you must typically wait a few minutes before you can start using it. This is because your Mac is performing its *startup sequence*. For you, this may simply represent an opportunity for a coffee break; for your Mac, however, it's a critical period during which a multitude of events occur that determine the success or failure of everything that follows.

An audiovisual overview of the startup sequence

When you turn on your Mac, you should hear the startup chime—typically before your display screen even lights up. Shortly thereafter, a gray screen appears with a darker gray Apple logo in the center (yes, the old Happy Mac icon has been retired!). At this point, you'll see a sundial cursor (which also looks like wheel spokes endlessly turning). Eventually, this screen is replaced by a blue screen with a white box in the center, containing the Mac OS X logo and the message, "Starting Mac OS X…" Next to appear will be either the Login window or (if you enabled automatic login) the Finder's Desktop. If you get the Login window, you enter your name and password and then click the Log In button to log in—at which point you're taken to the Finder's Desktop. In either case, you must now wait for items that load at login. Once this has occurred, the startup sequence is complete.

If a sequence other than the one just described occurs, you most likely have a problem. The following details what happens behind the scenes during the startup sequence, what can go wrong, and what you can do to fix problems when they occur.

Boot ROM and Open Firmware

Boot ROM and Open Firmware refer to two components of Macs (built into the hardware) that function before Mac OS X begins to load.

Boot ROM: Power-On Self-Test (POST). Boot ROM is software code stored within the circuitry of the Mac's logic board. Because the data does not reside on a hard drive, it can run even before a startup hard drive has been chosen. Thus, this code is just about the first thing that gets checked when you turn on your Mac. This software is also independent of what OS version you're using.

Boot ROM's initial function is to perform the Power-On Self-Test (POST).

This test checks the Mac's hardware and RAM (random access memory). It resides in the Mac's ROM (read-only memory) and runs at startup (though only from a currently shut-down Mac; it won't run if you simply restart a running Mac). If POST detects a problem, the startup sequence will probably halt almost instantly. In addition, you'll hear one of the following sounds:

- **One beep.** Indicates that no RAM is installed or detected.
- **Two beeps.** Indicates that an incompatible RAM type is installed.
- **Three beeps.** Indicates that no RAM banks passed memory testing.
- **Four beeps.** Indicates there's a bad checksum for the remainder of the Boot ROM. (*Checksum* refers to a method of determining whether data is corrupt.)
- **Five beeps.** This means there's a bad checksum for the ROM boot block.

Most often, an error here will indicate a RAM problem (one, two, or three beeps). If you've installed additional RAM on your Mac (and especially if it is third-party RAM from a vendor of unknown reliability!), it's time to check to see if it's defective or otherwise incompatible with your system. The simplest way to do so is to remove the RAM and see whether the POST warning goes away. If so, contact your RAM vendor about getting a replacement.

Four or five beeps suggest other hardware-related problems. Your next step should be to try the diagnostic software that came with your Mac:

Apple Hardware Test software. If the problem isn't with RAM and your Mac shipped with Hardware Test software, now's the time to use it. If you can't start up from the Hardware Test CD/DVD, you almost certainly have a hardware problem—which means it's probably time to take your Mac in for repair.

TECHNICALLY SPEAKING ▶ The Apple Hardware Test Software

Each Mac type (iBook, iMac, PowerBook, and so on) uses its own version of Apple's Hardware Test software—that is, don't try to use a Hardware Test disc with a Mac other than the model for which it was intended!

To start up from a Hardware Test CD, turn on your Mac, insert the CD, and hold down the C key.

If your Mac came with a single DVD, the Hardware Test software should be included on it. To start up from the Hardware Test component, insert the DVD and then restart while pressing down the Option key. From the list of bootable volumes that appears, select Hardware Test.

After your Mac has booted from the CD/DVD, Hardware Test will automatically load. Follow the instructions for the Quick and Extended tests, which examine components like AirPort, Mass Storage, and Memory. You can also use this software to diagnose hardware problems beyond startup ones, such as failures of USB and/or FireWire ports.

If the software detects an error, it displays an error code (for example, "ata1/6/3 HD:2,1"). You can then search Apple's Knowledge Base (http://kbase.info.apple.com) for documents that mention the error. You may find one that identifies the error and tells you how to fix it. Or simply enter the term into a Google search and hope you get lucky. If your search comes up empty, contact Apple directly.

Other symptoms of hardware failure include the following:

- If you don't hear the hard drive spinning, but everything else appears normal, your hard drive may be damaged. In this case, you should still be able to start from a CD, but you will likely need to replace the hard drive.

- If you don't hear any noise (not even the fan) and the Mac is plugged in and has power, the power supply has probably failed. You will need to replace it.

None of this information is specific to Mac OS X, so I'm not going to delve into these topics further here; for more detailed help when it comes to determining if you have a hardware failure, go online to sites such as MacFixIt (www.macfixit.com) or Apple's own support site.

Other hardware-based diagnostics. Some Mac models and displays have hardware diagnostics beyond the Boot ROM. These include the following:

- **Diagnostic LEDs on the logic board.** The iMac G5 has a new hardware feature: four diagnostic LED lights on the logic board. To access them, you need to remove the back cover of the Mac. If things are running normally, the first three lights will be on and the fourth one will be off. See this Apple Knowledge Base document for more details: http://docs.info.apple.com/article.html?artnum=86815.

  I expect these LEDs to pop up in other Mac models over time.

- **Display flashes.** Apple's new flat-panel displays can alert you to display-related problems via flashes of the power LED. For example, three short flashes means "The display is detecting wrong video format or an unsupported resolution." If this happens, make sure your display settings are correct and the display you are using is compatible with your Mac model. If they are correct, try resetting the PRAM (as described below). See this Apple Knowledge Base document for more details: http://docs.info.apple.com/article.html?artnum=88366. (Note: As with all computer peripherals, also make sure its cables are properly connected.)

Open Firmware. In essence, Open Firmware chooses the operating system you use. It also makes first contact with (or *initializes*) hardware beyond the Mac itself, such as external drives. You access Open Firmware directly by holding down Command-Option-O-F immediately at startup. From its simple command-line interface, you can type Open Firmware commands to carry out actions beyond what Open Firmware does by default at startup. You'll normally have little need for this; however, you may occasionally want to run a specific Open Firmware command to solve a troubleshooting matter. Or, due to a bug, your Mac may briefly display the Open Firmware screen at startup, even if you *do not* press Command-Option-O-F. Even more rarely, startup may halt at the Open Firmware screen.

Beware!

Note: When Apple comes out with Intel-based Macs in 2006, they will reportedly not support Open Firmware! Among other things, this means you will no longer be able to use Open Firmware passwords for security protection.

SEE: • "Take Note: Firmware Updates," "Technically Speaking: Open Firmware Commands," and "Technically Speaking: Open Firmware Password," below, for details on troubleshooting Open Firmware.

TAKE NOTE ▶ Firmware Updates

Apple periodically releases software called *firmware updates*. These updates are different for each Mac model. That is, an iMac firmware update is useless on a PowerBook. You can download the latest firmware updater for your particular Mac from Apple's Web site (www.info.apple.com/support/downloads.html). Once you have located and downloaded the appropriate updater, run it.

When you successfully run a Mac model firmware updater, it updates the Open Firmware software. Exact instructions on how to install these firmware updates may vary from computer model to model but are included with each update. Don't worry if you're unsure whether you need a given update: If you already have the same or a newer version installed, the utility will alert you and refuse to install the update. If you need the update, simply follow the instructions that appear.

You can also tell which firmware version you currently have installed by launching System Profiler and checking the Boot ROM Version line in the Hardware section.

Be careful not to interrupt a firmware update—doing so could leave the firmware nonfunctional, and you might not be able to start up again. If this happens, there's no easy way to reinstall the firmware. A trip to an Apple Service Provider will probably be needed.

In general, I recommend installing firmware updates: They fix bugs from the preceding version, and they may add new features. Occasionally, however, problems occur. As with any type of update, it pays to check online for reports of potential problems before deciding whether to install a particular firmware update.

All of the above refers specifically to updating Apple's Open Firmware on a Mac. Other peripheral devices, from Apple's AirPort Base Station to Bluetooth modules, have their own firmware, which may also be updated via firmware updaters. These are separate from Open Firmware updates.

SEE: • Chapter 3 for coverage of firmware updates and installing and updating Mac OS X.

TECHNICALLY SPEAKING ▶ **Open Firmware Commands**

If you hold down Command-Option-O-F immediately at startup, you get dumped into the Open Firmware environment, where you can run Open Firmware commands. To get a command to run, type the command and press Return. Open Firmware includes dozens of commands, which are summarized in the Apple Knowledge Base document located at http://docs.info.apple.com/article.html?artnum=60285. For most troubleshooting, however, you need to know only a small subset of these commands. The ones I've found to be most useful include the following:

eject cd and shut-down. Typically, to start up from a CD or DVD, you need to hold down the C key at startup with the disc inserted in the drive. Occasionally, the Mac may attempt to start up from the disc even if you aren't holding down the C key (for example, if you have selected the disc as the startup disk in System Preferences). Usually, holding down the mouse/trackpad button or the Media Eject key at startup will force the disc to eject before it's selected as the startup device. However, if even this method fails, you can boot into Open Firmware and type eject cd. This command will get the optical drive's tray to open, at which point you can remove the disc.

Alternatively, you may want to start up from a disc that is not in the optical drive. If, due to a system crash, you cannot access the drive before restarting, you're faced with a challenge: You need to get the drive tray to open (unless it's a slot-loading drive, like the one found in iMacs), insert the disc, close the tray, and hold down the C key—all before the Mac selects the hard drive as the startup device. If this is too much to do in so short a time, use Open Firmware. Open the tray via the eject cd command, insert the disc, and close the tray. Then type shut-down. This command does what its name implies: shuts down your Mac. Now you can restart as normal, holding down the C key, to use the disc as the startup disc.

reset-all. There's been some confusion among Mac users as to what the reset-all command does. Some people believe it resets the Open Firmware code to some default state—possibly all the way back to when your Mac first shipped, thus erasing any subsequent firmware updates. This is *not* the case. The command makes no changes in Open Firmware itself. Instead, it initiates the same sorts of changes that would occur if you pressed the Mac's Reset button or even simply restarted as normal. It rechecks the peripheral devices attached to your Mac, for example. Thus, if your Mac appears to not recognize a device such as a FireWire drive, using reset-all could help.

printenv, reset-nvram, and set-defaults. Though rarely necessarily, these commands can be lifesavers when you *do* need them. Typing printenv gets you a list of all the configuration settings in the Mac's nonvolatile RAM (NVRAM). These settings are stored in a special type of RAM on the Mac's logic board. You can modify their contents, as you can with ordinary RAM, but the contents are preserved even after you shut down the Mac. Among other things, NVRAM maintains the setting for the default startup device, called *boot-device*.

continues on next page

TECHNICALLY SPEAKING ▶ **Open Firmware Commands** *continued*

You use the reset-nvram and/or set-defaults command to return the NVRAM settings to their defaults if you ever need to do so. These commands can come in handy if you can't get your Mac to attempt to start up from your internal hard drive, no matter what you do. The command combination of reset-nvram and set-defaults is similar to a well-known Macintosh troubleshooting technique called *zapping the PRAM* (parameter RAM). Among other things, using these commands may fix problems where a Mac fails to go to sleep or wake from sleep.

The reset-nvram command followed by reset-all (or just zapping the PRAM) should also eliminate the symptom in which Open Firmware appears at startup even when you do not press the Command-Option-O-F keys.

bye or mac-boot. Whenever you want to exit Open Firmware and start up from the selected startup device, simply type bye, mac-boot, or reset-all to restart; or type shut-down to shut down.

SEE: • "Take Note: Zapping PRAM and Resetting the Power Manager," later in this chapter.

TECHNICALLY SPEAKING ▶ **Open Firmware Password**

The latest versions of Open Firmware software (4.1.7 and later) allow you to add a password requirement. With this option enabled, you won't be able to start up from any device other than the default boot device, nor will you be able to start up in any way that bypasses the normal startup procedure (such as attempting to enter single-user mode). If you do try, you will be dumped into Open Firmware, or (in some cases) the bypass attempt will be ignored and the normal startup sequence will proceed. The only way to circumvent this is to enter the Open Firmware password in the Open Firmware window or (as a more permanent solution) disable the password. With certain settings, the protection prevents any startup at all without entering the password.

An Open Firmware password is thus the ultimate startup security protection and may be especially useful in public and semipublic environments where you're concerned about users' bypassing Mac OS X's other, more vulnerable, protections. For example, a user could bypass normal Mac OS X accounts security by starting up via a bootable CD or DVD; Open Firmware protection would block this.

Enabling password. To create a password, enter Open Firmware and type password. You will not be asked to use this password at startup, however, until you enable the password-checking feature. To do this, type setenv security-mode *mode*, where *mode* is none, command, or full.

- The none mode (the default) means no password protection is enforced.

- The command mode, likely the most useful and common setting, allows you to start up (from the volume selected in Startup Disk only) without a password; however, you can't make any Open Firmware changes without entering the password. It also prevents starting up from devices other than the default boot device without the password. If the password is needed, you typically get a screen at startup where you can enter it. You then click the arrow button and startup proceeds.

- The *full* mode prohibits you from starting up under any circumstances without entering the password.

continues on next page

TECHNICALLY SPEAKING ▶ Open Firmware Password *continued*

Type reset-all after making a change to enable that change. Once you've done this, you cannot change password-enforced settings without first entering your Open Firmware password.

Note: Do not use the capital letter *U* in an Open Firmware password. If you do, certain Mac models (including any iBook, recent iMac models, and Power Mac G4s) will not recognize the password.

What password protection blocks. Here are the complete details regarding what operations are blocked by Open Firmware password protection. In command mode, the following operations are blocked:

- Use of the C key to start up from a CD-ROM disc.
- Use of the N key to start up from a NetBoot server.
- Use of the T key to start up in Target Disk mode.
- Use of the Shift key to start up in Safe Boot mode (including disabling user-level login items)
- Use of Command-V to start up in verbose mode.
- Use of Command-S to start up in single-user mode.
- Use of Command-Option-P-R to reset the PRAM.
- Use of the Option key to access the Startup Manager and choose a different startup device. (Actually, you can choose a different startup device here, but only if you enter the Open Firmware password when asked.)

In full mode, all of the same actions are blocked. In addition, when you try to start up your Mac, you will be required to provide the Open Firmware password; if you do not provide the correct password, your Mac will simply shut down.

Enabling password protection does not prevent access to Open Firmware itself (via Command-Option-O-F), but it requires entering the Open Firmware password before you can make any changes.

To perform any of the above actions, you need to disable the password requirement, as described in the following sections.

Disabling password protection. To disable Open Firmware password protection, simply re-enter Open Firmware (by holding down Command-Option-O-F at startup) and change the security mode back to none by typing setenv security-mode none and entering your password when requested.

Apple's Open Firmware Password utility. If you want to enable or disable command mode, there is an easier alternative to using the above password commands in Open Firmware: Apple's Open Firmware Password utility. This utility is located on the Mac OS X Install disc, tucked away in the /Applications/Utilities folder located at the root level of the disc. If you run it and enter your administrative password, you will be able to create an Open Firmware password and enable or disable its use. You can run this utility directly from the CD or copy it to your hard drive and run it from there. (The utility does not allow you to enable/disable full mode.)

continues on next page

TECHNICALLY SPEAKING ▶ **Open Firmware Password** *continued*

Using reset-nvram. Using the reset-nvram command followed by the reset-all command will also allow you to start up from a bootable CD or via single-user mode, even if the Open Firmware password is enabled.

Force-disabling password protection. The biggest risk of using Open Firmware password protection is that when full mode is enabled, if you forget your password (or the Mac refuses to accept it), you're locked out of your Mac. In such cases, you can remove Open Firmware password protection by installing an additional RAM module in your Mac or (assuming you have more than one) removing one—and then restart in Open Firmware. Password protection may now be disabled without your needing to enter a password.

If the above doesn't work, restart again and reset (zap) the PRAM by pressing Command-Option-P-R on startup; do not release the keys until the Mac has chimed three times. Note: The ability to do this without a password is enabled when you change your RAM configuration.

You should now be able to shut down your Mac, return your RAM configuration to its previous state, and restart again as normal. You can later re-enable password protection, if you wish, selecting a new password as desired.

Of course, the fact that the above procedure exists also means that Open Firmware password protection isn't 100 percent safe. However, if you physically secure your Mac so that no one can open it and change the amount of RAM inside, you can prevent anyone from taking advantage of this "back door."

Figure 5.1

The Open Firmware Password utility.

Figure 5.2

The dialog that appears at startup if you must enter your Open Firmware password.

TAKE NOTE ▶ Zapping PRAM and Resetting the Power Manager

The following information is not specific to Mac OS X; however, it can still be helpful for solving various startup problems as described in the main text.

Zapping, or resetting, the PRAM. Zapping the PRAM resets your Mac's *parameter* RAM and NVRAM settings to their default values. PRAM holds such information as your time zone setting, startup-volume choice, speaker volume, recent kernel panic information, and more. To reset it, shut down your Mac and then turn it on again while holding down the Command, Option, P, and R keys. When the Mac has chimed three times, release the keys and let startup proceed. For additional details, see these Apple Knowledge Base documents: http://docs.info.apple.com/article.html?artnum=86194 and http://docs.info.apple.com/article.html?artnum=2238. You can also check out the section on this topic in my book *Sad Macs*. In addition, you may be able to zap the PRAM via Open Firmware, as noted in "Technically Speaking: Open Firmware Commands," above.

Apple warns, "If you have a RAID setup, your computer may not start up if you reset parameter RAM (PRAM) when you restart. To fix this, restart your computer while holding down the Option key to select your startup system. If this doesn't work, restart your computer while holding down the Command-Option-Shift-Delete keys."

Resetting the Power Manager. On laptops, resetting the Power Manager accomplishes the same thing as zapping PRAM—with one additional bonus: It also resets the laptop circuitry responsible for power management (mainly sleep and battery use). Exactly how to perform this reset varies with each Mac laptop model; the following Apple Knowledge Base document provides the details: http://docs.info.apple.com/article.html?artnum=14449. On most recent PowerBook models, for example, you reset the Power Manager by shutting down the PowerBook, removing the battery and disconnecting the AC adapter, and then pressing and holding the Power button for 5 seconds.

Even some desktop Macs include a Power Management Unit (PMU). However, recent desktop Macs include instead a similar feature called the System Management Unit (SMU). One difference between the SMU and the PMU is that the SMU does not reset the PRAM. Exact details on how to reset the PMU and SMU vary by model. In all cases, resetting the management unit can resolve certain issues where the computer does not start up or has problems with issues such as video display, sleep, and fan noises.

See the following Apple Knowledge Base articles for more details: http://docs.info.apple.com/article.html?artnum=300574, http://docs.info.apple.com/article.html?artnum=300908, http://docs.info.apple.com/article.html?artnum=300341, and http://docs.info.apple.com/article.html?artnum=301733.

Startup Manager: Option key at startup

Holding down the Option key immediately on startup invokes Startup Manager. You can use this feature to select a startup volume different from the one selected in the Startup Disk System Preferences pane. Changes here

— enables select Windows XP on MacBook Pro.

don't modify the default selection: The next time you restart *without* holding down the Option key, your Mac will again start up from the device chosen in System Preferences.

Invoking Startup Manager brings up a screen with icons for the various volumes (drives, discs, and/or partitions) from which you can boot your Mac. The following details what you'll see in this screen and how to proceed once it appears:

- You will see one icon for each bootable volume. If a bootable CD or DVD is in the CD/DVD drive or a bootable external hard drive is attached, you should see icons for these as well.

- If you have a Mac that can still boot from Mac OS 9, and Mac OS X and Mac OS 9 are installed on the *same* volume, only one of them can be *blessed* (available as a bootable OS) at a time—which means that only one of them will ordinarily be shown in Startup Manager. Thus, when you hold down the Option key at startup, you will see either the Mac OS X icon or the Mac OS 9 icon for that volume, but not both. Which one you see will depend on which one was most recently selected as the bootable OS. If you have Mac OS 9 and Mac OS X installed on different volumes, you should see an icon for each OS.

- If you do not see a volume that you expect to see, click the curved-arrow button and the Mac will check again for potential startup volumes.

- Click the icon of the volume that you want to use as the startup volume. Then click the straight-arrow button, and startup will proceed.

- If you press Command-. (period) at this screen, the Mac's CD/DVD drive tray should open, allowing you to mount a CD or DVD for use as the startup disc. This screen also allows you to eject a CD or DVD at this point—another option for accessing the optical-drive tray at startup (as described in "Technically Speaking: Open Firmware Commands," earlier in this chapter).

Startup Disk System Preferences vs. Startup Manager. Using Startup Manager to change a startup-disk selection does not change the default startup drive. That is, if you normally boot into Mac OS X on your internal drive but select an external bootable volume in Startup Manager, you will boot from the internal drive the next time you restart normally, even if the external drive is still mounted. To change the default setting, go to the Startup Disk System Preferences pane and select the desired volume (and the OS within the volume, if more than one is listed).

Unlike Startup Manager, the Startup Disk System Preferences pane also allows you to choose among multiple bootable operating systems (such as Mac OS 9 and Mac OS X) on the same volume.

I recommend using Startup Disk to change your startup-disk selection. Only use Startup Manager if the standard methods either don't work or aren't accessible (perhaps because you can't start up successfully).

TAKE NOTE ▶ Keyboard Startup Options

Various keys and key combinations (beyond the Option key used to invoke Startup Manager) can be used to modify the startup process. The following describes some of them:

C key at startup. You can hold down the C key at startup to start up from a bootable CD or DVD already in the drive.

Command-Option-Shift-Delete. Holding down this combination of keys forces the Mac to bypass the typical default startup drive (your internal drive) in favor of an alternative bootable device, such as an external FireWire drive. This may succeed in cases where holding down the Option key does not access the drive you wish to use.

Command-D. Using this key combination, the Mac attempts to start from the internal drive or, if that drive is divided into partitions, the first partition on that drive. The first partition is the one at the top when viewed in Disk Utility's Partition pane.

X key at startup. By holding down the X key at startup, you can make a Mac that normally boots into Mac OS 9 boot into Mac OS X instead (assuming that both operating systems are located on the same volume, and you last started from the Mac OS 9 System Folder on that volume). This technique allows you to work around the problem whereby the Option-key method does not list Mac OS 9 and Mac OS X at the same time if they are on the same volume. Also, unlike the Option-key method, holding down the X key saves the change—that is, the next time you start up normally, you will again start up in Mac OS X.

Other options. Other keyboard startup options—Open Firmware, single-user mode, verbose mode, Safe Boot, and target disk mode—are covered elsewhere in this chapter.

SEE: • "Boot ROM and Open Firmware," "Single-user mode," "Verbose mode," and "Safe Booting," elsewhere in this chapter.

• "Sharing via Target Disk Mode," in Chapter 9.

BootX

If you elected to start up in Mac OS X, have passed through the Boot ROM stage successfully, and are not starting up from a CD, the next file that the Mac looks for is called the BootX booter, which is located in /System/Library/CoreServices. Its primary job is to load what is called the *kernel environment*.

It is at this point that the Apple logo on the gray screen should appear.

Without a BootX file in your Mac OS X System folder—or, more precisely, somewhere on the volume—your Mac will not start up. Even though you can boot the volume if the file isn't in the System folder, per se, I can think of no reason to move it. In fact, I've found that if you simply copy this BootX file onto any volume—even one with no other Mac OS X software—the Startup

Disk System Preferences pane will be fooled into thinking you can start up in Mac OS X from that volume. (This attempt will fail, of course, if you do try.)

Figure 5.3

The CoreServices folder with BootX highlighted.

Kernel extensions. During this phase, the kernel extensions (*kext* items) are loaded. Kernel extensions are mainly device drivers that support possible attached hardware, such as PCI cards, an AirPort Base Station, graphics cards, or an iPod. They are stored in /System/Library/Extensions.

It is at this point that the spinning cursor should appear on the gray screen.

Figure 5.4

The /System/Library/ Extensions folder (highlighted), with the Extensions. kextcache and Extensions.mkext files to the right. Partial contents of the Extensions folder are also shown.

TECHNICALLY SPEAKING ▶ Understanding Kernel Extensions

One of BootX's jobs is to determine which kernel extensions should be loaded at startup and then load them. Two Unix utilities assist with this: kextcache (which creates the mkext cache file described in the next paragraph) and kextd (which loads and unloads specific kext items, as appropriate for the startup in progress). Each individual kernel extension file/package contains information (in the OSBundleRequired key in its Info.plist file) describing its loading requirements.

BootX first attempts to load a previously cached set of device drivers—an mkext cache file named Extensions.mkext that's located at the root level of the /System/Library folder. A related file, called Extensions.kextcache, is also located here.

If these two files are missing or corrupted, BootX will create new ones by rechecking the extensions in /System/Library/Extensions for drivers and other kernel extensions set to be loaded at startup. In fact, deleting these files (which requires root access) occasionally fixes system crashes and/or kernel panics related to peripheral devices that use kext drivers.

Installing a new kext item. You typically install new kernel extensions indirectly via a Mac OS X update or third-party software installer. During the installation process, a script in the installer .pkg file should force the cache to be updated so that the OS recognizes the presence of the new extension the next time it starts up.

Getting the Mac to recognize a newly installed extension is one reason you may need to restart your Mac immediately after installing a Mac OS X update. In fact, if you have problems with a hardware peripheral after installing new software (even if the software installer claims not to require a restart), it's a good idea to try restarting (or, even better, shutting down and restarting).

If even restarting doesn't get the extension to work, try deleting the Extensions.mkext item and restarting. You will need root access (explained in Chapter 4) to delete this file (as covered in chapters 4 and 6). Alternatively, you can force-update the mkext item by changing the modification date of the Extensions folder. To do so, launch Terminal and type sudo touch /System/Library/Extensions.

Another approach would be to type sudo kextload /System/Library/Extensions/{*name of kext item*} to load a single extension (presumably the newly installed one)—which doesn't require you to restart your Mac. Still, given that you don't install new kext items every day, I advise playing it safe and restarting.

Third-party kext files that do not load at startup. Due to the complexities of Mac OS X's rules that determine when and if a kext file loads, it is possible that a third-party kext file for a peripheral hardware device is not correctly written and thus may refuse to load at startup. As a result, the peripheral device will not work. In such cases, unplugging and replugging the device (hot-swapping) after startup is over will usually get the kext file to load—and thus allow the device to work. The ultimate fix for this is for the third-party developer to revise its kext file.

continues on next page

TECHNICALLY SPEAKING ▶ Understanding Kernel Extensions *continued*

Working with kext items via Terminal. You can get information about, load, and unload specific kext items by entering any of the following commands in Terminal:

- `kextstat` provides information about currently active kext items.
- `kextunload` allows you to unload an active kext item.
- `kextload` loads a currently inactive kext item.

Type `man {name of command}` to get more details about each command.

System initialization

During the next phase of startup, several technical activities take place.

It is at this point that the gray screen should turn to blue, and the Mac OS X logo should appear.

For troubleshooting purposes, the details are not important; the following provides a brief summary of what occurs:

- **The core software (kernel) of the Unix/BSD basis for Mac OS X loads.** This is initiated by a process called mach_init, which in turn initiates the BSD init process. Note: Loading of processes via mach_init, as with all other loading processes, is being superseded by the use of `launchd` in Tiger.

- **The system checks to determine whether the user is booting from a CD-ROM or via single-user mode.** If either is the case, a special loading procedure takes over.

- **Special initialization scripts and commands are run.** These scripts handle the final initialization tasks, determining whether to run `fsck` at startup (as described in more detail later in the chapter), creating the swap file for virtual memory, and running the `kextd` process (which unloads kext items not needed for this startup).

  Scripts and commands that run here include `launchd`, `rc` (located in the /etc folder), and `SystemStarter`. These processes in turn launch various system daemons—processes launched before a user logs in and that generally run in the background.

  Note: If you're starting up from a bootable CD, the critical information for booting is in a similar file called `rc.cdrom`, rather than `rc`.

More details about most of these features are described in remaining sections of this chapter, especially the ones that immediately follow.

TECHNICALLY SPEAKING ▶ Hostconfig and Other Configuration Files

The rc scripts check the "hostconfig" file, located in the /etc directory. This file lists which system services should be started. To locate hostconfig in the Finder, select the Go to Folder command and enter /etc.

Hostconfig is a text file, which you can edit—for example, with Bare Bones Software's TextWrangler (www.barebones.com) (opened via root access) or in Terminal (for example, by opening the pico text editor as root using sudo pico)—to modify what services (startup items) load at startup. Typically, you modify this file indirectly by changing a setting in a System Preferences pane. However, in some cases you may need to modify it directly.

You can also use third-party Aqua utilities, such as Infosoft's MOX Optimize (www.infosoft-sw.com), to modify which startup items are enabled or disabled at startup.

SEE: • "Take Note: Why and How to Use Archive and Install" and "Technically Speaking: Custom Config Files After a Mac OS X Update," in Chapter 3, for related information.

• "Modifying invisible Unix files from Mac OS X applications," in Chapter 6, for more information on editing config files.

Startup daemons

During the next phase of startup, various items (usually called *daemons*) are launched. These are primarily used to start services (such as file sharing and Web servers) that must run at startup in order to have these services automatically available to users. These daemons typically load during the time when the blue screen and Mac OS X logo appear at startup (prior to logging in).

Exactly what types of daemons launch and what they do has varied a lot over the many versions of Mac OS X. Apple keeps changing the rules. In Tiger, Apple has shifted its emphasis to a new type of daemon called LaunchDaemon files. In previous versions, Mac OS X used Bootstrap Daemons and/or Startup Items. These latter two options are actually still available in Tiger, although they are being phased out (especially Bootstrap Daemons, which Apple has advised developers to avoid, although Apple itself still uses them).

In this section, I cover the basics of all these different types of daemons. I know—it's probably difficult enough to comprehend how just one of these methods works. Having to understand multiple methods of accomplishing the same tasks, and trying to figure out which method is doing what, can seem beyond difficult. The good news is that, for troubleshooting purposes, you need to know only a bare minimum of what is going on. That's what I emphasize here.

launchd: LaunchDaemons. The launchd command (located in the /sbin directory) is new in Tiger. Actually, it is now the first Mac OS X command, after the kernel, to run at startup. As Apple states: "During boot, launchd is invoked by the kernel to run as the first process on the system and to further bootstrap the rest of the system." Apple wants developers to launch their startup processes via launchd rather than by modifying the rc file or adding a startup item (using SystemStarter, discussed below). The intent is for launchd to eventually replace all other types of launch daemons. As Apple states: "At some point in the future, we hope to completely phase out the use of rc."

The launchd command launches files, called *control files*, that are stored in the LaunchDaemons and LaunchAgents folders in both the /Library and /System/Library folders. As a rule, the /System/Library folders contain items installed as part of Mac OS X, while the /Library folders contain third-party items. Additionally, you may have a LaunchAgents folder in your home Library; items here are invoked only when you are the logged-in user.

The Unix maintenance scripts, handled via the cron daemon in previous versions of Mac OS X (as covered more in "Technically Speaking: Terminal Commands to Monitor and Improve Performance," in Chapter 10), are good examples of notable tasks that are now handled by launchd in Tiger. To see the files involved, check out com.apple.periodic-daily.plist, com.apple.periodic-monthly.plist, and com.apple.periodic-weekly.plist in the /System/Library/LaunchDaemons folder.

Launchctl: Beyond startup. A related command, launchctl, which interacts with launchd, can be used for loading daemons/agents (typically stored in the LaunchAgents folder) at times other than at startup.

This is a very flexible system overall. Without too much effort, you can create items that force an application to launch at any time based on almost any conceivable criterion. For example, you could have a given application launch every hour on the hour or whenever you open another related application.

Startup items. Startup items are the oldest of the features for launching programs at boot. Mac OS X installs startup items in /System/Library/StartupItems; startup items installed by third parties are located in /Library/StartupItems, typically placed there by the installers for the applications that use them (that is, you're not expected to manually place them in the correct folder).

The Unix command SystemStarter (in the /sbin directory) handles the loading of these items at startup. You may also run this command from Terminal (at any time) to restart or stop individual startup items (as described in "Technically Speaking: SystemStarter," later in this chapter).

The following are some examples of items in the /System/Library/StartupItems folder:

- **Apache.** Starts the Personal Web Sharing server (if enabled).
- **AppleShare.** Starts Apple File Service (needed for Personal File Sharing).
- **NetworkTime.** Sets the OS to check for time and date.

Each startup item is itself a package or bundle folder that contains at least two items: the startup executable code and a .plist file.

Note: A big disadvantage of startup items is that they need to launch at startup and remain running (using CPU time and consuming memory) the entire time you are logged in, even if they are only briefly needed. launchd-compliant items can be launched on demand and quit as needed.

Note: Many of the items in the StartupItems folder no longer function; they have been replaced by launchd-compliant items. However, there may still be Startup Item files inside the folder, serving as empty "placeholder" items, for the benefit of other still-functioning startup items that may check for the presence of a prerequired Startup Item (technically called a "dependency") before launching.

SEE: • "Technically Speaking: Create Your Own Startup Daemons," later in this chapter, for more details.

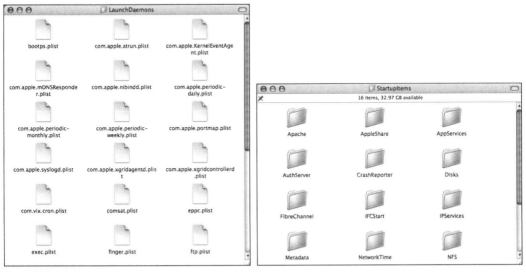

Figure 5.5

Left, *partial contents of the /System/Library/LaunchDaemons folder;* right, *the /System/Library/StartupItems folder.*

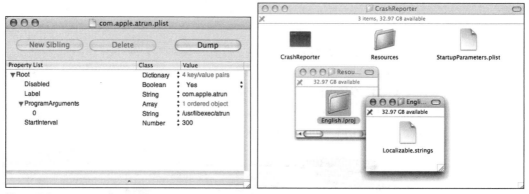

Figure 5.6

Left, *the contents of the com.apple.atrun.plist LaunchDaemon;* right, *the CrashReporter Startup Item.*

TECHNICALLY SPEAKING ▶ SystemStarter

The Unix SystemStarter command—which you can run from Terminal after startup is complete—provides one potential way of resolving startup-item problems *without* truly restarting your Mac. In its basic form (that is, with no options enabled), this command restarts all startup items (as would normally occur when you restart your Mac).

To run SystemStarter, launch Terminal, type sudo SystemStarter, and enter your password when requested.

For a list of additional features (such as starting or stopping individual startup items), type man SystemStarter. For example, if AppleShare stopped (due to some error), you could restart it by typing sudo SystemStarter AppleShare start. Be careful, however: Stopping an essential item could crash your Mac. In most cases, simply restarting your Mac is a simpler solution.

If there's a problem with a startup item, a diagnostic error message will appear in the Terminal window output when running SystemStarter. This can be especially useful for debugging a startup item you created yourself.

If you're using SystemStarter as a quick way to restart, be cautious: Using SystemStarter and actually restarting your Mac are not exactly the same processes. Unlike what happens with a true restart, all open applications *remain* open and functional after you use SystemStarter. Also, kernel extensions are not reloaded via SystemStarter (you use the kextload and kextunload commands for that). If problems occur, you should actually restart your Mac.

You can also use various third-party utilities, such as MOX Optimize, to individually turn on or off startup items and kernel extensions—a more user-friendly alternative to SystemStarter and kext Terminal commands.

Note: I could not always get SystemStarter to work as expected in the initial release of Tiger. However, its man file is still available, suggesting that the function still exists. Hopefully, this will be resolved in an update to Tiger.

Bootstrap daemons. Bootstrap daemons look to have only a brief life in Mac OS X. They were introduced in Mac OS X 10.3 Panther with a goal similar to launchd's: allowing daemons to launch only when and for how long they were needed. However, Apple now advises developers, "The use of boostrap daemons is deprecated and should be avoided entirely. Launching of daemons through this process is currently limited to some Apple-specific programs and may be removed or eliminated in a future release of Mac OS X. If you need to launch daemons, use launchd. If you need to launch daemons on versions of Mac OS X prior to 10.4, use a startup item."

So let me be brief here. Those bootstrap daemons that still exist are run at one of two different points in the startup sequence:

- **When the rc scripts are run.** This is comparable to when startup items are run. The rc script loads all of the files (*daemons*) found in the following directory: /etc/mach_init.d. These include system daemons such as configd and lookupd.

  SEE: • "Technically Speaking: System Daemons," later in this chapter, for more details.

  • "Optimize/update_prebinding," later in this chapter.

- **When the loginwindow application is run.** These items are stored in /etc/mach_init_per_user.d. Many of them simply instruct Mac OS X to run a specific system-level process. For example, MirrorAgent.plist and CrashReporter.plist result in the loading of the MirrorAgent and Crash Reporter applications (located in /System/Library/CoreServices). The former is involved in mounting iDisks; the latter is the application behind the "unexpectedly quit" message that appears when an application crashes.

The items in mach_init.d normally load only when you start or restart your computer. Thus, if you simply log out and then log back in (or another user logs in), these items won't be reloaded. The items in mach_init_per_user.d are loaded whenever a user logs in (a process described next).

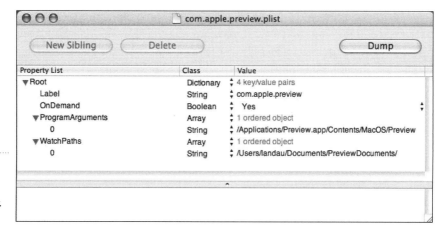

Figure 5.7

The contents of a LaunchAgent file I created, named com.apple.preview. plist.

TECHNICALLY SPEAKING ▶ Create Your Own Startup Daemons

As a troubleshooter, you won't have much reason to create your own startup items or bootstrap daemons. However, they're easy enough to create that it's worth knowing how. You could, for example, create one to run a function at startup that you wished to be in effect regardless of who was logged in to the machine. (Adding an item in the Startup Items pane of a given user, in contrast, affects only *that* user.)

Startup items. First, create a folder with the name of your startup item (for example, MyStartupItem). Each startup item folder contains the following components:

- **Executable file/script.** Create a text file (using BBEdit or another editor that can maintain Unix line endings) with the same name. Store this file inside the folder. This is the executable file that contains the instructions performed by the startup item. Typically, this is a shell script file—in essence, a file containing commands like those you would normally run in Terminal. A simple shell script might look like the following:

```
#! /bin/sh
. /etc/rc.common
ConsoleMessage "Starting MyStartupItem"
touch /Users/tedmac/Desktop/testfile
```

  The first line tells the Mac to run the sh shell. The second line causes rc.common to run. (This is shell-script code that Apple recommends running prior to your own startup-item code; it contains routines that are useful for processing command-line arguments.) The third line causes the text *Starting MyStartupItem* to appear during the blue-screen phase of startup. The final line describes what the startup item actually does—in this case, the touch command simply creates a file called "testfile" on the Desktop of my own account (or updates the modification date of the file if it already exists). (In Chapter 10, I discuss some other simple shell scripts of more practical value.)

- **StartupParameters.plist file.** This file includes the data that determines if and when the startup item runs. The simplest way to create this file is to copy one from another startup item and then modify it by loading it in Property List Editor.

  For example, the OrderPreference attribute can have a value of First, Early, None (default), Late, or Last. These determine when in the load order the item will load.

  The Requires attribute tells Mac OS X that the startup item requires that *another* specific startup item be loaded first.

- **Resources folder.** Optionally, if you want to localize a startup item for different languages, add a Resources folder and include an .lproj folder for each desired language (for example, English.lprog for English). Each .lproj folder will include a Localizable.strings file.

When done with all of the above, place the folder in the /Library/StartupItems folder.

You can optionally add a line to the /etc/hostconfig file (as noted in "System initialization," earlier in the main text) that determines whether the item loads at startup. To get this to work, you have to write code in the executable file that instructs the startup item to check this file. See the Apache file in the Apache startup item, in /System/Library/StartupItems, for an example.

continues on next page

TECHNICALLY SPEAKING ▶ Create Your Own Startup Daemons *continued*

See the following Apple document for more details on how to create startup items: http://developer.apple.com/documentation/Darwin/Conceptual/howto/ system_starter_howto/system_starter_howto.html. For more general background, see http://developer.apple.com/documentation/MacOSX/Conceptual/BPSystemStartup.

LaunchDaemons and LaunchAgent items. In Tiger, you can create special .plist files that run at startup if placed in the LaunchDaemons or LaunchAgents folder in the various Library folders. Items in the LaunchAgents folder launch at the login phase of startup. This means that LaunchAgents items are run each time a user logs in. LaunchDaemons items launch prior to login, which means that they run again only when you restart your Mac. All of these items are run using the launchd Unix command, also introduced in Tiger.

To get a feel for how things work, examine some of the preinstalled items, using Property List Editor to view the files. The first thing to note is the ProgramArguments array property/key; the 0 child property/key of this array is the name of the program to be run by the daemon. An optional key in this array may indicate how often the program is to be run (for example, daily or weekly). Several other optional properties (not in the ProgramArguments array!) can further determine when and how the program is launched. Here are a couple of examples:

- WatchPaths, an array that causes the listed process or job to be started or launched if any one of the paths in a value field of "children" in the array gets modified.

- StartInterval, with a value of N, causes the job to be started every *n* seconds.

- StartCalendarInterval is a dictionary of integers that causes a job to be started every calendar interval as specified. The semantics are much like those of crontab.

As one example, you could create a LaunchAgent that would cause Preview to launch every time the contents of a folder called PreviewDocuments was modified (for example, by adding a file to the folder). To do so, use Property List Editor to create a file, called com.apple.preview.plist, and place it in /Library/LaunchAgents. Again using Property List Editor, add properties to the file so that it looks like the listing in Figure 5.7 (except substituting the name of your home directory for "landau"). Next, launch Terminal and type the following: launchctl load /Library/ LaunchAgents/com.apple.preview.plist. This loads the LaunchAgent file so that it starts working. Now drag any file into or out of the PreviewDocuments folder and watch Preview launch! To stop this from working, repeat the Terminal command, except change load to unload.

To learn more about these commands, type man launchd and man launchctl in Terminal. Type man launchd.plist to learn more about how to create and edit the launchd .plist files.

continues on next page

TECHNICALLY SPEAKING ▶ **Create Your Own Startup Daemons** *continued*

One more way to create a global startup item: /Library/Preferences/loginwindow.plist.
There is an alternative way to get a program, such as Preview, to run at login no matter which
user logs in. To do so, use Property List Editor to create a file called loginwindow.plist (if you
don't already have one) and place it in the root-level /Library/Preferences folder (not the
Library/Preferences folder in your home directory). Use the structure of the loginwindow.plist
file in your home directory as a template for this file (in fact, you can just make a copy of the file
in your home directory and move it to the root Library folder, to use as a starting template, if you
wish). In particular, create an array called AutoLaunchedApplicationDictionary and add child
properties to it that represent the applications you want to launch. Such applications will now
launch at login for all users. (Note: Either do not include the AliasData fields or give them a value
of 0; items will load without this field.)

However, this is not a preferred solution, as these items run only at the initial login at startup. If a
user logs out and logs back in again, or another user logs in via Fast User Switching, the items in
this list will not load again. That's why a better solution is to use the launchd feature.

SEE: • **"Preferences Files," in Chapter 4, for more on creating and editing .plist files.**

• **"Startup daemons," "Login," and "Take Note: Solving Problems with Login Items,"
elsewhere in this chapter, for related information.**

• **"Using a shell script," in Chapter 10, for related information.**

Login

The last stage of the startup process begins with the appearance of the Login
window. However, if you checked the "Automatically log in as" box in the
Login Options of the Accounts System Preferences pane, and named yourself
as the person to be logged in (as described in Chapter 2), you will bypass
this window.

The Login window is, appropriately enough, handled by the loginwindow
application, located in /System/Library/CoreServices. When loginwindow is
launched during startup, the following things happen:

• **Your password is checked against information in Directory
Services (typically obtained from the NetInfo database, unless
modified via the Directory Access application).** The SecurityAgent
application (located in /System/Library/CoreServices) handles this
authentication.

Note: Tiger and Panther, by default, use a more secure method for
authenticating than was used in Jaguar. Called Shadow Hash, it's used
only on accounts created in Panther or Tiger, or accounts created in Jaguar
that have had the password changed since upgrading to Panther or Tiger.
Older accounts that haven't had their password updated still use the older

method (called Basic). It's doubtful that any of this will affect your troubleshooting; however, if you need to know more, check out the document titled "Open Directory Overview," available from Apple's Developer Web site: http://developer.apple.com/documentation/Networking/Conceptual/ Open_Directory/Chapter1/chapter_2_section_2.html.

- **Daemons in the /etc/mach_init_per_user.d are loaded, as described in the previous section.**

- **Your customized environment (based on the preferences settings in your home directory) is set up.** This includes launching items listed in the Login Items portion of the Accounts System Preferences pane (as explained more in Chapter 2).

- **Files are set to show the appropriate permissions and privileges for your account and status.**

- **Unix-style environment variables (which are listed in the environment.plist file in the invisible .MacOSX directory in your home directory) are checked and executed.** Note: This folder and document are present only if an environment value has been changed from its default state.

  SEE: • "Technically Speaking: What's a Shell?" in Chapter 10, for information on environment variables and the setenv command.

- **Other typical login tasks (such as displaying alerts) are completed.**

When you enter your correct user name and password, Mac OS X completes its startup sequence by launching the Finder, Dock, and applications in your personal account's Login Items list.

The loginwindow program continues to run while you're logged in. It manages the Force Quit window and the logout process. It also relaunches the Dock and Finder automatically (as well as the SystemUIServer background process), should they quit. Note: If you quit the loginwindow process, such as by force-quitting it using Activity Monitor, you're immediately logged out.

SEE: • The coverage of the Accounts System Preferences pane, in Chapter 2, for more details.

Login hooks. You can create a Unix shell script (as described more in Chapter 10) and have it run automatically, as root, at login (or even at logout). These are called *login* (or *logout*) *hooks*.

Note: In most cases, for login you could accomplish the same result, with less hassle, by adding the item to your Login Items list (in the Accounts System Preferences). Perhaps that is why Apple has stated, "In Mac OS X v10.4 and later, support for these hooks is deprecated and their use should be avoided." Despite this, Apple offers details in other documentation (http://docs.info.apple.com/article.html?artnum=301446) for how to use these hooks in Tiger. Go figure.

To add a login hook to run at subsequent logins, type the following in Terminal (or use Property List Editor to make the same change to the com.apple.loginwindow.plist file):

```
sudo defaults write com.apple.loginwindow LoginHook {absolute path
to script}
```

This modifies the /var/root/Library/Preferences/com.apple.loginwindow file.

To make this easier, you can use the third-party utility LoginWindow Manager, by Bombich Software (www.bombich.com), which offers additional customization options for the Login window.

Recovered Items in the Trash. After starting up and logging in to your account, you may find in your Trash a folder named Recovered Items (which is new in Tiger). Don't be concerned. Mac OS X periodically deletes unneeded files that had been located in its temporary (/tmp) directory. You can safely delete the Recovered Items folder.

Replacing the Finder. The loginwindow process is what causes the Finder to always launch at login. You can assign a different application to replace the Finder, if you wish.

SEE: • "Technically Speaking: Completely Hidden Properties: Changing the Finder," in Chapter 4, for details.

TECHNICALLY SPEAKING ▶ System Daemons

If you launch Activity Monitor—especially if you view Administrator Processes or All Processes—you will see many running processes that are not end-user applications and are not listed anywhere else you would typically see running applications (such as the Force Quit window, described later in this chapter). In general, these are *background processes*—that is, processes that have no user interface and thus are not visible in the Finder. Many of these processes are launched automatically early in the startup process or when you log in and are generally referred to as *system daemons*. Typically, you will have little need to interact with them. However, the following are some noteworthy items that should give you an idea what these processes are and do:

- configd. Automatically configures and maintains the network.
- kextd. Loads and unloads device drivers as needed.
- lookupd. A name resolver that expedites requests to NetInfo and DNS.
- update. Periodically flushes the system cache to help prevent data loss in the event of a crash. (For more on this, see "Technically Speaking: Connecting Remotely to a Frozen Mac: Killing Processes, Running Sync," later in this chapter.)
- pbs. Handles the clipboard and clippings files.

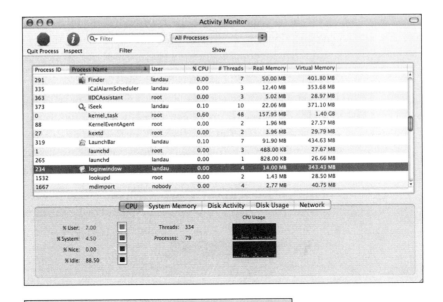

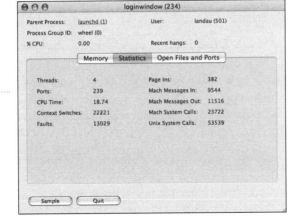

Figure 5.8

Activity Monitor:
top, *All Processes*
selected and
loginwindow
highlighted;
bottom, *the Info*
window for the
loginwindow
process.

Alternative Mac OS X Startup Paths

I've already covered a couple of deviations from the normal startup procedure, such as starting up from a CD or DVD or booting into Open Firmware. Those methods function prior to the launch of Mac OS X itself. What follows are several more startup deviations that are specific to Mac OS X.

Single-user mode

If you press and hold Command-S at startup, you start up in what is called *single-user mode*. In essence, this mode drops you directly into Mac OS X's command-line interface. The screen will turn black and begin to fill with a series of text lines in white (perhaps with some text in yellow). You can generally ignore this text. Eventually, the screen will stop at a command-line prompt, where you can enter text commands. If you've used Mac OS X's Terminal application, you should feel right at home.

The text that appears prior to the command-line prompt will sometimes provide clues as to the nature of a problem. For example, as covered in "Mounting and unmounting/ejecting media," in Chapter 6, doing this identified a FireWire port problem for me. If you only want to view text messages, rather than type in commands, you can use verbose mode instead, as described next.

Running fsck. For troubleshooting purposes, your main use for single-user mode will be to attempt disk repairs, especially when your Mac won't otherwise start up. From the single-user-mode screen, you can run a Unix utility called fsck (for *File System Check*), essentially the same as running the First Aid component of Disk Utility—which means it may be able to repair the startup (or other) problems.

SEE: • "Enabling and disabling journaling" and "Running fsck," later in this chapter, for more details.

Running Mac OS X from single-user mode. Another useful function you may invoke from single-user mode is the following: sh /etc/rc. After entering this command, you remain in single-user mode, but all normal Mac OS X processes are launched. The result is as if you are logged in as the root user. The effect is similar to logging in normally, launching Terminal and using the su command to become the root user in Terminal (as described in Chapters 4 and 10)—except that you have none of the Aqua graphical interface; all you have is the command line.

The main difference between the initial single-user mode and running the rc command is that in the latter case you have loaded all the extensions and startup items that would normally run. This is an advantage if you want to perform actions, such as networking-related functions, that would not work without these other items' being loaded. However, if you are having a problem that would prevent Mac OS X from starting up normally, this command may not succeed.

Other information about single-user mode. When you are done using single-user mode, you can type reboot (to restart the Mac) or logout or exit (to continue a normal booting of Mac OS X).

Beyond running fsck, the most common reason for using single-user mode is to delete or move files. This is critical, for example, if you have a corrupt file, such as a preferences file, that is otherwise preventing a successful startup of Mac OS X. I give an example of this procedure later in this chapter.

If you get the idea that starting up in single-user mode bypasses Mac OS X's admin password protections, you would be correct. A user in single-user mode has the same authority as a root user. If you want to block unauthorized users from single-user access, you need to enable Open Firmware password protection.

Verbose mode

If you press Command-V at startup, you start up in verbose mode, which at first looks very similar to starting up in single-user mode. The main difference is that in verbose mode, the Mac never stops for you to enter commands. Verbose mode also provides continuing feedback about the startup sequence (for example, what processes are loading) that does not appear in single-user mode. After you see all the white (and sometimes yellow) text, a normal Mac OS X login process begins at the blue screen.

Thus, verbose mode is used mainly to check for error messages contained in the initial text. This information is usually of interest only to software developers. The white text, for example, provides information about the progress of the initialization process; the yellow text usually comprises an alert about a possible problem with a kext item. You could view most of this information from Console logs after logging in; however, verbose mode can be of use if the error in question is preventing a normal startup and thus preventing you from accessing the Console application.

For everyday troubleshooting you will almost never need verbose mode; however, if you're familiar with Unix jargon, verbose mode may provide some clues about the source of a problem. One user, for example, was able to confirm that a problem with his Date & Time setting was due to a failure of the Network Time software loading at startup, as determined by a getGMTTimeOfDay error message in verbose mode. Shifting to a different server, as accessed from the Date & Time pane of the Date & Time System Preferences pane, solved the problem.

Verbose mode may also indicate a problem with a startup or kext item. This would alert you to use a Safe Boot (described next) to bypass loading of kext items, allowing startup to proceed. At this point, you could replace or disable the problem file.

SEE: • "Checking for extension (kext) problems," later in this chapter, for an example of a problem with the IOUSBFamily.kext file.

If you start up in verbose mode, your Mac should also return to verbose mode when you shut down—thus providing the same feedback for shutdown as it did for startup. Of course, once the Mac shuts down, the output is gone, so read it quickly!

Safe Booting

If you're having problems starting your Mac, the first troubleshooting technique you should try is a *Safe Boot*. A Safe Boot accomplishes several things:

- **It forces the Mac to run the fsck disk-repair utility at startup.** A Safe Boot is thus an alternative to running it via single-user mode. Running fsck is apparently done even if journaling is enabled. If directory damage is the source of the startup problem, a Safe Boot should fix it.

  SEE: • "Enabling and disabling journaling" and "Running fsck," later in this chapter, for more details.

- **It prevents nonessential kext items (stored in /System/Library/ Extensions) and third-party startup items (located in /Library/ StartupItems) from loading.** In essence, only Apple-installed items will run (and maybe not even all of them). If a third-party item is causing trouble here, this will bypass it.

- **It disables all fonts except those in the /System/Library/Fonts folder.** This feature, new in Tiger, is useful in case a corrupt font is causing the startup problem.

- **It moves font cache files stored in the folders in /Library/Caches/ com.apple.ATS/ to the Trash.** This feature, also new in Tiger, can resolve font-related problems. Note: There is a subfolder here for each user with an account. Only the folder of the user who logs in gets moved to the Trash.

- **It disables login items.** Login items are a potential source of problems; this feature (also new in Tiger) makes it unnecessary to separately disable login items at startup (as described below).

Overall, this means that most of the common causes of a startup problem are either bypassed or fixed via a Safe Boot.

The downside of a Safe Boot is that some features that require what has been disabled will now not work. For example, you won't be able to use your AirPort card or the DVD Player application. That's why you should only do a Safe Boot when it's needed to fix a problem.

Note: All the items that get "deleted" during a Safe Boot remain in the Trash after you restart. Thus, you can drag them out again and reinstall them in their original locations, should you want to do so. However, this would rarely be advisable.

Invoking a Safe Boot. To invoke a Safe Boot, *immediately* after you hear the chimes at startup (ideally not before), hold down the Shift key until the Mac logo appears on the blue screen. The text below the blue screen should read, "Starting up Mac OS X." Eventually, the Login window will appear. Note that the Login window will appear even if you have enabled the option to automatically log in (in Accounts System Preferences, as described in Chapter 2).

If you have successfully invoked a Safe Boot, the words *Safe Boot* should appear below the words *Mac OS X*. At this point, enter your name (if needed) and password to log in, just as you normally would.

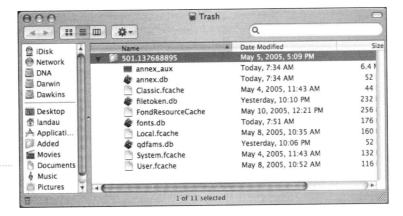

Figure 5.9

The files moved to the Trash after a Safe Boot.

Safe Boot takes longer. When you do a Safe Boot, you'll notice that startup takes considerably longer than normal. This is usually because fsck is being run. In addition, a Safe Boot ignores the cache of kernel extensions (/System/Library/Extensions.kextcache) used to speed startup.

Does the Safe Boot solve the problem? Simply running fsck or deleting the font cache files—both actions performed during a Safe Boot—may resolve your startup issue. Thus, if a Safe Boot allows startup to proceed, immediately try restarting your Mac without a Safe Boot. If it works, your problem is solved.

To be extra cautious, you could also run Disk Utility's First Aid (by starting up from the Mac OS X Install CD) or manually run fsck via single-user mode at startup (as covered more later in this chapter). This would allow you to see the results of running the repair function.

If, after all this, you still encounter the startup problem, the culprit may be a nondisabled startup item, a "safe" kernel extension (one of those that load even during a Safe Boot), or a font. Otherwise, it is likely to be a problem with either core Mac OS X system software or your Mac hardware.

Deleting or disabling files to prevent a startup problem. Beyond running fsck, the main advantage of a Safe Boot is that it can circumvent a startup crash or kernel panic caused by one of the bypassed files. Once you've started up successfully, you can then locate the problem file and remove it from its folder.

If you have no idea which file is the culprit, you should begin by checking recently added and/or third-party startup files and kext files; starting up in verbose mode and checking for error messages may help identify the problem file.

You can use a utility like MOX Optimize to disable problem files. Once you've disabled the suspect item, you can restart normally. Contact the vendor of the problem file for further advice.

If this does not help, try removing fonts from the /Library/Fonts and ~/Library/Fonts folders. If Mac OS 9 is installed, also remove fonts from the /System Folder/Fonts folder.

SEE: • "Technically Speaking: Understanding Kernel Extensions," earlier in this chapter, for related information.

• "Checking for extension (kext) problems," later in this chapter, for more troubleshooting advice.

• "Checking fonts," later in this chapter, for more details.

• "Deleting cache files," later in this chapter, for more details.

Disabling login items

By holding down the Shift key when you click the Log In button in the Login window, you can prevent login items from loading. This also will move your font cache files to the Trash. As just mentioned, doing a Safe Boot similarly disables login items and trashes your font cache files (plus does more!); this approach allows you to disable login items without having to do a Safe Boot.

As you might guess, disabling these items comes in handy when one of them is causing a startup crash. (A login item is a likely culprit for crashes that don't occur until *after* you've logged in or until the Desktop background has appeared.) Reminder: Login items are different from the systemwide startup items described earlier in this chapter.

Here are the details on using this feature, depending on whether or not you've enabled the option to log in automatically:

• To disable login items if you *have not* enabled the option to automatically log in (as set via Login Options on the Accounts System Preferences pane): Wait for the Login window to appear. In this window, enter your name and password as usual, or (if you're presented with a list of users) click your name and enter your password. Now hold down the Shift key and click the Log In button. Continue to hold down the Shift key until the Desktop background appears.

• To disable login items if you *have* enabled the option to automatically log in: Press and hold down the Shift key after the startup blue screen appears. Don't do this earlier, or you may invoke a Safe Boot (unless of course you want to do a Safe Boot). This will force the Login window to appear. Now proceed as above, pressing andholding down the Shift key again when you click Log In.

If you've already logged in and want to disable login items, simply choose Log Out from the Apple menu. This brings up the Login window. Once it appears, hold down the Shift key as you log in again; you do not need to restart. You do, however, need to restart if you want to do a Safe Boot.

SEE: • "Take Note: Solving Problems with Login Items," later in this chapter, for more on troubleshooting login items.

• Coverage of the Accounts System Preferences pane, in Chapter 2, for background on login items.

TAKE NOTE ▶ Bypassing Automatic Login

Suppose you have enabled the option to automatically log in at startup (via Login Options on the Accounts System Preferences pane), but you want the Login window to appear (perhaps to log in to a different account or to disable login items). The typical way to do this would be to log in normally and then log out, bringing up the Login window. You could then log in as another user and/or hold down the Shift key to disable login items.

However, especially if you are having problems successfully logging in to the automatic account, it can be difficult to get to the Login window using the above method. One alternative is to do a Safe Boot, which (as noted in the main text) forces the Login window to appear. Alternatively, you can instead wait to hold down the Shift key until after the blue screen appears at startup. This too forces the Login window to appear, but without doing a Safe Boot.

Logging in as console

When you get to the Login window, you typically log in with your own user name. As covered in Chapter 4, however, you may also occasionally choose to log in as the root user, using *root* as the user name instead. To do so, you need to either have the Login window set for Name and Password or select the Other option from the List of Users. Note: The Other option appears only if you have enabled use of the root user (as described in Chapter 4).

As it turns out, you can also use another name here: >*console*. (Note: This name is unrelated to the Console application in the Utilities folder.) There is no need to use a password here; just press Return after entering the term, including the > character, in the Name field. You'll reach a screen that's very similar to Terminal—except that the text is white on black (as it is in single-user mode). You will need to log in at this screen, providing your Mac OS X user name and password before you proceed.

When you're logged in via the >console option, it's just like being in Terminal. If you log in as the root user, it is very similar to what happens when you run the rc command from single-user mode, as described above. A primary reason to log in via this method is if you want to use Terminal to solve a problem, but the problem itself prevents you from logging in via normal methods (thus prohibiting normal access to Terminal).

One example in which logging in as console could help is if a corrupt font or preferences file is causing an Aqua-related crash. In this case, logging in via console would allow you to remove the file because the Finder's Aqua environment does not load at this point, and thus there would be no crash. The exact steps for logging in as console are as follows:

1. Type >console in the Name field at the login prompt (leave the Password field blank).

   If you selected "List of users" rather than "Name and password" in the Accounts System Preferences pane, you will not see a Name field. One solution is to choose the Other option; however, this option appears only if you've enabled the root user. If "Other" does not appear, press Shift-Option-Return and then click any name in the list. This should get the Name and Password fields to appear.

   Note: You cannot log in as console if another user is currently logged in via Fast User Switching.

2. At the next prompt, log in with your normal name and password.

3. Using the rm or mv command, remove, move, or rename the corrupt file so that it no longer loads at startup.

   SEE: • Chapter 10 for more on using these commands.

4. Type logout or exit to return to the normal Login window.

5. Log in as yourself, and hopefully all should be well.

TAKE NOTE ▶ Other Login User-Name Options

In addition to the >console command, a few other special commands work when you type them in the Login window's user-name text box. These commands include the following:

• >restart: Restarts the Mac

• >power: Shuts down the Mac

• >exit: Quits and relaunches the Login window

TAKE NOTE ▶ Forgot Your Password?

If you have forgotten your login password or other related passwords, don't despair. Mac OS X offers several ways to get up and running again:

• If you created a hint for your password, the hint will appear after three failed attempts to log in. Hopefully, that will jog your memory.

   Note: To see password hints, you should also enable "Show password hints" in the Login Options section of the Accounts System Preferences pane.

continues on next page

TAKE NOTE ▶ Forgot Your Password? *continued*

- If you're not an administrative user, get an administrative user to log in; he or she can reset your password via the Password pane in the Accounts System Preferences pane.

- If you are an administrative user and there's more than one admin account, get the other administrative user to log in; he or she can reset your password via the Password pane in the Accounts System Preferences pane. Just click the Reset Password button.

  Note: This will not work if you are the initial administrative user to create an account; other administrative users cannot change the password on this account. In this case, you should start up from the Mac OS X Install disc and use the Reset Password utility (as noted later in this list).

- After three failed attempts to log in (and after failing again with the password hint, if you set a hint), and if you previously set a master password in the Security System Preferences pane, you will be given an opportunity to enter your master password. If you do so, you will reset the password for that account (and unlock FileVault if it was enabled).

  Note: This does not change the password for the account's original login keychain (which is usually the same as the account password). Instead, a new login keychain is created; the original login keychain is saved (in the Library/Keychains folder of the account's home directory). If you later want to access the old keychain and the password information it contains, you will still need the old password.

- If you're the only administrative user, or you are unable to get the other methods to work for any reason, start up from a Mac OS X Install disc (by inserting the disc, restarting, and then holding down the C key), and access the Reset Password utility (as described more in Chapter 3). Locate the name of the account you want to fix and reset its password.

  Note: You cannot start up from the disc if Open Firmware password protection has been enabled. If this is the case, you will first need to turn off this protection (as discussed earlier in this chapter).

  Note: After resetting a password, if you previously enabled "automatic login," it may no longer be enabled. To fix this, simply log in and go to the Login Options of the Accounts System Preferences pane to re-enable it.

- You can also reset forgotten passwords from Terminal—even the root user password—as long as you know your administrator password. For example, to reset the password for the root user, type sudo passwd root. Provide your administrator's password when asked. You will then be prompted to enter a new password for the root user.

  Note: Doing this will enable root access, even if you have not previously enabled it in NetInfo Manager.

  If you forgot your master password, you can reset it, but only if FileVault is not turned on for the logged-in account. To do so, launch Terminal and type sudo rm/Library/Keychains/FileVault*. Enter your administrative password when asked. The FileVault files are now [de]leted. You can also delete these files from any admin-level account by authenticating [usin]g your account password. In either case, the master password will now be cleared and [you] will have the option to create a new one (via the Security System Preferences pane) [withou]t having to know the old one.

continues on next page

Larry D. Greller, Ph.D.
Chief Scientific Officer
Founding Director

Biosystemix, Ltd.
313 Victoria St., Kingston, Ontario, Canada K7L 3Z2
Tel.: 613-542-4554
ldgphud@earthlink.net   (Canada Corporation 6090690038)

biosciences; data-mining, analysis; mathematical modeling

TAKE NOTE ▶ Forgot Your Password? *continued*

Note: If you use this procedure to create a new master password, existing user passwords are not automatically stored with the new master password. Thus, the ability to change a forgotten password via the master password option in the Hints window (as described above) will not work. To get this working again, log in to each user's account with his or her current password and change that password to a different password (or use an admin-level account to change each user's account via Accounts preferences—just be sure to give users their new passwords!). This stores the new passwords with the new master password.

Warning! If you forget *both* the master password and the login password for an account that is currently FileVault-encrypted, there is no way to log in to your account! Period. You can't even use the Mac OS X Install disc's Reset Password command to change the password on a FileVault-encrypted account, as this procedure doesn't change the password on the FileVault disk image. This is a good reason to always have a second admin-level user account just for troubleshooting.

SEE: • **"Technically Speaking: Inside FileVault," in Chapter 2, for more on using the master password to reset your login password.**

• **"Keychain Access," in Chapter 2, for more Keychain Access.**

• **"The Installer menu," in Chapter 3, and "Logging in as root," in Chapter 4, for details on using Reset Password.**

TAKE NOTE ▶ NetBooting

NetBooting refers to a process whereby a client computer running Mac OS X starts up from system software located on a central server. Thus, you need at least one computer running Mac OS X Server to use this feature.

Client computers typically use the BootP protocol set in the TCP/IP pane of the Network System Preferences pane.

To start up via NetBooting:

• Select Network Startup from the Startup Disk System Preferences pane, and restart.

  or

• Restart and hold down the N key. (You do not need to use the N key to NetBoot if the server has been previously selected.)

NetBoot HD appears as a volume on the client's Desktop if NetBoot has been successful.

Note: Beginning with Mac OS X 10.3, you can NetBoot from a server even if your Mac does not have Mac OS X installed (called *diskless NetBooting*).

Further details about NetBooting, such as how preferences and permissions are handled, are beyond the scope of this book. For more details, see Apple's "Inside NetBooting" document (available from the following Apple Knowledge Base article: http://docs.info.apple.com/article.html?artnum=50055).

Figure 5.10

The Network Startup option, highlighted in the Startup Disk System Preferences pane. The question mark indicates that the Mac will search for a network volume at startup. Note: For starting up in Target Disk Mode, see Chapter 9.

Startup Crashes

One of the hallmarks of Mac OS X is its stability. Once the operating system is up and running, you'll rarely experience a crash that requires you to restart the computer—small comfort, though, if it crashes or freezes during startup. This section explores the various types of startup crashes and explains what you can do about them.

In addition to the advice contained in the following sections, check "Techniques for Solving Mac OS X Crashes," later in this chapter, for a laundry list of common fixes. Many of them can be applied to startup problems, especially if you're able to start up from a Safe Boot. Finally, check the following Apple Knowledge Base document for another overview of startup problems and solutions: http://docs.info.apple.com/article.html?artnum=106464.

Gray-screen crashes

Figure 5.11

The prohibitory symbol indicates that a startup failure has occurred.

During the gray-screen phase of startup, instead of getting the expected Apple logo symbol, you may get no symbol (just a blank gray screen) or the *prohibitory symbol* (a circle with a line though it).

Causes. Gray-screen crashes can typically be attributed to one of four things: (1) hardware failure; (2) the intended startup drive is not recognized as valid and bootable; (3) essential Mac OS X software is missing, incorrectly moved or renamed, or corrupt; or (4) a firmware update is needed.

The following describes a few of the things that can precipitate a gray-screen crash:

- **Memory.** If you've added memory (RAM) to your Mac, that RAM might not be compatible with your Mac model. Since there are subtle variations in the types of RAM available for Macs, your module could appear to be the correct type even when it's not. Or even if it is the correct type, you could have a defective module. Either situation can cause a crash.

   Note: Incompatible or damaged RAM might not show up in Apple System Profiler. Instead, ASP may indicate that the RAM slot is empty.

   Sources such as Apple's own "Specifications" page (http://www.info. apple.com/support/applespec.html) offer details about the precise memory specifications for each Mac. In most cases, however, if you use a reputable vendor, you should get the correct memory simply by telling the vendor what Mac you have. If problems occur, the vendor should replace the memory for free or a nominal charge.

- **AirPort card.** An improperly installed AirPort card (for example, one that's not fully inserted in the slot) can cause a startup crash. Check the documentation that came with your AirPort card and/or your Mac for how to install it correctly.

- **External devices.** Any device added to the Mac's other ports (USB, FireWire, or PCMCIA) can precipitate a startup crash. Most such devices should work fine; however, those that have not been updated to work with Mac OS X may remain a problem.

- **Missing Mac OS X software.** If you delete a critical Mac OS X file (such as mach_kernel), you will get a startup failure, typically at the gray-screen stage. Similarly, do not delete the /etc or /var folder that may be visible on the Desktop when booting from Mac OS 9. (These items are invisible by default in Mac OS X, to make it more difficult to accidentally delete them.)

What to do. Consider the following suggestions when troubleshooting a gray-screen crash:

- Make sure you have the latest firmware update installed. If you need to update the firmware, and problems continue after you do so, you should reinstall Mac OS X afterward.

   SEE: • "Take Note: Firmware Updates," earlier in this chapter.

- Try a Safe Boot. If this succeeds, the problem is most likely related to a kernel extension for a peripheral device, such as a SCSI card. Deleting or disabling the extension may prevent the crash, but it will also disable the card. A better alternative is to get an updated version of the file that fixes the error. Alternatively, replacing the file from a backup may help if the file has simply become corrupt.

   More generally, deleting the Extensions.mkext and Extensions.kextcache files may be all you need to do to fix a crash that occurs on a normal boot.

   SEE: • "Safe Booting" and "Technically Speaking: Understanding Kernel Extensions," earlier in this chapter, for more details.

- If the problem occurs only when you're trying to start up from an external volume, it may be caused by the way Mac OS X is installed on the drive.

  SEE: • "Take Note: Startup Failure When Starting Up from an External Device," later in this chapter.

- If you believe the problem can be traced back to a deleted critical file, such as mach_kernel, boot from another Mac OS X volume and drag the mach_kernel file at the root level of a Mac OS X Install CD/DVD (or from a backup of the current Mac OS X volume) to the root level of the Mac OS X volume. Now restart in Mac OS X. Your only other alternative would be to reinstall Mac OS X.

  Note: This assumes that the CD/DVD contains the same version of Mac OS X (and thus the same version of the mach_kernel file) that's currently installed on the drive. If not—for example, if your hard drive is running 10.4.2 and your Mac OS X Install DVD includes 10.4.0—you can get the needed mach_kernel file from a previously made backup, or you can reinstall Mac OS X and then install the necessary updates.

- If you believe the problem is due to a moved or renamed file, you can start up in single-user mode and use Unix commands to move and/or rename the file. You can also use this approach to re-create a missing alias or symbolic link.

  SEE: • "Blue-screen crashes and stalls," later in this chapter, for some examples of this technique.

- To further check for problems with peripheral devices, such as SCSI cards or external drives, or even USB or FireWire devices, remove all peripheral devices and cards from your Mac and restart. If the Mac starts up successfully, one of those devices may have caused the crash. Start adding devices back, one at a time, restarting after each. When the crash reoccurs, the most recently added device is the likely culprit. The incompatibility could be in the firmware on the device or in the item's kext device-driver software. If so, updating the firmware or driver software of the device may fix the problem. Contact the vendor of the device or check sites such as MacFixIt to determine whether such fixes exist or you need to abandon using the device in Mac OS X altogether.

- If the problem is caused by a USB or FireWire device, you may be able to work around it by not plugging in the device until *after* startup is complete. In other cases, switching from connecting the device through a USB or FireWire hub and using the port directly on the Mac (or vice versa) may help.

- If you have incompatible or defective RAM, replace it. Note that in some cases, updating the Mac's firmware, though generally recommended, may cause a startup failure due to a RAM incompatibility—even though the Mac worked prior to the upgrade.

- To check for other hardware problems, use the Hardware Test disc that came with your Mac. Problems turned up via this method will generally require taking your Mac in for a repair.

  SEE: • **"Technically Speaking: The Apple Hardware Test Software," earlier in this chapter.**

- If none of these fixes work, you may have a disk problem. If so, try to repair it.

  SEE: • **"Techniques for Solving Mac OS X Crashes," later in the chapter, for more on disk repairs and related fixes.**

TAKE NOTE ▶ Startup Failure When Starting Up from an External Device

CD/DVD drives. In some cases, a hardware conflict may prevent you from starting from a bootable CD (or DVD) even though you can start up normally from your hard drive. In such cases, the solution may be simple, if a bit inconvenient. If a USB device is the cause, remove the device, boot from the disc, and do what you need to do (such as install the software from the disc). Then shut down, reattach the device, and restart from your hard drive.

If your Mac refuses to start up from the disc, shifting instead to the hard drive, and the cause is not a connected device, the disc may not be a bootable disc—a situation that's especially likely to occur if you burned the disc yourself (since burning a bootable disc requires more than simply copying files from one disc to another). In this case, the solution is to reburn the disc correctly (as described in "Bootable CD or DVD" in Chapter 3).

In some cases, the latest Mac models will start up only via the Mac OS X software that came with that model (or newer versions). In other words, if the disc contains system software that predates your Mac model, it may not work. This is a particular problem for third-party software (such as Alsoft's DiskWarrior) that requires a bootable CD (or alternate startup volume) to work. Contact the vendor for advice if you get stuck in this situation.

External drives. Assuming the problem is not with the Mac itself or with the software installed on the drive, check with the drive vendor for possible firmware updates for the drive. In some cases, the fix may require that a hardware component of the drive be replaced. When you purchase a FireWire drive, make sure that it uses the Oxford 911 or newer chipset, which generally is needed for full Mac OS X compatibility.

For FireWire and USB startup drives, if selecting the drive in the Startup Disk System Preferences pane does not result in starting up from the drive, restart and hold down the Option key at startup; then select the drive from the choices that appear in the Startup Manager window.

(In one case, not only was I unable to start up from an external FireWire drive, but attempting to do so prevented any startup at all—that is, a gray-screen crash occurred. Further, no startup volumes were listed if I held down the Option key at startup. The only solution was to disconnect the FireWire device from the Mac and restart.)

continues on next page

TAKE NOTE ▶ Startup Failure When Starting Up from an External Device *continued*

Pressing Command-Option-Shift-D immediately at startup may force the Mac to attempt to boot from an external device that it otherwise would not boot from. You can also try turning off the power to the external drive briefly (especially if you're stuck at startup with no drive mounting) and then turning it back on. Based on my own experience, the probability of success here is low, but these tactics are worth a shot.

Occasionally you may find yourself unable to start up from an external drive because Mac OS X has been installed on it incorrectly—and thus the drive has not been "blessed" as bootable and/or permissions are not set correctly. There are several potential solutions to this situation, as described elsewhere in this book.

Finally, after updating to Panther, if you restart your Mac with a FireWire drive connected, you may fall victim to a bug that renders your FireWire drive unusable until you reformat it. Data on the drive will be difficult, if not impossible, to recover.

SEE: • "Take Note: Blessed Systems and Starting Up," later in this chapter, for more on blessing a drive.

• "Troubleshooting Tips and Hints: Installing Software," "Bootable CD or DVD," and "Take Note: Backups of Bootable Volumes Don't Boot," in Chapter 3, for more information on potential causes of startup problems.

• "Mounting and unmounting/ejecting media," in Chapter 6, for related information, including more information on the Panther bug that can corrupt external FireWire drives.

Blinking question-mark icons

A variation on gray-screen startup problems is a gray screen containing a folder icon with a blinking/flashing question mark inside. Typically, this means that your Mac cannot locate a volume with a valid version of system software from which to boot.

In the benign variation of this problem, the question mark is soon replaced by the Mac OS X logo, and all proceeds normally. In the malignant variation, the blinking icon persists.

What to do. Consider the following suggestions when troubleshooting this symptom:

• The benign variation typically means that no default startup device is selected or that the default device is not connected to the Mac. In such cases, the Mac will search through the available startup devices and select one; it is this search that causes the delay.

If this problem occurs each time you start up, you usually can fix it by opening the Startup Disk System Preferences pane and selecting a startup volume. The next time you restart, the blinking question-mark icon should no longer appear.

- To deal with the malignant variation, hold down the Option key at startup. In the Startup Manager window that appears, select a volume other than the one that is giving you trouble (assuming there is such a volume listed). When you reach the Desktop, select the desired Max OS X volume on the Startup Disk System Preferences pane and restart. The selected Mac OS X volume should now boot.

   Alternatively, try starting up from a Mac OS X Install disc. Once your Mac is booted, use the Startup Disk utility to select your desired default startup disk.

- If the Startup Disk System Preferences pane does not allow you to select a Mac OS X installation as the startup OS, the OS software on that volume may be damaged or a critical file may be missing. You can try repairing the disk with Disk Utility's First Aid. If this does not work, you will likely need to reinstall Mac OS X at this point.

- You may be able to fix things by using the `reset-nvram` command in Open Firmware (as described in "Technically Speaking: Open Firmware Commands," earlier in this chapter). Similarly, resetting the PRAM may do the trick.

- You may be able to start up normally by repairing permissions in single-user mode, as described in the "Recover files before reinstalling" section of "Reinstalling Mac OS X," later in this chapter.

- If you can't start up from a hard drive under any circumstance, and if (after starting up from a CD or DVD) your hard-drive volume or volumes do not mount, your hard drive is probably in need of repair or replacement.

Blinking globe icon. If you get a blinking globe icon instead of a blinking folder icon, this means your Mac is trying to start up via NetBoot but cannot find a bootable OS on the network. Typically, within a few seconds the Mac should shift to booting from your default local startup drive. After startup is complete, you can change your startup-disk selection, if desired, to prevent this symptom from occurring on future restarts. Of course, if you expect to return to NetBooting on your next restart, leave things as they are.

If you get a malignant variation, where the blinking globe remains indefinitely, follow the same advice as just described for the blinking folder icon.

SEE: • "Take Note: NetBooting," earlier in this chapter.
      • "Take Note: Blessed Systems and Starting Up," below, for related information.
      • "Techniques for Solving Mac OS X Crashes," later in this chapter, for advice on disk repairs.

TAKE NOTE ▶ Blessed Systems and Starting Up

A System folder that the Mac recognizes as one it can use for startup is referred to as a *blessed* folder.

BootX file. Located in /System/Library/CoreServices, the BootX file is an essential piece of software for booting from Mac OS X. If it is deleted, you will get the blinking question-mark icon at startup.

In some cases, the Mac OS X System folder may become unblessed. You will know that this is the case if the *X* icon that appears on the System and CoreServices folders disappears. (This *X* is visible only when you boot in Mac OS X.) If this occurs, dragging the BootX file out of the System folder and returning it to its original location in CoreServices may help. However, to do this, you must somehow be able to boot your Mac and access files! Typically, you would boot from Mac OS 9 or from another drive that contains Mac OS X (for example, an external FireWire drive).

Note that a BootX file by itself is not sufficient to start up in Mac OS X. The rest of the Mac OS X software must also be present and in working order.

Blessing a volume via Terminal. You can use the `bless` command to bless a Mac OS X volume (typically an external drive)—which may just be the ticket for making the drive bootable. To do so, type the following (all in one line), where *volumename* is the name of the volume from which you want to boot:

```
sudo bless -folder /Volumes/volumename/System/Library/CoreServices
```

Apple has documented a variation of this problem in which newer Macs (the ones that can no longer boot into Mac OS 9) may be unable to start up from a (presumably external) hard drive that was previously used with an older (Mac OS 9–compatible) Mac or that was restored via an image file created on an older Mac. The solution (if the problem volume or drive is now connected to the newer computer) is to type the following (all in one line, with a space between `-bootinfo` and `/usr`):

```
sudo bless -folder /Volumes/volumename/System/Library/CoreServices -bootinfo
/usr/standalone/ppc/bootx.bootinfo
```

See the Apple Knowledge Base document http://docs.info.apple.com/article.html?artnum=25506 for more details.

continues on next page

TAKE NOTE ▶ Blessed Systems and Starting Up *continued*

Blessed folder in Mac OS 9. Just for the record, a similar situation exists in Mac OS 9. For the Mac to start up from Mac OS 9, it typically must locate a blessed System Folder. A blessed System Folder has a mini-Mac-face icon (as you see when you boot in Mac OS 9). If Mac OS 9 and Mac OS X are on the same volume, however, and Mac OS X was the startup OS the last time you started up from that volume, you may not see this icon on the folder because the Mac OS 9 System Folder gets unblessed when Mac OS X is selected as the startup OS from that volume. You typically can re-bless the System Folder by selecting it as the startup OS in the Startup Disk control panel. Otherwise, dragging the System file out of the System Folder and dragging it back in again should re-bless the System Folder.

I mention this to emphasize a point I alluded to in the main text: If the Mac cannot find *any* blessed Mac OS 9 or BootX Mac OS X System folder, you will get the persistent blinking question mark at startup.

Making matters a bit more confusing, the Mac OS 9 System Folder that is currently selected for use when you launch the Classic environment will have a *9* icon in it when viewed in Mac OS X. This icon is a separate issue from whether or not the folder is "blessed" for startup.

Figure 5.12

Icons on System folders for Mac OS X and Mac OS 9.

System

System Folder

Dumped into Unix

A rare startup problem can occur in which you go from the gray screen directly to the command-line black screen that you normally see when booting into single-user mode.

In this case, you typically see the following line of text: "File system dirty, run fsck." You can run `fsck` directly at this point (that is, you don't need to restart and hold down Command-S to restart in single-user mode).

SEE: • "Running fsck," later in this chapter, for more details.

If running `fsck` doesn't correct the problem, it's likely that critical Unix files are missing or corrupted. Unix experts may be able to figure out exactly what went wrong and fix the problem from the command line; however, for most Mac users the solution at this point is to reinstall Mac OS X.

In some cases, the problem may be that one or more Unix files have incorrect permissions. You may be able to fix this by using the AppleJack utility to repair permissions (as described in "Running fsck," later in this chapter) or by modifying permissions well enough to start up successfully before reinstalling Mac OS X (as described in "Reinstalling Mac OS X," at the end of this chapter).

Blue-screen crashes and stalls

If Mac OS X successfully navigates the gray screen, next the screen will turn blue, followed shortly by the appearance of the Mac OS X logo. Within the logo box, you will see the message, "Starting Mac OS X…" When this process is complete, the Mac will either halt at the Login window or (if you've enabled automatic login) proceed directly to launching the Finder and Dock.

If a crash (or freeze) occurs at the blue-screen stage, it's likely to be related to a service that failed to load—the symptom of which is generally a blank blue screen and the failure of the Login window or Desktop to appear. Here are some of the most common causes of such problems, along with advice for what to do about them.

Stalled Network Services. One of the most common causes of a blue-screen freeze is a problem with network services. If your network connections have changed from those you set in the Network System Preferences pane, you may get a long stall. This could happen, for example, if the OS looks for an Ethernet network that no longer exists. Usually, the OS will eventually make it past this type of freeze—you just need the patience to outlast it (which can take several minutes). However, if it doesn't become unstuck, you may be able to modify your hardware network connections. In particular, if you have an Ethernet cable attached to your Mac, disconnect it. Conversely, if an Ethernet cable is normally connected to your Mac but for some reason is disconnected, reconnect it. If you use a cable modem and have disconnected it or turned it off, make sure the cable modem is active and connected. And so on.

If this technique works, the stall will end and login will proceed immediately. In any case, when you finish starting up, if you intend to maintain whatever arrangement led to the stall, you may need to modify your settings in the Network System Preferences pane to prevent the stall from happening again.

In particular, make sure you have a valid DNS address in the Domain Name Servers field (see Chapter 8 for details). Next, disable any Ethernet or AirPort ports (in Network's Network Port Configurations list) that will not be accessible at startup. For example, if you disable AirPort, your Mac won't search for or locate any wireless networks at startup.

If none of these measures help and you're still stalled at the blue screen, keep reading.

TAKE NOTE ▶ Network Stalls Beyond the Blue Screen

One of the changes in Tiger, as described in the main text (see "Startup daemons," earlier in this chapter), is the use of the launchd process to control the loading of services. One of the advantages of launchd is that it does not have to actually load requested processes at startup; it just registers them. They are then loaded later on, when needed. This is why the progress bar during the blue screen no longer indicates what individual services are loading. The progress bar is now mainly an "empty shell," indicating that various processes are being registered rather than launched.

The result is that the network services stall described in the main text may not occur during startup in Tiger (in earlier versions of Mac OS X it would occur when the text on the blue screen said, "Starting network services"). Instead, it may occur (as once happened to me) after login has started but before the Finder loads. This makes the stall more difficult to diagnose. But the cure is the same (that is, disconnect the "unused" Ethernet cable).

Other stalls and slowdowns. There is an assortment of other causes of stalls and slowdowns that may occur at this stage of startup. Here are a few examples:

- Selections in the Directory Access application can contribute to an unusually slow or stalled startup. In particular, if services (such as LDAP) are enabled that do not exist on your network, startup will be slowed while the Mac searches in vain for the nonexistent service.

- Similarly, if your Mac is set to search for a specific server at startup, but that server is not currently available (for example, the network connection is down), startup will be slowed. However, this slowdown will happen only for the first startup after the server loss.

- A bug in Mac OS X 10.3.2 can cause a significant stall at startup—at least for some users. The cause is that a Unix executable file, called BootCacheControl, is missing from the /usr/bin directory. This file creates a cache that speeds up the startup process. Because the file is missing, the cache is not created and the speedup does not occur. The solution is to place a symbolic link (a type of alias, as described in Chapter 6) in the /usr/bin directory that points to a copy of the missing file located in /System/Library/Extensions. To do this, launch Terminal and type (all in one line) the following:

```
sudo ln -s /System/Library/Extensions/BootCache.kext/Contents/
Resources/BootCacheControl /usr/sbin
```

On your second restart after doing this, startup time should be reduced.

This bug was fixed in Mac OS X 10.3.3. However, it is still useful to be aware of the general cause and solution for this slowdown. Problems with this file may occur in other situations.

Corrupt files and permissions errors. An assortment of files (mainly Unix and /System/Library software) can become corrupt or acquire incorrect permissions—both of which can cause blue-screen crashes. In such cases, performing a Safe Boot may allow startup to proceed. Alternatively, if you can start up your Mac in Mac OS 9—for example, by holding down the Option key at startup—do so. If not, you can start up in Mac OS X from a custom bootable CD or DVD (as described in Chapter 3) or an external drive. If none of these options are available, you may be able to solve the problem by starting up in single-user mode (as described in the auto-dial problem example that follows). In all cases, your next step is to locate and delete or replace the problem files or to fix permissions. Otherwise, you're looking at reinstalling your OS software. The following are some examples of problems that can be caused by corrupted files or permissions errors:

- **Disk corrupted; repairs needed.** A good general first step is to launch Disk Utility and from the First Aid section run the Repair Disk Permissions and Repair Disk functions.

  However, you will not be able to run Disk Utility from your hard drive if you're getting a crash at startup. The solution is to start up from an Install CD or DVD and run Disk Utility from there. You can also run fsck via single-user mode (or via a Safe Boot).

  If none of this works, you can try using a third-party repair utility.

  SEE: • "Performing repairs with Disk Utility (First Aid),""Enabling and disabling journaling,""Running fsck," and "Using third-party disk-repair utilities," later in this chapter, for more details.

- **Preferences-file problems.** In some instances, problems with preferences files in the /Library/Preferences folder, including com.apple.loginwindow.plist and com.apple.windowserver.plist, and files in the SystemConfiguration and DirectoryService subfolders can prevent a successful startup.

  To work around an issue with one of these .plist files, you need to rename or remove the file via single-user mode. This will prevent the problem files from loading at startup.

  Here is one specific example: The PPP pane of the Internal Modem pane of the Network System Preferences pane includes a button called PPP Options. In the dialog that appears if you click this button is a check box for "Connect automatically when needed." Under certain conditions, if this auto-dial option is enabled, it may cause a blue-screen crash at login. Since you can't start up in Mac OS X to disable the option at this point, you must instead work in single-user mode. From here, you can delete the preferences file (preferences.plist) where these and all other Network System Preferences settings are stored. This causes a new default preferences.plist file to be created at startup. You lose all of your Network System Preferences, but the problematic option is disabled, which should allow you to start up. You can then go back and re-enter your customized settings when you finally log in. To perform this procedure, follow these steps:

  1. Hold down Command-S at startup to enter single-user mode.

  2. Type mount -uw / and press Return.

3. Type `mv /Library/Preferences/SystemConfiguration/preferences.plist preferences.old` and press Return.

4. Type `reboot` and press Return.

This renames the existing preferences.plist file to preferences.old (in case you want to view it later), which forces a new default copy of preferences.plist to be created at the next startup.

See this Apple Knowledge Base document for more details: http://docs.info.apple.com/article.html?artnum=106464.

- **Corrupt Mac OS 9 fonts.** To check for problematic Mac OS 9 fonts, remove the Fonts folder from the Mac OS 9 System Folder, used by Classic, and drag it to the Desktop. Also consider removing any fonts in the Fonts folders of Mac OS X that you may have added since installing Mac OS X—especially older fonts originally used in Mac OS 9. (See Chapter 4 for details on Fonts folders.) Restart again from the problem drive. If the crash no longer occurs, one of the fonts you removed is the likely cause. You can start replacing fonts and restarting to isolate the file. If removing fonts did not eliminate the crash, you can return all fonts to their respective locations.

   SEE: • "Checking fonts," later in this chapter, for solutions to these problems.

- **Problem kext items or third-party startup items.** Crashes caused by these items may be prevented by a Safe Boot. After starting up successfully, you can remove or replace the problem item.

   SEE: • "Checking for extension (kext) problems," later in this chapter, for more details.

Hardware issues. If all else fails, the problem may be hardware related. Refer to the preceding sections on gray-screen crashes for more advice.

SEE: • "Logout, Restart, and Shutdown Stalls and Crashes," later in this chapter.

  • "Techniques for Solving Mac OS X Crashes," especially "Logging out, restarting, and resetting," and "Performing repairs with Disk Utility (First Aid)," later in this chapter.

Kernel panic

The most serious type of system crash you can get with Mac OS X is a *kernel panic*. Because kernel panics can occur at startup, I discuss them here. (If a kernel panic does occur at startup, it's most likely to happen during the gray-screen phase, since this is when the kernel extensions load.) However, they may also occur after startup is complete—most often when you launch an application or choose a command from one of its menus. The logic for finding a solution is the same in either case.

According to Apple, "A kernel panic is a type of error that occurs when the core (kernel) of an operating system receives an instruction in an unexpected format or that it fails to handle properly. A kernel panic may also follow when the operating system is not able to recover from a different type of error. A kernel panic can be caused by damaged or incompatible software or, more rarely, damaged or incompatible hardware."

Among other things, a kernel panic can be caused by renaming, modifying, or deleting files or folders in the /System folder or in the Unix directories.

> You need to restart your computer. Hold down the Power button for several seconds or press the Restart button.
>
> Veuillez redémarrer votre ordinateur. Maintenez la touche de démarrage enfoncée pendant plusieurs secondes ou bien appuyez sur le bouton de réinitialisation.
>
> Sie müssen Ihren Computer neu starten. Halten Sie dazu die Einschalttaste einige Sekunden gedrückt oder drücken Sie die Neustart-Taste.
>
> コンピュータを再起動する必要があります。パワーボタンを数秒間押し続けるか、リセットボタンを押してください。

Figure 5.13

The kernel panic screen.

Kernel panic message. If a kernel panic occurs, a message box will appear on your screen that reads (in several languages), "You need to restart your computer. Hold down the Power button for several seconds or press the Restart button."

At this point, everything halts. The good news is that you're not responsible for the crash; the bad news is that you can't do anything to fix the problem except avoid the action that caused it and wait for a permanent fix from Apple (or the third-party developer that makes the offending software).

Once you have successfully restarted, you are likely to get a message that says in part, "Mac OS X quit unexpectedly."

SEE: • "Technically Speaking: 'Unexpectedly Quit' Under the Hood," later in this chapter, for more details regarding this "unexpectedly quit" message.

Figure 5.14

The "Mac OS X quit unexpectedly" alert that appears when restarting after a kernel panic.

The computer was restarted after Mac OS X quit unexpectedly.

Click Report to see more details or send a report to Apple.

(Report...)   (OK)

Kernel panic log. After a kernel panic has occurred, details of what happened are recorded in the panic.log file in /Library/Logs. How can this file record the data if a kernel panic has crashed the Mac? It works because kernel panic information is temporarily saved in NVRAM and written to the log file at the next startup. If you can't find this log file, you probably didn't experience a kernel panic and have never had one previously.

Because kernel panics are both serious and rare, Apple is always interested in getting user feedback about how and when such panics have occurred and what the error text said. Such information will help Apple figure out why the problem occurred and how to fix the bug that caused it. Check your panic.log and post relevant information and details at Apple's Discussion Boards (www.apple.com/support).

Hardware causes. Peripheral hardware devices (such as external USB and FireWire devices, PCI cards, and PC Cards) are by far the most common kernel panic culprits. Many of the causes and fixes described in the section on gray-screen crashes (such as doing a Safe Boot, updating firmware, and so on) apply here as well.

SEE: • "Gray-screen crashes" and "Verbose mode," earlier in this chapter, for related details.

• "Checking for extension (kext) problems," later in this chapter, for a specific example of a kernel panic problem.

Mac OS X software causes. The second major cause of kernel panic at startup is altered Mac OS X system software that prevents the OS from starting up properly. As you search for the culprit, you should be aware of the following:

• **Third-party kext items can cause kernel panics.** The solution is typically to contact the vendor and get an upgraded version of the problematic kext item that works with the current version of the OS.

• **Apple reports that simply adding too many kext items to the /System/Library/Extensions folder can precipitate a startup crash.** The reason: insufficient memory to run BootX.

A Safe Boot can bypass this cause of a kernel panic; once you're up and running, you must determine the culprit file(s).

SEE: • "Safe Booting," earlier in this chapter.

• "Checking for extension (kext) problems," later in this chapter.

• **In general, you should avoid removing, deleting, or editing any files in the System directory.** Although you can make some changes inside this folder without causing harm (which you will occasionally need to do to fix certain problems), you must know what you can and can't do—any speculative troubleshooting in this area could easily lead to disaster.

• **Modifying (especially deleting) the contents of the normally invisible Unix folders (/bin, /var, and so on) can also lead to system crashes, kernel panics, and other problems.** Again, it's *possible* to modify or delete files here without causing harm, but you need to know what you're doing. In other words, *avoid experimentation*.

- **Moving Applications, System, Library, or any other OS-installed folder from its default location is strongly discouraged.**

- **Modifying permissions and ownership of critical Mac OS X files can cause kernel panics.** Changing a file's access so that the OS cannot use it when needed can be functionally equivalent to deleting it. Thus, don't even think about permanently modifying the permissions settings for files in the /System/Library folder. If you want to limit or expand access to these files, there are other ways to do so (which are discussed in Chapter 6).

If you made any of the above-described modifications and can undo them (possibly via starting from another Mac OS X volume), do so. Then try to restart in Mac OS X from the problem volume. Ideally, the startup will work. If not, you're looking at reinstalling the OS.

SEE: • "Techniques for Solving Mac OS X Crashes," later in this chapter.

   • "Checking for extension (kext) problems," later in this chapter, for related advice.

Third-party software causes. Occasionally, third-party software can be the cause of a kernel panic. The work-around solution here is to do a Safe Boot and/or disable Login Items at startup. Assuming this allows a successful startup, you can now disable or uninstall the offending software.

SEE: • "Safe Booting," earlier in this chapter, for more details.

Other examples. With each Mac OS X update, Apple fixes bugs that caused kernel panics in previous OS versions. Thus, whenever you describe specific causes of kernel panics, you must do so in reference to a particular version of Mac OS X. Here are two examples of kernel panics—and suggestions for fixing them:

- You may get a kernel panic after installing an AirPort Extreme card, if the AirPort software on your drive is too old to work with the Extreme card. This should not happen if you are running Tiger, as it will install compatible software, but may happen with older versions of Mac OS X or if you somehow wind up with an older version of AirPort software on your Tiger drive.

  To fix this problem, shut down the Mac, remove the AirPort Extreme card, and restart. Now get on the Internet (obviously via a wired connection!) and download the latest AirPort software. Install it. Shut down again and replace the AirPort Extreme card. All should now work.

- You may get a kernel panic as a result of optimizing a disk or after updating to a newer version of Mac OS X. In such cases, the panic.log file displays the following message: "Kernel loadable modules in backtrace com.apple.BootCache (with dependencies)." You can fix the problem by restarting while holding down the Shift key (to do a Safe Boot) and logging in as the root user. When startup is complete, use the Go to Folder command to go to /var/db. From here, delete the BootCache.playlist file. Restart as normal, and all should be well.

For more in-depth technical details about kernel panics, get Apple's Developer Technical Note titled "Understanding and Debugging Kernel Panics" (http://developer.apple.com/technotes/tn2002/tn2063.html).

Login crashes and failures

Login crashes are ones that occur after you've logged in, typically after the Desktop background appears. These are almost always caused by one of three things:

- **A login item that loads at login.** This is the most common cause. The initial work-around is to disable the loading of startup items.

    SEE: • "Disabling login items," earlier in this chapter, for more details.
    - "Take Note: Solving Problems with Login Items," later in this chapter, for additional details.

- **A corrupt preferences file is accessed at login.** If your Mac crashes just as the Desktop appears and no user-level login item appears to be the culprit, you may have a corrupt preferences file. (For example, the ~/Library/Preferences/com.apple.scheduler.plist file, used by iCal, is a common potential culprit.) The solution is to log in as the root user, locate the .plist file in your own User directory, and delete the file. (As alternatives to logging in as the root user, you could log in to another account and use the sudo command in Terminal to delete the file, or delete the file from within single-user mode at startup.)

    If you cannot easily diagnose the problematic .plist file, the ultimate solution is to log in as the root user and move the entire contents of your Preferences folder or even the entire Library folder from its current location to another folder (such as your Desktop). You should now be able to log in to the problematic account. A default set of Library files will be created in the active Library folder. Assuming you want to restore those files in your Preferences or entire Library folder that *weren't* responsible for the problem, you will need to do traditional trial-and-error troubleshooting to locate the problem file. If it isn't a preferences file, it's most likely a font.

    SEE: • "Logging in as another user," later in this chapter, for additional advice on this topic.

- **Short name of home directory was changed.** Never change the name of your home directory (folder) directly in the Finder. That is, don't go into the /Users folder and change the name of any of the folders contained within. Doing so may prevent you from logging in to your account (or the account associated with any folder you rename). The quick fix, if you have already done this, is to log in as the root user and change the name of the folder back to its original name.

    Alternatively, a new default empty home directory may be created if you change the name of your home folder and then log in to your account. The old one is still present (with the modified name). To get back to using your prior home directory at this point, rename the current folder by adding text to it (such as the word *new*) and then rename the old folder back to its original name. Log out and log back in.

See this Apple Knowledge Base document for more information: http://docs.info.apple.com/article.html?artnum=107854. If you really need to change the name of your home directory, Apple offers advice in this article: http://docs.info.apple.com/article.html?artnum=106824.

SEE: • "Take Note: Accounts Problems," in Chapter 2, for additional advice.

TAKE NOTE ▶ Solving Problems with Login Items

Login items (typically applications) load automatically when you log in—and are thus specific to each user, with each account maintaining its own list of these items. As described in Chapter 2, users can add items here, and some software installers do so automatically.

The list of login items is found in the Login Items pane of the Accounts System Preferences pane. To find it, click the name for your account and select Login Items from the row of tabs.

Unknown items. When you check your list of Login Items, you may find one or more with a Kind of "Unknown." If so, you need to fix this. It means that Mac OS X can no longer locate the "unknown" Login Item and so it is not loading at login, despite the fact that its name is still in the list.

This can happen for several reasons. The most common reasons are: (a) You deleted the item or the software package that contained the item, or (b) you moved the relevant software to a new folder.

In the former case, the solution is simply to delete the item from the Login Items list (as you presumably no longer use the software). To do so, select the item and click the Delete (–) button. (Note: If the software is still on your drive, deleting its name from the list does not delete the software from your drive; it just removes it from the Login Items list.)

In the latter case, you probably want to reassign the item to its new location. To do so, delete the existing Login Item, locate the item in its new location, and use the Add (+) button to re-add it.

Load order problems? Suppose it turned out that a Login Items conflict occurred, such that if Item B loaded before Item A, there was a problem, but not vice versa. The solution would be simple: reorder the load order so that Item A loads first. On the assumption that load order is determined by the order in which the items appear in the Login Items list, the solution would seem to be as simple as dragging the item to its desired location in the list.

And everything did appear to work pretty much this way prior to Tiger. In Tiger, attempts to drag an item to a new location have no effect. It's hard to even initiate a drag. Most attempts simply select multiple items in the list. The only "success" I had was if I click-held on the right side of an item's listing (to the right of where its Kind is listed). While I could drag the item around, the item was deleted as soon as I let go, rather than moved to the dragged location.

continues on next page

TAKE NOTE ▶ Solving Problems with Login Items *continued*

While this drag-delete is probably a bug, the general inability to rearrange items appears to be intentional. The reason is that login items load asynchronously, starting in Tiger. In brief, this means that login item B will launch immediately after login item A has launched, even if A has not yet completed its launch (and so on for other items). This is similar to what happens if you click several items in succession from the Dock. Depending on what the items are, Item B may actually finish launching before Item A. This makes the exact sort order largely irrelevant.

If you still want to have login items load in a specified order (perhaps because Item B needs information from Item A in order to launch successfully), you do have a few options. These include the following:

- Bypass using login items except for a single Automator workflow application. Have the Automator workflow set up to launch the desired items in the order you wish. Using primarily the Finder's Launch Application action, this should be easy to do.

- Assuming you believe that changing the order of the items in the Login Items list will have a beneficial effect, you can delete and re-add items. Each added item appears as the last item in the list, allowing for a crude but effective method of reordering items.

Some items, if added to the Login Items list, may cause problems no matter where they fall in the list or how many other items the list includes. In such cases, the only solution is to remove the login item from the list or replace it with a bug-fixed update.

Too many items. If you have too many login items (the exact number will vary with different Mac OS X installations), some may not load successfully. To get around this problem, you can delete items from the list and launch the removed items manually when needed.

If you have too many items in the list, you may find that in some cases when you try to open an application from the Dock—especially if login items are still loading—it will fail to open. In fact, it may even stall permanently, with an endlessly bouncing Dock icon. At this point, even a force-quit may not get the application to quit. Your only resort is to restart. Then disable login items as described next.

Disable login items at login. In worst-case scenarios, conflicts with login items can prevent the startup process from completing. If this happens, you will not be able to disable the item from the Accounts System Preferences pane because you cannot access System Preferences. The solution here is to disable all such login items at startup by holding down the Shift key (as described earlier in this chapter). You can then remove items as needed.

A login-items manager. Mac OS X stores the Login Items list in ~/Library/Preferences/loginwindow. plist. The list is contained under a subhead under the AutoLaunchedApplicationDictionary property of this file. Assuming that your problem doesn't prevent you from starting up, you can edit this list via Property List Editor as an alternate way to delete a login item.

continues on next page

TAKE NOTE ▶ Solving Problems with Login Items *continued*

On a related note, one of the weaknesses of the Login Items pane in the Accounts System Preferences pane is that, after removing a login item via the Delete (–) button, there's no automatic way to undo the removal. That is, if you delete a login item and later want to add it back, there's no button to help you do so. Yes, there is an Add (+) button, but because almost anything can be a login item, it can be hard to know where to look to find the item you want to restore. In particular, some programs add login items when they're installed, and these items may be buried within the .app package for the application. If you remove the item and don't know where it's stored, locating it again will be difficult. Even the Finder's Find feature will not locate it, because Find does not search within packages.

You have a couple of work-arounds here. For starters, if you pause the pointer over the item you plan to remove, a yellow tool tip will appear with the login item's path; save this as a record of where the item is located.

A more general solution would be to make a copy of ~/Library/Preferences/loginwindow.plist, which contains the paths to all of your current login items. That way, if you want to locate an item that you've removed, you can find out its path from this backup copy. To re-add an item with the least amount of hassle, do the following:

1. With the LoginItems.plist file open, double-click a desired path (in the Values column) and select/copy all but the last section (the one that contains the name of the item).

2. Go to the Login Items pane (in Accounts System Preferences pane) and click the Add (+) button.

3. Press Command-Shift-G. This brings up the Go to Folder window.

4. Paste the copied text into the text box and click Go. This will take you directly to the location needed to select and re-add the login item.

Whenever you add new login items (and you're sure you won't want to add back any previously deleted items), make a new backup copy of the loginwindow.plist file.

Alternatively, when trying to determine which login item is causing a problem, you can remove items from the list one by one until you locate the culprit. Once you've done this, you can replace the loginwindow.plist file with the backup copy to restore your list as it was before you began removing items—this time removing just the culprit item (if you found one).

You can also install the third-party utility Tiger Cache Cleaner, by Northern Softworks (www.northernsoftworks.com), which includes an option to create a LogIn Items folder in the Library folder of your home directory. (The feature itself is a login item.) If you enable this option, any item you place in the Login Items folder will launch at login, as if it had been added to the Login Items list. Remove an item from the folder (via the Finder), and it no longer launches at login. This won't necessarily help for items that are automatically added to the list when installing software; however, it does provide a way to work around some re-adding hassles.

continues on next page

TAKE NOTE ▶ Solving Problems with Login Items *continued*

Login items that require passwords. Apple states:"If you set up an application or file that requires a password as a Login Item, it will not open, but will appear in the Dock. You must click its icon in the Dock and enter its password in order for it to finish opening. Examples of such items include certain e-mail applications, encrypted files, and server administration applications."

Listed login items not hiding? When you check the Hide box for an application in the Login Items list, the application should open as hidden at login (as if you had used the Hide command for the application). Occasionally, however, this may not work. As far as I can tell, this is a bug in Mac OS X that will hopefully be fixed in a future update.

Auto-loading Classic. On a related note, to launch Classic automatically at startup, use the Classic System Preferences pane setting (no need to use the Login Items list here!).

SEE: • "Technically Speaking: Create Your Own Startup Daemons," earlier in this chapter, for more on the loginwindow.plist file.

• "Disabling login items," earlier in this chapter, for how to use the Shift key at startup to disable login items.

• "Logging out, restarting, and resetting," later in this chapter, for related information.

• "Preferences Files," in Chapter 4, for more information on .plist files and Property List Editor.

• The Classic chapter, online at Mac OS X Help Line (www.macosxhelpline.com), for more information.

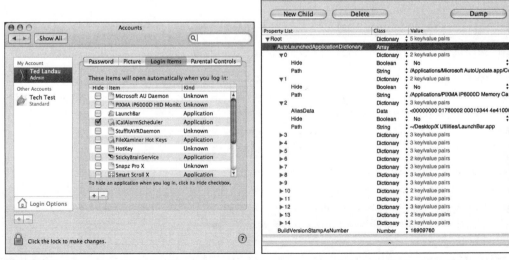

Figure 5.15

Left, *the Login Items list in the Accounts System Preferences pane;* right, *the contents of the loginwindow.plist file with detailed listings for the first three startup items.*

Startup Items security alerts

Apple wants to protect you from malicious startup items, possibly installed surreptitiously by software you downloaded from the Web. As of Tiger, Mac OS X checks for possible security problems with these third-party startup items (located in /Library/StartupItems). Apple calls this an "Automatic Security Check." If a startup item does not have what Mac OS X considers to be a "valid security clearance," you get an alert message at startup, stating, "The startup item {*name of item*} has problems that reduce the security of your computer." This message appears after you log in to your account, but before login is complete. The alert includes three buttons (you will need to enter an administrator's password after you click any of them):

- **Fix.** This is the default choice. It changes the settings for the startup item so that Mac OS X will not flag it again in the future. Do this only if you are confident that the item is indeed safe. If you do so, you will see the following message (or one similar to it): "The security settings for some startup items have been fixed. To use the items, you must restart your computer." If you click Cancel at this point, the item will not start up on this launch but will do so on future launches. Otherwise, click the Restart button.

- **Decide Later.** If you choose this, the item will not be launched on this startup. However, the next time you start up, you will see this same alert again. Ideally, before your next restart, you should investigate (perhaps by doing a search on the Web or calling the software vendor that appears to have created the file) to determine its safety. You can then select Fix or Disable, as appropriate.

- **Disable.** This "permanently" disables the item. The potential problem here is that if the item is really safe, it may be important for the use of some installed application. Disabling the item may prevent the application from working.

Checking the Startup Items folder itself. Mac OS X (Tiger) also checks the settings of the Startup Items folder. If it finds problems, you will get a message that states: "The Startup Items folder ('/Library/StartupItems/') does not have the proper security settings." You can choose to fix this as well. If not, none of the items in the folder will launch.

Re-enabling. What if you disable an item and later decide it was a mistake to do so? Can you re-enable it? Yes. One way would be to reinstall the application (which would presumably install a new copy of the Startup Item).

Otherwise, you can do so by deleting an invisible file, named ".disabled," that was created and placed inside the disabled Startup Item's folder when the Startup Item was disabled. To do this via Terminal:

1. Type cd /Library/StartupItems/{*name of startup item*} and press Return.

2. Next type sudo rm .disabled and press Return. Provide your administrative password when asked.

3. Restart your Mac.

What exactly does Mac OS X check to determine if a startup item is secure? It checks the permissions for the file or folder. In particular, as stated by Apple: "Directories and executable files should have permissions of '0755,' with the owner set to 'root' and group set to 'wheel.' Other (non-executable) files should have permissions of '0644,' with the owner set to 'root' and group set to 'wheel.'" Any other settings will trigger the alert. This means that only the owner (root) has write access to the startup item's contents, although anyone can read them (or run them, if they are executable).

Although it might seem that having root as the owner of a potentially rogue startup item would be a security risk in itself, this is not really the case here. These startup items can have no user interface and cannot directly affect a user process (although they can accept requests from user processes). Still, it does not strike me that these warnings are a particularly strong form of protection.

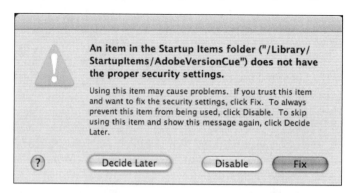

Figure 5.16

Top, *the Startup Items Security alert;* bottom, *the message that appears after you select to fix the listed item(s).*

SEE: • **"Startup daemons,"** earlier in this chapter, for more on startup items.

• **"Understanding Image, Installer Package, and Receipt Files,"** in Chapter 3, for more on packages.

• **"Ownership & Permissions,"** in Chapter 4, for more on permissions.

• **Chapter 6,** for more on invisible files.

TAKE NOTE ▶ Miscellaneous Crashes

The following is a collection of causes and potential solutions for a variety of crashes not specifically described in the main text.

Display-related crashes. Some Mac OS X crashes are directly related to the display software. Here is one example:

- If, in the Displays System Preferences pane, you uncheck the Show Modes Recommended by Display box and then choose a non-recommended resolution, the display may go blank. One solution is to boot into Mac OS 9 and delete the com.apple.windowserver.plist file in Mac OS X's /Library/Preferences folder. If your Mac cannot start up in Mac OS 9, you can start up in single-user mode and use Unix's `rm` command to delete the file.

Sleep-related crashes and problems. A host of potential problems can occur when your Mac wakes from sleep. These include crashes, kernel panics, and simple failures to wake (that is, the screen remains black); no sound or no AppleTalk connection in Classic; and loss of a network connection.

The following are some things to be aware of (and do) when a crash or failure occurs when waking from sleep:

- If a peripheral cable (such as a USB, FireWire, or Ethernet cable) is connected to the Mac, disconnecting it may bring the Mac out of its coma.

  Disconnecting these devices *before* you put the Mac to sleep and keeping them disconnected until you wake the Mac up may prevent the problem in the first place.

- A wake-from-sleep crash could be caused by a problem with a specific screen saver, especially a third-party one (as selected from the Desktop & Screen Saver System Preferences pane). In this case, the obvious work-around is to select a different screen saver.

- More generally, selecting the "Wake for Ethernet network administrator access" option, in the Energy Saver pane's Options pane, can prevent some of these problems. Otherwise, if you get a wake-from-sleep crash, you will need to do a hard reset of your Mac to get it working again.

- Using the commands `reset-nvram` followed by `reset-all` in Open Firmware may fix the problem.

- The ultimate solution is to wait for and/or get the Mac OS X update (or third-party software update) that fixes the problem.

Directory Services crashes. Incorrect settings in the Directory Access utility, or corrupted preferences used by this utility, can cause startup crashes and login failures.

SEE: • "Technically Speaking: Open Firmware Commands," earlier in this chapter.

- "Take Note: Sleep Problems," in Chapter 2, for related information.

- "Technically Speaking: Restoring and Replacing NetInfo and Directory Access Data," in Chapter 4, for more on Directory Services–related problems.

- "Sleep problems," in the Classic chapter online at Mac OS X Help Line (www. macosxhelpline.com), for more information on sleep problems specific to Classic.

Application Crashes

Most application crashes in Mac OS X will not bring down your entire system, nor will they require you to restart your Mac. Thus, in many cases the cure for an application crash is to simply ignore it, relaunch the crashed application, and hope the crash does not occur again (or at least happens only rarely). If this is not sufficient, consider the solutions described in the following sections.

Freeze/hang

Applications occasionally stop functioning—often while attempting to perform some action, such as opening a document or receiving an e-mail. In such cases, the spinning wait cursor appears and just remains; the intended action is never completed. At the same time, attempts to otherwise interact with the program (such as choosing menu commands) also fail to work. This is your standard application freeze.

Occasionally, issuing a Cancel command (Command-. [period]) will end the hung action and return control of the application to you; however, I've had only rare success with this technique in Mac OS X. Also occasionally, waiting and doing nothing will succeed—which means the application was just taking an unusually long time to complete its task. (See also Chapter 6 for some suggestions about how to improve application performance.) More likely, though, something has gone awry, and simply walking away from your Mac won't fix it.

The silver lining is that the effects of these freezes are almost always limited to the affected application. That is, if you simply click the window of another application, the spinning cursor vanishes and your Mac is working normally again. Return to the problem application, and the symptom returns. Still, on the assumption that you would like to use the frozen application again, you'll want to fix the problem. To do so, try the following:

- Force-quit the application.
- If force-quitting doesn't work, but you can still access the Apple menu, choose Log Out from there. When you log back in, things should work normally.
- If the Log Out command doesn't work, try choosing Restart. The logic is the same.
- Occasionally, an application will fail to launch, leaving its Dock icon to bounce endlessly. At this point, it's possible that no menu commands will work. Even so, you should still be able to force-quit the application.

Systemwide freeze. Occasionally, a frozen application will cause the entire system to hang—that is, you get no response from any application, the Finder, or the Dock. In addition, the pointer may no longer respond to the mouse and the Force Quit command fails to bring up the Force Quit window. When this happens, there's typically been a freeze or crash of some critical process, such as loginwindow.

Two well-known cases where you may get a systemwide freeze:

- **File sharing.** If an attempt to connect to a server is unsuccessful, or if you are unexpectedly disconnected from a server from which you had already connected, a systemwide freeze can occur.

- **Web browsing.** What starts as a simple failure to load certain Web pages may spread to a systemwide freeze. The most likely cause is the freeze of a process called lookupd (used to match network domain names to their IP addresses).

If you can still get the Force Quit command to work, force-quitting the Finder (and/or your Web browser) may be sufficient to get things working. If the freeze has not progressed to the point that you can no longer use Terminal, you may be able to fix the problem by killing and restarting the lookupd process. Otherwise, disconnecting and reconnecting the network hardware (such as a router or cable modem) may work. As a last resort, you will need to hard-restart/reset your Mac.

SEE: • "Force-quitting" and "Logging out, restarting, and resetting," later in this chapter.
• "Killing processes from Terminal," later in this chapter, for more on using the kill command.
• "Troubleshooting Sharing," in Chapter 9.
• "Fix DNS-related problems," in the "Troubleshooting Safari (and other Web browsers)" section of Chapter 9.

Diagnosing the freeze. In many cases, a freeze is isolated, meaning it may not occur again once you've escaped the freeze via one of the procedures described above. Even with consistently recurring hangs, however, you often won't able to diagnose the cause beyond saying, "It happens when I do this." Thus, the most common solution is to *not* do "this" and/or to wait for a bug-fixed upgrade of the relevant software to be released.

However, if you're determined to track down the precise cause of a freeze, you have a few more technical options:

- **Console.** Launch the Console utility and check the console.log output that appears by default. Also check any other log files that include the name of the hung application. Look for text that might suggest a cause for the freeze. (Note: Sections of log files usually include the date and time of each event; you can narrow down your search by looking for log entries that correspond to the approximate date and time when the application started misbehaving.)

Additionally, if you view the log files in /var/log/cups, you may find one called error.log. Check this for error messages related to printing.

SEE: • "Console," in Chapter 2, for more on using this utility.

- **Sample feature in Activity Monitor.** To use this feature, launch Activity Monitor, select the frozen application, and press Command-I. In the Info window that opens, click the Sample button and then check the text output that appears.

  If you're lucky, you may find a term in the output that indicates a potential cause of the freeze. For example, if you see the word *CUPS* in the sample for a frozen application, it suggests that the CUPS printing software may have indirectly precipitated the freeze. Perhaps the CUPS software itself crashed. The quickest solution is a common one: Restart your Mac; however, understanding the cause of a crash may provide clues about how to prevent it.

- **Spin Control.** The Spin Control application in the /Developer/ Application/Performance Tools folder (assuming you installed the Developer software) also provides sample output for apparently hung applications.

- **The fs_usage command.** The Unix fs_usage command, entered in Terminal, may similarly help diagnose the cause of a frozen process (as described in "Technically Speaking: Terminal Commands to Monitor and Improve Performance," in Chapter 10).

Check the next section for related information, including further advice that can help you diagnose a cause so that the freeze/hang does not happen again.

TECHNICALLY SPEAKING ▶ Connecting Remotely to a Frozen Mac: Killing Processes, Running Sync

Even when nothing appears to be working, your Mac may be running normally beneath the surface. What I mean is that the Aqua interface may have gone belly-up temporarily, but its Unix underbelly may still be working—if only you can get to it. This most often occurs when the loginwindow process freezes, often causing even a force-quit to fail. The only apparent option is to restart.

You may, however, be able to access your Mac remotely via another Mac on your network—that is, if you previously enabled the Remote Login option in the Services pane of the Sharing System Preferences pane on the now-frozen Mac. If such is the case, you may be able to connect to the frozen Mac via an application that provides SSH (Secure Shell) access. If the connecting computer is also running Mac OS X, you can use Terminal (or a third-party utility like MacSSH) to initiate such a connection. You'll need to know the IP address of your Mac.

continues on next page

TECHNICALLY SPEAKING ▶ Connecting Remotely to a Frozen Mac: Killing Processes, Running Sync *continued*

I discuss the details of how to connect remotely to a Mac (frozen or not) via SSH in "SSH and SFTP," in Chapter 9. Once you're connected, here's what you can do:

Kill a process. If a particular process is causing a freeze, killing it may provide the cure. Elsewhere in this chapter, we cover using Activity Monitor to kill processes; however, you can't use Activity Monitor if your Mac is frozen. The solution, in this case, is to issue a kill command remotely, via the SSH connection, as described later in this chapter. After doing so, you may be able to use your Mac again without having to restart—a valuable technique if you have unsaved files in other running applications that you would have lost via a restart (unless the process you kill results in the unsaved document being destroyed).

Run sync. Another command you could run is sync. In essence, this command takes all data in the RAM cache and makes sure that it is written to disk—a technique that's also known as *flushing the cache*. Normally, the Mac does this on its own when restarting or shutting down—as well as periodically when the Mac is idle. But when you perform a hard restart (such as by pressing the Reset button on the Mac), the Mac does not get a final chance to flush the cache. In such cases, data in the cache may not get written to disk, which can result in corrupted files that could cause new (and potentially more serious) problems when you try to restart. Although this scenario is not very common, it is more likely to occur in Mac OS X than in Mac OS 9, because Mac OS X flushes the cache on its own less often than Mac OS 9. Issuing a sync command remotely to a frozen Mac eliminates the potential danger.

If remote login is not possible and you're worried about sync problems, let the Mac sit idle for a minute or two before restarting. Assuming that the Unix subsystem is still running, it may sync on its own during that time. Alternatively, if you still have sufficient access to your Mac that you can run Terminal locally, try typing sync in the command line.

SEE: • "Killing processes from Terminal," later in this chapter, for more on using the kill command.

   • Chapter 9 for more on remote access and other networking issues.

Application quits

The most common type of crash in Mac OS X occurs when an application "unexpectedly quits." When this occurs, you typically get a message in the Finder informing you of the "quit."

"Unexpectedly quit" dialog. When an application unexpectedly quits, the "unexpectedly quit" dialog/alert typically appears. In its default variation, it includes three buttons:

• **Close.** Click this to close the dialog and continue your work in other applications.

- **Report.** Click this to open a new dialog. The new dialog contains two parts. In the top part, "Problem and System information," is a copy of the crash.log for the application (as described in the next section). In the lower part, "Please describe what you were doing when the problem happened," you can type in your own description of what led to the crash.

  If you're connected to the Internet, you can click the Send to Apple button. Doing so sends all the information from this dialog to Apple. Given how many of these reports Apple is likely to get each day, I'm not sure how much use Apple makes of a particular report. Also, clicking this is almost certainly of little value if the crashed application is not from Apple. However, I suspect that if Apple sees a clear pattern (for example, thousands of people reporting the same bug), it could help speed up diagnosing and fixing the problem.

  Once you click the Send to Apple button, any text that you typed in the dialog is gone. There is no automatic way to save this text.

- **Reopen.** If you click the Reopen button, the application that crashed is immediately relaunched. This is a convenient way to check if the crash will recur and to do further troubleshooting as needed.

  SEE: • "Technically Speaking:'Unexpectedly Quit' Under the Hood," below, for further details about the workings of this dialog.

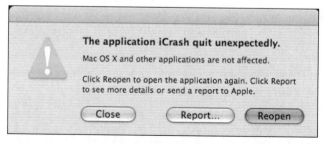

Figure 5.17

The "unexpectedly quit" error alert: top, *with the Reopen button;* bottom, *with the Try Again button.*

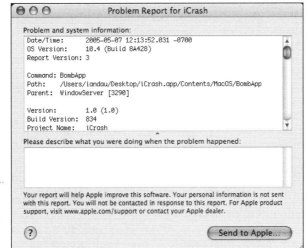

Figure 5.18

The dialog that appears if you click the Report button in the "unexpectedly quit" dialog.

TECHNICALLY SPEAKING ▶ "Unexpectedly Quit" Under the Hood

The "unexpectedly quit" dialog, always part of Mac OS X, adds several new options in Tiger to assist in your troubleshooting. Here are the details.

Reopen vs. Try Again. If you click the Reopen button in the "unexpectedly quit" dialog, a property called ApplicationCrashedAfterRelaunch (with a value of 1) is added to the application's preferences (.plist) file (typically located in ~/Library/Preferences). For example, if Safari crashed, you could open the com.apple.Safari.plist file (typically via Property List Editor, as described in Chapter 4) to see this added property.

Mac OS X uses this property to track that the application has previously crashed and that you have previously used Reopen to relaunch it. The result is that if the application should crash again, there is a change in the dialog: A Try Again button replaces the Reopen button. (Note: If you were to manually delete the ApplicationCrashedAfterRelaunch property before the next crash, the "unexpectedly quit" dialog would still show the Reopen button.)

If you click the Try Again button, the application again relaunches. If it crashes again, the dialog with the Try Again button appears again … ad infinitum.

Safe Relaunch. At this point, you may be saying, "Who cares?" That is, what does it matter whether the dialog says Reopen or Try Again? As it turns out, it matters quite a bit. When you click Try Again, the application relaunches, but in a special way that Apple calls a Safe Relaunch. This does not happen when you click the initial Reopen button.

In a Safe Relaunch, Mac OS X bypasses the use of the application's .plist file altogether when the application launches. This is the automatic equivalent of manually deleting or disabling the .plist file, as described in "Deleting or removing preferences," later in this chapter. If a corrupt .plist file was the cause of the crash, this means that the crash will now be prevented!

continues on next page

TECHNICALLY SPEAKING ▶ **"Unexpectedly Quit" Under the Hood** *continued*

If this disabling of the .plist file is successful, and the application does not crash, you will presumably quit the application normally at some later point. When you do so, yet another dialog will appear. This one asks if you want to keep the "new settings" that were created for the application. You can click either Yes or No.

- If you click No, the ApplicationCrashedAfterRelaunch property is deleted from the .plist file and the file reverts to how it was before. This means that if the .plist file was truly the source of the problem, the problem is likely to recur on your next launch of the application.

- If you click Yes, the ApplicationCrashedAfterRelaunch property is again deleted from the .plist file. In addition, the file itself is renamed, with a .saved extension added to the end. Thus, a .plist file called com.apple.safari.plist would now be called com.apple.safari.plist.saved. This permanently disables the .plist file (during the Safe Launch, the disabling was only temporary). The next time you launch the application, a new default .plist file will be created. This means you will no longer have any of the customized settings from your old .plist file (which is the price you pay for no longer getting the crashes that the file was causing!). In some cases, this will also mean losing settings and/or data that is either time-consuming or impossible to re-create. If this loss is critical, you can try copying and pasting data from the disabled .plist file to the new one, as needed. Or you can simply remove the new .plist file from the Preferences folder and delete the .saved extension from the old file to revert back to what you had before (although doing so again risks the return of the crash). Otherwise, you must redo your customized settings as best you can.

Safe Launch limitation. As implied above, a Safe Relaunch occurs only after clicking the Reopen button followed by clicking the Try Again button on the next appearance of the dialog. It will not happen if you use a force-quit to quit a frozen application. Nor will it occur if you click the Report button instead of the Reopen or Try Again button.

User-interface quirk. When the Reopen button is in the dialog, it is the far right button and the one that is the default choice (that is, it is the button that has color, which means it represents the action that will be taken if you simply press the Return key). When the Try Again button is in the dialog, it moves to the left. Now the Report button is the default choice in the far right. This can be a bit confusing and is something Apple should probably change.

"Unexpectedly quit" dialog after a kernel panic. After you restart following a kernel panic (as described in "Kernel panic," earlier in this chapter), at the end of the restart sequence (after you have logged in) an "unexpectedly quit" dialog will appear that says: "The computer was restarted after Mac OS X quit unexpectedly." There will be Report and OK buttons. At least when I tried it, the Report button did not work; no additional dialog appeared.

The com.apple.CrashReporter.plist file. There is a process called Crash Reporter, located in /System/Library/CoreServices, that runs in the background and is responsible for the "unexpectedly quit" dialog messages. You can modify the behavior of these messages by modifying the com.apple.CrashReporter.plist file (located in ~/Library/Preferences) that the application uses. In particular, you need to modify the value of a property called DialogType.

continues on next page

TECHNICALLY SPEAKING ▶ "Unexpectedly Quit" Under the Hood *continued*

Different values are available with Panther and with Tiger.

- **Panther options.** You have three options when modifying the "unexpectedly quit" dialog in Panther:

  prompt. The "unexpectedly quit" dialog appears as normal after a crash. The Submit Report button is present. This is the default if no option is selected.

  crashreport. The initial "unexpectedly quit" dialog is bypassed and you go directly to the Report dialog after a crash.

  none. No dialogs appear after a crash.

- **Tiger options.** The Panther options will still work in Tiger, but they are not the preferred ones. Instead, use one of the following three options:

  basic. The "unexpectedly quit" dialog appears as normal after a crash. It appears only for standard applications—typically, ones launched by a user. The Report and Reopen buttons are present. This is the default if no option is selected.

  developer. Additional debugging information, a brief "summary" version of what would appear in a crash.log in Console, appears in the "unexpectedly quit" dialog. In addition, the dialog appears for crashes of system and background processes as well as for standard applications. A new Attach Debugger button is present; it replaces the Reopen button that is in the basic dialog. Click this button to launch Terminal and get further debugging information (primarily of value to developers).

  server. As with the none option in Panther, no dialogs appear after a crash, allowing for unattended operation on a server. Still, the crash reports are logged in the relevant crash.log files.

Modifying the com.apple.CrashReporter.plist file. There are several ways to make the desired modifications to the .plist file. You can edit the .plist file in Property List Editor (general guidelines are covered in "Modifying a .plist file," in Chapter 4), use the `defaults` command in Terminal, or use a special utility that does all the work for you.

- **Using Property List Editor.** To enable one of the above options using Property List Editor:

  1. Open the com.apple.CrashReporter.plist file, located in ~/Library/Preferences. If this file does not exist, create one in Property List Editor. If you create a new file, immediately click the New Root button and then proceed.

  2. Add a property (via the New Child button) called `DialogType`, with one of the above options as its value.

- **Using Terminal.** To instead select one of the above options using Terminal, enter the following command:

  ```
  defaults write com.apple.CrashReporter DialogType value
  ```

  where *value* is one of the above options.

continues on next page

TECHNICALLY SPEAKING ▶ "Unexpectedly Quit" Under the Hood *continued*

• **Using a utility.** As a final alternative, you can use a utility to make the desired changes. With Panther, you can use a third-party System Preferences pane, CrashReporterPrefPane, to select either the prompt or crashreport option. With Tiger, if you have installed the Developer software, there is an application called CrashReporterPrefs (located in /Developer/Applications/Utilities) from which you can make your selection.

Value of the developer option. The main value of the developer option (in Tiger) for trouble-shooters is that the "unexpectedly quit" dialog appears after crashes of background processes. This means that, for crashes of background processes, you get notifications that you would otherwise not get. For example, I got one of these dialogs for StickyBrainService (a component of the Sticky Brain application) when I logged in. This suggested that this service feature was not working (it turned out that the problem was that an out-of-date version of the service was still installed). Deleting all old Sticky Brain software and reinstalling the latest version of Sticky Brain fixed things. But I would not have been alerted to the fact that the crash was even occurring if the developer option had not been enabled.

The downside of this option is that it does not include a button to get to a Safe Relaunch.

Bomb.app. Apple's Developer software, in Jaguar and earlier versions, included a small utility called Bomb.app. If you still have a set of Jaguar CDs, you can install the utility on your drive. It still works in Tiger. When you run it, it crashes itself, giving you a chance to check out the "unexpectedly quit" dialogs described above.

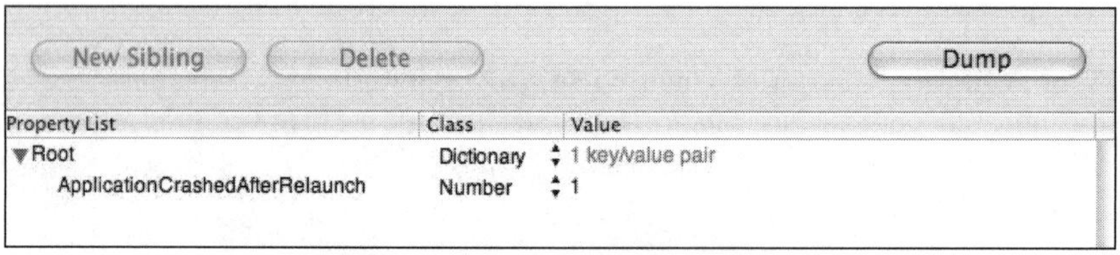

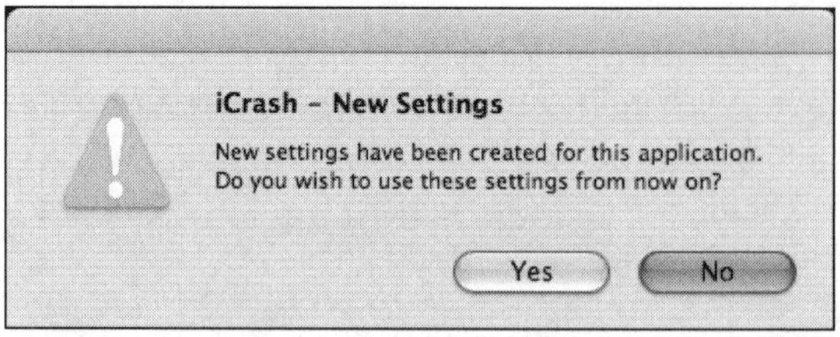

Figure 5.19

Top, *the property that gets added to an application's .plist file after clicking Reopen in an "unexpectedly quit" dialog; bottom, the message that appears after selecting to quit an application that has been relaunched (in a Safe Relaunch) a second time via the Try Again button in an "unexpectedly quit" dialog.*

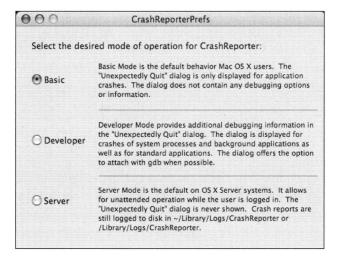

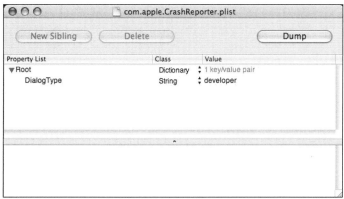

Figure 5.20

Top, *the CrashReporterPrefs application;* middle, *a view of the com. Apple.CrashReporter .plist file modified to enable the developer option;* bottom, *an "unexpectedly quit" dialog with the developer setting enabled (for a background process).*

Crash.log files. You can potentially learn more about a crash, such as an unexpected quit, by checking the log created or updated when the crash occurred. You can view these logs via the Console utility. Mac OS X maintains several logs simultaneously; the one you're most interested in after a crash is the log specific to the application that crashed. For example, if Safari crashed, you would look for Safari.crash.log. These files contain detailed information about the cause of the crash and are updated with new information at each subsequent crash.

To locate these crash.log files, launch the Console utility and then click the Logs icon in Console's toolbar; a list of logs will be displayed in the left column. Go to either ~/Library/Logs or /Library/Logs and look for a CrashReporter subfolder. Inside one of these folders will be a crash.log with the name of the crashed application. If an application is listed in both locations, start with the one in ~/Library/Logs. Click it to view it.

SEE: • "Console," in Chapter 2, for more on using this utility.

• Chapter 4 for background information on logs, extensions, and frameworks (especially "Technically Speaking: Log Files and cron Jobs," for more on logs).

Information about a crash, as viewed in a crash.log file, will usually begin with text like the following:

```
Command: Microsoft Word
PID: 551
Exception: EXC_BAD_ACCESS (0×0001)
Codes: KERN_INVALID_ADDRESS (0×0001) at 0×25000000
```

This is typically followed by many lines of technical jargon, detailing the state of the Mac at the time of the crash.

Unless you're a software developer, this text will often be of little use in figuring out what went wrong. And even if you are able to glean information from it, the likely fix will require updating the culprit software (which only the developer can do).

However, this information can occasionally be of value—especially the first few lines of text and particularly when the crash is caused by something other than the crashed application itself. For example, these lines may reference a font or fonts in general, suggesting that a corrupt font is the cause. In this case, deleting the font should eliminate the crash. This information could also reference a background process—for example, something loaded as a login item. As with the above example, disabling the user-level login item should allow you to work around the crash.

SEE: • "Take Note: Solving Problems with Login Items," earlier in this chapter.

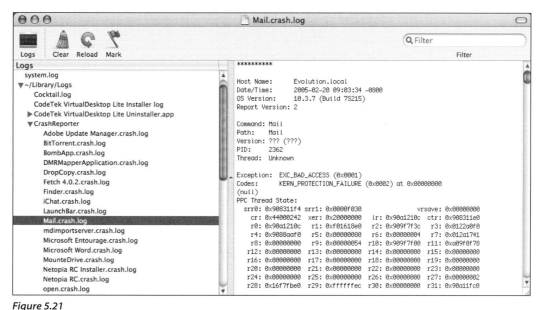

Figure 5.21

The Console utility with a crash.log file displayed.

Background-process crash. A background process (that is, a process with no icon in the Dock) can also crash—though you may not get an error message or any immediate indication of the crash. Symptoms will occur when the crashed process is needed. Console may be especially useful here. Its console.log, its system.log, and/or a CrashReporter log may indicate which process just crashed. For example, if background or Unix software essential for networking crashes, you may lose your Internet connection. In such cases, you may be able to restart the process (for example, by using SystemStarter, as described earlier in this chapter), assuming you can figure out exactly what crashed. More likely, your best solution is to restart the Mac.

Will a crash reoccur? After a crash has occurred (and you've decided whether to submit a report to Apple), the first thing you should do is determine whether it will happen again. In many cases, a specific crash will happen so rarely that it's not worth trying to determine the cause. To check for this, follow these steps:

1. Relaunch the application and try to replicate the action(s) you were performing when the crash occurred. Hopefully, the crash will not happen again.

2. If the crash does recur, log out and log back in. Again, the crash may not happen again after you do this.

3. If the crash persists, restart your Mac. Again, the crash may not happen again after you do this.

Diagnosing the crash. If the crash still recurs, it's time to try to further diagnose its cause and search for a solution:

- **Pay particular attention to recent changes you've made to your system.** To cite one example, some users experienced an increase in system crashes (even kernel panics) after installing iTunes 2 (in Jaguar). The cause was the iTunesHelper file that was added to the Login Items list when iTunes was installed. Removing this item from the list eliminated the crash. In such cases, it remains for the developer (Apple, in this case) to fix the software so that you don't need to perform this type of work-around.

- **Check the state of the Mac at the time of the crash for possible clues.** A program may crash only if Classic is active, for example. In that case, quitting Classic before running the application could be a work-around.

- **If the crash.log file indicates the involvement of software other than the application itself (such as a font), disable or remove the other software.**

   SEE: • "Take Note: Solving Problems with Login Items," earlier in this chapter.

- **The crash may be caused by a preferences file used by the application.** If so, delete the preferences file.

   SEE: • "Deleting or removing preferences" and "Logging in as another user," later in this chapter.

- **Does the application crash immediately on launch?** If so, this typically occurs if the application is incompatible with the installed Mac OS X version. To fix this, get a newer or older version of the application, as needed. Otherwise, it may be due to a permissions-related problem. This can usually be fixed by using the Repair Disk Permissions feature in the First Aid section of Disk Utility.

- **Do you have multiple versions of the same application on your drive?** If so, when you double-click a document, the Mac may try to open a version of the creating application that's incompatible with the version of Mac OS X you are using—thus causing the application to crash. Here are two examples:

   If you perform an Archive and Install, the Mac may attempt to launch an application from the resulting Previous Systems folder instead of from the active system software folders (for example, /Applications).

   If you have two mounted volumes with different versions of Mac OS X installed (or otherwise have different versions of the same application available), the Mac may try to launch the "wrong" version. For example, I had a setup where Panther and Tiger were installed on two separate partitions. When running Panther, if I double-clicked a document that required a Mac OS X application (such as TextEdit), the Tiger version of the application opened instead of the Panther version. This happens because the Mac typically opens the newer version by default if it finds two versions of the same program. The result was a crashed application.

The immediate work-around for these problems is to (a) launch the correct application manually before double-clicking the document or (b) drag the document icon onto the correct application icon. A more long-term solution is to change the default application via the "Open with" option in the document's Get Info window (as described in Chapter 4). The permanent, surefire fix is to delete the duplicate software (assuming you need only one version).

SEE: • "Document opens in the 'wrong' application," in Chapter 6, for more information.

- **Reinstall, upgrade, or downgrade the application software.** If the crash occurred after you upgraded to a new version of the software, a bug may have been introduced in the update. Reverting to the older version may eliminate it. Otherwise, check to see whether an even newer version fixes the problem.

  More generally, it can't hurt to reinstall the *existing* version of the application, just in case there was a problem with installation. If it is a Mac OS X application, you can typically reinstall it via a Custom install option from the Mac OS X Install disc.

- **Consider a hardware-related cause and work-around.** For example, a crash may occur only when the Mac is waking from sleep, which in turn may happen only when peripheral devices are attached to the Mac. If so, the work-around is to disconnect the devices before putting the Mac to sleep.

- **Occasionally, an application crash will result in a kernel panic.** If this happens, you will need to restart. At this point, troubleshooting advice is virtually identical to what it would be in the event of a kernel panic at startup.

  SEE: • "Kernel panic," earlier in this chapter.

- **Check sites (such as Apple's support site and MacFixIt.com) for possible solutions for specific problems.**

- **Consider other troubleshooting techniques, such as running repair utilities.**

  SEE: • "Performing repairs with Disk Utility (First Aid)," "Running fsck," and "Using third-party disk-repair utilities," later in this chapter.

  • "Techniques for Solving Mac OS X Crashes," later in this chapter, for more advice.

If nothing works, you may have to give up on using the crashing software until an update is released that fixes the problem.

TAKE NOTE ▶ Classic Crashes and Freezes

Programs running in Classic may crash, just as they could if you were booted into Mac OS 9. When they do, what happens is similar to what happens if you were booted into Mac OS 9—that is, you may get a freeze, a Type 2 crash, or whatever. When such problems occur, there's a good chance that the entire Classic environment will crash (although Mac OS X and Mac OS X applications will generally be fine). This means that you will lose all access to other applications open in Classic at the time. You will also need to restart Classic to use it again. The only good news is that you should not need to restart Mac OS X itself.

If you're trying to work with a Classic application and it freezes (or you otherwise can't use applications in Classic), try force-quitting the application. You will get a message warning that force-quitting a Classic application is likely to quit the entire Classic environment—and indeed this is almost always the case.

If Classic does not quit after an application freezes or crashes but it does not work, you will need to quit it manually. To do so, choose Quit or Force Quit in the Classic System Preferences pane. After Classic quits, you can restart it and hope that the problem does not recur.

I've found that problems with Classic are most likely to occur after I wake the OS up from sleep or when I wake up Classic from its sleep mode (as set in the Advanced pane of the Classic System Preferences). If you intend to work in Classic for an extended period of time, it's probably best to keep those options set to Never.

If you have problems with a crash or freeze when Classic launches, you probably have an old-fashioned extensions conflict with the extensions and control panels in the Mac OS 9 System Folder. Some files that work fine when you boot into Mac OS 9 do not work in Classic.

There is also a known issue whereby if the Startup Items folder in the Mac OS 9 System Folder contains aliases to servers that are not currently available, a hang can occur when launching Classic.

SEE: • **The Classic chapter, online at Mac OS X Help Line (www.macosxhelpline.com), for more information.**

Logout, Restart, and Shutdown Stalls and Crashes

When you choose Log Out, Restart, or Shut Down from the Apple menu, you get a dialog asking if you're sure you want to do this. If you don't click Cancel, the operation will occur automatically after 2 minutes. Note: To bypass this dialog, hold down the Option key when you choose the appropriate command from the Apple menu.

SEE: • **"Take Note: The Apple Menu and the Option Key," later in this chapter, for more details.**

When you choose Log Out from the Apple menu, Mac OS X quits all user processes and returns you to the Login window. You can now log in again as yourself or as another user (assuming you know the needed password), or another user can log in.

When you choose Restart or Shut Down, Mac OS X quits *all* open processes, including system-level processes that were opened at startup prior to your logging in (such as kernel extensions and startup items). With Restart, another startup is initiated immediately after everything has quit. With Shut Down, the Mac shuts down until you start it up again via the Mac's power button.

Quitting open user processes is handled primarily by the loginwindow process (as mentioned in the "Login" section, earlier in this chapter). It quits foreground processes (such as user-opened applications) first, then background ones. If successful, logout (followed by restart or shutdown, if selected) occurs.

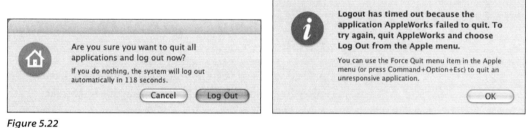

Figure 5.22

Left, *the standard logout message;* right, *a "logout canceled" error message.*

Logout stalls

If an application or process refuses to quit after you've chosen Log Out (or Restart or Shut Down), logout (or restart or shutdown) stalls. If the stall lasts long enough, you will eventually get an error message stating that logout has canceled and indicating which process is responsible.

In rare cases, an application or the entire OS may crash during logout. In such cases, you won't get a cancel message. Instead, for example, you may get an empty blue screen without the spinning-wait cursor, and the Mac will not subsequently shut down or restart as expected.

What to do. If you get a logout stall or crash, here's what to do:

- A stall may occur if an application is waiting for you to save a modified document. In this case, simply save the document; logout should proceed automatically. (If, however, logout has been officially canceled, you'll need to reinitiate it.)

- You can usually get around a stall by quitting the application manually and then—if necessary—choosing Log Out, Restart, or Shut Down again.

- If the application or background process remains stuck, try to force-quit it via the Force Quit window, the application's Dock icon, or Activity Monitor.

  SEE: • "Force-quitting," later in this chapter.

- Force a logout, using methods such as quitting the loginwindow process, as described in "Logging out, restarting, and resetting," later in the chapter.

- If problems persist, try pressing the power button on your Mac. Although this will trigger sleep or shutdown in some Macs, in others it may initiate a logout.

- If all else fails, you can reset your Mac by pressing Command–Control–power button, pressing the Reset button, and/or pressing and holding the power button, depending on your Mac model.

  SEE: • "Logging out, restarting, and resetting," later in this chapter.

Restarting and shutting down with Fast User Switching enabled

In the Login Options section of the Accounts System Preferences pane, you'll find an "Enable fast user switching" option. If you enable this option (as explained in Chapter 2), more than one user can be logged in to your Mac at once. To switch from user to user, you access the user menu in the upper-right corner of the menu bar (which contains the names of all users).

When you select Log Out from the Apple menu, you will see that the name of the currently logged-in user is included as part of the Log Out command. Thus, in my case, it would say Log Out Ted Landau. If I choose this command, everything works as described at the start of this section.

However, if you choose to shut down or restart when more than one user is logged in, an extra step is required. For example, if you choose Restart from the Apple menu and then click the Restart button in the dialog that appears, you will get a new message stating, "There are currently logged in users who may lose unsaved changes if you restart this computer." Before you're allowed to proceed, you must enter an administrator's name and password. After you've done this, the Mac will restart. (Note: As the warning states, any other user with unsaved changes to documents will lose those changes; if possible, you probably want to have that user log out before you shut down or restart.)

SEE: • The description of the Accounts System Preferences pane in the "System Preferences" section of Chapter 2, for more on Fast User Switching.

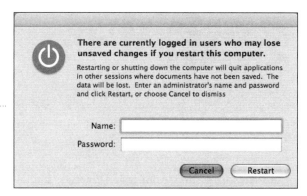

Figure 5.23

The message that may appear when you try to restart or shut down with multiple users logged in.

Other logout, restart, and shut-down problems

The following are some less common problems relating to log out, restart, and shut down.

Auto-logout crash. Occasionally, you may be logged out unexpectedly. That is, even though you did not choose Log Out, you're effectively logged out and either sent to the Login window or (if you enabled the option to automatically log in) returned to the Finder with all previous open processes now quit. This is caused by a loginwindow process crash (which was likely caused by conflicting processes' running simultaneously). As noted previously, whenever loginwindow is quit, you are logged out.

SEE: • "Login," earlier in this chapter.

Typically, no fix is needed here. Just log in, if needed, and continue. This is a rare problem that is not likely to recur any time soon.

Software Installer bug and loginwindow. You may have a problem with loginwindow when you're running a third-party installer utility that insists on quitting all open applications before installing the software. In such cases, you may get the following message: "Warning! Quitting 'loginwindow' will log you out." The OS prevents loginwindow from quitting (so you're not logged out), or it does quit (and you are logged out). In either case, this situation prevents the software from installing.

If you're lucky, simply quitting loginwindow (and logging back in, if needed) will resolve the issue. If you're having problems getting loginwindow to quit, launch Activity Monitor and then force-quit the process. Or, if you prefer to use Terminal, you can obtain the Process ID (PID) # from Activity Monitor and type kill *PID* to kill loginwindow and log out.

SEE: • "Killing processes from Terminal," later in this chapter, for more details.

Otherwsie, the application's installer will need to be fixed by the developer before you can get the installer to work.

Techniques for Solving Mac OS X Crashes

This section covers general techniques you can use to recover from and fix most common freeze and crash problems. The items are listed more or less in the order in which I recommend trying them, barring any specific information that would indicate which one to try first.

SEE: • "Startup Crashes" and "Application Crashes," earlier in this chapter, for more specific advice.

Force-quitting

The Force Quit command accomplishes exactly what its name implies: It gets an application to quit when the normal Quit command fails. You can use this technique to quit applications in which the menu commands are inaccessible or do not respond.

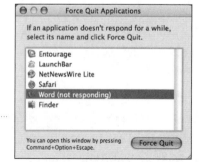

Figure 5.24

A Force Quit Applications window.

Figure 5.25

The Force Quit option in the Dock menu for an application.

You can force-quit an application in several ways:

• **Force-quitting from the Force Quit window.** To do this, press Command-Option-Escape, or choose Force Quit from the Apple menu. This brings up a window that lists all currently running user applications. Select the one you want to quit—this can be any application in the list, not just the currently active one—and then click the Force Quit button.

- **Immediately force-quitting the front-most application.** If you hold down the Shift key when accessing the Apple menu, the Force Quit command changes to Force Quit {*name of active application*}. Choose it and the named application is force-quit, bypassing the Force Quit window. Note that Carbon applications (such as AppleWorks) may not respond to this command.

- **Force-quitting from the Dock.** Click the icon of an application in the Dock and hold down the mouse button to get the contextual menu. If you then press the Option key, the menu's Quit command becomes Force Quit.

  Note: If you hold down the Option key while accessing the Finder's Dock icon menu, a Relaunch command will appear (even if the Finder is not frozen). If the Finder is frozen, the Relaunch command should appear automatically.

  One advantage of selecting Force Quit from the Dock is that it bypasses the Force Quit window—allowing the action to succeed in situations where the Force Quit window itself is not responding properly.

TAKE NOTE ▶ Application Not Responding

If an application is frozen, Mac OS X typically identifies it as an application that is "not responding." More specifically, the phrase "Not responding" will appear next to the name of the application in the Force Quit window.

If you access the Dock menu for a frozen application, the Force Quit option will appear by default (that is, you don't need to hold down the Option key). Similarly, you will get a message stating, "Application not responding" at the top of the Dock menu. This message typically appears in the Dock before it appears in the Force Quit window. Therefore, I would check the Dock menu first when seeking to confirm a freeze.

A word of caution: This message may also appear for a nonfrozen application if it's taking a very long time to complete a task and other actions in the application cannot be accessed during this time. For example, if you were to select a modification in Adobe Photoshop that takes a few minutes to complete and other Photoshop commands don't work while the modification is in progress, Mac OS X may indicate that the application is not responding. If you assume that Photoshop is hopelessly frozen and force-quit it, you end up terminating a process that would have successfully completed if left alone. Bottom line: Exercise some patience before electing to force-quit.

TAKE NOTE ▶ Force-Quitting from the Dock to Cancel an Application Launch

Suppose you accidentally click an application's Dock icon so that it launches (or you otherwise unintentionally launch an application). You may want to cancel the launch immediately rather than waiting for it to finish and then quitting it—especially if that program takes a long time to open (as Photoshop does on my Mac).

You can cancel the launch by force-quitting from the Dock. Just click and hold on the bouncing icon for the launching application. The command that normally reads Quit will now read Force Quit. Choose it, and the launch will be instantly terminated.

- **Force-quitting from Activity Monitor.** The Activity Monitor application lists all running processes—including background processes not listed in the Force Quit window. To force-quit a running process here, highlight it and click the Quit Process icon in the Activity Monitor toolbar (or choose Quit Process from the View menu or press Command-Option-Q). This brings up a dialog that asks if you "really want to quit" the selected process. Click Quit or Force Quit to do so.

  When using Activity Monitor, you should be extremely cautious about quitting Administrator Processes (you can see the full list of these processes by selecting the term from the Processes pop-up menu at the top of Activity Monitor's main window), because these often carry out essential tasks that, if quit, could precipitate an OS crash. However, there are occasions when quitting from Activity Monitor can be useful. The Dock, for example, is listed in Activity Monitor but not in the Force Quit window. If you force-quit it from Activity Monitor, the Dock disappears briefly and then relaunches. Doing this can eliminate problems specific to the Dock.

  Similarly, force-quitting certain administrator processes can resolve certain freezes. For example, force-quitting SystemUIServer can end a freeze that may occur when you're trying to mount a CD.

  SEE: • Chapter 2, for more information on Activity Monitor.

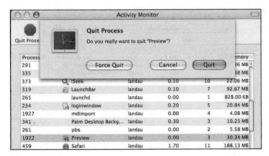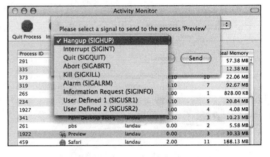

Figure 5.26

Left, *click the Force Quit button to force-quit an application from Activity Monitor;* right, *the options in the pop-up menu that appears after you select Send Signal to Process from Activity Monitor's View menu.*

- **Using the Send Signal to Process command in Activity Monitor.** New in Tiger is the Send Signal to Process command in Activity Monitor's View menu. To use it, select a process and then choose the command. A dialog drops down, containing a pop-up menu. The choices in the menu include a variety of kill-signal options, including Hangup, Abort, and Quit. Selecting these commands is an alternative to using Terminal to issue them (as described next and in "Technically Speaking: Kill Signals," below). They are all essentially variations on a force-quit. You should rarely need to use them, but it's convenient for those times when you do.

- **Killing processes from Terminal.** You can kill processes from Terminal—in essence the same thing as force-quitting from Activity Monitor, and a necessary alternative if Activity Monitor is not working. To do so, follow these steps:

  1. Launch Terminal and type `top`. You will get a list of running processes that pretty much duplicates what Activity Monitor displays. The first column provides the Process ID (PID) of the processes listed in the second column.

  Note: If you don't see the process you want, try enlarging the window to view processes not visible in the smaller window. Otherwise, you can get a complete list of processes by typing `ps -aux` (or by using Mac OS X's Activity Monitor, if it's accessible).

  2. Note the PID of the process you want to quit.
  3. Type `q` to quit `top`.
  4. Type `kill` *`PID`* to kill the process with the PID number you enter. (Note that if a process is owned by another user, such as the System or root user, you'll need to precede the `kill` command with `sudo` to run the command as root.)

  Alternatively, you can use the `killall` command; it works similarly to `kill` except that you enter the name of a process rather than its PID. This allows you to skip the step of locating the PID number. For example, you could type `sudo killall lookupd` to kill the `lookupd` process.

  Type `man kill` and `man killall` for more details.

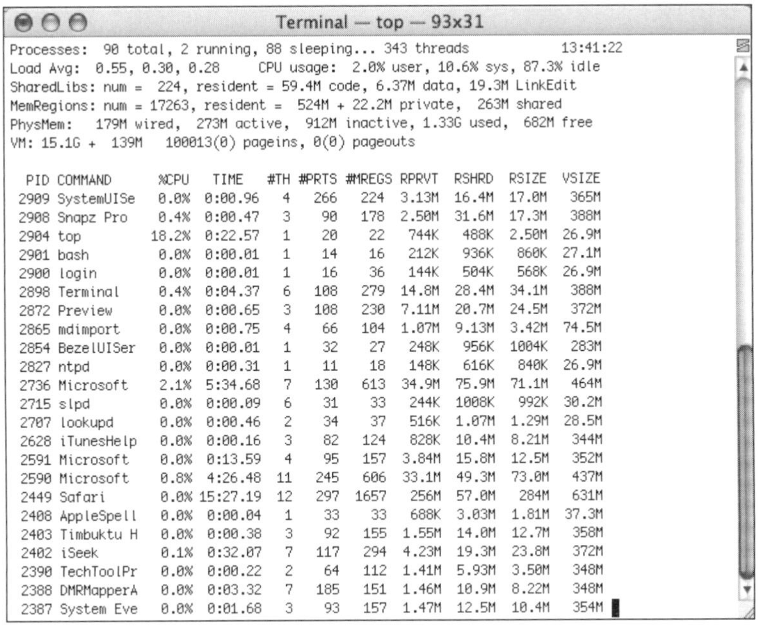

Terminal — top — 93x31

```
Processes:  90 total, 2 running, 88 sleeping... 343 threads            13:41:22
Load Avg:  0.55, 0.30, 0.28     CPU usage:  2.0% user, 10.6% sys, 87.3% idle
SharedLibs: num =  224, resident = 59.4M code, 6.37M data, 19.3M LinkEdit
MemRegions: num = 17263, resident =  524M + 22.2M private,  263M shared
PhysMem:   179M wired,  273M active,  912M inactive, 1.33G used,  682M free
VM: 15.1G +  139M   100013(0) pageins, 0(0) pageouts

  PID COMMAND      %CPU   TIME    #TH #PRTS #MREGS RPRVT  RSHRD  RSIZE  VSIZE
 2909 SystemUISe   0.0%  0:00.96   4   266    224  3.13M  16.4M  17.0M   365M
 2908 Snapz Pro    0.4%  0:00.47   3    90    178  2.50M  31.6M  17.3M   388M
 2904 top         18.2%  0:22.57   1    20     22   744K   488K  2.50M  26.9M
 2901 bash         0.0%  0:00.01   1    14     16   212K   936K   860K  27.1M
 2900 login        0.0%  0:00.01   1    16     36   144K   504K   568K  26.9M
 2898 Terminal     0.4%  0:04.37   6   108    279  14.8M  28.4M  34.1M   388M
 2872 Preview      0.0%  0:00.65   3   108    230  7.11M  20.7M  24.5M   372M
 2865 mdimport     0.0%  0:00.75   4    66    104  1.07M  9.13M  3.42M  74.5M
 2854 BezelUISer   0.0%  0:00.01   1    32     27   248K   956K  1004K   283M
 2827 ntpd         0.0%  0:00.31   1    11     18   148K   616K   840K  26.9M
 2736 Microsoft    2.1%  5:34.68   7   130    613  34.9M  75.9M  71.1M   464M
 2715 slpd         0.0%  0:00.09   6    31     33   244K  1008K   992K  30.2M
 2707 lookupd      0.0%  0:00.46   2    34     37   516K  1.07M  1.29M  28.5M
 2628 iTunesHelp   0.0%  0:00.16   3    82    124   828K  10.4M  8.21M   344M
 2591 Microsoft    0.0%  0:13.59   4    95    157  3.84M  15.8M  12.5M   352M
 2590 Microsoft    0.8%  4:26.48  11   245    606  33.1M  49.3M  73.0M   437M
 2449 Safari       0.0% 15:27.19  12   297   1657   256M  57.0M   284M   631M
 2408 AppleSpell   0.0%  0:00.04   1    33     33   688K  3.03M  1.81M  37.3M
 2403 Timbuktu H   0.0%  0:00.38   3    92    155  1.55M  14.0M  12.7M   358M
 2402 iSeek        0.1%  0:32.07   7   117    294  4.23M  19.3M  23.8M   372M
 2390 TechToolPr   0.0%  0:00.22   2    64    112  1.41M  5.93M  3.50M   348M
 2388 DMRMapperA   0.0%  0:03.32   7   185    151  1.46M  10.9M  8.22M   348M
 2387 System Eve   0.0%  0:01.68   3    93    157  1.47M  12.5M  10.4M   354M
```

Figure 5.27

The top display in Terminal.

TECHNICALLY SPEAKING ▶ Kill Signals

Although the term *kill* implies an all-or-nothing action, there are actually a number of degrees of "killing" when it comes to processes and applications. If the kill command (described in the main text) refuses to work in its default form, there are added kill options, called *signals*, you can try; the format for such commands is kill *signal*.

The default signal is sigterm. You do not need to specify this one when using kill. It causes an immediate and graceful termination (that is, temporary files get deleted prior to the kill).

For resistant processes, try the kill signal (for example, kill -KILL). For root-owned processes, you will also want to precede this with sudo. This is the *non-ignorable* kill (which implies that it should work even if the standard kill does not). This is essentially what happens when you force-quit an application.

To mimic the kill that occurs routinely when you log out of your Mac, use the HUP (hang-up) signal. The process should automatically restart after the kill—desirable if you have a problem you believe you can fix by simply restarting the process. One case in which the kill HUP signal can be useful is when you're connected to the Internet via a broadband connection and almost all applications appear to be frozen or running very slowly. If possible, check your Console log: If it's filling up with error messages that reference localhost lookupd, you need to kill the lookupd process. To do so, type the following:

```
sudo kill -HUP {PID of lookupd}
```

or

```
sudo killall -HUP lookupd
```

Typically, the process will quit and automatically restart, hopefully without the Console log errors and with your Mac back to normal. Otherwise, you will need to restart the Mac.

You can also call these signals by their respective numbers. For example, the non-ignorable kill number is 9 and the hangup (HUP) kill number is 1. Thus, to issue a non-ignorable kill for a root process with a PID number of 513, you would type sudo kill -9 513. Then enter your administrative password when prompted.

SEE: • **"Technically Speaking: Editing the Completed Jobs List," in Chapter 7, for another example of using** kill **with** HUP.

TAKE NOTE ▶ Why Force-Quit (Relaunch) the Finder?

You can press Command-Option-Escape to bring up the Force Quit window and then select Finder to force-quit the Finder. However, once you do this, the Force Quit button changes to Relaunch (since the Finder must be running for the OS to function normally). Similarly, as described in the main text, if you hold down the Option key prior to selecting the Dock menu for the Finder, a Relaunch command will appear instead of Force Quit. This relaunch technique can be useful in the following situations:

- **When the Finder freezes.** If you get a never-ending spinning wait cursor in the Finder, it's time to relaunch it. To me, this happens most frequently with file sharing. For example, it might occur when trying to access a volume mounted via file sharing that has disconnected and is no longer available.

- **To fix problems with the Finder itself (such as icons that don't display correctly).**

- **To make changes that would otherwise require logging out.** For example, if you make invisible files visible (as described in Chapter 6), you need to relaunch the Finder before the change takes place.

- **When the Finder crashes and does not relaunch automatically.** At this point, your Desktop will vanish, and the Finder will not be listed in the Force Quit window. You can typically relaunch the Finder from its Dock icon. However, if the Dock is also inaccessible, quit all other applications listed in the Force Quit window, and the Finder should reappear in the list. You can then relaunch it.

Finder Quit command. You can add a Quit command to the Finder menu. Numerous third-party utilities, such as TinkerTool, by Marcel Bresink Software (www.bresink.de), let you do this. And you can even do it yourself by adding a property called PutMenuItem with a value of True to the com.apple.finder.plist file in ~/Library/Preferences.

If the Finder is frozen, you won't be able to use this command. However, for situations in which you simply want to quit the Finder, it works as an alternative to Force Quit. To get the Finder back, simply click its Dock icon.

Figure 5.28

Three ways to relaunch (force-quit) the Finder: left, from the Force Quit Applications window; center, from the Apple menu; right, from the Dock.

Logging out, restarting, and resetting

As noted previously (in the "Application quits" section), a common way to solve a problem with a crash is to start over—by logging out, restarting, or (if necessary) doing a reset. Many problems occur only infrequently or under rare conditions. Logging out and/or restarting may clear those conditions, thereby eliminating the problem.

Start first by logging out via the Log Out command in the Apple menu. If that fails, choose Restart instead.

Logout and Restart shortcuts. If you can't get the Apple menu commands to work, you can try a keyboard shortcut to access these options (note: Some of these shortcuts may not work on all Mac models; in particular, they are more likely to work on desktop Macs than on laptops):

- **Command-Shift-Q.** This is the keyboard equivalent of the Log Out command. You can also try to log out by quitting the loginwindow process in Activity Monitor.

- **Command-Option-Shift-Q.** This key combination automatically logs you out without issuing the normal warning (asking whether you're sure you want to log out). It quits all open processes, including Classic if it is running (as long as a Classic application is not the current active application).

  Note: Except for the lack of warning, this is a normal logout. This means, for example, that if you have an unsaved document in an application, you will still be prompted to save the document before logout occurs.

- **Command–Control–Media Eject.** This should initiate a restart instantly (although it may give you a chance to save changes in open documents). (Note: The Media Eject key is the one that has a triangle with a line underneath it, typically in the upper-right-hand corner of the keyboard.)

- **Command–Control–Option–Media Eject.** This works the same as the above key combo, except that it shuts down the Mac instead of restarting it.

- **Control–Media Eject.** This brings up a dialog that says, "Are you sure you want to shut down your computer now?" Click Cancel, Sleep, Restart, or Shut Down.

- **Control–Option–Media Eject.** This puts the Mac to sleep instantly. (Although it's not useful for solving a crash problem, I included it here to make the list complete!)

- **Quit loginwindow.** Launch Activity Monitor, locate the loginwindow process, and choose Quit Process from the View menu. Quit the process to immediately log out, again without having a chance to save unsaved documents.

TAKE NOTE ▶ The Apple Menu and the Option Key

The Command-Option-Shift-Q command is actually a variant of the Log Out keyboard shortcut listed in the Apple menu. It is one of a trio of things that occur in this menu when you hold down the Option key. To see what I mean, pull down the Apple menu and then press the Option key. When the key is pressed, you will see that the ellipses disappear from the end of the Restart, Shut Down, and Log Out commands. In addition, the symbol for the Option key is added to the Command-Shift-Q shortcut for Log Out. This means that holding down the Option key when selecting any of these commands will bypass the normal warning messages that would otherwise occur.

Note: The third-party software FruitMenu, by Unsanity (www.unsanity.com), can also eliminate the ellipses from the Restart and Shut Down commands—in other words, cause the commands to be executed without requesting confirmation.

Figure 5.29

The Apple menu without the Option key held down, left, and with it held down, right.

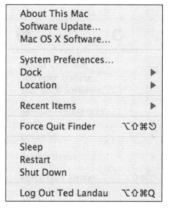

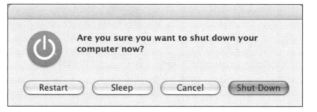

Figure 5.30

The dialog that appears when you press Control–Media Eject.

Hard restart/reset. If you cannot get any of the above commands to work, you will need to do what's called a *hard restart*, or a *reset*. The way you do this varies a bit by model, but here are some things to try:

- **Press Command–Control–power button.** On laptops and older Macs that don't use a USB keyboard, this should restart your Mac instantly. It doesn't work on current desktop Macs—primarily because their keyboards don't include power buttons!

- **Hold down the power button for several seconds.** The power button has a circle with a vertical line coming out of its top. Its location varies: On flat-panel iMacs, it's located on the base unit, near the ports in the rear. On Power Macs, it is on the front of the machine. On laptops, it is typically to the right of the keyboard. On most (all?) recent Mac models, if you hold down the power button for about 5 seconds or so, the computer will shut down.

- **Press the Reset button.** Only some Mac models have a Reset button, and even if the model has one, it may be internally located. Therefore, you should generally use the power button in preference to the Reset button. Use the Reset button (especially the internally located ones, described below) only if the prior methods fail. When you press the Reset button, the Mac should restart instantly. The exact location and appearance of the Reset button varies by Mac model. For example:

  - On older desktop Power Mac G4s, the Reset button is a small button with a triangle on it on the front of the machine. It is next to yet another small button, the Interrupt button (which you can ignore in this situation).

  - On newer Power Macs, the Reset button is located internally, on the logic board.

  - On most older iMacs, the button is on the right side of the machine by the ports. (Flat-panel iMac models do not have an external Reset button.)

  - On iBooks and some PowerBook G4s, it is a small hole near the ports; you'll need a straightened-out paper clip to access it. The PowerBook G3 does not have a Reset button; on this model press Control–Shift–Function–Power button.

  For more details, see the following Apple Knowledge Base documents: http://docs.info.apple.com/article.html?artnum=86225 and http://docs.info.apple.com/article.html?artnum=88330.

Before doing any of these resets, give the Mac an opportunity to sync by letting it sit idle for a few minutes after a crash.

SEE: • "Technically Speaking: Connecting Remotely to a Frozen Mac: Killing Processes, Running Sync," earlier in this chapter.

• "Technically Speaking: SystemStarter," earlier in this chapter, for a way to partially restart.

Checking fonts

The selection of fonts accessible while you're running Mac OS X depends on the contents of the Fonts folders in the main Library folders on your drive (/System/Library, /Library, and ~/Library). In addition, Mac OS X accesses the fonts in the Mac OS 9 System Folder used for Classic.

Although the fonts in the /System/Library/Fonts folder should generally remain untouched, the ones in the /Library/Fonts folder—and especially those in the

~/Library/Fonts folder (in your home directory)—may contain fonts added by application installers or by you or other users. In some cases, these fonts can cause a crash at startup or when you're using certain applications. Even though a font may work in Mac OS 9, it may be incompatible with Mac OS X.

Bitmap fonts are especially likely to be a problem. These fonts should be needed only to display PostScript printer fonts, which are generally imported from Mac OS 9 systems. Mac OS X does not come with any bitmap or PostScript fonts, relying almost entirely on TrueType fonts instead.

More specifically, Mac OS X prefers to use fonts in a Mac OS X format called *.dfont*. These fonts have a *.dfont* file extension and are identified in the Get Info window as having a Kind of Data-Fork TrueType Font. The main difference between these fonts and the older TrueType fonts used in Mac OS 9 is that the older font format used both a resource fork and a data fork, whereas the new format uses only a data fork.

SEE: • "Technically Speaking: Type/Creator vs. Filename Extensions vs. Others," in Chapter 4, for more information on resource forks and data forks.

Mac OS X can still read and use the older TrueType font formats, but they're more likely to be a source of trouble than the newer .dfont format. Fonts in Mac OS 9 font suitcases (especially when the suitcase includes more than one font type) are also a likely source of problems when imported to Mac OS X Fonts folders.

To check for problems, you can remove these font types from their folders and see whether the symptoms vanish. If so, one of the removed fonts is most likely the culprit. You can return the fonts one by one to determine which is the problem (assuming you need all the fonts).

Checking fonts and a Safe Boot. When you do a Safe Boot, as described earlier in this chapter, it temporarily disables all fonts except those in the System Folder and moves relevant font cache files to the Trash.

Mac OS 9 (Classic) fonts. Since Mac OS X also reads the fonts in the Fonts folder of the Mac OS 9 System Folder used by the Classic environment, cor-rupted or outdated fonts here can cause a crash—even a startup crash—when the OS attempts to load them. To test for a startup problem here, reboot in Mac OS 9 if possible, or from another Mac OS X bootable volume; drag the Fonts folder to the Desktop; and restart in Mac OS X.

If you *can* start up in Mac OS X, launch Font Book to disable Mac OS 9 fonts. Click the disclosure triangle next to the All Fonts item in the Collection col-umn. Next, select the Classic Mac OS item and click the Disable button at the bottom of the column.

Once the fonts are disabled, relaunch the problem application and/or restart the Mac. If the problem vanishes, a font in the Fonts folder was the cause. If you want to use these Mac OS 9 fonts, you'll need to do some trial-and-error testing to determine the offending font. Otherwise, you can simply leave all these fonts disabled.

Duplicate fonts. Having more than one copy of the same font installed, especially in the same fonts folder, can also be a source of problems.

Validating fonts. You can use Font Book to validate the integrity of fonts.

SEE: • "Viewing and Managing Fonts" and "Working with Fonts," in Chapter 4, for more information on adding and removing fonts, resolving problems with duplicate fonts, and using Font Book and other font utilities.

Deleting or removing preferences

Most applications maintain preferences files in the Preferences folder inside the Library folder of your home directory. These files contain the settings that you modify via the application's Preferences command. They may contain additional settings as well. Because such files are frequently modified, they are at risk of becoming corrupted.

If preferences files associated with an application become corrupted, they can cause problems with the application, including a freeze or crash on launch. They can also cause other, less serious problems specific to certain features.

Diagnosing a preferences file problem. The quickest way to tell if your problem is due to a preferences file is to remove the entire Preferences folder from your home Library folder. To do so,

1. Quit the problem application.

2. Drag the Preferences folder from the ~/Library folder to a new location, such as the Desktop. Do not delete the folder.

3. Log out and log back in. A new Preferences folder will be created in the ~/Library folder, containing fresh copies of the preferences files needed at login.

   Note: An alternative to Step 3 would be to maintain a separate user account with just default settings, and use this to test whether the application problem occurs in that account, which would indicate that files in your account are at fault. Using a test account simultaneously checks for potential problems with preferences, cache, and any other files in your Library folder.

   SEE: • "Logging in as another user," later in this chapter, for details.

4. Launch the problem application. A new default preferences file for the application will be created.

5. Check to see if the problem has vanished. If so, a corrupt preferences file in the original Preferences folder is almost certainly the cause of the problem. (If the problem still occurs, chances are good that it's not a problem with a file in your Preferences folder.)

If a preferences file does appear to be the culprit, your next task is to identify and delete it. To prepare for this, follow these steps :

1. Quit the problem application, if it's open.

2. Drag the newly created Preferences folder from the ~/Library folder to the Trash.

3. Drag the original Preferences folder back to the ~/Library folder.

4. Log out and log back in.

You are now ready to isolate and delete the problem file, as described in the next sections.

Figure 5.31

A peek into the contents of a Preferences folder, with com.apple.print files highlighted.

Preferences file problems and unexpected quits. If you are getting an application crash (unexpected quit), check out the Try Again button in the "unexpectedly quit" dialog—it automates the process of testing (and removing, if desired) a potentially corrupt preferences file.

SEE: • "Application quits," earlier in this chapter, for details.

Determining the problem preferences file. If a problem is with a specific application, the most likely culprit is the preferences file that includes the name of the application. Many preferences files have names like com.{*developer name*}.{*name of application*}.plist.

To find all such files, open the Preferences folder and type the name of the application in the Search field of the window's toolbar. This will generate a results list of all files in the folder that include the name of the application.

Occasionally, an application may use a preferences file that does not include its name. For example, Printer Setup Utility uses a file called com.apple.print. PrintingPrefs.plist (in addition to com.apple.print.PrinterSetupUtility.plist).

These atypically named files have been implicated in problems that are solved by deleting the files. How can you identify these atypically named files as the cause? If there's a preferences setting you can enable and disable to make the problem vanish and return, change the setting. Then sort the Preferences column by Date Modified (or use the Finder's Find command to search for items with a *date modified is today* criterion). Locate the most recently modified item, which is likely to be the culprit.

Check also in the ByHost folder inside the Preferences folder: It can contain the troublesome .plist file.

If you have little or no idea what the problem preferences file might be, launch the Console utility and view the system.log file (located in /var/log). From the Edit menu, choose Find, and search for all instances of *parse failed*. If a .plist file is mentioned in reference to this failure, it is the likely culprit. Delete the file from your Preferences folder.

Using diagnostic software. The Unix command `plutil` and third-party utilities that serve as a front-end for this command (such as Preferential Treatment, by Jonathan Nathan [http://homepage.mac.com/jonn8/as/html/ pt.html]) can be used to test the syntax of .plist files, reporting any errors that are found.

SEE: • "Running Mac OS X software from Terminal," in Chapter 10, for details.

Deleting the problem preferences file. Once you've identified the likely culprit, follow these steps to delete it:

1. Quit the problem application.
2. Drag the suspected preferences file to the Trash.
3. Log out and log back in.
4. Launch the problem application. A new default preferences file is created.
5. If the problem is gone, empty the Trash to delete the old preferences file.

The new preferences file will contain default settings—which means you may need to make some changes in the application's preferences to get the application back to the state you desired.

6. If the problem remains—indicating that the preferences file was not the problem—drag the original file from the Trash back to the ~/Library/ Preferences folder. This saves you the hassle of re-creating preferences settings unnecessarily.

   A variation on this theme would be to rename the preferences file (such as to *name*.plist.old) rather than drag it to the Trash. A new default copy will still be created when needed. If it turns out that this fixes the problem, you can now delete the .old file. Otherwise, delete the newly created file and rename the old file back to its original name.

If your first attempts at identifying a problem preferences file does not lead to success, you'll have to get more creative. Consider preferences files that were last modified around the time the problem started. Or look for preferences for software that interacts with the problem application (such as a spelling checker or font utility that's active within a word processor that's crashing). Try moving these files to the Trash, following the same procedure as described above.

Tips for deleting preferences files. The following is a collection of tips for troubleshooting problem .plist files:

- **Log out.** In general, you should log out and back in before relaunching the problem application and forcing a new preferences file to be created. Otherwise, Mac OS X may re-create the corrupted .plist file from data cached in memory (rather than create a new default copy).

  In certain cases, you may need to log out and temporarily log in as the root user (or at least another user), deleting the preferences file from here in order to avoid this caching problem. This is important, for example, when deleting the com.apple.finder.plist file (to fix odd Finder-related symptoms): You need to log in as another user because you normally can't quit the Finder while logged in.

  Note: If you have Fast User Switching enabled, just switching to another user is not sufficient in these situations; you need to log out from your account and log back in.

  An alternative is to add a Quit command to the Finder, using a utility like TinkerTool. Once you've done this, drag the com.apple.finder.plist file to the Trash and immediately quit the Finder. Finally, empty the Trash via the Trash icon in the Dock and relaunch the Finder. Just to be safe, I'd also log out and back in again.

  SEE: • "Logging in as another user," later in this chapter, for related information.

- **Stay home.** In general, you should only delete preferences that are in the Preferences folder within the Library folder of your home directory. Leave preferences files in /Library/Preferences alone unless you're specifically advised to modify or delete them (such as via a support document on Apple's Web site). You'll need administrator access to modify files in this folder, in any case.

- **Get permission.** Occasionally, you may be unable to replace a particular preferences file in your home directory due to insufficient permissions. In most cases, although you cannot replace the preferences file with a copy, you can still delete the original file. In these instances, the solution is to drag the problem file to the Trash and *then* drag the replacement to the Preferences folder. Otherwise, use any of the other methods described in Chapter 6 for dealing with files that cannot be deleted.

  SEE: • "Deleting and moving instead of replacing," in Chapter 6, for more details.

- **Lock or unlock preferences.** Occasionally, preferences settings get reset to their default values when you log in—even if you don't delete the preferences file. You may be able to prevent this by locking the relevant .plist file after making the change. To do this, open the Get Info window for the file and check the Locked box.

  Note that you will be unable to modify the preferences file unless you unlock it again. And keep in mind that other unusual and undesired symptoms can result from a preferences file being locked; if so, you will need to unlock it.

  In some cases, a preferences file may become locked even though you did not lock it. This situation can cause various symptoms, including an inability to install an update to the software. Sometimes, simply unlocking the file will cure the problem. Otherwise, unlock and delete the file.

Disabling preferences files at startup. In some cases, you may need to disable a preferences file at startup, via single-user mode, to get the Mac to successfully start up. I covered this in "Blue-screen crashes and stalls," earlier in this chapter.

SEE: • "Preferences Files," in Chapter 4, for more details about these files.
  • "Modifying or deleting the .GlobalPreferences.plist file," in Chapter 6, for related information.

TAKE NOTE ▶ **Utilities to Delete .plist and Cache Files**

For problems with .plist and cache files that are not obviously linked to a specific application, you may prefer to use a utility to delete these files rather than to manually diagnose the problem. Various shareware utilities, such as Kristofer Szymanski's Cocktail (www.macosxcocktail.com) and Northern Softworks' Tiger Cache Cleaner, automatically delete the cache files (and, in some cases, .plist files) most likely responsible.

Make sure you're using a version of the utility that's compatible with your Mac OS X version.

SEE: • "Take Note: Launch Services Files and Beyond," in Chapter 6, for related information.

TAKE NOTE ▶ Utilities to Disable Startup Items, Preferences Panes, and More

At various places in this chapter (and elsewhere in this book), I suggest that solving a problem may require disabling a startup item, preference pane, font, or other type of Library folder file. Although any of this can be done manually in the Finder, you may find it easier to use a utility to do so. Here are a few examples:

- Diablotin (http://s.sudre.free.fr/Software/Diablotin.html), which functions as a System Preferences pane, allows you to disable a variety of items, including contextual menus, startup items, fonts, and preference panes.

- Services Manager (www.pure-mac.com/sys.html#servicemanager), another third-party System Preferences pane, allows you to enable and disable items that appear in the Services menu (the menu that appears in each application's {*application name*} application menu, as covered more in Chapter 4).

- MOX Optimize (www.infosoft.sw.com) is an application that allows you to enable and disable kext extension files (as stored in /System/Library/Extensions), as well as several other types of files. It has not been updated for a while but still appeared to work in Tiger when I tried it.

- Font Book (as covered in Chapter 4) is Mac OS X's preferred utility for disabling fonts.

Deleting cache files

Cache files (stored in the ~/Library/Caches folder) are used by certain applications to store frequently accessed data. Items here typically have names that identify the application that uses them (such as iPhoto Cache). Through normal use, it's possible for these files to become corrupt. As with preferences files, deleting relevant cache files can solve application problems.

New cache files will be re-created as needed after old ones have been deleted. However, be cautious: In some cases, cache files contain information that cannot be easily re-created. Maintain a backup of cache files before deleting any (or remove the file from the Library folder instead of deleting the file immediately). That way, if you discover that a cache file is not the culprit, you can restore the originals.

Figure 5.32

Partial contents of my ~/Library/Caches folder.

 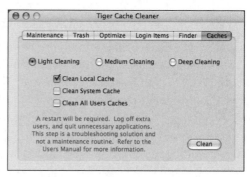

Figure 5.33

Utilities that can delete potentially corrupt cache files: left, Cocktail; right, Tiger Cache Cleaner.

Figure 5.34

Partial contents of my ~/Library/ Application Support folder.

Checking for other corrupt files

Sometimes a program will crash on your computer when the same program seems to run fine on an almost identical machine. Why is this? Corrupted preferences or cache files, as just described, could be one cause. But there are other potential culprits as well. Consider the following:

- **The application itself could be damaged or corrupted.** Files within the application package may have been deleted or modified, accidentally or deliberately. The typical solution is to trash and reinstall the application. In the case of applications installed by the Mac OS itself, however, this can be tricky since you won't likely have easy access to individual files installed by the OS update.

SEE: • "Selectively Installing Mac OS X Files," in Chapter 3, for details.

- **There could be problems with support files.** Sometimes problems can occur with accessory files for an application that get stored in locations separate from the application itself, such as the Application Support and InputManagers folders in the ~/Library and /Library folders. These accessory files may not get updated properly when an update installer is run, for example. If you know that this has happened, you can usually correct the problem by deleting the out-of-date software and reinstalling the latest version.

    If you use the third-party Application Enhancer (APE) utility, by Unsanity (www.unsanity.com), items in the Application Enhancers folder, in your ~/Library folder, are another potential source of problems. In some cases, the problem is with the software that's accessed by the APE modules: the APE Preferences pane and ApplicationEnhancer.framework (both located in the /Library folder). Reinstalling or updating this software may fix the problem.

    Note: You may find that a folder mentioned here is not in your Library folder. This is because such folders are only present if they would not be empty. If you have not installed any software that places something in such a folder, you may not have the folder at all.

- **Permissions and ownership of the file may have changed.** As discussed in Chapter 4, each file has a set of privileges/permissions, as well as an owner and a group name. If these settings change, a file may not open, or you may not be able to save documents in the file. Repairing permissions with Disk Utility may help (as described later in this chapter). Otherwise, see Chapter 6 for solutions to this problem.

Logging in as another user

As indicated in the previous sections, rather than removing files from your ~/Library folder to test for problem files, you can log in as another user. In fact, I advise creating a test user just for this purpose. Once you create this user account, don't add any third-party software or change the default settings. This way, the user's directory remains "clean." If changes you've made to your own directory are the source of a problem, the problem should not occur when you switch to this other user.

If the problem vanishes when you're logged in as another user. If the problem does not occur when you're logged in to the test user's account, you can be almost certain that the cause of the problem is either a file in your home directory (in the Library folder or in a folder in the Documents folder maintained by an application) or an item you've added to your user-level Login Items list.

If a problem in your account is indicated, and you haven't already checked for problems with user-level Login Items, fonts, preferences, and cache files (as described in previous sections), these would be the most likely culprits. Otherwise, it's time to look elsewhere, starting with recently modified files in the Library folder.

SEE: • Chapter 2 for more details on how to use the Accounts System Preferences pane to create a new user.

If you identify the problem file, delete or replace it as appropriate. Otherwise, as a last resort, create yet another user account and transfer all of your critical files to it, deleting the original account when you're finished. As long as you're an administrator and owner of both accounts, you should have no problem doing this.

If the problem remains when you're logged in as another user. If the problem remains when you're logged in as a different user, the problem is at a more systemwide level, either in the Applications folder (if the problem is specific to a given application) or in one of the main Library folders (/System/Library or /Library). If you have some idea about what the problematic file may be (and can work around any permissions hassles), you can try replacing it (assuming you have a good copy as a backup). Otherwise, you're probably looking at reinstalling the entire OS.

There could also be a problem with one of the files in the invisible Unix folders. Unless you're familiar with Unix or have specific advice from a reliable source (such as this book!), diagnosing and fixing problems here can be very difficult. In most cases, you will more likely wind up reinstalling Mac OS X.

Logging in as another user and Fast User Switching. Prior to Panther, one hassle of logging in as another user to test for problems with your account was that you had to log out of your own account before you could log in to another one. This meant that all open files in your account were closed or quit on logout and needed to be reopened when you logged back in.

With Panther and later, however, you can avoid this hassle by enabling Fast User Switching (via the check box in the Login Options section of the Accounts System Preferences pane). Now, just choose the name of your test account from the menu in the upper right corner and log in. This allows you to log in to the test account without logging out from your own account first.

Figure 5.35

The menu for Fast User Switching.

Checking for extension (kext) problems

While kernel extension problems most often lead to startup crashes or kernel panics, these files can also be the root cause of a variety of other symptoms. Here are three examples (none of which affect Tiger, thankfully!):

- In the initial (Build 6R65) version of Mac OS X 10.2.8, a buggy kext file (AppleGMACEthernet.kext) caused many Mac users to lose their Ethernet connections.

- On some G3 Macs with more than 192 MB of RAM installed, the ATIDriver.bundle file (located in the AppleNDRV folder in the same Extensions folder that contains kext files) in Mac OS X 10.2.8 could cause the screen to go black when running certain applications (for example, Disk Utility and Microsoft Entourage).

  Removing the ATIDriver.bundle file was Apple's recommended solution for problems with this file that persisted even after updating to a later build (Build 6R73) of Mac OS X 10.2.8.

- The IOUSBFamily.kext file can cause startup problems in some versions of Mac OS X. In these cases, you need to find a way to start up successfully before you can solve the problem. If a Safe Boot doesn't work, start up from another volume. As a last resort (and if you feel up to the task), start up in single-user mode to delete or replace files as needed.

  In one specific case, kernel panics occurred a few minutes after startup as a result of certain USB hubs' being connected to a Mac running Mac OS X 10.2.5. The panic.log file referenced the IOUSBFamily.kext file. Abandoning use of the hub often solved the problem. Otherwise, the solution was either to downgrade to an older version of the IOUSBFamily.kext file or to upgrade to Mac OS X 10.2.6 or later. Details regarding these types of fixes are described below.

Expect similar glitches to occasionally pop up in Tiger. Checking for error messages in verbose mode may help identify a problem kext file. Figuring out the best solution for kext problems, however, can be a bit tricky. Consider these alternatives:

- **Updating the kext cache.** A general potential fix for problems here is to delete the Extensions.mkext and/or Extensions.kextcache items. Typically you would do this in Terminal by typing the following:

  ```
  sudo rm /System/Library/Extensions.kextcache
  ```

  and

  ```
  sudo rm /System/Library/Extensions.mkext
  ```

  Restart immediately after doing this by typing reboot in Terminal.

  SEE: • "Technically Speaking: Understanding Kernel Extensions," earlier in this chapter, for more information.

- **Removing or disabling the kext file.** Select the file in the /System/ Library/Extensions folder, and drag the file to the Trash. A dialog will appear, asking you to enter an administrator's name and password. After you do this, the file is moved.

  Alternatively, you can use a utility such as MOX Optimize to disable (and later re-enable) kext files.

  Just be careful about what you remove or disable: Disabling an essential Mac OS X–installed kext file can make startup failure a near certainty.

  To check the "essential" status of any kernel extension, use the Show Package Contents contextual menu for the extension, and locate its Info.plist file. Open the file with Property List Editor. One of the properties may read OSBundleRequired. It has several possible values. If its value is Safe Boot, the extension will load even if the Shift key is held down at startup. This means it is required. If it has another property, or there is no OSBundleRequired property at all, the item will not load during a Safe Boot; it is thus not an essential file. In the rare case that an essential kext item causes a crash, you will need to start up in single-user mode to fix it or (more likely) reinstall the entire OS.

  If in doubt, contact Apple or the vendor of the problem software for advice.

  A potential disadvantage of removing any kext file is that you lose whatever function the removed file provided. For example, if the file provided support for a PCI card that you have installed, you can no longer use the card.

- **Replacing the kext file.** It may be that a kext file has become corrupt and needs to be replaced. If you have a backup copy, just drag it to the Extensions folder. A dialog with an Authenticate button will appear. Click it, and you're on your way. Alternatively, you may be able to replace the file by rerunning the installer that first installed the kext file. If in doubt, check with the software vendor for advice.

- **Downgrading to an older version of the kext file.** When the Ethernet problem with the 10.2.8 update first appeared, users found they could solve the problem by replacing the buggy kext file with the version of the file used in 10.2.6. To do this downgrade, you need to either have the older file in your backups or be able to extract it from the previous version of the Mac OS X Update package using a utility such as Pacifist, by CharlesSoft (www.charlessoft.com), as described in more detail in Chapter 3. Once you've done this, you can replace the newer file as just described. A similar solution worked for the IOUSBFamily.kext problem.

  However, be aware that there's always a risk when mixing kext files from different versions of Mac OS X. If they don't play together well, you may wind up with more problems than you solve. In particular, avoid replacing a Tiger file with a Panther or Jaguar one. On the other hand, if no other solution presents itself—meaning you're going to have to reinstall Mac OS X anyway—it's worth a shot.

A safer alternative is to reinstall Mac OS X entirely (using the Archive and Install feature of the Installation disc), and then update back to the most recent symptom-free version as needed. However, this is a much bigger hassle than downgrading a single file.

- **Upgrading to a new version of the kext file.** This is the ideal solution. For example, Apple resolved the Ethernet problem with Mac OS X 10.2.8 by releasing a new version of 10.2.8 that included a bug-fixed version of the file.

    While you await a bug-fix upgrade, you may be able to work around a symptom by modifying your hardware setup rather than fiddling with kext files. For example, if a problem occurs only when you're using a USB hub, you can temporarily give up the hub and connect all USB devices directly to your Mac.

Whenever you make a change to the Extensions folder (other than via an Installer utility), delete the Extensions.mkext and Extensions.kextcache files (at the root level of the /System/Library folder) or change the modification date of the Extensions folder, and then restart This gets Mac OS X to recognize that the change has been made.

TECHNICALLY SPEAKING ▶ Using Terminal to Diagnose and Fix a kext File Problem

If you are having trouble related to kext files, the most likely source of a problem is a third-party kext file (that is, one not developed by Apple). The hitch is that the names of the files often give little indication as to what the files do or whether they are Apple-developed files (although the naming system is considerably improved in Tiger). So identifying these third-party files can be difficult. One solution is to use Terminal. Here's what to do:

1. Type kextstat | grep -v apple.

    Some text output will appear.

2. Next, type (all on one line)

    grep -rl {*name from the last section*} /System/Library/Extensions

    For {*name from the last section*}, substitute the text that appears before the numbers in parentheses in the output from Step 1. For example, if the text is com.SuperDuper.driver.HIDDevices, type

    grep -rl com.SuperDuper.driver.HIDDevices /System/Library/Extensions

    What you'll now get is output that includes the names of .kext files that reside in /System/Library/Extensions. The list may look something like this:

    /System/Library/Extensions/SuperDuperUSBHIDevices.kext/Contents/Info.plist

    /System/Library/Extensions/SuperDuperUSBHIDevices.kext/Contents/MacOS/
    SuperDuperUSBHIDevices

continues on next page

If more than one item appeared after the kextstat command, you should repeat the above command once for each item.

Assuming your kext problems are due to a third-party kext file, at least one of the identified kext files is the likely culprit. In the above example, SuperDuperUSBHIDevices.kext is the only name of a kext file that appears. The solution is to remove the file from its current location. To do so, you have to do something that Apple generally advises users not to do: remove files from the /System directory. Problems using the affected device may still remain, however, unless you replace the removed file with an updated one available from the third-party vendor. Still, if the kext file was causing a system crash, which is now fixed, you have improved the situation.

For those unfamiliar with Unix, here is what these commands are doing: The first typed line results in a search through all of your currently active extensions, displaying the status of those that do not come from Apple. Or, more accurately, those extensions whose internal name—not the name in the Finder—does not contain the word *apple* (this "name" is actually the CFBundleIdentier name as listed in the extension's Info.plist file contained within the file's package). These are thus files that were installed by third-party software and are the likely candidates for causing the problem. Unfortunately, the command's output does not include the actual Finder-level names of these kernel extension (kext) files. That's what the second command should provide.

SEE: • "Technically Speaking: Understanding Kernel Extensions," earlier in this chapter, for more background information.

• "Beyond the Basics," in Chapter 10, for more on the Unix grep command.

Performing repairs with Disk Utility (First Aid)

Whenever you encounter otherwise inexplicable problems, a standard bit of troubleshooting advice is to run a disk-repair utility. These utilities check and, if need be, repair critical portions of a disk that can affect its ability to open and even locate files. In extreme cases, such problems can prevent a Mac from starting up, which poses a risk that data on the drive may be irrecoverable.

It's a good idea to run a repair utility periodically, perhaps once a month, even if you aren't having problems: It may detect and fix subtle problems that, while not causing symptoms at the moment, may precipitate more obvious and serious problems as time passes.

Disk errors are especially likely to occur whenever data is copied to the disk improperly—for example, during an improper shutdown (such as turning off the Mac without using the Shutdown command, or after a kernel panic), a forced restart, or any power interruption. Installing new software or updates can also cause problems. If problems occur after such events, you should attempt to repair the disk. Apple includes one such repair utility as part of Mac OS X: Disk Utility. It's the first repair utility you should try. It may not always succeed, but it will almost never make the problem worse.

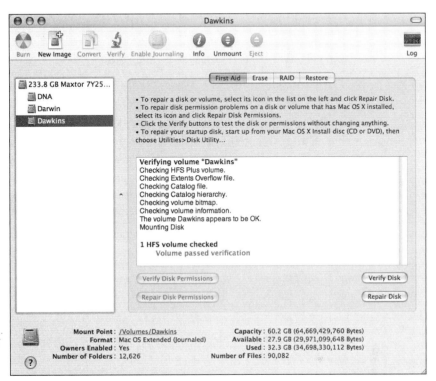

Figure 5.36

The First Aid pane of Disk Utility, after clicking Verify Disk.

Located in the Utilities folder, Disk Utility combines several disk-formatting, disk-copying, and disk-repair features. It is the disk-repair (First Aid) component that's the focus here.

You can use the First Aid functions of Disk Utility to repair permissions on the startup volume; however, you cannot use First Aid to repair the current startup volume's directory (see below for more information). This means that to use these functions, you will need to reboot and start up from another volume, either a Mac OS X Install disc or another mounted bootable drive.

SEE: • "Disk Utility," in Chapter 2, for an overview of Disk Utility.

• "Backing up Mac OS X: Utilities for volume backups" and "Bootable CD or DVD," in Chapter 3, for additional details about Disk Utility features.

Accessing Disk Utility's First Aid. To access the First Aid component of Disk Utility, follow these steps:

1. Launch Disk Utility. Select a disk, volume, or image from the column on the left side.

2. Click the First Aid tab at the top of the area to the right.

Near the bottom of the right side of the window, you should see four buttons: Verify Disk Permissions, Repair Disk Permissions, Verify Disk, and Repair Disk.

Verify vs. repair. The Verify options check for and report problems but do not repair them. The Repair options check for and make any needed repairs.

The main reason to choose Verify is that occasionally there may be problems you don't want to fix (at least not right away) for fear that doing so may cause even more problems. For example, if Verify reports serious problems and you have files that are not backed up, you should back up those files before proceeding with repairs. This is because an attempt to repair the drive could potentially fail and result in an inability to restart the Mac at all.

For simplicity, in the examples that follow, I assume that you're ready to proceed with repairs and will thus omit further discussion of the Verify option.

Depending on the volume you select, one or both of the Repair buttons may be dimmed and unselectable. The following sections provide details about how to proceed.

Repair Disk. The Repair Disk function repairs the drive's directory. To repair a disk, click the Repair Disk button.

As the repair check proceeds, feedback will appear in the scrollable text area above the button. You will see lines such as "Checking Catalog file" and "Checking volume bitmap." A progress bar will also appear in the window. When the work is complete, the progress bar will vanish.

If any errors were detected, they will be listed in the report text. In addition, the final lines of the text will indicate the overall result. If no problems were detected, it will say something like the following:

```
The volume {name of volume} appears to be OK.
Repair attempted on 1 volume
HFS volume repaired
```

If errors were detected, the final text will indicate that problems were found and that either repairs were made successfully or the volume could not be repaired. Here's what to do next:

• If First Aid reports problems and fixes them, run First Aid again. Keep doing this until First Aid no longer reports any problems. Sometimes a repair may uncover another problem that the next repair cycle will detect.

- If First Aid reports no problems or reports problems and fixes them, but your symptom persists, you could try another repair utility (just in case it could detect problems that First Aid cannot). Otherwise, disk issues are not likely to be related to the cause of the problem.

- If you get a message that says, "Volume not repaired," as opposed to "Could not be repaired," there is more reason for hope. Try the repair again. It may succeed on the next try or two.

- If First Aid reports problems but cannot fix them, definitely try another repair utility. Otherwise, erasing and reformatting your drive is the only likely way to repair the damage.

Error messages. You may wonder what First Aid's sometimes-cryptic error messages mean. In general, they're concerned with problems with an invisible area of the drive called the Directory, which is the main component that First Aid checks and repairs. The Directory has nothing to do with Unix directories or folders; it mainly keeps track of where every file is located on the drive. In addition, because a file may be stored in several segments in different locations on the drive, the Directory contains the information needed to tie these segments together so that the application can run or the file can be opened. Obviously, if this information gets corrupted, it can prevent an application from working or a file from being usable. If the corrupted software is critical for startup, such damage can prevent the OS from starting up. If this sort of error cannot be repaired, your only choice is to reformat the drive.

Note: If you get an "overlapped extent allocation" error in First Aid (or fsck), it means that two files have been assigned the same space on your hard drive. Since it is not possible for both files to do this and still be intact, it means that at least one of the files has permanent data loss. If the file is critical to the operation of the OS, it may also lead to system crashes and startup problems. Obviously, this is a potentially serious error. The best solution here is to make sure your data is backed up and then erase your volume and start over by reinstalling Mac OS X. Then restore other files from your backup. However, starting in Mac OS X 10.4.2, First Aid and fsck can help your system recover from such errors, fixing the volume without having to erase it. You will still lose the data in the file that was "overlapped," but, assuming it was not a critical file, you will be otherwise OK. When making this type of repair, First Aid may create a folder called DamagedFiles that will typically contain symbolic links to the potentially damaged files. You can use this to check on the condition of the files after repairs have been made. See this Apple Knowledge Base article for more details: http://docs.info.apple.com/article.html?artnum=25770.

Similarly, if you get an error message that states, "The underlying task reported failure," this means the problem is one that Disk Utility cannot fix. Third-party utilities may be successful. Otherwise, you will need to erase your volume and reinstall Mac OS X and all your (hopefully backed-up) data.

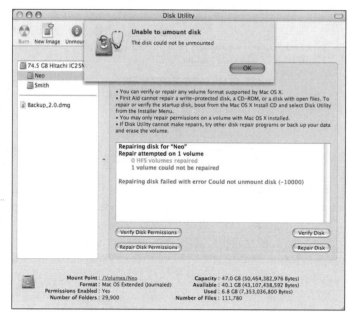

Figure 5.37

An error message that appears in First Aid if you try to check a volume that cannot be unmounted (perhaps because it has open files on it).

Verify/Repair Disk won't run. You cannot repair the current startup volume. If the volume is selected, the Repair Disk button is dimmed.

Prior to Mac OS X 10.4.3, you could similarly not select Verify Disk for the current startup volume. In Mac OS X 10.4.3 or later, however, Verify Disk is enabled, if journaling has been enabled for the volume. For more on this Live Verification feature, see this Apple Knowledge Base article: http://docs.info. apple.com/article.html?artnum=302672.

You also cannot repair any write-protected or read-only media, nor can you repair a volume that's in use (for example, one that contains open or launched files)—including the volume that contains Mac OS 9 (if Classic is active) or any partition that contains an open application or document (including Disk Utility itself). If you try to do so, you will get an error message after clicking the Verify or Repair button. You can repair any other volume (assuming the volume's format is supported by Mac OS X)—even ones without Mac OS X installed on them.

The fact that you can't repair the startup volume is a significant obstacle to using First Aid, since the startup volume is by far the most likely volume you'll want to repair (in fact, for many Mac users, it's their *only* volume). There are several ways around this problem:

- **Boot from the Install CD/DVD.** The typical way to use First Aid to check the startup drive is to start up from the Mac OS X Install disc. When the Installer opens, from the Utilities menu choose Disk Utility. As described above, go to the First Aid pane, select your normal startup volume, and click Repair Disk.

A potential problem here occurs if Mac OS X has been updated since the version that's on your Install disc. Say you have Mac OS X 10.3.0 on your disc, but you're now running Mac OS X 10.4. If the updated version of Mac OS X includes an updated version of Disk Utility, the version you run when booted from the disc is no longer the latest version. Obviously, you want to use the latest version because it presumably includes bug fixes and checks for problems not present in the older version. If this is a relevant issue for you, consider one of the remaining alternatives.

> SEE: • "Take Note: Determining the Disk Utility Version," later in this chapter, for related information.

- **Boot from a customized disc.** You can create a custom bootable CD or DVD and place the latest version of Disk Utility on it. The simplest way to do this is to make an editable disk image of the Mac OS X Install disc, replace the old copy of Disk Utility with the new copy, and burn the new disc.

  > SEE: • "Bootable CD or DVD," in Chapter 3, for more details.

- **Boot from another volume that contains Mac OS X.** If you have an external drive with Mac OS X installed, boot from it. You can now check your normal startup drive. You can even use an iPod this way (if you've installed system software on it).

- **Boot from another Mac.** If you have two Macs, you can connect them via Target Disk Mode, and then start up from the Mac you do not intend to repair. This procedure makes the target computer mount as though it were an external drive—at which point you can run First Aid on it.

  > SEE: • "Sharing via Target Disk Mode," in Chapter 9, for more information.

- **First Aid and FileVault.** You can use First Aid to verify or repair a home directory encrypted with FileVault, as long as it is not the currently open account. Thus, to do this for your own account, you would first have to log out and log in to another account. Then launch Disk Utility and, using the Finder's Go to Folder command, go to /Users. Then locate the folder with your name and open it. Inside will be a file with a name that ends in .sparseimage. Drag it to the Disk Utility window to add it to the list of volumes (providing your password if asked). You can now verify or repair the image.

- **Run fsck automatically (at startup).** Starting up via a Safe Boot forces the fsck utility to run at startup. This is equivalent to running First Aid to repair a disk.

  Alternatively, if you restart the Mac without first selecting Restart or Shut Down (such as after a kernel panic, power failure, or any crash that requires a reset), the Mac should similarly run fsck at startup. Startup will take longer than usual because of this check.

  The main disadvantage here is that you get almost no feedback as to whether repairs were needed and made. However, if the problem disappears, you can assume fsck was successful.

  There is one potential feedback indicator: If repairs were needed and made, the Mac should restart on its own. That is, before startup is completed, you will hear the startup chimes a second time, and the boot process will start over. This means repairs were made and were likely successful.

Another alternative is to start up in single-user mode and run fsck. This has the advantage of providing feedback much as if you were running First Aid.

Finally, the fsck_hfs command, run in Terminal after startup is over, may be able to check the current startup volume, thus working around the First Aid restriction. However, as explained a bit later in the chapter, be cautious about using it.

SEE: • "Safe Booting," earlier in the chapter, for related information.

• "Enabling and disabling journaling," later in this chapter, for an option that reduces the need to do First Aid repairs and prevents fsck from running at startup.

• "Running fsck," later in this chapter, for more information about fsck, especially with respect to single-user mode and the fsck_hfs option.

Repair Disk Permissions. Due to a variety of causes (most notably errors introduced during Mac OS X updates), some system-level files and folders on your drive may acquire incorrect permissions. When this happens, you may be unable to access a needed file or folder because you lack sufficient permission—however, it may not be obvious that this is the cause of a problem. For example, an application may fail to launch but display no error message due to a permissions problem with an accessory file used by the application. This makes it especially difficult to fix the permissions problem directly (such as via the file's Get Info window): You won't know that a permissions problem is definitely the cause, and you certainly won't know with any certainty which file needs fixing.

Other "mysterious" permissions-related problems include -108 errors in Printer Setup Utility, –192 errors when trying to mount a disk image, and certain locked files that cannot be unlocked.

To repair these disk permissions, click the Repair Disk Permissions button. This forces all system-level Mac OS X files to revert to their default settings (ownership and access), eliminating any introduced errors. It should have no effect on files you created or added by any means other than a Mac OS X Installer or Apple-provided software updater. While the repairs are in progress, the scrollable text box will generate a list of errors as they're detected and fixed. When they're complete, you should see a message resembling the following:

`The permissions have been verified or repaired on the selected volume. Permissions repairs complete.`

The hoped-for result? All permissions-related problems have vanished!

Note: The Verify Disk Permissions and Repair Disk Permissions buttons are enabled only if you're attempting to check a volume that has Mac OS X installed. Unlike the case with Repair Disk, you can use these buttons with the current startup volume. In fact, in older versions of Mac OS X, it was preferable to do so, because Repair Disk Permissions used the receipt files in the /Library/Receipts folder on the current boot volume to determine the correct permissions for system-level files. Thus, running Repair Permissions for your startup hard drive when booted from the Install Mac OS X CD may not work as expected, because it would search (in vain) for a Receipts folder on the CD. However, in newer versions of Mac OS X, including all versions of Tiger, Repair and Verify Permissions uses the Receipts folder on the drive you selected to check, so you should be OK no matter what your boot volume is.

SEE: • "Technically Speaking: Repair Disk Permissions and Receipts," later in the chapter.

Preventing problems by using Repair Disk Permissions. It's good preventive medicine to repair disk permissions before and (especially) immediately after installing any Mac OS X update—even if you haven't noticed problems. This can prevent update-related symptoms that might otherwise occur.

Occasionally, First Aid may "repair" a setting that was already correct, *causing* rather than fixing a problem. However, the risk of this is low. Thus, periodically repairing permissions remains a good idea.

Repair Disk Permissions error messages that are repeated. You may find that Repair Disk Permissions occasionally reports the same errors more than once, sometimes claiming to re-fix a problem it claimed to fix in a previous run. In most cases, you can ignore this repetition and assume that the repairs were correctly made, or that it is a "status" message that can be ignored.

In particular, if you see the following type of message, you can ignore it:

We are using special permissions for the file or directory *{path to directory}*. New permissions are *{five-digit number}*.

Fix Mac OS 9 permissions. Separate from the Repair Disk Permissions buttons, there is a command in Disk Utility's File menu called Fix OS 9 Permissions. If you choose this option, First Aid will check for and repair Classic System Folder permissions that might otherwise prevent Classic from launching.

If it's dimmed, you have not selected a system folder to be the Classic System Folder. To do so, go to the Classic System Preferences pane and select a system folder. Once you've selected it, quit and relaunch Disk Utility. The button should now be selectable.

SEE: • "Permissions settings and running Classic," in the Classic chapter, online at Mac OS X Help Line (www.macosxhelpline.com), for more information.

Figure 5.38

The message that appears after you've successfully run Fix OS 9 Permissions.

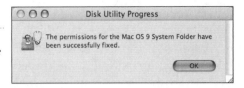

Disk Utility log. Disk Utility maintains a log of all your actions and their results. You can view this log by any one of the following methods: choosing Show Log from Disk Utility's Window menu, clicking the Log icon in the toolbar, or launching Console and accessing the DiskUtility.log file in ~/Library/Logs.

Match Disk Utility and Mac OS X versions. Ideally, assuming you are running the latest version of Mac OS X, make sure you are also using the latest version of Disk Utility.

Suppose you boot from Panther but want to check a volume that is has Tiger installed. Is that OK to do? Only in certain cases. Apple cautions to make sure that you are running Mac OS X 10.3.9 in order to check a Tiger volume. If you are running 10.3.8 or earlier, false errors will be reported. In extreme cases, ignoring this advice can lead to Disk Utility's attempting repairs that could lead to data loss!

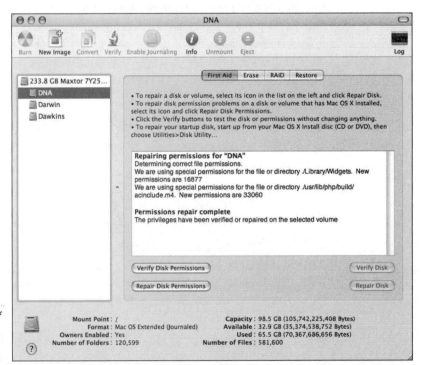

Figure 5.39

The First Aid pane of Disk Utility, after clicking Repair Disk Permissions.

Figure 5.40

Pacifist opens a receipt file. Note that the right-hand column lists the permissions settings for each item (using the Unix format as described in Chapter 10).

TAKE NOTE ▶ Determining the Disk Utility Version

You can determine whether your Install disc contains an older version of Disk Utility than the one on your hard drive by comparing the version numbers for each copy.

On your hard drive, you'll find Disk Utility in the Utilities folder. On the Install disc, you can locate Disk Utility by double-clicking the disc icon after it has mounted. In the window that appears, open the Applications folder and the Utilities folder contained within it. Inside you'll find at least nine applications. One of them will be Disk Utility.

To determine the versions of these two copies of Disk Utility, check the Version line in each application's Get Info window in the Finder, or launch each utility and check its About box. The version number will be something like 10.5 (198); the higher the number(s), the newer the version.

TECHNICALLY SPEAKING ▶ Repair Disk Permissions and Receipts

Disk Utility obtains its information about permissions settings from the receipt files located in the /Library/Receipts folder. These receipt files—which are created when .pkg files are opened via Apple's Installer utility and software is installed—will typically include among their contents an archive.bom file, which Disk Utility uses to check permissions. Even third-party software may have receipt items in this folder if Apple's Installer was used to install the application.

The initial stage of the verify or repair process entails determining correct file permissions. It is at this stage that First Aid checks the receipt files. After this, it begins to verify or repair permissions, as needed.

continues on next page

TECHNICALLY SPEAKING ▶ Repair Disk Permissions and Receipts *continued*

Bottom line: *As a general rule, do not move or delete the files in the Receipts folder.*

As an extreme example, if you were to remove all the .pkg files from the Receipts folder and then click Repair Disk Permissions, you would get an error message stating, "First Aid failed… No valid packages." Actually, the key file here is BaseSystem.pkg. If only this file is removed from the Receipts folder, you will still get this error message.

Viewing default permissions in Terminal. To view the default permissions settings of all files that were installed via a .pkg file, use the lsbom command in Terminal. It reads and displays the relevant contents of the archive.bom file. In particular, type the following command in Terminal:

```
lsbom -p FUGM /Library/Receipts/name.pkg/Contents/Archive.bom
```

This generates a list in which each line contains the name of a file or directory that was installed via the original .pkg file, followed by the item's owner name, its group name, and its permissions settings. It will separately list each file within a package (such as all the files in an .app package). For example, the first four lines from the receipt for iCal.pkg will be something like this:

```
"." root admin drwxrwxr-t
"./Applications" root admin drwxrwxr-x
"./Applications/iCal.app" root admin drwxrwxr-x
"./Applications/iCal.app/Contents" root admin drwxrwxr-x
```

Alternatively, the third-party utility Pacifist also shows the default permissions for files included in a package.

SEE: • "Receipt files," in Chapter 3, for more on receipt files.

• "Ownership & Permissions," in Chapter 4, for more on these terms.

• "Unix: Modifying Permissions," in Chapter 10, for more on Terminal commands and output regarding ownership and permissions.

Enabling and disabling journaling

Starting in Panther, Mac OS X provides a new file-system feature in Disk Utility called *journaling*.

Journaling is a method of quickly repairing a drive on restart after a system crash, power failure, or any other nonstandard restart (that is, any time fsck would normally run at restart). On such occasions, read and write processes get interrupted—which in turn can cause discrepancies between the file-system directory and the actual location and structure of stored files. Journaling automatically fixes these inconsistencies via data tracked in its journal file—a faster and more reliable method than trying to repair a disk via First Aid's Repair Disk option or via fsck at startup.

A bit more technically, Apple explains journaling as follows:

> Journaling helps protect the file system against power outages or hardware component failures, reducing the need for repairs.... It both prevents a disk from getting into an inconsistent state and expedites disk repair if the server fails. When you enable journaling on a disk, a continuous record of changes to files on the disk is maintained in the journal. If your computer stops because of a power failure or some other issue, the journal is used to restore the disk to a known-good state when the server restarts.

> With journaling turned on, the file system logs transactions as they occur. If the server fails in the middle of an operation, the file system can "replay" the information in its log and complete the operation when the server restarts. Although you may experience loss of user data that was buffered at the time of the failure, the file system is returned to a consistent state. In addition, restarting the computer is much faster.

Note: Apple recommends using journaling, to prevent problems, in preference to depending on First Aid or fsck to repair a disk after it has developed problems. If problems develop even with journaling enabled, however, you may still use First Aid or fsck. Also, keep in mind that journaling is *not* a substitute for backing up your data: You should still back up data to protect against damage that journaling cannot undo.

A notable advantage of enabling journaling is vastly improved speed on restart. On a large multiterabyte RAID-array server with many files, journaling can reduce restart time after a crash from hours (needed to check the entire file system) to just seconds (because the OS needs to replay only recent transactions in the journal, bringing the system up-to-date and resuming operations that were interrupted during the failure).

The downside of journaling is the performance penalty after restart is complete. Because journaling is a continuous background operation, it can cause slowdowns when you're using your Mac. However, this should not be significant with today's faster Mac models.

On balance, at least if you have a newer, faster Mac, I would go with using journaling—and Apple agrees. That's why when you install Panther or later, journaling is automatically enabled by the Installer. In particular, if you select the Erase and Install option, you will see that the only Mac OS X format choice for the disk is Mac OS X Extended (Journaled). Even if you select to Archive and Install or Upgrade/Install Panther or Tiger, journaling gets enabled.

Note: There is no harm in enabling and/or disabling journaling after a disk has been in use. The process takes only a few seconds. However, when you disable and re-enable journaling, you lose whatever journaling data was previously maintained, thus losing the prior protection offered by journaling as well. When you re-enable it, you start over with a blank slate.

Figure 5.41

Disk Utility's File menu.

Enabling journaling. If you've installed Tiger and want to use journaling, do nothing: Journaling is already enabled for your Tiger startup volume. To enable journaling for other volumes (or to re-enable journaling on any volume on which it was disabled), do the following:

1. Launch Disk Utility.

2. In the list along the left side of the Disk Utility window, click the volume you want to modify.

    Keep in mind that you can select a volume other than the startup volume; however, doing so will have no effect unless (and until) you use the other volume as a startup volume.

3. In the toolbar, click the Enable Journaling icon. Alternatively, from the File menu select Enable Journaling (Command-J).

Disabling journaling. From Disk Utility's volume list, select the volume for which you want to disable journaling. If journaling has indeed already been enabled for that volume, the Enable Journaling icon in the toolbar will be dimmed and will not be accessible. However, the command in the File menu may have toggled to read Disable Journaling. If so, select the command to disable journaling. In Tiger, it seems this command (as with the toolbar icon) may be dimmed and not selectable. In this case, you can disable journaling via a Unix command. To do so, launch Terminal and type

```
sudo diskutil disableJournal /Volumes/volumename
```

To disable the current startup volume (also called the *root volume*), substitute / for Volumes/*volumename*.

As usual, there are also a variety of third-party utilities that can easily enable and disable journaling (such as Micromat's TechTool Pro; www.micromat.com).

Is it journaled? You can quickly tell if a volume has had journaling enabled by checking the Format line at the bottom of the Disk Utility window. The Format line for a selected volume will include *(Journaled)* if this feature is enabled; the full text will likely read "Mac OS Extended (Journaled)."

Alternatively, in Terminal, type

```
diskutil info /Volumes/volumename
```

Again, use / instead of /Volumes/*volumename* to check the startup volume. If the output contains the text **File System: Journaled HFS+**, then the volume is journaled.

Journaling, fsck, and First Aid. With journaling enabled, I would avoid using fsck or First Aid to repair a drive as a maintenance option. Reserve their use only for when you suspect there is a problem that needs repair. This maximizes the effectiveness of the journaling record. In fact, if you select fsck in single-user mode, you will get the following message:

```
fsck_hfs: Volume is journaled. No checking performed.fsck_hfs: use
the -f option to force checking
```

If you insist on checking your drive in single-user mode with fsck, I recommend using both the -n and -f options (fsck -nf), at least for a first run, so that it simply verifies the drive without making any changes.

If and when journaling is enabled, fsck may report "benign" errors that can be ignored. These include "Volume bitmap needs minor repair," "Invalid volume free block count," and "Volume header needs minor repair." Note: This has supposedly been fixed in Tiger, and these messages should no longer appear.

However, there may be times when you need to truly repair even journaled volumes (for example, to fix a problem not automatically handled via journaling). To do so, you can run fsck in single-user mode (using just the -f option, as described above), use Disk Utility's First Aid (for a volume that is not the current startup volume or to repair the normal startup volume when booted from a Mac OS X Install disc), or use the fsck_hfs -f command (described in the next section). In general, if problems persist after restarting when journaling is enabled (and verifying with fsck or First Aid reports problems), I would do the repairs. In such cases, repairing the drive will erase the existing journaling record. As long as journaling remains enabled, a new blank record will be created and tracking will proceed.

See the following Apple Knowledge Base documents for additional information: http://docs.info.apple.com/article.html?artnum=107248 and http://docs.info.apple.com/article.html?artnum=107250.

Journaling tips and hints. If you decide to enable journaling, you need to be aware of the following:

- When using a third-party disk repair utility, make sure it's a journaling-compatible version. If it has not been upgraded to recognize journaled volumes, it may disable journaling when repairing a volume. This doesn't cause any harm; you just need to remember to re-enable journaling after using the repair utility. The latest versions of all major repair utilities have upgraded to work with journaling. In fact, DiskWarrior actually uses the journaled data, if available, to help diagnose problems.

- After a journaled volume has been mounted on an older Mac OS X system that does not support journaling or on a system running Mac OS 9, the journal file may be invalid. To prevent problems here, once you're back on your journal-supported system, disable journaling and re-enable it.

For more details on journaling, see the following Apple Knowledge Base document: http://docs.info.apple.com/article.html?artnum=107249.

Running fsck

The fsck (File System Check) command-line utility is a Unix program that checks for problems with Unix files and attempts to correct them. Apple has modified it so that it also includes the Mac-specific directory checks done by First Aid. Thus, in most cases, running fsck is a viable alternative to running First Aid.

The most common situation in which you would use this utility would be from single-user mode. What makes this alternative especially attractive is the fact that you can use fsck to check your default startup drive without needing to start up from a separate volume (as described in the preceding section). This means you can do the check without getting out and booting from your Mac OS X Install disc.

Still, for reasons that Apple has not specified, it especially encourages you *not* to use fsck in single-user mode in Tiger except as a last resort. It recommends that you instead run Disk Utility's First Aid (such as by booting from a Mac OS X Install disc) or do a Safe Boot (which runs fsck automatically, as described earlier in this chapter).

Running fsck via single-user mode. Here's what to do:

1. To run fsck from single-user mode, restart your Mac and immediately press and hold Command-S until the single-user-mode screen appears.

    SEE: • "Single-user mode," earlier in this chapter.

2. When the initial text scrolling has stopped and you can enter text, type /sbin/fsck -fy (or simply fsck -fy), and press Return.

    The fsck utility will run. The -y flag tells fsck that you want to answer yes to all questions, ensuring that the process continues without further halts.

The -f option forces the utility to run even when it might otherwise refuse to do so (such as if journaling is enabled).

SEE: • "Journaling, fsck, and First Aid," earlier in this chapter, for details.

As fsck is running, you will see text feedback that mimics what you would get from running First Aid from the Disk Utility application (for example, "Checking HFS Plus volume," "Checking Catalog file," and "Checking Volume bitmap").

3. If fsck makes any repairs, you will get a message that says: **File System was modified**.

   If you get this message, run fsck again, because the first run may uncover additional errors that will require a further run to fix.

4. Repeat Step 3 until the **modified** message no longer appears and you instead just get the one that says: **The volume *volumename* appears to be OK**.

5. Type reboot, and press Return. Or type exit to continue with the normal startup process.

   Note: I've read that it may be better to type reboot -nq than just reboot, if modifications were made during a repair. The additional -n option in particular prevents syncing from occurring (a process described in "Technically Speaking: Connecting Remotely to a Frozen Mac: Killing Processes, Running Sync," earlier in this chapter). Normally, running sync is recommended. However, in this case, that could undo changes that were just made by replacing the changed data with corrupted data that remained in RAM. However, Apple's instructions, and other advice I have read, states that just typing reboot or exit is sufficient.

Ideally, the symptoms that led you to run fsck will be fixed by fsck. If fsck cannot repair the problems it finds, or if it finds no problems but the symptoms persist on restart, your best bet is to try other repair utilities, as described in the next sections. Running First Aid will do no good since it's essentially the same utility as fsck.

The fsck utility does not have the options to repair permissions that Disk Utility includes.

Running fsck_hfs via Terminal. If you launch Terminal and try to run fsck, you will be unable to do so—for the same reason that you cannot use First Aid's Repair Disk option on the startup volume. However, there is an alternative command, called fsck_hfs, that partially works around this restriction. The fsck_hfs command will verify all volumes, even the current startup volume. It will even repair journaled volumes (if you use the -f option). However, it will not make repairs to the active startup volume, reporting, **Cannot repair volume when it is mounted with write access**.

Here is how to use it:

1. Launch Terminal.

2. Type mount or df and press Return. The diskutil list command is yet another command that will provide the same device information. These commands will generate a list of mounted devices. For example, the initial lines of output from the mount command on my system looks like this:

```
/dev/disk0s10 on / (local)
devfs on /dev (local)
fdesc on /dev (union)
<volfs> on /.vol
/dev/disk0s9 on /Volumes/Jedi (local, journaled)
```

The first term in the top item (**/dev/disk0s10**) is the device name for the current startup volume. The exact name can vary on different systems, which is why you need to check what it is. Copy this term to the clipboard.

3. Type sudo fsck_hfs. Follow this with a space and then paste the device name. To have the best chance of getting errors repaired, especially if journaling is on, add the -f and -y options/flags. To verify (rather than attempt to repair) a disk, add the -f and -n options instead. Thus, the final result for a repair request will look something like this:

```
sudo fsck_hfs -f -y /dev/disk0s10
```

4. Press Return. Enter your password when asked, and press Return again.

5. At this point, the check and verification or repairs will be performed. You will get feedback output similar to what you would see in First Aid or when running fsck via single-user mode.

6a. If verification of the startup volume indicates that repairs are needed, you will need to reboot from another volume (or use single-user mode) to make the repairs. For non-startup volumes, when repairs are complete, the text will either read **Repairing volume** or something like **The volume appears to be OK.** As is standard practice, if you get the **Repairing volume** message, run the utility again. The quickest way to do this is to press the up arrow key. This will bring back the command you just typed. All you need to do is press Return, and the command will run again.

6b. In some cases, the **Repairing volume** line may be followed by two additional lines:

```
** Repairing volume.
***** FILE SYSTEM WAS MODIFIED *****
***** REBOOT NOW *****
```

In such cases, the repairs are deemed sufficiently serious to require an immediate reboot to prevent problems that might occur if you continue using your Mac. Reboot by selecting the Restart command from the Apple menu. At this point, you should strongly consider checking the disk again, either with fsck via single-user mode (on a non-journaled system) or with First Aid via the Mac OS X Install CD. Do so until a run reports no more errors.

Using AppleJack: An alternative to fsck. AppleJack, by Apotek (www.applejack.sourceforge.net), is a third-party utility designed to be accessible in single-user mode. After running its installer, you can access the utility from single-user mode simply by typing `applejack`. This utility allows you to repair disks (just as `fsck` does). In addition, it can repair disk permissions, delete cache files, remove swap files, and validate preferences files. These latter functions can potentially address startup problems that would otherwise require more specific knowledge of Unix commands to address. Check out its read-me file for more details. I highly recommend installing this utility.

Note: If a corrupt preferences file is detected, you can delete it while still in single-user mode (as described in "Blue-screen crashes and stalls," earlier in this chapter).

Using third-party disk-repair utilities

When Mac OS X's built-in repair functions fail to do the job, it's time to consider third-party solutions. Before describing the specific utilities, here are a few general points to keep in mind:

- All of these utilities assume that you have formatted your Mac OS X volume with HFS Extended (also called HFS Plus), not the rarely used UFS.

- Make sure you're using the latest versions of these utilities. If you are running Tiger, for example, make sure the version you are using is compatible with Tiger.

- Unless a utility includes a specific option to repair permissions, you can assume that it does not do so.

- If the utility is on a CD—likely because it cannot repair the startup volume, so you need to boot from the utility's own disc to repair your Mac's hard drive—you may need to order a new CD when an updated version is released or if you purchase a new Mac that requires a newer version of Mac OS X than is on the CD. Alternatively, you may be able to create your own bootable CD.

    SEE: • "Select a Destination," in Chapter 3, for more information on UFS.

    • "Creating an Emergency Startup Volume," in Chapter 3, for information related to using alternative drives to run repair utilities, including creating a bootable CD.

DiskWarrior. Alsoft's DiskWarrior (www.alsoft.com) works by completely rebuilding the drive directory rather than attempting to repair an existing one. This is key to why it's often more successful than other repair utilities. You can even mount a preview version of the repaired volume at the same time that the original volume is mounted. This permits you to compare the two volumes, seeing what changes will be made. If repairing the volume appears to make matters worse (for example, deleting many files), this gives you the option of trying other solutions before doing the repair. In Mac OS X, using Preview mode requires a separate DiskWarrior Preview application when running DiskWarrior from the CD, because the special version of Mac OS X included on the CD does not allow you to access the Finder and thus cannot be used to see mounted volumes.

As with First Aid, DiskWarrior cannot repair the current startup volume. Thus, you will need to restart from a CD (or another bootable volume) to use DiskWarrior on your startup volume. To help out, DiskWarrior has a feature that allows you to create a new bootable CD, with the latest version of the application that you download from the Web (eliminating most of the need to separately purchase a new CD). However, if this does not work for your Mac, you will have to purchase a new CD from Alsoft, run DiskWarrior from a second hard drive, or create a custom bootable CD (using an application such as BootCD) to run the updated version.

DiskWarrior also includes a background daemon that monitors the SMART status of internal IDE and SATA hard drives to check for and monitor possible hardware problems.

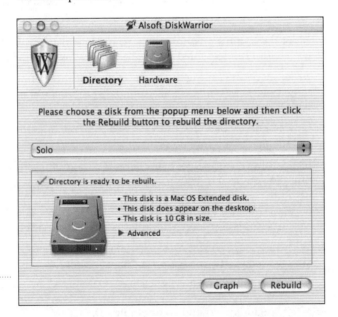

Figure 5.42

DiskWarrior's main window.

DiskWarrior has an excellent reputation for fixing problems that no other utility can repair. If Disk Utility alone is not sufficient, DiskWarrior remains my preferred alternative.

TechTool Pro. Micromat's TechTool Pro 4 (www.micromat.com) is a multi-featured utility that performs more tasks than DiskWarrior does. In addition to its directory-repair options, it includes numerous hardware tests, for everything from your Mac's memory to its network ports. It can also optimize/defragment a drive, potentially providing better performance. It includes a special Protection feature, to facilitate data recovery from a damaged volume. And it sports a cool feature called eDrive, which allows you to create an invisible partition on your drive that you can use as a startup volume in emergencies (just hold down the < key at startup). This can be done without having to erase your drive, and you won't need to run TechTool Pro from a CD to repair your normal startup volume. Finally, TechTool Pro 4 supports the same SMART tests included with DiskWarrior.

TAKE NOTE ▶ Get SMART

SMART—which stands for *Self-Monitoring Analysis and Reporting Technology*—is a technology built into newer hard drives that allows software on your computer to monitor those hard drives for problems, alerting you if it detects one. The idea is to provide an alert *before* the problem becomes so serious that the drive "dies" and data recovery is either very difficult or impossible.

In order for it to work, you need two components: (1) an internal hard drive that has SMART support (most recent EIDE and SATA drives, which are the most common drives used in Macs, include it); and (2) software that can monitor the drive and report possible problems. DiskWarrior and TechTool Pro 4 both support SMART. (Note: Even though the hard drives inside most recent FireWire and USB hard drives include SMART support, the FireWire and USB bridges used in these drives do not pass SMART data to your computer. In other words, you can't rely on SMART technology to monitor external hard drives.)

Disk Utility can tell you whether or not a drive supports SMART. To check, click the Info button for the selected drive and look for the "S.M.A.R.T. status" line.

Drive Genius. Prosoft Engineering's Drive Genius (www.prosofteng.com) is the newest entry in this field. It offers an array of features similar to what you get with TechTool Pro, including directory repair, defragmenting, and testing your hard drive. In addition, it offers the options to create a duplicate (clone) of a drive and to repartition a drive without having to erase it! Finally, for your inner geek, it sports a Sector Edit feature, allowing you to view and modify the hexcode at virtually every location on your drive.

Data Rescue II. Prosoft's Data Rescue II does not attempt to repair a drive. Rather, it attempts to recover files from a drive so damaged that nothing you try will fix it. It's especially useful for recovering important documents you had not backed up.

Norton Disk Doctor is gone! Norton Disk Doctor was one of the first repair utilities available for the Mac, dating back to the mid-1980s. However, Symantec (www.symantec.com) has decided to end development of it. There is no Tiger-compatible version of Disk Doctor. You should no longer use Disk Doctor (or Norton Utilities or Norton SystemWorks) on a drive running Tiger.

Defragmenting/optimizing Mac OS X volumes

Defragmentation and optimization are designed more to improve performance than to fix crash-related problems. Occasionally, however, they can solve or prevent a crash problem as well.

What exactly are defragmenting and optimizing? In essence, a file on a drive may be stored in several locations on your drive. For example, a 10 MB file may have 5 MB stored in one location, 3 MB in a second, and 2 MB in yet a third. Mac OS X, using information stored in the drive directory, tracks these file segments (or fragments) so that when you view or access the file, it looks like and behaves as if it were a single file. Defragmenting a drive takes all of these fragments and combines them, so that the number of segments for each file is reduced to a minimum (ideally, one). The optimization process then relocates the segments, typically into categories such as system files and documents, and groups all files so that all unused space is confined to a single large block. This may prevent problems that occasionally occur due to a file's otherwise being divided into a large number of fragments. It also may improve the speed with which files are accessed from the drive. With some utilities, you may be able to choose to defragment without optimizing. Normally you would do both, if possible.

Is defragmenting really needed in Mac OS X? Exactly how much benefit you derive from defragmenting and optimizing continues to be a matter of some debate. The growing consensus, however, is that defragmenting/ optimizing is of little or no value in Mac OS X, with a few possible exceptions. Among the reasons:

- The benefits of defragmenting are greater when your drive is nearly full. Because today's hard drives have much more capacity than older ones, most users have a lot of free space on their drives, which thereby reduces the need to defragment.

- Mac OS X avoids reusing small spaces from deleted files, if possible, to minimize fragmenting.

- Mac OS X includes *delayed allocation*. This means that small segments of the drive will be combined into a single, larger allocation when possible.

- Mac OS X includes "Hot-File-Adaptive-Clustering." This means that it will automatically defragment a file as the file grows in size (such as with a document that keeps increasing as you add more text). For example, if you open a small to moderate-sized file (less than 20 MB), Mac OS X checks to see how fragmented the file is. If it is broken into eight or more segments, Mac OS X will defragment the file automatically (unless the file is simultaneously in use by another process).

Security note: If this defragmenting happens when opening a file as part of an attempt to delete it with Secure Empty Trash, the original fragments will not be securely deleted; only the newer ones will be overwritten. See this Knowledge Base document for more information: http://docs.info.apple.com/article.html?artnum=25668.

Personally, I've never noticed any significant effect from defragmenting a disk in Mac OS X. Still, it may be useful for applications in which unsegmented files and large amounts of contiguous free space are beneficial, such as when working with digital video. Defragmenting utilities typically offer the ability to view the level of fragmentation of your drive, before you decide whether or not to defragment. If you check a drive with one of these utilities, and fragmentation appears high, it may pay to defragment it.

Before defragmenting, check your disk with First Aid. Defragmenting a drive that is usable but damaged can turn it into one that's no longer usable at all!

Optimizing with repair utilities. TechTool Pro and Drive Genius can defragment/optimize drives. Check the manuals that come with these utilities for details.

Note: DiskWarrior performs a kind of defragmenting/optimizing, but only for the invisible Directory area of the drive, not for the entire drive. If you're using DiskWarrior, this occurs as part of the normal repair process.

Note: If you back up, erase, and restore your hard drive, it will typically get defragmented as well. Or it may not. It depends on the backup utility you use. Check the documentation for your backup utility to find out.

Optimize/update_prebinding. When you install software via Mac OS X's Installer utility, you will likely notice that the last step claims to be "optimizing" the newly installed software. Sometimes this is the most time-consuming step of the entire installation.

This optimization is different from the optimization/defragmenting performed by utilities such as TechTool Pro or Drive Genius. The Installer's "optimizing" refers to a Unix-based process that can also help speed performance. Actually, you can perform optimizing at any time you choose. To do so, launch Terminal and run the Unix command update_prebinding. Several Aqua-based utilities, such as Yasu (www.jimmitchelldesigns.com), do the same thing without requiring Terminal.

However, starting in Mac OS X 10.2, the need to separately run the `update_prebinding` command has largely been eliminated. The optimizing is done on the fly, as needed, when an application is launched. There are a few exceptions to this. For example, automatic prebinding will not occur for a file that contains type/creator codes or a resource fork. It also may not occur if an application was drag-installed instead of Apple's Installer utility being used.

To manually update the prebinding information for just a single application, launch Terminal and use the `redo_prebinding` tool. To update prebinding information for one or more applications or frameworks, use the `update_prebinding` tool. Apple's Installer utility typically issues the following command to force prebinding of all files at the end of the installation:

`update_prebinding -root /`

In any case, prebinding affects only application launch times and works only for native Mac OS X applications, so there should not be much of an overall performance hit even in the worst cases. Still, I've seen a couple of reports indicating that `update_prebinding` fixed some odd symptoms (especially ones that occurred at application launch) that otherwise would not go away.

SEE: The following sidebars, all earlier in this chapter, for related trouble-shooting techniques:
- "Technically Speaking: Open Firmware Commands"
- "Take Note: Zapping PRAM and Resetting the Power Manager"
- "Technically Speaking: Understanding Kernel Extensions"
- "Technically Speaking: Connecting Remotely to a Frozen Mac: Killing Processes, Running Sync"

SEE ALSO:
- "Maximizing Performance," in Chapter 6, for related information.
- "Technically Speaking: Terminal Commands to Monitor and Improve Performance," in Chapter 10, for more on exactly what `update_prebinding` does.

Checking for "bad" memory (and other hardware problems)

Any hardware you add to your Mac, either a peripheral device (such as an external drive or a scanner) or an internal addition (such as additional memory or a PCI card) can be a source of problems if the device is defective or incompatible with your Mac or with the version of Mac OS X you are running. As mentioned earlier (see, for example, "Technically Speaking: The Apple Hardware Test Software"), you can run a check of your hardware to determine if you have a problem (assuming you can start up your Mac to do so).

Probably the most difficult-to-diagnose problem like this is an intermittent memory problem. What happens is that you have defective memory, but the memory performs fine most of the time. The failure may occur only occasionally and appear to be temporary. This can lead to almost any sort of odd symptom (varying as a function of what your Mac is trying to do when the failure occurs). Failures during installation of new software are especially likely.

The chance that you have bad memory is minimal if you use just Apple-supplied memory. The odds go up if you purchased third-party memory from an unreliable dealer. Because the problem is intermittent, even software like Apple's Hardware Test may not pick it up. A better alternative is a utility called Memtest, as discussed in "Utilities for monitoring and improving performance," in Chapter 6. To confirm a bad memory problem, remove the suspect memory (replacing it if necessary with other memory) and run your Mac for several days. If the problem vanishes, you can assume that bad memory was the cause.

Adding memory

No matter what's wrong with your Mac, if you don't have an abundance of physical memory (RAM), get more! Insufficient memory can cause numerous symptoms. Ideally, you should have at least 512 MB of RAM (and preferably more). Anything less than 256 MB is asking for trouble.

Even if you have more than enough memory, you can still run into trouble if you start opening too many applications at once or if a given application has a bug that causes it to use an excessive amount of memory (called a *memory leak*). Quitting open applications does not always solve these problems. In such cases, restarting your Mac is a good idea.

SEE: • "Not enough memory," in Chapter 6, for related information.

Reinstalling Mac OS X

If none of the actions previously described in this chapter are able to solve your Mac OS X problem, it's time to reinstall Mac OS X. You can do this with or without erasing your drive. Erasing your drive improves your odds of success but is more of a hassle, since it requires that you back up all files not included with Mac OS X and restore them after the reinstall. Reinstalling using the Installer's Archive and Install feature, on the other hand, allows you to maintain most of your customizations and added software while reinstalling the software that's the most likely cause of the problem.

Any reinstallation replaces most of the Mac OS X files—especially the files in /System/Library and /Library, as well as the invisible Unix files that work behind the scenes—with fresh default copies. Thus, if you were having a problem due to corruption of any of these files, a reinstallation would fix it. If only one file is corrupted, of course, this process can be like using a tank to shoot a fly. However, if you don't know which of hundreds of potentially corrupt files is the culprit, you may have little other choice.

When reinstalling Mac OS X, if your original Mac OS X Install disc is not the latest version of Mac OS X, you will need to reinstall the subsequent updates as well. In these cases, it is preferable to use a *combo updater* that combines several or all updates into one updater (such as an updater that goes from Mac OS X 10.4.0 to 10.4.3 in one step) rather than a series of single-step updaters.

SEE: • Chapter 3 for details on reinstalling Mac OS X.

Recover files before reinstalling. If you intend to reinstall Mac OS X because you cannot start up from your drive, and there are files on your drive that are not backed up, you can try a utility such as Prosoft Engineering's Data Rescue II to recover the files before reinstalling.

Otherwise, try the following:

1. Start up in single-user mode and run fsck, as described earlier in this section.
2. After fsck has made its repairs and while still in single-user mode, type mount -uw / and press Return.
3. Type chmod 1775 / and press Return.
4. Type reboot and press Return to restart.

If a permissions error was preventing startup, this technique changes the permissions settings on all files in such a way that startup should be successful. It does not necessarily restore permissions settings to what they were when Mac OS X was first installed, however, so a reinstallation is still advised—after you recover your un-backed-up files.

TAKE NOTE ▶ Mac OS X Maintenance, Diagnostics, and Repair: A Workflow

Throughout this chapter, I've suggested procedures that are useful not only to fix problems but also to *prevent* them. That is, they're useful for routine maintenance. Here's a quick summary:

- Restart your Mac periodically (at least once a week, even if you're not having obvious problems). This is especially good for remedying problems related to virtual memory.

- Run Disk Utility's Repair Disk and Repair Disk Permissions functions every month or so.

- Run Mac OS X's Unix maintenance scripts, just in case they were not automatically run recently. You can use a utility such as Brian Hill's MacJanitor (http://personalpages.tds.net/~brian_hill/macjanitor.html) to do this (see "Technically Speaking: Log Files and cron Jobs," in Chapter 4).

- Consider deleting preferences files and cache files that are a known common source of problems. The easiest way to do this is via a utility such as Cocktail. Do this every few months, or any time you suspect a problem.

- Consider defragmenting and optimizing your drive.

- Consider checking log files, using the Console utility, to see if any error messages suggest a chronic problem that needs your attention.

When the time comes that you do need to make repairs, consider the following sequence for deciding the order in which to try the various fixes:

1. Focus on files in your home directory first, such as .plist files.

2. Focus on application software, such as reinstalling a problem application.

3. Focus on Mac OS X software, such as using a disk-repair utility or reinstalling Mac OS X.

4. Focus on serious hardware problems last, such as taking the Mac in for repair.

In addition:

- Disconnect any peripheral devices when troubleshooting (unless the peripheral device is part of the problem that needs to be solved).

- Do quick fixes that minimize modifications to your software first (such as a simple restart of the Mac), saving longer and more invasive procedures (such as reinstalling Mac OS X) for last.

6

Problems with Files: Opening, Copying, Deleting, and Beyond

This chapter covers the most common problems you're likely to face as a Mac OS X user: those that occur when opening and saving files, copying and moving files, and deleting files. It also covers related issues regarding mounting and ejecting volumes. It concludes by examining various ways you can maximize your Mac's overall performance.

When Mac OS X is working as it should, the actions mentioned above are easy to accomplish. However, things don't always go as planned. Sooner or later, problems will occur. When they do, this chapter is the place to turn.

In This Chapter

Opening and Saving: Opening Files

This section covers the basics of opening files.

From the Finder

There are several ways in which you can open a file from the Finder:

Double-click the icon. To open any file (be it an application, folder, or document), simply select its icon (or name, if you're in List view) in a Finder window and from the File menu choose Open (or press Command-O). You can also simply double-click the file's icon or name in the Finder window. Whichever method you choose, the file will open.

- **Applications.** If you choose to open an application, it simply launches. Its icon appears in the Dock (if it's not already a permanent member of the Dock) and bounces until the application has finished opening. Thanks to Mac OS X's preemptive multitasking, if an application is taking a long time to launch, you needn't wait for it to finish before doing something else; you can still work with other applications. (If the application is already open, you'll simply switch to it.)

- **Documents.** If you choose to open a document, Mac OS X will also open the application needed to work with the document (assuming the application is not already open). Thus, double-clicking an AppleWorks document, for example, will cause AppleWorks to launch and the document to open within it.

Note: To view all currently open applications and quickly choose the active application, press Command-Tab.

SEE: • "Take Note: Dock and Finder Shortcuts," in Chapter 2.

Drag a document icon to an application icon. You can also open a document by dragging its icon to an application's icon—especially helpful when you want to open a document in an application other than the one that would be used if you double-clicked the document icon.

Use the Open With command. You can open a file by choosing Open With (rather than Open) from the Finder's File menu. If you choose this method, a submenu will appear listing all of the applications that the Finder *knows* can open the document. (The top item is the current default choice.) Choose an application in which to open the document.

You will also see an Other item in the list, which allows you to select applications that the Finder *does not* include. In the dialog that appears, navigate to the application you want to use. If you want to select an application that's dimmed (and thus unselectable) when the default recommended application is in effect, from the Enable pop-up menu choose All Applications. Be careful, however: The All Applications option allows you to use applications that aren't necessarily compatible with your document—which means you may cause a launch failure or crash if you try.

If you hold down the Option key when you're in the Finder's File menu, Open With changes to Always Open With. You'll also find an Always Open With check box at the bottom of the Choose Application window. If you select this option and then choose an application that's different from the current default one, the document will from that point on always open in the newly assigned application when you double-click it. Of course, if the selected application isn't capable of opening the document, this change won't work very well. In any case, the change *does not* affect other similar documents. If you want to change the default for *all* documents of a specific type (for example, to get all Preview documents to open in Adobe Reader), you need to use the Change All button in the document's Get Info window.

SEE: • "Open With," in Chapter 4, for more details on this option.

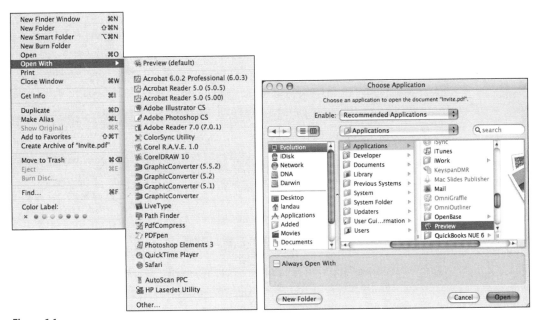

Figure 6.1

Using Open With: top, *the Open With menu when a .pdf file is selected;* bottom, *the window that appears when you choose Other from the menu.*

From the Finder's contextual and Action menus

You can access the same Open and Open With commands that are found in the Finder's File menu from contextual menus (which you access by Control-clicking an icon) and from the Action menu in the toolbar of Finder windows. The Open With command is available only for documents.

Choose Open, and the item will open (as described above, documents will open in their default applications; applications will launch). Choose Open With to open the document with a different application.

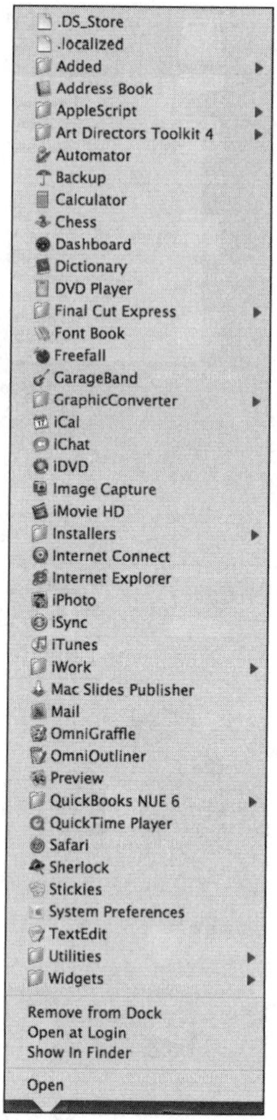

From the Dock

Single-click any application, document, or folder icon in the Dock, and the item will open. Similarly, for items listed in the Dock menu of an item (such as for a folder in the Dock), choosing the item will open it.

If an application has an icon in the Dock—either a permanent icon or one that's there because you launched the application—you should be able to open a document with that application by dragging the document icon to the application's icon in the Dock.

If a folder icon is in the Dock, its Dock menu (accessible by holding down the mouse button when selecting the folder) will provide a hierarchical list of that folder's contents; you can open any item in the menu by choosing it.

From the Recent Items menu

You can choose applications or documents from the Apple menu's Recent Items submenu to launch (or open) them.

From third-party utilities

You can also use an assortment of third-party utilities to launch (or open) items. These offer ways to sort and access files that are, at least to some users, more convenient than using the Finder. Three of the most popular of these are James Thomson's DragThing (www.dragthing.com), Sig Software's Drop

Figure 6.2

The applications in the /Applications folder, as accessed from its Dock menu.

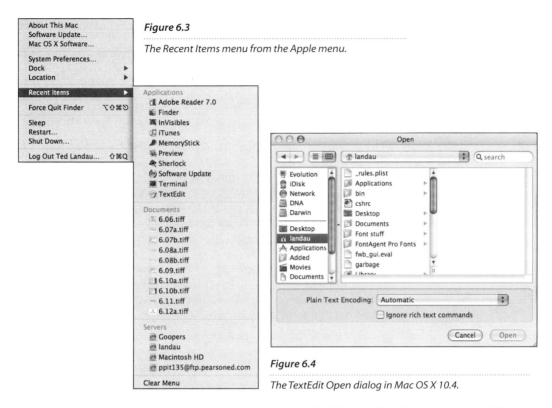

Figure 6.3

The Recent Items menu from the Apple menu.

Figure 6.4

The TextEdit Open dialog in Mac OS X 10.4.

Drawers (www.sigsoftware.com), and Objective Development's LaunchBar (www.obdev.at). There's even a utility called Path Finder (by CocoaTech; www.cocoatech.com) that acts as a complete replacement for the Finder, offering additional features such as the ability to create symbolic links or disk-image files.

From within an application: The Open command

For documents, a final option is to open a document via the Open command in the File menu of an open application. You can use this command only to open documents that the application believes it is able to open. Other documents either will not be listed or will be dimmed and unselectable.

The exact style of, and options available from, the Open dialog vary by application, but all versions of the dialog have some basic elements in common. I'll use the Open dialog in TextEdit as an example.

Toolbar. At the top of the Open dialog is a toolbar. Moving from right to left, the toolbar includes the following:

* **Search field.** Enter text here to initiate a Spotlight search directly in the Open dialog.

  SEE • "Spotlight," in Chapter 2, for more on this feature.

- **Pop-up menu.** This shows the name of the current folder (such as Desktop or Documents). By accessing the menu, you can navigate back along the hierarchy from the folder's location to the computer name. From the hierarchical menus that appear with each folder in the list, you can navigate to anywhere else.

  For example, if I were in the Movies folder of my home directory in a volume named DNA, the menu would appear as seen in Figure 6.5.

- **List and Column icons.** These icons allow you to switch the display between List and Column view.

- **Back and Forward arrow buttons.** The Back button allows you to retrace your steps to locations you've visited since opening the Open dialog. The Forward button moves you in the opposite direction. Exactly what locations appear when you click these buttons will depend on how you arrived at your current location (for example, from the pop-up menu, by clicking an item in the file list, or by clicking an item in the sidebar). I won't try to explain all the "rules" here. Suffice it to say that clicking the Back button immediately after making a change should always take you back to your prior location. It's like an Undo button (and similar to how the Back arrow button in a Web browser works). This is the most common use of these buttons.

Sidebar. Below the toolbar, on the left side of the window, is the sidebar, which mimics what you see in all Finder windows in Mac OS X 10.4 Tiger (as described in Chapter 2). Click any item here and the file list shifts to display the contents of your selection.

File list. The file-list area is the main section of the Open dialog. This is where the files and folders in the currently selected location are displayed.

If you're using List view, you can click a disclosure triangle for a folder (or double-click the folder) to reveal its contents.

If you're using Column view, you can click a folder to view its contents in the column to the right. You can use the horizontal slider along the bottom to navigate to columns that are shifted out of view.

Click a file that the application can open, and the Open button at the bottom of the window becomes the default button. Click the Open button (or simply double-click the filename), and the file opens.

You can also open a document by dragging its icon from its Finder location to the Open window, which shifts the view to that file's location and highlights the file. Or you can drag the icon of the folder that contains the item you wish to locate or open, which shifts the file list to the relevant folder. As above, once the file is highlighted, click Open, and the document opens. Why do this instead of simply double-clicking the file in the Finder? Some documents can be opened in several applications. If you want the file to open in an application other than the one in which it normally opens when you double-click it in the Finder, this method is one way to do so.

Command-key shortcuts (Desktop, "Go to the folder," and more). Press Command-D in an Open dialog and the file list instantly shifts to your Mac OS X Desktop.

Similarly, all of the Command-Shift-key navigational shortcuts in the Finder's Go menu work here as well. For example, pressing Command-Shift-C takes you to the Computer window.

Of special note, Command-Shift-G opens a "Go to the folder" dialog. In its text box, you can enter the path to any folder, including invisible ones, to instantly shift to that location. This is especially useful for navigating to invisible folders that would not otherwise be listed in the file list. For example, to see the contents of the Unix /etc directory, simply type /etc in the "Go to the folder" text box.

The bottom of the Open dialog. Along the bottom of the dialog are the Cancel and Open buttons. In addition, there may be application-specific options. For example, in TextEdit, there is a pop-up menu to choose Plain Text Encoding (which in almost all cases you should leave in its default Automatic setting).

Other options. If the document you want to open is not visible in the window, or its filename is dimmed and cannot be selected, you may be able to access and open it by changing a selection in various application-specific options that appear in the Open dialog.

For example, in Microsoft Word you would use the Enable pop-up menu at the top of the dialog. You could shift from All Office Documents to a more inclusive choice, such as All Documents. Just be aware that trying to open a document that is not intended for an application can have unpredictable results. The document window may be blank, for example, even though the file contains data. Or the file may be composed of an almost nonsensical string of characters (as might happen if you tried to open graphics files as text in a word processor).

Some applications may have a separate Import command to open files in formats other than the one(s) native to the application.

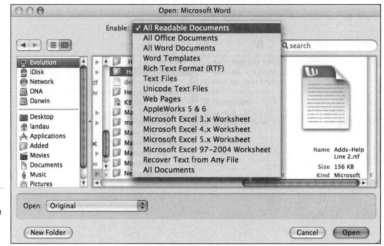

Figure 6.6

The Open dialog in Microsoft Word, with the Enable pop-up menu open.

Opening and Saving: Saving Files

When you're finished working with a document—or even *while* you're working with it—you will want to save it. Here's how.

From Save and Save As

To save an existing document that you have edited, simply choose Save from the File menu (or press Command-S) . It is saved, in its current location, without any further interaction.

To save an existing document as a new file (possibly with a different name), choose Save As. For an untitled, not-yet-saved document, choose either Save or Save As. In these cases, a dialog will drop down from the document's title bar.

In this dialog's Save As text box, you can provide a name for the document. Typically, for a new untitled document, a default name with a default filename extension is provided.

From the pop-up menu, you choose the location where you want to save the document. The default choice for a previously unsaved document is usually the Documents folder in your home directory. For choices not listed in the menu, click the disclosure triangle to the right of the Save As text box. This reveals a display almost identical to the Open dialog. From here, you can navigate to any location, just as you can in the Open dialog.

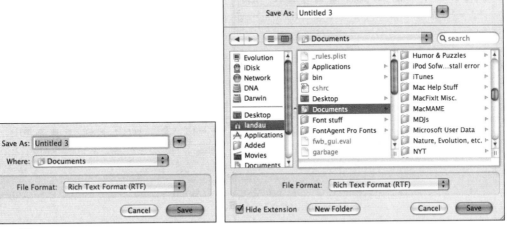

Figure 6.7

Left, *a dropped-down Save dialog (taken from a TextEdit document);* right, *the same Save dialog after the disclosure triangle is clicked.*

If you like, click the New Folder button at the bottom of the window to create a new folder in the current location.

If the application lets you save documents in more than one format, you will also have the option to select a format. TextEdit, for example, has a File Format option at the bottom of the dialog, from which you can select Rich Text Format (RTF) (TextEdit's default format), HTML (useful if you are creating a Web page), Word Format, or Word XML Format. The latter options save the document as Microsoft Word–formatted files.

Note: To save a file as plain text, you need to use the Make Plain Text command in TextEdit's Format menu. There is no option to do this in the Save dialog.

Some save dialogs will also have an option to Hide Extension. If you check this box, the file will still be saved with the appropriate file extension in its name, but that extension will be hidden in the Finder.

When everything is the way you want it, click the Save button.

The Save dialog is attached to the document to be saved. This makes it easy to track what document you're saving if multiple documents are open within the application. (A few applications that have been ported via Carbon from Mac

OS 9 versions may still use the old Mac OS 9–style Save dialog, which is a separate window independent of a specific document.)

A document with unsaved changes will have a black dot in its close button. If you try to close the document without saving it, you will be prompted to save the document first.

SEE: • "Take Note: Filename Extensions," in Chapter 4, for more on hidden file extensions.

From Export

If you want to save a document in a format other than the application's native format, but the format you want is not listed in the application's Save dialog (such as in a File Format pop-up menu), check if the application has an Export command in its File menu. For example, Preview's Save dialog has no options to convert formats. But if you choose Preview's Save As command, you'll be able to save a file in a variety of graphics formats, including TIFF, JPEG, PICT, and Photoshop.

SEE: • "Take Note: TextEdit: Format Options Beyond Show Fonts," in Chapter 4, for more on using TextEdit.

TAKE NOTE ▶ Filenames in Mac OS X

Related to the subject of saving files, here's an assortment of items regarding the limits of what you can and cannot do with filenames in Mac OS X:

Can't rename a file in the Finder. Normally, if you click the name of a file in the Finder (or simply click the file's icon and press Return), the name is shifted to an editable text box that allows you to change the file's name. If this text box does not appear, either you do not have the permissions required to make such a change, or the file is locked.

Long filenames. Mac OS 9 has a 31-character limit for filenames. In Mac OS X, a filename can be as long as 255 characters and span several lines.

Still, a couple of glitches are possible:

*   In many applications (especially non-Cocoa ones), the Open and Save dialogs show only the first 31 characters of a filename. In these applications, if you simply open and save a document that already has a longer name, the full name is preserved even though you don't see it in the Open and Save dialogs. If you use the Save As command to save a file under a new name, however, you will be limited to 31 characters (although you can add extra characters in the Finder later).

*   Some applications may truncate a long name to 31 characters when saving a file. Some compression utilities may do this when compressing a file or folder.

continues on next page

TAKE NOTE ▶ Filenames in Mac OS X *continued*

Do not use a forward slash (/) in filenames. The forward slash (/) is used in Unix as a separator for directories. Thus, Library/Fonts means the Fonts folder inside the Library folder. Adding the forward-slash character to the name of a file can confuse Unix into thinking that the slash refers to a subdirectory. It can also confuse the Finder. For example, if you use the Finder's "Go to the folder" command to go to a folder with a forward slash in its name, the command will not succeed. The solution is to avoid using the forward-slash character in filenames.

Do not use a colon (:) in filenames. If you try to use a colon in a filename, the colon may be converted to a hyphen. More likely, you will get an error message stating, "The name cannot be used. Try another name with fewer characters or no punctuation marks." This is a carryover from a naming restriction in Mac OS 9, in which the colon was the separator for directories (much as the forward slash is used in Mac OS X).

Do not use a period (.) at the start of a filename. As discussed in "Invisible Files: What Files Are Invisible?" later in this chapter, a dot (.) at the start of a filename indicates that the file should be invisible, so the OS typically blocks you from naming a file in this way. Unless you are deliberately attempting to create an invisible file, do not attempt to work around this block.

Other issues. Including a space in a filename is normally fine. However, if the file might be used on another platform (such as Windows or Unix), a space in a name could be misinterpreted. Thus, try to avoid spaces in names if you intend to export the file to another platform.

Finally, nonalphanumeric characters in names may cause problems. Hyphens and underscores work well, but be cautious of others. Apple's Knowledge Base lists most of these instances. For example, one article states, "Apple is unable to make prints of photos that have a question mark (?) in their filename."

SEE: • "Copying and Moving: Permissions Problems" and "Deleting: Problems Deleting Files," later in this chapter, for more details.

• "Take Note: Filename Extensions," in Chapter 4, for related information.

Opening and Saving: Problems Opening and Saving Files

The two most common problems that can occur when opening a file are: (1) The file opens in an application other than the one you wanted (or expected) when you attempt to open it from the Finder; and (2) a file fails to open entirely, yielding an error message instead.

Similarly, when saving a document, you may encounter an error stating that the file either cannot be saved at all or cannot be saved in the format you selected.

This section covers what you need to know if any of these problems occur.

SEE: • **"Opening and Saving: Permissions Problems," later in this chapter, for coverage of problems related to ownership and permissions settings.**

"Item {*name of item*} is used by Mac OS X and cannot be opened"

Many files, particularly ones in the /System/Library and /Library folders, are not intended to be opened, at least not by typical end users.

In general, when you're trying to open a file from the Finder, if you get a message that says, "Item {*name of item*} is used by Mac OS X and cannot be opened," leave the file alone. To see an example of this message, go to /System/Library/CFMSupport and try to open CarbonLib.

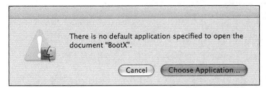
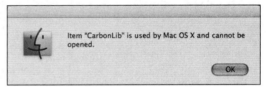

Figure 6.8

Two examples of error messages that may appear when you try to open a file from the Finder.

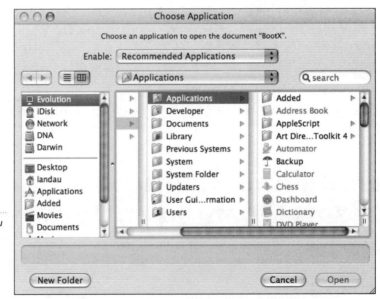

Figure 6.9

What appears if you click the Choose Application button in the first error message shown in Figure 6.8.

"There is no default application specified to open the document"

If, when you're trying to open a file from the Finder, you get a message stating, "There is no default application specified to open the document {*name of document*}," this typically means one of two things:

The file should probably be left alone. Go into the /System/Library/Extensions folder, for example, and double-click any kext file there. Or go into almost any other folder in /System/Library and try to open any file with a blank icon. You are likely to get this message. In most cases, unless you really need to see the contents of a selected file, simply click Cancel and go about your business.

If you really need to see the contents of the file, however, click the Choose Application button that appears in the error-message window, and select the desired application—assuming you know what application is needed to view the file.

Dragging the icon to the application you want to use may also work to open the document.

The Finder cannot find the needed application. It may be that the file is intended to be opened by an application that's not installed on your Mac—say if you've downloaded a document from the Internet (for example, a Microsoft PowerPoint slide show) but don't own the creating application (PowerPoint). In such cases, you would either

• Acquire (purchase, if necessary) the needed application.

or

• Determine whether a free reader application can open the document. If so, obtain the reader application (the Web would be one source).

The remaining possibility is to open the file with some application you already own. This method may succeed because certain types of files can be opened by multiple applications. A TIFF document that appears as an Adobe Photoshop document, for example, can usually be opened in Mac OS X's Preview application. In fact, Preview can open most graphics formats.

More generally, your options include the following:

• **Drag the file icon to the icon of the application you want to open it with (such as Preview), or open the application and then try to open its document via the application's Open dialog.**

• **Access the "Open with" section of the document's Get Info window, choose Open With from the Finder's File menu, or use the Open With contextual-menu item to select the desired application.**

SEE: • "Opening and Saving: Opening Files," earlier in this chapter, for details on Open With options.

- **Click the Choose Application button in the error dialog that appears when you double-click the document icon.** Select the desired application from the browser, navigating to it as needed. (You get the same file browser if you choose the Other item from an Open With pop-up menu.)

  With Recommended Applications chosen in the Enable pop-up menu (as it is by default), only applications that Mac OS X thinks should work with your document are selectable. If you're not content with the choices, choose All Applications instead. Now you can select virtually any application from the browser list. As noted earlier in this chapter, be cautious with this option. If you try to open a document in an incompatible application, you can get unexpected results—from the document opening but displaying gibberish to the document not appearing at all or the application crashing.

- **Convert the document.** Some applications let you convert a document from one format to another when saving or opening it. For example, TextEdit can open Microsoft Word documents as well as save documents in Word format so that Word can open these documents without having to convert them. You make these selections from the File Format pop-up menu in TextEdit's Open and Save dialogs. Other applications may use special Import and Export commands to accomplish similar conversions. These may work even if Open does not. Finally, DataViz's MacLinkPlus (www.dataviz.com) is a standalone utility that specializes in these conversions. If your application does not have the needed conversion built in, MacLinkPlus may be the solution.

SEE: • "From Export," earlier in this chapter.

If none of the preceding tips help and you have no idea what remaining applications on your drive might open a given document, how can you start narrowing down your choices? Here are some guidelines:

- For preferences files (files that end in .plist), it's typically best to open them with Property List Editor, which is installed with the Developer Tools software. If you have this application on your drive, double-clicking a .plist file should launch it automatically.

- For log files (files that end in .log), try Console. If double-clicking the file does not open Console automatically, drag the file's icon to the Console application.

- For font files (in the Fonts folder), try Font Book.

- For text files, including many of the files in the Library folders and the invisible Unix directories, try a text editor such as Apple's TextEdit or Bare Bones' TextWrangler or BBEdit (www.barebones.com).

It's a Unix application. Some "applications" on your hard drive are Unix programs that run only in the Unix environment (as accessed via Terminal). Most such applications are normally invisible; thus, there's little chance you'll attempt to open them accidentally. Occasionally, however, you might download a Unix program from the Web, thinking it's a normal Aqua-based Mac OS X application. In addition, Developer Tools contains a folder called Tools, located in the /Developer folder, that contains Unix programs.

Such applications are most often listed as Unix Executable Files and will launch Terminal if double-clicked from the Finder.

SEE: • "Unix: Executing Commands," in Chapter 10, for details on how to run Unix software.

Document opens in the "wrong" application

In some cases, if you double-click a document in the Finder, it will open in an application other than the one you want to use. For example, a PDF document may launch in Preview rather than Adobe Reader, or vice versa.

A similar problem occurs if you have more than one version of an application on your drive. In such cases, when you double-click a document in the Finder, the document may open with a different version of the application than the one you intended. This can cause a variety of symptoms, including a crash of the application. For example:

• If you have both Classic-only and Mac OS X versions of an application, when you try to open a document created by that application, it may launch the Classic version erroneously (rather than the Mac OS X version).

• After you use the Archive & Install option in the Mac OS X Installer (as described in Chapter 3), a document is opened with a different version of an application, still residing in the Previous Systems folder, rather than the currently installed version.

• If you have both a beta version and a release version of an application available, the beta version may launch instead of the current version.

• If you have different versions of the same application (such as Mac OS X 10.3 Panther and Mac OS X 10.4 Tiger versions)—especially likely if you've got two drives or partitions, each with a version of Mac OS X installed— the wrong version may open (for example, the Tiger version may open when you're running Panther).

• When you double-click a document icon, the Finder will generally prefer to launch a local copy of the associated application over launching to the same version located on a network volume. However, if the network copy is a newer version, it may be launched in preference to the local copy.

This section covers what to do in such situations. Some of the solutions are the same as those in the preceding section for documents that do not open.

SEE: • "Problems with applications," later in this chapter.

   • "Application quits," in Chapter 5.

   • "Problems launching applications" and especially "Take Note: Applications Packages Containing Two Application Versions," in the online Classic chapter, available at Mac OS X Help Line (www.macosxhelpline.com), for related information on Classic.

Delete unwanted additional and/or Classic copies of applications.
The simplest—and permanent—solution is to delete the additional versions, assuming you no longer need them and have access to delete them.

For example, if the problem is that there are applications in an Applications folder of the Previous Systems folder that are being incorrectly accessed, the solution is to delete the undesired applications. Similarly, if there are any third-party programs in Previous Systems that you still want to use, drag them out of this location and into your current /Applications (or other) folder location.

In the most extreme cases, you may need to uninstall all traces of all versions of an application and then reinstall the latest version. To do this, do a search for all files that include the name of the application and then drag all of them to the Trash. Hopefully, this search will also identify software that was installed with the application but is not part of the application itself (such as software in the ~/Library/Application Support folder). You may find that some accessory software cannot be moved to the Trash because you do not have permission; if so, you will need to get permission (as described elsewhere in this chapter). If the application came with an uninstaller, use it; this should save you the hassle of having to do a search and deal with permissions issues.

After doing all this, restart your Mac and empty the Trash. Now reinstall the latest version. One reason for restarting is that some applications leave background processes running even after you delete the main application. This method ensures that they're turned off and deleted as well.

Note: Some Apple applications interact with files in the Frameworks and PrivateFrameworks folders of the /System/Library folder. If the version of the framework is different from the version of the application, the application may not work properly. The preferred solution here is to make sure you have updated to the latest versions of Mac OS X and all other Apple applications. Otherwise, you will need to make sure that the version of the application you are using is a match for the version of Mac OS X you have installed (check Apple's Web site for help here); delete any application versions that do not match.

If none of this is helpful to your particular problem, proceed with the advice that follows.

Compress the unwanted version of the application. Compress the unwanted version (using the Finder's Create Archive command) so that the Mac no longer treats it as an application. If it is an .app file, removing the .app extension may be sufficient. With these options, you can still revert to the older version later, if desired.

Launch the application first. In some cases, if you simply launch the desired application before double-clicking the document, the document will open correctly. This works, for example, if the problem is that the document otherwise would launch with another (older or newer) version of the desired application.

Drag and drop. If you're unconcerned about *why* the wrong application was used and simply want to get the document to open in the desired application, drag and drop the document icon onto the icon of the desired application—either in its enclosing Finder window or in the Dock.

One of these methods usually solves the problem. Occasionally, a document may still refuse to open, even if you're certain the application can access it. For example, I've seen Adobe GoLive refuse to open HTML files downloaded from the Internet when I tried to open them by dragging the document icon to GoLive's Dock icon. In such cases, continue exploring the following options until you find one that works.

Open from within the application. Launch the application and open the desired document via the application's Open dialog. This method almost always works. If the Open dialog includes a pop-up menu of the types of documents it lists as available for opening, choose the one that matches what you're trying to open. If all else fails and you see an All Documents option, choose it and then open the document.

Use the Open With options. We've been over this already.

SEE: • "Opening and Saving: Opening Files," earlier in this chapter, for details.

For even greater flexibility in assigning documents to open with specific applications, use a utility like Rainer Brockerhoff's XRay (www.brockerhoff.net/xray) or Gideon Softworks' FileXaminer (www.gideonsoftworks.com). These utilities not only allow you to make the same sorts of changes you can make in the Get Info window, but they also allow you to change type and creator settings.

SEE: • "Technically Speaking: How Mac OS X Selects a Document or Application Match," later in this chapter, for more information.
• "Get Info," in Chapter 4, for much more background information.

Change the file's extension. Changing the filename extension for a document (or adding an extension if one does not exist) can change the default application that opens the file and possibly the type of the document as well. Sometimes, however, the document may still open in the same application, although the application treats it as a different type of document.

SEE: • "Technically Speaking: How Mac OS X Selects a Document or Application Match," later in this chapter, for more details.
• "Troubleshooting e-mail," in Chapter 9, for a successful example of this fix with an e-mail attachment file.

Delete Launch Services files. If you have two Mac OS X versions of the same application on your drive, you may find that double-clicking documents created by the newer application incorrectly launches the older version. If the icons are different in the two versions, the documents may also display the older version's icons. You may even be unable to get a document to open by dragging the document icon to the application's Dock icon.

The most likely culprit is a problem with Mac OS X's Launch Services database. The solution is to close all open applications and fix the database.

SEE: • "Take Note: Launch Services Files and Beyond," below, for details.

TAKE NOTE ▶ Launch Services Files and Beyond

Mac OS X's Launch Services files maintain important data—such as which documents are linked to which applications. For example, if you change the default application for opening a document (via the Change All command in the "Open with" section of a document's Get Info window), the change is stored in these files.

Deleting these files is a possible solution if any of the following problems occur:

- Documents fail to launch or fail to launch with their matching applications.

- Package items (such as .app applications) appear and function as folders or otherwise fail to launch correctly.

- Files lose their custom icons.

- Duplicates of contextual-menu items appear in contextual menus, or contextual menus fail to appear at all.

- Other launch-related problems occur.

Unfortunately, Apple keeps shuffling the names, the locations, and even the exact functions of these Launch Services files.

In Mac OS X 10.4 Tiger, the important files to know about are the com.apple.LaunchServices.plist file in ~/Library/Preferences and the com.apple.LaunchServices-####.csstore (where #### is a series of numbers) files in /Library/Caches/. There should be at least two such files in the Caches folder. One should be called com.apple.LaunchServices-0140.csstore and is owned by the System. This is the key file used by all users. In addition, there will be a file for every local user on your Mac. If you are the only or first user on your Mac, your user ID is probably 501, and the name of your "personal" LaunchServices file will be com.apple.LaunchServices-014501.csstore.

You can fix the types of symptoms described above by deleting the com.apple.LaunchServices.plist and .csstore files. To delete the .csstore file, however, you need to be an administrator. When you drag the file to the Trash, a dialog will appear, asking you to *authenticate* by entering your administrative password. Do so, and the file will be deleted. You don't need to authenticate to delete the .plist file (because it resides in your home directory).

Alternatively, you may delete these files via the following sequence of commands in Terminal (the last command restarts the Mac):

```
rm ~/Library/Preferences/com.apple.LaunchServices.plist
sudo -s (and give password when asked)
rm /Library/Caches/com.apple.LaunchServices-*.csstore
```

continues on next page

TAKE NOTE ▶ Launch Services Files and Beyond *continued*

Default versions of these files will be re-created automatically when you restart. In fact, you should restart immediately after deleting these files to prevent a cached copy of the data in memory from being used to re-create the file (and thus the problem).

As a final variation, you can use a "hidden" Terminal command called `lsregister`. To do so, enter the following command (all on one line) in Terminal:

```
/System/Library/Frameworks/ApplicationServices.framework/Versions/A/Frameworks/
LaunchServices.framework/Versions/A/Support/lsregister -kill -r -domain system
-domain local -domain user
```

Executing this command will delete the relevant ls cache files and rebuild new ones based on the applications on your drive. To learn more about the options available with this command (such as the dump option, used to view all data in the cache file), just type the path for the command itself, with no options.

The Terminal methods are especially recommended if it appears that the data in the file is being cached such that the deleted data is restored in the newly created files, rather than a default copy being created.

More files to delete. If you're unable to drag and drop an item in the Finder and/or Dock, try deleting the com.apple.dock.plist and com.apple.finder.plist files in ~/Library/Preferences. Note that doing this will mean that you have to reset all your customized preferences for the Dock and Finder.

Cache-cleaning utilities. Kristofer Szymanski's Cocktail (www.macosxcocktail.com), computer-support.ch's Xupport (www.computer-support.ch/xupport), and Northern Softworks' Tiger Cache Cleaner (www.northernsoftworks.com) are examples of utilities that can automate the deletion of the above-described cache files. These utilities often include other functions as well (which vary by utility), such as the ability to delete virtual-memory swap files, optimize network performance, or create a RAM disk.

Note: Make sure you update to the latest Tiger-compatible versions of these utilities before using them in Tiger.

`launchd`. New in Tiger, Apple has implemented a Unix command called `launchd`. This is a replacement for the several different ways of launching files in prior versions of Mac OS X. As most of this takes place behind the scenes, a typical user can be happily unaware of all these changes—except for the benefits it provides. The major benefit is faster and more reliable launches, perhaps most notable during startup.

SEE: • "Technically Speaking: Type/Creator vs. Filename Extensions vs. Others," in Chapter 4, and "Deleting cache files," in Chapter 5, for related information.

• "Startup daemons," in Chapter 5, for more details on `launchd`.

TECHNICALLY SPEAKING ▶ **How Mac OS X Selects a Document or Application Match**

Here is what you need to know about how Mac OS X decides which application to use when trying to open a document:

Priorities

Mac OS X uses a technology called Launch Services to do what its name implies (launch files). It is responsible for launching applications and their associated documents. Launch Services uses the following rules to decide which application should be used to open a document:

1. The document is opened via the application specified by the user in the Get Info window, if the user has made a nondefault selection.

2. If the document has a creator assigned to it, the file will be opened with the application indicated by the creator.

3. If no creator is present and a filename extension is included, the file will be opened with the default application for that file extension.

4. If neither a creator nor a filename extension is present, Launch Services will check for a file type. If a file type is present, the default application for that type of file will be used to open it.

5. If no default application is set for the document in Step 3 or 4, and more than one application is found that can open that type of file, preference is given to Mac OS X applications, then to Classic ones; preference is also given to newer versions.

In brief, Mac OS X will use creator information over extensions if the creator information is present. This is why Mac OS X may appear to ignore extensions in some cases; it trusts the creator type instead. If you want Mac OS X to use the extension, you can use a utility to eliminate the file's creator code.

In fact, you can remove a document's type and/or creator codes altogether. After doing this, the Finder would rely on its extension to determine how to treat the file.

Some applications may override these rules when opening documents. So, with third-party applications, you cannot automatically assume that the above rules apply—although they most likely will.

Priority conflicts. In some cases, two or more of the data sources above may be in conflict. For example, a graphic image may have a .gif filename extension but a JPEG Type code. Certain applications may have trouble opening such files, despite the priority rules cited above. This is especially likely if the application opens the document using the wrong criteria; that is, the application may open a JPEG file as if it were a GIF file. In such cases, deleting the type code and (if needed) renaming the file with the proper extension should get things working.

continues on next page

TECHNICALLY SPEAKING ▶ **How Mac OS X Selects a Document or Application Match** *continued*

Using Utilities Such as XRay and FileXaminer

XRay and FileXaminer are two of a number of utilities that allow you to change a file's settings in ways that exceed what you can do with Get Info. I use these utilities for two main functions:

• To extend the options accessible via the Get Info window's "Open with" section.

• To extend the options available via Get Info's Ownership & Permissions section.

Here, I focus on the first of these two functions. The second function is covered in "Opening and Saving: Permissions Problems" and "Copying and Moving: Permissions Problems," later in this chapter.

If you want to stick with just Mac OS X software, there are ways to make these changes, such as by using the Developer Tools' SetFile command in Terminal. But using these shareware utilities, as I show in the following examples, is easier. Maybe someday Apple will provide a similar utility or functionality with Mac OS X. But for now, I highly recommend getting the needed shareware.

XRay basics. To use XRay to change the Type and/or Creator for a document, follow these steps:

1. Drag the icon for the document you want to modify to the XRay icon (or, if XRay is open, drag the icon to the XRay window). Alternatively, if you've installed XRay's contextual-menu plug-in, you can access the contextual menu for the document and choose the XRay item.

2. Choose Type, Creator & Extension from the Show pop-up menu.

3. In the window that appears, make whatever changes you want to these settings (as described in the following paragraphs).

4. Close the window.

5. Save your changes when prompted to do so.

Modifying Type, Creator, and Extension settings. The Type, Creator & Extension window includes four categories you can modify, listed in the order in which Mac OS X checks them. That is, when deciding which application matches a given document, the Finder first checks the top item in the list. If it does not find a match there, the Finder moves to the second item in the list, and so on. If it finds no match anywhere, the Finder is likely to tell you that it cannot identify an application to open the document. Following are the details on the four categories:

• **"Bind this item to."** This category is equivalent to the Get Info window's "Open with" option. XRay presents pop-up menus listing every native and Classic application on your drive and lets you pick the one you want.

  If you make a selection, the Bind All Similar Items button at the bottom of the window is enabled. This button works similarly to the Get Info window's Change All button. Any other documents that match the creator, extension, and type settings of this document will be "bound" to open with the selected application.

continues on next page

TECHNICALLY SPEAKING ▶ How Mac OS X Selects a Document or Application Match *continued*

- **Creator.** The *creator* refers to the four-letter code that typically tells the Finder what application goes with what document. If you don't know what code to use, don't worry; XRay will help you out. Simply choose the desired application from the pop-up menu, and XRay will fill in the correct code. If you have not selected a specific application for the "Bind this item to" option, the Finder will use the creator code to decide what application goes with the document.

- **Extension.** This category refers to the file extension—typically, three or four letters that appear after a period (.) in the file's name. Changing the extension here changes the extension in the file's name (as you can also do in the Name & Extension pane of the Get Info window or in the Finder directly). In XRay, a pop-up menu lets you choose an extension that works with the application specified by the creator or binding option.

  Note: By removing a file's creator (such as choosing No Specific Creator from the Creator pop-up menu), you force the Finder to rely on the extension to determine a matching application (assuming that you didn't bind a specific application). This method can be useful if you do not want a given file to open with the application designated by the creator.

  Note: FileXaminer includes optional contextual-menu items that you can install via its preferences dialog. One of them is a Clear Type & Creator contextual-menu item that makes this task especially easy.

  Note: XRay also includes the same Hide Extension option that is available in the Get Info window's Name & Extension section.

- **Type.** Type is another four-letter code, often forming a pair with the Creator code. Type identifies the format of the file; however, it does not necessarily specify an application to work with that format. Microsoft Word, for example, can open files of many formats and types: Word documents, plain text documents, Rich Text Format documents, and so on. Thus, Type overlaps with File Extension, with which it should ideally match. That is, a document with an extension that specifies plain text format should also have a plain text type code. If a disparity occurs, the order of priority comes in: The extension takes precedence over the type. Again, XRay gives you a pop-up menu listing all the types associated with the creator or extension you selected.

If you don't choose a Binding or Creator option, the OS will search for any applications that claim the extension (if one is listed) or type (if one is listed and there is no match for the extension). If a match is found, that application will be listed at the bottom of the window. If more than one matching application is found, the OS will select native applications over Classic ones and newer versions over older ones.

Some document types are associated with a particular application. This is considered the default application for this type. If no creator or extension information is present, the document will open in this default application.

When even this fails to get a match, you will get an error message stating that the Finder cannot find a default application for the document.

continues on next page

TECHNICALLY SPEAKING ▶ **How Mac OS X Selects a Document or Application Match** *continued*

To understand what *claimed types* and *claimed extensions* are, click the XRay Application button at the bottom of XRay's window. This opens the application listed to the left of the button. Go again to the Type, Creator & Extension window for the application, which will be quite different from what you see when you select it for a document. You will not be able to change much of anything; however, the two pop-up menus (Claimed Extensions and Claimed Types) show you what the application will accept as a document that it can and will open.

To learn more about what XRay can do, play around with it. As long as you work with a copy of the file you're modifying (or don't save your changes), you can't do any harm.

Putting It Together: Print Preview Opens Acrobat in Error

When you click the Preview button in the Print dialog of most applications, Mac OS X should create a PDF version of the file and open the file in the Preview application. In some cases, however, the file may open in Adobe (Acrobat) Reader instead (perhaps even the Classic version of Acrobat, if you have that on your drive). To get the file to default to open in Preview instead:

1. Allow Adobe Reader to open the document after clicking Preview.
2. Save the document, using Adobe Reader's Save command.
3. Locate the saved file, and open it with a utility that can modify type and creator data. For this example, I dragged the document icon to the FileXaminer icon.
4. From the pop-up menu, choose Type/Creator (Command-3).
5. From the Favorites pop-up menu, choose Generic PDF Document.
6. Click the Apply button.
7. Quit FileXaminer.
8. In the Finder, open the Get Info window for the same file, and open the "Open with" section.
9. From the pop-up menu, choose the Preview application.
10. Click the Change All button.

Now, when you click Preview in the Print dialog, the document should open in Preview rather than Adobe Reader. Also, the icon for the document should shift from the icon for Adobe Reader documents to that of Preview documents.

Putting It Together: System Preferences Window Does Not Open

Suppose you choose Dock > Dock Preferences from the Apple menu, and the Dock System Preferences pane does not open. In one such case, Mac OS X attempted to launch iDVD instead, as though System Preferences files were iDVD documents. The likely reason was that the link between the Dock System Preferences pane and the System Preferences application was broken.

continues on next page

TECHNICALLY SPEAKING ▶ **How Mac OS X Selects a Document or Application Match** *continued*

File corruption that occurred during the installation of a Mac OS X update (or another software update) could have been the cause of this problem. To fix it, you would follow these steps:

1. Go to the /System/Library/PreferencePanes folder.

2. Click Dock.prefPane, and choose Get Info.

3. Go to the "Open with" section of the Get Info window.

4. If the pop-up menu reads anything other than System Preferences, choose the Other item from the menu.

5. In the window that appears, select the System Preferences application. (If it is dimmed, in the Enable pop-up menu change Recommended Applications to All Applications.)

6. Click Add.

7. A dialog will appear, stating, "You don't have privileges to change the application for this document only. Do you want to change all your System Preferences documents to open with the application 'System Preferences'?" Click Continue.

At this point, the Dock preference pane, and any other preference panes with this symptom, should open correctly.

Uniform Type Identifiers (UTI). Starting in Tiger, Apple has introduced a new type of file identifier system, called Uniform Type Identifiers (UTIs). These are intended to replace filename extensions, type and creator codes, and everything else as the ultimate criteria for a file's type. For now, even in Tiger, these older methods are still recognized. But expect them to be eliminated ("deprecated," to use Apple's terminology) in future revisions of the OS.

SEE: • "Take Note: Filename Extensions" and "Technically Speaking: Type/Creator vs. Filename Extensions vs. Others," in Chapter 4, for more background information.

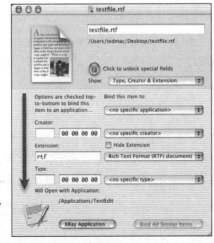
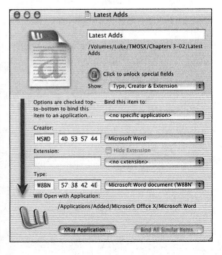

Figure 6.10

XRay's Type, Creator & Extension window for documents: two examples.

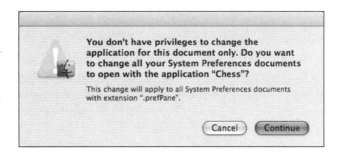

Figure 6.11

An example of a message that may appear when making changes in the "Open with" section of the Get Info window for files in the /System/Library folder. Unless you know you want to make the change (such as to fix a problem), click Cancel.

An application takeover. Sometimes, after you install an application, you may find that the application is opening documents that previously opened with something else (or would not open with any application).

You can choose to ignore the problem, which has an effect on what happens only when you double-click a document. If you need to open an affected document in a different application, follow the general advice from the earlier section on documents that open in the "wrong" application.

SEE: • "Technically Speaking: How Mac OS X Selects a Document or Application Match," earlier in this chapter, for another example and solution for this problem, involving iDVD and System Preferences.

File is corrupt

Occasionally, a file will not open because it is corrupt. That is, the contents of the file have changed in such a way that the file no longer works. If this happens, the tactics used to fix the problem are a bit different, depending upon whether the file is an application or a document.

Applications. Typically, this problem occurs with applications you've downloaded from the Internet—either because the file was only partially downloaded or because an error occurred during the download process. In either case, missing or corrupt data prevents the file from opening.

For downloaded files, the most common solution is to simply re-download the file. In some cases, you may have greater success by holding down the Option key when you download the file. Otherwise, try switching to a different browser. If the URL begins with *ftp* (rather than *http*), you may also have better luck by switching to an FTP client, such as Fetch Softworks' Fetch (http://fetchsoftworks.com), rather than a Web browser. And if an FTP client fails to work initially, shift to passive FTP transfer and try again—you will find a Use Passive FTP Mode (PASV) option on the Proxies pane of Network System Preferences (accessed by selecting a port from the Show menu and then clicking the Proxies tab); your FTP client application may include a similar option.

SEE: • "Download files and save content," in the "Troubleshooting Internet Applications" section of Chapter 9, for more on this issue.

If the problem persists, there may be a problem with the server containing the file. If so, you might check MacFixIt (www.macfixit.com) for possible confirmation and a solution. Otherwise, check with the site's Webmaster for advice.

Sometimes an application you've been using for a while becomes corrupted during normal use. When this happens, the solution is either to download a fresh copy or to reinstall it from your install discs, depending on how you first obtained the application.

If the problem occurs when you're copying files from one volume to another, the drive itself may have a corrupted directory or a hardware problem. In this case, it's time to attempt disk repairs.

SEE: • **Chapter 5 for more information on repairing disks.**
• **Chapter 9 for more information on Internet-related problems.**

Documents. For a damaged document, the easiest solution is to use an undamaged backup copy. If you don't have such a backup, the solutions just described for applications may apply. Otherwise, there are several things to try before relegating the document to the Trash. I'll use a damaged Word document as an example here, but the principles are the same for other applications. Note that some options may not exist or may have different names in other applications.

To recover text from a damaged Word document, try the following:

- If you can open the document, do so. Then convert the document to another format (such as an older version of Word or AppleWorks or whatever). The converted document may open undamaged.

- If you can open the document but not save it, copy and paste any undamaged text into a blank document. In the case of Word, first try this by copying all but the very last paragraph marker. (Microsoft claims it is this last marker that is often the source of the problem.) The paragraph marker is an invisible character at the end of each paragraph. If needed, you can show all these nonprinting characters by clicking the paragraph icon (¶) in the standard toolbar or pressing Command-8.

- If the document cannot be opened, create a new document and then choose File from Word's Insert menu; select the problem file in the dialog that appears. The text may still insert correctly into a new blank document.

- From the File menu, choose Open. Then, from the Open pop-up menu (at the bottom left side of the window) choose Copy and try to open the document. If that fails, from the Enable pop-up menu choose Recover Text from Any File and try again.

- If all else fails, try a third-party recovery utility such as Echo One's File Juicer (www.echoone.com) or Prosoft Engineering's Data Rescue Mac (www.prosofteng.com).

File is compressed or encoded

Files—especially those from the Internet—may download in a compressed or encoded format. Without the proper application to decompress or decode the file, you won't be able to open it.

The StuffIt Expander utility, which you can download from Allume's Web site (www.allume.com), is able to expand many compressed file formats (for example, files with .sit, .hqx, and .bin extensions). If the file does not expand automatically on download, drag it to Expander, or launch Expander and select the file via the Open command.

There are, however, a few file-compression formats that Expander cannot open. In these cases, try the shareware utility OpenUp, by Scott Anguish (www.stepwise.com/Software/OpenUp).

Files with a .dmg or .img extension are disk images, which you typically mount by double-clicking them in the Finder (the process uses a background application called DiskImageMounter, as described in Chapter 3). This method opens a virtual volume that behaves as though it were a physical disk. The application or document you seek is actually on the image. Thus, you have to open the image window, locate the file, and either open the file directly from the image or copy it to your hard drive and then open that copy.

Figure 6.12

Left, *a .dmg file;* right, *the mounted volume that opens when you double-click the image. You can open the mounted volume to access its contents, just as though it were an external drive.*

Backup_2.0.dmg

Backup 2

Occasionally, a compressed or encoded file may be erroneously downloaded as a text file. Double-clicking it may open it in a text editor, such as TextEdit or TextWrangler. You can work around this problem by dragging the file to the required application (such as DiskImageMounter or StuffIt Expander). If this problem happens with many files, you may want to make a change, via the "Open with" option in the Get Info window or a utility like XRay, so that similar files open correctly in the desired application.

Finally, sometimes when you click a download link on a Web page, you may get a message stating that your browser does not recognize the file type of the file you're attempting to download. It may offer to search for a needed plug-in or other helper file. If you just want the file to download, the best advice is to choose whatever option allows you to ignore the warning and download the file; then drag the downloaded file's icon to the desired decompression utility. The cause of these problems is either at the server end (someone mislabeled the file, for example, in which case you can do nothing to fix the problem) or, possibly, with your browser settings (especially the Helper settings). The latter problem can be fixed by changing a browser preference. I cover this topic a bit more in Chapter 9, but it quickly gets beyond the Mac OS X–specific scope of this book.

SEE: • "Image (.dmg) files" and, especially, "Technically Speaking: Internet-Enabled Disk Images," in Chapter 3, for related information.

   • Chapter 9 for more information on Internet problems.

Problems with applications

You're generally less likely to have problems launching applications than launching documents. There are, however, a few instances in which things may go wrong.

Most Mac OS X applications are actually package files (also referred to as *bundles*). A package (covered in Chapter 3) is actually a folder. You can view the folder's contents by choosing Show Package Contents from the contextual menu that appears when you Control-click the application's icon. If Show Package Contents does not appear, the application is not a package.

Note: Most Open dialogs, as well as the Finder itself, will not allow you to navigate inside packages. This is consistent with maintaining the illusion that a package is really a single application file. The Show Package Contents option is the main way to access these files. Exceptions are Bare Bones' BBEdit and TextWrangler applications, which include an Open Hidden command that allows you to navigate to almost every location on your drive, including inside a package.

The .app extension. Package applications have an .app extension. The Finder keeps this extension invisible unless you select the Finder preference to show all file extensions. The other way to confirm that the extension exists is via the Name & Extension pane of the Get Info window. If you do this for the Mail application, for example, you will see that its real name is Mail.app.

Figure 6.13

The Get Info window for the Mail application, showing that its true name is Mail.app.

If you were to eliminate the .app extension via the Get Info window, the Finder would change the application to a folder, which also means that the "application" would no longer launch. Clearly, you would not ordinarily want to do this. Fortunately, if you add the extension back, the folder reverts to an application, its icon returns, and it will launch properly when you double-click it.

Note: Turning a folder into a functioning .app package by adding the .app extension works only if the folder already contains the elements it needs to function as an application: the Contents folder with the .plist files, and so on. Thus, simply adding an .app extension to a folder with several Word documents in it will not turn the folder into a functioning application. I assume this is obvious, but you never know.

Applications as folders. Occasionally, applications may appear as folders rather than applications, even though you made no apparent change to cause this. If this problem occurs, you usually can fix it by deleting the relevant preferences and/or cache files. Another possible fix—if only a single application is affected—is to reinstall the offending application.

SEE: • "Take Note: Launch Services Files and Beyond," earlier in this chapter.

If that fails to work, you will likely need to create a new User account for yourself or completely reinstall Mac OS X.

The application is in the "application." The fact that the .app file is really a folder implies that the actual application that launches when you double-click an .app file is contained within the folder/package. This is true. In fact, sometimes more than one application is contained in the folder.

The folder may have two versions of the same application (such as Classic and Mac OS X versions, as with AppleWorks). In such cases, you may want to occasionally launch an application directly from within the package, rather than by double-clicking the package file itself.

SEE: • "Take Note: Application Packages Containing Two Application Versions," in the online Classic chapter, available at Mac OS X Help Line (www.macosxhelpline.com), for an example.

  • "Take Note: Opening Mac OS Applications from Terminal," in Chapter 10, for related information.

In other cases, there may be a secondary "helper" application inside the package with the main application. If you were to want to directly launch such applications (which you should rarely need to do), you would have to delve inside the .app package to do so. Once inside, double-click the application to launch it.

For details of a rare case where helper-type applications may not launch, check out this Apple Knowledge Base article: http://docs.info.apple.com/article.html?artnum=107672.

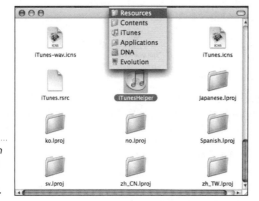

Figure 6.14

The hidden location of the iTunesHelper application inside the iTunes package.

.app files and installing Mac OS X updates. Suppose you decide to move the Mail application in the /Applications folder to your Desktop. If a Mac OS X update comes out and you run the updater, an updated version of Mail will be installed with the updated OS. Will the Installer locate the Mail application at its new location? Or will it have problems because the application is not in its default location, where the Installer expected it to be?

The answer is mixed. In older versions of Mac OS X, this was a significant problem. Starting in Mac OS X 10.2, however, as noted in Chapter 3, Apple claims to have fixed it—that is, the Installer will search for the application wherever it may be on your drive. Despite Apple's assurances, though, I've seen instances where problems still occur.

What happens if things go wrong? The application will likely not get updated properly. In particular, if only some of the files in the application package are being updated, and only those files are included in the Mac OS X update, those files—and only those files—will be placed in the /Applications folder, where the Installer expected to find the old version of the application. The old version of the application, located wherever you moved it, remains untouched. Thus, you wind up with a non-updated version of the application and a partially updated version that doesn't work. What are your options? You can choose from the following:

- You can delete the partially updated application, move the original Mail.app application back into the /Applications folder, and attempt to reinstall the update. Occasionally, however, this method doesn't work: The updater refuses to run because it believes the update has already been installed. If this happens, you can try to work around it by fooling the Installer into running (as described in Chapter 3). Or you can downgrade to a version of Mac OS X that you can install, and then re-update from there.

- You can open the packages of both the updated/partial and old/complete Mail.apps. Copy the new files from the updated application to the old one. Now you should have a complete application that will work.

- In some cases, the updater may contain a complete copy of the application, but the installation messed up something anyway. In this case, you can simply extract the complete .app application from the update package file. The easiest way to do this is via the shareware utility Pacifist (by CharlesSoft; www.charlessoft.com), which lists all files contained in an update package file and lets you extract the one(s) you want. However, be aware that many Mac OS X update packages, especially ones obtained via the Software Update application, may not contain a complete version of included applications. Extracting and using such "applications" via Pacifist will cause more problems than it solves!

  SEE: • Chapter 3 for more information on fooling the Installer, selective reinstallations, and using Pacifist.

- As a last resort, you can completely reinstall Mac OS X, with or without erasing your hard drive.

Wrong or damaged version of application. An application may fail to open on launch. There may be no error message; instead, its Dock icon bounces a few times and then stops without the application opening. In such cases, you typically do not even get the "unexpectedly quit" error. There are several reasons why this could happen:

- Extending what we covered in the previous section (".app files and installing Mac OS X updates"), this could happen due to an incompatibility between the version of the application and the version of Mac OS X in use. For example, after you do a downgrade reinstall of Mac OS X using the Archive and Install option, you may wind up with two versions of the same application on your drive. When you double-click a document, it may attempt to launch the newer version of an Apple application (still on your drive in the Previous Systems folder) instead of the version that was installed with the downgrade of Mac OS X. If the newer version of the application is incompatible with the older version of the OS, the failure occurs.

- Conversely, an older program may crash on launch because it is not compatible with a newer version of Mac OS X that you have installed.

- If a file is removed from the application's package, or if such a file gets corrupted, the same symptom may result. In some cases, you may get an error that states that the application is "damaged or incomplete."

- An incorrect permission setting for a file within the application package could also cause this failure.

The latter two causes might especially occur after an attempt to copy or move the application (as covered in the next two and in later sections of this chapter). Potential solutions vary with the precise cause, but include the following: reinstalling the application, updating Mac OS X or the application so that their versions match; deleting the incorrectly launching version of the application;

launching the desired version of the application before double-clicking the document icon; dragging the document to the icon of the desired version of the application; using Disk Utility to repair permissions.

SEE: • "Application quits," in Chapter 5, especially "Do you have multiple versions of the same application on your drive?" for related information.

• "Document opens in the 'wrong' application," earlier in this chapter, for more advice.

• "Technically Speaking: How Mac OS X Selects a Document or Application Match," earlier in this chapter, for related information.

Application must be in required folder. Some applications will not launch unless they remain in the folder where they were first installed. In rare cases, the application will work only if it's installed in a specific folder, most often the /Applications folder. In such cases, the read-me file for the software, or its installer utility, should inform you of this. But it may not.

Can't open a copy of an application. If you Option-drag an application package to another folder on the same volume or drag it to a new volume, the Finder creates a copy of the application. Similarly, pressing Command-D makes a duplicate of the file. Ideally, in all these cases the resulting application should launch and run identically to the original. Problems occasionally occur, however.

SEE: • "SetUID attribute and the 'Items could not be copied' error," later in this chapter, for details on these problems.

• Chapter 5 for more information on what to do if a file crashes on launch.

Applications that require a serial number. Some applications will not launch until you enter the serial number assigned when you purchased the application. In certain cases, the application may not be able to locate the serial number information, even after it has been correctly entered, for users other than the user who installed the software and/or administrative users. This is because the serial number information is stored either in the wrong location (for example, in a user's home directory rather than in a location accessible by other users) or in a folder with restricted permissions (so that non-administrative users cannot access it). Exactly what to do to fix this varies by incident: Check with the software's vendor or Web sites like MacFixIt for advice about a given application.

Background applications. Some applications open in the background—which means their icons don't appear in the Dock when they're running, nor will they show up in most other application-switching utilities. You need a utility such as Activity Monitor to see that the application is open at all. Some login items work this way. If you come across one of these applications and double-click it, the application may not appear to launch. This is normal; it really has launched or is already running. But if you're concerned, check Activity Monitor to verify.

SEE: • "Technically Speaking: Type/Creator vs. Filename Extensions vs. Others," in Chapter 4, for more on Info.plist files and background applications.

Application will not open in more than one account. If you enabled Fast User Switching (as first described in Chapter 2), you may not be able to open an application that's already been opened by another logged-in user. Of special note is the fact that you can launch Classic for only one user at a time.

The easiest solution here is to have the other user quit the needed application. However, if that's not possible and you're an admin user, you can quit the application yourself via Activity Monitor. To do so, from Activity Monitor's pop-up menu choose Other User Processes, and then select the application name from the list. Now, from the Process menu select Quit. (Note that any unsaved changes the other user has in that application will be lost.) If all else fails, you can quit the loginwindow process for the other user: This instantly logs out the other user—not a very friendly thing to do, though, since any unsaved changes in any application that user is running will be lost.

Opening .app files from within Terminal. Sometimes, if you're having problems launching an application from the Finder, you may have success by using Terminal.

SEE: • "Take Note: Opening Mac OS Applications from Terminal," in Chapter 10, for details.

Delete preferences/repair/reinstall. For almost any other problems involving opening applications, it's a good idea to quit the application (if it's running) and then locate its .plist file (by entering the name of the application in the Search field of the ~/Library/Preferences window) and delete the file.

Actually, it's safer to rename the preferences file (such as to *name*.plist.old) than to delete it immediately. A new default copy will still be created when you launch the application. If it turns out that this fixes the problem, you can go ahead and delete the old file. Otherwise, delete the newly created file and rename the .old file back to its original name. (This way, you don't lose your preferences unnecessarily.)

If this doesn't work, try repairing disk permissions via Disk Utility's First Aid pane. Your next step should be to remove all traces of the application and its preference and support files, and then reinstall the application altogether. If even this fails, you will probably need to create a new User account for yourself and delete the old account (after transferring files you want to save).

Microsoft Word advice. If Microsoft Word crashes on launch, Microsoft advises that you do the following:

1. Move the file named Normal from the Templates folder in the Microsoft Office folder to your Desktop.

2. Remove all files from the Microsoft Office/Office/Startup/Word folder. (Note: The Microsoft Office folder will be wherever you installed it, most likely in /Applications.)

3. Restart Word.

4. If the problem persists, delete com.microsoft.Word.plist and the entire Microsoft folder from the ~/Library/Preferences folder in your home directory.

   SEE: • **"Preferences Files," in Chapter 4, for related information.**

   • **"Techniques for Solving Mac OS X Crashes" and "Deleting or removing preferences," in Chapter 5.**

   • **Chapter 8 for details on creating a replacement account for yourself.**

Losing track of saved files

When you're choosing Save (for a new file) or Save As, and you let the application select the location in which to save the file, be sure to note the name of the destination folder. The location will often be the Documents folder but can also be something else.

If the file was not saved in the location you expected, you may have trouble locating it later should you want to move, delete, or reopen it. If this happens, use Spotlight or the Finder's Find command to track it down.

Note: If you have multiple partitions or volumes mounted, be careful when you save a file to the Desktop. If the application is located on a non-startup volume, the document may be saved to the Desktop folder of that partition rather than to the Desktop folder in your home directory. In this case, the file will not appear on your Desktop. The solution is to open the non-startup volume's root window, locate the folder called Desktop Folder (or Desktop), and open it. The file will be in there.

SEE: • **"File does not appear after being moved," later in this chapter, for related information.**

Copying and Moving: Copying vs. Moving vs. Duplicating Files

In this section, I cover the details on how to copy and move items in Mac OS X.

The basics

The primary ways to move a file from one location to another on your Mac include the following:

• **Copy via drag and drop.** Copying, as its name implies, places a copy of the original item in the new location while leaving the original item intact in its original location.

If you want to make a copy of an item on a *different* volume or partition than the original, the simplest way is to drag its icon to the new location.

If you want to copy an item to a new location on the same volume, Option-dragging the icon copies it to the new location. (If you don't hold down the Option key, you simply move the item instead.)

When dragging an item to a folder, if you continue to click-hold, the folder will "spring" open. This allows you to continue to navigate to a folder within the folder, until you get to your desired destination.

When dragging a file to be moved or copied, the pointer changes to reflect the status of the operation. If the copy/move can be completed successfully at the pointer location, a plus (+) symbol appears next to the pointer. If not, a prohibitory symbol appears.

- **Copy via Copy {*name of item*}.** If you highlight an item in the Finder and from the Finder's Edit menu choose Copy {*name of item*}, you've "copied" the entire item (document, application, or folder) to the clipboard. You can now go to any other location on any volume and choose Paste. (The command in the Edit menu will now read *Paste Item* rather than just *Paste*.)

Choosing Paste Item copies the item to the new location—more convenient than drag and drop if the destination location is nested within several folders.

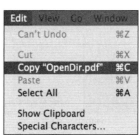

Figure 6.15

The Copy {name of item} command.

The Copy Item and Paste Item options are also available via contextual menus. Thus, if you Control-click an item, a Copy {*name of item*} command will appear. If you choose this item, you can then Control-click the destination location and choose Paste Item from the contextual menu.

- **Duplicate.** This command is almost the same as Copy, except that the copy is created in the same location as the original and assigned a new name. To make a duplicate, select a file in the Finder and from the Finder's File menu choose Duplicate (Command-D). The copy of the file will have the word *copy* appended to its name.

- **Move.** This command moves the item to the new location (without retaining a copy in its original location).

To move an item to a different location on the same volume, drag the item to its intended location.

To move, rather than copy, an item to a different volume, you can Command-drag the item. A word of caution, though: If the move fails, the OS may delete the original without creating the copy, leaving you with no file. For this reason, if you get an error message when using Command-drag, choose Stop rather than Continue. Or, to be even safer, avoid this feature and just copy the file. Then delete the original after you know that the copy was made successfully.

TAKE NOTE ▶ Copying from Within a Document

In the main text, I cover copying and moving items in the Finder. Just for the record, I review here the basics of copying and pasting selections within a document:

Copy and paste. From within most documents (for example, those created in word-processing programs), you can highlight a portion of text or a graphic image, and copy it (by choosing Copy from the Edit menu or pressing Command-C). This places the text or image on the clipboard (which you can view by choosing Show Clipboard from the Finder's Edit menu). If you now click elsewhere in the document, or in another document altogether, and choose Paste from the Edit menu (or Command-V), the selected content will be pasted into the new location.

Using Cut instead of Copy is the equivalent of moving the content rather than copying it.

Clippings files. In many applications, you can drag and drop selected content from a document to the Finder (such as to the Desktop). What happens when you do this depends on the nature of the content. Here are three common examples:

- With general text, you create a text clipping. Double-click the clipping to directly view the text in a window, independent of any separate text application. For applications that support clippings, you can paste the content of a clipping by dragging it to a document window.

- If the item is a graphic, you will create a graphic clipping file that works similarly.

- If the text is a URL (such as from the Address bar of a Web browser), you create an Internet Location file. It will have a different icon than a text clipping. If you double-click this Location file, the URL will open in your default Web browser.

    SEE: • "Take Note: Location Files and Browser Links," in Chapter 9, for related information.

Beyond the basics

Beyond the basics, you should know several additional variations on the theme:

Copy/replace. When you attempt to move or copy a file to a location where a file of the same name already exists, you typically get an alert message warning you that the action will replace the existing file—in essence deleting it. Be careful about clicking OK. If the files have different content, you could erase something you wanted to save.

If you're replacing a single item, the message will tell you whether the file you are about to delete is older or newer than the file you are moving. This can help you decide whether you really want to make the replacement. For example, if you were trying to synchronize two locations so that both have the latest version of a file, you would not want to replace a newer version with an older one.

In some cases, such as when you're downloading files from the Internet, rather than offering to replace a file with the same name, the Internet software may instead append an extension to the duplicate file so that both files are saved.

Thus, if you download the file CoolApp twice to the same location, the second download will likely have the name CoolApp.1.

Move results in a copy. If you attempt to move a file from a folder where you don't have sufficient permission to modify the folder contents, dragging the file typically results in a copy being placed at the new location rather than the file being moved. The original file remains intact, even if that was not your intention. Typically, no error message will appear. In some situations, the copy may fail completely, and an error message will appear.

SEE: • "Copying and Moving: Permissions Problems," later in this chapter, for more details.

Copy results in an alias. When you drag the icon of one volume to another or drag a mounted disk-image icon to a folder on a hard drive, an alias of the original volume is created rather than a copy. This is not an error. Mac OS X assumes that when you drag a disk image or a volume to a new location, you want to create an alias of it. You rarely would copy these typically large volumes except for backup purposes.

 If you truly want to copy the actual volume contents, select the volume and choose the Copy Item command, followed by the Paste Item command, from the Finder's Edit menu, as explained in the preceding section; Option-drag the volume; or open the window for the originating volume, choose Select All from the Edit menu, and then drag the selected files to the new location.

Actually, to make a true backup of a volume, you would be better off using a backup utility, as noted in the next section.

SEE: • "Aliases vs. symbolic links," later in this chapter, for more information.

Move to Trash. The other common variation of moving of a file is moving the file to the Trash. This special case deserves a section of its own, which you'll find later in this chapter.

Copying to back up

Backing up your entire hard drive, or at least the most critical files on your drive, is a form of copying. If you're wise, you'll regularly do this. Backing up provides protection against software or hardware damage that could result in the loss of the contents of your drive. Backing up a drive in Mac OS X—especially if you want to make a backup that can restore a volume, including making it bootable—presents some challenges. I cover this important topic in Chapter 3.

SEE: • "Backing Up and Restoring Mac OS X Volumes," in Chapter 3, for coverage of this issue.

Copying and Moving: Problems Copying and Moving Files

This section covers the problems that can occur when you attempt to copy, move, or duplicate an item.

SEE: • "Copying and Moving: Permissions Problems," later in this chapter, for coverage of problems related to ownership and permissions settings.

Insufficient space

If you try to copy a large file to a volume that has less free space than the size of the file, you will be unable to do so. Not a surprise.

The solution is to delete unneeded files from the destination volume in order to free up space. Alternatively, you could move the unneeded files to a volume with more free space.

Occasionally, a volume may seem to have less space than you expected, based on the files you installed. This usually occurs because an OS-related file (sometimes an invisible one) is taking up more than the usual amount of space. Examples include the Console log files. If these files are not "cleaned up" periodically, or if a recurring error is filling them rapidly, they can become very large. Microsoft Internet Explorer cache files can also become quite large.

The simplest solution is to locate the files and delete them. You can use Spotlight (via the Finder's Find command) to search for files by size. This technique will help you spot unexpectedly large files. (Note: Unfortunately, some large files may be invisible or located in folders that Spotlight does not search. There are ways to work around this, if needed, as discussed in the "Spotlight" section of Chapter 2.)

The swap files used by virtual memory are yet another example of large files on your Mac. To delete swap files, restart your Mac.

SEE: • "Spotlight," in Chapter 2, for more on this feature.
• "Technically Speaking: Dividing Up Mac OS X's memory," in Chapter 4.
• "Technically Speaking: Log Files and cron Jobs," in Chapter 4, and "Application quits," in Chapter 5, for more information on Console.
• "Technically Speaking: Swap Files and RAM Disks," later in this chapter.

File is corrupt

Sometimes you will be unable to copy a file because the file is corrupted and the Finder is unable to read the file's contents. In general, your best bet is to delete the file and start over with a fresh download, backup copy, or new document.

If you absolutely need to recover the information in the file, you can try opening it in its creating application (such as Microsoft Word for a Word document), and then copying what you can to a new document and saving the new document. In other cases, a text editor such as BBEdit may allow you to at least view the text within the document, allowing you to save it even if nothing else can be saved. A third-party utility, such as Echo One's File Juicer, may allow you to extract/recover critical data.

Otherwise, attempting disk repairs (such as with Disk Utility) may recover the item, or you can restore a copy from a backup. Barring that, give up on the file and delete it.

SEE: • "Opening and Saving: Problems Opening and Saving Files," earlier in this chapter, for related advice.

File does not appear after being moved

Occasionally, when you're copying a file, especially to the Desktop, the file may not appear at the location once the copy is complete. This situation most often occurs when you're decompressing a file from an archive or downloading a file from the Internet, or when the file is being moved or created from an application other than the Finder itself.

Figure 6.16

The magnifying-glass button in Safari's Downloads window; click it to reveal the downloaded item in the Finder.

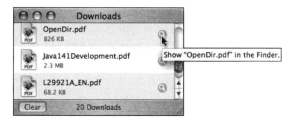

In almost all cases, the file is there; the Finder just hasn't been updated to reveal it. You need to give the Finder a bit of a push. Happily, Apple has addressed this issue in Tiger. So you should rarely, if ever, be bothered by it anymore.

But if you do find you need to give a push, locating the file with Spotlight and double-clicking the filename in the search-results window usually forces the Finder to update and show the file. Often, just typing the first letter of the filename, while you're on the Desktop (assuming the file is on the Desktop), is sufficient to get the file to appear.

For files that don't appear after being downloaded from Safari, you should be able see the file by clicking the magnifying-glass button next to the name of the file in Safari's Downloads window.

More generally, you may be able to take advantage of the fact that your Desktop is simply a folder in your home directory to reveal the new file. Open a new Finder window and navigate to ~/Desktop; when you open the Desktop folder, you'll most likely find the document inside, even if it isn't showing up "on" the Desktop.

As a last resort, choose Force Quit and reload the Finder. This procedure should always get the file to appear.

One related possibility, for files "saved to" or "copied to" the Desktop, is that the file was copied to a Desktop other than your Mac OS X Desktop. The file may have been copied to a Mac OS 9 Desktop that resides on the same volume as Mac OS X, for example. In this case, double-click the Desktop (Mac OS 9) icon that should be on your Mac OS X Desktop if Mac OS 9 and Mac OS X are on the same volume. When Mac OS 9 is on a separate volume, simply open the Desktop folder on the Mac OS 9 volume. You'll find the missing file there.

Opening and Saving: Permissions Problems

Some files will not open or will refuse to be saved (after being modified) because you do not have sufficient permissions to perform that action. If you try, you get an error message to that effect. Permissions settings here refer to the Ownership and Access settings as viewed and modified in the Ownership & Permissions section of the item's Get Info window. Similar (and more frequent) problems can occur when attempting to copy or move a file (which I cover in detail in "Copying and Moving: Permissions Problems," later in this chapter).

SEE: • "Ownership & Permissions," in Chapter 4, for background information.
 • "Unix: Modifying Permissions," in Chapter 10, for background information.

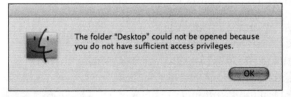
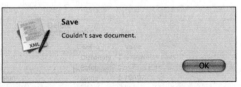

Figure 6.17

Left, the permissions-related error message that appears when you try to open another user's Desktop folder in the Finder; right, the message that appears when you try to save a document owned by the root user.

Examples of permissions-related problems

The following are some examples of the permissions problems that can occur when opening and saving files.

Can't access secondary folder or file. If launching an application requires accessing files or folders beyond the application itself, such as a preferences file or a file elsewhere on your hard drive, you may not be able to launch the application if you do not have permission to access the required additional folder or file.

In one example of this, a user was unable to launch iTunes, getting an "insufficient permissions" error when she tried. There didn't seem to be a problem with the permissions settings for iTunes itself, so I looked elsewhere. I found the answer in the iTunes folder located in the Documents folder of the user's home directory. Somehow, the owner of that folder was listed as the user's son (who also had an account on the system).

A similar situation may occur when you're trying to install an update to an application on your drive. I know of a case in which the owner of the Adobe folder located in /Library/Application Support was somehow changed to "unknown." This change prevented the successful update of an Adobe application that needed to access this folder but did not have permission to do so. The solution was to change the owner of the Adobe folder to System or to the name of the administrator trying to install the software.

No-entry folders. More generally, certain folders on your drive will have a small no-entry (prohibitory) icon in the lower right corner of their folder icon. These include most of the folders that reside in the home directory of any user other than you. There are also folders in the Unix directories that include this icon. For example, use the Go to Folder command to go to the /var directory. There you will see at least two no-entry folders: "backups" and "root." If you try to open these folders, you will be told you do not have sufficient privileges/permissions to do so. If you view the Get Info window for these folders, you will see that you do not own them and that Group and Others access is set to No Access. If you know that one of these folders includes a document you want to open, you will not be able to do so directly.

SEE: • "Accessing other users' folders," later in this chapter, for details on solutions to this problem.

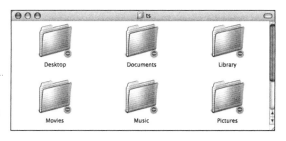

Figure 6.18

No-entry icons as seen on the folders for a user other than the logged-in user.

Document is owned by root. Most of the documents used by system software, including the vast majority of the files in the /System/Library folder and all of the files in the invisible Unix folders (such as the /etc directory), are owned by the root (System) user. As an administrator, you typically have "Read only" access to these files. This means you can open them and view their contents. But if you try to make any changes to them, you will get an error when you try to save those changes.

You would have a similar problem opening a file owned by any other user; however, the root user problem is more common.

Item access set to No Access. Virtually all applications should have access assigned to Everyone (as set in the Ownership & Permissions section of the file's Get Info window) of at least "Read only." This access is the minimum level of access needed to launch the application. If the permissions setting for Others is No Access, you may not be able to launch the application, especially if you are not an administrator. If you find this to be the case, you need to change the Others access to "Read only."

Problems for "standard" users. There are certain problems that can occur when opening files that occur only if you're a standard (non-administrative) user. In one example I know of, an application kept asking if I wanted to register online every time it was opened. This happened even though it was supposed to show this message only on its initial launch. The cause was that the preferences file for this application, where the application kept track of whether or not this was an initial launch, was in the /Library/Preferences folder, and non-administrative users cannot modify files in this folder. Thus, when the application was launched by a standard user, the file was never changed to indicate that an initial launch had occurred.

In another example, a standard user could not launch an application at all because its permissions had been set so that only administrative users could access it.

Sometimes, the solution to this type of problem will require a fix from the application vendor (changing the application to use a preferences file in the ~/Library/Preferences folder, for example). In other cases, having an administrative user launch the application once will be sufficient. Otherwise, you will need to use solutions as described in the next sections.

Cannot open files in your Drop Box. In some cases, you may be unable to open or edit a file in your Drop Box. This can be avoided if the person dragging the file to your Drop Box holds down the Option key while dragging. Otherwise, you will need to modify the file's permissions, as described in the following sections.

Using Get Info: Basics

To solve most of the above-described problems, you must modify the settings in the Ownership & Permissions section of the Get Info window for the relevant item. If, for example, the problem is a file or folder that you can't access, you need to (a) change the owner of the item to yourself, and/or (b) change Access settings (such as changing the Others access from No Access to "Read only"). You need to be an administrative user to do all this. Here are the steps to follow:

1. Select the file or folder and open its Get Info window (Command-I).

2. Go to the Ownership & Permissions section.

3. Click the padlock and enter your password when requested, to unlock access to the settings. (It's possible that you may not be prompted for your password until after you attempt to make a change.)

4. Change the Owner from whomever it is (probably System) to your own account name.

5. If you also want to change the Group name or modify any Access settings, do so via the pop-up menus that are now accessible.

6. When you've finished making your changes, close the Get Info window.

Figure 6.19

The Ownership & Permissions settings of iPhoto (located in the /Applications folder), as viewed from the Get Info window.

Once you've changed its ownership, you can now open a prohibited folder by double-clicking it from the Finder—even if the no-entry icon is still present. You will similarly be able to open documents or launch applications that you could not open or launch before.

Note: At least as of Mac OS X 10.4.2, there is a bug in Tiger such that, when you are changing the owner of a file in the System folder from System to yourself, the change will appear not to take. That is, after you close and reopen the Get Info window, the owner will have reverted to System. However, if you log out and log back in to your account, you will find that the owner has indeed changed!

Ownership of file vs. enclosing folder. Occasionally, you may not be able to save a file even though you have Read & Write access to the file. There is a two-part explanation for this: (1) You do not have write access to the folder that contains the file, and (2) the application that saves the file creates a "temporary" version of the document as part of the Save process. The result is that the temporary file cannot be created because you do not have permission to modify the contents of the folder. To solve this, you would either have to log in as root or temporarily change ownership of the folder to yourself via Get Info.

Using Get Info: Concerns and caveats

There are caveats you should bear in mind when using, or considering using, Get Info to change permissions:

When changes should be temporary. Unless you're correcting an erroneous permission setting, any changes you make to files or folders in the System or Unix directories should be temporary. To ensure that Mac OS X can access the software when needed, return permissions to their original state when you are done.

Thus, if you change the owner of a folder from System to yourself (in order to access a file in that folder), change it back to System when you're finished.

To avoid problems, a simpler solution may be to temporarily log in as the root user. You can now access the needed files without having to change their permissions—which means you don't need to worry about changing them back correctly.

When changes should be permanent. For other cases, such as the iTunes folder example above, you probably want to make the change permanent. In some of these cases, you may also want to change the access permissions for Group and Others. For example, if the access for Group and Others is set to No Access, you may want to change it to "Read only" or Read & Write, if you want other users beside yourself to have access to these files.

Batch changes. In some cases—again, using the iTunes example above—the problem may go beyond the permissions settings of the folder itself. The same permissions issue may exist for all files and folders *within* the initial folder. In this case, a potential solution is to click the "Apply to enclosed items" button at the bottom of the Ownership & Permissions section of the Get Info window for the folder. However, while this will change Access settings, it will not change the name of the owner or group. So this may still not solve your problem.

One solution is to open the folder, select All (Command-A), and then open the Get Info via the Inspector option (Command-Option-I). This opens a batch version of the Get Info window so that any changes you make will affect all of the selected items. (Note: If you use Command-I in Tiger for ten or fewer items, you will get a separate Get Info window for each, rather than one batch window; however, if you select more than ten items, you will get a batch window.)

Even this may not work, however, if there are subfolders within the folder: Ownership of items in the subfolders will not be properly updated.

In the end, a simpler solution may be to use a shareware utility, such as Arbysoft's BatChmod (http://macchampion.com/arbysoft) or Gideon Softworks' FileXaminer, that allows you to make changes, including nested ownership changes, in batch mode.

You can also make batch changes via the Unix chmod and chown commands in Terminal (as described in Chapter 10).

Alternatives to Get Info

To open, modify, and save documents owned by root, I recommend considering an application such as Bare Bones Software's TextWrangler (or its big brother BBEdit). It includes an option to open files that you would otherwise not have permission to access (assuming you're an administrator; you'll be prompted for your admin-level password to make changes).

Alternatively, you can use the Pseudo utility, from Brain R. Hill (http://personalpages.tds.net/~brian_hill/pseudo.html), to open any application with root access. To do so, drag the application icon to the Pseudo icon and provide your password when prompted. If you do this for a text editor, such as TextEdit or TextWrangler, you can then modify any document you open within the application.

SEE: • "Get Info" and "Root Access," in Chapter 4, and "Modifying invisible Unix files from Mac OS X applications," later in this chapter, for more background.

Repair Disk Permissions

If you believe that at least some of the permissions settings for files and/or folders in the essential Mac OS X directories (such as the System directory) are not correct, rather than trying to fix them yourself (assuming you even know exactly what to fix), go to the First Aid pane of Disk Utility and click Repair Disk Permissions. Only if this does not fix the problem will you need to use Get Info.

SEE: • "Performing repairs with Disk Utility (First Aid)," in Chapter 5, for more on Repair Disk Permissions.

Figure 6.20

The Ownership & Permissions settings of iPhoto (located in the /Applications folder) as viewed from XRay.

TAKE NOTE ▶ A Primer on Ownership and Access

The following is an overview of how different ownership and access settings (as viewed in Get Info windows) affect your ability to copy, move, delete, and open items.

Default permissions settings. Files and folders in different locations have different default permissions. For example, items in the System folder have different permissions than items in the Applications folder, which in turn have different permissions than items in your home directory. As one example, here are the default permissions for items initially installed in the Applications folder (as displayed in the Get Info window):

- Owner: system
- Owner access: Read & Write
- Group: admin
- Group access: Read & Write
- Other access: Read only

Because you (as an administrative user) are a member of the admin group, the access listed at the top of the section for "You can" is also Read & Write.

As displayed in XRay:

- Owner and Group: Read, Write, and Search (Execute, if a file instead of a folder) all enabled
- World: Read and Search (Execute, if a file instead of a folder) enabled
- Owner is "root (System Administrator)"
- Group is "admin"

Settings viewed in Terminal are essentially the same as those seen in XRay.

Item access. To view the contents of a file, you must have at least Read Only access to it. The access can be in any category (Owner, Group, or Others), as long as you belong to that category. (For example, if you are a member of the listed group and the group has Read Only access, you can view the contents of the file—even if Others has No Access and you do not own the file.)

To edit a file (such as to change the contents of a word-processing document), you must have Read & Write access for that file. If you have such access, you can modify the file even if you are limited to "Read only" access to the folder that contains the file. This is because to Mac OS X, changing a file's contents does not modify the folder's contents.

Enclosing folder access. To move items from one folder to another, you need Read & Write access for each folder whose contents will be modified. This is because you must be able to both view the contents of the original folder (Read) and modify its contents (Write). You also need Write or Read & Write access to the destination folder. If you want to copy a file to another folder, you need at least "Read only" access to the original folder, and either Read & Write access or "Write only" access to the destination folder. (With just Write access, you can add items to a folder but not view the contents.)

continues on next page

TAKE NOTE ▶ **A Primer on Ownership and Access** *continued*

Note that folder and file permissions are independent of one another. You can move an item to and from a folder even if you don't own the item and have only "Read only" access to it (or even No Access), as long as you have Read & Write access to the folder that contains the item. This means, for example, that you could move a file that you do not own and for which you have no "access" to the Trash—as long as it's located in a folder for which you do have access.

Unix directories. If you found the previous section confusing, you may find it helpful to look at how Unix conceptualizes directories, because Mac OS X bases its own behavior on these Unix concepts.

In Unix, a directory is not really a folder in the way that a folder appears in the Finder—that is, a Unix directory is not a container but rather simply another file that lists the contents of what's considered to be in that directory. Thus, the permissions settings for a directory only determine the extent to which you can modify the listing, not your ability to modify the files themselves. The latter capability is determined by the permissions set for each file. In other words, a lack of read access for a directory means you can't read the directory listing. It does not mean you cannot read the contents of files within the directory. Nor does it mean that you cannot change the contents of the listing (a lack of write access would mean this).

Administrator access. Administrators, because they are members of the admin group, have more access to files and folders than non-administrative users. This is the reason why non-administrative users cannot move files into or out of the Applications folder, while administrative users can—the Applications folder is owned by System, with the admin group having Read & Write access while Others have "Read only" access.

The reason why you cannot easily move things in and out of the System folder, even as an administrator, is that the group assignment is "wheel" (with "Read only" access). Admin users are not members of the wheel group in Tiger (and would have only read access even if they were members).

Of course, as an administrator, you can still change any of these access settings by unlocking the padlock in the Get Info window.

Ownership of moved files vs. copied files. When an item is moved, it generally maintains its permissions. For example, an application in the Applications folder is owned by System. If you move it to your Desktop, it is still owned by System.

In contrast, when an item is copied, it generally adopts the default permissions of its destination location.

For example, if you copy an application from the Applications folder to your Desktop, you now own the copy. Similarly, if you copy a file (owned by System and with wheel as the Group) from the System folder to your Desktop, you become the owner of the copy, and all categories will have Read & Write access.

continues on next page

An important implication of this copy versus move principle is that if you *copy* a file from Applications, for example, and then delete the original (in the Applications folder) and *move* the copy back, the item now in the Applications folder will still be owned by you instead of by System (its original owner). If some later access to this application requires that it have its original owner (System), you will have problems. For example, you could wind up with an application in the Applications folder that has permissions preventing non-administrative users from launching it.

Beware!
Beware!

Conversely, if you *copy* a file you own from your home directory to the Applications folder, its owner *may* change to System. You would thus no longer be the owner of the file you just copied. However, in some cases of this situation, the file will be retained with yourself as owner.

Creating new files. When you create a new file (for example, via an application's Save command) or a new folder (such as via the Finder's Command-Shift-N command), you are assigned the owner of the item by default. The group assignment for the item is typically the same as that of the folder containing the item. Thus, items created in the Applications folder would belong to the admin group.

"Ignore ownership on this volume." On all mounted volumes except the Mac OS X startup volume, the Ownership & Permissions section of the Get Info window includes an "Ignore ownership on this volume" option. If you select this option, it does what its name implies: Anyone will be able to access files on this volume, even if they otherwise would not have the permissions to do so.

SEE: • "Ownership & Permissions," in Chapter 4, for more details, such as how and why you would use the "Ignore ownership" option.

• "Technically Speaking: Group Settings Explained," in Chapter 4, for more background information.

• "Technically Speaking: Access Control Lists and Extended Attributes," in Chapter 10, for related information about ownership of files.

Copying and Moving: Permissions Problems

Permissions issues can cause problems with copying and moving files. The problem can be with either the Access settings or the Ownership, as viewed and modified via Get Info windows.

Examples of permissions-related problems

The following are several examples of problems that can arise when copying and moving files.

Item is copied instead of moved. As mentioned earlier in the chapter, this is a permissions-related problem. The typical reason you can't move the file is that you don't have modify (write) access for the folder that contains it—meaning you can't change the folder's contents by moving a file out of it. If you attempt to move an item from that folder, Mac OS X does the best it can—which means creating a *copy* of it in the destination folder instead. In such cases, no error message appears. This assumes, of course, that you have sufficient access to the destination folder. If not, you cannot even copy to the destination.

As one example of this, you can't move anything out of the Mac OS X System folder—in this instance, a good thing (meaning you typically *should not* try to work around the restriction). Removing items from the System folder is a bad idea—unless you know exactly what you're doing or want to see your Mac crash.

Occasionally, usually due to some bug in an installer package or utility, the ownership of a file or folder may be erroneously modified. In one example, the Applications folder permissions were modified such that even administrators no longer had write access to the folder.

SEE: • "Take Note: A Primer on Ownership and Access," earlier in this chapter, for an important implication of this copy versus move issue.

Item cannot be moved, copied, or replaced. When you try to move or copy certain items, you may get a message that says, "This operation cannot be completed because you do not have sufficient privileges for {*name of item to be moved*}". In this case, the problem is that you do not have sufficient permissions to access the item to be copied or moved. This may happen, for example, if you try to move a folder with a no-entry (prohibitory) icon on it.

When attempting to copy or move certain items, you may get a message that says, "The item {*name of item*} cannot be moved because {*destination location*} cannot be modified." In this case, the likely problem is that you don't have access permissions to modify the destination location.

Such messages were common in older versions of Mac OS X. In Panther and Tiger, however, most of them have been replaced by new authentication messages, as explained in the next section.

Using the Finder's Authenticate dialog

Prior to Panther, solving problems of the sort described in the previous section could be a bit of a hassle, since they often involved modifying an item's permissions settings and then restoring them after you had completed the copy or move.

Starting in Panther, Apple has made dealing with such problems much simpler—perhaps too simple. It's now so easy to circumvent these restrictions that inexperienced users are more likely to move or delete files they shouldn't—

which could lead to serious trouble. If you're confident you know what you're doing, though, these changes represent a big step forward in terms of ease of use.

Exactly what messages you now get—or do not get—when trying to copy or move files in Tiger varies, and it's not always immediately obvious what determines these minor variations. Happily, the overall theme remains the same. The following provides an overview of the types of messages you can expect to see.

Authenticate messages. When you try to delete or move an item to a location for which you do not have permission, you will likely get the following message: "The item {*name of item*} cannot be moved because {*destination location*} cannot be modified." This message box includes two buttons: Authenticate and OK. If you click OK, no action is taken. If you click Authenticate, an Authenticate dialog appears. Here, you're prompted to enter an administrator name and password. If you do so, the selected action (for example, moving the item) takes place.

When you try to move an item from a location for which you *do not* have modify permission to a destination for which you *do* have access, you typically get either the Authenticate dialog immediately or a message warning that leads to the Authenticate dialog if you continue.

The above actions eliminate the need for changes to permissions settings in the Get Info window, use of Terminal, or use of any third-party utility.

Note: Although I am emphasizing Authenticate dialogs in the Finder here, they can and do appear within any application that wants to restrict access.

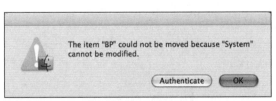

Figure 6.21

Left, *a message that appears when you try to move a file to a location that cannot be modified;* right, *the window that appears (with Details displayed) after you click the message box's Authenticate button.*

Figure 6.22

A message that appeared when I tried to drag a folder from another user's home directory to my Desktop.

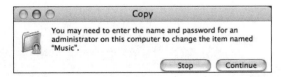

Command-drag to move; Authenticate. If you drag an item to move it from a folder for which you do not have write permission, the item may be copied instead (as previously explained). However, if you Command-drag the item, this forces an attempt to move it—in this case, presenting you with the Authenticate dialog. Again, enter the appropriate admin-level name and password, and the move will occur.

There are a variety of other messages you may get, depending on whether you're trying to move, copy, or replace a file and the specific permissions. In all cases, however, you will ultimately arrive at the Authenticate dialog. This is the key that unlocks all access for you. Only if the Authenticate option does not appear, or does not work, will you need the more tedious alternatives covered in subsequent sections.

Command-drag from the System directory. In Tiger, there is a notable exception to the above generalizations about the effect of a Command-drag. If you Command-drag an item out of most folders in the /System/Library directory, it will be copied instead of moved (just as if you had not held down the Command key). In Panther, this would have resulted in the appearance of the Authenticate dialog, after which the move would succeed. In Tiger, not only does the move not succeed, but you don't even get an alert message informing you of this fact. My guess is that Apple made the change, as a safety precaution, to reduce the odds that a user would inadvertently move items from this location.

The basis for the difference in behavior between Panther and Tiger is in the access for the folders, not for the files themselves. In Tiger, even an administrator is limited to "Read only" access to folders such as CoreServices. In Panther, administrators had Read & Write access to such folders.

If you truly need to move something out of (or into) the System directory in Tiger, you still have ways to do so. You can, for example, temporarily modify the ownership of the folder via the Get Info window for the folder, making yourself the owner. Or you can log in as the root user.

SEE: • "Using Get Info: Basics," and "Using Get Info and beyond," elsewhere in this chapter, for more details.

Note: This problem is likely to crop up when you attempt to remove items from any folder where you do not have write access. You can tell this is the case by checking in the lower right-hand corner of the folder's window. If you do not have write access, there will be a Pencil icon with a line through it.

Oddly, there is an exception to the above exception. If you Command-drag an item from a restricted System folder to the Trash, an Authenticate dialog will appear and you will be able to move, rather than copy, the item.

The grace period. After you enter your password in an Authenticate dialog, you may occasionally find that you no longer need to re-authenticate to perform the same or similar action again for a period of time (typically 5 minutes). However, don't expect to see this happen very often. In the later versions of Panther and in Tiger, almost all of these 5-minute grace periods have been eliminated. Instead, you will have to re-authenticate with each attempt. Again, the rationale here is for security. For example, with the 5-minute grace period, any user with access to your computer would have 5 minutes of access to otherwise password-protected actions.

Still, if you would like to avoid repeated Authenticate dialogs, you do have some options. For modifying secure System Preferences panes, for example, you can go to the Security pane and uncheck the box for "Require password to unlock each secure system preference." More generally, if you are willing to sacrifice security for convenience, and are technically up to the task, you can modify the underlying authorization software that determines whether or not you have a grace period.

SEE: • "Technically Speaking: Authorization Services," below, for more details.

TECHNICALLY SPEAKING ▶ Authorization Services

To be clear: When you authenticate in the Finder, as described in the main text, you are not invoking Unix's su or sudo command (as covered in Chapter 10), nor are you running as the root user (as covered in Chapter 4). Despite some similarities, this Authenticate window uses an entirely separate and independent Mac OS X feature. The details of how it all works are explained in documents available from Apple's Developer site. See especially "Security Overview" (http://developer.apple.com/documentation/Security/Conceptual/Security_Overview) and "Performing Privileged Operations with Authorization Services" (http://developer.apple.com/documentation/Security/Conceptual/authorization_concepts/index.html). What follows are some key points regarding Authorization Services, especially as they apply to the Authenticate feature in the Finder.

Note: There are a few exceptions to this rule—when some third-party applications ask you to authenticate, they may be accessing the Unix sudo command instead of what's described here.

Authenticate vs. authorize. Users are often confused by the difference between authenticate and authorize. *Authenticate* means to prove you are who you say you are. For example, I need to enter my password to prove I am really Ted Landau. Authentication is typically determined via settings in the Authentication pane of Directory Access (as covered briefly in Chapter 4). *Authorize* refers to the rights I have after I have authenticated. That is, even after I prove I am really Ted Landau (and an administrator), I may still not be authorized to remove a file from the System folder. It is the /etc/authorization file that determines these rights.

continues on next page

TECHNICALLY SPEAKING ▶ Authorization Services *continued*

The Details section of an Authenticate window. Clicking the Details disclosure triangle in an Authenticate window (that appears while in the Finder) reveals the following two lines:

```
Requested right: com.apple.desktopservices
Application: Finder
```

The word *Finder* is actually a button. If you click-hold the button, or click the triangle that appears when you move the pointer over the button, a pop-up menu appears listing all the folders in the hierarchy, from the file's location to the root level of the drive. Select a folder to open it in a Finder window.

The Authenticate window also appears in other applications and situations. Exactly what is shown in the Details section varies depending upon the situation. For example, if you try to make a restricted change in the Finder's Get Info window, the Finder is once again listed as the application, but the requested right is com.apple.finder.ChangeGroup.

If you get an Authenticate window while in System Preferences, it will state:

```
Requested right: system.preferences
Application: System Preferences
```

In each example above, what is listed is the name of the application requesting authorization (in the Application line) and the specific privilege (right) that is being requested.

The /etc/authorization file. The rights are maintained in a file called "authorization," located in the /etc directory. This is sometimes referred to as the *policy database*. You can open this file conveniently in Property List Editor.

A comment line in the file offers advice on how the file is to be used. It states in part: "The name of the requested right is matched against the keys. An exact match has priority, otherwise the longest match from the start is used. Note that the right will only match wildcard rules (ending in a '.') during this reduction."

Thus, the exact right (and rule) invoked can vary as a function of what right an application requests, what rights are listed in the authorization file, and whether a wildcard match gets involved. If no match is made, rights and rules revert to their default selections (as I'll explain in more detail in a moment).

Note: If you're using Property List Editor, you may need to copy the comment text and paste it into a text editor to read it.

continues on next page

TECHNICALLY SPEAKING ▶ Authorization Services *continued*

Rights and Rules. The authorization file contains two main categories: "rights" and "rules." Rights refer to what a user is allowed to do. Rules are a bit harder to define. They are similar to macros—a set of instructions that are combined under one heading. One rule, for example, may contain the instructions needed to check if a given user is an administrator. Rules are typically called by rights. Thus, a right that is given only to administrators may call the rule to check if a given user is an administrator.

The only rule I will specifically mention here is the *default* rule. This contains the rights that will be invoked if there is no specific authorization right that can be found. For example, if an application's authorization request called for a right that was somehow not listed in the authorization file, the default rule would be used.

In the rights section, you will find the com.apple.desktopservices and system.preferences rights referred to above. If you open the disclosure triangle for a right, it reveals a list of its properties. The properties of most interest for this discussion are "class," "shared," and "timeout."

- **class.** This property can have several different values. I will mention three: "allow," "deny," and "user." If the allow value is set, it essentially means that any user has access. In fact, the Authenticate dialog will likely not even appear in such cases. Conversely, if the deny value is set, users will have no access at all. Instead of the Authenticate dialog appearing, you will see an error message (such as one that states, "Sorry, the operation could not be completed"). If user value is set (which is the most common choice), the authenticate dialog appears and the user is given the opportunity to enter his or her password.

- **shared.** The shared property can have a value or Yes or No. If it is set to Yes, it means that an authentication can be shared with certain other applications. That is, if applications A and B have the shared property enabled, and you enter your password to authenticate in application A, you would also automatically be authenticated in application B.

- **timeout.** The timeout property has a numeric value that represents a number of seconds. If present, this property limits the authentication period to the time interval indicated. Thus, if timeout is set to zero, you will have to reauthenticate each time you attempt an action that requires authentication in the specified application. If timeout is set to 300, it means that you have a 5-minute grace period before you have to reauthenticate.

The com.apple.desktopservices right has class set to "user"; this means that authentication will be required for actions that access this right. The group is set to "admin"; this means that a user will need to authenticate as a member of the admin group to get the access he or she is seeking. Shared is set to No and timeout is set to 0. Thus, there is no sharing and no grace period. This is why you need to reauthenticate every time you attempt an otherwise-prohibited action in the Finder.

continues on next page

TECHNICALLY SPEAKING ▶ Authorization Services *continued*

Modifying rights. You can edit the authorization file's rights and rules to suit your fancy. To do so, first launch Property List Editor as the root user (via the Pseudo utility, as explained in Chapter 4); this allows you to save any changes. You can change a right's grace period from 0 to 300, for example, so that you have a 5-minute grace period after authenticating. Or you can change the class from user to allow; this would eliminate the need to enter your password at all. After making and saving changes, launch the affected application and the new rights should be in effect. For the Finder (and the com.apple.desktopservices right), you would need to relaunch the Finder (or log out and back in again) for the change to take effect.

Bear in mind that although such changes may make it more convenient for you to perform otherwise restricted actions, they also compromise your security. Do these only if your Mac is in a secure environment where you are not concerned about users' potentially having unauthorized access to your data.

Also, before making changes to the authorization file, save a copy of the original, so that you can revert to it if anything goes wrong. In addition, because your modified file may be replaced by a subsequent update to Mac OS X, you should save a copy of it, as well, so that you have a record of your changes.

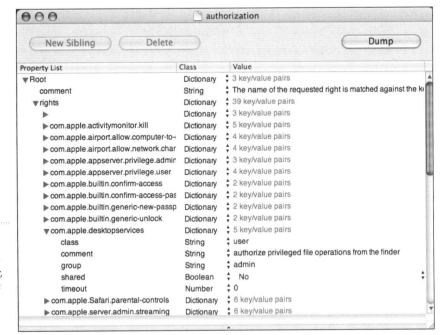

Figure 6.23

A peek at the /etc/authorization file, as viewed from Property List Editor, with the properties of the com.apple.desktopservices right visible.

Using Get Info and beyond

Assuming you're certain you want to override the Mac OS X restrictions for copying and moving files, a solution to these permissions issues is to temporarily or permanently change the permissions of the relevant files or folders.

Using Get Info. You can make most of the required changes via Get Info, as described in "Using Get Info: Basics," earlier in this chapter.

For example, if you find an application in the Applications folder that *you* own and you want the system to own it instead, you can use Get Info to change the owner.

If you own a file (or make yourself its owner), you can change any of its other settings.

In general, to *move* an item that Mac OS X prohibits you from moving due to permissions restrictions, you will need to change the ownership and permissions of the original enclosing or destination folder so that you have Read & Write permissions. In some cases, you may also need to similarly change the permissions of the item itself.

Beyond Get Info. If Get Info is not sufficient for your purposes, you can use a third-party utility that provides options for modifying permissions. My preferred choices are XRay and FileXaminer.

One advantage of using a utility like XRay rather than the Finder's Get Info window is that such utilities provide more complete access to the permissions settings. The Finder's Get Info, in contrast, provides access to only a subset of the settings. (For example, Get Info does not provide separate access to the execute bit.) Although you won't often need to modify settings in ways that exceed Get Info's capabilities, it's good to know you can do so when needed.

To access permissions settings via XRay:

1. Open the file in XRay (for example, by dragging its icon to the XRay icon).

2. From the Show pop-up menu, choose Permissions. To view all permissions options, click the Show Obscure Options button. You can now change all ownership and permissions settings. For folders, XRay includes a Change Enclosed button that works similarly to the "Apply to enclosed items" button in Get Info.

3. Save your changes.

Other options for changing permissions (beyond using Get Info) include (1) using the permissions-modifying commands in Terminal; (2) logging in as the root user (to bypass restrictions); and (3) using Disk Utility's First Aid to repair disk permissions (which may eliminate the need for more specific fixes). Details regarding these choices are covered in the following sections.

Figure 6.24

XRay's Permissions settings (with the pop-up menu for changing owners visible).

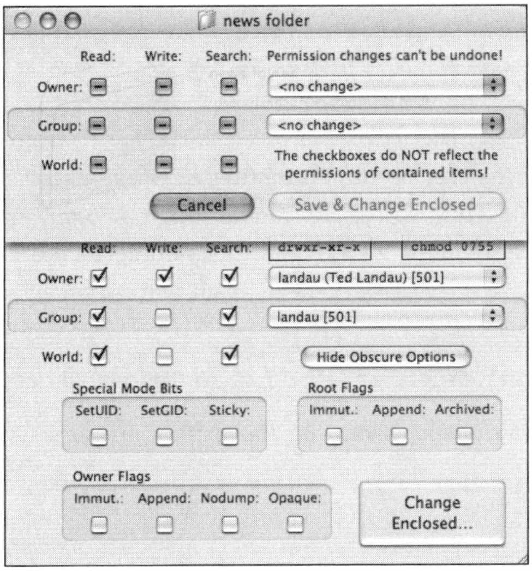

Figure 6.25

XRay's Permissions settings (with its Changed Enclosed window open) for a folder.

Deleting and moving instead of replacing

Occasionally, when you try to replace a file with a file of the same name from a different location, an error message appears, stating, "There was an error reading this file from disk." Alternatively, you may get a message stating that you don't have sufficient permissions to perform the replacement. The usual cause is incorrectly set permissions (in essence, a lack of read and/or write access). This permissions error prevents the to-be-replaced file from being replaced. This can happen even for files in your own home directory, for which you should presumably have the necessary access to replace.

The same error will appear if you try to replace an entire folder that contains one or more of these problem files with another folder of the same name. In this case, you will need to determine which files are the cause (by sequentially removing files from the folder and repeating the replace attempt each time) before you can fix the problem. The most likely cause is that the permissions were incorrectly set by the applications that created the files.

A simple solution is to drag the problem files to the Trash. You can typically delete such files even if you can't get the Replace option to work. Once you've done this, you should be able to move or copy the items that you were previously unable to, since you're no longer attempting to replace anything.

The same settings errors may also prevent backing up these files, such as via Apple's Backup utility for .Mac accounts. In this case, the best solution is to modify the permissions settings of the problem files using Get Info, as described previously. Keep in mind that you may need to modify permissions of the files on the backup copy as well as the ones in your current home directory.

SEE: • "Take Note: A Primer on Ownership and Access," earlier in this chapter, for more on how permissions work.

Accessing other users' folders

As an administrative user (which you are by default if you initially installed Mac OS X), you can set up additional user accounts (such as for other family members or colleagues, or as a troubleshooting resource). Therefore, there may be times when you want to check the contents of those users' home directories. Can you do this? Of course—though you may have to overcome some obstacles to do so.

SEE: • Chapter 9 for more on setting up additional user accounts.

Obstacles and exceptions. The above-mentioned obstacles vary by folder:

• **No-entry folders.** If you open the home directory folder for another user, you will find that most folder's icons include the no-entry icon. These include Desktop, Documents, Library, and most of the other folders created by Mac OS X when it set up the directory (see Figure 6.18). The no-entry icon means just that—*no entry!* If you try to open folders with this icon, you will get the following message: "The folder {*name of folder*} could not be opened because you do not have sufficient access privileges" (see Figure 6.17).

  The reason this message appears is that these folders have permissions settings of No Access for Group and Others, as can be seen in the Ownership & Permissions section of the folders' Get Info windows. Thus, at least for the moment, only the owner of each /Users directory can access the contents of these folders.

  Note: This is a case where an Authenticate button does not appear as an override option.

• **Public and Sites folders.** Exceptions to this no-entry rule include the Sites folder (where you would store a Web site used by Web sharing, which needs to be available publicly) and the Public folder (which is where you store files that you want anyone to be able to access, such as other local users on your Mac or people who access your Mac with guest access via Personal File Sharing). These two folders have the Group and

Everyone permissions set to "Read only" (as opposed to No Access), so you can open and view the contents of the Public folder of any other user. However, what you can do with the viewable contents will depend on the permissions settings of each file and folder:

If a document has Read & Write permissions enabled for Everyone, you will be able to open and modify the file.

If the document's permissions are set to No Access, you won't be able to open the file, even though you can see its icon in the Finder.

If permissions are set to "Read only," you will be able to read but not modify the file. If you open the file, make a change, and try to save the file, you will get an error message. You will be able to copy the file to your own home folder, however, and modify the copy there. You will also be able to use Save As to save a copy to a folder for which you have Write access.

- **Drop Box.** Within each user's Public folder is an additional folder, named Drop Box. This folder is designed so that any users can add to its contents but not view those contents—the opposite of the rest of the Public folder, which is designed to allow any users to see but not modify the contents.

The permissions settings for the Drop Box are "Write only (Drop Box)" for Group and Others.

The Drop Box allows any user to leave files for the user who owns the Drop Box without being able to see or access what other people may have left. When you drag a file to another user's Drop Box, you get a message that states, "You do not have permission to see the results of this operation." Similarly, if you double-click the Drop Box, you will get the "You do not have sufficient access privileges…" error message.

Note: To be safe, before dropping a file in a user's Drop Box, make sure you've assigned privileges to the file that will allow the user to view and modify it.

Figure 6.26

The Permissions settings of your Public Info folder, left, and Drop Box Info folder, right, as viewed in the Get Info window.

TAKE NOTE ▶ **The Shared Folder**

Inside the /Users folder, in addition to the home folders of each user, is a folder called Shared. The permissions of this folder are set in such a way that everyone has Read & Write access. Thus, this folder is like a community folder: Any local user can view, modify, copy, or move items to or from the folder. Although this setup is not very secure, it's convenient for low-security items—for example, to set up a common iTunes library so that all users can share the same music.

Some applications also install items in this folder. Applications use it to store accessory files that need to be accessed by multiple users but are not stored with the application itself. Extensis's Font Reserve uses this folder for its Font Reserve database, for example, and America Online Instant Messenger (AIM) uses it for its icon and sound files. This can present a problem if you ever want to move the application. For starters, to copy the application to another volume, you would also need to remember to copy the files in the Shared folder. In some cases, however, simply moving the application from one location to another on the *same* volume can break the application's link to the files in the Shared folder, leading to problems with using the application. If this happens, use the application's installer to install the application in another folder rather than copy it.

Note: The contents of the Shared folder are not available to non-administrative users when logged in remotely (a topic covered in more in Chapter 9).

Solutions. In the preceding examples, being an administrator did not directly give you access beyond what any other user would have. As an administrator, however, you can still acquire this access by doing any of the following:

- **Modifying permissions.** You can "unlock" a folder by modifying its permissions via its Get Info window so that you either make yourself the owner or otherwise give yourself Read & Write access. Once you're finished, however, you'll want to return the settings to their original values. Since this can become a hassle, I prefer one of the following solutions.

- **Logging in as root.** When you log in as root, you can access all no-entry folders and protected files. You can then not only view their contents but modify them as well.

  SEE: • "Root Access," in Chapter 4.

- **Using Terminal.** You can also use the sudo command to accomplish your goals. For example, a simple way to view a list of the contents of a no-entry folder is as follows:

  1. In Terminal, type sudo ls, followed by a space; don't press Return.

  2. Locate the prohibited folder in the Finder and drag its icon to the Terminal window. The pathname for the folder should now appear in the command line.

  3. Press Return, and then enter your password when prompted. The list of contents will appear.

  SEE: • Chapter 10 for more on using Terminal.

If you know the other user's password, you could also log in as that user—for example, you could switch to the other user's account via Fast User Switching. Alternatively, as an administrative user, you could go to the Accounts System Preferences pane and create a new password for the user, and use that password to log in. Of course, with the latter method, the original user would then be blocked from his or her account until you revealed the changed password.

Note: If a user has enabled FileVault, and you know his or her password, you can decrypt the FileVault disk image in the user's home folder to gain access to his or her home directory. In this case, the folders will not have no-entry icons.

Sticky bits and the Drop Box

In this section, we'll take a closer look at Drop Box permission settings. Along the way, I'll also explain some generally relevant tidbits about the Unix permission setting called the *sticky bit*.

Drop Box permissions. As noted earlier in the chapter, the Get Info window's permissions for a Drop Box folder are set to "Write only (Drop Box)" for Group and Others. You might think that this setting means what it says— that is, that no one except the owner (or someone with root access) can read or modify the files in that folder. But you would be wrong.

As implied in "Take Note: A Primer on Ownership and Access," earlier in this chapter, you can modify the contents of a file in someone else's Drop Box (such as deleting text within a word-processing document) if you have write access to the file, even though you can't view the folder's contents. You might be able to do this, for example, if you enter the full path to a document in the Go to Folder text box of the Open dialog of an application that can open the document. Similarly, because you have write access to the folder, you can even delete a file in another user's Drop Box, such as by using Terminal, assuming you know the pathname to the file. Thus, files in a folder such as the Drop Box are less secure than they may seem.

Typically, this situation is not much of a concern, because to modify or delete a file in a Drop Box that you do not own, you must at least know the name of the file. And since you can't view the Drop Box folder's contents, it's unlikely that you'll have this information (unless it's a file you put there). Even the Find command won't help because it doesn't list results from folders for which you don't have read access. However, if you know the name of the file, you can probably read it and (depending on the file's permission settings) modify or delete it as well.

Of course, as an admin user, you can always gain access to another user's Drop Box by changing the ownership of the folder to yourself (using the folder's

Get Info window). This would solve the problem of not knowing the name of a file in a Drop Box.

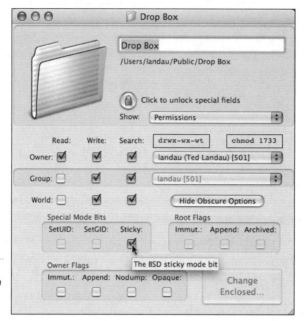

Figure 6.27

The permissions of the Drop Box, shown in XRay, with the sticky bit enabled.

The sticky bit. So is there a way you can improve the security of the Drop Box? Yes. To further restrict access to the contents of this (or any other) folder, you can set the *sticky bit* for the folder. A *bit* is essentially another word for a setting. The sticky bit is a special Unix attribute setting that goes beyond the standard read, write, and search/execute ones.

If the sticky bit is set for a folder, anyone can add files to the folder, but only the owner of the folder can directly remove or rename items from it. (Actually, a file's owner should also be able to remove or rename that particular file.) This situation does not prevent someone from opening and reading a file in a Drop Box (assuming that person knows the name of the file and has read access to it), but it does prevent that person from renaming or removing the file. In some cases, the setting will also prevent modifications to the file. To guarantee that no intruders can read or modify a file in your Drop Box, you need to modify the permissions of the file itself (setting Group and Others to No Access), not of the folder that contains it.

Setting the sticky bit. If you decide you want to set the sticky bit for your own Drop Box, you can do so in one of two ways: using Terminal or via a utility such as XRay. I'll explain both alternatives briefly.

SEE: • "Unix: Modifying Permissions," in Chapter 10, for background information on using Terminal for Unix permissions settings.

To use Terminal to add the sticky bit to the Drop Box folder, follow these steps:

1. Launch Terminal, and type cd Public.

2. Type ls -l.

   The permissions for the Drop Box should read drwx-wx-wx, which means that you have a directory (d); that the owner has -rwe (read, write, execute) permission; and that Group and Everyone have just -wx permission.

3. Type chmod 1733 "Drop Box"

   or

   Type chmod go=wxt "Drop Box"

   For the initial chmod (*change mode*) command, a 0 as the first digit means that the sticky bit is off; a 1 means that it's on.

   The latter chmod command has the same net effect as chmod 1733. Briefly, it sets the access for Group (g) and Other (o) to be equal to (=) write, execute, and sticky bit but provides no read access (-wxt).

4. Type ls -l again.

   The permissions should now read drwx-wx-wt. The last t indicates that the sticky bit is set.

To use XRay to add the sticky bit to the Drop Box folder, follow these steps:

1. Open the folder you want to modify (Drop Box, in this example) in XRay. (Using XRay's contextual-menu command is probably the easiest way to do this.)

2. From the Show pop-up menu, choose Permissions.

3. Click the Show Obscure Options check box (after which the name toggles to Hide Obscure Options).

4. In the Special Mode Bits section, check the Sticky box.

5. Save your changes.

Note: Examine the boxes just below the Show pop-up menu in the XRay window. You will see the same sort of attribute listing for the folder that you can see in Terminal when you list files by using ls -l. When you check the Sticky box, the last letter in the listing will change from x to t. For Drop Box, it will change from drwx-wx-wx to drwx-wx-wt. Again, this change indicates that the sticky bit has been set. The contents of the adjacent text box in XRay will similarly change from chmod 0733 to chmod 1733.

The sticky bit and the root volume. The sticky bit is enabled automatically for the root-level directory when you install Mac OS X. The root level is the level that has the name of the volume as its window name in the Finder (where you see System, Library, Users, Applications, and other folders). Thus, anything that is copied to that window cannot later be moved via a simple Finder drag by anyone other than the item's owner or by someone who has root access. Thus, if another user on your Mac adds a file to that window when he or she is logged in, you will not be able to drag the item to the Trash, for example, even though you are an administrator.

The simplest way to get rid of the file is to do a Command-drag and use the Authenticate dialog when it appears. In some cases, this alone will be sufficient for the move to work.

Otherwise, use Get Info to make yourself the owner of the file or folder (as described in "Copying and Moving: Permissions Problems," earlier in this chapter). Then you can move or trash the file as desired.

More generally, for almost any problem that involves moving a file from a folder with the sticky bit enabled, you can turn off the sticky bit temporarily, complete your move, and then turn the sticky bit back on.

To do this via XRay for the root directory, drag the icon for the Mac OS X startup volume to XRay and uncheck the Sticky box. Alternatively, you use the following command in Terminal: `sudo chmod 775 /`.

After returning to the Finder and completing whatever you wanted to do, recheck the Sticky box via XRay, or return to Terminal and type `sudo chmod 1775 /`.

SetUID attribute and the "Items could not be copied" error

Occasionally, when you attempt to copy an application, you may get the following error message: "One or more items can't be copied. Do you want to skip them and copy the remaining items?" Or you may get a similar message that refers to "special permissions." If you click Continue, you will get what appears to be a copy of the application, but if you try to launch it, it won't work. Typically, you won't get an error message. Instead, the application will simply start to launch and then quit.

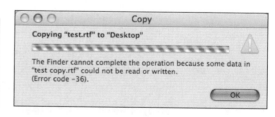

Figure 6.28

Two messages that may appear when you attempt to copy a file for which the SetUID bit has been set.

If it seems odd that attempting to copy an application brings up a message referring to multiple items' being copied, remember that most Mac OS X applications are actually packages, which contain multiple files and folders.

As to the reason for the error message, it usually occurs because at least one of the files within the .app package has its SetUID (*set user ID*) attribute enabled. The following sections provide more detail on this as well as instructions for working around the problem.

TECHNICALLY SPEAKING ▶ **SetUID and SetGID**

The `SetUID` command in Unix has little to do with copying .app packages in the Finder (as described in the main text). Instead, Unix users occasionally need it to access functions they would otherwise be prohibited from accessing. To change your password, for example, you need to access the function that changes passwords. However, such access is restricted to the root user (otherwise, any user could change someone's password). Unix works around this dilemma by providing an option that allows a user to access the password function just to change his or her own password—accomplished by enabling the SetUID bit for the function. This bit has a similar effect on any other command for which it is set.

When SetUID is enabled for a command, the command is run as though the person running it has the permissions of the file's owner (root, in the password example) for the action attempted. As long as you have permission to access the other files needed to complete your request, the command should work. Thus, any user can change his or her own password.

The SetGID bit works similarly, except that the normal group permissions are shifted temporarily to those of the group that owns the command in question. This bit has a somewhat different effect when applied to a directory rather than a file. In any case, you will have no need for this command; I mention it only for the sake of completeness.

Finding the problem file. For simplicity, I'll assume that only one file in the .app package has this problem. How do you locate the file? By comparing the original application's package contents with the copy. You need to use the Show Package Contents contextual-menu command to open the .app packages so that you can examine their contents. The one item missing in the copy but found in the original is the culprit.

For example, I encountered this problem when attempting to copy Mail.app. (I have no idea how the sticky bit came to be set here, since it's normally not.) A search revealed that the file missing in the copy had the following pathname: Mail.app/Contents/MacOS/Mail. Since this file contains Mail's program code, it's no wonder the copy didn't work!

Note: Some applications deliberately have the SetUID bit enabled for certain files within their packages. Typically, it would be used as one solution for the application to perform an action that requires root access. In such cases, disabling the bit could prevent certain features of the application from working.

Disabling the SetUID bit. To confirm whether the Mail file (in our example) has its SetUID bit enabled, you can open the file via a utility like XRay or by using Terminal.

SEE: • Chapter 10 for more on using commands in Terminal.

If you're using XRay, first use the Finder's Show Package Contents contextual-menu command to access the contents of the Mail.app package; locate the Mail file; and then open it in XRay. The SetUID bit is listed in the same Special Mode Bits section of the Permissions settings as the sticky bit. If its box is checked, it's enabled.

If using Terminal, you would type the following:

```
ls -l /Applications/Mail.app/Contents/MacOS/
```

Or, more simply, type `ls -l` (followed by a space) and then drag the MacOS folder icon from within the Mail.app package to the Terminal window. Now press Return. If the SetUID bit is enabled, the Mail file listed in the output will have its attributes listed as `-rwsrwxr-x`. Note the `s`, instead of the more common `x`, at the end of the first trio of letters (`rws` instead of `rwx`). This `s` indicates that SetUID has been enabled for the owner.

If a file has its SetUID bit enabled, it cannot be copied in the Finder. In Unix, the file would be copied with the SetUID bit stripped off. In Mac OS X, the file refuses to copy at all.

Thus, the solution to the problem is straightforward: Disable the SetUID bit for the file, and the file will copy successfully. The copy should also run successfully with SetUID still off, so you don't need to re-enable it (though if you have problems, you *can* re-enable the SetUID bit if necessary).

To disable (or re-enable) the SetUID bit, you can once again use a utility (such as XRay) or Terminal.

If you decide to use XRay, follow these steps:

1. From the contextual menu of the application that contains the SetUID-enabled file, select Show Package Contents.
2. Open the SetUID-enabled file with XRay.
3. Click the padlock icon, and enter your administrator's password when requested.
4. From the Show pop-up menu, choose Permissions and click the Show Obscure Options button.
5. Uncheck the SetUID check box.
6. Save your change.

You can reverse the change later, if necessary.

If using Terminal, follow these steps:

1. Type `sudo chmod u-s`.
2. Press the spacebar and drag the Finder icon of the SetUID-enabled file (in the application's package) to the Terminal window.

    This enters the pathname for the file.

3. Press Return.

4. Provide your administrator password when prompted.

   To verify that the change has been made (assuming you're still at the MacOS directory level), just type `ls -l` again. The permissions for the file should now read `-rwxrwxr-x`.

After using either method, if you attempt to copy the original application from the Finder, it should now copy successfully.

Unix commands such as `ditto` and `CpMac` may allow you to make the copy even with the SetUID bit enabled. However, if you want to copy the file from the Finder, the steps described above are the way to go.

Note: Enabling SetUID can be an effective form of copy protection. If you enable the SetUID bit for a file located on a volume for which a user does not have administrative access, there's virtually no way that user can copy the file—launch it, yes, but not copy it.

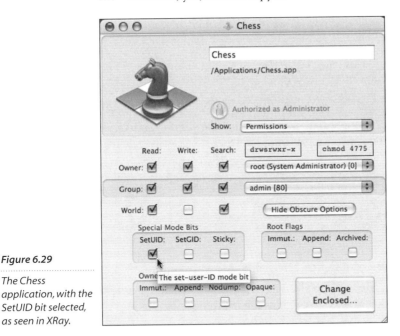

Figure 6.29

The Chess application, with the SetUID bit selected, as seen in XRay.

TAKE NOTE ▶ Package Contents Folder Won't Open

After making a copy of an .app application, if you try to access the contents of the package (by choosing the Show Package Contents command from the contextual menu), you may meet with resistance: Although the Show Package Contents command opens the package normally, the Contents folder inside is dimmed and cannot be opened.

Solution? Just log out and log back in. All should be well.

Deleting: Using the Trash

Deleting an item in Mac OS X is a two-step process. First you put the item in the Trash; then you empty the Trash. I discussed the basics of this process in Chapter 2; the following provides an overview of Trash essentials:

Placing items in the Trash

To place an item in the Trash, do one of the following:

- Drag the file's icon to the Trash icon in the Dock.
- Click the item, and from the Finder's File menu choose Move to Trash.
- Click the item and use the keyboard shortcut Command-Delete.

Until you empty the Trash, files placed there are not really deleted. You can view the contents of the Trash by clicking the Trash icon in the Dock to open its window. Any item in the window can be dragged out again. You can also place an item in the Trash by dragging it to this open window.

Each user maintains his or her own Trash. Thus, you will not see items in other users' Trash when you log in. (The Trash contents for that user will be visible to the user the next time he or she logs in.)

Mac OS X does not include a feature that allows you to create a Trash icon on the Desktop separate from the Dock. However, several shareware utilities, such as Northern Softworks' Trash X (www.northernsoftworks.com), provide a means to do this.

Emptying the Trash

To empty the Trash, do one of the following:

- From the Finder's application menu, choose Empty Trash.

   To overwrite the file data with meaningless information (so that there's little chance of the data being recovered), choose Secure Empty Trash instead.

- From the Trash's Dock menu, choose Empty Trash.
- Press Command-Shift-Delete (a shortcut for the Finder's Empty Trash command). This is especially convenient (combined with Command-Delete to get the file to the Trash) as a quick way to delete a file. Just click the file's icon and press Command-Delete followed by Command-Shift-Delete. The file is gone.

Files that will not delete. Mac OS X will prevent you from deleting certain files, such as those critical to the running of the OS. This is a good thing. However, it sometimes prevents you from deleting items that are safe to delete. Later in this chapter, I explain how you can get around this prohibition.

Show warning

If you have the "Show warning before emptying the Trash" option selected in the Advanced section of the Finder's Preferences window, every time you try to empty the Trash, you will get the following warning message: "Are you sure you want to remove the items in the Trash permanently?" This is useful because Empty Trash is one of the very few Finder commands that *cannot* be undone via the Finder's Undo command (Command-Z).

If you choose Empty Trash from the Trash's Dock menu, the Mac will empty the Trash without warning, even if the Finder warning option is enabled.

Changes in the Trash icon

Depending upon what you're dragging, the Trash icon in the Dock may change to indicate a change in its function or status. For starters, if there are items in the Trash, the icon indicates this by appearing to have crumpled paper inside.

If you drag a volume or server icon to the Trash, the Trash icon will change to an Eject icon. This indicates that placing the volume in the Trash will unmount, disconnect, or eject the volume—not delete its contents.

If you drag to the Trash the icon of a CD-R that has been set up for burning, the Trash icon will change to the Burn icon to indicate that placing the CD-R icon in the Trash will initiate the burn.

SEE: • "'Mounting and unmounting/ejecting media," later in the chapter.

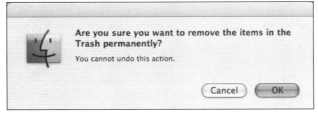

Figure 6.30

Talking Trash: left, *the Trash's Empty Trash option;* center, *the Empty Trash warning;* right, *the Trash icon when it's transformed into an Eject icon.*

Deleting: Undeleting Files

After you delete an item in Mac OS X, there's no easy way to recover it. The Finder's Undo command will not bring it back.

However, if you're desperate to recover deleted files, there are third-party utilities that may allow you to do so. For example, consider SubRosaSoft's FileSalvage (http://datarecoverymacosx.com) and Prosoft's Data Rescue II (www.prosofteng.com). Be aware that, in some cases, to use these types of utilities, they need to be installed and running *before* you need to use them to recover a file.

Note: Prosoft used to market a utility called Data Recycler X, designed specifically to instantly undelete deleted files (as opposed to a more general "search and rescue" operation performed by most other recovery utilities). However, rather than update the product for Mac OS X 10.4, they decided to drop it.

Deleting: Problems Deleting Files

This section explores the most common reasons (and a few uncommon ones) why you might have trouble deleting a file and explains what you can do to fix the problem and delete the file.

Locked files

The most basic reason a file refuses to delete is that it is locked, via the Locked check box in the General section of the file's Get Info window.

If a file is locked, a small padlock symbol is visible in the bottom left corner of the file's icon.

In addition, if you attempt to move a locked file to the Trash (or even to another folder on your drive), you typically get the following error message: "The operation could not be completed because the item is locked." (Note: If you attempt to move a locked file, you may find that you create a copy, rather than actually move the file; in such cases, no error message appears.)

Thus, to delete a file that's locked, you must open the Get Info window for the file and uncheck its Locked box. Once you've done this, you can drag the item to the Trash and empty it. Unlocking a file also allows you to move it to a different folder location, other than the Trash, if you wish.

Note: If the Locked check box is dimmed, this means that you do not have sufficient access to modify the file. In such cases, your first move would be to modify the Ownership & Permissions settings to give yourself access.

If a file is already in the Trash, you can still check the Locked box, but doing so will have no effect in this case. If you empty the Trash, the file will be deleted.

Occasionally, you may find that a locked item makes it into the Trash and refuses to be deleted (as discussed more in "Item cannot be placed in Trash or Trash cannot be emptied," later in this chapter). In such cases, you may not even be able to drag the item out of the Trash. Apple claims that pressing and holding down the Shift and Option keys while selecting Empty Trash (from the Finder) should work here. However, I have found that this does not always work. If you have problems, try unlocking the file and deleting it again.

Note: In Mac OS X, a locked file is the same as a file whose Unix immutable bit has been set (as covered more in "Using Unix to delete files," later in this chapter.

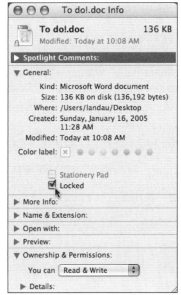

Figure 6.31

Left, *the Locked check box in a Get Info window;* right, *the locked symbol in the file icon.*

Figure 6.32

The "item is locked" error message that appears when you try to place a locked file in the Trash.

Batch-deleting locked files. If you select several files and then choose Show Inspector (Command-Option-I) from the Finder's File menu, you will get one Multiple Item Info window for all the selected items. The top of the window will indicate the number of items selected. Any change you make (such as unlocking) will affect all selected files simultaneously. When the files are unlocked, they can be deleted.

SEE: • "Using Unix to delete files," later in this chapter, for related information.

Figure 6.33

The Multiple Item Info window for a collection of items that have been batch-selected.

TAKE NOTE ▶ How to Lock Folders

Mac OS X currently does not permit folders to be locked or unlocked via the Get Info window. Although the Locked check box appears, it is dimmed and cannot be selected. This means you can't lock Mac OS X applications that are packages, because a package is actually a special type of folder (as I explained in Chapter 3). Neither can you lock certain types of documents, including .pkg and .rtfd documents, that are also packages.

You can circumvent this restriction by using Terminal's chflags command. Alternatively, you can lock folders from Mac OS X by using (yet again!) a utility like XRay, which allows you to enable the Locked option for any item, including folders (as well as the invisible and package attributes, also not available in Get Info windows).

SEE: • "Take Note: TextEdit: Format Options Beyond Show Fonts," in Chapter 4, for more on .rtfd packages.

• "The chflags Command," in Chapter 10.

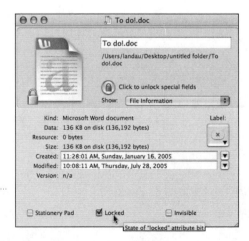

Figure 6.34

The XRay window with the Locked option indicated.

"In use" files

A file cannot be deleted from the Finder if it is "in use" or "open." The following are some examples of documents that would be considered "open" or "in use."

- **The file is a running application.** In this case, you probably won't even be able to place it in the Trash.

- **The file is a document that is currently open in an application.** Most often, a document is listed as "in use" only if it has unsaved changes. Mac OS X is inconsistent here, however. For some documents open in some applications, you can delete the document at any time. For other documents and applications, however, you can't delete the document (even once you've closed it) until you've quit the application.

- **The file is an accessory file for an open application or process.** For example, a preferences file for an application may refuse to delete while the application is running.

- **The file is a disk-image file, and its image is mounted.** In this case, you will probably be able to move the disk image to the Trash, but you won't be able to empty the Trash until you unmount the image volume.

- **A partially downloaded file may be considered in use even after the downloading application has quit.**

The easiest way to delete an in-use file is to quit the application or process that's keeping the file in use. Thus, for a document, quit the opening application; for a disk image, unmount the image. If the problem involves a background process (that is, a process not shown in the Dock), you may need to use Activity Monitor to quit that process. After quitting the process, the file should delete.

If this doesn't work, from the Finder's application menu select Secure Empty Trash. This should do the trick, bypassing any warning about the file's being in use. However, avoid doing this if the file you want to delete is truly in use. For example, if you use this to delete a document that is currently open in an application, the application will likely crash (unexpectedly quit) when you next access it. Instead, first quit the application. Only if you cannot delete the document at this point should you try Secure Empty Trash.

If the file still does not delete, or if you're unsure which process is causing the problem, log out and log back in. If that fails, restart. At this point, it's almost 100 percent certain that you'll be able to delete the file. If not, proceed to the next section!

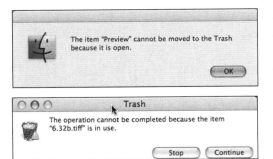

Figure 6.35

Examples of error messages that appear when you drag an open application to the Trash, top, *and when you try to empty the Trash if it contains a document that is still open,* bottom.

Item cannot be placed in Trash or Trash cannot be emptied

You may get an error message when you try to place an item in the Trash, stating that you are prohibited from placing the item in the Trash for some reason. Or you may succeed in placing the item in the Trash but get an error message when you try to empty the Trash.

This can happen if the item is locked or in use (as just described); however, it can also occur with unlocked files that are not in use.

Causes. For files that are not locked or in use, the most common cause of these types of Trash errors is a permissions restriction—similar to the ones that can prevent files from being moved. For example:

- If you have "Read only" access (the folder has a "pencil-with-slash" icon in its open window) or No Access (the folder has a no-entry icon on the folder icon itself) to a folder that contains the file you want to delete, you won't be able to move the file out of the folder (and into the Trash). Actually, with No Access, you won't even be able to open the folder to see the file.

  Note: Having "Read only" access for the file itself will not prevent you from deleting it. The settings for the containing folder are what matter. Further, you can probably delete the entire folder, even though you may not be able to drag an item out of it!

- If the sticky bit is set for a folder, and you're neither the folder's nor the item's owner, you likely will not be able to move items from the folder into the Trash.

In principle, if an item's permissions settings do not prevent you from moving it to the Trash, the settings should not prevent you from deleting the item once it's in the Trash. After all, you have Read & Write access to the Trash. In most cases, this is exactly how it works. There are, however, a few exceptions, which I describe in the following text.

Regardless of what the permissions settings are, how they got that way, why they cause trouble, or even whether they're the root cause of the problem, your goal is the same: to delete the file. It's often simpler to bypass the permissions settings altogether and focus on the task at hand: deleting the task directly, as described in the next section.

Solutions. Whether you cannot place the item in the Trash or cannot empty the Trash, try one of the following to see which solution works best for you:

- **Authenticate.** If an action (such as dragging an item to the Trash) is prohibited, an Authenticate dialog may appear. If so, enter your administrator name and password when prompted. The item(s) should now move to the Trash and delete.

SEE: • "Using the Finder's Authenticate dialog," earlier in this chapter, for more on the Authenticate dialog.

- **Use a delete utility.** If an Authenticate option does not appear, there are numerous utilities that will "force-empty" the Trash. That is, they force a file in the Trash to be deleted even if the Finder's Empty Trash command fails. For example, Kristofer Szymanski's Cocktail includes a Force Empty Trash option that works well (in the System > Misc pane), as well as an option to delete locked files (in the Files > Locked pane).

  There are a few utilities that can even delete files that aren't in the Trash—great for occasions when you can't move a file to the Trash. For example, Findley Designs' Delete It (www.drewfindley.com) offers a window with navigable access to anywhere on your drive. Simply select files from the list that you want to delete and then click the Delete button. Similarly, if you've installed Gideon Softworks' FileXaminer and its contextual-menu plug-ins, you can simply Control-click a problem file or folder and choose Super Delete from the resulting contextual menu. After you've provided your admin user name and password, the file(s) will be deleted outright.

  Once again, I advise caution: Some files, such as those in the System folder, may refuse to be moved to the Trash and deleted via this method—a good thing because they're critical to running the OS. *Do not* try to figure out how to delete these files—leave them be!

- **Use Unix.** The just-cited utilities typically work as front ends for Unix commands; the commands do the dirty work. If you want, you can bypass these utilities and use the Unix commands directly via Terminal. Using Unix commands (primarily the rm command) to delete a file will almost always succeed, whether the problem is that the file is locked, is in use, or has restrictive permissions, or whatever else you can imagine.

  SEE: • "Using Unix to delete files," below, for details.

- **Modify permissions.** Another workable solution is to modify the permissions of the item (and/or its enclosing folder) so that it can be deleted. To do so, you would assign yourself as the owner and give yourself Read & Write access. To make these changes, you can use the Finder's Get Info command, Terminal commands (such as chmod), and utilities like XRay, as appropriate.

  SEE: • "Opening and Saving: Permissions Problems" and "Copying and Moving: Permissions Problems," earlier in this chapter, for more details.

  • "Take Note: Adding or Deleting a User," in Chapter 2, for details on how to completely delete the home directory of a user who will no longer be using your computer.

- **Log in as root user.** You should almost never need to do this, but it will work: Simply log in as the root user and delete the files from there.

  SEE: • "Root Access," in Chapter 4, for more details.

- **Empty the Trash before placing the item in the Trash.** If you try to drag a file to the Trash when a file of the same name already exists there, the Finder usually renames the file that's already in the Trash (for example, by adding a *1* to the name) so that the new file can be added. However, the Finder may balk at doing this and block you from adding a file with the same name. If so, empty the Trash and *then* drag the file to the Trash.

- **Rename the volume or folder.** If a file to be deleted contains a slash (/) in its name—or any other unusual character (such as a copyright symbol)—it may fail to delete. The solution is to change the name to remove the character(s). Further, if the volume that a file is on contains these characters, the file may also refuse to delete. The solution here is to change the name of the volume. If necessary, you can change the name back after deleting the file.

- **Remove aliases from the Trash.** If you have too many alias files in the Trash, you may be unable to delete them. The solution is to drag the alias files from the Trash and return them in smaller groups (one at a time, if necessary), deleting each group separately.

- **Create a new folder.** Create a new folder; place the uncooperative item in it; move the folder to the Trash; and then empty the Trash. This will usually work even if you weren't able to delete the file by dragging it to the Trash directly.

    SEE: • "Take Note: The Locations of Trash Folders," in Chapter 4, for related information.

- **Repair the disk.** Use Disk Utility's First Aid both to repair the disk and to repair disk permissions. First Aid may repair a problem that is preventing a file from being deleted. If First Aid does not work, you can try other repair utilities, such as Alsoft's DiskWarrior (www.alsoft.com).

    In my opinion, it's rare that these repairs will be needed to delete a file, but they are worth a shot.

    SEE: • "Performing repairs with Disk Utility (First Aid)," in Chapter 5 for details.

Using Unix to delete files

Although I prefer Aqua-based solutions, there are times when the only and/or quickest path to success is through Terminal. For problems with deleting files, there are two Unix commands you can try: chflags and rm. If one fails, try the other. I have never failed to have success with them.

SEE: • "Unix: The sudo and su Commands," "The chflags command," and "The rm command," all in Chapter 10, for more information.

Using chflags. The chflags (*change flags*) command is used to turn file attributes on and off. In this case, you'll use it to turn off an attribute called the *immutable flag* (or *immutable bit*), which is the Unix equivalent of locking a file. The file resists being deleted until the flag is turned off. In most cases, the status of this flag will match that of the Locked check box in a file's Get Info window. However, it may happen that this flag is on even if the Locked check box is unchecked. By turning this flag off in Terminal, you can then return to the Finder and delete the file. To do this, follow these steps:

1. In the Terminal window type chflags -R nouchg.

2. Press the spacebar.

3. Locate the files and/or folders you want to delete. Drag the icon of each file to the Terminal window. (You can drag multiple files at once.) The files' pathnames should be appended to the line following the space.

4. Press Return.

Alternatively, if all the files you want to delete are in one directory, such as your home directory's Trash, you can type the following:

chflags -R nouchg {*name of directory*}

For example, for your Trash directory, the name would be ~/.Trash. The -R option (which stands for *recursive*) causes the flags of all files in the directory to be changed, not just the directory itself. (Again, you can drag a directory's icon to the Terminal window to add its pathname to the end of the command.)

If the flag was on for any problem file, it should now be off. You can now return to the Finder and delete the files via the Empty Trash command. If that doesn't work, try using the rm command, as described next.

Note: There is a special immutable flag called the *system immutable flag*. If this is set for a file, none of the procedures described here are likely to work. One way to delete such a file is via single-user mode (see Chapter 5 for more on this mode). The XRay utility includes an option to set this flag, via an Immut check box in the Root Flags section of the Permissions pane. Before it turns the flag on, it warns you of the need to enter single-user mode to undo this. Basically, I see no reason to ever enable this flag—which means it's unlikely that you'll confront this problem. For this reason, I'm skipping over single-user-mode details here. If you want more details, check out this Apple Knowledge Base document: http://docs.info.apple.com/article.html?artnum=106237.

Using rm. The rm (*remove*) command deletes files in Unix. In most cases, if the rm command would work, choosing the Empty Trash command in the Finder would have worked just as well—so there would be no point in bothering with rm. The need for the rm command arises when you want to delete an item for which you are not the owner, or in any other situation in which permissions restrictions prevent Empty Trash from working. In this case, using the remove command with root access (via the sudo command) will do the trick. To do this, follow these steps:

1. From Terminal, type sudo rm -R.

2. Press the spacebar.

3. Locate the files you want to delete. (In most cases they should already be in the Trash.) Drag the icon of each to the Terminal window. (You can drag multiple files at once.) The files' pathnames should be appended to the line following the space.

4. Press Return.

5. When prompted, enter your password and press Return again.

The files and folders should be deleted. You will not need to choose Empty Trash from the Finder. Even if the files you selected to remove were not in the Trash, they're now gone. And, they're gone forever (barring a potential recovery via a third-party utility, as covered earlier in this chapter)!

Be very cautious about using this command. If you make a mistake in typing, you could delete files you did not want to delete, possibly eradicating most of the contents of your drive!

SEE: • "Take Note: Using rm: Risk Management," in Chapter 10, for more details regarding the potential dangers of using the rm command.

TECHNICALLY SPEAKING ▶ More Trash Talk

If deleting files in the Trash individually via the rm command, as described in the main text, doesn't work, you can delete the entire Trash directory. Don't worry: A new one is created automatically the next time you drag an item to the Trash icon in the Dock.

Actually, there are several Trash directories you may want or need to delete. As covered in "Take Note: The Location of Trash Folders," in Chapter 4, there is a separate .Trashes directory at the root level of each volume, as well as a .Trash directory at the root level of each user's home directory. There is also a Trash directory at the root level of every volume that contains Mac OS 9 (although these should not be affected by the problems described here, so I will not include them in the examples that follow).

To delete your own .Trash directory plus the .Trashes directory at the root level of the startup drive, type the following two commands in Terminal:

```
sudo rm -R ~/.Trash/
sudo rm -R /.Trashes/
```

For any .Trashes directories on volumes other than the startup volume, you need to enter the volume information in the pathname. For example, for a volume called Matrix, you would type the following:

```
sudo rm -R /Volumes/Matrix/.Trashes/
```

Repeat this as needed for as many volumes as you have.

Note: These directories maintain separate subdirectories for each user. The name of each subdirectory is the user ID for that user. The user ID of the initial administrator of the Mac is typically 501. In some cases, you may want or need to specify this ID in the rm command. For example, you could type the following:

```
sudo rm -R /Volumes/Matrix/.Trashes/501
```

This deletes any trash you put in the .Trashes directory, while leaving items placed by other users untouched.

Mounting, Unmounting, and Burning Media

I have never been quite sure where the best place is to include this section of the book. As it has more to do with discs than with files, it does not quite fit here. However, I am talking about how to deal with media to which you copy files. Also, unmounting media and burning media share a potential common step with deleting files: All can be accomplished via dragging items to the Trash icon. So perhaps this is the best place.

Mounting and unmounting/ejecting media

This section outlines the ways you can mount and unmount a volume in Mac OS X, the problems that can occur when doing so, and the solutions to those problems.

Ejecting/unmounting disks. To eject removable media or unmount a server volume or disk image, assuming no problems, try any one of the following, as appropriate:

- Drag the volume's icon to the Trash.

  Note that you *cannot* use Command-Delete as an alternative here.

- Select the volume icon and, from the Finder's File menu, choose Eject (Command-E).

- If you have ever installed the Eject Menu Extra, select the desired device from its menu.

- For external media, such as a drive connected to the FireWire port or a remote network volume, click the Eject icon to the right of the volume's name in the sidebar of a Finder window.

- If your keyboard has a Media Eject key (or uses F12 as a Media Eject key), pressing that key should cause a CD or DVD to unmount and then eject from the internal drive. If there is no disc in the drive, the tray will simply open.

If you have multiple removable devices mounted, select the one you want to eject before pressing the Media Eject key. Otherwise, you might eject/unmount multiple devices.

Important: Do not disconnect a peripheral drive (such as a FireWire drive) before you unmount it from the Finder. Doing so can potentially damage data on the drive.

SEE: • "Take Note: Eject Options," in Chapter 2, for still more ways to eject removable media.

Eject/unmount problems: "In use" error. If you get a message that says a volume cannot be ejected (or put away) because it is "in use," this typically means that some document or application on the volume is still open. Thus, the fix is to close the open file or quit the open application. In the case of a document, you may need to quit its application as well, not just close the file. If these methods don't work, consider the following:

- If you get this message when you've quit all applications and closed all files on the volume, try to unmount/eject the volume again. It will usually succeed. Otherwise, relaunch (force-quit) the Finder and try yet again.

- If you get an "in use" error when trying to eject a disk that contains files that were in use (but are not in use anymore), choose Apple menu > Recent Items > Clear Menu and try again.

- If you cannot unmount a network volume because of an "in use" error, the cause may be a process that remains open (the Office Notifications feature of Microsoft's Entourage is one example) even if the parent application (Entourage, in this example) is quit. If the application has been used to access data on the mounted network volume, the unmounting problem will occur. In such cases, quitting the process (by choosing Turn Off Office Notifications from the Entourage application menu, for example) should work.

    Note: You may also be able to use Activity Monitor to see if a process related to the application is still open (for example, checking the list of processes for a name that suggests it's the process you're seeking); if so, quitting it from within Activity Monitor may allow you to unmount the volume.

- When sending files via iChat, if you send a file located on a non-startup volume, you will subsequently be unable to eject any removable media due to an "in use" error. The work-around is to log out and log back in.

    SEE: • "'In use' files," earlier in this chapter, for related information.

Eject/unmount problems: Other errors. If the preceding methods do not work or do not apply, try the following until one works:

- Use Disk Utility to unmount and/or eject a volume.

    To unmount a volume, select the volume/partition from the list in the sidebar along the left side of the window. Then choose Unmount from Disk Utility's File menu or toolbar.

    Sometimes, while in the Finder, after you drag the icon of a removable-media volume (such as a CD or DVD) to the Trash, the volume's icon vanishes (that is, the volume unmounts), but the removable media does not eject. In such cases, choose the Eject command in Disk Utility's File menu or toolbar. It may still work to eject the media.

    Alternatively, you can use the `diskutil` command in Terminal, which is the Unix equivalent of Disk Utility. For starters, try `drutil tray eject`. If that fails, try `diskutil unmount {disk name}` or `diskutil eject {disk name}`. The disk name should be the full path (for example, /Volumes/DiskOne).

- For an iDisk that will not unmount via standard methods, go to the /Volumes folder (via the Finder's Go to Folder command) and delete the iDisk volume listing there.

  SEE: • "Duplicate volumes in /Volumes," later in this chapter, for related information.

- Try the Eject button in iTunes or DVD Player, as appropriate. It may work even if the Finder fails.

- Log out and log back in. Now try to unmount/eject the media. This almost always gets the media to eject.

- For ejectable media, such as CDs and DVDs, restart and hold down the mouse button until the media ejects.

- Use the eject cd command in Open Firmware at startup.

- Press the Eject button on the drive itself, if one exists. Normally, this will not work if media is in the drive. However, it's worth a try.

- If an ejectable disc is stuck in a drive, you may be able to eject it manually, typically by inserting an straightened paper clip into a hole located near the drive opening. Check with Apple or the drive's vendor for specifics.

  SEE: • "Technically Speaking: Open Firmware Commands," in Chapter 5, for more information on ejecting a CD or DVD at startup.

How to remount a volume. Occasionally, the opposite problem may arise: You unmount a volume that you did not intend to unmount. For removable media or remote volumes, the solution is simple: Reinsert the ejected media or reconnect to the server. But what if you have a hard drive (especially a multiple-partition one), and you unmount a partition by mistake? (Typically, if you unmount one partition, you unmount all of them, unless one is the startup partition.) To get the volume back on the Desktop, follow these steps:

1. Launch Disk Utility.

2. Select the partition or volume you want to remount.

3. Choose Mount from the File menu or toolbar.

In rarer cases, a connected but unmounted volume may not be listed in Disk Utility. This has happened to me with my iPod (which may unmount when my Mac goes to sleep). Disconnecting and reconnecting the drive or iPod should get it to remount. But there is a faster way. Use the Finder's Go to Folder command to go to the /Volumes directory. An icon for the iPod (or other improperly unmounted volume) should be there. Double-click the icon and the volume should remount—assuming it is still connected to your Mac, of course.

Duplicate volumes in /Volumes. If your Mac goes to sleep while connected to an external volume, the volume may unmount when you wake the

Mac up, and you may have problems remounting the volume. The main solution is to use the Disk Utility methods just described.

However, in some cases (due to the sleep issue as well as other problems), you may have multiple copies of the same volume (external or remote) listed in the /Volumes directory. These duplicate copies may persist even after the volume is disconnected from your Mac. These duplicates can lead to mounting and unmounting problems. To check for (and fix) this issue, use the Finder's Go to Folder command to go to the /Volumes directory. If you see several copies of the same volume (they will have similar names, such as iPod, iPod 1, and iPod 2), you can delete all duplicates that have a plain folder icon (the folder will be empty). Do not delete any items that have an server alias or drive volume icon! Doing so could delete the contents of an actively mounted volume. You will need root access to delete these folders; you should be able to solve this by authenticating when asked.

Problem with data loss on a mounted external FireWire drive.
A much more serious problem can occur if an external FireWire drive remains connected to the Mac when you restart or shut down. In such cases, the directory of the drive may become so corrupted (due to incorrect writing of data to the drive during the shutdown sequence) that all data on the drive is essentially lost! Using a repair utility such as Prosoft's Data Rescue or sending the drive to a repair service such as DriveSavers (www.drivesavers.com) is about your only chance for recovering the data. The drive hardware itself remains fine, and you can reformat the drive to use it again.

This problem is not universal; it affects some drives but not others (for reasons that are not entirely clear). FireWire 800 drives (with the Oxford 922 bridge) are especially vulnerable, though some FireWire 400 drives have also been bitten.

Note: The Oxford bridge chip is not part of the drive itself but rather sits between the drive and the external casing. It is needed to allow what is most likely an ATA drive to connect to the Mac via a FireWire port.

To be safe and to avoid this data-loss problem, unmount and disconnect all external FireWire drives before restarting or shutting down your Mac.

As to a permanent fix, Apple claims that updating to Mac OS X 10.3.1 or later eliminates at least most causes of the problem. However, it may also be necessary to upgrade the firmware for your drive. Contact the drive's vendor for information about such firmware updates.

External ports lost. Occasionally, you may find that a given port appears dead. That is, no device connected to the port (USB or FireWire) mounts. Devices don't even get listed in System Profiler. In fact, the port itself (for example, USB or FireWire) may not be listed. Most often this is because the relevant port is not active and so the device is not recognized (assuming that your hardware is working, the ultimate cause of this is usually a software bug in the OS itself, hopefully one that will be fixed in an update). More generally, try the following:

- Try the standard troubleshooting techniques and hope that one works: (a) Unplug and replug the device; (b) shut down the computer and disconnect all peripherals after the computer is shut down, wait several minutes, and then start it up again, reconnecting peripherals after startup is over; (c) bypass hubs if in use; (d) switch to an alternate port (if your Mac has more than one of the same port); and so on. Also note: Non-bus-powered external drives need to be connected to AC power before connecting to a Mac or they will not mount.

- Try (a) repairing disk permissions with Disk Utility; (b) zapping the PRAM; (c) resetting the Power Manager (as covered in Chapter 5). If none of these work, repeat the PRAM zap with all third-party RAM removed. Make sure that the needed kext files (for USB and FireWire) are installed (also as covered in Chapter 5). As a last resort, reinstall Mac OS X using the Archive and Install option (re-updating to more recent versions of Mac OS X if needed).

- "Reset" your FireWire ports using the following procedure, described in an Apple Knowledge Base article (http://docs.info.apple.com/ article.html?artnum=88338):

  1. Shut down your computer.

  2. Disconnect all FireWire devices and all other cables, except the keyboard and mouse.

  3. Disconnect your computer from the power outlet (and remove the battery from laptops), and wait for 5 minutes. (Some hard-drive manufacturers recommend up to 15 minutes.)

  4. Plug the computer back in (and replace the battery on laptops) and turn it on.

  5. Reconnect the FireWire device(s) (one at a time if there is more than one) and test. Test with each FireWire port if you have more than one.

- If all of this fails, you're probably looking at a hardware repair. In fact, if you can determine that the port is not working even before Mac OS X begins to load, it's almost certain you have a hardware problem. For example, if you have an external bootable FireWire drive, connect it at startup and hold down the Option key. If the drive does not appear as a bootable drive (especially if it did appear before the problem started), it's probably time to take your Mac in for a repair.

  Checking the Mac with the Hardware Test software (as described in "Technically Speaking: The Apple Hardware Test Software," in Chapter 5) can also help diagnose hardware problems.

  Still another way to check for a hardware problem is to start up in single-user mode. If the first few lines of text reference a FireWire failure, for example, a hardware repair is needed. When this happened to me, I got a message that referred to a broken "FireWire PHY." To fix this, Apple told me, I needed to replace the logic board. If you have a desktop Mac that's no longer under warranty, a cheaper alternative is to get a FireWire PCI card. Note: The most frequent cause of this FireWire problem is incorrectly inserting a FireWire cable and thereby damaging the port.

SEE: • "Technically Speaking: Hard-Drive Sleep," in Chapter 2.

• "Take Note: Zapping PRAM and Resetting the Power Manager," in Chapter 5.

• "Single-user mode" and "Verbose mode," in Chapter 5.

Problems with copy-protected audio CDs. Some audio CDs are now copy-protected. Such CDs usually have a sticker on them that reads, "Will not play on PC/Mac." And indeed, they won't. Even worse, the CD may get stuck in your drive, refusing to eject when you press the Media Eject button. In some cases, it can even result in a gray-screen crash at startup.

If any of these things occur, first make sure you've installed the Apple SuperDrive Update (if appropriate for your Mac). Check the following Web page for details: www.apple.com/hardware/superdrive.

Next, try the procedures outlined previously in this section, especially: (a) holding down the mouse button at startup; (b) using the manual eject hole (if one exists for the drive); or (c) typing eject cd in Open Firmware at startup. If you can get the Mac to start up in Mac OS X (holding down the X key at startup may help), you can also try using the Eject command in iTunes or DVD Player. If none of these fixes work, you should probably bring the Mac to a service representative to get the CD removed. See the following Apple Knowledge Base document for further details: http://docs.info.apple.com/article.html?artnum=106882.

Problems mounting .dmg and .img files. If you attempt to mount a disk image, such as one downloaded over the Internet, you may get an error stating, "[*Filename*] failed to mount due to error -95 (no mountable file systems)." The most common cause is that the image was incompletely downloaded or otherwise damaged. The solution here is to re-download the file. If this fails to work, and you're confident the problem is not with the original file, try the following:

• Restart your Mac and try to mount the disk again.

• If StuffIt software is accessed at any point in the download-and-mount process, it could be the culprit. Check to see if an update is available that fixes the problem.

• Delete the com.apple.frameworks.diskimages.diskimagesuiagent.plist file in the /Library/Preferences folder for your home directory (assuming that such a file has been created on your drive).

• As a last resort, reinstall Mac OS X.

Image keeps remounting. Mac OS X 10.2 and later will attempt to remount any disk-image files that were still mounted when you last logged out. However, an apparent bug in the OS can sometimes result in an inability to unmount the image. Instead, the image remounts within a minute or so of each attempt to unmount it. Even after you unmount the image and restart the Mac, the image remounts. To fix this permanently, delete the image file from the drive (backing it up to another volume first, if desired) and restart. After doing this, you can return the file to the drive without the problem reoccurring.

Note: The software that regulates this automounting is the Unix program /sbin/autodiskmount.

Burning discs: CDs and DVDs

One of the more common things to do with a Mac is burn CDs and DVDs. You might do this to back up data from your hard drive, create your own bootable disc, or make an audio CD from music in your iTunes Library. Most often, you will be burning to a CD-R. Once you burn to one of these discs, you cannot erase and reuse it. There are rewritable CD-RWs; however, because they are more expensive and slower in speed than CD-Rs, it is often more convenient and economical to burn and discard a CD-R than to reuse a CD-RW. Also, some standard CD and DVD players, especially older models, cannot read CD-RWs.

Note: You can erase a CD-RW via the Erase pane in Disk Utility.

CD-burning basics. When you insert a blank CD-R or CD-RW into a CD-RW drive, what transpires next depends on the options you've selected from the CDs & DVDs System Preferences pane. In particular, you can select what you want Mac OS X to do when you insert a blank disc—that is, ask what to do, or automatically open a selected application. Personally, I prefer the "Ask what to do" option because it gives me the flexibility to make a different decision each time I insert a CD. I will assume this option is in effect for the discussions in this section.

Alternatively, you can launch any application that can burn CDs and insert a blank CD while the application is active. This bypasses the initial Finder dialog described here, but the process otherwise works the same.

When you insert a blank CD with the "Ask what to do" option selected, a dialog appears that states, "You inserted a blank CD. Choose what to do from the pop-up menu." The Action pop-up menu presents several options:

- **Open Finder.** Choose this option and a CD icon appears in the Finder with the name selected in the Name text box ("untitled CD" by default).

  You can now drag files from your hard drive to the CD. (Although you can drag audio files to the CD, you would not use this method to create an audio CD that you intended to play in a stand-alone CD player. Files copied in this way would be recognized as music files by computer software, such as iTunes, but not by a separate CD player.)

When you're finished adding files, you burn the CD by either (a) choosing Burn Disc from the Finder's File menu, (b) dragging the CD icon to the Trash (at which point the Trash icon changes to a Burn icon), or (c) clicking the Burn icon next to the CD's name in a Finder window's sidebar. Any of these choices causes another dialog to appear. This one reads, "Do you want to burn the disc?" You can choose a Burn Speed here. Faster speeds mean the burn takes less time to complete; however, they also increase the risk that an error may occur during the burn. Still, in most cases, using the Maximum speed works fine.

Click the Burn button, and a disc is burned in the HFS Plus/ISO 9660 hybrid disc format. You can mount the disc on PCs running Windows as well as Macs.

Click Eject instead, and the disc is ejected without being burned. In this case, nothing you selected is copied to the CD. The CD remains unused and can be used later to burn something else.

- **Open iTunes.** Choose this option, and a dialog may immediately appear, offering basic advice on how to burn a playlist via iTunes. Click OK to continue.

  To burn a CD, select a playlist. You cannot burn a CD simply by selecting songs from the Library. If necessary, create a playlist to burn by choosing New Playlist from the File menu. Add the desired songs to the playlist—either by dragging files already in the iTunes Library to the playlist or by adding new files from audio CDs via iTunes' Import option.

  With a playlist selected from the left column, the icon in the upper-right corner turns from Browse to Burn Disc. If the iris of the icon is closed, click the iris to open it. The yellow-and-black Burn icon will now be visible. Click this icon to initiate the burn. Note: If a CD is not already inserted, you can insert one at this point.

  This burns a disc in Audio CD (playable in a standard audio CD player), MP3 (ISO 9660, playable by most computers and many MP3-compatible CD players), or data CD (simply a disc with data files) format, as specified in iTunes Preferences.

- **Open other application.** If you choose this option, you can select any third-party software you may have that can burn CDs. Roxio's Toast Titanium (www.roxio.com) is a popular choice and is especially useful for copying CDs when you have two CD drives. With two drives, you can use it to directly copy an entire CD mounted in one drive to a CD-R or CD-RW mounted in the other drive.

  You can also use Mac OS X's Disk Utility.

  SEE: • Chapter 3 (especially "Creating an Emergency Startup Volume") for more on using Disk Utility to burn CDs, including details on making a bootable copy of a startup CD.

- **Run script.** If you've created or downloaded an AppleScript file that automates a sequence of events for burning a CD, you would choose this option.

Click OK to carry out your selected action. Or you can decide that inserting the media was a mistake and click the Eject button. Last, you can choose Ignore; this leaves the media in the drive but does not mount it in the Finder. If you later launch iTunes, for example, you can still burn songs to the CD.

Finder's New Burn Folder command. In the previous section, I explained how to set up and burn data to a blank disc that you have already inserted and mounted. Prior to Tiger, this was the only way to do a burn. But what if you want to set up the data to burn without having a disc inserted at the time? You can do this now in Tiger.

To do so, select New Burn Folder from the Finder's File menu. A folder (with a burn icon) will be created on your Desktop. Name the folder whatever you wish and then add to the folder whatever files you want to burn. You can keep the Burn Folder, or even multiple Burn Folders, around until you're ready to burn a copy. When you are ready, open the window for the folder. In the upper right there will be a Burn button. Click it and you will be prompted to insert a disc for burning.

Note: When you drag an item to a burn folder, an alias of the item is added; the item itself is not moved or copied. This is done to conserve space (you don't need to maintain two copies of each file prior to burning). However, it also means that if you double-click an alias to access a file, you are accessing the original file on your drive, not a copy in the burn folder.

Note: You can see how much space your items take up by selecting Get Info (Command-I) for the Burn Folder, expanding the Burning panel, and then clicking the Calculate button.

See this Apple Knowledge Base article for more information: http://docs.info.apple.com/article.html?artnum=302276.

Disk-image creation when burning. Prior to Tiger, when you burned data (other than a disk-image file) to a disc, Mac OS X first created a temporary disk image of what you selected. It then burned the image. This meant that (a) a successful burn required twice the free space of what was selected to burn, and (b) the burn process was significantly slowed due to the time it took to create the disk image. Starting in Tiger, the temporary disk image is no longer created or needed; the burn occurs directly, thereby saving space and time!

SEE: • "Finder's New Burn Folder command," above, for related information.

Multisession CDs. Although you cannot erase and reuse a burned CD-R, you can set it up so that only a portion of a CD-R is burned, leaving the remaining unused portion to be burned on a later occasion. This is called *creating a multisession CD*. To do this, (1) create an image file of what you want to burn, using Disk Utility (as described in Chapter 3); (2) from the Images menu in Disk Utility choose the Burn command and then select the image you want to burn; (3) in the window that appears, check the "Leave disc appendable" box from the choices in the Burn Options section (click the disclosure triangle on the right side of the window if Burn Options are not visible); and (4) click the Burn button.

When you later remount the CD, the multisession option remains enabled and can be used to burn additional files to the CD. Each subsequent burn session will mount as a separate volume in the Finder.

Disc-to-disc burning. If you have two disc drives, at least one of which is writable, you can easily make a duplicate of an existing disc (CD or DVD) by inserting the disc in one drive and inserting a blank disc in the writable drive. This works especially well if you have third-party disc-burning software such as Toast.

If you have only one drive, the way to make a disc-to-disc copy is to create an image of the disc (using Disk Utility) and then burn the image.

Troubleshooting CD burning. In most cases, burning a CD will work without hassles—especially when using an internal CD-RW or SuperDrive drive that shipped with the Mac. If problems do occur, consider the following:

- **CD drive not compatible.** After you insert a blank CD, Mac OS X may not recognize that a CD has been inserted. This could be because you have an external CD-RW drive that's not compatible with Mac OS X. Check with the vendor for details. Also make sure you have the latest firmware update for the drive.

  Another possible cause of this symptom is that you inserted a blank CD into a non-writable drive (for example, you put a DVD-R in a drive that can only write CDs).

- **External drive not connected properly.** If drive compatibility doesn't appear to be the issue, but you still can't get an external CD-RW drive to work, launch System Profiler and select USB or FireWire (from the Hardware section in the left column) to see if the drive is listed.

  If the drive is not listed, no CDs will mount when inserted. To fix this, make sure that all cables to the drive are connected properly (including power cables). Also make sure the drive is turned on! If you're using a USB or FireWire hub, try bypassing the hub and connecting the drive directly to the Mac.

  If the drive is listed in System Profiler, restart the Mac with the drive already on.

  SEE: • "Mounting and unmounting/ejecting media," earlier in this chapter, for more advice.

- **Interrupted burns.** Once a burn has started, the CD will be unusable if the burn is canceled or otherwise interrupted! So be careful: Once you start a burn, there's no going back.

- **Burn fails.** You may get to the point where you can click a Burn button and the burn is initiated, but the resulting CD-R does not mount or play as expected. Or you may get an error message during the burn, indicating that the burn has failed or "could not be completed."

  For starters, you may have problems if you are trying to burn files that are "in use" (as described earlier in this chapter). If you cannot stop using the relevant files (perhaps because keeping them "in use" is essential for you to be logged in to your account), the solution would be to log in to another user's account (assuming it is one from which you still have access to the needed data) and burn the CD from there.

  Otherwise, retry using a new CD-R and making sure to keep other CPU activity to a minimum. (Do not try to play a QuickTime movie while burning a CD, for example.) Quit any unneeded open applications to make sure you have enough memory (add more physical RAM as a last resort here). These precautions are especially important on older Macs that don't have the horsepower of newer models.

  If you're using software that allows you to adjust the burn speed, make sure you choose a speed that does not exceed the maximum specification of either your optical drive or the media being used; lower the speed if you're unsure. Otherwise, the burn may fail. Toast Titanium has a feature that allows you to test the maximum allowable speed.

  Burning requires a certain amount of space on your hard drive. If you do not have sufficient space, you will get an error message indicating that the "disc is full." Again, the burn will not be successful.

  Note: Ideally, before attempting to burn a disc, set Energy Saver's computer sleep setting to Never to disable any sleep that might otherwise occur during a burn. If your Mac goes to sleep during a burn, the burn will likely fail.

- **QuickTime needed.** QuickTime 6.2 or later is needed to work with the AAC (Advanced Audio Coding) format used by the iTunes Music Store.

- **Unwanted files and folders copied.** In older versions of Mac OS X, when you're burning a data CD (not intended to be bootable), certain (usually invisible) files and folders used by Mac OS X bootable volumes (such as a Temporary Items folder, a Desktop folder, or Desktop DB files) might get copied to the CD. These files are not needed to use the CD and are a minor annoyance when the CD is mounted on a Windows system (where they will be visible). Starting in Mac OS X 10.2.3, these files should no longer get copied to a burned CD.

- **Disk Utility and images with MS-DOS–formatted volumes.** Disk Utility will not burn disk images that contain MS-DOS–formatted volumes (such as FAT-12, FAT-16, and FAT-32). The only work-around for now is to save the image in a format that Disk Utility can use.

- **Problems specific to iTunes.** If none of the above advice helped and you're trying to burn a CD using iTunes, check the following Apple Knowledge Base article: http://docs.info.apple.com/article.html?artnum=61102. Titled "You're unable to burn a CD in iTunes," it offers additional tips for solving problems that may occur.

- **iTunes songs do not burn via Toast.** Older versions of Toast would burn audio CDs containing music downloaded from the iTunes Music Store. In doing so, the copy protection of the songs was removed. To prevent this, the latest versions of Toast will no longer burn iTunes Music Store songs.

DVD burning. Although specifics vary, the principles involved in burning a DVD (via the Finder or software like iDVD) are essentially the same as those for burning a CD. For example, the Burn Disc and New Burn Folder commands work as well for a DVD as they do for a CD. The essential difference is that you need a drive that can burn DVDs as well as CDs.

If your Mac came with one of Apple's SuperDrives, you are good to go. It is a DVD burner (and can burn CDs as well, although not as fast as a CD-only burner).

Note: iLife's iDVD application will burn only to an Apple SuperDrive. If you do not have this drive, you can instead choose the Save as a Disc Image command from iDVD's File menu. You can then burn the resulting image to a DVD via any DVD writer.

DVD formats and burning DVDs. Writable DVDs come in several different formats, most notably DVD-R, DVD-RW, DVD+R, and DVD+RW. Prior to Panther, Mac OS X only supported the DVD-R(W) format. Panther and Tiger add support for DVD+R(W). (To see which formats your Mac's optical drive can handle, type the command drutil info in Terminal; the resulting output lists those formats.) However, to be safe, your best bet is still to get DVD-Rs when purchasing blank discs for an Apple SuperDrive.

Commercial movie DVDs are typically double-layer DVDs (DVD+R DL media). Among other things, this means that a double-layer disc has almost twice the capacity of a "standard" DVD (8.5 GB instead of 4.7 GB). This presents a problem when attempting to make a copy of a movie DVD. Splitting the movie DVD across two standard DVDs typically does not work well. There are several potential solutions:

- Use software such as Roxio's Popcorn (www.roxio.com). This compresses the data (at some loss in quality) so that an entire movie DVD fits on a single standard DVD. It only does this for nonencrypted (that is, not copy-protected) discs.

- Get a drive that can burn double-layer discs. Apple's latest Power Mac G5s already include a SuperDrive that does this. Expect all of Apple's computers to eventually include such a drive. (However, again note that without third-party software, you will only be able to copy nonencrypted DVDs.)

Can you actually make a duplicate of a commercial copy-protected DVD? Yes. There is software that breaks the protection. There is no 100 percent guarantee of success, however, as copy-protection methods keep changing. I have had good success with MacTheRipper (www.releasethedogs.com/mtr). Another utility, HandBrake (http://handbrake.m0k.org), can convert a DVD movie to an MP4 file, so that you can include it in your iTunes Library. The legality of such copies remains an open question. My position is that it should be legal if you are just doing it for your personal use.

SEE: • "Running Mac OS X software from Terminal," in Chapter 10, for more on the Terminal commands that handle disc burning: `hdiutil` and `drutil`.

• Chapter 11, for more on iTunes, iDVD, CDs, and DVDs.

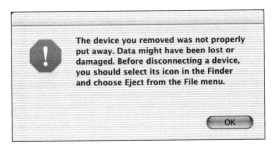

Figure 6.36

Unmounting errors: left, *the error message that appears if you disconnect an external device before unmounting it;* right, *an error message that may appear in the Finder if a volume is unmounted by a means other than the Finder.*

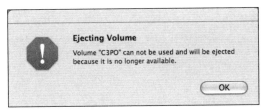
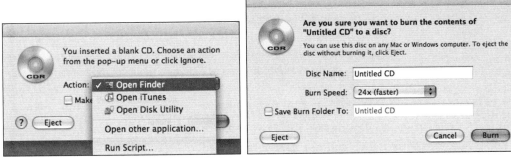

Figure 6.37

CD-related messages: left, *a message that appears in the Finder when you insert a blank CD if you've set the CDs & DVDs System Preferences pane to "Ask what to do";* right, *a message that appears when you attempt to eject a CD-R that has not yet been burned.*

Burn Folder

Figure 6.38

Burning from the Finder: left, *a Finder window for an "unburned" CD— note the Burn icon in the sidebar and the Burn icon below the toolbar;* right, *a Burn Folder, as created by the Finder's New Burn Folder command.*

Figure 6.39

The upper right portion of the iTunes window, with the Burn Disc icon (currently closed).

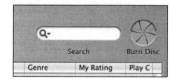

Aliases and Symbolic Links

An *alias* is a file that is a pointer to a real file (called the *original*) located somewhere else. Thus, when you double-click an alias, the other (original) file opens. No matter how big the original file is, its alias is never more than about 4K to 50K in size. By using aliases, you can list the same file in many locations without needing real copies in each location. This provides flexibility in organizing files on your drive without wasting disk space by duplicating the full-size files.

For example, suppose you have a collection of applications at various locations on your drive, and you want to bring them together in the same folder for a specific task. However, you also want to retain them in their original locations. You can do both by creating aliases of the application files and placing the aliases in the new folder. Whenever you double-click an alias in that folder, it launches the original application, as though the application were in two locations at the same time.

The following are some other ways you can use aliases:

• Sometimes a program may look for a preferences file in the System Folder used for Classic. If you have different Mac OS 9 System Folders, the preferences may be different in each. You can prevent this problem by placing an alias of the original preferences file in each of the other System Folders. Now all of the folders will use the same preferences file, no matter what changes you make at what time.

- If you place an alias of a folder in a new location, when you open the alias folder, the original folder actually opens. By placing such an alias in a convenient location (such as on the Desktop), you get instant access to folder contents, even though the actual folder may be nested several folders deep in some other location.

- Making an invisible folder visible temporarily and making an alias of it is a useful trick for maintaining easy access to folders that are normally invisible. You can use this technique to maintain access to the invisible /tmp folder, for example.

How to recognize an alias

The icon for an alias appears identical to that of the original file, except that a small arrow appears in its bottom left corner.

If you open the Get Info window for an alias, you should find that the Kind setting for the file is Alias. I say *should*, because in what appears to be a bug, an alias file may sometimes list the original file's kind as its own.

In addition, the Get Info window will list the location of the original file, in a field called Original. Right below that will be a button called Select New Original. Clicking this button allows you to change the file attached to the alias. You should not need to do this unless the original file has been deleted or the link to it has been broken.

To do!.doc

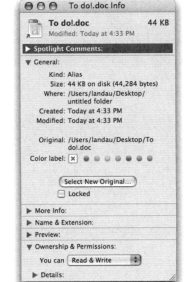

Figure 6.40

An alias file and its Get Info window.

How to locate an original via its alias

What if you want to locate the original file from its alias? To do so, first click the alias's icon, then choose Show Original (Command-R) from the Finder's File menu or the alias's contextual menu. The Finder will go directly to the folder where the original is located and display that folder with the file selected.

Alternatively, after noting the path in the Original field of the alias's Get Info window, you can navigate there yourself.

How to create an alias

To create an alias, click the original file, and from the Finder's File menu or the file's contextual menu choose Make Alias (Command-L).

Whichever method you select, an alias will be created in the same location as the original file, with the word *alias* added to its name (before its extension, if the file has one). You can then rename or move the alias. The alias's relation to the original file will be preserved no matter where you move either file, at least as long as both stay within the same volume (there is one exception to this rule, as described in "Aliases vs. symbolic links," below).

Often more conveniently, you can hold down the Command and Option keys and drag the file's icon to a new folder location. This technique creates an alias file at the new location with the same name as the original (the word *alias* is not added); the original file remains in its original location. This is likely the quickest way to create an alias in a location other than where the original file resides.

Fixing a broken alias link

If you delete the file to which an alias is linked, or if you move or modify the original file so that the alias can no longer locate it, you will get an error message when you double-click the alias file. This message will state the following: "The alias {*name of file*} could not be opened because the original item cannot be found." This is called a *broken alias*.

At this point, the dialog provides you with three choices: (1) OK (thereby ignoring the issue for the moment); (2) Delete Alias (with the obvious result); or (3) Fix Alias. This last option opens a window similar to the one that appears when you click Select New Original in the Get Info window. From here, you can navigate via a file browser to the desired original file and select it as the new destination for the alias.

Figure 6.41

The broken-alias error message.

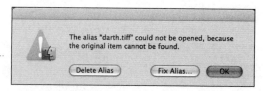

Note: One way to wind up with a broken alias is to copy an alias to a CD or other removable media, where the alias refers back to an item on your hard drive. If the disc is later mounted on another computer, the alias will not work.

Aliases vs. symbolic links

If you're familiar with Mac OS 9 (Classic), much of this alias discussion probably has a familiar ring to it, since aliases work in similar fashion in Mac OS 9. However, Mac OS X introduces a new wrinkle, compliments of Unix. Unix includes something similar to aliases: *symbolic links*. When you're in the Mac OS X Finder, a symbolic-link file looks and acts almost identically to an alias file, with the following exceptions:

- **Symbolic links refer to a specific path.** Thus, for example, a symbolic link to a file called Testing in your Documents folder will work only if Testing remains in the Documents folder. Move it anywhere else, and the link is broken. Symbolic links never link to an original file that has been moved from the location it had when the link was created.

  Just as important, if you move or delete the original file and create a new one with the same name in the original location, the symbolic link will point to that new file (because it has the same path).

- **Aliases**, **in contrast, are generally linked to the file or folder to which they originally point.** If you move the original file to a new location, the alias is able to keep track of this situation and maintain the link. When you double-click the alias, the moved original file still opens.

  However, starting in Mac OS X 10.2, this difference is no longer exactly true. Now, if you move an original file to a new location *and* create a new file with the same name at the original location, an existing alias will point to the newly created file, just as a symbolic link would. Only if that attempt fails (perhaps because you failed to create a file with the same name at the original location) will Mac OS X look to match the alias with the moved original file.

  The idea here is to provide greater consistency between how aliases and symbolic links work. To quote Apple: "If you replace a file with an identically named file, moving the old file to a new location, both aliases and symbolic links point to the new file. However, if you move a file without replacing it, symbolic links to the file break, while aliases do not."

When you install Mac OS X, the OS places symbolic-link files in various locations, such as inside the Library folders, inside application packages, and in the invisible Unix directories. Because these locations are off the radar of most users, the typical Mac user rarely needs to work with symbolic links. Symbolic links may also appear in more commonly visited locations, where they will seem to be ordinary aliases. As I'll describe a bit later in this chapter, there may be one such symbolic link to your Mac OS 9 Desktop.

If you want to create a new alias, I recommend that you stick with the traditional Mac variety. Aliases are easier to create than symbolic links, and they generally work more like you would expect. About the only reason to use a symbolic link is if the link must be recognized as such by Unix software. (Unix does not recognize traditional Mac OS X aliases as links.) Still, an understanding of the distinction is useful for when links don't work as expected.

Finally, if you format a drive using UFS (which I *do not* recommend) rather than HFS, Mac OS X will *not* recognize aliases; it will recognize only symbolic links.

SEE: • "Select a Destination," in Chapter 3, for more information on UFS versus HFS.

Determining whether a file is a symbolic link or an alias

You can't tell from Finder icons whether a file is an alias or a symbolic link—both file types have the same curved-arrow icon. Even the Get Info window for the two types of files does not offer an obvious solution, because both types may be identified with a Kind setting of Alias.

Still, the Get Info window does provide a critical clue. For a symbolic link, the Select New Original button is dimmed and cannot be selected.

Another way to determine whether a file is an alias or a symbolic link is to move the original file and then double-click the alias. If the original file still launches, you have a traditional alias. If you get a message that says the original could not be found, you have a symbolic link. Note: If this broken alias message contains a Fix Alias button, don't bother clicking it; it will not work with a symbolic link.

As described in the next section, symbolic links also differ from aliases in terms of how they're listed in Terminal.

Warning about deleting a symbolic link. In most cases, if you delete a symbolic-link file, the item is removed. End of story. No change is made to the original item itself (just as is the case when you delete an alias). However, if you delete a symbolic-link item from a folder for which you have "Read only" permission, you will be asked to authenticate before the Finder permits you to trash the item. After you enter your password to get permission, the original item (whatever folder or file the symbolic link references) may be deleted instead of the link itself! This was certainly the case in Panther; the bug may or may not still exist in Tiger.

How to create a symbolic link

Any alias you create via the Finder's Make Alias command is a traditional alias. What do you do if you want to create a symbolic link instead? You have two choices: You can use Terminal, or you can use a third-party utility like XRay or Cocktail.

Terminal. To create a symbolic link in Terminal, follow these steps:

1. Launch Terminal.

2. Type the following:

`ln -s {original file path} {symbolic-link path}`

Note: Use an absolute pathway for the original file, not a relative one. As always, a shortcut for adding the absolute pathway is to drag the Finder icon of the original file to the Terminal window after typing `ln -s`.

> **SEE:** • "Take Note: Finder Folders vs. Unix Directories," in Chapter 4, for back-ground on absolute versus relative pathnames.
>
> • Chapter 10 for more information on pathnames and shortcuts in Unix.

You can now use the `cd` command to navigate to the directory where you created the link; then type `ls -al`. This displays a list of all items in the directory, including symbolic links. Notice two things in the list:

*   In the File Attributes column (where permissions are indicated), the first letter listed for a symbolic-link file is `l` (rather than `d` for directory or a hyphen for files).

*   For symbolic-link files, the path to the original file is listed to the right of the filename.

Traditional Mac aliases have neither of these attributes.

Now if you go to the Finder, the symbolic-link file should appear in the same directory as listed in Terminal. If it does not, search for it via Find and then double-click its name in the Search Results output. This method forces it to show up. As a last resort, log out and log in again.

Cocktail. Probably the easiest way to create a symbolic link is with Kristofer Szymanski's Cocktail. To do so, click Files in Cocktail's toolbar. Then click the Links tab. From here, click the Choose button—a symbolic link to the selected item is created at the destination location you specify.

XRay. To create a symbolic link with Rainer Brockerhoff's XRay, follow these steps:

1. Open the original file with XRay, and from XRay's File menu choose Make Alias.

2. In the window that appears, from the Alias Format pop-up menu choose either Absolute Symbolic Link or Relative Symbolic Link.

    With an absolute symbolic link, moving the original file to a new location will break the link. With a relative symbolic link (most commonly used for files inside Mac OS X packages), the link is maintained as long as the link file and the original file are in the same relative locations within a folder (even if that enclosing folder is moved). This arrangement allows you to move an .app package file—which is actually a folder and contains symbolic-link files to other files within the package—without breaking the links.

Again, the link file should appear in the Finder at this point.

Note: The current version of XRay cannot show the permissions for an alias or symbolic link correctly; instead, it lists the permissions of the original file.

A word of warning: This alias/link confusion is rooted in Mac OS X itself and can affect functions in any utility. For example, some delete utilities, when you try to delete an alias or a symbolic-link file, will delete the original instead of the alias/link file. Be sure to test how a utility works with aliases before using it to delete an alias to anything that you would not want deleted.

 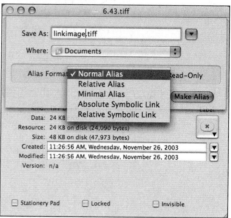

Figure 6.42

Create a symbolic link: left, via Cocktail; right, via XRay. With Cocktail, there is a related option to create a new alias to the Mac OS 9 desktop.

Fixing a broken symbolic link

What do you do if you click a symbolic-link icon and find that it's broken (you get an error message stating that the original file cannot be found)? As I said before, don't bother with the Fix Alias button (if present); it won't work. Instead, to fix the link, create a new symbolic-link file (for example, by using the ln command in Terminal, as just described).

A potentially more serious problem involves the multitude of symbolic links that exist in package files, Library folders, and invisible Unix directories. For example, the (normally invisible) tmp, var, and etc folder icons at the root level of a Mac OS X volume are actually symbolic links to the identically named folders in the /private directory.

If any of these symbolic links get broken, you may have problems ranging from application failure to the inability to start up Mac OS X—serious problems that you will no doubt want to fix.

For example, if for any reason the symbolic link to /tmp is missing, you can expect symptoms such as an inability to print using Classic, as well as problems with file sharing, burning discs, updating software, connecting via PPP, repairing privileges, and more. To fix this problem, type the following:

```
sudo ln -s /private/tmp /tmp
```

In other cases, fixing such links is a far-from-trivial task: You may have trouble locating the problem files and reestablishing the links correctly, especially if the problem is preventing you from starting up your Mac.

To fix these problems, try the following methods:

- **Run disk-repair utilities.** You may get some help from disk-repair utilities, such as Disk Utility's First Aid. Not likely, but worth a try.

- **Add link in single-user mode.** If a missing symbolic link is preventing a normal startup of Mac OS X, you may be able to fix the problem by starting up in single-user mode and adding the link back. See this Apple Knowledge Base article for details: http://docs.info.apple.com/article.html?artnum=106908.

- **Reinstall.** If all else fails, you'll likely need to reinstall the problem applications or Mac OS X itself.

    SEE: • Chapter 3 for advice on reinstalling Mac OS X.

How, you may ask, do these links get broken in the first place, assuming you made no obvious change to cause the breakage? There are several possibilities, including the following:

- If you back up and restore files via a backup utility, symbolic links may get broken unless the backup utility specifically knows how to restore them.

    SEE: • Chapter 3 for advice on backing up Mac OS X. All utilities recommended there work correctly with symbolic links.

- Archiving a folder or directory and later expanding it can cause problems unless the archiving utility knows how to handle the process. For example, StuffIt Deluxe may have some problems here.

- If designed incorrectly, an installer for an application can move files during the installation in such a way that symbolic links get broken.

    There's a relatively rare but significant problem with the .pax files contained in installer packages (see Chapter 3). If an installer .pkg file (likely one from a third party) writes to the invisible Unix folders on your drive (such as the /etc directory), it may do so in such a way that it breaks existing symbolic links to these directories. In extreme cases, this situation can result in the failure of your drive to start up, ultimately requiring a reinstallation of Mac OS X (unless you're skilled enough to recognize and fix the broken symbolic links or have a third-party utility that can do the job for you).

There's no sure way to prevent these problems other than not using the software in question or checking online (such as at the software vendor's Web site) before using a backup/archiving/installation utility to determine whether it has any known problems with symbolic links.

"Desktop (Mac OS 9)" file is a symbolic link

As described in "Take Note: The Location of Desktop folders," in Chapter 4, an alias file called Desktop (Mac OS 9) is created automatically at startup, at the root level of the Mac OS X startup volume—but only if there are items on the Desktop for a Mac OS 9 system on the same volume as Mac OS X.

Note: If you add items to a currently empty Mac OS 9 Desktop Folder, the alias will not appear until your next restart. Normally, items would get added to this folder only if you were booted in Mac OS 9 or via certain applications that run in Classic.

This alias is of value because the Mac OS 9 and Mac OS X Desktops are entirely independent. That is, what you place on the Mac OS 9 Desktop (when you're booted in Mac OS 9, for example) and what you place on the Mac OS X Desktop are stored in different locations. Thus the items from one Desktop are not visible when you're viewing the other. Furthermore, accessing the contents of the Mac OS 9 Desktop when you're booted in Mac OS X is complicated by the fact that the Mac OS 9 Desktop folder—located at the root level of the startup volume—is invisible in Mac OS X. The Desktop (Mac OS 9) alias allows you to work around this situation. When you open it, a window appears, showing the contents of the invisible Mac OS 9 Desktop. The contents are visible even though the folder itself is not.

If you have partitioned your drive into multiple volumes, you will not need a separate similar alias for the Desktop Folders of the other volumes, because the Desktop Folders for these volumes remain visible. These folders contain the files from these volumes that appear on the Desktop when you're booted in Mac OS 9. Thus, the Desktop (Mac OS 9) folder shows only the Desktop items that are stored on the Mac OS X boot volume.

Why am I mentioning all this here? Because the Desktop (Mac OS 9) alias is actually a symbolic link. I'm not sure what Apple's rationale was in making it such (perhaps Apple didn't want the link to continue to work if you moved the Desktop Folder), but if you delete this alias/symbolic link accidentally, it should be re-created automatically the next time you restart. If this does not happen, you can still re-create the symbolic link yourself, by following a procedure similar to that described in "How to create a symbolic link," earlier in this chapter. In this particular case, you would type the following in Terminal:

```
ln -s '/Desktop Folder' ~/'Desktop (Mac OS 9)'
```

The fact that the Desktop Folder is invisible presents no problems when using this command.

Cocktail. Once again, the third-party utility Cocktail provides a user-friendly alternative. To use it, click the Files icon in the Cocktail toolbar and then click the Links tab. From here, click the Create button next to the text that reads, "Create alias to Mac OS 9 desktop."

TECHNICALLY SPEAKING ▶ Unix Hard Links

A *hard link* in Unix is a duplicate directory entry for a file. Even if you delete the original file, the hard link will still access the file's contents, because the original file and all its hard links point to the same data. Think of the data as being stored somewhere on your drive and the original file as being just a pointer to the data; a hard link is another pointer to the same data.

I'm not aware of any case in which a hard link is used in the Finder, so hard links are relevant mainly for the workings of the invisible Unix files. About the only time they may become relevant for troubleshooting is when you're attempting to copy a Mac OS X volume to another drive. As is the case with symbolic links, the copy procedure will need to be able to maintain the hard links correctly.

Invisible Files: What Files Are Invisible?

Numerous files on a Mac OS X volume are deliberately set to be invisible. The general rationale for this is that invisibility minimizes the chance that users will meddle with them. Users should rarely need to modify, move, or delete these files. That said, however, there are occasions when you will need to do such things.

In this section, I explore what these invisible files are and how they are set to be invisible. I also explain why and how to access them.

Files that begin with a period (.)

If the first character of a filename is a period/dot (.), Mac OS X interprets that to mean the file should be invisible. Some invisible files of interest that begin with a period include the following:

- **.DS_Store (Directory Store file).** This file, which is likely to pop up in virtually every folder you access, stores various data about the items in a folder, such as the location of icons in the Icon view window for that folder.

Should you want to delete some of these files (such as for a folder to be copied to a non–Mac OS X system where these files are not used), various utilities—such as FinderCleaner (www.boswortels.tk) or Kristofer Szymanski's Cocktail (www.maintain.se/cocktail)—make it easy to do. Otherwise, you can delete the files directly in the Finder, as explained later in this chapter.

Finally, you can configure your account so that .DS_Store files are not created on remote volumes to which you may connect and transfer data, even though the .DS_Store files remain on your drive. Doing so requires making a change to the com.apple.desktopservices.plist file in ~/Library/Preferences. One way to do this is to launch Terminal and type

```
defaults write com.apple.desktopservices DSDontWriteNetworkStores true
```

• **.Trash.** This directory contains items you place in the Trash and is located at the root level of your home directory.

There are numerous other files that begin with a period. I mention some of them elsewhere in this book, as relevant. Most of these invisible items are text files.

Files with the Invisible (Hidden) bit set

The Invisible bit was first employed in Mac OS 9 but is still used in Mac OS X. Turning on this bit (also called an *attribute* or *flag*) makes the file invisible in the Finder. Some files may have the Invisible bit set and also have their names begin with a period. Perhaps this setup makes them doubly invisible?

Accessing and modifying the Invisible bit requires special utilities, described in the next section, "Invisible Files: Making Invisible Files Visible (and Vice Versa)."

TAKE NOTE ▶ The .hidden and hidden_MacOS9 Files

In Mac OS X 10.3 Panther and earlier versions of Mac OS X, there was a method for making files invisible that is not covered in the main text. Although this method is no longer used in Mac OS X 10.4 Tiger, a related method is still in use. This sidebar covers what you need to know about both methods.

The .hidden file. In versions of Mac OS X prior to Tiger, there is a file named .hidden, located at the root level of a Mac OS X volume. Because the filename begins with a period, the file itself is invisible. The .hidden file is a text document that simply contains a list of files and folders, mainly ones found at the root level of the volume. They include the Unix folders (such as /bin, /sbin, /var, and /etc) as well as the mach files (mach, mach_kernel, and mach.sym).

This list also includes the Mac OS 9 Desktop database files (Desktop DB and Desktop DF) and the Mac OS 9 Desktop Folder. These files appear at both the root level of your startup volume and the root level of your home directory. They are used only if you run Classic or boot from Mac OS 9.

continues on next page

TAKE NOTE ▶ The .hidden and hidden_MacOS9 Files *continued*

The files and folders listed in this file are invisible in the Finder, regardless of the item's name or other attributes. This is because the Finder checks this list as a means of determining whether or not an item should be visible.

You can modify the contents of the .hidden file and thus change the invisibility of the listed files. However, I recommend not doing so. There are better ways to change the invisibility of a file, as described in the main text.

Note: Some of the items in the .hidden list may be visible by default if you've booted from Mac OS 9. Also, some files in this list are invisible on the Mac OS X startup volume but visible if present on other volumes, even when you're booted in Mac OS X. The invisible Desktop and Temporary Items folders, for example, are visible in all partitions except the Mac OS X partition.

Note: Although you may have a .hidden file on your Tiger volume, it is not used by Tiger.

SetHidden and hidden_MacOS9 files. On the Tiger Mac OS X Install DVD, navigate to /System/Installation/Packages/OSInstall.mpkg. Now use the Show Package Contents command to open the package and navigate to Contents/Resources. In this folder, you will find two files named SetHidden and hidden_MacOS9.

The hidden_MacOS9 file is actually a text file that contains a list similar to the .hidden file just discussed. However, it lists a few additional items, including the Finder (located in /System/Library/CoreServices).

The SetHidden file is a Unix program. It runs as part of the Tiger installation process. Its function is to set the Invisible bit for all the items in the hidden_MacOS9 list. Thus, all of these items will now be invisible, whether you boot in Mac OS X or Mac OS 9, without any need for a separate .hidden file.

Technical note: If you restore a Mac OS X volume from a disk image, the SetHidden file will not run (as you are not using the Install DVD that contains the file). As a consequence, the files in the hidden_MacOS9 list will be visible on the restored volume. A quick fix for this is to locate the SetHidden command on the Install DVD and run it in Terminal. You must also make sure that the disk image is in read-write format (so that you can modify its contents). The exact command to use (assuming you are currently in the directory where the SetHidden and hidden_MacOS9 files reside) is

```
sudo ./SetHidden /Volumes/{name of mounted disk image} hidden_MacOS9
```

This runs the SetHidden command as root, and sets as invisible the files on the disk image that are listed in the hidden_MacOS9 file. You can now use the image for a successful restore. Further details are available in this Apple Knowledge Base article: http://docs.info.apple.com/article.html?artnum=301677.

SEE: • "Technically Speaking: What and Where Are the Unix Files?" in Chapter 4, for more details on these items.

```
automount
bin
cores
dev
etc
mach
mach_kernel
private
sbin
tmp
Trash
usr
var
VM Storage
Volumes
Desktop DB
Desktop DF
Desktop Folder
lost+found
mach.sym
opt
.hidden
.Trashes
.vol
Network
Mac OS 9/Desktop Folder
System/Library/CoreServices/Finder
Applications/Utilities/Print Center.app
```

```
automount
bin
cores
Desktop DB
Desktop DF
Desktop Folder
dev
etc
lost+found
mach
mach_kernel
mach.sym
opt
private
sbin
tmp
Trash
usr
var
VM Storage
```

Figure 6.43

Left, *the contents of the .hidden file;* right, *the contents of the hidden_MacOS9 file.*

TECHNICALLY SPEAKING ▶ Files That Begin with "._"

Built into Mac OS X is a mechanism called Apple Double that allows Mac OS X to work with disk formats that do not use resource forks, such as remote NFS, SMB, and WebDAV directories, or local UFS volumes. Apple Double does this by converting files with resource forks into two separate files. The first file keeps the original name and contains the data fork of the original file. The second file has the name of the original file prefixed by "._" and contains the resource fork of the original file. If you see both files on a non-Mac volume, the ._ file can be safely ignored. Sometimes, when you're deleting the data-fork version of the file, the ._ component does not get deleted. If this occurs, you can safely delete the ._ file.

Invisible Files: Making Invisible Files Visible (and Vice Versa)

Should you ever need to locate, view, modify, or delete an invisible file, this is the section that explains how to do it.

Making all invisible files visible in the Finder

The simplest and most general way to work with invisible items is to make all invisible items visible in the Finder. To do this, you need to modify a setting in the com.apple.finder.plist file located in the Preferences folder of the Library folder in your home directory. Then invisible items will be visible regardless of what method was used to make them invisible (that is, whether their names begin with a period or their Invisible bits are enabled).

Note: In Panther and earlier versions of Mac OS X, when all items are made visible, the icons for the normally invisible items are a shade lighter than the icons for the other items. This was a convenient cue for distinguishing visible from invisible files. In Tiger, this appears to have changed: All icons (normally visible or invisible) take on the lighter shade.

Note: I recommend making this change only on a temporary basis. Keeping all normally invisible files visible permanently may eventually cause problems. For starters, it makes it easier to inadvertently move or delete these files. Also, some applications may not work as expected when these files are visible.

Using Property List Editor. To edit the com.apple.finder.plist file, use Property List Editor. The specific property you need to modify is called AppleShowAllFiles. Changing its value (for example, from 0 to 1) toggles whether or not normally invisible files are visible in the Finder.

Note: If you start off with a new "default" copy of the com.apple.finder.plist file, it may not include this property. In fact, it will likely have very few properties at first, adding more as you use the Finder. In this case, you will need to create the property and set its value as desired.

Relaunch the Finder for the change to take effect. Reverse the procedure to undo the change.

SEE: • "Modifying a .plist file," in Chapter 4, for step-by-step instructions on how to edit AppleShowAllFiles in com.apple.finder.plist.

Using Terminal. If you prefer to use Terminal, the defaults command can be used to make the same changes in a .plist file. For example, to make all invisible files visible, type the following:

```
defaults write com.apple.Finder AppleShowAllFiles 1
```

Relaunch the Finder for the change to take effect. To reverse the process, repeat the same command, using 0 instead of 1 as the value at the end of the command line; relaunch the Finder again.

Using a third-party utility. There are numerous third-party utilities that automate this .plist file change. All you have to do is click a button or two. My favorite choices here are TinkerTool (from Marcel Bresink Software; www.bresink.de), Cocktail (by Kristofer Szymanski; www.macosxcocktail.com), and InVisibles (by Mac4ever; www.mac4ever.de).

- With TinkerTool, check the Show Hidden and System Files box from its Finder options. Then click its Relaunch Finder button.

- With Cocktail, check the "Show invisible items" box from the Interface > Finder pane.
- With InVisibles, launch the utility and click its Visible button.

In all cases, after you have done what you want with the (normally) invisible file(s), reverse the procedure to make these now-visible files invisible again.

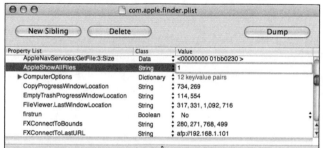

Figure 6.44

You can make invisible files visible by modifying the AppleShowAllFiles property in the com.apple.finder.plist file (in ~/Library/Preferences) as viewed in Property List Editor, left, or running InVisibles, right.

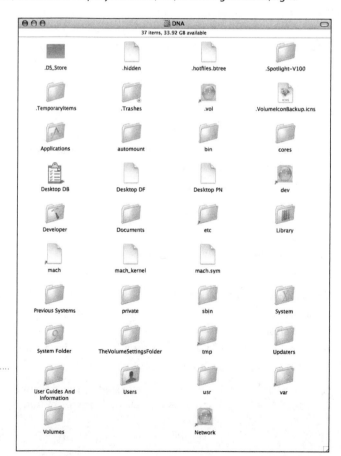

Figure 6.45

The root level of a Mac OS X volume, as seen in the Finder, with invisible items visible.

Using the Finder's Find command

You should be able to use Spotlight via the Finder's Find command to search for and (usually) open invisible items. However, due to an apparent bug in Tiger still present as of Mac OS X 10.4.2, invisible items do not currently appear in Spotlight's results—even when you specifically select to show them. Until this is fixed, you will not be able to use this method.

Note: You can apparently have at least partial success here by using Spotlight's Unix command-line tools (or by using the Raw Query option from Spotlight's Other criteria) and entering the correct query for searching invisible files. However, this hardly seems worth the effort to me. I'd rather use an alternate method while I wait for Apple to fix this.

Assuming Spotlight is eventually fixed so that it can locate invisible files, the following describes how you can locate and open an invisible file via Spotlight:

1. Choose Find (Command-F) from the Finder's File menu. In the toolbar at the top of the window, click the Computer icon, so that you are searching at the root level of the drive.

2. From the pop-up menu (most likely, Kind) in the first row of criteria, choose Other. From the list in the dialog that drops down, select Visibility. Click OK.

3. From the adjacent pop-up menu, change Visible or Invisible to Invisible Items.

4. From the pop-up menu (most likely Last Opened) in the second row of criteria, choose Name. Type {*name of invisible file*} in the text box to the right.

5. The invisible file should appear in the Search Results window. If it is a text file, you can double-click it to open it. If it does not launch directly (probably via TextEdit), select the appropriate application in the dialog that appears.

   SEE: • "Spotlight," in Chapter 2, for related information.

Using the Finder's Go to Folder command

In some cases, files within a folder are set to be visible, but the folder itself is invisible. Most of the files in Mac OS X's invisible Unix folders (located at the root level of the Mac OS X volume) work this way. For these folders, you can use the Finder's Go to Folder command to open a window showing the visible contents of the invisible folder. This bypasses the need to use the Find command to locate the item. However, it assumes you know the name and location of the invisible folder you wish to access.

To use this command, enter the folder's absolute pathname in the Go to Folder text box. For an example of how this works, see "Invisible Files: Working with Invisible Files," later in this chapter.

Using an application that lists and/or opens invisible files

Occasionally, you may want to edit the content of an invisible file. You can do this without making the file visible. TextEdit, for example, can be used to open invisible text files even when the file remains invisible in the Finder. However, third-party applications have features that allow you to do this with more ease than you can with TextEdit. My preferred choices here are Bare Bones' TextWrangler and BBEdit applications (www.barebones.com). For example, here's how you would use TextWrangler to view the contents of the .lpoptions file (a file that lists the name of your default printer):

1. Launch the application, and from the File menu choose Open Hidden.

2. In the window that appears, slide the browser's scroll bar all the way to the left.

3. Select the root level of your home directory in the left-most column.

   The .lpoptions file should be listed in the column immediately to the right.

4. Double-click the file to open it. If you cannot select it, first choose All Files from the Enable pop-up menu (rather than the default choice of All Readable Files).

   SEE: • "Take Note: Editing Text Files via Terminal," in Chapter 10, for other ways to open invisible files with text editors.

Toggling a file's Invisible bit

What if, rather than making all invisible files visible in the Finder or opening an invisible document in a text editor, you want to "permanently" change the visibility status of an individual file? You can do so.

If a file is invisible because its Invisible bit is enabled, you can disable the bit to get the file to appear in the Finder. Conversely, you can enable the bit to get any normally visible file to "disappear."

Unfortunately, Mac OS X's Get Info window does not include an option to enable or disable the Invisible bit for a file. However, several utilities, such as Rainer Brockerhoff's XRay (www.brockerhoff.net/xray), Gideon Softworks' FileXaminer (www.gideonsoftworks.com), and Bare Bones Software's Super Get Info (www.barebones.com), do include an Invisible bit option.

Making a visible item invisible. Open a visible item in FileXaminer (or a similar utility, such as XRay); locate the check box for the Invisible bit (it's in FileXaminer's Advanced section); and check it. Then click the Apply or Save button. When you go back to the Finder, the item should have vanished. As always, you may need to relaunch the Finder for this effect to take place.

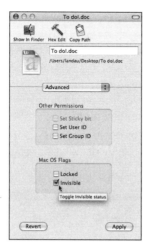

Figure 6.46

A file's Invisible bit option enabled via FileXaminer.

Making an invisible item visible. Changing the Invisible bit of an invisible file is trickier to do than changing it for a visible file. This is because the invisibility of the file makes it more difficult to access in the Finder. The problem is not insurmountable, however. Here's what to do:

1. **Access the invisible file.** There are several ways to do this:
   - You can make all invisible files visible in the Finder (as described above).
   - If you know the exact or approximate name of the file you're seeking, you can search for it via the Finder's Find command with the criteria set to search for invisible files (also as described above). With this method, you do not need to first make all invisible files visible.

     Note: The Find command will not list items in folders for which you do not have access (such as another user's home directory). If you want such items listed in search results, you should use the third-party utility Locator (which is a front end to Unix's locate command), by Sebastian Krauss (www.sebastian-krauss.de/software).

     Note: As mentioned above, as of Mac OS X 10.4.2, searching for invisible files via the Finder's Find command does not work. However, I include this method here because I am assuming Apple will eventually fix this bug.

   - If you're unsure of the name of the file you want, you can instead use a utility such as SkyTag Software's File Buddy (www.skytag.com) or CocoaTech's Path Finder (www.cocoatech.com). These list all invisible files on your drive. File Buddy even includes an option not to include the ubiquitous .DS_Store files in such lists. Assuming you're not looking for a .DS_Store file (which is likely to be the case), this reduces the number of files you need to sift through to locate the desired file.

2. **Modify the Invisible bit.** Once you've located the file, open it in a utility such as XRay or FileXaminer and disable the Invisible bit. For example, if you're using the Find command, when the file you want appears in the Results window, select it and access its contextual menu. Choose the XRay

{*filename*} item if you're using XRay; select Open in FileXaminer if you're using FileXaminer. (You can also drag the file from the Results window onto the icon or window of the utility.) With the file now open in the utility, you can disable the Invisible bit to make the file visible.

Alternatively, if you're using a utility like File Buddy or Path Finder instead of the Find command, you can modify the Invisible bit using options provided directly within the utility.

Note: The SetFile command (included with Apple's Developer Xcode Tools software) can be used to change the invisibility attribute of a file via Terminal.

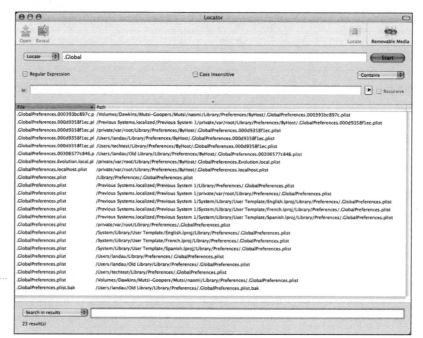

Figure 6.47

Locator finds all copies and versions of an invisible file and their paths.

Figure 6.48

File Buddy's option to search for invisible files.

SEE: • "Finding files: The find, locate, and mdfind commands," in Chapter 10, for related information.

• Chapter 10 for background information on how to use utilities such as SetFile.

Adding or removing a period at the start of a filename

You can make a visible file invisible by adding a period (.) to the start of its name. Conversely, for a file that's already invisible because its name starts with a period, you can make it visible by removing the period.

Although infrequent, there are occasions when you may want to do this. For example, I once downloaded a file from a remote Web server, via FTP, to my local Desktop. The filename began with a period. The result was that the file was invisible after the download was complete. To locate and work with the file, I wanted to eliminate the period (at least temporarily) so that I could more conveniently see the file in the Finder—without having to keep all invisible files visible.

Adding a period to the beginning of an item name from the Finder.
Adding a period to the beginning of an item's name in the Finder is a bit trickier than it sounds. If you try to do this directly, you will get an error message that states the following: "You cannot use a name that begins with a dot '.', because these names are reserved for the system."

The solution is to first make all invisible files visible in the Finder (as described above). Now, when you try to add the period to the file's name, you will get a warning message but will be allowed to make the change. The warning message asks, "Are you sure you want to use a name that begins with a dot '.'?" Click OK. When finished, make all invisible files invisible again. The file with the name change will become invisible.

Removing a period from the start of an item name from the Finder.
To remove a period from the start of a filename, the simplest solution is, once again, to make all invisible files visible in the Finder (as described above). Once you've done this, locate the now-visible file and remove the period from its name. When finished, make all invisible files invisible again. The file with the name change will remain visible.

Figure 6.49

The error message that appears if you try to add a dot to the start of a filename in the Finder without first making invisible files visible.

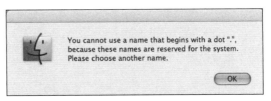

Figure 6.50

The warning message that appears when you add a period to the start of a filename while invisible files are visible in the Finder.

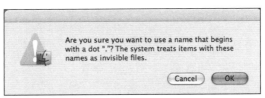

Adding or removing a period to or from the beginning of an item name using third-party utilities. Any utility that can list invisible files (such as File Buddy and Path Finder) can be used to add or remove a period from the start of a file's name, without your needing to first make all files visible in the Finder.

SEE: • "Toggling a file's Invisible bit," earlier in this chapter, for more details on how to access invisible files via these third-party utilities.

Adding or removing a period to or from the start of an item name using Terminal. You can use Terminal to add or remove a period from a file's name quickly. To do so, launch Terminal and type the following:

mv {/path/*filename*} {/path/.*filename*}

As I've said before, the easiest way to designate a file location in Terminal is to drag the file's icon from the Finder to the Terminal window. This enters the file's absolute path (/path/filename) to the command line. Once you've done this, enter a space and enter the same text a second time (either via the same dragging of the icon or via copy and paste). Then backspace to the start of the filename, type a period followed by whatever you want to name the file, and press Return. This creates a new file (with a period as the first character of the filename) to replace the original file in the same location. If you check the Finder, the file icon will have vanished.

You can later make the now-invisible file visible again by typing the opposite:

mv {/path/.*filename*} {/path/*filename*}

To make a visible *copy* of the file, instead of renaming it you could use the cp command.

Note: In Terminal, only items that begin with a period are considered invisible. Other items that are invisible in the Finder are listed as visible when using a command such as 1s. To see a list of all files in the current directory, including invisible files, type 1s -a. This lists the names of all files in the directory (including ones that start with a period).

SEE: • Chapter 10 for background information on using commands such as 1s, cp, and mv.

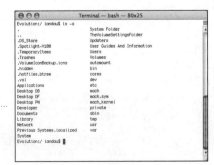

Figure 6.51

Viewing invisible files in Terminal via the 1s -a command.

Invisible Files: Working with Invisible Files

Here are three examples of situations in which the ability to work with invisible files can help solve problems.

SEE: • "Take Note: Where Is My Music?" in Chapter 11, for another example of working with invisible files: accessing the invisible location of music files on an iPod.

Modifying or deleting the .GlobalPreferences.plist files

The .GlobalPreferences.plist files contain various settings that are "global" to your account or to the system in general. There are at least three such files active in Mac OS X. The first one is in /Library/Preferences; the second one is in ~/Library/Preferences (that is, your home directory); and the third one (and the one least likely to need to be modified or deleted) is in ~/Library/Preferences/ByHost (this one has letters and numbers added to its name that are derived from your Mac's Ethernet/MAC address).

Each of these files contains different settings.

The one in the root-level Library folder contains your Mac's Energy Saver settings, time zone settings, list of ColorSync devices, and more.

The one in your home directory Library folder contains your AppleID, text highlight color selection, default system-font selections, file-sharing default settings (such as the idle time-out period), and more.

If you wish, you can directly modify these settings from the .plist file, rather than from System Preferences, by using Property List Editor.

SEE: • "Modifying a .plist file," in Chapter 4.

Alternatively, if problems occur with items related to the files' settings (such as problems with your Mac's date and time), you can simply delete the relevant file and log out. A new default copy will be created when you log back in. Hopefully, this will fix the symptoms.

The main problem with doing any of these things is that these files are invisible, due to the period prefix in their names. To work around this, you can use almost any of the solutions described in the previous sections of this chapter.

More specifically, to modify the file, the simplest approach is to make invisible files visible in the Finder (such as via InVisibles). Then open the file in Property List Editor.

To delete the file, you can use the same technique to make the file visible—and then drag the file to the Trash. Or you can use the rm command in Terminal (because the file is accessible in Terminal even though it's invisible in the Finder).

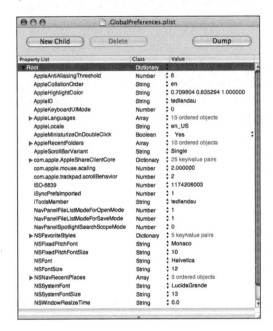

Figure 6.52

The contents of the .Global-Preferences.plist file in ~/Library/ Preferences.

Hiding personal files in an invisible folder

You can use invisibility as a minimal form of security to prevent prying eyes from accessing files that you wish to keep private. It won't deter a determined user from locating these files, but it will work effectively to prevent their casual discovery. The basic idea is to create an invisible folder to hold your private files. To do so:

1. Use a utility such as InVisibles or TinkerTool to make all invisible items visible.

2. Use the Finder's New Folder command to create a new "untitled" folder. You can locate it anywhere (such as on your Desktop or at the root level of your home directory).

3. Rename the folder with a name that starts with a period (such as .Private).

4. When the dialog that asks if you are sure you want to do this appears, click OK.

5. Place any files you want to keep hidden in this new folder.

6. Using the same utility as in Step 1, make all invisible items invisible again.

In the future, to add or delete files from the folder, you can temporarily make invisible items visible. Alternatively, you can access documents in the folder via

Open and Save dialogs of applications—by using the "Go to the folder" option (Command-Shift-G) and entering the full pathname to the folder in the text box (for example, ~/Desktop/.Private).

Modifying invisible Unix files from Mac OS X applications

Mac OS X keeps its essential Unix directories invisible in the Finder. These directories include /bin, /etc, /sbin, /tmp, /var, /usr, and /Volumes. In both Chapter 4 ("Take Note: What and Where Are the Unix Files?") and Chapter 10, I provide more details about the items in these directories and how to use Terminal to access their contents. For now, I want to focus on how and why to edit some of these Unix files using Mac OS X applications instead.

Unix uses configuration (config) files to determine the settings and preferences of a variety of features (such as network settings and Web server settings). In some cases, when you change a System Preferences setting, you're modifying the contents of one of these Unix config files. These files are mainly text files in Unix's /etc directory. Occasionally, you may want to change a setting in one of these files that cannot be changed via System Preferences or any other Mac OS X interface. The solution is to edit the configuration file directly.

To do so, you open and edit these config files in a Mac OS X text editor. In most cases, the permissions settings for the files will require that you have root access to modify the file.

You can edit these files in Terminal, using an editor such as nano in combination with the sudo command. Alternatively, you can edit these files directly in Mac OS X applications, such as TextEdit, by logging in as the root user. You can also modify these files directly in Mac OS X applications, even when logged in via your normal administrative account. The following sections provide some examples.

SEE: • "Take Note: Opening Mac OS Applications from Terminal" and "Take Note: Editing Text Files via Terminal," in Chapter 10, for related information.

Using TextWrangler. A program that makes it easy to edit config files is Bare Bones' TextWrangler (or its even more feature-packed sibling, BBEdit). To use it, follow these steps:

1. Access the desired file by choosing TextWrangler's Open Hidden command. In the Enable pop-up menu in the dialog that appears, select All Files. Navigate to the desired directory (for example, /private/etc) and select the desired file.

2. If the file requires root access, the initial Pencil icon in the toolbar at the top of the document will have a line through it. Click this icon.

You will get a message stating, "The document '{*document name*}' is owned by 'root.' Are you sure you want to unlock it?" Click Yes.

3. The line through the Pencil icon is removed. You can now modify the document and save your changes—you'll be asked for your admin-level user name and password when you save, of course.

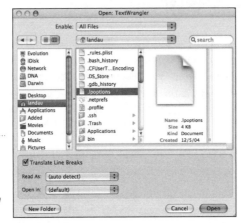

Figure 6.53

TextWrangler displays invisible files (in my home directory) available to open via its Open Hidden command.

Using Pseudo and any text editor. If you don't have TextWrangler or BBEdit, you can alternatively open almost any application with root access. Having done this, you'll find that all documents you open from within that application are automatically modifiable, even if they would otherwise require root access to do so. The easiest way to do all of this is with the freeware utility Pseudo, by Brian R. Hill (http://personalpages.tds.net/~brian_hill/pseudo.html). To use it, follow these steps:

1. Launch Pseudo.

2. Drag the icon of the application you want to open to the Pseudo window, and enter your admin-level password when prompted. The application is now open with root access.

   Apple's TextEdit is a fine choice for an application to open in this way. The config files described here will be listed in TextEdit's Open dialog because the files are visible, even though the enclosing folder is invisible.

3. Open the desired file. To do so, choose Open from the application's File menu and press Command-Shift-G to access the "Go to the folder" option. Enter the path to the folder you wish to access (for example, /var/log/cups). You will now see a list of all files in the selected folder. Double-click the file you want to open.

4. Edit and save the file, as desired.

   SEE: • "Root Access," in Chapter 4, and "Take Note: Opening Mac OS Applications from Terminal," in Chapter 10, for ways to open Mac OS X applications with root access using Terminal instead of Pseudo.

   • "Using shell-configuration files," in Chapter 10, for a discussion of Unix line breaks and text editors.

Using Terminal to delete .AppleSetupDone. There is an invisible file named .AppleSetupDone, located in the /var/db directory. If you delete this file, the next time you launch your Mac, Setup Assistant will run again, just as it does the first time you boot a new Mac (or erase your drive and reinstall Mac OS X). It is not often that you will have a practical need for doing this, but I thought it would be interesting to know about.

You will need root access to delete this file. Probably the easiest way to do so is to launch Terminal and do the following:

1. Type cd /var/db.

2. Type sudo rm .AppleSetupDone.

Note: If needed (perhaps because you have a startup problem that you believe will be helped by getting Setup Assistant to run), you can also do this via single-user mode. In this case, the sudo command is not required; after mounting the hard drive for write access, type the first command as listed and then just start the second line with the rm command.

Config files that may need editing. Following are three examples of Unix config files you might want or need to modify at some point.

- **inetd.conf.** Mac OS X uses SSH for making Telnet connections over a network. The SSH protocol provides greater security than the older Telnet. However, if you want or need to use the less secure Telnet, you need to change the /etc/inetd.conf file. To do so, open the file in BBEdit and then follow these steps:

  1. Locate the lines that read #telnet; #shell; and #login.

  2. Remove the # character from the start of each line.

  3. Save the file.

  4. Restart your Mac.

  SEE: • "Network Security," in Chapter 9, for more on SSH.

- **httpd.conf.** This is the Apache Web server configuration file. Modifying Web-related operations (such as starting PHP), although more likely to be done with Mac OS X Server than with the client, require editing this file. See the following Apple Knowledge Base article for an example: http://docs.info.apple.com/article.html?artnum=107292.

- **hostconfig.** This file contains a list of processes (CUPS printing software, Web server, file sharing, Crash Reporter, and more) that typically are enabled at startup. By changing values from YES to NO (and vice versa), you can determine whether or not a given process loads.

  SEE: • "Technically Speaking: Spotlight Indexes," in Chapter 2, for an example of modifying this file.

Note: Future updates to Mac OS X may provide more user-friendly ways of making these changes, eliminating the need to directly access these config files. Still, it's likely that there will always be some actions that require this direct access to the files.

SEE: • "Take Note: Why and How to Use Archive and Install" and "Technically Speaking: Custom Config Files After a Mac OS X Update," in Chapter 3, for related information.

• "Technically Speaking: Hostconfig and Other Configuration Files," in Chapter 5, for related information.

• "CUPS," in Chapter 7, for several examples of config and related files used by the CUPS printing software.

Maximizing Performance

Most computer users are never completely satisfied with how fast their computers run. They always want their Macs to run just a little bit faster. Although hardware and software place certain limits on a computer's speed, computers often don't run as fast as they're capable of. In this section, I describe some ways you can make sure you're getting the best performance from your Mac.

Several utilities, most notably Micromat's TechTool Pro (www.micromat.com), can be used to evaluate the overall performance of your Mac. Unless you know from experience or by comparing performance data generated by applications that run such tests, like TechTool Pro, it may be difficult to determine if your Mac is truly running slower than it should. Still, if you believe your Mac's speed is sluggish, consider the following causes and solutions.

SEE: • "Technically Speaking: Terminal Commands to Monitor and Improve Performance," in Chapter 10, for related information.

Not enough memory

Due to Mac OS X's dynamic memory, you will rarely, if ever, get "out of memory" messages, no matter how many applications you have open. This is because Mac OS X assigns an increasing amount of the memory load to virtual memory, as needed—which can make it appear that your Mac has unlimited memory. This is not the case. At some point, as you open more and more applications, the overall performance of every aspect of your Mac will slow. Keep pushing the memory envelope, and you will likely precipitate a crash. Otherwise, you might eventually get a memory-related error message, advising you to close windows and quit applications to free up more memory.

Following are the three surest solutions:

- **Quit unneeded applications.** The quickest solution, although often the least effective, is to quit any open applications you don't need (as the potential error message advises). Quitting Classic, if you don't need to use it, is always a good idea.

  Different programs use different amounts of memory. Thus, quitting Application A may have little effect, whereas quitting Application B may have a tremendous effect.

- **Log out or restart.** If a problem has become severe, you may need to log out and log back in before performance improves. Even better, restart your Mac. This is the surest way to free up memory that may have been causing a problem. It also resets the swap files(s) back to a default state (as discussed more in "Technically Speaking: Swap Files and RAM Disks," below).

- **Add more memory.** The best solution to memory problems, especially if they happen frequently, is to purchase more memory. How much? As much as you can afford and/or your Mac can hold. You can't have too much. Mac OS X devours whatever RAM you give it. And the less RAM you have, the more performance slowdowns you'll have.

About This Mac and MemoryStick. How do you know how much memory you have and how much you're using? The About This Mac window, which you open from the Apple menu, tells you how much physical memory (RAM) you have installed. A utility such as Matt Neuburg's MemoryStick (www.tidbits.com/matt) can show you how your RAM is being used; more important, it will let you know how many swap files and *pageouts* are occurring. If MemoryStick alerts you about frequent pageouts and swap files, you'll benefit from installing additional RAM.

SEE: • "Technically Speaking: Swap Files and RAM Disks," below.

  • "Utilities for monitoring and improving performance," later in this chapter, for more on memory issues, including memory leaks.

  • "Technically Speaking: Dividing Up Mac OS X's Memory," in Chapter 4, for more on virtual versus physical memory, and related issues.

TECHNICALLY SPEAKING ▶ Swap Files and RAM Disks

What and where is a swap file? When Mac OS X doesn't have enough physical memory (RAM) for what it needs to accomplish, it pages out some of the least-used contents of RAM to your hard drive as virtual memory. These pageouts are stored in swap files, located in /var/vm on your hard drive. Initially, there is one swap file, named "swapfile0." Its size may vary, depending on your computer setup, but will typically be about 64 MB to 80 MB. If additional space is needed, additional swap files are created, named "swapfile1," "swapfile2," and so on. MemoryStick is a useful utility that displays the current number of swap files, updated every few seconds.

If you find that you frequently have more than one swap file, this is a sure sign that you're pushing the memory limits of your Mac.

continues on next page

TECHNICALLY SPEAKING ▶ Swap Files and RAM Disks *continued*

Once additional swap files have been created, they aren't automatically deleted when no longer needed, nor should you attempt to delete them manually. The simplest and surest way to reset back to a lone swap file is to restart your Mac. A utility such as Cocktail can delete all swap files without forcing a restart, but I strongly recommend against this, as it will likely result in applications' no longer working correctly or, even worse, a major system crash. I would use this function only if (as occasionally happens due to some bug) restarting the Mac fails to delete additionally created swap files. Even so, after deleting all swap files, I would restart as soon as possible.

Moving swap files to a separate partition. Fragmentation of a hard drive occurs when a file is stored in several segments in different locations on the drive, typically because no single free section of the drive is large enough to hold the entire file as one segment. As more files become fragmented, the overall level of disk fragmentation increases. If the fragmentation level gets high enough, drive performance can start to decline. Disk optimizers such as Drive Genius's Defragment option (ProSoft Engineering; www.prosofteng.com) are designed to reduce this fragmentation.

Larger files are more subject to fragmentation than smaller ones. Thus, because swap files are large, they're especially vulnerable to fragmentation. Moving swap files to a separate volume (presumably one with lots of free space) from the one that contains Mac OS X can help reduce fragmentation. This change may in turn improve virtual memory performance and, especially, disk performance.

At least that's the theory. I'm not convinced that the benefit is worth the effort, especially because, as covered in "Defragmenting/optimizing Mac OS X volumes" in Chapter 5, Mac OS X already works to keep fragmentation to a minimum. I certainly don't do it myself. There are several utilities (such as Swap Cop) that automated this task for you, but I have not found any that have been updated for Tiger. The alternative solution—which requires considerable work in Terminal and/or with Unix files—is beyond the scope of this book.

RAM disks. RAM disks mimic the behavior of a mounted disk, except there's no physical media; it's all in memory. A mounted image (.dmg) file is a bit like a RAM disk. RAM disks were a supported feature in Mac OS 9; however, Mac OS X offers no equivalent feature. Indeed, developers report that writing a program that creates RAM disks in Mac OS X is a much more difficult task than it was in Mac OS 9. In addition, Mac OS X's virtual memory works so well that the speed benefits associated with a RAM disk in Mac OS 9 are not nearly as great as in Mac OS X. As a result, you won't see much use of RAM disks in Mac OS X.

Still, if it's a RAM disk you want, you can get one via third-party utilities like Clarkwood Software's ramBunctious (www.clarkwood.com). Because Apple does not directly support RAM disks (unlike disk images), they're more prone to problems—especially after an update to the OS. Be cautious in using them.

SEE: • "Technically Speaking: Dividing Up Mac OS X's Memory," in Chapter 4, for related information.

   • "Defragmenting/optimizing Mac OS X volumes," in Chapter 5, for more on fragmentation.

   • "Technically Speaking: Technical Commands to Monitor and Improve Performance," in Chapter 10, for still more information on memory and swap files.

Processor or graphics card is too slow

If your Mac is more than two years old, getting a new Mac will likely give you significantly better performance; however, upgrading the processor or graphics card on your existing Mac may be a more cost-effective solution. Keep in mind, though, that with the rapid rate at which computers advance, it's often a better deal to get a new computer than it is to spend hundreds of dollars upgrading an old one—even if it costs a bit more to do so.

A Mac with a G4 or G5 processor, for example, will be noticeably snappier than one that uses a G3. The difference in processor speed is usually more noticeable when you're running Mac OS X than it is in Mac OS 9, because Mac OS X places more demands on the processor. Mac OS X also includes dual-processor support for some OS functions; Mac OS 9 did not. Thus, if you have a dual-processor Mac, it should seem faster in Mac OS X than it does in Mac OS 9.

A faster graphics card (ATI and nVidia are always coming out with new and improved models) can also enhance speed in specific situations, such as when you're using multimedia or playing games. They do not, however, increase the overall speed of your Mac.

Note: Quartz Extreme is a hardware-accelerated update to Mac OS X's Quartz graphics engine, included in Mac OS X 10.2 and later. The good news is that it's faster at drawing graphics onscreen. The bad news is that some of its acceleration features work only with newer graphics cards from nVidia (such as GeForce2 MX, GeForce3, GeForce4 Ti, GeForce4, or GeForce4 MX or newer) and ATI (any AGP Radeon card). In addition, Tiger includes a new graphics technology called Core Image. However, the list of graphics cards that support Core Image is even smaller than the list supporting Quartz Extreme; see Apple's Core Image Web page (www.apple.com/macosx/features/coreimage) for a list of compatible cards.

Drive is too small

As a rough estimate, you should always keep at least 10 percent of your drive free. Thus, for a 60 GB drive, try to keep at least 6 GB unused. Even on smaller drives, I don't recommend going below 3 GB of "free" space. If you do, you're likely to see performance decline. At some point, as free space continues to decline, you will get error messages stating that you're almost out of disk space and advising you to delete files from the drive. You may even be prohibited from performing some action, getting a message that claims you don't have sufficient free space to perform it. This can occur even if it seems as if you have a good deal of free space. In such cases, this is usually because the operation requires more space than it will ultimately use. Some software updates work this way, for example, by maintaining a copy of the old software until after the new software has been completely installed. Thus, unless you have enough free space to hold both the old and new software simultaneously, the operation is prevented.

An increase in the number and size of certain files maintained by the OS itself (such as swap files and cache files) may cut into the amount of free space that was available when you first booted, even though you aren't saving any new files to the drive. In this case, simply restarting and/or deleting the cache files could free up enough space to solve an immediate crisis.

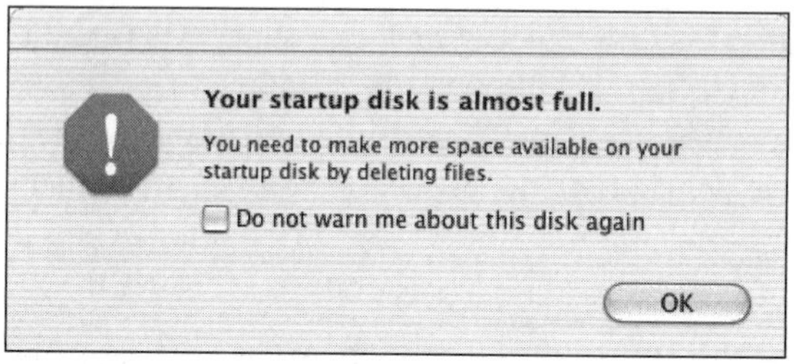

Figure 6.54

The error message that appears when your startup disk is almost full.

> **Your startup disk is almost full.**
>
> You need to make more space available on your startup disk by deleting files.
>
> ☐ Do not warn me about this disk again
>
> OK

Too little free space can also prevent additional virtual memory swap files from being created when needed. Actually, even with a minimally sufficient amount of space, fragmentation of swap files (which increases as free space declines) can lead to a performance decrease.

To solve problems associated with too little disk space, try the following:

- Delete large and unneeded files from your hard drive.
- Defragment your hard drive to create more contiguous free space.
- Purchase a larger hard drive to replace your existing one or as an additional drive to offload rarely used files. Newer hard drives also tend to be faster than their predecessors.
- Reduce the need to access virtual memory by (a) decreasing the number of processes and applications running and/or (b) adding more physical memory.

    SEE: • "Technically Speaking: Swap Files and RAM Disks," earlier in this chapter, for related information.

    • "Insufficient space," earlier in this chapter, for related information.

    • "Defragmenting/optimizing Mac OS X volumes," in Chapter 5, for more on fragmentation.

Internet connection is too slow

If your speed problems are primarily restricted to surfing the Internet (for example, Web pages are slow to load) and you have a dial-up modem connection, it's time to think about moving to a broadband connection (cable or DSL). Not only will speeds be much increased, but also you'll have a 24/7 connection with no need to log on and no dropped connections.

If you already have a broadband connection, there are still ways you can improve performance. The utility MOX Optimize (by Infosoft; www.infosoft-sw.com), for example, includes an option to speed Ethernet networking by optimizing buffers—in essence a front end for an operation you could otherwise perform in Terminal. Utilities like Cocktail and Northern Softworks' Tiger Cache Cleaner (www.northernsoftworks.com) have similar network-optimization features.

If you're plagued by slow launch times for your Web browser, check the /Library/Internet Plug-Ins folder and make sure there are no unneeded or out-of-date plug-in files. If you find any, delete or update them. If you're not sure whether you want a certain plug-in, remove it from the folder but don't delete it. You can always return it later if you want.

Want to see how your Internet download and upload speeds compare with what is typical for your type of connection (for example, a cable modem)? There are several Web sites that allow you to do this, such as Toast.net Performance Test (http://toast.net/performance) and PC Pitstop (www.pcpitstop.com/internet).

SEE: • Chapters 8 and 9 for more information on network and Internet issues.

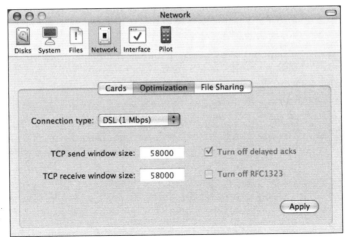

Figure 6.55

Cocktail's Network > Optimization pane.

Utilities for monitoring and improving performance

With so many possible causes of suboptimal performance, how can you best diagnose whether your Mac is performing up to par? And if it's not, what's the quickest way to determine the primary cause? The answers to both of these questions reside in a host of utility software.

For starters, Mac OS X comes with several performance-related utilities. For example:

Activity Monitor. Activity Monitor is located in the Utilities folder. I first mentioned this utility in Chapter 2, where I explained its basic features. In Chapter 5, I discussed this utility again, primarily as a means to force-quit processes. Here, I focus on several features specifically related to monitoring performance.

The values described here are updated at an interval you choose via the Update Frequency submenu in the View menu. The default is every 2 seconds.

- **Real Memory and Virtual Memory.** These two columns in the main Activity Monitor window list how much real (physical) memory and how much virtual memory are used by each listed process.

  You can sort the list by the values in any column by clicking the column name. Thus, to see which applications are using the most memory, click the Real Memory or Virtual Memory title at the top of a column. Processes that move to the top of the list are the ones that are the most likely culprits in any memory-related performance problems. (If the list shows smaller numbers first, click the column head again to reverse the sort order.) Quitting one or more of these processes is likely to have the biggest effect. However, regardless of what the results may be, do not quit any processes that you do not recognize, especially administrator processes (which you can view by changing the selection from My Processes in the pop-up menu)—quitting certain processes can cause you to be logged out or crash your Mac.

  You can also use memory listings to determine whether a process has a *memory leak* bug. In a memory leak, a process uses an increasing amount of memory over time—even if it's sitting idle. In extreme cases, memory use may get so enormous that it bogs down the entire Mac. By watching changes to the Memory columns in Activity Monitor, you can determine if a leak is likely and which process is the culprit. About the only solution at this point is to restart. The ultimate long-term solution is to get a bug-fixed version of the application that does not leak.

  Note: Classic applications are not listed separately in Activity Monitor but are instead included under the TruBlueEnvironme process. For a list of each open Classic application and its memory use, check out the Memory/Versions section of the Classic System Preferences pane.

- **% CPU.** The percentages in the % CPU column list how much of the processor's activity is used by each listed process. If overall CPU demand gets too high, the Mac's apparent performance may slow significantly. Use this column to determine which processes are placing the most demand on the CPU. Look especially for ones that have a sustained high number here, not just a brief peak.

- **Performance monitors.** As noted in Chapter 2, the bottom section of the Activity Monitor window contains five tabs: CPU, System Memory, Disk Activity, Disk Usage, and Network. Click each one to get data regarding these matters.

CPU. CPU provides information about CPU usage. The graphs show the ever-changing rise and fall of CPU usage. Don't be alarmed if the level occasionally gets to 100 percent; that's OK as long as it doesn't stay there for a sustained period. If the level remains at its peak for an extended time, you are likely trying to do too many processor-intensive activities at the same time. Quitting some applications (especially ones showing a high CPU percentage) or reducing how many tasks you have going simultaneously is likely to help.

You will see that CPU usage is broken into four categories: % User, % System, % Nice, and % Idle. The distinction between User and System is essentially the same as between User and Administrator processes, as described in the "Activity Monitor" section in Chapter 2. A *niced* process is one whose CPU priority has been modified from its default value, so as to take up more (or less) CPU time than it otherwise would (as explained more in "Technically Speaking: Terminal Commands to Monitor and Improve Performance," in Chapter 10).

Note: You can also see CPU graphs by choosing the CPU History or Show Floating CPU Window command from Activity Monitor's Window menu.

System Memory. System Memory shows how memory is divided up into its four main categories: Wired, Active, Inactive, and Free. It also shows "Page ins/outs." All of this is covered more in "Technically Speaking: Dividing Up Mac OS X's Memory," in Chapter 4.

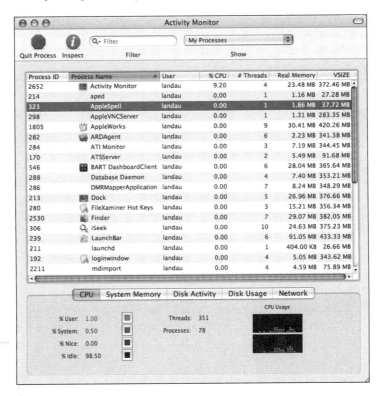

Figure 6.56

Activity Monitor's main window with CPU display.

Disk Activity. Disk Activity provides data regarding hard-disk access, including transfer speed (Reads in/sec and Writes out/sec).

Disk Usage. Disk Usage provides information about the amount of space on each volume that's utilized versus free.

Network. Network provides basic information that indicates when network data is being transferred to and from your Mac and the speed of the transfer.

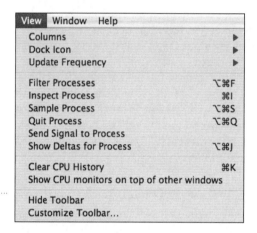

Figure 6.57

Activity Monitor's View menu.

Network Utility. Network Utility, also in the Utilities folder, provides additional statistics about network performance, particularly in its Info and Netstat panes.

SEE: • "Using Network Utility," in Chapter 8, for more on this utility.

• "Technically Speaking: Terminal Commands to Monitor and Improve Performance," in Chapter 10, for coverage of the netstat command accessed from Terminal.

Terminal commands and third-party utilities. The information provided by utilities such as Activity Monitor is also available via Unix commands entered in Terminal. For example, much of the information listed in Activity Monitor overlaps with what you get via the Unix top command.

Advanced users should also check out the sysctl command (type man sysctl in Terminal for information on this rather arcane tool).

Other utilities, primarily from third parties, are front ends for Unix commands, providing a graphical Aqua-based interface for what would otherwise require the use of Terminal.

As one example of this, Raging Menace's MenuMeters (www.ragingmenace.com) provides a quick view of a variety of performance-related data. In its default view, you get a constantly updated look at CPU use, system load, memory use (including pageouts), network ins and outs, and disk reads and writes.

SEE: • "Technically Speaking: Terminal Commands to Monitor and Improve Performance," in Chapter 10, for more details on Terminal commands and front-end utilities related to performance.

Also check out utilities such as Cocktail and Xupport (by computer-support.ch; www.computer-support.ch/xupport). For example, Cocktail (mentioned several times already in this chapter and illustrated in Figures 6.42 and 6.55) allows you to perform a variety of actions that would otherwise require several Mac OS X and third-party utilities. Here is a partial list of what Cocktail can do:

- Show invisible files in the Finder
- Add a Quit command to the Finder
- Enable the debug menu in programs such as Safari
- Renew a DHCP lease
- Optimize network settings for broadband versus dial-up
- Set Ethernet speed, duplex, and MTU values
- Delete locked or otherwise undeletable items
- Delete .DS_Store files
- Delete archived log files
- Delete cache files
- Perform the Unix optimizing/prebinding function
- Run cron scripts
- Create symbolic links
- Re-create the "Desktop (Mac OS 9)" symbolic-link file
- Enable disk journaling
- Set hard-drive spin-down times

SEE: • "Take Note: Launch Services Files and Beyond," earlier in this chapter, for more on Cocktail and related utilities.

Hardware-testing software. As discussed in Chapter 5, to check for hardware-related causes that may be at the root of performance problems, you can use the Apple Hardware Test software that came with your Mac. Micromat's TechTool Pro is also useful here.

To test specifically for memory-related problems, however, use the third-party Unix command-line tool called Memtest (www.memtestosx.org). Alternatively, use the Aqua application called Rember, by KelleyComputing (www.kelleycomputing.net:16080/rember), which is a front end for Memtest.

The main limitation of Rember, compared with Memtest itself, is that Rember cannot run in single-user mode. This means that you cannot use it to test for problems that may be preventing your Mac from starting up. In addition, because both utilities can only test RAM that is not in use, Memtest's ability to be run in single-user mode means it's able to test *more* of your RAM for problems. Either way, these are the best tools available for checking for bad RAM. For details on how to use these programs, check the documentation that comes with them.

Other miscellaneous performance tips

Finally, you can do a host of other minor tweaks to bring about incremental improvements in performance.

Turn off unneeded Finder and Dock features. Turning off certain Finder and/or Dock features can reduce overall CPU usage and thus improve performance. It's up to you to decide whether the trade-off is worthwhile. Any one feature is not likely to have a big effect, but turning off a combination of items may be significant. Such actions are likely to have the greatest effect on older hardware. Features to consider turning off include the following:

- Genie effect for minimizing folders to the Dock (use Scale instead)
- Dock magnification (keep to a minimum)
- Bouncing icons in the Dock
- Languages for searching file contents (turn off all but the language you use)
- Text smoothing (set it to be off for the largest font size available)
- Zoom rectangles
- Window shadows

The on/off switches for these features can be found in the Finder's Preferences, the Dock and Appearance System Preference panes, Get Info windows, and various third-party utilities that provide access to some settings not available via Apple's Mac OS X software. Infosoft's MOX Optimize has an especially rich selection of options, including the capability to increase the Finder's Unix nice priority (see "Technically Speaking: Terminal Commands to Monitor and Improve Performance" in Chapter 10). Other potentially useful utilities include Marcel Bresink's TinkerTool, Kristofer Szymanski's Cocktail, and Unsanity's ShadowKiller and Dock Detox (www.unsanity.com/products/free).

Remove unneeded login and startup items. Check the applications and processes listed in the Login Items list in the Accounts System Preferences pane. You may have some items for software that you no longer want to use. In such cases, remove the item. Otherwise, the item continues to launch at login and may contribute to a decrease in performance.

Don't put hard drives to sleep. Uncheck the Energy Saver System Preferences pane's "Put the hard disk(s) to sleep when possible" option. This can significantly improve performance related to hard-drive access, especially for external FireWire drives. However, keep in mind that disabling this option on a laptop will lead to reduced battery life.

Speed up application launches. To improve application launch times, Mac OS X maintains certain information about each application in /var/vm/app_profile. The files here are typically re-created on restart. If application launch times become unusually slow, and especially if the app_profile directory is very large, deleting the directory may return speeds to normal. You need root access to do this. To do so via Terminal, type the following:

```
sudo rm -R /private/var/vm/app_profile
```

Then restart your Mac by typing reboot.

Disconnect from remote servers before installing software. This is especially recommended if you're installing software that uses the VISE installer software. Being connected to a server (even your iDisk) while installing can significantly slow the computer's response.

Check the Web. Various Mac Web sites post frequently updated tips for enhancing Mac OS X performance. One good site is Mac OS X speed FAQ (www.index-site.com/Macosxspeed.html).

7

Troubleshooting Printing

Given the Mac OS's historically strong position in the graphics and publishing industries, you might assume that Mac OS X would include advanced printing features—and you would be right! Mac OS X provides Mac users with a high-tech printing engine that includes built-in support for many printers and tools for managing your print jobs. In this chapter, I'll show you how printing works in Mac OS X and what to do when it doesn't.

In This Chapter

TAKE NOTE ▶ Printing: A Behind-the-Scenes Introduction

As with Fonts folders (described in Chapter 4), there are multiple Printers folders in the various Library folders on your drive. Each folder serves a different function.

/System/Library/Printers. This folder is the main location for the non-Unix printer software installed by Mac OS X. Within this folder is a collection of other folders. In general, you should not modify any of the files here. The folders of most interest include the following:

- **PPDs.** This folder contains (buried in /PPDs/Contents/Resources) the .lproj (language-specific) folders containing the PostScript Printer Description files for Apple's LaserWriter printers. The en.lproj (English-language) folder must be there in order for the system to work; the rest of the folders are optional, based on the language support you've installed with Mac OS X.

   The PPDs are archived as .gzip files. If you double-click one, it will be uncompressed by the Finder. From here, you can save the expanded copy to your Desktop for viewing. The PPD is a Unix Executable File (see Chapter 10 for more on this term) and can be opened in a text editor.

   Note: The active PPD files for the printers added to your Printer List in Printer Setup Utility are stored (uncompressed) in the Unix directory /etc/cups/ppd.

- **PBMs.** This folder contains Printer Browser Modules files, which determine most of the options available in the pop-up menu of Printer Setup Utility's Add Printer dialog. The names of the files mirror the options they provide: PB_AppleTalk.plugin, PB_Bluetooth.plugin (Bluetooth printing), PB_SMB.plugin (printing to Windows printers), and PB_Advanced.plugin.

/Library/Printers. This folder is primarily for third-party printer software (Brother, Canon, Epson, and so on) installed by Mac OS X or the user. It includes PPDs for PostScript laser printers, as well as separate vendor-specific folders for inkjet printers.

~/Library/Printers. This folder, located in each user's home directory, can contain the same sorts of folders and files as /Library/Printers. The main difference is that files in this folder are accessible only when the user of that name is logged in, whereas files in /Library/Printers are accessible to all local users. In Mac OS X 10.3. Panther and later, this folder is also where printer proxy applications are stored (as described later in this chapter in "Take Note: Printer Queue (Proxy) Applications").

If matching files that correspond to the same printer appear in more than one of these folders, Mac OS X will use the one in your home directory over the one in the /Library directory, which in turn overrides the one in the /System/Library folder.

Classic. Mac OS X also looks in the Printer Descriptions folder (inside the Extensions folder) of your Classic Mac OS 9 System Folder for additional PPD files, but only if it has not already found a match in the Mac OS X Library folders. In addition, starting in Tiger, any printers you've set up in Mac OS X will automatically be available to applications running in Classic.

continues on next page

TAKE NOTE ▶ Printing: A Behind-the-Scenes Introduction *continued*

On the other hand, when you're booted into Mac OS 9, none of the Mac OS X folders described here are directly checked—Mac OS 9 checks for PPDs only in the Mac OS 9 System Folder and uses the Chooser (rather than Printer Setup Utility) to select a printer.

SEE: • **"Printing from Classic," later in this chapter, and the online Classic chapter, available at Mac OS X Help Line (www.macosxhelpline.com), for more information on printing in Classic.**

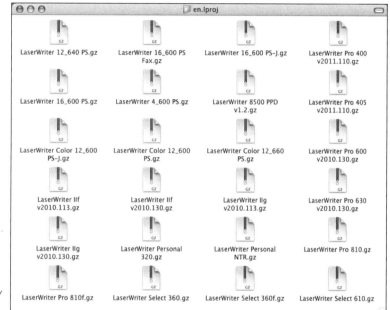

Figure 7.1

The PPD files (compressed) in /System/Library/ Printers/PPDs/ Contents/Resources/ en.lproj.

Printer Support in Mac OS X

Before I begin talking about setting up printing in Mac OS X, I'm going to go over the types of printers and connections that are supported, as well as the differences between these printer types.

One of the problems with older versions of Mac OS X was that they didn't support many of the most common printers—especially inkjet printers. In addition, they provided little, if any, support for connecting to printers over an AppleTalk network. These limitations have largely been addressed via the latest versions of Mac OS X and the various printer updates released by Apple and printer vendors. Thus, if you're having printer problems, the first thing you should do is make sure you're using the latest software available for your printer.

What types of printers does Mac OS X support?

Mac OS X supports both PostScript (Level 2 and Level 3) and non-PostScript printers. The nature of that support, however, differs.

PostScript printers. *PostScript* is an Adobe-developed programming language that allows the operating system to describe the appearance of a printed page precisely to the printer. PostScript has long been the standard for professional publishing and printing, but as technology has advanced, PostScript support has also become fairly common among home- and small-office printers. Because PostScript is a standard language, all PostScript-compatible printers receive the same basic instructions from the operating system on how to print the same document, so a single PostScript driver can provide basic printing support for *any* PostScript printer. Mac OS X has a built-in PostScript driver, so it supports any PostScript 2 or 3 printer on a supported connection right out of the box.

SEE: • **"What types of printer connections does Mac OS X support?" below.**

If a particular PostScript printer provides added features or functionality (multiple paper trays, various resolutions, different paper sizes, and so on), the printer manufacturer provides a *PostScript Printer Description* (PPD) file. A PPD tells the PostScript driver what is different about (or what additional features are provided by) that printer. Mac OS X includes PPD files for many PostScript printers from Apple and third-party vendors.

Note: Mac OS X cannot print to older PostScript Level 1 printers, such as the Apple LaserWriter NT and LaserWriter Pro 400 and 405.

SEE: • **"Take Note: Why and How to Create PDF Files," later in this chapter.**

Non-PostScript (raster) printers. Other recent printers (such as most inkjet printers) commonly use *Printer Control Language* (PCL) rather than PostScript. Because such printers don't support a universal printing system, each printer requires its own model-specific driver. On the other hand, because these drivers are printer-specific, PPD files aren't necessary; the printer driver itself usually includes all of the information the OS needs for full feature support. Mac OS X comes with drivers installed for many inkjet printers, such as Apple, Canon, Epson, and Hewlett-Packard models.

QuickDraw printers. In what may be disappointing news for some users, Mac OS X does *not* support older QuickDraw printers. Some older Apple printers (such as the ImageWriter series, StyleWriter series, and a few LaserWriter models) use Apple's own QuickDraw printing technology to communicate between the OS and the printer. Unfortunately, these printers are currently unsupported, and there's no indication that Apple will support them in future versions of Mac OS X.

If your printer is advertised as being Mac OS X–compatible, but Mac OS X does not come with a driver or PPD for it, you'll probably need to install the appropriate support files manually. Luckily, with each new release of Mac OS X, more and more printer drivers and PPD files are included.

SEE: • "Installing Printer Drivers," below.

What types of printer connections does Mac OS X support?

Mac OS X supports several connection types for printing. You can connect a non-AppleTalk printer directly to your Mac, using USB (Universal Serial Bus), Ethernet, FireWire, or (on older Macs) serial/printer/modem ports. You can also connect non-AppleTalk serial-port printers to newer Macs using third-party serial-port adapters.

If you have an older AppleTalk printer, your options for direct connections are a bit more limited. Because Mac OS X does not support LocalTalk (AppleTalk via serial/printer/modem ports), and because AppleTalk is generally not supported over USB or FireWire, your only real option is Ethernet. If you have a LocalTalk printer, you would need to purchase a third-party LocalTalk-to-Ethernet adapter. Unfortunately, these adapters cost approximately $100, so unless your LocalTalk printer is worth a lot of money, your best bet may be simply to get a newer printer that has a supported connection type.

In addition to the direct connections described in the preceding paragraphs, Mac OS X fully supports network printing to both AppleTalk and non-AppleTalk printers. If your Mac can "see" a printer, it can print to it. You can use any printer on a local or AirPort (wireless) network, as well as any printer anywhere on the Internet that has its own IP address (by using LPR, described later in this chapter).

The type of connection you use is largely determined by the printer itself. If it requires a USB connection (as most current inkjet printers do), that connection is how you connect the printer to the Mac. Some printers have multiple connection options. An inkjet printer, for example, may include a USB port and—via a network card—an Ethernet network connection. This card may come with the printer, or you can purchase it as an add-on.

Unfortunately, Mac OS X does not support IrDA printing to printers with infrared ports. On the plus side, if your Mac has a Bluetooth module, you will be able to print wirelessly to Bluetooth-supported printers. A Bluetooth Printers item will be added to the Printers pop-up menu in the Print dialog. (Note: To print via Bluetooth on older Macs—those that didn't come with Tiger preinstalled—you need to make sure you've installed Bluetooth Firmware Updater 1.0.2 or later, as well as Bluetooth Update 1.5.)

SEE: • "Using Bluetooth," in Chapter 8, for more details.

Installing Printer Drivers

As mentioned earlier in the chapter, Mac OS X comes with drivers and/or PPD files installed for many Apple and third-party printers. If you have a recent printer model, you should be able to configure Mac OS X to use your printer right out of the box. However, if your printer is Mac OS X–compatible but a driver is not already installed, you'll need to install it.

How do I tell if my printer is already supported?

There are several ways you can determine whether Mac OS X already supports your printer. For newer USB printers (both PostScript and non-PostScript), the easiest way is to connect the printer to the Mac via the USB ports on both devices. Mac OS X can recognize a supported USB printer automatically, select the appropriate PPD file (for PostScript printers) or driver (for non-PostScript printers), and set up a print queue for it in Mac OS X's Printer Setup Utility, which is where all printer and print-queue management is coordinated (as described in detail later in the chapter). Mac OS X should similarly auto-discover and set up printers on your local network that use Bonjour.

For other printers, you can see whether or not support is included by checking the printer support files on your hard drive.

For non-PostScript printers, check /Library/Printers/{*name of printer vendor*}. Within these directories, you'll find support files listed by model number. Drivers for Canon printers, for example, are in /Library/Printers/Canon/BJPrinter/PMs. Drivers for Epson inkjet printers are in /Library/Printers/EPSON.

You may also find manufacturer-specific printer utilities in these directories. These are used for ink-level checks, nozzle checks, head cleaning, and head alignment of the relevant printer. Inside /Library/Printers/Canon/BJPrinter/ Utilities is Canon's BJ Printer Utility, for example. Epson printers have a similar-functioning EPSON Printer Utility in /Library/Printers/EPSON/ Utilities. While you can double-click the application icons to open them, it is more convenient to launch them by selecting the relevant printer in Printer Setup Utility and clicking the Utility icon in the toolbar.

PPD files for third-party PostScript printers are located in the /Library/ Printers/PPDs/Contents/Resources/*name*.lproj folders. English-language PPD files, for example, are in the directory en.lproj—listed by printer manufacturer (for example, HP LaserJet and Lexmark Optra) and model number.

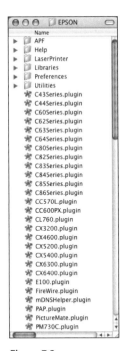

Figure 7.2

Partial contents of the
/Library/Printers/Epson folder.

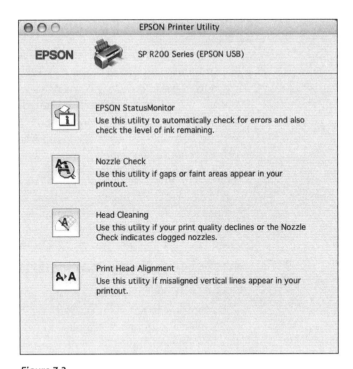

Figure 7.3

Epson's EPSON Printer Utility.

Note: You can also copy PPD files from a Mac OS 9 System Folder to the appropriate .lproj folder in Mac OS X. The files will work in Mac OS X. In addition, if Mac OS X cannot find a PPD file for your printer in the preceding directories, it will search for PPD files in the Mac OS 9 System Folder.

SEE: • "Take Note: Printer Models with Drivers Built Into Mac OS X," below.

TAKE NOTE ▶ **Printer Models with Drivers Built Into Mac OS X**

Mac OS X includes printer drivers and PPD files for many popular printers. The list of printers that Mac OS X supports out of the box is too long to print here, but you can view this list on Apple's "Mac OS X Printer Support" page (www.apple.com/macosx/upgrade/printers.html). Also check out this Apple Knowledge Base article for information on Mac OS X compatibility from third-party printer vendors: http://docs.info.apple.com/article.html?artnum=25407.

Note: The list on the "Mac OS X Printer Support" page doesn't include printers supported by the Gimp-Print drivers included with Mac OS X, described later in this chapter.

In addition, a third-party Web site (www.index-site.com/printersx.html) has compiled a list of printers supported by Mac OS X, which includes drivers not provided by Apple, and gives troubleshooting information.

SEE: • "Take Note: Using Gimp-Print," later in this chapter.

Updating via Software Update?

When you update to a new version of Mac OS X, it may include support for new printers and/or fixes to software for already supported printers. In older versions of Mac OS X, Apple occasionally posted vendor-specific printer updates via Software Update (for example, an update that just contained printing software for certain Epson printers). Apple no longer does this. Instead, for support beyond what's included with Mac OS X, Apple refers users to the printer vendor's Web site.

Apple may, however, include updated or additional printer-support files in a general Mac OS X update. In fact, on some Macs, I've seen a "Check for printer updates" item in the Printer pop-up menu in the Print dialog; choosing the item launches Software Update.

Installing third-party drivers

If Mac OS X doesn't include the appropriate support files for your printer and you aren't able to get them via Software Update, you'll have to install them manually using an installer application provided by the printer manufacturer. Some printers include a CD with the driver installer; others will tell you to go to the manufacturer's Web site to download the installer. (Going to the Web site is probably a good idea either way, because the drivers available from the Web site are often newer than those that come with the printer.) After you've obtained the appropriate installer, installation usually involves simply double-clicking the installer application and following its instructions.

SEE: • "Troubleshooting Printing: Checking Printer Drivers," later in this chapter, for more details.

Using CUPS software

As explained later in this chapter, Apple completely overhauled its printing architecture in Mac OS X 10.2 Jaguar, shifting to using CUPS. One advantage of this is that users familiar with Unix can configure the CUPS software to support printers that are otherwise unsupported by Mac OS X. For those unfamiliar with Unix, Gimp-Print software (which is mainly a collection of printer drivers) does most of the work for you. Gimp-Print is included as part of Panther and later and is installed by default.

SEE: • "CUPS" and "Take Note: Using Gimp-Print," later in this chapter, for details.

Deleting unused printer drivers

If you use a single printer and don't plan on getting a newer one for a while, you can reclaim quite a bit of hard-drive space (possibly over 1 GB) by deleting unused printer drivers and PPDs in the /Library/Printers folder. The easiest (and safest) way to do so is to simply delete the folders belonging to other manufacturers' support files. (If you have an Epson printer, for example, delete the Canon and HP folders.) If you're using only the U.S. English version of the Mac OS, you can also delete all of the folders except en.lproj within the /PPDs/Contents/Resources folder (since the other folders provide support for non-English languages). To make these deletions, you'll need to be an administrative user.

As a side note, even if you *don't* use the U.S. English version, the en.lproj folder must be present; if it's not, Mac OS X won't be able to find the non-English versions of your printing software automatically. You will still be able to use non-English versions, but you will have to select them manually in Printer Setup Utility.

The downside to removing these files is that if you ever need to support other printers or languages, you'll need to reinstall the support files.

Note: If you're a laptop user, it might be worth leaving drivers for all printers installed—you never know where you'll be and what printers will be available when you need to print on the road.

Note: If you plan ahead, you can mostly avoid the need to delete unused printers: When first installing Mac OS X, if you elect to do a Custom Install, you will have the opportunity to *not* install selected brands of printers (for example, Epson). Since they never get installed, you don't need to worry about deleting them later.

SEE: • "Take Note: How to Reinstall the Mac OS X Printer Drivers," below.

TAKE NOTE ▶ How to Reinstall the Mac OS X Printer Drivers

If you've deleted any of the printer drivers or printing support files that come installed in Mac OS X (perhaps to save hard-drive space) and later need one or more of them, there is an easier way to get them back than reinstalling Mac OS X.

If you have multiple Mac OS X Install CDs, the solution is to mount Mac OS X Install Discs 2 and 3. From here, you will see several .pkg files (inside the Packages folders on the CDs) with names that refer to printers: CanonPrinterDrivers.pkg, EpsonPrinterDrivers.pkg, HewlettPackardPrinterDrivers.pkg, LexmarkPrinterDrivers.pkg, and Gimp-PrintDrivers.pkg. Double-click the file with the brand name that you want.

Note: On Disc 1, there is an AdditionalPrinterDrivers.mpkg file (in /System/Installation/Packages) that you can use to reinstall all printer drivers at once. Once the Installer has launched, enter your password when asked and select the desired Mac OS X volume as your destination volume. Then click Upgrade or Install, as indicated. You do not need to restart from the Install disc to do this.

continues on next page

TAKE NOTE ▶ **How to Reinstall the Mac OS X Printer Drivers** *continued*

If you have a Mac OS X Install DVD—most common for Tiger—simply double-click the Optional Installs.mpkg package. When you get to the Custom Install window, check the Printer Drivers option, and then click the disclosure triangle and choose the driver package(s) for the printer vendor(s) for which you want to install drivers.

Note: On the Install (Restore) DVD, the driver package files are hidden. If desired, you can view them by using the Finder's Go to Folder command and going to /Volumes/{*name of DVD*}/System/ Installation/Packages.

Print & Fax System Preferences Pane

To access the Print & Fax System Preferences pane, either (a) open Printer Setup Utility and from the Printer Setup Utility application menu select Preferences; (b) open System Preferences and choose Print & Fax; or (c) in any Print dialog, choose Print & Fax Preferences from the Printer pop-up menu.

The Print & Fax pane includes three main tabs—Printing, Faxing, and Sharing. Click a tab and the pane shifts to display the matching options. The explanations that follow reference aspects of printing and faxing that are covered in more detail later in the chapter. Check the relevant sections if you need more detailed information.

Printing pane

The Printing pane displays a list of currently set-up printers along its left side.

Next to each printer name is an In Menu check box. Uncheck this option (assuming it is not the default printer) to remove the printer's name from printer menus (such as in Print dialogs). This does not uninstall the printer; it just removes its name from such menus. You can easily re-enable this option later. Note: The same option appears in the Printer List in Printer Setup Utility.

The Printing pane includes a number of other options:

- **Add (+) and Remove (–) buttons.** Selecting a printer from the printer list and clicking the – button removes the printer from the list—you will not be able to print to it until you set it up again. If you click the + button, Printer Setup Utility launches and provides you with the Printer Browser window to allow you to add or set up a printer.

- **Printer info box.** When you select a printer from the list, the box to the right of the list displays information about that printer: the printer's name, location, kind, and status. Clicking the "Supplies for this printer" button takes you to the Apple Store online, where you can purchase supplies.

- **Print Queue.** Selecting a printer from the list and clicking Print Queue will launch the printer proxy application for that printer, as described in "Take Note: Printer Queue (Proxy) Applications," later in this chapter.

- **Printer Setup.** Selecting a printer from the list and clicking Printer Setup will launch Printer Setup Utility and then open the Printer Info window for that printer.

- **Selected Printer in Print Dialog.** From this pop-up menu, you can choose which printer should appear as the default printer in Print dialogs. If you choose Last Printer Used (the initial choice), the default printer will always be whatever printer you last used. However, suppose you want to occasionally use an alternate printer (say a color printer) but want the Print dialog to revert back to your standard printer automatically the next time you Print. In this case, select the name of the "standard" printer from the menu.

- **Default Paper Size in Page Setup.** The default paper-size choice in Page Setup dialogs is typically US Letter. To change the default selection, choose your desired size here. If you want to choose a different size for a particular print job, use the Page Setup dialog.

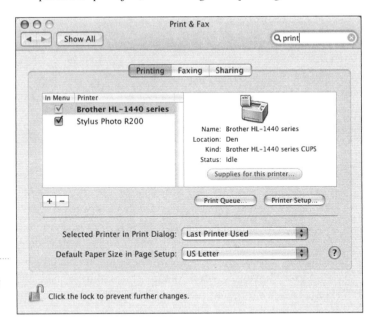

Figure 7.4

The Print & Fax System Preferences pane: the Printing pane.

Faxing pane

You can use the options available from the Faxing pane to set up to receive faxes. The main options include the following:

- **"Receive faxes on this computer" check box.** Check this box if you want to be able to receive faxes.

- **When a Fax Arrives.** Select options here to tell the Mac what to do with an incoming fax.

- **Set Up Fax Modem button.** Click this button to open the Fax List window in Printer Setup Utility.

- **"Show fax status in menu bar" check box**. Check this box to add a Fax status menu to the menu bar.

SEE: • "Faxing," later in this chapter, for details.

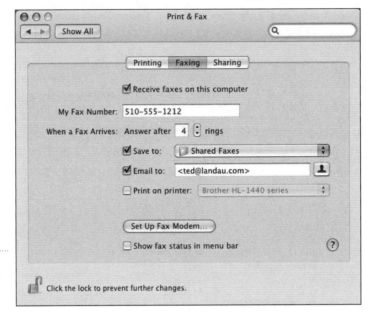

Figure 7.5

The Print & Fax System Preferences pane: the Faxing pane.

Sharing pane

On this pane, new in Tiger, you can enable Printer Sharing, just as you can via the Printer Sharing option in the Sharing pane of System Preferences. By default, with Printer Sharing enabled, all printers in your Printer List (in Printer Setup Utility) are shared, whether they're directly connected to your computer (for example, via a USB port) or connected over a network. In most cases, however, you would use this option to share a USB- or FireWire-connected printer. For printers on an Ethernet network, other users would likely already have access because they are on the network as well.

The two advantages to using this pane, as opposed to simply enabling Printer Sharing in the Sharing System Preferences pane, are that (1) you can enable and disable sharing for individual printers; and (2) you can decide whether or not to share your fax "printer." The latter option (selected by checking the "Let others send faxes through this computer" box) lets other computers on your network send faxes using *your* fax modem.

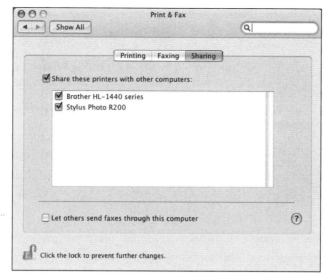

Figure 7.6

The Sharing pane of the Print & Fax System Preferences pane.

Using Printer Setup Utility: An Overview

Printer Setup Utility is an application installed by Mac OS X and located in the /Applications/Utilities folder. You use it to set up the communication between a printer and the OS. You also use it to set up a modem for faxing. For printing, the utility also manages the queue of documents printed on each printer. The following sections assume that your printer's required printer drivers and PPD files have already been installed on your drive (as described previously).

Printer Setup Utility menus

The following provides an overview of the most important commands in Printer Setup Utility's menus:

Printer Setup Utility application menu. Two important commands are found here:

- **Preferences.** This opens the Print & Fax System Preferences pane.
- **Reset Printing System.** New in Tiger, the Reset Printing System feature is—as Apple calls it—a "last resort" troubleshooting step when you're having printing problems. If you choose this command, the entire printing system is reset to its default configuration: All printer queues (set-up printers) are deleted (along with any pending print jobs); all printer-configuration files are deleted; and the /tmp directory is checked

for correct permissions. This procedure can fix many printing issues; however, because it's such an extreme step, I recommend first trying less invasive procedures.

SEE: • **"Troubleshooting Printing: Checking Printer Setup Utility and Desktop Printers" and "Printing Quick Fixes," later in this chapter.**

As noted before, choosing the Preferences command here takes you to the Print & Fax System Preferences pane.

TAKE NOTE ▶ Showing and Hiding Printers

Printers being shared by computers elsewhere on your network are displayed in Printer Setup Utility by default; there is no option *not* to display them in the Printer List. You can't even use the Delete Selected Printer command. However, if you don't want a printer to appear in Print and Page Setup dialogs, you can uncheck the box next to its name in the In Menu column (enabled via the Columns submenu of the View menu, as described in the main text).

View menu. There are two pairs of commands of interest here, as well as a useful submenu:

- **Show Printer List and Show Fax List.** These commands open the two main windows of Printer Setup Utility. The former displays a list of all printers that are available to your computer; the latter shows a list of all available fax modems.

- **Hide Toolbar and Customize Toolbar.** As in most Mac OS X applications that include toolbars, you can select to hide or modify the toolbar by choosing between these options. By default, the Printer List toolbar contains Make Default, Add, Delete, Utility, ColorSync, and Show Info icons. The Fax List toolbar contains Delete, Show Info, and Stop Jobs.

- **Columns submenu.** The Columns submenu lets you choose which columns—and thus which information—to display in the Printer List and Fax List windows. For example, by default the Printer List window displays Kind and Status columns; you can also choose to display In Menu, Host, Location, and Jobs.

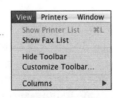

Figure 7.7

Left, *Printer Setup Utility's View menu;* right, *the utility's Printers menu.*

Printers menu. If no printers have been added, or if you haven't selected a printer from the list, the only choice that will be enabled is Add Printer.

Otherwise, the available options depend upon what printer(s) you have selected. The following provides a brief overview of the available commands:

- **Make Default.** You use this command to change the default printer (that is, the one that appears as the initial choice in Print and Page Setup dialogs). This is essentially the same as choosing the printer in the Selected Printer in Print Dialog pop-up menu in Print & Fax preferences.

   Note: The name of the default printer is stored in an invisible file called .lpoptions, located at the root level of your home directory.

- **Add Printer.** You can use this command to add a new printer to the Printer List. (The details of how to do this are the focus of the next few sections of this chapter.)

- **Delete Selected Printers.** You can use this command to delete printers from the list. However, because the driver software is not deleted when you select this command, you can still re-add the printer later, if you wish.

- **Pool Printers.** To use this command, first select more than one printer; then select the command. In the window that appears, drag the printer names in the order in which you prefer each printer to be used. Give the pool a name and select Create. The pool you just created will appear in the Printer List just as if it were another printer. If you choose this printer in a Print dialog, the document will print to the first printer on the list, if it's available. If that printer is busy, it will try the next printer—and so on until it finds an available printer.

   If all printers are busy, the document should be queued for printing in the first printer on the list. The Printer Pool item in the Printer List will display the icon for this first listed printer. This printer is also the one that will determine which printing options are available in Print and Page Setup dialogs when the pool is selected.

   You cannot rearrange the order of printers in a pool after you create it. Instead, you must delete the pool and create a new one with the desired order. Note: You can view and possibly edit the order of printers in a pool via the Classes page of the CUPS interface.

   SEE: • "Accessing CUPS from a Web browser," later in this chapter.

- **ConfigurePrinter.** This command is used to access printer-specific utilities. For example, if I choose it for my Canon inkjet printer, a window appears in which I can click a Maintenance button. Doing this launches Canon's BJ Printer Utility, where I can clean the print heads, print a test page, check ink levels, and more.

   Note: This command duplicates what happens if you click the Utility icon in the Printer Setup Utility toolbar.

   Note: This command is dimmed unless the currently selected printer has a separate configuration utility available. To configure options for printers that do not have a separate utility, or for options not available from the separate utility, select instead the Show Info command.

- **Supply Levels.** On supported printers, this command checks the ink/toner levels. Even if it reports Information Not Available, you can still click the Supplies button to go to a page on Apple's Web site that lists supplies for the selected printer.

- **Print Test Page.** This command does exactly what its name implies. It provides a useful way of determining whether a printer is correctly connected and working. If the test page prints and you're otherwise having problems getting a document to print from an application, this suggests that the problem is with the document, the application, or some other Mac software rather than with the printer itself.

- **Show Info.** This command is used to configure a selected printer's options.

  SEE: • " Changing printer configurations (Show Info)," later in this chapter, for details.

- **Show Jobs.** This command opens the queue for the selected printer. The same thing happens if you double-click the name of the printer in the Printer List.

  SEE: • "Take Note: Printer Queue (Proxy) Applications," below for related information.

- **Stop Jobs.** This command stops any jobs that are currently in the queue of the selected printer. You can also do this via the Stop Jobs icon in the toolbar of the printer queue (if the queue is open).

- **Create Desktop Printer.** This creates an alias of the selected printer on the Finder's Desktop. If you double-click this icon, it opens the queue window/application, just as if you had selected Show Jobs from Printer Setup Utility's Printers menu. Even more useful, if you drag a document icon to a desktop printer, it immediately prints the selected document in its default application, bypassing the need to open the application and select the Print dialog!

  SEE: • "Using Printer Setup Utility: Managing Print Jobs" and "Printing," later in this chapter, for more on these menus and on desktop printers.

TAKE NOTE ▶ Printer Queue (Proxy) Applications

If you choose Show Jobs for a selected printer or double-click the name of a printer in Printer Setup Utility's Printer List, a queue window for the printer opens. Each queue window is actually a separate application, often referred to as a *printer proxy application*.

You can tell that the window represents a separate application because when it launches, a separate icon opens in the Dock with the name of the printer. In addition, the menus in the printer application's menu bar shift from those available in Printer Setup Utility. For example, there is now a Jobs menu, from which you can choose to delete, hold, or resume a job.

These printer proxy applications are stored in your ~/Library/Printers folder.

Creating a desktop printer. If you create a desktop printer for a printer, all you're really doing is creating an alias to the proxy application. You can delete these aliases from the Finder and re-create a new one any time you wish.

continues on next page

TAKE NOTE ▶ Printer Queue (Proxy) Applications *continued*

Deleting proxy applications. When you delete a printer via Printer Setup Utility's Printer List, its proxy application in ~/Library/Printers should also get deleted. If you created a desktop printer for this printer, however, that icon *does not* get deleted. If you double-click it, you'll get an error message stating that the original for the alias can no longer be found. The obvious solution is to delete the desktop printer.

Occasionally, you may find that a proxy application remains even after you've deleted the printer in Printer Setup Utility. This can cause immediate glitches because some Mac OS X features continue to access the proxy application, not realizing that the printer has been deleted from Printer Setup Utility. Similarly, if you later re-add a printer with an identical name, this can cause confusion, as well. Thus, I recommend making sure that the printer proxy application in the ~/Library/Printers folder has been deleted after you delete a printer from Printer Setup Utility.

If you accidentally delete the proxy application for a printer that is still listed in the Printer List, delete the printer from the list and re-add it. Otherwise, it will no longer work.

Shared printers. When you access the queue of a shared printer, a proxy application is created for that printer. You can even create a desktop printer for the shared printer. Obviously, if the host computer later turns off Printer Sharing, you will no longer be able to print from the desktop printer. Instead, you will get an error stating the network host is busy (as shown in Figure 7.44).

SEE: • "Printer Sharing" and "Printer queue window," later in this chapter, for related information.

Figure 7.8

Left, *printer and fax proxy applications in my ~/Library/Printers folder;* right, *desktop-printer icons on the Desktop.*

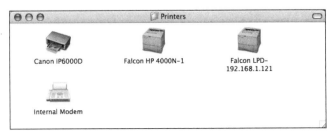

Figure 7.9

An example of a printer queue window that appears if you open a printer proxy application— by double-clicking the proxy application file itself, double-clicking a desktop printer file you created, or double-clicking the name of the printer (or selecting Show Jobs) in Printer Setup Utility.

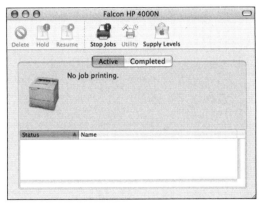

Printer Setup Utility toolbar

Printer Setup Utility includes two main windows, one for Printer List and the other for Fax List, each with its own toolbar.

Printer List. The Printer List toolbar includes icons that mainly duplicate options available from Printer Setup Utility's menus. For example, you can choose Show Info from the toolbar or from the Printers menu.

The only exception is ColorSync, for which there's no equivalent menu command. If you click this icon while a printer is selected, the ColorSync Utility (which is described briefly in Chapter 2) launches. From here, you can choose a specific ColorSync profile for your printer. This can help improve the accuracy of printed color documents. Details of how this works, however, are mostly beyond the scope of this book.

SEE: • "Printing," later in this chapter, for related information on selecting ColorSync settings in the Print dialog.

Fax List. In the Fax List toolbar, you can choose Delete, Show Info, or Stop Jobs. These commands are specific to faxing and are separate from the same commands for the Printer List.

SEE: • "Printer Setup Utility and faxing," later in this chapter, for more details.

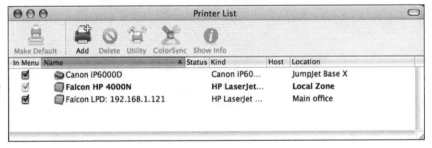

Figure 7.10

Printer Setup Utility's Printer List window, with its toolbar displayed.

Printer Setup Utility's Printer List window

The Printer List window lists every printer that you've added manually or that's been automatically added. There are several columns in the list—you can determine which columns appear by the selections you make in the View > Columns submenu. The default columns include the following:

- **Name.** The Name column lists the name assigned to the printer (automatically or by you, as described in the next section).

- **Status.** The Status column typically remains empty unless a print job is in progress (in which case it reports the current status of the job; for example, "Printing") or you have stopped all jobs via the Stop Jobs command (in which case it will say "Stopped").

- **Kind.** The Kind column lists the model name as selected via the Printer Model option (as described in the next section). For PostScript printers, this is determined by the PPD file.

Other commonly selected columns:

- **In Menu.** If you uncheck the In Menu box for a printer, its name no longer appears in Print and Page Setup dialogs. Note: You cannot deselect this item for the default printer.

- **Host.** The Host column provides information about the Host computer to which the printer is connected, if applicable. This is useful in identifying the source location of a shared computer.

  SEE: • "Printer Sharing," later in this chapter.

Using Printer Setup Utility: Adding and Configuring Printers

Even if your printer's required software is installed on your drive, you can't print until you've added your printer to Printer Setup Utility's Printer List. Exactly how you do this depends on what type of printer you have. The following sections provide the details.

Note: Mac OS X locates and adds many printers automatically via its Bonjour technology (see "Take Note: Printing and Bonjour/Rendezvous," below), thus bypassing the steps outlined in this section. However, you still may need to follow these steps to manually *reinstall* a printer (for troubleshooting reasons, as described throughout the chapter) or if a printer, for whatever reason, isn't automatically added.

The first thing you do to add a printer is launch Printer Setup Utility. If no printers have been added yet, a dialog will appear asking if you want to add a printer. If you're ready to do so, click Add. Otherwise, click Cancel. This will leave an empty Printer List window. You can then add a printer at any later time by clicking the Add icon in the window's toolbar.

Once you've added printers, those printers are listed in the Printer List window. From here, you can further configure them.

> **TAKE NOTE ▶ Printing and Bonjour/Rendezvous**
>
> Bonjour—called Rendezvous in Panther and earlier versions of Mac OS X—is Apple's zero-configuration networking protocol, which means it eliminates the need to enter the IP address of a network-accessible printer. Instead, the Mac discovers the printer on its own and lists it in Printer Setup Utility—all the work is done for you. However, for this magic to occur, the printer must be "Bonjour enabled." All major printer vendors have announced their support for this technology, and many such printers are already available. Expect this to be a common feature of Mac-compatible printers in the years ahead. (Note that by connecting a printer to an AirPort Base Station, or to another Mac OS X computer with Printer Sharing enabled, your printer is automatically accessible via Bonjour.)
>
> In most cases, a Bonjour-enabled printer will be automatically detected and set up in Printer Setup Utility—that is, you won't need to manually add the printer. However, it's important to note that this feature works only for printers on the same *subnet* of the same local network as your Mac. Printers on another subnet of your network, or on a remote network, will not be automatically connected via Bonjour, even if they're Bonjour enabled.
>
> If a printer you expected to see via Bonjour does not appear, you can add it manually, as described in the main text.
>
> **SEE:** • Chapter 8, for more on Bonjour.

Adding a printer: An overview

To add a printer to the Printer List, click the Add icon in the toolbar. This brings up Mac OS X's Printer Browser window.

Default Browser. In most cases, the Default Browser—which is, as its name suggests, the default view—is where you will start. It should list any printers connected to your Mac, as well as any network or shared printers on your local network. If so, simply selecting the desired printer from the list and then clicking the Add button will set that printer up for use.

Note: If you'd like to customize the printer name and location—for example, *Epson Printer* in *The Den*—you can do so before clicking Add, by filling in the Name and Location text boxes. Similarly, if you have a specific reason to use a different printer driver or PPD file than the one automatically picked by Mac OS X, you can choose it from the Print Using pop-up menu before adding the printer.

The Printer Browser also includes a Search field. Click the magnifying-glass icon to access a menu from which you can restrict the search to certain categories of printers (such as AppleTalk, Bonjour, or Shared).

More Printers. If your printer doesn't show up in the Default Browser window, click the More Printers button. A dialog drops down. From the pop-up menu at the top, you can choose from among different types of printer connections. At the top of the menu, you will see at least three options: AppleTalk, Bluetooth, and Windows Printing. The bottom part of the dialog includes choices for specific printer brands, such as Canon BJ Network, EPSON AppleTalk, HP IP Printing, and Lexmark Inkjet Networking. (The printer brands listed here vary according to whether you installed all the printer software when Mac OS X was installed.)

In most cases, the choice should be obvious: If your printer is an AppleTalk-only printer, you would select AppleTalk; if you're connecting to a printer via a Windows computer sharing that printer (or if you're trying to print to a Windows network printer), you would select Windows Printing; and so on.

However, if your printer fits one of the categories included among the bottom choices, choose it over a preference in the top section. (For example, use the Epson AppleTalk option to add an Ethernet-connected Epson 900N printer; otherwise, for an AppleTalk-connected printer, pick AppleTalk from the top choices.)

After you choose the desired item from the printer connection menu, any connected printers that fit the chosen category should automatically appear in the list below. Select the printer you wish to add. Next, if the window includes a Printer Model pop-up menu, select the precise model from the menu choices. If your printer model is not listed, it probably means that the necessary printer-driver software was not installed by Mac OS X. If this is because you did a Custom Install of Mac OS X and chose not to install the specific printer software, you should go back and install it (as described in "Take Note: How to Reinstall the Mac OS X Printer Drivers," earlier in this chapter). If the problem is that Mac OS X does not include the driver software, contact the printer vendor for the needed software or for other assistance. Further details on how to add a specific type of printer (such as USB or AppleTalk) are covered in the sections that follow.

Note: Some USB printers don't work properly when connected to a USB hub (including the hub built into Apple USB keyboards). If your supported USB printer does not show up in the Printer Browser, make sure that it's connected directly to one of the USB ports on your Mac. Also make sure that the printer is connected and powered on.

Note: If you're adding a printer accessed via an AirPort Extreme network, you need to add it via Bonjour (Rendezvous in Panther), as discussed later in this chapter.

SEE: • "Take Note: AirPort and Printer Sharing," later in this chapter, for more details.

IP Printers. One situation that might be confusing is if your printer uses IP printing. If the printer has its own IP printing driver—such as HP IP Printing—choose that item from the pop-up menu in the More Printers dialog. If the printer does not automatically appear, click the tab to switch from the Auto to Manual mode; then manually enter the IP address of the printer.

For all other instances of IP printers, use the IP Printer icon in the toolbar of the main Printer Browser window. This switches the display from the Default Browser mode to IP Printer mode. In the pane that appears, choose a protocol from the pop-up menu and then fill out the rest of the items. If you are uncertain as to what settings to enter, seek help from the manual that came with your printer, from the printer's vendor, or from your network administrator (assuming you have one!).

SEE: • "Adding a printer via IP printing" and "Take Note: How Do You Determine the Printer's IP Address?," later in this chapter.

Option key. If you hold down the Option key while clicking the More Printers button, an Advanced option appears at the bottom of the pop-up menu. If you're knowledgeable about printer settings or have found the required information (such as from tips posted to Mac Web sites), you can use this option to configure a selected printer, including a USB, Bluetooth, or FireWire printer, that might not otherwise work. The Advanced option can also be used to enable an otherwise unsupported AppleTalk printer (although you will more likely be able to do this simply by accessing the Gimp-Print driver Gimp-Print directly from the main choices).

SEE: • "Take Note: Using Gimp-Print," later in this chapter, for details.

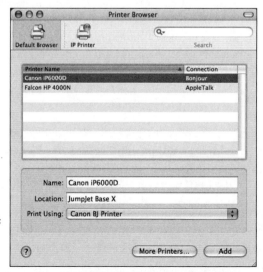

Figure 7.11

The Printer Browser dialog that appears after clicking the Add (printer) icon in Printer Setup Utility's toolbar. The Default Browser pane is shown.

Figure 7.12

The dialog that drops down from the Printer Browser when the More Printers button is clicked. In this case, the Option key was held down to make the Advanced option appear.

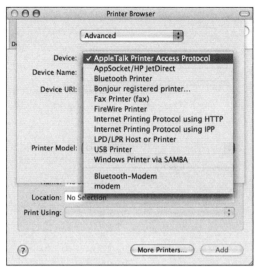

Figure 7.13

The dialog that appears after choosing Advanced from the More Printers dialog in the Printer Browser of Printer Setup Utility; the Device pop-up menu is shown.

Adding a USB printer

The most common connection type for Mac printers today is USB. In almost all cases, a USB printer will be automatically recognized in the Printer Browser, typically via Bonjour. To add it, just follow the instructions outlined above.

One exception may be for older Epson USB printers; in this case, you may need to choose EPSON USB from the More Printers pop-up menu. Otherwise, the following sections walk you through the steps necessary to add other particular types of printers. These instructions assume that, for whatever reason, Mac OS X doesn't automatically set up your printer, or that your printer doesn't appear in the Printer Browser.

Adding an AppleTalk printer

If you have an AppleTalk printer, here's what you need to do to get it to work with Mac OS X:

Enable AppleTalk. The first thing you need to do is make sure that AppleTalk is enabled for the appropriate network type. To do this, go to the Network System Preferences pane, and from the Show pop-up menu choose the network port configuration by which your printer is connected (for example,

Ethernet or AirPort). Switch to the AppleTalk pane and make sure that the Make AppleTalk Active box is checked. Note that AppleTalk can only be enabled for one configuration at a time; thus, you cannot enable AppleTalk for both Ethernet and AirPort simultaneously.

In Panther and later, you may also need to enable AppleTalk in the Directory Access utility (in /Applications/Utilities). After you launch Directory Access, click the padlock icon at the bottom of the window to unlock it (if necessary), and then provide your admin-level user name and password when prompted. Make sure that AppleTalk is checked, and click the Apply button.

SEE: • Chapter 8 for much more on Network settings.

Use Printer Setup Utility. Once you've enabled AppleTalk, follow these steps:

1. Make sure the printer is on and connected, then launch Printer Setup Utility.

2. Click the Add button in the dialog that may appear; otherwise, click the Add icon in the toolbar.

3. In the Printer Browser window that appears, the printer should be automatically listed. If so, select it and click Add. Otherwise, click More Printers and, from the pop-up menu, choose AppleTalk. (If you're on a large, multizone AppleTalk network, you'll also need to select the appropriate zone from the second pop-up menu.) Your printer should appear in the list.

4. In the Printer Model pop-up menu, if the appropriate driver or PPD file is not auto-selected via the default Auto Select option, it may list "Driver not installed" or "Gimp-Print." In the latter case, you can usually leave this as is. Otherwise, locate the brand for your printer from the Printer Model menu and select it.

   If your printer brand or model isn't listed at all, choose Other from the pop-up menu and navigate to the appropriate driver/PPD for your printer (in the /Library/Printers folder). As a last resort, you can select the Generic option.

5. From the Character Set pop-up menu at the bottom of the box listing available printers, make sure that Western (Mac) is selected, assuming you're using English. Otherwise, the printer's name may be garbled in the Printer List window.

6. Select the printer name and click the Add button.

   This takes you back to the Printer List window, where the printer should be listed.

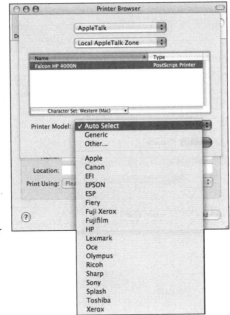

Figure 7.14

The AppleTalk option in Printer Setup Utility's Printer Browser. In most cases, you can use the Auto Select option from the Printer Model menu as shown.

Adding a printer via IP printing

Mac OS X supports IP printing via various TCP/IP protocols, the most common being Line Printer (LPR or LPD). The LPD protocol provides a way to print to a networked or Internet-accessible printer via a TCP/IP connection. Printers without built-in networking hardware will not work via this method.

If your networkable printer is connected to your Mac via an Ethernet cable, you can likely use this option. Alternatively, if your printer and your Mac are both connected to a Ethernet hub or router, via Ethernet cables, you should also be able to use this option. If you have a printer (or print server) that supports LPR/LPD, and is properly connected, here is how to set up the software:

1. Make sure the printer is on and connected, then launch Printer Setup Utility.

2. Click the Add button in the dialog that may appear; otherwise, click the Add icon in the toolbar.

3. In the Printer Browser window that appears, click the IP Printer icon in the toolbar. (Note: As described above, there are a couple of IP options in More Printers; try them first as relevant, as they may auto-list your printer. Assuming they fail to do so, continue with the next step here.)

4. From the Protocol pop-up menu, choose your desired printer type. I'm assuming Line Printer Daemon-LPD as the most likely choice; however, if this does not work, you can experiment with other choices (Internet Printing Protocol and HP Jet Direct).

5. In the Address text box, enter the IP address or domain name of the printer or printer queue (see "Take Note: How Do You Determine the Printer's IP Address?" below).

6. If you want to give the printer queue a custom name, or if your printer requires it, enter it in the Queue text box. If you're accessing a printer on a larger network, you may need to use a specific name; check with the network administrator for assistance.

   Do not use spaces in a queue name; if you need to represent a space, use an underscore character instead.

   Note: If you don't specify a name, the printer's default queue is used—which is usually fine. However, on certain PostScript printers, if your printer's firmware does not specify a default queue, leaving this blank can cause print jobs to fail. In this case, the solution is to delete the printer from Printer Setup Utility and re-add it, this time including a known queue name. Refer to your printer's manual for a list of proper IP or LPR queue names.

7. If you'd like the printer's name in Printer Setup Utility to differ from its queue name, or if you did not enter a Queue name, enter the desired name in the Name text field. You can also enter an informative Location tag (for example, Main Office).

8. Ideally, the appropriate printer name appears automatically in the Print Using pop-up menu, after you enter a valid and complete IP address in the Address field above. If not, it typically means either that the printer is not properly connected to the network or that the printer is not one that Mac OS X automatically recognizes. In the latter case, ideally select a PPD for the printer other than the default Generic setting—assuming an appropriate one is listed (typically a PPD with the same name as your printer model). Doing so may enable specialized printer features not available via the generic PPD.

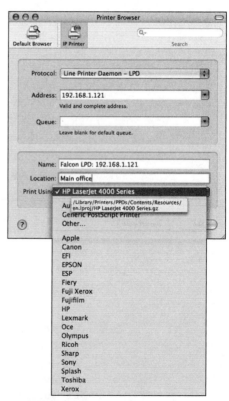

Figure 7.15

The IP Printer pane of Printer Setup Utility's Printer Browser. Use this to set up an LPD printer, as shown. Note: The tool-tip text shows the location of the PPD file of the printer.

9. Click the Add button.

   This brings you back to the Printer List window, where the printer should now be listed.

   In many cases, a printer connected to an Ethernet network may work via either AppleTalk or IP printing. In this case, choose which method you wish to use when you set up the printer. Keep in mind, however, that using IP printing is generally faster and more reliable than using AppleTalk, which is a legacy technology that may eventually be phased out of Mac OS X.

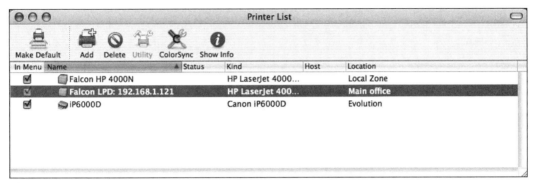

Figure 7.16

An LPD printer, as set up in the dialog shown in Figure 7.15, has been added to the Printer List window. It's the same HP 4000–series printer listed above in the Printer List; the first listing is an AppleTalk connection to the printer.

TAKE NOTE ▶ How Do You Determine the Printer's IP Address?

If your printer supports IP printing, you will need to enter its IP address (or domain name, if it has one) in the Address text box within Printer Setup Utility's IP Printer settings. How do you find out what your printer's IP address is? The procedure varies, depending on your printer and network setup. Here are two methods that worked for me with my HP LaserJet 4000N printer:

Use the HP LaserJet Utility. Locate and launch the HP LaserJet Utility that came with the printer (and that currently runs only in Classic). Then do the following to create a new IP address:

1. In the window that appears, click the Settings button in the column on the left and then choose the TCP/IP option from the "Please select a setting" list.

2. In the TCP/IP dialog that appears, choose the option to manually specify a TCP/IP configuration.

3. Enter the information necessary to set up the printer as a device connected to your network, just as you would do for the Mac itself in the Network System Preferences pane (as described in Chapter 8). See Figure 7.17 as an example.

4. Launch Printer Setup Utility, click the Add button, and in the Printer Browser window click the IP Printer button. Configure the printer as described in the main text, using the IP address you set up as the one you enter in the printer's Address text box.

continues on next page

TAKE NOTE ▶ How Do You Determine the Printer's IP Address? *continued*

Note: If the printer already has an IP address assigned, and you don't care to create your own, you should be able to obtain it by selecting one of the "Automatically obtain" options in the TCP/IP dialog.

Print a Configuration page. This HP printer includes options to print several types of information pages. Start by clicking the Menu button on the printer itself and navigating to the Information menu. Then print the Configuration page. The output will include the printer's IP address, assuming one has been assigned.

Whatever method you choose, once you set or determine the address, enter it in Printer Setup Utility.

Note: If you enter an incorrect (for your printer) but valid IP address in Printer Setup Utility, the printer will still be added to the Printer List; you just won't be able to print to it.

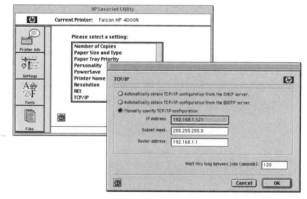

Figure 7.17

Setting up an IP address via the HP LaserJet Utility (running in Classic).

Adding a Windows printer

With Mac OS X, you can print to a printer shared by a Windows computer via SMB, by doing the following:

1. Launch Printer Setup Utility.
2. Click the Add button in the dialog that may appear; otherwise, click the Add icon in the toolbar.
3. In the Printer Browser window that appears, click the More Printers button.
4. From the first pop-up menu, choose Windows Printing.
5. From the Workgroup pop-up menu, select the desired network workgroup, or select Network Neighborhood to find a local workgroup and then select it from the list that appears. Click the Choose button.

    Any Windows printers in your selected network should now appear in the Printer List.

    SEE: • Chapter 9 for more on SMB sharing and workgroup selections.

Adding and using unsupported printers

If the default drivers that come with Mac OS X don't support your printer, you may simply need to install additional software from your printer's vendor: Check for software that came with the printer or go to the vendor's Web site.

Some printer models that have no specific driver software will still work in Mac OS X if you choose a similar printer driver from the Printer Model pop-up menu or (for PostScript printers) if you choose the generic PPD file. Some Epson inkjet printers that don't have Mac OS X drivers, for example, work fairly well with the drivers for similar Epson printers. Keep in mind, though, that if you try this method, you may not get your printer's full functionality and you might experience problems printing. If this is the only way you can use your unsupported printer, however, it's worth a try.

In some cases, advanced users have hacked a driver designed to work with one printer so that it works with similar printers. Such hacks are available on the Web. Again, use such methods with caution: They may cause problems due to the unintended way in which they are used.

Finally, you can use the Print Browser's Advanced option and/or Gimp-Print drivers to get an unsupported printer to work.

SEE: • "Adding a printer: An overview" and "Take Note: Using Gimp-Print," elsewhere in this chapter, for more information.

TECHNICALLY SPEAKING ▶ Creating a PostScript File for Printing

Although most people choose to print directly to a printer, it's sometimes useful to save a file in PostScript format. This way, the file is saved in the language of PostScript printers, which means you can later send it to a printer without opening any application.

You can save a Microsoft Word file as PostScript, for example, and later send the file to an LPR printer via Terminal without opening Word. Similarly, you can save a document from within a Mac OS X application and then boot into Mac OS 9 (or, in some cases, use Classic) to print the document on a printer that does not support Mac OS X. In the latter case, however, it's probably simpler to save the file as a PDF document, as described in "Take Note: Why and How to Create PDF Files," later in this chapter.

Creating a PostScript file. To create a PostScript file, open the document you want to convert, then follow these steps:

1. From the File menu of a Mac OS X application, choose Print.
2. In the Print dialog that appears, from the Printer menu choose your desired PostScript printer.
3. From the PDF pop-up menu at the bottom left of the Print dialog, choose Save PDF as PostScript.
4. Save the file, which will be in PostScript format, in the desired location.

continues on next page

TECHNICALLY SPEAKING ▶ Creating a PostScript File for Printing *continued*

PostScript files saved in this manner will automatically open in Preview when double-clicked from the Finder; Preview then converts the PostScript files to PDF documents.

Printing PostScript files from Terminal. You can send a PostScript file directly to an LPR printer for printing. If you have an LPR printer set up, launch Terminal and type the following:

```
lpr -P printername filepathname.ps
```

Changing printer configurations (Show Info)

After you've added a printer, you may later want to change some of its settings. To do so, you can use the Show Info command.

Show Info also gives you access to some options not available when you first set up the printer. And if you want to make changes that even Show Info does not allow, you may be able to do so via the CUPS Web interface, described later in this chapter. In some cases, you may be able to make changes via a separate utility accessed by the Configure Printer command, as described earlier in this chapter. Otherwise, your last resort is to delete the printer, making the desired changes when you re-add it.

Using Show Info. To use Show Info, follow these steps:

1. In Printer Setup Utility's Printer List, select the printer you want to modify.

2. From the Printers menu choose Show Info, or click the Show Info icon in the toolbar. The Printer Info window opens.

3. From the pop-up menu at the top of the window, choose among the following options:

    • **Name & Location.** You can rename a printer from here or give it a location. Assigning a location (such as a room number) can be useful if people using the printer may not know where to collect their output.

      This window also lists the driver and/or PPD file version—useful if you need to determine whether you're using the latest version.

    • **Printer Model.** This allows you to change the printer model (for example, PPD file for PostScript printers) from what you initially selected when you added the printer. To make a change, select a vendor from the pop-up menu and then select a model from the list that appears. (You can instead choose Other to navigate to a specific driver or PPD.)

    • **Installable Options.** The options available here depend on the printer model selected. If your printer supports optional features, such as Duplex Printing or an Envelope Feeder (and you have those features installed), this is where you enable or modify them.

You may also find some software options in this window, such as what the printer should do if a document is too big to fit on a page (for example, prompt user for a choice versus automatically shrink to fit versus automatically crop).

If you don't see the options you expected to find, you may not have selected the correct vendor and model when you first added the printer. To fix this, select the Printer Model option noted above.

4. Click the Apply Changes button.

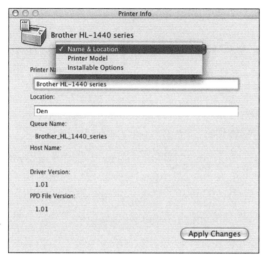

Figure 7.18

Printer Setup Utility's Printer Info window.

Limitations of Show Info. You will not be able to use Show Info to change settings for printers that are shared by other Macs on your network. To change settings for such printers, you must access Printer Setup Utility from the computer to which the printer is connected directly.

You also cannot use Show Info to configure a USB printer connected to your computer via an AirPort Extreme or Express base station (although you can change the Name and Location fields). You must connect the printer directly to your computer to make configuration changes (after which you can reconnect it to the base station).

Setting and changing the default printer

If you've added more than one printer, you'll notice that one printer's name is in bold in Printer Setup Utility's Printer List window, while the rest are in plain text. The bold text indicates the default printer.

If you have multiple printers set up in Printer Setup Utility, the default printer is the one that's used when you print unless you switch to another printer by choosing it from the Printer pop-up menu in the Print dialog (as described in "Printing," later in the chapter).

If you want to change the current default printer, select the desired printer in Printer Setup Utility and then click the Make Default icon in the toolbar, or choose Make Default (Command-D) from the Printers menu.

Note: If you switch to a different printer in the Print dialog, the selected printer may become the new default printer. To prevent this switch, you need to go to the Print & Fax System Preferences pane and select the name of the desired default printer from the Selected Printer in Print Dialog pop-up menu rather than the Last Printer Used option (as described in "Print & Fax System Preferences Pane," earlier in this chapter).

Deleting printers from Printer Setup Utility

You can also delete printers from Printer Setup Utility. When you select a printer and click the Delete button, that printer is removed from Printer Setup Utility and will no longer be available for printing. (Don't worry: If you delete a printer you wanted to keep, you can always re-add it.)

If a printer that you're attempting to delete has queued print jobs, you will be asked whether you would like to wait for them to finish before deleting the printer, or cancel them and delete the printer immediately.

You can select multiple printers to delete at once if you wish.

The main reason to delete a printer is because it's no longer connected or you no longer intend to use it. However, occasionally you may want to delete a printer (and re-add it) even when you do intend to use it. One reason to do this is if you change languages for Mac OS X (via the International System Preferences pane). Deleting and re-adding the printer ensures that dialogs related to the printer appear in the newly selected language. Another reason to delete and re-add a printer is to fix problems with the printer, as described in "Deleting and re-adding a printer," later in this chapter.

SEE: • "Take Note: Printer Queue (Proxy) Applications" and "Take Note: Showing and Hiding Printers," earlier in this chapter, for important related information about deleting printers from Printer Setup Utility.

TAKE NOTE ▶ Updating PPD Files

Printer manufacturers often provide updated or improved printer drivers and PPD files (often via a software download). If you have already installed and are using a PostScript printer in Mac OS X and later install an updated PPD file, you probably won't be able to simply select the new PPD file. You need to delete and re-add the printer in Printer Setup Utility.

SEE: • "Deleting corrupt print jobs," later in this chapter, for related information.

Printer Sharing

In Mac OS X, you can share printers that are connected to your computer with other computers on your local network. This works with any type of printer connection—USB, IP, whatever.

Enabling Printer Sharing

To allow other computers on your local network to share your printers, open the Print & Fax System Preferences and click the Sharing tab. From here, check the "Share these printers with other computers" box and choose which of your connected printers you wish to share.

Alternatively, you can enable printer sharing from the Services pane of the Sharing System Preferences pane. To do so, either (a) check the box next to Printer Sharing or (b) select Printer Sharing and click the Start button. With this option, however, you cannot select specific printers to share; it is all or none.

Whatever method you chose, your shared printers will now appear in the Printer List of the Printer Setup Utility of other Macs on your network.

When someone prints a document to your shared printer, *your* hard drive holds the queue information for the document. Thus, someone cannot print to a shared printer unless the computer to which it is connected is turned on. This also means that if problems occur with printing the document, those problems will likely need to be diagnosed from the Printer Setup Utility application on the computer to which the printer is connected, not the computer that is doing the printing.

Figure 7.19

The Printer Sharing option selected in the Sharing System Preferences pane (compare with Figure 7.6).

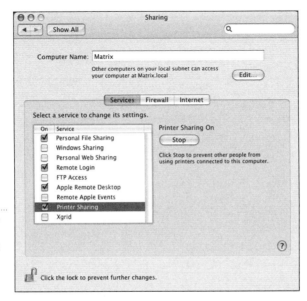

To access shared printers from your Mac

If Printer Sharing has been enabled on another Mac OS X computer on your network, any sharable printers connected to that computer should appear automatically in the Printer pop-up menus of Print dialogs, without any special setup needed. Look for an item called Shared Printers; its submenu should contain a list of all available shared printers on your local network. If you pause the pointer over a printer name, a yellow tool tip will appear, indicating the printer's location.

When you select to print to a shared printer, a desktop printer will be created for the printer on your system (stored in ~/Library/Printers). If you open the desktop printer's queue window, you will be able to delete a job you have selected to print (if it has not yet been printed), but no other toolbar options will be enabled. Additionally, the printer will now be listed in your Printer Setup Utility Printer List.

Prior to Tiger, a list of all available shared printers showed up in Printer Setup Utility's Printer List, even before you selected any of them. In such cases, you would see a heading called Shared Printers. If you clicked the disclosure triangle next to the Shared Printers heading, you would get the complete list of shared printers. If you chose the Show Jobs command for a listed shared printer, a queue window opened for the printer. You could monitor the progress of print jobs from here. You could also delete a job waiting to be printed. However, similar to what I just described in the previous paragraph, you could not access the Hold Job or Stop Jobs command; you could choose these only from the computer to which the printer was directly connected. Printer Setup Utility still works this way on computers running Panther, even if the printer being shared is connected to a computer running Tiger.

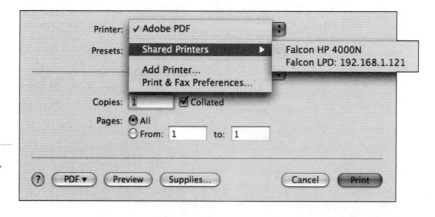

Figure 7.20

Shared printers listed in the Printer pop-up menu of a Print dialog.

Beyond Mac OS X–to–Mac OS X sharing

Users not running Mac OS X (for example, those running Mac OS 9, Windows, or Unix) can also access shared printers connected to a computer running Mac OS X. Here are a few tips to bear in mind:

- **Windows sharing.** To make a printer available to Windows users (via SMB), the Mac OS X computer must enable Windows File Sharing as well as Printer Sharing in the Sharing System Preferences pane.

- **Unix sharing.** Shared Mac OS X printers are automatically available to Unix users who are using the Common Unix Printing System (CUPS). However, Unix users can only print PostScript print jobs.

- **Mac OS 9 sharing.** If you want Mac OS 9 users to be able to access a USB printer on your Mac OS X Mac, you need to make sure that Classic is running, and then separately enable this feature via Mac OS 9's USB Printer Sharing control panel in Classic. Turning on Printer Sharing in Mac OS X has no effect on Mac OS 9 sharing. The Mac OS 9 user will need to access your printer via the Desktop Printer Utility. (You can see more information on this procedure at http://docs.info.apple.com/ article.html?path=Mac/10.4/en/mh1868.html.)

  Unfortunately, you can't easily enable both Mac OS X and Mac OS 9 printer sharing. If you need such functionality, you'll need to do a bit of extra homework. See the following Apple Knowledge Base document for details: http://docs.info.apple.com/article.html?artnum=107060.

For more details on these sharing variations, check Mac OS X's Help files and enter *printer sharing* as the search term.

SEE: • "Take Note: Troubleshooting Shared Printers," later in this chapter.

TAKE NOTE ▶ AirPort and Printer Sharing

Apple's latest versions of its AirPort Base Station are AirPort Extreme and AirPort Express. Both include a USB port to which you can connect a USB printer. This printer can then be accessed by all users on the wireless network. Although this setup works similarly to the Printer Sharing feature described in the main text, it has the advantage that the printer is available to all users on the network without their having to go through another computer (and thus without having to worry whether or not that computer is currently on).

When first set up, the printer can be accessed by all users on your local network—it should automatically appear in Printer Setup Utility as a Bonjour-connected printer. Unfortunately, not all printers work with the USB port on AirPort Base Stations, and Apple no longer provides a list of printers that are officially compatible; you'll need to try your printer out to see if it works.

continues on next page

> **TAKE NOTE ▶ AirPort and Printer Sharing** *continued*
>
> Note: Printer-specific utilities, such as Canon's BJ Printer Utility and EPSON Printer Utility, will not work when the printer is connected via AirPort Extreme or Express. To access the utility's features, you will need to make a direct USB connection between the printer and the Mac. Similarly, certain printer-specific error messages may not appear when the printer is connected via an AirPort Extreme or Express base station.
>
> Computers connected via the Base Station's WAN port cannot access the shared printer by default. However, using the AirPort Admin Utility, you can configure the Base Station so that the printer can be accessed in Printer Setup Utility via Bonjour. The simplest method is to turn on WAN-LAN bridging: To do so, make sure that Details is selcted from Admin Utility's View menu; then, in the Network pane, uncheck the Distribute IP Addresses box. For more details, see the following Apple Knowledge Base article: http://docs.info.apple.com/article.html?artnum=107511.
>
> **SEE:** • **"Setting Up System Preferences: Sharing," in Chapter 9, for more on Printer Sharing and sharing in general.**
>
> • **Chapter 8 for more on AirPort and wireless connections.**

Determining the hostname and location (unshared and shared)

To find out the computer to which a given printer is connected, you can pause the pointer over the printer's name in the Printer pop-up menu of the Print dialog—a tool tip with the information will appear. You need to click-hold to bring up the menu for these notes to appear.

For printers connected to your computer or connected on your local network but not shared by another Mac—for example, connected to an AirPort Base Station—the Host should say Local. For shared printers, the Host name indicates the shared host to which the printer is connected. For example, if you're sharing a printer connected to a computer named Yoda on your local network, the Host name will read Yoda.local.

If a location was assigned to a printer (via the Show Info window in Printer Setup Utility), it will appear in the tool tip as well. This is a quick way to determine a printer's physical location.

Figure 7.21

The Printer pop-up menu in the Print dialog for unshared printers. Host information, such as printer location, is shown in the yellow tool tip.

SEE: • **"Changing printer configurations (Show Info)," earlier in this chapter.**

Alternatively, you can access this same host information from the Host column of the Printer List in Printer Setup Utility. For printers directly connected to your computer or connected to your network but not shared by another Mac, the Host column will either be blank or read Local (as in the yellow notes described above). Otherwise, the Host name will again indicate the host to which the printer is connected.

If you do not see a Host column, you can enable it by choosing Host from the View > Columns submenu in Printer Setup Utility.

You cannot delete a shared printer from the Printer List. If you try, it will momentarily vanish and then return. However, via the In Menu column, you can prevent a given printer from showing up in Print and Page Setup dialogs.

SEE: • "Printer Setup Utility's Printer List window," earlier in this chapter.

Printing

After you've set up your printer(s) in Printer Setup Utility, you're ready to print. You have two main options:

You can print a document from an application. In most cases (assuming you don't want to modify default settings and no problems occur), printing is as simple as choosing Print from the File menu of an application that can open the desired document. In the standard Print dialog that appears, enter the number of copies you want and (optionally) the desired page range. Then click the Print button. That's it. If desired, you can choose additional options in the Print and Page Setup dialogs (which I describe in following sections).

Once you've clicked the Print button, the printer queue application for the selected printer (or the default printer if you didn't choose a different one) launches, and its icon appears in the Dock. Your document is then printed. When it's no longer needed for the selected job(s), the printer queue application closes automatically and its icon disappears from the Dock (unless you manually placed it in the Dock, in which case it will remain there).

You can print a document from the Finder or Printer Setup Utility. You can print a document directly from the Finder if you previously created a desktop printer for the desired printer. To do so, simply drag the document icon to the desktop-printer icon.

If instead you drag the document icon to the Printer Setup Utility icon, it also prints—using the default printer. Similarly, if you launch Printer Setup Utility, open the printer queue window for any listed printer, and drag a document to the queue window, the document will print to that printer.

If you have two or more printers, you can even drag a pending print job from the queue list of one printer to that of another printer. This works in most cases, although it may fail if the printers are of different types (from example, non-PostScript versus PostScript).

Finally, you can highlight a document icon in the Finder and choose Print from the Finder's File menu. This too should lead to the document's being printed. However, I have found this to be a bit buggy; it does not always work.

In most cases, what happens next is that the creating application opens, the document itself briefly appears, and printing is initiated; the Print dialog is bypassed. In some cases, such as with a PNG document created when you take a screen snapshot, no application is opened; printing proceeds directly to the printer queue for the selected printer.

SEE: • "Take Note: Printer Queue (Proxy) Applications," earlier in this chapter.

• "Printer queue window," later in this chapter.

TAKE NOTE ▶ Printing Finder Windows

Because the Finder doesn't include a Print command, there's no automatic way to print a list of the contents of a Finder window. There are, however, work-arounds; try these:

• Drag a folder icon to the Printer Setup Utility icon. If a Printer Setup Utility icon is in the Dock, you can just drag the folder to the Dock icon.

• If you've created a desktop printer for the desired printer, you can alternatively drag the folder icon to the Desktop Printer icon.

A Print dialog will appear. Click the Print button, and you should get a text listing of all items at the top level of the folder, including their names, sizes, and date last modified. Note: Even invisible items are printed.

Page Setup

You can access the Page Setup dialog from the File menu of any application that can print. Usually, you'll need to use the Page Setup dialog only if you want to modify the default layout settings; for example, the main occasion when I need to switch settings here is when I shift from printing 8.5-by-11-inch documents to 4-by-6-inch photos.

Basic options. The first item in this dialog is the Settings pop-up menu. Although its options vary depending on the application, these are the two most common:

• **Page Attributes.** With the Page Attributes item selected (which is what you see when the Page Setup dialog first opens), you can choose from several options in the remainder of the window:

Format for—The default selection here is Any Printer. Some printers have special formatting requirements for a page to print correctly. If documents are printing oddly with the Any Printer option, choose the printer name from the pop-up menu that matches the printer you will be using. You can also open the Print & Fax System Preferences pane from here.

Paper Size—For choosing a size other than the current selection. Use this, for example, to shift from "US Letter" to "4 x 6 in (borderless)." Choose "Manage Custom Sizes" to create a size not included in the default list.

Orientation—For choosing between portrait, landscape, and reverse landscape.

Scale—For reducing or enlarging the copy by a given percentage.

SEE: • **"Take Note: Why and How to Create PDF Files," later in this chapter, for related information.**

The changes you make to these attributes will be applied to all documents that are currently open in the application containing the selected document, as well as to any new documents that you create in the application (while it's still open).

• **Save As Default.** After choosing your settings, you can save them as the default by choosing this item.

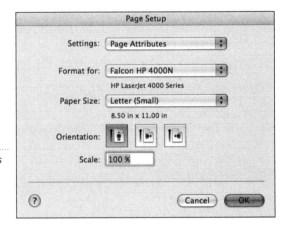

Figure 7.22

The Page Attributes option of the Page Setup dialog, formatted for an HP printer.

Application-specific options. Applications may provide additional options in the Settings menu. For example, Microsoft Word adds an item called Microsoft Word, which provides unique options (for example, for margins), and allows you to apply the Page Setup settings to only part of the document, if desired. Word also adds a Custom Paper Size item to the Settings menu.

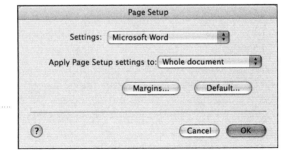

Figure 7.23

Microsoft Word's additional Page Setup options.

Print

As already mentioned, when you're ready to print a document, you can simply choose Print from the application's File menu. In the Print dialog that appears, you can choose from a variety of options before printing the document. Note that unlike changes to settings in the Page Setup dialog, changes in the Print dialog apply only to the document about to be printed. The following paragraphs describe the options. For basic printing, you can ignore all of these options and immediately click the Print button.

Printer. If you have more than one printer connected to your Mac, you can use the Printer pop-up menu to choose a printer other than the default printer. Any printer you set up in Printer Setup Utility will be available in this menu. If you want to use a printer that is not listed, you can choose Add Printer to open the Printer Setup Utility and then add or delete printers as needed. You can also choose Print & Fax Preferences from the Printer pop-up menu to open that System Preferences pane.

SEE: • **"Determining the hostname and location (unshared and shared),"**
earlier in this chapter.

Note: If an exclamation point precedes the name of a printer, it means you have stopped printing for that printer, via Printer Setup Utility or the printer queue window.

Presets. The Presets pop-up menu lists the Standard settings by default. If you have a particular group of settings (which you created by modifying the following options) that you use frequently, you can save it as a custom preset and choose it at any later time from this menu. From this menu you can subsequently choose Rename or Delete for a saved setting. Note: Unfortunately, there is not a way to save a paired set of Page Setup and Print settings; each is saved separately.

Printing options. Just below the Presets pop-up menu is an unnamed pop-up menu, commonly called either Printing Options or Copies & Pages (because it is the default item in the menu). The options in this menu vary by application and printer. The following options are almost always listed:

- **Copies & Pages.** These options allow you to enter the number of copies to print (and, if you print multiple copies, whether they should be collated or printed by page), as well as whether to print the entire document or a subset of pages.

- **Layout.** These options allow you to print multiple document pages on each piece of printer paper, as well as to arrange the pages. You can also choose to include a thin border around each page. On the left is a sample printer sheet that shows you how document pages will be printed.

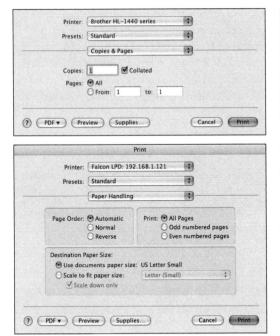
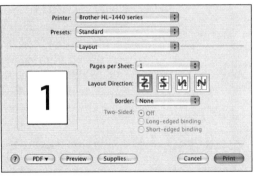

Figure 7.24

Several of the option panes in the Print dialog (as accessed from TextEdit): top left, *Copies & Pages;* top right, *Layout;* bottom left, *Paper Handling;* bottom right, *Color Sync.*

- **Scheduler.** This is where you can set a document to be printed at some specified later time—useful if the printer you wish to use is not currently available but will be later.

- **Paper Handling.** Use this option if you want to print only odd- or even-numbered pages, or to print in reverse order. You can also designate the size of paper on which the document will be printed and, if necessary, choose to have the document scaled to fit that paper size.

- **ColorSync.** ColorSync is Apple's technology designed to ensure that the color of an image remains consistent, whether it's viewed onscreen or printed to a printer. This is accomplished by creating ColorSync profiles, matched to your display and other devices, via the ColorSync utility and the Displays System Preferences pane. If your color printer is "ColorSync aware," it can take advantage of this technology to maintain color consistency.

  Note: If there is also a Color Options item (as described below) and you want to use ColorSync for your printer, select the ColorSync option from there.

  Note: You can use the ColorSync option to reduce the size of PDFs created using the Print dialog, as described later in this chapter.

  SEE: • "Take Note: Why and How to Create PDF Files," later in this chapter.

- **Cover Page.** This option lets you print a cover page for your document. For example, you can choose from several cover-page templates, such as Standard, Classified, and Confidential; the job ID, document title, and user name of the person printing the document will be included. You can also include a billing code or text.

- **Summary.** This pane presents a table that summarizes all of your settings in the different option panes.

TECHNICALLY SPEAKING ▶ Using ColorSync

The details of how to use the ColorSync printing options not only are largely beyond the scope of this book, but they're also beyond the needs of most Mac users. However, if you do need these features, check the Help files for ColorSync Utility for assistance.

For starters, here are two tips regarding the ColorSync option in the Print dialog:

- From the Color Conversion pop-up menu, choose Standard if you want the application you're using to control the color management of the printed output, or choose In Printer if you want the printer you're using to control the color management of the printed output.

- From the Quartz Filter pop-up menu, select a filter to vary the appearance of a specific document (for example, adding a sepia tone). The filters are stored in /System/Library/Filters. You can modify a filter, create a new one, or view how a file will look with a filter selected via the Filters option in ColorSync. Choose Add Filters from the Quartz Filter pop-up menu to directly open a PDF preview of your document in ColorSync; you can select different filters from here.

Other common options available in this pop-up menu, depending on the chosen printer, include the following:

- **Error Handling.** For PostScript printers, you can choose to ignore the reporting of PostScript errors or to have your printer create a detailed report. This pane also provides printer-specific options such as Tray Switching, which specifies what to do when a tray runs out of paper on a multiple-tray printer.

- **Paper Feed.** If your printer has multiple paper trays or feeds (an envelope feed, a manual-feed slot, and so on), you can specify which tray you want to use. You can even have the first page come from one source and the rest of the document come from another source. (This option is frequently used for printing the first page of a multipage document on letterhead.) The options here may vary because they're typically provided by the printer driver or PPD for the printer chosen in the Printer pop-up menu.

- **Printer Features.** This pane, which is common for laser printers, allows you to modify other printer-specific features, such as the type of paper used and printing resolution.

- **Image Quality (or Quality & Media).** This is another option where you may find menus for choosing a printer's resolution or levels of gray, as well as the type of paper used.

- **Color Options.** This includes printer-specific options for adjusting how screen colors are translated to printed colors.

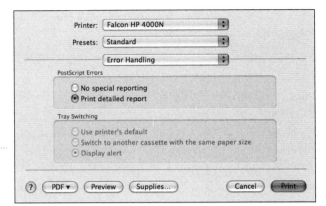

Figure 7.25

The Error Handling pane in the Print dialog (as accessed from TextEdit).

Applications may also provide a menu choice, usually named after the application, that provides extra options specific to the application. Most of these application- and printer-specific options are determined by the PPD and/or PDE files that are installed.

Note that a few applications, such as iPhoto, may initially display a completely customized Print dialog. In the case of iPhoto, you can still get to the standard options by clicking the Advanced button.

SEE: • "Take Note: PDE Files," below, for details on PDE files.

• "What types of printer connections does Mac OS X support?" and "How do I tell if my printer is already supported?" earlier in this chapter, for more information on PPD files.

TAKE NOTE ▶ PDE Files

PDE (*Printer Dialog Extension*) files allow an application or printer (PostScript or non-PostScript) to add application- or printer-specific options in the Print dialog. (Note: These files differ from the PPD files described earlier in this chapter. PPD files allow Mac OS X's built-in PostScript driver to support features specific to a particular PostScript printer.)

PDE files determine what options are available in the Printing Options pop-up menu—such as the Paper Handling and Error Handling options noted in the main text. A standard suite of these files is installed with Mac OS X. Additional ones may be installed by other software.

Mac OS X–installed PDE files are buried in a framework within the System folder. A separate set of these files exists for each language installed. For example, in Tiger, English-language PDEs can be found in the following location: /System/Library/Frameworks/Carbon.framework/Versions/A/Frameworks/Print.framework/Versions/A/Plugins/PrintingCocoaPDEs.bundle/ContentsResources/English.lproj/.

continues on next page

TAKE NOTE ▶ PDE Files *continued*

The files here have names like ErrorHandlingPDE.nib and PaperHandlingPDE.nib, which correspond to options of the same name in the Print dialog. If you double-click one of these files, it opens up in Interface Builder (assuming you have the Developer software installed). From here, you see the same layout that's visible in the Print dialog. For example, if you open PaperHandlingPDE.nib, you will see the Page Order option, and so on.

Printer-specific PDE files. Printer-specific PDE files for most non-Apple printers (PostScript and non-PostScript) are stored in various subdirectories of the /Library/Printers directory. For example:

- PDEs for several brands of PostScript printers (for example, Lexmark and Hewlett-Packard) are stored in the /Library/Printers/PPD Plugins folder in this directory. These plug-in files are packages, so you can use the Show Package Contents command to examine their contents.

- For non-PostScript Hewlett-Packard DeskJet printers, there is a PDE file called hpdjPDE. plugin, located in the /Library/Printers/hp/deskjet/ directory. There is also a separate /Library/Printers/hp/PDEs directory that contains several separate .plugin files representing different PDEs.

- For Epson printers, inside /Library/Printers/EPSON is a .plugin file for each supported printer. Select a file (SC900.plugin, for example) and use Show Package Contents to navigate to Contents/PDEs. Inside this folder you will find the PDE .plugins file for the named printer.

Application-specific PDE files. Some applications add their own PDE-file-based options to the Print dialog. These application-specific PDEs are typically located inside the application package. Microsoft Word is one exception: Its PDE file, WordPDE.plugin, is located in the Office folder inside the Microsoft Office folder.

Bottom buttons. The bottom of the Print dialog contains at least five buttons: PDF, Preview, Supplies, Cancel, and Print.

- **PDF.** The PDF button opens a pop-up menu that allows you to save your document as a PDF or PostScript file, fax your document, or process a PDF of your document using Mac OS X's PDF Workflow feature (see "Take Note: Why and How to Create PDF Files," below).

- **Preview.** This option creates a temporary PDF file of the current document and opens it in Mac OS X's Preview application.

  This feature is especially useful for applications that don't provide their own Preview command. It allows you to see exactly how the document will look when printed. If you like what you see, you can close the preview and return to the Print dialog to print the document.

  You can actually print the preview directly from the Preview application, but your document will be printed with the preferences you set there rather than in the Print dialog of the original application. To get the best-quality printed output, it is preferable to print the original document in its creating application. If you select Preview and then print the PDF file in the Preview application, print quality may be decreased.

Note: If your initial application is Preview (used to open an existing PDF file, for example), don't use the Preview button from its Print dialog. This creates a PDF of a PDF, which, again, is likely to decrease the quality of the output.

- **Supplies.** Clicking this button will open Safari to the online Apple Store, displaying any available supplies for the printer you had chosen in the Print dialog.

- **Cancel.** Click this button to exit the Print dialog without printing.

- **Print.** You click this button to print your document.

Figure 7.26

The bottom row of buttons in the Print dialog (with the PDF pop-up menu visible).

SEE: • "Take Note: Why and How to Create PDF Files," below, for more details on the PDF and Preview buttons.

TAKE NOTE ▶ Why and How to Create PDF Files

PDF stands for *Portable Document Format*. Adobe created the format as a way to distribute documents so that they display consistently on any computer platform.

Why to create PDF files. Saving a document as a PDF file can be useful for two related reasons:

- PDF files can be viewed on almost any platform via the free Adobe Reader (formerly called Acrobat Reader) application or any other PDF-compatible application (such as Preview in Mac OS X)—great if you need to send a document to someone who does not have the application you used to create it. For example, Windows users can open a PDF file created on a Mac without any need for file conversion.

- A PDF file can be created from any document. All text, graphics, and formatting are embedded within the PDF file. This means that the PDF file of the document can be viewed just as it looked in the original application. You don't even have to worry whether the file's recipient has the appropriate fonts or styles installed.

The one (admittedly small) drawback is that PDF files are formatted for the specific printer you choose when you "print" them. If the recipient prints a PDF file on a printer that is drastically different from yours, he or she may experience minor margin or spacing issues; however, this is generally not a significant issue. (Note: The "Format for" option in the Page Setup dialog may help prevent problems here. For example, if you know what printer the recipient has installed, and you have the same printer, choose it here before creating the PDF file. Otherwise, use Any Printer.)

continues on next page

TAKE NOTE ▶ Why and How to Create PDF Files   *continued*

How to create PDF files: The PDF pop-up menu. The key to creating PDF files in Mac OS X is the PDF pop-up menu in the Print dialog. To access it, click-hold on the PDF button; then choose from the following options:

- **Save as PDF.** This is the option you will most commonly choose. In Mac OS 9, creating PDF files required separate applications, such as Adobe Acrobat. You can still use Acrobat in Mac OS X—and, in fact, you may need to if you intend to create PDFs with advanced features (such as a table of contents) or if you wish to edit an existing PDF document. However, because PDF support is built into Mac OS X, you can create a basic PDF file of any printable document. No additional software is needed.

  Thus, to create a PDF file of almost any document, open the document and choose the Print command from the application's File menu, just as if you intend to print the document. From the PDF button's pop-up menu, choose Save as PDF. Then use the standard Save dialog to name the PDF and choose the destination to which the PDF should be saved. You now have a cross-platform PDF file of your document.

  (Note: An alternative to selecting Save as PDF is to click the Preview button, just to the right of the PDF button in the Print dialog. As described in the main text, this opens a temporary PDF of the document in Preview—then, from Preview's File menu, choose Save As to name and save the PDF.)

- **Save PDF as PostScript.** I covered this PDF menu option in "Technically Speaking: Creating a PostScript File for Printing," earlier in this chapter.

- **Fax PDF.** This command creates a PDF of the document and allows you to fax it, using the fax settings in the dialog that appears.

- **PDF Workflow items.** The remaining options in the PDF pop-up menu are referred to as the PDF Workflow commands. They are used to post-process PDF files created from documents. The default options include

  Compress PDF—Creates a smaller PDF than the standard Save as PDF command does by compressing images contained in the document.

  Encrypt PDF—Creates a password-protected PDF.

  Mail PDF—Creates a PDF and then e-mails it using your default e-mail client.

  Save as PDF-X—Creates a PDF in PDF-X format, a subset of the PDF format that contains the minimum amount of information needed to print the document later. This format is common in the printing industry.

  Save PDF to iPhoto—Creates a PDF of the document and then adds it to your iPhoto Library.

  Save PDF to Web Receipts Folder—Creates a PDF of the document and then adds it to ~/Documents/Web Receipts, using the name of the document or Web page as the PDF name. This is a handy way to save receipts from online purchases—you simply choose the Print command in Safari while viewing the receipt, and then choose this command from the PDF pop-up menu.

continues on next page

TAKE NOTE ▶ **Why and How to Create PDF Files**   *continued*

Adding PDF Workflow items. You can also add your own PDF Workflow options by placing folders, applications, AppleScripts, or shell scripts—or aliases to these items—in /Library/PDF Services (to make them accessible to all users) or ~/Library/PDF Services (to restrict them for use in only your own account). Here is what you can add to the folder and what the resulting menu item will do:

- **A folder or alias to a folder.** When you choose the folder from the PDF pop-up menu, a PDF version of the document is automatically saved to that folder, using the name of the document as the PDF name; no Save dialog appears.

- **An application or an alias to an application.** If you choose the application, a PDF file is created and opened in the selected application. You can use this, for example, to open the PDF in Acrobat or Adobe Reader rather than Preview.

- **An Automator workflow document.** These are documents created via the Automator application. (Note: The default items placed in the /Library/PDF Services folder when you install Mac OS X are workflow documents.)

- **A Unix tool or an AppleScript (or an alias to either).** If this option is chosen, the actions specified by the Unix tool or AppleScript file will be performed on the created PDF file. This is the most powerful option; however, it requires more advanced skill to create the tool or script needed. For example, you can use this option to automate a series of actions, such as a sequence of scriptable actions in Adobe Photoshop or Illustrator. Check the Web for free or shareware "canned" scripts to use here.

Note: In versions of Mac OS X 10.2 Jaguar starting with Mac OS X 10.2.4 and in all versions of Panther, you can get a similar set of PDF Workflow options. However, this feature is not enabled by default. To get the menu to appear, you must first manually create a PDF Services folder in the /Library or ~/Library folder. This changes the PDF button in Print dialogs to a pop-up menu.

Using Printer Setup Utility: Managing Print Jobs

Each printer you set up in Printer Setup Utility has a corresponding printer queue.

SEE: • "Take Note: Printer Queue (Proxy) Applications," earlier in this chapter.

After you click the Print button in an application, your document (now known as a *print job*) is sent to the printer queue for the appropriate printer, where it's spooled to the printer or (if other documents are already waiting to be printed) waits in line for its turn (is *queued*). From the printer queue for a printer, you can view and manage print jobs.

Printer List and Status

The Status column of Printer Setup Utility's Printer List window indicates the current printing status of each listed printer.

SEE: • "Printer Setup Utility's Printer List window," earlier in this chapter.

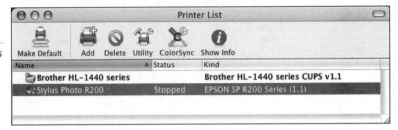

Figure 7.27

Printer Setup Utility's Printer List window. The Status column indicates that the Epson printer has stopped jobs.

Printer queue window

To get a more complete picture of the status of a given printer's print jobs—not to mention more control over their progress—double-click the name of the printer in Printer Setup Utility's Printer List window. This opens the printer queue application for that printer. You can do the same thing by (a) clicking the name and then from the Printers menu choosing Show Jobs (Command-O) or (b) double-clicking the desktop printer for the printer (assuming you've created one).

SEE: • "Take Note: Printer Queue (Proxy) Applications," earlier in this chapter.

The window that appears goes by various names: queue window, desktop-printer jobs window, show jobs window, or even the name of the printer itself. Whatever you call it, you will find that it contains two tabs:

- **Active.** This pane displays a list of all documents currently printing or waiting to be printed. If there are no such documents, it simply states, "No job printing." By default, documents are listed in the order in which they will be printed. The document that is being printed will be listed by name at the top of the scrollable text area, and the entry in the Status column will read Printing.

- **Completed.** This pane displays a list of documents that were printed to this printer in the past, including the date and time each was printed. The list even includes documents that you started to print and later canceled.

The printer queue window has its own toolbar, with Delete, Hold, Resume, Stop/Start Jobs, Utility, and Supply Levels icons. The Utility icon functions identically to the Utility icon in the Printer Setup Utility toolbar. The Supply Levels icon will show you the current level of supplies (such as ink) in your

Figure 7.28

The printer proxy (also called a desktop printer or printer queue) application's Active pane for an Epson printer, showing Jobs Stopped.

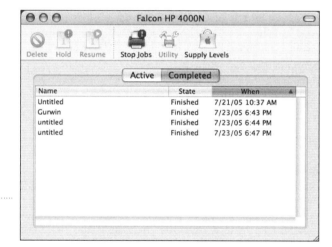

Figure 7.29

The printer queue window's Completed pane.

Figure 7.30

Left, *a printer queue window's Printer menu;* right, *its Jobs menu.*

printer, assuming that your printer's software supports use of this feature. The other toolbar icons function as follows:

- **Delete.** If you decide that you do not want to print a job (perhaps after clicking Print, you discovered that you selected more pages than you intended or used the wrong formatting options), you can select the job in the queue and click the Delete icon in the toolbar or choose Delete Job (Command-Delete) from the Jobs menu. Note that if your printer has already spooled the job in question, it may still print even if you've "deleted" it from the queue.

- **Hold /Resume.** If there's more than one job in the queue, you can stop a particular job from printing while allowing the remaining items to continue. To do this, simply select the item you want to halt and then click the Hold icon in the toolbar of the printer queue window or choose Hold Job from the application's Jobs menu.

  When you want to resume printing, select the held item and then click the Resume icon in the toolbar or choose Resume Job from the Jobs menu.

- **Stop Jobs/Start Jobs.** You can halt the entire queue for a printer by clicking the Stop Jobs icon in the toolbar of the printer queue window or by choosing Stop Jobs from the application's Printer menu. (Alternatively, you can choose Stop Jobs from Printer Setup Utility's Printers menu while the desired printer is selected in the Printer List window.)

  When you want the queue to resume, use the toggled Start Jobs option.

  Note: When a printer is stopped, an exclamation point appears next to its name in the Printer pop-up menu of the Print dialog. The exclamation point also appears in the printer's icon in the Dock.

  Stopping jobs can be useful, for example, if you notice that your printer is about to run out of paper—you can stop all jobs until you've added more paper. It can also be helpful to stop jobs if you're not connected to your printer continually. When you're using a laptop, for example, you can stop the print queue while you're on the go; any documents that you "print" will be sent to the queue and held there. When you connect to your printer later, you can start the queue, and the documents will print.

  Unfortunately, Mac OS X does not yet allow you to set or change the priority of print jobs here. Using the Hold icon to delay the printing of less important documents is the closest you can get for now. There is a Priority pop-up menu in the Scheduler options of the Print dialog, but this setting does not appear to be available in the printer queue window.

All of these options come in handy when you get a printing error. A printing error may prevent a job from being printed, automatically holding or stopping the queue. If the problem is something you can fix, you can make the necessary adjustment and then click Resume or Start Jobs. Otherwise, you can delete the problem job and at least allow other documents to print.

Transferring print jobs. If you have a print job in a queue, you can open up another printer's queue window and drag the job from one window to the other. This transfers the job to the new queue (and thus a different printer).

SEE: • "Nothing prints," later in this chapter, for related information.

TAKE NOTE ▶ When You Need to Delay a Print Job

Suppose you want to print a document but either you don't want it to print immediately or you can't get it to print immediately. In such cases, you can do any of the following:

- **Use Scheduler.** From the Printing Options menu in a Print dialog, choose Scheduler. From the options that appear, choose the desired print time. The print job is added to the queue and will print at the designated time. The On Hold option places the document on indefinite "hold." You can resume the job whenever you wish via the printer queue window.

  Finally, you can assign a Priority level here. If multiple jobs are scheduled to print at the same time, the higher-priority jobs will print first.

- **In the printer queue window, select Hold Job.** This works the same way as choosing On Hold from the Scheduler options. The advantage of the Scheduler route is that for a small document, the document may print before you can even get the printer queue window to appear.

- **In Printer Setup Utility or the printer queue window, click Stop Jobs.** This halts all print jobs—useful if you're not currently connected to the desired printer (such as while working with a laptop computer while traveling). If you select Stop Jobs, any documents you print will be queued until you select Start Jobs (assuming the printer is connected).

  When jobs are stopped, after you click the Print button, an alert dialog appears informing you that you cannot print at the moment. Click the Add to Queue button to add the document to the queue for later printing.

- **Create a PDF or PostScript file.** As a last resort, instead of printing at all, you can save the document as a PDF or PostScript file (as described elsewhere in this chapter) and then print the PDF or PostScript file at any later point.

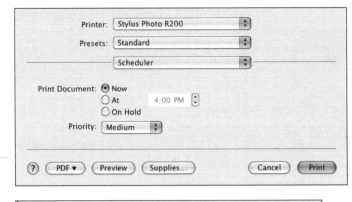

Figure 7.31

The Print dialog's Scheduler pane.

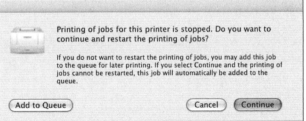

Figure 7.32

The alert that appears when you select to print a document when jobs have been stopped for the printer.

Printing from Classic

As long as you have a printer supported by Classic, you can print directly from Classic applications. In fact, in Tiger, any printers available in Mac OS X should be available to Classic applications just as if they were set up in Mac OS 9. However, if you can't get a Mac OS X printer to appear in a Classic application, you may be able to access the printer by setting it up within Classic using the following procedure.

Setting up USB and AppleTalk network printers in Classic is pretty much identical to how you select them in Mac OS 9. In essence, you use the Mac OS 9 Chooser just as you would do if booted from Mac OS 9. See this Apple Knowledge Base document for related information, specific to inkjet (raster) printers: http://docs.info.apple.com/article.html?artnum=300849.

If you use an LPR printer in Mac OS X and want to use it in the Classic environment as well, use Desktop Printer Utility (installed by Mac OS 9) and follow these steps:

1. Launch the Mac OS 9 Desktop Printer Utility. This will launch Classic if Classic is not already running.

2. A New Desktop Printer window should appear by default. If not, from the File menu choose New.

3. From the list in the window, select Printer (LPR) and click OK. A new window, named Untitled 1, opens.

4. In the new window, click the upper Change button to select the appropriate PPD file for your LPR printer.

5. Click the lower Change button to enter the IP address or domain name of the printer and the queue name.

6. Click the Create button.

   With the newly created desktop printer set as the default in Classic, you will be able to print to the LPR printer from Classic applications.

Finally, some printers are supported in the Classic environment but will not print in Mac OS X. If you have one of these printers, you can save a document as a PDF file in Mac OS X and then print it in Classic using an application such as Adobe Reader for Mac OS 9.

SEE: • "Printing problems," in the online Classic chapter, at Mac OS X Help Line (www.macosxhelpline.com), for more information on printing from Classic.

CUPS

Apple completely revised Mac OS X's underlying printing software in Mac OS X 10.2 Jaguar, moving from the original printing architecture to one that depends on a Unix printing architecture called *CUPS (Common Unix Printing System)*. Mac OS X 10.3 and 10.4 use the same CUPS software.

Mac OS X's printing software, notably Printer Setup Utility, uses the CUPS software for printing but gives you an Aqua interface to it. This section provides an overview of how CUPS works with Mac OS X and how to use it to solve problems. You can obtain more background on CUPS at the Common Unix Printing System Web site (www.cups.org).

Where CUPS software is stored

The CUPS software for Mac OS X is located in the invisible Unix directories. The software consists of numerous files stored in several different locations. The following provides an overview of the CUPS software locations of most interest:

/private/etc/cups. This is where you'll find the CUPS software you're most likely to access for troubleshooting.

 Open the ppd subdirectory located here, for example, and you will see a .ppd file for each printer listed in Printer Setup Utility's Printer List.

 Also important here is the cupsd.conf file, which contains configuration data, such as where the CUPS log files are stored.

SEE: • "Accessing CUPS from a Web browser" and, especially, "Technically Speaking: Editing the Completed Jobs List," later in this chapter, for related information.

/private/var/spool/cups. The spool directory contains various subdirectories for holding spooled printing files. One subdirectory is named cups.

You cannot open the /cups subdirectory without root access. To view a list of its contents via Terminal, use the sudo command (that is, sudo ls /private/var/spool/cups). Alternatively, from the Finder, open Get Info for the cups folder and change the owner from "system" to yourself. Then change the access for Others from No Access to Read & Write. Finally, change the owner back to system. You can now enter the folder whenever you wish (although it's unlikely that you'll have much need to do so). Note: If you're concerned about the security risk involved in making this change, you can instead enter the folder after you've changed the owner to yourself and then change the owner back to system when you're finished.

SEE: • "Ownership & Permissions" and "Root Access," in Chapter 4, for related information.

• Chapter 6, for more on problems opening and saving files due to permissions restrictions.

/private/var/log/cups. This directory holds the log files created by CUPS.

/usr/libexec/cups and /usr/share/cups. These directories contain various CUPS interface software, including the user-interface files for when you access CUPS from your Web browser, as described in the next section. (Note: The cover pages you generate in Print dialogs are actually stored in /usr/share/cups/banners.)

The /usr/share/doc/cups directory holds CUPS documentation. Gimp-Print software is located in /usr/share/cups/model.

/usr/sbin and /usr/bin. These locations contain the printing commands used when printing from Terminal. These include cupsd and lpadmin (in /sbin) and the more general printing software, lp and lpr (in /bin). See the CUPS documentation, described in the next section, for details on using these commands.

The non-CUPS printing software, as described in the previous sections of this chapter (for example, the software in /System/Library/Printers and /Library/Printers), works in coordination with the CUPS software described here. Both are needed for Mac OS X printing to function.

~.ppd stored in
/usr/share/cupsd/model
- see p. 380 J. & Wm. Ray, MacOSXTiger
unleashed, SAMS, 2006

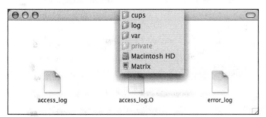
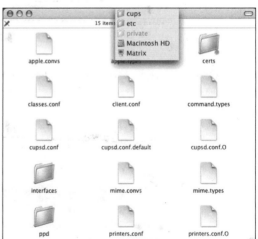

Figure 7.33

Two examples of Unix directories that contain CUPS software.

Accessing CUPS from a Web browser

Many of the options accessed from Printer Setup Utility and from Print dialogs actually call up CUPS routines. Although I won't discuss this much, you can also access CUPS via commands in Terminal (not surprisingly, since CUPS is Unix software). However, you can directly access the CUPS software more conveniently via a Web interface built into CUPS. From here, you can even access CUPS options that are not available from Printer Setup Utility or Print dialogs.

To load this Web interface, enter one of the following local addresses in your browser: http://127.0.0.1:631/ or http://localhost:631/. (These are actually variations of the same address.) This will load the CUPS main page, with links to several other locations. You can also access these links from the buttons at the top of the CUPS window. The following provides an overview of the various links:

Do Administration Tasks. This takes you to the Administration page. From here, you can use the Add Class and Add Printer functions. You can also access the same Manage pages more directly accessed via the Manage links listed below; however, note that some features require administrator access (that is, you will need to enter a name and password), which can be gained via this link but not the others.

SEE: • "Technically Speaking: Access Restrictions in the CUPS Web Interface," later in this chapter, for details.

Manage Printer Classes. This takes you to the Classes page. If you've created classes (for example, via Printer Setup Utility's Pool Printers command), you will be able to perform such tasks as modifying or deleting the class. The Modify Class command is of particular interest because it allows you to change the printers included in the class. You cannot do this from Printer Setup Utility. In fact, Printer Setup Utility does not even tell you what printers are in the class.

Note: A *class* is a group of pooled printers (as described in "Printer Setup Utility menus," earlier in this chapter).

On-Line Help. This takes you to the Help page. From here, you can access CUPS documentation and learn just about everything there is to know about CUPS—including how to access printing via Terminal commands (such as lp, lpr, and lpstat).

Manage Jobs. This takes you to the Jobs page. Here, you can hold, release, or cancel a currently active print job, just as you can in the printer queue window.

Click the Show Completed Jobs button to get a list of all recently completed print jobs. (Note: This is essentially the same list, combined across all printers, that you can get by accessing the Completed pane in a printer queue window, as discussed earlier in this chapter.

SEE: • "Technically Speaking: Editing the Completed Jobs List," later in this chapter, for related information.

Manage Printers. This takes you to the Printer page, where you will see a list of all added printers (similar to what you would see in Printer Setup Utility's Printer List window). In each case, you have several options, including Print Test Page, Modify Printer, and Configure Printer. Most of what you can do here can also be done via Printer Setup Utility.

Download the Current CUPS Software. This takes you to the CUPS Web site (www.cups.org), where you can check for a newer version of the CUPS software. In general, however, I recommend ignoring this option. Let Apple update the CUPS software, as needed, via Mac OS X updates.

There's a good deal of redundancy built into these pages. For example, if you click the link for a printer's name from any page where it's listed, you go to a page that contains both the Manage Jobs and Manage Printers information for just that printer.

Troubleshooting printing from CUPS Web pages. The CUPS Web interface provides an opportunity to do some troubleshooting you could not otherwise attempt. Here are two examples:

- **Enabling options.** Suppose you try to add an option such as an additional paper tray via the Installable Options selection in Show Info from Printer Setup Utility and it doesn't work; you can try to accomplish the same thing from the CUPS software instead. To do so, on the Manage Printers page click the Configure Printer button and then choose the desired options from the resulting list. This may succeed even when an attempt from Printer Setup Utility does not. You may also find options, such as one for printing a cover page both before *and* after a document, not listed in Printer Setup Utility.

- **Canceling jobs.** You cannot stop jobs from a shared printer via Printer Setup Utility or a printer queue window on the client computer (you can only do this from the computer to which the printer is physically connected). However, you may be able to do so via the CUPS Web interface: Go to the CUPS Jobs page, find the problem job, and click the Cancel Job button. This may get the job to delete.

Note: Not all CUPS Web-interface options will work from the browser—at least not by default. You may need to enter a password first. And, in some cases, even that will not work.

SEE: • "Technically Speaking: Access Restrictions in the CUPS Web Interface" and "Technically Speaking: Editing the Completed Jobs List," below, for details.

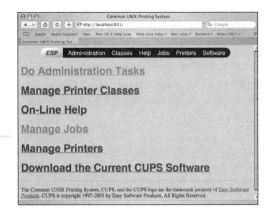

Figure 7.34

The main page of
the CUPS software
as accessed via its
Web-browser
interface.

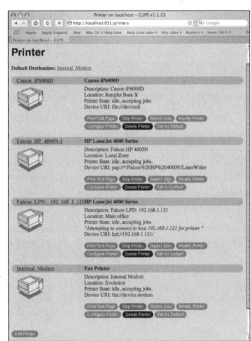

Figure 7.35

The page that
appears after
clicking Manage
Printers on the
CUPS main page.

Figure 7.36

The page that
appears after
clicking the Show
Completed Jobs
button on the CUPS
Manage Jobs page.

TECHNICALLY SPEAKING ▶ **Access Restrictions in the CUPS Web Interface**

When using the CUPS Web interface, if you try to perform some actions—for example, canceling a print job—you may see an error stating, `client-error-forbidden`. The reason for this is that you're trying to make a change that requires administrative access. Unfortunately, you're not given an opportunity to provide your admin-level user name and password. The solution is to go back to the main CUPS Web page and then click the "Do Administration Tasks" link. This will bring up a name and password dialog. Provide your Mac OS X user name and password to authenticate. After doing this, you'll be on the Admin page, from which you can access the various administrative dialogs. (Note: You can also go back to the main CUPS page and access any functions from there; once you've authenticated, you'll no longer see "client-error-forbidden" errors.)

TECHNICALLY SPEAKING ▶ **Editing the Completed Jobs List**

As stated in the main text, if you click the Show Completed Jobs button on the Manage Jobs page of the CUPS Web interface, you get a list of all recently printed documents, along with Restart Jobs buttons that seem to imply that you can reprint past jobs. Unfortunately, the features on this page may not always work the way you want. To fix this, you will need to manually edit the cupsd.conf file, mentioned earlier in this chapter.

Keep the completed-jobs list empty. The completed-jobs Web page can be easily accessed by any local user. In fact, if your Mac is on the Internet and other users know your computer IP address, they can access any part of the CUPS Web interface for your Mac by typing `http://{your_IP_address}:631/`. They can do this remotely, even if Web Sharing is not enabled (assuming that you have not blocked the 631 port via a firewall). You may well consider this a security risk or a privacy invasion (for example, you may not want others to know what you've been printing).

To keep others from viewing your completed jobs via a Web browser, you need to delete the items listed here and prevent new items from being added. Here's a way to do so that bypasses using Terminal to edit files:

1. Using the Finder's Go to Folder command, go to /private/etc/cups.

2. Open the cupsd.conf file in a text editor, such as TextEdit or Bare Bones Software's TextWrangler. You will need root access to save changes to the file. With TextEdit, use Pseudo (a utility described in Chapter 4) to accomplish this.

3. Use the Find command to locate `PreserveJobHistory`. Go to the line that reads as follows: `#PreserveJobHistory Yes`. Change that line to the following: `PreserveJobHistory No`.

   Note: Be sure to remove the # at the beginning of the line; this changes the line from a comment to an active setting.

   Note: There is also an option, called `MaxJobs`, used to adjust the maximum number of print jobs saved. The default limit is set at 500; changing this to zero means there is no limit, rather than none being saved.

continues on next page

TECHNICALLY SPEAKING ▶ Editing the Completed Jobs List *continued*

4. Save the modified file. Now, subsequent print jobs will not be saved in the completed-jobs listing of the browser display. However, this does not get rid of any completed jobs already listed. To do that, proceed to the next step.

5. Launch Terminal and type the following:

`cancel -a {name of printer}`

For the name of the printer, use the name as listed in the CUPS Web pages (for example, my HP LaserJet was listed as Falcon_HP_4000N). Press Return.

Repeat this for any other printers that still show completed jobs listed.

Note: /var/log/cups/page_log retains a record of completed print jobs but not the name of each document. The data that's actually used to generate the Completed Jobs Web page is located in /private/var/spool/cups. There is a separate file (beginning with the letter *c* and followed by a series of numbers) for each job listed on the Web page. The only problem here is that the cups folder is owned by root. Thus, even as an administrator, you cannot directly open this folder from the Finder. You can work around this by changing the owner in the folder's Get Info window (as described in "Where CUPS software is stored," in the main text above). However, it is probably simpler to use the cancel command, as described above.

6. Restart your Mac.

To save yourself the hassle of restarting the Mac, you should be able to instead launch Terminal and type sudo `killall -HUP cupsd`. At least in Tiger, however, this may not work here as a substitute for restarting the Mac.

 In any case, the purpose of the restart is to relaunch the CUPS software so that the change to the .conf file takes effect. Once you have done this, all existing completed jobs for that printer are no longer listed when you select Show Completed Jobs.

You have now wiped the Completed Jobs record clean and turned off the option to add new jobs to the list. Note: These changes will also affect the jobs listing in the Completed pane of printer queues.

Enable the Restart Job command. If you change the #PreserveJobFiles No line in cupsd.conf to PreserveJobFiles Yes, you should now be able to use the Restart Job button in the Completed Jobs dialog to reprint a previously printed document. However, it will only work for jobs saved after you enable this option and then restart.

Note: The Restart Job command may still not work, even after following the above procedure. Instead you will get an error that states, client-error-not-possible. This is because, starting in Mac OS X 10.3, Apple employed a new type of password encryption called ShadowHash (the old method was called Basic). If you have upgraded your account from Jaguar, you may not be using ShadowHash for your password, even though you are running Panther or Tiger. New accounts, created in Panther or Tiger, however, use ShadowHash. You can check what method is being used for your account by opening NetInfo Manager and going to /users/{your account name}.

continues on next page

TECHNICALLY SPEAKING ▶ **Editing the Completed Jobs List** *continued*

At the bottom of the window, check the authentication_authority line. If it has a value of `;ShadowHash;`, then you are using that method. The problem is that CUPS cannot decrypt a ShadowHash password here, so the Restart Job feature will not work. There is no ideal solution for this; the ultimate solution is for Apple to modify the software so that CUPS works with ShadowHash. In Panther, I was able to get Restart Job to work after modifying the `AuthType` lines in the last section of the cupsd.conf file from `AuthType Basic` to `AuthType None` (thereby eliminating the password check altogether). But in Tiger, nothing I tried would work. For some reason, this works differently than the password issues described in "Technically Speaking: Access Restrictions in the CUPS Web Interface" (where your admin password is accepted without problem).

Note: As noted above, the actual print jobs are stored in the /var/spool/cups directory. You will find two types of files here: ones that begin with a *c* (such as c00212) and ones that begin with a *d* (such as d00212-001). The latter files are the actual print jobs. If you drag one of these files to BBEdit or TextWrangler, it will open and correctly display the print job output—much like a Print Preview feature. (Other applications will likely display either raw code or nothing at all.) You can then choose to print the document, if desired.

In case it isn't obvious, you can't combine both of the procedures (disabling completed jobs and restarting jobs) described here—if you disable completed jobs, you can't restart them, because they won't exist.

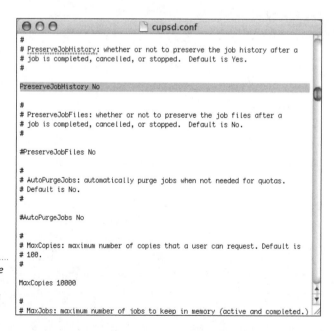

Figure 7.37

A partial view of the cupsd.conf file; the PreserveJobHistory line is highlighted.

TAKE NOTE ▶ Using Gimp-Print

One plus to having CUPS in Mac OS X is that it's relatively easy for Unix-savvy developers to write driver software for printers. These drivers can support printers whose manufacturers have not updated their drivers to work in Mac OS X 10.2 or later.

However, you don't have to know any Unix to take advantage of these drivers. With Gimp-Print, any Mac user can benefit from this approach. Gimp-Print is a collection of drivers that provide support for, or a way to work around problems with, a variety of printers and printer drivers.

Gimp-Print is installed automatically as part of the standard printing software when you first install Mac OS X. The drivers (.ppd files) can be found in the following location: /usr/share/cups/model/Gimp-Print (look especially in the C folder).

If you want a newer version of the drivers than the ones that came with your copy of Mac OS X, you need to download Gimp-Print, available from SourceForge.net (http://gimp-print. sourceforge.net) and install it. Checking for a newer version is useful if you're having any problems printing via the current version of the Gimp-Print drivers. A newer version may have fixed bugs or added support for a previously unsupported printer.

Note: Gimp-Print may be unable to print files that contain PostScript code opened in Carbon applications (such as most Adobe applications and AppleWorks). You can work around the problem by saving the file as a PDF document and printing the PDF file. Otherwise, you can use a program called ESP GhostScript (see "ESP Ghostscript"; www.cups.org/ghostscript.php), which allows Gimp-Print to work with these otherwise Gimp-Print–resistant applications.

Using Gimp-Print drivers. In Tiger, using Gimp-Print drivers for an "unsupported" printer works just like using official drivers: You set up the printer as explained in the main text, except that when you access Printer Setup Utility's Printer Browser, if the correct driver is not automatically chosen, you choose the appropriate Gimp-Print driver via the Print Using pop-up menu. For example, for an Epson Stylus C45, you would choose EPSON from the pop-up menu and then select EPSON Stylus C45–Gimp-Print v5.0.0 from the list of drivers shown. (The version number may differ, of course, depending on which updates you've installed.) Then click Add to create the new printer queue.

Faxing

Included as part of Mac OS X is the ability to fax documents. To get you started, here's some general information:

- To receive a fax, you must be connected—via the Modem port on your Mac—to the phone line that people will be using when sending you a fax. To send a fax, you can be connected to any phone line.

- You can't be connected to the Internet via your modem and send and receive faxes at the same time.

- You can receive a fax even if you're not logged in to your account at the time it arrives. However, you cannot receive faxes when the computer is asleep or shut down.

The following sections cover the remaining essential information on faxing.

Setting up Print & Fax to receive a fax

Before you can receive a fax, you must first set up the preferences on the Faxing pane of the Print & Fax System Preferences pane (see Figure 7.5). To do so, follow these steps:

1. Launch System Preferences and open the Print & Fax pane. Click the Faxing tab.

2. Check the "Receive faxes on this computer" box.

3. In the When a Fax Arrives section, specify the number of rings before the fax feature "answers." In addition, check one (or more) of the following boxes to set what to do with a fax after it arrives:

   - Save it as file to a specified folder.

   - E-mail it to a specified address. For this to work, you should ideally be connected to the Internet via a separate line from the phone/modem (for example, via a cable modem).

   - Print it to the chosen printer.

4. Enter your fax number in the My Fax Number text box. This is used only for identification purposes when sending and receiving faxes.

Optionally, you can check the "Show fax status in menu bar" box to have easy access to your fax status right from the menu bar.

Assuming you have a fax modem set up and connected to a phone line, this is all you need to do to receive a fax. To modify the settings for a fax modem, click the Set Up Fax Modem button; this takes you to the Fax List in Printer Setup Utility. Otherwise, to send a fax, read on.

Sending a fax

If you have a modem that's currently connected to a phone line, you're ready to send a fax. No other settings need be adjusted in advance. To send a fax (such as an AppleWorks, Pages, or Microsoft Word document):

1. From the current application's File menu, choose Print.

2. In the Print dialog that appears, click the PDF button to open the PDF pop-up menu; choose Fax PDF.

3. In the dialog that appears, fill in the options as indicated. The most important of these options are the following:

   To. Enter the phone number (and name if desired) where the fax is to be sent. You can alternatively select a fax number from your Address Book by clicking the icon to the right of the text box. If your phone line requires a dialing prefix that is not part of the phone number, enter it in the Dialing Prefix text box.

   Modem. If you have more than one available phone line/modem (such as your own internal modem and a mobile phone paired with your Mac), choose the one you want to use.

4. From the pop-up menu below the Presets menu, you can optionally specify settings in the following categories:

   Fax Cover Page. If desired, check the Use Cover Page box and enter the text you want to appear on the cover page.

   Modem. Choose the desired dialing settings.

   Scheduler. Use this if you want to send the fax at some later time (useful, for example, if you are currently connected to the Internet via your modem).

5. Click the Fax button. The fax will be sent. If your phone line is currently in use, the fax will be sent as soon as the phone line is free.

Managing fax jobs. If all goes well when you send a fax, a modem icon (which looks like a fax machine) will appear in the Dock. This is similar to the printer icon that appears when you print a document. If you click it, it opens a queue window that is again similar to what appears if you click a printer icon. From here you can monitor the status of a fax. If a problem occurs, a message will appear here. It will also indicate when the fax is complete. If desired, you can stop or delete a queued fax job from here. Otherwise, when the modem icon vanishes from the Dock, you can assume that the fax has been sent.

Fax sharing. Just as you can share your printers with other computers on your local network, you can also share your fax modem so that others on the network can send faxes using your computer. You enable this feature on the Sharing pane of Print & Fax preferences—check the "Let others send faxes through this computer" box. (Note: Printer Sharing does not need to be enabled to share your fax modem.) Your modem will now automatically appear (to other computers on your local network) in the Modem pop-up menu in the Fax PDF dialog. Similarly, if a user on your local network enables fax sharing on his or her computer, that user's modem will appear in your Modem menu.

Note: If a document needs to be temporarily stored on a hard drive while waiting to be faxed, it is stored on the drive of the computer sharing its modem (not the drive of the user sending the fax).

Note: Although Windows users can access your shared printers if Windows Sharing is enabled in Sharing preferences, they cannot access shared fax modems.

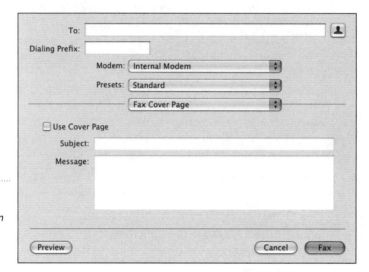

Figure 7.38

The options that appear when you select Fax PDF from the PDF pop-up menu in the Print dialog.

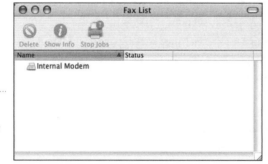

Figure 7.39

The window that appears when you select Show Fax List from Printer Setup Utility's View menu.

Multipurpose fax devices do not receive faxes sent from a Mac.
If you send a fax to a multipurpose device (such as one that acts as both a telephone and a fax machine), the fax may not be received. As a work-around, have the recipient either set the device to receive a fax manually or set the device's receiving mode from auto-recognition to fax-only.

Printer Setup Utility and faxing

After the first time you send a fax from a Print dialog, the modem you used will be listed in the Fax List window of Printer Setup Utility. Via the Fax List window's toolbar, you can delete a selected modem, stop jobs for a modem, or choose Show Info (which I just about never use for a fax modem; it's really designed for printers). There is no Add icon here. Modems are added as just described in "Sending a fax." If your Mac came with an internal modem, Internal Modem should be listed here as a fax modem.

Double-clicking a modem name in the list opens up its queue window.

When the Fax List is the active window, the commands in Printer Setup Utility's menus shift, as appropriate, to access Fax List options instead of Printer List options. For example, if you choose Customize Toolbar, the settings will apply to the Fax List toolbar rather than the Printer List toolbar.

Troubleshooting Printing: Overview

This section covers a variety of printing problems as well as the solutions required to get things working again.

Nothing prints

Perhaps the most common and frustrating printing problem is when a printer refuses to print at all—regardless of what document or application you're using. There are at least three variations of this problem:

- The printer responds in some manner to the Print request, but nothing is every printed.

  This symptom usually means there's a problem with the printer itself. For help, start with the section below titled, "Troubleshooting Printing: Checking Printer and Connections."

- Nothing prints, no error message appears, and the printer does not appear to acknowledge receiving the Print request. In other words, the Mac and printer behave as if you had never selected to Print.

  This, too, often means a problem with the printer. However, it can also mean a problem at the Mac end. For help, start with the section below titled, "Troubleshooting Printing: Checking Printer and Connections." Then proceed to "Troubleshooting Printing: Checking Printer Setup Utility and Desktop Printers."

- An error message appears when you try to print.

  In this case, the message text should help you identify the problem and determine what to do. For more help, check the following sections for the particular error message or a similar one. Otherwise, look for any section that best describes your specific symptom.

Other printing problems

A common printing problem is an inability to add a new printer to Printer Setup Utility's Printer List.

Finally, there is an assortment of problems where some documents print but others don't, or you get printed output but there's something wrong with it (garbled text, incorrect format, and so on).

These issues are all addressed in the sections that follow.

Troubleshooting Printing: Checking Printer and Connections

There are numerous hardware-related reasons why things may go wrong with printing. Although these are not necessarily Mac OS X–specific issues, this is a good place to start your troubleshooting.

In general, there are two types of solutions to hardware-related printing problems: Either you can fix the problem yourself (for example, by replacing a cable or turning on the printer), or you will need to repair or replace the printer.

In all cases in this section, I am assuming that you previously successfully added the printer in Printer Setup Utility.

Checking the printer

To check for printer-related problems, consider the following:

*   Turn your printer off and back on again. This alone may be enough to fix the problem.
*   Make sure the printer is turned on, with paper and ink/toner in place.

    For most inkjet printers, you can check ink levels via a utility accessed from the Utility button in Printer Setup Utility. These utilities may also be used to clean the print nozzles and check for printer-head alignment. If your document is printing but the output quality is poor, check these options. For example, as mentioned earlier in this chapter, my Canon printer comes with an excellent such utility called BJ Printer Utility.

    Note: In some cases, a lack of ink prevents the printer from even attempting to print. In such cases, you may get an error message indicating a printing problem but not specifically describing this as the cause.

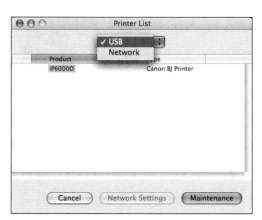

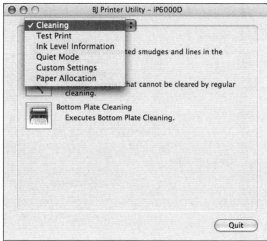

Figure 7.40

Canon's BJ Printer Utility: Left, in the initial window that appears, select a printer and click the Maintenance button; right, in the window that next appears, select the desired function.

- Make sure that any optional hardware additions you made to your printer are correctly installed.

- If you have more than one printer, check to see if a document will print to other printers. If so, this isolates the original printer or its connection to the Mac as the cause. Check with the documentation that came with your printer for troubleshooting advice, and proceed to the sections below.

- Make sure that the problem is not specific to a particular document or application, rather than a general problem with the printer itself. Try printing other documents and printing from other applications.

   SEE: • "Document or application problems," later in this chapter, for more specific advice.

Printing a test page

Try printing a test page directly to your printer. The best way to do this will vary according to printer. Try one or more of the following, as appropriate:

- Select the printer in Printer Setup Utility's Printer List, and from the Printer menu choose Print Test Page. The CUPS Web interface described previously in this chapter includes the same test-page option.

- Select the printer in Printer Setup Utility's Printer List, and click the Utility icon in the toolbar (if available). Check to see if the utility includes a test-page option. If so, try it.

- There may be a test-page button on the printer itself. To determine if this is the case, check the documentation that came with your printer.

If you can successfully print a test page, it indicates that the problem is a Mac OS X software problem. If you can't print a test page, it indicates a hardware problem. In either case, continue with the sections below for more specific advice. Note: Successfully printing a test page from a button on the printer itself does not rule out a problem with the connection from the printer to the Mac; it just rules out a problem with the printer.

Checking USB and FireWire hardware connections

For USB- or FireWire-connected printers, launch System Profiler to see if the printer is listed as being connected to the relevant port. If not, you have a problem with the printer itself or the connection to the Mac.

In any case, make sure your printer is connected to the proper port (USB or FireWire) with the correct cable and that the cable is not faulty (for example, by trying a different cable). Make sure the printer's status lights or other indicators indicate a normal status.

Note: Apple has confirmed that there are potential printing failures when using a USB-to-parallel cable or adapter. You should use a USB cable whenever possible.

If your computer is connected via a USB or FireWire hub, connect the printer directly to the Mac instead. If it still does not work, leave the printer connected and restart the Mac. Try to print again.

Checking Bluetooth connections

If your printer is connected to the Mac via Bluetooth, make sure that Bluetooth is working correctly and that your printer is recognized.

SEE: • "Using Bluetooth," in Chapter 8, for more details.

Checking Ethernet network connections

If your printer is connected to an Ethernet network, make sure it is a networkable printer and is connected to the network with the correct cable. In addition, consider the following:

- Use Network Utility to *ping* the printer to determine whether the printer is available after being connected. You need the DNS name or IP address of the printer to do this. Check Printer Setup Utility to get this information. If there's a problem with the printer connection, you may see a message such as "Host is down" when you ping the printer.

- Make sure that all settings in the Network and Sharing System Preferences panes are correct. If you're using AirPort and/or Printer Sharing, check these settings. Details on these issues are covered in other sections of this chapter and in Chapter 8.

- For shared printers, make sure the user who owns the computer to which the printer is connected still has the printer and computer turned on, and has Printer Sharing enabled.

- For a Bonjour-connected printer, make sure it is still on your local network.

- If you're using an AppleTalk printer, make sure AppleTalk is enabled in the Network System Preferences pane and, if necessary, in the Services list in the Directory Access utility.

  If you're using AppleTalk and you get the message "No AppleTalk printers are available because AppleTalk is currently disabled" in an error or in Printer Setup Utility, it probably means that you did not enable AppleTalk for the appropriate network (the one on which your printer is located). The solution is to select the appropriate network (Ethernet or AirPort) in the Network System Preferences pane, click the AppleTalk button, and then check the Make AppleTalk Active box in the AppleTalk pane.

  Note: Prior to Mac OS X 10.2, you could have AppleTalk enabled on multiple network configurations (for example, both Ethernet and AirPort). This could also cause a problem. However, this option no longer exists in Mac OS X 10.2 or later.

  Note: AppleTalk is turned off by default and is normally not needed for USB printers.

  Sometimes, you may not be able to add an AppleTalk printer in Printer Setup Utility, even if you have correctly enabled AppleTalk in the Network System Preferences pane. In this case, open Network System Preferences and from the Location pop-up menu choose New Location. Type a name for the location, and click OK. Click Apply, and then change the location back to your original location (Automatic, if you're using the default choice) and click Apply again.

  In addition, from the Show pop-up menu select Network Port Configurations, and make sure that the port with AppleTalk enabled is the top choice. I once had a problem where I could not connect to an AppleTalk printer until I had made this change.

  You should now be able to add and print to the AppleTalk printer.

  Check out the following Apple Knowledge Base document for more advice on AppleTalk and printing problems: http://docs.info.apple.com/ article.html?artnum=106613.

If nothing you try succeeds, you may be able to get the printer to work by adding the printer via IP printing rather than via AppleTalk.

SEE: • **Chapter 8 for more on Network Utility and the Network System Preferences settings.**

• **Chapter 9 for more on Sharing System Preferences.**

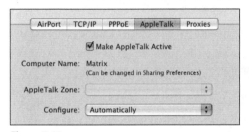
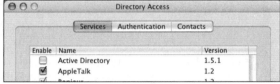

Figure 7.41

Left, *the AppleTalk options in the Network System Preferences pane;* right, *the AppleTalk option in the Directory Access utility.*

Troubleshooting Printing: Checking Printer Drivers

The first step in using a printer in Mac OS X is to add the printer to the Printer List in Printer Setup Utility. I covered the basics of doing this earlier in this chapter.

SEE: • **"Using Printer Setup Utility: Adding and Configuring Printers" and "Using Printer Setup Utility: Managing Print Jobs," earlier in this chapter.**

Even if you previously added a printer successfully, many problems can be resolved by updating, reinstalling, or deleting printer-driver software. You need to be an administrative user to do this; in some cases, you may need root access as well.

"Driver not installed" message

If you see your printer listed in Printer Setup Utility but a "Driver not installed" message is next to its name in the Printer List, or the message appears when you try to add the printer, it generally means that the necessary driver software is not installed. This is probably because it was not installed as part of Mac OS X. Assuming that you did not prevent installation of the needed software by unchecking options in a Custom Install of Mac OS X, you will need to obtain the driver software and install it.

Start by checking for software that may have come with the printer. Otherwise, check the printer manufacturer's Web site. Once you locate the software, install it and return to Printer Setup Utility.

If you get this message even though you believe you have the software installed, it typically means that you have to specifically select your model from the Printer Model pop-up menu in the Printer Browser.

If neither of these fixes works, you probably have an unsupported printer. Using the Gimp-Print driver for that printer, if available, may help. Otherwise, you may not be able to use the printer with Mac OS X.

Getting updated or third-party printer software

If you upgrade to a new version of Mac OS X and your printer software is not among the software that gets updated automatically as part of the Mac OS X upgrade, you may have printing problems if your current driver is incompatible with the new version of Mac OS X. In this case, contact the printer vendor about getting a new version of the driver software, and then install it. In particular, you should note the following:

Install updated PPD. For PostScript printers, an update usually consists of a PPD file that you're instructed to manually install. Here is a typical set of instructions for updating the PPD file of a printer already listed in Printer Setup Utility:

1. After obtaining the updated PPD file (typically from the vendor's Web site), install it in the /Library/Printers/PPDs/Contents/Resources/en.lproj folder.

2. Launch Printer Setup Utility, select the printer in the Printer List, and click the Show Info icon in the toolbar.

3. From the pop-up menu, select Printer Model.

4. Select Other as the model.

5. Navigate to the en.lproj folder where you just installed the PPD file and select the file.

6. Click the Apply Changes button.

If the driver still appears not to be recognized by Printer Setup Utility or other applications, it may be that the PPD file has incorrect permissions. For example, you may be incorrectly listed as the owner of the file rather than "system." Disk Utility's Repair Disk Permissions function is not likely to help here. Instead, you should check the permissions of another file in the same folder and change the permissions of the newly installed file to match it.

Otherwise, use Fixamac Software's Printer Setup Repair utility (www. fixamacsoftware.com/software/psr) to install the PPD files. This utility makes sure they are installed with the correct permissions.

SEE: • "Using Printer Setup Repair," later in this chapter.

If the software comes with its own installer utility, it will likely take care of these permission issues automatically.

Use third-party drivers. For PostScript printers, you can resolve some problems by replacing the printer's "official" PPD file with a modified one created by a third party, as obtained from the Web. To do so:

1. Manually install the PPD file (in the relevant en.lproj folder, as described in the previous section).

2. Launch Printer Setup Utility. Select the problem printer and click Delete in the toolbar.

3. Click Add in the toolbar. Locate the printer you want to add. From the Printer Model menu in the add dialog, select Other rather than Auto Select. Then select the modified PPD file.

Reinstalling corrupt printer software

Occasionally, a printer driver or PPD file becomes corrupt and needs to be replaced. This is especially likely to be the case if you're unable to print to a printer that previously worked fine.

Deleting and re-adding the printer won't solve the problem because you'll still be using the corrupted software.

In most cases, it will be enough just to reinstall the software.

SEE: • "How do I tell if my printer is already supported?" and "Take Note: How to Reinstall the Mac OS X Printer Drivers," earlier in this chapter, for more details.

For other drivers, check the software that came with your printer or the vendor's Web site. In some cases, you may need to manually remove the problem software (typically from /Library/Printers) before you can reinstall it. The instructions that come with the software should indicate whether this is required.

Note: Unless you believe this is the likely cause of your problem, I recommend first trying some of the less "invasive" fixes in the section "Troubleshooting Printing: Checking Printer Setup Utility and Desktop Printers," below.

Removing incompatible printer-support files

The software for one printer may prevent printing on another brand of printer—possibly because of corrupt printer software, improperly installed software, or software that otherwise causes a conflict with the printer in use. For example, in some cases, printing to an Epson printer does not work if Canon printer software was installed, and vice versa.

If the problematic software is for a printer you don't own (for example, it was included in a standard Mac OS X installation), an obvious solution is to delete the unneeded software. To do so, go to /Library/Printers and delete the folders for the printers you don't own. You can also use Printer Setup Repair to completely remove the drivers for particular printer brands.

SEE: • "Installing Printer Drivers," "Using Printer Setup Utility: Adding and Configuring Printers," and "Take Note: Using Gimp-Print," earlier in this chapter, for related advice.

Troubleshooting Printing: Checking Printer Setup Utility and Desktop Printers

This section explores Printer Setup Utility problems and the diagnostic techniques and fixes that require Printer Setup Utility. It assumes you have ruled out a general problem with the printer, its connections, or its driver software, as described in the previous sections.

Note: For shared printers, you will probably need to work with the computer to which the printer is attached, not your own Mac.

Checking for printer queue window (desktop printer) error messages

Whenever you have a problem printing that you cannot otherwise diagnose, go to the printer queue window to check for error messages. You can do this by clicking the icon for the desktop printer in the Dock (it probably automatically launched when you selected to print). If a printing problem has occurred, the icon will likely have a yellow triangle with an exclamation point in it. Otherwise, to launch the desktop printer: (a) Launch Printer Setup Utility and double-click the printer's name in the Printer List; or (b) double-click the printer's desktop printer icon (if you created one).

In the middle area of the printer queue window (to the right of the printer icon), you see a message that indicates an attempt to print the selected job. It may say, "Attempting to connect to . . . printer" or "Starting job" or "Waiting for job to complete." Note: The last message appears when attempting to print to a shared printer.

A separate error message box may appear eventually. For example, you may get one that says, "Unable to connect to printer . . . Operation timed out" or "The printer does not respond," with options to delete or stop the job(s).

Any of these messages suggest a problem with the network connection or cables, or perhaps that the printer is not even turned on, as the most likely causes.

The Status column of Printer Setup Utility's Printer List window may sometimes include a similar error message. However, even if the Status column says Printing, you should still check out the printer queue window. If the message suggests a likely solution, try it. Otherwise, try the suggestions that follow.

TAKE NOTE ▶ More on Printing-Related Error Messages

Prior to Mac OS X 10.2, when you tried to print a document and it failed, you would typically get an error message briefly describing the problem. Often, the message would include a Show Queue or Retry button . Clicking the Show Queue button would take you to Printer Setup Utility, where you would be greeted by yet another error message, with more details of the error and the opportunity to perform some of the same actions (such as stopping a job) that you can do in the printer queue window.

In Mac OS X 10.2 and later, probably due to the shift to CUPS, most of these error messages have vanished. The main sign of trouble will be a change in the appearance of the Printer Setup Utility icon or desktop-printer icon in the Dock. For example, it may shift to a triangle icon with an exclamation point over it, indicating that there is a printing problem and that the print queue has stopped as a result. Additional error information, such as "Printer not responding" or "Unable to make connection," may be displayed if you open the printer queue window. However, in Tiger, even these messages have largely disappeared.

Beyond that, the main way you'll know you have a problem is simply that nothing happens, and nothing is printed.

One bit of good news: Even if no error messages appear in the Aqua interface, you may still find useful error messages in Console logs (as covered more "Checking Console," later in this chapter).

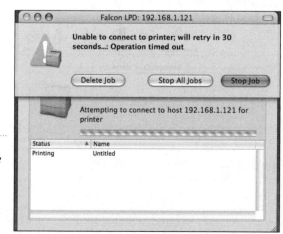

Figure 7.42

The "Operation timed out" message that appears if you try to print to a printer that is currently turned off or disconnected.

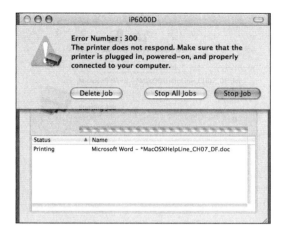

Figure 7.43

The "Printer does not respond" error message. This one appeared when I tried to print to my inkjet printer with the printer turned off.

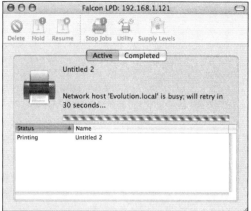

Figure 7.44

An error that appeared when I tried to print to a shared printer, one that had been successfully set up previously but could not be located now because Printer Sharing had been turned off.

Checking the basics

If you're having a general problem with printing, start with these basic Printer Setup Utility troubleshooting techniques:

- Make sure the Printer Setup Utility application is in the /Applications/ Utilities folder. If you moved your /Utilities folder out of the /Applications folder, moved the application out of the /Utilities folder, or renamed either folder, printing may not work.

- In the Print dialog that appears when you choose Print from the File menu of an application, make sure that the chosen printer is the one you intended to use. If the default printer has been changed, you may not be using your desired printer. Also, if your default printer is a shared printer and it isn't currently available, Printer Setup Utility automatically chooses a different printer for you.

  To check for this if you have already started to print, choose Print again and check the name of the printer in the Printer pop-up menu.

- If the printer you want is not in the list in the Print dialog, from the pop-up menu choose Add Printer. This takes you to Printer Setup Utility.

  If the printer is not listed in Printer Setup Utility, add it via the Add Printer command. If it is listed, make sure the box next to its name in the In Menu column is checked.

  SEE: • "Take Note: Showing and Hiding Printers," earlier in this chapter.

- If the printer is correctly listed in the Printer List, check whether jobs have been stopped for the printer.

  If the Printer List window's Status column, the printer queue window, or a message that appears when you select to print indicates that jobs have been stopped (see Figures 7.27 and 7.28), select Start Jobs (for example, in the printer queue window's toolbar). Actually, it's worth toggling Stop Jobs and Start Jobs even if jobs are not stopped; it may still get things working.

If jobs are automatically stopped again after you select Start Jobs, it indicates a problem with the document or printer. Whenever printing fails, jobs are stopped even though you did not select the command to do so. In this case, delete the current job (as described next) and start over.

- If a specific document is listed as on Hold, in the printer queue window's toolbar select Resume to get the document to print.

- For related problems specific to shared printers, see "Take Note: Troubleshooting Shared Printers" and "Take Note: Troubleshooting a Printer Connected to an AirPort Express," below.

TAKE NOTE ▶ Troubleshooting Shared Printers

If you're having problems accessing or using a printer made available to your Mac via Printer Sharing, note the following:

- To manage print jobs with Printer Setup Utility, you need to use Printer Setup Utility on the computer to which the printer is connected.

- A shared printer will vanish from your Printer List if any of the following occurs: The computer that is hosting the printer is turned off, the printer is turned off, or Printer Sharing is turned off.

- If the owner of a computer hosting a shared printer changes the name of the computer (in Sharing preferences), print jobs sent from a client computer to the shared printer will fail until the sharing computer is restarted. After the host computer has been restarted, clients should then delete and re-add the printer in Printer Setup Utility.

- In a more specific case, if you change your Bonjour name in Sharing, any users connected to a printer you are sharing via Printer Sharing may have certain printing preferences corrupted. To fix this problem in Panther or later, delete the following files from the ~/Library/Preferences folder of the computer with printing problems:

  com.apple.print.PrintSetupUtility.plist

  com.apple.print.custompresets.plist

  com.apple.print.PrintingPrefs.plist

  To avoid this problem completely, turn off Printer Sharing before changing your Bonjour name.

- If applications crash (unexpectedly quit) when attempting to print to a shared raster printer, the problem may be a conflict between the printer-driver software on your computer and on the host computer. To fix this, make sure that both computers have the latest software available (or at least the same version). Check the printer vendor's Web site for the latest updates.

To view the driver version of a non-PostScript (inkjet, raster) printer, launch Printer Setup Utility, select the printer in the Printer List, and then click the Show Info icon in the toolbar (or choose Show Info from the Printers menu)—the printer-driver version will be displayed at the bottom of the window. You can use the same technique to view the PPD version number, which will be displayed beneath the PPD File Version label.

TAKE NOTE ▶ Troubleshooting a Printer Connected to an AirPort Express

There are a number of reasons why a printer made available to your AirPort network via an AirPort Express Base Station's USB port might become inaccessible—or simply refuse to print—even though the printer appears to be connected to the AirPort Express properly and the AirPort Express appears to be connected to your wireless network. For example, I've found that if the AirPort Express loses power and then reconnects to my wireless network, other AirPort Express features work fine, but I can often no longer print to the printer. Whichever particular issue you're experiencing, the following should restore printing functionality:

1. Unplug the AirPort Express for a few seconds, and then plug it back in.

2. Open Printer Setup Utility on your computer—the one having trouble printing—and delete the printer queue in the Printer List for the printer connected to the AirPort Express.

3. After the AirPort Express has successfully reconnected to your AirPort network—in other words, after it provides a solid green light—re-add the printer via Printer Setup Utility.

If this does not work, you should perform a "soft reset" of the AirPort Express Base Station in lieu of Step 1, and then follow Steps 2 and 3. For instructions on soft-resetting an AirPort Express, see this Apple article: http://docs.info.apple.com/article.html?artnum=108044.

SEE: • "Take Note: AirPort and Printer Sharing," earlier in this chapter, for related information.

Deleting corrupt print jobs

If a print job file has become corrupt, Printer Setup Utility may stall indefinitely as it tries and fails to print the document. The solution is to delete the print job causing the block.

To delete a print job, choose Show Jobs for the printer or otherwise access the printer's queue window. In the window that appears, if the Status column and/or error-message area indicate a problem with a document, select the document and click the Delete button.

Remember that deleting a print job does not delete the document itself; it deletes only the temporary spool file created to print the document.

If you have more than one item in the queue and more printing problems occur, it's a good idea to delete all queued jobs. After all jobs have been deleted, make sure that the queue is started, and try to print the document(s) again.

Checking for Printer Setup Utility memory problems

Sometimes, Printer Setup Utility claims to be printing a particular document, yet the document isn't printing. Other documents may print without problems. If you can print simple documents but not larger or more complex documents, the problem may be memory-related. Despite Mac OS X's superior memory-management skills, Printer Setup Utility may have insufficient memory to print. Unfortunately, no error message appears to indicate that this is the case.

If you suspect this problem, cancel the print job, quit all open applications that you don't need at the moment, and try to print again.

Deleting and re-adding a printer

If problems with a printer remain, delete it from the Printer List altogether and then re-add it.

When re-adding the printer, make sure that all settings are correct. For example, for IP printing, make sure you have the correct IP address.

If you have to use the Printer Browser's More Printers dialog, be sure to make the correct choice from the pop-up menu. For example, to add an Epson USB printer, select EPSON USB. Otherwise, you may have problems such as the printer names' not appearing in the Printer List or appearing with a question mark on the printer icon.

SEE: • "Using Printer Setup Utility: Adding and Configuring Printers" and "Deleting printers from Printer Setup Utility," earlier in this chapter, for details.

• "Troubleshooting Printing: Checking Printer Drivers," earlier in this chapter.

Deleting Printer Setup Utility's preferences

Some printing problems can be attributed to corrupt Printer Setup Utility preferences (.plist) files. To fix such problems, delete the appropriate preferences file by following these steps:

1. From Printer Setup Utility, choose Stop Jobs for the problem printer.

2. Make sure all jobs currently in its printer queue are deleted, then quit Printer Setup Utility.

3. Go to the ~/Library/Preferences folder and delete the file named com.apple.print.PrintCenter.plist (yes, it says Print Center, not Printer Setup Utility—in Jaguar and earlier, the utility was called Print Center and the preferences file name never changed).

4. Log out and then log back in.

5. From Printer Setup Utility, choose Start Jobs for the printer. Try again to print.

Other printing preferences. If deleting the PrintCenter.plist file doesn't solve your problem, try deleting all files in ~/Library/Preferences that begin with *com.apple.print*. These may include com.apple.print.custompresets.plist, com.apple.print.favorites.plist, com.apple.print.PrinterProxy.plist, com.apple.print.PrintingPrefs.plist, com.apple.print.PrinterSetupUtility.plist, and a separate .plist file for every named printer and fax in your printer and fax lists. Also delete the printing-related .plist files in the ~/Library/Preferences/ByHost folder.

SEE: • "Take Note: Troubleshooting Shared Printers," earlier in this chapter, for related information.

• "Deleting or removing preferences," in Chapter 5, for more general advice.

TAKE NOTE ▶ Print-Related Crashes

If Printer Setup Utility crashes when you try to add a printer, launch Disk Utility and click the Repair Disk Permissions button in the First Aid pane. If this fails, there may be a conflict with software running in the background, launched as a login item. To test for such a conflict, start up with these items disabled.

If a crash of Printer Setup Utility occurs whenever you try to print to a particular printer, try deleting and re-adding the printer software in Printer Setup Utility. If most of your applications quit whenever you print, (a) make sure you are using the latest version of the printer driver(s), and (b) delete the com.apple.print.custompresets.plist file in ~/Library/Preferences (you'll have to re-create any custom presets after doing this).

SEE: • "Getting updated or third-party printer software," earlier in this chapter, for related information.

Question-mark icon in Printer Setup Utility

If a question-mark icon appears next to a printer's name in Printer Setup Utility, you need to install or reinstall the printer's software. The problem is that (a) the needed software is not included as part of Mac OS X, (b) you did not make the correct connection selection (for example, USB or AppleTalk) when you added the printer to the list, or (c) you deleted the needed driver software after adding the printer.

SEE: • "Take Note: How to Reinstall the Mac OS X Printer Drivers," "Adding and using unsupported printers," and "Troubleshooting Printing: Checking Printer Drivers," earlier in this chapter, for more information.

Using Printer Setup Repair

Fixamac Software's Printer Setup Repair, a third-party utility, includes a variety of options for fixing problems that may occur when using Printer Setup Utility (for example, the application will not launch or printers cannot be added), as well as when printing any documents.

If you use this utility, first make sure you're using the latest version; in particular, note that there are different versions of this utility for each major version of Mac OS X: Jaguar, Panther, Tiger, and so on.

Everything that Printer Setup Repair does can be done "manually" with just Mac OS X software. The utility simply automates and simplifies the process (which is a big advantage for many users!). The documentation that comes with Printer Setup Repair details the symptoms it can fix and exactly what it does to fix them. The utility can repair the spool directory, repair the CUPS directory, delete temporary files, fix printing-related permissions, delete printing-related preferences, and install PPD files.

SEE: • "Getting updated or third-party printer software," earlier in this chapter, for related information.

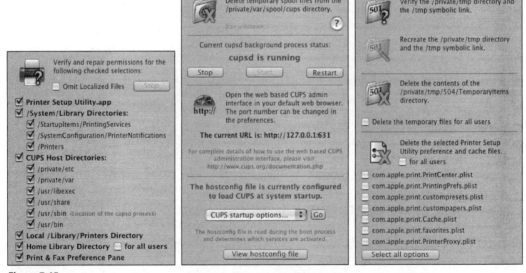

Figure 7.45

A peek at just some of the things you can do via Printer Setup Repair's various panes: left, *File Permission Verification & Repair;* center, *CUPS Tools;* right, *Temporary & Preference File Management.*

Figure 7.46

The message that appears if you choose Reset Printing System from the Printer Setup Utility menu.

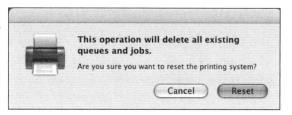

This operation will delete all existing queues and jobs.

Are you sure you want to reset the printing system?

Cancel   Reset

Resetting the printing system

As mentioned earlier in this chapter, Mac OS X 10.4 offers a new option in Printer Setup Utility's application menu: Reset Printing System. This command resets the entire printing system to its default configuration: All printer queues are deleted (along with any pending print jobs); all printer-configuration files are deleted; and the /tmp directory is checked for correct permissions. If none of the steps above solve your printing problems, this feature is worth a try. However, because you lose all settings and printers, as well as all pending print jobs, I recommend this as a last resort.

Printing Quick Fixes

This section covers a variety of fixes that did not fit into the preceding sections.

Document or application problems

If a document in a given application does not print (or prints incorrectly), try printing another document from within the same application. Ideally, create a new test document and type just a few characters, then try to print it.

If this fails, try printing a document from a different application that currently has no documents in the print queue.

If either of these attempts succeeds, it suggests that the problem is with the application or document rather than the printer software or OS.

What do you do if this is the case? Try the following:

*   If testing indicates that the application is at fault, try quitting the application, deleting its preferences file(s), and then relaunching it. If that doesn't work, try deleting and reinstalling the application itself. Make sure the application and its accessory files have the correct permissions and are installed in their required locations (if such requirements exist). In general, the read-me file for the software should inform you of any requirements. Otherwise, follow the guidelines you would use if the application failed to launch, as covered in Chapter 6.

- See if you can print the problem document from another application. This is especially useful for documents that can be opened in several applications, such as plain-text files, graphics files, and PDF files.

- If testing indicates that the document is at fault and thus possibly corrupted, try copying the text from the document into a new blank document. If you were using any unusual page layouts, fonts, or graphic inserts, avoid them in the new document, if possible. With luck, this work-around should eliminate the need to start from scratch and retype the text.

- If the document is being printed in the Classic environment, try printing it from an application that runs natively in Mac OS X instead. This works around the possibility that the problem is specific to the Classic environment.

- Apple notes, "When you print a document, Mac OS X sends a 'Digital Master' PDF file of your document to the printer to ensure good quality. This file is larger than a typical PDF file because the resolution of images in the file is not scaled down."

  Because of the large size of this file, printing may slow. This is especially likely if your print job contains numerous, large, and/or high-resolution graphic images. Solutions include (a) lowering the resolution of the images (if this is acceptable to you); (b) splitting the document into several separate documents (if feasible); or (c) choosing the Reduce File Size or Black & White Quartz filter from the ColorSync options in the Print dialog (especially the latter, if printing a color document to a black-and-white-printer).

- For general problems printing from Adobe Reader, Adobe suggests clicking the Advanced button in the Print dialog and checking the Print as Image box. See the following support document for more advice: www.adobe.com/support/techdocs/a9da.htm.

- If none of this works, check the remaining sections of this chapter for more printer-related advice.

Page Setup issues

If a document prints but formatting is incorrect, recheck your Page Setup and Print dialog settings to make sure they're as you intended.

In particular, from Page Setup's "Format for" pop-up menu, choose the printer you're using rather than the default Any Printer option.

In some cases, selecting a paper size is also important. For example, to get duplex printing to work in an HP DeskJet 970C printer, you need to choose the printer in the "Format for" menu and choose A4 in the Paper Size pop-up menu; selecting A4 as the size in the Print & Fax System Preferences pane is not sufficient.

SEE: • "Margin errors," later in this chapter.

Font problems

Occasionally, a printing problem may have nothing to do with the document itself, the application being used, or the printer software. Instead, the culprit may be a font selected for use in the document. The font file may be corrupt or otherwise incompatible with Mac OS X—with the result being that printing fails when you select the problem font in your document.

The work-around is to select a different font. Be especially suspicious of older fonts located in the Classic System Folder or transferred from a Mac OS 9 System Folder to a Mac OS X Library/Fonts folder (most likely, the one in your home directory). To prevent a repeat of the problem, delete the font after you've identified it as the cause. If you need the font, check with the font vendor to see whether a newer version of the font may prevent the problem.

SEE: • **The sections on fonts in Chapter 4, for other font-related information.**

Preview problems

If you click the Preview button in a Mac OS X Print dialog, the Classic or Mac OS X version of Acrobat Reader or the Mac OS X version of Adobe Reader may launch instead of Mac OS X's Preview application. The solution is to access the "Open with" section of the Get Info window of any PDF file. From here, choose Preview as the application in the pop-up menu and click the Change All button. Preview is now the default PDF application. It should launch the next time you click the Preview button in a Print dialog.

SEE: • **"Technically Speaking: Type/Creator vs. Filename Extensions vs. Others," in Chapter 4, for more details on how to make these changes.**

Checking for PostScript errors

If you're using a PostScript printer, you may have printing problems that are specific to PostScript. In such cases, knowing the exact nature of the error may assist in finding a solution.

To get a printout of PostScript errors that may have occurred when you were trying to print, go to the Print dialog and from the Printing Options pop-up menu select Error Handling. Then check the "Print detailed report" box. If a PostScript error occurs the next time you try to print, you should get a printed report of the problem. If the report does not suggest a solution, contact the printer vendor for advice.

Classic problems

Some printers will not print in Mac OS X when Classic is running. In this case, the usual solution is to quit Classic before attempting to print.

SEE: • "Printing problems," in the online Classic chapter, at Mac OS X Help Line (www.macosxhelpline.com), for additional information.

Checking Console

You may be able to track down the cause of a printing failure by using the Console application. Launch Console before printing. The error text that is generated when the print job fails may provide a clue to the source of the problem. If the error message refers to fonts, for example, a font selection in the document may be the cause of the problem.

In particular, check the following:

*   **console.log and system.log** for messages that may pertain to printing.
*   **The log file in ~/Library/Logs/CrashReporter and/or /Library/Logs/CrashReporter** that contains the name of the application you are using, if the application crashed when you tried to print.
*   **/var/log/cups/error_log** for printing-related error messages generated through the CUPS software. This turned out to be especially valuable in one case where a Lexmark printer that was not working left the following message in error_log: "[Job 6] fatal: The printer has detected a cartridge change. We recommend that you align the ink cartridges from the 'Lexmark Solution Center.'" This message suggested that realigning or replacing the ink cartridges would fix the problem. As it turned out, replacing the cartridges was the cure.

    SEE: • Chapters 2 and 5 for coverage of the Console application, especially the Crash Reporter feature.

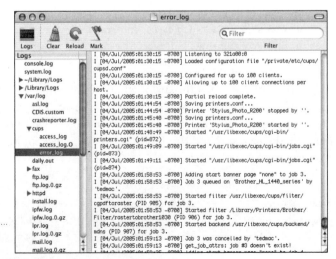

Figure 7.47

The error_log file in /var/logs/cups.

Margin errors

If text along the right margin of a document appears to be cut off when printed, determine whether your application has a preference to enable fractional (character) widths. If so, enable it. This should fix the problem. For example, in AppleWorks, go to General Preferences and choose the Text topic. A Fractional Character Widths check-box option will appear.

More generally, if you get a printing-related error message that says something like, "Some margins are smaller than the minimum allowed by the printer. Your document may be clipped," make sure the margins are big enough. In AppleWorks, these settings are in Format > Document. Margin limits vary from printer to printer; however, they usually cannot be smaller than one-half inch.

If the error message persists even though it appears that margins are set correctly, ignore the message and try printing. It may succeed. If not, check the paper size (as listed in Page Setup) and the default paper size (as selected in the Print & Fax System Preferences pane). Make sure they are set as you intended. If so, delete the com.apple.print.custompresets.plist file in ~/Library/Preferences. Try printing again.

Permissions errors

The initial version of Mac OS X 10.3 contained a bug in which certain system users (lp and postfix) that are needed to print and (especially) to fax are not properly created. This happens only if you choose the Upgrade option when running the Installer from the Mac OS X Install CD to upgrade an existing installation of Mac OS X 10.2.x to 10.3. You may not have symptoms until after you run the Repair Disk Permissions function of Disk Utility. Receiving a fax may also trigger this problem. The result is printing and faxing failures. A typical error message states, "Can't open /private/var/spool/cups/{*spool file name*}."

The simplest solution is to upgrade to Mac OS X 10.3.1 or later, which fixes the problem. Alternative solutions exist, though I don't see why anyone would prefer them to installing the Mac OS X update.

Although Tiger users should not have this specific problem, you may see related permissions problems. The permission-repair feature of the aforementioned Printer Setup Repair utility is excellent for fixing these problems.

Printer software and CPU slowdowns

Users of certain Hewlett-Packard printing and scanning devices (for example, All-in-One and ScanJet models) may experience an overall slowdown in the performance of their Macs. The precise cause is an increased processor (CPU) usage attributable to the HP Communications item included with the ScanJet Manager software (which is installed in the /Printers/Library/HP folder). HP confirmed this, noting, "When the ScanJet Manager software conflicts with another piece of software which also manages the USB ports, increased processor usage will result as the ScanJet Manager is forced to increase polling to detect button presses. HP Communications (version 4.6.3) is the cause of the slowdown. Killing the process can help."

This problem should largely be fixed with the versions of the software included in Tiger, eliminating the need to kill any process. However, if you believe you are seeing this problem, you can try killing the process (using Activity Monitor to do so, for example). The problem with killing the process is that you have to do so each time you restart the Mac. A more general solution is to try any one of the following:

- Downgrade to a prior version of Mac OS X that does not have the symptom (at least until the problem is fixed in an update).

- Revert to a prior version of the Mac OS X IOUSBFamily.kext file (located in /System/Extensions). Note: You can use CharlesSoft's Pacifist (www.charlessoft.com) to extract this file from an update package, as needed. This has some risk of mixing and matching software from different versions of Mac OS X, but users report success.

- Delete the HP software and use an alternative driver that works with the printer.

- Upgrade to a version of the Mac OS X and/or HP software that fixes the problem (assuming that such an upgrade exists).

Note: Similar problems and solutions may occur with other software. For example, HP confirmed that a version of "the HP Communication application used by the Photosmart printer may interfere with printing to the LaserJet 1200 printer." The solution in this case is to kill the process when using the LaserJet and relaunch the application when using the Photosmart printer. Similar solutions continue to be cited for a variety of other USB problems, including those with devices such as Palm PDAs.

SEE: • "Force-quitting," in Chapter 5, for more on killing processes.
- "Checking for extension (kext) problems," in Chapter 5, for more information on the IOUSBFamily.kext file.
- "Maximizing Performance," in Chapter 6, for related information.

TAKE NOTE ▶ Scanners and Mac OS X

There are Mac OS X drivers for almost all popular scanners that work with a Mac, especially Epson and Canon scanners. There are also shareware drivers, such as Hamrick Software's VueScan (www.hamrick.com), that work with a variety of scanner models for which the vendors do not offer Mac OS X support.

Scanner drivers work via either a plug-in for Photoshop (most commonly) or a separate scanner utility.

Note: When you upgrade to a new major version of Mac OS X, your scanner software may need to be updated to work properly. As always, check with your scanner vendor for specific advice.

Even if a Mac OS X driver does not yet exist for your scanner, you may be able to use the scanner in Mac OS X. You just have to use it via Mac OS 9 software, which you access from the Classic environment.

Checking for other Mac OS X software problems

If none of the preceding suggestions helped, try the following general software fixes:

- Is Fast User Switching enabled (as described in Chapter 2)? Are two or more users currently logged in? If so, you may find that only the first user to log in can print to a USB printer. If you are not the first logged-in user, the solution is to get the user who *was* first to log out, so that you can print.

- Restart your Mac. This is a potential panacea for a variety of ills, including printing problems.

- Launch Disk Utility and run the Repair Disk Permissions function. Some general printing problems (primarily associated with Printer Setup Utility) are permissions-related and are fixed by repairing them. For example, doing this fixed a problem with a −108 error that was known to occur when trying to print in earlier versions of Mac OS X.

- As a last resort, reinstall Mac OS X. If you still can't print, it's time to seek out a witch doctor to remove the spell from your Mac.

8

Troubleshooting Networking

You can merrily run Mac OS X independent of the rest of the computing universe, creating documents in your word processor, listening to music with iTunes, and much more. In fact, flying solo was the norm for Mac users until the Internet explosion of the early 1990s. Now it's the exception. These days, almost all Mac users are on some type of network.

For most Mac users, there are two primary reasons to network their Macs:

- **To access the Internet.** This is what you need to do to use e-mail, browse the Web, or connect to remote servers. In networking terms, the Internet is a form of *wide area network* (WAN).

- **To access and share data over a local network.** Computers that are in the same general physical location (for example, a room, an office, or a building) and are linked to one another through a network make up a *local area network* (LAN). Computers on the same LAN can be set up so that files and devices (such as printers) can be shared among them. To accomplish this, you must know (1) how to access the other computers on the LAN, and (2) how to set up your computer so that other users can access it.

These interrelated topics are the subject of the next two chapters. This chapter focuses on setting up your Mac to access data over the Internet and/or a local network, using various System Preferences panes and other software. Chapter 9 focuses on the most common practical applications of these networks: file sharing, Web browsing, e-mail, and the like.

In This Chapter
. . . .

Network and Connection/Port Types

A *network* can generally be defined as a setup where multiple computers or computing devices are interconnected. A network may consist of two computers and a printer in an office, a classroom of computers connected to a central server, a corporate network that extends to several locations across the country, or the Internet itself (which is essentially a global network). Regardless of the arrangement, the purpose of a network is to allow computers to communicate with each other and/or peripheral devices.

Network *connection types*, on the other hand, refer to the ways in which computers connect to each other or to a larger network. Mac OS X calls these different connection types *ports* or *network ports*, and supports a good number of them: Ethernet, modem, AirPort, Bluetooth, and, most recently, FireWire. If you think of a highway system as a network among cities, consider a network port in Mac OS X the vehicle you choose to travel the roads.

I make this distinction between *networks* and *network ports* because it's important to understand that *network type* and *connection type* are not intimately linked. That is, the same connection type can be used for more than one network, and, conversely, multiple computers can connect to the same network using different types of connections. As a common example, an Ethernet connection can be used for both a local network and a connection to the Internet.

Although this situation can be a bit confusing, it means that Mac OS X is incredibly flexible in its networking capabilities. You can use Ethernet to communicate with other computers in your home or office while at the same time using a modem to connect to the Internet. Or you can use an AirPort Base Station for both local networking and Internet access. In addition, if your connection and network types change frequently (for example, if you travel with a PowerBook and connect in different ways at different locations), Mac OS X allows you to set up *Locations* that store groups of network settings; you can switch between Locations when necessary.

In the sections that follow, I'll explain each type of network connection and how to set it up for local and Internet connectivity.

Setup Assistants. The first time you start up Mac OS X after installing it, the (Mac OS X) Setup Assistant and/or Network Setup Assistant software (located in /System/Library/CoreServices) automatically launches and offers to walk you through setting up your network and Internet connection. In answering its questions, you're actually editing your Mac's Network preferences, just as if you had entered the appropriate information in the Network pane of System Preferences. This arrangement simplifies the setup process—especially welcome for novice users. However, if you ever want to alter these settings, or if you opted out of using the Setup Assistants, you will need to know how to interact directly with Mac OS X's networking software, as described in this chapter.

Setting Up Network System Preferences

The Network pane of System Preferences is where you manage network settings—a task that can seem overwhelming at first because of the myriad combinations of panes and settings. To simplify things, consider first that this preferences pane includes just three basic categories of network settings:

- **Network port configurations.** These settings show which connection types (*ports*) are enabled by you for use (*active*), and the order (*priority*) in which Mac OS X tries to use them.

- **Connection-specific settings.** These are the settings for each type of connection/port. Exactly which options appear will depend on your connection type.

- **Locations.** These are different combinations (groups) of network ports and port-specific settings for different network environments. For example, if you use a laptop, you can have one group of settings for home, a second group for work, and a third group for when you travel. Creating different Locations facilitates these switches.

In the bottom right area of the Network System Preferences pane you will find two buttons:

- **Assist me.** Click this button and a dialog appears that asks whether you "need assistance setting up a new network connection or solving a network problem."

    If the former, click the Assistant button. This launches the Network Setup Assistant application, which walks you through the steps needed to set up Network preferences. (This is the same assistant that launches automatically when you first start up into a new installation of Mac OS X.)

    If the latter, click the Diagnostics button; this launches the Network Diagnostics utility (as described later in this chapter).

- **Apply Now.** Anytime you make a change to a setting in Network preferences, clicking this button saves the change (modifying the configuration file where the settings are stored, as I discuss later in this chapter). This is an essential final step before closing the pane, assuming that you made changes you want to save.

At the top of the pane you will find two pop-up menus:

- **Location.** I discuss this in detail in the "Locations" section, later in the chapter. Its initial selection is Automatic. Unless you create a new Location, this will be the only selection you ever use.

- **Show.** Your selection from this menu determines what the main part of the preference pane displays. You can choose a particular network port, an option called Network Port Configurations, or an option called Network Status. The Network Status option is typically the default option when you first access the pane. All of these choices are explained in the following sections.

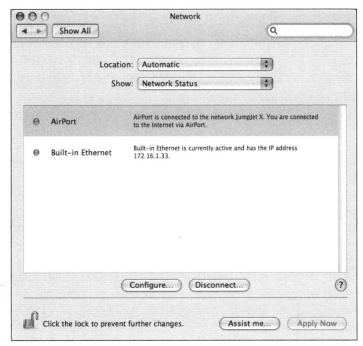

Figure 8.1

The Network System Preferences pane with Network Status selected.

Network Status

The Network Status pane (which you access by choosing Network Status from the Show pop-up menu) lists all currently active and enabled ports (as set from the Network Port Configurations pane—such as AirPort, Ethernet, and Internal Modem), as well as the current status of each. For example, if you were connected to the Internet via AirPort, the summary next to AirPort would say something like, "AirPort is connected to the network {*name of network*}. You are connected to the Internet via AirPort." Similarly, if you had the FireWire port enabled but no cable plugged into it, the FireWire port item would state, "The cable for Built-in FireWire is not plugged in."

In some cases, even if a port is enabled in the Network Port Configurations pane, it may not appear in the Network Status pane. Or it may initially appear, with an error message, and then vanish. For example, this may happen if Built-in Ethernet is enabled but there is no cable plugged into the Ethernet port.

Also, just because the Network Status pane says, "You are connected to the Internet . . . ," it doesn't really mean that you are. This pane indicates the port that is currently being attempted to use for Internet access. If there are problems elsewhere in the connection sequence, such as a defective router, such problems may not be detectable here.

To modify the settings for any listed port, you have three choices, all of which bring you to the same pane: (a) Double-click the name of the port in the Network Status pane; (b) select the name of the port in the Network Status pane and then click the Configure button near the bottom of the window; or (c) go to the Show pop-up menu and choose the desired port.

To return to the Network Status pane at any time, choose it from the Show pop-up menu.

Finally, next to the Configure button is a Connect/Disconnect button. This button is active only if the currently selected item can connect or disconnect (for example, a modem connection, a PPPoE connection via Ethernet, or an AirPort connection). If the selected item is currently connected to the Internet, the button will read Disconnect. If the selected item is not connected to the Internet but is set up so that you can attempt to connect via the port, the button will read Connect. What happens *after* you click this button depends on the type of port: Often, the Internet Connect application is launched; from there you can select to disconnect from an AirPort or modem connection.

Network Port Configurations settings and port priority

I have a PowerBook that's connected wirelessly to my cable modem via an AirPort Base Station. At times, however, I would prefer to connect the Power-Book via an Ethernet cable as part of my wired local network. Alternatively, if my cable modem goes down, I am also set up to access the Internet via the PowerBook's internal dial-up modem. With Mac OS X, I can set up all three of these connection types, and have them active simultaneously, via the Network Port Configurations settings. Technically, this process is called *multihoming*. Mac OS X users just call it *great!*

Additionally, you can prioritize connection ports in Mac OS X. This means that the OS will try each port automatically, in the order you specify, until it obtains a working connection. In the scenario above, for example, if the AirPort software is disabled, the PowerBook automatically skips AirPort and tries Ethernet instead. Mac OS X requires no modification of settings for this switching to work. You can have multiple ports active at the same time, even for the same network type. (In truth, the switching doesn't *always* work as well as intended. I cover what to do in those situations in "Troubleshooting Internet Applications" and "Troubleshooting Sharing," in Chapter 9.)

Figure 8.2

The Network System Preferences pane with Network Port Configurations selected.

Adding, deleting, enabling, and disabling ports. To set up your Network Port Configurations, follow these steps:

1. Launch System Preferences. Select the Network pane, and from the Show pop-up menu choose Network Port Configurations. The window will change to show a list of all available ports, with a check box next to each.

   Note: If you add a new port via an alternate method (such as by adding a Bluetooth adapter to your Mac, as described later in this chapter), you will typically get a New Port Detected message when you next launch Network preferences. It is automatically added to the Network Port Configurations list.

2. Turn on each port you plan to use. Similarly, turn off ports you won't be using.

   To turn on a port, also called *enabling* the port, check the box next to its name.

   To turn off a port (that is, *disable* the port), uncheck the box by its name. If you will be using your modem and AirPort card, for example, but not your Ethernet port, you can uncheck the Built-in Ethernet box.

If you're sure you'll *never* want to use a certain port, you can delete the listing by clicking the Delete button on the right side. Although a warning appears saying that this cannot be undone, you can always re-add the port via the New button, as described next. However, you will then need to reenter the settings for the port. Thus, I recommend making a port inactive rather than deleting it—unless you're 100 percent certain you'll never want to access it again.

Note: With some ports, clicking Delete will not work. Instead, the port is immediately re-created and added to the bottom of the list. This occurs, for example, with ports that remain always active (such as AirPort when an AirPort card is installed).

An enabled port that is connected to (or configured to be connected to) a network is an *active* port. Active ports are listed in the Show pop-up menu. From here, you can choose each item to configure its settings (more on that in a bit).

3. If a port type that you know you have isn't listed in Network Port Configurations, add it by clicking the New button.

   If you have an internal modem, for example, but there's no listed port configuration for Internal Modem, click New and then choose Internal Modem from the Port pop-up menu in the dialog that drops down. You can name the connection type anything you want, but for clarity I recommend something obvious (such as Internal Modem).

   The ports that are available in the Port menu will vary depending on what hardware is connected to or built into your Mac. For example, unless you have a Mac with built-in Bluetooth support or have added a USB Bluetooth adapter, Bluetooth will not be listed as an option. Similarly, if your Mac did not come with an internal modem, and you have not added one, Internal Modem will not be an option.

   SEE: • **"Technically Speaking: Lesser-Known Ports,"** below, for related information.

4. For some ports, you can create additional ports for the same type of connection.

   Suppose, for example, that you have more than one dial-up Internet service provider (ISP). You can create a separate Internal Modem port for each ISP. To do this, click the New button and create a new Internal Modem port (in addition to the one that's presumably already present). To distinguish between them, give each a different name.

   Alternatively, if you want to create a new port configuration that uses the existing Internal Modem settings as a starting point, select Internal Modem from the list and click the Duplicate button. You can then change the name of the duplicated port by selecting it and clicking the Edit button.

   You are now set to modify the settings of each Internal Modem port, as needed, by choosing each port from the Show pop-up menu.

   New in Mac OS X 10.4 Tiger, you can create multiple AirPort ports, allowing you to access separate AirPort settings (such as for work and home) without needing to switch to a different Location setting.

5. Drag the ports to rearrange their order in the list, as desired.

The order in which ports are listed in this dialog represents a priority ranking. If you try to initiate a network connection (local or Internet), Mac OS X first tries to connect via the port listed first. If it connects, it stops there. If the connection is unsuccessful, Mac OS X tries the next port. This process continues down the list until a successful connection is made, or until all ports have been tried, to no avail (at which point you generally get an error message). What this means for you is that if you have both DSL and dial-up Internet access and want your computer to try to use the DSL connection first, using the modem only if DSL is not available, you should drag Built-in Ethernet *above* Internal Modem. Likewise, if you want your laptop to attempt to dial up your ISP only if it cannot find your AirPort network, make sure that AirPort is listed above Internal Modem.

Once you have created and enabled the ports you wish to be active, your next step is to enter the settings for each port type.

TECHNICALLY SPEAKING ▶ Lesser-Known Ports

Many Mac users are familiar with ports such as Built-in Ethernet, AirPort, Internal Modem, and even Built-in FireWire. However, there are two ports found in the Port menu (accessed by clicking the New button in the Network Port Configurations pane of Network System Preferences) that are not commonly used and probably not familiar to you:

• **Link Aggregate.** New in Tiger, Link Aggregate allows you to create a single virtual port that combines two or more separate Ethernet ports—for example, two Ethernet ports or one Ethernet port and one AirPort port.

Note: The AirPort port, in this situation, is treated as an Ethernet port (for example, the AirPort Base Station is connected to a WAN via Ethernet). This has two advantages: (a) It combines the bandwidth of the two ports, allowing for faster transmission; and (b) if one port fails, traffic is automatically routed to the second one, providing uninterrupted connection. This is more likely to be used with Mac OS X Server, but technically it can work with Mac OS X client, as well.

Note: If you do not have at least two active ports that can be linked, the Link Aggregate option will not appear in the list at all.

To set this up, choose Link Aggregate from the pop-up menu, give the port a name (such as "Link Aggregate"), and select at least two ports from those listed. Click OK. You will get a warning that the existing configuration ports will be "lost" (disabled) if you create this new aggregate. Go ahead and click Create anyway. The port configurations remain in your list and can be re-enabled later if you decide to abandon the Aggregate connection. Finally, click the Apply Now button. You should now be good to go.

For information about the linked ports, select the Link Aggregate port from the Show pop-up menu; then, in the pane that appears, click the Status tab.

continues on next page

TECHNICALLY SPEAKING ▶ **Lesser-Known Ports** *continued*

Unfortunately, this connection type may not always work well. I have both a cable modem and a DSL modem (yes, I want to make sure I always have an Internet connection!). I have the DSL modem connected directly to my Mac's Ethernet port and the cable modem connected to my AirPort Base Station. I used Link Aggregate to combine these two ports: the Ethernet port on the back of my Mac (en0) and the Ethernet port on my AirPort Base Station (en1). I wound up with no Internet connection at all. Checking the connection's Status window, I found error messages indicating that my AirPort link was "not valid" and that my Built-in Ethernet link did not have "802.3ad Link Aggregation enabled." My guess was that either the DSL modem or the AirPort Base Station do not support Link Aggregation. I confess I did not investigate this further. To get things working again, I deleted the Aggregate port and re-enabled the separate AirPort and Built-in Ethernet ports.

- **6 to 4.** This port is used to connect to an IPv6 address from your Mac (assuming that your Mac is using an IPv4 address). I cover this more in "Technically Speaking: IPv4 vs. IPv6," later in this chapter.

In addition, a few ports may show up in your Network Port Configurations list that are not included in the Port menu (that is, the menu you access in the dialog that drops down when you click New). How did these items get added? Typically, in one of three ways:

- **Mobile phones.** Certain devices, when connected to the Mac, may cause a new port to be created. For example, certain mobile phones (primarily those from Motorola) connect to a Mac via a special USB cable (which you purchase from a mobile-phone vendor). When you open the Network System Preferences pane with such a phone connected, it creates a new modem port and names it using the model name of the phone (for example, Motorola T720c). The port name is dimmed and unselectable unless the phone is attached.

  Note: Setting up a Motorola phone port, such as just described, is necessary to sync the data on the phone with your Mac via iSync (as covered in Chapter 11). Theoretically, you could also set up the phone to act as a modem, and thus use it to connect to the Internet. However, this would require having a modem script for the phone that works with the Mac.

  I am aware of one such script, offered by Verizon (called Verizon_Wireless_STD_driver), designed to work specifically with Verizon's CDMA-2000-1XRTT service (also known as its Express Network). However, as of this writing, I have been unable to get my Motorola phone, using this or any other script, to act as a modem for any other dial-up ISP. This will often be the case (that is, a mobile phone will connect to the Internet only via its own proprietary method).

- **VPN.** Certain selections in Internet Connect result in the creation of a new port. For example, if you select New VPN Connection and then select the radio button for PPTP, a new port called PPTP or VPN (PPTP) will be created in the Network System Preferences pane. When this happens, a message will appear that says, "Your network settings have been changed by another application."

- **Bluetooth.** Devices connected to "serial ports" set up in Bluetooth Serial Utility may also appear in the Network System Preferences list.

  SEE: • "Modem" and "Using Internet Connect," later in this chapter, for more details on Internet Connect, VPN, and modem scripts.

  • "Bluetooth Serial Utility," later in this chapter, for more on this utility.

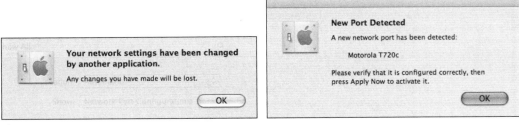

Figure 8.3

Two examples of messages that may appear after a new port (established outside of Network System Preferences) is detected by Network System Preferences.

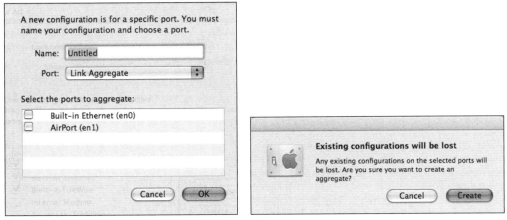

Figure 8.4

Left, the Link Aggregate Port options, accessed in the dialog that drops down when you click the New button in Network Port Configurations; *right,* a message that may appear when you choose to aggregate.

Ethernet (including cable and DSL Internet)

The Ethernet port is the one you use if you're connected to any type of network (including the Internet) via an Ethernet cable. The most basic Ethernet connection is one that goes from the Ethernet port on the back of your Mac to a cable modem or DSL modem. More-complex setups involve the use of an Ethernet hub or router to join multiple devices on the same local network.

To configure the Ethernet port settings, go to the Network System Preferences pane, and from the Show pop-up menu choose Built-in Ethernet. From here, you will be able to configure the various types of connections you'll be using over your Ethernet port.

Note: If you've added extra Ethernet ports via third-party Ethernet PCI cards, the configuration for them will be the same, and you will be able to choose each port's configuration pane from the same Show pop-up menu (each will have something other than *Built-in* in its name).

The Ethernet port settings include five main tabs: TCP/IP, PPPoE, AppleTalk, Proxies, and Ethernet.

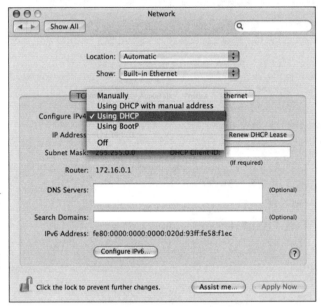

Figure 8.5

The Network System Preferences pane with the TCP/IP tab of the Ethernet port selected—and Using DHCP selected from the Configure IPv4 pop-up menu.

TCP/IP. If you access the Internet via a DSL or cable modem or through a company network, you typically enter the required settings in the TCP/IP pane. There are too many settings to cover all the possibilities here: Either you know what you're doing (and thus don't need this book to advise you), or you don't (in which case you'll simply enter what your network provider tells you to, or the settings will be entered automatically as explained below). Still, it's worthwhile to provide a broad overview of these settings.

From the Configure IPv4 pop-up menu, you determine whether you will be entering IP addresses and related information manually or a server will provide the information. There are five options:

*   **Manually.** If you have a *static IP address* (that is, one that always remains the same), you would generally select Manually. You would then enter the IP address and other ISP information (subnet mask, router, and DNS servers) in the fields below the pop-up menu.

*   **Using DHCP.** This is the most common option used by cable and DSL providers, as well as many large networks. Typically, after making this selection, you're finished! All remaining settings in the TCP/IP pane, including the IP address, are automatically assigned via your ISP or office network's DHCP server. (In some cases you may be asked to provide a DHCP Client ID or domain name server.)

This setting typically uses a *dynamic IP address* (that is, one that can change over time due to reassignment by the DHCP server).

With this option selected, an additional button appears in the window: Renew DHCP Lease. Your DHCP address is set to renew after a certain period of time. Renewing a lease typically results in your getting a new IP address; however, sometimes your current address is retained after a renewal. In either case, your ISP has rechecked your connection as part of the renewal process. If you click this button, you force an immediate renewal of the lease. If you're having problems with your DHCP connection, clicking this button may help you reconnect successfully.

- **"Using DHCP with manual address."** This option is a less common variation of DHCP, in which you need to enter a static IP address but the DHCP server provides the rest of the settings.

- **Using BootP.** BootP works much like DHCP; however, it uses a BootP server (common mostly in large office environments) to assign IP addresses and other settings. (If your network administrator asks you to enter DNS information, you enter it here.)

- **Off.** Select this option if you will not be using an IPv4 address at all but will instead be using an IPv6 address exclusively.

Speaking of IPv6, at the bottom of the window, no matter which Configure IPv4 option you select, you'll find a button labeled Configure IPv6. You may need to click this if you're using an IPv6 address.

SEE: • "Technically Speaking: IPv4 vs. IPv6" and "Take Note: What Are the TCP/IP settings?" below, for more details on IPv6 and on the other settings shown in the TCP/IP pane.

Note: If you have cable or DSL Internet access but are using an AirPort card with an AirPort Base Station or third-party wireless router/access point, you should enter your TCP/IP settings in the AirPort pane rather than the Ethernet one.

SEE: • "AirPort," later in this chapter.

TAKE NOTE ▶ What Are the TCP/IP Settings?

The entries in the TCP/IP pane of Network System Preferences are vital to a successful Internet connection. Unfortunately, most users have no idea what they mean. If you're curious, here's a quick primer.

IP Address. If you want a friend to be able to write you a letter, you give him or her your street address. Likewise, if you write a letter to a company, you generally include a return address so that the company can reply to you. The Internet works in much the same way. For someone to contact you, that person needs to know your address, and if you contact someone else, you must provide your address so that he or she can send data back to you.

continues on next page

TAKE NOTE ▶ **What Are the TCP/IP Settings?** *continued*

Your IP (Internet Protocol) address is that address. An IPv4 address is a unique string of numbers (in the format xxx.xxx.xxx.xxx, in which each *xxx* is a number from 0 to 255) that identifies your computer to the rest of the Internet. If you request a Web page, your Web browser provides your IP address to the Web server; the Web server sends the content of that Web page back to your IP address.

If you have a *static* IP address (generally entered manually in Network preferences), your IP address is always the same. In most other cases, as with most DHCP connections, your ISP (Internet service provider) assigns a temporary IP address when you connect; it lasts until you disconnect or for a certain amount of time set by the ISP or your network administrator (generally days or weeks). This type of address is called a *dynamic* IP address.

Subnet Mask. As just mentioned, an IP address is a string of numbers in the format xxx.xxx.xxx.xxx. The address actually has two parts. The first part identifies the specific local network on which the IP address resides; the second is the particular node (location) of the computer in question on that network. A *subnet mask* delineates which part of your complete IP address refers to the local network and which refers to the node. For a hypothetical IP address of 148.152.168.02, a subnet mask of 255.255.255.0 indicates that the 148.152.168 part of the address refers to the local network, and the .02 refers to the node. A subnet mask of 255.255.0.0 means that the local network is described by 148.152, and that .168.02 refers to the node. These delineations are also referred to as *subnet classes*.

Router. An Internet router generally provides a gateway between your computer and the Internet. You send data to the router, which then forwards it on the appropriate path to its destination; data sent to your computer first hits your router and is then directed to you. Unless you have selected Manually from the Configure menu, the router address (if needed), as well as the IP address and subnet mask, are typically assigned for you by your ISP or network administrator.

If you're using a locally connected Internet router, you generally enter a specific, local-only "private" router address, as described in "Using a Router," later in this chapter. An address of this type is used for LAN connections because it has been arbitrarily assigned for this purpose. These addresses will never be assigned to any device on a WAN, so there is no chance for confusion between LAN and WAN IP addresses.

Domain Name Servers. The DNS Servers section of the Network System Preferences pane is where you enter the numeric addresses for any DNS servers you use. You obtain these addresses from your ISP, just as you do for the previously covered settings. Entering one or more addresses here is usually optional, because for most types of connections, the ISP connection (for example, DHCP) provides them automatically. Some setups (notably Manually), however, require that an address be entered.

continues on next page

TAKE NOTE ▶ What Are the TCP/IP Settings? *continued*

Troubleshooting tip: Entering the wrong DNS server address can prevent a successful Internet connection. For example, when I switched from @home to Comcast for my cable connection, the DNS address that I had been using (which was still entered in the DNS Servers field) was no longer valid. Until I realized this fact and deleted the previous address, I was unable to connect to the Internet!

If you're using an Internet router (especially if you selected Manually as the Configure option in the TCP/IP pane of Network System Preferences), you may circumvent certain connection problems by entering your router's IP address (that is, the same address shown next to Router) in the DNS Servers field rather than entering your ISP's DNS server address or leaving the field blank. Note: Your ISP's DNS address(es) will still be listed in the router's settings, as covered in "Configuring a router," later in this chapter.

Here's what a DNS server does and why you need one:

It would be a hassle to have to remember the actual IP address of every computer or server to which you want to connect; instead, many servers use *domain names*, such as apple.com, to identify their location on the Internet. This Web address is actually a "readable" substitute for the site's true numeric IP address. Special software on the Internet, on *domain name system* (DNS) servers, converts this domain name to the appropriate IP number. More specifically, domain name system servers host databases that translate the readable-text domain name to the specific IP address to which it corresponds. Thus, when you enter www.apple.com, your computer contacts the DNS server(s) listed in this field and retrieves the actual IP address of that domain name; then it contacts the IP address directly.

This is all necessary because the connection requires the true IP address, not the domain name. The domain name system allows you to use an easy-to-remember URL without having to know the IP address. It similarly means that a Web site can change its IP address without your needing to relearn it. If the DNS server is not working correctly, however, you may find that you cannot access a Web page via its domain name (though you can still access it via its IP address).

What if you don't know the IP address of a Web site? You can find it in several ways. One method is to use the *ping* function of the Network Utility included with Mac OS X (though you need to do this before a DNS problem appears in order for the function to work). Enter www.apple.com as the address to ping, and the results window will show you the IP address (17.254.0.91 or 17.254.3.183, at the time of this writing). You can test it yourself by entering http://17.254.0.91 in your Web browser. This action should take you to the Apple site (unless Apple's IP address has changed since I wrote this, which is always a possibility).

Search Domains. If you frequently access servers or Web sites that reside within a single larger domain (*sales*.domain.com, *finance*.domain.com, and so on), you can place the local network name (*domain*.com) in this field. The contents of this field will be added to the end of any incomplete domain names (*sales, finance*). Most users will not need to use this option.

SEE: • "Technically Speaking: IPv4 vs. IPv6," below, for more on this topic.

TECHNICALLY SPEAKING ▶ **IPv4 vs. IPv6**

There's a problem with IPv4 addresses that no one could have anticipated back when the system was created and before anyone knew how popular the Internet would become: We're rapidly running out of IP addresses! The IPv6 configuration solves this by increasing the address size from IPv4's 32 bits to 128 bits. The longer addresses also allow for simpler auto-configuration—which means you rarely need to enter your own settings with this protocol.

IPv6's use is currently limited, primarily to large research and educational institutions, so it's unlikely that you'll be using it. In addition, in most cases when it *is* used, your ISP will automatically assign your IPv6 addresses—which means you don't need to do anything extra. Thus, most Mac users can ignore the entire IPv6 issue for now.

For those rare cases in which you need to manually set up an IPv6 address, click the Configure IPv6 button at the bottom of the TCP/IP pane, and from the Configure IPv6 pop-up menu choose Manually. Then enter the Address, Router, and Prefix Length data supplied by your network administrator.

The default IPv6 setting is Automatic. This is why you do not even need to click the Configure IPv6 button if your address is automatically assigned.

Note: To completely disable IPv6, choose Off from the pop-up menu.

Note: The current IPv6 address is listed in the IPv6 Address line (below the Search Domains setting in the TCP/IP pane)—assuming an Ethernet cable is currently plugged into the Ethernet port or an AirPort card is installed in your computer. The automatically calculated IPv6 address adds your Ethernet or AirPort MAC (Media Access Control) address to the tail end of the IPv6 address. (Compare the similarity of the MAC address, as listed in the Ethernet or AirPort pane, to the IPv6 address.)

"6 to 4" network port configuration. If you need to connect to an IPv6 address and your Mac is using IPv4, you can still do so; simply follow these steps:

1. From the Show menu for the Network System Preferences pane, choose Network Port Configurations.

2. Click the New button.

3. From the Port pop-up menu, select "6 to 4."

4. Assign a name to the selection (for example, *6 to 4*) and click OK.

5. Turn on the "6 to 4" port in the Configuration list, if not already on, by checking its On box.

6. If you need to manually set up a relay address, choose the "6 to 4" port from the Show pop-up menu, and from the Configure pop-up menu select Manually.

Figure 8.6

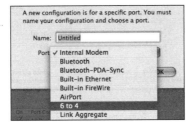

The "6 to 4" port, as listed in the Port pop-up menu in the dialog that appears after you click New in Network Port Configurations.

TAKE NOTE ▶ Ethernet Hubs, Switches, Routers, and Cables

Before you take even the first steps in setting up your Ethernet network, you should be familiar with some basic terminology.

Hubs, switches, and routers. If you have only two Ethernet devices, your network is very simple: a single cable connects the two devices. If you have more than two devices with Ethernet ports (multiple computers, printers, and so on), you need a way to connect them. Hubs, switches, and routers provide such functionality in different ways. By far, the most common device in use today is the router. As such, it will be the focus of the coverage in this chapter. The following, however, provides a brief description of each type:

- **Hub.** A hub takes incoming data from one Ethernet port and broadcasts it to every other Ethernet port on the hub. This setup is fine for small networks, but when it's used in larger networks with many devices, performance can degrade, because every device attached to the hub has to filter through the data being sent by every other device.

- **Switch.** Switches are similar to hubs, but instead of sending incoming data back out to every connected device, a switch checks the destination address contained in the data (usually the MAC address of the appropriate Ethernet port) and forwards the data only to the appropriate machine. In addition, if the destination address is not valid (doesn't exist on any devices connected to the switch), the data basically dies at the switch. Switches learn the MAC address of connected devices by examining the data that passes through the switch.

- **Router.** Routers are similar to switches, but instead of directing traffic based on hardware (MAC) addresses, routers rely on network addresses (IP addresses). Unlike switches, which generally configure themselves, routers need to be configured by the user. Because routers can isolate parts of your network on different subnets, they allow you to share a single IP address among several network devices.

  An Internet router, used for sharing a broadband or modem connection to the Internet (discussed elsewhere in this chapter), is a specific type of router.

  A wireless router is a combination of a traditional router (which uses Ethernet cables to connect devices) and a *wireless bridge* (which *bridges* a wired network with a wireless one). An AirPort Base Station is an example of a wireless router (albeit one with fewer Ethernet ports than a traditional router has).

Note: These devices, as well as the Macs to which they connect, may operate at different speeds, such as 100 Mbps or 1 gigabit. In general, the slowest device in the chain determines overall speed. Thus, data traveling between two Gigabit Ethernet Macs connected via a router with a maximum speed of 100 Mbps will travel at 100 Mbps.

continues on next page

TAKE NOTE ▶ Ethernet Hubs, Switches, Routers, and Cables *continued*

Ethernet cables. Devices on an Ethernet network are connected by Ethernet cables. Two kinds of Ethernet cables are available: standard and crossover. The difference between the two has to do with how the strands of wire in the cable are arranged.

- **Standard.** This type of cable has the strands of cable used for sending and receiving data in the same location on both ends. You generally use this type of cable to hook devices to a hub, switch, or router in a multiple-device network: computers to hubs, printers to hubs, hubs to routers, and so on. As data passes through the hub, switch, or router, it is transferred from the send wires of the incoming cable to the receive wires of the outgoing cable. Most printers with Ethernet ports also use a standard cable to connect to a computer.

- **Crossover.** This type of cable has its send and receive wires switched (so that the signal "crosses over"), and is often used to network two computers directly (without any kind of hub, switch, or router).

Because most users can't easily visually distinguish between the two cable types, cables are a frequent source of trouble when connecting computers. Using a crossover cable where a standard cable is needed (or vice versa) will result in a failed connection. Note that many hubs, switches, and routers have an Ethernet port marked Uplink. This port is designed to accept a crossover cable rather than a standard cable. The port for an Internet connection on a router may also use a crossover cable.

The latest Macs use Ethernet ports that sense the type of cable and automatically adjust to work with either type. If your Mac has this capability, it will be listed as such in the technical-specifications section of the documentation that came with the computer. Alternatively, check the following Apple Knowledge Base article to see which Macs still require a crossover cable: http://docs.info.apple.com/article.html?artnum=42717.

SEE: • "Using a Router," later in this chapter, for more information on routers.

• "Take Note: What Are the TCP/IP Settings?" earlier in this chapter, for related information.

PPPoE. Some ISPs that provide DSL or cable Internet access use a protocol called *PPPoE* (short for *Point-to-Point Protocol over Ethernet*). This protocol is a variation of the older modem-style Point-to-Point Protocol (PPP) that has been adapted for use for broadband connections. If your ISP uses this protocol, PPPoE verifies your user name and password when you connect to its servers.

Enabling "Connect using PPPoE" in the PPPoE pane allows you to connect via PPPoE. It also changes your settings in the TCP/IP pane: The only options now available from the Configure pop-up menu will be Manually and a new option, PPP. Generally, you will want to use PPP, which gets the rest of the needed settings from the PPPoE server.

Back in the PPPoE pane, you need to enter an account name and password for your ISP account. These are used to determine your status when you attempt to connect, in what amounts to a login procedure. Thus, until you connect and log in, you will not have an active Internet connection (even though your Network settings are correct). Typically, you connect via a menu bar item or the Internet Connect application, as described two paragraphs below.

If you click the PPPoE Options button, a dialog drops down, from which you can select different session options. These options determine whether Mac OS X automatically attempts to connect when needed (for example, when an Internet application such as a Web browser is launched), and whether the OS should disconnect automatically (for example, after a designated period of idle activity). A few advanced logging and connection options are also presented.

If you enable "Show PPPoE status in menu bar" back in the PPPoE pane, a PPPoE item is added to your menu bar. From there you can connect or disconnect from the PPPoE server. The menu will also indicate the current status of your connection (for example, idle, connected, or disconnected). The Internet Connect application similarly lets you initiate a PPPoE connection and monitor its status, as long as you have selected PPPoE and enabled Ethernet as an active network port.

Note: If your ISP requires a PPPoE connection, but you use an Internet router to connect to your ISP, you will most likely configure your router to use PPPoE and then set up your Mac's Network preferences to connect to the router (in other words, *not* using PPPoE).

SEE: • "Using Internet Connect," later in this chapter.

AppleTalk. This legacy Mac OS protocol is used primarily to connect multiple local devices, such as a few Macs and a printer. However, a TCP/IP connection can accomplish the same task (without using AppleTalk), and, in general, Mac OS X prefers it. In fact, future versions of Mac OS X may not even support AppleTalk.

To enable AppleTalk, check the Make AppleTalk Active box in the AppleTalk pane.

The other AppleTalk settings are generally only applicable if you're on a large network, such as at a university. If your network has multiple AppleTalk zones, you can select the zone in which you want your computer to appear. In addition, if you need to change your AppleTalk node or network IDs (which you should do only if you've been told to do so by a network administrator), you make the change by choosing Manually from the Configure pop-up menu. Note that the Computer Name option in this pane is set in the Sharing pane of System Preferences.

Starting with Mac OS X 10.2, you can enable AppleTalk for only one network port at a time. Thus, if you have AppleTalk enabled for Ethernet, you cannot also enable it for AirPort. If you try to enable AppleTalk on a second port, you will get an error message stating that AppleTalk can be active on only one port and that if you continue, AppleTalk will be disabled on its currently enabled port.

In addition, if you use PPPoE on an existing Ethernet port, you cannot enable AppleTalk on that port. If you try, you'll get the following error message: "AppleTalk cannot be used with PPPoE. To use AppleTalk, select the Advanced pane and create a new Ethernet configuration." You can create multiple configurations of the same Ethernet port to allow access to AppleTalk.

SEE: • "Setting Up System Preferences: Sharing," in Chapter 9.

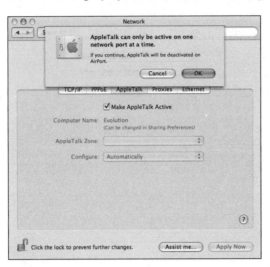

Figure 8.7

The Network System Preferences pane with the AppleTalk tab of the Ethernet port selected—and the error message that appeared when I tried to enable AppleTalk here (because it was already enabled for AirPort).

Proxies. A proxy is generally a server that sits on a network (or is implemented by an ISP) and intercepts requests from individual computers before they go out to the Internet at large. There are separate proxy-server settings for different Internet services (for example, FTP and Web).

Acting as an intermediary between the computers and the Internet, the proxy server typically works with a firewall to provide protection for computers on the local network. More specifically, proxies limit what you can do from your Mac when accessing the network, whereas firewalls protect your Mac against incoming actions (such as attempts to hack into your account).

Proxy servers, for example, often implement content filters that allow or restrict access to particular data or Web sites. Also, most proxy servers cache data so that multiple or repeated requests for the same Web page from within the network require only a single external request (the proxy requests the remote page and then stores it and "serves" it to every computer on the local network that requests it).

Most users will not need to deal with proxies. If your network is served by a proxy, your network administrator will supply the information you need to fill in the fields in the Proxies pane.

If you do need to enable proxies, you may have difficulties accessing some network features. For example, accessing the iTunes Music Store was blocked by certain proxy settings when using iTunes version 4.0 (this problem was fixed with iTunes 4.0.1).

SEE: • "Download files and save content," in the "Troubleshooting Internet Applications" section of Chapter 9, for one example of using this Proxies pane.

Ethernet. The Ethernet pane contains two items:

• **Ethernet ID.** An IP address is assigned in software and can be changed at any time. By contrast, an Ethernet ID (also called a *MAC address*) is a hardware address that identifies your computer uniquely and is hard-coded into the Ethernet port on your computer before it ships. ISPs and network administrators may use your Ethernet address for verification purposes (such as to make sure that it really is you trying to connect via your DSL connection). If your ISP uses such verification, this can be a problem if, for example, you purchase a new computer; the result can be no Internet connection until you contact your ISP and get it to update its records to include the ID for your new hardware.

The Ethernet ID is also used in IPv6 addresses, as well as for machine-specific preferences (for example, the ones located in the ByHost folder of the Preferences folder in your ~/Library folder).

SEE: • "Preferences Files," in Chapter 4, for more on ByHost preferences.

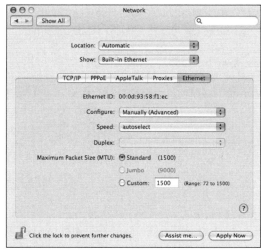

Figure 8.8

The Network System Preferences pane with the Ethernet tab of the Built-in Ethernet port selected—and Manually (Advanced) selected from the Configure pop-up menu.

• **Configure menu.** The default setting in the Configure pop-up menu is Automatically. If, like most users, you use this setting, you'll never need to access this pane. If, however, you select Manually (Advanced) from the Configure menu, a set of modifiable options appears. These include Speed, Duplex, and Maximum Packet Size (MTU). The only time you will need to change these settings is to solve certain troubleshooting problems.

SEE: • "Technically Speaking: Ethernet Speed, Duplex, and MTU Problems," below, for more details.

TECHNICALLY SPEAKING ▶ Ethernet Speed, Duplex, and MTU Problems

The options that appear when you select Manually (Advanced) from the Configure menu in the Ethernet pane of Network's Ethernet port settings allow you to modify the speed, duplex, and MTU of your Ethernet connection. Although it's unlikely that you'll need to make changes in this pane, the following explains what the settings mean and when you might need to alter them.

Speed. Changing this setting from its default of autoselect forces your Ethernet port to use a particular supported speed (10base, 100base, or 1000base) for sending and receiving data. You should change this setting only if your Mac does not seem to be selecting the correct speed automatically.

SEE: • "Take Note: Ethernet Hubs, Switches, Routers, and Cables," earlier in this chapter, for more background.

Duplex. This setting can be changed from its default of auto only if you select a specific speed option in the setting above. You have two choices: full-duplex and half-duplex. *Full-duplex* means that data can travel both to and from a computer at the same time. *Half-duplex* allows only one direction at a time and is thus slower. In most cases, you would select full-duplex. You're likely to need half-duplex only if you're connected to certain large networks where a full-duplex connection cannot be configured automatically.

MTU. This setting, which stands for *maximum transmission unit*, controls the size of the largest packets of data that your Mac will send over a network. You can select Standard (the default), Jumbo, or your own Custom value. You may need to change the MTU rate when connecting to certain ISPs that don't work correctly with the default MTU rate—as in the following example:

If you're using Internet Sharing to share your Internet connection with other computers (as covered in Chapter 9), you may find that your Internet connection is working fine with the primary computer (the one connected to the Internet) but not with the machines that are getting their Internet access via Internet Sharing. Symptoms may include failure of Web pages to load, an inability to use Sherlock, or an inability to use iTunes' radio (streaming audio) feature. The cause may be a somewhat obscure issue involving the MTU used by certain ISPs. When the problem occurs, the Internet Sharing client computers are probably attempting to use an MTU of 1500, whereas your ISP may be maxing out at a lower number, such as 1454 or 1492. The result is that packets are not received correctly. Fortunately, the major cause of this problem was a bug with Mac OS X 10.2 through 10.2.4; thus, you can avoid it by upgrading to Mac OS X 10.2.5 or later (including 10.3 or higher, of course). If you continue to have this problem in Mac OS X 10.3 or later, you can modify the MTU rate (so that the Mac's value matches your ISP's) by selecting the Custom radio button and entering the desired MTU value.

Note: If you use a router, the router software may include an option to vary the MTU value, especially when using a PPPoE connection (which is when this issue is most likely to be relevant). You can use this option instead of the MTU option in the Network System Preferences pane, if you prefer.

AirPort

If you have an AirPort card installed in your Mac and you want to use it to connect to a wireless network, you will need to set up Network System Preferences for AirPort. (Note: In general, I will be assuming that you are using an AirPort Extreme card and an AirPort-branded Base Station. With other configurations, some of the options described here may be different or absent.)

If you're connecting to a wireless network that has already been set up, the Network System Preferences pane is your starting point: From the Show pop-up menu choose AirPort. Setting up the TCP/IP, AppleTalk, and Proxies data for AirPort is very similar to the procedure just described for Ethernet. The one tab that's not found in the Ethernet settings is called, appropriately enough, AirPort.

Note: If you intend to connect to your own wireless network and have not yet set it up, your initial step is to set up your AirPort Base Station, compatible wireless router, or software router connection.

SEE: • **"Take Note: Setting Up an AirPort Base Station and Network" and "Using a Router,"** later in this chapter, for information on setting up a router prior to using the AirPort settings in Network System Preferences.

• **"Using Internet Connect,"** later in this chapter, for related information.

AirPort. The AirPort tab is the first one in the row of five tabs. The settings here determine how your Mac connects to a wireless network.

There are four items of note in the AirPort pane:

• **AirPort ID.** This sequence of letters and numbers uniquely identifies your AirPort card. In essence, it's the MAC address of the card.

Note: An AirPort Base Station also has an AirPort ID, which you may need on occasion (such as when setting up a wireless distribution system). You can find it on the bottom of the Base Station next to the AirPort symbol. For AirPort Extreme Base Stations, it is also listed in (a) the initial pane of the AirPort Admin Utility (in the pane on the right after you select the Base Station from the list on the left); and (b) the AirPort pane of the Internet Connect utility.

• **"By default, join" pop-up menu.** This menu offers two choices: "Automatic" and "Preferred networks."

With Automatic selected: AirPort should attempt to join the network you last joined (if it is still available). Otherwise, it will attempt to join the network with the strongest signal it can find. If you have never joined the network before, you will be asked if it's OK before joining it. If a password is required to join the network, you will be prompted to enter it (unless you have previously entered it into your keychain).

With "Preferred networks" selected: A text box appears with a list of all networks you have previously joined. AirPort will attempt to connect to them in the order in which they are listed. You can reorder the list, if desired, by dragging items. To permanently delete a listed network, select it in the list and then click the Delete (–) button. To add a network that you have not previously joined or that is a closed network (which means it does not automatically appear as available to join), click the Add (+) button and enter the network's name and password in the dialog that drops down. To edit the name or password of a listed network, select it and click the Edit button. Of special note: If you forgot a network's password, check the "Show password" box to view it in clear text.

Troubleshooting tip: If you see "Specific network" listed instead of "Preferred networks," and you are running Tiger, something went awry when you upgraded from Panther and the Network pane is still using the old Panther option. To fix this, go to Network Port Configurations and delete the AirPort port. A new one will likely be created automatically. Otherwise, create a new one. In either case, the newly created port should have the newer Tiger features.

Note: If you're setting up your own AirPort network, you can create passwords via the AirPort Setup Assistant application.

SEE: • **"Locations," later in this chapter, for details on setting up multiple locations.**

 • **"Take Note: Setting Up an AirPort Base Station and Network," later in this chapter, for more on closed networks.**

 • **"Take Note: Passwords and Joining a Wireless Network," later in this chapter, for more information regarding passwords.**

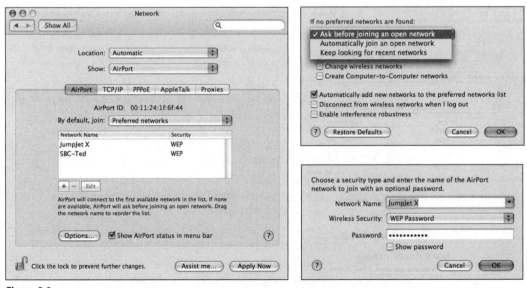

Figure 8.9

Left, *the Network System Preferences pane with the AirPort tab of the AirPort port selected;* top right, *the dialog that drops down if you click the Options button at the bottom of the pane;* bottom right, *the dialog that drops down if you click the Edit button (located below the "Preferred networks" list) for a selected network.*

Figure 8.10

The message that appears if the only accessible AirPort network is one you have never joined before, it is not on Network System Preferences' "Preferred networks" list, and you have selected "Ask before joining an open network" in AirPort's Options dialog.

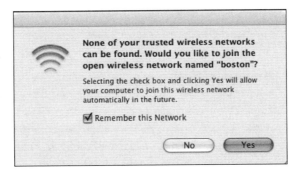

None of your trusted wireless networks can be found. Would you like to join the open wireless network named "boston"?

Selecting the check box and clicking Yes will allow your computer to join this wireless network automatically in the future.

☑ Remember this Network

No   Yes

- **Options.** If you click the Options button, a dialog drops down with a list of various AirPort-related selections. Most are self-explanatory. For example, if you don't want to be asked before joining a new network, or if you don't want new networks that you do join to be added to your "Preferred networks" list, select the relevant option.

  If you want to allow only administrators to be able to set up a computer-to-computer wireless network, select the option that requires an administrator password to do this.

  Finally, if you are having trouble connecting to the desired network, consider choosing the "Enable interference robustness" option. This is especially worth trying if you suspect that interference from a nearby wireless device, such as a cordless phone, may be causing problems with your AirPort connection. Note that with interface robustness enabled, overall wireless speed is reduced; however, this is likely to be preferable to intermittent connections or no connection at all.

  SEE: • The "AirPort" section of "Using Internet Connect," later in this chapter, for more on computer-to-computer wireless networks.

- **"Show AirPort status in menu bar."** If you check this box, an AirPort menu is added to the right side of the menu bar. This is used to turn AirPort on and off, check signal strength, and/or join an AirPort network.

  SEE: • "Take Note: The AirPort Menu and Joining an AirPort Network," "Take Note: Setting Up an AirPort Base Station and Network," and "Using Internet Connect," later in this chapter, for more details.

TCP/IP. When using AirPort or another type of wireless router to access the Internet, you will enter your TCP/IP settings here. (These settings work just like the corresponding ones in the TCP/IP pane for Ethernet port configurations, described earlier in the chapter.) If your wireless router is set up to use DHCP or BootP, you can simply choose the appropriate setting from the Configure pop-up menu, and the router will take care of the rest. If your router is set up for static IP addresses, you will need to enter each setting manually. (Your IP address will usually be something like 192.168.1.x, 172.16.1.x or 10.0.0.x, and the router address will generally be 192.168.1.1, 172.16.1.1 or 10.0.0.1.)

SEE: • "Take Note: Setting Up an AirPort Base Station and Network," later in this chapter, for how to set up an AirPort Base Station.

If your ISP requires that you use certain domain name servers, you may need to enter their addresses as well (see "Take Note: What Are the TCP/IP Settings?" earlier in the chapter, for more details).

AppleTalk. If you plan to use AppleTalk over an AirPort network, this pane is where you enable it (by checking the Make AppleTalk Active box). An AirPort AppleTalk network does not require an AirPort Base Station; you can create a network between two AirPort-equipped computers directly. You can also choose an AppleTalk zone (if applicable) and manually configure your AppleTalk node ID and network ID.

Note that some third-party wireless routers do not support AppleTalk over AirPort/wireless connections. If your wireless router is one of those, you'll need to create a computer-to-computer network to communicate with another computer via wireless AppleTalk.

SEE: • "Using Internet Connect," later in this chapter, for more details.

Proxies. If your ISP or network requires proxies, you enter proxy information in this pane.

TAKE NOTE ▶ Setting Up an AirPort Base Station and Network

An AirPort Base Station is not the only hardware device for creating a wireless network to use with Macs. You can use AirPort cards with third-party wireless routers instead of an AirPort Base Station. In fact, you can even use wireless PC cards instead of AirPort cards in PowerBooks with PC Card slots. However, the AirPort Extreme Base Station (and its AirPort Express cousin) are the only such devices made by Apple—and the only ones to have software support built into Mac OS X. Therefore, this sidebar provides some details on how to set them up.

Base Station models. Apple currently makes two AirPort Base Station models (I will not be discussing older Graphite and Dual Ethernet Base Station models here):

• **AirPort Extreme.** AirPort Extreme uses a newer version of the wireless transmission protocol (802.11g, as opposed to 802.11b) that can transmit data five times faster (54 Mbps). To get this speed bump, you must use new AirPort Extreme cards (which fit only in the AirPort Extreme slots on newer Macs). However, the Extreme Base Station is backward-compatible, so it can still connect to the original 802.11b cards. The Extreme Base Station includes a USB port that allows you to connect a printer and share it with computers connected to the wireless network. AirPort Extreme also supports Bonjour, for quickly finding and making connections to compatible devices.

Finally, if your AirPort Extreme Base Station has a built-in modem (it's optional), and if you are not set to connect to the Internet via an Ethernet port, the Base Station automatically attempts to make a connection to your dial-up ISP whenever you launch an Internet application, and then shares that modem connection with connected Macs. (Note: You can also call in to the modem while on the road and gain access to your entire wireless network.)

continues on next page

TAKE NOTE ▶ Setting Up an AirPort Base Station and Network *continued*

This model also has dual Ethernet ports: one for LAN connections (with the double-arrow Ethernet icon) and the other for WAN connections (with the circle-of-dots icon). In general, you connect to your cable or DSL modem via the Base Station's WAN port, and you connect to other Macs on your local network via the LAN port. This is especially helpful for troubleshooting a Base Station when the wireless connection is not working; you can still connect to the Base Station via the LAN Ethernet port while your broadband modem remains connected to the WAN port.

Troubleshooting tip: If you connect to the Internet via a wired router, you may decide to attach an AirPort Base Station to the network, so that AirPort-connected Macs can access the Internet. In this case, the Base Station's LAN Connector (port) connects to the router, which in turn connects to the Internet. The WAN Connector remains unused. This is called a *bridge* connection. In such cases, you may get an Internet Connection Warning message when you first connect to the Base Station. The warning states that you should be connected via the WAN port instead of the LAN port. In this setup, you can typically ignore this warning; actually, I have found that connecting via either port usually works. For other setups, if you get this message, follow its advice. In general, use the WAN port to connect to whatever device connects to the Internet; use the LAN port to connect to wired clients.

- **AirPort Express.** The AirPort Express is a smaller version of the "flying saucer" Extreme model. In fact, it looks similar to the AC power adapters that come with Apple's laptop computers. It can do most of what an Extreme Base Station can do, although it comes with only one Ethernet port. However, one of its biggest attractions is that it includes an audio port. With the proper cables, you can connect the Express to a sound system. Now, via iTunes' AirTunes feature, you can play the music in your iTunes Library over any sound system that is in AirPort network range of your Mac.

Base Station software. This software contains two primary components:

- **AirPort Admin Utility.** This utility, located in the Utilities folder in Mac OS X, allows you to connect to a Base Station and input the settings needed for connecting the Base Station to the Internet—or otherwise modify your AirPort network settings.

- **Base Station firmware.** The Base Station itself has firmware code built into it. Occasionally, Apple will release an update to the firmware, usually as part of a general update to the Admin Utility. If when installing the new Admin Utility you're not asked to update the firmware, you can manually update it via the Upload command in the Base Station menu of the Admin Utility. (You first have to access the Base Station, as described below.)

AirPort Setup Assistant and AirPort Express Assistant. In addition to the Base Station software, there's one more set of AirPort-related software: AirPort Setup Assistant and AirPort Express Assistant (located in the Utilities folder). AirPort Setup Assistant can be used with either type of Base Station; the Express version works only with AirPort Express Base Stations. Both provide the simplest and most user-friendly way to set up an AirPort Base Station network.

For example, after launching Setup Assistant, you initially select "Set up a new AirPort Base Station" or "Change settings on an existing AirPort Base Station." Simply follow the prompts to complete the setup, and then click Update to upload the information to the Base Station.

continues on next page

TAKE NOTE ▶ **Setting Up an AirPort Base Station and Network** *continued*

Note: If you are setting up a new Base Station, you probably don't have a wireless network already in place. If so, you'll need to connect the Base Station to your Mac via an Ethernet cable in order to set it up. The assistant walks you through the steps, including setting up the initial network. When you're finished, the assistant uploads the information to the Base Station. You're now ready to set up and join a network. You can use the same setup to troubleshoot a Base Station with which you cannot communicate via an existing wireless network.

If you use AirPort Setup Assistant, your Base Station will only be able to use DHCP (as set in the Internet pane of the Base Station and in the TCP/IP for AirPort pane of Network System Preferences for the client computer) to communicate with other devices on the network. If you want to assign IP addresses manually, you must use the AirPort Admin Utility to set up the Base Station. In fact, if you used the Admin Utility to set your Base Station *not* to use DHCP but then connect to the Base Station using Setup Assistant, you will receive an error message warning that Setup Assistant cannot configure the Base Station until DHCP is turned on. Depending on the version of the software you're using, the assistant will either offer to change your settings (turning on DHCP) or instruct you to use the AirPort Admin Utility instead. Thus, if you want to make changes beyond what Setup Assistant can handle, you will need to use the Admin Utility.

The assistant utilities work only if you have an AirPort card installed in your Mac. If you want to configure a Base Station from a Mac that does not have an AirPort card installed (using a wired Ethernet connection, for example), you will (again) need to use the more full-featured but somewhat less-user-friendly AirPort Admin Utility. Also, although this is unlikely to be an issue for most users, for the assistant utilities to work, the following ports must not be closed by a firewall: 192, 5009, 5353. Personally, I use the Admin Utility exclusively—at least after the initial setup is complete.

continues on next page

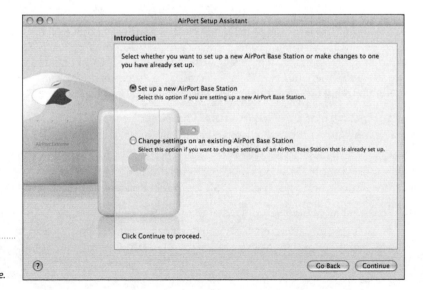

Figure 8.11

The AirPort Setup Assistant's Introduction pane.

TAKE NOTE ▶ Setting Up an AirPort Base Station and Network *continued*

AirPort Admin Utility. The first time you launch this utility on an AirPort network, you'll get a list of all Base Stations within range (with the IP address of each). If you click the name of the Base Station, the installed version of the Base Station firmware is listed at the bottom of the data to the right.

If the Base Station you're looking for is not listed, click the Rescan button to try again. If that technique fails, and you know the IP address of the Base Station, click the Other button and enter the IP address and password. If neither of these approaches works, you need to check your basic network connections (as described in "Setting Up Network System Preferences," in the main text) to make sure that the Base Station is correctly connected to the network.

Note: As mentioned earlier, if you're using a Base Station for the first time and thus have no AirPort network setup, or if you're accessing the Base Station from a Mac that simply does not have an AirPort card, the Base Station must be connected to the computer running the Admin utility via an Ethernet connection. In such cases, only the Base Station(s) connected via Ethernet will be listed in the AirPort Admin Utility window. Recall that if your AirPort Base Station has both WAN and LAN ports, you typically connect it to the Mac via the LAN port.

When the appropriate Base Station is listed, double-click it (or select it and then click the Configure button) to access its settings. If the Base Station has already been configured, you will have to enter its password. (Even if it has not been configured before, you may need to enter a default password: *public*.)

Note: If you select to add the password to your keychain (via the option in the Password dialog), you won't be prompted to enter the password in the future.

Note: If you enter the wrong password, you will get an error message that states, rather ambiguously, "An error occurred while reading the configuration." Note also that the Base Station password is separate from the password you use to join a network. Each network can have its own unique password, separate from other networks as well as from the Base Station.

continues on next page

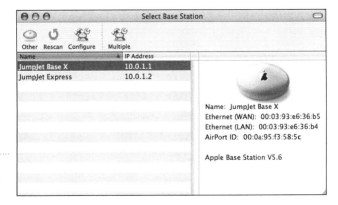

Figure 8.12

The AirPort Admin Utility's Select Base Station window.

TAKE NOTE ▶ **Setting Up an AirPort Base Station and Network** *continued*

After you connect to a Base Station using the Admin Utility, the window that appears will typically have a toolbar at the top with a row of tabs immediately below.

Toolbar icons. Listed in the toolbar are the following icons:

- **Restart.** Restart (also called a *soft reset*) is the AirPort equivalent of restarting your Mac; it may fix temporary connection problems.

- **Upload.** If you want to upload a newer firmware version to the Base Station (such as an update released by Apple), click the Upload icon and then select the update file in the dialog that appears. (Note: In most cases, after you install an update of the AirPort software on your Mac, the Admin Utility will prompt you to update the Base Station immediately after you click the Configure button, making use of this Upload icon unnecessary.)

continues on next page

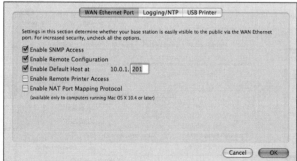

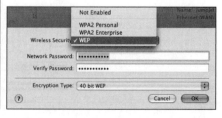

Figure 8.13

The AirPort Admin Utility: top, *the AirPort pane;* bottom left, *the AirPort pane's Base Stations Options dialog;* bottom right, *the AirPort pane's Change Wireless Security dialog.*

TAKE NOTE ▶ Setting Up an AirPort Base Station and Network   *continued*

- **Default.** Default uploads the default version of the AirPort Base Station firmware to the Base Station. This is the version that is "built into" the current version of the Admin Utility.

- **Password.** Clicking the Password icon reveals the form of the WEP or WPA password (if enabled) that computers using wireless software other than AirPort need to use. For example, you'll need to know this password information if you're connecting to a Base Station using a third-party wireless card (rather than an Apple AirPort card).

- **Profiles.** This option is enabled only for the AirPort Express. Because the Express is designed to be portable, you may take it with you when you travel. Thus, you may want to have different settings for the Express in different locations. The Profiles option allows you to create up to five different configurations. It is similar in concept to the Locations settings in Network System Preferences. Use the Profiles icon to create, edit, or switch between profiles.

Tabs. Click each tab to change the window to display a different set of options. The following is a summary of the many options available from these panes. For more complete coverage, check the Utility's Help files and Apple's Knowledge Base (especially the documents on designing AirPort networks, such as the ones available at www.apple.com/support/airport).

- **AirPort.** This is the default pane that appears when you first access the Base Station. It is divided into two sections: Base Station and AirPort Network.

  Base Station. In the Base Station section, you can set the name of the Base Station and change the password needed to access it (via the Change Password button). Of special interest is the Base Stations Options button. After clicking it, a dialog drops down with three new tabs: WAN Ethernet Port, Logging/NTP, and USB Printer.

  In the WAN Ethernet Port pane, you can uncheck the default-selected options for Enable SNMP Access and Enable Remote Configuration. Doing so makes it more difficult for others to "see" your AirPort; however, it also provides greater security—particularly in protecting against denial-of-service (DoS) attacks (a hacker's attempt to bring down your network by flooding it with data). Checking the "Enable Default Host at" box and assigning an IP address is done to set up one of the computers on your local network as a DMZ host (as discussed in "Internet routers and port mapping," later in this chapter).

  In the Logging/NTP pane, you can set whether or not the Base Station gets time and date information from the network.

  On the USB Printer pane, you can give a name to the USB printer connected to your Base Station.

  AirPort Network. Returning to the main window, let's turn our attention to the AirPort Network section at the bottom. Here you can name the network (this is the network's SSID) and set whether or not it is a closed network. If a network is closed, it will not automatically be listed in the AirPort menus of computers within range. To access the network, users have to enter its exact name and password (via the dialog that appears after you choose the Other command in the AirPort menu or in Internet Connect). This option makes it harder for unauthorized users to find your network.

continues on next page

TAKE NOTE ▶ Setting Up an AirPort Base Station and Network *continued*

Click the Change Wireless Security button in the lower section to set or modify the network password. In the dialog that opens, choose the desired type of password from the Wireless Security pop-up menu. If you don't want any password, choose Not Enabled. With any other password option enabled, users seeking to join the network will be required to enter the password.

If you want to use WEP, you can select either "40 bit WEP" or "128 bit WEP" (this affects the length of the encrypted password). (Note: You cannot join a 128-bit encrypted network from a wireless card that only has 40-bit support.)

continues on next page

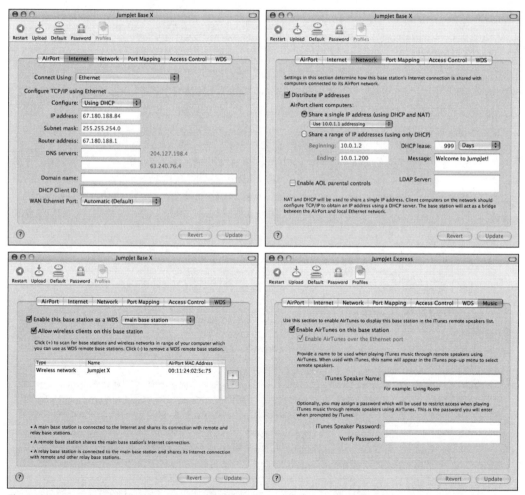

Figure 8.14

The AirPort Admin Utility: top left, *the Internet pane;* top right, *the Network pane;* bottom left, *the WDS pane;* bottom right, *the Music pane (available only with an AirPort Express).*

TAKE NOTE ▶ Setting Up an AirPort Base Station and Network *continued*

For WPA (which offers greater protection than WEP), you will almost certainly want to select WPA Personal; the WPA Enterprise option is needed only by systems that use a RADIUS server. For WPA, you can also choose between a Password (your most likely choice) and a Pre-Shared Key. A Pre-Shared Key must be 64 hexadecimal characters; this is more protection than most users will care to bother with.

Provided that all of the devices on your wireless network support WPA, I recommend WPA as your encryption method. However, some devices—such as many third-party products with wireless capability—do not support WPA. For example, at the time of this writing, TiVo units with wireless network adapters supported only WEP.

The remaining options in this pane (the Channel and Mode pop-up menus and the Wireless Options button) are settings that primarily affect the network's performance. Therefore, you would use them if computers were having difficulty locating or maintaining a connection to your Base Station. Selecting a specific channel may allow you to improve your signal strength if your current channel isn't responding well. Use the Mode menu to determine whether the Base Station can connect to AirPort cards that use the older (slower) 802.11b protocol, the newer (faster) 802.11g protocol, or both. (Note: If all of your wireless devices support 802.11g, choosing the 802.11g Only setting should provide you with better performance than the Compatible mode.) Click the Wireless Options button to access still other options, including "Enable interference robustness" (as covered in the main text).

SEE: • **"Take Note: Passwords and Joining a Wireless Network," later in this chapter, for additional information on WEP and WPA.**

• **Internet.** This is where you set up the Base Station for connecting to the Internet. In general, you enter the settings you would have entered in the TCP/IP pane of Network System Preferences if you were connecting to the Internet directly from your computer (most likely, simply select Using DHCP from the Configure pop-up menu). If you're using a router (rather than the Base Station itself) to connect to the Internet, you will likely enter the TCP/IP settings to connect to your router here.

Note: From the "Connect using" pop-up menu, you can choose a few options that are unique to AirPort setups. In particular, AirPort (WDS), together with Using DHCP (from the Configure pop-up menu), is used when setting up a *wireless distribution system* (WDS) consisting of two or more AirPort Extreme Base Stations. You would use this setting to connect the currently accessed Base Station to a main Base Station that is, in turn, connected to the Internet (as described later in this sidebar).

• **Network.** This critical pane determines how the Base Station works with the other computers on your local network. The most common choice is to select "Distribute IP addresses" together with "Share a single IP address (using DHCP and NAT)." From the pop-up menu, you can also select the range of local addresses to be used by NAT. This setup allows you to share an Internet connection among several computers and provides IP addresses to connected computers. (Users on those computers will be able to select the DHCP setting in Network System Preferences and have the settings provided automatically.)

Alternatively, if you have a separate Internet router that is assigning IP addresses manually or via DHCP, you may choose to disable the "Distribute IP addresses" option. This setup lets the router handle the address sharing that would otherwise be performed by the Base Station.

continues on next page

TAKE NOTE ▶ **Setting Up an AirPort Base Station and Network** *continued*

Whatever choice you make, the text at the bottom of the pane provides a summary of what you've done and how other computers must be configured as a result. This information can help you decide whether or not you have made the correct decision.

Admittedly, making the correct decisions here can be difficult if you're not familiar with how computer networks work—especially so if you get into using manually assigned IP addresses. To find help, check the PDF documents describing how to design AirPort networks at http://docs.info.apple.com/article.html?artnum=52002.

- **Port Mapping.** I cover Port Mapping in general (which would likely be used only if you had manually assigned IP addresses, rather than using DHCP) in "Internet routers and port mapping," later in this chapter.

- **Access Control.** With this option, you can limit access to your AirPort network to just the computers listed in this pane. Computers not on this list will be unable to access your network, even if they know the password. This provides an additional level of security to your network. If no computers are listed here, Access Control is ignored, and all computers that can provide the needed password will have access to your network.

  To add a computer to the list, click the Add (+) button and enter its AirPort ID (MAC address) where indicated. For the computer you are currently using, you can simply click the "This computer" button. Otherwise, you can find the AirPort ID in the AirPort section of the Network System Preferences pane for the computer.

- **WDS.** This is a very cool option if you have two or more Base Stations. For example, I have an AirPort Base Station and an AirPort Express. While I use the Express mainly to allow me to play iTunes music via my sound system in the lower level of our house, I can also use the Express to extend the strength of my wireless network; this provides stronger and more reliable wireless connections when using a laptop computer in the lower level. To do this, in the settings for the AirPort Extreme, I selected the "Enable this base station as a WDS" option and chose "main base station" from the pop-up menu. From the same pop-up menu in the settings for the AirPort Express, I chose "remote base station." I enabled "Allow wireless clients on this base station" for both units. I then needed to "connect" the two via the Add (+) button on the AirPort Extreme. See AirPort's Help files and http://docs.info.apple.com/article.html?artnum=107454 for more details, including the remaining "relay base station" option in the pop-up menu.

- **Music.** This option appears only on an AirPort Express. Click "Enable AirTunes on this base station" if you want to use it to play your iTunes music. You can also choose the name of the Express as it appears in iTunes, and you can require that anyone trying to play music through the Express first provide the correct password. That's it. Of course, for this to work, the Express must be connected to a sound system.

- **Menus.** Although AirPort Admin Utility has the typical set of menus in the menu bar, you will rarely if ever need to access any of the commands there (as they are duplicated in the toolbar or elsewhere). There is one pair of items worth mentioning, however: In the View menu, you can toggle between Details (the choice I have assumed is selected) and Summary. The latter command hides all the tabs and instead displays a simple summary of the Base Station settings.

continues on next page

TAKE NOTE ▶ Setting Up an AirPort Base Station and Network *continued*

Finishing up. When you've finished making changes to your Base Station settings, remember to click the Update button at the bottom of the window. This action saves the changes, uploading them to the Base Station and restarting it. If you are worried that you made any mistakes, you can always close the window without updating and start over.

After you finish setting up a Base Station and wireless network, your next step (if you have not already done so) is to input the AirPort settings in Network System Preferences, as described in the main text. Remember that what you enter here will vary depending on how you configured the Base Station's Network settings and what type of network you have. Fortunately, once you've established these settings, you won't need to refer to them again unless problems occur.

Finally, you need to turn on your AirPort card and choose the desired network (usually via the AirPort menu bar item or Internet Connect). Congratulations—you're now on a wireless network!

Performing a hard reset of the Base Station (for Base Station problems). If you're having problems with your Base Station, perhaps congratulations *weren't* in order! Perhaps you're unable to access your Base Station, or maybe things worked for a few days but don't any longer. Or perhaps the flashing lights on the Base Station are showing a color or a pattern other than what's "normal." Whatever the case, it's time to do a hard reset of the Base Station.

To do this with an AirPort Extreme or Express Base Station, using an unbent paper clip, push and hold the Reset button, located on the Base Station itself, for 5 seconds. Note: On an AirPort Express, a hard reset does not erase saved Profiles. To do this as well, you use a third option— factory default: Start with the Express unplugged; plug it in while holding down the Reset button; continue holding it down for about 5 seconds.

After performing a hard reset or factory default, the initial password will be *public*. You will need to reenter all settings, just as you did the first time you set up the Base Station.

Performing a soft reset of the Base Station (for a forgotten password). If the problem is only that you forgot your Base Station password, the solution is to do a soft reset. To do this, hold down the Reset button for only 1 second. Then, go to the AirPort Admin Utility, access the Base Station, and create a new password when prompted. You must do this within 5 minutes of the reset, or settings will revert to what they were before.

For more details on resetting Base Stations, including how to locate the Reset button, see these Apple Knowledge Base articles: http://docs.info.apple.com/article.html?artnum=107451 and http://docs.info.apple.com/article.html?artnum=108044.

Figure 8.15

The AirPort Admin Utility's Internet Connection Warning message.

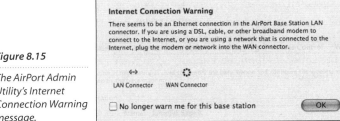

Internet Connection Warning

There seems to be an Ethernet connection in the AirPort Base Station LAN connector. If you are using a DSL, cable, or other broadband modem to connect to the Internet, or you are using a network that is connected to the Internet, plug the modem or network into the WAN connector.

LAN Connector   WAN Connector

☐ No longer warn me for this base station   OK

Modem

You may not think of a dial-up connection to your ISP (AOL, EarthLink, and so on) as being a network connection, but it is. Just as with an Ethernet- or AirPort-based Internet connection, the modem is linking your computer to other computers on the Internet. As a result, the settings for modem connections are located in the Network pane of System Preferences. To set up your Mac's built-in modem, from the Show pop-up menu choose Internal Modem. (If you have a USB or Bluetooth modem attached, the port configuration will have the name you assigned when you created a new port configuration for that modem.)

Note: The Internet Connect utility and the Internet Connect menu both let you *initiate* dial-up connections. Before you can do so, however, you must go to the Network System Preferences pane and *set up* a modem port configuration, select Internal Modem (or whatever the name of that modem configuration might be), and then enter the appropriate settings in the Modem port panes.

SEE: • "Using Internet Connect," later in this chapter.

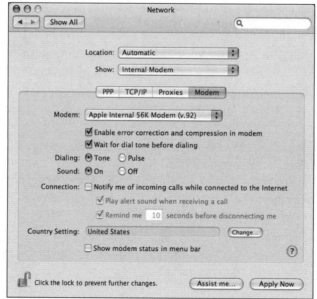

Figure 8.16

The Network System Preferences pane with the Modem tab of the Internal Modem port selected.

PPP. This pane is where you enter the information required to connect to your dial-up ISP. To do so, follow these steps:

1. In the Service Provider field enter your ISP's name. Although this step is optional, the name you input here shows up in Internet Connect—helpful in determining the current default if you have multiple dial-up ISPs.

2. In the Account Name field, enter your account name. This is your ISP account name, not your Mac OS X login name. For some ISPs, your account name is simply your user name; other ISPs require your entire e-mail address. Check with your ISP to determine which it is.

3. In the Password field enter your ISP account password.

4. In the Telephone Number field, enter the phone number your computer dials to connect to your ISP.

5. If you have a second number, enter it in the Alternate Number field. (If the first number is busy or not responding, Mac OS X will try the second number.)

6. If you want Mac OS X to remember your password so that you don't have to type it each time you connect, check the "Save password" box.

7. You can now click the Dial Now button to immediately connect, or use the Internet Connect application and/or menu as a more convenient way to connect at any later time.

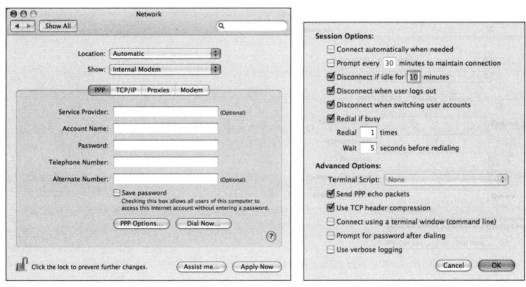

Figure 8.17

Left, *the Network System Preferences pane with the PPP tab of the Internal Modem port selected;* right, *the PPP Options dialog, as accessed from the PPP pane.*

8. (Optional) If you click the PPP Options button, you can enable or disable a variety of PPP settings. Most users will be content to leave these options at their default settings. However, two choices in this dialog are worth special mention:

"Connect automatically when needed." With this option enabled, Mac OS X will automatically initiate a connection—if you aren't already connected—when you launch an application (such as a Web browser) that requires Internet access.

"Disconnect if idle for __ minutes." You can set this option to automatically disconnect you from your ISP if you have not used the connection for the specified period of time. This option can be useful if you leave your computer with your connection still active, especially if your ISP charges you according to the time you're connected. However, it can be annoying if you want to maintain the connection despite an idle period. Note that some dial-up ISPs may disconnect you after a period of idleness regardless of how you set this option.

TCP/IP. As with AirPort and Ethernet, this pane is where you enter your ISP's TCP/IP settings. The Configure pop-up menu offers three options: Manually, Using PPP, and AOL Dialup. If you're one of the few people who have a dial-up connection with a static IP address, choose Manually. However, if you're like most users, you'll choose Using PPP. The only additional data you may have to enter is the address of your ISP's domain name server.

AOL users may select AOL Dialup. This disables almost all other options for the Internal Modem settings. It is designed to allow you to dial up via AOL's own custom software—you then enter your dial-up settings in that software instead. If you try to connect via Internet Connect with AOL Dialup selected here, you will get a PPP error message. See the following Apple Knowledge Base article for more on connecting to AOL in Mac OS X: http://docs.info.apple.com/article.html?path=Mac/10.4/en/mh2065.html.

TAKE NOTE ▶ When Connecting Automatically Is Not a Good Idea

Although enabling "Connect automatically when needed" can be convenient, it can also mean that a connection will be attempted when you do not want it to be. For example, if you're not connected to a phone line and you launch your Web browser (perhaps to view a page offline), the Mac will attempt to make a connection and fail to do so.

To avoid this situation, you can simply not enable this option. The other alternative is to create a separate network Location for those times when you are not connected to any network or phone line. You would disable all ports for this Location and then switch to this Location at times when you are not connected.

A slightly different variation: If you have File Sharing or Web Sharing enabled, and you have the "Connect automatically" option enabled, your Mac may try to initiate a dial-up connection at startup. To prevent this situation, follow the same suggestions I just described or turn off the sharing options (via the Sharing pane of System Preferences). If you need to use Sharing Services, simply turn them off before shutting down or restarting, and re-enable them after startup.

SEE : • "Blue-screen crashes and stalls," in Chapter 5, for coverage of a problem with the "Connect automatically" option that can cause a crash at startup.

• "Locations," later in this chapter, for more information on network Locations.

Proxies. If your ISP requires proxies, you enter proxy information in this pane.

Modem. This pane is where you configure your modem for PPP connections. The Modem pop-up menu is where you choose the modem model. (Note that for most recent Apple computers, the model is chosen for you: Apple Internal 56K Modem—typically V.90 or V.92.) If you have an older Mac or are using a third-party modem, choose the appropriate model. Other options available in this pane include "Enable error correction and compression in modem," "Wait for dial tone before dialing," and "Show modem status in menu bar." (The menu bar item is a useful way to connect, as well as to tell whether your dial-up connection is active; this is the same menu bar item you can enable from Internet Connect.) Other options include Sound (determines whether or not you can hear through your speakers the modem dialing and connecting), Dialing (for selecting tone versus pulse dialing), and Country Setting (useful for international dial-up connections). Some systems may also include the option "Notify me of incoming calls while connected to the Internet."

Once again, after making any changes to your Network settings, click the Apply Now button to save your changes.

TAKE NOTE ▶ Modem Scripts and Terminal Scripts

When setting up a modem, you may see references to two types of scripts: *modem scripts* and *terminal scripts*. Here's what you need to know about them:

Modem scripts. When you select a modem model/type in the Modem pane of Network System Preferences, you're actually telling Mac OS X which modem *script* to use when initiating a dial-up connection. Because every modem is slightly different, these scripts (located in /Library/Modem Scripts) tell Mac OS X how to interact with each modem. A modem script generally describes the modem's initialization string, maximum data speed, buffer size, data-compression settings, error-correction settings, and any other special features the modem supports. You can open and view any of these modem scripts in a text editor such as Bare Bones Software's BBEdit (www.barebones.com). (You can even edit them, though I advise against it unless you really know what you're doing.)

Generally, all you need to do is choose your modem's name from the Modem pop-up menu and connect. At times, however, the "right" script for your modem may not work as well as it should. Your modem may try to connect at a speed your phone line can't sustain, for example, resulting in frequent disconnects. Or maybe you have a V.90 modem, but your ISP supports only the slower V.34 standard. Choosing a different modem script from the Modem pop-up menu may help. In particular, for the Apple Internal Modem, shifting from "Apple Internal 56K Modem (v.90)" to "Apple Internal 56K Modem (v.34)" may help.

continues on next page

TAKE NOTE ▶ Modem Scripts and Terminal Scripts *continued*

In addition, modem manufacturers sometimes release updated scripts for their modems. In this case, you simply place the updated script in the Modem Scripts folder (/Library/Modem Scripts) and then choose it from the Modem pop-up menu in the Modem pane.

Terminal scripts. Sometimes called *connection scripts*, these have nothing to do with the Terminal application. (They are so called because years ago all dial-up connections were initiated via a terminal connection between your computer/modem and the ISP's servers/modems.) These scripts contain a series of commands needed to log in to your ISP. It's rare for such scripts to be needed nowadays, but some dial-up ISPs still require them. If your ISP supplies such a script file, here's how you install and use it:

1. Create a folder called Terminal Scripts in the root-level Library folder (/Library), if one does not exist. Place the script file in this folder.

2. Go to the Network System Preferences pane, and from the Show pop-up menu select Internal Modem.

3. Click the PPP tab and click the PPP Options button.

4. From the Terminal Script pop-up menu that appears in the dialog that drops down, select the name of the script you installed.

5. Click OK, and then click Apply Now.

Bluetooth modem

If your Mac came with internal support for Bluetooth, or if you connected a third-party USB Bluetooth adapter, you can use a Bluetooth-enabled mobile phone to connect to the Internet via a dial-up connection (assuming your mobile-phone provider offers data connection and Internet support). Because Bluetooth is wireless technology, you're actually getting a "double wireless" connection—one wireless connection between your Mac and your mobile phone, and another between your mobile phone and your ISP (which means you should expect slower network speeds than if you were using a standard phone line).

SEE: • "Using Bluetooth," later in this chapter, for more details on Bluetooth and its software.

If you've never used Bluetooth and you attach a USB Bluetooth adapter to your Mac, the first time you open Network System Preferences, you'll get a message saying that a new port has been detected and added. If your Mac has Apple's Bluetooth internal hardware installed, the port should already exist.

Using a Bluetooth-enabled mobile phone as a modem requires two steps: (1) "pairing" your phone with your Mac, and (2) configuring Network System Preferences to connect to the Internet using your Bluetooth modem.

To pair your phone and your Mac, follow these steps:

1. Using the documentation that came with your phone, make your phone *discoverable.* This makes your phone available for pairing with your Mac.

2. Open the Bluetooth System Preferences pane. (Note: Don't worry about whether or not your Mac is discoverable, if all you want to do is use the phone to connect to the Internet.)

3. In the Bluetooth System Preferences pane, click the Devices tab.

4. Assuming your phone is on and near your Mac, the phone may already appear in the list of Bluetooth Devices. If not, click the "Set up new device" button. This will launch the Bluetooth Setup Assistant software. Select "Mobile phone" as the device type and follow the prompts to pair the device with your Mac.

5. In the Sharing pane of Bluetooth System Preferences, make sure that Bluetooth Serial Port (sometimes called Bluetooth-PDA-Sync) is enabled and that Modem is chosen from the Type pop-up menu.

Your Bluetooth-enabled mobile phone is now available as a modem and should appear as a port configuration in Network System Preferences.

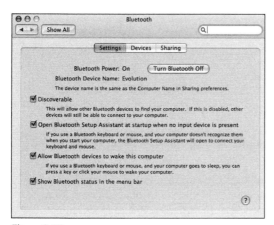

Figure 8.18

The Bluetooth System Preferences pane: left, *the Settings pane;* right, *the Devices pane.*

To configure the phone to connect to the Internet, follow these steps:

1. In the Network System Preferences pane, choose Network Port Configurations from the Show menu and make sure that Bluetooth is enabled (that is, the On box for the Bluetooth port is checked).

   Note: If this port is not in the menu, click the New button; from the Port pop-up menu choose Bluetooth; name the port; and click OK to create the port. Alternatively, you could have selected the "Show in Network Preferences" option of the Bluetooth System Preferences pane.

2. From the Show pop-up menu select Bluetooth.

3. Configure the TCP/IP and PPP panes as you would for any non-Bluetooth modem. In the Bluetooth Modem pane, select the name of your Bluetooth-enabled phone from the Modem menu (rather than the name of your Mac's internal modem).

   Note: Some mobile phone service providers provide "data" services specifically designed to allow you to use your mobile phone for network connections; some of these require you to use a domain name (such as wap.voicestream.com) instead of a phone number in the Telephone Number field. Check with your mobile phone service provider for the appropriate settings.

   The "Show modem status in menu bar" and "Show Bluetooth status in menu bar" options are at the bottom of the window. I recommend selecting both.

4. Open Internet Connect (or use the modem-status menu bar item) and click Connect.

For assistance in setting up a Bluetooth modem or any other Bluetooth device, you can always directly launch Bluetooth Setup Assistant (located in /System/Library/CoreServices).

For more information on using a Bluetooth-enabled phone as a modem, check the Help files that came with Tiger.

FireWire

You can make an IP connection over FireWire. To set up a FireWire IP connection:

1. In Network preferences, choose Built-in FireWire from the Show pop-up menu.

   Note: If this port is not listed in the menu, choose Network Port Configurations; click the New button; choose Built-in FireWire from the Port pop-up menu; name the port; and click OK to create the port. Then check the box for Built-in FireWire, if needed.

2. With Built-in FireWire enabled and selected, click the TCP/IP tab and enter the settings, much as you would in an Ethernet TCP/IP pane (as described previously in this chapter). In most cases, simply select Using DHCP. Click Apply Now to save your changes.

To get an Internet connection directly over FireWire, you need a device (such as a router) that connects to the Internet and allows connections from a Mac via a FireWire cable. Currently, such devices are rare.

However, there are other, more common, uses of a FireWire IP connection:

- **Exchange data between Macs connected via a FireWire cable.** This can be an especially convenient and speedy way of sharing files between two nearby Macs. This is separate from connecting two computers via Target Disk mode, as described in Chapter 9. To use a FireWire IP connection, you do not need to restart your Mac. It can be many times faster than sharing files over an Ethernet connection.

To do this, both Macs must have set up a FireWire port in Network System Preferences and be connected to each other via a FireWire cable. You must also enable Personal File Sharing in the Services pane in the Sharing System Preferences pane of the Mac that is to be shared.

- **Share an Internet connection among FireWire-connected Macs.** To do this, you need to set up Internet Sharing in the Sharing System Preferences pane of the Mac that is to be shared, as well as set up FireWire as a port configuration in the Network System Preferences pane of both the Mac sharing the Internet connection and the Mac accessing that shared connection.

    SEE: • "Take Note: Setting Up and Using Internet Sharing and File Sharing," in Chapter 9, for more details.

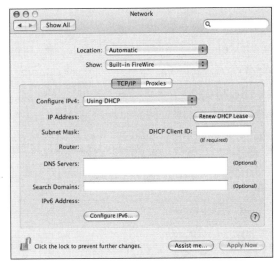

Figure 8.19

The Network System Preferences pane with the TCP/IP tab of the Built-in FireWire port selected.

Locations

The discussion up to this point has assumed that, for the most part, you use your Mac or PowerBook in an environment where your network settings remain unchanged. In many situations, however, you may have multiple groups of network settings. Perhaps you use your PowerBook at work and at home, and each location requires different network settings.

Mac OS X addresses these situations through network Locations—groups of network settings that you set up based on the environments in which you'll be using your computer. You can create any number of Locations.

All of your initial network settings are part of a default location called Automatic, which is really no more or less "automatic" than any other Location you may set up. Apple simply calls the first Location by this name.

To create a new Location, follow these steps:

1. From the Location pop-up menu in the Network System Preferences pane, choose New Location.

2. Give your new Location a name, and click OK. The new location is selected automatically.

Next, you need to configure the new Location. To do so, follow the steps previously outlined for Network System Preferences (that is, configure and prioritize the ports and then configure the settings for each port).

To instead create a new Location that's based on, or similar to, an existing Location, follow these steps:

1. From the Location pop-up menu choose Edit Locations.

2. Select the existing Location on which you want the new Location based.

3. Click the Duplicate button, and give the new Location a name.

4. Click Done.

5. From the Location pop-up menu, choose the new Location.

6. Make any necessary changes in your network settings.

When you've created multiple Locations, you can switch among them easily. To do so, do either of the following:

*   Open the Network pane of System Preferences and choose a location from the Location pop-up menu; click the Apply Now button.

*   Choose Location from Mac OS X's Apple menu and choose the desired Location from the hierarchical menu.

Figure 8.20

The Network System Preferences pane's edit Locations dialog.

Using Internet Connect

If your Mac is not set to automatically connect to the Internet when it starts up or when you use an Internet application (Web browser, e-mail client, and so on), you will need to manually connect to the Internet (or perhaps to an AirPort network that provides access to the Internet).

For such occasions, it's convenient to use Mac OS X's Internet Connect utility (located in the Applications folder). Internet Connect allows you to manually initiate a modem, AirPort, PPPoE, or VPN connection. It gets its default settings from Network System Preferences, but you can also manually enter ISP telephone numbers as well as your ISP account user name and password (assuming you've chosen not to have the latter remembered by the OS).

After you launch Internet Connect, select the pane for the connection type you want to use by clicking the desired icon in its toolbar. The options that appear in the toolbar are generally determined by which ports are active in Network System Preferences. The following sections cover the main options.

Summary

This pane summarizes the status of the different devices you can currently access from Internet Connect. For example, it will tell you whether you're connected to an AirPort network, as well as list the status of a modem and include a toggled Connect/Disconnect button for the modem or a VPN connection.

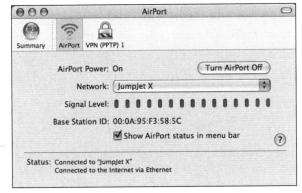

Figure 8.21

The Internet Connect utility: the AirPort display.

AirPort

If you have an AirPort card in your Mac and have set up AirPort in Network System Preferences, you can click the AirPort icon in Internet Connect's toolbar to switch to the AirPort pane.

The first option you're presented with is AirPort Power, which states whether AirPort is currently on or off. If it's on, you can click the Turn AirPort Off button to shut down your AirPort card; if it's off, you can click the Turn AirPort On button to turn it on. You can conserve a good deal of battery power on a laptop by turning your AirPort card off when you're not using it.

From the Network pop-up menu, you choose an AirPort network. If a network is within range and is not a closed network, its name should appear automatically. If you're in the vicinity of multiple networks, you can choose which one you want to join. If a network is not listed (that is, it's closed), choose Other and enter the appropriate network name and (if needed) password.

If a network is password-protected, you will be asked to enter the appropriate password when you attempt to join it. Before entering a password, you may need to select the correct type of password from the Wireless Security pop-up menu.

SEE: • "Take Note: Passwords and Joining a Wireless Network," later in this chapter, for more details.

This pane also shows (a) a meter indicating the signal level of the AirPort connection; (b) the ID of the Base Station to which you're currently connected; and (c) if your AirPort Base Station includes a dial-up modem, and, if you have set it up to connect to your ISP, a Connect button. (Note: To temporarily use a different number than the one set in the AirPort Admin Utility, hold down Option when clicking Connect.)

Create a computer-to-computer network. Also in the Network pop-up menu is an almost-hidden gem: Create Network. This option lets you create a direct, wireless, computer-to-computer network between two AirPort-equipped computers (that is, no Base Station required). To do so, follow these steps:

1. From the Network pop-up menu choose Create Network.

2. In the Name field, enter the name of your network. This is the name the other computer will display in its Network menu.

3. Choose the AirPort channel you want to use. You can generally stick with the default selection (Automatic), but if you have problems connecting due to interference, you can choose another channel. Choosing a different channel does not affect the ability of other computers to connect to your network.

4. If desired, click the Show Options button. This expands the dialog to display options for adding a password. If you want the network to be private, select "Enable encryption (using WEP)" and enter a password; you can also choose the type of WEP key.

    SEE: • "Take Note: Passwords and Joining a Wireless Network," later in this chapter, for information about WEP keys and passwords.

5. Click OK.

    The other computer can now use its own Internet Connect utility to connect to your newly created network.

Airport menu bar item. The AirPort pane of Internet Connect includes the same "Show AirPort status in menu bar" option as is available in Network System Preferences. This menu provides all of the same options as the AirPort pane of Internet Connect. You can use the menu bar menu as a shortcut to many of the options otherwise available via Internet Connect. It is the generally preferred way to join a network that you do not automatically join.

SEE: • "Take Note: The AirPort Menu and Joining an AirPort Network," below, for more details.

TAKE NOTE ▶ **The AirPort Menu and Joining an AirPort Network**

The AirPort menu (enabled via either the option in Network System Preferences or Internet Connect, as described in the main text) is a nearly essential menu if you use wireless networks. Its most common use is to let you join an AirPort network, either because you did not join one automatically or because you want to switch to a different one than you are currently using. The menu shows a list of all currently available open networks.

The AirPort menu's icon is also a convenient indicator of the current signal strength of your wireless connection, shown by the number of bars that are black (indicating increasing strength) instead of gray.

More specifically, the menu includes options to (a) turn AirPort on or off (turning AirPort off prevents AirPort connections, as well as conserves battery power on laptops, until you turn it back on); (b) join an existing AirPort network, either via a Base Station (or other wireless router) or via a computer-to-computer network—you either select one of the networks listed or choose Other to connect to a closed unlisted network; (c) create your own computer-to-computer network (via the Create Network command); (d) open Internet Connect; and (e) enable Use Interference Robustness. The latter two options are described more in the main text.

Sometimes, even if you expect to automatically join an AirPort network, the connection may not occur (such as when waking up from sleep). In such cases, the simplest work-around is to choose the network from this AirPort menu.

Note: Connecting to an AirPort network is a separate issue from connecting to the Internet. Thus, you may successfully connect to an AirPort network, but unless the network to which you're connecting is itself successfully connected to the Internet, you still won't be able to access Internet services such as e-mail or Web browsing.

Note: If you purchased an AirPort Extreme Base Station that contains a modem, and set up the Base Station to connect via that modem, you should see submenu off of the network name in the AirPort menu. This submenu includes options to connect to or disconnect from the Internet via the modem.

SEE: • **"Troubleshooting wireless connections," later in this chapter, for more on Use Interference Robustness and other options for improving the quality of an AirPort connection.**

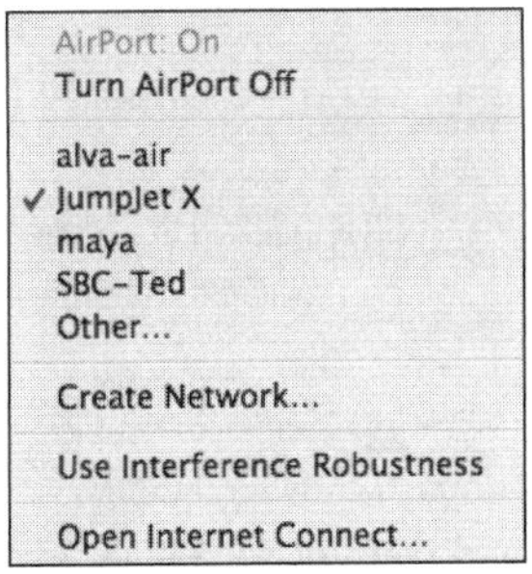

Figure 8.22

The AirPort menu in the menu bar.

```
AirPort: On
Turn AirPort Off

   alva-air
✓  JumpJet X
   maya
   SBC-Ted
   Other...

   Create Network...

   Use Interference Robustness

   Open Internet Connect...
```

TAKE NOTE ▶ Passwords and Joining a Wireless Network

A wireless network, AirPort or not, may require a password in order for you to join it. Here are some guidelines for entering a password correctly:

AirPort card to AirPort Base Station. For Mac users, this is the most common situation: You're connecting from a Mac with an AirPort card to an AirPort Base Station. A network password may have been set up in the Base Station via the AirPort Admin Utility, using either *wired equivalency privacy* (WEP) or (starting in Panther and with an AirPort Extreme Base Station) *Wi-Fi Protected Access* (WPA). WPA provides greater data protection than WEP.

If the Base Station has been set up to require a password, you will need to enter it when you first attempt to join the network (for example, from the AirPort menu or via Internet Connect, as described later in this chapter). Before typing the password in the Enter Password dialog that appears, you must first select the type of password from the Wireless Security pop-up menu.

Note: If you choose a listed network name, the Wireless Security menu will only list options relevant to that network (for example, WEP or WPA). If you choose Other, the pop-up menu in the resulting window will always show the full range of choices (for example, WEP and WPA).

For a WEP password, for example, you will have three options: WEP Password, WEP 40/128-bit hex, and WEP 40/128-bit ASCII. Your best bet in this case is usually WEP Password. You can take advantage of the latter options only if the password meets the 40- or 128-bit restriction in password length. Thus, a 40-bit password must be exactly 5 ASCII characters or 10 hexadecimal digits. For 128 bit, the password must be 13 ASCII characters or 26 hexadecimal digits. If the password, as entered in Admin Utility, is shorter or longer than this number of characters, you cannot use the ASCII option when attempting to connect. However, you can still use the hex option if you have the hexadecimal equivalent password (which you obtain by clicking the Password icon in the AirPort Admin Utility's toolbar). With the plain WEP Password, you just enter whatever ASCII text was entered in the Admin Utility—length does not matter.

continues on next page

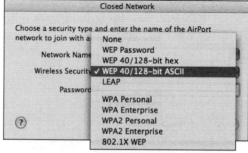

Figure 8.23

Left, *the Enter Password dialog for a network that uses WEP (be sure you select the correct option here or the password will not be accepted); right, the Enter Password dialog for a closed network (accessed via the Other command in the AirPort menu).*

TAKE NOTE ▶ Passwords and Joining a Wireless Network *continued*

For WPA Personal, on the other hand, you will be presented with only one choice: WPA Personal. Much simpler! However, WPA is available only with AirPort Extreme cards and Base Stations (and Mac OS X 10.3 Panther or later). You cannot join a WPA-protected network from a Mac with a non-Extreme AirPort card.

Note: ASCII characters are the plain text you're familiar with using in creating passwords and typing in general (that is, the full alphabet and the numerals 0 to 9). Hexadecimal characters are restricted to the following: abcdef0123456789.

Note: If in the Enter Password dialog you select the Add to Keychain option, you shouldn't get asked to enter the password again.

Mac with AirPort card to non-AirPort network. If you have an AirPort card installed in your Mac, you can use it to connect to almost any wireless network, not just ones that use an AirPort Base Station. (*AirPort* is simply Apple's name for the 802.11b wireless protocol; *AirPort Extreme* is similarly Apple's name for 802.11g.) It is becoming increasingly common to connect to publicly accessible "hot spots" in coffee shops and airports, for example. If you want to join a wireless network that does not use AirPort and requires a password, you can typically use the same method as just described: Select the type of password from the Wireless Security menu and enter the password.

Note: You may need to ask the network's administrator to find out what type of password is being used. The AirPort software does not automatically detect this when connecting to non-Apple wireless networks. For example, if the network uses a WEP password with encryption keys (such as optionally used by Linksys wireless routers), you will have to manually enter the active key. The Apple software does not automatically generate the correct key from the pass phrase.

Note: Prior to Panther, when entering passwords for third-party networks, you typically needed to employ some special tricks. In particular, you had to precede a hexadecimal password with a dollar sign ($)—referred to as the *Hex Escape*—and you had to enclose ASCII passwords in quotation marks (for example, *"password"*). Although you shouldn't need to employ such tricks in Panther or Tiger, if you're having trouble getting a password accepted, it may be worth a try.

Check out various Apple Knowledge Base documents (such as http://docs.info.apple.com/article.html?artnum=106424) and AirPort Help (on your Mac) for additional advice.

Non-AirPort computer to an AirPort Base Station. If you have an AirPort Base Station network that requires a password, a person using a computer with wireless software other than AirPort may not be able to use the password in its plain text version to access the network. Instead, that person may need to use an encrypted form of the password, especially if using WEP.

You can always obtain the form of the password needed for non-AirPort computers by clicking the Password icon in the toolbar of the AirPort Admin Utility.

SEE: • **"Take Note: Setting Up an AirPort Base Station and Network,"** earlier in this chapter, **for additional information on WEP and WPA.**

Built-in Ethernet (PPPoE)

If you have a DSL or cable-modem connection using PPPoE, and you have set up Network System Preferences for PPPoE, click the Built-in Ethernet icon in the Internet Connect toolbar. You can use the options that appear to manually connect and disconnect from the network.

Your PPPoE Service Provider and Account Name are entered automatically, using the values you supplied in Network System Preferences (as is your password, if you told Mac OS X to save it). If you didn't choose to save your password, you can enter it here each time you connect. Click the Connect button to connect.

The Status section typically provides your current IP address, the time you have been connected, and a graphical representation of data being sent and received over your connection.

PPPoE menu bar item. You can choose to show your PPPoE status in the menu bar. If you do so, a PPPoE menu item appears, from which you can select to connect or disconnect to your PPPoE connection.

Internal Modem

To connect via your Mac's internal modem, click the Internal Modem icon in the toolbar. Note: If you named your modem port configuration something different, that name will appear in the toolbar rather than *Internal Modem*.)

From the Configuration pop-up menu, you can select the dial-up settings you created in the PPP pane of the Internal Modem section of Network System Preferences. You can create still other dial-up settings by selecting the Other item in the menu and entering the telephone number, account name, and password in the fields below the menu (you will be prompted to name and save this configuration before closing Internet Connect). Each new configuration you create is added to the pop-up menu. This is a handy way to save different dial-up numbers; for example, my ISP offers local dial-up numbers for cities around the country.

Finally, if you choose Edit Configurations from the pop-up menu, a dialog opens in which you can (a) edit existing configurations (you even get a few options not available in the main Internet Connect window, such as selecting a specific modem script), and (b) add a new configuration or delete an existing one (via the Add [+] and Delete [–] buttons in the lower left).

Note: You cannot edit the configuration set up in Network System Preferences via Internet Connect; edit that one directly in Network preferences.

Note: The first time you choose Edit Configurations, if you have not already created additional configurations via the Other command, a default configuration called Modem Configuration is created.

Note: The password for the configuration set up in Network System Preferences will appear for this configuration only if you checked the "Save password" box in the Network System Preferences pane. Otherwise, you need to enter it manually each time you connect via Internet Connect.

Through all of these options, you can maintain a set of phone numbers to use for dial-up (which you may need if you travel and dial up using different local numbers in different locations). Simply choose the preferred configuration from the pop-up menu and then click Connect.

In the Status section at the bottom of the window, you can see your connection speed (or at least the speed you had when you first connected), the length of time you've been connected, your current IP address, and a graphical representation of data being sent and received. Note: If these graphs indicate no activity, you probably no longer have a connection, even if other settings indicate you are still connected.

Figure 8.24

The Internet Connect utility: the Internal Modem pane after a successful dial-up connection has been made.

Modem menu bar item. You have the same "Show modem status in the menu bar" option here as is available in the Network System Preferences pane. The menu bar icon is used to open a menu from which you can choose Connect (or Disconnect, if connected), which eliminates the need to open Internet Connect at all (assuming you intend to use its current default settings). You can also switch between modem configurations (including Internal Modem and Bluetooth) from the Modem Status menu.

The "Show time connected" and "Show status while connecting" options, located in the Modem Status menu (assuming that a phone number has been entered for the modem), can be enabled to provide feedback directly in the menu bar.

Bluetooth modem

If you have a Bluetooth-enabled mobile phone, and you've set up Network System Preferences to use it as a modem (as explained earlier in the chapter), you can connect to the Internet via this phone.

The settings in this pane are virtually identical to those just described for internal modems.

SEE: • "Bluetooth modem," earlier in this chapter, and "Using Bluetooth," later in this chapter, for more details on Bluetooth and its software.

VPN connections

A *virtual private network* (VPN) allows a remote user to connect to a private network (such as the internal network at a large company or even a small home-office network) via the Internet. It does this by creating a secure tunnel between the two: Data is encrypted as it travels through the tunnel so that anyone who might intercept it as it travels over the Internet will not be able to access it. A VPN thus ensures that all communication between the remote computer and the network remains private. The idea is to allow you to connect to your base network from a public environment without worrying that you are exposing yourself (or your network) to hackers trying to intercept your transmission.

To set up a VPN port and connect to a VPN:

1. Click the VPN icon in the toolbar or select New VPN Connection from Internet Connect's File menu. In the window that appears, you have two choices: L2TP over IPSec and PPTP. The one you select will depend on the network to which you're connecting; check with your network administrator for this information.

   Note: *PPTP* refers to Microsoft's popular Point-to-Point Tunneling Protocol. The IPSec protocol is common on many Unix systems. Some networks use proprietary Cisco VPNs. Cisco provides its own Mac OS X VPN client for use on these networks. Your system administrator should provide you with this client; use it instead of Internet Connect.

   After making your selection, click Continue. Internet Connect's VPN window will appear.

   A new port called VPN (PPTP) or VPN (L2TP) will be added to your Network Port Configurations in Network System Preferences (the System

Preferences icon in the Dock will likely start bouncing to indicate that this change has occurred, generating a message informing you of this). In most cases, you will not need to configure this port; you simply make sure it is enabled.

SEE: • "Technically Speaking: Lesser-Known Ports," earlier in this chapter.

2. Select the newly added VPN icon in Internet Connect's toolbar (if it's not already selected).

The options that appear are almost the same as those for the Internal Modem settings described above. The main difference is that there is a Server Address field instead of a Telephone Number field. In this field, enter the VPN server's IP address or domain.

Choose a configuration from the Configuration pop-up menu. If none is listed, you need to either (a) choose Edit Configurations from the Configure menu and fill out the fields as instructed by your network administrator; or (b) choose Import Configurations from Internet Connect's File menu and import the configuration file as supplied by your network administrator.

Note: Some VPN servers require that you enter your account name as *domain/username*, where *domain* is the network domain of the part of the remote network to which you are connecting.

3. Click Connect. After connecting via VPN, you should be able to browse Mac or Windows shares on the remote network as if your Mac were actually on the network.

Note: Some VPN servers do not allow connections from users behind Internet routers. If you're having problems connecting to a supported VPN from behind an Internet router, you have two choices: The first is to connect directly to the Internet when you need to connect to the VPN (in other words, disconnect the router temporarily and connect to the Internet directly from your Mac). The second is that some routers include their own PPTP clients—you can set up your router to connect to the VPN and then access the VPN through your router. Check with your Internet router's manual to see if it supports PPTP connections.

VPN menu bar item. Select "Show VPN status in menu bar" to add a VPN menu. It functions in a manner similar to how the modem menu functions for modems (as described above).

Additional toolbar icons

If you have an external USB modem attached to your Mac and set up in Network System Preferences, a separate icon for this modem should appear in the Internet Connect toolbar. Similarly, you can create more than one VPN-connection icon—for example, if you connect to multiple VPNs using different protocols (PPTP versus IPSec).

If your Mac is equipped with infrared technology, there will be an IrDA icon in the toolbar. Click it to connect to another IrDA device or computer.

Menu bar items

Most of Internet Connect's connection choices include the option "Show {*name of connection method*} status in the menu bar." These items are noted separately in the preceding sections for each choice. More information on these (and related) menu bar items is also located in other parts of this chapter (for example, "Setting Up Network System Preferences," earlier in this chapter, and "Bluetooth System Preferences," later in this chapter).

Figure 8.25

Left, *menu bar items for Modem;* right, *for Bluetooth. See Figure 8.22 for the AirPort menu.*

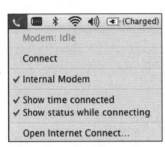

Internet Connect's menus

Internet Connect's menus offer a few useful options not accessible from its main window:

- **New VPN Connection (in the File menu).** As discussed in the previous section, you use this to create a new VPN-connection port.

- **New 802.1X Connection (in the File menu).** This protocol is designed to provide increased security for local networks. It can be used to connect to an existing Ethernet or AirPort network. When you select New 802.1X Connection, an 802.X icon is added to the toolbar. Select it to configure the connection and connect. Your network administrator should provide the data you need to fill in the configuration fields.

- **Import Configurations and Export Configurations (in the File menu).** Select these items to export a set of configurations as a separate file or to import a previously saved set. This could be useful, for example, for transferring a set of configurations from one computer to another. (Note: This menu item is available only when viewing a connection type that supports configurations—for example, VPN or modem.)

- **Connection Log (in the Window menu).** The Connection Log tracks the details of every modem or VPN connection you make. As such, it can be helpful in troubleshooting a problematic dial-up connection. You can view your Connection Log by choosing Connection Log in this menu.

- **Options (in the Connect menu).** This item, available for VPN connections, presents a dialog with several options: You can force the VPN connection to disconnect whenever you log out or switch to another account. You can also force all network/Internet traffic over the VPN (rather than attempting to send Internet traffic over your standard Internet connection, with only VPN-specific data going through the VPN). Finally, you can select verbose mode for the VPN connection log.

Using Bluetooth

Bluetooth is the odd name given to a multiplatform wireless technology that facilitates short-range, direct connections between a variety of digital devices, including mobile phones, mice, keyboards, other computers, personal digital assistants (PDAs), printers, scanners, and digital cameras.

Think of Bluetooth as the offspring of a union between infrared and AirPort wireless technology. With Bluetooth, as with AirPort, you can connect to any device within a given range (10 to 100 feet with Bluetooth, which is generally smaller than the 50-to-150-foot range for AirPort), and the connection is omnidirectional (that is, you don't have to point two devices directly at each other). However, unlike AirPort and more similarly to infrared, Bluetooth doesn't require you to set up a TCP/IP network to use it. Any two Bluetooth-compatible devices can almost instantly talk to each other.

I said above that Bluetooth is designed for *direct* connections. Unlike AirPort, which allows multiple devices to form a common wireless network, Bluetooth works by "pairing" devices: a computer and a printer, a cellular phone and a laptop, two computers. With Bluetooth software version 1.5 or later, you can even connect a Mac to Bluetooth headphones. Devices must be paired before they can communicate; but, once paired, they can remember each other indefinitely to facilitate easy connections in the future. (Note: In some cases, a device can be paired with more than one other device at a time.) Thus, if AirPort is the wireless equivalent of Ethernet (a full-featured networking protocol), then Bluetooth is the wireless equivalent of USB (intended for direct device-to-device "paired" connections).

All current Mac models either include a built-in Bluetooth hardware module or have it available as an option. For older Macs, you can add Bluetooth compatibility via a third-party Bluetooth adapter that attaches to any available USB port.

Note: For Macs without built-in Bluetooth, Apple's Bluetooth mouse and keyboard require a D-Link DBT-120 USB Bluetooth adapter (hardware version B2 or later). Older D-Link DWB-120M adapters are not supported. You can also use USB Bluetooth modules from other manufacturers.

Note: Bluetooth and AirPort both use the 2.4 GHz frequency band. In some Mac models with built-in Bluetooth, Bluetooth and AirPort also share the same antenna. Thus, they may interfere with each other's reception. If you're using either AirPort or Bluetooth but not both, turn off the one you are not using.

See the following Apple Web page for more background information on Bluetooth: www.apple.com/bluetooth.

Bluetooth System Preferences

Assuming that your Mac has Bluetooth hardware installed (built in or via an adapter), typically the first thing you need to do to connect to another Bluetooth device (or to allow a device to connect to your Mac) is open the Bluetooth System Preferences pane and configure it as desired. (This pane won't appear in System Preferences unless your Mac has the requisite Bluetooth hardware installed or connected.) The pane has three main tabs: Settings, Devices, and Sharing.

Settings. The Settings pane provides general Bluetooth preferences. Here are the options:

- **Turn Bluetooth On/Off.** Use this button to do what it says.

- **Discoverable.** If you check this box, the Mac broadcasts a signal over Bluetooth frequencies so that other Bluetooth devices within range can see it. If you don't enable the Discoverable option, other Bluetooth devices will be able to initiate a connection to your Mac only if they have previously been paired with it. Note that although you may want your Mac to be discoverable at a specific moment (to allow another device to connect to it), you do not have to keep it discoverable all the time. In fact, you can use the Bluetooth menu item (discussed below) to enable Discoverable mode, and then disable it immediately after the pairing is complete.

- **Open Bluetooth Setup Assistant at startup when no input device is present.** This feature is useful if you use a Bluetooth keyboard or mouse. If your Mac doesn't detect the presence of such devices at startup, it will automatically launch Bluetooth Setup Assistant and attempt to find your keyboard and/or mouse.

- **Allow Bluetooth devices to wake this computer.** This is useful if you are using a Bluetooth keyboard and/or mouse. It allows you to wake your Mac via a Bluetooth keyboard or mouse—something you wouldn't otherwise be able to do if your only keyboard and mouse are connected via Bluetooth!

- **Show Bluetooth status in the menu bar.** If you use Bluetooth devices, you will almost certainly find it convenient to enable this option. It creates a Bluetooth menu in the menu bar.

  From this Bluetooth menu, you can (a) turn Bluetooth on or off; (b) enable and disable Discoverable mode; (c) set up a Bluetooth Device (by launching Bluetooth Setup Assistant); (d) open the Bluetooth System Preferences pane; and (e) use the Send File and Browse Device items to access the Bluetooth File Exchange utility (this utility is described more in the next section). In addition, any Bluetooth keyboard or mouse paired with your Mac will appear in this menu; choosing one will open the Keyboard or Mouse pane of Keyboard & Mouse System Preferences, as applicable.

  Note: The icon for the Bluetooth menu will change depending on the current status of Bluetooth and Bluetooth connections. For example, if the icon is dimmed, it means that a Bluetooth adapter is connected but Bluetooth is turned off. If you turn Bluetooth on, the icon turns black. See the following Apple Knowledge Base article for details of other icon variations: http://docs.info.apple.com/article.html?artnum=107679.

Devices. This is the key pane where you pair Bluetooth devices so that they can work with each other. The Devices pane also lists all paired devices, including ones that are currently connected to your Mac.

Click the "Set up new device" button to initiate a new connection with a device (or to reestablish one that you deleted). This launches Bluetooth Setup Assistant, from which you can search for discoverable devices that are within range and pair with them. Once paired, the device is added to the list on the left side of the Devices pane. You should now be able to use and contact the Bluetooth-connected device.

To "unpair" a device, select it in the list and click the Delete button.

When a device is selected, you can click the Add to Favorites button to add that device to your Favorites list. Making a device a favorite means that if you temporarily lose your connection to the device (for example, due to low battery power or moving the device out of range), the Mac will automatically seek to connect to it again when it becomes available (for example, when the batteries are replaced or the device is moved back in range). For such items, the Add to Favorites button will toggle to Remove from Favorites.

Items that are favorites have a heart icon next to their name. If a key icon appears next to a device name, this means that data will be encrypted when transferred to and from that device.

Sharing. A default list of names appears in the Service Name column. To the left of each name are two check boxes—one for turning the service on and off, and the other for determining if "require pairing for security" is enabled (meaning that a password will be needed to use the service). Clicking a service name reveals its options on the right side of the window. Among other things, you can duplicate the effects of the check boxes from the choices available here. The buttons to Add and Remove (virtual) Serial Port Service are rarely used, and I will skip over them here.

Here are the three main service names:

- **Bluetooth File Transfer.** Click the Start button here to allow other users to browse files on your computer (for example, via the Browse Device command in the Bluetooth menu, allowing files to be downloaded or uploaded via the Bluetooth File Exchange utility). The default selected folder available for others to browse is the Public folder in your home directory. Note: Prior to Security Update 2005-005, the default folder was the Shared folder in the /Users directory. In either case, you can change the designated folder via the pop-up menu.

- **Bluetooth File Exchange.** This section is where you decide how files sent to your Mac from other Bluetooth devices (for example, via the Send File command in the Bluetooth menu, which opens the Bluetooth File Exchange utility) are treated. This type of file transfer is different from uploading files via Bluetooth File Transfer, which allows a Bluetooth device to browse a folder on your computer and search for available files; Bluetooth File Exchange simply sends an individual file to your Mac, and it is then accepted according to your preferences. Here are those options:

  "When receiving items." This pop-up menu lets you decide whether you want to automatically accept items sent to your Mac, automatically refuse all items, or be prompted to accept or refuse each item.

  "When PIM items are accepted" and *"When other items are accepted."* Once an item is accepted, the settings available from these two pop-up menus determine what happens to it: You can choose to have items automatically saved to your hard drive or automatically opened with the appropriate helper application, or you can be asked for each item. Note: *PIM* stands for *personal information manager* (such as Address Book or iCal).

  "Folder for accepted items." Items that are saved to the hard drive are automatically saved to the directory you choose via this menu.

- **Bluetooth-PDA-Sync.** This port should be on if you intend to sync a Bluetooth cell phone or PDA with your Mac.

  If you enable the Show in Network Preferences option, Bluetooth-PDA-Sync will appear as a Network Port Configuration. You can then customize settings to allow a connection to the Internet via Bluetooth. This essentially does the same thing as if you had set up a Bluetooth port directly in Network System Preferences.

SEE: • "Take Note: Problems Pairing Bluetooth Devices," later in this chapter, for related information.
    • "Bluetooth Setup Assistant," later in this chapter, for more on this utility.

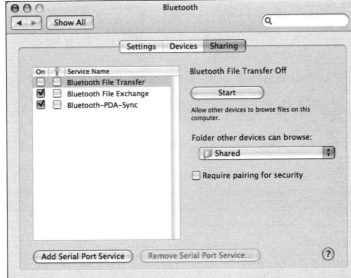

Figure 8.26

The Sharing pane of the Bluetooth System Preferences pane. See Figure 8.18 for views of the other panes.

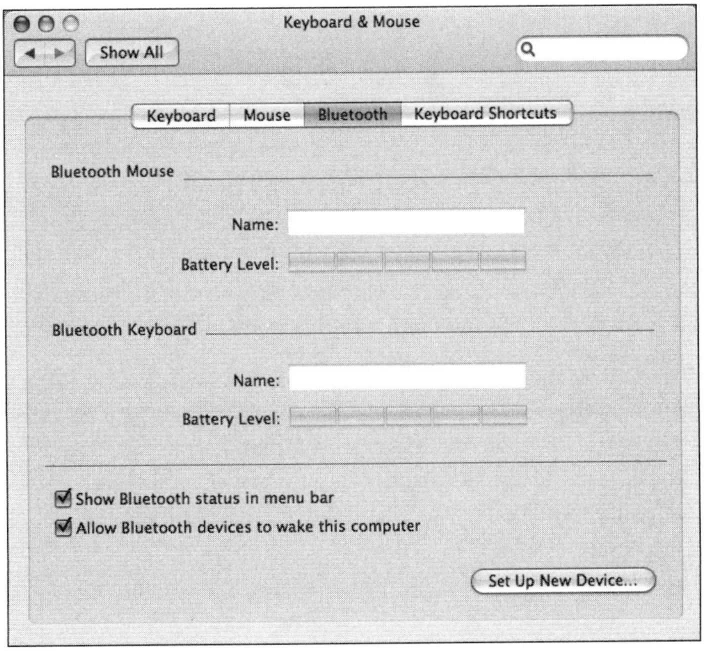

Figure 8.27

The Bluetooth pane of the Keyboard & Mouse System Preferences pane.

TAKE NOTE ▶ **Setting Up and Using a Bluetooth Mouse and/or Keyboard**

Apple sells a Bluetooth wireless keyboard and mouse, as do a number of third-party vendors. For connecting (pairing) these two pieces of hardware to a Mac, Mac OS X offers an alternative procedure in addition to the Bluetooth options described in the main text. Follow these steps:

1. Select the Keyboard & Mouse System Preferences pane (not Bluetooth!).
2. In this pane, select the Bluetooth tab.
3. In the Bluetooth pane, click the Set Up New Device button. This launches Bluetooth Setup Assistant. Click the Continue button, and select Mouse or Keyboard from the next pane (as appropriate). The assistant should now guide you through the process of finding and pairing the device with your Mac.
4. When you're finished, the device's name will appear in the Bluetooth pane of the Keyboard & Mouse System Preferences pane. In addition, if you're using an Apple-branded Bluetooth keyboard or mouse, the battery level of the device will be indicated (to help you know when it's time to replace the batteries).

If you enabled the Bluetooth menu bar menu, the device name will also be listed there; select the name to return to the Keyboard & Mouse System Preferences pane.

The following are some tips for using a Bluetooth mouse and/or keyboard.

Battery issues. Bluetooth mice and keyboards run on battery power. Apple's Bluetooth mouse, for example, runs on two AA batteries. The mouse also has a slide switch to turn the mouse power off; this conserves battery power but breaks the connection of the mouse to the Mac. Turning the mouse back on automatically reestablishes the connection (assuming it is a favorite). Some devices may also have their own power-saving modes that kick in when they're idle for a period.

Discoverable issues. A Bluetooth mouse or keyboard can be paired with only one Mac at a time. This makes sense, since it's unlikely that you'd want to move the pointer on two Macs at the same time. However, this means that if you want to transfer the use of a Bluetooth mouse from your desktop Mac to your laptop, for example, you must first delete the pairing to your desktop Mac (via the Bluetooth System Preferences pane's Delete button in the Devices pane) and then pair the mouse with the laptop.

Pairing and connect issues. To re-pair an unpaired Bluetooth mouse or keyboard, you may temporarily need to use a wired mouse and/or keyboard (to open the needed software and click the relevant buttons and so on). Thus, you should retain your wired devices even if you shift to using a Bluetooth device all the time.

continues on next page

TAKE NOTE ▶ **Setting Up and Using a Bluetooth Mouse and/or Keyboard** *continued*

Startup issues. As described primarily in Chapter 5, your Mac (and Mac OS X) supports numerous special startup modes that require holding down keys at startup (for example, holding down the Shift key at startup to perform a safe boot). A potential problem here is that these startup modes cannot be initiated via keyboard commands from a Bluetooth keyboard if the Bluetooth connection to the keyboard is not established until after the time to enter the keyboard commands at startup has passed. Apple has solved most problems here via updates to the Bluetooth firmware (especially version 1.0.2 and later).

Note: Macs released in 2004 or later should have the needed firmware already installed; for older Macs, or to get any firmware update newer than what you have installed, download the relevant Bluetooth Firmware Updater from Apple's Web site. To find out the version of Bluetooth that is installed, as well as other tech specs on Bluetooth, launch System Profiler and select Hardware > Bluetooth. The first line of the output is the firmware version number.

Once you've installed this firmware update, most startup functions are supported with Bluetooth devices. For example, holding down the mouse button at startup ejects a CD from the internal drive. And from the keyboard, Command-Shift (for safe boot), Command-S (for single-user mode), C (to start up from a CD), Option (to access the Startup Manager screen), T (for Target Disk Mode), and Command-Option-O-F (to access the Open Firmware screen) all work.

In some cases, however, your success with these startup modes may be short-lived. For example, prior to Mac OS X 10.4.3, after you start up in single-user mode or via a safe boot, the Bluetooth keyboard and mouse would not function. Similarly, after you start up from a bootable disc, a Bluetooth mouse or keyboard may not function—because the pairing information (set in Bluetooth System Preferences) is not present on the CD. The solution, in such cases, is to switch to a wired keyboard and mouse.

With the latest versions of Mac OS X, however, a screen may appear at startup indicating a problem with a Bluetooth-device connection and how to fix it (for example, install fresh batteries).

TAKE NOTE ▶ **Problems Pairing Bluetooth Devices**

The following describes a few common problems with pairing devices—as performed via Bluetooth Setup Assistant or Bluetooth File Exchange—and their solutions:

- **Device not found.** If a search does not list a device you expected to find, make sure that the device is on, Bluetooth is enabled, and the device is discoverable. Thus, for connecting to another Mac via Bluetooth, go to the Bluetooth System Preferences pane of the other Mac and check the just-cited settings.

continues on next page

TAKE NOTE ▶ Problems Pairing Bluetooth Devices *continued*

- **Passkey problem.** When you attempt to pair with certain devices, such as another Mac, you may be prompted to enter a passkey. For two Macs, this can be almost any short string of letters and numbers. The important thing is that after entering it, you will be prompted to enter the same passkey on the other device. This is a security protection against unwanted pairings. If the passkey is not entered on the second device, the pairing will fail.

  These passkeys will be requested if you have selected "Require pairing for security" in Bluetooth's Sharing pane.

- **Validation fails.** Your Mac may successfully locate a device for pairing but then claim that validation failed after you click the Pair button. If this happens, check all of your Bluetooth-related settings on both devices to make sure that everything is as it should be. Try again. If that fails, restart your Mac and try yet again. On one mysterious occasion, I couldn't make this error go away regardless of the changes I made. Later that day, I tried again, and it worked immediately. Go figure.

- **Device does not have the necessary services.** If this message appears in the Bluetooth File Exchange utility, it generally means that the necessary Sharing service (as described in the main text) has not been enabled. You need to go to the other computer and turn on the service to prevent the error.

There is a good deal of redundancy built into the various Bluetooth connection methods. That is, there are multiple paths to the same goal. For example, I could connect my two Macs via Bluetooth Setup Assistant, as described in the main text. If I had previously done this, I would not need to enter a passkey when selecting Browse Device, because a passkey would already have been entered. On the other hand, I could select Browse Device without first using Bluetooth Setup Assistant. In this case, the Mac to be browsed would likely require a passkey and the browsing computer would then have to enter the same key before browsing was permitted. Obviously, the two users have to be in some sort of communication for this to occur (so that one user can tell the other what the passkey is).

To be frank, Apple needs to do some work on the Bluetooth interface. It is simply too confusing and inconsistent. For example, sometimes the Passkey Options button appears in Bluetooth Setup Assistant and sometimes not, for reasons I could not determine. Similarly, I have had a request to give a passkey even when the option to require one has been turned off in the Sharing pane of Bluetooth System Preferences. Also, you can pair to a device even if all of its Sharing services are turned off; but when you try to connect to the device via Bluetooth, you will get an ambiguous error message about not having the "necessary services" (as just described). Plus, there are many different paths to the same end point (via Bluetooth Setup Assistant, Bluetooth File Exchange, Bluetooth menu, and so on), and it is not always clear that the options overlap.

The good news is that if you simply try to do what you want to do and follow the prompts, it will generally work. Whatever route you try, Mac OS X attempts to find a path that leads to success!

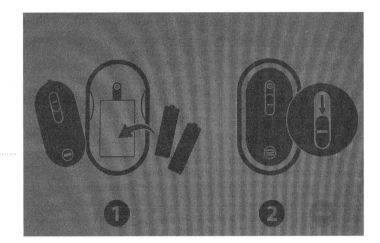

Figure 8.28

The screen that may appear at startup if your Bluetooth mouse needs fresh batteries.

Bluetooth utilities

In the Utilities folder, you should find three Bluetooth utilities: Bluetooth Setup Assistant, Bluetooth File Exchange, and Bluetooth Serial Utility.

Bluetooth Setup Assistant. This utility, which I've already mentioned several times in this chapter, walks you through the steps entailed in setting up new Bluetooth devices for use with your Mac. You can launch it in several ways: by clicking the Set Up New Device button in the Devices pane of the Bluetooth System Preferences pane, by clicking Set Up New Device in the Bluetooth pane of the Keyboard & Mouse System Preferences pane, or by choosing Set Up Bluetooth Device from the Bluetooth menu bar menu.

Once Setup Assistant has launched and you've selected Continue to move past the first pane, you will be asked to select which type of device you're setting up (Mouse, Keyboard, Mobile Phone, Printer, Headset, or Other Device). Then click the Continue button to move to the next pane.

From here, the assistant then searches for and lists discoverable Bluetooth devices (of the type you selected) that are in range. You select the device from the list and click Continue again; a connection is initiated.

For some devices, particularly if you select Other Device, there will be a Passkey Options button at the bottom of the pane. If you click it, a dialog drops down, in which you can select the type of passkey security you wish to use. In general, select the option that matches what is required for the device to which you are connecting (as stated in the device's documentation). Otherwise, select whatever type of security you prefer, and see if it works. In other cases, you will simply get a dialog in which to enter a self-selected passkey (no Passkey Options button appears), as described more in "Take Note: Problems Pairing Bluetooth Devices," elsewhere in this chapter.

As one example, I tried connecting my desktop Power Mac to my PowerBook via Bluetooth, using "Automatically generate a passkey option" from Passkey Options. After I clicked Continue, a numeric passkey appeared on my Power Mac. At the same time, a Pairing Request dialog appeared on my PowerBook. I filled in the Passkey field with the number that was displayed on my Power Mac and clicked the Pair button, and a successful pairing occurred. At this point, I could use the Send File and Browse Device commands in the Bluetooth menu to send and receive files from the other computer.

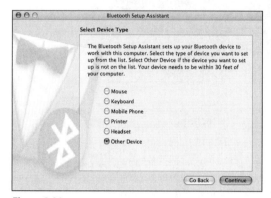 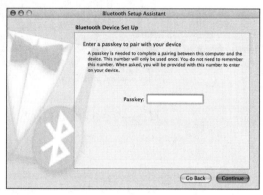

Figure 8.29

Bluetooth Setup Assistant: left, the Select Device Type pane; right, the passkey pane.

Figure 8.30

Bluetooth File Exchange: the Browse Files window.

Bluetooth File Exchange. This utility provides a way to exchange files with users of other Bluetooth-equipped Macs. You can launch it manually, or by selecting either Send File or Browse Device from the Bluetooth menu. If you launch it manually, these same two commands are accessible from Bluetooth File Exchange's File menu.

- **Send File.** If you choose Send File, you will be asked to select a file from your mounted volumes (via a standard file dialog) to send to the connected Bluetooth device.

  After you've selected to send a file, you will be prompted to select a Bluetooth device to which the file should be sent.

  After selecting a device, click Send to send the file. A dialog will display the status of the sent file. The way in which the transfer is initiated will depend on how the receiving device is configured to receive files. For example, if the receiving device is another Mac, those settings are configured in the Sharing pane of the Bluetooth System Preferences pane—these options are covered earlier in this chapter. If "Prompt for each file" is set for the other Mac, the recipient user will get a dialog in which he or she must either accept or decline your transfer request. If accepted, the file will be placed in the folder designated to receive accepted items.

  Note: The Send File option is opened by default when you launch Bluetooth File Exchange. You can change this behavior via File Exchange's Preferences settings.

  Note: You can drag a file onto the Bluetooth File Exchange icon in the Finder or the Dock to send the file; you'll be asked immediately to select a device as the recipient.

  Note: The Select Bluetooth Device pane lets you view devices by Device Type (Phones, PDAs, Computers, and so on) or by Device Category (Discovered, Favorites, Recent), which can be useful if you've set up a number of Bluetooth devices and want to restrict your search.

- **Browse Device.** If you choose Browse Device, you again get the Select Bluetooth Device pane, used to select a Bluetooth device. After you select a device from the list and click the Select button, a window appears that displays a list of the contents of whatever directory is available for Bluetooth browsing on the other device. For example, if the other device is another Mac, you'll be able to browse the folder that was selected in the Sharing pane of the Bluetooth System Preferences pane on that Mac (as described earlier in this chapter). The Public folder is the default selection.

  You can now get a file from this folder or send a file to this folder via the Get and Send buttons at the bottom of the window. Selecting a file in the browser and clicking the Get button brings up a dialog that lets you save that file to any location on your own computer. Clicking the Send button lets you choose a file from your own computer to be saved to the currently selected folder on the Bluetooth device.

  There are four additional buttons to the left of the Get and Send buttons: The back arrow takes you to the previous folder (assuming you've navigated to another folder); the home icon button switches from the current directory to the default folder (assuming you've navigated to another subfolder from the list above); the folder icon button lets you create a new folder in the current directory; the Trash icon button allows you to delete an item. If a button is dimmed, it means you do not have the authority to perform the operation.

Bluetooth Serial Utility. This utility is used to add emulated (virtual) serial ports to your Mac. You would use this functionality to enable connections with devices such as Bluetooth-equipped personal digital assistants (such as a Palm handheld organizer). A device called Bluetooth-PDA-Sync should be present by default.

Note: This overlaps with the Bluetooth-PDA-Sync option available by default in the Sharing pane of Bluetooth System Preferences.

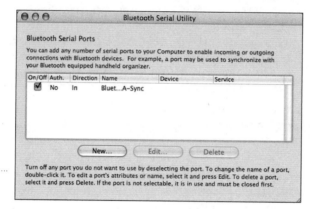

Figure 8.31

Bluetooth Serial Utility.

The utility's main options include the following:

- **New.** To add a Bluetooth serial port, click the New button. In the dialog that drops down, provide a name for the port (for example, *Palm Tungsten* if you're going to be connecting to a Palm Tungsten PDA). You have the option to select Incoming or Outgoing as the Port Direction. However, it's easier to instead click the Select Device button and then choose the actual Bluetooth device; this automatically selects the right setting for you.

  Note: After you click Select Device, a window appears; click the desired device in the list. At this point, you may be given a list of services for that device (to the right of the device-name list). If so, select the service that most closely resembles the one for which you intend to use the device (for example, Fax for a Bluetooth-enabled mobile phone that you intend to use as a fax line).

  In the New dialog, you can also select Require Authentication and Require Encryption, as well as choose to have the device show in Network preferences. Finally, choose the port type. If you'll be using this new port with other software or hardware (such as a PDA), be sure to read the documentation to see which options you should choose.

  Finally, click OK to add the new port.

- **On/Off.** You can temporarily disable a port by unchecking the On/Off box next to its name.

- **Edit and Delete.** To edit or delete a serial port, select the port in the list and then click the Edit or Delete button, respectively. Unfortunately, the Edit dialog doesn't provide you with all of the same options you had when you first added a serial port. Specifically, you cannot change the incoming/outgoing status of a port, nor can you switch between different services for a device (the additional options that appear when first selecting a device, described above). If you need to change one of these settings, you'll need to delete the port and re-create it.

Note: If you delete a device that was added to the Network System Preferences list, you will also need to separately delete it from the Network pane of System Preferences.

TAKE NOTE ▶ Bonjour

Bonjour is Apple's new name for what was called Rendezvous in Panther.

What is it? Bonjour is a new industry standard for automatic discovery (zero configuration) of computers, devices, and other services on *local* IP networks. With Bonjour, you can browse a network, find other Bonjour-enabled devices, and connect to those devices without having to fiddle with TCP/IP settings. I emphasize *local* because Bonjour's magic is limited to devices on the same subnet of your local network.

Bonjour is actually used in a number of places in Mac OS X. Printer Sharing, discussed in detail in Chapter 7, uses Bonjour to make shared printers available to other Mac OS X computers on the local network. Even Personal File Sharing, discussed in Chapter 9, supports Bonjour: If you have Personal File Sharing enabled, other Mac OS X Macs will be able to connect to your computer without needing to worry about your IP address. You can also use Bonjour in iChat to connect to other users on your local network (as an alternative to the Buddy List method). Selecting Log Into Bonjour from the iChat menu makes you available to chat with other local users and displays other users in your iChat Bonjour window.

Bonjour is also used in iTunes: If in the Sharing pane of iTunes' Preferences you select "Share my music," any Bonjour-capable computers on your local network will automatically discover your iTunes music when they launch iTunes. Your music files will be listed in their iTunes Source list, under the name you provided in your iTunes Preferences. No special network configuration settings or IP addresses need be entered for this to work.

Finally, Bonjour is also supported in many newer printers, allowing them to be discovered on a network without users' having to enter any configuration settings. When you open Printer Setup Utility and click Add, these printers automatically show up in the Default Browser pane of the Printer Browser window. Select a printer and click the Add button, and you're ready to print.

The beauty of Bonjour is that it requires very little setup, and it works over your existing network (AirPort, Ethernet, FireWire, and so on). The only prerequisite is that a network port configuration be active in the Network System Preferences pane for the type of network (Ethernet, for example) to which you're connected and intend to use for Bonjour. You don't even need to fill in any of the settings for that port if all you're doing is using Bonjour! To enable Bonjour for sharing services, for example, simply open the Sharing System Preferences pane and enable the desired Sharing service(s).

continues on next page

TAKE NOTE ▶ Bonjour *continued*

How does it work? When your Mac connects to a network, Mac OS X selects an IP address from a specific subset of available addresses that have been set aside for Bonjour/zeroconf networking. (This IP address is *separate* from any IP address you may have already given your Mac, or that has been given to your Mac by your ISP for Internet access. It is also a local-only address, meaning that it cannot be used to connect to your computer from outside of your own subnet on your local network.) After choosing this local IP address, your Mac uses the Address Resolution Protocol (ARP) to query the rest of the subnet and see if any other device is already using that IP address. If not, Mac OS X claims that address as its own. If the address is already taken, another address is chosen, and then another query is sent out, and so on, until an unused address is found.

Once your Mac has claimed one of these local IP addresses, it uses a technology called *Multicast DNS* (a variant of the DNS protocol used on the Internet at large) to equate that IP address with its own Bonjour (.local) name. However, instead of connecting to an actual DNS server to resolve a Bonjour name into an actual IP address, each Mac knows its own Bonjour name and responds to requests directly via IP multicast (basically a kind of "broadcast" over the entire local network).

If you look at the Sharing pane of System Preferences, beneath the Computer Name field you will see the following sentence: "Other computers on your local subnet can access your computer at *ComputerName*.local." You can modify the name by clicking the Edit button. Technically, this local hostname name is not the same thing as the Bonjour name. Instead, it is a DNS name (which is why the name cannot contain spaces, as DNS naming conventions do not allow it). However, at a practical level, it is useful to think of it as the Bonjour name, and I will often refer to it that way in the discussions that follow.

A local hostname is needed because the DNS protocol requires that domain names include an identifiable top-level domain, such as .com, .net, or .edu. The .local domain has been assigned to Bonjour, so all local Bonjour-enabled devices will have domain names that take the following form: *BonjourName*.local. Services provided by that device will have an address of *Service@BonjourName*.local. For example, when you connect to a printer that is being shared by another Mac, if you use Printer Setup Utility to get information about the printer, you'll see that the Host name of a shared printer is *OtherComputerName*.local. If you select Show Info for this printer, you will see that its Queue Name is listed as *PrinterName@OtherComputerName*.local. In another example, if you have Personal Web Sharing enabled, other local users will be able to connect to your Mac's built-in Web server by pointing their Web browsers to http://*BonjourName*.local.

Because all Bonjour-enabled devices will end in .local, if you enter .local in the Search Domains field in the TCP/IP pane of the Network System Preferences pane (for the port configuration used for your local network, of course), you can then avoid having to type .local as part of a server name. This would apply, for example, when connecting to a Bonjour-enabled Web server or file server.

SEE: • **Chapter 11, for more on iChat and iTunes.**

• **Chapter 7, for more on Printer Sharing.**

Using a Router

Earlier in this chapter I talked briefly about *routers*—devices that connect multiple network devices together. As home networks proliferate, routers have become increasingly common. Many users, otherwise unfamiliar with the details of networking, purchase routers to manage their local networks and share Internet connections.

Internet routers—the most common router type (and the only one I cover here)—typically (a) allow you to interconnect multiple local devices on a common network; (b) allow you to connect to the Internet (via a broadband device such as a cable or DSL modem connected to the router); (c) provide firewall protection (preventing unauthorized access to your computer from outside the network); and (d) allow you to share a single Internet connection between multiple computers.

Some routers require Ethernet cables for all connected devices, whereas others support both wired and wireless connections (an AirPort Base Station is actually a router in this sense).

I covered issues specific to wireless routers in the section on AirPort, earlier in this chapter. Here I cover general router issues, especially those relevant to wired routers. It is beyond the scope of this book to provide extended coverage of router and networking issues, which could easily fill a book of their own. Instead, I focus on issues relevant to Mac OS X troubleshooting.

Connecting to the Internet via a router

Most Internet routers are broadband-based devices, meaning they're designed to work with cable or DSL Internet connections. Linksys (www.linksys.com), for example, makes routers that are quite popular for use with Macs. Instead of hooking up your DSL or cable modem to your computer, you hook it up to a special WAN port on the router. Then you connect multiple computers to the additional Ethernet ports on the router. In the case of wireless routers (including Apple's AirPort Base Station), additional devices may be hooked up via a wireless connection (see "Take Note: Setting Up an AirPort Base Station and Network," earlier in this chapter). Then the Internet router directs Internet traffic between your ISP and each computer on the network, typically using Network Address Translation (NAT) to share one address among multiple machines. All of your computers get Internet access, but it appears to the outside world that only a single computer is accessing the Internet.

Some Internet routers may also include dial-up modems; Apple's AirPort Base Station is one. These routers are useful to people who have only modem-based (dial-up) Internet access. Internet routers using a modem work the same way as those using a broadband connection, except that when someone on the network tries to access the Internet, the router dials up the ISP just as you would when you use a modem on your own computer. When the router connects to a dial-up ISP, everyone on the network can access the Internet (although at much slower speeds, because multiple users are sharing a single modem line).

Note: Although almost any router will work with a Mac, some routers are not entirely Mac-compliant. In particular, some will not work with devices connected via AppleTalk and/or Bonjour. Check with the vendor before purchasing a router if this is of concern to you.

TAKE NOTE ▶ Software Routers: Software AirPort Base Station and More

In addition to the hardware-based Internet routers described in the main text, several software-based Internet routers are also available. This type of software is installed on the computer that is connected directly to the Internet, and you then connect other computers to the base computer via an Ethernet hub or switch or an AirPort/wireless connection. The base computer routes Internet traffic to and from the client computers so that all of the computers on the network have Internet access.

Mac OS X includes a software Internet router, called Internet Sharing, which you can access via the Internet pane of the Sharing pane of System Preferences. You can set up Internet Sharing with almost any type of network.

Software routers are commonly used to allow multiple devices with AirPort cards to connect to the Internet via the base computer without a hardware Base Station. The advantage of this capability—called a Software Base Station in Mac OS 9 but now simply a feature of Internet Sharing—is that you eliminate the expense of a separate hardware device. (That is, you need purchase only an AirPort card for each connected device.) The main disadvantage is that the computer sharing its Internet connection must always be up and running, and connected to the Internet, for the AirPort network to be active. Internet Sharing also uses the sharing computer's CPU, possibly reducing performance of other processes on the computer.

Sustainable Softworks' IPNetRouter (www.sustworks.com) is a third-party example of a software Internet router, which could be used instead of Mac OS X's built-in Internet Sharing feature.

SEE: • "Take Note: Setting Up an AirPort Base Station and Network," earlier in this chapter, for more on using AirPort.

• "Take Note: Setting Up and Using Internet Sharing and File Sharing," in Chapter 9, for more on Software Base Station setups.

Network Address Translation

When you have a dial-up or broadband connection, you generally have only a single IP address assigned to your household or connection. If you were connecting a single computer to the Internet, that IP address would be assigned to that computer. However, many Internet routers allow you to share a single IP address among multiple computers, using a feature called Network Address Translation (NAT). An Internet router using NAT masquerades as that single IP address and then manages all traffic between the various computers on your network and the Internet. It does this by assigning each computer on the network an *internal* IP address (such as 192.168.1.x or 10.0.1.x) and then translating that address to the single IP address that is supposed to represent your Internet connection. For example, when you request a Web site, your coworker or family member checks an e-mail account, and the computer down the hall requests a file to download, the router uses Network Address Translation to keep track of which computer requested what, and then to send these requests out to the Internet. Conversely, when the Web page, the e-mail, and the file are sent back to your IP address, the router knows which computers on your network to send them to.

As explained earlier in the chapter, Mac OS X's Internet Sharing feature is simply a software implementation of an Internet router. Therefore, it uses Network Address Translation to share your Internet connection, just like a hardware router.

SEE: • "Internet" in "Setting Up System Preferences: Sharing," in Chapter 9, for more details.
       • "Network Security," in Chapter 9, for more information on NAT.

Configuring a router

The following provides a brief overview of what to expect when you set up a router. For more details, see the instructions that came with your router.

Routers include built-in settings that you access via either a special utility designed to work with the router or a Web-based interface (also built into the router) that you access from your Mac's Web browser.

For example, to access most Linksys routers, which use a Web-based interface, you would type `http://192.168.1.1` in any Web browser. This brings up a dialog asking for the router's administrative password (if this is the first time you're accessing it, the router expects a default password; you need to check the router's documentation to get it). After entering the correct password, you get a Web page that provides access to all of the router's settings.

What settings do you enter here? For starters, you will want to provide the information necessary for making a WAN connection to the Internet; in other words, how to connect to your ISP. This includes telling the router whether you're using a static IP address (and if so, what it is), a DHCP dynamically generated IP address, or a PPPoE address (which requires entering a name and password). Your ISP should tell you which option to choose and what data (if any) to enter.

You will also instruct the router whether and how you want IP addresses to be distributed to other computers on your local network (in other words, if you want to manually assign IP addresses to each computer (via each computer's TCP/IP System Preferences settings), or if you want the router to automatically assign IP addresses). Typically, you will have the router assign IP addresses to computers dynamically, via DHCP. To use DHCP with a Linksys router, you would click the DHCP link in the router's browser display and select the DHCP server. Otherwise, you can leave DHCP disabled and have each computer use a local IP address (such as 192.168.1.101, 192.168.1.102, and so on), entered for each client computer via its TCP/IP settings. (Note: If these settings sound similar to those discussed earlier in the chapter when I talked about setting up an AirPort Extreme Base Station, they should—the Base Station is simply a wireless Internet router.)

If you connect to the Internet via a dynamic IP address (such as via a cable modem using DHCP), the router settings are also where you go to determine your current IP address. For example, with a non-wireless Linksys router for which "Obtain an IP automatically" has been selected on the Setup page, click the Status link to view your WAN IP address and DNS Server addresses. On the Status page, you can also renew or release your DHCP IP address. With an AirPort Base Station, this same information is accessed via the Internet pane of AirPort Admin Utility.

Finally, the Linksys router interface allows you to perform more advanced actions, such as port forwarding and mapping, enabling a DMZ host, and MAC address cloning. Note: Linksys continues to update its software; the software on your router may be a newer version than what is covered here.

SEE: • "Take Note: What Are the TCP/IP Settings?" and "Take Note: Ethernet Hubs, Switches, Routers, and Cables," earlier in this chapter, for related information.

• "Internet routers and port mapping," below, for information on port mapping.

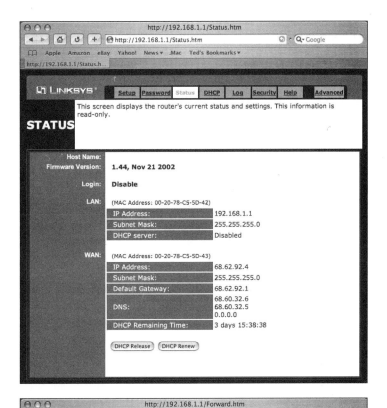

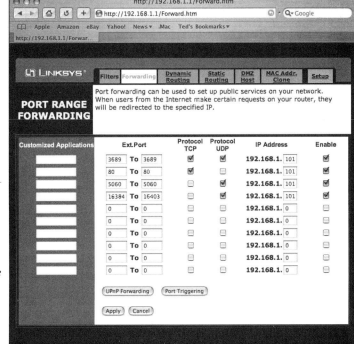

Figure 8.32

Two pages from a Linksys router's software: top, the status page, showing the current LAN and WAN settings; bottom, the port forwarding page, showing various ports opened for the Mac with an IP address of 192.168.1.101.

TECHNICALLY SPEAKING ▶ Upgrading the Firmware on a Linksys Router

Your router's vendor may occasionally release firmware upgrades, usually available from the Web. These upgrades add features and bug fixes to the existing firmware. Unfortunately, not all vendors provide a Mac interface for performing these firmware upgrades. For example, Linksys router upgrades use the TFTP (Trivial FTP) protocol. In Mac OS 9, the main way to install these upgrades was typically via a third-party TFTP utility. In Mac OS X, however, you have a built-in alternative: the tftp command, included as part of Mac OS X's Unix software and accessible via Terminal.

To update the firmware of a Linksys router, follow these steps:

1. Go to the router's Web interface (that is, 192.168.1.1). On the Password page, remove the router password. Apply the change.

2. In Terminal, use the cd command to go to the directory where the firmware upgrade file is located. You're looking for a file called code.bin.

3. Type tftp and press Return. This should change the prompt to tftp>.

4. At the prompt, type the following four lines, pressing Return after each:

```
connect 192.168.1.1
binary
put code.bin
quit
```

5. Quit Terminal, return to the router's Web interface, and restore your password.

Your firmware has now been updated. The firmware version on the status page should indicate the new version number.

Note: Recent versions of the Linksys firmware include an Upgrade Firmware option, available on the Help page of the Web interface. If this works (and I have found that it sometimes does not), you can use it instead of the above method.

After upgrading the router's firmware via the tftp command, you may find that many of your settings have been reset to default values. Confirm that all of your settings are correct before continuing.

Internet routers and port mapping

Using a router to allow multiple computers to share an Internet connection generally works very well. However, if you plan to enable any type of file sharing and want to share files with users who are not on your local network (for example, users connecting from elsewhere on the Internet), an Internet router complicates things a bit. The problem is that whereas your Internet router knows where to send incoming Internet data that has been requested by a computer on the local network, it doesn't know what to do with "unrequested" incoming data—data that is not in response to a specific request the router previously sent out. To put it another way, if a router receives a request from a remote computer to access files, the router may not be able to determine which computer on the local network to route the request to. Typically, this happens when someone outside your home or office tries to initiate contact via your external IP address—which basically is your router. Your router has to decide which computer should receive the incoming data, but it doesn't know where to send it. Although this may sound serious, the good news is that most modern Internet routers have addressed such scenarios by adding support for what's known as *port mapping* (or *port forwarding*).

In addition to its IP address, every server has *ports* that are reserved for different types of connections. When you point your Web browser to www.*servername*.com, for example, you're actually connecting to www.*servername*.com:80. Port 80 is the network port that generally receives requests for Web pages on a Web server.

Because each sharing service uses specific ports, you can use port mapping to tell the router that any incoming requests for a particular port should always be directed to a specific computer on the internal network. For example, AFP (Apple Filing Protocol, used for Personal File Sharing in Mac OS X) uses port 548. If you "map" port 548 to one of the computers connected to your router, all File Sharing requests from the Internet will be directed to that computer.

Note that port mapping requires that the computers on your network have manually assigned IP addresses; you cannot assign addresses via DHCP. Also, each port can only be "mapped" to a single computer (meaning that, for example, remote users can only access Personal File Sharing on a single computer on your local network).

A list of ports used by various Mac OS sharing services is available in the following Apple Knowledge Base document: http://docs.info.apple.com/article.html?artnum=106439.

The specifics of enabling port mapping and forwarding vary a bit from router to router. In general, there will be a location in which you can specify the port(s) you wish to forward, as well as a location for specifying the IP address of the computer to be mapped to that port. Thus, to map port 80 (used for Web sharing) to a specific computer, you would enter 80 as the port to be mapped and the IP address of the computer you wish to share (listed in that computer's TCP/IP pane of Network System Preferences) as the target.

Note: These ports are the same ones that are opened and closed via firewall software, such as Mac OS X's firewall (accessed in the Firewall pane of Sharing System Preferences). Mac OS X's firewall is discussed in Chapter 9.

TCP vs. UDP. Your router's Port Sharing or Port Forwarding window will likely include separate options for TCP and UDP, for each port listing. TCP is used for services that require a persistent connection, such as for an FTP transfer. UDP is a "connectionless" method that is used when only a brief connection is needed, such as to check a domain name. If in doubt, when you open a port, open it for both TCP and UDP.

DMZ host. Some routers offer an additional solution: You can specify one computer to be the DMZ host, which is akin to enabling port mapping for *every* port, all forwarded to that one computer. The computer will then receive all incoming data requests of any type. This feature has two significant drawbacks: First, if the DMZ Host option is enabled for a particular computer, you cannot enable port mapping for any other computer on the local network—all unrequested data is "mapped" directly to the computer specified as the DMZ host. More important from a security point of view, designating a computer as a DMZ host allows *all* external requests, on *all* ports, to be passed on to that particular computer, thus negating the firewall value of the Internet router itself. The main reason you should use the DMZ Host option is if you need to use port mapping on many different ports and your Internet router's port-mapping settings do not accommodate them all (for example, some routers allow you to specify a maximum of ten ports for port mapping). You may also need to use this to play certain games over the Internet.

Network System Preferences settings vs. router settings

After setting up your Internet router, you'll need to enter the appropriate settings in Network System Preferences on each computer. Your settings will differ from what they would be for a direct connection to the Internet, especially if you're using a manually assigned IP address. In particular, note the following when entering data in Network System Preferences:

• **Ethernet router.** For a DHCP address—the most common setup—just choose Using DHCP in the TCP/IP pane of the Built-in Ethernet port configuration.

  For a manually entered IP address, enter a local IP address (usually 192.168.1.x, 172.16.1.x, or 10.0.1.x, where *x* varies for each computer on the network). The IP address entered in the Router field will typically be 192.168.1.1, 172.16.1.1, or 10.0.1.1. The Subnet Mask is typically something like 255.255.255.0. Again, the router instructions will provide specifics.

• **Wireless router.** The logic is the same, except that you enter the information after choosing AirPort from the Show pop-up menu. You will be accessing the Internet via an AirPort card through the router.

The important general principle here is that the settings entered into your router are typically the settings you would enter in the TCP/IP pane of the Network System Preferences pane if you were not using a router. These settings having been entered in the router, the TCP/IP settings on each computer on the local network refer to the router rather than to a direct connection to your ISP.

SEE: • "Firewall" and "Firewalls," in Chapter 9.

TECHNICALLY SPEAKING ▶ Internetconfig Preferences

Although applications like Safari and Mail have their own preferences files (for example, com.apple.Safari.plist and com.apple.mail.plist), many preferences settings for these applications (especially ones that would be common to any e-mail or Web-browser application) are stored in a special preferences file called com.apple.internetconfig.plist, located in ~/Library/Preferences.

This .plist file thus also holds some of the data that you access via the Preferences command in applications such as Microsoft Internet Explorer and Entourage—including the settings for Internet Explorer's File Helpers and Protocol Helpers. (These settings determine the applications used to open certain types of files, such as StuffIt compressed files.)

Preventing preferences changes from being overwritten. When you change com.apple.internetconfig.plist via an application's preferences, be cautious if you have two applications that use this file (such as Entourage and Internet Explorer) open at the same time. In such cases, any changes you make via Application 1 may get eliminated when you quit Application 2—especially if you quit Application 2 before quitting Application 1. What appears to happen is that when Application 2 quits, it overwrites the changes you made via Application 1. The workaround is to quit all applications that could affect the .plist file *except* the one in which you intend to make changes. Then quit that application before opening any other relevant applications. After that, all should go well.

The com.apple.internetconfig.plist file and Internet settings. This file stores the default homepage selection made in Safari. (It's listed in the WWWHomePage key, as most easily viewed in Property List Editor.) It also stores the default homepage selection for Internet Explorer. However, the latter is stored in a separate key called 4d534945•WWWHomePage (which stands for MSIE•WWWHomePage, because *4d, 53, 49*, and *45* are the hex codes for the ASCII characters *M, S, I*, and *E*). Thus, even though both applications use the same file to store this preference, the default preference need not be the same for each application. Other applications have the option to do this as well.

The com.apple.internetconfig.plist file and crashes (unexpected quits). If applications that obtain some of their settings from com.apple.internetconfig.plist are crashing, try removing the file from the Preferences folder. A new version with default settings will be created the next time you launch any application that uses this file. You will have to re-create some of your preferences, but the crashes will likely disappear. Still, just in case this technique doesn't fix the crashes, save the .plist file in a different location (rather than deleting it right away). You can move it back if you conclude that removing it didn't fix the problem.

File Mappings and Protocol Helpers. Internet Explorer's preferences allow you to view and modify the File Mappings and Protocol Helpers lists. These lists, if changed in Internet Explorer, will affect Safari as well—because they share the common internetconfig.plist file. However, Safari includes no options to edit these lists directly. If you use Safari and don't want to bother with Internet Explorer to edit these settings, you can use a third-party System Preferences pane called More Internet, from Monkeyfood Software (www.monkeyfood.com), or an application such as iCab's MisFox (www.clauss-net.de/misfox/misfox.html) or Rubicode's RCDefaultApp (www.rubicode.com).

continues on next page

TECHNICALLY SPEAKING ▶ Internetconfig Preferences *continued*

Note: File Mappings interpret a file's "content-type" or name extension so that the Mac knows what to do with the file (post-process) after it is downloaded (for example, unstuff a .sit file or open an AAC file in iTunes). Protocol Helpers are used to match a specific Internet protocol to its appropriate application (for example, specifying which application should be used for FTP access, mailto URLs, and so on). One of the things you can do when editing a File Mapping, for example, is change what post-processing does (for example, from opening a file in iTunes to just saving the file to disk without opening any application).

Launch Services vs. internetconfig.plist. The third-party preference pane called Default Apps (RCDefaultApp) includes features similar to More Internet. In many cases, however, it is superior to More Internet. In particular, More Internet limits itself to checking the internetconfig.plist file, whereas RCDefaultApp also checks Launch Services data—which (as indicated in this Apple document: http://developer.apple.com/documentation/Carbon/Conceptual/LaunchServicesConcepts) can "[i]dentify the preferred application for opening a document or URL." The Apple document goes on to state, "Launch Services' facilities for dealing with URLs were formerly implemented through the Internet Config API. Launch Services replaces and supersedes the Desktop Manager and Internet Config with a new API providing similar functionality, but designed to operate properly in the Mac OS X environment." In other words, we can expect internetconfig.plist to be eliminated altogether in a future revision of Mac OS X.

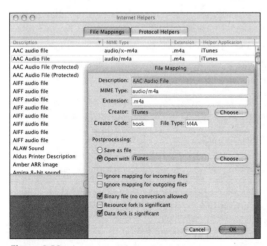 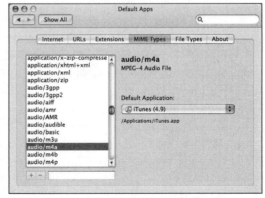

Figure 8.33

Left, *MisFox: editing the post-processing of a File Mapping;* right, *Default Apps: a similar listing.*

SEE: • Chapter 9, for more on Web-browser and e-mail issues.

Using .Mac

Provided by Apple, .Mac is an Internet-based subscription service that offers a wide range of features. The most useful are a mac.com e-mail account and access to an Internet-based server (called iDisk) on which you can store files for backup or for others to access. You can also use .Mac's HomePage feature to create sophisticated-looking Web pages with very little effort. You can send e-mail greeting cards (called iCards) to your friends and relatives.

Your .Mac account interacts with several other Mac OS X utilities. For example, iCal works with .Mac to post calendars to the Web that anyone can access. You can post photos in your iPhoto Library directly to a Web page via your .Mac account. The Backup utility, available to .Mac members, can be used to back up files on your drive to your iDisk.

SEE: • Chapter 11, for more on iCal and iPhoto.

Apple has also released free utilities designed to work with .Mac: Mac Slides Publisher, for example, can post a collection of photos as a slide show to your iDisk (which you can then share over the Web).

Membership costs $100 per year. For additional fees, you can increase your e-mail and/or iDisk storage limits, as well as provide e-mail–only access (via individual e-mail addresses) for individuals other than the primary member. For more details on .Mac and access to other .Mac features, such as HomePage and iCards, go to www.mac.com or click the .Mac button on Apple's homepage.

.Mac System Preferences

Mac OS X's .Mac System Preferences pane is where you set up local preferences related to your .Mac account. The pane includes four tabs: Account, Sync, iDisk, and Advanced. The following sections provide details about each pane.

Note: Most of the features will work only if you have a .Mac account and are currently connected to the Internet.

Account. If you have a .Mac account, the Account pane is where you enter your .Mac member name and password—information used when you access .Mac features from any application. For example, Mail can use this information to receive e-mail from your .Mac account.

If you do not have an account, a Learn More button will be at the bottom of the window. Click this to go to the .Mac homepage in your Web browser. You can open an account from there.

Figure 8.34

Top, *.Mac's Account pane;* bottom, *the Account Settings Web page for a .Mac account.*

If you already have an account, and have entered your name and password, the button at the bottom is named Account Info. Click it and your personal Account Settings page will open in your default Web browser. From there, you can modify your account, such as changing your credit card info or your password. Note: The bottom of the Account pane will also tell you how long before your current annual membership expires. If it expires in less than 30 days, the Account Info button will change to Renew Now, which takes you to the .Mac-renewal Web site.

Of special interest: When viewing your account settings in your Web browser, click Mail Preferences to set various options for your e-mail account; click Storage Settings to customize how your total amount of online storage (1 GB by default) is divided up between e-mail storage and iDisk storage.

Sync. In the Sync pane, you can select to upload various data to your .Mac account's iDisk and then keep that data synchronized with the data on your computer—either manually (by clicking the Sync Now button) or at pre-determined intervals that you set. Such data includes Safari bookmarks, iCal calendars, and Mail accounts.

If you have more than one Mac, you can keep the data synchronized across all of your Macs, so that all of your Macs always have the same and most up-to-date data. To do so, simply set up each Mac's .Mac Sync preferences identically.

Finally, to get a Sync menu to appear in the menu bar, enable the "Show status in menu bar" option. From the menu, you can manually select to sync at any time. This will also sync any connected devices synced via iSync.

SEE: • "Troubleshooting iSync," in Chapter 11, for more on syncing.

Figure 8.35

.Mac's Sync pane.

iDisk. iDisk is an online storage space that allows you to store documents, music, pictures, Web sites, and movies—basically, any kind of file you desire. In addition, Apple stocks each iDisk with software updates and a selection of third-party software (applications, music files, and even drivers for third-party peripherals). The iDisk pane of the .Mac System Preferences pane includes three sections:

• **iDisk Storage.** This section features a bar graph showing how many megabytes of your iDisk are currently being used. You have a default maximum of 1 GB of combined e-mail and iDisk storage. If you need more iDisk storage than is currently shown as the maximum on the graph, you can get it by shifting it from your e-mail storage (as described in the Account section above), assuming you don't need the space for e-mail. Otherwise, click the Buy More button; it takes you to a Web site where you can make a purchase.

- **iDisk Syncing.** If you click the Start button, a local copy of your iDisk is created on your hard drive (which may take a while, depending on the amount of data on your iDisk and the speed of your Internet connection). This local copy will appear as a volume in the sidebar of Finder windows as well as all other locations where volumes are listed. Open the volume window to access the iDisk's contents.

  Note: The actual volume is stored as a disk image (.dmg file) in the ~/Library/Mirrors folder. Check the General section of the Get Info window of the iDisk icon on your Desktop for the exact location.

  The advantage of this arrangement is that once the local copy is created, you can copy items to or from your iDisk at the speed of your hard drive rather than the slower speed of your Internet connection. You can also access your iDisk's content even when you aren't connected to the Internet. Of course, when you make changes to the local copy, those changes aren't immediately reflected in the "real" copy on the server. For this to happen, you must synchronize the local copy with the server copy. The iDisk pane offers two options for doing this: Automatically and Manually. Apple recommends Automatically. With this set, syncing is done in the background at set intervals as long as you are connected to the Internet. A manual sync is performed only when you specifically request it.

  To manually sync an iDisk at any time (even if you selected Automatically), click the Sync icon (which looks like two arrows chasing each other in a circle) located next to the iDisk listing in the sidebar of any Finder window. When you do this, the arrows will rotate until the syncing is complete. If you open the window for the local iDisk volume, the phrase *Syncing iDisk* will appear in the status bar at the bottom of the Finder window. A progress bar indicates how much syncing is left to be done. When syncing is finished, the status bar will indicate the time of the last sync.

  Note: This is an entirely separate feature from the syncing done via the Sync pane.

- **Your Public folder.** One of the folders on your iDisk is called Public. By default, anything you place in this folder can be accessed by anyone with an Internet connection. You can set it so that this folder has "Read only" or Read & Write access. If you don't want the folder to be completely public, you can also elect to require that a password be used to access your Public folder.

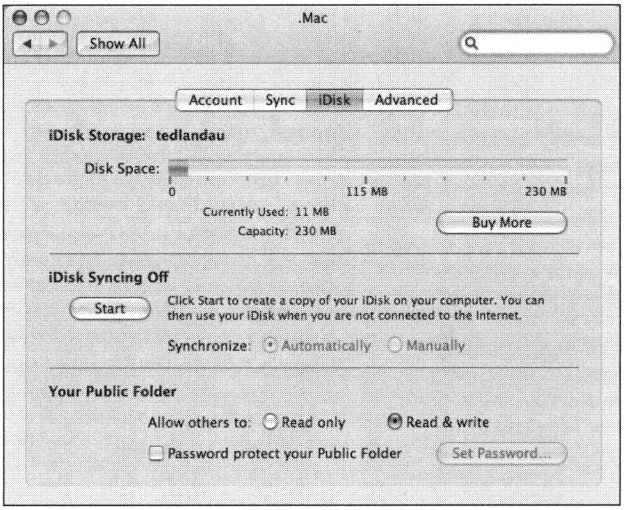

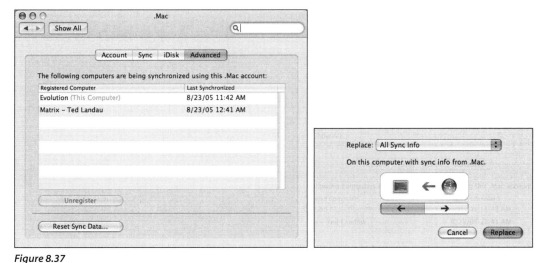

Figure 8.36

.Mac's iDisk pane.

Figure 8.37

Left, .Mac's Advanced pane; right, the Reset Sync Data dialog.

Advanced. The Advanced pane displays a list of all computers that have been "registered" to sync with the data in your .Mac storage, as well as the last time each was synchronized. To remove a Mac from the list, select its name and click the Unregister button. Note: To add a computer to the list, you must be using the computer to be added and check the "Synchronize with .Mac" box in the .Sync pane of .Mac System Preferences.

If you click the Reset Sync Data button, a dialog drops down, in which you can select a direction for syncing. That is, you can select whether to replace all data on .Mac with data on the currently used computer, or vice versa. From the pop-up menu, you can select which data you want to be replaced. A reset erases all information in the selected categories on the receiving device and replaces it with the data from the sending device.

You could use a reset, for example, if your .Mac data synced with computer B and you have decided that was a mistake. To remedy this, you could reset your .Mac data to match what is currently on computer A.

Figure 8.38

A message that appears the first time you sync files via .Mac's Sync pane.

Figure 8.39

You can use the iDisk command in the Go menu to mount your own iDisk as well as the iDisks and Public folders of others.

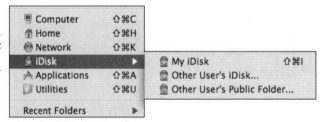

Figure 8.40

After a local copy of your iDisk is mounted, the iDisk appears in the Finder's sidebar with a Sync icon next to its name.

.Mac and iSync

Prior to Tiger, .Mac syncing was handled via Mac OS X's iSync utility. In Tiger, this function has shifted locations to .Mac's System Preferences pane. If you open iSync, you will still see a .Mac icon in the toolbar. But if you click it, you will be referred back to the .Mac System Preferences pane.

Nevertheless, iSync's Preferences settings still affect .Mac's syncing. Here are three examples:

- **Reset Sync History.** The first time you select to sync a computer with .Mac, you are asked how you want the initial sync to work. In particular, from a pop-up menu you can select "Merge data on this computer and .Mac" (thus combining the data from the two sources), "Replace data on .Mac," or "Replace data on this computer." You normally never see this dialog again. However, you can bring it back by clicking the Reset Sync History button. Note: The latter two functions are similar to what you can do by using the Reset Sync Data option in the Advanced pane of the .Mac System Preferences pane.

  Simply resetting will not delete the synced data on any device. This occurs only when you actually select to sync.

- **"Show Data Change Alert when more than __% of the data on this computer will be changed."** If you enable this option, a warning will appear when more than the selected percentage of data will be modified by a sync. This allows you to cancel a sync if you believe that it is about to do something you did not intend (as indicated by an unexpectedly large % change). As a safeguard, you can have this warning appear with every sync by selecting "any" as the percentage.

- **"Enable syncing on this computer."** If you check this box, it simultaneously checks the "Synchronize with .Mac" box in .Mac's Sync pane.

TAKE NOTE ▶ Troubleshooting .Mac Syncing

Here are some useful troubleshooting tips regarding syncing via the Sync pane in .Mac's System Preferences pane:

- **Conflict Resolver.** After the initial syncing of a computer to .Mac, subsequent syncing is done as a merge. That is, the data on both the .Mac account and the computer are updated with new information from each source. Occasionally, especially when syncing multiple devices, this can lead to a situation where the same record gets stored more than once, such as two slightly different Address Book records for the same person. When this is detected, a utility called Conflict Resolver kicks into gear (it is located in /System/Library/CoreServices). It will allow you to review each conflict and decide which of the multiple records to keep and which ones to discard.

  Note: If you have enabled the Sync menu in the menu bar, it will alert you to conflicts and offer to launch Conflict Resolver.

  After resolving all conflicts, it would be wise to sync again, just to be sure everything is up-to-date and no new conflicts are spotted.

continues on next page

TAKE NOTE ▶ Troubleshooting .Mac Syncing   *continued*

- **SyncServices.** Inside the ~/Library/Application Support folder is a folder called SyncServices. It maintains information important for accurate syncing of your data. Do *not* modify the contents of this folder in any way.

- **Not enough space.** If you get a .Mac Sync Error Code 5006 or other unusual error, the problem may be that there is not enough space on your iDisk to complete the sync. A potential solution is to select Reset Sync Data in the Advanced pane of .Mac's System Preferences, with data going from the computer to .Mac. Otherwise, you will need to make more space available, by either deleting other data on your iDisk or adding more space (as described in the main text). See this Knowledge Base article for more details: http://docs.info.apple.com/article.html?artnum=301377.

- **Multiple users on a Mac.** If you have multiple users on your Mac, each one will need his or her own .Mac account in order to use .Mac's Sync feature. One exception to this is if you use a single .Mac account to, for example, sync the same bookmarks, contacts, and calendars between different family members' accounts.

- **iDisk Sync icon does not appear.** If the iDisk Sync icon (in the sidebar of Finder windows) does not appear as expected, relaunch the Finder (by holding down the Option key and selecting the Relaunch command from the Finder's Dock menu).

- **Mac OS X applications and syncing.** Preferences and controls regarding syncing of information from Mac OS X applications, such as Address Book and iCal, are stored within the application itself and its related files. Therefore, the preferences settings for an application may include a sync option that overlaps with the option presented here. That is, enabling or disabling one will have the same effect on the other.

  Exactly what can be synced, and restrictions on how it gets synced, varies as a function of the individual applications involved. For one example, whereas you can sync contacts from Address book, you cannot sync Address Book's Smart Groups. Similarly, when syncing Address Book data, a contact's "preferred" e-mail address (if he or she has more than one) may change when synced to another computer. See Tiger's Help files for more examples of these types of restrictions.

  SEE: • "Troubleshooting iSync," in Chapter 11, for more on syncing.

TAKE NOTE ▶ Mounting and Working with iDisks

This sidebar provides details about mounting and working with an iDisk (either a network or a local copy).

Mounting a server-connected iDisk: Go > iDisk. To mount your own server-connected iDisk volume, go to the Finder's Go menu and select iDisk; from the hierarchical menu, choose My iDisk (or simply press Command-Shift-I). If your member name and password aren't already entered in the .Mac System Preferences pane, you will be prompted to enter them now.

continues on next page

TAKE NOTE ▶ Mounting and Working with iDisks *continued*

This mounts the active server copy of the iDisk, which will use your member name as the name of the volume and appear in your Computer window, in your sidebar, and on your Desktop (if the preference to mount volumes on your Desktop is selected)—just as if it were an external drive.

For other users' iDisks, from the same iDisk hierarchical menu you can choose either Other User's iDisk (which will require that you know the name and password for the account; this gives you full access to the iDisk as if it were your own) or Other User's Public Folder (which typically requires only the user name but restricts access to just the Public folder).

If you can no longer access your mounted iDisk (for example, when you click to open a window, nothing happens), the iDisk may have "crashed." To check for this, launch Activity Monitor and search for a process named mount_webdev. If you cannot find it, the iDisk has crashed. To get it going again, restart your Mac.

Unmounting a server-connected iDisk. To unmount (disconnect from) a server-connected iDisk, drag the iDisk icon to the Trash, or Control-click the volume's icon and choose Eject *volumename* from the resulting contextual menu.

Mounting a local copy of your iDisk. As described in the main text, to do this: Click the Start button in the iDisk Syncing section of the iDisk pane of the .Mac System Preferences pane. After doing this, wait a short while, and a copy of your iDisk will mount on your Desktop (typically with the name *iDisk*).

Unmounting a local copy of your iDisk. You cannot unmount a local iDisk copy by typical means (such as dragging the icon to the Trash). To unmount a local copy, you must click the Stop button in the iDisk pane of the .Mac System Preferences pane (it replaces the Start button after you mount the iDisk).

When you do so, the local copy is unmounted, but left behind is a disk-image file called "Previous local iDisk for *membername*.dmg." To mount this image file, double-click it. You can now copy files from the mounted image to your hard drive. However, the mounted image will no longer sync with the server copy. To re-create a new synced copy, you must click the aforementioned Start button again. Thus, once you have decided there is nothing in the "previous" disk image that you want to copy to your drive, you can and probably should delete the image file.

Using the local copy of your iDisk. Here are some tips for using a local copy of your iDisk:

- If you have chosen to sync manually, in addition to being able to sync the iDisk contents by clicking the Sync icon in the Finder's sidebar (as noted in the main text), you can choose Sync Now from the iDisk icon's contextual menu.

- To temporarily toggle automatic syncing on and off, choose the Automatic Syncing command from the iDisk's contextual menu.

continues on next page

TAKE NOTE ▶ Mounting and Working with iDisks *continued*

- The local copy of your iDisk does not include *all* files on the server version. In particular, software maintained on the iDisk by Apple is not copied to the local version—nor are the Library, Software, and (if you used the Backup utility) Backup folders and their contents. These folders are represented on your iDisk as aliases. If you double-click them, you are taken to the content on the server (assuming you have an active Internet connection at the time, so that the server copy is accessible).

- When a local copy of your iDisk is mounted, there is no command or button that can be used to access the server copy directly. For example, if you choose My iDisk from the Finder's Go menu, it will open the local copy, not the server copy.

  However, you can access the server copy indirectly via the folder aliases just described. To do so, select Show Original from the contextual menu for the alias. This opens up a new folder window (with your member name as the name of the window). This is the actual server copy of your iDisk. Changes made to this folder immediately modify the folder (no syncing required).

  Actually, the server copy is mounted even before you do this; it just remains invisible in the Finder. For example, you can see the server copy by launching Terminal and typing `ls /Volumes`. Thus, you could also access this copy by choosing Go to Folder from the Finder's Go menu and entering `/Volumes/`*membername*.

- Where is the actual local copy of your iDisk stored? That is, where on your hard drive are the files that are contained in the local copy? They are maintained in an image file named *membername*.dmg, located in ~/Library/Mirrors/*hexcode*, where *hexcode* is a hexadecimal code.

- If you have more than one Mac, try not to maintain a local copy of your iDisk on each one and then make different changes to each local copy. If this does happen, the Mac will ask which version of the file you want to save. Select either the version on the computer or the version on the iDisk, and click Keep Selected. To save both versions to your iDisk, click Keep Both.

- The program used to create and perform syncing of your local copy of iDisk is called MirrorAgent. It is located in /System/Library/CoreServices. If MirrorAgent detects any problem with syncing, it will send an alert message. Examples of such messages include the following: "Creating the iDisk on your computer failed (Not enough free space)" and "There is a problem deleting the file."

  Note: If you get persistent unexpected error messages from MirrorAgent, try quitting MirrorAgent (from Activity Monitor) and relaunching it (by double-clicking the file in CoreServices).

Alternative ways of mounting an iDisk. If, for some reason, you don't want to or can't use the above-described methods of mounting an iDisk, there are alternatives:

- **Connect to Server.** In the Finder's Go menu, choose Connect to Server. In the Address field, enter `idisk.mac.com`. When you click the Connect button, enter the user name and password of the .Mac account you want to access.

  Alternatively, you can type `http://idisk.mac.com/`*membername* in Connect to Server. Clicking Connect brings up a WebDAV dialog, in which you similarly enter the name and password of the selected account.

  In either case, the selected iDisk will mount as a server-connected volume.

continues on next page

TAKE NOTE ▶ Mounting and Working with iDisks *continued*

- **iDisk Utility.** Apple's iDisk Utility (downloadable from Apple's .Mac site) allows you to mount your own iDisk using the Open iDisk button. You can also mount the Public folder of another user's iDisk via the Public Folder Access button. You would only be likely to need this on a Mac running a version of Mac OS X prior to Panther or on a Windows PC.

- **Alias files or Dock icons.** Once an iDisk is mounted, you can create an alias to the volume. Similarly, you can drag the mounted iDisk icon to the Dock, placing a Dock icon for the iDisk there. In either case, after unmounting the iDisk, you can remount it by double-clicking the alias or clicking the Dock icon. You will likely be prompted to enter a name and password at this point.

- **Internet Location files.** You can create Internet Location files (which are described in Chapter 9) that allow you to quickly mount an iDisk or iDisk Public Folder.

- **WebDAV utilities.** Finally, because iDisk uses WebDAV technology for its access, you can mount an iDisk via any WebDAV-capable utility. For example, the third-party utility Goliath, by WebDAV (www.webdav.org), includes an Open iDisk Connection command in its File menu. Choose it, enter the name and password of the account, and you're in! Rather than having the iDisk mount as a volume on your Desktop, however, Goliath opens its own directory window that lists all of the files and folders on your volume. With Goliath, performance is typically faster than with Mac OS X's native iDisk access.

- **HomePage.** You can use .Mac's HomePage option to create a Web page that gives anyone access to the Public folder on your iDisk. To access this Web page, use the following URL format: http://homepage.mac.com/*yourname*.

As is always the case, these methods won't work if you are not connected to the Internet, the desired server is not on the network at the time, or you don't have access permissions for the server.

SEE: • "Using Network Browser and Connect to Server," in Chapter 9, for related information.

• "Take Note: Connecting to Servers via Aliases and Location Files," in Chapter 9.

Troubleshooting Networking and Internet Problems

I've divided the troubleshooting tips in this section into separate categories, such as wireless connections and modem connections. This division is difficult to achieve cleanly, however, because categories overlap—for example, you can connect to the Internet via a dial-up modem, which may be part of an AirPort Base Station. Thus, if you don't find the answer you seek in one of the sections below, try the one that seems closest.

To help you get started, here are some general guidelines:

- If you're having trouble with File Sharing or Web Sharing over the Internet, you should troubleshoot your network and Internet connections first. If all seems well, then troubleshoot File Sharing or Web Sharing.

- If your problem is limited to your Internet connection, concentrate on Internet troubleshooting, because services such as File Sharing and Web Sharing are not relevant to getting on the Internet.

- If you have a working Internet connection but are having problems with your Web browser or e-mail client, your problem is most likely with the browser or client. Focus your troubleshooting on the application's settings.

Specifics regarding troubleshooting file sharing, Web browsers, and e-mail are all covered in Chapter 9.

Checking the basics

Regardless of the specific likely source of your networking problem, it often pays to start with these basic steps:

- **Check your hardware connections.** Disconnect and reconnect all cables (Ethernet cables, modem cables, power cables, and so on). Make sure that all needed hardware is on and connected properly.

  To test whether a problem is with a cable or the Mac, try swapping: Connect a suspected defective cable to another Mac, for example, and see whether the problem still occurs. Alternatively, try a new cable with the problem Mac.

- **Check the Network System Preferences settings.** In the Network System Preferences pane, check and double-check that you've entered all of your settings correctly. A single incorrect number or letter can prevent you from accessing the Internet. Having AppleTalk disabled will prevent any AppleTalk connections.

  Be sure to go to the Network Status pane. If there's a basic problem with your connection (such as a cable that's not plugged in), you'll find a message there indicating the problem.

  Note: If you maintain a local network and assign IP addresses manually, make sure that no two devices have the same address. If a conflict does exist, you should get an IP Configuration error message when you start up (or wake up) a Mac with a conflicting address.

- **Switch Locations and Network Port Configuration settings.** Changing Locations and/or Network Port Configuration settings in the Network System Preferences pane may clear up an assortment of connection problems. I give specific examples in the sections that follow.

- **Check various Console logs.** OK, this is a bit beyond the basics, but still worth doing. Various log files, as accessed from the Console utility (as described more in Chapter 2), may contain error messages that can point the way to the cause and/or solution of a networking problem. For example, check DirectoryService.error.log.

SEE: • "Setting Up Network System Preferences," earlier in this chapter, for information on how to determine your correct settings and switch Locations.

Using the Network Diagnostics utility

Network Diagnostics is a utility primarily designed to help you diagnose Internet-connection problems. It is located in /System/Library/CoreServices. As such, it is not intended to be directly launched by users (as is the case for utilities in /Applications/Utilities). Instead, it is launched via options that appear in other applications. The two most common places to access Network Diagnostics are (a) via the "Assist me" button in Network System Preferences (as described earlier in this chapter) and (b) via the Network Diagnostics button in the "Failed to open page" page that appears in Safari if you are not connected to the Internet.

Figure 8.41

Click the Network Diagnostics button to launch the utility from Safari.

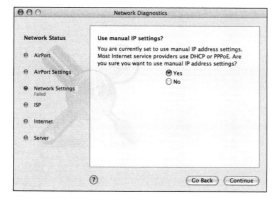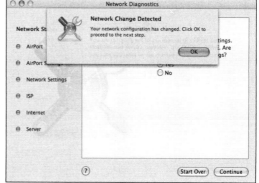

Figure 8.42

Left, a view of the Network Diagnostics utility before fixing the problem; right, after fixing the problem (changing the Network System Preferences pane's TCP/IP settings from manual to DHCP, in this case).

Once launched, the utility will test your Internet connection at various stages (for example, AirPort settings, Network settings, ISP) and determine where a failure first occurred. From this information, it will suggest potential solutions. All you need to do is answer the questions in each window that appears and click Continue to move to the next window. It won't be able to diagnose (and it certainly won't be able to offer solutions for) all possible Internet-connection problems. But it is a great place to start.

Using Network Utility

Apple's Network Utility (located in /Applications/Utilities) can help you diagnose various Internet problems. It is a much more technical (meaning less user-friendly!) tool than Network Diagnostics. The tradeoff is that it can supply much more detailed information. You can use it to check whether a failure to get to a Web site is due to a problem with the site or a more general Internet-connection problem. Although the scope of all that Network Utility can do is too broad to cover here, the following provides a brief overview.

SEE: • "Technically Speaking: Terminal Commands to Monitor and Improve Performance," in Chapter 10, for more on commands accessed from Terminal that overlap with what you can do via Network Utility.

Info. This pane provides information about your local network connections. The pop-up menu allows you to choose which network port the information refers to (en0 is the built-in Ethernet port; en1 is your AirPort card, if applicable, or a second Ethernet card; fw0 is for the FireWire port). The hardware address is the unique number (the media access controller, or MAC, address) that identifies your computer. Your IP address is either your local IP address (if you're using an Internet router) or the IP address assigned to you by your ISP.

The Transfer Statistics section of this pane provides information about errors that occur when transferring data over the network. A high number of errors indicates a problem with your network connection.

Netstat. To get various types of feedback about your network, including summaries of the different types of network traffic (TCP, UDP, IP, and so on), select an option here and click the Netstat button. This is fairly technical stuff that most users will rarely (if ever) need.

For more details about this command, enter man netstat in Terminal. Note: You can similarly use the man command in Terminal to get more information about most of the other commands cited in the next sections (for example, appletalk, ping, and so on).

SEE • "Technically Speaking: Terminal Commands to Monitor and Improve Performance," in Chapter 10, for more on netstat and related Terminal commands.

AppleTalk. AppleTalk can be used to get diagnostic information for troubleshooting AppleTalk connections. I discuss this elsewhere in the chapter.

SEE: • "Troubleshooting AppleTalk connections," later in this chapter, for examples of using the options in Network Utility's AppleTalk pane.

Ping. Ping is one of the most useful tools for testing an Internet connection. If you type the IP address or domain (for example, 66.179.48.115 or www.macfixit.com) of a remote server and click the Ping tab, Network Utility will send a special signal to the server and request a response. If the server answers, you know that your Internet connection is functioning properly. If it doesn't, try several other servers; all you need is a single successful ping result to verify your connection.

If you cannot get the Web page of a certain site to load, and you can't ping to that site—but other sites load and ping successfully—this suggests that the Web site is temporarily unavailable. That is, the problem is at the site's end, not yours. In such cases, there is little you can do except wait for the site's Webmaster to fix the problem.

If you cannot ping any site successfully, there's likely a connection problem on your end. Note that some servers have disabled ping responses, meaning that even if your network connection is working fine, you'll never get a response to a ping to that server. Thus, if you don't get a response from a particular server, be sure to try a number of other servers before deciding that your network connection isn't working properly.

Note: Pinging a site is also a quick way to learn its numeric IP address. For example, when I pinged www.macfixit.com, I quickly learned its IP address: 66.179.48.115. Entering this address in a Web browser loads the Web site just as well as the domain name does.

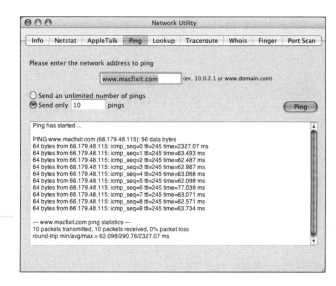

Figure 8.43

A successful ping to a remote server using Network Utility.

Lookup. This feature allows you to determine information about a particular Web address (for example, who "owns" it). This can be useful in detecting if a particular Web address is a spoof or not. For example, if a URL you receive in an e-mail is supposed to be the address of the Web page for your bank, the bank should be the owner of the page. This can also help in troubleshooting problems with Web browsers loading pages.

SEE: • "Network Security" and "Troubleshooting Safari (and other Web browsers)," in Chapter 9, for related information, including an example of using Lookup.

Traceroute. Traceroute is similar to ping. However, in addition to indicating a successful connection, it displays all of the routers and computers your connection must pass through on its way to the destination computer. If there's a problem with your connection to a remote server, knowing at exactly what point the stoppage occurs can help determine the cause. (For example, a stop at the start indicates a problem at your end; a stop at the end indicates a problem at the destination end; a stop in between indicates a problem elsewhere on the Internet that is preventing a connection.)

Note that some Internet routers do not allow traceroutes to function properly. Specifically, when starting a traceroute, you'll see a response from the router itself but not from any device beyond the router. If you attempt a traceroute and it "dies" at the router, keep this fact in mind—it may not be a symptom of a network problem.

Whois and Finger. These panes are useful for searching for information about a Web address (Whois) or an e-mail address (Finger). For example, you can use Whois to find out the administrative and technical contact people behind any Web site.

Port Scan. In this pane, you can check what ports are open at a particular IP address, including your own address. I discuss one example of how you might use this function in the "Firewalls" section of Chapter 9's "Network Security" section.

An alternative to Network Utility is the shareware program IPNetMonitorX, by Sustainable Softworks (www.sustworks.com). It contains features that go beyond what Network Utility can do.

Troubleshooting AppleTalk connections

If you're having trouble connecting to a device (such as a printer or another computer) via AppleTalk, the following steps will be useful in helping you isolate the cause of the problem.

In general, be aware that Apple is phasing out support for AppleTalk. Tiger, for example, no longer supports AppleTalk as the primary protocol for AFP File

Sharing. This means that you can no longer use AppleTalk to make a file-sharing connection from a computer running Tiger to another computer. You *can*, however, connect via file sharing from an older Mac (not running Tiger) to a newer Mac running Tiger, via AppleTalk, even though you cannot connect in the other direction.

In any case, if you prefer to use AppleTalk in ways that are still supported, or if you have devices that can connect *only* via AppleTalk (such as a Mac running an older, Classic version of the Mac OS that does not support TCP/IP sharing, or an Ethernet printer that is AppleTalk-only), you will need to enable AppleTalk over the Ethernet port.

Make sure that AppleTalk is active—and only on a single port.
Make sure that you have enabled AppleTalk on at least one of your active network ports. The way to do this is to check your port configurations in the Network System Preferences pane. Check the AppleTalk pane for the desired configuration, and make sure that Make AppleTalk Active is selected.

Starting with Mac OS X 10.2 Jaguar, AppleTalk can be enabled on only one port at a time. Thus, for example, you cannot enable AppleTalk simultaneously for both AirPort and Ethernet. If you try, you will get an error message.

If you require AppleTalk to be active on multiple ports at different times, the best solution is to create multiple Locations (as described earlier in this chapter), each with AppleTalk active on a different port. Switch Locations when you need to use AppleTalk on a different port.

If you're using an older version of Mac OS X, you may be able to enable AppleTalk on two or more ports at one time. However, you should not do so, because it's likely that some or all AppleTalk-connected devices will not work. See the following Apple Knowledge Base article for details: http://docs.info.apple.com/article.html?artnum=106614.

If the Network System Preferences pane claims that AppleTalk is active for your selected port, but it's not working, proceed to the next sections of this chapter.

Enable AppleTalk in Directory Access. AppleTalk printers and related devices should be able to work even if AppleTalk is not enabled in the Directory Access utility (in /Applications/Utilities). In general, disabling a service in Directory Access only prevents its auto-discovery. This might affect an attempted computer-to-computer connection via AppleTalk. AppleTalk may still be automatically accessed by other services or by a manual connection attempt.

Still, if you are having AppleTalk problems, and AppleTalk is not enabled in Directory Access, give it a try. It can't hurt.

SEE: • "Directory Access," in Chapter 4, for details on how to use this utility.

• "Take Note: Connect to Server vs. Network Browser: What's the Difference?" in Chapter 9, for related information.

Use Network Utility or Terminal to determine if AppleTalk is active and if Mac OS X can see AppleTalk devices. If AppleTalk appears to be enabled on the desired port, but you're still having problems, the Network System Preferences pane may be displaying AppleTalk information incorrectly. To get additional feedback about AppleTalk, you can use the AppleTalk pane of Network Utility or employ Terminal commands.

- **`appletalk -s` or Network Utility.** To confirm which port is using AppleTalk and whether or not AppleTalk is active, type `appletalk -s` in Terminal. The active AppleTalk interface will be listed, along with other information about the port (network number, node ID, and current zone) and some statistics on AppleTalk traffic.

  The interface designations provided by `appletalk -s` correspond to specific ports on your Mac:

  en0: This corresponds to the built-in Ethernet port.

  en1: This corresponds to the AirPort card (if no AirPort card is installed, it refers to the second Ethernet port).

  en2: This corresponds to the second Ethernet port (or third Ethernet port, if an AirPort card is installed).

  Alternatively, if you select "Display AppleTalk statistics and error counts" in the AppleTalk pane of Network Utility and then click the Get AppleTalk Information button, you will get essentially the same output.

- **`atlookup`.** To confirm that your Mac is actually seeing connected peripheral devices (such as printers) via AppleTalk, type `atlookup` in Terminal. You should get a list of all AppleTalk-connected devices. If the command does not list any peripheral devices (listing nothing or only your own computer), this generally means that AppleTalk is active and that you are connected to an active AppleTalk network, but that the other devices on the network are not communicating properly (or that there are no other AppleTalk devices on the network). In other words, the problem is not with your computer settings. Otherwise, you would get an error message; for example, if AppleTalk is not really enabled, you'll see the error, "The AppleTalk stack is not Running."

  Again, you can use Network Utility as an alternative—at least in theory. If you select "Display all AppleTalk zones on the network" and then click the Get AppleTalk Information button, you should get essentially the same output as with `atlookup`. However, since upgrading to Tiger, when I do this I get no output, just messages that say lookup has "started" and then "completed."

The additional options in the AppleTalk pane of Network Utility match other variations of the `appletalk` and `atlookup` commands (check the `man` output in Terminal for details).

If, when using either command, you get a message that states, "The AppleTalk stack is not running," either AppleTalk is disabled or the port on which it is enabled has not experienced any network activity (so AppleTalk has not been initialized on that port). If you connect an Ethernet cable directly to an AppleTalk device or try to initiate a direct AirPort connection to another AirPort device, this action should initiate AppleTalk traffic on the port. If you run the command again and still get an error, AppleTalk is simply not active. You will need to reset AppleTalk, as described next.

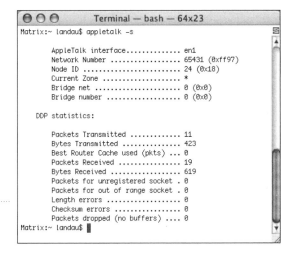

Figure 8.44

Output from *appletalk -s* in Terminal.

```
Matrix:~ landau$ appletalk -s

        AppleTalk interface............. en1
        Network Number ................. 65431 (0xff97)
        Node ID ........................ 24 (0x18)
        Current Zone ................... *
        Bridge net ..................... 0 (0x0)
        Bridge number .................. 0 (0x0)

    DDP statistics:

        Packets Transmitted ............ 11
        Bytes Transmitted .............. 423
        Best Router Cache used (pkts) .. 0
        Packets Received ............... 19
        Bytes Received ................. 619
        Packets for unregistered socket . 0
        Packets for out of range socket . 0
        Length errors .................. 0
        Checksum errors ................ 0
        Packets dropped (no buffers) .... 0
Matrix:~ landau$
```

Figure 8.45

Output from *atlookup* in Terminal.

```
Matrix:~ landau$ atlookup
Found 8 entries in zone *
ff01.04.9d      Falcon HP 4000N:LaserWriter
ff01.04.08      Falcon HP 4000N:SNMP Agent
ff01.04.9e      Falcon HP 4000N:HP LaserJet
ff97.18.80      Matrix:Darwin
ff97.18.81      Matrix:AFPServer
ffb3.bd.80      NaomiMac:Darwin
ffce.90.81      Yoda:AFPServer
ffce.90.80      Yoda:Darwin
Matrix:~ landau$
```

Reset AppleTalk connections. If you've checked every aspect of your AppleTalk connection and still aren't getting connectivity, try the following steps to reset your AppleTalk settings. After each step, test your AppleTalk connection. After you have regained connectivity, you can ignore the subsequent steps.

1. In the AppleTalk section of the port for which AppleTalk is active in the Network System Preferences pane, disable Make AppleTalk Active. Click the Apply Now button, and then re-enable AppleTalk by reselecting the option. Click the Apply Now button again.

2. Log out and then log back in. Sometimes, the AppleTalk settings in the Network System Preferences pane don't "take" until you do this.

3. Create a new network Location (using the steps outlined earlier in the chapter), switch to that Location, and then switch back to your original Location.

    The simplest way to perform a Location swap is to create a new Location that has no active ports (name it Nothing Active, for example) and then switch to it. Wait a few seconds and then switch back to the Location that's giving you problems. With luck, the problem will be gone.

4. Create a new Location, and set it up with the same network settings as the original Location.

    If the new Location works properly, delete the original Location item.

5. Assuming you got the "stack is not Running" error in Terminal (as described in the previous section), type `sudo appletalk -u en0` (that's a zero at the end), entering your password when asked. Next, type `appletalk -s`. If this fix worked, you should get a screen full of AppleTalk info instead of the error message.

    Note: Enter en1 or en2, as appropriate (instead of en0), depending on the port identified as using AppleTalk.

6. Zap the PRAM on your Mac by restarting and holding down Command-Option-P-R until you hear three chimes. Thereafter, your Mac will start up normally.

    Some AppleTalk settings are stored in PRAM. Thus, if your PRAM gets corrupted, it can cause problems with AppleTalk connections.

7. Delete the Network Preferences file, or all files in the SystemConfiguration folder, as described in "Take Note: Deleting SystemConfiguration Folder Files," later in this chapter.

Troubleshooting wireless connections

If you have a wireless or AirPort network for local networking or Internet access, and you are having connection problems, the following suggestions can help you isolate the problem. If you use AirPort or a wireless Internet router for Internet access and are having connection problems, try the steps suggested here before troubleshooting your Internet connection itself.

Note: To help in your diagnosis, first try to determine whether the problem affects all wireless clients or just some. Similarly, does the problem prevent Internet access only, or does it prevent all wireless access (for example, Internet *and* file sharing between local computers)? The answers to these questions will help you locate the specific cause. For example, if a problem affects all clients, it is most likely with the Base Station software or hardware; if it is instead with just one client, it is most likely with that client's software or hardware.

Switch Locations. In Network System Preferences, switching to a new Location and back again—or creating and using a replacement Location—can fix a variety of AirPort-related problems:

•   It may allow you to choose Turn AirPort On from the AirPort menu, which would not work before.

- It may get an AirPort network to appear in the AirPort menu or Internet Connect application, when it would not show up before.
- It may get AirPort to be listed in the Show pop-up menu in the Network System Preferences pane when it was not present before, even though it was enabled in the Network Port Configurations section.

Figure 8.46

The Locations pop-up menu in the Network System Preferences pane. See also Figure 8.20.

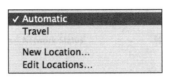

Check Network Port Configurations. You might think that the most reliable way to set up a Location for AirPort would be to make it the only port configuration enabled in the Network Port Configurations section. However, I've encountered cases in which an AirPort connection would not work unless Ethernet was also enabled.

This situation leads to another variation on this theme: The problem may be specific to how you set up Network Port Configurations in Network System Preferences. For example, if you have two ports enabled, and the port you want to use is listed second in the Network Port Configurations list, the connection may not work. More specifically, if Ethernet is at the top of the list (especially if you have an Ethernet cable that does not lead to an active network, connected to the Mac's Ethernet port), the Mac may not make the AirPort connection. The solution is to switch the order of the network ports, placing AirPort at the top.

The same solution applies if Internet Connect claims you have a valid AirPort connection, but you cannot access the Internet.

Remove AirPort configuration files. As with all preferences (.plist) files, a corrupt file can cause problems. Deleting the file is the general solution. You will need to reenter settings in Network System Preferences after doing this.

SEE: • "Take Note: Deleting SystemConfiguration Folder Files," later in this chapter, for details on the specific files for AirPort.

Restart the Mac. As is the case with a variety of symptoms, restarting the Mac may get AirPort working properly again. Restarting is especially likely to be helpful if your Mac can locate a network, but when you select to join it, you get an error message that says, "There was an error attempting to join the network {*name of network*}."

Unplug the AirPort Base Station (or wireless router) and plug it back in. This can fix an assortment of ills, such as renewing a dead DHCP lease issued from your ISP.

There is also a reported problem when using some versions of AirPort Extreme Base Station firmware, whereby a Mac with an AirPort card spontaneously loses contact with the Base Station; contact typically returns again in a few minutes. Unplugging and then replugging the Base Station can speed recovery.

Downgrading or upgrading to a different version of the Base Station firmware is the long-term fix. After doing this, I would again unplug the Base Station, leave it unplugged for at least 20 minutes, and then plug it back in. Check Apple's discussion boards for the latest specific advice.

Check software versions. The preceding firmware problem aside, it's generally advised that you use the latest available versions of software for your Base Station and AirPort cards. As one particularly nasty example, if you install an AirPort Extreme card in your Mac without first updating to an Extreme-compatible version of the AirPort software (as included on the CD that comes with the Extreme card), you can get a kernel panic on startup.

Remove wireless from the equation. If you're having trouble connecting to an AirPort or wireless network, and you're also set up to connect via Ethernet, switch to Ethernet (adding the cable, if needed) to see whether you can connect.

If you are able to connect, you know that you have a wireless-connection problem. However, if you aren't able to connect via Ethernet either, you have a more general connection problem—one that is not specific to your AirPort connection.

Conversely, if you're able to connect to other local computers via AirPort but can't get Internet access via AirPort, this confirms that the problem is not with the AirPort Base Station directly but rather with the Internet settings or connection.

SEE: • "Troubleshooting routers," later in this chapter.

Check that your AirPort card(s) are seated properly. If the problem appears to be with AirPort, but with only one Mac or Apple laptop, check to see that the computer's AirPort card is installed and seated properly. This procedure is an especially important first step for PowerBooks and iBooks, because the added movement and bumping that occur with a laptop are more likely to cause an AirPort card to come loose than on a desktop Mac.

Check that your AirPort card is active. Launch Internet Connect and verify that your AirPort card is active. If it is, the Internet Connect window should read AirPort Power: On. If not, click the Turn AirPort On button.

Alternatively, if you launch Network Utility and select Network Interface (en1)—or whichever interface corresponds to AirPort—from the pop-up menu on the Info pane, you can check the AirPort connection. Note: You can tell which setting is for a wireless connection by looking at the last (Model) line of the informational display, which will read Wireless Adapter (802.11) or something similar. If the Link Status line states Active, your AirPort connection is working.

SEE: • "Using Network Utility," earlier in this chapter.

Check for AirPort signal-level strength and channel interference.

As signal strength weakens, your AirPort connection will slow. Thus, a Web page that takes a few seconds to load when the connection is at full strength may take a minute or more to load when strength is reduced. If signal strength gets too low, you lose the connection altogether—even if all settings and connections are correct. Thus, it is desirable to keep the signal as strong as possible. You can check the signal level via either the AirPort menu bar icon or the Signal Level graph in Internet Connect.

To increase the signal strength of your AirPort connection, try one or more of the following:

- In the simplest cases, a weak signal level may mean that your computer is too far from the Base Station or that the Base Station is not facing in an ideal direction. Moving your Mac closer to the Base Station and/or rotating the Base Station slightly may fix this. If you have both an AirPort Base Station and an AirPort Express, you can use WDS settings to use the Express to extend the range of your network (as described in "Take Note: Setting Up an AirPort Base Station and Network," earlier in this chapter).

- The cause of the weak signal may be wireless-channel interference. More specifically, the technology behind AirPort and wireless networking uses a narrow range of radio frequencies around 2.4 GHz. Unfortunately, this range is close to that used by many wireless telephones and other consumer wireless devices (as well as being similar to the range of frequencies used by Bluetooth). Some users have reported problems with their AirPort and wireless connections when in the vicinity of other consumer wireless devices. If you experience such problems and verify the cause, the obvious solution is to avoid such wireless devices or turn them off (including Bluetooth if you're not using it) when you're using your AirPort connection.

- If you are using an AirPort Base Station, launch the AirPort Admin Utility and select different channels from the Channel pop-up menu until you find one that provides better connectivity. Each channel has a slightly different transmission frequency. If you're in the vicinity of other AirPort networks and these networks are using the same AirPort channel, your connection reliability and data-transfer rates can vary greatly, depending upon the channel you select. Client computers connecting to the router or Base Station will switch to the appropriate channel automatically. Note: Non-AirPort wireless routers typically also offer ways to change channels.

- Choose Use Interference Robustness in the AirPort menu. This option is used to minimize connection problems due to the presence of interfering devices nearby (such as a microwave oven, a cordless phone, or anything else using the 2.4 GHz band). However, enabling this option is likely to reduce the overall range of your AirPort connection—which means you shouldn't use it unless you're already having connection problems. To use this feature, the Enable Interference Robustness option may also be enabled in the Wireless Options pane of the AirPort Admin Utility. The difference is that enabling the option on the Base Station uses Interface Robustness for *all* connections to the Base Station; enabling it on your computer uses the feature only for your own computer.

Use third-party software. Third-party tools are also available to monitor AirPort signal strength. These include korben's MacStumbler (www.macstumbler.com) and Chimoosoft's AP Grapher (www.chimoosoft.com). Some of these tools are also useful for checking for nearby wireless networks, including the name, signal strength, and type of security for each network located. Note: Apple offered a similar utility at one point, called AirPort Management Utility, but appears to have removed it from its Web site.

Do general AirPort troubleshooting. If all else seems well, it's time to recheck your initial AirPort setup. You also may need to reset the Base Station. If even this fails to locate a solution, you may need a hardware replacement or repair; contact Apple.

One final bit of advice: I recently had an odd problem, running Mac OS X 10.4.2, where I would periodically get an error message that said, "There was an error joining the AirPort network." It was immune to any logical diagnosis. It occurred on only one of my three Macs (indicating that the network and the Base Station were otherwise fine); it was not a signal-strength issue; and none of the advice listed above fixed the problem. What happened was that, an hour or so later, the error message spontaneously vanished and the network was restored. I never did figure out the cause, although I suspect a bug in Mac OS X that may be specific to Power Mac G5s. If so, hopefully this issue will be fixed in a future update to Mac OS X.

SEE: • "Take Note: Setting Up an AirPort Base Station and Network," earlier in this chapter.

• "Troubleshooting Sharing," in Chapter 9, for related information.

Figure 8.47

An AirPort-related error message.

Troubleshooting routers

If you're using a router, wireless or wired, checking whether it's the cause of an Internet-connection problem is one of the first things you should do. If you have set up your router incorrectly, or if your ISP has taken steps to prevent the use of such routers, no amount of other troubleshooting will solve your connection problems.

A first step is to reset your router. You typically do this by turning it off (unplugging it if necessary) for a few seconds and then turning it back on (or plugging it back in). Sometimes, this alone will fix a problem. Alternatively, if the router has a reset button, use that.

Otherwise, the best way to determine whether the router is the problem is to disconnect it; connect your computer directly to your phone, cable, or DSL line; and set up your computer to access your ISP directly. For most dial-up modem connections, this procedure means connecting the phone wire to the phone port on the Mac (to access the internal modem). For broadband connections, connect your broadband (cable/DSL) modem directly to your Macintosh via the Ethernet port.

You will likely have to change the settings in Network System Preferences to reflect this change. For example, if you had been using a manual Ethernet setting to connect your Mac to your router (probably with an IP address such as 192.168.1.101), you may need to shift to DHCP (if that's what your cable or DSL modem setup requires), or—if you have a static IP address—you may need to enter that. Similarly, if you were using a wireless router but are now connecting a cable modem directly to your Mac (rather than to the router), you will need to switch from AirPort to Ethernet.

To make it easier to switch back to the original router configuration later, set up a separate Location with these alternative settings in advance of any problems. This allows you to switch back and forth easily.

If, after connecting directly, you're able to establish a working Internet connection, the problem is not with your computer or with the connection itself, but with your router or the way you have your Mac configured to access the router. In such cases, consider the following:

Check router TCP/IP settings. I'm assuming you already checked the TCP/IP settings in Network System Preferences. However, with a router you also need to check whether the router's TCP/IP settings are correct.

SEE: • "Configuring a router," earlier in this chapter.

Check for firmware updates. The router may need a firmware update to correct some bug; check with the vendor to see whether a newer version is available. One firmware version of Apple's AirPort Base Station, for example, had a problem connecting to Comcast's cable Internet services. The fix required an update to the AirPort Base Station firmware.

Check for the MAC address and other ISP/router interaction problems. The cause of a problem may be the interaction between your ISP and your router. For example, some broadband ISPs check the computer's MAC address before allowing a connection. If the ISP is looking for the MAC address of your Mac and instead finds the MAC address of your router, the connection will fail. One solution is to contact your ISP and request that it update the MAC address in its database. Otherwise, your router may include a feature called Mac Address Cloning, which allows you to enter your computer's MAC address in a special field in your router's software. The router sends this address to the ISP, fooling the ISP into thinking that the router has the MAC address it's seeking.

SEE: • "Using a Router" and "Take Note: What Are the TCP/IP Settings?" earlier in this chapter, for related information.

If you still can't connect to the Internet, even after taking the router out of the equation, the router is not the direct cause. In this case, proceed with the troubleshooting advice in the following sections. You can reconnect your router after you have determined the cause and solution.

TAKE NOTE ▶ Self-Assigned IP Addresses

As discussed at several points in this chapter, if your Mac is connected to the Internet via a server or router using DHCP (such as an AirPort Base Station), your Mac's IP address (as found in the TCP/IP section of Network Preferences for your configuration port) will likely be in the form of 10.0.1.x, 172.16.1.x, or 192.168.1.x (where x changes for each device on the network, up to a maximum of 255). If you are using manually assigned local addresses, you will still likely be using an address in one of these ranges. Anything else suggests a problem.

If, on the other hand, you have a direct wired connection to your DSL or cable modem (with no intervening router), the address in the TCP/IP section should be your WAN IP address (either a DHCP-generated address or a manually entered address). The exact format here can vary, but it should *not* be in one of the above address ranges (as these are reserved for "local" addresses on LANs). If the expected WAN address does not appear, that too suggests a problem.

If a problem does occur, one of two things will likely be the case: (a) the IP Address field will be empty; or (b) it will contain a *self-assigned* address. A self-assigned address on a Mac is typical in the 169.x.x.x range. This means that a valid DHCP-generated address could not be obtained and you are thus not successfully connected to the Internet.

If this happens, for starters try renewing the DHCP lease, by clicking the Renew DHCP Lease button in the TCP/IP pane. Otherwise, follow the advice, as relevant, in the main text.

Note: Even though you are not connected to the Internet, you may still be able to use the self-assigned addresses for local connections, such as for file sharing between Macs on the same network.

169.254.x.x and AirPort. If you are using an AirPort Extreme or Express Base Station, a self-assigned address in the range of 169.254.x.x will appear if your Mac is attempting to connect to the Base Station but has not yet succeeded or is simply unable to do so. See the main text for troubleshooting suggestions.

For further information, see also these Apple Knowledge Base articles: http://docs.info.apple.com/article.html?artnum=58618 and http://docs.info.apple.com/article.html?artnum=106879.

SEE: • "Take Note: Setting Up an AirPort Base Station and Network," earlier in this chapter.

Troubleshooting dial-up modems

Despite the proliferation of broadband, dial-up connections are still a common way for home users to access the Internet. These days, most dial-up connections are made via the internal modem included with nearly every Mac. If your modem fails to connect (or if it appears to connect but no Internet applications can access the connection), and the advice in the preceding sections didn't solve your problem, here are some additional steps specific to standard dial-up modems.

Check your Modem screen settings. In addition to verifying that the TCP/IP and PPP settings are correct in the respective panes in the Internal Modem configuration of Network System Preferences (you did that already, right?), make sure that the settings are correct in the Modem pane. If you don't have the correct modem model selected, for example, you may experience poor connections or may not be able to connect at all. In addition, make sure that you've selected the correct dialing method (tone or pulse).

Finally, some phone systems provide a voicemail beep when you have messages instead of the standard dial tone. If you use such a system, uncheck the "Wait for dial tone before dialing" box.

SEE: • "Take Note: Modem Scripts and Terminal Scripts," earlier in this chapter.

Check Network Port Configurations and Location settings. I discussed the troubleshooting value of switching Locations and Network Port Configuration settings in previous sections of this chapter. Here is yet one more variation on the theme.

Once, when my cable modem went down, I decided to use my internal modem via a dial-up ISP account that I maintained for just such emergencies. It seemed to work OK—Internet Connect indicated that I had successfully connected. But no services worked. I couldn't load Web pages or get e-mail. It turned out that the problem was caused by a glitch in how network ports work. Even though I was dialing in to my ISP using the modem, the network software was still trying to connect through the Ethernet port to the nonfunctional cable modem.

The reason for this is that Mac OS X considered my Ethernet connection to have priority over my modem: Because it detected a valid connection to the cable or DSL modem, it refused to let the dial-up modem provide Internet access—despite the fact that an apparently good dial-up connection had been made.

The solution is to do one of the following:

- Unplug the Ethernet cable (that goes to your cable modem) from your computer.

- Temporarily move Internal Modem to the top of the ports list in the Network Port Configurations pane (accessible from Network System

Preferences' Show pop-up menu). You can change the order back when the cable modem is working again.

- Create a separate Location for the modem in which only the Internal Modem setting is active. Switch to this Location.

Use Internet Connect's Connection Log. If you're having trouble figuring out why your modem connection is not working, checking the error messages in the Connection Log may provide a clue. To do this, follow these steps:

1. Launch Internet Connect.
2. In the toolbar, click the Internal Modem icon (if it's not already selected).
3. From the Window menu choose Connection Log.

You can view information about past connection attempts, or you can use Internet Connect to attempt a dial-up connection and watch the log generate in real time. Even if *you* aren't able to identify the problem, if you end up contacting your ISP for technical support, this log may be useful.

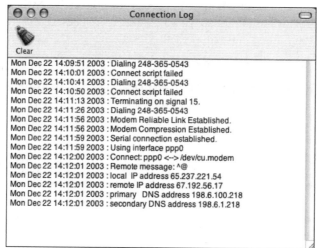

Figure 8.48

An example of the output that appears in the Connection Log, as selected from Internet Connect's Window menu.

Use verbose logging. If the standard Connection Log doesn't provide enough helpful information, you can enable a more detailed logging procedure called *verbose logging*. To do so, follow these steps:

1. Open the Network System Preferences pane.
2. From the Show pop-up menu, choose the modem configuration you have set up (for example, Internal Modem).
3. Click the PPP button to access the PPP pane.
4. Click the PPP Options button.
5. In the Options dialog (see Figure 8.17), check the "Use verbose logging" box.

6. Click OK.

7. Click the Apply Now button to apply your new settings.

   If you already had an Internet Connect window open, this step will generally cause it to close and then reopen.

From this point on, when you choose Connection Log in Internet Connect, the log will contain much more detail about every step of the connection process.

Deselect echo packets. In some cases, the PPP connection to the Internet will not succeed if a PPP server does not reply to LCP Echo packets. The solution is to deselect "Send PPP echo packets" in the PPP Options dialog (from the PPP pane of the Internal Modem settings) in the Network System Preferences pane.

Deselect error correction. Deselect "Enable error correction and compression in modem" in the Modem pane of Network System Preferences if a modem connection cannot be established or is unreliable.

Deactivate phone-line features. Many phone lines have features such as call-waiting that can cause frequent disconnects. If you have such features, check with your phone company about how to disable them when you're online.

End hanging disconnects. After selecting to disconnect from your modem, you may occasionally find that the Mac declines your request and remains connected. This "hanging disconnect" can be solved by quitting certain background processes (pppd, modemd, AppleModemOnHold) in Terminal or Activity Monitor. A simpler solution is to get a freeware application called End Hanging Disconnect, from Useful Software (www. shopperturnpike.com/usefulsoftware), and run it. Otherwise, the only solution is to restart your Mac.

Check your phone line. Unplug your modem from the phone jack and hook up a telephone to the jack, to verify that you have a dial tone and can dial out. This step will also allow you to figure out whether other phones in the house are in use or off the hook, thus preventing your Mac from connecting.

Have your phone line checked. If you are able to connect only intermittently and experience frequent dropped connections, it's possible that the phone lines in your home, or in the area around it, are simply of poor quality. You can contact your phone company to check your phone line quality.

Contact your ISP. If you've gone through every step mentioned here and *still* can't access the Internet, it's probably time to contact your ISP and see whether it can figure out the problem.

Troubleshooting DSL, cable, and PPPoE connections

Broadband connections are the fastest-growing type of Internet connection. They tend to be more reliable than dial-up modem connections, they are much faster, and they are available 24/7. Whenever your Mac is on, you're on the Internet (or can get on immediately without having to wait through a lengthy connection/login procedure). Things can still go wrong, however. If the more general advice in the preceding sections didn't help, here are some additional steps specific to standard broadband modems.

Reset your modem. Turn your DSL or cable modem off (or unplug it), and leave it off for 2 to 3 minutes. (If your DSL or cable modem has a reset button, press it first.) After turning it back on, wait a few minutes for it to resynchronize with your ISP, if necessary. Many times, this step will fix a finicky Internet connection.

Restart your Mac. If the reset of your DSL/cable modem had no beneficial effect, shut down your Mac and restart it.

Fix "configd not available" error. If the system-configuration server process (configd) on your Mac unexpectedly quits, DHCP and BootP choices may not be available in the TCP/IP pane and/or you may not be able to change any other settings in Network System Preferences. If this happens, the following alert message will appear when you click the Apply Now button: "The System Configuration server (configd) is not available." The solution is to restart your Mac.

Make sure your computer is properly connected to the DSL or cable modem. Most broadband modems have an indicator light (or lights) that verify that your computer is connected properly. If these lights aren't on, or are blinking (or not blinking) in an unexpected way, recheck the connecting cable. Try a different cable, if possible.

Access your modem's settings directly. In most cases, there is a way to directly interface with the cable/DSL modem (or router) that you use to connect with your broadband ISP. This is a local connection that uses the software built into the device itself. Typically, you access it through a Web browser. For example, to access the cable modem that I use for my Comcast connection, I would enter the following URL in my Web browser: http://192.168.100.1. Similarly, to access my SBC wireless router/modem, I enter http://172.16.0.1/. (Note: For these URLS to work, you must either have a wired connection to the modem or be on the wireless network that the modem uses. You may also need to enter a name and password to access the settings.)

Once the Web page has opened, you will be able to check and/or modify its various settings. Exactly what you can do is obviously determined by the exact modem and ISP you are using. With my Comcast modem, for example, I can run several diagnostic status checks that tell me whether the cable connection is working properly and, if not, what is the likely cause of the problem. With my SBC modem, I can check and monitor the Internet-connection speed. In most cases, if any problem is found, the next step is to call the ISP (for example, Comcast) for further advice.

Use Internet Connect's Connection Log for PPPoE connections. If your ISP uses PPPoE, you can use the Connection Log that Mac OS X keeps in order to see detailed information about your connection attempts. The log often includes error messages that indicate the source of the problem, which hopefully provide direction as to the solution. To set this up, click the Built-in Ethernet icon (used for PPPoE) in Internet Connect's toolbar before opening the Connection Log from the utility's Window menu.

Fix automatic PPPoE connection failures. If you click the PPPoE Options button (located in the PPPoE pane of the Ethernet port of Network System Preferences), a dialog drops down; it contains several options, including "Connect automatically when needed." If you enable this option, PPPoE should automatically make a connection when you launch an application, such as a Web browser, that requires an Internet connection. This may fail to work if you manually disconnected the last time an automatic connection occurred. Automatic connection is also disabled after three failed connection attempts. The solution is to manually start your PPPoE connection and (if needed) re-enable the automatic option.

Contact your ISP. In my experience, 99 percent of broadband problems (beyond those fixed by resetting your modem) are not your fault—and you cannot fix them. This is especially true of problems that occur spontaneously (that is, when you haven't made any changes or additions to your Mac setup). In such cases, the first thing I recommend is contacting your broadband ISP. The ISP will often inform you that there's a temporary problem with the service in your area and that it's working to fix the problem. In such cases, there's nothing to do but wait. Occasionally, the ISP may need to *reprovision* your modem (a technique the cable company can perform via the Internet). This task is usually accomplished within a few hours of your call. As a last resort, the ISP may need to make a service call to check your connection or replace your modem.

Note: If your modem is connected via a router or any sort of wireless connection, some broadband ISPs will refuse to help you with potential router-related problems, claiming that they don't support or (in some cases) even permit the use of such connections (although that attitude is thankfully increasingly rare!). If this happens, temporarily removing your router from your setup may facilitate getting help from your ISP. The fact that you use a Mac may make matters worse, as many ISPs are less skilled in dealing with Mac setups than with Windows PC setups. If your ISP proves unhelpful, and the advice in this book is not sufficient to solve your problem, you may want to seek help from a consultant or other technical-support professional.

Optimize your broadband network. Software such as Enigmarelle Development's Broadband Optimizer (www.enigmarelle.com/broadbandoptimizer.py), a startup item, and Kristofer Szymanski's Cocktail (www.macosxcocktail.com), an application, allow you to increase the memory buffers used for TCP transfers so that data comes in bigger chunks at a time. Ideally, this should result in faster transfers when using a broadband connection, which should translate into faster loading of Web pages, downloading of files, and so on. To confirm that this "optimization" has occurred, type the following command in Terminal before and after enabling the optimizing: sysctl -a. From the long list of output, check the values (##) in the following four items; they should change after optimizing:

```
net.inet.tcp.sendspace: #####
net.inet.tcp.recvspace: ##
net.inet.tcp.delayed_ack: ##
net.inet.udp.recvspace: ##
```

TAKE NOTE ▶ Deleting SystemConfiguration Folder Files

In the /Library/Preferences folder is a folder called SystemConfiguration. Inside this folder are several .plist files. Most of them have to do with networking settings. These include NetworkInterfaces.plist, com.apple.airport.preferences.plist, and preferences.plist. If you're having networking-related problems, deleting one or more of these files (or even the entire folder) may fix them. Any administrator has access to these files.

If you delete them, new default copies are created—which means you lose your customized settings. For that reason, it's best to save a copy of the original files in another location before deleting them. If it turns out that removing them has no effect, you can replace the new copies with the originals rather than re-create your custom settings. Even better, make a backup copy of this folder when everything is working properly; if you have problems later, you can replace the problem copy with the good backup. You can store the backup copy anywhere you're able to access, ideally somewhere in your home directory.

continues on next page

TAKE NOTE ▶ Deleting SystemConfiguration Folder Files *continued*

Note: If you're reinstalling Mac OS X—and choose not to select the Archive and Install option to preserve network settings, as described in Chapter 3—saving a copy of this SystemConfiguration folder will still allow you to preserve network settings. Just replace the newly installed copy with the copy you saved.

Note: Mac OS X 10.2 Jaguar and earlier used a different format for SystemConfiguration files; thus you could not use a saved folder from Jaguar to replace a Panther or Tiger folder.

The following represents some more specific information and advice regarding the SystemConfiguration folder.

preferences.plist. If you cannot connect to the Internet from your Mac, and you are able to verify that your Internet connection is functional (perhaps because you can connect to the Internet via a second Mac), the problem could be that the preferences.plist file has become damaged. This preferences file can cause a number of networking problems, including network loss after sleep, an inability to log in, and even an inability to start up.

In such cases, assuming you can log in, you should go ahead and remove or delete this file—though not until after you've saved a copy of all of your settings. After deleting the file, log out (or restart) and log back in. Reenter your network settings (using the information from the saved file, if needed). Now try to connect to the Internet as you normally do. Assuming the problem was with the preferences.plist file, you should now be able to connect. Note: See "Blue screen crashes and stalls," in Chapter 5, for an example of how to address this problem if you *cannot* log in.

NetworkInterfaces.plist and com.apple.airport.preferences.plist. If just deleting the preferences.plist file fails to work, you may have success if you additionally delete NetworkInterfaces.plist and (if the problem involves an AirPort connection) com.apple.airport.preferences.plist. After doing this, again open the Network System Preferences pane and reenter settings as needed.

Good preferences, bad connections. In some cases, the preferences.plist file is in good shape and your connections are correct, but for some reason Mac OS X just gets "confused" (for lack of a better term). In these situations a simple restart will often solve the problem. However, you may be able to avoid the need to restart by instead resetting the interface/port used for the connection having problems. To do so, follow these steps in Terminal:

1. Type ifconfig -a, and then locate the interface that is giving you problems.

   This interface will likely be en0 for the internal Ethernet port or en1 for an AirPort card. If the Terminal output indicates that the port in question is inactive (when you believe it should be active), move on to Step 2.

2. Type sudo ifconfig en0 inet up (or replace en0 with en1, if applicable).

3. Type ifconfig -a and look at the interface entry. The port should be active, and various data should now be listed for it. If so, networking should work.

TAKE NOTE ▶ **Network Connection Setting Causes Stall at Startup**

If your network is set up to access the Internet via a cable or DSL modem over Ethernet, and that connection is not working at startup, you will likely get a significant delay at startup, at the point where an attempt is made to access the network. Prior to Tiger, you could confirm that this was the case because a status message referring to networking would appear on the Startup screen. No such status messages appear in Tiger, so you lose this feedback. Still, if you are getting an unusual startup delay and networking is a suspect, try these solutions as appropriate:

- Make sure that your cable/DSL modem connection is working. If it's not, use the advice in this chapter to determine whether the problem is something you can fix (such as a domain name or number entered incorrectly in the TCP/IP settings) or something that the ISP needs to fix.

- As a temporary work-around until your Internet connection is fixed, disconnect the Ethernet cable from the Mac. Also disable Built-in Ethernet in Network System Preferences' Network Port Configurations settings. Doing this should eliminate the startup delay.

I have used this slowdown as a diagnostic tool to quickly determine whether a change I made helped or hurt my attempt to fix a connection problem. If I restart and get this delay, I already know that I still have problems.

Note: Using manually assigned IP addresses instead of DHCP for a local network can also help avoid this type of network stall at startup.

SEE: • **"Take Note: What Are the TCP/IP Settings?" earlier in this chapter, for related advice.**

• **"Startup items" in the "Startup daemons" section, and "Blue-screen crashes and stalls," in Chapter 5, for related information on startup problems related to network settings.**

9

Troubleshooting File Sharing and the Internet

In Chapter 8, I covered the basics of setting up and troubleshooting a network, whether it be Ethernet, AirPort, Bluetooth, or dial-up. In this chapter, I cover the most common practical applications of having set up a network. In particular, I focus on file sharing and accessing the Internet for e-mail and Web browsing.

In This Chapter

Setting Up System Preferences: Sharing

The Sharing pane of System Preferences is your one-stop shop for almost any sort of file/computer sharing that you intend to do. It is where you control whether (and how) users on other computers can access your computer and its contents. After the Network System Preferences pane, it is the most critical pane to configure if you're using the Internet.

For starters, you enter your computer name at the top of the window. A matching local hostname (.local) name—used to identify your computer on the local network—is automatically created (though you can change this hostname by clicking the Edit button). Note: The computer name can have spaces in it; the local hostname cannot. You use the local hostname, as described in Chapter 8, when attempting to locate computers via the Bonjour protocol.

SEE: • "Take Note: Bonjour," in Chapter 8, for more details.

TAKE NOTE ▶ Sharing and the Accounts System Preferences Pane

Creating users in the Accounts System Preferences pane, though not covered in this chapter, is an important prerequisite for using certain Sharing services, such as Personal File Sharing, since anyone who wants to connect to your computer via Sharing services must have an account. In other words, you use the Accounts settings to create a list of users who can locally log in to your Mac, as well as to determine who can access your Mac remotely via Sharing. If you want someone to be able to access files on your computer over the Internet or a local network other than as a guest, that user must have an account on your computer—even if he or she will never use the computer in person.

SEE: • "Take Note: Using SharePoints," later in this chapter, for an exception to this restriction: File Sharing Only users.

• "System Preferences," in Chapter 2, for details on setting up and using the Accounts System Preferences pane.

The Sharing System Preferences pane has three tabs: Services, Firewall, and Internet. I describe each in the sections that follow.

Services

Sharing, in the general sense used here, means allowing users on other computers to have at least some access to your computer. You can provide this access in a variety of ways. It could be a direct link—where your computer mounts on the Desktop of the other computer almost as if it were an external hard drive. Or it could be access only via a Web browser—where the user can access files you set up as part of a Web site.

The Services pane is used to enable or disable the various methods by which users are permitted to connect to your Mac. To enable a desired Sharing service, simply check the box next to its name (or select its name and click the Start/Stop button). To turn off the service, uncheck the box (or select the service and click the Start/Stop button).

SEE: • "Sharing Services: A Closer Look," later in this chapter, for more details than in the overview provided in this section.

The services available from the Services pane include the following:

• **Personal File Sharing.** This service provides a way for users (specifically, those with accounts and, in a more limited capacity, those who are guests) to directly access files on your Mac from another Mac. Your computer mounts as a volume on the other computer.

 Mac OS X users connect to your Mac via the Finder's Connect to Server command or the Network (Browser) window.

 A maximum of ten users can be connected simultaneously via Sharing. If you need more than that, you need Mac OS X Server.

 SEE: • "Personal File Sharing" and "Using Network Browser and Connect to Server," later in this chapter, for more details.

• **Windows Sharing.** This service makes it easy for Windows users to access files stored on your Mac using the SMB/CIFS protocol (a Windows/Unix file-sharing standard). After enabling this feature, you will also need to create accounts for the Windows users in the Accounts System Preferences pane. Note that because SMB/CIFS is also a Unix standard, enabling Windows File Sharing also allows Unix users to connect to your Mac.

 SEE: • "Windows File Sharing" and "Using Network Browser and Connect to Server," later in this chapter, for more details.

• **Personal Web Sharing.** This service allows users to access files (such as HTML files) in the Sites folder of your home directory via a Web browser.

 SEE: • "Personal Web Sharing," later in this chapter, for more details.

• **Remote Login.** This option allows access to your computer via the encrypted SSH protocol. SSH can be used via Terminal or specialized third-party SSH applications. It also allows SFTP (Secure FTP) access to your Mac.

 A remote login can be useful in certain troubleshooting situations—that is, you may be able to access an apparently frozen Mac remotely via SSH from another Mac. In this case, despite the freeze, you could access the computer via Terminal from another Mac on the network, which in turn might allow you to modify or delete files that are preventing the Mac from starting up without freezing.

 SEE: • "Network Security," later in this chapter.
  • "Technically Speaking: Connecting Remotely to a Frozen Mac: Killing Processes, Running Sync," in Chapter 5.

- **FTP Access.** This service enables users with local accounts to connect to your Mac via any FTP client software, including a Web browser. These users just need to know the IP address for your Mac (which would be entered in the format *ftp://192.168.1.878*, for example, followed by a user name and password when asked).

  SEE: • "FTP Access," later in this chapter, for more details.

- **Apple Remote Desktop.** This service makes it possible for other users to control (or at least "watch") your Mac via the Apple Remote Desktop application (see www.apple.com/remotedesktop for details). You can also use third-party VNC software, such as Chicken of the VNC, by Geekspiff (www.geekspiff.com/software). With this option, you can "take over" control of another user's computer almost as if you were physically seated in front of it.

  SEE: • "Take Note: Remote Sharing via VNC," later in this chapter, for more details.

- **Remote Apple Events.** Enabling this option allows applications (including AppleScripts) running on remote computers to interact with your computer. Unless you have a specific reason to allow such scripts and applications from a trusted user, you should keep this option turned off: People can do some very malicious things to your computer by using Apple Events.

- **Printer Sharing.** This option lets users on your local network print to printers connected directly to your Mac. You can share any printer that is listed in Printer Setup Utility (whether connected via USB, Ethernet, FireWire, or AirPort).

  SEE: • "Printer Sharing," in Chapter 7, for more details.

- **Xgrid.** This option is mainly used in educational and research environments. It allows computers to join together in a "grid" so that the processing load of computer-intensive tasks is shared. I will not be discussing this option further.

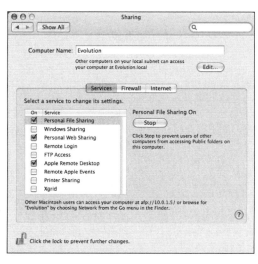

Figure 9.1

The Services pane of the Sharing System Preferences pane.

TAKE NOTE ▶ When Services Addresses Are Not Correct

When you click a service name, a brief description of its function appears below the Start/Stop button in the Services pane. If you enable the service, the address information needed to access your computer via that service is summarized at the bottom of the pane, if applicable. For example, after you enable Personal File Sharing, that description will read something like the following: "Other Macintosh users can access your computer at afp://68.60.48.4 or browse for '*computer-name*' by choosing Network from the Go menu in the Finder." A similarly appropriate message appears, citing the URLs needed for Web access, if you enable Personal Web Sharing. And so on.

If you attempt to use an address listed in the Services pane and it does not work, there are two likely explanations:

Addresses and routers. If your Mac is connected to a hardware router (including an AirPort Base Station) using network address translation (NAT), the URL will be incorrect for anyone outside of your local network. The address shown in Services will be the local IP address, which will work for users connecting from elsewhere on your local network but not from remote locations. For example, if the address is something that begins with 192 or 10, it's good only for local machines connected to the same router.

To access your Mac from remote locations, you need to use the WAN IP address of the router itself. For an AirPort Base Station, for example, you can access the WAN IP address by launching AirPort Admin Utility, choosing the option to configure the Base Station, and then clicking the Internet tab. If you don't want to bother checking the router directly to find out your true current IP address, there are various shareware utilities and even Web sites that provide this information. For example, try WhatIsMyIPAddress.com.

You will also likely need to use your router's port-mapping functionality to map the relevant port used for the service to your computer. For example, to get Web Sharing to work, you would need to map port 80 from your router to your computer.

Dynamic IP addresses. An IP address may be correct when you check it (either via the Sharing System Preferences pane or via your router software, as appropriate). However, unless it is a static IP address (which is unlikely for users with a dial-up or DHCP connection), the IP address will change periodically. Thus, if you later try to use the address from a remote location, it may not work (if it has changed since you last checked). This means you can't use these dynamic IP addresses as permanent addresses—frustrating if you want to give other people a "permanent" URL for accessing your Web site, for example.

One solution is to get a static IP address—if your ISP provides this option. In fact, if you're able to get a static IP address, you can even register a domain name, such as www.*yourname*.com, via one of the main domain registration services, and provide that domain name instead of the IP address. This is desirable if you expect frequent access to your computer or Web site. Otherwise, you may be able to use a *dynamic DNS service*. These services assign your machine a permanent domain name that remains linked to your machine despite changes in the IP address. One site that offers this service is DynDNS (www.dyndns.org).

SEE: • "Take Note: What Are the TCP/IP Settings?" and "Internet routers and port mapping," in Chapter 8, for more details.

Firewall

Click the Firewall button in Sharing's tab bar to access its firewall pane. In brief, a firewall is software (which can run on your own computer, a router, or dedicated firewall hardware) that prevents incoming data that has not been specifically requested from reaching your computer. Firewalls exist primarily to prevent hackers from accessing your computer without permission. However, there may be times when you *want* unrequested data to get through a firewall. Why? As described in the previous chapter (in discussions about port mapping) and in "Take Note: When Services Addresses Are Not Correct" in this chapter, Sharing services count on remote users' being able to connect to your Mac without your first contacting them. If you enable Personal File Sharing, for example, it means you want incoming data from remote Sharing users passed to your computer. Thus, if you turn the firewall on in general, you would still want to selectively disable it for Personal File Sharing.

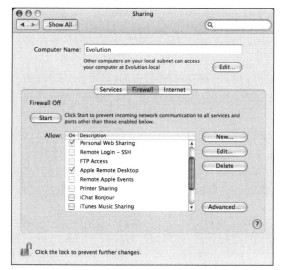
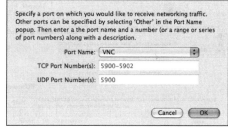

Figure 9.2

Left, *the Firewall pane of the Sharing System Preferences pane;* right, *the dialog that drops down if you click the New button in the Firewall pane.*

To understand how you can "open up" a firewall for certain services, refer back to the discussion of ports in Chapter 8. I explained that each service on a server (for example, Web Sharing, Personal File Sharing, and FTP in Mac OS X) uses a specific port. File Sharing, for example, uses ports 427 and 548. Thus, if you allowed incoming traffic destined for ports 427 or 548, your firewall would remain largely effective, but remote users would be able to access Personal File Sharing.

The Firewall options available in the Sharing System Preferences pane are essentially a graphical front end to the Unix firewall ipfw command. It does not provide access to all the features of ipfw, so there may be times when you will want to run ipfw in Terminal. However, for most users this should be rarely needed. There are also third-party applications, such as Brian R. Hill's BrickHouse (http://personalpages.tds.net/~brian_hill/brickhouse.html), that provide a more complete front end to ipfw.

To enable and modify the firewall in the Sharing System Preferences pane, here's what to do:

- **Enable/disable.** To turn on the firewall, click the Start button. Once the firewall is running, you can selectively enable or disable specific ports and services. Well . . . almost.

  Note: To turn off the firewall completely, click the Stop button (which was the Start button before you turned the firewall on).

  Mac OS X includes a collection of preinstalled firewall rules. (A *rule* instructs the firewall to allow or deny specific kinds of traffic.) The names of the rules (together with their respective port numbers) are provided in the Allow list in the Firewall pane. All of these rules *allow* the named service. Thus, if the Personal File Sharing rule is enabled, the ports for Personal File Sharing are open even when the firewall is running. A rule is enabled (or active) when the On box next to its name is checked.

  Most of the preinstalled rules pertain to the services listed in the Services pane of Sharing System Preferences. You do not enable or disable these rules in the Firewall pane. Instead, they are automatically enabled when you turn on the service in the Services pane. For example, if you enable Personal File Sharing in Services and then switch to the Firewall pane, you'll see that the Personal File Sharing rule has been activated. In other words, Mac OS X's firewall is smart enough to automatically open those ports needed for the services you've activated.

  Mac OS X 10.4 Tiger's preinstalled list also contains several rules that don't correspond to services from the Sharing list: iChat Bonjour, iTunes Music Sharing, Network Time, and iPhoto Bonjour Sharing. You will need to enable these rules to use the services for which they are named.

  When making any changes to rules (as described next), turn the firewall off. Turn it back on when you are done with your changes. Otherwise, the change may not take effect immediately.

- **Create new rules.** To create a new rule (that is, one that's not prein-stalled), click the New button. A dialog drops down that includes a Port Name pop-up menu and TCP and UDP Port Number fields. The pop-up menu includes some services that Tiger already knows about (MSN Messenger, Timbuktu, and VNC, for example). If you choose one of them, the Port Number fields are filled in automatically. Click OK, and the new rule is created. It is automatically added to the list of rules in the Allow list; it is also enabled (that is, its On box is checked). This means that the port for the service is open even when the firewall is running.

  If you want to create a firewall rule for a service that is not listed in the Port Name pop-up menu, choose Other from that same menu. This allows you to manually provide the port (or range of ports) that need to be "open" for the service to work. Give the new rule a descriptive name and then click OK to create it. I provide more details on how to do this just below.

- **Edit/delete existing rules.** To edit an existing rule, select the rule and click the Edit button. This causes the same dialog to drop down that appeared when you selected New—except that the settings for the selected port are already present and accessible for editing. Even if you don't intend to edit the rule, this is a useful way to check to see the precise ports that a listed rule opens. For example, you would learn that the iTunes Music Sharing rule opens port 3689.

  Note: You can also see what ports a rule affects by placing your pointer over the rule name and waiting for the yellow tool tip text to appear.

  To delete an existing rule, select the rule and click the Delete button.

  One exception: You cannot edit or delete a rule that's linked to services from the Services list (such as Personal File Sharing). If you try, you will get the following error message: "You cannot change the firewall settings for this service." You also cannot change the port numbers for a port (such as iTunes Music Sharing) selected from the Port Name pop-up menu.

Advanced options. New in Tiger, you have additional control over Mac OS X's firewall settings via the Advanced button. In particular:

- **Block UDP Traffic.** UDP stands for *User Datagram Protocol*. It is an alternative to TCP as a means of transmitting data over the Internet, especially smaller units that do not require dividing up into packets and thus do not require a formal "connection" between the two computers. In most cases, you would leave your computer open to UDP traffic, as various applications (such as iChat) use it. However, there is a risk that a hacker can then use this path as an entry to your computer. To protect against this, enable this block. If, as a result, you find that some Internet-related actions that you need no longer work (such as iChat AV), you may have to unblock UDP.

  SEE: • "iChat AV and UDP ports," later in this section.
  - "Internet routers and port mapping," in Chapter 8, for more on TCP versus UDP.

- **Enable Firewall Logging.** This enables a log that keeps track of all firewall-related events, such as if and when someone tries to breach your firewall and is blocked. To see the log, click the Open Log button. It launches Console and opens a log file called ipfw.log.

- **Enable Stealth Mode.** This provides an extra layer of security. If a user is trolling for computers that he can potentially hack, he can send out commands that yield a reply if a computer is located at a given address. This can occur even if your firewall is enabled. But it won't happen if you also enable Stealth mode. To uninvited guests, it will be as if your computer does not exist. Note: As you might guess, hackers have figured out ways to potentially circumvent this protection, so you cannot count on this as being 100 percent secure.

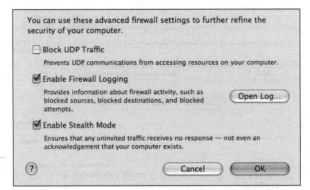

Figure 9.3

Firewall's Advanced options.

Figure 9.4

The message that appears when you launch iChat AV if Sharing's firewall is on, the iChat Bonjour rule is not enabled, and Bonjour is enabled in iChat AV.

Opening specific ports. When you're unable to connect to another computer or a user is unable to connect to your computer, and the connection settings appear correct, the cause may be the firewall. The quickest solution is to turn the firewall off temporarily. Alternatively, and more securely, you can leave the firewall enabled but create and/or open the port that's needed for the sharing to work. Here are a few suggestions about ports you might want to create or enable:

•   **iChat AV Bonjour text messaging.** If you're having trouble receiving iChat messages over Bonjour, and Sharing's firewall is on, make sure you've enabled the iChat Bonjour rule to open ports 5297 and 5298.

•   **iChat AV file transfers.** If you're having trouble sending or receiving files via iChat when the firewall is enabled, the solution is to create a new rule that opens port 5190. To do so, follow these steps:

   1. Open the Sharing System Preferences pane and select the Firewall tab.

   2. If the firewall is running (which it presumably is), click the Stop button.

   3. Now click the New button.

   4. From the Port Name pop-up menu, choose Other.

   5. In the TCP Port Number field, type 5190.

   6. In the Description field, give the new rule a name (such as *iChat File Transfer*).

   7. Click OK to create the new rule.

   8. Click the Start button to restart the firewall.

- **iChat AV invitations.** Port 5060 is used for the signaling and initiating of AV iChat invitations. If you're having trouble getting this feature to work, open this port. To do so, you could include port 5060 in Step 5 above. That is, type 5060, 5190.

  Combining this advice with the first two items above, you should open a total of four ports to ensure access to all services in iChat AV when Sharing's firewall is on: 5060, 5190, 5297, and 5298. The other alternative, of course, is to turn the firewall off while using iChat AV.

- **iChat AV and UDP ports.** With its default settings, the firewall component of the Sharing System Preferences pane only blocks TCP ports. Thus, it is generally not necessary to use Sharing's firewall to create rules to open access to UDP ports; such ports are open by default. Apple states that all iChat AV traffic is UDP-only except for ports 5190 and 5298, which need to be open for both TCP and UDP. This seems to imply that opening ports 5060 and 5297 (as described above) should not be necessary with Sharing's firewall. However, Apple recommends opening these ports anyway. You can experiment to see exactly what's needed for your setup.

  In addition, if you enable the Block UDP Traffic option in Firewall's Advanced settings, this will likely prevent iChat from working.

  If you use firewall software other than Sharing's firewall, it will likely block both TCP and UDP traffic. Thus, you may need to open additional ports for iChat AV to work. For example, iChat AV uses ports 16384 to 16403 to send, receive, and optimize AV streams. I had to open this range of ports (for UDP) in my Linksys router's Port Forwarding settings before I could get iChat AV to work. Note: If you use a router, you may have to open the same ports (TCP and UDP) on your router as you do in Sharing's firewall.

  Check out this Apple Knowledge Base article for more on iChat and firewalls: http://docs.info.apple.com/article.html?artnum=93208.

- **iTunes.** To enable locally connected users to share your iTunes music library and to access other users' music, enable the "Look for shared music" and "Share my music" options in the Sharing section of iTunes' Preferences. If, after doing this, you still cannot get this feature to work, the problem may be caused by the firewall's running on one or both of the interacting computers. To fix this, enable the iTunes Music Sharing rule.

  SEE: • "Network Security," later in this chapter, for more on firewalls and related topics.

  • "Technically Speaking: Using ipfw," later in this chapter, for the solution to a problem where you get a message that says, "Other firewall software is running on your computer."

  • "Take Note: File Sharing: It's Your Choice," later in this chapter, for related information.

  • "Internet routers and port mapping," in Chapter 8, for more on ports, including TCP versus UDP issues.

  • Chapter 11, for more on iChat, iTunes, and iSync, including other firewall-related issues.

Internet

The final of Sharing's three tabs is Internet. In Chapter 8, I talked about using software Internet routers to share a single Internet connection with multiple computers. Mac OS X includes such a router, which you can access via the Internet pane of Sharing preferences. With Internet Sharing, you can share your primary Internet connection (such as a cable modem connected to your desktop Mac via Built-in Ethernet) with other computers on your Mac's network (via AirPort, for example, if all the Macs have AirPort cards). Note that if you already have a router or an AirPort Base Station, you need not bother with this feature. Indeed, trying to do so may even cause a conflict that interrupts Internet access.

SEE: • "Using a Router," in Chapter 8, for related information.

If you don't have an Internet router or AirPort Base Station, and you have more than one computer on your local network, you will almost certainly want to use this feature. For users who have AirPort cards but no Base Station, the most exciting thing about Internet Sharing is that it can serve as a Software Base Station—a method of sharing an Internet connection from your Mac to all other computers via an AirPort network.

SEE: • "AirPort" and "Take Note: Software Routers: Software AirPort Base Station and More," in Chapter 8, for related information.

Figure 9.5

The Internet pane of the Sharing System Preferences pane.

The first time you open the Internet pane of Sharing System Preferences, it will say Internet Sharing Off. To get Internet Sharing running, follow these steps:

1. From the "Share your connection from" pop-up menu, select the port to which you will be connected to the Internet when Internet Sharing is on.

2. The "To computers using" list will include all ports that can be used to share your Internet connection with other computers. For a port to be used, it must be enabled in the Network System Preferences pane, and the needed cables or other hardware must be connected. If your desired port meets these requirements, check its On box. Note: You can enable more than one port from this list, if you wish.

One caveat: Be careful about using the same port for sharing to computers and your Internet connection. For example, if you choose Ethernet in both the "Share your connection from" pop-up menu and the "To computers using" list, you will get a warning message that states: "If you turn on this port, your Internet Service provider might terminate your service . . ." Even if your ISP doesn't object, your Sharing connection may not succeed. More significantly, there are only a few cases where you would even want to do this (for example, I can't see why you would ever choose AirPort for both ports). Note: There appears to be some inconsistency in how Sharing works here: When I choose AirPort as the shared connection, sometimes AirPort disappears from the Sharing list below, making the dual selection impossible; other times AirPort remains in the list and can be selected.

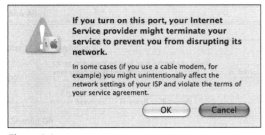 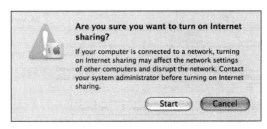

Figure 9.6

Two Internet Sharing warning messages that may appear when you enable this feature, as described in the text.

3. If you will be connecting to computers via AirPort, click the AirPort Options button. From here, you can set up a name and password for your network (as you would normally otherwise do via the AirPort Admin Utility, if you had a hardware Base Station).

4. The Start button should now be enabled. Click it to turn Internet Sharing on.

After clicking the Start button, you will get a warning that you may potentially disrupt your network by using Internet Sharing, asking, "Are you sure you want to turn on Internet sharing?" This should only be a concern if you are already part of a larger network, such as at a university. For your own home, even if something goes wrong, you can correct it without annoying anyone simply by turning Sharing off again.

Note: If you selected AirPort in the "To computers using" list, you will see a change in the AirPort status menu: An arrow will appear in the menu bar icon, and the menu will shift to state that Internet Sharing is on.

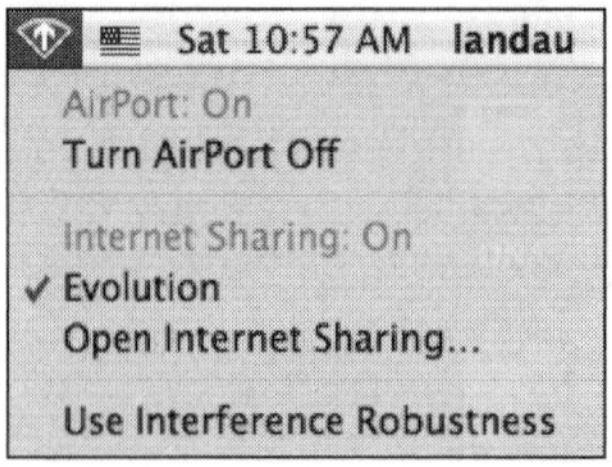

Figure 9.7

The AirPort menu with a Mac set up as a software AirPort Base Station.

Note: You cannot make further changes to Internet Sharing settings until you click the Stop button to turn Internet Sharing off again.

Troubleshooting tip: If you have problems getting Internet Sharing to work, turn Sharing off. Next, go to Network System Preferences and move the port for the Internet connection to the top of the Network Port Configurations list, with the Sharing port enabled and second in the list. Then turn Internet Sharing back on. Similarly, on the Macs that will be sharing the connection from the Internet-connected Mac, the Sharing port should be at the top of the list.

SEE: • "Take Note: Setting Up and Using Internet Sharing and File Sharing," below, for a more detailed example, using Internet Sharing over a FireWire connection.

TAKE NOTE ▶ Setting Up and Using Internet Sharing and File Sharing

This sidebar provides two different examples of ways that Sharing options can be used. It shows how to set up two locally connected computers to (1) use Internet Sharing so that one can get an Internet connection from the other, and (2) use Personal File Sharing to share data between the two computers. A FireWire connection will be used as the connection method in both cases. We will additionally assume that the host Mac is an iMac connected to the Internet via Ethernet; an iBook is the Mac that seeks to share.

Internet Sharing. To set up Internet Sharing for FireWire, you first have to establish a FireWire network connection between the two Macs. Follow these steps:

1. Connect a FireWire cable between the two Macs.

2. In the Network System Preferences pane on the iMac, make sure that a FireWire port configuration is listed and enabled.

Note: It doesn't appear to matter what's chosen from the Configure IPv4 menu in FireWire's TCP/IP pane—it can even be Off. The important thing is for the port to be enabled in the Network Port Configurations list.

continues on next page

TAKE NOTE ▶ **Setting Up and Using Internet Sharing and File Sharing** *continued*

3. In the Sharing System Preferences pane of the iMac, click the Internet tab. Assuming that the iMac is connected to the Internet via Ethernet, from the "Share your connection from" pop-up menu choose Built-in Ethernet.

4. From the "To computers using" list, choose the FireWire port. To do this, check the On box next to the FireWire port.

5. Click the Start button to turn on Internet Sharing. If and when a warning message appears, click Start again. Internet Sharing is now active.

   Note: Once you've done this, the Start button will change to a Stop button.

   You are now set to share the iMac's Internet connection with the iBook.

6. On the iBook, go to the Network System Preferences pane. Enable the FireWire port in Network Port Configurations (if it's not already enabled).

7. Choose the FireWire port from the Show pop-up menu. In the TCP/IP pane that appears, choose Using DHCP from the Configure pop-up menu. Click Apply Now.

8. The shared Internet connection should now be established. To confirm this, from the Show pop-up menu on the iBook choose Network Status. The listing for the FireWire port should now read, "You are connected to the Internet via Built-in FireWire." If so, all is well!

   You should now be able to use the shared connection, such as to browse the Web in Safari.

Note: You can follow the same general rules to set up other network variations. For example, if you want to connect the iMac and the iBook using AirPort: (1) The two computers would need AirPort cards; (2) AirPort should be on and should be enabled in Network System Preferences for both computers; and (3) you would select AirPort rather than Built-in FireWire in Step 4 above. After starting Sharing, select the name of the network (as determined by the setting in AirPort Options) from the AirPort status menu in the menu bar of the iBook.

File Sharing. To set up Personal File Sharing via FireWire, follow these steps:

1. On the host Mac (the iMac in the above example), in the Services pane of the Sharing System Preferences pane, turn on Personal File Sharing.

2. Both computers (the iMac and the iBook in this example) must be actively connected to the shared port. For connecting via FireWire, for example, a FireWire cable must be connected between the two computers; Built-in FireWire must be enabled in the Network System Preferences pane.

   Note: Internet Sharing *does not* also need to be enabled for File Sharing to work. However, you can enable both if you want to share file access and Internet access over the same cable.

continues on next page

TAKE NOTE ▶ Setting Up and Using Internet Sharing and File Sharing *continued*

3. From the Finder's Go menu on the iBook, choose Network. An icon for the iMac should be present. Double-click it to mount the computer (you will need an account name and password to mount the computer other than via guest access).

Troubleshooting tip: If the computer icon does not appear in the Network window, select Connect to Server from the Go menu. From here, for the Server Address, enter the local hostname name of your computer (for example, *computername*.local) or its IP address (as listed in the Services pane of the Sharing System Preferences pane). Click Connect. This may work even if the Network window method does not.

4. The iMac should now be mounted on the iBook. You can transfer files back and forth, as desired.

SEE: • Numerous other sections of this chapter and Chapter 8 for more general information regarding the Sharing and Network System Preferences panes, as well as the Network and Connect to Server items in the Finder's Go menu.

Sharing Services: A Closer Look

In this section, I explore further details of some of the services you can enable via the Services pane of the Sharing System Preferences pane.

SEE: • "Services," earlier in this chapter, for short descriptions of available services.

Personal File Sharing

Other than via guest access, only those users who have accounts set up on your Mac can access it remotely via Personal File Sharing. Further, access limitations are determined largely by user level (admin versus non-admin).

SEE: • "Using Network Browser and Connect to Server," later in this chapter, for details on how to connect to a computer via File Sharing.

Non-administrative users. What a standard (non-administrative) user can access on a Mac depends on whether the user is physically logged in to the Mac (that is, using the Login window on the Mac itself) or connected over a network from another Mac (via Personal File Sharing).

A logged-in non-administrative user can access files in his or her home directory and the Shared directory, and has at least read-only access to files in other users' Public and Sites folders. This non-administrative user can also run applications in the Applications folder, and open and read many other system files; however, he or she cannot edit or move those files.

SEE: • "Accessing other users' folders," "Take Note: The Shared Folder," and "Sticky bits and the Drop Box," in Chapter 6, for more on access to shared and other users' folders.

This same user, connected via Personal File Sharing, however, has much more restricted access. The user will be able to access only his or her own user directory (home folder) and the Public folders of other users. The user will not be able to access other directories outside his or her home folder (not even the Shared user folder), nor will the user be able to access other mounted volumes. This means that if you want to make a file available to a remote File Sharing user, you should place it in your or the other user's Public folder.

Administrative users. Administrative users have virtually the same access whether they're logged in to their accounts locally or connected via Personal File Sharing. In fact, in some cases they have even more access when connected via Personal File Sharing.

More specifically, when connecting to the Mac via Personal File Sharing, an administrative user will see a list of all available volumes on the shared computer (included CDs and DVDs, iDisks, and external drives); the user can choose to mount any or all of them. In addition, there will be a separate share for the user's own home directory.

To access files from your own home directory, choose the home share. You can (as an administrative user) mount the startup volume share instead and navigate to your home directory via the /Users folder. However, if you mount *both* your home share and the startup-volume share, you will probably be unable to access your home directory via the /Users folder; if you try, you will get a message that says you do not have sufficient permissions. Even if this error message does not appear (and it sometimes does not, in my experience), you should avoid this dual access anyway. It prevents problems that might occur if you tried to perform different actions via the two different routes to your home directory.

If you choose to mount the boot drive rather than just your own home directory, you can also navigate, via the /Users folder, to the home directories of other users (as well as the Shared directory). As when logged in locally, you are prohibited from opening all but the publicly accessible folders within another user's home directory.

As an administrative user, you may be able to bypass this prohibition and gain full access to another user's files when connecting via Sharing. To do so, when prompted for a name and password, enter the user's name but your *own* admin password. Mac OS X should log you in as if you actually were that other user—which means you'll have the same level of access as that user would have. In other words, you will have complete access to the user's home folder and the same limitations on accessing any other files and folders. Note: Even with the AttemptAdminAuth value set to "yes," as described in "Technically Speaking: Modifying Apple File Server Preferences," I sometimes find that my admin password is rejected here; I have been unable to determine why.

This "feature" (when it does work!) is a remnant of traditional Unix administration, in which the administrator always has access to other accounts on the system so that he or she can verify operations and fix problems. By logging in as another user, the administrator can see and do exactly what that user can, making it a good way to test accounts. This may seem like a security hole, but since an administrative user can technically access any "private" files (by changing permissions to the prohibited folders) or even log in as root, it's not a unique risk. However, it does underscore the risk of giving too many people admin-level access to your Mac.

Another way to access other users' accounts locally is to log in as the root user. This gives you complete access to all accounts in a single login. Note: You cannot log in as root via Personal File Sharing without enabling this feature, as described in "Technically Speaking: Modifying Apple File Server Preferences."

SEE: • "Using Network Browser and Connect to Server," later in this chapter, for details on how an administrative user can connect to a Mac remotely.

• "Root Access," in Chapter 4, for details on logging in as the root user.

Guests. When accessing a Mac via Personal File Sharing, there is a Guest button in the dialog that requests your name and password. If you click this button, you are immediately connected to the Mac. However, access is limited to the Public folders of all users on the Mac.

Note: Although Mac OS X has guest access enabled by default, other operating systems (Mac OS 9, Windows) may not permit guest access or may have it turned off. In such cases, the Guest button, even if enabled, will not work.

TAKE NOTE ▶ Create a "Guest" Account

For logging in locally (not using Sharing), Mac OS X doesn't provide a guest account. If you want one, however, you can create it yourself. To do so, create a Standard account (via the Accounts System Preferences pane) and name it Guest (or something like that), and do not assign it a password. Now anyone can log in to your Mac using that account, without having to know a password. Once logged in, users will have the same status as any Standard (non-administrative) user. If you want to further limit this guest access, use the Parental Controls pane in the Accounts System Preferences pane. For starters, I would enable Finder & System; then click Configure and, in the window that appears, enable Simple Finder. The account is now listed as a "Managed" account rather than a Standard one.

Any user can now also access this account remotely, as an alternative to File Sharing's "built-in" guest access. Another alternative is to create a File Sharing Only account via the third-party utility SharePoints (as described in "Take Note: Using SharePoints," later in this chapter).

That said, for security reasons—especially if you have Sharing services enabled—I would recommend giving the guest account a password. Another layer of security can never hurt.

TECHNICALLY SPEAKING ▶ Modifying Apple File Server Preferences

Suppose you wanted to enable Personal File Sharing but prevent anyone from having guest access to your computer—that is, you would prefer that the Guest button be removed from or dimmed in the dialog where it normally appears.

Or suppose you wanted to turn off the feature that allows administrative users to log in to other users' accounts with their administrative password (as described in the main text).

Or suppose you wanted to enable AppleShare logging and determine who's currently connected to your Mac.

Can you do these things? Yes, assuming you are an administrator. The solution is to edit the com.apple.AppleFileServer.plist file in /Library/Preferences.

Note: If you delete this .plist file, a new default copy is created. Where do the default settings come from? They're stored in the AppleFileServer application in /System/Library/CoreServices. Use the Show Package Contents command for the application package and navigate to the Resources folder. In here are two defaults files: Defaults.plist and PFSDefaults.plist; the latter is the one that is applicable.

To change settings here, do the following:

1. Turn Personal File Sharing off.
2. Launch Property List Editor with root access (using the Pseudo utility, as described in "Root Access" in Chapter 4).
3. Open the /Library/Preferences/com.apple.AppleFileServer.plist file in Property List Editor.
4. Make the change to the desired value(s) as indicated in the following sections.
5. Save the change and quit Property List Editor.
6. Turn Personal File Sharing back on.

Here are some of the specific things you can do:

Disable guest access. In the com.apple.AppleFileServer.plist file, locate the property named guestAccess. Change the Value of this property from Yes to No.

The next time you attempt to access an account, the Guest option will be dimmed and unselectable.

Note: You can instead use the third-party utility SharePoints to disable guest access.

Enable AppleShare logging. In the com.apple.AppleFileServer.plist file, locate the property named activityLog. Change the Value of this property from No to Yes.

continues on next page

TECHNICALLY SPEAKING ▶ Modifying Apple File Server Preferences *continued*

Mac OS X has the capability to keep a log of all File Sharing activity, but it is turned off by default. Doing the above turns it on. The next time someone logs in to your Mac remotely via File Sharing, a log file named AppleFileServiceAccess.log will be created in the /Library/Logs/AppleFileService directory. The log's contents will be updated as it logs all File Sharing activity. You can best view the contents by opening the log file in the Console application or any text editor.

One use of this log is to determine who's currently connected to your computer via File Sharing. This was much easier to check in Mac OS 9 (you simply viewed the Activity Monitor in the File Sharing control panel). Otherwise, the third-party utility AFS Monitor, from HornWare (www.hornware.com), can be used to display a list of connected users. Maybe in the next Mac OS X upgrade Apple will make this a more accessible feature.

Note: You can instead use the third-party utility SharePoints to enable logging.

Disable admin logins to other accounts. In the com.apple.AppleFileServer.plist file, locate the property named AttemptAdminAuth. Change the Value of this property from Yes to No.

After this change, administrators can no longer use their own password to log in to other users' accounts via Personal File Sharing (as described in the main text).

Login as root user. In the com.apple.AppleFileServer.plist file, locate the property named allowRootLogin. Change the Value of this property from No to Yes.

Assuming that you have enabled the root account (as described in "Root Access," in Chapter 4), you can now log in to that account via File Sharing, using the user name "root" and the root account password (as set up in NetInfo Manager).

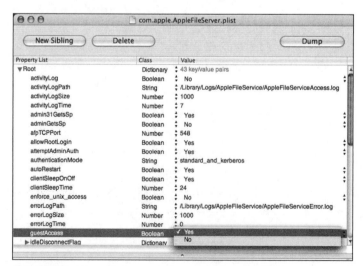

Figure 9.8

You can disable guest access via the highlighted setting in the com.apple.AppleFileServer.plist file.

Sharing and FileVault. If FileVault is enabled for your account and you connect to your computer when your account is not currently logged in locally, all you will see in your home directory is the FileVault sparseimage file. To access your files, double-click the sparseimage file and enter your password when requested. The sparseimage will mount on your Desktop. You can now read and write to the mounted volume.

Other users who connect via File Sharing will not be able to access your account (not even the Public folders) if FileVault is enabled and you're not logged in locally (unless they know your password, of course!). At most, they will see the sparseimage file. In theory, if you're an administrative user and know the FileVault master password, you should be able to use it to mount sparseimage files of other users. However, this does not work—or at least not as of this writing.

SEE: • "FileVault," in the "Personal" section of Chapter 2, for more on this feature.

Sharing individual folders. A significant limitation of Personal File Sharing in Mac OS X is that you cannot easily share individual folders (or *shares* or *share points*, as they're technically called)—useful, for example, if you wanted to make your Pictures folder accessible to other users. Mac OS X actually includes the ability to modify the default Sharing settings and access share points directly. However, the Sharing System Preferences pane does not provide access to this capability. If you want to separately assign sharing for individual folders, you need to do so via either NetInfo Manager (or Terminal commands that access NetInfo) or third-party software, such as SharePoints. The latter is much easier and the method I recommend.

SEE: • "Take Note: Using SharePoints," later in this chapter.

Stopping File Sharing with users connected. To turn off Personal File Sharing, select its name in the Services pane and click the Stop button.

If you stop Sharing when other users are connected to your Mac, a dialog drops down, stating, "There may be users connected to this machine. How many minutes until File Sharing is turned off?" The turn-off time is set to 10 minutes by default. If you select this, users on connected computers will get a warning message about the impending disconnect. This gives those users a chance to unmount the shared volume before they're disconnected. However, you can bypass this warning by entering 0 as the time delay, thus disconnecting users immediately (and causing them to lose any unsaved changes in documents opened from your computer—which is why I recommend against this).

Similarly, if you shut down or restart your shared Mac, a disconnection occurs. Again, you should get a warning message first, such as the following: "Apple File Sharing Users Connected. There are # AFP user(s) still connected. Are you sure you want to restart?"

SEE: • "Host (or client) unexpectedly disconnects," in "Troubleshooting Network Browser and Connect to Server," later in this chapter, for related information and figures.

TAKE NOTE ▶ Using SharePoints

By default, Personal File Sharing in Mac OS X shares only the Public folder of each user's home directory. However, you can share other folders by creating other *share points*—Mac OS X's term for a shared directory. The "official" way to create and modify share points is by using NetInfo Manager. An easier (and safer) way, however, is to use one of several third-party utilities that simplify this process. My favorite is HornWare's SharePoints (www.hornware.com).

SharePoints is available as a stand-alone application or as a System Preferences pane. Although both versions operate identically and provide the same functionality, the pane version is a bit more accessible—you generally have the System Preferences window open when you're working with Sharing, anyway. However, the screen shots shown here are of the application window.

Before making any changes, click the padlock icon to unlock the settings (to do so, you must provide your administrator user name and password when prompted).

Adding share points. To add a share point, follow these steps:

1. Choose the "Normal" Shares tab.

2. Enter a name for your share point in the Share Name field.

3. In the Directory field, enter the path to the folder you want to share (or click the Browse button to navigate to the folder).

4. Click the Show File System Properties button. From the Owner, Group, and Permissions pop-up menus, enter your desired settings. If you set permissions for Everyone to Read or Read/Write, any remote user will be able to view the new share point.

   Note that the permissions you set here apply only to the top-level folder; enclosed files and folders will keep their original permissions for security reasons. If you want enclosed files and folders to reflect the new permissions, you'll need to set them separately, using the Finder's Get Info window or a utility such as Rainer Brockerhoff's XRay (www.brockerhoff.net/xray). However, if you check the "Inherit permissions from parent" box, items later added to the share point folder will acquire the permissions of the share point (parent) folder.

5. From the AppleFileServer (AFS) Sharing pop-up menu, choose "Shared (+)."

6. Click the Create New Share button to create the new share point.

If you want to add another share point, repeat these steps.

To remove a share point from the list, select it and then click the Delete Selected Share button. This will not undo changes made to Owner, Group, and Permissions settings, nor will it actually *delete* the folder in the Finder; however, it will prevent the folder from being accessed via File Sharing.

To edit an existing share point, make the desired changes and click the Update Share button.

continues on next page

TAKE NOTE ▶ Using SharePoints *continued*

Unsharing a Public share point. SharePoints also allows you to *prevent* a user's Public folder from being shared. If you want to disable Public-folder sharing, follow these steps:

1. Choose the Users & "Public" Shares tab.

2. In the User column on the left, select the user whose Public folder you *do not* want to share.

3. In the "Public Directory Shared?" pop-up menu, change Yes to No.

4. Click the Update User button. Note: The Add New User button in Figure 9.9 becomes Update User if and when you select a user in the column on the left.

File Sharing Only users. A handy SharePoints feature allows you to create File Sharing Only users—users who can log in *only* via File Sharing. (In other words, they can't log in locally, nor can they log in via a Terminal connection, FTP, or any other service.) The advantage of File Sharing Only users is that you don't have to clutter up your Mac with accounts for users who will never use it locally. To create a File Sharing Only user, follow these steps:

1. Select the Users & "Public" Shares tab, but *do not* choose an existing user. (If a user is already chosen, click in the empty space in the users box to deselect it.)

2. Fill in the information for the user in the Full Name, Short Name, Group, and UID fields. (You should click Get Next UID if you're unsure what number to assign, and choose "staff" as the group.)

3. Click the Add New User button. You will be asked whether you're sure that you want to add a File Sharing Only User. Click Yes; you will then be asked to enter a password for the new user.

Creating new groups. As discussed in Chapters 4 and 6, each file and folder in Mac OS X is assigned to a group. You can view an item's group by opening the Get Info window for the item and viewing the Ownership & Permissions section. You can change the group assignment for an item from here, but you cannot create or delete groups. You *can* do this via SharePoints— something you can otherwise accomplish only via NetInfo Manager. To do so, follow these steps:

1. Choose the Groups tab, but *do not* choose an existing group. (If a group is already chosen, click in the empty space in the Groups box to deselect it.)

2. In the Group field, type a name for the new group.

3. Click the Get Next GID button to have SharePoints find the next available group ID number.

4. Click the Add New Group button.

5. To add users to the group, select the group in the groups list on the left; then add users by selecting user names in the Users list on the right and clicking the Add (+) button.

6. Once you've added the desired users, click the Update Group button. Note: The Add New Group button in Figure 9.9 becomes Update Group if and when you select a group in the column on the left.

Changing AFS Properties. The AFS Properties pane provides options such as Allow Guest Access and "Enable logging" (as noted in "Technically Speaking: Modifying Apple File Server Preferences").

SEE: • "Technically Speaking: Windows File Sharing: Custom Options and SharePoints," later in this chapter, for related information.

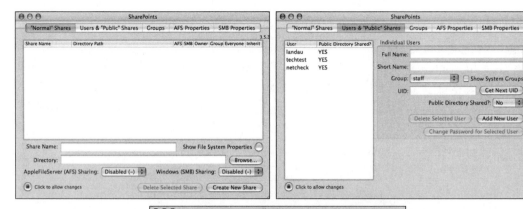

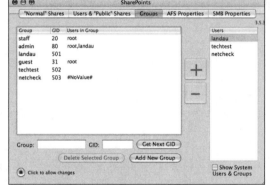

Figure 9.9

The SharePoints utility: top left, *the "Normal" Shares pane;* top right, *the Users & "Public" Shares pane;* bottom, *the Groups pane.*

TAKE NOTE ▶ Remote Sharing via VNC

Apple Remote Desktop is one of the services listed in the Services pane of the Sharing System Preferences pane. It is primarily designed to work with Apple's Remote Desktop software. This software is designed especially for classroom environments, allowing an instructor to access the computers of all students in a class or lab. This access includes the ability to view and control the display of another computer on your computer, almost as if you were physically sitting in front of it. It is not limited to a local lab setup; you can connect to remote computers (even to a Mac from a Windows PC) in other locations as well, over the Internet. You can observe and/or manipulate the remote computer for monitoring activity, for collaborative work, or for providing troubleshooting help. You can also send messages back and forth. See this Web page for details about Apple Remote Desktop: www.apple.com/remotedesktop.

What is less known is that you can perform similar magic via third-party utilities, eliminating the need to purchase the Apple Remote Desktop package. This is because Apple Remote Desktop is now based on the VNC (Virtual Network Computing) open protocol. The following instructions explain how to do this using a third-party VNC viewer application called Chicken of the VNC.

continues on next page

TAKE NOTE ▶ Remote Sharing via VNC *continued*

From the computer to be controlled (assume it is an iBook for this example), do the following:

1. Open the Sharing System Preferences pane. In the Services pane, select Apple Remote Desktop and click the Start button (or check its On box). A dialog will drop down. If not, click the Access Privileges button.

2. Almost all of the settings here can be ignored, as they are specific to the Apple Remote Desktop software (which is not being used in this example). All you need to do is (a) choose the option "VNC viewers may control screen with password" and enter a password; and (b) select at least one user in the User list. There is no need to enable any of the Allow options.

3. Click OK. Enter your admin password if and when you're asked.

4. The line at the bottom of the window now reads something like this: "Others can manage your computer using address 10.0.1.3."

    In principle, this is the address that others can use to access the computer. However, if the iBook is connected to the Internet via a router (such as an AirPort Base Station), this address is probably a local address. It will work for other computers on the same LAN as the iBook. However, for a computer trying to access the iBook over a WAN, it will not work. Instead, you will need to use the "public" WAN IP address (as found in the Internet pane of the AirPort Admin Utility, if you are using an AirPort Base Station). If you have a dynamic, rather than a static, IP address, you also need to make sure that the address is still current when you try to use it. In addition, you may have to go to the Port Mapping pane of the AirPort Admin Utility and open port 3238; or, if your router has this option, you may instead set the iBook as the "DMZ host" on the network.

    SEE: • "Take Note: When Services Addresses Are Not Correct," earlier in this chapter, as well as several sections of Chapter 8, for more details.

    To keep things simple in this example, I will assume that the address listed in the Sharing pane is one that will work with no further manipulation needed.

On the computer to be doing the controlling (assume it is an iMac), do the following:

1. Launch Chicken of the VNC.

2. In the Host field, enter the IP address (10.0.1.3 in this example).

3. In the Password field, enter the password that you entered on the iBook.

4. Click the Connect button.

If all goes well, the iBook's screen should now appear in a window on the iMac. Using this screen, you can actually control the iBook, including launching applications, opening documents, editing text, and so on. Cool! If the connection fails to work, and you have Sharing's Firewall running, make sure you have opened the VNC port, as described in "Firewall," earlier in this chapter.

Timbuktu Pro. Timbuktu Pro, from Netopia (www.netopia.com), offers another alternative for gaining similar "control" of another user's computer. It is an independent application that does not work via Apple Remote Desktop.

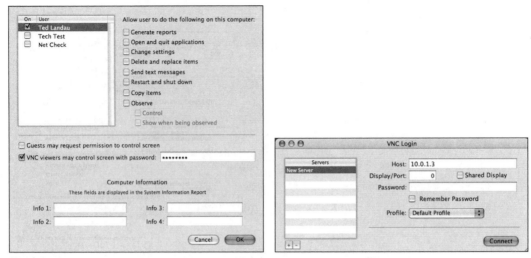

Figure 9.10

Left, *the Access Privileges settings, as accessed from the Apple Remote Desktop listing in the Services pane of the Sharing System Preferences pane;* right, *Chicken of the VNC, a VNC viewer that can work via the Apple Remote Desktop VNC setting.*

Personal Web Sharing

With Personal Web Sharing enabled, anyone—regardless of whether or not he or she has an account on your Mac—can use a Web browser on any computer connected to the Internet to access Web pages stored in the special Web-site folders located on your computer. Each user on your computer has his or her own Web directory, called Sites, located in his or her home folder. In addition, your computer has a general Web directory located at /Library/WebServer/ Documents. Enabling Personal Web Sharing permits Web-browser access to your personal site and to the main computer site.

To access the contents of the pages in a user's Sites folder, type `http://` followed by the IP address of the computer, a slash, a tilde, and the user's short name. For example, to access the Sites folder contents for a user named landau on a computer with an IP address of 68.62.15.134, you would type `http://68.62.15.134/~landau/`.

When using Personal Web Sharing, you should be aware of the following:

- You can find the URLs needed to access the computer site and your personal site at the bottom of the Services pane of Sharing System Preferences when Personal Web Sharing is selected. On my Mac, for example, it currently lists http://10.0.1.5/ and http://10.0.1.5/~landau.

  However, if you use a router, this is probably not the address you need. It is a local address that will work only inside your local network. More likely, you want the current WAN IP address, as listed by your router.

If, however, you want to check out how your own Web pages look in a browser via Web Sharing, you can do so via the above local addresses. Alternatively, you can substitute either localhost or 127.0.0.1 (the default IP local address) for the numeric address cited in Sharing. You can even omit the local IP address altogether, just typing http:///~landau/ (notice the third slash).

Note: Using the local hostname of your computer (for example, matrix.local and evolution.local for my laptop and desktop computers) instead of local-host should also work. However, this was not always successful for me (but it hardly matters, as there are all the other alternatives I just cited).

Note: If you have not placed anything in your personal Sites folder, a default index.html page supplied by Apple will appear.

SEE: • **"Take Note: When Services Addresses Are Not Correct," earlier in this chapter, for more details.**

- If you type just http:// followed by the WAN IP address for your machine, *without* your account name (http://68.62.15.134, for example), you will get whatever Web pages are stored in /Library/WebServer/Documents. This folder can be used for a site that you do not want linked to a particular user on your Mac.

  To access this site locally, you can instead type http://localhost or http:///.

  Note: If you have not placed anything in your main WebServer/Documents folder, a default index.html page supplied by Apple will appear.

Figure 9.11

Default (index.html) pages for Personal Web Sharing.

- If a Web-site folder has a document named index.html at the root level of the folder used for Web Sharing, that document will be used as the home-page of the Web site; Mac OS X includes such a default index.html file in every Web-site folder. If such a document does not exist in a Sites or

WebServer/Documents folder, anyone trying to view the default page will receive an error message. The default setting for Mac OS X's Web Server is to *not* display directory contents when a default page is not present.

- If you're using a router, accessing Personal Web Sharing will likely require that you forward port 80 to the computer with Personal Web Sharing enabled. This is done via the router's port-mapping/forwarding feature. In such setups, only one of your local computers can be set as a Web server at any one time.

  SEE: • "Internet routers and port mapping," in Chapter 8.

- When accessing a user's Web page, you should ideally place a slash after the name in the URL. That is, for example, type /~landau/, not just /~landau. If you leave off the last slash, you may get a localhost error (it may attempt to connect to 127.0.0.1 and fail), though this appears to be fixed in the latest versions of Mac OS X.

- As opposed to the broader access typical with Personal File Sharing, a remote user connecting to Personal Web Sharing cannot access *any* files outside the Sites folder or the computer's WebServer/Documents folder, which makes Web Sharing a more secure way to share files with the public. In addition, users can access only files linked from a Web page that's accessible from the homepage, or via a specific URL that points to a file in the Sites folder. Thus, if a user of the "naomi" account placed a file called myapp.zip in her Sites folder, a user could download it via a URL to access that file, such as http://68.62.15.134/~naomi/myapp.zip.

- When you enable Web Sharing, you're actually activating a full installation of the widely used (and feature-rich) Apache Web server for Unix, which is included in Mac OS X. If you are familiar with Unix, you can access many more advanced Web Sharing features (such as working with Perl scripts and CGI commands) by entering Apache commands in Terminal and by modifying the Apache configuration files.

.Mac HomePage. A simpler but more limited way to create a Web site, if you have a .Mac account, is to set it up via .Mac's HomePage feature. This method has the advantage of providing a permanent URL, and access does not require that your computer be on and connected to the Internet.

FTP Access

If you check the FTP Access box in the Services pane of the Sharing System Preferences pane, Mac OS X's built-in FTP server starts up. Anyone with an account on your computer and an FTP client (such as Fetch, Transmit, or RBrowser) will be able to connect and browse files by entering the IP address or domain name of your computer, along with a valid user name and password. Users can also connect via FTP from another Mac OS X computer by using the Connect to Server command and entering ftp:// as the address prefix (as opposed to the default afp:// used for Personal File Sharing). This mounts a volume on the Mac, similar to what would happen if you mounted a network file via File Sharing. However, as of this writing, using Connect to Server (instead of a dedicated FTP client) means you'll only be able to download files; you will not be able to upload files or perform any other "write" actions.

Otherwise, FTP Access limits users to the same access they would have if they were physically sitting at the computer, logged in to their accounts. They will have full read-and-write access to their own home folders in the /Users folder, as well as read access to other users' Public and Sites folders, but they will also have read access to most other system-level files. Because read access via FTP means the ability to view and download, FTP users will be able to download system, application, and settings files located outside private folders in the /Users folder. They won't be able to alter or delete these files, but you should stop to consider whether you have sensitive files or information in nonprivate areas of your computer.

One other (serious) caveat to FTP Access is that FTP is not a secure protocol: When you connect to an FTP server, your user name and password are sent over the Internet in plain text, so anyone who might be able to intercept your connection attempt will be able to see your user name and password—and thus may be able to use them to gain access to your Mac via FTP Access or even another service. A secure alternative to FTP is Secure FTP (SFTP), discussed later in the chapter in "SSH and SFTP."

Web browsers and FTP. Because most Web browsers support the FTP protocol, you can also connect via FTP using a Web browser. For example, typing `ftp://IPaddress` or `ftp://domainname` should work.

If you try to access any FTP account that requires a name and password, you should be prompted to do so. In most Web browsers, if you successfully log in, you will get a directory listing of the home directory of the account. Each directory item will be a link; click a link to view the contents of the directory. If you click a file, it is downloaded to your computer.

Safari works a bit differently: The FTP account opens as a volume in the Finder, independent of the browser itself. Further, you have only read access to the volume, even if you would have write access had you used an FTP client. In other words, you cannot upload files via FTP using the Safari connection.

Windows File Sharing

Whereas Personal File Sharing allows you to share files with other Macs, Windows File Sharing is designed to let you share files with Windows and Unix computers via the SMB/CIFS (*Server Message Block/Common Internet Filesystem*) protocol. (The actual server software is called *Samba*.) If you enable Windows File Sharing in the Sharing System Preferences pane, anyone with a user account on your Mac will be able to connect from a Windows (or Unix) computer and access his or her home directory. (By default, there is no guest access via Windows File Sharing.)

To let Windows users access your Mac, all you need to do is enable Windows Sharing in the Services pane of the Sharing System Preferences pane. If you have more than one account on your Mac, you will be prompted to indicate which one(s) can use Windows Sharing; you must enable at least one account in order to enable Windows Sharing at all.

As with Personal File Sharing, a user must have an account on your Mac to access the Mac via Windows File Sharing (unless you enable guest access, as described later).

By default, Windows File Sharing allows remote users to access their own home directories; however, unlike with Personal File Sharing, these users won't be able to access other users' Public folders. This means that to share a file with a remote Windows user, you'll need to place it in *that user's* Public folder (which means you must place it in his or her Drop Box).

Note: Although it sounds odd, you can also connect two *Macs* via Windows Sharing, just as you can via Personal File Sharing. This is because Mac OS X is designed to allow access to Windows shares. In fact, if a Mac on your local network has both Windows File Sharing and Personal File Sharing enabled, it may appear twice in the Network Browser. If so, choose only one server icon to access the Mac. If you want to connect to another Mac via Windows File Sharing using Connect to Server, you precede the address of the Mac with *smb://* (as described more in "Connect to Server," later in this chapter). Of course, this feature also works to connect to a Windows PC from a Mac, which is its more common function!

SEE: • **"Network Browser," later in this chapter, for more on this feature.**

Figure 9.12

The login dialog that appears on a Mac after you access a computer (either a Windows machine or a Mac with Windows File Sharing enabled) via an smb:// URL in Connect to Server.

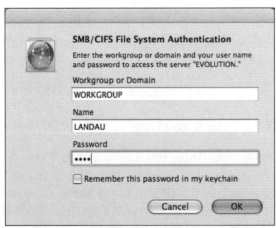

Connecting from a Windows machine to a Mac. The procedure that Windows users employ to connect varies depending on whether they're connecting from a local network or over the Internet, and on which version of Windows they're using.

For a user on the same local network, follow these steps:

1. From the Start menu, open My Network Places (called Network Neighborhood in older versions of Windows).

2. Provided that your Mac's Workgroup name—by default, *Workgroup*— is the same as the one for the Windows computer, your Mac will be visible in the Network Neighborhood or Places window. (On XP, the user may need to click View Workgroup Computers in the Explorer bar.)

   or

   If your Workgroup name differs, the user should open Entire Network and find your Workgroup. In XP, the user should click Microsoft Windows Network in the Explorer bar. If the user still does not see your Mac, he or she should click "Add a network place" in the Explorer bar and follow the onscreen instructions to add the Mac to My Network Places (when asked for a server address, enter your Mac's network address).

   Note: If Workgroup names are not the same, an easier solution may be to change the Workgroup name on your Mac, via the Directory Access utility or the third-party utility SharePoints, so that they match.

3. Double-click the desired computer/share. Enter the short user name and password of the account on your Mac when requested.

Users connecting over the Internet need to use a slightly different procedure (which also differs depending on the version of Windows being used):

1. Do one of the following: Open My Computer and choose Tools > Map Network Drive (Windows XP); open My Computer and choose Tools > Map Network Drive, and then click "Web folder or FTP site" (Windows 2000); or open the Web Folders icon and then double-click the Add Web Folder icon (Windows 98).

2. Enter *IPaddress**sharename*, where *IP address* is the IP address of your Mac, and *sharename* is the name of the share they want to access (by default their short user name, since they can only access their home directory).

   SEE: • "Using Network Browser and Connect to Server," later in this chapter, for details on how to connect to a Windows machine from a Mac.

   • "Technically Speaking: Windows File Sharing: Custom Options and SharePoints," below, for related information.

   • "Directory Access," in Chapter 4, for more on changing a workgroup name.

TECHNICALLY SPEAKING ▶ Windows File Sharing: Custom Options and SharePoints

By default, the Windows File Sharing option in the Sharing System Preferences pane shares only each user's home directory, and with only that user. However, you can customize the Samba server settings to share other directories, as well as to make a few other useful changes. Although you can edit the Samba Preferences file (/etc/smb.conf) directly, an easier method is to use the SharePoints utility, mentioned earlier in this chapter.

Using SharePoints to share additional folders with Windows users is almost identical to the procedure for sharing additional folders with other Mac users. Simply follow the instructions in "Take Note: Using SharePoints," earlier in this chapter, but instead of choosing "Shared (+)" from the AppleFileServer (AFS) Sharing menu, choose the same option from the Windows (SMB) Sharing menu. In fact, if you already have additional Personal File Sharing share points that you want to also share with Windows users, simply open the "Normal" Shares pane of SharePoints, select an existing share, and then choose "Shared (+)" from the Windows (SMB) Sharing menu to add Windows sharing for that folder. You would then click the Update Share button to begin sharing it. Note: To allow Windows guests (users without a password), click the Show File System Properties button, and select the Allow Windows Guests option.

SharePoints' SMB Properties window allows you to customize various properties of the Samba server:

- In the SMB Properties pane, you can change your Mac's NetBIOS name, which is the name that Windows computers see when connected to your Mac. More important, you can also change the Workgroup name; if you're on a local network, it is easier for everyone if your Workgroup name is the same as that of the computer that will be connecting to your Mac. (If you're on a Windows NT network, your Workgroup name *must* be the same.)

- In the File Visibility pane, you can hide or prevent access to certain files. By placing names of files in the Hide Files field (separating multiple filenames with slashes), you ensure that these files will not be visible to connected Windows users. The Hide Files Starting with a Period option hides files that have names beginning with a period (files that are usually invisible in Mac OS X). However, these two options only *hide* files—they don't prevent access. A Windows user who has chosen to view hidden files can still get to these files. You can prevent files from being accessed at all by placing their names in the Veto Files field (again, separating multiple filenames with slashes). Note that this field supports the wildcard (*) character; to prevent Windows users from accessing normally invisible files, include the following: ".*". You could also prevent Windows users from accessing Microsoft Word files by including "*.doc".

- In the Home Directories pane, you determine how users can interact with home directories. The Shared option, when unchecked, disables home directory sharing altogether; Windows users will be able to connect to only those shares you've specifically created in the "Normal" Shares pane. The Browseable option, when disabled, prevents local Windows users from seeing home directories in My Network Places or Network Neighborhood; to connect, they'll instead need to use the procedure listed in the main text for connecting over the Internet. The Read Only option, when enabled, restricts users connected from a Windows computer to only copying files from their home directory; they won't be able to save files to the directory or edit files in it.

SEE: • "Take Note: Using SharePoints," earlier in this chapter, for the basics of using this utility.

Sharing access from non-Mac computers: Beyond Windows File Sharing. If you want to share files with users on non-Mac computers, you can also use Personal Web Sharing, FTP Access, or SFTP. Because each of these protocols is platform-independent, any user on a Windows, Unix, or other computer can connect by using a Web browser, FTP client, or Telnet/SSH client, respectively. Accessing a Mac via Personal Web Sharing (as with guest access via Personal File Sharing) doesn't even require the user to have an account on the Mac. Conversely, since Mac OS X supports connecting to SMB/CIFS volumes via the Connect to Server dialog, you can enable Windows File Sharing to allow access to Windows users, Unix users, and Mac users running Mac OS X, all via a single service.

Using Network Browser and Connect to Server

I've talked at length about the various ways you can allow other users to share files on your computer. But what about your access to shared files on *other* computers? And, related to this, how do other Mac OS X users connect to your computer?

I have touched on this a bit in previous sections (such as connecting via VNC or using a Web browser). In this section, I explore the details of how to access a computer or server.

Mac OS X offers two means of connecting to these servers: Network Browser, which is primarily for accessing devices on your local network, and the Connect to Server command, which you can use to connect to any device, local or otherwise. This section covers both methods.

Note: A *server* in this context typically refers to any other computer to which you can connect via some type of file-sharing service. It does not have to be a "true" server, such as one running Mac OS X Server software. Any Mac, Windows, or Unix computer that is sharing files is technically a "server." Even an iDisk is considered a server in this context.

Network Browser

To access Network Browser, simply click the Network icon, if visible, in the sidebar of any Finder window. Alternatively, from the Finder's Go menu choose the Network command (Command-Shift-K), or choose the Computer command (Command-Shift-C) and select Network in the window that appears.

If you do any of these things, a window named Network will appear. This is called Network Browser.

At minimum, and assuming you are now or have previously been connected to a network, the Network window will contain an item called Servers, which is an alias file. If you open this, an alias to your computer appears: *computername*.local. Open this alias, and you arrive at the root level of your startup volume. If you're on a large network that uses a server (such as Mac OS X Server), the server volume may also be listed here. My focus in this chapter, however, is in connecting to shared computers, not actual servers. For these types of connections, return to the root level of the Network folder.

If you have a local network (such as one that includes several computers connected via an AirPort Base Station or an Internet router), all other Macs on the network that currently have Personal File Sharing enabled should appear as alias items in your Network window.

This ability to browse local servers and shares is not limited to Macs with Personal File Sharing enabled. Mac OS X includes support for SMB browsing, so if there are Windows file-sharing servers on your local network, the Network window should also show Windows workgroups and computers in those workgroups. You can connect to them just as you can connect to other Macs.

Note: Icons in the Network window may show up as either server icons or folders. Don't worry about this. Both are OK. The difference depends on how your Mac and the server to which you want to connect are set up. For example, Windows file-sharing servers (SMB) will likely be contained within a WORK-GROUP folder.

SEE: • "Take Note: Connect to Server vs. Network Browser: What's the Difference?" later in this chapter, for more details.

Connecting. There are two basic ways to connect to any of the shared computers in the Network window.

- If you're using the Finder's Column view, click the icon for the shared computer in the Network window. In the column to the right, a Connect button will appear. Click it, and you will be presented with a Login window.

- If you're using Icon or List view, simply double-click the desired icon in the Network window; you will be presented with the same Login window noted above.

In either case, you will have a choice to log in as a registered user or as a guest. If you choose Registered User, you will need to enter your name and password—the name and password for your account on the *server*, not on your own computer. Choose the option of your choice and click Connect.

You will next be presented with a Volumes window that lists every volume, user account, and/or folder that you have permission to mount. Exactly what items wind up appearing there depends on the account you accessed and the privileges for that account (for example, whether you're logged in as an admin). For admins, the list will typically include every mounted volume/ partition on the shared computer, as well as an additional item for the home directory of your account on that machine.

When you select the desired volumes/accounts and click OK, the items will mount. Assuming that you previously enabled the Finder Preferences' options to show "Connected servers" on your Desktop and in Finder sidebars, the mounted items will appear in these locations. The items will also show up in your Computer window (accessed via Command-Shift-C or the Computer item in the Finder's Go menu).

Once connected, you can browse the contents of these items in the Finder, just as you would a volume physically connected to your Mac.

If you double-click a server icon in the Network Browser window after already mounting one or more volumes from the server, the server's volume list will reappear (allowing you to mount additional shares, if any).

Disconnecting. To disconnect from the volume: (a) Drag the server icon on the Desktop to the Trash; (b) click the Eject icon next to the name of the server in a Finder window's sidebar; or (c) select the server icon and then choose the Eject command either from the Finder's File menu (Command-E) or from the server icon's contextual menu.

Do not attempt to disconnect by dragging the server icon in the Network Browser window to the Trash. This will not work.

SEE: • "Personal File Sharing" in "Sharing Services: A Closer Look," earlier in this chapter, for details on admin versus standard access, and so on.

• "Connect to Server: The Connect/Login window," "Connect to Server: The Volumes window," and "Connect to Server: Connection completed," later in this chapter, for more details on those features of Network Browser that are the same in Connect to Server.

• "Troubleshooting Network Browser and Connect to Server," at the end of this chapter, for advice on what to do if you cannot connect or disconnect successfully.

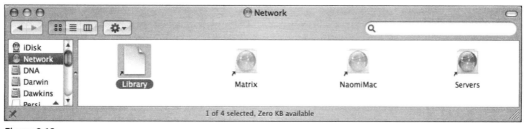

Figure 9.13

The Network Browser window. Matrix and NaomiMac are two Macs connected on the local network.

TAKE NOTE ▶ Connect to Server vs. Network Browser: What's the Difference?

How do you decide whether to attempt to connect to a shared computer or server via Network Browser or via the Connect to Server command? What are the key differences, advantages, and disadvantages of each method? This sidebar provides the answers.

A quick comparison. Here are the two key differences between the two methods:

- With Network Browser, you can connect only to servers that are shown in the Network window.

  With Connect to Server, you can connect to any server accessible over your network, provided you know the server's address.

- With Network Browser, you can connect to a server without knowing the address (URL) for the machine.

  With Connect to Server, you must enter a server address (unless you're returning to a previously entered address, in which case you may find it in the Recent Servers or Favorites listing).

Which method should you use, and why? In general, the Network Browser method is quicker and easier to use, assuming that the server you want is listed. It's also desirable when you don't know what's available on your local network and literally wish to "browse." The Connect to Server method is essential only when you need to connect to a server not listed in Network Browser—typically only for servers outside your local network.

If a server is listed in the Network Browser window, you can choose to connect to it via either method. Most often, you will choose Network Browser because of its simplicity. You may occasionally find, however, that a connection error occurs when you try to use Network Browser, whereas using Connect to Server succeeds (although this should be less common when using Tiger than it was in earlier versions of Mac OS X).

What items appear in Network Browser? The following explains in more detail what determines whether a server or shared computer on your network appears in Network Browser. In brief:

- **The server must be accessible on the local network.** The volume must be accessible via your connection to the network. Thus, if you're connected via Ethernet to a specific network, only computers on that network are accessible. Typically, if you're on a large network, browsing is restricted to a local *subnet* of the larger network. The nature of your subnet is determined by a network administrator.

  Note: It is possible that a server accessible via Ethernet cannot be seen when using AirPort (or vice versa), because they are set in Network System Preferences to access different networks.

- **The server must be discoverable.** Thus, for a Mac, Personal File Sharing must be enabled. In addition, it must broadcast a signal announcing its availability. Mac OS X does this most commonly via the Bonjour technology. Other services in Directory Access also support dynamic service discovery (as described next).

continues on next page

TAKE NOTE ▶ Connect to Server vs. Network Browser: What's the Difference? *continued*

- **Your computer must have the needed service enabled.** You will not see a particular server in the Network Browser window if the needed service is not enabled via the Directory Access application on your computer (located in the Utilities folder, as covered in Chapter 4). In most cases, particularly for just local networks in your home, you needn't worry about this, because the default settings should suffice. Still, if you have unexpected problems, especially when connected to a larger network, pay a visit to Directory Access. Make sure the service being used by your network is enabled. These services are Bonjour, AppleTalk, SLP, and SMB. If you are unsure what service is required, check with your network administrator.

Network Browser aliases. The Network Browser window (listed as just Network in the window's title bar) employs aliases in an atypical way. In particular:

- All of the server icons in the Network Browser window are alias files. If you choose the Show Original command from the contextual menu for one of these items, you are not taken to an "original" file elsewhere on the drive. Instead, you are typically taken to the Login or (if the server already has a mounted volume) Volume list dialog. The alias may also disappear briefly and return in a new location of the Network Browser window after you access the contextual menu.

- The Servers item in the Network Browser window behaves a bit differently: If you select the Show Original command for *this* alias, you're taken to the Computer window. Similarly, if you choose Go to Folder from the Finder's Go menu and enter /automount, you will see another alias called Servers. This alias behaves the same as the one in the Network Browser window.

Note: If you drag any of these alias files to the Trash, you may succeed in deleting them. However, I don't recommend doing so because problems connecting to servers may result. Still, I've never found any permanent harm caused by doing this. In the worst case, restarting the Mac restores things back to normal.

Getting the "old" Connect to Server window. The format of the Connect to Server window changed dramatically in the upgrade from Jaguar (Mac OS X 10.2) to Panther and Tiger (Mac OS X 10.3 and 10.4). If, for some reason, you want to use the old-style Connect to Server window, you can. In fact, the "new" old-style version is even better than the original: It adds a Show pop-up menu from which you can show different types of servers (for example, Web servers, FTP servers, and Telnet hosts). To access this window, follow these steps:

1. Open Script Editor (in the AppleScript folder in /Applications).
2. In the Untitled document that appears, enter the following:

   ```
   open location (choose URL)
   ```
3. Click the Run button.

The Connect to Server window should now appear. If you wish, choose Save in Script Editor to save the script so that you can more easily get back to this window in the future. For example, if you save it as an application, you can simply double-click the resulting item to instantly access the window. If you place the saved application in the ~/Library/Scripts folder, the script will appear in your Scripts menu with whatever name you assigned to it.

SEE: • "Take Note: AppleScript," in Chapter 4, for more details on using AppleScript and the Scripts menu.

Connect to Server

To mount any server or shared computer (whether or not it's listed in Network Browser), choose Connect to Server (Command-K) in the Finder's Go menu. The Connect to Server window will appear.

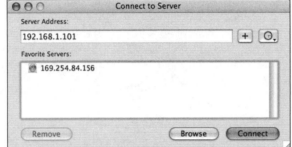

Figure 9.14

The Connect to Server window, as accessed from the Go menu.

The basic activity you perform in this window is entering a server address. You can enter either a local addresses or a remote one (for a server located outside your local network, such as one you access over the Internet). Here are some details.

Local (LAN) connections. Normally, you would use Network Browser to connect to a local address; however, you can do so here as well. Thus, for a local hostname of BobsMac, you would enter BobsMac.`local`. Alternatively, if you know the device's IP address (provided in the Sharing System Preferences pane if it's a Mac running Mac OS X), you could enter *that* into the Server Address field instead. For example, if the local address for BobsMac is 192.168.1.112, you could type `afp://192.168.1.112` (where *afp* is the protocol; in this example, *afp* tells Mac OS X to connect via Personal File Sharing).

Remote (WAN) connections. To connect to a remote computer, you need to enter its address in the Server Address field. To do so, you will need to know the exact public address of the computer (typically supplied by the owner of the computer to which you want to connect). For some types of servers, you also need to know the name of the share point you wish to access.

In either case, you generally also provide the *protocol* you want to use for the connection. In the Server Address field, type your information in the following format: `protocol://{IPaddress or domainname}`. Mac OS X supports several protocols. For example:

- AppleShare, via AppleTalk or TCP/IP: `afp://{IPaddress or domainname}`. Note: This is the protocol that Connect to Server assumes by default if you do not enter one.

- WebDAV (*Web Distributed Authoring and Versioning*), an extension of HTML that provides read/write functionality: `http://{IPaddress or domainname}/path/`.

- SMB/CIFS, the native sharing protocol for Windows: smb://{*IPaddress or domain name*}/*sharename*/.

  Note: You may need to provide the Windows Workgroup in the address, such as in the following: smb://*workgroup*;{*IPaddress or domainname*}/*sharename*/.

- NFS exports, a common way that Unix computers share directory trees: nfs://{*IPaddress or domainname*}/*path*.

- FTP: ftp://{*IPaddress or domainname*}.

Fortunately, once you enter an address, the Connect to Server window offers some assistance for recalling it again later:

- **Favorites.** Click the Add (+) button to the right of the Server Address field to add the address that is currently in the field to the Favorite Servers list. To remove an item from the list, select it and click the Remove button.

To connect to a favorite, double-click its name.

- **Recent.** Click the Clock button to the right of the Add (+) button to bring up a pop-up menu with a list of recently accessed servers. Choose the one you want, and its name will appear in the Server Address field.

- **Browse.** Clicking the Browse button opens the Finder's Network Browser window (covered in the previous section).

- **Connect.** To connect to the server entered in the Server Address field, click the Connect button. Assuming that a connection is made with the server, this should bring up the Connect/Login window.

Connect to Server: The Connect/Login window

If all goes well after clicking Connect, either via Network Browser or Connect to Server, a Connect/Login window will appear. In this Connect/Login window, you decide whether to log in as a guest or as a registered user via the two radio buttons. As a registered user, you need to enter the name and password for your account on the shared computer (not the one on the computer you're currently using!). Some additional choices appear for registered users:

- You can check the box next to "Remember password in keychain." Do this and Mac OS X will automatically fill in the Password field the next time you try to log in to this particular server.

- An Action button appears in the lower left corner. Click it to access a pop-up menu with two choices: "Change password" and Options.

  Choose "Change password" to change the password needed to log in; you need to know the old password to do this.

  Choose Options to access some security-related choices. For example, "Allow sending password in clear text" is less secure but may be needed for certain accounts. "Allow secure connections using SSH" increases security but may not be supported by the account you are trying to access. If you enable the warning options for clear text or SSH, a warning message may appear when you attempt to log in to a server that does not support SSH. However, if you click Continue in the warning alert, login will still proceed.

- If you're connecting to a Windows computer via SMB, you may be asked to provide the workgroup name of the computer and, possibly, the name of the share you're trying to access.

When finished, click the Connect button.

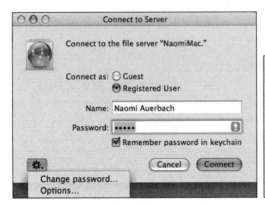

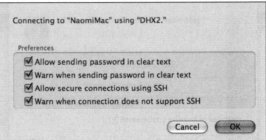

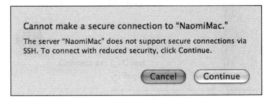

Figure 9.15

Above, *the Connect to Server Login window;* top right, *the Options dialog, as accessed from the Connect to Server Login window's Action menu;* bottom right, *the warning that may appear if the option "Warn when connection does not support SSH" is enabled.*

SEE: • "SSH and SFTP," later in this chapter, for more on SSH.

Connect to Server: The Volumes window

If all continues to go well, after you click Connect in the Connect/Login window, the Volumes window appears. This window lists all volumes, folders, and user directories—the *shares*—that you can access.

- If you connected as a guest via Personal File Sharing, all you will see are the names of users with accounts on the computer (if they have enabled File Sharing). If you select a user, you will have access to that user's Public folder (the only type of access a guest is allowed).

- If you're a non-admin registered user, the result is the same. However, selecting your own account provides you with your normal access to your home directory.

- If you're an admin user of the computer to which you're connecting, you will see your home directory listed but not those of other accounts. Instead, you'll see the server volume to which you connected. If the server volume has been divided into partitions, you will instead see each partition listed separately. You should also see any external mounted volumes currently connected to the computer.

If you select a volume (as opposed to your home directory), you will have the same access to items on that volume as if you were logged in locally as an administrative user. For example, you'll be able to access the /Applications folder, the root-level Library folder, and so on. You'll also be able to access other user accounts via the /Users directory.

Note: If an administrator of the remote computer has used a utility like SharePoints to set up additional custom shares, these directories will also be listed for guest and non-admin users. Admin users will not see custom shares when connecting; this is because they can access the entire volume.

You can connect to more than one volume or account (by Command-clicking your choices). However, you should not connect to both your home directory and the volume that contains that directory at the same time. Doing so would allow you to try to move a file from a folder in your home directory to the same folder on the full volume, potentially resulting in the loss of the file.

Once you have selected a share (a user directory, share point, or volume), click OK.

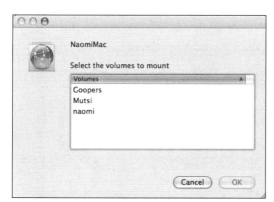 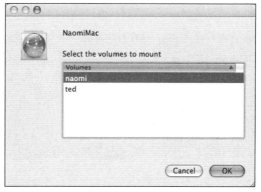

Figure 9.16

Connect to Server: left, *the Volumes window after logging in as an administrator (naomi), which shows all mounted volumes;* right, *the Volumes window after selecting Guest from the Login window.*

Connect to Server: Connection completed

After you click OK in the Volumes window, each selected item will show up as a separate volume in the Finder's Computer window, on your Desktop (if you have chosen to show connected servers on the Desktop via the Finder Preferences dialog), and/or in Finder sidebars (if you've chosen this option in Finder Preferences).

Double-clicking your own User account's share opens the home directory from the shared computer. Double-clicking another user's account share opens that user's Public folder. You will be able to view any files in the user's Public folder, as well as to drop files in the user's Drop Box. (As discussed in Chapter 6, you can drop files into another user's Drop Box, but you cannot view its contents.) For volumes you access as an administrator, you will be able to access just about the same things you could if you were logged in locally to the computer.

Disconnect. When you're finished, you typically disconnect from any connected item by doing the following: (a) dragging its icon to the Trash; (b) clicking the Eject icon next to its name in Finder window sidebars; or (c) selecting the volume in the Finder and then choosing Eject (Command-E) from the File menu. You can also choose the Eject command from the contextual menu or the Action menu for the server icon.

Before you disconnect, you may wish to make an alias of the server icon via the Finder's Make Alias command (Command-L). You can then use this alias as a shortcut to connect to the server.

SEE: • "Take Note: Connecting to Servers via Aliases and Location Files," below, for more details.

• "Troubleshooting Network Browser and Connect to Server," at the end of this chapter, for advice on what to do if you cannot connect or disconnect successfully.

TAKE NOTE ▶ Connecting to Servers via Aliases and Location Files

If you expect to access the same server(s) repeatedly, you can speed things by creating a file that mounts the server automatically when you double-click it in the Finder. This probably isn't necessary for servers that would normally appear in Network Browser; however, it can be useful otherwise. You can use two approaches: aliases and (for AppleTalk servers) AFP Internet Location files.

Aliases. The basic idea is to make an alias of a server or share to which you're already connected. Once you've done this, double-clicking the alias will mount the volume automatically. Here's how to set this up:

1. Connect to the volume or share via the Connect to Server window.

2. When the Connect/Login window appears, click the Options button and choose Add Password to Keychain. Click OK.

   Note: If you skip this step, double-clicking the alias you create will take you back to the Connect/Login window rather than mount the volume immediately—still faster than going back to the Connect to Server window, but I prefer the express route.

3. Enter your name and password, and then click Connect.

4. Mount the volume as usual.

5. Select the volume icon from any location where it is displayed (such as on the Desktop or in the Computer window).

6. Holding down the Option and Command keys, drag the server's icon to the Desktop. Or, if the server icon already appears on the Desktop (because you have chosen to show connected servers on the Desktop), you can select the icon and choose Make Alias (Command-L) from the Finder's File menu. In either case, an alias is created.

continues on next page

TAKE NOTE ▶ Connecting to Servers via Aliases and Location Files *continued*

Now, after you disconnect from the volume, you can reconnect at any time (assuming that the volume remains on the network) simply by double-clicking the alias. If you would rather connect directly to a certain directory on that volume, you can create an alias to that directory (rather than to the main volume).

Note that you can even use this tip to connect to iDisks. If you do, however, be aware of a potential problem: If you use an alias to connect to an iDisk, then connect to a *second* iDisk (while the first iDisk is still mounted), and then disconnect the *first* iDisk, your alias file may update automatically to point to the second iDisk. There's no work-around for this problem other than avoiding connecting to multiple iDisks at the same time.

AFP Internet Location files. Although aliases usually work well, some servers do not allow you to add your password to the keychain, forcing you to enter it every time you connect.

For these cases, a better alternative solution is to use AFP (*Apple Filing Protocol*) Internet Location files. These files allow you to include the server address, user name, password, and even a volume or share name. The location file then connects automatically when you double-click it.

Unfortunately, creating a location file is not quite as convenient as creating an alias. The easiest method is to use a text editor such as TextEdit and follow these steps:

1. Open TextEdit, and create a new blank document.
2. Type the address of the server, using one of the following formats (substituting the specifics for your server):

    AppleShare servers: afp://*username:password*@{*IPaddress or domainname*}/

    Specific volumes on AppleShare servers: afp://*username:password*@{*IPaddress or domainname*}/*volume*

    Specific share points on AppleShare servers: afp://*username:password*@{*IPaddress or domainname*}/*sharename* (if the share name has a space, replace the space with *%20*)

3. Select the entire address in the text window, and then drag it to the Desktop or any folder on your hard drive. An Internet Location file with the extension .afploc is created. This is the same sort of file that is created if you drag a URL from your Web browser to the Desktop.

You can place this file anywhere you like (in the Dock, in a folder, and so on). When you double-click it (or click it in the Dock), it will automatically connect to the server and mount in the Finder. You can create location files for every iDisk and server you access. You can even put all of these location files in a folder and drag the folder to the Dock to have a pop-up menu of all the servers you use frequently.

Note: You can use a similar method to create location files for services other than AFP, such as FTP. You simply need to change the URL format.

continues on next page

TAKE NOTE ▶ **Connecting to Servers via Aliases and Location Files** *continued*

Connecting to servers at startup. If you want to automatically connect to an AppleShare server at startup, you can do so via the just-described Internet Location files. After you create the desired location file, open the Accounts System Preferences pane. Choose the Login Items tab for your account. Drag the location file into the Login Items list. The next time you log in, the server should be mounted automatically.

SEE: • "Take Note: Location Files and Browser Links," later in this chapter, for related information.

• "Take Note: Mounting and Working with iDisks," in Chapter 8, for more on iDisks.

Sharing via Target Disk Mode

If you have two or more computers connected on a local network, enabling File Sharing is a convenient way to transfer files. You can use this method to transfer files from a desktop computer to a laptop before going on a trip, for example.

However, if the two computers are physically next to one another, you have another choice. Using a FireWire connection between two computers, you can mount one of the computers as if it were an external drive connected to the other one. This is called Target Disk Mode. You can then transfer files between the two computers at full FireWire speeds.

True, Target Disk Mode won't be much faster than file sharing via a FireWire network connection (as detailed in "Take Note: Setting Up and Using Internet Sharing and File Sharing," earlier in this chapter). The difference is that, with Target Disk Mode, the mounted computer is connected without any need to start up the Mac or configure its network settings. This can be especially important if you are trying to access a computer that has a problem that prevents it from starting up successfully.

Mounting the drive

There are two basic ways to mount a drive in Target Disk mode. The first is the "old" way, used in all versions of Mac OS X. To use it, follow these steps:

1. Turn off the computer you want to use as the target ("FireWire hard drive") Mac.

   Note: Make sure that you actually choose Shut Down on the target Mac, not Restart.

2. Turn on the target Mac and hold down the T key until the FireWire symbol appears on its screen. The computer is now in Target Disk Mode.

3. Using a FireWire cable, connect the target Mac to a Mac that is currently started up and logged in to your account. The target computer should now mount and be accessible on the other computer.

An alternative method, new in Tiger, is as follows:

1. Startup the computer that you want to use as the target Mac. Open the Startup Disk System Preferences pane.

2. Click the Target Disk Mode button. In the dialog that appears, click the Restart button. The computer will restart in Target Disk mode.

3. You can now connect it to another Mac as described in Step 3 above.

Note: A disadvantage of the latter method is that you cannot use it to access a Mac that cannot successfully start up.

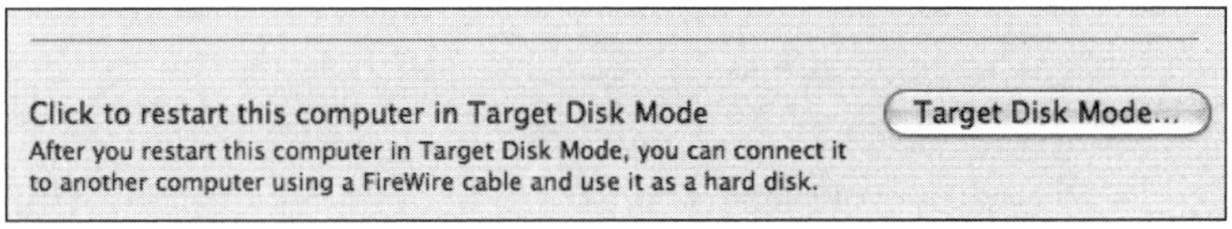

Figure 9.17

The Target Disk Mode button in the Startup Disk System Preferences pane.

Click to restart this computer in Target Disk Mode
After you restart this computer in Target Disk Mode, you can connect it
to another computer using a FireWire cable and use it as a hard disk.

[Target Disk Mode...]

Unmounting the drive

To stop using Target Disk Mode, follow these steps:

1. On the main computer, drag the Target Disk Mode–mounted volume's icon to the Dock's Trash icon (which will change to an Eject symbol), or select the mounted volume and press Command-E to unmount it.

2. Press the power button on the target Mac to turn it off.

3. Disconnect the FireWire cable.

It's important not to turn off or disconnect the target computer before you unmount it. Doing so risks damaging the data on your drive.

TAKE NOTE ▶ File Sharing: It's Your Choice

When Apple dropped the floppy-disk drive from the original iMac back in 1998, there was concern about how users would transfer files between computers—since at that time, the most common way to do so (at least for small files like word-processing documents) was via a floppy disk.

Mac OS X offers a multitude of choices for sharing files (most of them far more convenient and faster than a floppy disk). The following summarizes your more common options (more details on these and other options are discussed elsewhere, primarily in this chapter and in Chapters 6 and 8). Specifically, to transfer a file to another computer, use any of the following:

• Send the file as an attachment via e-mail.

• Burn the file to a CD-R or DVD-R (assuming that you have a CD-RW or DVD-RW drive).

continues on next page

TAKE NOTE ▶ **File Sharing: It's Your Choice** *continued*

- Put the file on a portable FireWire or USB hard drive. Connect the drive to the destination computer to transfer the file.

- Put the file on a USB keychain (flash) drive. Connect the drive to the destination computer to transfer the file.

- If two computers are within close physical proximity of one another, connect them via FireWire Target Disk Mode—in essence, setting up one computer to act as an external drive connected to the other.

- Enable Personal File Sharing in the Sharing System Preferences pane, and access the Mac via File Sharing (for example, using Network Browser). For the most general access, make the file available in your Public folder.

- Set up Web Sharing in the Sharing System Preferences pane, and make the file available via a personal Web site.

- Enable FTP Access, allowing other users to access your data via an FTP client.

- Use Bluetooth for supported devices in close proximity to each other.

- Use iChat, Mac OS X's implementation of instant messaging. When a chat window for a buddy is open, you can exchange files by choosing the Send a File command from iChat's Buddies menu. Because iChat supports Bonjour, you don't even need to be connected to the Internet—two Macs connected locally can use iChat to communicate by using the Login to Bonjour command in the iChat menu.

    SEE: • **Chapter 11 for more on iChat.**

Network Security

Historically, personal computers have not needed much in the way of protection from network attacks, hackers, and the like—primarily because they were connected to the Internet either via a dial-up connection (making the computer difficult for a hacker to nail down and preventing high-bandwidth data transfers) or via a company network (which was protected behind an industrial-strength firewall managed by an IT person).

The widespread use of broadband connections for home use, however, means that more and more computers are permanently connected to the Internet, which means more availability and greater bandwidth. In addition, computer users are becoming more and more Internet-savvy, and the increased bandwidth has led many people to use the various sharing technologies discussed in this chapter, creating more openings for malicious people to try to exploit.

Traditionally, Mac OS computers have been among the least vulnerable to security breaches. Mac OS X continues this trend. Although Mac OS X's Unix base has the potential to be more vulnerable than the classic Mac OS—if only because hackers have spent many more hours trying to break into Unix servers than Mac servers—Mac OS X ships with most remote services (File Sharing, FTP Access, Remote Login, Web Server, and so on) disabled. Thus, you're not vulnerable unless you choose to be. If you *do* decide to enable any sort of sharing, you will likely want some firewall protection.

There are three types of network protection you need to be concerned about: (a) protection of information you *send* over the Internet (typically via e-mail or to a Web site); (b) dangers lurking in material you *receive* via e-mail (such as e-mail that contains a virus or HTML-formatted e-mail with code that attempts to upload data from your Mac); and (c) unauthorized access to your computer (such as by a hacker attempting to gain access via an Internet connection). This section presents an overview of the tools available to protect against all of these dangers.

Note: This section is about protecting your Mac from the dangers present when connected to the Internet and/or a network. For protection of your Mac and its data from people who have physical access to your Mac, check out "Take Note: Securing Mac OS X," in Chapter 10.

Security updates

Your first line of defense should be to make sure you're using the latest version of Mac OS X. This includes "Security Updates" that are separate from the more familiar updates (such as 10.4.3). Over time, Apple has gotten much better at responding rapidly to security issues that affect the OS. As one example, Apple released a security update for Panther less than a week after Panther's release. These security updates most often fix newly identified vulnerabilities in Mac OS X's underlying Unix software. For more details on available updates, check out the following Apple Knowledge Base article: http://docs.info.apple.com/article.html?artnum=61798.

Note: A security update typically does not change the build number for Mac OS X (as a standard Mac OS X update does).

SEE: • **"Take Note: About This Mac," in Chapter 2, and several sections in Chapter 3 for more on build numbers.**

Network Address Translation and security

In Chapter 8, I discussed Network Address Translation (NAT) in the context of Internet routers. In addition to its value in sharing a single Internet connection among multiple computers, NAT offers a weak form of security protection. Because all data coming into your network must pass through the router, which then directs it to the appropriate computer, computers behind the router are not exposed to the Internet directly. What's more, since only data that has specifically been requested by a computer behind the router actually makes it past the router, hackers will generally not be able to reach any of your computers— the exception, of course, being ports that you have specifically opened using port mapping.

SEE: • "Network Address Translation" and "Internet routers and port mapping," in Chapter 8, for more details.

Firewalls

The single best form of protection is a firewall. As explained earlier in this chapter, a firewall sets up a barrier between your computer and the outside world. The main job of a firewall is to prevent contact with your computer that you did not initiate. For example, when you attempt to load a Web page, the data for that page is sent to your Mac. This does not typically trigger a firewall reaction, because it is understood that you initiated the request when you clicked a link, or entered a URL, to load that page. On the other hand, if an attempt is made by a computer outside your firewall to send data to your computer that has not specifically been requested (other than legitimate access to Sharing Services that you've enabled), the firewall should block the data before it reaches your computer. (A firewall can also block unauthorized data going the other direction—such as covert attempts by software on your computer to connect to the Internet and send data. However, most users don't take advantage of this feature because setting it up is not a trivial task.)

If the firewall detects anything it believes is malicious, it blocks it. Depending on the firewall in use and your settings, it may or may not alert you of this block. In any case, if you're using Mac OS X's "built-in" firewall, the system log, which you can access from Console, should list any firewall-generated activity. If you've enabled Firewall logging (as described earlier in this chapter), opening the ipfw.log file will provide still more details.

Under Mac OS X, you have several potential firewall options:

- The Firewall pane of Sharing System Preferences enables the firewall protection built into Mac OS X.

  SEE: • "Firewall," earlier in this chapter, for details.

- The Firewall pane is actually a front end to the robust Unix firewall software ipfw. A few shareware utilities, such as the excellent BrickHouse, allow you to more fully customize and configure ipfw.

- Firewall software for Mac OS X that is completely independent of ipfw, such as Symantec's Norton Personal Firewall (www.symantec.com), is also available. Personal Firewall's most recent version (3.0) includes some very cool features, such as one that allows you to visually track an intruder. The Norton Internet Security package includes Personal Firewall and Norton Privacy Control—the latter of which is one of several available utilities that include parental controls for Web access as well as the ability to block ads that may attempt to obtain data from your drive (typically via JavaScript).

A firewall's protection need not be "all or nothing"—that is, it's not as simple as an on/off switch. Occasionally, you will want to allow certain types of data or access that would otherwise trigger a block, while still preventing other types of access. This is exactly what Sharing's Firewall feature does when the firewall is enabled but you activate Personal File Sharing: The firewall is active, but it lets Personal File Sharing data through.

How does a firewall determine what it will and won't let through? By opening and closing what are called *ports*. As discussed earlier, different types of data intended for different services travel through varying ports. By opening some ports and not others, you can achieve a finer level of control over your firewall. (These ports are different from the network ports discussed earlier in the chapter and in Chapter 8. In this context, a *port* is a particular network interface that deals with a particular type of data.)

Note: If you have an Internet router, you can typically open and close ports through router settings rather than via Mac OS X software. As much as possible, create settings in only one location or the other; if not, you run the risk of having contradictory commands that lead to unpredictable results. One potential advantage of using router firewall settings over Mac OS X software settings: Router settings affect *all* devices connected to the router as opposed to just one Mac.

SEE: • "Internet routers and port mapping," in Chapter 8, for more details.

Note: Using default settings, a firewall lets in most or all traffic originating within your local network (LAN), as opposed to traffic from the Internet (WAN). This is typically what you would want. However, using ipfw or a utility such as BrickHouse, you can block local access as well.

Proxy settings (as set via the Proxies pane of Network System Preferences) also serve as a form of firewall protection. However, proxies are typically only used in large network environments. To find out if you need or can use proxies, check with your network administrator.

SEE: • "Proxies," in Chapter 8, for more details.

Finding the problem port. One caution about using a firewall: You can be overzealous in your firewall protection, blocking things you don't really want to block. For example, if you're having trouble loading some but not all Web pages, the problem may be caused by your firewall. Assuming you know that the Web page you want to load is safe, try disabling your firewall temporarily.

If the page now loads properly, it means that a firewall setting was blocking the page. If this happens, it generally means there's a closed port that you need to open. How do you find out what this port is? The easiest way is to contact the vendor whose service is being blocked. Otherwise, you can use the Port Scan pane of Network Utility. To do so, set the IP address to 127.0.0.1 (which indicates your local machine) and click the Scan button. Now attempt to perform the action that's blocked by the firewall. With a bit of luck, the port in use will appear in the scan at the same time. That's the port you need to have open.

SEE: • "Firewall," earlier in this chapter, for examples of specific port problems.

Note: New in Tiger are the Advanced options to block all UDP traffic and enable Stealth mode. Selecting these will increase your security but may occasionally cause problems as just described.

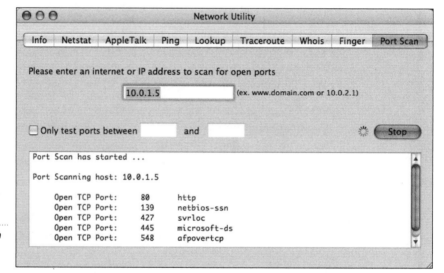

Figure 9.18

Using the Port Scan pane of Network Utility.

Little Snitch and MacScan. Objective Development's Little Snitch (www.obdev.at/products/littlesnitch) is a specialized firewall utility that I have come to rely on. It uses ipfw software but in a different way than most other firewall software does. It alerts you every time an application on your Mac attempts to connect to the Internet "on its own." Typical firewall settings often overlook this, because the connection attempt is coming from your Mac rather than the outside. The firewall typically cannot distinguish between a connection attempt made with your awareness and one that is not. Little Snitch makes this distinction. The goal here is to protect you from any application that might try to upload data you would prefer kept private (for example, your e-mail address). When Little Snitch detects an attempt, a message appears, and you can either deny the connection or allow it. If you repeatedly get a warning about the same connection, you can create a rule that will permanently allow or deny that specific connection.

Note that in many cases, connection attempts are harmless (such as when iTunes attempts to contact its Music Store) and thus should be allowed.

SecureMac.com's MacScan works differently. It scans your drive and locates known examples of keystroke loggers (which record everything you type), spyware, and Trojan horse software that may have been surreptitiously installed there.

Figure 9.19

A warning message from Little Snitch. In this case, you would choose to allow "until NetNewsWire quits" (you want NetNewsWire to be able to connect to the Internet; that's its function!).

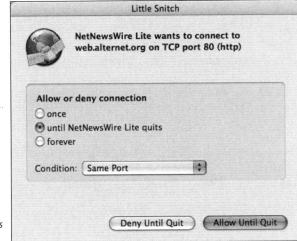

TECHNICALLY SPEAKING ▶ Using ipfw

The Firewall feature of Sharing System Preferences is designed to be easy to use—which leads to some significant limitations. For example, you can only specifically *open* a port via a rule; there's no way to close a specific port. On the plus side, new in Tiger, you can selectively determine the opening of both TCP and UDP ports; prior to Tiger, you only had control of TCP ports.

If you're unsatisfied with the limitations of Sharing's Firewall options, you can explore the full range of functionality available via the ipfw command in Terminal. Using ipfw's arguments, such as add and deny, you can customize your firewall. The output from the man ipfw command will explain exactly how to use ipfw (though not in a very user-friendly way). A friendlier introduction (although it was written for Mac OS X 10.2 specifically) can be found at www.macdevcenter.com/pub/a/mac/2002/12/27/macosx_firewall.html.

continues on next page

TECHNICALLY SPEAKING ▶ Using ipfw *continued*

Even if you don't intend to use ipfw as your main firewall software, there are two basic commands you should know:

- **sudo ipfw list.** The output of this command shows every firewall rule in effect. Changes you make in the Firewall pane of Sharing System Preferences will be reflected here, as will those you make directly using the ipfw command or a third-party utility such as BrickHouse.

  A typical line looks like this:

  `02070 allow tcp from any to 80 in`

  This means the following: Rule No. 02070 allows incoming TCP transmissions from any IP address to port 80 on your computer.

- **sudo ipfw -f flush.** Use this command to delete all added firewall rules and return the firewall to its default state.

  One occasion where you will find this useful is if you go to Sharing's Firewall pane and get a message that says, "Other firewall software is running on your computer. To change the Apple firewall settings, turn off the other firewall software." This message typically appears because you (or perhaps some third-party software you used) made changes to the ipfw firewall. To avoid potential rule conflicts, when Mac OS X detects that changes have been made to firewall rules outside of the Sharing preferences pane, it turns its own firewall access off. To regain access via Sharing preferences, and invoke just the rules listed in the Firewall pane, flush the firewall settings with the above command and then restart the firewall via Sharing System Preferences.

Note: Using the ipfw command in Terminal requires root access. This is why all commands are preceded by sudo and will request a password.

Figure 9.20

The output from the ipfw list command showing the rules that are in effect when the firewall is enabled via the Firewall pane of the Sharing System Preferences pane of my Mac.

```
                    Terminal — bash — 80x21
evolution:~ landau$ sudo ipfw list
02000 allow ip from any to any via lo*
02010 deny ip from 127.0.0.0/8 to any in
02020 deny ip from any to 127.0.0.0/8 in
02030 deny ip from 224.0.0.0/3 to any in
02040 deny tcp from any to 224.0.0.0/3 in
02050 allow tcp from any to any out
02060 allow tcp from any to any established
02070 allow tcp from any to any dst-port 3238 in
02080 allow tcp from any to any dst-port 548 in
02090 allow tcp from any to any dst-port 427 in
02100 allow tcp from any to any dst-port 407 in
02110 allow tcp from any to any dst-port 80 in
02120 allow tcp from any to any dst-port 427 in
02130 allow tcp from any to any dst-port 443 in
02140 allow tcp from any to any dst-port 139 in
12190 deny log tcp from any to any
20000 deny log icmp from any to me in icmptypes 8
65535 allow ip from any to any
evolution:~ landau$
```

Figure 9.21

The message that appears in the Firewall pane of the Sharing System Preferences pane if you have modified the firewall via ipfw.

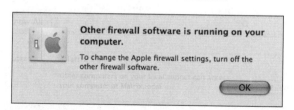

Other firewall software is running on your computer.

To change the Apple firewall settings, turn off the other firewall software.

OK

SSH and SFTP

It used to be that if you wanted to connect to a Unix-based computer, you used common protocols such as FTP or Telnet. One problem with these methods is that all data, including passwords, is sent as clear text, making it a bit too easy for hackers to grab your address and password. These methods are especially risky in a Mac OS X environment, where knowing your password could give someone administrative access to your computer.

The solution is something called SSH (*Secure Shell*), a secure substitute for Telnet, and its file-transfer counterpart SFTP, a secure alternative to FTP. Programs that use the SSH protocol transmit all data in an encrypted format, making it harder to crack. Mac OS X supports SSH via Unix software called OpenSSH. You enable both SSH and SFTP access via the Remote Login service in Sharing System Preferences' Services pane.

Note: Enabling FTP Access in Sharing System Preferences (as described earlier in this chapter) is not required to enable SFTP. Conversely, enabling FTP Access does not enable SFTP; only Remote Login does this. Enabling FTP Access enables the less-secure FTP protocol.

SSH. To access another computer via SSH, you would open a command-line application, such as Mac OS X's Terminal, and type ssh *servername*. The *servername* can be the domain name or IP address of the server. This attempts to log you in to the remote computer using your current user name. If your user name on the remote system is different from your user name on your current system, type the following instead:

```
ssh servername -1 {remote username}
```

or

```
ssh {remote username}@servername
```

Note: Instead of *servername*, you can use the remote computer's IP address. When trying to connect to Macs on your local network, add .local to the *servername* (for example, use evolution.local rather than evolution). Also, if you initially get a message that says, "Authenticity of host '*servername*' can't be established," don't worry. Just continue, and you will still be able to log in.

Once connected via SSH, you will basically have the same capabilities you would have via Telnet or, in the case of Mac OS X computers, via Terminal if you were logged in locally.

Should you want to enable access to your Mac via the less-secure Telnet protocol, you can do so by opening the file /etc/inetd.conf in a text editor (or via pico or vi in Terminal), and then deleting the # symbol in front of the #telnet,

#shell, and #login lines of this file. Anyone can then use the telnet command to access your Mac. Otherwise, for a computer running Mac OS X 10.2 or later, Telnet is inaccessible altogether; you can only use SSH. I don't recommend this, however; you can generally do everything you could do via Telnet using the more secure SSH.

SEE: • "Modifying invisible Unix files from Mac OS X applications," in Chapter 6, for related information.

• "Connect to Server," in the "Terminal's menus" section of Chapter 10, for related information on a simpler method for connecting via SSH.

• "Take Note: Editing Text Files via Terminal," in Chapter 10, for details on editing Unix files.

SFTP. As a secure alternative to FTP, SFTP can be used in two ways. If you're a fan of the command line, you can use the sftp command in Terminal. However, a much easier way is to use a dedicated SFTP client, such as RBrowser (www.rbrowser.com), Research Systems Unix Group's Fugu (http://eq.rsug.itd.umich.edu/software/fugu), or Panic's Transmit (www.panic.com/transmit). These clients allow you to work with files much as you would in the Finder, via drag and drop. You simply enter the IP address of the remote computer and then provide your user name and password (for the remote computer, not your own).

Security issues with SSH. One thing to be aware of with SSH is that an admin user connected to your Mac via SSH has unfettered access to your system. For example, an admin user could enable the root user via SSH and then log in to any other sharing services as the root user. Or the user could simply use the sudo command to execute nearly any command via SSH. The point here is that if you decide to enable Remote Login (SSH/SFTP), you should be extremely careful who (if anyone) has an administrative-level account.

Note: The telnet and ftp commands still work in Terminal in Mac OS X to access other servers from your Mac. The restrictions described here are for accessing your Mac from other locations. Type man telnet, man ftp, man ssh, and/or man sftp to get more information about the use of these commands.

Note: Sometimes the term *telnet* is used generically to indicate a remote terminal connection, whether by the actual Telnet protocol or by SSH.

VPN

A VPN (or *virtual private network*) is a type of secure network connection used mainly by large companies. The idea is to provide a secure way for employees to connect to the mother ship when they're on the road. Mac OS X has a built-in client for two VPN protocols, Microsoft's Point-to-Point Tunneling

Protocol (PPTP) and the newer Layer 2 Tunneling Protocol (L2TP) over IPsec. Using Internet Connect, you can connect to a VPN that uses one of these protocols.

For a good discussion of the security issues involved in VPN connections, check out this article from TidBITS: http://db.tidbits.com/getbits.acgi?tbart=08209.

SEE: • "VPN connections," in Chapter 8, for more details.

Web and e-mail security

When you send private information to a Web site, such as a credit card number to make an online purchase, you want that transmission to be protected from snoopers who might try to steal the information. With most Web browsers, you're made aware that your data is protected by a message that appears stating that the page you are entering is secure. There may be a graphical indication as well, such as the locked-padlock icon that appears in the upper right corner of the Safari window when connected to a secure Web server. In such cases, the Web page is likely using SSL (Secure Socket Layer) technology, a form of encryption. You should never send private information over the Web unless the connection to the Web server is secure.

Some e-mail programs, such as Apple's Mail and Microsoft's Entourage, also include SSL options that you can enable for sending and receiving e-mail (check the options in the Accounts dialog for each e-mail account). In general, using these options works only if the mail server you're contacting is set up to use SSL.

Web browsers also include numerous other security-related features, typically accessed from the Preferences window. For example, go to Safari's Preferences and click the Security icon in the toolbar. From here, you can turn off Java and JavaScript as well as block pop-up windows. You can also restrict access to cookies. E-mail clients generally offer similar security measures, such as those noted in "Take Note: Dealing with Spam," later in this chapter.

New in Tiger is Safari's Private Browsing command (in the Safari application menu). If you use this, a history of your Web-browsing actions is no longer preserved. For example, viewed Web pages are not added to your History list, and search terms are not saved to the Google pop-up menu. In addition, cookies (discussed below) are not allowed. This helps preserve your privacy, preventing others from potentially viewing where you have been surfing. Although you can turn all of these features off to gain security, you're likely to end up blocking features you may actually want to use in the process. Thus, be prepared to turn one or more of these features back on, at least temporarily, if a problem loading a page occurs.

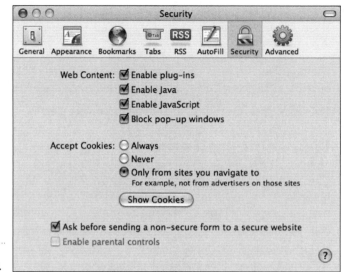

Figure 9.22

Safari's Security Preferences settings.

Cookies. Cookies are a technology used by Web sites primarily to track your previous visits. They can be used to remember a password for the site or to keep track of when you last visited the site (helpful for forums that track "new" posts). This information is stored in a cookie file on your drive. The potential risk of cookies is that a site could use them to place data on your hard drive that might allow them to have otherwise unauthorized access to your drive. No legitimate well-known sites do this. However, if you're browsing the backwaters of the Web, you might want to refuse to accept cookies.

To disable cookies in Safari, for example, go to Safari's Preferences > Security pane. From here, you can select Never from the Cookies section. This will prevent all future creation of cookies on your drive.

A useful compromise is the "Only from sites you navigate to" option. This setting allows cookies for sites you visit directly, but not from other sites. This prevents, for example, advertisers on sites you visit from setting cookies.

To delete a previously created cookie, click the Show Cookies button; from the list that appears, select the desired cookie file(s) and click the Remove button.

Spoofing. Have you ever gotten an e-mail that purports to come from eBay or AOL or some similar service and includes a request to go to a Web site to update or confirm your confidential account information? If so, be wary!

In many cases, despite the legitimate look of the e-mail, it is a fraud—a sneaky attempt to get you to divulge your password or credit card information to the perpetrator. Be especially wary of e-mail that comes from a domain that's slightly different from a company's typical domain. For example, *apple.com* is the domain of Apple; *apple.{somedomain}.com* is not. In some cases, the Web

URL or e-mail address may look exactly like the legitimate URL or address (for example, it may be www.ebay.com for eBay) and yet still be a fake. These phony addresses and URLs are said to be *spoofs*.

To determine whether a suspicious e-mail is legitimate, check its full header. To do this in Mail, for example, select the message and from the View menu select Show All Headers. The From, Reply To, and Return Path lines, in particular, should indicate if the supposed source is the true sender.

Here is a way to check whether a Web URL is a spoof:

1. Go to the suspect page (but do not enter any of the requested info!). (Note: As an added precaution, make sure you have cookies disabled when doing this.)

2. Enter the following JavaScript code in the address field of your browser:

```
javascript:alert("The actual URL is:\t\t" + location.protocol
+ "//" + location.hostname + "/" + "\nThe address URL is:\t\t" +
location.href + "\n" + "\nIf the server names do not match, this
may be a spoof.");
```

3. Press Return. A dialog should appear that lists both the address URL and the true *actual* URL. If the domains are not the same, play it safe and assume that the address is a spoof. Close the Web page immediately!

To do this spoof checking in the future without having to retype the JavaScript code, make it a bookmark. Such JavaScript bookmarks are often referred to as *bookmarklets*. For example, if you are using Safari, drag the icon for the JavaScript text from the address field to the Bookmark bar below; rename the bookmark SpoofCheck when prompted. Now, whenever you want to run a check on a currently loaded Web page, just click the SpoofCheck bookmarklet.

SEE: • "Troubleshooting Safari (and other Web browsers)" and "Troubleshooting e-mail," later in this chapter, for related information.

TAKE NOTE ▶ Certificates

Certificates are essentially documents that are used to confirm the authenticity of other documents and Internet communications. They are thus a form of security, ensuring that information you receive is really coming from the claimed source.

They can be used, for example, to confirm the authenticity of a digital signature added to an encrypted e-mail message or a PDF file. Or they may be used to confirm the authenticity of a secure (SSL) network connection accessed via your Web browser. This all works by matching private encrypted information (such as a digital signature included in a document) with publicly available information in a certificate. If the proper match occurs, authenticity is confirmed.

continues on next page

TAKE NOTE ▶ **Certificates** *continued*

For all of this to work, the certificate itself must be valid. The validity of a certificate is determined by its trust policy (as described more below). Mac OS X ships with a number of certificates of confirmed validity. You may get other certificates as you surf the Web or get e-mail.

For most Mac users, these certificates function in the background, without the user's needing to interact with them or even be aware of them. Still, as a troubleshooter, you'll benefit by learning some basics about how they work and what to do if things go wrong.

Certificates and Keychain Access. New in Tiger, you can view and manage your certificates via the Keychain Access utility. To do so, launch Keychain Access. If the Keychains list is not visible on the left side, click the Show Keychains button in the lower left corner. Then, in the Keychains list in the upper left, select the keychain you wish to access—most likely your personal keychain, named either "login" or your short user name. Next, click Certificates in the Category list at the lower left. All certificates in the selected keychain will now appear in the list to the right.

Note: The X509Anchors keychain is made up entirely of certificates, installed mainly by Mac OS X itself. Although not in your personal keychain, certificates here can be used to authenticate documents that you access. Certificate information for this X509Anchors keychain is stored in two documents, both located in /System/Library/Keychains.

Certificate validity. If a certificate is valid, when you select it in the list, you will see a check-mark icon followed by the words "This certificate is valid" at the top of the window.

Certificates have expiration dates. If a certificate has expired, you will see an *x* icon followed by the words "This certificate has expired." If this happens, you will need to get an updated certificate in order to keep using it. You may get this update either via an update to Mac OS X or, if needed, by contacting the source of the certificate.

If a certificate has not expired but cannot be confirmed as valid, you will see a message after the *x* icon, such as "This certificate was signed by an unknown authority." Using such certificates will usually lead to errors, as described later in this sidebar.

Viewing and editing a certificate's trust policy. You can view much more detail about each certificate —more than you probably care to know!—by double-clicking its name in Keychain Access or by clicking the Info (i) button at the bottom of the Keychain Access window for a selected certificate. In the window that opens, there will be two sections: Details and Trusts Settings. Click the disclosure next to each section title to reveal its contents. In particular, if you select Trust Settings, you get a list of policy settings with pop-up menus.

The top setting is "When using this certificate." In most cases, the selection here will be Use System Settings. Making a different selection from the pop-up menu (such as Always Trust or Ask Permission) changes all the settings below to match. Alternatively, you can override the default for an individual setting (such as Secure Sockets Layer or iChat Security) from its pop-up menu.

continues on next page

TAKE NOTE ▶ Certificates *continued*

As already indicated, it is *very* rare that a typical Mac user would ever need to make changes here. Still, if you want to know more about what each setting is and how it determines if a certificate can be trusted, click the question mark (?) button to the right of the "When using this certificate" pop-up menu. A Help document called "Certificate trust policies" will appear.

Note: For Keychain Access to recognize a separate file as a certificate, it must have a certificate file extension, such as .cer, .crt, .p12, or .p7c. You can import such files into Keychain Access by dragging them to the main window. You can delete a certificate by selecting it and choosing the Delete command from the Edit menu.

Using Certificate Assistant. Perhaps you intend to send encrypted e-mail that you want to have validated via a certificate. To do so, you will need to have your own certificate. Mac OS X facilitates doing this via the Certificate Assistant utility. It is stored in /System/Library/CoreServices. However, you most easily access it by selecting Certificate Assistant from Keychain Access's Keychain Access menu.

Using Certificate Assistant, you can create your own "self-signed" certificate. Or you can request that a certificate be created for you from a Certificate Authority (CA). You can also use Certificate Assistant to evaluate the validity of existing certificates.

To learn more about how all of this works, click the Learn More buttons in the windows of Certificate Assistant. Or choose Mac OS X Help from the Finder's Help menu and search on the keyword *certificate*.

Note: Adobe Acrobat includes its own routines from creating and validating digital signatures in PDF documents. For example, check out the Digital Signatures command in Acrobat's Document menu and Manage Digital IDs in the Advanced menu.

Certificate-related errors. If you get any error message with the word *certificate* in it, and you have no idea what to do to fix it (which will usually be the case), copy the message text and send it to your ISP or network administrator. Let them try to figure it out.

However, in some cases, Mac OS X provides the tools you need to potentially fix a certificate error yourself. Here is one example:

You may have a mail account set up in the Mail application that uses what is called a "self-signed Secure Sockets Layer (SSL) certificate." In this case, whenever you attempt to check mail from that account, you will likely get an "Unable to Connect" error message that states: "There is no root certificate for this server."

One work-around here is to just click the Continue button. This tells Mac OS X that you are not concerned about possible security risks and you want to get the mail anyway. The only problem with this solution is that you will keep getting this message every time you check this account.

continues on next page

TAKE NOTE ▶ Certificates *continued*

The ultimate solution is to permanently accept the self-signed certificate as valid. According to Apple, you can do this as follows:

1. Click the Show Certificate button in the Unable to Connect message.

2. Hold down the Option key. Drag the certificate icon (in the upper left of the scroller that appears) to the Desktop. This creates a certificate file on the Desktop.

3. Double-click the certificate file. An Add Certificates dialog appears. From the Keychain pop-up menu in the dialog, choose X509Anchors.

4. Click the OK button. Enter your admin password when asked.

The certificate should now permanently be accepted as valid (Always Trust will be the Trust setting). If things went as expected, the next time you check mail for the problem account, the error should no longer occur. Unfortunately, in the one case where I actually had this problem, doing all of the above had no effect. I still kept getting the error. My guess is that this is due to a bug in Mail that Apple will need to fix.

In any case, for more details on this subject, choose Mail Help from Mail's Help menu and enter *certificate* as the keyword.

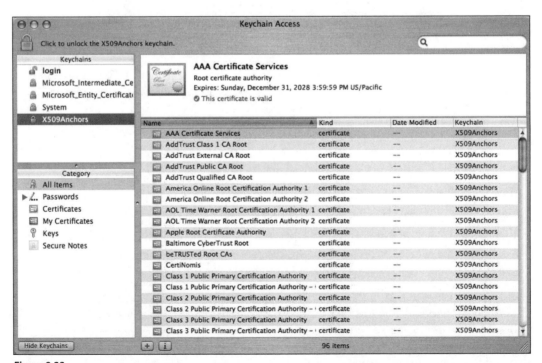

Figure 9.23

Keychain Access, showing the X509Anchors keychain.

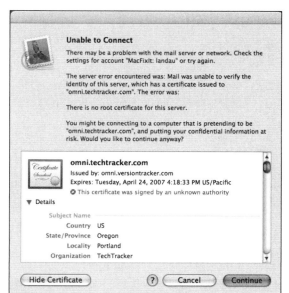

Figure 9.24

Left, *a certificate error message I received in Mail;* right, *the Add Certificates dialog.*

Viruses

Because many viruses arrive at your computer via e-mail messages or down-loaded files that you deliberately permit past your firewall, a firewall doesn't necessarily protect against computer viruses. As a result, it's wise to have some sort of anti-virus software on your computer. Two of the more popular such programs are Symantec's Norton AntiVirus (www.symantec.com) and McAfee's Virex (www.mcafeesecurity.com/us/products/mcafee/smb/antivirus/virex_smb.htm). Whichever one you use, make sure you keep it current by installing updated "definitions" files that are periodically released by the vendor. That said, there are currently no known viruses that target Mac OS X. Your vulnerability to and involvement with viruses will stem more from your exposure to Microsoft Word and Excel macro viruses and your Mac's potentially passing viruses to PC users via e-mail.

Note: Many claims of potential virus attacks are actually hoaxes. There are several Web sites where you can learn more about viruses, both real and false. Symantec's Security Response site (www.sarc.com) is a good place to start.

Troubleshooting Internet Applications

In this section, I cover the more common problems that can occur with Internet applications—primarily Web browsers and e-mail clients.

Troubleshooting Safari (and other Web browsers)

Although there are several popular Web browsers you can use with Mac OS X, there is only one that ships with Tiger: Safari. Therefore, although some of the advice in this section applies to all Web browsers, when solutions for different Web browsers diverge, this section focuses only on Safari.

This section also assumes you are familiar with the basics of using a Web browser (for example, how to enter Web addresses, such as www.apple.com, or how to use links). As always, the emphasis here is on troubleshooting.

One general note: The familiar acronym for most Web addresses is URL (*Uniform Resource Locator*). Today, there is an increasing use of the URI (*Uniform Resource ID*) acronym instead. Although there are technical differences in the two terms, for our purposes they mean the same thing.

"You are not connected to the Internet" error. The most common problem with a Web browser is that pages do not load. Of course, if you are not connected to the Internet, no Web pages will load. Instead, you will get an error message that says, "You are not connected to the Internet." The solution is equally obvious: Connect to the Internet.

However, there may be times when you believe you are already connected to the Internet even though your browser says you are not. In such cases, if you are using Safari, click the Network Diagnostics button that appears as part of Safari's error message. This takes you to the Network Diagnostics utility (described in Chapter 8), which can help you figure out the cause of the problem. For further help, check out the related troubleshooting sections of Chapter 8.

"Can't find the server," "Safari cannot open the page," and related errors. You may find that you can't access a certain Web site but *can* access others—a symptom that may be accompanied by an error message similar to one of the following: "Safari can't find the server" or "Safari cannot open the page." If the problem truly is limited to a specific site, the cause most likely lies with the site itself, not your connection.

The same logic holds true if a particular site loads significantly slower than most other sites (or if it keeps trying to load but does not ever succeed)—even if you don't get any error messages.

If you get a "404" or "Page not found" error message when trying to load a Web page, this means that the browser was unable to find that particular page. However, since these particular errors are returned by the Web server itself, it means you've at least succeeded in connecting to the server (or *a* server), so the problem is not connection related. If other pages from the same site load successfully, you may have simply entered the URL incorrectly. Otherwise, the Web-site administrator may have deleted the page or changed its URL.

The next section, on DNS-related problems, covers another cause of these symptoms.

SEE: • "Maximizing Performance," in Chapter 6, for related information on Internet application performance.

• "Using the Network Diagnostics Utility" and "Using Network Utility," in Chapter 8, for related advice.

Figure 9.25

Three Safari error messages: Top, *a message that may appear if your Internet connection is broken (note the button to launch Network Diagnostics);* middle, *a message that may appear if you typed a Web address incorrectly or the site's server is down (note the spelling error in the URL);* bottom, *a message that may appear for any of the cited reasons.*

Fix DNS-related problems. You may have a valid connection to your ISP and the Internet, yet still have trouble accessing some or all Web sites by domain name. In such cases, using Network Utility, you may be able to ping an IP address but not be able to ping or browse the corresponding domain name. Assuming that the problem doesn't originate with Web pages that are not loading, as covered in the previous section, the problem is most likely with your DNS settings or DNS lookup. (*DNS* refers to the process by which domain names are converted into numeric addresses.)

SEE: • "Take Note: What Are the TCP/IP Settings?" in Chapter 8.

Another symptom of DNS problems is significant delays before a Web page will begin to load (however, the page then loads at normal speed).

If you suspect you have a DNS problem, try one or more of the following:

- **Use an IP address to diagnose a DNS problem.** One way to confirm that a problem is specific to domain *names* (rather than an Internet connection problem in general) is to attempt to load a Web page in a browser via its numeric IP address instead of its domain name. If, for example, Apple's IP address (at the time of this writing, http://17.254.0.91) works just fine, but www.apple.com does not, you have a DNS problem.

  Of course, you need to know the numeric IP address of the problem Web site to test this out. Assuming that you can get to the Web site (which may not be the case), you can obtain the IP address via the Ping pane in Network Utility (as described in Chapter 8, in "Using Network Utility").

  If this happens with almost all sites that you try, you probably have a DNS problem on your end. If it only happens with one specific site, the source of the problem is likely at the site's end (which you cannot fix; you just have to wait and hope that they fix it).

  Note: Sites may have more than one IP address, and the addresses may change over time. The above IP address for www.apple.com worked at the time of this writing; however, it may not by the time you read this.

- **Check that your domain name server is listed correctly.** A DNS problem at your end may mean that your DNS server information, as listed in the Network System Preferences pane, is incorrect. To check, open the Network System Preferences pane and click the TCP/IP tab for the port you use to access the Internet. Verify that the values entered in the Domain Name Servers box, if any, match the settings given to you by your ISP (or that the box is blank, if your ISP has instructed you to leave it blank). Because domain name servers convert domain names to numerical IP-address equivalents, mistakes in this setting may prevent you from accessing domain names.

  Note that if you switch network locations in Mac OS X, and the location contains multiple network configurations (modem, Ethernet, and AirPort), it generally takes a few seconds for Mac OS X to determine which of the configurations it will use. During this delay, you will not be able to resolve domain names properly. This is a good reason to disable unused network interfaces and configurations in the Network Port Configurations section.

  SEE: • The "Domain Name Servers" section of "Take Note: What Are the TCP/IP Settings?" in Chapter 8, for important related information.

- Use Network Utility's Lookup pane or Terminal's host command. If the DNS problem is specific to just one Web site, sometimes you can fix it by "waking up" the lookup for that domain.

  One way to do this is via Network Utility. To do so, go to the Lookup pane of Network Utility; type the name of the problem domain (for example, www.macfixit.com); and click Lookup (typically with Default

Information chosen from the pop-up menu). The numeric address will be listed in the output as follows:

```
;; ANSWER SECTION:
www.macfixit.com.     3975 IN A      66.179.48.115
```

In the above example, 66.179.48.115 is the numeric IP address for www.macfixit.com.

Alternatively, you can use the host command in Terminal. In particular, for the MacFixIt example, you would type the following:

```
host -a www.macfixit.com
```

This would result in nearly identical output to what you get in Network Utility.

- **Renew your DHCP lease.** If your ISP uses DHCP to provide you with an IP address, procuring a new dynamically assigned IP address from your ISP may help with DNS issues (in fact, it may also help connection problems that extend beyond DNS issues). To do this, click the Renew DHCP Lease button in the TCP/IP pane of the Ethernet or AirPort section of the Network System Preferences pane.

    SEE: • "Ethernet (including cable and DSL Internet)," in Chapter 8, for
    more details.

    There are also shareware utilities, such as Kristofer Szymanski's Cocktail (www.macosxcocktail.com), that include an option to renew your lease.

    Note that if you use a router, this approach won't work—you need to request a new DHCP lease using the router itself. Your router's internal software may include an option to renew the lease.

- **Flush the lookupd cache.** The lookupd daemon maintains a cache on your hard drive of recently accessed information of all sorts (not just for domain names). If the cache becomes corrupted, this can cause DNS-related symptoms. The solution here is to flush the cache. To do so, launch Terminal and type the following:

```
lookupd -flushcache
```

Note: The lookupd -statistics command provides a summary of lookupd information. Use this command before and after a flushcache command to confirm that the cache has actually been emptied. If the cache did empty, the number in the Total Memory line of the output (for example, # **Total Memory: 58448**) should be substantially lower than it was before.

In most cases, flushing the cache will fix the lookupd problem. In rare circumstances, however, you may need to kill the lookupd process altogether from Terminal (it will be restarted automatically). The cache gets flushed as part of this process, but other settings are set to a default as well. I especially recommend getting a utility called Unlockupd (http://www.dshadow.com/software/unlockupd). If lookupd fails for any reason, Unlockupd will discover this and force a restart of lookupd.

    SEE: • "Killing processes from Terminal," in the "Force-quitting" section,
    and "Technically Speaking: Kill Signals," in Chapter 5, for details.

Use Safari's Activity window. In Safari's Window menu, choose Activity to reveal a list of all links (for example, to other Web pages, image files, and so on) for the currently displayed page. Double-click any link to load it. If you're having trouble accessing a specific component of a Web page (for example, an image will not load), open this window. It should indicate which links are causing the error. Try double-clicking these links. If you're lucky (this works for me maybe 50 percent of the time), the linked items will now load—problem solved!

Reset Safari. Occasionally, some of Safari's accessory files, such as the browsing-history list, may become corrupt and lead to problems. Or you may simply wish to erase this data for privacy reasons.

To erase Safari's browsing history, list of prior downloads, cookies, and autofill text, choose Reset Safari from Safari's application menu. About the only thing you don't lose is your bookmarks file.

Note: If you want to save your cookies (which may store items such as passwords for a Web site that you select to keep remembered) so that you can restore them—in case it turns out that resetting Safari does not fix the problem—save a copy of the ~/Library/Cookies/Cookies.plist file. To restore your cookies, drag the copy back to the Cookies folder and allow it to replace the newly created file.

For more manual control, you can locate and delete an individual file from the Finder. For example, Safari's bookmarks and history files are ~/Library/Safari/Bookmarks.plist and ~/Library/Safari/History.plist.

Note: Third-party utilities such as Cocktail provide another means of deleting these files, including some that the Reset command may not remove.

SEE: • "Web and e-mail security," earlier in this chapter, for more about what cookies are and how to delete them.

Empty Cache. To empty Safari's cache files, select Empty Cache from Safari's application menu.

These cache files are stored in ~/Library/Caches/Safari and are generally used to speed up loading of previously loaded Web pages. However, cache files may occasionally cause problems. For example, a page may refuse to load because of an error in the page's content. After the error has been corrected, if Safari tries to load the page from its cache, it may still refuse to load. Sometimes, Option-clicking the Reload icon in the toolbar or quitting and relaunching Safari is sufficient to bypass the cache error. If not, you will need to empty the cache.

Note: Third-party utilities such as Cocktail can be used to delete cache files.

Figure 9.26

Safari's application menu, with Private Browsing, Reset Safari, and Empty Cache options.

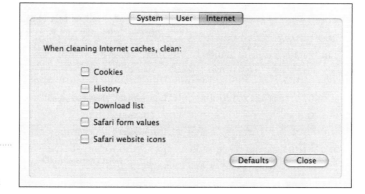

Figure 9.27

Cocktail's options to delete Internet cache-related files.

Delete corrupt preferences files. A corrupt browser preferences file can prevent a Web browser from working properly. In such cases, deleting the corrupt file (or simply removing it from the Preferences folder) should solve the problem. Before removing/deleting these files, quit Safari. Relaunch it after the file has been removed/deleted.

Removing the file instead of deleting it allows you to restore the file if it turns out that removing it doesn't solve the problem. This avoids unnecessarily losing, and having to re-create, all of the information contained in the file.

Safari's main preferences file is called com.apple.Safari.plist and is located in ~/Library/Preferences/.

Occasionally, some other preferences files may cause problems for Safari. The preferences file for the QuickTime plug-in is one example. Again, the solution is to delete the file. The file is named com.apple.quicktime.plugin.preferences.plist and is located in ~/Library/Preferences.

SEE: • "Preferences Files," in Chapter 4, and "Deleting or removing preferences" and "Deleting cache files," in Chapter 5, for more details.

Remove/Add Internet plug-ins. Plug-in files are designed to add features to Safari that are not built into the application itself. They are stored in Library/Internet Plug-Ins and ~/Library/Internet Plug-Ins. As with any accessory component, these plug-ins (especially ones from third parties) may cause problems with Safari (due to bugs in the software or updates to Safari that make it incompatible with particular plug-ins). The solution (assuming that you have several plug-ins installed) is to remove the entire Plug-ins folders from their respective Library folders. If this eliminates the symptom, return the folders and use trial and error (removing one plug-in at a time) to determine the offending plug-in. If the removal of the folders has no effect, simply return the folders to their respective locations and look elsewhere for the cause of the symptom.

On the other hand, sometimes problems are caused by not having a needed plug-in. The symptom here is that you will not be able to do whatever function the plug-in provides. In such cases, you will often get an error message informing you that you need to obtain a specified plug-in. Third-party plug-ins can usually be found and downloaded from the Web.

The QuickTime Plug-in.plugin file is a plug-in from Apple. It is located in /Library/Internet Plug-Ins. You need it to play QuickTime movies in Safari. It is also used to provide support for an assortment of other file types, such as sound files (for example, AIFF and MP3) and graphic files (for example, PICT and TIFF). You can see the full list of supported (MIME) file types, as well as enable and disable the ones you want, by accessing the QuickTime System Preferences pane and clicking the "MIME settings" button in the Plug-In pane.

Modify Web Content settings. Some Web-site features may not work properly if you have disabled a relevant setting in the Security > Web Content section of Safari's Preferences (as shown in Figure 9.22).

For example, while it is generally desirable to check the box for "Block pop-up windows" (which are usually annoying ads), a Web site may use a pop-up window for important content. In such a case, you would want to uncheck the box for "Block pop-up windows"—at least temporarily—when using that site.

Similarly, although you would normally want to enable Java and JavaScript, Safari may crash when trying to load some Web pages that use Java or JavaScript. To determine whether this, or a related issue, is the cause of the crash, go to the Security pane of Safari's Preferences and uncheck the Enable Java and Enable JavaScript boxes in the Web Content section. If the problem goes away, Java or JavaScript was likely the cause. If this happens, make sure you're using the latest version of Apple's Java software (available from Apple's Web site or via Software Update). The initial implementations of Java for Mac OS X had numerous bugs, which continue to be fixed in updates. Otherwise, contact the owner of the problematic Web site for further advice.

As an alternative to methods described in the previous section, you can uncheck the box for Enable Plug-ins in the Web Content section to temporarily disable all plug-ins.

Mimic other browsers (using the Debug menu). Some Web sites may be incompatible with Safari but work with other browsers. Symptoms include the following: Specific features on a page don't work; pages refuse to load altogether; or, in extreme cases, Safari crashes.

One solution, of course, is to try another Web browser, such as Microsoft Internet Explorer or Firefox.

A potential work-around is to get Safari to mimic the identity of another browser. To do this requires that you first enable Safari's "hidden" Debug menu. This menu adds several technical features to the browser—one of which allows Safari to mimic a different browser.

To enable the Debug menu, do one of the following (preferably while Safari is not running):

Figure 9.28

Safari's "hidden" Debug menu.

- Open ~/Library/Preferences/com.apple.Safari.plist in Property List Editor. Change the IncludeDebugMenu property value from No to Yes. If this property does not exist, you will need to add it.

- Launch Terminal and type

  ```
  defaults write com.apple.Safari IncludeDebugMenu 1
  ```

- Use a third-party utility. For example, using Cocktail, select "Show Debug menu" in Interface > Safari options.

After the Debug menu is enabled, launch Safari, select the Debug menu, choose User Agent, and then choose the desired browser (such as Mac MSIE 5.22 for Internet Explorer) from the hierarchical menu. Safari will identify itself as the desired browser when it connects to Web servers.

Note: A very few Web sites may be incompatible with the Mac platform altogether. In that case, you may be able to access the Web site by using Virtual PC (Microsoft's Windows emulator). Otherwise, you'll need to use an actual PC.

Reimport bookmarks in Safari. The first time you launch Safari, it automatically imports bookmarks from Internet Explorer and Netscape Navigator. It never does this again. A potential problem here is that if you still use Internet Explorer (for example) and continue to add bookmarks, at some point you might want to import your updated list. One way to do this is to delete the com.apple.safari.plist file in ~/Library/Preferences (while Safari is not open). Safari should reimport bookmarks on its next launch. However, this also loses any preferences changes you've made via Safari's Preferences command. For a more elegant solution, just modify the lines in the .plist file that tell Safari that the importing has been done. For example, for Internet Explorer:

1. Quit Safari.

2. Open the com.apple.Safari.plist file in Property List Editor and locate the property called IEFavoritesWereImported. Note: There's a related one for Netscape called NetscapeAndMozilla-FavoritesWereImported; however, I'm focusing on Internet Explorer here.

3. You have two equally good options at this point: Either select the IEFavorites property and click the Delete button, or access the pop-up menu in the Value column for the IEFavorites item and change Yes to No.

4. Save your changes and close the document.

The next time you launch Safari, it will import Internet Explorer's current bookmarks; and the IEFavoritesWereImported property will be re-added (if you deleted it) and its value set to Yes. If you previously imported bookmarks from Internet Explorer and did not delete them, the newly imported URLs will merge with the existing list.

Note: There are third-party utilities, such as Cocktail (Interface > Safari tab), that similarly allow you to reimport bookmarks. Alternatively, the Import IE/NS/Mozilla Bookmarks command in Safari's Debug menu (assuming that you activated this menu, as just described) should do the trick.

Note: Safari may only partially import bookmarks from Internet Explorer, stopping at some point in the process as if there were a maximum number of bookmarks that can be imported. If this happens, you can work around the problem by deleting all of the successfully imported bookmarks from Internet Explorer and repeating the above procedure with the .plist file. The remaining bookmarks should now import. Save a copy of the ~/Library/Preferences/Explorer/Favorites.html file before doing any of this (and use it to replace the active copy when done with the import), if you want to preserve in Internet Explorer the bookmarks you will be deleting.

Download files and save content. Besides surfing, the thing you're mostly likely to do with your Web browser is download software or save page content. Here's a brief collection of tips to assist you when you run into trouble downloading or saving in Safari:

- If a download attempt results in text appearing in your browser window, rather than a file in your normal download location, it usually means the Web server is configured improperly. Several work-arounds are available.

  First, hold down the Option key when clicking the download link; the file should now download correctly.

  If that doesn't work, Control-click the download link to bring up its contextual menu; from the menu, choose Download Linked File.

  If neither of the above works, it's potentially time to edit your Internetconfig settings (as described in "Technically Speaking: Internetconfig Preferences," in Chapter 8). Otherwise, you will need to contact the Web site to request that they fix the problem at their end.

- If you get an error message indicating that you're missing a plug-in or other software needed for the file to download, make sure that the needed plug-in is present (check ~/Library/Internet Plug-Ins, as described earlier in this section). If not, locate it on the Web and download it.

- After you click a link to a PDF file in Safari, the PDF will open in a Safari window. If you wish to save the PDF file as a separate document, you have several options:

  (a) After opening the PDF file in a Safari window, choose Save As from Safari's File menu.

  (b) Before opening the PDF file in Safari, Option-click the link to the PDF file on the original page. The PDF file will download directly without first opening in a window.

  (c) Before opening the PDF file in Safari, choose Download Linked File from the contextual menu of the link to the PDF file. This will also download the PDF file directly without its first opening in a window.

  (d) If you know that you *always* want to download PDF files, rather than have them open in Safari windows, you can make a change to Safari's .plist file that disables Safari's PDF support. To do this from Terminal, for example, type

  ```
  defaults write com.apple.Safari WebKitOmitPDFSupport Yes
  ```

- You can save any HTML Web page in Safari by selecting the Save As command. The Save dialog includes a Format pop-up menu with a choice of Web Archive or Page Source. Assuming that you want to save images together with text (as would be most common), choose Web Archive. Note: To view this Web Archive, you'll need to use Safari; other Web browsers cannot open a Safari Web Archive.

- If a download is interrupted for any reason, you may not need to start over to download it. Instead, open Safari's Downloads window (Command-Option-L). Locate the name of the file in question. To the right should be two icons. On the far right is a magnifying-glass button; click this to show the downloaded (or partially downloaded) file in the Finder. More important, just to the left should be a button with a curved arrow; click this to resume downloading. Assuming that the resume attempt works, this saves the time required to re-download the entire file from scratch.

Note: In some cases, you may use Mac OS X's Software Update to download software (as covered in Chapters 2 and 3), rather than downloading it directly from a Web browser. As with Safari, this application also supports resuming of interrupted downloads.

• Many Web-site downloads use the FTP protocol. You will know that this is the case for a specific download if the URL of the link to download the file begins with *ftp://* instead of *http://*. In such cases, using passive (PASV) mode can be the ticket to preventing download problems. Fortunately, most Web browsers use passive mode automatically. If problems occur, you can ensure that this mode is in use by going to the Network System Preferences pane, clicking the Proxies tab for the Network port used for Internet access, and making sure the Use Passive FTP Mode (PASV) box is checked.

With Safari, if you enter the address of an FTP server, rather than the address of a particular file on that server, as a URL, the FTP site mounts as a volume on your Desktop rather than as a Web page. Thus, it works about the same as if you had entered the address in the Finder's Connect to Server window. If an FTP site does not mount as expected, delete ~/Library/Preferences/com.apple.LaunchServices.plist and try again.

Note: If you enter an FTP URL in Safari that points directly to a file on a server, the file will be downloaded immediately, and the server won't be mounted as a volume.

Note: I have occasionally had problems downloading software from the members-only Apple developer site at http://connect.apple.com. In such cases, the solution is either: (a) turn off the Firewall in the Sharing System Preferences pane; or (b) if you want to keep the Firewall on, make sure that you have enabled FTP Access in Sharing's Services list. Otherwise, downloads may keep getting stuck when the server tries to enable FTP passive mode. I believe this problem has now been fixed; but just in case it pops up again, you now know what to do.

If you still have problems with FTP downloads via a browser, you can instead try using an FTP client, such as Fetch (Fetch Softworks; www.fetchsoftworks.com), RBrowser, or Transmit. To do so, launch the FTP client and enter the domain name or IP address from the file's URL (the portion between *ftp://* and the first slash) where the client asks for an address. Assuming that the FTP server is a public server, no password will be needed. Once you're connected, you can navigate to the directory that contains the file you want to download. Note: Some FTP clients let you simply paste the entire URL into the Server field; they automatically access the appropriate directory and download the file without any further navigation from you.

SEE: • "Technically Speaking: Internetconfig Preferences," in Chapter 8, for related information regarding unexpected quits in Web browsers.

Downloaded files and security. In versions of Mac OS X prior to Tiger, a serious security risk was discovered that involved a vulnerability when down-loading and/or running applications from a Web browser. In brief, the problem was that other applications on your drive could be opened and, to some extent, controlled from a Web browser. For example, if you type `help://` in Safari's address field, Mac OS X's Help Viewer application launches. In addition, Help Viewer includes an AppleScript function that could be exploited so that Terminal could be launched and a harmful command (such as one to erase your home directory) could be executed. This could all be exploited by a Web page that contains the needed malicious code. When you went to load the Web page, the damage would be done, typically without any warning to you or a way to prevent it.

The initial work-around for this problem was to disable vulnerable URL schemes (such as help://) using a utility such as Rubicode's RCDefaultApp (www.rubicode.com) or Unsanity's Paranoid Android (www.unsanity.com). However, Apple soon released security updates that patched the leak for Help Viewer as well as other applications, eliminating most (if not all) of the need for these separate utilities.

However, there remains some risk any time you download files from the Web. More specifically, there is a risk that you may be fooled into downloading a hidden malicious application when you think you are doing something more benign (such as downloading a text document). That's why, when downloading software from Safari, you should now get a message such as "*filename*.dmg contains an application. Are you sure you want to continue downloading?" or "The safety of this file cannot be determined. Are you sure you want to download *filename*?" If you did not expect the download to contain an application, click Cancel.

Similarly, if an application on your drive is launched for the first time via double-clicking a document handled by that application, you may get a message that alerts you that this is the application's initial launch. Again, you have an opportunity to choose Continue or Cancel. Normally, this happens when you try to open such a document yourself. In such a case, just click Continue. However, this message also protects against an application that has been surreptitiously installed on your drive and indirectly launched (for example, via a remote download and command) with the intent to do something malicious. In this case (that is, if the message appears even though you are unaware of launching any application), click Cancel until you can figure out what is going on.

Note: After downloading software, Safari will automatically attempt to open files that it considers to be "safe" (although you will still get a warning message if an application is detected as part of the download). To be extra-cautious, uncheck the "Open 'safe' files after downloading" box on Safari's Preferences > General tab. Now files will be opened only manually, when you decide to do so.

Bottom line: Any time you get a message regarding an application's being downloaded or launched, and you did not expect an application to download or launch, click Cancel. Then check the Web (on sites such as MacFixIt [www.macfixit.com]) for advice about the safety of the software. If it appears OK, launch it again and click Continue.

See this Apple Knowledge Base article for additional information: http://docs. info.apple.com/article.html?artnum=301191.

Figure 9.29

Messages that may appear when downloading software from the Internet via Safari.

Figure 9.30

The series of three messages that may appear when downloading a Dashboard widget from the Internet.

Downloaded widgets and security. With the initial release of Tiger, a security risk, similar to what was just described for applications in general, was discovered that was specific to Dashboard widgets. This was because all widgets were treated as "safe" by default and thus bypassed the protection given for applications. This was changed in Mac OS X 10.4.1. The result is that, when downloading widgets via Safari (and assuming you have Safari's Preferences enabled to "Open 'safe' files after downloading"), you now get several warning messages. The first is the general application warning, informing you that "*widgetname*.wdgt is an application." If you click Download, the widget will download and Safari will attempt to open it. You will then see a message asking if you want to install the widget (in ~/Library/Widgets) and open it in Dashboard. If so, click Install. At this point, Dashboard will become active and the new widget will appear. You will now be given the option to Delete or Keep the widget (this message appears anytime you double-click a .wdgt file to install it, whether just downloaded or not). This gives you three opportunities to prevent a rogue widget from getting installed.

Note: Starting in Mac OS X 10.4.2, you can disable or delete widgets via the Manage Widgets Widget.

SEE: • "Web and e-mail security," earlier in this chapter, for related security information.

• "Technically Speaking: How Does Mac OS X Decide if a File Is 'Safe'?" below, for related information.

• "Dashboard & Exposé," in the "Personal" section of Chapter 2, for more on Dashboard widgets.

TECHNICALLY SPEAKING ▶ How Does Mac OS X Decide if a File Is "Safe"?

The main text mentions Safari's Preferences setting to open "safe" files after downloading. You may be wondering what the criteria are that Mac OS X uses to decide if a file is "safe" or not—and where these criteria are stored.

The criteria are buried in a file in the following package: /System/Library/CoreServices/CoreTypes.bundle/. From here, open this package and go to Contents/Resources/. In this folder is a file called System. It is an XML-formatted file that will open in Property List Editor. This is where the criteria are stored.

The file contains properties with names such as LSRiskCategorySafe and LSRiskCategory UnsafeExecutable. An examination of the values of these properties shows that safe files are primarily identified by filename extension (for example, .midi, .mp2, and .key are considered safe) and content type (for example, com.adobe.pdf files, com.apple.pict files, com.apple.quicktime-movie, and com.real.realaudio are considered safe). Unsafe files are determined exclusively by content type.

A final field, MIMETypeToExtensionMap, allows MIME types to be used to determine the safety of a file.

The result is that files such as pictures, movies, sounds, text files, PDF documents, and disk images are usually considered safe. Applications, shell scripts, frameworks, and widgets are typically considered unsafe.

Note: In some cases, Safari's download warning message states that a file *may* contain an executable application, as opposed to claiming it for certain. This message appears for files that are in the LSRiskCategoryMayContainUnsafeExecutable category. As of now, only one type of file is contained here: public.archive. This refers to archived files, such as .zip files created with the Finder's Create Archive command. This is because Safari cannot tell for sure whether or not an archived (for example, .zip) file contains an application.

Remember: "Unsafe" does not mean "guaranteed to be dangerous." It's just a warning to proceed with caution when downloading these files. Most files initially considered "unsafe" are probably OK.

Can you edit this System file to change the rules as to what is considered safe? Yes, but I would not do so. Aside from the general risk in making any changes to a System file, Apple may replace this file as part of a general Mac OS X update, effectively "erasing" whatever changes you made.

Get a longer Downloads list. If, in Safari's General preferences, you have selected Manually in the "Remove download list items" pop-up menu, be aware that Safari maintains a longer list of downloaded files than it shows in its Downloads window. To access the complete list, open the Downloads.plist file located in ~/Library/Safari.

Installation and reinstallation of Safari. If you are having general problems running Safari, you may wish to reinstall it as a potential solution. If so, do not attempt to install Safari simply by dragging a copy of the application from one volume to another. Always use the Mac OS X Installer. Otherwise, Safari may not work properly.

If you have more than one version of Safari on your drive, and you run the Installer, it will upgrade the first copy it finds. This may not be the copy you use. The easiest way to avoid this is to delete all but one copy of Safari from your drive.

Safari crashes. If Safari crashes (unexpectedly quits) repeatedly and none of the above advice has helped, try more general troubleshooting fixes for unexpected quits, as covered in Chapter 5.

Check the basics. Finally, if you are having problems getting your browser to perform as expected, it always pays to make sure that you understand how its different features work and that you have set options as desired. I can't begin to go into all the details (it would take a separate book!), but here are a few guidelines specific to Safari:

- **Work with bookmarks.** Bookmarks are the standard way to save the URLs of Web sites so that you can return to those sites more easily. You can add a bookmark for a currently displayed site by choosing Add Bookmark from Safari's Bookmarks menu.

   To edit your Bookmarks list, choose Show All Bookmarks from the Bookmark menu. In the display that appears, you can add, remove, or edit bookmarks, whether in the Bookmarks menu, the Bookmarks Bar, or listed but not in either location.

   This view also includes your History listing.

- **Enable tabs.** Tabs allow you to have more than one Web page loaded simultaneously in the same window. You can shift from page to page via tabs that appear at the top of the window. This can be more convenient than having a separate window for each page. You can turn this feature on or off, and modify how it works, via the Tabs section of Safari's Preferences.

   Press Command-T to open a new blank tab. Click the question-mark button in the Tabs preferences pane to get more help about using tabs.

- **Use RSS feeds.** RSS feeds offer a convenient way to scan a summary of articles from many Web sites via a single display. Safari 2.x added RSS support, with a collection of RSS feeds built in. You can see the full list by choosing Show All Bookmarks from the Bookmarks menu and selecting All RSS Feeds in the Collections list.

To view the most recent articles for any RSS feed in the list, double-click the item. In the window that appears, you can modify which articles are listed (for example, just today's or just this week's) using the options in the column on the right side.

If a Web site provides an RSS feed, there should be a link to that feed on its Web page. Even easier, an RSS button should appear at the right end of Safari's address field. In either case, clicking the button/link loads the RSS feed page (typically with a *feed://* URL).

You can bookmark the RSS feed page to return it more easily. To view the summaries for all articles in RSS feeds currently in your Bookmarks list, assuming you have at least one, choose View All RSS Articles from the Bookmarks menu. A similar command exists in the hierarchical menu for the Bookmarks Bar; it will load all RSS summary feeds listed in the Bookmarks Bar.

In the RSS section of Safari's Preferences, you can modify how RSS feeds work, such as how often Safari checks for updates. Of particular note, you can choose to have an application other than Safari be the Default RSS Reader. If you do so, that application will launch, rather than Safari, when you click an RSS feed link. NetNewsWire (http://ranchero.com/ netnewswire) is an especially popular RSS reader.

Click the question-mark icon in the RSS preferences pane to get more help about using RSS.

TAKE NOTE ▶ Location Files and Browser Links

A Web page may include several types of links. Most will link to other Web pages (using the http:// protocol). Others may open your e-mail application and open a message to a particular address (using the mailto:// protocol). Homemade Web pages may even have links to files on your Desktop (using the file:// protocol).

If you click-hold a link in Safari and then drag it to the Desktop, an Internet Location file will be created. This file is simply a marker that, when opened, performs the same action that would occur if you had clicked the link on the Web page—that is, it goes to the selected Web site, e-mail address, or file on your drive.

Each of these different location files has its own filename extension. These extensions are hidden in the Finder (unless you enabled the Finder's "Show all file extensions" option). For example, the extension for http links is .webloc; the one for e-mail addresses is .mailloc; and the one for files on your drive is .fileloc. If the link is an FTP site, an .ftploc file is created. If the link is an Apple File Sharing server address (using the afp:// protocol), the file will have an .afploc extension. (I covered .afploc files earlier in this chapter in their capacity to quickly access File Sharing servers.)

continues on next page

TAKE NOTE ▶ Location Files and Browser Links *continued*

These location files can be created any time a valid URL is dragged to the Desktop or a Finder window. For example, if you select a URL in a text document in AppleWorks or Safari's address field and drag it to the Desktop, a .webloc (Web Internet Location) file will be created. This is similar to creating text clippings (which have a .textClipping extension) and graphic clippings (which have a .pictClipping extension).

If you select and drag a URL from Safari's address field to create a .webloc file, the file's name will be the URL (for example, http://www.apple.com). However, if you select and drag the mini-icon to the left of the URL, the file's name will be the title of the Web page that appears at the top of the Safari window (for example, Apple).

If the extension is not visible in the Finder, and you don't want to enable the Finder preference to make it visible, the extension for a given file can always be viewed via the Name & Extension field of the Get Info window for the file.

Note: If you drag the icon of a location file to a Terminal window, the pathname of the file *will not* appear (as is typical, and explained more in Chapter 10). Instead, you get the "path" for what the file represents. Thus, for a .webloc (http) file, what appears will be the http URL that the .webloc file represents.

SEE: • **"Take Note: Connecting to Servers via Aliases and Location Files,"** earlier in this chapter, and **"Technically Speaking: Internetconfig Preferences,"** in Chapter 8, for related information.

Figure 9.31

Left, *a .webloc file icon in the Finder;* right, *an Info window for a .webloc file for Apple's homepage (www.apple.com).*

Apple.webloc

Troubleshooting e-mail

Assuming that your network connection is working, most e-mail problems can be traced to incorrect e-mail settings or problems with your ISP's e-mail server. The emphasis in this section is on using either Mac OS X's Mail or Microsoft's Entourage as your e-mail client. I am assuming that you have already set up your e-mail client to get and receive e-mail and are familiar with the basic commands for doing this.

Connection Doctor. If you are using Mail, and you are having general trouble receiving or sending e-mail for one or more accounts, your first stop should be to Mail's Connection Doctor (accessed from Mail's Window menu). After you select Connection Doctor, a window opens that lists all the e-mail accounts you have created. An attempt is made to log in to each account; the results of the attempts (success or failure) are reported, with advice as to what to do to fix any problems.

Checking your e-mail settings. If you're using an e-mail client such as Mac OS X's Mail or Microsoft's Entourage and are having problems sending or receiving e-mail from one or more accounts, compare the settings you entered in your e-mail client's Preferences dialog or Account Setup dialog with the settings provided by your ISP or e-mail provider. At the very least, you will need to know your user name, your password, and the mail server addresses— including whether you're using a POP or IMAP server for receiving mail.

In Mail, for example, you access this information by choosing Preferences from Mail's Mail menu; then you click the Accounts icon in the toolbar. Choose the desired account (if you have more than one) from the Accounts list. The essential information for each account is in the Account Information pane.

POP servers download e-mail to your drive—providing you with a permanent copy that you can read even when you're offline. With IMAP, e-mail is stored on and accessed from a server (until and unless you specifically copy it to your hard drive). The advantage of IMAP is that you can access your e-mail, even messages you have already read, from any computer. The disadvantage of IMAP is that you need to have an active connection to access your previously read e-mail (unless you have stored a copy of the e-mail offline).

If you're using Web-based e-mail (such as Yahoo) instead of an e-mail client, the situation is usually simpler. You need only enter your name and password in fields on a Web page to access your e-mail. If you're using AOL, you need to set up and access your e-mail either directly from the AOL software or via AOL's Web site.

Figure 9.32

The Accounts pane of Mail's Preferences window; the MacFixIt IMAP account is selected.

Storing messages on a POP server. What if you check and download your e-mail at work, on a POP account, but also want to download those messages on your home computer? You can do so in Mail, for example, via the settings for the desired account as accessed from Preferences (as described in the previous section). Choose the Advanced tab. From here, enable the "Remove copy from server after retrieving a message" option. From the pop-up menu, choose the desired interval for doing so (for example, "After one week"). Downloaded e-mail will now stay on the server for the selected interval before it gets removed. Thus, if you chose a one-week interval, the e-mail you downloaded at work during the day will still be available for you to download again once you get home. At any time, you can click the "Remove now" button to instantly remove all previously downloaded mail from the server (your local downloaded copies are not affected). To always have e-mail immediately deleted from the server when you download it, select "Right away" from the pop-up menu. Note: These settings do not appear for IMAP accounts.

Skipping messages that are too large. If you don't want your e-mail program to get bogged down downloading large attachments sent to your POP account, most e-mail programs allow you to automatically skip messages that are over a user-specified size. Again, in Mail, this option is located in the Advanced pane of the Accounts preferences pane. Note: These settings do not appear for IMAP accounts.

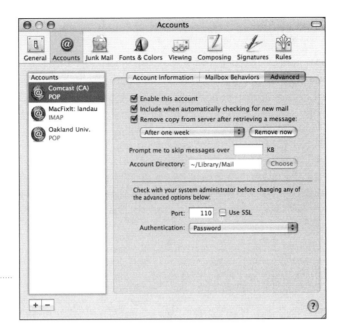

Figure 9.33

The Advanced settings for a POP account in Mail.

Authentication, spam blockers, and sending e-mail. Many e-mail providers, in an attempt to block spammers from using their servers, require special procedures for sending e-mail. For example, you may need to check for new e-mail received before you can send e-mail. Or you may need to enable an SMTP authentication option. Thus, if you get an error message when trying to send e-mail, check for new e-mail first, and then try again to send. Otherwise, check with your ISP concerning other authentication options that may be in use and how to enable them in your specific e-mail client.

In Mail, you typically enter these settings in the Account Information pane of the Accounts preferences pane—click the Server Settings button in the Outgoing Mail Server (SMTP) section. Enter Server port numbers and Authentication settings from here.

As one example, my DSL ISP (SBC/Yahoo) blocks the standard SMTP port (port 25) so that mail can be sent only via SBC's SMTP server, which uses a different port (specifically, 587). If I want to send e-mail from other accounts that have other SMTP servers, I have a few options:

- The easiest solution is to use SBC's SMTP server as the Outgoing Mail Server in all accounts. People who receive e-mail will still see the correct reply address. That is, if I send e-mail from my ted@tedlandau.com account, ted@tedlandau.com will still be listed as the reply address regardless of the SMTP server used.

- I could contact the ISPs of my other accounts to see if they allow using port 587, rather than 25, to send authenticated e-mail. If so, this should work. I then need to enter 587 as the port in the Server Port field of Server Settings for each account.

- I can request that SBC turn off its port filtering, which it will do in certain circumstances.

Spam blockers and "bounced" e-mail. Some ISPs and individual users institute protections against receiving spam—which can result in an e-mail you send to them getting bounced back. For example, Apple states that its .Mac service will refuse messages sent to it if the DNS server(s) for the e-mail address provider are not available or are incorrect. The sender will get an error message that says, "Cannot resolve PTR record . . ."

These spam blockers do not reside on your Mac, so you cannot directly remove or modify them. If you suspect that legitimate e-mail is being treated as spam by your own ISP (and you are thus not receiving certain messages), contact your ISP for advice as to how to modify the spam blocker's behavior.

SEE ALSO • "Take Note: Dealing with Spam," below.

TAKE NOTE ▶ Dealing with Spam

Spam refers to the junk e-mail you receive, be it about pornography, Viagra offers, or con artist scams. Usually it's just an annoyance, as you try to wade through dozens (or even hundreds) of unwanted e-mail messages each day. Occasionally, however, it may raise serious security issues, because some of these messages may contain viruses (as discussed next) or include HTML/JavaScript code that tries to perform surreptitious actions behind your back.

You typically have two goals when it comes to spam: keeping it to a minimum, and quickly separating it from "legitimate" e-mail. Here are a few guidelines for achieving these goals:

- To automatically separate spam from real e-mail, you can use a spam filter. These filters sort spam into a separate folder so that it doesn't clutter up your main mailbox and can be deleted more easily. The dilemma with spam filters is a classic signal-detection problem: The better the filter gets at correctly identifying spam as spam, the more often it will falsely identify a legitimate e-mail as spam. There's no easy way to avoid this problem, and no spam filter is perfect; however, some are much better than others. The junk-mail filter built into Mac OS X's Mail application is one of the best I have ever seen; the filter in Microsoft Office 2004's Entourage is also quite good. There are also third-party spam filters that can work with an assortment of e-mail applications. In general, the ones that claim to use "Bayesian logic" work best; Michael Tsai's SpamSieve (http://c-command.com/spamsieve) is one example.

- Most spammers get your e-mail address because you have either posted it someplace public or sent it to someone who sells it to a spammer. Your best defense against spam is to be vigilant about providing public access to your e-mail address. For example, don't include your address with postings on online forums, and don't register for anything that requires that you provide your address—unless you're confident that your privacy will be maintained. I actually use a phony e-mail address in cases where privacy is not assured and a real e-mail address is not required for what I want to do.

continues on next page

TAKE NOTE ▶ Dealing with Spam *continued*

- If you have your own Web page, putting your e-mail address on the page (so that visitors can contact you) is asking for spam. Many spammers use automated "crawlers" or "spiders" that scour Web pages for e-mail addresses. However, if you want visitors to your site to be able to contact you, you have no choice but to provide your address. Still, there are some precautions you can take. One technique is to create an encoded e-mail address that gets decoded when someone clicks the e-mail link. Several Mac OS X utilities, such as RAILhead Design's SpamStopper (www.railheaddesign.com/pages/software/spamstopper/spamstopper.html), can automatically create such a link, using either HTML or JavaScript. When you use an encoded e-mail address, most crawlers will not be able to grab your true address.

- If you get a spam message that instructs you to send a message back if you wish to be removed from the spam list (presumably so that you no longer get spam from this source), you may not want to do so. The reason is that when you send a message back, you're telling the spammer that you actually opened and read the e-mail. This just encourages the unscrupulous spammer to send you more spam or to sell your e-mail address to other spammers as a "confirmed" address. Recent legislation to require legitimate "remove" options in spam have increased the likelihood that the option now works as intended, but I still avoid it unless I know the origin of the e-mail and I am confident that it's legitimate.

- Some spam, especially spam sent as HTML rather than plain text, may include code that attempts to automatically send a message back to the sender when you open/read the message (thus verifying that your e-mail address is "real" and allowing the spammer to sell it to other sellers as a "good" address). You can often prevent this by using an e-mail option, available in some e-mail clients, that prevents HTML code (and graphic images) in e-mail messages from being rendered, or that prevents online access to links within e-mail messages. In Mac OS X's Mail application, for example, uncheck the "Display images and embedded objects in HTML messages" box (found in Viewing preferences). Alternatively, a firewall that has been configured to detect this sort of activity (for example, set up via a utility such as Little Snitch) can help here, as discussed in previous sections.

- Some e-mail programs, such as Mac OS X's Mail, give you the ability to bounce e-mail from a specific address. For example, if you get frequent, unwanted e-mail "newsletters" from a company—and you can't find a place to tell the company to stop—you can choose Bounce from the Message menu in the Mail application. The sender then receives a "bounce" e-mail indicating that your address is not valid (sort of a "white lie"). Hopefully, this will discourage further e-mails from being sent to you. However, this will not work for most spam, as the return addresses for most spam messages are not valid, so your bounce message will get bounced back to you!

SEE: • "Web and e-mail security," earlier in this chapter, for additional information.

Junk-mail filtering fails. Occasionally, the junk-mail filter for Mac OS X's Mail application may stop working. That is, junk mail is no longer recognized as junk. If this happens, choose Preferences from the Mail menu and click the Junk Mail icon in the toolbar. In the dialog that appears, click the Reset button. After resetting, all your previous junk-mail rules will be lost. You will need to "retrain" the filter. However, the filter should start working again.

Note: This symptom was especially common after selecting a blank message as Junk. To avoid this result, send such messages directly to the Trash, rather than to Junk. In any case, this bug supposedly no longer occurs in Tiger.

Firewall block. If you're running any firewall software, it may block the sending and receiving of e-mail (although this is rare, because most firewalls are configured to allow e-mail). To determine whether this is the case, turn the firewall software off and see if the problem disappears.

Pinging the e-mail server. If you're having trouble sending mail and your e-mail client returns an error message such as "Cannot contact server," use Network Utility to ping the SMTP server address listed in your e-mail preferences (this is the server that's used to send mail).

If you cannot retrieve mail (and your e-mail client tells you that it cannot contact the server), ping the POP or IMAP server that you access to receive mail.

If you have Internet access (for example, you can successfully surf the Web) but the server does not respond to your ping, it may simply be that your e-mail server is having problems. Contact your ISP for details.

For example, over the past year, .Mac's mac.com e-mail server has been hampered by periodic server failures. During these periods—which have occasionally lasted for days—users have been unable to send or receive e-mail. There's little you can do in such situations except wait for the problem to be fixed.

SEE: • "Using Network Utility," in Chapter 8, for more on using ping.

Problems with attachments. Attachments that cannot be opened by the recipient represent one of the more common e-mail problems—especially if you're a Mac user sending files to a PC user. The solution, in brief, is to make sure that the compression and encryption used for the attachment can be decoded by the recipient machine. For example, when sending a file to a PC via Entourage, access the pop-up menu below the Attachment box in the message window. In the mini-window that appears, in the "Encode for" options section choose "Any computer (AppleDouble)" or "Windows (MIME/Base64)." Then, as the Compression option, choose None.

Make sure that documents you send have the appropriate filename extension (for example, Word documents should end in .doc, or they will likely not open on a PC). Conversely, for attachments you receive, you may need to add an extension for them to open properly (such as adding .jpg to the name of a graphic file that otherwise opens as a text document).

When receiving files from Microsoft Exchange or Microsoft Outlook, the attachment may be named winmail.dat and/or have a MIME attachment type of application/ms-tnef. To read or use these files, get a utility called TNEF's Enough, from Josh Jacob (www.joshjacob.com/macdev/tnef).

Problems with a corrupt account database. If you have problems accessing most or all of your e-mail, you may have a corrupt database affecting one or more of your e-mail accounts. If so, there is some chance that you can repair the damage. To do so:

- If you use Mail, select a problem mailbox (in the left column) and then choose the Rebuild command from Mail's Mailbox menu. If that does not work, try restoring Mail's preferences file, com.apple.mail.plist, from a recent backup (assuming that you have a backup).

- If you use Entourage, hold down the Option key when launching the application. This will launch Database Utility; a window will appear from which you can select to rebuild the Entourage database. This often fixes the problem.

These rebuilds should also reduce the size of your e-mail database files, especially if you have deleted large amounts of e-mail since the last rebuild.

Corrupt received messages. Occasionally, an e-mail message will arrive corrupted or otherwise conflict with your e-mail application, causing it to freeze or crash when you attempt to access or read the message. This may also appear to prevent you from deleting the e-mail (since attempting to do so results in a crash). The quickest solution here is to select multiple messages for deletion (typically by making a selection that brackets the corrupt message). Because this does not cause the corrupt message to be displayed, the crash should not occur—and you can now delete the selected e-mails.

Duplicate messages in Mail. If you are getting duplicates of your received mail (for POP accounts) in Apple's Mail application, a potential solution is to delete the MessageUidsAlreadyDownloaded file(s), located in the POP folders inside the ~/Library/Mail directory.

Backing up. It's always a good idea to maintain a backup of your e-mail, especially if you don't maintain frequent backups of your entire drive.

- To back up the e-mail for Mac OS X's Mail, make a copy of the Mail folder in ~/Library. Your account information is stored in the ~/Library/Preferences/com.apple.Mail.plist file, so save that as well. You can also back up your account via .Mac syncing (as noted in Chapter 8).

- For Entourage, back up ~/Documents/Microsoft User Data/Office {*X* or *2004*} Identities.

Mac OS X Mail's Activity Viewer. If you're having problems sending or receiving e-mail using Mac OS X's Mail, and none of the above advice helps, choose Activity Monitor in Mail's Window menu to get detailed feedback on what's happening when Mail attempts to send or receive e-mail (especially useful if you're receiving e-mail from more than one account at a time). If something goes wrong, messages here may help to diagnose the problem. Stop buttons also allow you to terminate a hung connection (such as when an attempt to get mail from an IMAP server remains hung in the "fetching headers" stage).

TAKE NOTE ▶ Troubleshooting Web Browsing and E-mail: More Help

I know—there are many troubleshooting issues for Web browsers and e-mail programs that I have not covered in the main text. Similarly, there are many basic features of these programs that I have barely mentioned, if at all. For example, for e-mail, if you are wondering about the difference between forwarding and redirecting e-mail, how and why to create mailboxes in Mail, or how to use rules and signatures, you won't find it here.

The reason, as stated before, is that this book focuses mainly on general aspects of troubleshooting Mac OS X. To include detailed coverage of specific applications such as Safari and Mail (and possibly other Web browsers and e-mail clients) would add several hundred more pages. My publisher would not permit this even if I wanted to try.

If you do need more help, the Help files for a given application are always a good place to start. Vendor Web sites (such as Apple's Support site, at www.apple.com/support) are also excellent sources of help.

Troubleshooting Sharing

If, despite following all the advice earlier in this chapter as well as in Chapter 8, you still have problems with File Sharing, the following sections should provide the solution.

Checking the basics

For starters, consider these two basic steps:

- **Restart Sharing service.** *On a host/server computer:* If any changes have been made to the Sharing, Accounts, or related settings (such as to change privileges settings for any items), you may need to stop and restart the relevant Sharing service (for example, Personal File Sharing) in the Services pane of the Sharing System Preferences pane, before the changes take effect.

  Even if you haven't made any changes, this is worth a try if you're having Sharing-related problems. The problem may be that some underlying Unix software has crashed. Restarting the Sharing service will typically fix this.

  Note: Doing this restart requires physical access to the host machine. If you're on the client machine but have access to the host machine (for example, both are in the same room), this probably won't present a problem. If, however, you're dealing with a remotely connected host computer, you will need to contact someone who has access to it.

- **Log out and back in; restart.** *On either a host/server or client/connecting computer:* Log out of your account and then log back in again. If this fails to fix the problem, restart your Mac.

If you still have a problem, consider these additional basic tips:

Make sure that the server you want to locate is active, is on the network, and has the desired Sharing service enabled. Before you can connect to a host computer, that computer must be active (that is, not asleep or turned off), must be on the network (for example, connected to a router for a local connection or to the Internet for a remote connection), and must have the desired Sharing service enabled (as set in the Services pane of the Sharing System Preferences pane). All of these issues are covered earlier in this chapter.

Note: To avoid a host computer's going to sleep unintentionally, temporarily set sleep to Never in the Energy Saver System Preferences pane whenever Sharing services are in use. You don't need to do this for the client computer; in most cases, the client computer can sleep without affecting a connection.

Make sure that the client is using the correct protocol and application. If you're a client computer, make sure you are using the correct protocol and application for connecting to a host. As described earlier in this chapter, Mac OS X provides several methods for sharing files over a network or the Internet. Each method is accessible only when you use certain applications or protocols. For example:

- **Personal File Sharing.** The connecting user (client) must be using a Mac OS computer that supports File Sharing. If the "server" is running Mac OS X 10.4 or later, the connecting computer must support File Sharing over TCP/IP.

- **Web Sharing.** The connecting user can access your computer only via a Web browser.

- **FTP.** The connecting user must use a dedicated FTP client, a Web browser, or a command-line shell that supports the ftp command (such as Mac OS X's Terminal application).

- **Remote Login/Terminal access.** The connecting user must be using a Terminal-like application and SSH to connect. Again, Mac OS X's Terminal works here.

Make sure that the client has an account and the correct settings. If, when attempting to connect to a host, you get to a point where you're asked to enter your name and password as a registered user, but doing so leads to a "Login failed" or similar error message, it could be for one of the following reasons: The password may have been changed; you may be entering the wrong password; or the account may have been deleted (or modified in some way that prevents you from logging in successfully) since you last accessed it.

Make sure that Internet router or Firewall settings are not blocking access. The settings used to prevent unwanted access to your computer sometimes prevent intended access as well. For example, if you use a router, make sure that the port to your computer from your router is open, so that the computer can be accessed for sharing. Similarly, make sure that the Firewall settings in the Sharing System Preferences pane are not blocking the needed access.

SEE: • "Network Security," earlier in this chapter, and "Using a Router" and "Troubleshooting routers," in Chapter 8, for more details on these issues.

Make sure the computers have correct IP addresses. The exact IP address you need depends on whether you're having problems with a local (LAN) or an Internet (WAN) connection.

For a LAN connection over TCP/IP, both computers must have an IP address. Depending on your setup, you may need the other computer's local address, not its Internet address. Otherwise, if a computer typically connects to the Internet via PPP or DHCP and has not yet connected to the Internet, it may not have an IP address at all. A solution here is to assign the computer an IP address. To do so, you can set up an Ethernet port to be used just for sharing. Set this port to be configured manually (by creating a new port or a new location). Then assign an IP address in the TCP/IP settings; this address should be a local private address, such as one in the 10.0.0.1–10.0.0.255 range or the 192.168.1.xxx range. The subnet mask should be 255.255.255.0. Of course, if the computers involved support Bonjour (as covered in "Take Note: Bonjour," in Chapter 8), they should be able to find each other even without an established IP address.

For WAN connections, similarly make sure you are using the correct IP address for the computer to which you're trying to connect. For example, for dynamically assigned IP addresses, make sure you're connecting to the remote computer's current IP address—it may have obtained a newer address since the last time you connected. If you will be trying to connect to your home or office computer while on the road, a utility called Ipanema (from If Then Software; www.ifthensoft.com) can automatically e-mail your current IP address each day, allowing you to track potential changes to your home/office computer's address.

SEE: • "Take Note: What Are the TCP/IP Settings?" in Chapter 8, for more on IP addresses and related information.

Troubleshooting Network Browser and Connect to Server

This section describes an assortment of problems and solutions related to connecting to servers via either Network Browser or the Connect to Server command.

Finder freeze/hang. In several of the situations described below (for example, unexpected disconnect, disconnect fails, alias could not be opened), the Finder may hang or freeze when you try to access an open window for the problem server or access an (alias or Desktop) icon of the server. The primary symptom is a spinning wait cursor (just in the Finder) that continues indefinitely. Sometimes, if you wait long enough, the Finder unhangs itself and an error message appears. If so, follow the advice for that message (as described below). Otherwise, if the freeze persists, relaunch the Finder (for example, by holding down the Option key and accessing the Dock menu for the Finder, and then choosing Relaunch). If even this fails, it's time to log out of your account or restart the Mac (if the freeze does not prevent access to these commands), or, as a last result, to do a hard restart of the Mac.

If the hang recurs when you're accessing the server after a restart, the source of the problem is most likely on the host machine. A common fix is to restart Personal File Sharing on the host/server computer (assuming that you have access to it).

Network command dimmed. If the Network command is dimmed in the Go menu, the Network icon in the sidebar will likely still work. Use it, instead of the Go menu command, to get to the Network Browser window. Otherwise, relaunch the Finder (for example, by holding down the Option key and accessing the Dock menu for the Finder, and then choosing Relaunch); the Network command in the Go menu should now be active.

Server does not appear in Network Browser window. Occasionally, you may have a problem in which one or more local servers that you know have been set up correctly do not appear in Network Browser. If this happens, here's what to do:

- Assuming that you know the server's IP address, enter it in the Address field of the Connect to Server window and try to connect this way.

- Often, although Computer A can't locate Computer B, Computer B can locate Computer A. Thus, if you have access to both computers, you can make the File Sharing connection go the other way (assuming that you have an account set up to do so). If all you want to do is copy files back and forth, the direction of the connection usually doesn't matter (but see "Copying goes in only one direction," later in this chapter, for one exception).

- If two servers on your local network have the same name, only one (or none) of them may appear in Network Browser. The solution is to change the name of one. If you don't have the necessary access to do this, contact the person who does.

- Make sure the necessary service (such as AppleTalk for AppleTalk-connected servers) is enabled in Directory Access. If the needed service is already enabled, disable it and re-enable it to restart the service via the Directory Access application.

Note: A crash of the DirectoryService process on your Mac may prevent servers from appearing in the Network window. In this case, restarting your Mac may be the simplest solution. If you want to check whether or not a crash has occurred, you'll typically find a message noting that such a DirectoryService quit in the log files (console.log or system.log) accessible via Console.

SEE: • "Take Note: Connect to Server vs. Network Browser: What's the Difference?" earlier in this chapter, for more specific advice.

• "Directory Access," in Chapter 4, for background information on this application.

• It's possible—especially when attempting to connect via FTP—that you won't see any volumes listed in this window, or that the window won't even appear. If this happens, make sure that you entered the address, name, and password correctly. If you did, for FTP, try a third-party FTP utility, such as Fetch or RBrowser. If that fails to work, the problem is probably at the server end (in which case you have to wait for the server administrator to fix the problem).

• Otherwise, it's time to check the basics (for example, is the computer on and awake; is it connected to the network; is Sharing enabled; did you restart Sharing; and more), as described earlier in this section.

Alias could not be opened. You attempt to connect to a server via Network Browser or an alias (or location) file that you created for a server. Instead of connecting or getting a Login window, however, you get an error message that says, "The alias could not be opened, because the original item could not be found." If this happens, simply try again; the connection may succeed. Otherwise, if using Network Browser, trying going to the Browser window via a different method (such as via the Computer window instead of the Finder sidebar); try again. If this, too, fails, it's time to check the basics, as described above.

Connection failed or timed out. After you click a Connect button, a Connecting to Server alert may appear (especially if you used the Finder's Connect to Server command to attempt to connect to a remote server). If the connection is unsuccessful, this may soon be followed by an "AFP Connection Status" (or similar) alert. In both alerts, you will have an option to cancel the connection attempt.

If a connection is not made after some period of time, you will get the "Connection failed" (or similar) error message. This means that Mac OS X could not locate the selected server. The most likely cause is that either the server you want to access is not currently on the Internet, you're not on the Internet, or the appropriate Sharing services have not been enabled. Check the basics, as described above.

More generally (either with Connect to Server or the Network Browser), you may get a "Connection failed" error (which includes some generic advice) or a more specific message explaining the reason for the failure. Or you may get no message at all—but still a connection fails. Here's what may be going on and what to do about it:

- **You may not have waited long enough.** Wait at least 30 seconds before you assume that you have a problem. Especially if you are opening a window from a server for the first time after making a connection, it may take a few seconds before the contents of the window appear. Until this happens, the Finder window may erroneously say that there are zero items in the window.

- **The two Macs are on different networks.** If you are trying to connect via AirPort, for example, and there are two or more available AirPort networks within range, you may be on one network and the other computer may be on a second network. You both need to be on the same AirPort network to connect locally.

- **You're using Connect to Server and the address you entered in the Server Address field does not exist (because you mistyped it, for example).** The fix is to find the correct address and use it.

- **You're using an HTTP address to connect to a server, and the server does not use WebDAV.** The solution here is to use a Web browser to connect to the server.

    SEE: • "Take Note: Mounting and Working with iDisks," in Chapter 8, for more on WebDAV.

- **You may have selected a connection method that's not working for a reason you cannot diagnose.** To work around this, if possible (for example, for a server listed in the Network Browser window and for which you know its address), switch from using the Network Browser method to the Connect to Server method to connect. Or vice versa. Often one method works when the other does not.

- **There's some other unspecified network-related problem.** Check the basics (such as for the Network System Preferences settings), as described above. If everything you check appears to be OK, restarting the Mac may help clear up any temporary glitches.

Figure 9.34

The "Connection failed" error that may occur when you attempt to connect to a server.

Connection failed

The server may not exist or it is not operational at this time. Check the server name or IP address and try again.

OK

Host (or client) unexpectedly disconnects. As described earlier in this chapter, if the owner of a host machine decides to turn off Personal File Sharing while other users are connected to it, the other users will typically get a warning message alerting them of the impending disconnect. If the owner decides to bypass this warning or otherwise causes a disconnect to occur (for example, by changing network settings, allowing the computer to go to sleep, or removing the cable connecting the computer to the network), the connected user(s) will likely get a "Server connection interrupted" message, containing a Disconnect button. Although you have already been disconnected, click the button to get your Mac (especially the Finder) functioning normally again (otherwise you may get a Finder freeze/hang, as described above).

If a window to the now-disconnected server is still open, or an alias to the server remains in the Network Browser window, you may also get an error message (such as "No file services are available at the URL") if you try to use the window or icon to access the server. Or icons may vanish as soon as you select them. Otherwise, you may get a Finder freeze/hang, as described above.

A similar situation can occur if the client causes an unintended disconnect. For example, this may happen if the client's Ethernet cable accidentally comes loose, or if the client computer is a laptop connected via AirPort and moves out of AirPort range. The problem may remain even after you reconnect the cable or move back in range.

If the problem is a disconnect at the host or client end, the obvious solution is for the host or client to reconnect. For persistent problems at the client end, such as a freeze, logging out or restarting the Mac should fix things.

SEE: • "Stopping File Sharing with users connected," in "Personal File Sharing," earlier in this chapter, for related information.

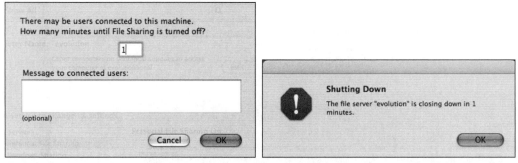

Figure 9.35

Left, a warning message that appears if you attempt to shut down Personal File Sharing on a server computer while a client computer is connected; right, a message that appears on the client computer before Sharing is shut down.

Figure 9.36

An example of a message that may appear on a client computer if a successful connection to a server computer is unexpectedly broken (for example, if the host server shuts down with no warning).

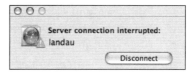

Disconnect fails. Occasionally, especially when using Network Browser in versions earlier than Mac OS X 10.3.3, you may be unable to disconnect from a server. Typically, you drag the server icon from the Desktop to the Trash and all appears to go well; however, you remain connected. If this happens, try the following until something works:

- Select the server and use the Finder's Eject (Command-E) command. I have found this to be more reliable than dragging the item to the Trash.

- Go to the Network System Preferences pane and switch to a different location or create a new one if necessary. In this new location, turn off the port to which you're currently connected to the network (for example, turn off AirPort if that's what you're using). This should break the connection to the server. Now you can return to your initial location.

- Physically disconnect from the network. For example, for an Ethernet connection, remove and then replace the Ethernet cable.

- If it additionally appears that the Finder has frozen as a result of your disconnect attempt, relaunch the Finder (via the Relaunch command that's available when you hold down the Option key while accessing the Finder's Dock menu). If that fails, restart the Mac. Simply logging out and back in again, or putting the Mac to sleep, is not likely to be sufficient.

SEE: • "Using Network Browser and Connect to Server" and "Take Note: Connect to Server vs. Network Browser: What's the Difference?" earlier in this chapter, for related information.

Miscellaneous Sharing problems

The following is a sampling of some less common, more specific problems (and solutions) than those in the previous sections.

File Sharing turned off at startup. Personal File Sharing is disabled at startup if you're not connected to a network (for example, via an AirPort card or network cable). The solution is to connect to a network and re-enable File Sharing in the Sharing System Preferences pane.

More generally, Sharing requires software in the Extensions and StartupItems folders of the /System/Library folder. For dealing with startup issues that may cause problems here, see Chapter 5.

Copying goes in only one direction. Typically, with Personal File Sharing, you have a choice of establishing File Sharing from Mac A to Mac B, or vice versa. In such cases, you may find that you can successfully copy a certain file (on Mac B, for example) when connected to B from A, but not when connected to A from B. Unfortunately, you may not get an error message indicating a problem. Instead, you simply get an incomplete copy of the file, with no error message at all. The simplest work-around is to connect via the direction that works.

This has happened to me, for example, when trying to replace the database file used by Microsoft Office's Entourage. When Sharing was set up so that the shared computer was the one receiving the copy, the problem occurred. When the shared computer was the one sending the copy, it worked.

Sharing and configuration priority glitches. In general, for Internet Sharing, the port you intend to use should be the one at the top of the list (highest priority) in the Network Port Configurations section of the Network System Preferences pane. Otherwise, Internet Sharing may not work. This is especially true for sharing over FireWire or sharing an AirPort Internet connection with wired Ethernet clients.

Similarly, for File Sharing, if a server is accessible only over wired Ethernet, and you have AirPort listed as your top preferred network port, you may not be able to connect to the server. The simplest solution here is to move Built-in Ethernet up to the top port in Network System Preferences' Network Port Configuration list—at least temporarily.

Internet Sharing disconnected, turned off, or blocked. If Internet Sharing is not running as expected, there could be several possible causes, including the following:

- If you change your Location in Network System Preferences while Internet Sharing is on, shared computers will no longer be able to connect. The solution is to stop and restart Internet Sharing.

- Internet Sharing will be turned off whenever you restart or shut down your Mac. You must restart Internet Sharing each time the computer is restarted.

- Turning on the firewall may block the use of Internet Sharing. If this happens, the solution is to turn the firewall off *before* starting Internet Sharing. In some cases, I've found that enabling Personal Web Sharing (in Sharing's Services pane) can get Internet Sharing to work with the firewall running when it would not otherwise work with the firewall on.

  SEE: • "Internet" and "Take Note: Setting Up and Using Internet Sharing and File Sharing," earlier in this chapter, for related information.

Problems making an SMB connection and/or copying files via Windows Sharing. If an attempt to copy a file to a Windows PC via the SMB protocol results in a corrupt file or a failure to copy (often with some error message), or if you're having any problems connecting to a Mac from a PC, try one or more of the following:

- Turn Windows Sharing off and then back on again.

- Disable and re-enable the SMB service in the Directory Access application. In addition, if your network uses a WINS Server, make sure you entered it in the SMB settings in Directory Access. (To access these settings, double-click the SMB service item in the Directory Access list.)

- Go to the Accounts System Preferences pane and change your password. If you like, change it back again to the original password. The important thing is to get the Mac's "attention" by making the change.

- Use a utility such as Cocktail to delete Sharing-related cache files.

- Do not use any of the following characters in the name of a file you want to copy to a PC: < > / \ | * ? " ".

- When viewed from a Mac, files copied from a Mac to a Windows PC may copy correctly yet not appear in the Finder immediately. Creating an empty folder on the Windows computer may force the Finder to update and show the copied items. Otherwise, relaunching the Finder or logging out and logging back in should do the trick.

  SEE: • "SMB/CIFS," in "Directory Access," in Chapter 4, for related information on using Directory Access (which can help if the PC does not show up in the Connect to Server or Network Browser window).

10

Unix for
Mac OS X Users

As first mentioned in Chapter 1, the core of Mac OS X is an operating system whose origins predate the Mac itself: Unix.

SEE: • Chapters 1 and 4 for a general background on Unix in Mac OS X.

For the majority of Mac users, the fact that Unix exists on the Mac is about as relevant as the fact that REALbasic exists as a programming language for Mac OS X. You don't need to bother with either just to use a word processor or a Web browser.

Troubleshooters, on the hand, don't have that luxury. When things go wrong and the standard Mac OS X techniques don't work, your ability to use Unix commands may represent your best or only chance of solving the problem. That's why I've peppered the preceding chapters with tips that demonstrate these commands' effectiveness. In case you missed them along the way, here are just a few prime examples:

- "Technically Speaking: More About Disk Utility's Image and Restore Features," in Chapter 3
- "Technically Speaking: Restoring and Replacing NetInfo and Directory Access Data," in Chapter 4
- "Technically Speaking: Connecting Remotely to a Frozen Mac: Killing Processes, Running Sync," in Chapter 5
- "Killing processes from Terminal," in the "Force-quitting" section, and "Technically Speaking: Kill Signals," in Chapter 5
- "Viewing default permissions in Terminal," in the sidebar "Technically Speaking: Repair Disk Permissions and Receipts," in Chapter 5
- "Using Unix to delete files," in Chapter 6
- "Modifying invisible Unix files from Mac OS X applications," in Chapter 6
- "CUPS," in Chapter 7
- "Technically Speaking: Using ipfw," in Chapter 9

For those users with little or no background in Unix, who may have felt a bit mystified by what was going on in the above examples, this chapter explains the basics.

In This Chapter

Understanding the Terminal Application

In Unix, the typical way to issue commands (in other words, run command-line Unix applications) is by typing text in a terminal application. Mac OS X provides such an application, called—appropriately enough—Terminal. Terminal has a *command-line interface* (CLI), as opposed to Mac OS X's more familiar *graphical user interface* (GUI). To be fair, though, Terminal does offer some handy GUI tools for working with the CLI via its menu bar items and menus.

The Terminal application is located in the Utilities folder of the Applications folder. When you launch Terminal, a window opens, into which you type commands. In this window, Terminal accepts only text input and produces only text output, making almost no use of the mouse.

What exactly does Terminal do?

Terminal is your window to the Unix world. Via Unix commands entered in Terminal, you can do almost anything in Mac OS X that you could do from a standard Unix (that is, non-Mac) machine. This includes creating and running Perl scripts (often used in conjunction with Web sites); setting up cron events (such as maintenance tasks); accessing FTP, Telnet, or Apache Web server software; and setting up your own mail server. It's no wonder that many advanced computer users have been almost drooling at the prospect of what can be done with Mac OS X's combination of Unix and a traditional Mac interface.

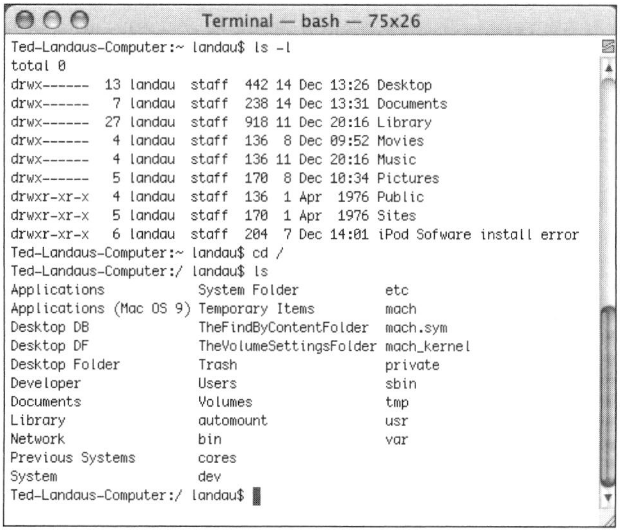

Figure 10.1

A Terminal window.

Terminal is also a potentially dangerous tool, especially if you're not familiar with how to use it. A small error could result in your deleting a good portion of the data on your drive without even getting a warning about the trouble that's about to occur. Thus, if you're new to Terminal, it pays to enter the pool at the shallow end, which is what we do in this chapter.

For starters, we'll take a look at the parts of Terminal that are most Mac-like: the menu commands, as accessed from the menu bar at the top of the screen (or via their Command-key equivalents). Admittedly, for the troubleshooting focus of this book, most users will never need to access any of these menu options—the default settings work just fine, and you can go directly to entering commands in the main window. Thus, you may decide to skip the next two sections (although I would still check out the sidebars). The chapter's remaining sections explore how to use the main Terminal window itself.

Terminal's menus

After you launch Terminal, its menus appear in the menu bar at the top of the screen. The following describes these menus.

Terminal. The main points of interest in the Terminal application menu include the following:

- **Preferences.** This command opens a window from which you can select several options. The first group of options modifies what happens when you open a new Terminal window. For example, if you wanted a new Terminal window to open a shell other than the default shell, you would select "Execute this command (specify complete path)" and enter the path to the shell in the text box.

    SEE: • "Technically Speaking: What's a Shell?" and "Take Note: Changing the Default Login Shell," below, for details.

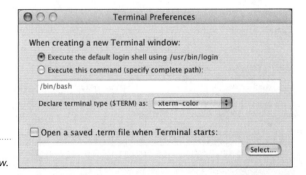

Figure 10.2

Terminal's Preferences window.

You can also declare your terminal type ($TERM) here. Unless you need to have your Mac emulate a specific terminal (a throwback to the days before desktop computers replaced terminals) other than the default, you don't need to make any changes here. (However, see "Scrollback," a bit later in this chapter, for one reason to use this option.)

Finally, you can also select a saved .term file to be opened by default when Terminal launches.

> **SEE:** • "Take Note: .Term Files," later in this chapter, for details.

- **Window Settings.** This command is one of several menu items you can use to access Terminal's Inspector window.

> **SEE:** • "Terminal Inspector," later in this chapter, for details.

TECHNICALLY SPEAKING ▶ What's a Shell?

A *shell* in Unix refers to a command-line interpreter: When you type a command (such as 1s), the shell determines the response to that command.

You can think of the Mac OS's graphical interface as a type of "shell"—a way to interact with the operating system—and different versions of the Mac OS as different shells. Thus, if you have both Mac OS 9 and Mac OS X on your Mac, and you shift between them, commands may work differently. Command-I, for example, opens a Get Info window in both operating systems; on the other hand, Command-N creates a new folder in Mac OS 9's Finder but opens a new Finder window in Mac OS X.

Changing shells in Unix can have the same effect. For the basic Unix commands described in this chapter, all shells work similarly—just as many Mac OS commands do the same thing whether you're in Mac OS 9 or Mac OS X—but there may be slight differences, depending on your shell.

In Mac OS X 10.3 Panther and later, the default shell is the *bash* shell (which stands for *Bourne Again Shell*). Other shells available from Terminal include the following: *tsch* (the *"TENEX" C shell*), which was the default shell in Mac OS X 10.2 Jaguar and earlier; *zsh* (called the *Z shell*), which is an enhanced version of *ksh* (the *Korn shell*); *csh* (called the *C shell*); and *sh* (called the *Bourne shell*). The sh and bash shells are preferred for running shell scripts (such as the .command files you can create, as described later in this chapter).

You can change to a new shell simply by typing its name in the Terminal window and pressing Return. For example, to shift to the csh shell, type csh and press Return. To revert to the preceding (parent) shell, type exit and press Return again (or open a new Terminal window).

Note: When you use the su command to get root access, as described later in this chapter, you similarly temporarily shift to a new shell.

If you want to have two shells open at once, it's simple: Just open another window (by selecting New Shell from Terminal's File menu). If you want the shell to be different from the default shell, type the command for the desired shell in the new window.

If Active Process Name is enabled in the Window section of the Terminal Inspector (as described in "Terminal Inspector," later in this chapter), the title bar will indicate which shell is currently active in that window.

continues on next page

TECHNICALLY SPEAKING ▶ What's a Shell? *continued*

Environment and shell variables. You can view the system default shell by typing env (for *environment*) in any Terminal window. From the several lines of output that appear, check the SHELL line to see the default. The env command also gives you a host of other basic environment information, such as the PATH listing.

When a shell is used, it stores important and frequently accessed bits of data in *variables*. Some of these variables are defaults, but you can also create your own variables.

There is a distinction between shell variables (which are not inherited by programs, such as subshells) and environment variables (which are inherited). The set command is for shell variables. The setenv command (in tcsh) and the env command (in bash) are used to modify environment variables. If you just type set with no arguments, you get a list of its variables. Similarly, if you just type setenv or env with no arguments, you get a list of its variables.

Note: Arguments are text added to a command that instructs the command what to do.

When someone creates a shell variable, he or she typically has an intention as to when it should run (for example, whether or not it should run in subshells). By choosing the "wrong" category (shell versus environmental), the shell's creator may have the shell run at times when unintended and/or not run when intended. As an end user, it is merely useful to have some awareness of this distinction so that you know how to search for all relevant variables.

Figure 10.3

Output from the env *command: The default shell name is listed in the* SHELL *line. On this Mac (running Mac OS X Tiger), it's /bin/bash.*

TAKE NOTE ▶ Changing the Default Login Shell

In Panther (Mac OS X 10.3) and later, new user accounts are assigned the bash shell. In Jaguar (Mac OS X 10.2) and earlier, the default is the tsch shell. To change the default login shell:

1. From Terminal's Terminal application menu, select Preferences.

2. From the "When creating a new Terminal window" option, switch from the default choice ("Execute the default login shell using /usr/bin/login") to "Execute this command."

3. In the text box, enter the complete path to the shell of your choosing. The shells you can use (for example, tcsh, bash, csh, and sh) are located in Unix's /bin directory. Thus, to select tcsh as the default shell, enter the following: /bin/tcsh. By default, the text box contains the path for the bash shell: /bin/bash.

continues on next page

TAKE NOTE ▶ Changing the Default Login Shell *continued*

Now, whenever you launch Terminal, it will use tcsh instead of bash. Note: This will not change the SHELL listing of the env command's output.

bash or tcsh: Which should you use? Which is used in this book? Perhaps it's just that I got used to tcsh as the default choice prior to Panther, but I prefer it to bash. Because I find it a bit more user-friendly (if you can use such a term to describe Unix!), I've made tcsh my default shell in Tiger. Although the bash shell is better for creating shell scripts, this has never been an issue for me. In any case, you can still create a shell script in bash and keep tcsh as your default shell.

However, in keeping with Apple's shift, the examples in this chapter refer primarily to bash—though I may on occasion refer to tcsh. With regard to the topics covered in this book, the differences between bash and tcsh are mostly minor to nonexistent. In the few cases where there are significant differences between the two shells, such as when using the alias command or setting up shell-configuration files, I describe the "rules" for both shells.

Note: If you try a command listed in this chapter and it doesn't work as expected, it's probably because it works in only one shell (and I perhaps forgot to specify this). Thus, if you're using bash, switch to tcsh and try the command again. It should now work.

tcsh may be the default shell after you upgrade to Tiger (or Panther). Despite the fact that bash is the default shell in Tiger (and Panther), you may find that tcsh is your initial default. This happens if your account was first created in Jaguar. In this case, Tiger retains tcsh as the shell for the accounts. If you create an account for a new user after upgrading, bash will be the default for that user.

SEE: • "Technically Speaking: What's a Shell?" above, and "Using shell-configuration files," later in this chapter, for more details.

File. This menu includes the typical New, Open, Save, and Print commands, plus a few more unusual ones. The following are the most important ones for you to know:

- **New Shell.** This command opens a new Terminal window.

- **Connect to Server.** This command provides a convenient way of accessing another computer via Terminal. For example, if another Mac OS X user has enabled Remote Login in his or her Sharing System Preferences pane and you have an account on that Mac, you can log in by choosing Connect to Server from the File menu, which opens a shell session *on that Mac* (instead of on your own Mac). You can also use this command to log in to any Unix server for which you have remote-login access. To do so, follow these steps:

  1. Select Connect to Server. In the window that appears, in the Services column select "Secure Shell (ssh)."

2. Select the server you wish to connect to in the Server column. Thanks to Bonjour, any computers on your local network will automatically appear in the Server column. If you want to connect to a computer across the Internet or at some other address, add a new server to the list by clicking the Add (+) button at the bottom of the Server column, enter the IP address of the remote computer, and then click OK to save it.

3. Type your account name (on the target computer) in the User text box. If the account name on the target computer is the same as your local account name, you can leave this blank.

4. Click Connect. A Terminal window will open. If the connection is successful, you will be asked for your password. If you give the correct password, you will be logged in to your account on that computer.

Note: After doing this, your login information is saved in the pop-up menu at the bottom of the window. The next time you want to access that computer, just select it; no need to re-enter your name. To enter a new name, delete any name in the User text box and reselect the IP address listed in the Server column; then enter a new name.

The Service column comes preconfigured with settings to connect to another computer using SSH (Secure Shell), STFP (Secure File Transfer Protocol), and the less secure FTP and Telnet. If you regularly use some other kind of shell, or shell-like, program, you can add your own definition of a Service by clicking the Add (+) button below the Services column.

- **Save** and **Save As.** Use these commands to save a Terminal settings (.term) file.

  SEE: • "Take Note: .Term Files," later in this chapter, for more on the Save command, as well as the Open, Library, and Use Settings as Defaults commands, also in the File menu.

- **Save Text As** and **Save Selected Text As.** Use these commands to save the text in a Terminal window to a text file.

- **Send Break (Ctrl-c).** Use this command (or the Send Reset and Send Hard Reset commands, if needed) to stop a process that appears to be hung.

  SEE: • "Take Note: Unix Problems and How to Fix Them," later in this chapter, for more information.

- **Secure Keyboard Entry.** Use this command to ensure that other applications on your computer (or on any computer on your network) cannot detect or record what you're typing. If you're worried about someone trying to steal your password, for example, you should use this command.

- **Show Info.** This command opens the Terminal Inspector (as does the Set Title command).

  SEE: • "Terminal Inspector," later in this chapter, for details.

Edit. This menu includes the typical Copy, Cut, and Paste commands, as well as a Find command. The Paste Escaped Text command adds a backslash in front of any spaces in the copied selection when pasting it so that the text is treated as a single selection (rather than multiple commands) when pasted into Terminal.

SEE: • "Take Note: Spaces in Pathnames," later in this chapter, for details.

Scrollback. This menu provides commands (such as Line Up and Page Up) for navigating the text output in the Terminal window.

Note: When using these commands (or the scroll bars on the right side of the window) to scroll back, you may note that the previous output *does not* appear— for example, if you're viewing man output. To work around this problem, use the up (and down, for scrolling forward again) arrow keys on the keyboard. You can also work around the problem by accessing Terminal's Preferences, and then, from the "Declare terminal type ($TERM) as" pop-up menu, select vt100. Once you've done this, all of the Scrollback commands should work as expected.

You can use the Clear Scrollback (Command-K) command to "erase" the window's currently displayed text. Note: Typing clear in the Terminal window accomplishes the same thing.

Font. This menu provides commands for customizing the size and look of the text in the Terminal window. The Show Fonts (Command-T) command opens the same Font panel described for TextEdit in Chapter 4.

Window. This menu includes commands for minimizing and enlarging a window as well as for rotating between windows or selecting a specific window (if you have more than one window open).

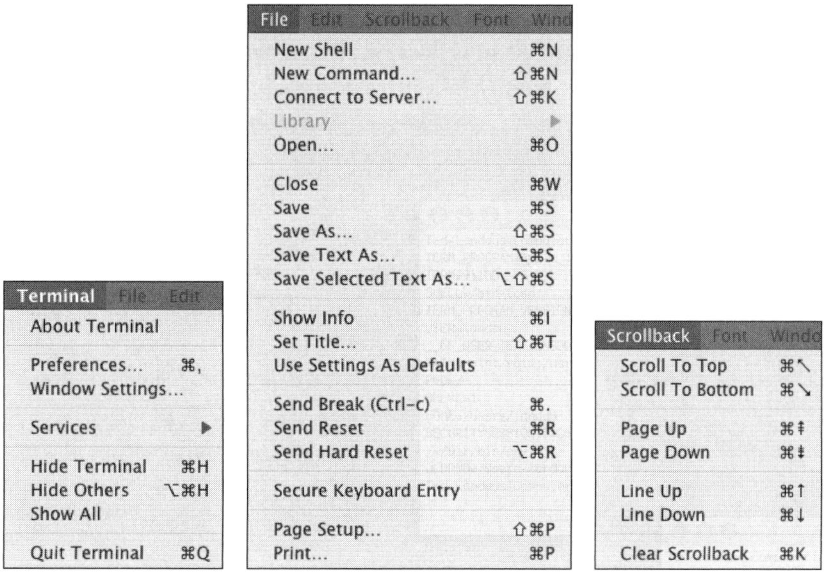

Figure 10.4

Terminal menus: left, Terminal application menu; center, File menu; right, Scrollback menu.

Terminal Inspector

You can open Terminal Inspector in any of the following ways: (a) by typing Command-I, (b) by selecting Show Info from the File menu, or (c) by selecting Window Settings from the Terminal menu.

The different panes in Terminal Inspector are accessed via the pop-up menu at its top. The choices are Shell, Processes, Emulation, Buffer, Display, Color, Window, and Keyboard. Any changes you make in the Inspector only affect the current shell window—unless you click the Use Settings as Defaults button.

The following is not a complete listing of all Inspector settings and options. They are the ones I believe you will use most often; feel free to experiment with others as desired.

Processes: Prompt before closing window. See "Quitting Terminal," later in this chapter, for coverage of this selection.

Emulation: Option click to position cursor. Select the "Option click to position cursor" option. Why? Consider this: When typing in a shell window, if you discover a typo ten letters back, you would normally press the Delete key ten times and then start over from that point. However, with the Emulation option enabled, you can Option-click to any location in the command line and instantly fix the typo. Once you've made the correction, Option-click back to the end of the line to return to your previous location.

Buffer: Unlimited scrollback. The Buffer Size option lets you adjust the size of the scrollback buffer. This is especially relevant when you execute a command that produces a large amount of output that quickly scrolls through your window. When the scrolling stops, you may want to scroll back to the beginning of the output. If the scrollback buffer is too small, the initial output will have disappeared. The default setting is for 10,000 lines—adequate for most situations. However, you may occasionally want to change this setting to "Unlimited scrollback."

Display: Enable drag copy/paste of text. This option allows you to select any text in a Terminal window and drag it to the current command line—convenient when you want to reuse a long selection of text without retyping it. You can even drag text from one shell window to another—or from any application that supports dragging of text.

Color: Transparency. You can use the Transparency slider to adjust the transparency of Terminal's windows to your liking.

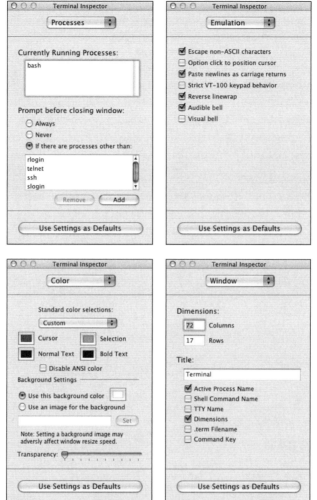

Window: Title. When you initially launch Terminal, it opens a shell window with a title that likely reads something like, "Terminal - bash - 80x24." In the Window pane, you can customize the title by choosing the options you wish to display.

- Active Process Name should be selected by default. If it's not, it's a good idea to select it because it identifies the active shell. Further, should you ever change your shell (such as typing the csh command to go from bash to csh), with this option enabled the change is instantly reflected in the title. In fact, if you enter certain temporary shell-modifying commands, such as su, the command name will temporarily appear in the title as the active process.

- If you select Command Key, you will be shown in each window title which Command-key shortcut (for example, Command-1 or Command-2) to type to make that window the active one (assuming more than one window is open).

- In the Title text box, enter text of your choosing—for example, Command & Control. Whatever you type will appear, instead of the word *Terminal*, at the start of the title of each window.

  SEE: • "Take Note: What's a Shell?" earlier in this chapter, for more details.

Keyboard. I don't use the options here, but I felt I should at least mention them. Most shells use a variety of keyboard shortcuts for common commands. If you wish to modify these shortcuts, this is where you do so. Check out "Creating custom control sequences in Terminal," in the Help Viewer files for Terminal, for more information.

Split window. One option not listed in any menu or Inspector option is the ability to split a window so that you can view and compare two sections of the Terminal output at the same time. To do this, click the torn-square icon just below the title bar on the right side of the window; you can change the relative size of the two panes by dragging the divider. This option is especially useful when you want to see the current shell prompt while viewing earlier output. To revert to a single window, click the solid square icon in the lower of the two panes.

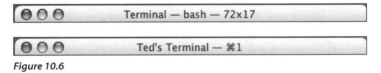

Figure 10.6

Top, *the title bar of a Terminal window before making customized changes in the Window section of the Inspector;* bottom, *after making changes.*

TAKE NOTE ▶ .Term Files

If you customize a Terminal window via Inspector and want to save those changes as defaults, you can usually do so by clicking the Use Settings as Defaults button (or by choosing the command of the same name in Terminal's File menu).

But what if you want to save several different sets of settings, none of which you necessarily want as the default? You can save any particular customization (font size, color, transparency, and so on) via a Terminal settings (.term) file.

To do so, make all of the changes you wish to save, and then select Save (or Save As) from Terminal's File menu. This creates a file of the current settings; the file will have the name you provide, with a .term extension appended to it. From options in the Save window you can also decide whether to (a) open this .term file when launching Terminal (which overlaps with the setting in Terminal's Preferences window); (b) save all currently open windows or just the active (main) one; and (c) add further options (again overlapping with preferences settings) for which shell and command to execute when opening the file.

continues on next page

TAKE NOTE ▶ .Term Files *continued*

If you do not enable the option to open the saved .term file by default when Terminal starts up, you can always open it later by choosing the Open command from Terminal's File menu.

Terminal is supposed to save .term files in ~/Library/Application Support/Terminal. However, in earlier versions of Mac OS X, when I tried this, Terminal instead elected to save the file in my Documents folder. If this happens to you, you can create your own Terminal folder in the Application Support folder and save the .term file there (or move any existing file there). After relaunching Terminal, subsequent saving of .term files should result in this Terminal folder's being selected by default in the Save dialog.

Once you've saved one or more .term files, you will see that the Library command in Terminal's File menu is no longer dimmed. Choose it, and you'll be able to access a hierarchical menu listing all .term files in the Terminal folder.

The .term file is a text file (in XML format). Therefore, you can open it in a text editor and add Unix commands to it. A popular use here would be to connect to a remote server via SSH on launch. The added commands run when the .term file is opened. For more details, see the following Apple Knowledge Base article: http://docs.info.apple.com/article.html?artnum=86134. (At the time of this writing, the article claims to be for Mac OS X 10.2; however, it applies to Panther and Tiger, as well.)

These .term files have a significant limitation: If set to run automatically when Terminal launches, a .term file affects only the initial shell window. To see what I mean, make a change to your default settings (such as choosing a larger font) and then save the change as a .term file (via the Save command). In the Save dialog, enable the "Open this file when Terminal starts up" option, then quit and relaunch Terminal. The window will indeed open in the modified font. But now select Command-N to open a second Terminal window. The second window will use the default font, *not* the one in the .term file. Sometimes this may be what you want: For example, if you're using the .term file to connect to a remote server, you may not want this action performed with each new window you open. However, if you do want to repeat the action, you can always use the Open command to select the .term file and run it a second time (or, even easier, choose the saved .term file from the Library submenu in the File menu). And for something like a font change, if you really wanted that change to occur in every shell window, you could select the new font as the default font in the Inspector window. Still, there are commands, beyond what can be set via Terminal's menus, where it would be more convenient if the commands were run automatically with each new window.

Although there's some overlap in function, a .term file is not the same as a shell script, a .login file, or a .tcshrc/.cshrc file. A .term file is a Mac feature and is primarily a way to select customized window settings, which would otherwise be set via Terminal's menu commands. A .term file, for example, is what you would use to change default settings for text color and font. The other types of files modify the Unix command-line environment, and are Unix features.

SEE: • **"Using shell-configuration files" and "Using a shell script," later in this chapter, for explanations of these other types of files.**

Launching Terminal

When you launch Terminal, a window opens that says, `Welcome to Darwin!` The next line is the command-line prompt—which in the bash shell typically reads as follows:

`computername:~ username$`

For example, on one of my Macs, which is named Yoda, when the logged-in user is landau, the command-line prompt reads as follows:

`Yoda:~ landau$`

In some cases, the name will simply read `localhost`.

In the tcsh shell, in contrast, the general format for the command-line prompt will typically read as follows:

`[computername:~] username%`

In either case, `computername` is the name of your Mac (as set up in the Sharing System Preferences pane), and `username` is the short name of the currently logged-in user (as shown in the Accounts System Preferences pane). If you're connected to a server, the server's computer name, and your user name on that computer, will appear instead of the local names.

The symbol and/or text that appears after the colon represents the name of the directory at your current location—which in this case is the root level of your home directory. The tilde (~) is a standard Unix abbreviation for this location. This is the default location when you open a new shell.

The % and $ symbols indicate that Terminal is ready to accept your typed input. The symbol may be different (perhaps a #), or absent, in other shells.

Quitting Terminal

To log out of a Terminal session, type `logout` or `exit`. However, you do not need to log out before quitting Terminal. When you quit Terminal (by pressing Command-Q) or even simply close a shell window, Terminal logs you out. Depending on the option selected in the Processes item of the Inspector window, you may get a Close Window dialog with the following warning: "Closing this window will terminate the following processes inside it . . . " (followed by a list of processes). If you get this dialog, click the Terminate button to close the window and truly log out.

To prevent the Close Window dialog from appearing, choose Never from the "Prompt before closing window" section of the Processes pane of the Inspector window. However, with certain processes active and Never selected, Terminal will refuse to quit when you select Quit from the File menu. If this happens, you can still force-quit Terminal by selecting Force Quit from the Apple menu.

You can avoid this hassle, however, by closing all Terminal windows before choosing Quit or by not using the Never option. If you type `logout` when done with a shell window, this also avoids any possible hassle with a force-quit or having active processes open when trying to quit Terminal.

Figure 10.7

An example of the Close Window message.

TAKE NOTE ▶ Learning What Commands Do

To get more information about almost any Unix command, you have three main options from within Terminal:

man. Type `man` (for *manual*), followed by a space and then the name of the command. To learn more about the `ls` command, for example, type `man ls`. You will be provided with details on the various options available for use with the `ls` command.

You can even type `man man` to find out about the `man` command itself.

The output of `man` requests often assumes you already know a good deal about how Unix commands work. Don't expect a tutorial! However, even Unix novices can usually glean some useful information from the output—especially about the various options that work with a command. Unlike the Mac, which has menus and check boxes, Unix gives you no easy way to guess what options are available. Without the `man` command to tell you what your options are, you might never know.

continues on next page

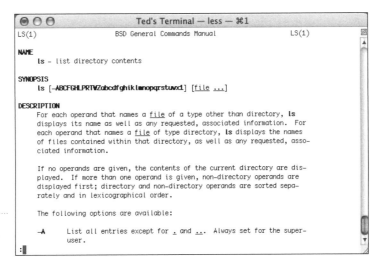

Figure 10.8

The initial output that appears if you type man ls.

TAKE NOTE ▶ Learning What Commands Do *continued*

Most man output exceeds what can fit on a screen. To see more, just keep pressing the Return key or the spacebar. If you want to exit before the output is complete, press the Q key.

Apple maintains an HTML version of all of Mac OS X's man pages, viewable from your Web browser, located at the following address: http://developer.apple.com/documentation/Darwin/Reference/ManPages.

Several Aqua-based utilities, such as Carl Lindberg's ManOpen (www.clindberg.org) and computer-support.ch's Xupport (www.computer-support.ch/Xupport), provide a graphical interface to the man output.

apropos and whatis. To search for a command by keyword, enter apropos *keyword* or whatis *keyword*. For example, to get a list of commands that include the word *Apple* in their names, or that directly refer to Apple, you would type apropos Apple. If the resulting list includes the command you seek, you can then use the man command to get more information about it. apropos finds any command description containing the characters you type; whatis finds only whole words. For example, while apropos cat will find commands dealing with *cat*alogs, appli*cat*ions, and communi*cat*ions, whatis cat will find only the command cat and commands that mention cat.

Usage. Many Unix commands work correctly only if an argument or option is added to the command. For example, the remove (rm) command performs an action only if you specify what you want removed. In this case, if you type rm—and nothing else—you get a usage summary of how the command works. Try this for the Apple-created diskutil command, for an even better example. This "usage" output is much shorter than the man information, but it can be a convenient reference if you already know the basics of how the command works. In some cases, where no man output exists for a command, there is still a usage summary available. So if you are looking for help, try both.

TAKE NOTE ▶ Unix Problems and How to Fix Them

If you think some of the error messages in Mac OS X are cryptic, you won't find any relief with Unix's error messages. They're usually worse.

Unix error messages. When Unix doesn't like what you've typed, it will often give you an error message—most commonly for incorrect commands. The causes can range from typographical errors (such as a misspelled word) to nonexistent paths to attempting to use an option that requires more information than you've provided.

If Unix has a good guess as to what went wrong, it may prompt you with its guess about the solution (for example, revising the input) and then ask, **OK?** If you like its guess, type y (for *yes*). If not, simply press Return or type n (for *no*).

Other error messages simply provide an indication of what went wrong. For example, if you mistyped a name, Unix might say, **No such file or directory**. This is your clue to make sure you didn't type the name incorrectly or attempt to access a nonexistent file.

continues on next page

TAKE NOTE ▶ Unix Problems and How to Fix Them *continued*

In other cases, Unix may offer a brief summary of the format of the command and some common options. This is essentially the same as the usage summary described in "Take Note: Learning What Commands Do." If you get this usage feedback, it usually means you used an invalid option or typed something incorrectly.

Stopping Unix. Sometimes, after typing a command, you may find yourself waiting indefinitely for the command-line prompt to reappear. This may be exactly what's supposed to happen: It means Unix has entered a mode in which the command line won't return unless you specifically instruct it to. Typically, typing q or exit will bring the prompt back. However, other times, it may just mean that Unix is doing some intensive processing: The command line will return when it's finished; you just need to be patient.

If neither of the above is the case, you may have the Unix equivalent of a freeze. To fix this, press Control-C or Command-. (period). This halts whatever process is in progress but allows you to enter further commands. (Choosing the Send Break command in Terminal's File menu is the same as pressing Control-C.) If none of this works, from the File menu choose Send Reset or Send Hard Reset, as needed.

You can use the same commands if the output from some earlier command continues to scroll and scroll, with no end in sight. At least one of these commands should bring the scrolling to a halt.

As a last resort, you can always close the window or quit Terminal.

To prevent such freezes or excessive scrolling from occurring the next time, make sure that you typed the initial command correctly. If you're not certain, use man to check the manual for the problem command to make sure you're using it correctly. Some commands normally produce an excessive amount of output; these usually have options to restrict the output as needed. If this still fails to turn on any light bulbs, you'll probably need to consult a book on Unix or seek other outside help.

```
Ted-Landaus-Computer:/ landau$ sp
-bash: sp: command not found
```

```
Ted-Landaus-Computer:/ landau$ cd ~/Dcouments
-bash: cd: /Users/landau/Dcouments: No such file or directory
```

```
Ted-Landaus-Computer:/ landau$ cp
usage: cp [-R [-H | -L | -P]] [-f | -i | -n] [-pv] src target
       cp [-R [-H | -L | -P]] [-f | -i | -n] [-pv] src1 ... srcN directory
```

Figure 10.9

Three examples of the feedback that Unix provides when something goes wrong: top, for typing a nonexistent command; middle, for entering a nonexistent path; bottom, for entering a command without its required additional parameters.

Unix: Listing and Navigating

In the remaining sections of this chapter, you'll learn about an assortment of Unix commands and files essential to troubleshooters. I'll start here by describing the basic commands used to list the contents of a directory (folder) and then show you how to navigate to any directory you want.

The ls command

The ls (*list*) command lists the contents of the current directory location. When you first launch Terminal, you arrive by default at the root level of your home directory (~). Thus, typing ls gives you a list of items in your home directory. You can compare this list with the Finder's view of the same directory by typing open . in Terminal to open a window for the current directory (in this case, your home directory) in the Finder. The items you see in the window should be very similar to those listed in Terminal. (Terminal may display a few additional items, such as Temporary Items.)

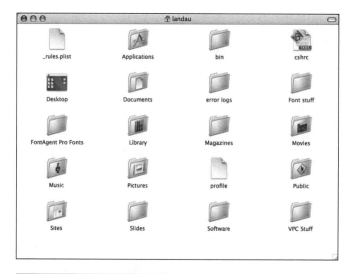

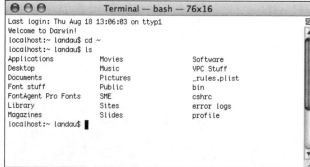

Figure 10.10

Top, *the items in my home directory as viewed in the Finder;* bottom, *as viewed in Terminal.*

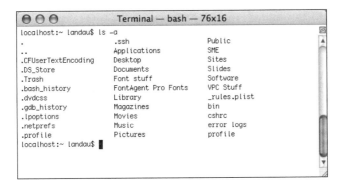

Figure 10.11

Top, *the same home directory, as listed after typing* ls -a; *bottom, after typing* ls -l.

Options. Most Unix commands have options that can be appended to them (see also "Take Note: Learning What Commands Do," earlier in this chapter). These options usually start with a hyphen, followed by an uppercase or lower-case letter. The ls command has three notable options:

- **-a.** With this option, the output of the ls command includes items that are normally invisible (for example, ones that start with a dot). Typing this command for your home directory, for example, will reveal the .Trash directory, which is where most of your files go when you drag them to the Trash.

- **-l.** This option outputs the *long* form of the directory listing. Each item is listed in its own row, followed by an assortment of additional information, including each item's permissions settings, owner, and group name. If you've read earlier chapters of this book (especially Chapters 4 and 6), you know what these permissions are used for. I also review the topic as it applies to Terminal in "Unix: Modifying Permissions," later in this chapter.

- **-F.** With this option, directory names end in a trailing slash (/). Thus, a directory named Documents will appear as Documents/ when you type ls -F. This makes it easy to distinguish between files and directories—a distinction you can't make based on the output of a basic ls command.

You can combine options in the same line, using only one hyphen if desired. Thus, to get a list that includes invisible items and is in the long form, you could type either `ls -a -l` or `ls -al`.

ls of any directory. If you want to see a list of items in a location other than your current one, you can type `ls` followed by the desired options and then the absolute or relative path to the directory you want to view.

Suppose, for example, you wanted to view the contents of the Documents directory of your home directory. Assuming you're still in your home directory, you could simply type `ls Documents`. This is what's known as a *relative-path command*. Unix assumes you're starting your path at your current directory location; thus, it looks for a directory called Documents in your home directory.

Suppose, however, you wanted to see the contents of the root-level Applications folder. The simplest way to do that would be to type the *absolute path*—that is, the pathway that starts at the root level of the volume itself. In this case, you would type `ls /Applications`. The initial slash instructs Unix to start the path at the root level of the volume.

By the way, Unix commands are almost always case sensitive. Thus, typing `ls /Applications` is not the same as typing `ls /applications`. If the name of the folder is Applications, using the lowercase *a* to begin its name will result in an error.

SEE: • **"The cd command and related commands,"** later in this chapter, for more on pathways and navigational commands.

• **"Take Note: Finder Folders vs. Unix Directories,"** in Chapter 4, for background on absolute and relative pathnames.

TAKE NOTE ▶ Unix Shortcuts

Having to type a long pathname and/or a string of command options can get to be a pain—especially when one typographical error can ruin the entire line and force you to start over. That's one of the reasons why a Mac-like interface is often preferred. Still, Unix offers a variety of shortcuts to help reduce typing. The following are the ones I use the most:

• **History.** Press the up arrow key at any point to make the last command you typed appear. You can then keep pressing the up arrow key to retrace your history for as many commands as Terminal tracks. You can use the down arrow key to return to your starting point. When you find the command you want to use again, simply press Return and it will execute. To modify the command, press Delete to backspace the needed number of characters, then type in the new characters and press Return.

If you type the `history` command in Terminal, you'll get a list of all commands entered since the shell was started, numbered sequentially and beginning with 1 for the first command entered. To re-enter a command from the list, type `!n`, where n represents that command's number in the history list. Thus, to re-enter the third command in the list, you would type `!3`. As an alternative method, you can type `!!` in order to re-enter the most recently used command.

continues on next page

TAKE NOTE ▶ **Unix Shortcuts** *continued*

• **Wildcards.** The asterisk (*) is a wildcard character—which means it provides a match for any number and sequence of characters. For example, suppose you're in your Documents directory and want to delete (remove) every item that ends in *.html*. Instead of typing each item separately, you could simply type *.html just once following the remove (rm) command (that is, rm *.html). The asterisk instructs Unix to match every file that ends in *.html*, no matter what precedes it.

   The question mark (?) is also a wildcard, except that it can substitute for only a single character. Suppose, for example, you wanted to match every file ending in *.dmg* or *.img*. You could type *.?mg. This command matches every file, no matter what precedes the period, as long as it ends in a period followed by any single character followed by *mg*. Assuming that no files end in some other combination of a character plus *mg*, this command would do the trick.

   Brackets ([and]), like the question mark, match a single character. But not just any character. Brackets match a character only if it is listed between the brackets. Thus [Cc]at will match the files cat or Cat, but not Rat or hat. A range of characters can be defined using a hyphen: [A-Z] will match any uppercase letter, [1-5] will match the numbers 1, 2, 3, 4, or 5. These can be put togther in any combination, in any order. [0-9Ca-f] will match a decimal digit; the lowercase letters a, b, c, d, e, or f; or the uppercase letter C.

• **Tab.** Whenever you start to type a pathname, pressing the Tab key fills in the remainder of the item name that matches what you're typing.

   For example, if you're in your home directory in Terminal and you type ls ~/Do and then press Tab, Unix will fill in the rest of the name (*Documents*) for you—a great time-saver for long filenames or names you can't remember precisely.

   If there's more than one matching item in a given directory (for example, if you type ls ~/D and press Tab, the D could represent either *Desktop* or *Documents*), you will hear a beep or be presented with a list of all possible matches. In either case, continue to type letters, pressing the Tab key after each, until you have a unique match.

• **Drag or copy/paste a Finder item.** This trick is not a Unix one, as it depends on the Mac OS; however, it makes working in Terminal a bit easier. If you drag a Finder icon to the Terminal window, it pastes the pathname of the item into the current command line. Alternatively, numerous Aqua-based utilities allow you to select an item and copy its Unix pathname to the clipboard. Sebastian Krauss's Locator (www.sebastian-krauss.de/software) is one such utility: Once the item is in the clipboard, Locator lets you paste the pathname into Terminal.

   Thus, to list the contents of a particular directory in Terminal, including invisible items, type ls -a followed by a space, and then drag the Finder icon of the directory you want to list to the Terminal window. Its pathname will be added to the line. Press Return, and the directory list will appear.

   New in Tiger, you can copy the name of an item, via the Finder's Copy command, and paste the copy into a Terminal window. The file's path will appear in the command line, just as if you had dragged the item there. Note: Select the item itself to copy, not just the text name of the item.

• **Dragging text.** If you selected "Enable drag copy/paste of text" from the Inspector, as described in "Terminal Inspector," earlier in this chapter, you can drag any selected text to the current command-line location and Terminal will act just as if you'd typed that text at the prompt.

TAKE NOTE ▶ Spaces in Pathnames

When you type pathnames, Unix interprets a space as being the start of a new name. Thus, if you type Research Report as the filename to be used with some command, such as cp or rm, Unix will think you're referring to two separate file or directory names—one called Research and another called Report—rather than a single item called Research Report. To instruct Unix to include the space as part of a single name, you have two options:

• You can place a backslash before the space—that is, type Research\ Report.

  Preceding a character with a backslash (\) negates any special meaning it may have. Thus, preceding a space with a backslash says, "Treat the space as a space, not as a divider."

• You can put the name in quotes (ideally single quotes, though double quotes usually work as well)—that is, type 'Research Report'. Putting a pathname in quotes tells Unix to treat everything within quotes exactly as typed. This means that a space is treated as part of the name and not as a separator.

Note: If you copy the name of a file in the Finder (or copy text that represents a file path), you can make sure the text is pasted with backslashes as needed by choosing Paste Escaped Text from Terminal's Edit menu. This eliminates the need to enclose the pasted text in quotation marks. Unlike dragging an icon from the Finder, however, copying the name of a file or folder in the Finder does not copy the full pathname.

Auto-filling a pathname. To make sure you're entering a pathname correctly, with spaces treated as spaces, use the Tab key to complete a name or drag the Finder icon for the item to the command line, as explained in "Take Note: Unix Shortcuts," above. These techniques automatically fill in the pathname, correctly adding backslashes in front of each space as needed.

SEE: • "Unix: Copying, Moving, and Deleting," later in this chapter, for more on the rm command.

 • "Take Note: Using rm: Risk Management," later in this chapter, for a warning about how errors involving spaces in pathnames combined with the rm command can lead to disaster.

The cd command and related commands

Sometimes, it's not enough to list the contents of a directory; sometimes you need to *go* to the directory. Among other things, moving to the desired directory can simplify working with items there. For example, when you're working in a directory, just typing ls yields a list of its contents; you no longer need to enter the directory's path each time.

To move to a different directory, you use the cd (*change directory*) command. To move to the main Applications folder, for example, you would type cd /Applications.

The following are some further examples of using the `cd` command and the related `pwd` (*print working directory*, *present working directory*, or *path of working directory*, depending on whom you ask) command:

- To determine what directory you're in, type `pwd`.
- To move to the root level of the volume, type `cd /`.
- To return to your home directory quickly, type `cd` with no path specified.
- Use the ~ symbol to indicate the path to your home directory. Thus, to change to the Documents directory in your home directory, no matter where you're located, type `cd ~/Documents`.
- You can use relative pathways to navigate. This method saves time, because you don't have to type the longer absolute path. Thus, if you want to move to the Documents directory and you're in your home directory, just type `cd Documents`.
- You can use dots in pathnames to assist in navigating. For example, if you're in the Documents directory and want to return to your home directory, you can simply type `cd` to get there. However, there's a more general shortcut you can use to go up a single level in the file hierarchy, regardless of where you're located: Simply type `cd ..` and press Return. To go back more than one level, you can type this command multiple times. Or, to go back two levels with one command, type `cd ../..` and press Return.

  A single dot refers to the current directory. Thus, `cd ./Documents` tells Unix to go to the Documents directory within whatever directory you're currently in. In most cases, the single dot and slash are not needed; simply typing `cd Documents` would have worked just as well in this case. However, the dot is necessary for some commands other than `cd`. For example, as explained in "Unix: Executing Commands," later in this chapter, you may need the single dot when you're trying to execute a command located in the current directory.

Many of the examples described here apply just as well to Unix commands other than `cd`. Thus, the use of the dot shortcuts would work the same when entering a pathname for `ls` as for `cd`.

Unix: The sudo and su Commands

If you type a command in Unix and get a "permission denied" or "operation not permitted" error message, you probably need root access to do what you were trying to do. There are two means of obtaining this type of access: the `su` command and the `sudo` command.

Using su. To get root access, type `su`, then press Return. You will be prompted to provide the root password. Once you've done so, the prompt will change to something like the following (note that the computer and user names are from my own Mac; I was working in my home directory, called tedmac, on a computer named Yoda, when I typed the su command):

```
Yoda:/Users/tedmac root#
```

You are now a root user and will remain so until you type exit or logout.

Note: The password you provide here is the root user password, not your administrative password. This is the password you set in NetInfo Manager when you enable the root user. Still, you need to be an administrator for the root user password to work. If, after entering a correct password, you get a message that says, **Sorry**, this probably means that root user access has not been enabled for your Mac. To remedy this, launch NetInfo Manager and enable root access, as described in Chapter 4. Alternatively, you can enable root access in Terminal simply by setting a password for it. To do so, type sudo passwd root. Give your administrator's password when asked. You will then be prompted to enter a new password for the root user.

Note: After you use su to change to the root user, your home directory (in Terminal) changes to that of the root user. This means that shortcuts (such as the ~ symbol) that indicate a home directory now refer to a different home location (specifically, /var/root). To avoid errors when typing commands that include pathnames, you may thus want to enter the absolute path for a file rather than one that includes the ~ symbol or other shortcuts.

Using sudo. Alternatively, to get *temporary* root access, you can type sudo followed by the name of the command you wish to execute with root access, all on the same line. For example, to delete a file that requires root access to do so, you would type the following:

```
sudo rm filename
```

You will be asked for your administrator's password before the command will execute. (This is your account password, *not* the root user's password.) In this case, only commands entered on that line are executed with root access; you do not need to type exit to return to your own, non-root, command line. Also, unlike sudo, this command works regardless of whether you've enabled root access in NetInfo Manager.

Once you've executed the sudo command, you can continue to use the command for 5 minutes without having to re-enter your password; however, only commands preceded by sudo will be executed as root. So, for example, if you correctly execute a sudo rm command to delete a file, and next type rm otherfile, the second rm will work as if you'd typed it into your own shell; if, however, you typed sudo rm otherfile, the command would work as if typed into the shell of the root user. Once the 5-minute period has elapsed, if you try to use another sudo command, you will be asked to re-enter your password. There are, however, ways to extend or reduce this time limit—most notably, typing sudo -v to extend sudo privileges for an additional 5 minutes, or typing sudo -k to immediately revoke sudo privileges (called *killing*, or invalidating, the timestamp).

Finally, you can use a variation of the sudo command to mimic the effect of the su command. To do so, type sudo -s; no additional input is needed on the line. This gives you sustained root access via your administrator's password rather than the root user password, and, like sudo, it does not require that the root account be enabled. (It also offers the advantage of remaining in the current working directory, rather than changing to /var/root like su.)

Type man sudo for details on these and other sudo command options.

Note: Although sudo works with almost all common Unix commands, you cannot combine sudo with the cd command to move to a directory for which you do not have permission. To use cd in this manner, you need to first access a root shell via su or sudo -s.

Which to use? In general, you should use sudo rather than su so that root access remains as limited as possible. Even if you have the best of intentions, mistyping a command via root access can have devastating consequences—sometimes wiping out files that the OS needs to work or deleting an entire home directory. With the more limited sudo command, the risks are minimized because you are not "permanently" given root access.

The main reason to consider using su is if you need to retain root access over a series of commands, especially if you need to do so for more than 5 minutes. However, even in this case, you could use sudo -s instead of su. And with sudo -s, you don't need to first enable the root user in NetInfo Manager.

The sudoers file. The list of users who can use the sudo command, the time limit for re-entering your password (5 minutes by default), and other sudo-related options (such as a list of all user categories that can use the sudo command) are maintained in a file called sudoers (located in the /etc directory).

You can modify this file (in a text editor) to change how sudo works. For example, if you change the value of timestamp_timeout from 5 to 0, sudo will ask for a password every time you use it (eliminating the 5-minute grace period). Type man sudoers in Terminal for more information about this file.

Note: Opening and editing this file requires root access. In fact, the default setting is for the owner of the file (System) to have read-only access (so even the root user can't modify the file without first changing its permissions!).

Don't modify this file unless you're confident that you know what you're doing. Making a mistake here could prevent you from using sudo altogether.

SEE: • "Root Access," in Chapter 4, for much more information on this topic.

• "Using the Finder's Authenticate dialog," in Chapter 6, for a separate method of temporarily having privileged access in the Finder.

Figure 10.12

Using the sudo *command: Without* sudo, *the attempt to list the contents of a restricted directory fails. With* sudo, *the* ls *command succeeds. Note: A password is not requested here because it was entered during an immediately prior use of the sudo command.*

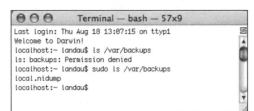

TAKE NOTE ▶ Securing Mac OS X

The requirement to use su or sudo in order to execute certain commands is intended to guard against unauthorized access to your Mac.

If your Mac is in your home, and only you and your family have access to it, your main security concern is that a thief might steal your Mac, not that an unauthorized user might gain access to your data. Although it's possible that your Mac's security could be breached via an Internet connection, it's doubtful that anyone would try—unless you have valuable information on your computer that some unscrupulous person knows about.

If you're in a more public environment, such as a university, data security is of greater concern. This book is geared toward users with more modest security concerns—which explains why I've been fairly lenient in my attitude toward root user usage, for example. Still, it's worth knowing what security options are available. The following reviews some data-security tips introduced elsewhere in this book:

• Creating separate user accounts represents the most basic form of security; for more on this, see Chapter 2.

   Tip: It's more difficult for people to log in illegally if they don't know the names of the valid accounts. You can hide these names by selecting "Name and password" from the "Display login window as" options in the Login Options section of the Accounts System Preferences pane (rather than selecting the "List of users" option). You can also download a utility from Apple's Web site called HideOrShowPreviousLogin (http://docs.info.apple.com/article.html?artnum=106691). Running this turns off the feature in which the name of the last person to log in is shown in the Login window by default.

• Obviously, if security is a concern, you don't want to enable automatic login.

   SEE: • "System Preferences," in Chapter 2, for coverage of the Accounts System Preferences pane.

continues on next page

TAKE NOTE ▶ Securing Mac OS X *continued*

- You can disable the root user if you have enabled it, using NetInfo Manager, as covered in Chapter 4. This makes it more difficult for someone to get unauthorized root access. In most cases, the sudo command, which does not require that the root user be enabled, will be sufficient for your root user needs in Terminal.

  You can always re-enable the root user temporarily if you need to, such as to log in as root from Mac OS X.

  Actually, if you've never enabled the root user, you should do so, and then enter a password (and then disable the user if you wish). Otherwise, by default there is no password for the root user, which itself is a security risk.

- You can encrypt your home directory (via the FileVault option in Mac OS X 10.3 or later) and/or require a password when waking up the computer from sleep (or a screen saver). To select these and related options, go to the Security System Preferences pane.

  SEE: • "System Preferences," in Chapter 2, for coverage of the Security System Preferences pane.

- You can set an Open Firmware password.

  SEE: • "Technically Speaking: Open Firmware Password," in Chapter 5.

- To protect against intruders coming over the Internet, you can enable the Mac OS X firewall (via the Sharing System Preferences, as described in Chapter 9). To safeguard privacy when transmitting data, you should use more secure methods, such as SSH instead of Telnet.

  SEE: • "Network Security," in Chapter 9, for more details on network security.

- From the Finder's Help menu, choose Mac Help, and search for Security Technologies. Double-click the Security Technologies result for a summary of all the security protocols used by Mac OS X.

Unix: Modifying Permissions

Ownership and permissions for a file in Unix refer to essentially the same settings you access via the Ownership & Permissions section of a file's Get Info window in the Finder—changing the settings in Get Info modifies the underlying Unix settings. The main difference is that you have access to settings in Terminal that are not available via the Get Info window. You can also access these additional settings via third-party utilities such as Rainer Brockerhoff's XRay (www.brockerhoff.net/xray) and Gideon Softworks' FileXaminer (www.gideonsoftworks.com). In general, I find these utilities to be more convenient and less time-consuming than going to Terminal, but for those who prefer not to invest in additional shareware, Terminal is the way to go.

I've discussed changing permissions settings in several other chapters of this book; the focus of *this* section is the basics of viewing and modifying these settings in Terminal.

SEE: • "Ownership & Permissions," in Chapter 4; "Opening and Saving: Permissions Problems," in Chapter 6; and "Copying and Moving: Problems Copying and Moving Files," in Chapter 6, for more background on these topics.

Unix assigns a minimum of nine permissions settings (or bits) to each item: a *read* (*r*), *write* (*w*), and *execute* (*x*) value for each of three categories—the *owner* of the item, the *group* assigned to the item, and *everyone else*. Each of these settings can be either *on* (you have the needed permission) or *off* (you don't). In brief, *r* refers to the ability to open and view a file, *w* refers to the ability to modify a file, and *x* refers to the ability to execute or run a program.

These settings are also used for directories/folders (in addition to individual files), but they have slightly different meanings in that context. For example, you can't *run* a directory, so the execute bit takes on a different meaning: The execute permission needs to be enabled for a directory before the *r* and *w* settings have an effect. In fact, when it's used with directories, the *x* bit is more often called the *search* bit than the *execute* bit, because it needs to be on before you can search or view the directory's contents.

```
drwxrwxr-x    3 root    admin    102 Aug  4 08:43 Stickies.app
drwxrwxr-x    3 root    wheel    102 Mar 20 19:44 System Preferences.app
```

Figure 10.13

The output of an ls -l *command for two files in the Applications folder (Stickies and System Preferences). Note that even though they're applications, Terminal correctly shows the files as directories. Compare the permissions, owner, and group settings here with those shown in Figure 10.11 (bottom), for items in a home directory.*

In Terminal, when you use the ls -l command to view a list of directory contents (see Figure 10.13 for an example), you see in the column at the far left the permissions settings for each item in the current directory. A drwxrwxr-x listing would be a common setting for applications located in the Mac OS X Applications directory, for example. Here's what this permissions listing means:

- **d**. The initial d means that the item is a directory (or folder in Mac OS X jargon). In this example, it may seem odd that applications are considered to be folders, but remember that most Mac OS X applications are really .app packages, which are simply special types of folders. If an item were a single file instead of a folder, the initial character would typically be a hyphen (-).

- **Owner rwx.** The first trio of rwx refers to the owner's permissions. In this case, the owner of the application has read, write, and execute permissions. As indicated in the columns to the right, for applications installed by Mac

OS X, the owner is "root." (Applications that you installed by drag and drop generally show your account as the owner.)

- **Group rwx.** The second rwx refers to the permissions for the members of the listed group. As indicated in the group column, for most applications installed by Mac OS X, the group is "admin" (most often) or "wheel." Because all administrative users are in the admin group, they all have the same access to the admin group items in this directory as does the owner. (Note: For most files in your home directory, the owner will be you, and the group will be one with the same name as your owner name or one named "staff.")

- **Everyone r-x.** The third trio, r-x (for *everyone else*), means that all other users can access and execute the application but cannot modify it.

The precise implication of having no modify access can get a bit tricky. (Can you move the application out of the Applications directory without modify access? Can you modify a text file within the .app package? Can you delete the application?) What you can or cannot do is determined by a combination of the permissions settings for the item itself and for its enclosing directory or directories. I cover most of the specifics in Chapter 6. In this chapter, my focus is not on the nuances of what these settings mean but on how to use Unix commands in Terminal to edit these settings.

The chmod command

You use the chmod (*change mode*) command to change permissions (also called *mode bits*). At any time, you can use the ls -l command to examine the current settings and confirm that your intended change was made.

Note: The following examples assume you're in the parent directory of the item you want to modify; thus, you need to enter only the name of the item. Otherwise, you would need to include a relative or absolute pathname for the item.

You can use the chmod command in two ways:

Octal method. The octal method requires entering numbers to indicate the permissions settings you want to use. This is called the *octal* method because it has eight possible values (0 to 7). A 0 implies no access, while 7 indicates all access (rwx) for the indicated category of user (owner, group, or everyone).

Each type of access (r, w, and x) has an associated numeric value: x is assigned 1, w is assigned 2; and r is assigned 4. If you want to assign more than one type of access (such as both read and write) to a given category of user, you add the numbers for each individual access type.

Thus, the octal notation for read and write but not execute access (rw-) is $4 + 2 = 6$. The octal notation for complete access (rwx) is $4 + 2 + 1 = 7$. And so on.

When using this form of the chmod command, you enter three of these numeric sums, one each for owner, group, and everyone—in that order. Thus, the octal notation for rwx access for owner and group, but r-x access for everyone else, is 775. To set this permission for an item called test.app, for example, you would type the following:

```
chmod 775 test.app
```

A minor disadvantage of the octal method is that if you want to make a single modification (perhaps removing write access for the group), you still need to re-enter all the octal values. Thus, to make the cited group-assignment change for test.app, you would need to type the following:

```
chmod 755 test.app
```

Symbolic method. In the *symbolic* method, you use an equation format that describes what you want to do. The equation has three parts:

• First, you pick which category of user the change will affect (*u* equals user, which is the same as owner; *g* equals group; and *o* equals other, which is the same as everyone).

• Second, you indicate whether you want to add (+), remove (–), or set (=) a permission for that user category.

• Third, you select one or more permission types (*r*, *w*, and/or *x*).

Again, suppose that you want to change the permission of the test.app item from rwxrwxr-x to rwxr-xr-x. With symbolic notation, you would type the following:

```
chmod g-w test.app
```

This command says, "For just the group setting, remove the w access."

Another example: To set rwx access for group and other, overwriting the current settings, you would type the following:

```
chmod go=rwx test.app
```

Special-mode bits. In addition to read, write, and execute, you may encounter some less well-known modes: the sticky bit, SetUID, and SetGUI.

SEE: • "Sticky bits and the Drop Box" and "Technically Speaking: SetUID and SetGID," in Chapter 6, for more information on these settings.

You can use the chmod command to change these special-mode settings. To do so via the octal method, you add a fourth digit in *front* of the initial three: 1 enables the sticky bit; 2 enables the SetGID bit; and 4 enables the SetUID bit.

Suppose, for example, you wanted to enable the sticky bit for a directory called myitems that currently has rwxr-xr-x access. To do so without changing existing rwx permissions, you would type the following:

```
chmod 1755 myitems
```

If you use ls -l to see the permissions settings after making this change, you will see that it now reads rwxrwxrwt. The t at the end, rather than an x, indicates that the sticky bit has been enabled. (Yes, it's confusing that you insert the octal digit setting special-mode bits to the beginning of the octal digits, but the status of these bits is noted at the end of the permissions display.)

As another example, to enable the SetUID bit for a file called myfile, precede the standard octal notation with a 4. That is, type the following:

```
chmod 4755 myfile
```

If you now use ls -l to see the permissions settings for the file, it will read rwsr-xr-x. The s at the end of the first trio of letters indicates that SetUID has been enabled for the owner (SetUID always applies just to the owner).

For those who prefer to use the symbolic method, you can make the same changes, though I'll omit the details here.

Viewing Terminal commands and output via GUI utilities. A reminder: If you don't want to bother with any of these techniques, you can use an Aqua-based utility such as XRay instead. A convenient tutorial feature of XRay is that it shows the ls command info (such as rwxrwxrwx) and chmod command input (such as chmod 777) for whatever change you make. You can then use this information to compare the changes you make in XRay with what you would have done in Terminal.

The chown and chgrp commands

Although the previously described methods allow you to edit the *permissions* of the owner and group of a given item, they don't actually change the owner or group themselves. To do that, you must use the chown (*change owner*) and chgrp (*change group*) commands.

The format is quite simple: You just type the command, the new owner or group, and the pathname of the item to be changed. To assign the group named staff to an item called testfile, for example, type the following:

```
chgrp staff testfile
```

Similarly, to change the owner of an item called test.framework from root to yourself (*your username*), you would type the following:

```
chown {your username} test.framework
```

OK, it's not quite *that* simple. You can't change the group assignment of an item unless you own that item. A greater obstacle is that no one but the root user can change an item's owner. In fact, you can't even change the ownership of a file you own. Thus, typing this chown command will lead to an "operation not permitted" error.

True, as I discussed in Chapter 6, copying a file from one directory location to another may modify the ownership of the file. But that's a separate issue from modifying the permissions of a file directly.

The solution—assuming you're an administrative user—is to use the sudo command, as described earlier in this chapter, to get temporary root access. To do so, type the following:

```
sudo chown {your username} test.framework
```

Enter your password when requested, and the change should be made.

Be aware that changing the ownership or group of an item could mean that you can no longer modify or even access the item via the Finder. For example, for a document that is owned by root, where the group is admin and has read and write access, if you change the group to one to which you do not belong, you will no longer be able to edit the item or even open it in the Finder. To regain access, you would have to modify permissions again (or possibly access the file with root access).

SEE: • "Root Access," in Chapter 4, for related details.
• "Ownership & Permissions," in Chapter 4, for how to make ownership changes from the Finder, via the Get Info window.

TECHNICALLY SPEAKING ▶ Access Control Lists and Extended Attributes

Here are two items of interest related to the basic Unix (BSD) permissions settings discussed in the main text:

Access Control Lists. Believe it or not, Unix's permissions, as described in the main text, are not sufficient to handle many situations. In particular, you are limited to assigning a file to just one owner and one group. But suppose, for example, that you wanted John to have the ability to read and edit a certain file that you own. Additionally, you wanted Jane to be able to read the file but not edit it. And you wanted no one else to even be able to read it. There is no way that the standard Unix permissions can handle this. If John and Jane are in the same group, they cannot have different permissions. And if they are in different groups, then only one of them can have permissions that are different from those assigned to Others. The solution to this dilemma, newly implemented in Tiger, is Access Control Lists (ACLs). These allow you to assign specific permissions to every user and/or group listed on your drive.

To do so, you use the same chmod command described in the main text, but you use some additional options specific to working with ACL settings. As one example, suppose you had a file called test.doc and you indeed wanted a user named john to be able to have write permission for this file, regardless of what group he was in and what other permission restrictions he might have. To do so, you would enter the following command in Terminal:

```
chmod +a "john allow write" test.doc
```

continues on next page

TECHNICALLY SPEAKING ▶ Access Control Lists and Extended Attributes *continued*

Note: If there are two ACL items that conflict with each other, in terms of what permissions are to be assigned, the one that is listed first is the one that is used. To see a list of all ACL items currently in use for the files in a particular directory, move to the directory and type

```
ls -le
```

The -e option is what instructs the command to list ACL information.

There's only one problem with all of this. If you try the above chmod command, it will probably not work. Instead, you will get an "operation not supported" error. Why is this? Because, at least for now, Apple has activated this feature only in Mac OS X Server. Actually, if you are running Mac OS X Server, you don't even really need to use this command at all. You can more easily create ACL items using the Workgroup Manager application included with Mac OS X Server.

Happily, there is a work-around. To enable ACL functionality in Mac OS X client, type the following in Terminal:

```
sudo /usr/sbin/fsaclctl -p / -e
```

If you later wish to undo this, type the following:

```
sudo /usr/sbin/fsaclctl -p / -d
```

If you are interested, type man chmod to learn much more about how ACLs work and additional options available.

Extended attributes. Each file on your drive has what is called *metadata* (or *attributes*) associated with it. This is, for example, where information is stored, such as the size of the file, the date it was created, the date it was last modified, and whether the file is locked. Much of a file's metadata in Mac OS 9 was stored in the file's resource fork. With resource forks largely gone in Mac OS X, the data is typically stored in the drive's directory (the same directory that Disk Utility's First Aid is designed to repair if needed). New in Tiger is the ability to include much more information as attributes. This information is called, appropriately enough, *extended attributes* (EA). ACLs are stored as a special kind of extended attribute. For now, extended attributes is another feature largely restricted to Mac OS X Server, and still in a preliminary stage even there, so I will not spend more time on it here. If you want more information, including a Unix program (called xattr) that will allow you to "see" extended attributes in Terminal, go to this Web page: http://arstechnica.com/reviews/os/macosx-10.4.ars/7.

Archiving files. One caution: If you archive a file (using the Create Archive command in the Finder's file menu), all EA and ACL metadata for that file are lost. The data will also likely be lost using any other archiving utility, unless and until the utility is specifically updated to support these options. However, unless you are connected to a Mac OS X Server, or have enabled the ACL feature yourself as described here, you should not have any such metadata to worry about.

Disk repairs. Apple warns: "A disk repair application that's not Mac OS X 10.4–aware may incorrectly report Extended Attributes as directory damage. You may get an error message such as 'Cannot be rebuilt. The original directory is too severely damaged.' That is untrue."

The chflags command

The chflags command is used to change flags, which are similar to Finder attributes. You can thus use this command to modify such attributes (bits) as whether a file is locked or unlocked, visible or invisible.

For example, if you type chflags nouchg myfile, you're turning off (no) the immutable flag (uchg) for the file named myfile (though, again, you can do the same thing via a utility like XRay).

Modifying the immutable flag is similar to locking and unlocking files from the Finder's Get Info window. Sometimes, however, the Finder may indicate that a file is unlocked even though this flag is set. That's when you may need to use this command.

SEE: • "Using Unix to delete files," in Chapter 6, for more details on using this command.

```
Ted-Landaus-Computer:~ landau$ ls -l TEST
-rw-r--r--  1 landau  staff  0 13 Dec 15:15 TEST
Ted-Landaus-Computer:~ landau$ chmod ugo+x TEST
Ted-Landaus-Computer:~ landau$ ls -l TEST
-rwxr-xr-x  1 landau  staff  0 13 Dec 15:15 TEST
Ted-Landaus-Computer:~ landau$ █
```

```
Ted-Landaus-Computer:~ landau$ ls -l TEST
-rwxr-xr-x  1 landau  staff  0 13 Dec 15:15 TEST
Ted-Landaus-Computer:~ landau$ chgrp admin TEST
Ted-Landaus-Computer:~ landau$ ls -l TEST
-rwxr-xr-x  1 landau  admin  0 13 Dec 15:15 TEST
Ted-Landaus-Computer:~ landau$ █
```

Figure 10.14

Examples of some permissions commands: top, *using* chmod *to give execute (x) access to owner (u), group (g), and others (o) for the file called TEST;* bottom, *using* chgrp *to change the group of the TEST file from staff to admin.*

Figure 10.15

Using the mv *command to rename a file:* TEST *is changed to* testy.

```
Ted-Landaus-Computer:~ landau$ ls
Desktop      Library    Music      Public    TEST
Documents    Movies     Pictures   Sites
Ted-Landaus-Computer:~ landau$ mv TEST testy
Ted-Landaus-Computer:~ landau$ ls
Desktop      Library    Music      Public    testy
Documents    Movies     Pictures   Sites
Ted-Landaus-Computer:~ landau$ █
```

Unix: Copying, Moving, and Deleting

In most cases, when you want to copy, move, or delete files, you will do so in the Finder. Occasionally, however, the Finder may not carry out the operation successfully; in such cases, you may find that using Terminal solves the problem. In addition, if you're already working in Terminal, you may sometimes find it more convenient to stay within Terminal to perform these actions.

Remember that any changes you make in Terminal affect the locations of these files in the Finder as well: These are two interfaces to the same environment, not two parallel universes.

SEE: • Chapter 6, for several examples of using Unix to copy, move, and delete files for troubleshooting purposes.

The cp command

The cp (*copy*) command is (almost) the equivalent of the Mac's Copy command. It creates a copy of the file without deleting or modifying the original. A simple format for this command is

```
cp {old filename} {new filename}
```

This example assumes that you're in the directory of the old file. In this case, a new copy of the original file is created in the same directory.

Note: A limitation of the cp command under Panther and earlier is that it does not copy the resource fork portion of a file (if present), as explained in "The CpMac and MvMac Commands," later in this chapter. This limitation has been fixed in Tiger.

Copying to a different location. If you want the new file to reside in a different directory than the old file, you need to specify its path. Thus, if you're at the root level of your home directory and want to copy a file called report.doc to your Documents directory, where you want it listed as report42.doc, you would type one of the following:

```
cp report.doc Documents/report42.doc
```

or

```
cp report.doc ~/Documents/report42.doc
```

or

```
cp report.doc /Users/{your username}/Documents/report42.doc
```

Copying with the same name. If you're content to have the name of the new file be the same as that of the original, you can leave off the filename in the second path. Thus, to move a file called song.mp3 from the root level of your home directory to your Music directory, you could type the following:

```
cp ~/song.mp3 ~/Music/
```

Batch copying. You can combine the cp command with wildcard notation (such as an asterisk) to copy several files at the same time. Thus, to copy all files at the root level of your home directory that end in .mp3 to the Music directory, you could type the following:

```
cp ~/*.mp3 ~/Music/
```

This represents a case where using Terminal is easier than using the Finder—that is, selecting and copying the same batch of files in the Finder would not be as simple.

Copying directories. So far, I've been talking about copying files. If you try to use the cp command to copy a directory—one called testfolder, for example—it will fail. You will get the following error message:

```
cp: testfolder/ is a directory (not copied)
```

To solve this problem, you need to type cp -R, followed by the pathname(s). The -R option is the recursive option. (Note: Using an uppercase or lowercase R works equally well here, though don't count on this being the case for all commands.) Thus, to copy testfolder from the current directory to the Documents directory, you would type the following:

```
cp -R testfolder ~/Documents/testfolder
```

In this case, you should end the second path with the desired name of the new directory—even if it's the same name as the original. If you're using wildcards in the name of the first path, however, you can just specify the destination directory in the second path. Thus, the following command copies all items, files, or directories in the current directory that begin with *test* to the Documents directory without changing any names:

```
cp -R test* ~/Documents/
```

Similarly, to copy an application, such as TextEdit, from the main Applications folder to the Applications folder in your home directory, you would enter the following:

```
cp -R /Applications/TextEdit.app ~/Applications/TextEdit.app
```

Note: The -R option was necessary here because, as discussed in Chapters 3 and 4, applications like TextEdit are actually packages, which Unix sees as folders. In addition, you need to use the .app extension because the full names of these application packages include that extension, even if it's not seen in the Finder.

In one example of how the cp command could help in troubleshooting, I once ran into a situation where I couldn't copy an application from a CD to my hard drive using the Finder. I kept getting a -50 error (which I later discovered was due to an oddity with one of the files inside the .app package). Using the cp command succeeded where the Finder failed.

The mv command

The mv (*move*) command follows almost exactly the same structure as the cp (*copy*) command. The main difference is that mv deletes the original file, so that only the moved version remains. As its name implies, you appear to move the file to its new location rather than copy it. Thus, if you wanted to move the previously cited report.doc file to the Documents directory, instead of copying it (and changing its name at the same time), you would type the following:

```
mv report.doc Documents/report42.doc
```

You can also use the mv command to rename a file without moving it. That is, if you left off Documents/ from the above command, it would simply rename report.doc to *report42.doc*, leaving the renamed file in its original location rather than moving it to the Documents folder.

The mv command works equally well with files and directories. Like the cp command, it can be used to move multiple items. Unlike the cp command, it doesn't need a -R option.

Note: A limitation of the mv command under Panther and earlier is that it does not copy the resource fork portion of a file (if present), as explained in "The CpMac and MvMac commands," below. This limitation has been fixed in Tiger.

SEE: • "Opening and Saving: Permissions Problems," and "Copying and Moving: Permissions Problems," in Chapter 6, for a discussion of how moving versus copying may affect permissions.

The CpMac and MvMac commands

As an alternative to copying files with cp, Apple includes a command in /Developer/Tools (installed with the Developer Tools software) called CpMac. For moving files, Apple similarly provides an alternative to the mv command: MvMac.

Note: If the CpMac or MvMac command does not run if you type just its name in Terminal, you need to enter its full pathname. For example, to copy the TextEdit application, as cited above, you would type the following:

```
/Developer/Tools/CpMac -rp /Applications/TextEdit.app ~/Applications/
TextEdit.app
```

Why have these commands at all? Here's why: Some Mac files are composed of two forks: a resource fork and a data fork. The use of resource forks is limited mainly to older Carbon applications (usually imported from Mac OS 9) that do not use the package (.app) format, as well as document files created by many applications in Mac OS 9. Most other Mac OS X files do not include a resource fork. Files created in the Unix environment never have resource forks; every Unix item consists only of a data fork. Apple originally provided the CpMac and MvMac commands because, under Panther (Mac OS X 10.3.x) and earlier, the included versions of cp and mv did not preserve resource forks. The Tiger versions of cp and mv have been updated to support resource forks, pretty much eliminating the need to use the special Mac alternatives.

SEE: • "Unix: Executing Commands," later in this chapter, for more on how to run the commands in the Developer directory.
      • "Technically Speaking: Type/Creator vs. Filename Extensions vs. Others," in Chapter 4, for background information on resource and data forks.

The ditto command

There are other times when the cp command is not sufficient to copy a file or directory exactly the way you would like, even under Tiger. The problem is that cp does not necessarily copy permissions and links accurately. This can be a real problem if you're trying to make an exact duplicate backup of a Mac OS X volume. In such cases, you can use the ditto command—which *does* copy permissions correctly, maintaining the same settings as the original file(s); it can even preserve resource fork information.

The man entry for ditto states the following: "The ditto command overwrites existing files, symbolic links, and devices in the destination when they are copied from a source. The resulting files, links, and devices will have the same mode, owner, and group as the source items from which they are copied. ditto preserves hardlinks present in the source directories and preserves setuid and setgid modes. Finally, ditto can also preserve resource fork and HFS meta-data (e.g., Type/Creator) information when copying files within or between file systems."

In other words, ditto copies everything exactly and correctly, which is why it's useful for volume backups. As I mentioned above, it will even preserve resource fork data, via its -rsrc option.

The ditto command requires root access when you're using it to back up an entire volume, as this procedure involves copying files that you would otherwise not have permission to copy, and to preserve setuid and setgid file modes, which only root can set. To get this access, use the sudo command. Since there's no harm in using sudo, even if it's not required, I typically use it whenever I employ the ditto command. For example, to copy a folder called BackUps in your home directory to an external drive called BackupDrive, you could enter the following:

```
sudo ditto -rsrc ~/BackUps /Volumes/BackupDrive/BackUps
```

No -R option is needed because ditto automatically copies a directory and its contents, if indicated.

When this type of industrial-strength copying is not essential, cp is simpler to use. The ditto command is used primarily for volume backups. Another command to consider using for volume backups is asr.

SEE: • "Backing up Mac OS X: Utilities for volume backups," in Chapter 3, for more on ditto, asr, and related commands.

The rm command

The rm (*remove*) command deletes files and directories. To use it, type rm plus the name of the item(s) you want to delete. If you want to delete a directory (and all of its contents), add the -R option. Thus, to delete a song.mp3 file from your Desktop, you would type the following:

rm ~/Desktop/song.mp3

To delete the Music directory and its contents from your home directory, you would type the following:

rm -R ~/Music

You can remove multiple items by typing them individually (separated by a space) or by using a name with a wildcard. You could thus delete both of the preceding files with one remove command. To do so, type the following:

rm -R ~/Music ~/Desktop/song.mp3

Remember that you can also add a pathname by typing rm followed by a space, and then dragging the Finder icon(s) of the item(s) you want to delete to the Terminal window.

When combined with the sudo command, the rm command can be used to delete files that are owned by root. But again: Be careful!

SEE: • "Take Note: Using rm: Risk Management," below, for the risks involved with the rm command and ways to minimize them.

• "Using Unix to delete files," in Chapter 6, for practical examples of using the rm command for troubleshooting.

The rmdir and mkdir commands. If a directory is empty, you can use the rmdir command to delete it. If you want to create a new directory, use the mkdir command. In both cases, follow the command with the pathname of the directory you want to delete or create. Thus, to create a directory called mp3files in your home directory, you would type the following:

mkdir ~/mp3files

A newly created directory will, by default, have the permissions determined by settings in a Unix feature called umask. The settings will typically be rwxr-xr-x.

An often overlooked feature of mkdir is its ability to create multiple, nested directories at once. The -p option causes mkdir to create all of the folders listed in the path:

```
mkdir -p ~'/Desktop/Vacation/Video/iDVD Projects/Snorkeling'
```

This command creates a folder named Snorkeling, inside a new folder named iDVD Projects, inside a new folder named Video, inside a new folder named Vacation, on your Desktop—all using a single command.

TAKE NOTE ▶ Using rm: Risk Management

You can delete a file via the rm command, even if the file is not in the Trash. In fact, unlike the Finder, Unix has no "interim" place for a file to go when you delete it. You can't "remove it from the Trash" if you change your mind—the file is deleted immediately. As you can imagine, this makes rm a potentially dangerous command—one with the ability to delete a file anywhere on your drive instantly. Even worse, most Mac OS X utilities that claim to be able to undelete files are not able to undelete files deleted via the rm command.

Combined with the -R option (which provides a way to delete files within folders, as described in the main text), the rm command becomes even more dangerous. Normally, rm will not delete a folder that contains files or folders. However, the -R option instructs the OS to override this restriction, deleting all listed files and folders, as well as all the files and folders contained within the listed folders.

Thus, you should be very careful when using the -R option: It can irrevocably delete everything in the directory you select—which means that even a simple typing error can have devastating consequences, especially if you invoked the rm command via the sudo command for root access.

Inadvertent spaces in pathnames represent the biggest potential source of problems. Suppose, for example, you wanted to delete your entire Applications folder (not that I recommend doing this): To do so, you would type rm -R /Applications, with no space between the slash (/) and the A. If, however, you accidentally placed a space there—that is, typing rm -R / Applications— Unix would interpret the slash and Applications as two separate items. Since the / character by itself refers to the root level of your volume, you would be requesting that the entire contents of your drive be deleted!! As I said, be *very* careful.

Even Apple is not beyond making an error here. As I noted in "Updating Mac OS X," in Chapter 3, Apple made an error of this type in a script file inside an iTunes Updater package back in the days of Mac OS X 10.1. Before Apple caught and corrected this mistake, hundreds of users ran the Updater and wound up deleting entire volumes.

If you need to use the rm command, there are several things you can do to minimize the risk:

• **Auto-fill a pathname.** Use the Tab key or drag the Finder icon of the desired item to the command line to automatically fill in the pathname, as described in "Take Note: Unix Shortcuts" and "Take Note: Spaces in Pathnames," earlier in this chapter. This minimizes the chance of inadvertently inserting a space in the command.

continues on next page

TAKE NOTE ▶ Using rm: Risk Management *continued*

For example, to delete a file you're having problems deleting from the Finder, type sudo rm -R followed by a space. Then drag the icon of the problem file to the command line and (after the pathname appears) press Return.

- **Use quotes.** Putting a pathname in quotes—even if you don't think you need to—similarly prevents a space in a pathname from being treated as a separator (as covered in "Take Note: Spaces in Pathnames," earlier in this chapter).

  If a space is typed intentionally within quotes, this is what you want. If a space is typed unintentionally, the intended file will not be deleted, but at least no unintended files will be deleted.

- **Use -i option with rm.** If you type sudo rm -Ri *pathname*, the use of the -i option results in a confirmation request appearing before anything is deleted. The following output will appear after you press Return:

  remove *pathname/filename*?

  Type y for *yes* or n for *no*. You can still end up in trouble here by saying yes when you should have said no. However, at least the command shows you what it intends to delete and gives you a chance to back out if you realize you made a mistake.

  Optionally, you can modify your environment so that typing rm is automatically treated as typing rm -i. This way, you don't have to remember to type the i. To do this, add an alias to your .profile or .cshrc file, as explained in "Using shell-configuration files," later in this chapter.

  However, most Unix experts advise against "permanently" modifying the actions of built-in commands like rm. Why? Because other Unix programs that include the command may no longer work. For example, the execution of a Unix program that includes the rm command may get "stuck" because the modified command invokes the request for user input and waits until it is given.

  Note: If you have a large number of files to delete, the repeated requests for confirmation can become annoying. Depending on a file's permissions, you may be asked for a confirmation, even if you don't use the -i option. In such cases, you may want to actively *prevent* confirmation requests. To do so, use the -f option. The -f option acts as the opposite of -i, instructing Unix to remove the indicated files without prompting for confirmation, regardless of the file's permissions. Use this option with care, though, as it removes a protection against deleting files in error.

  SEE: • "Using Unix to delete files," in Chapter 6, for related information.

Figure 10.16

Using the rm command to delete the testy file.

```
Ted-Landaus-Computer:~ landau$ ls
Desktop         Library         Music         Public         testy
Documents       Movies          Pictures      Sites
Ted-Landaus-Computer:~ landau$ rm testy
Ted-Landaus-Computer:~ landau$ ls
Desktop         Library         Music         Public
Documents       Movies          Pictures      Sites
Ted-Landaus-Computer:~ landau$ 
```

Unix: Executing Commands

When you type ls, cp, or most of the other commands discussed in this chapter, you're executing (or *running*) a built-in Unix program. However, you're not limited to what's "built in." Just as you can add software beyond what ships with the Mac OS, you can add new software to run in Unix.

Note: To see a full list of all commands available for you to run in Unix, launch Terminal and press Tab. A line will appear that states the following:

Display all ### possibilities? (y or n)

In the above output, ### represents the number of commands available. Type y to view the list.

To run a built-in Unix program, you don't need to precede the file's name with any special command. To run the ls command, for example, you don't need to type run ls. Neither do you need to include the relative or absolute path to where the ls command file resides. That is, you don't need to type /bin/ls, just ls. In general, Unix understands that you want whatever you type as the first term in a line to be treated as a command to be run and executed.

For commands to run in this manner, two conditions must be met:

- The execute (x) bit must be enabled for the item to be executed.
- The file must be in a directory that Unix searches when it looks for commands that match what you type.

When you type a command such as ls, the OS checks specified directories for executable files. If it finds a file that matches the name you typed, it executes and runs the file. Two of the directories where Unix looks, for example, are /bin and /sbin (both at the root level of the startup volume). Thus, all commands in these directories will work as described, just by your typing their names. Commands such as ls, cp, and kill are stored here.

PATH. To see a complete list of all directories searched by a Unix shell, type env. In the output that appears, examine the PATH line. All the searched directories are listed and separated by colons.

SEE: • "Technically Speaking: What and Where Are the Unix Files?" in Chapter 4, for more information on /bin, /sbin, and related directories.

You can also use the echo command to see a PATH listing. In its simplest form, echo prints to the screen whatever text follows the command. Thus, typing echo ls generates an output line that simply reads ls.

You can use echo in combination with the dollar sign ($), however, to print the value of a variable. Thus, if you type echo PATH, you simply get the word **PATH** as output. But if you type echo $PATH, you get a list of all directories searched by the shell, just as would appear in the PATH line of the env output. A colon separates each path.

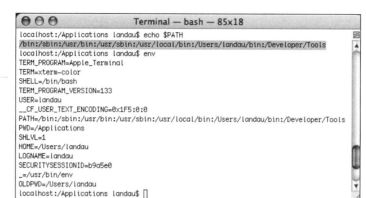

Figure 10.17

The output from the echo $PATH *command. Note that it's the same as the listing in the PATH line in the output from the env command that follows.*

Note: When searching for a command, Unix searches directories in the order listed in PATH. This means that if, for some reason, you have two executable files with the same name in two different directories, Unix will execute only the one it finds in the first directory it searches, ignoring the other. If the two command files perform different functions, this could be a problem. The simplest solution is to rename one of the files. Most Mac OS X users, however, will never encounter this problem.

Developer/Tools. If you installed the Developer software, you have a Developer directory at the root of your drive. Inside this directory is a Tools directory, which contains a collection of Apple-supplied Unix commands. CpMac and MvMac (discussed earlier in "The CpMac and MvMac commands") are two such commands.

SEE: • "Take Note: Developer Software," in Chapter 2, for more details on the Xcode Developer Tools software.

All the commands in the Tools directory have their execute bits set so that they have no problem meeting the first criterion cited above. Still, if you type just CpMac followed by the pathname(s) of the file(s) you want to copy, the command will not work (assuming the Tools directory is not in your PATH list, which it is not by default). Instead, the following error message appears: **CpMac: Command not found**. This is because Unix does not check the Tools directory for commands.

Note: The PATH listing in Figure 10.17 includes /Developer/Tools; this is because I separately added it to the PATH listing (as described later in this chapter under "Using shell-configuration files").

So how do you get a command like CpMac to run? There are several options. Some details are beyond the scope of this book, but the following sections should provide enough information for you to accomplish your goal. While we will use `CpMac` as an example, the same basic procedures will work for any command that does not execute by default.

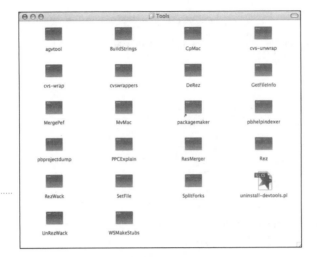

Figure 10.18

The /Developer/ Tools directory, as viewed from the Finder.

Typing the absolute or relative pathname

If you type a correct absolute or relative pathname for a command, Unix will execute it—even if that command doesn't reside in one of the default directories that Unix searches.

Thus, to run the `CpMac` command from any directory location, type the following:

`/Developer/Tools/CpMac`

If you're in the directory that contains the command file (/Developer/Tools, in this example), you can take a shortcut and just type the following:

`./CpMac`

TAKE NOTE ▶ Opening Mac OS Applications from Terminal

You can open almost any Mac OS application via Terminal: The application will launch, just as if you had double-clicked it in the Finder. To do this, type the following:

`open` *pathname*

Thus, to launch Mac OS X's Calculator, you would type

`open /Applications/Calculator.app`

Or, even simpler, assuming the application is in one of the Applications folders, just type this:

`open -a Calculator`

continues on next page

TAKE NOTE ▶ Opening Mac OS Applications from Terminal *continued*

The -a option tells the open command to search all the Applications folders on your drive for a match for the name given (in this case, *Calculator*). One possible glitch here: When I tried this on a Mac running Panther, Terminal tried to launch the version of Calculator it found in my Mac OS 9 Applications folder. A work-around is to instead type

```
open -a Calculator.app
```

There's usually no advantage to opening a file with the open command rather than double-clicking it from the Finder; however, if you're already working in Terminal, it may be more convenient. It can also be useful for opening a file visible in Terminal using a Mac OS X application, as explained in "Take Note: Editing Text Files via Terminal," later in this chapter.

Opening applications by selecting the "application" within the .app package. If (from the contextual menu or the Action menu) you select Show Package Contents for an application package and navigate to Contents/MacOS, you will typically find the actual application file.

In some cases, primarily for Carbon-based applications, it will be a "true" Mac OS application. AppleWorks 6.x is one application that works this way. If you double-click such files, they open just as if you had double-clicked the application packages themselves.

Most Mac OS X applications, however, work a bit differently. In these cases, when you navigate to the application package's MacOS folder, you'll still find a file with the name of the application there. However, the file will typically have the exec icon that represents a Unix executable file.

SEE: • "Take Note: Unix Executable Files and TerminalShellScript Files," below, for details.

If you double-click these application executable files, Terminal launches and executes a command. The result is that the application launches in the Finder, again just as if you had double-clicked the application package icon. Note: When Terminal launches in this situation, it opens a separate shell specific to that application; if you close this shell window, the application quits as well.

In some cases (especially if you are running an older version of Mac OS X), when you double-click one of these exec icons, you may instead get the following error message: "There is no default application specified to open the document." Despite this error, these files are probably Unix executable files and can still be used to launch the overall application. However, you must do so manually by entering a command in Terminal. For example, to launch the Calculator application this way, you would type the following:

```
/Applications/Calculator.app/Contents/MacOS/Calculator &
```

The ampersand is needed if you want Terminal's command-line prompt to return after launching the application. It tells Unix to run the application in the background. Just press Return in Terminal and the prompt should reappear. Otherwise, the prompt will not return until you quit the application you just launched.

continues on next page

TAKE NOTE ▶   Opening Mac OS Applications from Terminal   *continued*

Opening applications as root. Why bother with opening an application via its executable file in the package? As briefly discussed in Chapter 4 (under "Root Access"), you can use the sudo command to open applications as root. However, you cannot do this simply by using sudo in combination with open. If you try, the application opens, but not with root access. For Cocoa applications (and the Carbon ones that work similarly), you can work around this restriction by typing the following command (all in one line), modified for the application you want to open:

```
sudo -b /Applications/TextEdit.app/Contents/MacOS/TextEdit
```

This opens the Unix executable file directly, allowing the sudo option to work. The -b option here serves a similar function to the ampersand in the previous example (needed because the ampersand trick doesn't work with sudo).

For Carbon applications that won't work via this method (that is, ones that don't use the package format), there's still a way to use sudo to open the application with root access. To do so, type the following on one line (assuming the application you want to open is in the main Applications folder):

```
sudo -b /System/Library/Frameworks/Carbon.framework/Versions/Current/Support/
LaunchCFMApp '/Applications/{name of application}'
```

Note the space between LaunchCFMApp and '/Applications.

This command launches the LaunchCFMApp application with root access. Because the pathname to the actual application (in quotes, if needed, to handle spaces in its name) is used as an argument, the named application is indirectly launched with root access.

Note: You can use the Pseudo utility (from Brian R. Hill; http://personalpages.tds.net/~brian_hill/pseudo.html) to duplicate using sudo in this manner, thus eliminating the need for Terminal.

SEE: • "Take Note: Editing Text Files via Terminal," later in this chapter, for related information.

TAKE NOTE ▶   Unix Executable Files and TerminalShellScript Files

There are files you can access from the Finder (without having to delve into a package) that typically launch Terminal when double-clicked. I covered one such file type earlier in this chapter: the .term file (see "Take Note: .Term Files"). This sidebar focuses on the two other major types:

Unix software. These files are, in essence, executable files designed to run in Unix. Thus, for example, if you install the Developer software, all the items in the /Developer/Tools folder will be listed as Unix executable files. Similarly, all of the commands in Unix's invisible /bin folder are also of this type. These files all have an icon that looks like a Terminal window with *exec* printed on it. If you access the Get Info windows for these files, you will see that their Kind is listed as Unix Executable File.

continues on next page

TAKE NOTE ▶ Unix Executable Files and TerminalShellScript Files *continued*

If you double-click these files, they typically launch Terminal and execute. However, most commands require additional arguments in order to work. For example the cp (or CpMac in Panther or earlier) command requires that you indicate *what* you want to copy. When you just double-click the cp icon from /bin, you get the same usage summary that would appear if you typed cp while already in Terminal. Nothing will be copied. In contrast, typing the 1s command yields a list of the items in the current directory (because 1s doesn't require additional arguments). However, once you've executed a command in this manner, you will be logged out—which means you won't be able to execute additional commands without opening a new shell. Overall, double-clicking most of these files from the Finder is usually not very useful. The useful ones are commands that are interactive. That is, once started, they accept commands from the Terminal window until they are done. These would include any of the shells (zsh, tcsh, bash, csh), the ftp program, and even little utilities like dc, a calculator that accepts RPN expressions and performs very high-precision calculations. Another potential use is to open files in an .app package.

In some cases, you will not be able to directly open an executable file in the Finder, getting the following error message instead: "There is no default application specified to open the document." The most common reason is that the executable file is a script, rather than a binary program. In the shell, executable scripts and binary programs are synonymous. The Finder, however, treats binaries as applications and scripts as documents.

SEE: • "Take Note: Opening Mac OS Applications from Terminal," above, for a related example of this.

TerminalShellScript files. Terminal shell scripts are similar to Unix software. However, rather than containing compiled program code, they contain mainly a series of Unix commands in plain text. You can quickly see the difference by comparing a shell script and an executable file in a text editor, such as TextEdit. Terminal shell scripts often have a .command extension and have a Kind of TerminalShellScript in the Get Info window. The Finder will recognize and launch scripts that have the extension .command. If you have an executable script that you wish to launch from the Finder, give it the .command extension. This will not affect its use in the shell—except, of course, that you will have to use its full name. If you rename the script executeme to executeme.command, then you must invoke the command as executeme.command arguments when in the Terminal.

SEE: • "Using a shell script," later in this chapter, for more details.

Figure 10.19

The icons of a Unix executable file, left, and a TerminalShellScript file, right.

Using your home bin directory

As a rule, I recommend that you don't add files to the root-level Unix directories (such as /bin) because they may end up being eliminated in a Mac OS X update or otherwise cause problems. In addition, you need root access to add files there, which makes it less convenient. Thus, although moving the CpMac file to the /bin directory would allow CpMac to run without your having to type its pathway, I would not move it there.

Fortunately, an alternative exists that accomplishes almost the same goal, but without the risks or hassles: Move CpMac (or whatever software you wish) to a new bin directory in your home directory. The main glitches here are that (a) if you check your PATH listing, you will likely not find an entry for this directory; and (b) you will not find a bin directory in your home directory. Thus, to use this bin option, you must first set it up. Here's how:

1. Create a bin directory in your home directory. You can do this via either the Finder (by pressing Command-Shift-N while in your home directory and naming the folder *bin*) or Terminal (type mkdir ~/bin).

2. Add the ~/bin directory to your PATH listing via a set path command in the shell-configuration file for your shell type. This is necessary to make the PATH change permanent (so that you don't need to re-enter the set path command every time you launch Terminal).

   SEE: • **"Using shell-configuration files," later in this chapter, for details on how to do this.**

3. Copy or move the CpMac file (and any other similar Unix command tools you wish to use) from its location in /Developer/Tools to the newly created bin directory.

   Again, you can do this via either the Finder or Terminal. To copy just the CpMac command in Terminal, type the following (and note the space before the ~):

   ```
   cp /Developers/Tools/CpMac ~/bin/
   ```

4. Before trying to use the command, open a new shell window in Terminal (by pressing Command-N), or just quit and relaunch Terminal.

   Type CpMac.

   The command should now execute correctly. In this case, since you didn't specify any files, you'll get just the usage summary.

Using other directories

Perhaps you would rather not copy files from one location to another (for example, from /Developer/Tools to ~/bin). If so, there's an alternative that still allows you to run a command in /Developer/Tools, for example, by just typing its name: You simply instruct Unix, via your shell-configuration file, to add the relevant directory (/Developer/Tools, in this case) to the PATH list. This is what I did and why /Developer/Tools is listed in the PATH listing in Figure 10.17.

SEE: • "Using shell-configuration files," later in this chapter, for details on how to do this.

Multiple users and /usr/local/. A limitation of both prior solutions is that the Developer Tools commands still won't work via just their names when someone other than you logs in. If access by multiple users is important, you could repeat the same procedure (for example, modifying PATH listings) for each local user on your drive.

A potentially less tedious method, though it requires manipulating the root-level Unix directories, is to create a bin directory in the /usr/local/ directory. Files placed there are accessible to all local users. Actually, a bin directory (as well as others) may have already been created there if you previously ran installers for third-party Unix software. However, at least on my Mac OS X systems, these directories are not included in the PATH listing by default. Thus, you may still need to add this directory to the PATH listing of each user to run software installed in /usr/local—but at least you don't have to create and set up a separate bin directory for each user.

Note: Changes you make in locations like the /usr folder might be eliminated when you upgrade to a new version of Mac OS X. To protect against losing all of your work, make sure you've made backup copies of whatever files you modified or moved.

TAKE NOTE ▶ Installing Third-Party Unix Software

Some Unix software for Mac OS X includes an Aqua-based Installer utility. In such cases, the Unix software is likely to be installed in the /usr/local directory, especially /usr/local/bin.

Fink. Other Unix software may come without the benefit of an installer. Because the software may include a host of files that need to be installed in a variety of locations, it can be tedious to manually install it all.

A solution is to install Fink (by the Fink Project), software designed to help you install other Unix software. Note: Fink itself is installed in a directory named sw, created and located at the root level of your startup volume; see http://fink.sourceforge.net/faq/general.php for more background.

X11. Although Unix is essentially a text-only command-line system, there is a way to run a graphical user interface on Unix: It's called the X Window System, commonly referred to as X11. Apple has created a version of X11 designed especially run on a Mac OS X implementation of Unix. It features a level of integration with Aqua not available in non-Mac systems. With X11 installed, you can then install and run application software designed for X Window environments.

SEE: • "Terminal and X11," in Chapter 2, for more details.

Creating an alias

In Unix, the `alias` command is used to create a shortcut for another (usually longer) command. For example, almost every time I use the `ls` command, I use the arguments `-lAF` to display the long listing of all files (including normally invisible files) and to add special characters to their names to make different types easier to identify. Typing `ls -lAF` hundreds of times becomes tedious. I use the `alias` command to create a new, shorter command that does the same thing. Here's how you would do this:

- In the default bash shell, type

   `alias 'll=ls -lAF'`

- In tcsh or csh shells, type

   `alias ll 'ls -lAF'`

The only difference is that bash requires an equals sign (=), whereas the tcsh and csh shells work with just a space. (The single quotes are to prevent the space in `ls -lAF` from being interpreted as two arguments.) The following examples use the bash shell.

In either case, when you next type `ll` as a command, it will act as if you had typed `ls -lAF`.

The name you choose for the alias does not need to be similar to that of the original command; it can be anything you want.

Overriding existing commands. You can also use an alias to modify the meaning of an existing command. For example, if you are new to Terminal and nervous about the too-powerful `rm` command, you can type the following:

`alias rm='rm -i'`

Now whenever you type just `rm`, Unix will interpret it as `rm -i`. The `-i` option causes `rm` to ask for permission before deleting each file, greatly reducing the chance of deleting something by mistake. If you later want to invoke the original `rm` command while maintaining the alias, type `\rm`. The backslash tells Unix to interpret the command literally—meaning without substituting any potential alias. If you want to delete the alias and revert to the default use of the command, type `unalias rm`.

Note: If you ever want to override the `-i` option when deleting files, you can add the `-f` option to the command in Terminal. For example, to delete a folder full of files without getting the confirmation requests, you would type `rm -Rf {folder name}`.

Note: Unix experts advise against using the name of a built-in command for an alias (as described more in "Take Note: Using rm: Risk Management," earlier in this chapter). If you're concerned about this, using an alias such as `saferm` would be preferable to `rm` in the examples above.

Aliases vs. aliases. In Unix, an *alias* (as described here) has an entirely different meaning than the same term in Mac OS X. The Unix equivalent of a Mac OS X alias is a *symbolic link*.

SEE: • "Aliases and Symbolic Links," in Chapter 6, for more information on this distinction.

Aliases are not saved. One limitation of aliases is that they're forgotten as soon as you close the shell window. This means you have to re-create them each time you launch Terminal—or even open a new shell window.

There are, however, ways to circumvent this limitation—ways not only of preserving the aliases you've created but of automatically running any command (or sequence of commands) in Terminal. These impressively flexible methods are described in the next two sections of this chapter.

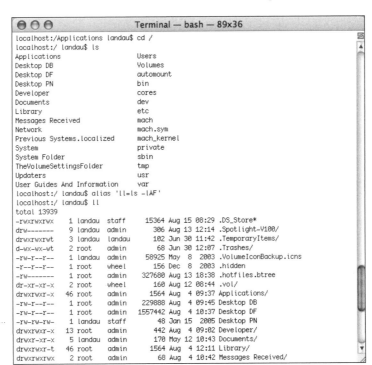

Figure 10.20

After creating `ll` as an alias, the command works.

Using shell-configuration files

Shell-configuration files refers to files that are accessed when launching Terminal or when logging in to and/or opening a new shell. Settings and commands, as listed in these files, are executed—modifying what would otherwise be the default behavior of the Terminal window.

.term files vs. shell-configuration files. I've already described a Mac OS X–specific method for modifying a shell: the .term file. However, when selected to run automatically when Terminal launches, this file affects only the initial shell window. Although you can add Unix commands to a .term file, the method for doing so is not quite as convenient as the other techniques described here. Overall, these .term files are primarily intended to be used for changes made via (Mac OS X) menu commands in Terminal. Overall, I recommend that you do not use .term files as a substitute for shell-configuration files.

SEE: • "Take Note: .Term Files," earlier in this chapter.

Logging in vs. starting a new shell. When you open a new shell window and see the `Welcome to Darwin` message, you are said to have logged in to the shell. In this case, you're logging in and starting a new shell at the same time. In contrast, if you type the name of a shell while in a shell window (for example, typing `bash` while in a tcsh shell), you open a new shell (referred to as a *subshell* or a child to the parent shell) but you do not log in again.

This distinction has consequences for the different configuration files described below. Some files work whether you're logging in or just opening a new shell. Others work in only one situation or the other.

.cshrc and .tcshrc configuration files. For the tcsh and csh shells, your personal shell-configuration files are called .tcshrc and .cshrc, respectively. The period at the beginning of their names keeps these files invisible in the Finder. These .tcshrc and .cshrc files do not exist by default in your home directory. If you want a shell-configuration file customized with your own commands, you must create it yourself and save it to the root level of your home directory.

The tcsh and csh shell-configuration files run each time you open a new shell or subshell of the appropriate type. In Terminal, this means that such files are run each time you open a new tcsh or csh window, or enter the appropriate shell command in an existing window.

More specifically, a .cshrc file runs when either a new csh or tcsh shell is opened. A .tcshrc file will run only when opening a tcsh shell (and is the only file run when opening a tcsh shell, should you have both a .tcshrc and a .cshrc file in your home directory). Overall, because it works for both types of shells, I prefer to use a .cshrc file rather than a .tcshrc file, even for tcsh shells. The only potential glitch here is that you cannot use a command in a .cshrc file that works only in the tcsh shell.

.login and .logout files for csh/tcsh. If there is a .login file at the root level of your home directory, Terminal will find it and execute the commands contained in the file, as appropriate, whenever you open a new window for a csh or tcsh shell. A .login file, however, is not executed if you open a subshell, as this does not represent a new login. As .cshrc and .tcshrc files are also run at login, you probably won't need to use a separate .login file, certainly not for the relatively simple troubleshooting-related examples described in this book.

Similarly, you can create a .logout file in your home directory. It will be executed whenever you enter the logout command. This, too, is rarely needed in a Mac OS X Unix environment.

bash configuration and login/logout files. In the tcsh shell, a .tcshrc or .cshrc configuration file is conveniently executed both at login and whenever a new subshell is otherwise opened. There is no comparable file in bash. For this shell, you have to choose between a file that runs only at login and one that runs only when a subshell is being opened, not both. In the examples described here, where subshells are rarely used, it's much more important to have the file run at login (for example, when a new window is open in Terminal). Thus, I focus almost exclusively on such files. To have a file run at login for bash, name it *.profile*, *.bash_profile*, or *.bash_login* (and place it in your home directory). For simplicity, I use just the name *.profile* in the examples later in this chapter.

If you do need a configuration file that runs when opening a subshell in bash, create a file called .bashrc. And here's a neat trick: If you want the commands in this file to also run at login (mimicking the way the .cshrc file works), create a .profile file and add the following line to it:

```
. .bashrc
```

Finally, should you want a file that runs at logout, create a file called .bash_logout.

Again, none of these files exist by default in your home directory. You must create them yourself, as described next.

Creating and using a shell-configuration file. We now return (finally!) to the issue of how to permanently save commands using a shell-configuration file. For the purposes of our discussion, I'll be creating a .profile file to run in a bash shell (because bash is the default in Panther and later). If you're using a tcsh shell, create a .cshrc file instead. Aside from the name change, the steps are almost identical; where differences do occur, I make note of them. Here's what to do:

1. Create the shell-configuration file (for example, .profile).

   You can't do this directly in the Finder because it will not let you create a file that begins with a period (since such files are invisible there). Given that you're using Terminal anyway, the simplest solution is to use Terminal to create the file. To do so, first make sure you're at the root level of your home directory (type cd and press Return to take you there). Next, type the following:

   ```
   touch .profile
   ```

   If you now type ls -a, you will see that the file is there.

2. Open the .profile file in a text editor.

   To do so, use a utility such as the free TextWrangler, from Bare Bones Software (www.barebones.com), or its commercial cousin, BBEdit. These applications include an Open Hidden command that you can use to locate and open invisible files like .profile. Note: When using Open Hidden, you should select All Files from the Enable pop-up menu that appears in the Open dialog.

   You can instead open the file in TextEdit by using the open command from Terminal:

   ```
   open -e ~/.profile.
   ```

   The line breaks (sometimes called the line endings) must be in a format that Unix understands (the standard Mac format will confuse the shell when it reads the file). In the BBEdit or TextWrangler Save dialog, click the Options button and access the Line Breaks pop-up menu. Make sure Unix is the chosen item. If you are using TextEdit, you can accomplish this by choosing Make Plain Text from the Format menu, then save the file using Western or UTF-8 encoding.

   You could also do all of this in Terminal, using a Unix text editor such as nano, but I prefer the easier-to-use Mac interface for text editing.

   SEE: • "Take Note: Editing Text Files via Terminal," later in this chapter, for more details on this subject.

3. Add commands to the .profile file. To add a command to this file, simply enter it as you would in Terminal. You can add as many commands as you like. The following are examples of some useful commands you may wish to add:

   • **Set path commands.** To set your home bin directory to be searched for commands (as noted in "Using your home /bin directory," earlier in this chapter), enter the following:

   ```
   PATH="$PATH:$HOME/bin"
   ```

To set the entire Tools directory in the /Developer folder to be searched for commands by default, enter the following:

```
PATH="$PATH:/Developer/Tools"
```

Note: If you are working with a .cshrc file, use these commands instead:

```
set path=("$path" ~/bin)
set path=("$path" /Developer/Tools)
```

- **Alias command for ls.** To save the alias that makes lls the equivalent of ls -lAF, enter the following:

```
alias ll='ls -lAF'
```

- **Alias command for rm.** To make sure that every time you type rm, you're asked for confirmation before anything is deleted (as described in "Take Note: Using rm: Risk Management" and in "Creating an alias," earlier in this chapter), enter the following:

```
alias rm='rm -i'
```

Alternatively, consider adding this more-advanced rm alias:

```
alias rm='mv \!* ~/.Trash'
```

This will cause any files you selected for deletion to be moved to your Trash folder instead, just as if you had dragged them to the Trash via the Finder. You can then later decide if you want to use the Finder's Empty Trash command to truly get rid of them.

- **Alias commands using absolute path.** As an alternative to changing the PATH variable to search for all commands in a folder, you can use an alias to redefine a specific command to one that uses an absolute path:

```
alias CpMac=/Developer/Tools/CpMac
```

Now you can use the CpMac command without adding /Developer/Tools to your PATH or to each command.

Or, let's say you want to use your own special version of the ps command, which you downloaded and compiled from an open-source project:

```
alias ps=$HOME/bin/specialps
```

Now every time you use ps, the program ~/bin/specialps will run instead.

Note: As explained earlier in the chapter, if you're working with a .cshrc file, use a space instead of the equals sign for the above alias commands.

4. Save the file. How you do this depends on what editor you're using, For Mac applications, simply select the Save command (making sure you save the document with Unix line breaks, if this option is provided).

That's it. To test out your newly created file, open a new shell (by pressing Command-N in Terminal). All of the commands you included in your .profile file should now be in effect. Congratulations!

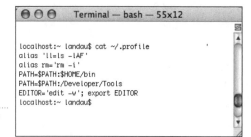

Figure 10.21

The contents of my .profile file.

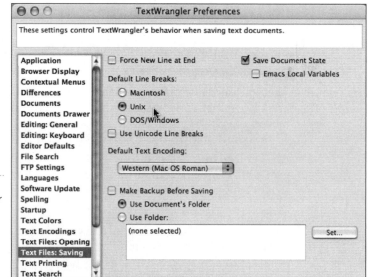

Figure 10.22

When using a utility like TextWrangler for creating shell-configuration files, make sure you have set files to be saved with Unix line breaks.

TAKE NOTE ▶ Editing Text Files via Terminal

Suppose you want to edit a text file, such as a .profile file. As suggested in the main text, one way to do so is to avoid Terminal altogether and instead open the text file in a Mac OS X text editor such as TextEdit or Bare Bones Software's TextWrangler.

Using the open command. Assuming you're starting in Terminal, you can switch from Terminal to a Mac OS X application without having to go to the Finder by using the open command in Terminal.

SEE: • "Take Note: Opening Mac OS Applications from Terminal," earlier in the chapter, for more on the open command.

continues on next page

TAKE NOTE ▶ Editing Text Files via Terminal *continued*

This is because the open command can open documents as well as applications. For example, type the following:

```
open ~/Documents/report.txt
```

This opens report.txt in the default application (as if you had double-clicked it in the Finder). In this example, it will most likely launch TextEdit, because that is the default application for .txt files (unless you changed the default via the Finder's "Open with" option).

Alternatively, you could type the following:

```
open -e ~/Documents/report.txt
```

The -e option forces the document to open in TextEdit, even if it is not the specified default. Thus, to go directly from Terminal to editing the .profile file in TextEdit, you would enter the following:

```
open -e ~/.profile
```

This has the bonus of allowing you to open invisible files in TextEdit.

Finally, you can also choose to open a document in any specified application; for example, you could type the following:

```
open -a {application name} ~/Documents/report.txt
```

In this case, the document will be opened in whatever application you specified. For example, to open it in AppleWorks, you would specify AppleWorks 6 as the application name. Note that if you're trying to open the file in an application *not* located in one of the Applications directories, you'll need to type the path to the application instead of just the application name.

Creating a text file in TextEdit. If you want to create a new Unix-compatible text document in TextEdit (as opposed to opening an existing document), make sure the new document uses plain text format rather than rich text. Because rich text is enabled by default, you will probably need to choose Make Plain Text (Command-Shift-T) from the Format menu before saving the document. If you don't, the document will be saved in Rich Text Format (with an .rtf extension) and cannot be used with Unix (for example, it will not work as a .profile file or a shell script). In addition, plain text files are saved with a .txt extension by default. For a .profile file, eliminate the extension. If you want to use the file as a shell script, you can change the extension to .command.

Using BBEdit's or TextWrangler's edit command. With BareBones' BBEdit and TextWrangler text editors, you have the option of installing a Unix command for working with files in the text editor. (The command gets installed in the /usr/bin directory.) The first time you launch either editor, you're asked if you want to install this Unix command; if you fail to install it at this time, you can install it at any later time via the Install Command Line Tools button in the Tools pane of either editor's preferences. If you own this software, you should install this command: It offers some convenient and powerful options.

continues on next page

TAKE NOTE ▶ **Editing Text Files via Terminal** *continued*

Once installed, these commands—bbedit for BBEdit, edit for TextWrangler—work just like any other command in Terminal. For example, for TextWrangler, you simply type edit plus arguments to use the command. Type man edit to get full details on its use. Here are the essentials:

- If you type edit {*text document name*}, the selected text document will open in TextWrangler.

- If you type edit -w {*text document name*}, the selected text document will open in TextWrangler, and the command-line prompt will not return (for example, edit remains open in Terminal) until you close the document. This allows TextWrangler to mimic the behavior of Unix editors such as nano and vi.

- If you type any command that produces output and add | edit to the end of it, this pipes the output of the command to TextWrangler. For example, suppose you wanted a text copy of the output of an ls command. To obtain it, you would type the following:

  ls | edit

  Note: The | symbol in the above command invokes the *pipe* feature of Unix. In essence, this says to use the output of the first command as the input for the second command. In this case, since edit opens up an untitled document in TextWrangler, the output of ls pipes into the untitled document as input.

- If you want TextWrangler to be your default text editor (that is, opened any time another Unix command would cause the default Unix text editor to open), you can add the following line to your .profile file:

  EDITOR='edit -w'; export EDITOR

  Note: If you're working with tcsh and a .cshrc file, add the following command instead:

  setenv EDITOR 'edit -w'

  Note: Adding this command will cause problems for a few commands that launch text editors, such as crontab. See the man pages for the edit command for a potential work-around.

Using nano, vi, or emacs. If you wish, you can avoid Mac OS X applications altogether and edit files directly in Terminal. Mac OS X comes with several different Unix text editors, including vim (vi in Jaguar and earlier), emacs, and nano. If you choose any of these, be sure to check out the text editor's man pages to find out how to use it. The nano editor (pico in Panther and earlier) is the most user-friendly for non-Unix folks.

For starters, to open any text file in nano, type nano *filename*. To open the file with root access, precede the command with sudo. Press Control-X to exit from nano.

The vim editor is the default text editor in Terminal. If you find yourself in vim and want to get out, type :q.

You can change the default editor from vim to nano, using the same sentenv command that I used to set TextWrangler as the default editor. To do so, add the following to your .profile file:

EDITOR=nano; export EDITOR

continues on next page

TAKE NOTE ▶ **Editing Text Files via Terminal** *continued*

Note: If you're working with tcsh and a .cshrc file, add the following command instead:

```
setenv EDITOR nano
```

To see what effect this addition has on your .profile or .cshrc file, type crontab -e before and after making the change (also open a new shell window after making the change). The crontab -e command opens your crontab file (or a blank file, if no crontab file exists) in the default text editor. Before the addition, the command will open the crontab file in vim. After the change, it will open in nano.

Note: You cannot set EDITOR to open -a TextEdit or open -e. The open tool does not wait until you have finished editing the file before it continues. This is a requirement of whatever command you set in the EDITOR variable.

Note: In Tiger, the pico text editor in previous versions of Mac OS X has been replaced with nano. nano is a "compatible but enhanced" clone of the pico text editor. It adds many new features, such as support for Macintosh line breaks, better scrolling, search history, and syntax coloring. If you are used to typing pico on the command line, fear not; Tiger includes a symbolic link that runs nano whenever you type pico. Visit www.nano-editor.org for more information.

SEE: • **"Modifying invisible Unix files from Mac OS X applications," in Chapter 6, for related information.**

• **"Technically Speaking: Terminal Commands to Monitor and Improve Performance," later in this chapter, for more on crontab.**

Figure 10.23

Using TextWrangler's edit command to pipe the output of an ls command to a TextWrangler document.

Using a shell script

A *shell script* is a text document that contains one or more Unix commands. When you run the script, the commands are executed. A shell script is not limited to any particular length, so you can use it to carry out what would otherwise require a long sequence of commands—which means it can save you from having to repeatedly re-enter the same series of commands at the command prompt. Think of shell scripts as the Unix equivalent of Mac OS X macro utilities, such as Automator or QuicKeys X.

Shell scripts can also get much more elaborate than just a string of commands that mimic what you might type in Terminal. For example, as with such Aqua macro utilities as QuicKeys (www.startly.com/products/qkx.html), you can add conditional statements to make the script perform different actions depending on what it finds when executing. For our purposes, however, I'm going to skip these complexities. Instead, let's walk through the creation and use of a simple example script, which is based on the following sequence of Unix commands (as first described in Chapter 6):

```
sudo rm -R ~/.Trash/
sudo rm -R /.Trashes/
sudo rm -R /Volumes/volumename/.Trashes/
```

SEE: • "Technically Speaking: More Trash Talk," and "Using Unix to delete files," in Chapter 6, for more details.

The third line refers to an additional mounted volume beyond the startup volume, named *volumename*. If you have no such volume, you can omit that line. If you have more than one such volume, you need a separate line for each one.

This sequence makes sure that everything in your Trash bin is deleted, regardless of where the Trash items are stored—a useful thing to try if you're having problems emptying the Trash from the Finder. However, if you use this sequence often, you would probably like to invoke it without having to retype the entire sequence each time—not only saving time but preventing problems that could result from mistyping it. A shell script accomplishes these goals.

Creating a shell script. To create a shell script for the above commands, follow these steps:

1. Create a new blank document in a text editor. For this example, I'll assume you're using a Mac OS X editor, such as TextEdit, BBEdit, or TextWrangler.

   SEE: • "Creating and using a shell-configuration file" and "Take Note: Editing Text Files via Terminal," earlier in this chapter, for more details on how to use text editors, including TextWrangler and TextEdit, with Unix.

2. For the first line, type #! /bin/sh.

   This line is optional if you want to use the default shell (bash). Otherwise, you will need to enter the path of the shell you want to use. Both sh and bash are shells commonly used for scripts. Apple primarily uses sh shells in its Mac OS X scripts, so I'm conforming to its example. Either alternative will work for the shell script in this example.

3. Type the sequence of sudo rm commands, pressing Return at the end of each line, including the last line.

   Remember: You may need to type several variations of the last line, one for every partition or volume you have mounted. Substitute the actual volume name where *volumename* is located in the command. If you're unsure what volumes are available, type ls /Volumes in Terminal to get a list.

   Note: If the script does not work when created as just described, try ending every line but the first (#!) line with a semicolon. With the semicolon, you should not need to press Return at the end of each line (though it won't cause a problem if you do); the semicolon is interpreted as a Return character. Some combinations of shell scripts and shell environments work better with this format.

4. Save the file—for now, anywhere in your home directory; the root level is fine. Later, I'll describe how to move the file to your home bin directory, if you created one.

   Ideally, the file's name should end in .command—for example, delete-trash.command. The .command extension is needed to run the command from the Finder via a double-click. Even without this extension, however, you could still run the command by opening it from within Terminal (as I explain in the next section, "Running a shell script").

   If you're using TextEdit, make sure you save the file as plain text (via the command in the Format menu). Also, after adding the .command extension, when you select Save, you will be asked if you want to append the .txt extension anyway. Choose Don't Append.

Figure 10.24

The message that appears when you save a plain text file ending in .command in TextEdit.

5. Using the chmod command (in Terminal) or a utility such as XRay (in the Finder), change the file's permissions so that the execute (*x*) permission is enabled for owner, group, and other (referred to as *world* in XRay). Note: This is one permissions change that cannot be done from the Get Info window for the file.

For example, if you're using Terminal and are in the same directory as the deletetrash.command file, type the following:

```
chmod ugo+x deletetrash.command
```

SEE: • **"The chmod command," earlier in this chapter, for details on using this command.**

• **"Technically Speaking:"How Mac OS X Selects a Document or Application Match" and "Copying and Moving: Permissions Problems," in Chapter 6, for more information on using XRay and similar utilities.**

6. Return to the Finder. If you want the script to launch and execute automatically when you double-click it in the Finder, you may have one more step to go. Do one or both of the following, as appropriate:

• If you did not add the .command extension to the end of the file's name, open the Get Info window for deletetrash, and in the "Open with" section, select Terminal as the application. (You may choose to do this, even with the .command extension added, in case you might later want to remove the extension.)

• If you used TextWrangler or BBEdit, you need to delete the file's creator. You can skip this step if you used TextEdit or a Unix text editor.

To do this using XRay, go to the Type, Creator, & Extension section and, from the Creator pop-up menu, select "no specific creator" (which leaves a blank creator code). If you use FileXaminer and installed its contextual-menu items, you will find an item called Clear Type and Creator. Use it for the deletetrash.command file. Without this modification, the file will open in the text editor (for example, BBEdit Lite or TextWrangler) when you double-click it, rather than Terminal, even with the .command extension.

Alternatively, you can do this in Terminal via the Developer Tools' SetFile command. To do so, enter the following:

```
/Developer/Tools/SetFile -c "" pathname
```

In the above, *pathname* is the relative or absolute pathname for the deletetrash.command file.

Note: To later re-edit this script file, you can still open it in a Mac OS X text editor, but you will have to use the application's Open command (or drag and drop the file to the editor's icon) rather than double-clicking it in the Finder.

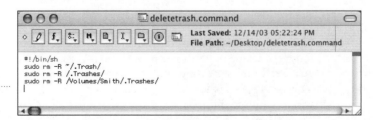

Figure 10.25

The completed shell script.

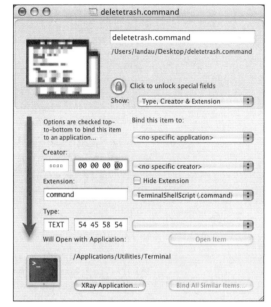

Figure 10.26

How a .command file's settings appear in XRay after making the changes to turn it into a double-clickable shell script: left, *Permissions pane;* right, *Type, Creator & Extensions pane.*

Running a shell script. You can run a shell script by doing any of the following:

- **Double-clicking the script file.** When you double-click a shell script file in the Finder (assuming you set it up as a .command file, as described in the previous section), the file will launch in Terminal in its own window (even if Terminal is already launched and a shell window is open), carry out the designated commands, and log out.

  Note: In the deletetrash.command example, Terminal should ask for your password before executing (because you're asking to run it as root).

  Note: If you get an error message that says, "No such file or directory," one or more of the Trash directories are empty. You can ignore this message. The script will still empty the other Trash directories.

  Note: After running this command, when you later drag items to the Trash in the Finder, you may get a message that says, "The item will be deleted immediately." If this message persists and you want to get rid of it, log out and log back in.

- **Dragging the script file icon to the Terminal icon.** Dragging the file icon to the Terminal icon will similarly launch the script. You only need to do this if you *did not* set the file to be double-clickable.

- **Using Terminal's New Command menu item.** You can run any command, shell script or otherwise, via the New Command item in Terminal's File menu. In the window that appears when you select the command, type the pathname to the command file in the text box. For the deletetrash example (assuming you saved the file at the root level of your home directory), type

~/deletetrash.command

Then click the Run button.

Optionally, if the script produces output that you want to view in Terminal, check the "Run command inside a shell" box before clicking Run.

- **Executing the script from Terminal's command prompt (script *not* stored in home bin directory).** Launch Terminal, and after the prompt appears, type the path to the command. If you saved the file in the root level of your home directory, for example, you would type

~/deletetrash.command

The command will run.

- **Executing the script from Terminal's command prompt (script stored in home bin directory).** If you created a ~/bin directory for running commands (as described in "Using shell-configuration files," earlier in this chapter), and added the ~/bin directory to the PATH variable, you can run these scripts a bit more conveniently. In particular, you can move the script file to your bin directory and then run the script just by typing its filename, rather than entering its full pathname.

For example, with the script file in the bin directory, you would only have to type deletetrash.command to run the script. Doing this, you may no longer care if the file is double-clickable in the Finder. If so, you can eliminate the .command extension from its name. With the extension gone, you can run the command from Terminal just by typing deletetrash.

One advantage of running the command from Terminal (rather than the Finder)—whether or not the file is in the bin directory—is that after the command is completed, you're not logged out. Thus, you can continue typing commands after the script is run without needing to open a new shell window. If the shell script deleted a file, for example, you can continue to work in Terminal, just as though you had deleted the file with an rm command rather than via the script.

However, even though you're not logged out, Terminal treats the script as an independent subprocess that opened and closed after it ran. The running of the script is described as a *child* of the initial *parent* process. After the script has run, you're back at the parent level. An important implication of this is that any changes made by the script that would get undone when you exited a shell will also be undone after the script is run. Therefore, you cannot use a shell script in this way to run a list of alias commands. The aliases will be forgotten after the script is run, just as they would be after you exited a shell or logged out.

Fortunately, there's a way to preserve the results of alias commands (or other commands with the same problem) *after* a script is run: You can use the source command.

- **Using the source (.) command.** Suppose you created a shell script, called `loadaliases`, to run a list of alias commands, such as the `alias ll=ls -lAF` command mentioned earlier in this chapter. That text might look like the following:

```
#! /bin/bash
echo 'enable aliases'
alias ll='ls -lAF'
```

The script could continue with as many additional alias (or other) commands as you wanted to include.

(The echo line is optional here. It provides feedback when you execute the shell, so that you can tell that it ran successfully. This is desirable because an `alias` command doesn't produce any immediate output on its own.)

You can create and run this shell script using the methods just described. Suppose, for example, you placed it in your home bin directory: When you type `loadaliases` in Terminal, the script will run successfully. However, when you next type `ll`, the alias will not execute. As just noted, this is because the alias change is not preserved after the script is run and its shell is exited. To solve this problem, use the `source` command: `. pathname`. In this case, you would type the following:

```
. ~/bin/loadaliases
```

Note: In some shells, notably tcsh and csh, you must use the command source instead of just a period (.) That is, you would type

```
source ~/bin/loadaliases
```

The `source` command runs the script in the current shell rather than in a separate subshell, preserving the changes. Try it!

One potential glitch here: The `source` command works as described only if the script is written in a shell that's compatible with the one that's active in the Terminal window. For example, the default bash shell in a Terminal window will correctly run scripts as source if they're written in the sh or bash shell but not if they're written using the tcsh or csh shell. The opposite is true for Terminal windows using the tcsh and csh shells.

In my view, a far better way to deal with this alias issue is to include the commands as part of a configuration file, such as .profile, as described above. (In fact, these files are often called *source* files for this very reason.) However, I wanted you to be aware of this alternative option.

Bottom line: This introduction should help you see how even simple shell scripts can be extremely valuable tools. Even if you only use Terminal occasionally, turning sequences of commands into scripts can save time and eliminate the need to remember what to type.

AppleScript and shell scripts. AppleScript includes a `do shell script` command that lets you run shell scripts via AppleScript. See the following Apple document for more details: http://developer.apple.com/technotes/tn2002/tn2065.html.

SEE: • "Take Note: AppleScript," in Chapter 4, for more on AppleScript.

The hash command. When you execute a command while a shell is open, the shell typically looks for the command in a cache it maintains, which is quicker than having to search all the locations in PATH. If you changed the PATH, redefined commands using aliases, or moved executable files around, the command may not work initially because it has not yet been added to the cache. Or, more correctly, the information in the hash is now inaccurate. To remedy this, enter hash -r. This causes the shell to re-create its cache.

If you are using the tcsh or csh shell, use the rehash command instead.

Unix: Creating, Viewing, and Finding Files

The following describes some additional commands for creating, viewing, editing, and locating files you may want to work with in Terminal.

Creating files: The touch command

To create a new blank document file or to update the modification time of an existing file, type the following:

touch *filename*

If no file with your selected name exists in the current location, Unix creates one (a simple text file). This command is especially useful for creating documents whose name begins with a period (since the Finder won't let you do this).

If the file already exists, Unix updates the "last modified" time for the file to the current time—it *touches* the file, hence the command's name.

As always, you can type a relative or absolute path to the file to create or modify a file in a location other than the current one. Alternatively, you can use text editors to create and edit documents.

SEE: • "Take Note: Editing Text Files via Terminal," earlier in this chapter, for more details.

Viewing files: The head, tail, cat, more, and less commands

If you want to view the contents of a text file related to troubleshooting, you can easily use Mac applications such as TextEdit and Property List Editor. If you're working in Terminal, however, it may be more convenient to examine a file's contents directly from that application. If you need to view the file's contents without editing it, you can use any of the following commands.

head and tail. These commands output the first and last 10 lines of a file, respectively. You can request to see more or fewer than 10 lines by adding a number option to the command. For example, to see the first 20 lines of a file called mydoc.txt, located in the current directory, you would type the following: head -20 mydoc.txt.

cat. Use the cat command, followed by a filename, to view an entire file (as long as it doesn't exceed Terminal's scrollback buffer). For example, type cat mydoc.txt to view the contents of the file.

more. Use the more command for long files, especially ones that exceed the scrollback buffer. The output of this command resembles that of the man command—that is, it stops when the screen is filled. To see more of the file, you need to keep pressing Return (to advance line by line) or the spacebar (to advance screen by screen). Type q at any point to quit the output display and return to the command prompt.

less. Yes, there is a matching less command. Contrary to its name, though, it actually provides more options than the more command. For starters, you remain in a separate process after entering the less command (where you can issue further commands) until you quit the less command by typing q. For example, if you type less mydoc.txt, the initial part of the document will appear (assuming the document is longer than can fit on one screen). Pressing the D key advances the document approximately one-half screen at a time. (You can also press Return to advance line by line). Press the B key, and the document will scroll backward; press V, and the entire document will open in the default text editor (where you can modify it). Type man less to reveal additional details about using the command.

SEE: • "Take Note: Editing Text Files via Terminal," earlier in this chapter, for more on editing files.

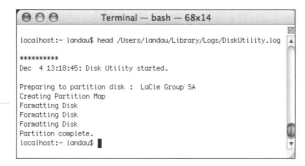

Figure 10.27

Output from the head command examining the file DiskUtility.log.

Finding files: The find, locate, and mdfind commands

Similar to the Finder with its Find command, Unix has its own commands to help you find items from within the Terminal application.

find. In its basic form, the find command displays a list of every item in the directory you specify. Thus, to display a list of *all* files and directories in the Applications directory, including items contained within subdirectories, type the following:

```
find /Applications
```

Because .app packages are considered to be directories in Unix, the resulting list will include the items within every .app package—probably much more than you want to see, which limits the usefulness of the command. In fact, you'll likely want to press Command-period to halt the scrolling output that results from the command.

You can get less output by limiting the scope of your search. For example, if you knew the item you wanted was in the Utilities folder inside the Applications folder, you could type /Applications/Utilities as the pathname, instead of just /Applications.

To further limit (or extend) your search, you can use wildcards in any part of the search term. Thus, you could type /Applications/Utilities/Air* as the pathname for the find command. With this expression, the command would match any item at the root level of the Utilities directory whose pathname (starting from the Utilities directory) begins with the word *Air*. In other words, it would match AirPort Admin Utility.app and AirPort Setup Assistant.app. However, it would also list all of the items *within* these two packages as matches. For example, /Applications/Utilities/AirPort Admin Utility.app/Contents/ Info.plist would be a match because AirPort Admin Utility.app matches the wildcard for the pathname.

You can also use the find command to limit matches to items in which the search term is in the actual filename (that is, the search term must be in the very last segment of the pathname). This more limited search will probably yield results closer to what you'll typically want. To perform this type of search, you need to use the -name option. You combine the -name option with the filename (or part of a filename, with wildcards added) that you're seeking. Thus, to find every filename in the /Applications directory that contains the word *Chess*, type the following:

```
find /Applications -name '*Chess*'
```

Similarly, to find all filenames that end in *.mp3* in your home directory, type the following:

```
find ~ -name '*.mp3'
```

You can also use the Finder's Find command to perform a similar search, but the results won't be the same: The Finder's Find command does not list files contained within packages; the Unix find command does.

Some further advice about using the find command:

- If you plan to use wildcards with the -name option, the filename should be in single quotes.

- Without wildcards (and without the -name option), the find command will only find exact matches. For example, the full name of the Chess application is Chess.app—even though all you see in the Finder is the word *Chess*. Thus, the application itself will not appear as a match in a search for the exact term *Chess*. A search for Chess.app or Chess*, on the other hand, *would* yield a match.

- Remember that Unix is case sensitive. Thus, in the Chess example, if I had wanted to search simultaneously for *Chess* and *chess*, it would have been better to search for **hess*.

- If you get "permission denied" messages for certain directories, and you believe that the item you're searching for does exist in those directories, you'll need to search again with root access (by preceding the find command with sudo).

The find command includes numerous options not described here. You can check out man find to see the full range of this command, but I don't recommend it. The rules that determine what output you get with find can be confusing even to experts. And no matter what you do, you'll often fail to turn up the item you're seeking. If you're unable to get the find command to yield the desired results using the advice presented here, you can try using the locate command instead. It works similarly to the find command but includes fewer options and is usually easier to use. Otherwise, search via Mac OS X and bypass Terminal altogether.

Figure 10.28

Output from a find command with the -name option selected.

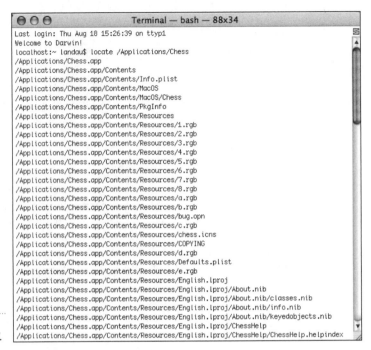

Figure 10.29

Partial output from a locate command.

locate. The `locate` command also finds (or *locates*) files. Since there are no options to select, it's simpler to use. In its basic format, you simply type the following:

`locate` *searchterm*

For example, if you type `locate /Applications/Chess`, you will get a list of all items (in the database that the `locate` command searches) that include the term *Chess* in the segment of their pathname that immediately follows the Applications segment.

Recall that typing `find /Applications -name '*Chess*'` yields a different and smaller subset of results. It lists just those items with *Chess* as part of the final filename or folder name in the path. Thus, the item /Applications/Chess.app/Contents will be a match for /Applications/Chess when you use `locate` but not when you use find with the `-name` option. You can get the `locate` command to provide results similar to the just-cited find command by typing `locate '*Chess'`. Again, note the use of single quotes to prevent the shell from interpreting the wildcard.

A few items of interest about how `locate` works:

- The `locate` command searches a database that is updated periodically. This database is likely to include information about any volume that was mounted at the time of the most recent update. In contrast, the find command, used with options such as `-name`, performs a real-time search of the current entire contents of the startup volume.

As a result, the locate command is typically much faster than the find command, especially for large volumes filled with files. However, it also means that locate may not match an item if the item was added after the last update to the database. You can update (or create, if the database does not yet exist) the database at any time by typing the following:

```
sudo /usr/libexec/locate.updatedb
```

Note: An update may take several minutes to complete.

- A command with no wildcards or other special characters is interpreted the same as if asterisks surrounded the search term. Thus, locate 'Chess' yields the same results as locate '*Chess*'.

- If you type locate '/Applications*Chess' (note the lone asterisk!), you'll get only a single match—that is, to the only file in which *Chess* comes at the very end of its pathname:

```
/Applications/Chess.app/Contents/MacOS/Chess
```

- Sebastian Krauss's Locator (www.sebastian-krauss.de/software) is a third-party Mac OS X utility that serves as a graphical front end for Unix's locate command. If you want to get the benefits of locate without using Terminal, this is the way to go. I use Locator, for example, whenever I want to search the contents of packages (because Mac OS X's Find options don't do this, unless you're within a given package and use the search box in a Finder window).

   SEE: • "Technically Speaking: Inside Packages," in Chapter 3.

mdfind. The traditional Unix method for searching the contents of a file is to use the grep command.

SEE: • "grep," in the "Running Mac OS X software from Terminal" section of "Beyond the Basics," later in this chapter, for details.

Tiger introduced the Spotlight search technology, which takes finding files to a whole new level. You can use Spotlight to search for files in Terminal using the mdfind command. In its simplest form, you can use mdfind to locate all files that match a given keyword:

```
mdfind chess
```

The keyword can also be an expression that searches for particular metadata (*metadata* is "data about data"—in this case, information about your document that is not contained *in* your document, such as the date it was last modified and how large a file it is). The full syntax of the mdfind command is

```
mdfind [-live] [-onlyin directory] query
```

where -live tells mdfind to update its results in real time (press Control-C to exit the results listing); -onlyin restricts the search to the specified directory; and query is the actual search you want to perform.

The query isn't limited to filenames; any kind of metadata associated with a file can be searched. To get a better idea of the types of metadata a file can have, type

mdls *filename*

where *filename* is the pathname or filename of a file on your hard drive. (mdls is the *metadata list* command—it lists all of the metadata associated with a given file.) Metadata have names that begin with *kMDItem*. For example, the metadata listing for an HTML document will include kMDItemKind = "HTML document".

You can limit a search to a specific type of metadata by using the format

mdfind [-live] [-onlyin *directory*] "*metadatatype* == '*query*'"

where *metadatatype* is the kind of metadata attribute you wish to search and *query* is the value of that attribute you want to find. For example, to have Spotlight find all of the items in your Documents folder that are HTML documents, enter

mdfind -onlyin ~/Documents "kMDItemKind == 'HTML document'"

As with any Unix command, you can find out more by typing man mdfind.

SEE: • "Spotlight," in Chapter 2, for details on the Spotlight searching technology.

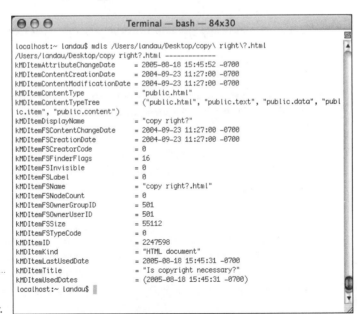

Figure 10.30

The output of an mdls command for an HTML document.

Beyond the Basics

This chapter is obviously not the last word on everything that might be said about using Unix in Mac OS X. For those who want to know more, the following information should set you on the right path.

Front-end Mac utilities and back-end Unix commands

Mac OS X software and Unix commands interact in several significant ways. The following describes some of those interactions.

Mac OS X front ends for Unix commands. When you're using Terminal, it's easy to forget that you're running Mac OS X (with a mouse/window interface) rather than a machine that only runs Unix. Mastering the use of Terminal is as difficult (or easy, depending on your bias) as mastering Unix itself. For those who would prefer to skip this mastery, Mac OS X offers an out: Many of its utilities and System Preferences provide indirect access to Unix commands via the traditional Mac-like menu and window GUI. For example, when you modify the Firewall settings in the Sharing System Preferences pane, you're really accessing Unix's ipfw command. You could do the same thing in Terminal by typing ipfw and adding the appropriate options. The ipfw command even provides access to options not available from the Sharing System Preferences pane. However, learning how to use ipfw is more of hassle for most users than learning how to use Sharing.

In addition, where Apple has left off, third-party developers have kept going. There are numerous third-party utilities (such as the ones mentioned in "Maximizing Performance" in Chapter 6) that similarly give an Aqua interface to Unix commands. The front-end utilities mentioned most frequently in these pages are for modifying permissions, such as XRay and FileXaminer.

Unix back ends for Mac OS X software. Conversely, there are some commands that were specifically created (typically by Apple) to serve as the underlying software of a Mac OS X utility. They have no general Unix function and would never be found on a non-Mac Unix machine. These specially created Unix commands are more commonly referred to as back ends to the Mac OS X software. This is the case for the asr, diskutil, and hdiutil commands, for example, which serve as back ends for Apple Software Restore, Disk Utility, and DiskImageMounter (formerly Disk Copy).

Unix commands created for Mac OS X. Finally, there are Unix commands created by Apple (or carried over from NextStep software) that are designed specifically to work with Mac OS X (Darwin) but have no direct match with corresponding Aqua-based software. As with the previous similar category, these commands would not be found in a non-Mac Unix system. Some of these commands are included as part of a basic Mac OS X installation. Others are available only if you install the Developer Tools software. Two examples of such commands are lsbom and CpMac.

To Unix or not to Unix: That is the question. You may well ask: Why should average Mac users bother with a Unix command when they can use an Aqua alternative instead? In many cases, there *is* no good reason. Unless you simply prefer the Terminal environment, the Aqua alternative is usually the better choice. However, the Aqua interface often provides only a subset of what's available via the Unix command. To access the full range of options (assuming you need them), you must use the Unix command. You may also run into troubleshooting situations (such as when connecting to a Mac via SSH) in which using Unix is your only option. And if you're willing to learn the basics of Unix, there are some situations where using Terminal is simpler and faster than accessing Unix commands from the Aqua interface.

Knowing how to use commands in Terminal frees you from dependence on Aqua-based utilities. If you can use Terminal, you can do anything that can be done with Unix on a Mac. Conversely, using Mac OS X front ends and other utilities frees you from having to learn how to use Unix and typically represents a more user-friendly solution. Take your choice.

Running Mac OS X software from Terminal

The following list represents my choice of the Mac-specific Unix commands—as well as some general Unix commands (serving as back ends for Mac OS X System Preferences and utilities)—that are of the most use to troubleshooters. Many of these commands are also mentioned in earlier chapters.

Some of these commands require root user status to run; in those cases, you must precede the command with sudo. I include examples of what you can accomplish with these commands that you *cannot* do from Mac OS X directly. (Remember, you can type—in Terminal—either man {*name of command*} or just the command name to get more details on how to use each.)

- **appletalk.** You can use this command to enable or disable AppleTalk. This can be done from the Network System Preferences pane as well; however, you have more options here. For example, you can type appletalk -n to find out the current AppleTalk interface (typically en0), Network Number, Node ID, and Current Zone. (In Panther and later, most or all of this information is available in the new AppleTalk pane of Network Utility.)

   The appletalk command is also useful for enabling AppleTalk in cases where turning it on from the Network System Preferences pane does not appear to work.

   SEE: • Chapter 8 for more on using this command to enable AppleTalk.

- **asr.** This is the back-end software used by the Apple Software Restore utility and the Restore functions in Disk Utility in Panther and later, as described in Chapter 3. It provides options not available via the Aqua version of either utility. It not only restores software from existing images, but can also be used to create new images for a subsequent restore. For example, you can clone an entire volume using a command like the following:

```
sudo asr -source /Volumes/Classic -target /Volumes/install
```

(This would make a clone of the volume Classic on the volume install.)

Although the Restore features in Disk Utility can now similarly clone a volume, the asr command offers more options.

> SEE: • "Technically Speaking: More About Disk Utility's Image and Restore Features," in Chapter 3, for more details.

- **bless.** Running this command enables a volume to be used as a startup volume. In most cases, such as when you install Mac OS X on a volume using the Installer utility, running this command is not required (because the Installer does the work for you). However, if you're having trouble getting a volume to boot, this could be the fix. One way to bless a volume with Mac OS X installed is to bless the CoreServices folder on the volume. Thus, for an external volume named HardDisk2, you would type the following:

```
bless -folder /Volumes/HardDisk2/System/Library/CoreServices
```

If you want the volume to be the default startup drive (that is, so that the Mac will attempt to boot from this drive at the next startup), add -setOF at the end of the above command. Presumably, you can duplicate the effect of the -setOF option by selecting the volume in the Startup Disk System Preferences pane.

> SEE: • "Take Note: Blessed Systems and Starting Up," in Chapter 5.

- **chmod, chown, and chgrp.** As discussed earlier in this chapter, these commands are the more full-featured Unix equivalents of what you otherwise do via the Ownership & Permissions settings in a file's Get Info window.

- **cupsd.** This is the basic CUPS software command. It serves as the back end for many of the features in Printer Setup Utility.

> SEE: • "CUPS," in Chapter 7, for more information.

- **defaults.** This command is used to modify the defaults for Mac OS X software. (In this context, *defaults* is synonymous with *preferences*.) Thus, this command duplicates what you can do via Property List Editor or (in a more limited way) by using the Preferences dialog for the relevant software.

Note: To make sure that changes you make are not "undone," do not modify the defaults of a currently running application.

> SEE: • "Modifying a .plist file," in Chapter 4.

- **diskutil.** You can use this command to verify, repair, mount, and erase volumes, as you would otherwise do via Disk Utility. You can also use it to unmount, mount, rename, or eject drives and partitions. There is no manual (man) entry for this command, but you can get a summary of its options by just typing the command and pressing Return.

  This command has some options that are not included in Disk Utility, such as to check RAID sets for errors, and to repair a damaged set.

  Note: To use diskutil, you use a device name, not a disk or volume name. Type diskutil list to find the device name for a volume. For example, when I did this, included in the output was the following line, which described a currently mounted non-startup partition:

  ```
  9: Apple_HFS Solo    10.0 GB    disk0s9
  ```

  This indicates that disk0s9 is the device name for the volume called Solo. Note: The Unix commands mount and df will similarly provide this device information.

  To unmount a mounted partition or volume (other than the startup volume, which cannot be unmounted), you would type diskutil unmount *{device name}*. To remount it, use the mount option.

  Note: disktool is a related command that can also be used for mounting and unmounting volumes.

  SEE: • **"Performing repairs with Disk Utility (First Aid)," in Chapter 5, for more on enabling journaling and other Disk Utility features.**

- **ditto.** This is one of several commands that can be used to copy a bootable volume to a backup.

  The third-party utility Carbon Copy Cloner, from Mike Bombich (www.bombich.com), relies on the ditto command as its back end.

  SEE: • **"Unix: Copying, Moving, and Deleting," earlier in this chapter, for more on ditto and related commands, like CpMac and MvMac.**

  • **"Backing up Mac OS X: Utilities for volume backups," in Chapter 3, for still more information.**

- **drutil.** This command accesses the DiskRecording framework to interact with CD and DVD burners. One interesting option here is bulkerase. With this option, after an initial -RW disc is erased, the Mac will eject the disc and prompt to insert another one. The next inserted disc will also be erased. This will continue until you terminate the process. You can type man drutil to get more details.

- **fsck_hfs.** This command is virtually identical to running Disk Utility's First Aid option on a volume. Unlike First Aid or diskutil, however, it may be usable on the current startup volume (although I generally don't recommend using it in this manner).

  SEE: • **"Running fsck_hfs via Terminal," in Chapter 5, for more details on using this command.**

- **grep**. grep scans text for something called *regular expressions.* In its simplest usage (which is all I am going to cover here), you can use grep to scan files for a keyword. Let's say I want to find which system-startup scripts run the fsck disk-repair tool. The command grep fsck /etc/rc* quickly scans the content of all of the rc files in the /etc directory (the scripts that are executed when the system boots) and lists each line that contains the word fsck.

  One of the more useful applications of the grep command is in combination with a *pipe* (where the output of one Unix command becomes the input for another command). You use the vertical bar (|) character to construct the pipe. For example, suppose you wanted a list of every file on your Desktop that was an application (that is, with a name ending in *.app*). To get this list, you could type

  ```
  ls ~/Desktop | grep '.app'
  ```

  This essentially says: "Take the output from the ls command and pipe it to the grep command. Now use the grep command to search for lines in that output that contain *.app.* Finally, list each line found by the grep command as output in the Terminal window."

- **hdiutil.** This is the back end for Mac OS X's DiskImageMounter background utility, as well as the source for Images functions in Disk Utility. Prior to Panther, this command served as the back end for Disk Copy. Most of what you can accomplish here can be at least as easily accomplished by using Disk Utility (in Panther and Tiger). Still, there are some options and features available only via hdiutil.

  For example, you can create a sparse image with Disk Utility in Panther or Tiger, but you have more options for doing so with hdiutil. The following provides a brief look:

  ```
  hdiutil create ~/Desktop/testcase -size 800m -type SPARSE -fs
  HFS+ -volname testcase
  ```

  The above command creates a disk image on your Desktop named testcase.sparseimage. If you double-click the file, it will mount an image called testcase (this is what the volname option establishes). The image will be in HFS Plus format. The testcase volume will be able to hold a maximum of 800 MB of data (as specified by size option). Most important, the -type SPARSE option means that the testcase.sparseimage file will start off at a minimal size (much smaller than its 800 MB limit) and grow only as needed to accommodate what you add to the mounted image.

  Note: Apple's man entry for hdiutil states the following: "Specifying SPARSE creates a read/write image which starts small and grows as more data is written to it. The default is to grow one megabyte at a time. SPARSE images (and shadow files) are designed to be used during intermediate steps in the process of creating other images when final image sizes are unknown. Such growable files should not be used for persistent storage because their internal structure exacerbates any fragmentation introduced by the filesystem."

An alternative is to create an image with the -stretch option. The resulting image is of a fixed size, but can later be changed via the hdiutil resize command or by using the Convert command in Disk Utility.

Another intriguing option is -shadow. The man entry says this about the option: "This option prevents modification of the original image and allows read-only images to be used as read/write images. When blocks are being read from the image, blocks present in the shadow file override blocks in the base image. When blocks are being written, the writes will be redirected to the shadow file."

You can also use the segment option to divide a single image file into multiple segments. This is especially useful if, for example, you need to divide a large image file over several CDs.

Finally, the makehybrid option can be used to create a disk image in hybrid formats such as a hybrid of HFS Plus, ISO9660, and Joliet. The image can later be burned to a CD, enabling audio CD tracks and computer data to exist on the same CD.

> **SEE:** • "Backing up Mac OS X: Utilities for volume backups," "Bootable CD or DVD," "Technically Speaking: More About Disk Utility's Image and Restore Features," and "Technically Speaking: Internet-Enabled Disk Images," in Chapter 3, for more on hdiutil options.

- **id.** This command gives basic ID information about your account: your user ID (and name), your group ID (and name), and the other groups to which you belong. This information is also available via NetInfo Manager, but not without a good amount of searching.

- **ifconfig.** This is a non-Apple Unix command that's used to configure network settings. It overlaps some with the settings on the Network System Preferences pane.

> **SEE:** • "Take Note: Deleting SystemConfiguration Folder Files" and "Technically Speaking: Ethernet Speed, Duplex, and MTU Problems," in Chapter 8, for examples of using this command.

- **installer.** This command can be used instead of Mac OS X's Installer utility to install .pkg files. Personally, I've never had a need for this utility, much preferring to use Installer instead. However, if you do decide to use the installer command, note that it does not issue a restart command automatically the way the Installer utility does. Thus, for software that requires a restart, type either /sbin/reboot or /sbin/shutdown -r after the installer is finished.

- **ipfw.** This is the back end for the firewall available via the Firewall pane of Sharing System Preferences. Third-party utilities such as Brian Hill's BrickHouse (http://personalpages.tds.net/~brian_hill/brickhouse.html) are also based on this ipfw software.

> **SEE:** • Chapter 9 for more on using this command to enable some settings that cannot be configured via the Sharing pane of System Preferences.

- **kill and killall.** These commands provide alternatives to Mac OS X's Force Quit command and the Force Quit option in Activity Monitor.

  SEE: • "Force-quitting" and (especially) "Technically Speaking: Kill Signals," in Chapter 5, for more information.

- **launchctl and launchd.** These commands are used by the new (in Tiger) method for launching processes, whether at startup or at any other time. Especially as it relates to startup, I covered details in "Startup Daemons," in Chapter 5. For other information, see the "launchd and crontab" section of "Technically Speaking: Terminal Commands to Monitor and Improve Performance," later in this chapter.

- **locate.** As mentioned earlier, locate is an alternative to the Finder's Find and Spotlight options. However, the two commands are not related; they work by separate means. (The third-party utility Locator is a front end for locate.)

- **lpr.** This command, followed by the pathname of a document, prints a document to the default printer just as if you had opened it and selected Print from the application showing the document.

  SEE: • "Technically Speaking: Creating a PostScript File for Printing," in Chapter 7.

- **lsbom.** This command lists the contents of a binary *bom* (bill of materials) file in text form. These bom files are often included in .pkg files and list the contents of all items installed by the .pkg file.

  SEE: • "Technically Speaking: Repair Disk Permissions and Receipts," in Chapter 5, for an example of how to use this command.

- **mdfind and mdutil.** The mdutil command can be used to control certain aspects of Tiger's Spotlight technology. For example, sudo mdutil -E /Volumes/Tiger will erase the Spotlight database on the volume "Tiger." (If indexing on "Tiger" is turned on, the database will be rebuilt automatically.) sudo mdutil -i *on/off volumename* will turn Spotlight indexing for a volume on or off. You can also check the status of indexing with sudo mdutil -s *volumename*. The mdfind command is a command-line equivalent of Spotlight searching.

  SEE: • "Unix: Creating, Viewing, and Finding Files," earlier in this chapter, for information on the mdfind and mdls commands, and "Spotlight," in Chapter 2, for more information on Spotlight itself.

- **niutil.** The niutil command is used to modify data in the NetInfo database. Related commands include nicl, niload, and nireport. In most cases, you can duplicate the actions of these commands by using NetInfo Manager. However, if a problem with the database is preventing a successful startup, it may be necessary to use these commands from single-user mode.

  SEE: • "NetInfo and NetInfo Manager" and, especially, "Technically Speaking: Restoring and Replacing NetInfo and Directory Access Data," in Chapter 4, for more details.

- **nvram.** This command can be used to modify Open Firmware variables. It provides an alternative to accessing Open Firmware via holding down Command-Option-O-F at startup.

  Type nvram -p to get a list of most Open Firmware variables and their current settings. As one interesting example, the boot-screen variable is what determines the graphic image displayed at startup.

  I'm not going to delve into using this command in Terminal, because in my experience it's rarely needed. I would rather work in Open Firmware directly. In any case, you should make changes to Open Firmware only if you know exactly what you're doing: Mistakes can lead to serious problems, including an inability to start up your Mac again! If trouble occurs, try resetting the PRAM (Command-Option-P-R at startup) and/or NVRAM; this should reset most Open Firmware values to their default states and allow startup to proceed.

  SEE: • "Technically Speaking: Open Firmware Commands," in Chapter 5, for more on Open Firmware commands.

- **open.** You've seen the open command used several times already in this chapter. But it has a few more tricks we haven't mentioned.

  open *directory*

  This will cause the Finder to display the directory in a window. Particularly handy is open ., which will open the current directory in a Finder window.

  somecommand | open -f

  The -f option causes open to gather the text from the pipe and then open it in a new editor document (usually TextEdit). For example, curl http://www.apple.com | open -f will download the HTML for Apple's homepage and pipe it to open, which will capture it and open it in a new TextEdit window.

  open -t *filename*

  opens the file using the system's default text editor (usually TextEdit).

  open -a *application filename*

  opens the file using the application specified. This is the command-line equivalent of the Open With contextual-menu command in the Finder.

- **pbcopy and pbpaste.** These are two more commands that allow you to integrate the Aqua world of applications with the command line. pbcopy transfers its input to the system clipboard (also called the "pasteboard" by programmers, which is where pbcopy gets its name). Let's say you want to paste a directory listing into a word processor. You could issue the ls command in Terminal, scroll up to find the beginning of the output, click and drag your mouse to select all of the filenames, and then choose Copy from the Edit menu to copy that text to the clipboard. Or you could simply use ls | pbcopy.

  Similarly, anything currently on the clipboard can be fed to a Unix tool via pbpaste (although pbpaste isn't very useful for images or other complex data). Let's say I want to know how many words are in the paragraph I just typed. I select the paragraph in my word processor, choose Copy from the Edit menu, switch to Terminal, and type pbpaste | wc -w.

SEE: • "grep," earlier in this section, for more about pipes.

• **plutil.** With this command, you can check if the content of a property list (preference) file uses the proper syntax. To use it, type plutil, followed by the pathname of the desired file. If a problem is reported, you should probably trash the file. This command won't detect every possible type of corruption, but it is a good start. Alternatively, Preferential Treatment, by Jonathan Nathan (http://homepage.mac.com/jonn8/as/html/pt.html), is an Aqua-based utility that employs this command. It can check all of your preferences files with one mouse click. I recommend reading the utility's Help file for a good overview of the issues involved here.

You can also use the plutil command to convert a .plist file from its binary format (the default in Tiger) to the older XML format (used in Panther and earlier, although still supported in Tiger). To do so, type

```
plutil -convert format pathname
```

For *format*, substitute either xml1 (to convert a file from its binary format to XML) or binary1 (to convert a file from XML format to binary). For *pathname*, enter the pathname for the .plist file you want to modify.

Note: You can also convert a binary-formatted .plist file to XML format via Property List Editor, using the Save As: XML Property List File option, as covered in Chapter 4). Additionally, you can use Property List Editor to save a .plist file as an ASCII file, by selecting ASCII Property List File from the File Format pop-up menu in the Save As dialog. These files are simple ASCII versions of the binary file, not converted to XML format. Further, at least in my experience, these ACSII files will not function correctly as .plist files in Preferences folders.

As examples of the different formats, the following three outputs are all of a com.apple.screencapture.plist file, as opened in TextEdit. The first is the default binary format, the second is the ASCII conversion of the binary format, and the third is the XML format.

(1) bplist00Ñ__TtypeSpng

(2) {type = png; }

(3)
```
<?xml version="1.0" encoding="UTF-8"?>
<!DOCTYPE plist PUBLIC "-//Apple Computer//DTD PLIST 1.0//EN"
"http://www.apple.com/DTDs/PropertyList-1.0.dtd">
<plist version="1.0">
<dict>
    <key>type</key>
    <string>png</string>
</dict>
</plist>
```

SEE: • "Preferences Files," in Chapter 4, for more on .plist file formats.

• "Deleting or removing preferences," in Chapter 5, for more on .plist file troubleshooting.

• **pmset.** You can use this command to modify the power-management settings, otherwise accessed from the Energy Saver System Preferences pane.

SEE: • "Technically Speaking: Hard-Drive Sleep," in Chapter 2, for an example of using this command.

Figure 10.31

Usage summaries of two of the commands listed in "Running Mac OS X software from Terminal": top, defaults; *bottom,* pmset.

- **reboot (and shutdown).** These commands duplicate what you can do by choosing Restart and Shut Down from the Apple menu. In particular, to shut down immediately, with no further warning messages or delays, you would type the following:

  ```
  shutdown -r now
  ```

- **screencapture.** This command duplicates what you can do via Command-key sequences (such as Command-Shift-3 and Command-Shift-4). I see no advantage to using Terminal for this, unless the Command-key equivalents are not working for some reason.

  SEE: • "Take Note: Screen Captures," in Chapter 2, for related information.

- **SetFile.** This is one of about two dozen Unix commands included in the /Developer/Tools directory (if you installed the Developer software). With this command, you can lock and unlock files, change a file's visibility, and modify file attributes that you would otherwise access from the file's Get Info window or via a third-party utility such as XRay or FileXaminer.

  For example, to make a currently visible file (as an example, a file called ReadMe located on your Desktop) invisible (by enabling its invisibility bit), type the following:

  ```
  SetFile -a V ~/Desktop/ReadMe
  ```

  (You will need to relaunch the Finder to make the file vanish.) To restore the file's visibility, use the same command, but use a lowercase v instead of an uppercase one.

  Note: GetFileInfo is a related command that displays but does not modify these settings. The chflags command, covered in the main text of this chapter, is a non-Apple Unix command that has some overlap with SetFile.

  SEE: • "Unix: Executing Commands," earlier in this chapter, for more on how to run software located in the /Developer directory.
  - "Take Note: Developer Software," in Chapter 2, and "The Mac OS X Install disc(s)," in Chapter 3, for more on the Developer software.
  - "Invisible Files: Making Invisible Files Visible (and Vice Versa)," in Chapter 6, for more on invisibility.

- **softwareupdate.** This is a simple and largely unnecessary command, unless you prefer to do from the Terminal what you can otherwise do from Mac OS X itself. In this case, the command checks for and allows you to install software updates that you would otherwise get via the Software Update System Preferences pane.

  For example, type softwareupdate -l to get a list of all currently non-installed updates (that is, the same list you would get by running the Software Update application).

  About the only case where I could imagine preferring this command to the application is if you wanted (or needed) to update software over a network. For example, you could use ssh to log in to another user's computer (assuming you had permission) and use `softwareupdate` to update that computer.

- **srm.** This command duplicates the effect of the Secure Empty Trash command in the Finder. That is, it overwrites all blocks that contain the to-be-deleted file with random data (so as to make it almost impossible for someone to later recover the deleted information). The `srm` command offers additional options not available from the Finder. For example, you can choose between `-s` (which only overwrites with a single pass) and `-m` (which overwrites with seven passes, as the Finder command does). A `-z` option zeros all data blocks after overwriting them, for even more security.

- **strings.** This command, originally designed to scan binary application files, will scan any file looking for ASCII strings. It is most useful in trying to extract some useful information from files that otherwise can't be read—for example, hidden data in JPEG images, or a document or data-base file written with a program you don't own and for which you have no translators. It looks for any sequence of four or more printable ASCII characters and simply prints them out. For instance, executing `strings IMG0164.JPG` (a snapshot I took with a pocket digital camera), I discovered all kinds of exposure and camera settings that aren't accessible with any other software. This is an old utility, and the logic for determining strings is primitive. It won't find any strings that are stored with the newer UTF-16 Unicode encoding, for example.

- **sw_vers.** This is a substitute source of the information otherwise available from the Apple menu's About This Mac command. It tells you the product name (Mac OS X), product version (for example, 10.4.3), and build version (for example, 8F46) of your current startup system.

- **SystemStarter.** This command allows you to restart all items in the /System/Library/StartupItems and /Library/StartupItems folders—possibly useful when doing so will fix a problem that would otherwise require a true restart, thereby saving you some time and inconvenience. However, with the changes Apple has made to the startup sequence in Tiger, this command is less useful than it was in prior versions of Mac OS X.

  SEE: • "Technically Speaking: SystemStarter," in Chapter 5, for more details.

- **tiff2icns.** This command allows you to take any TIFF graphic image and convert it to an icns file suitable for using as a Finder icon. Using it is quite easy: Just type `tiff2icns {filename.tiff}`. This creates an icns file named *filename*.icns at the same location as *filename*.tiff.

- **top.** This command overlaps with the information available via Mac OS X's Activity Monitor. It provides details about memory and CPU usage of all currently running processes.

  SEE: • "Technically Speaking: Terminal Commands to Monitor and Improve Performance," below, for more information on top and other performance-related Unix commands.

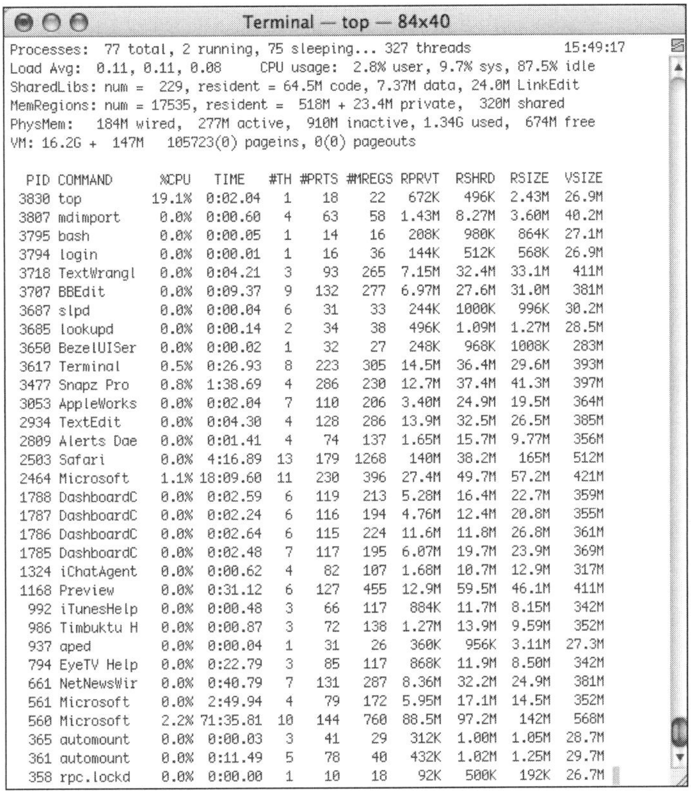

```
Terminal — top — 84x40
Processes:  77 total, 2 running, 75 sleeping... 327 threads           15:49:17
Load Avg:  0.11, 0.11, 0.08     CPU usage:  2.8% user, 9.7% sys, 87.5% idle
SharedLibs: num =  229, resident = 64.5M code, 7.37M data, 24.0M LinkEdit
MemRegions: num = 17535, resident =  518M + 23.4M private,  320M shared
PhysMem:  184M wired,  277M active,  910M inactive, 1.34G used,  674M free
VM: 16.2G +  147M   105723(0) pageins, 0(0) pageouts

  PID COMMAND      %CPU   TIME    #TH #PRTS #MREGS RPRVT  RSHRD  RSIZE  VSIZE
 3830 top         19.1% 0:02.04   1    18    22   672K   496K  2.43M  26.9M
 3807 mdimport     0.0% 0:00.60   4    63    58  1.43M  8.27M  3.60M  40.2M
 3795 bash         0.0% 0:00.05   1    14    16   208K   980K   864K  27.1M
 3794 login        0.0% 0:00.01   1    16    36   144K   512K   568K  26.9M
 3718 TextWrangl   0.0% 0:04.21   3    93   265  7.15M  32.4M  33.1M   411M
 3707 BBEdit       0.0% 0:09.37   9   132   277  6.97M  27.6M  31.0M   381M
 3687 slpd         0.0% 0:00.04   6    31    33   244K  1000K   996K  30.2M
 3685 lookupd      0.0% 0:00.14   2    34    38   496K  1.09M  1.27M  28.5M
 3650 BezelUISer   0.0% 0:00.02   1    32    27   248K   968K  1008K   283M
 3617 Terminal     0.5% 0:26.93   8   223   305  14.5M  36.4M  29.6M   393M
 3477 Snapz Pro    0.8% 1:38.69   4   286   230  12.7M  37.4M  41.3M   397M
 3053 AppleWorks   0.0% 0:02.04   7   110   206  3.40M  24.9M  19.5M   364M
 2934 TextEdit     0.0% 0:04.30   4   128   286  13.9M  32.5M  26.5M   385M
 2809 Alerts Dae   0.0% 0:01.41   4    74   137  1.65M  15.7M  9.77M   356M
 2503 Safari       0.0% 4:16.89  13   179  1268   140M  38.2M   165M   512M
 2464 Microsoft    1.1% 18:09.60 11   230   396  27.4M  49.7M  57.2M   421M
 1788 DashboardC   0.0% 0:02.59   6   119   213  5.28M  16.4M  22.7M   359M
 1787 DashboardC   0.0% 0:02.24   6   116   194  4.76M  12.4M  20.8M   355M
 1786 DashboardC   0.0% 0:02.64   6   115   224  11.6M  11.8M  26.8M   361M
 1785 DashboardC   0.0% 0:02.48   7   117   195  6.07M  19.7M  23.9M   369M
 1324 iChatAgent   0.0% 0:00.62   4    82   107  1.68M  10.7M  12.9M   317M
 1168 Preview      0.0% 0:31.12   6   127   455  12.9M  59.5M  46.1M   411M
  992 iTunesHelp   0.0% 0:00.48   3    66   117   884K  11.7M  8.15M   342M
  986 Timbuktu H   0.0% 0:00.87   3    72   138  1.27M  13.9M  9.59M   352M
  937 aped         0.0% 0:00.04   1    31    26   360K   956K  3.11M  27.3M
  794 EyeTV Help   0.0% 0:22.79   3    85   117   868K  11.9M  8.50M   342M
  661 NetNewsWir   0.0% 0:40.79   7   131   287  8.36M  32.2M  24.9M   381M
  561 Microsoft    0.0% 2:49.94   4    79   172  5.95M  17.1M  14.5M   352M
  560 Microsoft    2.2% 71:35.81 10   144   760  88.5M  97.2M   142M   568M
  365 automount    0.0% 0:00.03   3    41    29   312K  1.00M  1.05M  28.7M
  361 automount    0.0% 0:11.49   5    78    40   432K  1.02M  1.25M  29.7M
  358 rpc.lockd    0.0% 0:00.00   1    10    18    92K   500K   192K  26.7M
```

Figure 10.32

The top display in Terminal.

TECHNICALLY SPEAKING ▶ Terminal Commands to Monitor and Improve Performance

You can view (and, in some cases, modify) a variety of important performance measures via Unix commands entered in Terminal. The following are some examples:

top. When in Terminal, type top and you'll get a list of the currently running processes, sorted in the order of their PID numbers (with the largest number at the top). You will see only as many processes as fit in the window. To see more, enlarge the window; you cannot scroll the list. The list is constantly updated, in real time, to reflect changes in the data. To exit this display, type q (for *quit*).

Each column provides information about the specific processes. The PID column, for example, gives the Process ID number for a process; the COMMAND column displays the name of each process (limited to ten characters by default); and the %CPU column indicates current CPU use.

continues on next page

TECHNICALLY SPEAKING ▶ **Terminal Commands to Monitor and Improve Performance** *continued*

At the top of the `top` display are some important numbers not specific to an individually listed process:

- **Load Avg** is an indication of CPU use. The three load average numbers represent the most recent average and the two averages from minutes before. Generally, the load should stay below 2.0. If it gets higher and stays there, and performance slows, you may be trying to do something beyond what the processor can handle. If that task is essential to your work, you may need to upgrade to a faster processor. Otherwise, you need to try to do less at the same time.

- **CPU usage** numbers provide a different perspective on how the CPU is being used. These numbers indicate how much of the CPU is allocated to the system (kernel) versus the user and how much is not currently being used (idle). Be especially on guard as the idle percentage approaches 0, which is likely to correlate with performance slowdowns.

- **VM** (virtual memory) gives an indication of the Mac's memory use. The VM line will be formatted something like the following:

```
VM: 3.19G + 50.7M 25092(0) pageins, 24969(0) pageouts
```

If the initial number (3.19 GB in the example here) is getting close to the size of your remaining free hard-drive space, you're likely to see performance slowdowns. For further details on memory use, see the coverage of `vm_stat`, later in this sidebar.

The `top` display is Unix's version of Activity Monitor. Given the beefed-up Activity Monitor in Panther and later, I see little advantage to using `top` to get this information, unless you specifically want to be in the Terminal environment. Activity Monitor also provides a more user-friendly way to access the same information available from several of the commands listed below (such as `df` and `vm-stat`). (However, I have seen one example where `top`—or `ps`, discussed below—has an advantage over Activity Monitor: Under certain circumstances, Activity Monitor may show an application's name twice, and/or with the wrong PID. The correct PID is visible using `top` or `ps -aux`.)

launchd and crontab. The `cron` command has long been used on Unix computers (including Macs running Panther or earlier versions of Mac OS X) to perform routine background maintenance tasks. On Mac OS X machines, these tasks are primarily the daily, weekly, and monthly *periodic* scripts, which are run by `cron` in the early hours of the morning (assuming your Mac is left on at this time). Schedules of what `cron` should do and when it should do it are stored in crontab files, which are "read" by the `cron` command. To edit the crontab files (including adding new tasks, if desired), you would use the `crontab` command.

SEE: • "Technically Speaking: Log Files and cron Jobs," in Chapter 4, for more background information on Unix maintenance scripts.

continues on next page

TECHNICALLY SPEAKING ▶ Terminal Commands to Monitor and Improve Performance *continued*

All this has changed in Tiger. To see this, type `cat /etc/crontab`. In Panther, the resulting output will be a list of all tasks in the default system crontab file. In Tiger, the output states instead: "The periodic and atrun jobs have moved to launchd jobs." Yes, as described in "Startup Daemons," in Chapter 5, Apple has migrated `crontab` and numerous other functions to Tiger's new `launchd` command. Via `launchd`, Mac OS X runs assorted tasks, based on schedules determined by .plist files in folders such as /System/Library/LaunchAgents and /System/Library/LaunchDaemons.

For example, the daily Unix maintenance script is now run by `launchd` via the com.apple. periodic-daily.plist file, found in /System/Library/LaunchDaemons. This file tells `launchd` to run the daily script by executing the `/usr/sbin/periodic` command, using the argument `daily`, at 3:15 a.m. every day.

Note: Users who are comfortable with crontabs can still use `cron` to accomplish much the same thing; however, it's not clear if, or when, Apple might eventually phase out `cron` completely. You can also run the maintenance tasks manually via the `periodic` or `sh` command in Terminal. For example, to run the daily maintenance tasks at any time, type `sudo periodic daily` or `sudo sh /etc/daily`.

Finally, there are third-party utilities, such as Brian Hill's MacJanitor (http://personalpages.tds.net/~brian_hill/macjanitor.html), Atomic Bird's Macaroni (www.atomicbird.com), and abstracture's CronniX (http://h5197.serverkompetenz.net:9080/abstracture_public/projects-en/cronnix/), that allow you to run, schedule, and/or edit crontab tasks via an Aqua interface rather than having to deal with Terminal. Before using any of these utilities, however, make sure that the version is compatible with Tiger.

df. The `df -h` command tells you the amount of space used by every volume on your computer. The first row is for your Mac OS X startup volume. The various columns indicate the volume's capacity, the amount used, the amount available, and the percentage of capacity used.

Note: The `-h` option formats the listing in "human readable" (for example, KB and GB) form. This option also works with numerous other Unix commands.

The first column is the filesystem name of the volume, such as `/dev/disk0s10` (these names may be required when referencing the volume via certain other Unix commands, such as `hdiutil`). The last column ("Mounted on") lists the *mountpoints* and names of volumes (the name is the volume's name as displayed in the Finder; the mountpoint is the point on the filesystem at which the volume is mounted). The exception is the startup volume, which is listed simply as /.

continues on next page

fs_usage. The fs_usage command is useful for diagnosing problems with file usage in real time, providing a constantly updated running list of all filesystem activity. Each time a process is "used," it gets listed. This can be helpful in nailing down the causes of problems that appear linked to a specific process but you're not sure which. For example, suppose a logout fails due to some process's not quitting. The fs_usage listing should allow you to see which process is stalling the logout. Similarly, if a strange noise or visual artifact occurs about every 30 seconds, the fs_usage listing should allow you to see what process is being used at approximately the same interval and is thus the likely culprit. fs_usage must be run as root.

You can press Control-C to halt the output at any point.

To view the entire list of output, you may prefer to have it stored in a text file so that you don't have to scroll back through the Terminal screen. To store it in a text file, type the following:

```
sudo fs_usage -w -w > fsoutput.txt
```

At this point, no text will appear in Terminal. Instead, it's accumulating in fsoutput.txt. To stop the output, press Control-C. Then type open fsoutput.txt to view the file in TextEdit.

Note the following from the man entry for fs_usage: "The output presented by fs_usage is formatted according to the size of your window. A narrow window will display fewer columns of data. Use a wide window for maximum data display. You may override the window formatting restrictions by forcing a wide display with the -w option. In this case, the data displayed will wrap when the window is not wide enough."

Note: The > symbol in the command line above is an example of Unix's *file redirection*. It instructs the system to direct the output of the fs command to the file named fsoutput.txt. This serves a similar function to the pipe feature described in "Take Note: Editing Text Files via Terminal," earlier in this chapter.

lsof. This lsof (*list open files*) command is the basis for the output in the Open Files and Ports pane of the Inspector window of processes listed in Activity Monitor. For example, type the following in Terminal:

```
lsof -c Safari
```

This will produce the same output as seen in the Open Files and Ports pane in Safari. Of course, the lsof command has many more options than are accessible from Activity Monitor. Type man lsof to get the details.

continues on next page

netstat. The `netstat` command gives you a quick indication of whether your network connection is performing up to par. For starters, type `netstat -i`. In the listing that appears, you will get a separate line for each network connection. For your Internet connection, look for the address that represents your current IP address (as listed in the Network or Sharing System Preferences pane). If the incoming packet count (`Ipkts`) for that line is 0, you probably don't have an active connection. If your error counts (`Ierrs` and `Oerrs`) are greater than 1 to 2 percent of the total number of packets listed, there is likely to be some problem with your connection (perhaps a network issue at your ISP's end).

Type `netstat -i 10` to have the display updated every 10 seconds. This technique allows you to perform diagnostic tests. For example, you could start your browser to see whether the error counts change as the browser attempts a connection.

The Netstat pane of Network Utility (included in the Utilities folder of Mac OS X) offers functionality similar to Unix's `netstat` command's.

SEE: • **Chapter 8 for more information on networking issues.**

renice. Mac OS X's preemptive multitasking attempts to allocate the processor's attention such that the most important tasks get the most attention (generally giving greater attention to a foreground application than a background one, for example). Tasks that get the greatest attention are completed the most quickly. One way the OS makes these decisions is by assigning each process a priority ranking. When two processes are competing for the CPU's attention, the one with greater priority receives greater attention.

SEE: • **"Mach," in Chapter 4, for more background on preemptive multitasking.**

On occasion, however, you may want to override the OS's default priorities. Some users have found, for example, that they can give Microsoft Virtual PC a speed boost by assigning a higher priority to it. To do this, you use Terminal's `renice` command. The default nice level—basically, the priority for processor time—for most applications is 0. The potential range is between -20 and +20. To increase an application's priority, you lower its nice level from 0 to a lower number. (The lower the number, the more attention a process gets.) There are limits, of course. If you give everything a score of -20, for example, you won't be increasing the performance of anything. The benefits are always relative to the priorities assigned to other processes.

To change a nice value, type `sudo renice {`*`nice #`*`} {`*`pid`*`}`, where {*`nice #`*} is an integer from -20 to +20 and {*`pid`*} is the process ID number of the process you want to change. (You can determine a process `pid` from the `top` command or from Activity Monitor.) Unfortunately, these changes may not be saved after you quit the application and/or restart the Mac. Thus, you may need to re-enter your changes each time you use the application.

continues on next page

TECHNICALLY SPEAKING ▶ **Terminal Commands to Monitor and Improve Performance** *continued*

Northern Softworks' Renicer (www.northernsoftworks.com), Ryan Stevens' Nicer (http://homepage.mac.com/ryanstevens), and La Chose Interactive's Process Wizard (www.lachoseinteractive.net) are examples of Aqua-based utilities that allow you to modify the nice level of a process, bypassing the need to use Terminal.

Don't expect to see much difference after using this command. Mac OS X does a very good job of managing priorities on its own. It's not likely that your manipulations will result in much improvement.

ps. The ps command displays "process status." This overlaps some with the top command, but with two significant differences: It is not updated in real time, and it can provide a more complete list of all active processes (you'll probably need to scroll back through the Terminal window to see the complete listing). Thus, it provides a snapshot of all active processes at a moment in time. The best variations of this command to get the complete list are ps -aux and ps -auxc.

sysctl. Most users will rarely, if ever, need this technical command. Its function is to "retrieve kernel state and allow processes with appropriate privilege to set kernel state." One practical example of using this command is covered in "Optimize your broadband network," in Chapter 8.

tcpdump. This command performs a *packet analysis*. Utilities that do this are often called *packet sniffers*. Although there are Mac OS X utilities that do this (for example, WildPackets' EtherPeek for Mac OS X; www.wildpackets.com), for the price (free!) tcpdump can't be beat. In essence, what a packet sniffer does is report all incoming and outgoing traffic on your Internet connection. If you suspect that a hacker is trying to bust through your firewall, for example, the tcpdump output should provide the evidence. The command must be run with root access, so precede it with sudo. Also, the command requires that you specify which network interface you want to monitor. For example, to monitor an Ethernet connection, you would type

sudo tcpdump -i en0 -s 0 -w ~/Desktop/DumpFile.dmp

For an AirPort connection, type

sudo tcpdump -i en1 -s 0 -w ~/Desktop/DumpFile.dmp

For a modem connection, type

sudo tcpdump -i ppp0 -s 0 -w ~/Desktop/DumpFile.dmp

Press Command-C, if needed, to stop the output.

The problem with the tcpdump command is that its output is so overwhelming and obscure that anyone new to packet analysis will have a difficult time deciphering what he or she is seeing. Check man tcpdump to learn more, especially about all the optional arguments that are available. Apple offers information about using tcpdump at http://docs.info.apple.com/article.html?artnum=107952.

continues on next page

TECHNICALLY SPEAKING ▶ **Terminal Commands to Monitor and Improve Performance** *continued*

update_prebinding. This command does the same sort of optimization that is done when you install a Mac OS X update and get to the point where the Installer utility says that it is "optimizing." This optimizing updates the stored information about the links between related software components, allowing the Mac to run faster. However, there is almost no need to run this command in Tiger, as Mac OS X should do all the needed optimizations on its own.

vm_stat. The vm_stat command provides a more focused look at Mac OS X's memory use than that provided by top. Of particular interest is the number of pageouts (also listed in the top display). The pageout value is an indication that physical memory is being paged (swapped) to the swap file on your drive. The higher the number of pageouts, the greater the disk access and the worse your Mac's performance is likely to be. A performance problem is especially indicated if your pageouts steadily increase over time.

If pageouts equal 0, you're not using the swap file at all—this is ideal, since any use of the swap file is likely to slow performance. As long as the pageout number is near 0 and relatively stable, you needn't be too concerned about memory use, even if other statistics indicate that your memory use is at or near 100 percent.

SEE: • "Technically Speaking: Dividing Up Mac OS X's Memory," in Chapter 4, and "Not enough memory," in Chapter 6, for more background information on memory.

• "Technically Speaking: Swap Files and RAM Disks," in Chapter 6, for related information.

• "Utilities for monitoring and improving performance," in Chapter 6, for information on using Activity Monitor and other utilities as alternatives to these Unix commands.

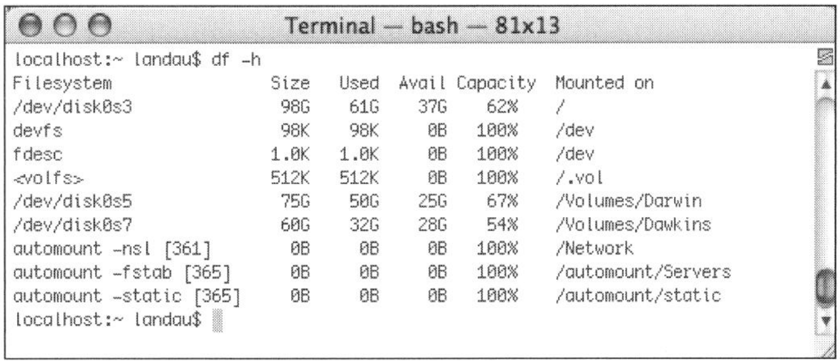

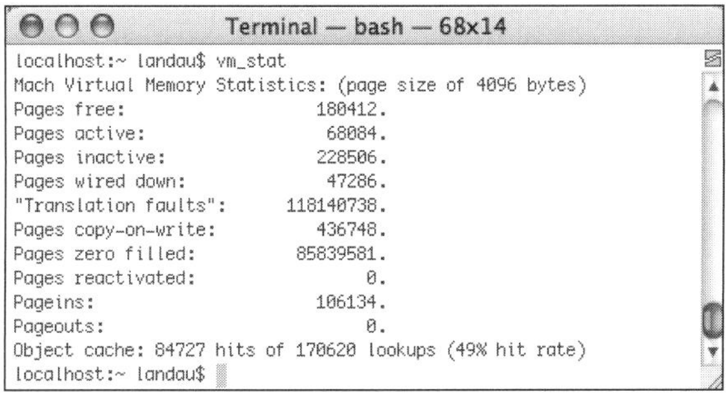

Figure 10.33

The output of two of the commands listed in "Technically Speaking: Terminal Commands to Monitor and Improve Performance": Top, the df command lists mounted volumes and/or partitions (the last item in the list is a network-mounted volume; "volumes" with a capacity of 100 percent can be ignored in most cases); bottom, the vm_stat command indicates memory usage.

```
localhost:~ landau$ df -h
Filesystem          Size   Used  Avail Capacity  Mounted on
/dev/disk0s3         98G    61G    37G    62%     /
devfs                98K    98K    0B    100%     /dev
fdesc               1.0K   1.0K    0B    100%     /dev
<volfs>             512K   512K    0B    100%     /.vol
/dev/disk0s5         75G    50G    25G    67%     /Volumes/Darwin
/dev/disk0s7         60G    32G    28G    54%     /Volumes/Dawkins
automount -nsl [361]   0B     0B    0B    100%     /Network
automount -fstab [365]  0B     0B    0B    100%     /automount/Servers
automount -static [365] 0B     0B    0B    100%     /automount/static
localhost:~ landau$
```

```
localhost:~ landau$ vm_stat
Mach Virtual Memory Statistics: (page size of 4096 bytes)
Pages free:               180412.
Pages active:              68084.
Pages inactive:           228506.
Pages wired down:          47286.
"Translation faults":    118140738.
Pages copy-on-write:      436748.
Pages zero filled:        85839581.
Pages reactivated:             0.
Pageins:                  106134.
Pageouts:                      0.
Object cache: 84727 hits of 170620 lookups (49% hit rate)
localhost:~ landau$
```

Unix information beyond this book

If you're motivated to learn still more about Unix, many resources are available.

Books. There are numerous books that provide valuable information on Unix. Some are specific to Unix's implementation on Mac OS X; others are more general. Some are for beginners; others are for advanced users. Here are four of my favorites:

- *Unix for Mac OS X 10.4: Visual QuickPro Guide*, by Matisse Enzer (Peachpit Press, 2005; www.peachpit.com). If you're new to Unix, this book is a good place to start your journey.

- *Mac OS X Tiger in a Nutshell*, by Andy Lester (O'Reilly, 2005; www.oreilly.com). This has the most complete listing of all Unix commands, including ones just found on Mac OS X systems, that I have seen anywhere.

- *Mac OS X Tiger Unleashed*, Third Edition, by John Ray and William Ray (Sams Publishing, 2005; www.samspublishing.com). If you want to learn how to do almost any advanced Unix procedure on Mac OS X, such as setting up a Web or FTP server, this is the book you want.

- *Unix Power Tools,* Third Edition, by Shelley Powers, Jerry Peek, Tim O'Reilly, and Mike Loukides (O'Reilly, 2002). This book is an exhaustive resource of just about every imaginable Unix tip and trick. It is not a Mac OS X–specific book.

Web sites. Numerous online tutorials and reference databases are available. Old ones disappear and new ones crop up periodically, so any list I can provide will soon be out-of-date. You are better off doing a Google search to find the latest and best sites. However, here is one good site that has been around for several years: UNIX Tutorial for Beginners (www.ee.surrey.ac.uk/Teaching/Unix).

11

Troubleshooting the iApps

Most of this book is concerned with Mac OS X as an operating system—specifically, how to solve problems with the OS and with applications in general. This chapter is an exception: It focuses on a specific collection of applications from Apple that are referred to as the *iApps*—because their names all begin with *i*. Some of these applications are included as part of Mac OS X. Others are sold separately (although they are included with the software that comes with a new Mac purchase).

The core of the iApps is a suite of excellent and popular multimedia applications, which Apple calls iLife: iTunes, iPhoto, iMovie, GarageBand, and (if your Mac comes with a SuperDrive) iDVD. Also included in the more general category of iApps are iCal (Mac OS X's calendar program), iSync (Mac OS X's synchronization utility), and iChat (Mac OS X's instant messaging and conferencing application). Closely related to iTunes is the iPod and its associated software. Finally, even though its name doesn't begin with an *i*, Mac OS X's Address Book utility works closely with several of these applications.

Although space constraints prevent me from going into detail about the use of each of these applications, this chapter covers their basic functionality and the problems you may experience when using them.

Troubleshooting tip: Right off the bat, two of the best things you can do to avoid problems with iApps are (1) make sure you have the latest versions installed (you can check for updates via Software Update or Apple's Web site), and (2) get the most Mac you can afford! The faster your CPU, the more RAM you have installed, the larger and faster your hard drive, the better the software will run. Apple's minimum requirements should be taken with a grain of salt. The programs will run with the minimum—but not necessarily well.

In This Chapter

TAKE NOTE ▶ iLife '05, iTunes 6, and Beyond

In January 2005, Apple released iLife '05, which is made up of iTunes and the latest versions of GarageBand, iPhoto, iMovie HD, and iDVD. These programs are included free on all new Macs and are also available for retail purchase as the iLife package. In addition, the latest version of iTunes is available separately as a free download.

This chapter is mainly based on the versions of the software included in iLife '05. In addition, it covers iTunes 5.0, which was released in September 2005 as an update to the 4.0 version included with the original iLife '05 suite. However, even if you're using older versions, most of the information presented in the main text applies. For a more complete overview of the iLife suite of software, see the following Apple Web page: www.apple.com/ilife. For information on iTunes, see www.apple.com/itunes.

iTunes 6.0 and video iPods. In October 2005, Apple introduced new full-size iPods with video capabilities. A new version—6.0—of iTunes was also released, primarily to support these new video capabilities.

Users can now download video, including music videos and television show episodes (all with a resolution of 320 by 240, the native resolution of the new iPods), for a fee, for playback via iTunes or a video iPod. To go along with this, a Videos category has been added to the iTunes Source list. There are, of course, new sections of the iTunes Music Store devoted to these video downloads.

In addition to viewing on a video iPod, downloaded videos can be viewed in iTunes 6 (either in a video viewer at the bottom of the Source column or in a separate window), as well as in QuickTime Player (version 7.0.3 or later). These videos are saved in a protected MPEG-4 or H.264 format. The filenames typically have an .m4v extension. Unlike audio files, these video files cannot be burned to a CD or DVD from iTunes. However, for backup purposes, you can burn them to a data CD or DVD from the Finder. You can convert movie/video files in other formats to the iPod video format via a Movie to iPod selection, as accessed from the Export command in QuickTime Player Pro—as well as from any application that supports QuickTime exporting (such as iMovie HD). iTunes can also play movies in formats, such as the standard MPEG-4 (.mp4) format, that cannot be uploaded to the video iPod.

As covered in the main text, older versions of iTunes already had limited video support, including access to free music videos and movie trailers that had been posted to the iTunes Music Store. The main change in iTunes 6 is formal support for the new video format that can be uploaded to the video iPod. iTunes 6 also has beefed-up support for movie trailers. It now duplicates the full selection of trailers available at Apple's QuickTime Web site. The iTunes Music Store also sports a few non-video new features; most significant is the ability to purchase items as gifts. In all other respects, iTunes 6 remains the same as the short-lived iTunes 5.

Note: If you are using iTunes 6 and sharing your music with other authorized computers, they too must be using iTunes 6.

The video iPods have a larger screen but are otherwise similar in function to the previous generation of iPods, aside from the video feature, of course. One notable change is that you can only update these iPods via a USB cable; FireWire is no longer supported, except for charging the battery.

continues on next page

> **TAKE NOTE** ▶ **iLife '05, iTunes 6, and Beyond** *continued*
>
> See this Apple Knowledge Base article for more details about playing and syncing videos in iTunes and on iPods: http://docs.info.apple.com/article.html?artnum=302758.
>
> **Photo Booth and Front Row.** Also in October 2005, Apple introduced a new iMac G5 that features a built-in iSight camera. Working together with this camera is a new application called Photo Booth, which lets you take instant still photographs, with a variety of special effects. The new iMac also includes a remote control that works with yet another new application, called Front Row. This application lets you listen to the music and view the photos, movies, and DVDs on the iMac via an interface designed to be used from across a room (much like the menus on a DVD or television screen).
>
> These October developments occurred just as this book went to press. Therefore, these products are not covered in the main text. Of course, within a couple of months of this book's hitting the shelves, iLife '06 will probably get released, with an entirely new set of updated applications. Such is life in the Apple fast lane.

Troubleshooting iTunes

iTunes is Mac OS X's audio hub: It plays audio files and CDs (and, in the latest versions, even movies); converts audio files from one format to another; organizes music; coordinates the music on your iPod; downloads and manages podcasts; and even allows you to purchase new music (via the iTunes Music Store). In addition, it serves as a music library for other users in your household (via iTunes Sharing) and for the other iLife applications: iPhoto, iMovie, iDVD, and GarageBand.

iTunes basics

Even if it didn't offer features for sharing and purchasing music, as well as interacting with the other iLife apps, iTunes would still be a full-featured music center. With it, you can play your favorite CDs, listen to audio files located on your hard drive (generally referred to as MP3s, though iTunes supports a number of other audio file formats as well), create MP3s from your CD collection, and listen to *streaming audio*—that is, live audio broadcast over the Internet. When listening to audio from your hard drive, you can create playlists that contain any combination and order of songs—and in doing so become your own DJ! You can even burn your own audio CDs for use in the CD player in your home or car.

The column on the left side of the main iTunes window displays the Source list with the currently selected source item highlighted (Country in Figure 11.1). The main section of the window contains the contents of the selected source—the song list with columns for name, artist, time, and so on. Playback and volume controls are in the upper left, information about the current track (such as remaining time) is in the upper center, and a Search field and Browse/Import/Burn Disc button are in the upper right. Along the bottom is a row of buttons for features such as creating a playlist, turning shuffle and repeat on or off, accessing the Equalizer window, ejecting a disc, and more. If you pause the pointer over any item, a yellow tool tip describing its function will appear.

If you double-click any item in the Source list, including the Music Store, a separate window opens for that source.

To begin playback, select a source, select a song, and then click the Play button. Alternatively, you can double-click a song in the song listing. You can adjust the volume using the volume slider and, if desired, click the Equalizer button to view the Equalizer, which lets you apply one of a number of EQ settings. The right and left arrow buttons in the upper left of the window skip forward or back one track, respectively; if you click and hold on either arrow button, you'll "scan" through the current song instead. Finally, the Play button doubles as a Pause button: Click it again to pause playback, and again to resume.

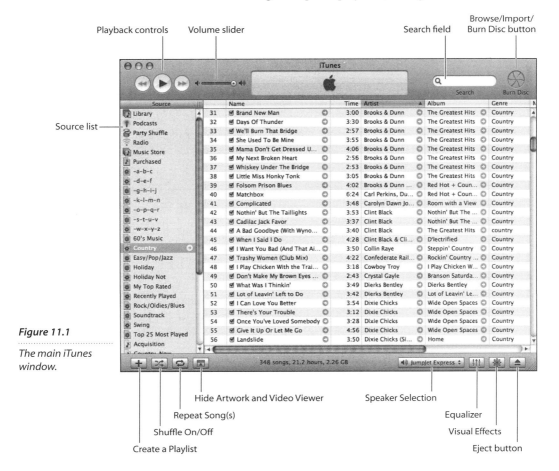

Figure 11.1

The main iTunes window.

Those are the basics of playback; however, there are a number of other play-back features that aren't immediately obvious:

Browsing. When your Library, the Music Store, or an iPod Library, rather than a playlist, is selected in the Source list, the icon in the upper right of the iTunes window is a Browse button. By clicking the Browse button, you can change the song list to a file browser that lets you browse by genre and/or artist, and then by album, allowing you to restrict playback to a certain type of music, a single artist, or even a single album.

Figure 11.2

iTunes' Browse mode.

Playback modes. In the lower left portion of the iTunes window is the Shuffle button (second from the left—the one with two arrows crossing, as shown in Figure 11.1). When this button is clicked, it turns blue, indicating that random-shuffle playback is enabled. Just to the right is the Repeat button (two arrows forming a circuit): A single click enables Full Repeat mode, mean-ing that once the current playback selection (your Library, a playlist, an album, and so on) finishes, it will repeat. A second click switches to Single Repeat mode, which repeats the currently playing track over and over. A third click disables Repeat mode.

Note: New in iTunes 5.0, you can modify the degree of randomness in a random shuffle, via the Smart Shuffle slider in the Playback pane of iTunes' Preferences. You can, for example, make it less likely than random that two songs in a row will be by the same artist.

iTunes visuals and artwork. If you click the Visualizer button (in the lower right portion of the iTunes window, it's the button that looks a bit like an asterisk, second from the right), iTunes' Visualizer activates to provide a graphical display that changes in time to the beat. If you click the Artwork button (fourth button from the left in the bottom left corner of the iTunes window; it looks like a triangle inside a box), an artwork panel is displayed below the Source list: If the currently playing track has embedded artwork, it will be displayed. Any tracks purchased from the iTunes Music Store include artwork (usually the album's cover); you can also drag your own artwork for a particular track into the artwork panel.

Enabling and disabling tracks. Each song in the Song list has an associated check box. If a track's box is checked, the song will be played when any playlist or album containing it is played; if it's not checked, the song will be skipped. (You can manually play an unchecked song by double-clicking it.)

Columns and sorting. You can add or remove columns in the Song list by opening the View Options dialog from the Edit menu, and then enabling or disabling the appropriate column types. (You can also Control-click any column head to bring up a list of possible columns. Select one to switch its current status—viewed or not.) When you click a column name in the Song list, the list is sorted by that column. For example, to group songs by album, click the Album column head.

Searching. By typing words into the iTunes window's Search field, you instruct iTunes to find—in real time—all music files that contain those words in their artist, composer, album, or song names. For example, if you type door, iTunes will find all songs that contain the word *door* in their titles, as well as any songs by the Doors or Three Doors Down. The songs it finds are listed in the Song list. The Search field is in effect a filter that determines which audio files are visible. If you click the magnifying-glass icon to the left of the Search field, you can elect to search only one of the available fields rather than all of them.

New in iTunes 5 is the Search Bar, which works much like the location bar in Finder window searches. Once you've typed in a search term, the Search Bar appears above the list of found items, allowing you to filter the search results by type of item (Music, Audiobooks, Podcasts, Videos, or Booklets) or track information (such as by Artist, Album, or Name). For example, if you're looking for a song called "Beatles and the Stones," but you also have many songs by the Beatles, you would type Beatles in the Search field and then click the Name button in the Search Bar—the resulting list of files would include only those with *Beatles* in the title.

Help. For more details on iTunes' features, check out iTunes and Music Store Help and Keyboard Shortcuts from iTunes' Help menu.

TAKE NOTE ▶ The iTunes Library and iTunes Music Folder

The Library item in iTunes' Source list represents the collection of audio files located on your hard drive (or on a connected volume) and "catalogued" in iTunes. Although you can create *playlists*, which are individual subsets of audio tracks, the Library always shows *all* files—providing, in effect, a database of your music.

By default, iTunes' main files are located in a folder called iTunes, located in the Music folder in your home directory (~/Music/iTunes). Inside this folder is the Library database, called iTunes Library. There's also a folder here called iTunes Music; by default, this is where the actual music and audio files are stored. You can change the location of the iTunes Music folder—for example, to store music files on a second hard drive (to conserve space on your boot volume) or to store files in a public directory (to make them available to all users).

SEE: • "Moving your iTunes Music folder to a different folder or volume," later in this chapter.

Although you *can* use the iTunes Music folder to store music files, iTunes doesn't *require* that you do so. Audio files created in iTunes—for example, files "ripped" from audio CDs or songs downloaded from the iTunes Music Store—are automatically placed inside the iTunes Music folder. However, files not created or downloaded by iTunes may reside elsewhere. You determine where they're placed via the "Copy files to iTunes Music folder when adding to library" setting in the Advanced pane of iTunes' Preferences. Regardless of this setting, when you double-click an audio file to play it in iTunes or drag it into the main iTunes window, the track is automatically added to your Library and made available for playback. However, if the above option is enabled, a copy of the file is placed in the iTunes Music folder (you can later delete the original, if desired); if it is not enabled, the file remains in its original location; if you delete it, iTunes will no longer be able to find it.

You determine how files are organized *within* the iTunes Music folder by adjusting another setting in iTunes' Advanced preferences: "Keep iTunes Music folder organized." If this option is disabled, files are stored loosely. If the option is enabled, iTunes examines each file's *ID tags* (which include such information as the track's name and the artist) and creates folders for each artist, subfolders for each album, and so on—in an effort to organize your music files.

If you previously chose *not* to keep the iTunes Music folder organized but later decide to take advantage of this feature, selecting Consolidate Library from iTunes' Advanced menu will place copies of every file in your Library in the iTunes Music folder—making your iTunes Music folder look as if you had the "Keep iTunes Music folder organized" option enabled from the start.

If you need to locate a particular audio file on your hard drive, you can select it in the Song list and then choose Show Song File from the File menu.

"Ripping" (converting) audio

If you're playing a CD via iTunes, it's obvious where your music is coming from. But how do you get music *onto* your computer—and, if you have one, onto your iPod? One way is to purchase music from the iTunes Music Store (discussed later in this chapter) or another online music service; the music is generally downloaded in the appropriate format. Many users also—rightly or wrongly—download music files shared by other users over the Internet via file-sharing services.

You can also copy (or *import*, as it's called in iTunes) music from a CD to your hard drive. The more common term for this procedure—copying music from a CD and converting it to a file format that can be stored on your computer and played back later—is *ripping*. As I mentioned earlier, iTunes includes everything you need to rip your own CDs. To do so, simply follow these steps:

1. Place an audio CD in your drive and wait for it to appear in the Source list in iTunes' main window. If you've chosen Show Songs from the On CD Insert pop-up menu in the Importing pane of iTunes' Advanced Preferences, iTunes will connect to the Internet and get the names of the tracks on the CD. It does this by connecting to an Internet CD database (CDDB), which uses the contents of the CD—the number of tracks and the exact length of each track—to determine which CD it is and then sends information about that CD back to iTunes. (As a side note, data for CDs you've previously "looked up" via the CDDB is stored in a file called CD Info.cid, located in your ~/Library/Preferences folder.)

2. Click the CD in the Source list to view the CD's song list.

3. To import the CD, click the Import button (in the upper right corner of the iTunes window; this button changes between Import, Burn, and Browse, depending on the context). If you don't want to import all of the songs on the CD, first uncheck the boxes for the unwanted songs in the song list, and then click the Import button.

By default, iTunes imports songs using the AAC file format at a bit rate of 128 Kbps. However, you can customize both the format and the settings for ripping in the Importing pane of the Advanced pane of iTunes' Preferences.

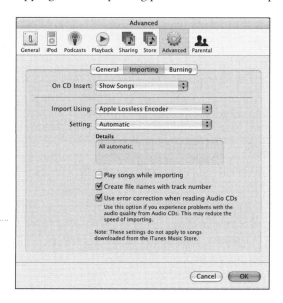

Figure 11.3

iTunes' Preferences window, with the Importing tab selected in the Advanced pane.

For example, from the Import Using pop-up menu, you can choose from among AAC, AIFF, Apple Lossless, MP3, and WAV formats. From the Setting pop-up menu, you can choose from among a few different quality settings for each format (or choose Custom to create your own settings). The Details box displays a summary of the current settings.

Note: In Mac OS X 10.3.2 and later, iTunes will continue importing songs from a CD even if you switch to another account, via Fast User Switching, while the import is in progress.

SEE: • "Take Note: Audio File Formats," below.

TAKE NOTE ▶ Audio File Formats

When you import files from CDs, iTunes uses the settings chosen in the Importing pane of iTunes' Advanced Preferences. You can choose from among five encoding formats: AAC, AIFF, Apple Lossless, MP3, and WAV. Since the differences between these file formats are a bit of a mystery to most users, the following provides a quick summary.

AIFF and WAV. These *uncompressed* encoding formats are basically identical, except that AIFF is a Mac file format and WAV is a Windows file format. Files typically appear in one of these formats on an audio CD mounted in the Finder. Extracting audio in these formats produces files of the same size as the original music files on the CD—basically, around 10 MB per minute of music. For both AIFF and WAV files, iTunes is set to "automatic"—meaning it figures out the settings of the original music file and imports using those same settings. Unless you're specifically trying to create a mono version of a stereo song, you should leave these settings alone.

You would generally use the AIFF or WAV format to make an exact copy of an audio CD. You would extract AIFF or WAV versions of the songs on the CD, and then burn them to a blank CD. Or, if you're a die-hard audiophile who refuses to listen to compressed audio (more on that in a second), you would import CDs in AIFF or WAV format to have the highest-quality audio files on your hard drive. (However, the next format offers an attractive alternative.)

Apple Lossless. This encoding format compresses audio files as it imports them—meaning that the resulting files take up less space than the original files (approximately half as much)—but does so with no loss in quality: The resulting audio file, when decoded, will be identical in every way to the original. If you're concerned with sound quality, Apple Lossless allows you to have your cake and eat it too: smaller file size with full quality.

AAC and MP3. The other two supported formats, AAC and MP3, are *lossy compression* formats. When importing using one of these formats, for each fraction of a second of audio, iTunes uses a process called *perceptual encoding* to estimate which parts of the spectrum the human ear won't be able to hear at all, or won't miss very much, and then discards that information. It then creates a new, much smaller, audio file. The result is that you can store much more music on your hard drive (or iPod) than you would if you had imported using *uncompressed* formats (such as AIFF or WAV). For example, a song that may have required 65 MB of hard-drive space if imported using the AIFF format may require as little as 3 or 4 MB using a low-quality MP3 format.

continues on next page

TAKE NOTE ▶ **Audio File Formats** *continued*

The drawback to AAC and MP3 is that in order to compress files so dramatically, they *lose* data (which is why they're called *lossy* encoders). Granted, the perceptual encoding process described above ensures that much of what is lost you'll never miss. However, if you have good ears and good audio equipment (for example, great speakers or headphones connected to your Mac), you may be able to hear a difference between the original CD and the compressed versions on your hard drive. This is where iTunes' Importing settings come in. The AAC and MP3 encoders both have a Settings dialog that allows you to decide how much of a trade-off you're willing to make between sound quality and file size. If you choose AAC or MP3 as the encoder, and then choose Custom from the Settings pop-up menu, you'll be presented with a dialog that allows you to customize the AAC or MP3 settings. The most important of these is the *bit rate*, which tells iTunes how much data you want to be used to represent each second of audio—the higher the bit rate, the better the quality but the larger the file.

Unfortunately, I don't have enough space to describe each setting for AAC and MP3 files. Your best bet is to play around with them, importing songs using each, until you find the best settings for you. If you have a small hard drive (or iPod), you may want to use lower-quality encoding in order to fit more music. On the other hand, if you have a huge hard drive with lots of free space, you may be more willing to use higher-quality encoding.

So what's the difference between MP3 and AAC? AAC is a newer encoder that uses MPEG-4 technology. It's not as widely used as MP3, but it works with iTunes and Apple's iPod, as well as a growing number of third-party playback devices. AAC is designed to offer better sound quality than MP3 at lower bit rates, whereas many users feel that MP3 files sound better at higher bit rates. In general, I would say that if you're looking for small file size, use AAC as the import format, with a 128 Kbps or 160 Kbps bit rate. If you're looking for better sound quality and don't mind larger files, use AAC at 192 Kbps or MP3 at 192 Kbps or higher. Or, even better, use Apple Lossless for the best sound quality while still saving space.

Creating playlists

Once you've downloaded and/or imported songs into your iTunes Library, you'll probably want to listen to them as you would albums—that is, as smaller subsets of songs. You can do this by creating playlists; iTunes features two types: standard and Smart.

Standard playlists. To create a standard playlist, you simply click the New Playlist (+) button in the lower left corner of the iTunes window (or choose New Playlist from the File menu). A new untitled playlist appears in the Source list, which you can name as desired. You then populate the standard playlist manually: You add songs to it by dragging them from the Library's Song list. You can re-create individual albums (by dragging all of the songs from a particular album) or make your own "mix" playlists. In other words, you decide exactly what songs should be in a playlist. When you click the playlist name in the Source list, the playlist's contents are displayed in the Song list. You can drag songs up or down to change their play order, and you can delete songs by selecting them and pressing the Delete key. (Deleting songs from a playlist does *not* delete them from your Library; it simply removes them from the playlist.)

Smart playlists. Smart Playlists are, well, *smart*. Instead of manually choosing which particular songs you want your playlist to include, you tell iTunes what *kinds* of songs to include, and iTunes automatically populates the playlists with every song that fits your criteria.

To create a new Smart Playlist, hold down the Option key and click the New Playlist button in the iTunes window (or choose New Smart Playlist from the File menu). A dialog will appear that lets you choose specific settings for the playlist. In the "Match the following rule" section, you can choose the criteria to be used to populate the playlist. For example, you could choose songs that you've rated as more than four stars, songs from 1960 to 1969, songs from the folk genre—any criteria that iTunes tracks. If you click the plus button at the far right of the section, you can add more criteria to fine-tune your playlist. If you want to limit the number of songs in the playlist, you can check the "Limit to" box and specify a number of songs/minutes/hours/MB/GB and designate how iTunes should choose those songs. If you want iTunes to update the playlist on the fly (for example, adding new songs to the playlist as you add new files to the iTunes Library), be sure to check the "Live updating" box. Finally, you can check the "Match only checked songs" box if you don't want songs you've unchecked in your Library to be included in the Smart Playlist.

When you click the OK button, your new Smart Playlist will appear in the Source list, with a name of either "untitled playlist" or one loosely based on the criteria you chose. (For example, if your criteria include "Artist contains Beatles," the Smart Playlist will automatically be called *Beatles*.) You'll also notice that the new, untitled playlist has a different icon than the one displayed by standard playlists; this helps you to quickly differentiate between the two.

You can edit a Smart Playlist's criteria at any time by selecting it in the Source list and then choosing Edit Smart Playlist from the File menu (or pressing Command-I).

Figure 11.4

The settings for an iTunes Smart Playlist.

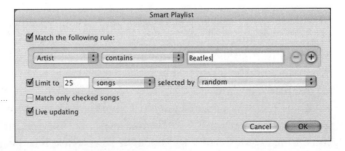

Smart Playlists are one of iTunes' shining features. With a bit of creativity, you can use them to create an infinite number of unique playlists to satisfy any music mood you might be in. You can even burn Smart Playlists—just like standard playlists—to CDs for listening at home or on the go.

Playlist folders. New in iTunes 5.0 are playlist *folders*: You can create folders in your Source list and then move multiple playlists to those folders. This can be a handy feature if you've got so many playlists that you have to scroll the Source list to see them all. For example, if you've got a number of playlists that are time based (1960s, 1970s, 1980s, 1990s, and so on), you can create a folder named *Decades* and then move those playlists into it.

The Party Shuffle "playlist"

There's one other type of playlist in iTunes: the Party Shuffle playlist. As the name implies, the purpose of this playlist—you have only a single Party Shuffle—is to quickly create a playlist for a party or gathering based on your iTunes Library or any other playlist. (It's also a nice way to generate a playlist for your own personal listening session.)

To use Party Shuffle, click its name in the Source list. Below the song list, from the Source pop-up menu, choose the playlist from which you want your Party Shuffle to be drawn—you can use one of your own playlists, or your entire Library. Then decide how many recently played and upcoming songs you want displayed. Finally, you can choose whether or not you want songs that you've ranked higher to be included in the Party Shuffle more frequently than those you've ranked lower.

The advantage of Party Shuffle over other types of playlists is that it's updated in real time like a Smart Playlist, but it can be managed manually—you can add and delete songs—like a standard playlist. And if you don't like the mix of songs selected by iTunes, you can click the Refresh button in the upper right of the iTunes window to get a new set of songs. (Tracks you've added manually will be preserved and moved to the top of the list.) Finally, by combining Smart Playlists with Party Shuffle, you can create a "mix" that's perfect for your gathering (or personal mood).

Listening to Internet radio

You can also use iTunes to listen to Internet streaming radio—that is, radio stations that broadcast over the Internet. You can browse a built-in list of stations or connect directly to a known station.

To browse stations, click the Radio item in the Source list. The song list changes to a list of available stations, organized by music type. Click the disclosure triangle next to a genre to reveal available stations in that genre. Double-click a station to connect to it (or select it and click the Play button).

To connect to a known station, choose Open Stream from the Advanced menu and then enter the station's URL.

iTunes basics: Tips and fixes

The following are a number of iTunes tips and fixes that should help you get the most out of the application, as well as overcome any trouble you might encounter. For even more tips, open iTunes and Music Store Help (via the Help menu) and type tips into the search field; one of the top results will be a document named Tips.

Viewing other types of media in iTunes. Recent versions of iTunes provide the ability to manage and view certain types of data other than music files. For example, some albums from the iTunes Music Store include a PDF file of the album's "liner notes." These files appear in your iTunes Library as any other supported file would; however, at the time of this writing, iTunes doesn't actually display PDF files, so double-clicking these liner-notes files opens them in Preview. On the other hand, iTunes does support QuickTime movie files. If you have a QuickTime movie in your iTunes Library, and you select it and play it, it will play directly in iTunes (either in the video viewer below the Source list, in a separate window, or in full-screen mode, depending on your setting in iTunes Preferences). This, for example, allows playing music videos and movie trailers, as well as the videos included with some albums you purchase from the iTunes Music Store.

SEE: • "Take Note: iLife '05, iTunes 6, and Beyond," earlier in this chapter, for information on the expanded video capabilities in iTunes 6.0.

Bookmarking files. New in iTunes 5, you can bookmark an audio or video file in your Library. This means that iTunes will keep track of where you left off the last time you listened to the file and pick up from there the next time you play it. This is especially convenient for long audio files (such as podcasts) and movie files, which you may not finish in one session. You set this option as follows:

1.   Select the file and choose Get Info (Command-I) from the File menu.

2.   In the window that appears, click the Options tab.

3.   Check the "Remember playback position" box.

Backing up your iTunes music and Library. To prevent losing music you have downloaded, and to avoid having to re-rip the music you transferred from CDs, you should back up your MP3s by copying them to an external hard drive or burning them to CDs or DVDs. Ideally, you should copy the entire ~/Music/iTunes folder. At the very least, copy the music files in ~/Music/iTunes/iTunesMusic. You can use Smart Playlists to make the process easier: Create a Smart Playlist with the criterion "Date Added is after {*date of* *your last backup*}" and then burn the contents of that playlist to CD or DVD. (Just make sure you set iTunes' Burning preferences to "Data CD or DVD.") Each time you back up your music files, change the Smart Playlist date to the date of your previous backup; the resulting playlist will contain only those tracks that have been added in the interim.

Note: Some users who previously used iTunes 2 or iTunes 1 may find that their iTunes folder is located at ~/Documents/iTunes.

SEE: • "Backing Up and Restoring Mac OS X Volumes," in Chapter 3, for more general advice on backing up.

Making batch changes to iTunes songs. Suppose you have a collection of several dozen songs, all of which you want to apply the same change to (perhaps changing the genre from Rock to Oldies). You can do this in one step by selecting all the songs in the Library list and then selecting Get Info (Command-I). This brings up the Multiple Song Information window: Any changes you make here will simultaneously affect all selected items.

Of course, to make changes to a single song, select just that track and choose Get Info. A somewhat different set of editing options appears.

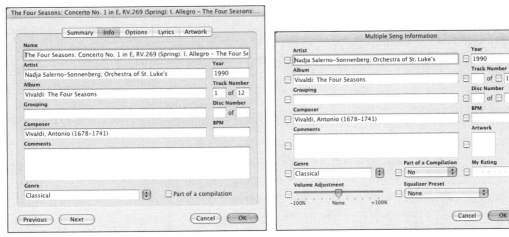

Figure 11.5

Left, *the Get Info settings for a single song;* right, *the settings for a selection of multiple songs.*

Moving your iTunes Music folder to a different folder or volume.
If you decide that you would rather have your iTunes folder in a different folder or on a volume other than the startup disk (say, because you want to make your music available to other users, save space on your startup volume, or ease backups), follow these steps:

1. Copy the iTunes Music folder from your startup drive to the alternative volume.

2. From iTunes' menu, choose Preferences, and click the Advanced button.

3. Click the Change button next to the "iTunes Music folder location" box.

4. In the window that appears, navigate to the *new* iTunes Music folder location, select it, and then click Choose.

Note: An alternative to the above procedure is simply to move the iTunes Music folder from its default location (in ~/Music/iTunes) to the desired location, create an alias of the folder, and put that alias in the iTunes folder in ~/Music. When you next launch iTunes, the application will correctly find your music.

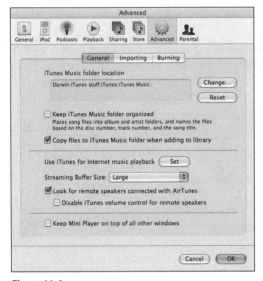

Figure 11.6

iTunes' Preferences window, with the General tab of the Advanced pane selected.

Apple has a Knowledge Base article (http://docs.info.apple.com/article.html?artnum=301748) that similarly describes how to move your iTunes Music folder. Oddly, it is much more convoluted than the above steps (including recommendations to enable the "Keep iTunes Music folder organized" option in the Advanced > General section of iTunes' Preferences, and to use the Consolidate Library command in iTunes' Advanced menu). However, assuming all of your music files are already stored in your iTunes Music folder, the simpler procedure described above should be sufficient. It's always worked for me; all songs, playlists, ratings, and play histories are transferred intact.

Note: If you move your iTunes Music folder to another volume, that volume must be connected and mounted for iTunes to play your music files.

Accessing another user's iTunes music. If another user has placed his or her iTunes Music folder in a public location (for example, his or her own Public folder or the Shared folder), you can add that user's music to your iTunes Library list by following these steps:

1. From iTunes' menu, select Preferences, and click the Advanced button.

2. Uncheck the box for "Copy files to iTunes Music folder when adding to library" and click OK.

   Note: If you don't uncheck this box, iTunes will copy the actual files (assuming they are not protected files for which you do not have authorization) to your own iTunes Music folder when you select to add them to your Library, rather than simply adding the names of the songs to your Library list. If this is what you want to do, then leave this option selected.

3. From the File menu, choose Add to Library.

4. Navigate to the other user's iTunes Music folder, highlight it, and click the Choose button.

The contents of the user's iTunes Music folder will be added to your Library list. You can play the songs as long as you have access to the other user's folder. Note: If you selected the "Copy files" option, then the songs will actually reside in your Music folder, so you will still be able to listen to them even if you no longer have access to the other user's folder.

SEE: • "iTunes Sharing," later in this chapter, for alternative method for sharing music, typically over a local network.

Playing music from an iPod. To play music in iTunes from any connected iPod, without otherwise modifying the iPod's contents, you must select "Manually manage songs and playlists" via iTunes' iPod Preferences. However, even this option will not work for an iPod shuffle.

Using AirPort Express. If you have an AirPort Express with the AirTunes feature enabled (as covered in Chapter 8), in order to play your iTunes music through the AirPort Express select the AirPort Express's name (rather than Computer) from the pop-up menu at the bottom right of the main iTunes window.

Music in iTunes Library disappears. If you launch iTunes and no songs and/or no playlists are listed, it typically means one of two things: iTunes has lost track of where your iTunes folder is located or the Music Library data has become corrupt. In either case, this can usually be fixed. You need to reconnect to or re-create the iTunes Library database.

To check for and fix the former cause, locate and reselect the "disconnected" iTunes Music folder via the Change button next to the "iTunes Music folder location" box in the Advanced pane of iTunes Preferences.

For the latter cause, you will need to re-create your iTunes Library. There are two ways to do this.

The first assumes that only your iTunes Library file has become damaged, and that your iTunes Music Library.xml file is still good.

1. Quit iTunes if it's open. Locate your iTunes folder. Unless you moved it from its default location, it will be in either ~/Documents or ~/Music.

2. From within the folder, delete the iTunes Library file (named iTunes 4 Music Library in iTunes 4).

   As discussed earlier (in "Take Note: The iTunes Library and iTunes Music Folder"), the deleted file is one of the files that keep track of where and how the songs are stored. It does not actually contain the songs.

3. Launch iTunes. From the File menu, choose Import.

4. In the resulting dialog, navigate to your iTunes folder and select the iTunes Music Library.xml file. Click Choose. This creates a new iTunes Library file based on the .xml file.

If this procedure does not work, chances are that both the iTunes Library and iTunes Music Library.xml files are corrupt. You'll need to rebuild your iTunes

Library from scratch. This will likely mean that all of your custom playlists will be lost, but your songs will be saved. To re-create the Library, do the following:

1. Quit iTunes if it's open. Locate your iTunes folder. Unless you moved it from its default location, it will be in either ~/Documents or ~/Music.

2. From within the folder, delete iTunes Library (named iTunes 4 Music Library in iTunes 4), iTunes Music Library.xml, and any other *files* (*not* folders) that may be in the iTunes folder. Whatever you do, do not delete the folder named iTunes Music. This is where your songs are stored.

    As discussed earlier (in "Take Note: The iTunes Library and iTunes Music Folder"), the deleted files are catalog files that keep track of where and how the songs are stored. They do not actually contain the songs.

3. Launch iTunes. From the File menu, choose Add to Library.

4. Navigate to the iTunes Music folder mentioned in Step 2. Click Choose. Your songs should now reappear.

Note: To ease the rebuilding process, you can also delete your iTunes Preferences file (~/Library/Preferences/com.apple.iTunes.plist). This resets iTunes Preferences, so that the next time you launch iTunes, it will ask whether it should search for all music files and add them to your music library, bypassing the need for Steps 3 and 4 above.

Note: If you've got a backup of your iTunes Music Library and iTunes Music Library.xml files, a better solution is to quit iTunes, replace the corrupt versions of these files in your ~/Music/iTunes folder with the backup versions, and then launch iTunes again. This preserves your playlists and other data (and is yet another example of why it's good to back up!). Actually, such backup files may be created automatically when you update to a new version of iTunes. If so, you will find them in the ~/Music/iTunes/Previous iTunes Libraries folder. If all of your songs disappear immediately after upgrading to iTunes 5, for example, do the following:

1. Quit iTunes and go to the Music/iTunes folder in your home directory.

2. Locate the iTunes Library file and remove it from the folder.

3. Open the Previous iTunes Libraries folder.

4. Locate a file called iTunes Library YYYY-MM-DD (where YYYY-MM-DD is the date you first opened iTunes 5). Rename this file *iTunes Library*. Drag it to the enclosing folder from which you just removed the iTunes Library file.

5. Launch iTunes. Your music and playlists should now be restored.

Original file could not be found. Songs in your iTunes Library may appear with an exclamation-point icon in front of their name. When you select to play the song, you get an error message that says the song "could not be used because the original file could not be found. Would you like to locate it?" Click Yes to locate the song; navigate to the location and select it.

Clicking Yes is useful for an occasional song that may not be stored in the default Library location. However, if this happens with many (or all) songs at once, it probably means that iTunes has lost track of the location of your entire Library. Again, this is likely because you are not using the default (Music folder) location for these files. To fix this, open iTunes Preferences and click the Advanced button; click the Change button to reset the "iTunes Music folder location."

Delete a song entirely. When you delete a song in iTunes, it is initially deleted only from the Library listing, not from your drive; you'll then see a dialog asking if you want to delete the file from your drive as well. To delete a track immediately without having to select further options, press the Option and Delete keys, rather than just Delete.

Finding matches via the arrow button. When you click the arrow button next to a name, iTunes takes you to the iTunes Music Store and shows matching items. If you Option-click the arrow button, it will show matching items in your own Library (such as all songs by the artist to the left of the arrow).

Note: If desired, you can invert what clicking and Option-clicking do by making a change to the iTunes .plist file. To make this change via Terminal, for example, type

```
defaults write com.apple.iTunes invertStoreLinks Yes
```

Opening lists in separate windows. To open the Music Store, Radio, or Podcast list in a separate window, double-click its name in the Source column.

"Error –208" message. If, when you launch iTunes, you see the message "Error –208 Cannot Open iTunes Music Library," your iTunes Music Library file may be corrupt. To fix this, follow the steps to re-create the iTunes Library, as described in the previous section.

AAC files won't play. Although iTunes generally supports the AAC file format, you may find that some AAC files won't play on your computer. There are a couple of reasons why this might happen:

- Some AAC files simply don't work with iTunes. If an AAC file won't play in iTunes, chances are it wasn't created in iTunes or QuickTime, or it wasn't purchased from the iTunes Music Store.

- A song was purchased from the iTunes Music Store, but your computer is not authorized to play it. To authorize a purchased song for your computer, double-click it; you'll be asked to provide the Apple ID and password of the person who purchased it.

   SEE: • "iTunes Music Store," later in this chapter, for more details.

Third-party plug-ins can cause problems with iTunes. If you're experiencing unexpected quits with iTunes, or if certain features (such as the Visualizer) don't work, the cause could be one or more third-party iTunes Plug-ins.

To diagnose and fix this, remove all plug-ins by following these steps:

1. Quit iTunes.
2. In the Finder, navigate to ~/Library/iTunes/iTunes Plug-ins.
3. Drag any files in this folder to the Desktop.
4. Launch iTunes.

If the symptoms have disappeared, isolate the plug-in that was the cause and contact the plug-in's vendor for further advice. The solution is usually to get a newer version of the plug-in. If the symptoms haven't disappeared, return the moved files to the iTunes Plug-ins folder.

You may also have iTunes plug-ins in /Library/iTunes. If the above procedure doesn't fix the problem, try using the same steps to determine if third-party plug-ins in this main Library folder are the cause.

Song titles include strange characters. If you've obtained MP3 files from sources other than your own CDs or the iTunes Music Store, some song titles may include strange characters that make the titles undecipherable. This generally happens when files are created in an application that uses a different language system for titling songs. It may also be indicative of songs with titles in non-Roman-character languages.

To update the titles, you can use iTunes' ID3 Tag feature. To do so, follow these steps:

1. Select the songs with titles you wish to update, and choose Convert ID3 Tags from the Advanced menu.
2. In the resulting dialog, enable the "ID tag version" option, and from the pop-up menu choose the desired version. Click OK. If appropriate, also select "Translate text characters" and choose an option from among the three choices presented.
3. If you're uncertain about which option you should select, you can try different ones, varying your selection until you find the combination that best fixes your filename problems.

If converting ID3 tags doesn't fix song names, you can always edit song information manually by selecting a track and then choosing Get Info from iTunes' File menu.

"Unsupported Compression Scheme" error message. If you use a proxy when accessing the Internet, inserting a CD while iTunes is running may prompt the appearance of an error message about an "Unsupported Compression Scheme." What's actually happening is that iTunes is attempting to connect to the online CDDB (CD Database) to retrieve information about the CD (track names and so on), but your proxy server is not properly passing CDDB data. This usually occurs with nonstandard proxy servers. If you can contact the proxy-server administrator, you can request that a more standard proxy be implemented, but an easier solution is usually to simply avoid using the proxy server (if possible).

iTunes Radio cannot connect. If you're using iTunes behind a firewall, you may find that you cannot connect to iTunes Radio (streaming audio) stations. This is because streaming audio uses ports that most firewalls close by default. Unfortunately, each station/stream can choose its own port, so it's difficult to suggest which ports you'll need to open.

If you are able to figure out which port(s) you need to open for a particular station or stream, you can open them in your firewall. If you're using a hardware or third-party firewall, check with the documentation for the firewall for how to open those ports. If you're using Mac OS X's Firewall, as accessed from the Sharing System Preferences pane, you can open the needed ports by creating a new rule.

SEE: • "Firewall" in "Setting Up System Preferences: Sharing," in Chapter 9, for details on how to create a new rule to open a port.

Streaming performance. The Advanced pane of iTunes' Preferences includes a pop-up menu for Streaming Buffer Size. To get the best performance out of streaming audio (for example, from Internet radio or iTunes Music Store), choose Small if you're using a DSL or cable modem or Large if you're using a dial-up modem. The default setting is a compromise: Medium.

Playlist too big to fit on disc. Beginning in iTunes 4.1, if the playlist to be burned to a disc contains more songs than will fit on the disc being used, iTunes will ask you to insert additional discs as needed. Older versions of iTunes will burn only as many as will fit on one disc. In these cases, you will need to create several smaller playlists, each containing only as many songs as will fit on the media being used.

After selecting a playlist, you can see the total size of the songs to be burned by looking at the bottom edge of the iTunes window. A CD-R or CD-RW will generally hold about 650 MB, whereas a DVD-R or DVD-RW will hold about 4.7 GB.

Problems burning CDs. Select the Advanced pane of iTunes' Preferences and select the Burning tab. Check the settings here to make sure they are as intended. In particular: (a) make sure the Preferred Speed is not faster than your CD burner can burn, and (b) confirm that the desired format for recording (for example, Audio CD versus MP3) is selected.

SEE: • "Burning discs: CDs and DVDs," in Chapter 6, for additional information.

iTunes Music Store

Via the iTunes Music Store, you can purchase and download music by thousands of artists from directly within iTunes. Music is encoded in AAC format at a 128 Kbps bit rate, so quality is quite good considering the small file sizes. To access the store, click Music Store in the Source list; the song list will change to the store.

Note: In recent versions of iTunes, you can also use the store to view certain movie trailers and music videos, and to subscribe to podcasts. The various options are listed below the Choose Genre pop-up menu.

To purchase music from the iTunes Music Store, you need an Apple ID and account. You can set one up in the online Apple Store (http://store.apple.com), or you can create one from within iTunes by clicking the Account button just below the Search/Browse area in the upper right corner of the iTunes window. In iTunes 4.2 and later, you can also use the Music Store via your AOL account.

Note: When you set up your account, one of the options is 1-Click ordering, which allows you to purchase and download a song with a single click. If you choose not to enable this option, you'll use the familiar shopping-cart approach provided by many online stores.

Figure 11.7

Top, *the iTunes Music Store main window;* bottom, *the Music Store with an album selected.*

The iTunes Music Store "storefront," if you will, presents special promotions, new releases, and other items of interest. However, most users will find the Search Music Store field to be the most-used feature; it works just like the regular iTunes Search field, only it searches the iTunes Music Store for available music that you can purchase. In addition, if you click the magnifying-glass icon on the left of the Search field, you can choose to search only artists, albums, composers, or songs, or you can switch to Power Search, which lets you search by song, artist, album, genre, and composer simultaneously. (You can also click the Browse button, which works just like the Browse function when viewing your own iTunes Library.)

When you find a song you like, you can double-click it (or select it and click the Play button) to play a 30-second preview. Click the right arrow next to the artist name to view that artist's page, or click the arrow next to the album name to view that album. (The Left/Right/Home buttons at the top of the Store pane work like the Back/Forward/Home buttons in your Web browser.) To buy a song, scroll to the right and you'll see the price as well as a button. If you have 1-Click ordering enabled, the button will say BUY SONG; clicking it purchases the song and downloads it to your computer. If you don't have 1-Click ordering enabled, the button will say ADD TO CART. Once you've selected all the songs you want to purchase, you can view your cart and then purchase them all in one transaction.

SEE: • "Take Note: iLife '05, iTunes 6, and Beyond," earlier in this chapter, for information on the expanded iTunes Music Store features in iTunes 6.0.

After you purchase music from the iTunes Music store, a new playlist is created called Purchased Music. Although all of your purchased music is automatically added to your main Library, this playlist contains *just* your purchased music. It provides a convenient way to see what you've bought, which can be very useful if you want to back up those files (see below).

Music purchased from the iTunes Music Store has two restrictions:

- **CD-burning limit.** You can burn an audio CD from a playlist containing purchased music seven times without altering the playlist somehow. This is Apple's way of preventing people from mass-producing audio CDs from purchased music.

- **Authorization.** Although you can transfer purchased music files to any number of iPods that connect to your Mac, you can listen to purchased music on only *five* computers, including the one used to purchase the song. When a user of another computer attempts to play any purchased song—via iTunes Sharing (discussed below) or by copying the song to the computer and then adding it to a user's iTunes Library—he or she will be required to provide the Apple ID and password of the person who purchased the song. This has significant consequences:

  First, unless you have physical access to the other person's computer to enter the ID and password yourself, it means you need to trust the person who wants to play the song enough to give him or her your Apple ID and password (which theoretically allows that person to access your Apple Store account as well as other confidential information).

Second, it allows Apple to enforce the five-computer policy. When a user provides your ID and password, his or her computer will access the iTunes Music Store over the Internet. If you haven't already reached the five-computer limit, that person's computer will then be "authorized" to play your purchased music. If five computers are already authorized, that user will be prevented from playing any such songs. To authorize this user, you must first deauthorize one of the other computers.

There is one other consequence of this authorization process. Apple authorizes *computers*, not users, and that authorization remains in place for each computer until you manually *deauthorize* it. Thus, if you sell your Mac, or one of the other four authorized computers is sold (or otherwise changes hands), you need to make sure that you deauthorize those computers as well *before* you sell them or give them away. You can do this by opening iTunes on the computer and, from iTunes' Advanced menu, choosing Deauthorize Computer. If you don't do this, that computer will continue to be authorized, and you won't be able to authorize another computer to take its place.

However, if you need to deauthorize a computer to which you no longer have access—for example, you sold it and forgot to deauthorize it first— you are not entirely stuck. Apple provides one last-ditch work-around. Assuming you've used up all five of your authorizations, if you go to your Music Store account (by clicking the Account button when viewing the Music Store), one of the options is Deauthorize All. Clicking this button will deauthorize *all five* computers in one fell swoop. There are two significant caveats, however. First, this button doesn't even appear unless all five of your authorizations are in use. Second, you can use this feature only *one* time every 12 months. So you should use this method only as a last resort.

iTunes Music Store: Tips and fixes

The following represent a number of iTunes Music Store tips and fixes for getting the most out of the store and solving some of the most common problems that can occur.

Backing up purchased songs. Even if you don't back up your entire iTunes Music Library, you may want to back up songs you've purchased through the iTunes Music Store, since Apple does not allow you to re-download songs (if you lose a song, Apple asserts that you must buy it again). Assuming that your Mac has a CD-RW drive or SuperDrive, the easiest way to back up these songs is to burn a data CD or DVD. To do so, follow these steps:

1. Open iTunes, and from the iTunes menu choose iTunes Preferences.

2. Click the Burning button.

3. In the Disc Format options, select Data CD, and then click OK. Note: Files purchased from the iTunes Music Store cannot be burned to MP3 CD format.

4. If you still have the Purchased Music playlist that was created automatically the first time you purchased music, select it. If not, create a new playlist, include all of your purchased songs in it, and then select it.

   Make sure the boxes next to all of the songs in the selected playlist are checked.

5. Click the Burn Disc button in the upper-right corner of the iTunes window.

6. Insert a blank disc (CD-R, CD-RW, DVD-R, or DVD-RW), and then click the Burn Disc button again.

Can't purchase or play songs. If you find you're unable to purchase music from the iTunes Music Store or play previously purchased music, it might be because the Shared user folder (/Users/Shared) is missing. (iTunes uses this folder to keep track of certain data on purchased music.) If this is the case, you can re-create the folder by following these steps (which require administrative access):

1. In the Finder, navigate to /Users; assuming the Shared folder does not exist, proceed to the next step.

2. From the File menu, choose New Folder.

3. Name the new folder *Shared*.

4. Select the new folder, and from the File menu choose Get Info.

5. Click the disclosure triangle next to Ownership & Permissions to reveal that section.

6. If the padlock icon is locked, click it to unlock it.

7. Using the pop-up menus, change the access for Owner, Group, and Others to Read & Write.

8. Close the Info window.

The next time you launch iTunes, you should be able to purchase music and play purchased music.

Can't play purchased songs. If you find yourself unable to play previously purchased music, and iTunes doesn't even prompt you to enter an Apple ID and password, the problem could be that the permissions on your hard drive are set incorrectly. To fix this, quit iTunes, open Disk Utility, highlight your startup disk in the column on the left, and in the First Aid pane click the Repair Disk Permissions button.

Can't connect to Music Store or play purchased songs. If attempting to connect to the Music Store or play music purchased from the Music Store results in a -9800, -9814, or -9815 error, the cause is most likely that the date and time on your Mac are set incorrectly. Quit iTunes and then set the correct date and time in the Date & Time pane of System Preferences.

Interrupted Music Store downloads. If something—quitting iTunes, restarting your Mac, a network problem, an iTunes or system crash, a power outage—interrupts your download of a purchased song, iTunes should automatically download it the next time you launch iTunes. If this doesn't happen, choose "Check for purchased music" from the Advanced menu to force iTunes to check for interrupted downloads.

Errors downloading songs. If you purchase songs from the iTunes Music Store but experience errors when iTunes attempts to download them (such as error -35, error -5000, or a more generic one like the following: "There was an error in the Music Store"), this is typically because (a) the iTunes Music Store is unable to locate your iTunes Music folder (because either the folder is not in the location where iTunes expects to find it or you are using an alias to the folder and the alias link is broken), or (b) the permissions for the iTunes Music folder are not set incorrectly.

For problems with the folder not being in its expected location or an alias not working, the solution is to set the correct location and/or create a new alias, as discussed in "Moving your iTunes Music folder to a different folder or volume," earlier in this chapter.

Figure 11.8

iTunes' Advanced menu.

If you have a recognized iTunes Music folder, and you still experience these errors, you should verify that permissions are set correctly for that folder. To do so, follow these steps (your account must have administrative access):

1. Select your iTunes Music folder in the Finder, and from the File menu choose Get Info.

2. Click the disclosure triangle next to Ownership & Permissions to reveal that section.

3. If the padlock icon is locked, click it to unlock it. Presumably, you are the owner, so this should not be a problem.

4. Using the pop-up menus, change Owner Access to Read & Write, Group Access to "Read only," and Others to "Read only."

5. Click the "Apply to enclosed items" button.

6. Close the Info window.

Can't burn Music Store songs to CD. First, make sure that this is not an authorization issue, as described above.

Otherwise, if you try to burn a playlist to a CD in MP3 format, and that playlist contains only songs you purchased from the iTunes Music Store, you'll get the following message: "None of the items in this playlist can be burned to disc." Likewise, if the chosen playlist includes both purchased songs and your own songs, the CD will be burned, but iTunes Music Store songs will be dimmed and will not be copied to the CD.

The reason for this is that the songs you purchase from the iTunes Music Store are in AAC format, not MP3 format. AAC files can be converted to standard Audio CD format but not to MP3 format.

There is a potential work-around for this: You must first burn your iTunes Music Store songs to CD in Audio CD format. Once you've done this, you can rip them *back* into iTunes using iTunes' MP3 encoder (at which point they'll be in MP3 format and can be burned to MP3 CDs). Note, however, that this procedure significantly reduces the sound quality of your song files. Because AAC files are already compressed, when you convert them to Audio CD and then to MP3, you're adding another level of compression. The result is an audio file that's been compressed twice.

On a similar note, third-party applications, such as Roxio's Toast (www.roxio.com), cannot burn iTunes Music Store tracks to audio CD. With versions of Toast prior to 6.0, burning a protected song to a CD would strip its copy protection. To prevent this, Roxio agreed to change Toast, starting in version 6.0, to prohibit copying of Music Store songs altogether. If you want use Toast to burn an audio CD containing songs you purchased via iTunes, you'll need to first convert those songs to a different format using a procedure like the one above.

Music Store previews are choppy. If song previews from the iTunes Music Store are choppy or distorted, the problem could be your Internet connection. Apple recommends a connection speed of at least 128 Kbps (more than twice that of a dial-up modem) for best results. However, you can improve performance over slow connections by opening iTunes Preferences, clicking the Store item in the toolbar, and then enabling the "Load complete preview before playing" option. This downloads the entire preview before playing it, instead of playing it as it downloads (streaming).

Hiding the Music Store. Although it's not really a troubleshooting issue, many users want to hide the iTunes Music Store—for example, to prevent their children from accessing it, to leave more room in the Source list for their own playlists, or even to remove the temptation to buy more music! To do so, open iTunes Preferences, click the Parental icon in the toolbar, and simply check the Disable Music Store option.

Blocking the Music Store. If you want to block all access to the iTunes Music Store, you must block traffic to and from the phobos.apple.com domain. Many Internet routers will allow you to "blacklist" particular domains (aka hosts) for your entire network. You can also add a rule to Mac OS X's built-in firewall using Terminal or a utility like Brian R. Hill's BrickHouse (http://personalpages.tds.net/~brian_hill/brickhouse.html) that blocks traffic to and from this host; this would prevent any user of your Mac from accessing the Music Store.

SEE: • Chapter 9 for more on firewalls.

Proxy servers and the iTunes Music Store. If your network requires you to use a proxy, note that not all proxy servers work with iTunes. According to Apple, Web (HTTP) and Secure Web (HTTPS) proxy servers work fine. However, SOCKS proxy servers and proxy servers that require authentication (a name and password) will not work. In addition, the "Bypass proxy settings for these Hosts & Domains" setting in the Proxies pane of the Built-in Ethernet section of Network System Preferences in Mac OS X does not work with the iTunes Music Store.

iTunes Sharing

Starting in iTunes 4, iTunes Sharing lets you share your music library with other local iTunes users (that is, other iTunes users connected to your local network). Specifically, when you have iTunes Sharing enabled, anyone located on the same *subnet* of your network can play music from your Library and access (but not modify) your playlists.

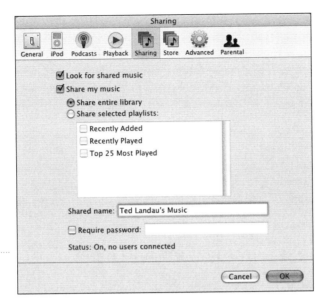

Figure 11.9

iTunes' Preferences window, with Sharing selected.

Allowing your music to be shared. To enable iTunes Sharing, follow these steps:

1. Open iTunes Preferences and click the Sharing icon in the toolbar.

2. Check the box next to "Share my music."

3. Choose either the "Share entire library" option (making your entire Library and all playlists available to other local users) or the "Share selected playlists" option (making only those playlists you select accessible).

4. Enter a name for your shared music in the "Shared name" field. This is how the shared music will be displayed in other users' Source lists.

5. If you want to require a password for users to access your iTunes music over the network, check the "Require password" box and enter a password.

A maximum of five other users can access your iTunes Library simultaneously; if a sixth user attempts to connect, he or she will be prevented from doing so. In fact, only five different users can access your Library in any 24-hour period. This, again, is to keep you from sharing your music with too many other people.

Note: QuickTime movie files and files purchased from Audible.com cannot be shared; they will not appear to other users connected to your Library.

Accessing music shared by others. To connect to other users' shared Libraries, follow these steps:

1. Open iTunes Preferences and click the Sharing button.

2. Check the box next to "Look for shared music."

When your Mac is connected to the local network and detects shared iTunes Libraries, those libraries will show up in the Source list—they'll appear with a blue icon to distinguish them from other Sources. If you click the disclosure triangle next to a shared Library, you'll see all shared playlists from that Library. You can play songs from any shared playlist or from the shared Library itself; if your computer has been authorized, you can even play songs the other user purchased from the iTunes Music Store. However, you cannot modify shared Libraries and playlists, nor can you copy files from another user's Library to your own Library or playlists.

To disconnect from another user's shared Library, from the Controls menu choose "Disconnect *libraryname*" (where *libraryname* is the name of the shared Library you're accessing).

iTunes Sharing: Tips and fixes

Below are a number of sharing tips and fixes for getting the most out of iTunes Sharing, as well as for getting out of some of the more common trouble you may encounter.

"Shared music library not compatible" error. If you try to access an iTunes Library being shared by another iTunes user and get an error message stating, "The shared music library *libraryname* is not compatible with this version of iTunes," the problem is that you and the person sharing the library are using different versions of iTunes (for example, 4.5 and 4.9). (Note: Apple implies that this should occur only if one user is using iTunes 4.0 while the other user is using 4.0.1 or later.) In any case, the solution is to update the earlier version to match the newer version.

Music Sharing not working due to firewall. If you're using iTunes behind a firewall and attempt to share your music, other computers will be able to see your iTunes Sharing name but may not be able to access your shared playlists. The iTunes application gets stuck at the message "Loading {*iTunes sharing name*}," or you get an error message that states, "The Shared music library '*name*' is not accessible for an unknown reason (-3259)." This is because iTunes Music Sharing uses a port (3689) that most firewalls close by default. If you have Mac OS X's Firewall enabled in the Sharing System Preferences pane, the solution is to go to the Firewall pane and either turn off the Firewall or enable the iTunes Music Sharing rule.

SEE: • "Firewall," in "Setting Up System Preferences: Sharing," in Chapter 9, for details on how to enable the iTunes Music Sharing rule.

Audiobooks

Another type of audio file that iTunes can play is audiobooks. Although the term *audiobooks* generally refers to any audio file that includes a spoken-word reading of a book—similar to "books on tape"—iTunes and the iPod can also play a particular type of AAC-encoded audiobook (most noticeable by the file extension *M4b*, instead of *M4a*). These audiobook files have two significant features. First, just like music from the iTunes Music Store, they can be encoded with Apple's FairPlay digital rights management (DRM) system. In fact, you can purchase these books from the iTunes Music Store, as well as from Audible.com. The second feature is that these files are *bookmarkable*. In other words, if you pause or stop an AAC audiobook during playback, the next time you play that file, it will pick up right where you left off.

You can actually make any standard AAC file "bookmarkable" by simply changing its file extension from *M4a* to *M4b*—including the trailing space ("M4b "). This can be done in the Finder, but if you plan to use this feature often, an easier way is to download the "Make Bookmarkable" iTunes AppleScript from Doug's AppleScripts for iTunes (www.dougscripts.com/itunes)—this script lets you quickly convert any standard AAC file to a book-markable one by simply selecting it in iTunes and choosing the script from the iTunes script menu.

Podcasts

Starting in iTunes 4.9, iTunes features the ability to subscribe to, download, and listen to *podcasts*. Put simply, most podcasts are radiolike audio programs that are published on the Internet as audio files (video podcasts are now also available). You can either download podcasts individually or subscribe to a podcast using the RSS protocol—in the latter case, whenever a new episode is published, your podcast application (such as iTunes) will automatically download it and make it available for listening. (Unlike iTunes' Radio programming, which is streamed to your computer—meaning you have to be connected to the Internet to listen—podcasts are downloaded to your Mac as individual files and can be listened to at any time; they can even be transferred to an iPod.)

iTunes makes it easy to both find and subscribe to podcasts. To access iTunes' podcast functionality, first select the Podcasts item in the Source list. You'll see the Podcast list (which will likely be empty the first time you open it). If you know the URL of a podcast (for example, you might have found the URL on a Web site), choose Subscribe to Podcast from the Advanced menu and then enter the URL. A podcast subscription will be added to the Podcast list.

If you instead want to find new podcasts, click the Podcast Directory arrow at the bottom of the list. This takes you to the Podcast section of the iTunes

Music Store, where you can browse and search for podcasts just as you can for music. Once you find a podcast you like, you simply click the Subscribe button next to the podcast name. Although the button looks just like the one used to purchase music, the vast majority of podcasts are free.

After you subscribe to a podcast, it appears in the Podcast list, and iTunes periodically checks for, and downloads, new episodes. Click the disclosure triangle next to a particular podcast to see a list of all available episodes; just as you would a music track, double-click a podcast to listen to it (or select it and click the Play button). You use the Podcasts pane of iTunes Preferences to set your preferences for how often iTunes checks for new episodes; how many to download (none, all, or just the most recent); and which episodes to keep on your hard drive (all, unplayed, or a specified number of the most recent ones). If you choose not to download and keep all episodes, you can always manually download a particular episode in the list by clicking the Get button next to it. To unsubscribe to a podcast, select it and then click the Unsubscribe button in the lower right; existing episodes will remain on your hard drive until you manually delete them.

Finally, when your iPod is connected, if you click the iPod button in the lower right of the iTunes window, you'll find that a new Podcasts pane has been added to the iPod Preferences window. Via this pane, you can decide which podcasts, if any, are copied to your iPod and which episodes.

Exclamation point appears next to podcast. If you see an exclamation-point icon next to a podcast episode or subscription, this could be due to one of a number of issues:

- If the podcast episode was previously downloaded to your Mac, iTunes can't locate the podcast episode file. If you moved it after downloading, you should move it back to its original location; otherwise, the easiest solution is to simply download it again using the Get button next to the episode title.

- iTunes can't download the podcast. If you click the exclamation-point icon, iTunes will give you more information on the problem. It could be that the podcast source server is down or that the URL to the podcast is wrong.

- You haven't listened to this particular podcast in a while. Specifically, if you have more than five unplayed episodes of a particular podcast, iTunes stops downloading new episodes and puts the exclamation-point icon in front of the subscription. If you click the exclamation point, you'll get the message, "iTunes has stopped updating this podcast because you have not listened to any episodes recently. Would you like to resume updating this podcast?" Click Yes to have iTunes continue downloading episodes as scheduled. (You can also simply listen to any exiting episode; iTunes will take that as its cue to resume downloading normally.)

Create your own podcast. When you are ready to create your own podcasts, Apple is ready to help you. It provides tutorials for making a podcast using either GarageBand (www.apple.com/support/garageband/podcasts/) or QuickTime Player Pro (www.apple.com/quicktime/tutorials/podcasting.html).

Parental controls

New in iTunes 5.0 are parental-control options. Accessible via the Parental pane of iTunes Preferences, these options allow a parent to control which options appear in the Source list and which content can be viewed in the iTunes Music Store. For example, you can disable podcasts, shared music libraries, and even the Music Store; once disabled, these items will no longer appear in the Source list for the current user. If you choose "Restrict explicit content," items that are marked by Apple as "Explicit" will not appear in the Music Store.

Parental controls must be enabled for each account individually. Once they're set—by clicking the padlock icon in the Parental pane—only an administrative user can change them.

TAKE NOTE: iLife Application Interactions

iLife applications interact with each other. For example, when you're in iPhoto, you can select music from your iTunes collection to be background music for an iPhoto slide show. You can similarly include iTunes selections in iMovie to add music to a sound track. However, you may occasionally find that the desired collection unexpectedly does not appear in the interacting application.

If this happens, first make sure that you are using the latest versions of all the applications (or at least make sure the versions are all from the same overall version of iLife). Next, make sure that all interacting applications have been opened at least once. Finally, make sure that the needed Library files are in their expected location. For example, your iPhoto Library should typically be in ~/Pictures/iPhoto Library.

If you are still having problems, here are two more specific examples of what to do to get things working again.

iTunes Library doesn't appear in other iLife applications. The solution is to re-create iTunes' Music Library file. To do so, follow these steps:

1. Quit all iLife applications.
2. In the Finder, navigate to your iTunes Music Library folder (located by default at ~/Music, though you may have relocated it manually).
3. Delete the file iTunes Music Library.xml (or move it to the Desktop).
4. Open iTunes.
5. Create one or more new playlists.
6. Quit iTunes.

The next time you open iPhoto, iMovie, or iDVD, your iTunes music should be available.

continues on next page

> **TAKE NOTE: iLife Application Interactions** *continued*
>
> **iPhoto Library doesn't appear in other iLife applications.** The solution is to re-create iPhoto's album file. To do so, follow these steps:
>
> 1. Quit all iLife applications.
> 2. In the Finder, navigate to ~/Pictures/iPhoto Library.
> 3. Delete the file AlbumData.xml (or move it to the Desktop).
> 4. Open iPhoto.
> 5. Create one or more new albums.
> 6. Quit iPhoto.
>
> When you next open iMovie or iDVD, your iPhoto albums should now be available.

Troubleshooting the iPod

If you've watched TV, read a magazine, or even just walked down the street in the past few years, you're familiar with the various iterations of Apple's portable music players. Depending on the size of your iPod and the encoding method you use for your audio files, you can store days, or even weeks, of continuous audio. (The 60 GB model, for example, can store as many as 15,000 songs at 128 Kbps—enough to play 24 hours a day for almost two months!)

What makes the iPod really stand out, though, is its integration with iTunes and the Mac OS. You simply connect it to your Mac—on older models, via a standard FireWire cable; on newer models, via a dock connector cable (connected to your Mac via either USB or FireWire, depending on which cable you use); or, with the iPod shuffle, by plugging it directly into a USB port—and iTunes launches. Your music (including custom playlists) is transferred (in a matter of seconds or minutes), and the battery charges. Accessing your music on the iPod is as simple as using the circular scroll wheel to navigate to a menu item and then pressing the Enter button in the middle of the wheel to select that item. Pressing the Menu button moves you back to the previous menu. It's as simple as that—and it's one of the reasons why the iPod is the most popular hard-drive-based player on the market. Note: The iPod shuffle, which doesn't include a screen, dispenses with the Menu and Enter buttons.

However, the iPod can do a lot more than simply play music. In addition to customizing what music and which playlists are stored on it, you can use it to store your calendar, contacts, and notes and other text information. Color-screen models can store and display your photos. You can even use it as an alarm clock and an ordinary external FireWire or USB hard drive, including (at least with some models) getting it to work as a bootable drive!

As always, Apple's Knowledge Base is a good source of more troubleshooting information than can be covered here. Check out these two documents for starters: http://docs.info.apple.com/article.html?artnum= 60920 and http://docs.info.apple.com/article.html?artnum=300657. For the latest on all the different iPod models and their names, check out this document: http://docs.info.apple.com/article.html?artnum=61688.

SEE: • "Take Note: iLife '05, iTunes 6, and Beyond," earlier in this chapter, for information on the video iPod.

Adding music (and data) to an iPod

With iTunes open, when an iPod is attached, the iPod appears in the Source list. If this is the first time your iPod is attached to your Mac, all of your iTunes music and playlists will be copied to the iPod (assuming your iPod is big enough, that is).

Let's assume that an iPod is connected to your Mac, and an iPod icon is thus in the iTunes Source list. If you click this icon, an iPod Eject button will appear in the lower right of the iTunes window (replacing the Eject button for your CD/DVD tray). If you select either this button or the Eject button next to the iPod name in the Source list, or you choose Eject *iPodName* from the Controls menu, the iPod disconnects from iTunes, and you can physically disconnect it from your computer. Each time you reconnect your iPod, iTunes compares its Library and playlists, and updates the iPod's music files to reflect any additions, deletions, or changes.

Note: If the iPod does not appear in iTunes after you connect it to your Mac, you may need to restore or reset the iPod, as covered later in this chapter.

In addition, you can use your iPod as a limited PDA: You can store calendars, contact info, and even text notes on it, and view this info on the iPod's screen. You won't be able to edit or add information—the iPod has no way to easily input text—but for those times when you need a phone number or address, need to check your schedule, or want to bring some text information along with you, the iPod is more than adequate and saves you from having to carry an additional gadget. With photo-capable iPods, you can also store and display photos.

iPod Preferences. You can modify the default automatic updating as well as other iPod-related settings via the iPod Preferences pane in iTunes. The pane is accessible when an iPod is connected and the iPod is selected in the Source list. To open it, click the iPod button in the lower right of the iTunes window; in the resulting iPod pane of the iTunes Preferences window, you'll see at least four tabs: Music, Podcasts, Contacts, and Calendars. You may also see a fifth,

Photos, if your iPod is capable of displaying photos. Each determines how its respective type of data is synchronized from your computer to your iPod:

- **Music.** The default selection is "Automatically update all songs and playlists." Choosing this results in the behavior I described in the previous section. Alternatively, you can choose "Automatically update selected playlists only," and then check the boxes next to the playlists you want copied to the iPod. Only those playlists, and the audio files contained in them, will be copied. Finally, you can choose "Manually manage songs and playlists." With this option chosen, you simply drag songs from your iTunes Library to the iPod icon in the Source list. If you drag a playlist to the iPod, that playlist and its songs will be copied. Note that with automatic updating, your iPod will only contain songs that are currently in your iTunes Library. If you want to keep *different* songs on the iPod—songs that aren't in your iTunes Library—you'll need to use the "Manually manage songs and playlists" option.

  You also have three or four other settings in the lower part of the iPod Preferences window: "Only update checked songs" will prevent tracks that you've manually unchecked in your Library from being copied to your iPod. In other words, iTunes will use the "all songs and playlists/selected playlists/manually" update setting, but will only copy songs in your Library (or in selected playlists) that are checked. "Open iTunes when this iPod is attached" causes iTunes to launch—if it's not already running—when you connect this particular iPod. If you uncheck this box, you will need to manually launch iTunes in order to update your iPod. This can be useful if you don't change your iTunes Library often but frequently connect your iPod to your Mac to recharge the iPod's battery. The "Enable disk use" option allows you to use your iPod as an external hard drive (see below).

  Finally, if you've got an iPod with a color screen, selecting "Display album artwork on your iPod" makes sure that album art is transferred to your iPod along with the corresponding music files.

- **Podcasts.** I described this pane above, in the "Podcasts" section.

- **Contacts.** With the "Synchronize Address Book contacts" box checked, iTunes will automatically copy your Address Book contacts to your iPod each time you synchronize. You can then view contact information by navigating to the Contacts item in your iPod's menu (by default, under the Extras menu). By default, all contacts are synchronized, but you can instead choose the "Synchronize selected groups only" setting and then choose only those groups you want copied to your iPod. For example, you can create a new contact group in Address Book called iPod Sync and then drag to that group only those contacts you want copied to your iPod.

  The main restriction of the Contacts feature (besides the fact that it's read-only—you can't update contacts on your iPod) is that it works only with Apple's Address Book. If you use a third-party contact application such as Microsoft's Entourage, to use this feature you would first need to copy your contacts into Address Book.

- **Calendars.** The Calendars pane works just like the Contacts pane; you choose whether or not you want your iCal calendars copied to your iPod and, if so, which ones (for example, just your "personal" calendar, not your "work" one). You can then view your calendars on your iPod via the Calendars menu item. You can even choose to have your iPod notify you of iCal alarms.

  Like the Contacts feature, the Calendars feature works with only Apple's iCal calendar program.

- **Photos.** Color-screen iPods—at the time of this writing, iPod photo, iPod with color display, and iPod nano models—have the ability to both store and present photos, either on their own screens or (for full-size color iPods) via a television. If you connect a color iPod to your Mac, a Photos tab will be included in the iPod Preferences pane. If you enable "Synchronize photos from," iTunes will copy photos to your iPod, making them accessible via the iPod's Photos menu. From the "Synchronize photos from" pop-up menu, you choose whether to copy photos from your iPhoto Library, from your Pictures folder in your home directory, or from a folder you choose. In any of these cases, you have the option to copy *all* photos or just photos from selected albums or folders.

  Note that you can't simply drag photos onto your iPod in the Finder and later view them on the iPod or a TV; you need to use iTunes' photo-syncing feature.

  By default, before iTunes copies your photos to your iPod, it creates smaller-sized versions that are more appropriate for storing on your iPod and displaying on a television. If you need full-resolution versions, enable the "Include full-resolution photos" option; your iPod will still display the lower-resolution versions of photos, but you'll be able to access the full-resolution versions—for example, to transport them to another computer—by placing the iPod in Disk Mode and navigating to the Photos folder.

  If your iPod doesn't have enough room to fit all of the selected music and the selected photos, it first copies your music; if there's room left over, it then copies photos, in the order shown in the list in this window, until your iPod is full. You can rearrange photo albums or folders in the list by dragging them up or down.

  You can view your photos on your color iPod by navigating to the Photos menu, choosing an album, and then pressing the Play button. If you've got Apple's AV cable or dock base for color iPods, you can connect your full-size color iPod to your TV via the AV cable or an S-Video cable, respectively, and "project" your photos on your TV.

  For more on photo syncing with the iPod, see this Apple Knowledge Base article: http://docs.info.apple.com/article.html?artnum=300265.

Note: If you have multiple iPods, *each* of them has its own settings, accessible via the iPod settings button.

Note: When the iPod is mounted as a hard drive, as described below, you also can drag .ics calendar files to the Calendars folder at the root level of the iPod, and drag vCard contact files to the Contacts folder. Most contact and calendar applications let you export calendars in ICS format and contacts in vCard format. These calendars and contacts will then be accessible from the Contacts and Calendars items, respectively, just as if you'd synced them via iTunes.

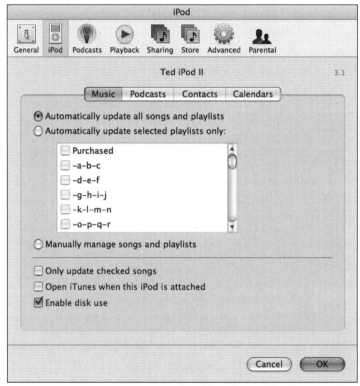

Figure 11.10

The iTunes iPod Preferences pane lets you customize your iPod syncing.

TAKE NOTE ▶ iPod Preferences for the iPod shuffle

When you connect an iPod shuffle to your Mac, you see a different set of iPod preferences than when you connect a full-size, mini, or nano iPod. Instead of a series of tabs for Music, Podcasts, Contacts, and so on, the iPod shuffle has a single settings pane, which includes the following options:

• **"Open iTunes when this iPod is attached" and "Only update checked songs."** These options are the same as those for larger iPods.

• **"Keep this iPod in the source list."** With this option enabled, your iPod shuffle's "playlist" remains in the Source list even when the shuffle is disconnected. You can edit the shuffle's contents as desired; the next time you connect the shuffle, it will be synced with this playlist.

continues on next page

TAKE NOTE ▶ iPod Preferences for the iPod shuffle *continued*

- **"Convert higher bit rate songs to 128 kbps AAC for this iPod."** If you check this box, when songs are copied to your iPod shuffle, iTunes will first check for tracks encoded at a bit rate higher than 128 Kbps AAC. It then creates *copies* of those tracks, re-encoded at 128 Kbps AAC to reduce their size, and copies the lower-bit-rate versions to the shuffle instead. (Your original files remain untouched.) This feature lets you keep higher-bit-rate (that is, larger) music files in your iTunes Library while allowing you to copy as many tracks to your iPod shuffle as possible.

- **"Enable disk use."** This feature is similar to the one of the same name for larger iPods, with one significant difference. Because the iPod shuffle's capacity is so small, iTunes requires that you decide *how much* of the shuffle should be used for music versus data. Below the "Enable disk use" check box is a slider with More Songs on the left and More Data on the right. As you slide the control left or right, the slider tells you approximately how many songs and how much data will fit on your iPod shuffle at each setting. After you choose the appropriate tradeoff and click OK, the iPod shuffle playlist in the Source list is updated to reflect the new "music" capacity.

iPod Note Reader. With iPod 2.x software and later, you can also store text notes on your iPod. To do so, first enable disk use in iPod Preferences in iTunes. Then copy your text notes to the Notes folder at the root level of the iPod. The notes will now be visible via the Notes item in the iPod's main menu. For more information on the iPod's Note Reader, check out the following PDF file: http://developer.apple.com/hardware/ipod/ipodnotereader.pdf.

iPod settings. The iPod itself has preferences settings that you access via the Settings menu on the iPod. These include, for example, the Shuffle, Repeat, and Sound Check settings. Because these are not Mac OS X–specific features, I won't be covering them in this book. For more help with these features, search Apple's Knowledge Base documents at www.apple.com/support.

iPod shuffle. The iPod shuffle, unlike other iPods, doesn't support contacts, calendars, or notes—mainly because it doesn't have the screen on which to view them! It also syncs your music a bit differently. When you connect an iPod shuffle and then select it in the Source list, you'll notice at the bottom of the Song list a few settings not visible for other iPods. The most significant is a button called Autofill. Because the iPod shuffle's capacity is so much smaller than that of other iPods, iTunes assumes right off the bat that it won't hold all your music. In addition, because the shuffle doesn't support multiple playlists, you don't get the same choices for syncing music. You could manually drag just those tracks you want to copy to your iPod shuffle, but the latest versions of iTunes include a feature specifically for the shuffle called Autofill. To use this feature, first you choose a playlist from the "Autofill from" pop-up menu; then you choose the settings for how iTunes should choose songs ("Replace all songs when Autofilling," "Choose songs randomly," and "Choose higher rated songs more often"). When you click the Autofill button, iTunes will automatically generate a new playlist of songs, small enough to fit on your iPod shuffle, based on the criteria you chose. (If you're not happy with the choices iTunes has made, click the Autofill button again to get a new sampling.) iTunes will copy those tracks to the iPod shuffle immediately or, if your shuffle is not currently connected, the next time you connect it.

This last part is also a feature unique to the iPod shuffle: Once you initially connect your shuffle, its icon remains in the Source list unless you choose to remove it. This allows you to modify your shuffle's content even if the shuffle is not connected (as covered in "Take Note: iPod Preferences for the iPod Shuffle," earlier in this chapter).

Multiple iPods, multiple Macs. You can sync an iPod with just one particular computer. The iPod is said to be *linked* to that Mac. If you connect it to another computer, when iTunes is launched, a dialog will appear, asking you if you want to associate the iPod with that computer, wiping out the iPod's music content and replacing it with the iTunes Library of the new computer!

If you say OK here by mistake, you will erase all the music on your iPod, so be careful. This feature also means there's no way to copy songs from different iTunes Libraries (from different Macs) to the same iPod (or, vice versa, to use your iPod to copy songs from one Mac to another, as noted below).

Figure 11.11

The message that appears in iTunes if you connect an iPod to a Mac other than the one to which it is "linked" in iTunes.

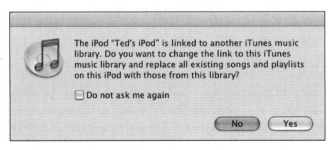

However, you can sync as many iPods with a single computer as you like. If you or your family has more than one iPod, you can all use the same iTunes Library. As mentioned above, each iPod will have its own iPod Preferences. The only caveat is that you need to make sure you give each iPod its own unique name. You can change an iPod's name by double-clicking its name in iTunes' Source list. Note: If you double-click the iPod's icon in the source list, iTunes will open a window showing that iPod's contents.

You can also add music to an iPod from more than one computer. The first computer you attach to your iPod is treated by the iPod as the "home" computer. It is the one that the iPod syncs with (getting new music each time you connect to it). When connecting to another computer, the iPod will offer to sync to it via Auto-Sync. Decline this invitation, or this new computer will become the "home" computer, and all existing content on the iPod will be erased and replaced (as described above). Next, open iTunes' Preferences and click the iPod icon in the toolbar. From here, select "Manually manage songs and playlists," if it is not already selected. You can now drag songs to the iPod from the iTunes Library. However, these songs will not be able to be transferred back to your home computer, automatically or manually. Also, if you later re-enable automatic updating on your home computer, the songs you placed on the iPod from other computers will be lost.

More generally, the iTunes application prohibits you from copying music from an iPod to a Mac. This is a form of copy protection, designed to prevent an iPod owner from using the iPod to transfer music to a friend's computer. While I am by no means suggesting that you break any copy-protection laws, it must be noted that this is a very weak form of copy protection. For starters, you could obviously transfer music to a friend's computer via an external hard drive, a burned CD, or any other portable media. Second, you can even use your iPod to transfer music files; there are two ways to do this:

- You can access and copy the invisible music files on your iPod. Once you've done this, you can install them in the iTunes Library just as you would any other music you added to your hard drive.

  SEE: • "Take Note: Where Is My Music?" later in this chapter.

- You can use a third-party utility that permits iPod-to-Mac copying. My preferred choice here is a utility called Senuti, from Whitney Young (http://wbyoung.ambitiouslemon.com/senuti). Others include Findley Designs' iPod Access (www.drewfindley.com/findleydesigns/ipodaccess/index.html), Sci-Fi Hi-Fi's PodWorks (www.scifihifi.com/podworks), and KennettNet's PodUtil (www.kennettnet.co.uk/software/podutil.php). These automate and simplify the procedure, allowing you to restore both songs *and* playlists from your iPod to iTunes.

Using an iPod on Macs and PCs: iPod formats. An iPod will function as a music player on a given platform only if it is formatted properly. It should be in either Mac OS X Extended (HFS Plus) format (for a Mac) or FAT32 format (for a Windows PC). Further, to ensure that all is done correctly, any reformatting/restoring of an iPod should only be done using the iPod Updater application for that platform, not utilities such as Mac OS X's Disk Utility.

Starting with third-generation iPods, the first time you connect most factory-default iPod models to a computer, they will be reformatted as needed for the computer's platform (Mac or Windows). That's why there is only one iPod model sold for both Macs and PCs. Once the iPod is formatted and used for one platform or the other, Apple implies that it can be used only with that platform. However, despite Apple's warnings, an iPod formatted with FAT32 should still work on a Mac (unless you try to use it as a bootable drive). And you can get a Mac-formatted iPod to work on a PC via third-party software such as Mediafour's XPlay 2 (www.mediafour.com/products/xplay).

In any case, you can always use the Restore feature of the iPod Update software to change the iPod's format if desired (although this will erase all your music on the iPod), and thus "officially" switch platforms. For example, the iPod nano comes preformatted for Windows (FAT32). Normally, the first time you connect it to a Mac, it will reformat itself automatically for the Mac platform (a dialog will appear that says it is "optimizing your iPod for Mac OS X"). However, if you connect an iPod nano to a Windows PC before ever connecting it to a Mac, this automatic reformatting does not occur when you later connect it to a Mac. To switch this nano to a Mac format, you will need to use the Restore function.

The iPod shuffle is another partial exception to the above rules. Whether used on a Mac or a Windows PC, it works as a music player only when formatted as FAT32. The FAT32 requirement for the iPod shuffle is related to why the shuffle does not mount in the Finder unless you've set aside part of the shuffle's storage for disk use.

Note: For details on how to check the current format of an iPod, see this Apple Knowledge Base article: http://docs.info.apple.com/article.html?artnum=61672.

SEE: • **"Take Note: iPod Preferences for the iPod shuffle," earlier in this chapter.**

Insufficient space on an iPod. If you have more music in your iTunes Library than can fit on your iPod, and you try to update your iPod using the "Automatically update all songs and playlists" or "Automatically update selected playlists only" option, you'll get an error message stating that your iPod doesn't have enough space to hold all of your songs.

If this is the first time you have tried to sync to the iPod, iTunes will automatically create a playlist (named "iPod Selection") that will fit, and will copy this playlist to the iPod.

On subsequent updates, you will instead get a message that says, "The iPod cannot be updated because there isn't enough free space." You should be given a similar option to create a playlist that fits.

However, you have no control over which particular music gets copied. If you want to decide which music to copy to the iPod, you have several options:

• You can use the "Manually manage songs and playlists" option. With this option activated, you simply drag songs and playlists until the iPod is full. Note: The bottom of the Song list for the iPod shows how much free space you have.

• If in "Manually" mode, you can delete songs from the iPod by selecting them in the Song list or selecting playlists from the iPod Playlist menu in the Source list, and pressing the Delete key.

- You can use the "Automatically update selected playlists only" option, and then choose as many playlists as will fit on your iPod.

- You can take advantage of Smart Playlists, limiting the Smart Playlists by size so that they contain only a specific number of songs or a limited number of megabytes of music.

See this Apple Knowledge Base article for more details: http://docs.info.apple.com/article.html?artnum=93656.

Songs won't copy to the iPod. When attempting to update the contents of an iPod, you may get a message that says, "Some of the songs in the iTunes music library … were not copied to the iPod, because they cannot be played on this iPod," or something similar. Typically, this occurs when there are items in your library, such as certain video files, that are in a format that will not work on an iPod, even though they may work in iTunes.

In one odd case, when I got this error message, it was because a few dozen of my .mp3 files had been mysteriously renamed to have an .mpg extension. These files would not copy. The fix was to rename the files from the Finder to have the correct extension. After that, iTunes still found the files just fine, and they successfully copied to the iPod.

Note: There are several other reasons why music may not transfer to an iPod. For each cause, a warning message should appear, describing the reason. The message will include a check box that, if checked, causes that particular message not to appear again. If you check these boxes but later decide that you want the warning messages to return, you can do so: After connecting your iPod to your Mac, access the contextual menu for the iPod in the Source list on the left side of the iTunes window, and choose the Reset Warnings item.

Music purchased from the iTunes Music Store won't play on the iPod. If you have an older iPod, and songs purchased from the iTunes Music Store and transferred to your iPod will not play, the problem is most likely an out-of-date version of the iPod software. iTunes Music Store tracks are encoded in AAC format, which is only supported by iPod Software 1.3 and later.

To fix this, install the latest version of the iPod software, as described in "Updating and restoring the iPod software," later in this chapter.

Artist names that begin with *The* appear alphabetized under *T*.
If you've updated your iPod to iPod Software 2.0 or later from a 1.x version, artists whose names begin with *The*—The Beatles, The Doors, The Cure, and so on—may appear under the letter *T* in the artist list. In iTunes, in contrast, the same artists are "correctly" alphabetized by the second word in their name (ignoring the *The*).

To fix this, you need to reset your iPod, as described in "Reset the iPod," later in this chapter, to force it to use the iTunes method of alphabetizing.

TAKE NOTE ▶ Where Is My Music?

If you put your iPod into Disk Mode and open it in the Finder, you may find yourself asking, "Where is all my music?" This is because, at first glance, it doesn't appear to be on the iPod. Your music is actually stored in a number of *invisible* folders on the iPod. Apple did this to prevent music piracy—the theory is that if you can't find the music on your iPod, you won't be able to connect it to a friend's computer and give him or her copies of it.

However, there are some legitimate reasons for accessing the music stored on your iPod from the Finder. For example, what if your Mac's hard drive crashes and you lose all of your iTunes music (and you don't have a backup!)? Or what if you're away from your Mac and desperate for some free hard-drive space on your iPod to transport files, so you need to delete a few songs? Or perhaps your computer's hard drive is getting full and you need to delete some music files. In this latter case, you would think you could later simply restore that music from your iPod to your hard drive. However, because the iPod doesn't normally allow you to copy music *to* your Mac, to do so you need to access these hidden folders.

The iPod stores your music in an invisible folder called Music, inside another invisible folder called iPod_Control. Inside the Music folder are *more* invisible folders that contain individual song files. Unlike songs stored on your hard drive, which (if you've selected "Keep iTunes Music folder organized" in iTunes' Preferences) are neatly stored in hierarchical folders in the format Artist/Album/Song, music on your iPod is stored randomly in a series of folders called F00, F01, F02, and so on. This, again, is to make it difficult to find and copy songs from your iPod to a computer.

So how do you get music files from your iPod to your computer? You can do so in any of the following ways:

- You can use a third-party utility, such as Senuti, as described in the main text. This is by far the easiest method.

- You can use a utility, such as Marcel Bresink's TinkerTool (www.bresink.de), that makes invisible files visible in the Finder.

- You can use Terminal to see your music folders. For example, type `cd /Volumes/iPodname/iPod_Control/Music/F00` and then press Return. Now type `ls` and press Return again. This will list all the music files in the F00 folder. You can use the `cp` (copy) command to copy them to your hard drive.

    SEE: • "Multiple iPods, multiple Macs," earlier in this chapter.

    • "Invisible Files: Making Invisible Files Visible (and Vice Versa)," in Chapter 6, for more on invisible files.

    • Chapter 10 for more on using Terminal and Unix commands.

Using an iPod as a hard drive

In addition to being impressive music players and limited PDAs, non-shuffle iPods can be used as portable hard drives. To do so, check the "Enable disk use" option in the Music pane of the iPod Preferences pane, as described in the previous section. Note: The iPod shuffle can serve a similar purpose, as noted in "Take Note: iPod Preferences for the iPod shuffle," earlier in this chapter; however, its capacity is much more limited, and, as noted earlier, it can be formatted only as a FAT32 volume.

Your iPod will now appear on the Desktop as a mounted volume. You can open it just like any other hard drive, copy files to and from it, and even run applications from it. This makes the iPod an excellent means of transferring documents and other data.

Figure 11.12

The Eject button for an iPod in a sidebar.

When you use your iPod as a portable drive, it is still updated by iTunes when you connect it (unless you have the "Manually manage songs and playlists" option enabled). Note: If you select to Manually manage songs and playlists, "Enable disk use" is selected automatically as well.

However, keep in mind that when you store other data on your iPod, this takes away from the amount of space available for storing music. In addition, it means that you must manually eject the iPod before disconnecting it—by either clicking the iPod Eject button in iTunes or ejecting the iPod in the Finder. (Without the "Enable disk use" option enabled, the iPod automatically unmounts when you quit iTunes.)

Disconnect advice. When your iPod is connected to your Mac and mounted, the "Do not Disconnect" message appears on the iPod's screen. Follow its advice. To disconnect the iPod, do one of the following:

* Drag the iPod's icon to the Trash in the Finder (assuming the icon is visible and that iTunes is not running).

* Click the iPod's icon on the Desktop and from the Finder's File menu choose Eject, or click the Eject button next to the iPod icon in the sidebar of a Finder window.

* Launch iTunes and click the button to eject the iPod at the bottom right of the window.

The iPod's screen should display either the main menu or an "OK to Disconnect" message. Now you can disconnect.

If you fail to follow this procedure, an error message will appear on the Mac, warning you that the "disk has stopped responding" or that the "storage device that you just removed was not properly put away." The message will further warn that data on the device may have been damaged. Actually, it's unlikely that any damage has occurred. Regardless, your next step should be to reconnect the iPod and then disconnect it properly. If all seems well with the iPod at this point, it should be fine.

Note: If you unmount an iPod but do not disconnect it from the Mac, you should also be able to remount it by launching Disk Utility, selecting the iPod in the list of volumes on the left, and then clicking the Mount button.

If you try to reconnect an iPod immediately after having one of these disconnect problems, it may appear to connect properly but not show up in the Finder. In such cases, relaunching the Finder typically fixes the problem.

iPod as a bootable drive. Apple concedes that you can install Mac OS X on a full-size iPod and use it as a bootable drive—a potentially great troubleshooting feature since it provides you with a portable emergency startup disk (for booting a Mac that will not otherwise start up from its internal drive) without needing to purchase an additional device. However, Apple also lists this feature as *unsupported*—and most recently warned that "you shouldn't use the iPod as a startup disk." In addition to meaning that Apple will not assist you if you have trouble with this option, it also means (at least with the current software) that you can anticipate having trouble. For starters, neither the iPod mini nor iPod nano will currently work as a bootable drive, even if you succeed in installing system software on it. It also seems that you can use an iPod as a bootable drive only via FireWire (via Apple's FireWire dock connector cable); I haven't been able to get this feature to work via USB. In addition, for the full-size iPod, expect one or both of the following problems:

- When you start up from a Mac OS X Install CD, the iPod is not listed as a device on which you can install Mac OS X.

  If this happens, you can work around the failure by bypassing the Installer and instead installing a backup copy of a bootable volume to the iPod via a utility such as EMC Dantz Retrospect (www.dantz.com), Mike Bombich's Carbon Copy Cloner (www.bombich.com/software/ccc.html) (as described in Chapter 3), or Shirt Pocket's SuperDuper (www.shirt-pocket.com/SuperDuper/SuperDuperDescription.html). This is not as convenient as using the Installer, but it works.

- Assuming that you succeeded in getting Mac OS X to install on your iPod, you may have a problem when later trying to install an updated version of the iPod software. In particular, the iPod update may fail, typically with an error message appearing. Exactly what the error message says may vary depending on the version of the OS you're running, but the net result is that the update will not install.

The main solution here is to select the Restore rather than Update option from the Updater utility (as described in the next section). This unfortunately erases all of the data on the iPod, including system software, but it succeeds where the Update failed. You can now try to reinstall Mac OS X and upload your music files from your iTunes Library.

If you would prefer not to use Restore, you can try simply removing all traces of Mac OS X (including invisible Unix files) from the iPod. However, I have not found this to work reliably; the Update may still fail. Restoring is a safer bet.

Figure 11.13

The iPod Updater application: the message that appears after an iPod is successfully restored.

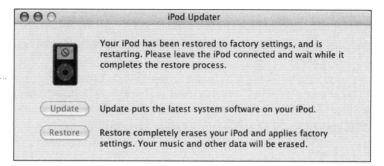

Updating and restoring the iPod software

Apple periodically releases updates to the iPod software. These are completely separate from the music files placed on your iPod via iTunes, and different from updates to iTunes itself. You will typically be notified of these updates when you run the Software Update application. Otherwise, you can always download the latest version of the updater from Apple's Web site at www.apple.com/ipod/download. It's a good idea to make sure your iPod has the latest software. When you download and install the update package, an application called iPod Updater (sometimes with a version number or date as part of the name) is installed in your /Applications/Utilities folder (in a folder called, oddly enough, iPod Software Updater) and automatically launched. You have two options here: Update and Restore.

Updating the iPod. To update your iPod's software, follow these steps:

1. With the iPod connected to your Mac, launch the iPod Software Updater (if it's not already automatically launched). Your iPod should be listed in the iPod Updater window.

2. Check the Software Version line; if it says "up to date," your iPod has the latest version and you don't need to update. If not, click the Update button and provide your administrator's name and password when prompted. The update will be installed, and your iPod will restart.

3. If you're updating iPod 2.0 or later, the update procedure is complete. Quit the Updater application.

   or

   If you're using an iPod with a software version prior to 2.0, disconnect the FireWire cable from your iPod and then reconnect it. A progress dialog will appear on the iPod's screen; once it finishes, the iPod will be updated.

Note the following issues regarding updating an iPod:

• If you already have the same or a newer version of the iPod software installed, the Updater application will alert you and refuse to update. The Update button will be dimmed.

• If you choose not to update when the Updater is launched, quit the application instead. You can relaunch the Updater and update at any future time.

• When an Updater is present in your Utilities folder, but you have not yet installed the update, iTunes will detect the Updater when you launch iTunes and will ask if you would like to install the new version of the software.

• In general, older iPods cannot install the latest versions of iPod software. To get new features that are included in newer iPod software, you will need to get a new iPod.

Restoring the iPod. Restoring an iPod is generally reserved for when you are having problems that cannot be fixed by less extreme measures. Such problems include the following: An attempt to update the iPod fails; resetting the iPod (as described below) fails to get the iPod working again; or an iPod connected to a Mac does not appear on the Mac's Desktop and/or in iTunes. Be aware that restoring your iPod erases the hard drive completely and then restores it to its original factory configuration, except that it installs the version of the software included with the Updater application. Thus, you will want to make sure that any files on your iPod are backed up *before* you attempt a restore.

To restore your iPod's software, follow these steps:

1. Launch the iPod Updater application.

2. Click Restore; provide your administrator's name and password when prompted.

3. If you're using an iPod with a software version prior to 2.0, disconnect the FireWire cable from your iPod and then reconnect it. A progress dialog will appear on the iPod's screen; once it finishes, the iPod will be restored. Otherwise, just continue to Step 4.

4. Your iPod will restart, and a progress dialog will appear on its screen. After this is complete, the iTunes Setup Assistant will appear. Provide a name for your iPod and then select your iPod updating preference.

5. Allow iTunes to update your iPod's contents, and then quit iTunes.

6. Disconnect the iPod from your computer and quit the iPod Software Updater.

7. Your iPod will show its setup screen; select a language using the scroll wheel and click the Select button.

Note: In certain rare cases, an iPod's disk icon may appear in the Finder but not in the iPod Updater and/or in iTunes. If you are running Tiger, and assuming you are using the correct cable connection, the likely solution is rather extreme: Reinstall Mac OS X using the Archive & Install option. See this Apple Knowledge Base article for more details: http://docs.info.apple.com/article.html?artnum=61937. For more general advice regarding iPods' not mounting on your Mac, see this article: http://docs.info.apple.com/article.html?artnum=60950.

TAKE NOTE ▶ iPod Sleep

If you leave an iPod idle for about 2 minutes, it automatically goes to sleep. This is the same thing that would happen manually, if you held down the Play/Pause button for a few seconds. Normally, when you wake the iPod (by pressing any button), it resumes at the point where you left it (such as in the middle of a song). However, for most iPod models, if the iPod has been asleep for more than 36 hours, it goes into a deep sleep (to conserve power). When you wake it from deep sleep, you will see the Apple logo briefly; when the iPod is done waking up, it will be at its main menu, rather than where you last left it. One exception is the iPod nano; it goes into a form of deep sleep called *hibernation* after 14 hours. However, when you wake up the nano from hibernation, it still remembers where you left off.

---

iPod: Problems starting up

The iPod is a rugged, reliable device. Still, you may occasionally hit a snag in which the iPod does not start up as expected. When this happens, you'll get an error message or alert symbol of some sort; the iPod may be unresponsive to its buttons and scroll wheel; or it may appear completely dead.

In a related situation, you may not be able to get an iPod to mount or be recognized when it's connected to a Mac. The result is that the iPod does not show up in the iTunes Source list. Also, you may see a "sad iPod" icon or an "exclamation point with folder" icon appear on the iPod screen. If this happens, start by checking that you are using the correct cable and it is connected to the iPod/dock and the Mac correctly.

Otherwise, try the following fixes, as appropriate for the specific symptom:

Turn the Hold switch on and off. If you have a third-generation iPod—the one with all touch-sensitive controls (with the Back/Menu/Play/Forward buttons arranged horizontally just below the screen)—under certain circumstances, waking the iPod from sleep results in the controls' being unresponsive. Specifically, if the iPod is asleep with the Hold switch in the On position, and you wake it by turning the Hold switch off while touching one of the other controls, the iPod's touch-sensitive controls may not respond. The reason for this is that this iPod model recalibrates its touch-sensitive controls whenever you turn the Hold switch off; if you're touching any of the controls when this recalibration occurs, the iPod doesn't recalibrate properly.

To fix the problem, turn the Hold switch on and then off again, making sure you aren't touching any of the touch-sensitive controls during the process.

Reset the iPod. If your iPod won't respond to any buttons or the scroll wheel, the first thing to do is to make sure the battery isn't simply dead. Plug it into your computer or the power adapter. If it responds, let the battery recharge.

If it doesn't respond, you probably need to reset the iPod. The procedure for doing so varies depending on the iPod model:

1. Connect the iPod to the iPod power adapter or your computer via the dock connector cable or the iPod dock.

2. Slide the Hold switch to the On position (the switch shows a bright orange color) and switch it back to Off.

3. For any iPod with the Click Wheel controller (for example, color iPods, "fourth-generation" iPods, iPod minis, and iPod nanos), press and hold the Menu and Select buttons simultaneously until the Apple logo appears.

    or

    For first-, second-, and third-generation iPods—those with a scroll wheel in the middle surrounded by physical buttons and those with horizontal, touch-sensitive buttons below the screen—press and hold the Play/Pause button and the Menu button simultaneously until the Apple logo appears.

All of your data (music, playlists, contacts, and so on) is saved. A few preferences set using the iPod's Settings menu, however, may be lost.

Note: See the following Apple Knowledge Base article for more details on resetting your iPod: http://docs.info.apple.com/article.html?artnum=61705.

Reset the iPod shuffle. If your iPod is an iPod shuffle, the procedure for resetting it is much different:

1. Disconnect the iPod shuffle from your computer, if connected.

2. Move the shuffle's Off/Play/Shuffle switch to the Off position.

3. Wait at least 5 seconds and then move the switch to the Play or Shuffle position.

The iPod shuffle is now reset.

Update and/or restore the iPod. If even the reset procedure described above doesn't bring your iPod back to life, you may need to update or (more likely) restore your iPod's operating software.

SEE: • "Updating and restoring the iPod software," earlier in this chapter, for details on how to update and restore.

Place iPod in Disk Mode. If the Apple logo appears when you turn on the iPod and then refuses to go away, you likely need to update or restore the iPod. However, with an Apple logo freeze, it's unlikely that the iPod will mount or otherwise respond when you connect it to a Mac (especially if you haven't enabled disk use in iTunes' iPod Preferences). To work around this problem, you need to *manually* put your iPod in Disk Mode. To do so, follow these steps:

1. Connect the iPod to the iPod power adapter or your computer via the dock connector cable or the iPod dock.

2. Slide the Hold switch to the On position (the switch shows a bright orange color) and switch it back to Off.

3. For color iPods, iPods with the Click Wheel control, iPod mini, and iPod nano models: Press and hold the Menu and Select buttons for at least 6 seconds until the Apple logo appears. (This resets the iPod, as described above.) Then release those buttons and immediately press and hold the Select and the Play/Pause buttons until the Disk Mode screen appears.

   or

   For first-, second-, and third-generation iPods—those with a scroll wheel in the middle surrounded by physical buttons and those with horizontal, touch-sensitive buttons below the screen—press and hold the Play/Pause button and the Menu button simultaneously until the Apple logo appears. (This resets the iPod, as described above.) Then release those buttons and immediately press and hold the Previous and Next buttons until the Disk Mode screen or FireWire logo appears.

4. Connect the iPod to your computer via the dock connector cable or the iPod Dock (or FireWire cable for first- and second-generation iPods).

5. The iPod should appear in iTunes and/or mounted in the Finder.

   Note: If at this point a message appears stating that the volume could not be mounted and asking if you want to initialize it, chances are your iPod's hard drive has suffered some sort of damage. Clicking OK will erase all of the data on your iPod—but your data is probably hosed at this point anyway. So click OK and then choose the Mac OS Extended/HFS Plus format.

6. Update or restore your iPod, as appropriate. If you erased the iPod's data, only a restore will work. You may also need to reset the iPod to get it working normally again. All of these procedures are described earlier in this chapter.

For more information on Disk Mode, see the following Apple Knowledge Base article: http://docs.info.apple.com/article.html?artnum=93651.

If your iPod is still not up and running, it's time to consider getting it repaired. You can take it to an Apple Store or visit Apple's online repair page at http://depot.info.apple.com/ipod.

"Disk scan" icon appears when iPod is turned on. If, when you turn on your iPod, a screen with a disk and a magnifying glass appears, this means that the iPod has found a problem with its hard drive and is in the process of examining and, if possible, repairing it. Once the procedure is complete (which can take as long as 20 minutes, so be patient), one of the following icons will appear:

- **Disc with check mark.** No problems were found.

- **Disc with right arrow.** Serious problems were found but repaired. You should restore your iPod using the procedure described above in "Updating and restoring the iPod software."

- **Disc with alert symbol (exclamation point).** Diagnostics failed and will be repeated the next time you turn the iPod on.

- **Disc with "x" symbol.** Diagnostics were canceled by the user and will be repeated the next time you turn on the iPod. You can cancel diagnostics by holding down the Select button for 3 seconds or longer.

- **iPod with alert symbol.** The iPod is damaged and cannot be repaired. You most likely will need to get it serviced by Apple.

Folder with alert symbol appears when iPod is turned on. If you see a folder with an alert symbol (exclamation point) when you turn on your iPod, this can indicate any of the following problems:

- **Near-dead battery.** To fix this, connect your iPod to the power adapter or to your computer to charge it. (You may see a battery icon with a warning sign over it; this also means your iPod's battery is dead.)

- **iPod needs to be reset.** Your iPod may simply need to be reset. To do so, use the procedure described previously in "Reset the iPod."

- **Hard drive has been reformatted or erased.** If you erased or reformatted your iPod from the Finder, the iPod software may be missing and/or you may have chosen an incorrect hard-drive format. Reformat the iPod in the Finder as Mac OS X Extended (HFS Plus) format and restore the iPod using the procedure described previously in "Updating and restoring the iPod Software."

- **Incorrect iPod software version.** You may have installed a version of the iPod software that is too old for your iPod. To remedy this, update your iPod's software using the procedure described previously in "Updating and restoring the iPod software."

- **Serious damage.** Your iPod may have a hardware failure or other serious damage that requires service.

Figure 11.14

Examples of iPod error screens: left, *Disk Scan icon;* right, *Disk Scan Failed icon.*

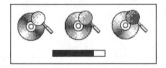

iPod: Battery issues

Among the most commonly reported problems with iPods—accurately or not—are battery issues, especially problems with charging and shorter-than-expected battery life. I don't have the space to discuss this problem in depth, but I do want to mention a few things. The first is that the batteries used in the iPod, just like any batteries, have a finite lifespan; they simply don't last forever. According to Apple, this lifespan is 300–500 *discharge cycles*, where a single cycle is a complete discharge of the battery. In other words, if you run your iPod's battery down halfway, charge it, and then run it down halfway again, that's only a single discharge cycle. If your iPod is more than a year or two old, or if you run the battery down very frequently, it will not have the same battery life it had when it was new—shortened battery life is to be expected.

For more on the iPod's battery, see www.apple.com/batteries/ipods.html and http://docs.info.apple.com/article.html?artnum=62018. For tips on getting the most life out of the battery, see http://docs.info.apple.com/article.html?artnum=61434. If, after reading this information and following the tips provided, you're convinced that your battery is not operating normally, you should contact Apple. I suggest taking your iPod to a local Apple Store, if possible—if your iPod is still under warranty, the Genius Bars have been known to replace truly defective iPods on the spot. If your iPod is out of warranty, and you didn't purchase an AppleCare protection plan (which also covers batteries), Apple has a battery-replacement service; more details are available at www.apple.com/support/ipod/service/battery. Numerous third-party vendors also provide battery-replacement services, as well as replacement batteries you can install yourself.

As for problems whereby your iPod battery won't even charge, Apple has a helpful Knowledge Base article describing a number of possible causes and solutions, at http://docs.info.apple.com/article.html?artnum=60941. Interestingly enough, only two are actually problems with the iPod; the rest are problems with low-powered and faulty computer ports, with faulty cables and adapters, and with computers' sleeping. (For example, the iPod should charge when connected to your Mac, even if the Mac is asleep. However, if this does not seem to be working, either wake up the Mac or connect the iPod directly to a power outlet, via Apple's iPod AC power adapter.)

Troubleshooting iPhoto

iPhoto is the image spoke of Apple's digital hub. It allows you to organize, edit, and share your digital images, and is one of the most widely used and praised iApps. However, it's also one of the most widely criticized—primarily due to a few quirks as well as its reputation (prior to iPhoto 4.x) for slow performance once you've acquired a large number of photos.

The first time you launch iPhoto, you'll see a "welcome" dialog asking, "Do you want to use iPhoto when you connect your digital camera?" If you click

Use iPhoto, iPhoto will launch whenever you connect your digital camera to your Mac. If you click Use Other, you can import photos from your camera using your camera's software or a digital-media reader, or by importing them manually (as described below). You can hold off on making a choice by clicking Decide Later.

Figure 11.15

iPhoto's initial setup dialog.

The main iPhoto window has five distinct areas: the Library/Album Source list in the upper left portion; the main image-viewing pane; the Information box just below the Library/Album list; the *control bar* items, which are listed horizontally below the Information box and image-viewing pane; and the *toolbar* along the bottom of the window. In many ways, iPhoto looks much like iTunes; it works similarly as well.

Note: iPhoto's interface seems to undergo significant changes with each version. I cover version 5.x here; new versions may have slight differences.

Source list and main image-viewing window. The Library/Album Source list on the left side of the iPhoto window provides quick access to your Photo Library (the main library containing all of your images), as well as any albums you've created.

- **Library.** Select Library to see all of your photos in the viewing window to the right. Click the disclosure triangle to see a sublist of photos, typically organized by year.

- **Last Roll.** Select Last Roll (Last Import in older versions of iPhoto) to view only those images you added to your Photo Library during the most recent import.

- **Albums.** Select any listed album, and the viewing pane shows just the images contained in that album. (For more about creating albums, see the discussion a bit later in the chapter.)

- **Trash.** The Trash item is the last item in the Library/Album list. It contains any images that you've deleted from your main Photo Library.

  The only time a photo is moved to the iPhoto Trash is if you delete it from your main Photo Library; deleting an image from an album *does not* move it to the iPhoto Trash. This is because when an image is added to an album, iPhoto references that photo from your main Photo Library; deleting an image from an album simply deletes the reference. The photo itself remains in your Photo Library. This also means that to permanently delete an image from iPhoto, you need to delete it from the Photo Library.

  The iPhoto Trash works independently of Mac OS X's Trash. To empty the iPhoto Trash, you must choose Empty Trash from the iPhoto menu.

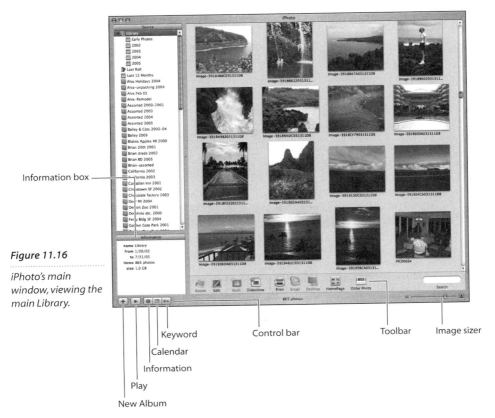

Figure 11.16

iPhoto's main window, viewing the main Library.

Information box. Just below the Library/Album list is the Information box, which displays information about whatever item is selected—an item from the Library/Album list or a photo in the viewing window. In the case of an album, it allows you to rename the album. In the case of an image, it lets you rename the photo as well as change the date and rating. (If you change the name or date on a photo, that information is changed everywhere that photo occurs within iPhoto—that is, in the main Photo Library as well as in any albums.) You can also use the Information box to add comments to an album or photo(s).

Control bar. The control bar provides a few important controls that let you work with albums and photos.

- At the far left, the New Album (+) button adds a new album to the Library/Album list. Just as in iTunes, holding the Option key down when you click this button instead creates a new Smart Album, discussed below.

- The Play button (the one with the side-facing triangle) starts a full-screen slide show using whichever album is selected above, including the main Photo Library. After clicking the button, you'll be presented with a dialog with two tabs (Settings and Music) for customizing options such as transitions, speed, and music selection.

- To the right of the Play button is a trio of related buttons.

  The Information button (the one with the lowercase *i*) toggles the Information box on and off.

  Next to that is the Calendar button—the one that looks like a small calendar. When you click this button, the Information box is replaced by a Calendar view that lets you navigate to a particular year, month, or even date; the contents of the main image-viewing pane are then *filtered* by that time period. For example, if you select your main Library in the Source list and then select December 2004 in the Calendar, the main image pane will show only those photos in your Library that were taken in December 2004. This filtering is based on the creation date of each photo as set by your digital camera, so if your camera's date and time are incorrect, this feature is much less useful. If you first selected an album, only images in that particular album taken during that time period will be shown.

  Finally, to right of the Calendar button is the Keyword button. It works just like the Calendar button except that it filters pictures by keywords that you've given them (see "Arranging and sharing your photos," later in this chapter).

- The text in the middle of the control bar tells you how many photos are in the currently selected album (or Library), as well as how many images are selected, if any.

- The slider at the far right end of the control bar changes the size of images in the viewing pane. If the slider is all the way to the right (largest), you'll only be able to view a single image at a time, and it will fill the entire viewing area. If the slider is all the way to the left, images will be quite tiny—you will be able to see many of them, but they may be too small to differentiate. You can choose any size in between to find one that offers you the best compromise between detail and number. You can quickly toggle the size of images using the keyboard: 0 moves the slider all the way to the left, 1 moves it to the far right, and 2 switches to iPhoto's "native" size, which is approximately ⅑ of full size.

TAKE NOTE ▶ The iPhoto Library

Like the iTunes Library, the Photo Library item in iPhoto represents your iPhoto image library. This library is actually a folder located in your home directory at ~/Pictures/iPhoto Library. Unfortunately, unlike in iTunes, this folder is not organized in a way that will make immediate sense to most people. Photos are organized in folders by year; within each year folder are month folders, and within each month folder are day folders. Within each of *those* folders are loosely stored images and a folder called Thumbs that stores thumbnails for these images. In addition, at the root level of the iPhoto Library folder are a slew of other folders and files that store data for keeping track of image information and changes made to those images.

Original vs. cropped images. If you make any changes to a photo using Edit mode, an additional folder will be added to that day's folder, called Originals. iPhoto makes a copy of the original image and moves it into this folder before making changes to the image. This is how iPhoto allows you to revert to the original photo (via the Revert to Original command in the Photos menu) if you decide you aren't happy with your edits.

Back in the main iPhoto Library folder, there's a file called AlbumData.xml and a folder called Albums. These two items contain all the information about albums that you create in iPhoto. Apple has a bit of information about this organizational structure in the following document: http://docs.info.apple.com/article.html?artnum=61262.

Backing up your iPhoto Library. If you want to back up your iPhoto Library, you can periodically copy it to another hard drive or burn it to CD or DVD. You can also use a dedicated backup utility to back it up regularly.

Moving your iPhoto Library to a different volume. If you decide you want your iPhoto Library on a volume other than the startup disk (perhaps because your startup disk is getting low on space or you want to put your iPhoto Library on an external FireWire drive so that you can take it with you), you can follow these steps to do so:

1. Navigate to your Pictures folder in the Finder (~/Pictures).

2. Drag the iPhoto Library folder to the destination volume, and wait for the copy to complete.

3. Rename the iPhoto Library on your startup disk (the original library) to something like Original iPhoto Library.

continues on next page

TAKE NOTE ▶ **The iPhoto Library** *continued*

4. Launch iPhoto; you'll see an error message dialog saying that your Photo Library cannot be found, asking if you want to create a new Library or choose an existing one.

5. Click the Choose Library button in the alert dialog.

6. Navigate to the iPhoto Library on the alternative drive (in other words, find the "new" Library you just copied).

7. After you've selected the new iPhoto Library folder, click the Open button.

Your new iPhoto Library, located on a different volume than your startup disk, should now be used whenever you launch iPhoto. After verifying that everything is working properly, you can delete the Original iPhoto Library by dragging it to the Trash.

Note: If you place your iPhoto Library on a different volume, you must make sure that the volume is accessible before you launch iPhoto or any other iLife application that accesses your iPhoto Library. For example, if you place your iPhoto Library on an external FireWire drive, make sure the drive is connected and mounted in the Finder.

Using multiple iPhoto Libraries. If you have so many photos that iPhoto is starting to slow down, one solution is to have more than one iPhoto Library. You can do this manually, or you can use a third-party utility. To manually use multiple libraries, follow these steps:

1. Make sure that iPhoto is not currently running.

2. Navigate to your current library at ~/Pictures/iPhoto Library.

3. Rename the iPhoto Library folder; use something meaningful that will allow you to differentiate between libraries once you have more than one (for example, Original Library or Library #1).

4. Launch iPhoto. You'll get a message stating that iPhoto cannot find your Photo Library and presenting you with three options: Quit, Create Library, or Choose Library. Click Create Library, and iPhoto will launch using a brand-new Photo Library. The new library will be located at ~/Pictures/iPhoto Library, just like your original.

5. After working with your new Photo Library, quit iPhoto, and then rename the *new* iPhoto Library folder.

6. If you want to create more iPhoto Libraries, repeat Steps 4 and 5 as necessary.

Now, whenever you launch iPhoto, you'll see the "Photo Library was not found" dialog. From this point on, click Find Library and then choose whichever library you want to use.

If you want to automate this process, a number of utilities have sprung up to make it easier. Some of the most popular are BubbaSoft's iPhoto Buddy (http://nofences.net/iphotoBuddy), Brian Webster's iPhoto Library Manager (http://homepage.mac.com/bwebster/iphotolibrarymanager.html), and Luc Regnault's MorePhotoLibs (http://regnault.luc.free.fr/MorePhotoLibs_1.0.html).

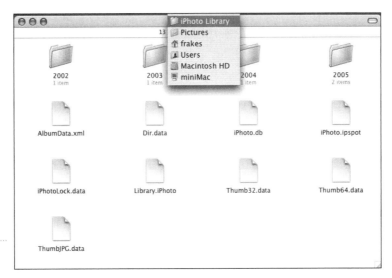

Figure 11.17

The iPhoto Library
folder in ~/Pictures.

Toolbar. The bar at the bottom of the main image-viewing area, which Apple
calls the *toolbar*, contains icons for tools and actions; its contents change depending on whether you're in standard or Edit mode. I'll discuss these contents
when I talk about arranging and editing your photos, below.

Figure 11.18

The toolbar area of iPhoto's main window.

Importing photos into iPhoto

iPhoto allows you to import photos into your Library in several ways; you can
choose the one that works best for you. If a photo is in JPEG (.jpg) format
when you import it, it will remain in that format. However, images that you
import in other formats (RAW, GIF, TIFF, PICT, and so on) will be converted
to JPEG.

Importing directly from a digital camera. You can import your photos
directly from your digital camera by connecting your camera to your Mac
(usually via a USB cable) and launching iPhoto. The latter may happen automatically, depending on your settings. Your camera will appear in the Source
list, and the main viewing area will show a camera and the text "Ready to
import # items" (where # is the number of photos on your camera). After
naming the "roll" to be imported and giving it a short description, you simply
click the Import button; iPhoto will copy photos from your camera to your
Library. During the transfer, a small preview window displays each photo as it

is being transferred; the progress bar shows how many photos remain to be transferred. Once importing is complete, the new photos will appear in your Photo Library. You can view them via the Last Roll item in the Source list. Alternatively, if you have chosen to view by Film Rolls (from the View menu), the newly imported photos will be listed within a new roll designated by the import date and the title you provided earlier.

The Import function provides the option "Delete items from camera after importing"; however, if iPhoto runs into a problem when attempting to add the imported photos to your Library, you could lose your photos. Thus, I recommend *not* using this option. Once you're sure that your photos have been imported successfully, you can delete them from your camera manually (using whatever procedure your camera uses to delete photos). Although iPhoto supports a wide range of digital cameras, it does not support every model on the market. A list of supported cameras is available at www.apple.com/macosx/upgrade/cameras.html. If your digital camera is not supported, chances are your camera uses some form of removable digital media (CompactFlash, Memory Stick, Microdrive, MultiMedia Card, SmartMedia, Secure Digital, and so on) that can be mounted in the Finder via an inexpensive digital-media reader (USB, FireWire, or PC Card). You can thus take advantage of the process explained in the next section ("Importing via the Finder") to import your photos into iPhoto.

Importing via the Finder. If you have an image, or a folder full of images, already on your Mac, you can import them into iPhoto by choosing Add to Library from the File menu and then navigating to an image or folder of images. Even easier, you can add photos to your Library by simply dragging them into the iPhoto Source list or onto the iPhoto icon in the Finder or Dock: Dragging a photo or folder of photos to the Library or to the iPhoto icon simply adds them to the Library; dragging to an existing album adds the photo(s) to that album; dragging images or a folder of images to an open area of the Source list creates a new album containing those images. In the latter two scenarios, the photos are also added to your Library, of course. (For more on albums, see "Arranging and sharing your photos," below.)

When you import images into iPhoto from the Finder, the original photos aren't modified. Instead, a copy of each photo is created in your iPhoto Library folder. The original photos remain untouched.

Each time you drag an image file, or folder of images, into iPhoto, a new "roll" is created. Thus, if you want a group of images to appear in the same roll, be sure to either drag them at the same time or place them in a folder and then import that folder. When you import a folder, the new "roll" is given that folder's name.

TAKE NOTE ▶ **iPhoto Image Formats**

iPhoto supports a number of image formats, but the support varies depending on whether you're importing, exporting, or editing.

iPhoto can *import* any photo format supported by QuickTime, including BMP, GIF, FlashPix, JPEG/JFIF, MacPaint, PICT, PNG, Photoshop, RAW, SGI, Targa, and TIFF.

iPhoto can *export* photos as JPEG, PNG, or TIFF images.

Finally, when editing a photo within iPhoto (including rotating it), GIF and RAW images are converted to JPEG images. All other images retain their original file formats.

Import warning. If you try to import formats other than the ones noted above (including non-graphic files, graphic files in an unsupported format, and damaged files), you will likely get a warning message when you try to import the file(s).

CMYK photos don't print properly. iPhoto can import photos created or edited using other photo and graphics applications; however, if photos have been saved using the CMYK format, you should convert them to RGB format before importing them. CMYK photos will not print properly from iPhoto (either directly to a printer or when ordering prints or books).

Importing using Image Capture. You can also import photos directly from your digital camera to your hard drive using Mac OS X's Image Capture application—you can then later import them into iPhoto via the Finder. Although most users will be content with using iPhoto, Image Capture offers a few features not otherwise available. For example, you can view all images on your camera before downloading, choose where to save images, and even *selectively* download only certain images. You can also automatically process images—to build a slide show, build a Web page, crop or fit to a specific size, or process with another application or AppleScript. There's not enough space to discuss all of Image Capture's features here, but be aware that it's an option.

Regardless of which method you use to import your photos, if iPhoto finds that the same photo already exists in your Library, it will present a dialog—displaying both the existing and new images—asking whether you want to proceed with the import or skip that image. If iPhoto finds multiple instances of duplicates, you can either handle each import/skip decision individually or choose to import or skip all the duplicates.

Arranging and sharing your photos

iPhoto main viewing area has two modes; the default View mode, designed to help you organize and share your photos; and Edit mode, which allows you to edit your photos. When in View mode (see Figure 11.16), you can browse your photos; selecting your Library or an album in the Source list displays the photos in the source in the main viewing window. From the View menu, you can choose to view photo titles, keywords, and ratings along with the photos themselves; show photos in rolls; and sort photos by roll, date, keyword, title, or rating.

Albums. As I mentioned earlier, you can create new albums by clicking the New Album button (or choosing New Album from the File menu) and then dragging photos from your Library or other albums into the new album. When viewing an album, you can rearrange the order of photos by dragging them around the viewing pane.

You can also create Smart Albums by holding down the Option key down as you click the New Album button. A dialog will appear allowing you to name the new Smart Album and choose the criteria that iPhoto should use to populate the album—image comments, filenames, dates, keywords, ratings, rolls, titles, and so on. Like iTunes' Smart Playlists, Smart Albums are updated in real time—if you create a Smart Album that includes all photos with a rating of 4 or higher, any photos you later rate with a 4 or 5 will automatically be added to that album. Note: You can edit a Smart Album's criteria at any time by selecting it and choosing Edit Smart Album from the File menu. New in iPhoto 5 is the ability to create *folders* in your Source list. Folders, which can hold only albums, are designed to help you better organize your photos. For example, I have folders for family vacation albums, work-related albums, albums of screen shots for books and articles, and so on.

Toolbar. iPhoto's toolbar provides you with a number of options for working with your photos beyond simple browsing. What follows is a brief overview of each icon as it appears left to right in View mode; some of the icons change iPhoto to other modes, each of which has its own toolbar layout:

- **Rotate.** Selecting an image (or multiple images) and then clicking this icon rotates the image(s) 90 degrees. The default rotation direction, clockwise or counterclockwise, is configurable in iPhoto Preferences; holding down the Option key as you click the button temporarily switches the rotation direction.

- **Edit.** This icon switches the main viewing area to Edit mode, discussed in the next section.

- **Book.** iPhoto allows you to order professional-looking bound books of your own photos. When you click the Book icon, a dialog appears, asking you to choose a book theme, a book type (the book's size), and either single- or double-sided pages. (Clicking the Options + Prices icon opens your Web browser to Apple's book-pricing page.) Once you click the Choose Theme icon, a new Book item appears in the Source list. If you were viewing an album when you clicked the Book icon, all the photos in that album will be included in the book; if you had selected a number of photos before clicking the Book icon, only those photos are used.

You then lay out your book the way you want it by dragging photos from the image area at the top of the window to the book layout in the main pane. (The two buttons to the left of the image area let you switch between viewing "unplaced" images or a preview of the book's pages.) Alternatively, if your images are already in the correct order, you can click the Autoflow button to have iPhoto place images automatically.

You'll notice that the toolbar changes when you enter Book mode. The icons available in Book mode allow you to change the theme, the current page type, the page design (if a theme includes multiple designs), and text settings. You can also add more pages. When you're finished, click the Buy Book button to order the book. (You must set up an Apple account to purchase books or photos; if you've already got an account with the online Apple Store or the iTunes Music Service, you can use it.)

Click any album or your main Library to exit Book mode. To go back and edit a book, simply select the Book in the Source list.

Figure 11.19

The toolbar area of iPhoto's main window, after the Book icon (shown in Figure 11.18) has been selected and a Book theme has been chosen from the dialog that appears.

- **Slideshow.** The Slideshow icon lets you create a slide show based on the currently selected album or, if applicable, the currently selected photos in an album or the main Library; the resulting slide show appears in the Source list and remains there until you delete it. When the slide show is selected in the Source list, the toolbar changes to provide you with options for the slide show—you get all of the settings available when you click the Slideshow icon in the control bar, with a few additions, such as the Adjust palette (discussed below) and better customization.

  You may be wondering why you would use this mode to create a "slide-show album" rather than just start a slide show from an existing album via the control bar; there are a few reasons. First, you can create a number of different slide shows, each with its own playback settings. (The Slideshow icon in the control bar requires that you choose your settings each time you start a slide show.) Second, each slide show is basically an album—you can reorder, add, delete, and adjust photos without affecting any other album or your Library. Finally, you can export these slide shows to iMovie and iDVD.

- **Print.** Clicking the Print icon is the same as choosing Print from the File menu. Instead of the standard Mac OS X Print dialog, iPhoto presents a simplified version (called the Standard iPhoto dialog) that allows you to choose the printer, printer presets (if any), iPhoto printing styles (contact sheet, greeting card, full page, and so on), margins, and number of copies. If you would rather use the general Mac OS X Print dialog, click the Advanced button (it's in the row of buttons at the bottom of the standard iPhoto Print dialog).

- **Email.** The Email icon lets you quickly e-mail photos. If you select one or more photos in the viewing pane and select the Email icon, a dialog appears, asking what size you want to use for the photos and whether to include photo titles, comments, or both. When you choose a size, you're shown the total size of the files to be sent. Click Compose, and iPhoto creates resized versions of the selected photos, switches to your preferred e-mail client (chosen in iPhoto Preferences), and then opens a new e-mail message with those photos enclosed as attachments.

- **Desktop.** If you select a photo and select the Desktop icon, Mac OS X will use the photo as your Desktop background. If you select a group of photos and select the Desktop icon, iPhoto chooses one to be the current Desktop image and then opens the Desktop & Screen Saver pane of System Preferences with the item iPhoto Selection chosen as the source for a rotating Desktop image. You then decide how often the Desktop should change—Mac OS X will cycle through all the photos in that selection, either randomly or in order.

- **HomePage.** If you have a .Mac membership, HomePage lets you publish photos as a Web page to your iDisk. Select a group of photos and click the HomePage button to bring up the Publish HomePage window. You can edit the title, as well as captions for each picture, and decide on the layout and columns (if any) you want to use. You can also place a link for e-mailing you, and a counter, on the page. If you've got multiple HomePage sites, you can also choose which one you want the new photo album published to. Click Publish to publish your photo page; you will be provided with the URL to the new page, which you can then share with others.

  Note: iPhoto will publish to the iDisk belonging to the .Mac account entered in the .Mac pane of System Preferences.

- **Order Prints.** The Order Prints icon lets you order professionally made prints of your photos via the Kodak Print Service. To order prints, select a group of photos in the viewing pane (use the Command key to select multiple photos) and then click Order Prints. A window will appear that allows you to select how many of each print, and at which size(s), you want to order. When you place your order, iPhoto will connect to the photo-ordering service via the Internet and then upload your photos and order information.

  Note that if you try to order prints (or a book) and one or more of your photos have a resolution too low to produce good-quality prints or pages, you'll see a warning icon. Apple provides more detail about this in the following Knowledge Base article: http://docs.info.apple.com/article.html?artnum=61025. Apple recommends certain resolutions and certain aspect ratios to get good results. See the following Knowledge Base articles for more information: http://docs.info.apple.com/article.html?artnum=93279 and http://docs.info.apple.com/article.html?artnum=93288.

- **Search.** The Search field lets you find photos in the currently selected album (or your main Library, if selected), based on text contained in each photo's title, filename, keyword(s), comments, or film roll.

There are three other toolbar icons that are hidden by default; you can enable any or all of these icons via the Show in Toolbar submenu of iPhoto's Share menu. Conversely, you can use the same menu to hide any toolbar icons you don't use. The other icons are the following:

- **.Mac Slides.** If you have a .Mac membership, you can publish photos to your iDisk as .Mac slides; other Mac OS X users will then be able to view your slide show as a screen saver by choosing the .Mac screen-saver option in the Desktop & Screen Saver pane of System Preferences and entering your .Mac member name in the Options dialog. Simply select a group of photos, select the .Mac Slides icon (or choose .Mac Slides from the Share menu), and iPhoto will create versions of your photos optimized for the .Mac slide-show feature and upload them to your iDisk. You will then be given the option to "Announce" your slide show; a new e-mail message will be created in your default e-mail client explaining how to view your slide show.

  Note: The images are stored in a folder on your iDisk named Public, located in the Pictures/Slide Shows folder.

- **Send to iDVD.** Selecting the iDVD icon launches iDVD—provided it's installed on your Mac—and creates a new photo DVD project using the selected pictures.

- **Burn Disc.** The Burn Disc icon lets you burn the selected photos to a CD.

Note that the functionality of the following toolbar icons is also accessible via the Share menu: Print, Email, Desktop, HomePage, .Mac Slides, Order Prints, Send to iDVD, and Burn Disc.

Editing your photos

Although iPhoto isn't a full-featured graphics application like Adobe Photoshop, it does provide limited but effective editing functionality. To switch to Edit mode, either select a photo in the viewer pane and select the Edit icon (in the toolbar) or double-click a photo. Depending on which option you've chosen in iPhoto Preferences, the photo will appear in the main iPhoto window and the toolbar will switch to Edit mode, or the photo will open in a new editing window. The main advantage of the "separate window" setting is that it allows you to open multiple images for editing simultaneously. Using Edit mode in the main window, on the other hand, provides a handy scrolling pane of all the photos in the current album/Library; clicking one presents it for editing in the main viewing area.

Note: You also have the option, via iPhoto Preferences, of opening the photo in another application when you double-click it—which means you can actually do your editing in Photoshop, GraphicConverter, or another application.

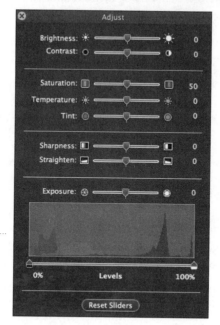

Figure 11.20

Top, *the toolbar area of iPhoto's main window after the Edit icon is selected;* bottom, *the Adjust palette.*

With many of the editing features, you typically start by clicking the desired area of the photo to select it.

- **Rotate.** Use the Rotate icon to rotate the photo 90 degrees.

- **Crop and Constrain.** Clicking the Crop icon crops the photo accordingly. You can use the adjacent Constrain pop-up menu to select a specific size or aspect ratio for cropping. This is useful if you want to prepare a photo for printing on a specific size of paper (such as 4 by 6 or 5 by 7).

- **Enhance.** Clicking the Enhance icon automatically adjusts the photo's color and contrast to match what iPhoto thinks they should be. On some photos, this feature works great; on others, it has little effect; and on still others, it makes the image worse. Try it out; if you don't like the result, simply choose Undo from the Edit menu to revert to the "unenhanced" version.

- **Red-Eye.** If someone in your photo has red-eye, select an area around the eyes and then click the Red-Eye icon. iPhoto will automatically fix it—this feature works quite well.

- **Retouch.** You can use the Retouch feature to "brush out" facial blemishes, cuts, bruises, and so on.

- **B & W and Sepia.** These icons are used for converting a color image to black-and-white or sepia tones, respectively.

- **Adjust.** Clicking the Adjust icon (new in iPhoto 5) brings up the Adjust palette. It provides the most extensive editing features available in iPhoto. You can customize an image's brightness, contrast, saturation, temperature, tint, sharpness, and exposure. (Note: In earlier versions of iPhoto, the only available adjustment options were brightness and contrast.) You can use the Straighten slider to rotate images in increments of 10 degrees or less—great for those photos that are just slightly off-kilter. Note that not all of these options will appear on all Macs; specifically, older Macs with slower processors and/or video cards may see only brightness and contrast controls.

You can always undo your last edit, so feel free to experiment. In addition, as mentioned in "Take Note: The iPhoto Library," whenever you make a change to a photo, iPhoto saves the original. Thus, if at any time you decide you want the original photo back, you can simply choose Revert to Original from the File menu, and iPhoto will delete the edited photo and restore the original.

Once you're finished editing, selecting the Done icon in the Edit mode toolbar to return to the standard viewing mode (or, if you've elected to have photos opened in a separate window for editing, simply close any editing windows).

If you edit a photo in your main Library or in any album, those edits will be reflected everywhere the photo occurs. In other words, if you have the same photo in three albums, changes to that photo in one album will also be reflected in the versions in the other two albums.

SEE: • "Take Note: The iPhoto Library," earlier in this chapter, for related information.

Exporting photos

iPhoto also has an export feature, hidden away in the Share menu (the File menu in older versions of iPhoto). If you select a group of pictures or an album, and choose Share > Export, you'll be presented with a dialog offering three choices: File Export, Web Page, and QuickTime.

- **File Export** exports the selected photos as files. You can choose the image format (Original, JPEG, TIFF, or PNG), the size (if you want them resized), and the naming convention (the filename in the Finder, the iPhoto photo title, or names based on the album name).
- **Web Page** creates a Web site that you can later upload to your Web server (or your iDisk Sites folder) and access via a Web browser. You can choose the title, layout, site colors, and image and thumbnail sizes. The difference between exporting images as a Web site and using the HomePage button is that this option lets you upload the resulting Web site to *any* Web server, whereas the HomePage button works only with a .Mac account.

- **QuickTime** saves the photos as a slide show in QuickTime movie format. You choose the movie-screen size, duration of each slide, background, and whether to add music.

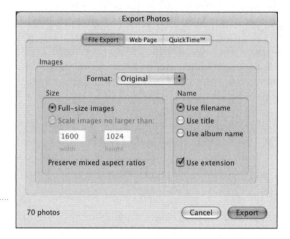

Figure 11.21

iPhoto's Export
Photos dialog.

iPhoto Sharing

In iPhoto 5, Apple introduced an iPhoto Sharing feature. Like iTunes Sharing, discussed earlier in this chapter, iPhoto Sharing lets you share your iPhoto Library with other iPhoto users connected to your local network—specifically, anyone located on the same *subnet* of your network can view photos in your Library and access (but not modify) your albums.

Allowing your photos to be shared. To enable iPhoto Sharing, follow these steps:

1. Open iPhoto Preferences and select the Sharing icon in the toolbar.
2. Check the box next to "Share my photos."
3. Choose either the "Share entire library" option (making your entire iPhoto Library and all albums available to other local users) or the "Share selected albums" option (making only those albums you select accessible).
4. Enter a name for your shared photo collection in the "Shared name" field. This is how the shared photo collection will be displayed in other users' Source lists.
5. If you want to require a password for users to access your iPhoto photos over the network, check the "Require password" box and enter a password.

Accessing photos shared by others. To connect to other users' shared Libraries, follow these steps:

1. Open iPhoto Preferences and select the Sharing icon in the toolbar.
2. Check the box next to "Look for shared photos."

When your Mac detects shared iPhoto Libraries on the local network, those Libraries will show up in the iPhoto Source list just as shared iTunes Libraries appear in the iTunes Source list. To distinguish them from other Sources, the icon displayed for shared Libraries looks like a blue version of our main Library icon and has a tiny lock on it (to indicate that you can't edit or otherwise change the Library's contents). If you click the disclosure triangle next to a shared Library, you'll see all shared albums from that Library. Selecting an album (or the main shared Library) displays its contents in the main viewing area, just as with any of your own albums.

Unfortunately, one limitation of iPhoto Sharing is that only "top-level" albums and folders will appear to users viewing your shared Library. In other words, if you keep most of your albums in folders to keep your Source area organized, those folders will appear to the people you're sharing them with, but the individual albums *in* those folders will not. (The photos contained in the albums will be visible, but they will all appear under the folder as a single "album.") In addition, movies taken with a digital camera—which can be viewed in your local iPhoto Library—are not shared over the local network.

Unlike iTunes Sharing, iPhoto Sharing lets you copy photos from a shared Library to your own. Simply drag the selected images from the shared Library to your own Library (or to one of your own albums); iPhoto will import the images just as if you'd dragged them from the Finder.

To disconnect from another user's shared Library, simply click the Eject icon next to the Library's name in the Source list.

Solving iPhoto problems

The following are some common iPhoto problems, with suggestions for avoiding or solving them.

Don't modify the iPhoto Library via the Finder. In general, to avoid an assortment of problems, do not change anything inside the iPhoto Library folder via the Finder. Use only the iPhoto application to make changes to the folder's contents.

Note: If a problem occurs with your iPhoto Library, fixing the problem may require making an exception to this rule, as evidenced in a few of the items that follow.

iPhoto performance slows. The more photos you add to your iPhoto Library, the slower iPhoto runs. Here are a few tips to help speed things up:

- **Update to the latest version.** With each new version of iPhoto, Apple takes steps to improve performance, so it's best to make sure you're using the latest version. Starting in iPhoto 4, performance improved dramatically.

- **Disable drop shadows.** In iPhoto Preferences, in the Appearance pane, disable all borders. Showing borders seems to slow things down a bit, and if you have a lot of photos, showing drop shadows can *really* slow things down.

- **Hide rolls.** When viewing your Photo Library, use the File Rolls option from the View menu; this groups your photos by roll. You can then use the disclosure triangles next to the roll names to hide any rolls you aren't currently using, which can dramatically speed iPhoto's performance.

- **Use multiple iPhoto Libraries.** If your Photo Library is very large, but most of those photos are ones you don't access frequently, you may want to consider having multiple Photo Libraries. For example, you can keep older photos in one library and newer, frequently accessed photos in another.

  SEE: • "Take Note: The iPhoto Library," earlier in this chapter, for more details on this option.

iPhoto Library disappears or becomes inaccessible. Although this is rare, some users have experienced problems in which their iPhoto Library "disappears"—that is, iPhoto doesn't show any photos in the Photo Library. However, if you look in your iPhoto Library folder in the Finder, all the photos seem to be there. If this happens to you, try the following procedures (in the order listed here) until one works:

- Quit iPhoto and then delete the iPhoto preferences file (~/Library/Preferences/com.apple.iPhoto.plist). Relaunch iPhoto and see if your photos reappear.

- Quit iPhoto and then drag your iPhoto Library folder onto the iPhoto icon while holding down the Command and Option keys. This forces iPhoto to use the selected Library.

- Restore your iPhoto Library from a backup, as some of your data may be damaged.

- If you don't have a recent backup, try iPhoto's built-in "rebuild Library" feature. To access this feature, hold down the Command and Option keys when launching iPhoto. (Note: In iPhoto 4, instead hold down Option and Shift.) You'll see an alert, warning you that you may lose data by using this procedure if there are any damaged photos or data files, but if the above procedures didn't help, this is better than nothing. Note that you *will* lose photo rolls and date information. (I recommend making a backup of your iPhoto Library before performing this procedure; if it doesn't help, you can then revert to the current Library.)

- If all else fails, some users have had excellent results with the freeware utility iPhoto Extractor, from Sean Butler (http://homepage.mac.com/butlers/iPhotoExtractor). Try it.

iPhoto Library doesn't appear in other iLife applications. You may find that your iPhoto Library does not appear in iMovie or iDVD.

SEE: • "Take Note: iLife Application Interactions," earlier in this chapter, for what to do to fix this.

"iPhoto Library not found" error message appears. You may get a message that says: "Your Photo Library was not found. Do you want to find your Photo Library? iPhoto can't continue without a Photo Library. Make sure the disk containing your Photo Library is connected." If you do, it may indeed mean that your iPhoto Library is on a volume not currently mounted. The solution, of course, is to mount the needed volume.

However, the symptom can also occur due to some unexpected causes. Whatever the cause, the solution is the same: Click the Find Library button and locate the desired iPhoto Library folder. Select the folder and click Open.

Duplicate photos imported. Normally, when you attempt to import photos into iPhoto that have already been imported, an alert will appear informing you of this fact. However, if the time/date settings on your camera change between the two imports, iPhoto will assume that the photos are actually different. The solution is to make sure that your camera's date/time settings are correct when you take pictures.

In general, whenever the date and/or time on your camera is incorrect, you may wind up with duplicate imported pictures.

"Unrecognized file type" error. When importing photos, you may get an error message listing files that cannot be imported because "they may be an unrecognized file type or the files may not contain valid data." There are a couple of possible reasons for this. The first is that some of the files may actually not be recognized as valid image files (because they aren't images, or because they're damaged). The other reason is that your hard drive may not have sufficient space available. Check to see if your hard drive has enough free space before importing.

SEE: • "Take Note: iPhoto Image Formats," earlier in this chapter, for more
         details.

Rotated photos not rotated when opened in other applications.
If you rotate a photo in iPhoto and then later drag that photo to another application (such as a word-processing document, an e-mail message, or another graphics application), you'll find that the document "loses" its rotation (that is, it appears in its original orientation). The reason for this is that iPhoto's Rotate command doesn't actually edit the photo; rather, it simply changes the way iPhoto presents the photo for viewing. If you want to use the rotated version of the image in another application, you need to export the photo from iPhoto. To do so, follow these steps:

1. Select the desired photo in iPhoto.

2. Rotate the photo to the desired orientation using iPhoto's Rotate command.

3. From the Share menu choose Export, and then click the File Export tab in the resulting Export Photos dialog.

4. Select your desired export options, and then click Export (provide a name and location for the exported photo when prompted).

5. Open the exported version of the photo in the other application or drag it into the desired document.

Can't access HomePage or .Mac Slides features. If you attempt to use the HomePage or .Mac Slides feature of iPhoto, you may get the following error message: "A connection could not be established at this time. Please ensure your network connection is active and try again." The cause could be that your computer's date and time are set incorrectly. Check to make sure that your date and time are correct in Date & Time System Preferences, and then try again.

Can't order photos from within iPhoto. If you attempt to order photos from within iPhoto, you may get the following error message: "There was an error while accessing your account information. Please check your network connection and try again." The cause could be that your computer's date and time are set incorrectly. Check to make sure that your date and time are correct in Date & Time System Preferences, and then try again.

Corrupt photos or thumbnails. Occasionally, a photo or a thumbnail of a photo may become corrupt. This can lead to crashes when accessing the photo or its thumbnail. Deleting the corrupted file and reimporting the photo (or re-creating the thumbnail) will fix the problem. If you need help with exactly how to do this, I suggest *iPhoto 5 for Mac OS X: Visual QuickStart Guide*, by Adam Engst (Peachpit Press, 2005). In particular, check out Chapter 7, on troubleshooting. It includes tips on this and an assortment of other problems.

TAKE NOTE ▶ Photo-Printing Tips

When you create an iPhoto book, order prints, or print photos on a printer, it seems fairly straightforward: What you see onscreen should be how it looks when printed, right? Not necessarily. A problem may occur if the size of the photo image is different from the size of the paper for the print, or if you have not selected the correct Page Setup and Print dialog settings.

General guidelines. Photos may be cropped or resized in unexpected ways when printed. To prevent this, crop the photo yourself to fit the dimensions of the photo-paper size prior to sending it to Apple or your own printer. Use the Constrain pop-up menu to select the desired aspect ratio. Then, using your mouse, select the desired area of the photo to print.

After selecting (and, if desired, cropping) the photo you wish to print, choose Print from iPhoto's File menu. The initial dialog that drops down should be iPhoto's Standard Print dialog (as noted in the main text). You can choose the Style (such as Standard Prints or Contact Sheet) and Size (such as 4x6 or 5x7) from here.

continues on next page

TAKE NOTE ▶ Photo-Printing Tips *continued*

In general, make sure that both the Page Setup and Print options are properly set up for your printer (and for printing photos) before proceeding. This is especially critical if you have two printers (such as a laser printer for text and a color printer for photos), as settings may have reverted to non-photo defaults since your previous printing from iPhoto. For example, if you are printing to 4-by-6 borderless paper:

1. In the Page Setup dialog, make sure that the desired Paper Size (for example, 4x6 Borderless) is chosen. Note: If the desired option does not appear, it may be because either your printer does not support it or you have not chosen the correct printer from the "Format for" pop-up menu.

2. In the Print dialog, choose the Full Page setting from the Style pop-up menu.

When printing an individual photo, if you still have problems after doing all of the above, click Print and then click the Preview button. This opens the photo in the Preview application. Print the photo from Preview.

Note: Although iPhoto's Book feature allows you to include photos that use any aspect ratio, Apple recommends using only the 4:3 ratio for photos added to a book. To change a photo's aspect ratio, select the photo in an album, click the Edit button, and from the Constrain pop-up menu choose either "4x3 (DVD)" or "4x3 Portrait (Book)."

Page Setup Scale setting does not affect printout. If you attempt to print a photo from within iPhoto, and you change the Scale percentage in the Page Setup dialog, you will find that the photo is printed at its original scale. The reason for this is that iPhoto does not honor the Page Setup Scale setting. To change the size of printed photos, you must access the standard Print dialog and do the following:

1. From the Presets pop-up menu in the Print dialog, choose Standard.

2. From the Style pop-up menu choose Standard Prints.

3. Select the desired printout size next to Size.

Alternatively, you can bring up the Print dialog and click the Preview button to create a preview of the printout in the Preview application. You can use Preview's Page Setup dialog to choose a Scale percentage and then print directly from Preview.

Third-party drivers. Some third-party printer drivers are incompatible with iPhoto's custom print dialog. If your printer is producing printouts that don't match the color, size, or other settings designated in the iPhoto print dialog, make sure you're using the newest version of your printer's driver software (as covered in Chapter 7). If that is not the issue, try using the standard Print dialog, rather than the iPhoto dialog, by clicking the Advanced button in iPhoto's Print dialog. Finally, if that doesn't work, yet again, you can use the Preview button in iPhoto's Print dialog to open a PDF version of the photo in Preview; you can then print from Preview.

SEE: • Chapter 7, for more general information on printing.

Troubleshooting iChat and iChat AV

iChat is Apple's instant-messaging and conferencing client. With it, you can communicate over the Internet with other users (both Mac users and users of other platforms). The original version allowed you to communicate via text messaging using a .Mac or AOL Instant Messenger (AIM) account. The newer version, iChat 3, included with Tiger, lets you communicate via audio and video as well. (iChat AV—aka iChat 2—which shipped with Mac OS X 10.3 Panther and was available as a separate purchase for Jaguar users, also supported AV chat, but with less functionality.) You can videoconference with other iChat users or with Windows users running AOL Instant Messenger.

This section assumes you're using iChat 3. However, older versions of iChat work similarly for text messaging, and iChat AV (2) is fairly similar when it comes to AV conferencing.

To use iChat, you need an account. If you're a .Mac member, you can use your .Mac account name as your iChat user name, in the form *username*@mac.com. (If you previously had a .Mac account but canceled it, you should still be able to use that account name and password for iChat.) Otherwise, you can get an iChat-only .Mac user name (see below), or you can use an AOL Instant Messenger (AIM) account, which you can sign up for at www.aim.com.

When you first launch iChat, you'll be asked to set up the application. Enter your first and last names, select the account type (.Mac or AIM), and provide your user name and password. (Note: If you want an iChat-only .Mac account, click the Get an iChat Account button.) After you click Continue, you'll be asked whether you want to enable Jabber Instant Messaging. (This is a separate messaging protocol from .Mac/AIM. Many organizations use Jabber as their internal messaging protocol; you'll need a separate Jabber account to use this.) You'll then be asked if you want to turn on Bonjour (formerly called Rendezvous) messaging. This allows you to communicate with other iChat users on your local network, even if you aren't connected to the Internet. I generally recommend enabling the "Use Rendezvous messaging" option. Finally, if you have a compatible video camera (such as Apple's iSight or a DV camcorder), you'll be able to see a preview of the camera's video shots.

On subsequent launches of iChat, you should connect (log in) automatically. If this does not happen, choose Preferences from the iChat menu and click the Accounts button; make sure your account name and password are entered correctly. If so, and you still don't log in, and assuming you have the minimum hardware requirements to run iChat, it is most likely a networking issue (as covered in "Solving general iChat problems," later in this chapter, and in Chapter 8).

Figure 11.22

iChat's setup
window.

Figure 11.23

iChat's Buddy
List window.

Chatting: Text, audio, and video

Depending on your setup, you can initiate a text chat, an audio-only chat, or an audio-video chat.

When you first launch iChat, you may automatically log in to your accounts or you may be listed as offline. Which option occurs depends on the setting you select in the Accounts pane of iChat's Preferences. In particular, to automatically log in, check the "When iChat opens, automatically log in" box for the desired account.

You'll see, at the minimum, a Buddy List window. This window lists any iChat buddies you've configured (as explained below) and displays the current status of each (online or offline, available, and so on). If you've enabled Bonjour messaging, you'll also see a Bonjour window. This window lists anyone—buddy or not—who is running iChat on your local network.

Also in iChat's Preferences, in the General pane, select "Show status in menu bar" to add an iChat menu to the menu bar; this menu lets you quickly change your iChat status, even if iChat is in the background. There are, in essence, three status options: Offline (you're not connected), Away (you're connected but away from your desk and thus not replying to requests), and Available (you're at your desk and ready to use iChat). You can initiate a chat if you're listed as Available or Away but not if you're listed as Offline. Your current status is reflected in the status line just below your name in the Buddy List or Bonjour window. If you click the status line, you can change your online status—just as you can with the menu bar menu. However, you can also customize the status message for Away and Available modes by choosing the Custom option in the appropriate section. Choosing Edit Status Menu lets you edit any of your custom changes. New in iChat 3 is the Current iTunes Track status item, which replaces your standard status message with the name of the song currently playing in iTunes, updated automatically whenever the song changes.

If you click your own picture at the top of your Buddy List or Bonjour window, a menu that includes all of your recently used pictures drops down. Choose one to switch to that picture. If you instead choose Edit Picture, you're presented with a dialog in which you can either choose a different picture from your hard drive (by clicking Choose) or take a picture (Video Snapshot) using a connected video camera. Alternatively, you can simply drag a picture onto the picture icon in the Buddy List or Bonjour window.

Note: iChat's Preferences and menus include many more options than covered here. I recommend exploring them to see what is available.

Text chat. To initiate a text chat with another user, from the File menu choose New Chat with Person, and then enter that person's .Mac or AIM address. Once the person accepts, a new iChat window opens, and you can communicate by simply typing a message and pressing Return to send it. You can read the other person's messages in the same window. Your message, and the person's response, are sent and viewed in real time, making messaging much faster than e-mail (assuming you're both online at the same time). Note: New in Mac OS X 10.4.3, .Mac members can enable encrypted chat sessions.

If you plan on communicating with a particular user in the future, a better option is to make that user a *buddy*. To do so, click the Add (+) button in the Buddy List window. This brings up a list of all contacts in your Address Book application's database. If the person is already in your Address Book and his or her contact information already includes an iChat user name, simply choose his or her name and click Select Buddy. Otherwise, click New Person and enter his or her information. That person is now added to your Buddy List: You can see when he or she is online and determine that person's current status (Available, Away, and so on). To initiate a text chat with that person, you simply double-click his or her name in the Buddy List. Alternatively, select a name and click the A (text) button at the bottom of the window.

To send a file to someone with whom you're chatting, simply drag the file into the chat window. (You can also choose Send File from the Buddies menu.) Once the recipient accepts the file, it will be transferred to the folder designated as that person's Downloads folder in Safari's Preferences.

Adding a new user to chat. If you have an active text chat session with someone, you can add people to the chat if you wish. To do so, click the Add (+) button at the bottom of the Participants list to the side of the active chat window. If the list is not visible, choose Show Chat Participants from iChat's View menu.

Audio chat. A Telephone icon next to a buddy's name indicates that the user has a microphone connected and can participate in an audio conference (which works like an Internet telephone)—assuming you have audio capability as well. If you have an iSight camera, you can use its built-in microphone, bypassing the video option. Macs with internal microphones will also work.

To initiate an audio chat, click the Telephone icon next to a buddy's name. That person will get a message that you're trying to initiate an audio chat. If the other user accepts, you can start talking. If that user rejects your invitation, you'll see a message indicating as much.

Note: You can alternatively select a name and click the Telephone icon at the bottom of the window: This will start an audio chat using an iSight camera, even though the Telephone icon is not listed next to the person's name.

Video chat. A camera icon next to a buddy's name indicates that he or she has a video camera connected and can engage in a video chat—again, assuming you have similar video capability, such as an iSight camera or any compatible digital video camera.

To initiate a video chat, click the camera icon next to a buddy's name. Alternatively, select a name and click the camera button at the bottom of the window. That person will get a message saying you're trying to initiate a chat. If your buddy accepts, you can start talking. If your buddy rejects your invitation, you'll see a message indicating as much.

If you have a video camera, but the other person only has a microphone, you can instead select Invite to One-Way Video Chat from the Buddies menu: Even though that person can only *talk* to you, he or she will be able to *see* and hear you just fine.

If you click the camera icon next to your picture at the top of the window, it opens a window that allows you to preview your appearance on camera.

Note: What *you* see is actually a mirror image of yourself. However, the user on the other end of the chat sees your image correctly (for example, text will be readable). This is not a bug; Apple assumes that people are more familiar with seeing themselves in mirror image.

Multiperson audio/video chats. New in iChat 3 is the ability to participate in multiperson audio and video chats. Provided you have a fast enough computer and Internet connection (see the next item), you can host up to three other people in a video chat or up to nine other people in an audio chat. To invite multiple people to an AV chat, you first select the buddies you want to invite, using the Command key to select multiple buddies simultaneously. Then you click either the microphone or camera button at the bottom of the window.

Audio/video system requirements. Sending and receiving audio and video requires more processing power and a faster Internet connection than standard text messaging does. To use the basic one-on-one audio chat mode, Apple recommends a 56K or faster modem connection; however, for video chats, you need at least a DSL or cable modem connection. In addition, you need a Mac with a 600 MHz G3 processor (at minimum) to do any audio or video chatting. Apple provides the following examples of quality versus requirements:

	Standard Quality	Enhanced Quality	High Quality
Window size	352 by 288 to full screen	352 by 288 to full screen	352 by 288 to full screen
Video resolution	176 by 144	176 by 144	352 by 288
Frames/second	15	30	20/30
Processor required	>600 MHz G3	>1 GHz G4	>Dual 800 MHz G4 or a G5
Bandwidth needed	100–500 Kbps	100–500 Kbps	>500 Kbps

Multiperson AV chats have even stricter requirements. To join a multiperson videoconference, you need either a G5 processor, a G4 processor of 1 GHz or more, or a dual-processor G4 of 800 MHz or more; you also need a broadband connection to the Internet. To *host* a multiperson videoconference requires either a G5 processor or a dual-processor G4 Mac of at least 1 GHz; your Internet connection must provide a minimum download speed of 384 Kbps and a minimum upload speed of 384 Kbps.

Solving general iChat problems

In this and the following section, I cover common iChat problems and their solutions. I then discuss a few issues concerning Apple's iSight and digital video cameras.

"Could not connect to Bonjour" error. If you get this error message, or if you can't connect to a buddy in your Bonjour List (even though you know you're connected to a local network), there are three possible causes:

- **You don't have Mac OS X's BSD Subsystem installed.** This should be an issue only if you manually installed Mac OS X, chose a Custom installation, and specifically deselected the BSD Subsystem. (This isn't even possible in Mac OS X 10.4 Tiger.)

- **One of the services Bonjour uses has quit (usually accidentally or unexpectedly).** Restarting your Mac will generally solve this problem.

- **Mac OS X's Firewall is blocking the port needed for iChat to communicate over a local network (ports 5297 and 5298).** If you have Mac OS X's Firewall enabled in the Sharing System Preferences pane, the solution is to go to the Firewall pane and either turn off the Firewall or enable the iChat Bonjour rule.

   SEE: • "Firewall," in "Setting Up System Preferences: Sharing," in Chapter 9, for details on how to open this iChat Bonjour port.

Can't send or receive files via iChat when Firewall is active. Similar to the previous problem, if Mac OS X's built-in Firewall is active, you may not be able to send or receive files to and from other iChat users. If you're only sending or receiving a single file, you can simply turn the Firewall off in the Sharing System Preferences pane, and then turn it back on after sending or receiving the file. If you want to be able to send and receive files at will, you should open the necessary port (5190) in Sharing's Firewall pane.

SEE: • "Firewall," in "Setting Up System Preferences: Sharing," in Chapter 9, for details on how to create a rule to open this port.

iChat and routers. iChat works seamlessly with most Internet routers, including Apple's own AirPort Base Stations. However, in some cases you may get a "network timeout" or "user did not respond" alert message when attempting to use iChat with a Mac connected via a router. If this happens, check to see if there is a newer version of the router firmware that may fix the problem. Otherwise, you will likely need to access the router's Port Forwarding feature and open the same 5297 and 5298 ports noted above.

SEE: • "Using a Router," in Chapter 8, and "Firewall," in "Setting Up System Preferences: Sharing," in Chapter 9, for more details.

iChat problems with proxies. If your Internet connection uses a proxy server, you must set up iChat for proxy use separately from Network System Preferences. In iChat Preferences, go to the Accounts pane and then click the Server Settings button. iChat supports SOCKS 4, SOCKS 5, HTTP, and HTTPS proxies.

Multiple logins. If you are logged in to an AIM account on a Mac running Tiger, and then try to log in to the same account on another computer, you will be automatically logged out from the Tiger-running Mac and logged in on the second computer. No warning message appears. Apple is likely to "fix" this in a future update to Mac OS X 10.4. If you initially log in to a Mac running Mac OS X 10.3.9 or earlier, you instead get a warning; you are given a choice of logging out of the other computer or being logged in at both computers simultaneously.

Additions to Buddy List fail to "stick." The AOL Instant Messenger network limits the number of AIM buddies any user can have. According to Apple, the stated limit is 150 buddies. If you try to add more, you may find that after quitting iChat and later reopening it, the most recently added buddies (those over the limit) either show up incorrectly or don't show up at all. You'll need to delete one or more buddies from your Buddy List in order to add more.

Can't eject a disk after sending a file via iChat. If you send a file located on a nonboot volume (that is, any volume or disk other than the Mac OS X startup disk) to another user via iChat, you may not be able to eject or unmount that volume. You're likely to get an error message to the effect that the disk is "in use." The work-around is to copy files to the startup volume *before* sending them via iChat. Otherwise, you will have to quit iChat and possibly even log out before you can eject or unmount the volume.

Solving AV problems with iChat

Videoconferencing requires open ports. If you're using iChat from behind a firewall, you may find that you can't establish a videoconference with another user outside the firewall. This is because iChat uses ports that most firewalls close by default. If you turned on the Firewall in the Sharing System Preferences pane, you will need to either turn it off or open the needed ports (5060, 5190, 5297, 5298). You should then be able to videoconference with users outside your firewall.

SEE: • "Firewall," in "Setting Up System Preferences: Sharing," in Chapter 9, for details on how to open these ports.

If you're using a hardware router or third-party firewall, you need to open ports 5060, 5190, 5222, 5298, 5353, and 5678, plus ports 16384–16403. Check the firewall's documentation to find out how to open these ports. Apple states, "If that does not work, try opening all ports from 1024 to 65535." However, I don't recommend this, as it opens up thousands of ports, negating much of the benefit of having a firewall at all. If you must do this, do it only temporarily— just while you're conducting the AV conference. For more on iChat's network port usage, see http://docs.info.apple.com/article.html?artnum=93208.

SEE: • "iChat AV and UDP ports," in "Setting Up System Preferences: Sharing," in Chapter 9, for more details.

Poor AV quality over AirPort, part one. If you attempt to audio- or videoconference over a wireless/AirPort connection, you may experience jumpy or choppy audio and/or video. You might even get a message stating that "no packets have been received for the last 10 seconds," followed by a disconnection of your audio- or videoconference. This is generally caused by packet loss, a symptom of a weak wireless connection.

If you open iChat's Connection Doctor—which you access from the Video (or Audio, if no camera is connected) menu—you can verify packet loss by looking at the Statistics section. If one or both of the Video and Audio meters show less than 100 percent, you're probably experiencing packet loss. If possible, connect your Mac to your network or Internet connection via a wired (Ethernet) connection, and try again. If the Quality meters show 100 percent, the problem was a less-than-ideal AirPort connection. If the Quality meters still show packet loss, the problem is most likely with your Internet connection (or a problem with your local network, if you're conferencing with another local user).

Poor AV quality over AirPort, part two. If you have an iBook and are using iChat to audio- or videoconference over an AirPort connection, *and* are using the iBook's internal microphone, you may hear popping noises or severe interference. According to Apple, the iBook's AirPort signal can interfere with its internal microphone. The solution is either to use an external microphone (USB, FireWire, or the microphone built into Apple's iSight camera), or to connect via Ethernet.

Poor audio quality, general. When video chats provide poor audio quality, many users have found success in opening iChat Preferences, clicking the Video button, and changing the selection in the Bandwidth Limit pop-up menu to 500 Kbps. This limits the amount of bandwidth used by the video portion of AV chats, freeing up more bandwidth for the audio portion. One consequence, of course, is that video quality may not be as good, but this is likely an acceptable tradeoff. You may also want to experiment with different values here until you find the one that works best for you.

Audio chats lag or go silent. Some users experience problems in which audio gets choppy and may even halt. One solution that works surprisingly well is for both chat participants to click the Mute button in the Chat window (to mute sound), and then click it again to unmute. This forces iChat to "resync" audio and often fixes the problem immediately.

CRT iMac microphones. The built-in microphones on some CRT-based iMacs do not provide enough gain for iChat audio conferences. Apple suggests using an external microphone or, if you're using Apple's iSight camera, the iSight's own microphone. You can choose between multiple microphones via the Microphone pop-up menu in the Video section of iChat's Preferences.

Disconnecting USB microphone crashes iChat. If you disconnect your USB microphone while iChat is running, iChat may crash. Unfortunately, the only solution seems to be to quit iChat before unplugging the microphone.

No sound from left speaker on PowerBooks and iBooks. If you have a PowerBook or iBook with stereo (left and right) speakers, only the right speaker will provide sound when iChat is in use. This is to prevent audio feedback, since the microphone on these computers is located near the left speaker. It doesn't affect sound quality, since iChat AV audio is transmitted in mono. However, if you wish to hear the audio better, you can connect external speakers or headphones to your PowerBook or iBook.

Solving iSight and other camera problems

iSight microphone not recognized. If you connect an iSight video camera to your Mac while iChat is running, the iSight's microphone may not be recognized by iChat. Quitting iChat and relaunching it generally fixes the problem.

"Your camera is in use by another application" message. If you try to use iChat with an iSight camera but get an error message that the camera is in use by another application, first quit all other applications that might be using iSight, and then quit and relaunch iChat. If that doesn't fix the problem, quit iChat, unplug the FireWire cable from the iSight and your Mac, and then reconnect everything and launch iChat again. The camera should now work normally.

Connecting iSight and DV cameras simultaneously freezes video editing software. If you connect both an iSight camera and a digital video (DV) camera to your Mac at the same time, video editing applications (iMovie, Final Cut Pro, Final Cut Express, and so on) may freeze. This is a known bug, and Apple recommends disconnecting your iSight camera before launching any video editing applications.

DV camera not recognized on G3. iChat does not support digital video (DV) cameras on Macs with a G3 PowerPC processor (older iMacs, iBooks, and PowerMac G3 computers). To use iChat for videoconferencing on these computers, you need to use a dedicated USB or FireWire video camera, such as Apple's iSight.

Problems with other FireWire devices. Many users have reported that having an iSight plugged into their Mac's FireWire port causes problems with other FireWire devices. (iPods connected via FireWire appear to be especially prone to such interference.) The solution is to unplug the iSight when it's not in use. Some users have also had luck purchasing a powered FireWire hub—similar to a standard FireWire hub except that it comes with its own AC adapter and provides power to FireWire devices connected to it—and plugging the iSight into the hub instead of directly into their Mac's FireWire port.

Troubleshooting iCal

iCal is Apple's take on the electronic calendar and "to do" list. In an onscreen calendar, it allows you to schedule events and keep track of tasks, schedule reminders, and publish your events and tasks to the Internet for other users to view. You can also subscribe to other users' calendars, making it a great way for families and small businesses to coordinate schedules.

When you launch iCal, you'll see the main window with the Calendars list and monthly calendar on the left, the current calendar view in the middle, and your To Do list on the right.

You can hide or show the monthly calendar using the New Calendar button in the lower left corner of the window. You can hide or show To Do Items by clicking the Show/Hide To Do List button (it looks like a thumbtack) in the lower right corner or by choosing Show/Hide To Dos from the View menu. You can switch the current calendar view between Day, Week, and Month views, as well as advance the calendar forward and backward in time, using the View menu or the buttons at the bottom of the main window.

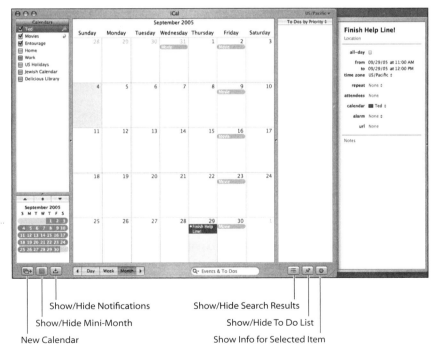

Figure 11.24

The main iCal window, with the Info drawer open to the right.

You can create as many independent calendars as you like. By default, iCal provides you with Home and Work calendars. Clicking the New Calendar (+) button in the bottom left portion of the window (or choosing New Calendar from the File menu) creates a new calendar. By checking or unchecking the box next to each calendar, you can view or hide them in the main calendar area. Selecting a calendar in the Calendars list and pressing the Delete key (or choosing Delete from the Edit menu) deletes it. If you select a calendar and click the Show Info for Selected Item button (the lowercase *i* button in the lower right corner of the main window), the Info drawer will appear on the right of the window. You can edit the calendar name, provide a description, and change the calendar's color scheme.

Calendar Groups. Calendar groups are a new feature in iCal 2. To create a group, either choose New Calendar Group from the File menu or hold down the Shift key as you click the New Calendar button. A new group will appear in the Calendars list. You can then drag calendars to add them to the group. The main advantages of groups are that (a) you can view/hide all the calendars in a group simultaneously, and (b) you can publish multiple calendars to a single calendar.

SEE: • "Publishing and subscribing to calendars," later in this chapter.

Calendar backups. New in iCal 2, you can easily back up your calendars. To do so, choose "Back up Database" from the File menu, and choose a location for the resulting backup (actually a package containing all your calendar data). If you later need to restore your calendars from this backup, use the Revert to Database Backup command, also in the File menu.

Creating, deleting, and editing events and To Do items

This section explains how to create a new event, edit an existing event, and create and edit To Do items.

Creating a new event. To create a new calendar event, follow these steps:

1. In the Calendars list, select a calendar (to determine *which* calendar the event will be part of).

2. From the File menu, choose New Event, or drag your pointer across the time span of the event (for example, from 10 a.m. to 11 a.m.). A new event is created with the name highlighted.

3. Type the name of the event and press Return to enter it.

Deleting an event. To delete an event, select it in the calendar and either choose the Delete command from the Edit menu or press the Delete key.

Editing an event. You can edit an event in two ways:

• To change the time or duration of the event, you can simply drag the event to another time slot, or click the top or bottom edge of the event and drag it to extend or reduce the duration.

- To get much more control over the event, click the Show Info for Selected Item button in the bottom right corner of the main window (or choose Show Info from the View menu).

  As shown in Figure 11.25, you can create and edit events in the Info drawer. From there, you can change an event's title; set the time and date (or set the event as an "all-day" event); set the repeat status (whether or not the event repeats, and, if so, the schedule); indicate whether to set up a reminder alarm, and what type (a pop-up message, audio, sending an e-mail, opening a file, or running a script); decide which calendar the event should belong to; put in a URL to associate with the event; and add any notes you want to include with the event. Note: You can also edit an event's title directly from its listing in the calendar itself.

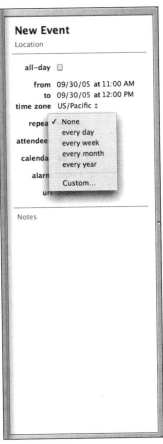

Figure 11.25

Creating an iCal New Event using the settings in the Info drawer; the Repeat pop-up menu is shown.

Creating and editing To Do items.

Creating a new To Do item works in much the same way as the above. However, the Info drawer contains a few different options: You can assign one of three priorities, set a due date, and "check off" the task once it's completed. In addition, by clicking the small icon to the right of a To Do item, you get a menu that allows you to set the item's priority: None, Very Important, Important, or Not Important.

Sending invitations. When you create an iCal event, you can e-mail invitations to the event. To do so, you need to add the e-mail addresses of the people being invited (or names, if their addresses are already in Address Book) to the "attendees" section of the event (accessed by clicking the Show Info for Selected Item button). Alternatively, if you open Address Book, you can drag contacts to the "attendees" space to add them to the event. Once you've added attendees, click the Send button at the bottom of the Info drawer to send out the invitations. Replies to your invitation will appear in the Notifications box (accessed by clicking the Show/Hide Notifications button—the one that looks a bit like an inbox—in the lower left of the calendar window). The Help files for iCal provide more details, if needed.

Searching iCal items. The search field at the bottom of the iCal window lets you quickly search for events and To Do items; the results of your search are displayed in a new pane that appears just above the search field. Click the magnifying-glass icon in the search field to limit your search to just titles or notes; events or To Do items; locations; or attendees.

Importing and exporting calendars

iCal can import calendars from other applications, as well as export its own calendars.

Importing calendars. If you're just starting to use iCal and have information stored in another calendar application, iCal can import a number of standard calendar formats. From the File menu, choose Import; iCal presents a dialog asking which type of calendar you wish to import: iCal file (iCalendar format), vCal file (vCalendar format), or Entourage data.

If you have Microsoft Entourage installed, choose Entourage, and iCal will automatically launch Entourage and import calendar information from it. Otherwise, choose iCal for data stored in the iCal format or vCal for vCal format, and then navigate to the appropriate calendar file. Many third-party applications, including the Palm Desktop application, can export their data in vCal format, thus allowing you to import the data into iCal.

New in Tiger, you can have iCal display all the birthdays listed in the Address Book application. To do so, simply check the "Show Birthdays calendar" box in iCal's Preferences. Any subsequent changes to birthdays must be made in Address Book; you cannot modify them from iCal. Note: If your Address Book contacts do not have a Birthday field, you can add it by choosing Add Field > Birthday from Address Book's Card menu.

Exporting calendars. iCal can also export its own calendars in the .ics format. Saved calendars will have the .ics extension in their names. To export a calendar, first select it in the Calendars list, and then choose Export from the File menu and choose a location to save the resulting .ics file to when prompted. You (or any other user) can then import that calendar into iCal or another calendaring application. (As mentioned above, if you want to combine multiple iCal calendars for export, first place them in a calendar group, and then export the group.)

Publishing and subscribing to calendars

In addition to exporting calendar files, you can publish your iCal calendars on a server on the Internet and allow other users to *subscribe* to them—those users won't be able to change a published calendar, but they will be able to view it and, if you allow them, be reminded by your reminders. You can also subscribe to calendars that others have published.

Publishing calendars. To publish a calendar, follow these steps:

1. Select the calendar you wish to publish in the Calendars list, and then choose Publish from the Calendar menu.

2. In the resulting dialog, provide a name for the published calendar and then choose your publishing options.

   You can choose to have the published version be automatically updated with any changes you make in iCal, as well as whether or not your To Do items, alarms, and/or notes are included in the published version.

3. Choose whether to publish the calendar to .Mac or to "a Private Server"; the latter must be a WebDAV server.

   If you choose .Mac, iCal will use the .Mac account set up in the .Mac pane of System Preferences.

   If you choose "a Private Server"—which really means a WebDAV server— you'll need to provide the URL, login name, and password to connect to the server.

   In either case, once the calendar has been published, iCal will provide you with the URL to give to other users who want to subscribe to your calendar. You'll also be provided with a standard HTTP URL that allows anyone to view your calendar in a Web browser—generally in the format http://ical.mac.com/*username/calendarname* (for those calendars published to .Mac). Once a calendar is published, a Broadcast icon will appear next to the calendar name in the Calendars list.

Figure 11.26

iCal lets you publish your calendars to the Internet for other users to view them.

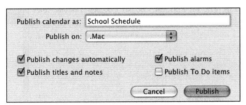

If you decide that you no longer want others to view your calendar, select it in the Calendars list and from the Calendar menu select Unpublish. You can also change the location where the calendar is published by selecting Change URL from the Calendar menu (or by opening the Calendar, clicking the "published" line, and choosing Change URL from the resulting menu).

Deleting a published calendar will also present you with a dialog asking if you want to also unpublish it.

Subscribing to calendars. Just as other users can subscribe to your calendars, you can subscribe to the calendars of other users. There are a couple of ways to do this:

- The first way is to choose Subscribe from the Calendar menu, and then enter the calendar URL in the dialog that drops down. In the next dialog, decide how often you want the calendar to refresh and whether or not to remove alarms and/or To Do items.

- The other way is to click a *webcal* URL (a URL that takes the form webcal://*serveraddress/calendaraddress*) in an e-mail or a Web browser. The same dialog will appear, with the URL already entered. In either case, click Subscribe and the calendar will show up in your Calendars list (with an arrow next to it).

  Where do you get webcal URLs? The most obvious source is other iCal users who have published their calendars. However, Apple provides a huge library of published calendars—holidays, sports schedules, concert dates, TV schedules, and more—to which iCal users can subscribe. To access these calendars, either choose Find Shared Calendars from the Calendar menu (which will open the calendar library in your Web browser) or switch to your Web browser and surf to www.apple.com/ical/library. Click a calendar link in your browser to subscribe.

Refreshing calendars. To refresh a calendar (to see if any changes have been made to it), select it and from the Calendar menu choose Refresh (or "Refresh all" to refresh all calendars). Alternatively, you can Control-click or right-click the calendar and choose Refresh from the contextual menu.

Unsubscribing from calendars. To unsubscribe from a calendar, select it and from the Calendar menu choose Unsubscribe. You can also simply select the calendar and press the Delete key.

Solving iCal problems

Although the most commonly reported iCal problem is sluggish performance, which you cannot do much about, there are a few known issues you can avoid or fix by using the following tips.

iCal's search doesn't find certain events. If your searches in iCal—using the search field at the bottom of the iCal window—aren't finding items that should obviously appear, it's possible that your iCal indexes have somehow become corrupt or otherwise damaged. This may also happen after you update to a new version of Mac OS X; in this case, search fails to find any items created prior to the update. The solution, in all cases, is to delete those indexes and let iCal create new ones. To do so:

1. As a precaution, first back up your iCal calendars via the Backup Database item in the File menu; then quit iCal.
2. Navigate to ~/Library/Application Support/iCal/Sources.
3. Each folder in the Sources directory contains a file named Index; delete each by moving it to the Trash.
4. Relaunch iCal; iCal will rebuild its indexes and the search command should function normally.

Can't edit published calendars if original is deleted. If you deleted a local copy of a calendar that you published on .Mac, changed computers recently, or had to reinstall Mac OS X, you won't be able to use iCal to change the published copy of your calendar. However, the calendar will still be visible to users who have subscribed to it.

To make changes, you will need to re-create the calendar and republish it, using the same calendar name you used the first time you published it; the newly published calendar will replace the previously published calendar of the same name. You can now edit the calendar. Alternatively, you can simply remove the calendar from .Mac. You would think you could use iCal's Unpublish command here, but that won't work if the original calendar file is no longer present. Instead, to remove published calendars from .Mac, follow these steps:

1. From the Finder's Go menu choose iDisk. Your iDisk will appear in the Finder. If your iDisk is already mounted, you can skip this step. If you're using a local copy of iDisk, remember that it needs to sync with the online copy before the change will take effect.

   SEE: • "Using .Mac," in Chapter 8, for details.

2. From the Go menu choose Go to Folder.

3. Type the following: /Volumes/*membername*/Sites/.calendars/ (where *membername* is your .Mac member name).

4. In the window that appears, drag the calendars you no longer want published to the Trash.

Login crash caused by iCal. If your Mac crashes *after* you log in but *before* the login process is complete, the culprit may be a loginwindow process crash triggered by a corrupt com.apple.scheduler.plist file, which is used by iCal and located in ~/Library/Preferences. Log in as root or using single-user mode at startup, and delete the file to fix the problem.

Can't send invitations or reminders via default e-mail client selected in Internet System Preferences. If you try to send an e-mail invitation to an iCal event or set up e-mail reminders, Mail opens—even if you have a different application selected as your preferred e-mail client. Unfortunately, iCal supports only Apple's Mail e-mail client, in conjunction with Address Book, for sending e-mail invitations.

You can get third-party software that modifies the scripts iCal uses so that it can access other e-mail programs, such as Entourage. For example, get ZappTek's "iCal via" utilities (iCal via Entourage, iCal via Eudora, and so on), available at www.zapptek.com/ical-mail. However, undoing this change requires reinstalling iCal or restoring it from a backup.

Invitees aren't notified if you delete an event. If you delete an event after previously inviting others via iCal's Invite feature, invitees will not be automatically notified. You'll need to notify them of the cancellation manually.

"This invitation is not correct" alert. If you receive an iCal invitation in Mail and receive an alert stating, "This invitation is not correct," the problem is that you haven't specified your *own* card in Address Book. You need to create an Address Book entry for yourself and then from the Card menu choose This Is My Card. Make sure that all of your e-mail addresses are listed in the card's contact-information area.

iCal can't read Entourage .ics files. Even though iCal and Entourage both support the iCalendar (.ics) standard, their .ics files are not compatible with each other. Apple claims it is "investigating this issue." However, you can import Entourage calendars using iCal's Import command (from the File menu); simply select the Import Entourage Data option in the Import dialog.

Alarm fails to go off as scheduled. A previously set alarm will likely not go off within the first hour after turning your computer on. Nor will it go off if your computer is asleep.

Troubleshooting iSync

The iSync application allows you to synchronize your iCal data (calendars and To Do items) and your Address Book contacts between your Mac and any number of devices, such as handheld computers (for example, Palm handhelds) and mobile phones. The only requirement is that the device be iSync-compatible. For a full list of supported devices, visit the following Web site: www.apple.com/macosx/features/isync/devices.html.

TAKE NOTE ▶ Syncing Across Computers and iPods

In Tiger, you no longer use iSync to sync information across computers via .Mac (as you did in Panther). Instead, you must use the .Mac System Preferences pane. Members of Apple's .Mac service can sync calendars, contacts, Safari bookmarks, keychains, and Mail between multiple Macs via the Internet.

For iCal calendars, for example, you would enable this feature either by selecting Calendars from the Sync pane of the .Mac System Preferences pane or by selecting "Synchronize my calendars with other computers using .Mac" in iCal's Preferences dialog.

Note: Synchronizing your calendar(s) via iSync is independent of publishing calendar(s) via iCal as described in the previous section. Whenever you use iSync, it updates the calendars on all synced devices. However, to update a published calendar, you need to update it from within iCal.

Similarly, syncing calendar and contact data with iPods is no longer handled by iSync in Tiger. Instead, you use the iPod Preferences settings in iTunes, as covered in "Troubleshooting the iPod," earlier in this chapter.

SEE: • "Using .Mac," in Chapter 8, for more on this service.

iSync Preferences. Before using iSync, your first step should be to examine its preferences, making sure that options are set the way you want. To do so, choose Preferences from the iSync menu. This opens a dialog with several choices:

- **"Enable syncing on this computer."** This enables iSync syncing.

- **"Show HotSync reminder when syncing Palm OS devices."** If you're syncing to a Palm OS device, choosing this option warns you, when syncing, that syncing with a Palm requires that you use the HotSync application or button on the device cradle, not the Sync Now button in iSync.

  SEE: • "Syncing with Palm devices," later in this chapter.

- **"Show status in menu bar."** This places a menu in the menu bar from which you can check when the last sync occurred or initiate a new sync. You can also launch iSync from the menu.

- **"Show Data Change alert when {*percentage pop-up menu selection*} of the data on this computer will be changed."** If you select this option, you will be notified before syncing if the upcoming sync is going to change more than the specified percentage of data on your Mac. This can prevent you from accidentally deleting information. For example, if you mistakenly erased your .Mac contacts when you first synced from another computer, the next time you synced this computer, iSync might think you wanted to delete all of those contacts on all registered computers. This option would notify you first, giving you an opportunity to avoid such a disastrous sync.

- **Reset Sync History.** Clicking this button doesn't affect your data, but it resets the history of syncs; the result is that the *next* time you use iSync, your Mac will act as if it's the first time you've ever performed a sync. This gives you the option—normally unavailable—to completely replace information on your Mac with information from another computer or device.

  SEE: • ".Mac and iSync," in Chapter 8, for related details.

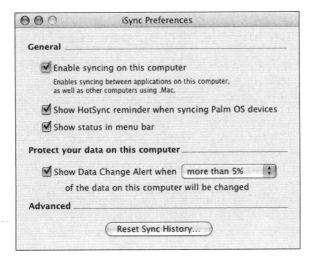

Figure 11.27

iSync's Preferences dialog.

iSync Log. The iSync Log, viewable by choosing Sync Log from the Window menu, displays a history of every sync operation. Clicking the disclosure triangle next to a particular sync provides you with details of that sync, including how many changes were made to which devices and any problems encountered.

If you ever have a failure after trying to sync, checking the log files is a good first step. The log should indicate the nature of the error, hopefully facilitating your ability to fix the problem.

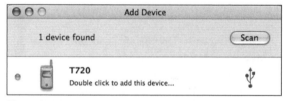

Figure 11.28

Left, *iSync detects my mobile phone;* right, *the main iSync window after my mobile phone has been added and selected.*

Adding and setting up devices

If you want to sync with a supported device, such as a Palm handheld or an iSync-compatible phone, you need to add it to iSync's device list.

Adding a device. To add a device, follow these steps:

1. Make sure the device is connected to your Mac. For USB-equipped Palms and mobile phones, connect to a USB port; for Bluetooth-enabled phones and handhelds, "pair" the device with your Mac.

    If your USB device requires a special software driver—some (not all) Motorola phones, for example, require a driver to connect via USB—make sure that driver is installed. Connecting a Motorola phone via USB also requires a special USB cable (which you purchase from Motorola). This is because the mobile phone itself does not have a standard USB port.

2. Launch iSync.

3. From the Devices menu choose Add Device. iSync will scan your Mac's ports and connections and present you with a list of the compatible devices it finds.

4. In the Add Device dialog, double-click the device you want to add. The device will be added to the iSync window.

Figure 11.29

iSync's Devices menu.

If you are still having problems adding a device (assuming it's an iSync-compatible one), recheck to see that all Bluetooth devices have been paired with your computer and that all USB mobile phones are listed in the Network Port Configurations section of the Network System Preferences pane.

SEE: • **Chapter 8, for advice on solving network-related problems.**
   • **"Syncing with Bluetooth devices," later in this section.**

Note: Some mobile phones, when added to iSync, need a special piece of software called iSync Agent installed before iSync can use the phone for syncing your data. If this is the case, a dialog will appear, alerting you to this; assuming you indicate your approval in the dialog, the software will be sent to your phone as a message. You should follow the appropriate procedures for your particular phone to view this message and install the attached software.

Removing a device. If you decide to remove a device, click its icon in the iSync window, and from the Devices menu choose Remove Device.

Device settings. Each device has its own customizable settings for what data should be synchronized between the device and your Mac. To access a device's settings, click its icon (at the top of the iSync window); a settings dialog will drop down. The various settings will differ slightly according to device type; however, they generally allow you to enable and disable syncing, and to decide whether you want to sync contacts, calendars, or both. Of particular note are the following settings:

• **Contacts.** In the Contacts section, you can choose to sync all Address Book contacts or just those in a particular group.

   SEE: • **"Take Note: Address Book Groups and iSync," below, for more details on using groups with iSync.**

   For some phones, iSync will give you the option of syncing only contacts with phone numbers. If your iSync doesn't give you this option for your phone, you can make a group in Address Book called *phone contacts*, drag all contacts with phone numbers into the group, and then synchronize only this particular group.

- **Calendars.** The Calendars section lets you choose to sync all or only selected iCal calendars. Some devices also give you the option of syncing calendar information for a selectable period of time (for example, the next four weeks). Finally, if you sync more than one calendar with your phone or Palm, you can choose in which calendar events *created* on the device will be placed when you sync.

TAKE NOTE ▶ Address Book Groups and iSync

To create a new group in Address Book, select New Group from Address Book's File menu. Give the new empty group any name you want by replacing the default Group Name in the Group column.

Alternatively, you can select a group of existing contacts and choose New Group from Selection. This immediately populates the new group with the contacts you selected.

Groups in Address Book play an important role in iSync. In particular, suppose you want to sync the contacts on your mobile phone. However, you have hundreds of contacts in Address Book and only a dozen or so on your phone. How can you sync your Mac with the phone so that the phone's contacts get copied to Address Book without having all of Address Book's contacts copied to your phone? The answer is, by using a group. To do so, follow these steps:

1. Create an empty group in Address Book, and name it for your phone (for example, Mobile).

2. Launch iSync, and click the icon for your phone to view its settings.

3. In the Contacts section of the phone settings, click the Synchronize pop-up menu and choose the name of your newly created group—this tells iSync to sync only that group's contacts with your phone.

4. Click the Sync Now button. The contacts on your mobile phone will be copied to the new Mobile group in Address Book. No Address Book contacts will be copied to the phone.

Syncing devices

In most cases, once you've selected the settings for a device, syncing the device is as simple as clicking the Sync Devices button in iSync, the Sync Devices command in iSync's Dock menu, or the Sync Now command in the Sync menu.

Note: Choosing Sync Now from this menu is designed to initiate a sync of .Mac (using the settings in the .Mac pane of System Preferences), any connected iPods (using the iPod settings in iTunes), and iSync—all via this single command. However, in what is probably a bug, it initiates the iSync sync *only* if the iSync application is open. As a work-around, you can use the freeware utility Sync Now, from JoolsG4 (http://mobile.feisar.com); it lets you initiate all three syncs from the menu bar, even if iSync isn't currently running.

Note: Third-party software has access to syncing services in Tiger. If written to use this feature, such software may sync with Mac OS X databases, such as iCal, or provide their own custom data for syncing.

Syncing with Palm devices. Syncing with a Palm OS device requires that you have the iSync Palm Conduit installed. With iSync 2 (included with Tiger), iSync will install this for you if needed. With prior versions of Mac OS X, you needed to download the Conduit from Apple's Web site. In fact, if you are using iSync 2, you should *not* use the prior version of the Conduit available from the Web; use only the version that comes with iSync.

To install the necessary software on your Palm device, simply choose Enable Palm OS Syncing from iSync's Devices menu. Then follow the prompts.

Before you add a Palm OS device to your list of iSync devices, you also need to install the Palm Desktop software 4.2.1 or later (which should have come with your handheld). Use Palm's HotSync option at least once before proceeding to use iSync.

To choose what information is synced with your Palm handheld, instead of clicking the Palm icon in the iSync window, launch the Palm HotSync Manager, and from the HotSync menu choose Conduit Settings. Double-click iSync Conduit, and then check the box next to "Enable iSync for this Palm device."

Some caveats to consider with Palm handheld syncing:

- When syncing with a Palm OS device, you must initiate the sync via the HotSync feature of the Palm device, not the Sync Device button in iSync. For faster syncing, make sure the HotSync Progress window is kept in front.

- Because neither iCal nor Address Book provides a notes application or functionality, your Palm Notes will still sync with Palm Desktop.

- Certain options in iCal for "repeating" events do not transfer properly to Palm handhelds. For details, see http://docs.info.apple.com/article.html?artnum=93172.

- If you're sure the Palm device is set up correctly and you're still having problems getting the device to sync, force iSync to do a *slow sync*. To set this, click the iSync device icon in iSync to access its settings. Check the "Force slow synchronization" box. Now sync the Palm as usual.

- Before removing a Palm OS device from the iSync list, make sure that the Palm HotSync application isn't running. Otherwise, the Palm device may reappear in iSync.

Syncing with Bluetooth devices. If your Mac has Bluetooth functionality (either built in or via a USB Bluetooth adapter) and you plan on syncing with a Bluetooth-enabled device, such as a Palm handheld or mobile phone with built-in Bluetooth, before you can add the device in iSync you need to pair the device with your Mac.

> **SEE:** • "Using Bluetooth," in Chapter 8, for more details on pairing a device and other Bluetooth-related features.

Likewise, if you want to use iSync to sync with a Bluetooth-enabled Palm device, you need to first disable the Palm conduits and install the iSync Palm conduit, as described above.

Resetting devices

The Reset Device and Reset All Devices commands, available from the Devices menu, erase all of the iSync-related data on a particular device or all connected devices (mobile phone, iPod, Palm, and so on), respectively, and replace it with the current data in Address Book and iCal. This can be a useful option if you're having trouble with the data in one of your devices; however, it can also result in data loss if you're not careful. Before using a Reset command, make sure that any new information added to the connected devices has been synced or added to Address Book or iCal, as well.

In addition, Apple warns that on some devices, the Reset command will erase information that is not synced by iSync, such as voice dial tags, speed-dial info, and custom-ring tags that are attached to contacts. In essence, any information stored on the device but not also stored on your computer will be lost. Thus, use this option with caution!

Note: The iSync Backup and Revert commands, included in iSync 1.x, are no longer included in Tiger's iSync 2.x version.

Solving iSync problems

This section lists a number of common problems that may occur with iSync, along with their solutions. Apple has also documented a number of specific issues that may occur with certain devices (particular phone models, for example).

You can find out more about these issues by visiting Apple's Support site at www.apple.com/support and doing a search on *iSync*. For additional help, you can also check out the various iSync Help topics included with Mac OS X. However, as of iSync 2.1, the Help files still refer back to iSync 1.x and thus include now-obsolete information!

Synchronization fails. If you ever get a message indicating that a synchronization attempt has failed, make sure the needed device (for example, mobile phone) is correctly connected to your Mac. Otherwise, if you cannot determine a cause, choose Sync Log from the Window menu. The log output should provide at least a clue as to what caused the failure.

Solving synchronization conflicts. If you're syncing multiple devices with your computer and you've made changes to the same item in more than one location (and the changes are not the same), iSync will prompt you via a dialog to indicate which data should be used when syncing. Select the source you wish to use.

Syncing devices to just one computer. If you add a device, such as a mobile phone, to more than one computer, the device may not sync correctly.

Crash on launch. iSync may crash on launch after you upgrade from Panther to Tiger. This is usually due to a damaged .plist file and can be fixed via general methods as described in Chapter 5. However, you can also fix things by going to /Library/Application Support/SyncService/5## (where ## represents numbers for the one folder here that you have access to, such as 501) and deleting any files with *iSync* in their name.

Note: There is a folder named SyncServices in ~/Library/Application Support. You should *never* delete files from this folder; syncing may no longer work if you do.

Syncing fails with some phones. When syncing data with some mobile phones—Sony Ericsson P800 phones are one example—you may get an error message stating that some data will not fit. This typically occurs because you're trying to synchronize more data than the phone's memory can hold. The solution is to sync less data, which you can do by choosing to sync fewer iCal calendars (or only recent data) or creating a smaller group of contacts in Address Book and then syncing only that group.

Similarly, with Symbian OS–based phones (which include Sony Ericsson P800 and P900 phones, plus several Nokia phone models), if the phone has less than 300 Kbytes of memory available, you will get an error that states, "An error occurred while copying iSync Agent to your phone." The solution is to free up more memory by deleting items, such as sounds and pictures, from the phone.

Can't sync to Motorola mobile phone because "device is unavailable." If, when you attempt to use iSync to synchronize data with a Motorola phone, you receive this error message, make sure your phone isn't locked (the phone's screen will show a "locked" message or a padlock icon if it is). If it is, unlock the phone and then sync again.

Restoring Palm HotSync conduits. When you install the iSync Palm Conduit, it automatically disables certain Palm HotSync conduits—that is, those that would conflict with iSync. If at some point you decide to use Palm Desktop instead of iCal and Address Book, you'll need to disable the iSync conduit and re-enable the Palm conduits. To do this, move the Apple conduit from /Library/Application Support/Palm HotSync/Conduits to /Library/Application Support/Palm HotSync/Disabled Conduits, and then move the contents of /Library/Application Support/Palm HotSync/Disabled Conduits to /Library/Application Support/Palm HotSync/Conduits. After this, you'll need to launch the Palm HotSync Manager and configure each of the restored Palm conduits.

Troubleshooting iMovie

iMovie is Apple's "consumer" movie editing application. (Final Cut Express and Final Cut Pro are Apple's professional-level editing applications.) It is included free with most new Macs and is part of the retail iLife package. The latest version of iMovie, part of iLife '05, is actually called iMovie HD, reflecting the fact that it can work with high-definition video content; I'll refer to it here simply as iMovie.

iMovie overview

To create a movie, you can import video directly from a digital camcorder, iSight camera, or existing movie files; include music from your iTunes Library; and even use images from your iPhoto Library. You can edit your movies and save them as movie files or export them to iDVD for use in iDVD projects.

Creating a project or opening an existing project. The first time you launch iMovie, you're given the option of opening an existing project or creating a new one. With iMovie, unlike most applications, when you create a new movie project, you need to save the file *before* you start to work on it; the default location is your Movies folder inside your home directory. On subsequent launches, iMovie opens the project you were using most recently.

When you first create a project, you are given the option of saving it in various video formats, via a pop-up menu in the Create Project dialog. In most cases, iMovie automatically selects the format compatible with the input device you have connected to the Mac (such as an iSight camera). Otherwise, you can make your own choice (potentially useful if no device is connected at the time of launch). DV is the default and most common choice.

You may instead choose to open an existing project.

The main iMovie window includes three distinct sections, as follows.

Viewing area and basic controls. The upper left portion of the iMovie window is the *viewing area*. Like a TV screen, it lets you view video as it is imported and preview the current status of your iMovie project.

Below the viewing area are the basic controls for viewing the video:

- **Scrubber bar.** Directly along the bottom of the viewing area is a scrubber bar. As with the Timeline Viewer, described below, you can use this to drag a pointer to any location in the current clip. You can also use the crop markers to define a section of a clip to be cropped.

  Note: If a specific clip is not selected in the Clip/Timeline Viewer below, the entire movie is included in the scrubber bar (rather than a single clip).

- **Clip/Timeline Viewer switch.** This switch is located below the viewing area on the left side. It consists of a pair of icons—a movie strip icon on the left and a clock icon on the right. Clicking each icon toggles the Viewer below between Clip and Timeline modes (as described below).

- **Camera/Scissors switch.** This switch is located to the right of the Clip/Timeline Viewer switch. It lets you toggle between Import (camera icon) and Edit (scissors icon) modes. Use Import mode when a camera is connected to the Mac and you're importing video; use Edit mode when editing an already imported clip.

- **Playback buttons.** In Edit mode, you'll see three buttons to the right of the Camera/Scisssors switch. Click the Play button (the large triangle button) to play the clip currently in the viewer. Use the Play Full Screen button (the button with the Play icon within the screen icon) for full-screen playback (press the Escape key to stop full-screen playback). The Rewind button takes you to the beginning of the selected clip.

  In Import mode, there are five buttons; they offer similar controls for the playback of a connected video camera. In addition, an Import (or Record) button will appear; clicking this button will import/record whatever is currently playing (or being viewed) on the camera.

- **Volume slider.** Located below the viewing area, on the right side, this is used to adjust playback volume.

Clip Viewer and Timeline Viewer. The lower part of the iMovie window contains either the Clip Viewer (which shows you the times and arrangement of individual movie clips) or the Timeline Viewer (which lets you view and edit your project on a Timeline).

When you use the Timeline Viewer, the area below the viewer provides a few Timeline-related controls:

- The *zoom control* lets you choose how much of the Timeline you see at any one time.

- The *volume slider* (or the adjacent Clip Volume field) allows you to specify different volume levels for each clip in your project.

Finally, you can view *available drive space* just below the viewer. The size of the Trash's contents is also shown.

Action pane. The right-hand pane of the iMovie window (which I call the *Action pane*) shows various options for adding content to or enhancing the content of a movie. The options that appear here depend on which mode is selected from the row of buttons below the pane: Clips, Photos, Audio, Titles, Trans (transitions), Effects, and iDVD.

SEE: • "Editing video," later in this chapter, for a brief description of each of these modes.

The following sections provide additional details about iMovie's basic functions. The last part looks specifically at solving iMovie problems.

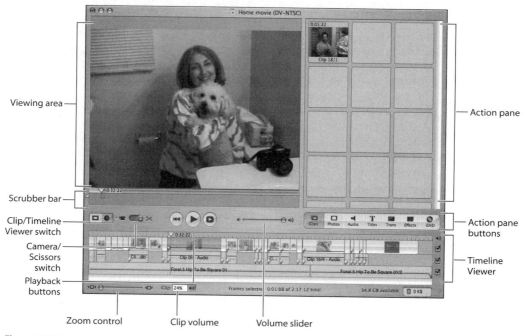

Figure 11.30

The main iMovie window: The initial part of the selected clip is set to be cropped in the scrubber bar; the Timeline Viewer is shown in the lower part of the window; Clips is selected in the Action pane.

Importing video

There are a number of ways to import video into iMovie:

- To import directly from an existing movie file on your hard drive, from the File menu choose Import and then navigate to that file.

- If you have a DV camera with a FireWire port, connect the camera to your Mac via a FireWire cable. Place your camcorder in Playback mode (often called VCR or VTR mode), and then place iMovie in Camera mode (via the Camera/Scissors switch below the main viewing area). To import an entire video, simply click the Import button. If you've enabled the "Automatically start new clip at scene break" option in iMovie Preferences, iMovie will create a new clip each time it detects a scene break—most DV cameras insert a scene break each time you pause or stop recording. You can also record from a stand-alone iSight camera (but not the one built into iMacs). To set this up, open the iSight's privacy shutter. Next, in iMovie HD, make sure that iSight is selected from the pop-up menu to the left of the Camera mode icon.

- To import selections of video, use the playback controls beneath the viewing window to find the beginning of the section to be imported, and then click the Import button (or press the spacebar); click it again to stop importing. iMovie shows the tape counter from your DV camera at the top of the viewing window.

Note: By default, newly imported clips are placed in the Action pane's Clips view. However, you can choose, via iMovie Preferences, to instead have them added directly to the movie Timeline.

TAKE NOTE ▶ iMovie Projects

When you create a project in iMovie, it's saved in an iMovie project package with the name that you gave it. By default, the project is saved inside your personal Movies folder. However, as discussed in the main text, you can choose to save your project anywhere.

To see inside the project package, select the item and use the Show Package Contents command from its contextual menu. The project package itself contains a few files and folders. These include folders named Media and Cache and files called *projectname* and *projectname*.iMovieProj. The *projectname* files contain a complete map of your project: which clips are used, in what order, using which transitions and effects; titles; and so on. The Media folder contains all of the imported video clips, photos, and other data files for your project. You'll also see a .mov file—probably in the Shared Movies folder—which is the currently rendered version of your movie (sort of a draft version). This is what iMovie uses to play the movie in the viewing area (you can double-click this movie file in the Finder to play it in QuickTime Player).

If you delete any file within the package, that project will likely no longer be usable, so work on a project only from within iMovie itself, not from the Finder. On the other hand, to get rid of a project, simply drag the project package to the Trash.

Note: Older versions of iMovie had a substantially different format for saving movie projects. For starters, the project was saved in a true folder in the Finder, rather than a "package."

Be aware that projects created with older versions of iMovie will need to be upgraded to work with iMovie HD. You will be prompted to do so when you open the projects; after doing so, the projects will no longer be usable with the older iMovie versions. Such upgraded projects apparently also remain in the folder rather than package format. The old *projectname* file will also remain, but be given a new name, such as *projectname*.iMovie2Project. When opening the movie, select the new *projectname* file rather than the old one.

Editing video

Apple has made editing video in iMovie extraordinarily simple. You just drag clips from the Clips pane to the Clip Viewer at the bottom of the window. To rearrange clips in a movie, simply drag them around in the Clip Viewer or (new in Tiger!) the Timeline.

Figure 11.31

iMovie's Clip/ Timeline Viewer in Clip Viewer mode.

You can trim a particular clip in the scrubber bar: To do so, use the two crop markers (found on the lower left edge of the scrubber bar below the viewer) to enclose the section of the clip to be cropped—that section will be highlighted yellow (instead of blue) on the bar. Now press the Delete key to cut the enclosed section. This change will be reflected in the Clip/Timeline Viewer at the bottom of the window. You can also use the Timeline Viewer to fine-tune your movie's audio and video tracks as well as to add audio tracks.

Note that for many editing actions, after you apply the action, the clip(s) will need to be *rendered*, meaning that the action (transition, effect, title, and so on) will need to be digitized into the existing video. Because this takes some time, the bottom of the clip image (in Clip Viewer mode) or video track (in Timeline Viewer mode) displays the progress of the current render. Once rendering is complete, you'll be able to play the finished clip in the main viewing area.

Other editing functions are available via the various editing modes you access from the Action pane buttons:

Clips. The Clips pane lists all of the video clips imported into the current project. These clips aren't necessarily included in the actual movie; they are simply available for use.

Photos. You can use this pane to access any photo in your iPhoto Library for use in your iMovie project.

If the Ken Burns Effect box is unchecked, you can use a static picture in your project. With the Ken Burns Effect enabled, you can pan and zoom around a photo, just as you see on TV (the effect is named after documentary film maker Ken Burns, who uses such an effect frequently). When you're satisfied with your photo, drag it from the photo list to the Clip Viewer to add it to your project.

Audio. The Audio pane works much like the Photos pane, except that you can browse any playlist from your iTunes Library and then choose a song. To add the song to your project, drag it to the Timeline's audio track or click the Place at Playhead button.

The Audio pane also lets you record audio via your Mac's built-in microphone (if applicable) or an external mike. Click the red Record button to begin recording, and a new audio track will be added to the Timeline. Click the button again to stop recording.

Titles. Using the Titles pane, you can add titles, credits, or any other text to your iMovie project. When you've completed your creation, drag the title from the list (actually, the name of the title effect—your text and settings will be used) to the beginning of any clip in the Timeline; make sure the clip you choose is longer than the duration of the title.

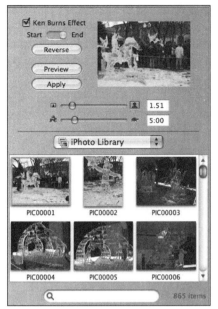 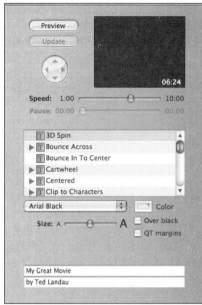

Figure 11.32

Two examples of iMovie panes: left, Photos; right, Titles. See Figure 11.30 for the Clips pane.

Trans(itions). You can apply transitions between clips using the Transitions pane. Select a transition from the list, and then choose a speed (you're actually choosing the duration of the transition). Once you're satisfied, drag it from the transition list to the divider between two clips—the transition will be rendered using those two clips.

Effects. iMovie comes with a number of built-in video effects that you can apply to clips via the Effects pane. To do so, select the clip to which you want the effect applied, and then select an effect from the list and choose your desired settings. (Each effect has its own settings; the Effects pane will change to reflect this each time you select a different effect.) If you're happy with the result, click Apply.

Note that if you apply an effect to a clip, any transitions you previously applied to that clip will be deleted; you must reapply the transition after the effect has been rendered.

iDVD. If you plan to export your iMovie project to iDVD for burning to a DVD, the iDVD pane lets you add chapter markers to your movie. As with the chapters in a commercial DVD, these markers allow viewers to use their DVD players' Forward and Reverse buttons to skip between "scenes" or to go directly to a particular chapter. When you export your project to iDVD, iDVD automatically creates menus and buttons for these chapter markers.

To add a chapter marker, move the scrubber (either in the Clip/Timeline Viewer or in the main viewing area) to the spot at which you want the marker to appear; then click Add Chapter in the iDVD pane. You can even name the chapter; iDVD will use this name when creating your DVD.

iMovie plug-ins

A number of third-party developers offer plug-ins that enhance iMovie (for example, check out those at www.geethree.com). Some work by simply dropping the plug-in file into ~/Library/iMovie/Plug-ins; others use an installer. If iMovie is running, you'll need to quit it and then relaunch it for the plug-in to take effect. These plug-ins usually provide additional transitions and effects, which will be available in the standard Transitions and Effects panes.

Exporting (Sharing) iMovie projects

When you've finished producing your movie, you can export it in a number of ways, all accessible via the Share command in iMovie's File menu. After you select Share, a dialog drops down from which you can choose from several options, to export the entire movie or just the currently selected clips.

Whichever Share option you choose, the dialog indicates the final size and compression of the exported movie.

Exporting to Email. This option compresses your movie to a size suitable for e-mailing. (In theory, that is; for example, a 6-minute movie I made was compressed to around 12 MB—a larger attachment than most people would want to receive.) When finished, your preferred e-mail client will open to a new message with the movie attached.

Exporting to HomePage. This compresses your movie to a size approximately 50 percent larger than the e-mail option, and then automatically publishes it to the .Mac account listed in the .Mac pane of System Preferences.

Exporting to Videocamera. This option automatically records your movie, at full resolution, to your digital video camera's tape. You simply insert a recordable tape and set the video camera to VTR mode. You have the option of inserting "black" space before and/or after the movie.

Exporting to iDVD. This sends your video, in full resolution, to a new project in iDVD.

Exporting to QuickTime. If you want to create a movie file to post on the Web, burn to a data CD, or keep on your hard drive, choose this option.

A "Compress movie for" pop-up menu will appear, allowing you to choose the type of QuickTime file/movie you want to produce: Web (creates a small, low-quality QuickTime .mov file); Email (creates a smaller but even lower-quality file); Web Streaming (creates a file suitable for a QuickTime Streaming Server); CD-ROM (asks you to insert a blank CD and creates a CD containing the movie that will be playable on any Mac or Windows computer via QuickTime); and Full Quality (provides the highest-quality QuickTime .mov file, but that file will be very large). Click the Export button, and then name the file and indicate the location to which the file will be saved.

Exporting to Bluetooth. This option creates the smallest—and thus lowest-quality—movie file and then attempts to send it to a connected Bluetooth device. After compression is completed, you'll see a dialog similar to Mac OS X's Bluetooth Send File dialog, in which you choose the Bluetooth device to which you want to send the movie.

Figure 11.33

iMovie's share/ export (to QuickTime) dialog.

Magic iMovie. iMovie also includes a feature, separate from the Share command, for quickly creating a movie from the video on your video camera with minimal intervention. When you choose Make a Magic iMovie from the File menu, iMovie will import the video into a new project and even create opening titles. You can also choose—via a dialog that appears when you choose the Magic iMovie command—the types of dissolves that should be used between clips and whether or not to add a music soundtrack (and, if so, which music to use). You can even have the resulting movie sent to iDVD automatically. Of course, using this feature means you don't get much input into how your movie will look, but it's a handy way to quickly archive all the videotapes sitting in your closet (although iDVD's OneStep DVD feature, discussed below, is an even better option). You can also use any Magic iMovie as a starting point for your own moviemaking.

Solving iMovie problems

The problems most users experience with iMovie seem to be more performance related than those seen with the most other iApps (with the exception of GarageBand, as covered later in this chapter). Typical symptoms are that iMovie's response to commands is too slow or movies are too choppy. There is no surefire cure for this. To try to improve iMovie's performance, do one or more of the following: (a) rebuild your project (as described in "'Your iMovie project is unreadable' message," below); (b) remove third-party plug-ins in ~/Library/iMovie/Plug-ins; (c) store your project in a folder not protected by FileVault; (d) gain free memory by quitting all open applications; (e) defragment your drive; (f) buy a faster Mac. See this Apple Knowledge Base document for further advice: http://docs.info.apple.com/article.html?artnum=93699.

The following represent some of the more common *non-performance-related* issues with iMovie.

Undo actions. If you make a mistake in the latest version of iMovie, iMovie HD, you have more recovery options than in previous versions of iMovie. For starters, items dragged to iMovie's Trash are not actually deleted until you double-click the Trash icon and select Empty Trash. Until then, you can still drag items out of the Trash. iMovie HD also supports multiple levels of Undo (Command-Z). And iMovie HD now features "non-destructive editing." Essentially, this means that if you cut part of a clip while making a movie, the entire clip (audio and/or video) still remains as part of the iMovie project and can later be restored if desired.

DV camera (camcorder) not recognized by iMovie. If your DV camera isn't recognized, make sure of the following:

- The camera is compatible with iMovie. Apple has a list of compatible cameras at www.apple.com/macosx/upgrade/camcorders.html.
- The camera is turned on and connected via FireWire. iMovie does not support USB.
- The camera is set to VTR/VCR mode, not "record/on" mode.
- The camera's date and time are set accurately.

See the following Apple Knowledge Base article for more advice on this matter: http://docs.info.apple.com/article.html?artnum=43000.

"Found files that don't belong" message. If iMovie finds files in a project's Media folder that don't correspond to any part of the project, you'll receive the following error message: "Found files that don't belong in project folder. Okay to move them to Trash?" These files are usually files that were created when iMovie crashed during rendering. Generally it's OK to click the Trash Unused Files button to move these files to the Trash. If you instead click Leave Files Alone, iMovie will leave them in the Media folder, but you will get the above-described error message each time the affected project is opened in iMovie.

Can't eject audio CD after importing. If you add an audio track into iMovie by importing it directly from the CD, you may find that you're unable to eject the CD afterward. The solution is to save your iMovie project and quit iMovie; you should then be able to eject the CD. You can relaunch iMovie and resume working on your project.

"Your iMovie project is unreadable" message. If your iMovie project becomes damaged or corrupt, you may be unable to open it in iMovie, instead seeing this message. It's sometimes possible to recover a project by following the steps outlined below:

1. Create a new project in iMovie.

2. Navigate in the Finder to the damaged iMovie project package and use the Show Package Contents command to access its contents.

3. Drag the file *projectname*.mov from the damaged project folder to the Timeline of the new iMovie project. This should import the original project contents as a single clip.

4. Save the new project, but do not delete the old project. The new project will still reference files in the older one.

Third-party iMovie plug-ins can cause iMovie to crash. If you're experiencing unexpected quits with iMovie, or you get error messages when iMovie is launched, the cause could be an incompatible third-party iMovie plug-in file. A related symptom that often has the same cause is a message that states, "Something is wrong with the plugin Localized.rsrc," when you launch iMovie.

To diagnose and fix this, remove all plug-ins by following the steps outlined below:

1. Quit iMovie.

2. In the Finder, navigate to ~/Library/iMovie/Plug-ins.

3. Drag any files in this folder to the Desktop.

4. Launch iMovie.

If the symptoms have disappeared, isolate which plug-in was the cause and contact the plug-in's vendor for further advice. The solution is usually to get a newer version of the plug-in.

Toast Video CD Export plug-in causes iMovie to crash. If you've installed Toast, the third-party CD-burning software from Roxio, you may have also installed the Toast Video CD Export plug-in for iMovie. This plug-in is an occasional source of problems—in particular, causing a crash when selecting iMovie Help. Unfortunately, it is typically installed directly inside the iMovie application package. Thus, the advice in the previous section will not work. Here's how to delete it:

1. Quit iMovie.

2. In the Finder, select Get Info for iMovie.

3. Click the disclosure triangle next to Plug-ins.

4. Find the Toast Video CD Export plug-in in the Plug-ins list, and then uncheck it to disable the file. Or click the Remove button to delete it completely.

5. Launch iMovie and see if the problem has disappeared.

Third-party QuickTime codecs cause iMovie to crash. If you've installed any third-party codecs for QuickTime, they can potentially cause iMovie to quit unexpectedly. To see if these codecs are responsible for problems, follow these steps:

1. Quit iMovie.
2. In the Finder, navigate to /Library/QuickTime; if any files exist in this folder, drag them to the Desktop.
3. In the Finder, navigate to ~/Library/QuickTime; repeat the above procedure.
4. Launch iMovie and see if the problem has disappeared.

If this fixes the problem, isolate which codec is the cause, and contact the vendor for further advice.

More generally: These codecs also affect the ability to play QuickTime movies in QuickTime Player. If a needed codec is missing, when you try to play the movie in QuickTime, you will get an error that states: "QuickTime is missing software required to perform this operation." The solution is either to (a) upgrade to a new version of QuickTime that includes the codec; (b) locate the needed codec on the Web to download and install it; or (c) switch to another application that supports the codec (if QuickTime does not).

Problems importing video formats. When importing video, make sure that the format you select from the Create Project dialog matches the format of the source video. Otherwise, you may get an "Incompatible Camera Video Format" error. It is possible, although not recommended, to combine more than one video format in the same project. See these Apple Knowledge Base articles for details: http://docs.info.apple.com/article.html?artnum=300829 and http://docs.info.apple.com/article.html?artnum=300830.

After reinstalling Mac OS X, the iMovie icon is generic and iMovie may not launch. If for some reason you reinstalled Mac OS X and are now experiencing problems with iMovie (for example, it won't launch, or its icon becomes generic), drag the damaged iMovie application to the Trash and then reinstall iMovie (via your Restore or iLife disc).

Moving iMovie projects to a different volume. If your boot drive is low on space, you may want to store your projects on another volume. When creating a new project, you can simply choose a different volume as the save location. However, if you want to move an existing project, you need to use the following procedure:

1. Quit iMovie.
2. Drag the existing project package from its current location to the desired location on the alternative volume.
3. Launch iMovie and open the project from the new location.

Note that you should always store iMovie projects on hard drives, rather than on slower media such as Zip drives, CD-RWs, or USB devices. In addition, iMovie requires that projects be stored on HFS (Standard or Extended/Plus) volumes. You cannot use projects stored on volumes formatted as UFS or any Windows file system.

"Disk responded slowly" alert message. If you use the audio recording feature of iMovie—for example, to record a voice-over—you may get the following message: "The disk responded slowly. It may have been interrupted by something, or it may not be fast enough for your movie. If you have a lot of audio clips, you might try muting the audio tracks to see if helps playback speed."

The problem here is that your hard drive is having trouble keeping up with iMovie. This doesn't mean, however, that your hard drive is inherently too slow. Rather, it's more commonly due to such factors as having too many applications open or virtual memory paging to disk too often. To fix this, try quitting other open applications, and don't switch to other applications while iMovie is recording.

Another cause may be that your hard drive is extremely fragmented, causing hard-drive access to slow down. The solution would be to defragment your hard drive (as described in Chapter 5).

Graphics import as blank clips. If you import PICT files into iMovie, they may appear as blank (white) clips after being rendered. The solution is to first convert the images to JPEG or TIFF. You can do this fairly quickly by opening them in Apple's Preview application and then choosing Export from the File menu.

More iMovie help. For help with an assortment of basic troubleshooting issues, be sure to check the Solving Problems section of iMovie Help (as accessed from iMovie's Help menu). Among the problems and solutions covered there are the following:

- **"I hear a sound when importing video."** Answer: The "Filter audio from camera" option in iMovie's Preferences is disabled. To fix this, enable it.

- **"I get a message about files that don't belong in my project."** Answer: This message may appear if iMovie crashed or was force-quit while it was rendering a file—or if you added files to the Media folder from the Finder. If you're sure you don't need the files, select Trash Unused Files.

- **"I don't see any photographs in the Photos pane."** Answer: Make sure you're using iPhoto 4 or later with at least one picture in the Library. You also must have launched iPhoto at least once.

Troubleshooting iDVD

iDVD is Apple's DVD-creation software. You can create custom DVDs using movies from iMovie, stand-alone video clips, and even photos. You then create your own DVD menus and burn your DVD content to a disc that can be played on any standard DVD player. The end result is a DVD that rivals what you get when you purchase commercial movies, in terms of the look and feel.

Note: The most recent versions of iDVD will install on a Mac that does not have a SuperDrive. However, to burn a completed project to a DVD, you will still need to transfer the project to a Mac with a SuperDrive.

The following sections provide a brief look at iDVD's features. However, I assume you are at least a bit familiar with how iDVD works and are mainly seeking troubleshooting help. If you've never used iDVD before, a good place to start is with the Help files that accompany iDVD.

iDVD overview

When you launch iDVD for the first time, the initial dialog gives you three options: Create a New Project, Open an Existing Project, and OneStep DVD. If you choose Create a New Project, iDVD will ask you to name the project and choose a location to save it to (it's saved in Documents by default). In the future, iDVD will always open the last project on which you were working, assuming that it is still available. Choose Open an Existing Project to reopen a project other than the one that opens by default.

OneStep DVD is a useful feature, new in Tiger, that takes all the video currently on the media in the camera attached to your Mac and creates a DVD playable on any standard DVD player. This feature is perfect for archiving your old videotapes.

Figure 11.34

iDVD's main window.

iDVD opens a new project using its default settings. The "screen" area in the main window lets you view your project in action as well as edit it. The window provides only a few options, via buttons across the bottom:

- **Customize** opens iDVD's Customize pane, which is where most of your project-editing tasks will occur.
- **Folder** adds a link for a folder on the currently viewed DVD screen.
- **Slideshow** adds a link for a slide show of images (typically taken from your iPhoto Library) on the currently viewed DVD screen.
- **Motion** lets you preview theme animation and animated video menus, as well as listen to background music.
- **Map** displays a diagram of your entire project, which you can use to navigate to a specific location.
- **Preview** switches iDVD to Preview mode—a DVD Player remote appears, and you can preview your project just as it would appear to someone who popped your finished disc into a DVD player.
- **Burn** allows you to burn your DVD to disc. However, before you do that, you're going to want to edit and customize your DVD, as briefly explained in the next sections.

TAKE NOTE ▶ iDVD Projects

When you create a project in iDVD, it's saved in a file called *projectname*.dvdproj. This file is actually a *package* (as explained in Chapter 3). If you look inside the package, you'll find a folder called Resources that contains a file called ProjectData—which contains the map of your project, including a catalog of all audio, video, menus, and other settings—and a bunch of folders that contain the actual data: Audio, Menu, MPEG, Overlay, Slideshow, and Thumbnails.

However, unlike iMovie project packages, iDVD packages don't actually contain all of the files used in the project. If you've used photos, movies, audio, and so on in your project, those files still exist wherever they resided before you used them in your project. For this reason, you can't move your iDVD project to another computer simply by copying the project file. You must also copy over all of the accompanying support files. Note: You can see a list of all the files in a project by choosing Project Info from the Project menu.

In iDVD 5, Apple introduced a new Archive feature that makes this process easier. When you want to move a project from one computer to another, open the project in iDVD and choose Archive Project from the File menu; then choose the name and location of the archive. The resulting archive contains copies of all the media files used in the project; you can copy it to another computer and open it normally.

Editing a DVD: Customize

You aren't limited to iDVD's default DVD design—not by a long shot! When you click the Customize button, the Customize drawer slides out, offering four editing panes: Themes, Settings, Media, and Status.

Themes. In the Themes pane, you can choose from a number of themes for your DVD. A *theme* consists of a coordinated set of background, buttons, menus, music, and so on. The pop-up menu lets you browse them by group: All, 5.0 Themes (themes added in iDVD 5), 4.0 Themes (themes added in iDVD 4), Old Themes (themes that came with the original version of iDVD), and Favorites (themes you've modified or created and saved for future use). Themes in the list that display a tiny icon of a person contain animated features.

Note that Old Themes—those from iDVD 1 and 2—will be available in newer versions of iDVD only if you upgraded from iDVD 3; if iDVD 3 was not installed on your hard drive before installing iDVD 4 or 5, you'll see only 4.0 and 5.0 Themes.

Click any theme icon, and your project will instantly switch to that theme. If a theme contains motion elements, click the Motion button in the main window to view them.

Figure 11.35

iDVD's Customize drawer lets you customize the look of your DVD creation: left, the Themes pane; right, the Settings pane.

A quick note about terminology: In iDVD, the term *menu* has two distinct meanings: As in all of Mac OS X, it can refer to a pull-down menu available via the menu bar; however, it can also refer to the graphical system for navigating a DVD (which the user employs when playing the DVD on a standard DVD player). I differentiate between the uses when there's any chance of confusion.

In addition to design elements, many iDVD themes contain *drop zones*—areas of a theme into which you can (guess what?) *drop* movies or photos. For example, iDVD's Projector theme has a drop zone on its main screen, into which you can drop a photo or movie. That photo or movie then becomes part of the background of your project's theme. You can even drop a group of photos; iDVD will rotate through them (click the Motion button to view this animation). Although drop zones represent a very cool feature, you need to be careful to drag your movies or photos into the correct positions. For example, if you want the movie to serve as one of the actual video portions of your DVD, you must make sure that you *don't* drop it into a drop zone but instead drop it into the main menu area.

SEE: • "Movies," later in this section, for further details.

Settings. The Settings pane lets you customize the settings for almost everything on your DVD. In fact, even though it's the second pane in the list, most people will end up using it *after* the Media pane, because it lets them edit buttons, text, and so on for each menu.

For each menu screen, you can remove any custom image, movie, and/or audio you may have added. If the menu includes animation (for example, built into the theme or added to a drop zone), you can use the Duration slider to determine how long that motion lasts before repeating. Using the Text section options, you can edit the position, font, color, and size of each menu screen's title. Using the Button section options, you can make similar editing changes for buttons on the menu screen.

Once you've completed your changes, click the Save as Favorite button to save your settings as a new theme. A dialog will appear, asking you to name the new theme.

TAKE NOTE ▶ Theme Favorites and Third-Party Themes

When you modify your theme settings in the Settings pane, you can save the current settings by clicking the Save as Favorite button. What this does is create a *new* theme inside /Library/iDVD/Favorites (if you choose the "Shared for all users" option in the dialog that drops down) or ~/Library/iDVD/Favorite (if you don't). If you want to use your custom theme on another Mac, you can copy the theme file to the same location on that computer. Likewise, if you want to share your custom theme with friends, you can simply give them a copy of that theme file, and they can place it inside their Favorites folders.

Along those lines, you can find lots of third-party themes—some free, some shareware, some commercial—on the Internet. If you find one you like, simply quit iDVD and place the theme file inside one of the folders mentioned above. The next time you launch iDVD, the theme will be available in the Themes pane.

Media. The Media pane provides quick access to music, photos, and movies on your Mac, which you can add to your iDVD project. You choose which type of media (Audio, Photos, or Movies) you want to browse via the pop-up menu at the top of the pane.

• **Audio.** You can add an audio track from iTunes to a menu screen or slide show. The box at the top displays all of your iTunes playlists, and the list beneath it shows all tracks in the selected playlist. You can also sample the selected song and search for a particular song using the controls at the bottom of the pane.

To add a song to a menu, simply drag it to an open area in the screen. To add a song to a slide show, switch the main screen to the Slideshow settings and then drag the song to the Audio icon. You can also drag audio files to iDVD from the Finder.

- **Photos.** As iTunes is to Audio, iPhoto is to Photos: You can add any photo or photos from your iPhoto Library to your DVD. Your iPhoto Library and any albums are listed at the top, and photos in the chosen album are shown at the bottom. You can add a group of photos to a drop zone in a menu, or in a slide show's or folder's screen. (The latter appear when you double-click a Slideshow or folder button, respectively). You can also drag photos to iDVD from the Finder.

- **Movies.** Finally, you can include any movies in your Movies folder in your DVD. Your Movies folder is listed at the top, and any movies contained in it—including iMovie projects (whose thumbnails include the iMovie icon)—are shown below. To preview a movie, select it and click the Play button.

  Note: If you want iDVD to look in other folders as well, open iDVD's Preferences, click the Movies button, and then add folders via the "Look for my movies in these folders setting."

  You can drag a movie to a drop zone to animate the menu or to the main menu area to add it as a "feature" for the DVD. You can also drag movie files from the Finder. If you drag a movie to the menu area, iDVD creates a menu button for you. If the movie already contained chapter marks (such as from an iMovie project for which you created chapter marks, as discussed in the iMovie section earlier in this chapter), iDVD adds a second menu button, called Scene Selection, which works just like the Scene Selection button on commercial DVDs.

  Note: Apple warns: "If you export an iMovie project as a QuickTime movie using the Full Quality option, iMovie HD doesn't include chapter markers in the QuickTime movie. To export your movie with chapter markers, export using the iDVD pane or by clicking the iDVD icon in the Share dialog."

Status. The Status pane shows you the status of your DVD, including how much space the project will take on a typical DVD (and thus how much space you have left to work with); and how many motion menus, tracks, and menus you've added. If you're doing something that requires that video be encoded, the Background Encoding box shows you the process of the encoding.

Editing a DVD: Folder and Slideshow

You use the Folder and Slideshow buttons to add content—generally *after* choosing a theme.

Folder. If you plan to use a single movie for your DVD, you won't need the Folder button. However, if you want another "screen" of options—for example, like a commercial DVD's Special Features screen—you must add a folder to your DVD. Click the Folder button, and a new folder button/menu item will be added to the menu screen.

If you double-click the new folder's icon or label, the screen will change to display that folder's menu (rather than the DVD's main menu). You'll now also see a Return button, which takes you back to the main menu. This folder is basically a subscreen that can do anything your main screen can.

To delete a folder from a menu, click its icon or label to select it and then press the Delete key.

Slideshow. The Slideshow button adds a Slideshow button/menu item to the menu screen. When you double-click the icon/label for the slide-show item, the screen area changes to a slide-show editor. Drag photos from the Finder or the Photos pane to add them to the slide show. Options here include the ability to set the duration for which each photo is displayed (or choose Manual for no automatic advance), choose a transition effect between photos, and add an audio background to the show (just drag an audio file to the Audio icon to do so).

Figure 11.36

The iDVD slide-show editor, which you access by double-clicking the Slideshow button in the project window.

To see what your slide show will look like, click the Preview button. When you're finished, click the Return button to go back to the previous menu.

Note: Slide shows, by default, fill the entire screen. However, since most TVs end up cropping the edges of images, you may not be able to see the entire image during a slide show viewed on a TV. To avoid this problem, from the iDVD menu select iDVD Preferences, select the Slideshow icon in the toolbar, and then in the Slideshow pane check the box next to "Always scale slides to TV Safe area."

Also in the Slideshow preferences pane is the option, "Always add original photos to DVD-ROM." This option adds a data section to the DVD that, when the DVD is placed in a computer, provides the viewer with access to the original photos—a nice feature if you're sharing the DVD with relatives or friends.

To delete a slide show from a menu, click its icon or label to select it and then press the Delete key.

Burning a DVD

When you've finished creating your DVD, you're almost ready to burn it to disc. Before you do so, however, click the Preview button to thoroughly test out your DVD. Make sure that all the buttons work and that everything is viewable. To help test things out, you can use the "DVD controller" that appears, much as you would a remote control for a DVD player.

Note: If your DVD will be viewed on a standard TV, choose Show TV Safe Area from the Advanced menu before selecting Preview. Since many TVs crop the edges of video, this allows you to view your DVD using the worst-case-scenario, cropped-TV view.

When you're ready to burn your DVD to disc, click the Burn button. It becomes a Burn *icon*, which you must click again. You will be asked to insert a blank DVD-R, at which time iDVD will encode your DVD and burn it to the disc. This process takes a bit of time, so you may want to find something else to do in the interim. Unless you have one of the most recent superfast Macs, I don't recommend doing anything else on the computer while iDVD is going through its thing.

When the DVD is finished, iDVD will eject it. You can now play it on any computer that plays DVDs or any standard DVD player.

Note: If the computer on which you're creating your DVD doesn't have an optical drive that can burn DVDs, you should instead use the Save as Disc Image command in the File menu. This creates a Mac OS X disc image of the final DVD, which can be copied to a computer that *does* have an appropriate drive, where the DVD can then be burned.

Cleaning up

iDVD projects can take up a lot of space, especially if they contain a lot of raw video or iMovie projects. Some people delete iDVD projects after they've been burned to DVD, but many people like to keep them around. If you want to keep them handy, there is a way to reduce the amount of hard-drive space they occupy: In iDVD Preferences, click the General button and then check the box next to "Delete rendered files on closing a project."

Now, when you click the Burn button and burn your project to DVD, iDVD first encodes it into a format used for DVD discs and then burns that data to the DVD. After burning, iDVD deletes the encoded files, freeing up quite a bit of space. If you don't choose this option, iDVD keeps both the original project files *and* the encoded DVD files on your hard drive. The drawback of choosing this option is that if you ever decide to burn another copy of a project, you'll have to wait for iDVD to re-encode the entire project again.

Solving iDVD problems

This final section lists a few of the most common problems users have with iDVD—and some suggested solutions.

Restoring iDVD. Unless you obtained iDVD by purchasing Apple's iLife bundle, it came preinstalled on your hard drive. Because iDVD cannot be downloaded for free from Apple, if you ever need to reinstall it, you'll need to use the Software Restore CDs or Software Restore feature on the Install DVD that came with your Mac.

SEE: • "Restoring Mac OS Software," in Chapter 3, for more details.

"Multiplexer preparation" error. You should have at least 10 GB of hard-disk space available before burning a DVD. Otherwise, you may get a "Multiplexer preparation" error message.

"Problems were found validating your project" message. If, after clicking the Burn button, you get a message stating, "Problems were found validating your project. A DVD must have at least one video track or one slideshow," you may have accidentally dragged all of your photos and/or videos to drop zones rather than to menus. As described earlier in the chapter, if you drag photos or movies to drop zones, they become part of the theme background rather than part of the slide show or a movie. If you don't have at least one actual slide show or movie in your project, iDVD will not be able to validate the project. The above error message is the result. The solution is to add a slide show or movie to your project, being careful not to place it in a drop zone.

Can't remove iDVD themes. iDVD allows you to save custom iDVD themes as Favorites. However, it doesn't allow you to delete or remove these themes from within iDVD. To delete a custom/favorite theme, quit iDVD, go to ~/Library/Favorites or /Library/Favorites (depending on whether or not you originally elected to make the custom theme available to other users of your Mac), and then drag the theme you want to delete to the Trash. The next time you launch iDVD, the theme will no longer appear.

Chapter submenus not created when importing movies. When you import a movie to iDVD that includes chapter markers, iDVD automatically creates a submenu containing buttons for each chapter. However, you can modify this default behavior by selecting Preferences from the iDVD menu, clicking the Movies button, and making a different selection from the "When importing movies" choices. Note: If you select "Ask each time" and import a movie that's more than 60 minutes long, you will not be asked whether to create a chapter submenu, and no menu will be created.

Importing iPhoto slide shows. You can import slide shows created in iPhoto into iDVD. However, to do so, you must first export the slide show from iPhoto as a QuickTime movie. Then import the slide show to iDVD as a movie file.

Not enough memory to burn a DVD. If you get an error message when trying to burn a DVD, stating that you don't have enough memory, make sure that you have at least twice as much free space on your boot volume as the size of the DVD project you're trying to burn.

Eliminating the Apple logo watermark. To get rid of the Apple logo watermark that appears on all iDVD screens, select Preferences from the iDVD application menu. In the General pane, deselect the "Show Apple logo watermark" option.

Characters you assign to a DVD name don't appear on the burned DVD. DVD names can include only the letters A through Z, the numbers 0 through 9, and the underscore character. Spaces in names will be replaced by the underscore character. All other non-alphanumeric characters will be ignored.

Troubleshooting GarageBand

GarageBand, Apple's entry-level music-creation software, is the newest addition to iLife (added with iLife '04). It allows you to (a) combine prerecorded sounds (called Apple Loops) to create your own "original" music; (b) use built-in "software instruments" (typically via an onscreen or external keyboard) to play and record music; and (c) play and record additional instruments (such as an electric guitar) or even your own singing voice (via a microphone). You can combine multiple tracks. In all cases, you can edit and save the music to create your own musical compositions.

GarageBand has the most limited audience of all the iLife applications, as it requires at least a minimum of musical knowledge to use it for anything beyond combining a few loops. Therefore, the following sections assume that you have this knowledge and are at least a bit familiar with how GarageBand works. The goal here is to provide some troubleshooting help.

To learn how to record your own music, control what tracks play and at what volume, edit an existing track, or delve into GarageBand's more advanced features, start with the wealth of information in the Help files that accompany GarageBand. Also be sure to check out the "Hot Tips" at www.apple.com/support/garageband/hottips, as well as the other topics at the GarageBand

Support site (www.apple.com/support/garageband) and main GarageBand site (www.apple.com/ilife/garageband).

GarageBand overview

In GarageBand's main window for a composition, the area at the top shows the tracks that you have selected to be part of your composition. At the left of each row is the name of the instrument (with buttons to access various track features (such as a muting button). From the middle section, you select volume level and balance for the track. (Note: A Master Track [with pitch and volume controls] allows you to adjust the overall sound of the composition.) The right section indicates the actual music Timeline to be played. Music is usually added here when you either record it yourself or drag a prerecorded loop to the track (in which case the name of the selected loop is shown).

Below the list of tracks is a row of buttons, including typical buttons used to record and play back the current composition. Of special note are the Track Editor (scissors icon) and Loop Browser (eye icon) buttons. Whichever one you select determines the content of the bottom part of the window (as covered later in this section).

No matter how you intend to use GarageBand, it will help immensely if you have two key concepts nailed down. These are (a) loops versus recorded music, and (b) software instruments versus real instruments. Your choices here have implications that cascade throughout the rest of GarageBand.

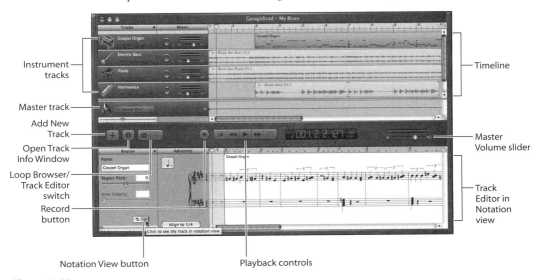

Figure 11.37

GarageBand's main window with the Track Editor shown at bottom. When you click the Notation View button, bottom left, the Track Editor displays the music of this software instrument as individual notes, as in standard sheet music. Notes can be changed, added, deleted, or moved. The top area shows the song's tracks in the main Timeline.

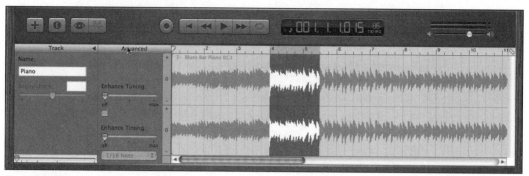

Figure 11.38

The Track Editor for a real instrument. You can select a region of the editor's Timeline (as shown) to be cut.

Loops vs. recorded music. GarageBand comes with a collection of prere-corded riffs called *loops*. These can be used to provide background rhythms for a main melody or, in some cases, combined to form a song all on their own.

To access loops, click the Loop Browser (with the eye icon) button in the middle area of the GarageBand window. You can view the available loops either in Button or Column view (shift views by clicking the desired button in the lower left of the window). Using the Loop Browser, you add loops as tracks to a song. To do so, in Button view do the following:

1. Click one or more buttons. The effect is additive. That is, by clicking both the Piano and Jazz buttons, you see only loops that are in both the Piano and Jazz categories.

2. A list of all loops that meet your selected criteria appear in the column on the right. Click a loop to hear it. Drag a selected loop up to a track in the Timeline to add it to the Timeline.

3. Drag the end of the loop's Timeline region to extend the loop, having it repeat as desired. Reverse the drag to shorten the loop.

Recorded music, in contrast, is any music that a user records. Most recorded music will be recorded in GarageBand itself, via some input device connected to the Mac (such as a keyboard, guitar, or microphone), typically using a USB or Audio In port. That's the whole point of GarageBand, after all. In brief, you do this by selecting a track for the audio input and clicking the Record button.

However, you can also import music files recorded outside of GarageBand. For example, audio files such as AAC or MP3 files will be added as real instrument tracks. MIDI files are imported as software instrument tracks. In either case, just drag the file from the Finder to the Timeline; GarageBand does the rest.

By clicking the Track Editor (scissors) button, you can get a more detailed view of, as well as the ability to edit, any selected track. Note that software instruments display as actual notes (or bars representing notes), while real instruments display as a graphic representation of the sound itself.

TAKE NOTE ▶ **What Is MIDI?**

MIDI stands for *Musical Instrument Digital Interface.* It is a standard format used by synthesizers and other electronic music instruments. Many such instruments have MIDI output ports. You use these outputs to send MIDI data created by the instrument to other devices, such as a Mac running GarageBand. However, doing this requires an intermediary MIDI interface or MIDI-to-Mac cable—that accepts the MIDI input and sends it to the Mac, via a USB or Audio In port. This is needed because the Mac does not have a MIDI port. Some instruments have a USB port and can send MIDI data to a Mac via a standard USB cable. This simplifies the instrument-to-Mac connection and saves the cost of additional hardware.

You can also create and save MIDI files via instruments that have this capability or via separate music software. Unlike MP3 and related audio files, MIDI files do not contain actual audio data. Instead, they contain the digital MIDI instructions that electronic instruments (and software such as GarageBand) can use to produce audio output.

Unfortunately, while you can import MIDI data and files to GarageBand, you cannot convert GarageBand files to MIDI files.

Note: You can gain additional control over how a Mac works with a MIDI device via the Audio MIDI Setup utility, located in the /Applications/Utilities folder.

Can you record a riff in GarageBand and then add it to the collection of built-in loops? Yes. To do so in GarageBand 2.x, simply select the desired region (that is, the precise portion of the riff that you want to make into a loop) in the Timeline (Shift-click to select multiple regions) and choose Add To Loop Library from the Edit menu (or simply drag the selection to the Loop Browser at the bottom of the window). Fill in the dialog that appears, as desired; then click the Create button.

Prior to version 2.x of GarageBand, doing this was more of a hassle. The hitch was that the riff had to be in Apple Loop format before you could import it. How did you get a sound file to be in Apple Loop format? By using Apple's free Soundtrack Loop Utility (available at ftp://ftp.apple.com/developer/Development_Kits/Apple_Loops_SDK_1.1.dmg.bin). Documentation is included and gets installed in /Developer/Apple Loops SDK; the utility itself is installed in /Applications/Utilities. Although designed to work with Apple's Soundtrack application, Loop Utility can produce loops that work with GarageBand as well. Essentially, you use it to add tags to an .aif sound file that provide the metadata needed for GarageBand to work with the file. Here's the way I did it:

1. Export a GarageBand song to iTunes (via the Export to iTunes command in the File menu). This converts the file to an .aif file.

2. Open the .aif file in Soundtrack Utility and enter a selection for at least one tag (such as Genre).

3. Save the file.

4. Drag the file's icon to the Loop Browser in GarageBand's window.

    A dialog will appear that states, "Adding Loops to the Loops Browser." Simply click the Move to Loops Folder button and you are done. This imports and indexes the file. A copy is stored in /Library/Application Support/GarageBand/Apple Loops/SingleFiles. It is now available for selection from the Loop Browser.

Note: Soundtrack Utility can be used for any .aif file, even ones not created in GarageBand.

Figure 11.39

Top, *the Loop Browser display;* bottom, *the dialog that appears when you drag a region from the Timeline to the Loop Browser.*

Software vs. real instruments. The distinction between software and real instruments is a bit more subtle—and ultimately much more significant. Both loops and recorded music can be based on either software or real instruments—creating a sort of two-by-two grid of all the different possibilities. For loops, Apple makes the distinction easy to see by assigning a separate color and icon for each instrument category (for example, a note icon for real and digital wave icon for software). In most cases, you can select loops without much concern for what type they are. But if you are connecting your own instrument to the Mac, the distinction becomes critical.

If you click the Add New Track (+) button in the middle region of the GarageBand display, a New Track window appears. The essentially same window appears, although it is called Track Info, if you click the adjacent Info button for an existing track. The window contains separate tabs for Real and Software Instruments:

 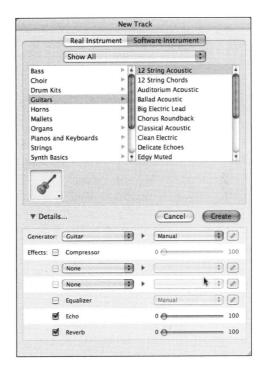

Figure 11.40

The New Track (Track Info) window with the Guitars options for Real Instrument selected, left, and options for Software Instrument selected, right. In the Details section, you can modify the instrument's default settings.

- **Software Instruments.** If you are using a MIDI/USB device, such as a digital keyboard, your selection must be from the Software Instrument list; Real Instrument selections will not work. Software instruments work with devices, such as digital keyboards, that generate MIDI digital signals rather than real sounds. Sometimes, these devices may be incapable of making sounds on their own; in such cases, GarageBand (together with the sound output of the Mac) can be used to produce sound from the data generated by the instrument.

  When GarageBand is launched, the keyboard should be detected (assuming it is a supported device). You are now ready for takeoff.

  Note: If you intend to use software instruments only occasionally, you may be able to get by with GarageBand's built-in virtual keyboards. To access them, select either Keyboard or Musical Typing from the Window menu. Keyboard requires that you use the mouse to click keys. This means you can play only one note at a time, and even that at a slow pace.

Musical Typing, new in GarageBand 2.x, lets you "play" from the Mac's keyboard, allowing for multiple simultaneous notes. Either one can be sufficient for listening to the different software instruments or adding filler notes to a composition (such as an occasional bass note). But for most anything else, these options are severely limited.

- **Real Instruments.** Real instruments refer to exactly that: real instruments. These include such common band mainstays as an electric guitar or bass. There are a variety of ways to connect a real instrument to GarageBand. It can be as simple as a cable that connects directly from your instrument to the Mac's Audio In port. Or it can require an intermediate MIDI audio interface device, costing hundreds of dollars. Once everything is connected, you select a Real Instrument track from GarageBand. Although you can mix and match Real Instrument selections to the actual instrument you are using, you will almost certainly want to select a Real Instrument that makes sense. Thus, if you are using a guitar, you'll select one of the guitar options (which mimic different types of amplifiers).

  Your own voice also qualifies as a real instrument. To use it, all you need is a microphone. If your Mac comes with a built-in microphone (all laptops and iMacs have one), GarageBand will automatically access it! Just set up a Vocals track (you have several options here, such as Male Basic and Female Basic), hit the Record button, and start singing. The sound quality is not great compared with using a good-quality external mike, but it's decent enough for just playing around. You don't need to limit yourself to recording a voice. With a microphone, you can record anything you want, from an acoustic instrument to your dog barking. If there is no matching track setting for what you want to record, select Basic Track. You can edit the exact setting parameters later, if desired.

Jam Packs. GarageBand comes with a minimal collection of loops and instruments. You can expand this by separately purchasing Jam Packs (there are currently four of them). New in GarageBand 2.x, you can select to show only loops from a particular Jam Pack. To do so, click and hold your mouse on the double arrows to the right of the word Loops, above the Loop Browser. A pop-up menu appears, allowing you to choose which Loops collection is displayed. You can restrict your choice so that, for example, you see just the loops available with Jam Pack 1.

GarageBand: Tips and fixes

The following is a collection of problem-solving tips for working with GarageBand:

Performance issues. GarageBand is the iLife component most likely to have processor- and memory-related problems. For starters, the maximum number of Software Instrument tracks a song can contain is directly related to the amount of RAM in your Mac. The more memory, the more tracks. In addition, the more tracks and instrument effects you use, the greater the demand on the processor. Having more than one note play at a time on a track also increases the processor load.

If the load gets too high, GarageBand cannot read and/or write data quickly enough to keep pace with the song that's playing. As the situation worsens, the triangle at the top of the playhead changes color (from white to orange to red) to indicate the demand on the processor. If it stays red too long, you will likely get a System Overload or "Disk is too slow" error message. The song will stop playing. If this happens, try one or more of the following:

- Add more memory to your Mac, get a CPU upgrade, or get a new, faster Mac. Especially if you have this problem often, this is the best and most permanent solution. For even minimal performance, you should have at least a G4 Mac with at least 512 MB of RAM.

- Quit other open applications to free up memory and processor access for GarageBand. Quit and reopen GarageBand itself.

- Do not have FileVault enabled for the account using GarageBand.

- Simplify the song: Mute, delete, or combine tracks as practical.

- Go to GarageBand's Preferences. Click the Audio/MIDI button, and choose "Minimum delay when playing instruments live."

- Go to GarageBand's Preferences. Click the Advanced button and select a low limit (no more than 16) for Maximum Number of Real Instrument Tracks, Software Instrument Tracks, and Voices Per Instrument.

- Real Instrument loops require less processing power than Software Instrument loops. You can Option-drag to convert a Software Instrument loop to a Real Instrument loop when you add it to the Timeline.

  Note: You can make this the default behavior (eliminating the need to use the Option key) by checking the Convert to Real Instrument box in the Advanced pane of GarageBand's Preferences.

- Lock tracks. To lock a track, simply click the Lock icon in the instrument's track line. Doing this shifts the track to being drive-based rather than RAM-based. This can improve performance on systems where you otherwise have too little RAM.

- If you have multiple users logged in, only one user can use GarageBand at a time. Similarly, for best performance, log out of all other user accounts when using GarageBand.

Apple provides its own tips for optimizing GarageBand performance, at http://docs.info.apple.com/article.html?artnum=93618. Although the article says it is for GarageBand 1, most of the advice applies to GarageBand 2 as well.

No sound from an instrument. If you connect an instrument to your Mac and cannot get GarageBand to produce the expected sound from it, consider the following:

- Make sure the instrument you are using has been correctly configured for sending output to the Mac. For some devices, such as the M-Audio

Keystation keyboards sold at the Apple Store, this is all automatic. For other keyboards, particularly ones that have their own speakers, you may need to make a setting switch so that sound goes to the external port rather than the built-in speakers. Check the documentation that came with the device for details.

- Make sure the device is correctly connected to the Mac (that is, you are using the correct cable and the correct ports). If GarageBand does not recognize a connected device, turn the device off and back on, or disconnect and reconnect the cable, or quit and relaunch GarageBand. Assuming that all other settings are correct, one of these actions should get GarageBand to detect the device.

- Make sure there is a track selected to play the device and that the sound for that track is enabled (for example, do not click the Mute button for the track; make sure the volume slider is not all the way to the left).

- If the instrument or microphone is connected to your Mac's Audio In port and you are having problems "hearing" the device on the Mac, check the Input pane of the Sound System Preferences pane. In particular, select Line In from the sound input list and drag the Input volume slider to the desired input level. You may also need to launch Audio MIDI Setup and modify settings there (details of how to do this are beyond the scope of this book).

Tempo, time signature, and key signature issues. Tempo, time signature, and key are set initially in the dialog that appears when you select New Song from the File menu. You can subsequently change these settings via the Master Track pane of the Track Info window, accessed by clicking the Open Track Info button (located on the left side of the middle section of the GarageBand window).

New in GarageBand 2.x, Real Instrument recordings will match changes you make to a song's tempo and key.

When you add a loop to the Timeline, GarageBand matches the loop's tempo and key to the tempo and key of the song. If the transposition is too great, the sound of the instrument can be "off." To prevent this, select "Filter for more relevant results" from the General pane of GarageBand's Preferences. This limits selections in the Loop Browser to only those close to the song's key.

Almost all of GarageBand's loops work best (or only) in 4/4 time. If you want 2/4, for example, the number of accessible loops drops to zero!

Are you having trouble keeping pace with the constant rhythm of a GarageBand loop? If so, open the Track Editor. For a Software Instrument (such as a digital keyboard), the Fix Timing (Align to) button (to the left side of the editor) can help remedy your worst miscues. For a Real Instrument, you can similarly use the Enhance Tuning and Enhance Timing sliders.

See this Apple Knowledge Base article for more information: http://docs.info. apple.com/article.html?artnum=150640.

Accessing more keywords and loops. When you select GarageBand's Loop Browser, some of the available keyword buttons may not be visible. To make sure you are seeing them all, do the following:

- Click-hold over the double-arrows to the right of the title word for the Loop Browser. As just described, this reveals a pop-up menu. Select Show All. Note: If Show All is already selected, Loops will be the title word.

- Click-hold the mouse when the pointer is directly to the left of the Record button. The pointer changes to a hand. Drag the hand up to enlarge the browser section, revealing additional buttons (if any).

- Control-click any of the listed keyword buttons. A pop-up menu appears, from which you can choose from a complete list of keywords. Select any item, and it replaces the keyword currently displayed on the button.

By default, GarageBand only lists loops that are within two semitones of the key and time signature of the current song. To show more loops, go to the General pane of GarageBand's Preferences and deselect "Filter for more relevant results."

Working with GarageBand's loop and instrument files. To add currently uninstalled loops to the Loop Browser, drag the loop files (or folder containing loops) to the Loop Browser section of the GarageBand window. You will typically get a dialog asking if you want to move the loops to the loop library location (as described below) or index them in their current location. Unless you specifically want to store the loop files in your own defined location, I recommend accepting the offer to move the files. Note: Some non-Apple loops may not appear in the Loop Browser even after you do this. To use them, you will need to directly drag the loop file from the Finder to the Timeline of the GarageBand song.

By default, GarageBand stores its loop and instrument files in /Library and ~/Library folders: Application Support/GarageBand and Audio/Apple Loops. For example, GarageBand 1 and Jam Pack 1, 2, and 3 store loop files in /Library/Application Support/GarageBand/Apple Loops. GarageBand 2 and Jam Pack 4 store loops in /Library/Audio/Apple Loops/Apple/. Third-party loops should install in their own folder within the default folder location of the current version of GarageBand. For user-installed files, such as Jam Pack Promotions offered to .Mac members, check out ~/Library/Audio/Apple Loops/User Loops.

In general, do not use the Finder to edit, add, or remove these folders and files. Work within GarageBand instead. Otherwise, GarageBand may no longer correctly list the affected loops and/or instruments. If problems do occur (for example, installed loops no longer appear in the Loop Browser), quit GarageBand and try one of the following as needed:

- If the Apple Loops Index folder has been removed, you can create a new folder with the same name in the same location. Then relaunch GarageBand

and re-index your loops by dragging all the folders containing loops (such as /Library/Audio/Apple Loops/Apple/Apple Loops for GarageBand) into GarageBand's Loop Browser. The Importing Loops dialog will drop down after each drag; wait for it to finish before dragging an additional folder. If duplicates are discovered, GarageBand will give you a warning message, with options to replace the existing item or not.

Check in all the /Library folder locations indicated above, as each one may have an Apple Loops Index folder.

- Apple Loop Index files may become damaged, with the result that no loops at all appear in the Loop Browser. If this happens, remove all the Search Index files from the Apple Loop Index folder(s). Then, as just described, drag the folders containing the loops into GarageBand's Loop Browser.

- Reinstall GarageBand (and any Jam Packs you installed). Do this especially if any Apple Loops or Instrument Library folders have been deleted or if the above fixes failed to work.

See the following Apple Knowledge Base article for what happens to loop locations, including exceptions to the above generalizations, after you upgrade from GarageBand 1 to GarageBand 2: http://docs.info.apple.com/article.html?artnum=300913.

Figure 11.41

GarageBand alerts you to duplicate items when importing loops. If you are re-indexing, you should probably select "Replace original with new folder."

Index

W